THE OXFORD COMPANION TO CHEESE

THE OXFORD COMPANION TO

CHEESE

EDITED BY CATHERINE DONNELLY

OXFORD

UNIVERSITY PRESS

OXFORD
UNIVERSITY PRESS

Oxford University Press is a department of the University of Oxford.
It furthers the University's objective of excellence in research, scholarship,
and education by publishing worldwide. Oxford is a registered trade mark of
Oxford University Press in the UK and certain other countries.

Published in the United States of America by Oxford University Press
198 Madison Avenue, New York, NY 10016, United States of America.

Library of Congress Cataloging-in-Publication Data

Names: Donnelly, Catherine W., editor.
Title: The Oxford companion to cheese / edited by Catherine Donnelly.
Description: New York : Oxford University Press, 2016. | Includes index.
Identifiers: LCCN 2016034026 | ISBN 9780199330881 (hardcover : alk. paper)
Subjects: LCSH: Cheese–Encyclopedias.
Classification: LCC SF270.2 .O94 2016 | DDC 637/.303—dc23
LC record available at https://lccn.loc.gov/2016034026

3 5 7 9 8 6 4
Printed in the United States of America on acid-free paper

CONTENTS

FOREWORD

When my brother Andy and I started Jasper Hill Farm in Greensboro, Vermont, in 2003 it was with the intent of satisfying three deep-seated needs: meaningful work, in a place that we love, with people we love. Beyond the nourishment of the body, cheese has provided a fount of meaning for us and for many who have come from near and far to participate in building something of significance in the Northeast Kingdom of Vermont. We are a bright spot of hope on a landscape that is battered by global market forces in its efforts to produce a commodity there is already too much of: milk. As cheesemakers we generate value not just in our ability to transform milk into money, but in our ability to reconnect consumers with a landscape through our work. There is a yearning for connection to the Land and to Place, and cheese is uniquely able to bridge this divide and to connect consumers to the landscape we distill every time we make a batch of cheese. In this way our customers have become co-creators and participants in a virtuous cycle that is transforming our community by bringing young people back into town, keeping kids in our schools and cows on the land, and we in turn offer the opportunity for connection through a sensory experience to something profoundly deeper than just a piece of cheese.

Cheese is primordial. It has spurred and fed human civilization from the Fertile Crescent and the inception of agriculture through the building of empire and beyond the Industrial Revolution. In its simplest form cheesemaking is the aggregation and preservation of protein; in its highest form cheesemaking is alchemy. With only four ingredients but a thousand iterations, every cheese embodies the particulars of history and the place and people that produced it in a way that few other products can match. Cheese is a form of capital, a store that increases in value over time and is the founding capital of a few European banking systems. Sunshine, banked in the form of cheese, held in darkness until that light captured in summer is revealed in the form of a thousand aromas, textures, and flavors.

And cheese is alive! It is one of the only truly living foods we consume. Every bite of cheese contains over 10 billion living microbes. The biochemical cascade of ripening is just beginning to be understood. The diversity of volatile aromas and the range of sensory attributes across the dizzying spectrum of products we call cheese is truly mind-boggling. The recent advent of molecular biology, whole-genome sequencing technologies, and microbiome research makes this an incredibly exciting time to be a cheesemaker.

But these technologies have also made pathogen detection easier than ever and while cheese has an exemplary history of safety, traditional practices and artisan and farmstead-scale production live in the shadow of an uncertain regulatory future. The complexity of the microbial ecology of raw milk and cheese along with the industrialization of the global food supply has created a regulatory paradigm that struggles to appreciate and comprehend the value that traditional cheesemaking has in the creation of social and economic good. Many traditional European cheeses are in decline or have disappeared. It is ironic that the United States is leading the resurgence of artisan cheese and is the fastest growing market for specialty cheese on the planet.

Can we Americans be the saviors of French terroir? Or will our efforts to reveal our own terroir be stillborn because of insurmountable regulatory hurdles?

I used to believe that the greatest threat to our business was a microbiological threat, but have learned the microbiological risk can be managed. I now believe that the biggest risk to the cheeses that are the foundation of our business is a regulatory risk. The Food Safety Modernization Act (FSMA) is the biggest change to food regulation we are likely to see in our lifetimes. It represents an opportunity and a hazard for cheesemakers. Twice in the past two years regulators have been forced to walk back on the implementation of rules that would have significantly damaged existing foreign and domestic businesses and limited traditional practices without providing a public health benefit. Regulators were caught off guard by the immediate, passionate, and decisive response from cheesemakers, retailers, consumers, politicians, and the media. It has been astounding to watch and participate in the defense of the cheeses and practices that are the link to our collective history. A broad alliance of scientists, academics, cheesemakers, cheesemongers, consumers and enthusiasts has emerged to confront regulators and hold them accountable as we move into rulemaking under FSMA. It is a community response and a reminder of why I really love cheese. The People.

The Oxford Companion to Cheese is a testament to the passion and an embodiment of the willingness of so many to participate and share their particular experience and special knowledge. Three hundred twenty-five authors from 35 countries penned 855 entries in what must be one of the greatest collaborations of any cheese book ever. Among the 325 contributors to this great book are many I count as friends and many whom I admire and have yet to meet. It is the people I have the privilege to interact with because of cheese on a daily basis or as part of my broader work that gives me hope and knowledge that the next thousand years of cheesemaking will be even more interesting and rewarding for humankind than the last.

Mateo Kehler

INTRODUCTION

Cheese is a paradox, a remarkably complex food that begins as one simple and humble ingredient: milk. When coupled with equally simple ingredients—bacteria, salt, enzymes—and manipulated under the right temperatures and conditions, a transformation occurs, resulting in a vast array of products of differing shapes, sizes, and colors, with a panoply of flavors, tastes, and textures. These are the great cheeses of the world. But there is nothing simple about cheesemaking. The hours are long and the labor backbreaking. Great care is required to lovingly tend the animals and landscapes that produce high-quality milk for cheesemaking. Once milk is collected, many hours, days, and months are required to complete the stages of cheesemaking and aging needed to produce great cheese. So much can go wrong. But when things go right, the result is over fourteen hundred named cheese varieties enjoyed throughout the world.

In approaching this book, it was necessary to explore the multitude of ways in which we interact with cheese. For many, our experience with cheese is limited to cheese as an ingredient—wonderful mozzarella topping a hot pizza, shredded cheese in tacos or on nachos or other Mexican foods, cream cheese on a bagel, Cheddar cheese in comfort foods such as macaroni and cheese, or cheese melted on top of that iconic Quebecois dish, poutine. Given consumer demand for fast food and prepared meals, the processed food industry is a major user of cheese as an ingredient throughout the world. The requirements in the processed food industry dictate that cheese function as a perfectly predictable ingredient—that it melt with consistency, brown in a predictable manner, appear as a perfect emulsion so

that oil does not separate from the cheese mass. As a result cheeses used as ingredients often contain products that help them behave consistently. There are many wonderful cheese products that have created great demand for milk and milk-derived ingredients, such as milk protein concentrates. Whey, once considered a byproduct of cheesemaking, is now valued industrially as an important source of highly functional proteins, immunoglobulins, and lactoferrin.

There is another world of cheese, one that shares rich cultural roots and traditions with varieties that have been manufactured in Europe for centuries. These age-old cheese traditions are now being embraced by US artisan cheese producers and, as a result, over the last thirty years a bona fide cheese culture has emerged within the United States. The cheeses produced in the United States now rival the very best produced throughout the world. These cheeses vary in consistency, depending on what starter culture was used, the aging conditions, the pastures or forages on which the animals were raised, and the animals used to produce the milk, ranging from sheep to goats to cows to water buffalo. These cheeses are living, breathing entities. They have in some cases a very short shelf life. Like fine wines, artisan cheeses have terroir, a connection to place. It is the search for uniqueness and often inconsistency that makes consumers crave these products.

In 1985 the American Cheese Society, founded by Cornell professor Frank Kosikowski, judged 89 cheeses entered by 30 cheesemakers at its annual meeting. In 2015 the ACS held its annual meeting in Providence, Rhode Island, where 1,799 cheeses made by 267 producers were entered in competition.

The Festival of Cheeses, during which all entries are displayed and available for tasting, pays tribute to the remarkable efforts of US artisan and farmstead cheesemakers. If Frank Kosikowski were alive today, I think he would be extremely proud to see what his initial vision has realized. Demand for artisan cheeses is growing remarkably in the United States and is providing income and opportunities during challenging times for dairy farmers and rural economies. The rise of the US artisan cheese industry was perhaps best illustrated for me when, in 2014, President Obama hosted a state dinner at the White House for French president François Hollande. What does the leader of the free world choose to serve to the president of the greatest cheese culture on earth? Instead of selecting from the enormous variety of exceptional French cheeses for the menu, the White House chefs featured as part of the main course an American artisan cheese, Bayley Hazen Blue, one of my favorite Vermont artisan cheeses. This moment was symbolic for me, representing how truly far the American artisan cheese industry has come.

The growth of the US artisan cheese industry and the renaissance of cheesemaking occurring throughout the world presents a tremendous opportunity to educate new populations of farmers, mongers, affineurs, students, scientists, cheesemakers, technologists, and cheese connoisseurs about the history, art, regulation, sales, marketing, and cultural impacts of cheese. We have tried our best to do justice to these many dimensions of cheese in the *Companion*.

Sadly, despite the exceptional growth and success of artisan cheese, the artisan cheese industry globally has come under regulatory scrutiny. Regulations that govern cheesemakers in the United States apply equally to large industrial cheesemakers and small farmstead producers who may milk as few as five cows. Increasingly industrial producers are requesting that standards of identity be changed for cheese varieties to reflect new technologies being used for cheese production. The Food and Drug Administration has long considered a ban on the sale of raw-milk cheeses, considering instead a mandatory requirement for use of pasteurized milk in cheesemaking. As my esteemed colleague and friend Paul Kindstedt states: "raw-milk cheeses are worth saving." At its essence, the raw-milk cheese debate highlights the fundamental difference in philosophy dividing the United States and Europe when it comes to regulation of raw-milk cheese and other traditional food production.

The European Union approaches cheese safety from the standpoint of hygiene, arguing that consumer safety is best protected when strict veterinary and sanitary practices (good animal health and regular inspections; collection, transportation, and transformation of milk in a short time period; education of consumers regarding shelf life) are followed from production to consumption for raw-milk cheeses. The French contend that these common hygiene provisions provide adequate public health protection without mandatory pasteurization. The quality of raw milk used for cheesemaking is perhaps the most important consideration when producing raw-milk cheeses. European cheesemakers pay great attention to raw-milk quality, knowing that this will in turn dictate cheese quality. Raw-milk quality decreases during refrigerated storage; therefore utilization of milk as soon as possible for cheesemaking protects cheese quality. In artisan cheesemaking, if milk is produced on farm, the reduced time from milking to cheesemaking ensures the manufacture of high-quality cheese. Immediate manufacture of milk into cheese without cooling reduces the opportunity for the growth of undesirable bacteria. Conversely, when milk is cooled and held in a bulk tank, the potential for growth of psychrotrophic (cold-loving) pathogens and other bacteria is increased. We seem to be incapable of connecting those dots within our US regulatory system, despite a vast body of science from around the globe that conclusively proves that raw milk cheeses can be safely produced.

At its essence, regulatory scrutiny may be driven more in response to the political threat of geographic protections as opposed to a bona fide food safety threat. Geographic indicators are trademark protections affecting European cheeses in global trade negotiations. The European Commission argues that natural, geographic, and human factors have combined to give protected cheeses their specific aroma and flavor. In Europe PDO (protected designation of origin) cheeses enjoy special protection as cultural treasures, with PDO described as "gastronomic precious heritage" by my friend and colleague Sylvie Lortal. It is of note that cheese names and geographic protections have arisen during recent Trans-Pacific Partnership Agreement negotiations. The politics, regulation, trade, and protection of cheese are all topics covered by entries in this *Companion*.

As a scientist and food microbiologist, I of course am biased toward and fascinated by the microbiology and chemistry of cheese. I can think of few other places in nature where microorganisms are more magnificently displayed than when associated with cheese. The blooms, veins, sticky surfaces, gooey interiors, crystals, wrinkles, strings, and, yes, for some, the strong olfactory notes, are all due to microbial action and growth. Entries in this book address the beneficial associations of microbes with cheese, from the perspective of the diversity of unique cheeses that arise due to the growth of the bacteria, yeasts, and molds that play a crucial role in cheesemaking. New scientific tools are greatly informing and forcing a re-examination of our knowledge of cheese microbiology. These discoveries provide insights into the complexity of the microbial biodiversity of traditional cheeses and will further advance our knowledge of some of the oldest traditional foods known on earth. I offer all due apologies to the non-scientists who are readers of this text, hoping to perhaps inspire that inner scientist in all of us.

Beyond the scientific, there are a multitude of other dimensions associated with cheese. The history and culture of cheese production and consumption commands a large part of the book. Archaeological evidence of cheesemaking goes back to Sumerian and Mesopotamian civilizations approximately seven thousand years ago, though it is believed that simple cheeses were made after the domestication of sheep and goats as far back as eleven thousand years ago. Entries on these subjects and others cover the history of cheesemaking, up through modern times, including the impact of the Industrial Revolution, which led to the invention of mass-market cheeses.

Cheeses have inspired writers and artists, poets and playwrights. Cheese is featured in Homer's *Odyssey* (the blinded Cyclops Polyphemus made cheese from sheep's milk), praised by the Roman author and naturalist Pliny the Elder, and often given symbolic import in the Bible ("The virgin will conceive and give birth to a son, and will call him Immanuel. He will be eating curds and honey when he knows enough to reject the wrong and choose the right." Isaiah 7:14–15). They have inspired historians and filmmakers, fed armies, and been used as sacraments to pay tribute during religious services. We have tried our best to capture these many dimensions of cheese, from ancient times to present. Many of the entries have been beautifully written

from places of pure passion, which has been deeply inspiring to me.

Approach and Features

I have always been humbled by education, realizing during my PhD studies how little I really knew about anything. I felt these same sentiments during the production of this book. I would therefore like to offer a few words about the scope, organization, purpose, and limitations of the *Companion*.

The Oxford Companion to Cheese is an A–Z encyclopedia composed of 855 entries signed by the authors, and each entry includes at least one reference or further reading suggestion. Entries range from fewer than 250 words to more than 2,500 words, depending on the specificity and importance of the topic. Entries are cross-referenced, providing the reader with suggestions for related topics, and there is also a lengthy index at the back of the book to assist readers in finding the topics they are most interested in. We hope readers will dip into one entry, only to emerge someplace else entirely, wandering along natural paths of discovery.

For a more structured exploration of the *Companion*, readers may consult the topical outline of entries at the beginning of the book, where, for example, all the "Regional" entries are listed in one place. The topical outline of entries reflects the organization of the book into fifteen broad areas: animal species, breeds, and nutrition; culinary uses of cheese; biographical entries; cheese styles and specific cheeses (i.e., Camembert de Normandie or Stichelton); cheese classification (i.e., blue cheeses or clothbound cheeses); cheese shops; historical and cultural entries; industry and cheese producers; microflora and starter cultures; the cheesemaking process; properties of cheese (i.e., shelf life or flavor); regional entries; regulation, designation, and safety concerns; schools, institutions, and associations; and technology and equipment used in cheesemaking.

More than 180 accompanying images—including three full-color inserts—capture, among other things, the culture, tradition, and vast array of unique cheese styles worldwide, showcasing both the products themselves and the beautiful geographic locales from which they arise. We were lucky that so many authors sent us photos from their personal collections, which has immeasurably improved our image program.

While we attempted to produce the most comprehensive reference work on cheese ever assembled, we could never hope to actually be comprehensive in the true sense—so we had to be choosy. The book is not an index of (for example) cheese styles, cheesemakers, or cheese shops, but includes representative and important examples of each. Naturally there will be omissions, both unintentional and intentional, since any one of the categories could easily be a stand-alone book. For example, we present 244 cheese style entries covering the history of the style, exemplary producers, common sensory qualities when eaten, any unique production techniques, and so on. If we covered all the fourteen hundred named cheese styles we wouldn't have space for anything else! At best, this is a starting point, a reference work dedicated to cheese that we hope will be carried forward in future editions. We welcome comments from learned readers, as these will surely inform and improve future editions of this work.

With Gratitude

The Oxford Companion to Cheese was very far from the work of one person, and there are plenty of thanks to go around. Jason Hinds, of Neal's Yard Dairy, got me involved in this project at the outset. My wonderful editor at Oxford University Press, Max Sinsheimer, was confident that I could indeed do justice to the *Companion*. He worked tirelessly over a period of several years to develop the conceptual foundation for the project, and to bring it to fruition. Among countless other ways in which Max kept us moving toward a finish line that sometimes seemed quite distant, he was unflappable in managing the complexities of developing a major new reference work, ensuring, for instance, that every entry was assigned to a knowledgeable author, and then submitted to the Editorial Board for review. In this Max had the cheerful support of Sara Rodgers, an editorial assistant at OUP, who also has my thanks.

I was so heartened when our illustrious group of Area Editors agreed to step forward and collaborate with me on this assignment, serving as the Editorial Board. They are (in alphabetical order): Montserrat Almena-Aliste, Kate Arding, Ed Behr, Ursula Heinzelmann, Paul Kindstedt, May Leach, Giuseppe Licitra, Sylvie Lortal, Heather Paxson, and Bronwen Percival. Their varied and impressive backgrounds in (among other fields) cheesemaking, microbiology, dairy science, cheese retailing, quality and sensory analysis, and the anthropology and history of cheese ensured that the editorial oversight of the *Companion* matched its ambitious coverage.

I also knew that it would be an injustice to approach the topic of cheese from anything other than a global context, so I made sure to reach out to my European and Latin American colleagues and friends who reached out to their international colleagues and friends. What materialized is something of a miracle: 325 authors from 35 countries, which I believe sets a high-water mark for an Oxford *Companion*. Many of the authors reside in Europe, where the traditional cheeses they study have been continuously produced for centuries. The sweeping international nature of this project is something of which I am enormously proud, and I am thankful to every one of the contributors.

I am also enormously grateful to my employer, the University of Vermont, which provided a sabbatical that I used to plan the scope of this encyclopedia.

I finally thank Professor Henry V. Atherton for his early inspiration of my interest in dairy science and cheese. As a professor myself, I see each day the difference I can make in the lives of students. He certainly made a difference in mine. It is to his memory that this book is dedicated.

Catherine Donnelly

TOPICAL OUTLINE OF ENTRIES

Entries in the body of *The Oxford Companion to Cheese* are organized alphabetically. This outline offers an overview of the *Companion,* with entries listed in the following categories:

Animal Species, Breeds, and
    Husbandry
Biographies
Cheese Families and
    Classification
Cheesemaking Process and
    Technology
Cheeses
Cheese Shops

Chemistry
Cultural
Equipment and Tools
Health and Safety
Historical
Microflora and Cultures
Organizations, Education, and
    Accreditation
Pairings and Cuisine

Producers
Regions
Regulations and Designations
Sensory and Functional
    Properties

Animal Species, Breeds, and Husbandry

alpage
Alpine (goat)
Ayrshire (cow)
bovine somatotropin
breeding and genetics
Brown Swiss (cow)
camel
cow
donkey
East Friesian (cow)
East Friesian (sheep)
goat
Guernsey (cow)
heritage breeds

Holstein (cow)
Jersey (cow)
lactation
Lacaune (sheep)
LaMancha (goat)
Latxa (sheep)
mare
Montbéliarde (cow)
moose
Murciana (goat)
Normande (cow)
Nubian (goat)
pastoralism
pasture

reindeer
ruminants
Saanen (goat)
Salers (cow)
Sarda (sheep)
sheep
shepherd
Shorthorn (cow)
silage
total mixed ration
transhumance
water buffalo
yak

Biographies

Androuët, Pierre
Archestratus of Gela
Canut, Enric
Cato, Marcus Porcius
Charles VI
Columella, Lucius Junius
   Moderatus
Ginzburg, Carlo
Hansen, Christian D.A.
Harding, Joseph
Harel, Marie
Hildegard of Bingen
Hodgson, Randolph

Homer
Hooke, Robert
Jones, Evan
Jossi, John
Kosikowski, Frank
Kraft, James L.
Le Jaouen, Jean-Claude
Leeuwenhoek, Antoni van
Marcellino, Sister Noella
Pasteur, Louis
Peluso, Franklin
Petite, Marcel
Pliny the Elder

Rance, Patrick
Saint Bartholomew
Saint Benedict
Saint Gall
Saint Uguzo
Schmid, Willi
Steele, Veronica
Varro, Marcus Terentius
Virgil
Willard, Xerxes Addison
Williams, Jesse

Cheese Families and Classification

Alp-style cheeses
artisanal
bark-wrapped cheeses
bloomy-rind cheeses
blue cheeses
brebis
brined cheeses
caillé doux and caillé acide
chèvre
clothbound cheeses
commodity cheese
concentrated whey cheese
cone-shaped cheeses
families of cheese
farmer cheese

farmstead
fermier
flavored cheeses
fresh cheeses
government cheese
green cheese
industrial
industriel
leaf-wrapped cheeses
Mexican cheeses
natural-rind cheeses
oil-marinated cheeses
pasta filata
pasteurized process cheeses
pot cheeses

pressed cheeses
raw-milk cheeses
Serbian white brined cheeses
sheep- and goat-skin cheeses
smoked cheeses
soft-ripened cheeses
sour skimmed-milk cheeses
specialty cheese
territorial
thermized milk cheeses
Tomme
triple-cream cheeses
truckle
washed-curd cheeses
washed-rind cheeses

Cheesemaking Process and Technology

accelerated ripening
acidification
Alp cheesemaking
annatto
ash
brining
brushing
buron
cave
cheddaring
cheese grading
clean break
coagulation or curdling
colostrum

continuous whey starters
curd mill
cutting
deacidification
demineralization
draining
dry salting
fleurines
flocculation
fossa
home cheesemaking
homogenization
ladles
larding

manual testing
maturing
membrane filtration
microfiltration
milk
milling
molding
morge
nettle
packaging
pasteurization
pH measurement
Piophila casei
pitching

prematuration
relative humidity
rinds
saffron
scalding
separator
shredding

skimming
standardization
stewing
stirring
stretching
syneresis
titratable acidity measurement

turning
ultrafiltration
vacuuming
waxing and coating
whey
whey powder
yield

Cheeses

Abbaye de Tamié
Abondance
Afuega'l Pitu
Anari
Anevato
Appenzeller
Arzúa-Ulloa
Asiago
Azeitão
Bandal
Banon
batzos
Beaufort
Bergkäse
Bitto
Bleu d'Auvergne
Bleu de Gex
Bleu des Causses
Bleu du Vercors-Sassenage
Boeren-Leidse met sleutels
Bohinjski sir
Bovški sir
Bra
Brânză de burduf
Brick
Brie de Meaux
Brillat-Savarin
Brin d'Amour
brocciu
burrata
burrini
Cabrales
caciocavallo
Caciocavallo Podolico
Cacioricotta
Caerphilly
Camembert de Normandie
cancoillotte
Canestrato di Moliterno
Canestrato Pugliese
Cantal

Casatella Trevigiana
Casciotta d'Urbino
Cashel Blue
Casieddu
Castelmagno
Castelo Branco
Cebreiro
Celtic Blue Reserve
Chabichou du Poitou
Chaource
Charolais
Cheddar
cheese curds
Cheshire cheese (U.K.)
Chevrotin
Classic Blue Log
Colby
Comté
cottage cheese
Cougar Gold
Coulommiers
cream cheese
Crottin de Chavignol
Crowley Cheese
Domiati
Edam
Emmentaler
Époisses
feta
Fiore Sardo
Fiore Sicano
Fontina Val d'Aosta
Formaella Arahovas Parnassou
Formaggella del Luinese
formaggio di fossa
Fourme d'Ambert
Fourme de Montbrison
Galotyri
Gamonedo
gaperon
Garrotxa

Ġbejna
Gloucester
Gorgonzola
Gouda
Grana Padano
Graviera Agrafon
Graviera Kritis
Graviera Naxou
Great Hill Blue
Grobnik
Gruyère
Halloumi
Havarti
Herzegovina sack cheese
Humboldt Fog
Idiazabal
Istrian
Jack
Jajikhli Panir
Jarlsberg
Kalathaki Limnou
kashkaval
Kasseri
Katiki Domokou
Kefalograviera
Kopanisti
Kraški kozji sir
Kraški ovčji sir
Krasotyri
Krk
Kupa Paniri
Ladotyri Mytilinis
Laguiole
Lancashire
Langres
Lankaaster Aged
La Serena
Lighvan Paniri
Limburger
lisnati
Livarot

Cheese Shops

Chemistry

Cultural

Equipment and Tools

Health and Safety

adulteration
ambient storage
cheese addiction
cheesemaker's lung
critical control points
cross-contamination
dairy allergy
environmental impact

equivalence of pasteurization
Generally Recognized As Safe
genetically modified organism
Hazard Analysis and Critical
    Control Point
health properties
hygiene
lactose intolerance

Listeria
outbreak
pathogens
post-process contamination
pregnancy advice
Salmonella
60-day aging rule

Historical

Alkmaar auction
ancient civilizations
archaeological detection
Aristaios
bog butter
Caseologia
cheese boxes
cheese cradles
cheese factor
Cheshire cheese (U.S.)
Congress of Vienna
counterculture
Customs of Corbie, The

dairymaids
Diocletian Edict
earthenware pottery
etymology
faiscre grotha
Hypata
Inanna
industrialization
latifundia
Luna cheese
manorial cheesemakers
Mesopotamia
military rationing

milk boiler
monastic cheesemaking
origin of cheese
plakous
Puritans
Rocamadour pilgrimage
Stresa Convention
trade (historical)
turnsole
World War I
World War II

Microflora and Cultures

adjunct cultures
asexual reproduction
bacteriocins
bacteriophages
biodiversity
biofilms
Brevibacterium linens
cheese mites
colony-forming unit
culture houses
dairy propionibacteria
Debaryomyces
ecological niche
ecosystem
exopolysaccharides
filamentous fungi

flower of the molds
fungi
Geotrichum candidum
hyphae
indigenous microorganisms
inoculum
jolie robe
lactic acid bacteria
Lactobacillus
Lactococcus lactis
microbial communities
microbial flux and succession
morphology
Mucor
mycelia
mycotoxins

non-starter lactic acid bacteria
opportunistic pathogen
Penicillium
phenotypic variability
plant-derived coagulants
ripening cultures
Scopulariopsis
spores
Staphylococcus aureus
starter cultures
strains
symbiotic relationship
synergistic effects
taxonomy
wild-type strain

Organizations, Education, and Accreditation

accreditations
advertising and promotion

apprenticeships
American Cheese Society

American Dairy Goat
    Association

Pairings and Cuisine

Producers

Regions

Regulations and Designations

Sensory and Functional Properties

Abbaye de Tamié is a washed-rind cheese produced from raw cow's milk by the monks at Abbaye Notre-Dame de Tamié in the Savoie department, France. The cheese has a thin disk shape and comes in two sizes, Grand Modèle (4 pounds [1.6 kilograms]) and Petit Modèle (21 ounces [600 grams]). About 882 pounds (400 kilograms) of the cheese is produced daily from the milk collected from eight surrounding farms.

The abbey was founded under Cistercian order in 1133 and located in an ideal dairy farming area with very well-established mountain pastures. The cheese was produced from the first day of the abbey's history, but many people believe that the original cheese was similar to Gruyère. The original recipe was lost during the French Revolution. When the monks came back in 1861 to resurrect the abbey, they had to work with the reduced milk production from abandoned pastures by adapting a Port-Salut recipe to produce a smaller and faster-aging cheese. Over one hundred years the monks have refined the recipe to produce the current style of Tamié. The abbey has one of the most successful monastic cheesemaking operations in Europe by mechanizing most of the cheesemaking process and maintaining a strict quality-control system from milk production to whey utilization for methane gas production. More than half the monks participate in the various cheesemaking-related activities, generating the most important economic resource for the abbey's community of seventy people.

Tamié belongs to a pressed, uncooked cheese category. To make it, raw whole milk is heated up to 93°F (34°C), and a small amount of starter culture and calf rennet are added. When the coagulation is complete, the curd is cut into pea-size pieces and moved into the perforated cylinder-shaped molds. The curds are turned several times and pressed for three to four hours before brining, which takes one to three hours, depending on the size of the cheese. The aging of the cheese is done in the vaulted cellars located at the basement of the abbey, which keeps the humidity between 85 and 90 percent and the temperature around 57°F (14°C). The aging process requires frequent washing and turning and takes up to forty days.

The finished cheese has 50 to 53 percent of solids nonfat content. The rind is light beige to saffron in color, with a very thin layer of white mold enveloping a softening interior, which develops a few small pea-size holes. The taste is nutty, milky, and delicate when young, and a typical washed-rind cheese flavor, full and strong, develops with age.

See also FRANCE; HAUTE-SAVOIE; and MONASTIC CHEESEMAKING.

Abbaye Notre Dame de Tamié. http://www.abbaye-tamie.com.

Soyoung Scanlan

Abondance is a semi-cooked pressed cheese, made in the Alpine region of Haute-Savoie in eastern France. In 1990 Abondance was awarded AOC status, which dictates it can only be made in the mountains of the Haute-Savoie using the ancient skills and methods and raw milk that guarantee its quality and authenticity. See HAUTE-SAVOIE.

The origin of this cheese is linked to the cow with the same name, famous for their distinctive brown

Abondance is a semi-cooked pressed cheese made in the alpine region of Haute-Savoie in eastern France.
© FRÉDÉRIQUE VOISIN-DEMERY

eye patches like "spectacles" on their white faces. Augustine monks began manufacturing Abondance in the Abbaye d'Abondance in the twelfth century (it was previously called Toupin). In 1381 Abondance was served at the papal conclave in Avignon at the election of the new pope.

Abondance is manufactured in dairy cooperatives (*laitier* label) or on farms (*fermier* label). For *fermier*, milk comes from one herd composed of Abondance (45 percent minimum in the herd), Tarentaise, or Montbéliarde cows. During summer Abondance can be made in the mountains ("alpage") from milk of cows grazing between 1,300 and 1,850 meters. See ALPAGE. In winter cows are kept in warm barns and feast on summer hay. There are about sixty-five farmhouse (*fermier*) producers using their own milk and fifteen cooperatives or *fruitières* using milk from about two hundred milk producers. In 2014 about 2,400 tons of Abondance were produced, with 800 metric tons consisting of Abondance *fermier*. See FERMIER.

A copper vat or cauldron is used to manufacture Abondance. Raw whole cow's milk derived from two milkings must be processed within fourteen hours maximum after the oldest milking (*fermier*) and before midday following the oldest milking (*laitier*). Milk may be heated only once, at the time of renneting, to a temperature of 86–95°F (30–35°C). Milk is inoculated with thermophilic starters (*Streptococcus thermophilus, Lactobacillus delbrueckii*, and *Lactobacillus helveticus*). During Abondance *fermier* cheese manufacture, certain processes must be done manually such as:

- Cutting of milk gel into curd grains with a "cheese harp" (so-called because it is strung with wires like the musical instrument). See CHEESE KNIFE.
- For each cheese, curd is removed with a linen cloth and directly put in a mold. See CHEESECLOTH.
- Turning of cheese must be done at minimum once within thirty minutes after molding and at minimum twice during the following twelve hours. See TURNING.

After cutting the curd, the mixture of curd particles and whey is warmed to 113–122°F (45–50°C) and held at this temperature for forty-five minutes maximum. The ripening period varies from one hundred days minimum to eight to twelve months, at a temperature of 50–55°F (10–13°C) and relative humidity of 90 percent minimum. Matured on spruce planks in caves or cellars, the cheeses are constantly turned and rubbed with salt to create the thin reddish-brown rind.

Abondance is produced in wheels (3 inches [7–8 centimeters] high, 15–17 inches [38–43 centimeters] diameter), which weigh 13–26 pounds (6–12 kilograms) and have a typically concave edge. The golden yellow to brown rind covers an interior that is ivory to slightly yellow in color, with small, regular, and well-distributed eyes. Abondance *fermier* cheese has a green oval casein nameplate, while a red square is used to distinguish the *laitier* label.

Abondance has a supple, fine grained texture. Its yeasty aroma carries through onto the palate, which is savory yet fruity with an intense "umami" taste when melted like Raclette. See RACLETTE. Scientific studies have shown that Abondance *fermier* cheeses manufactured from milk produced from mountain pastures (1,500–1,850 meters) were deemed to be more "fruity," "animal," "boiled milk," and "hazelnut" and less pungent and "propionic acidic" than cheeses made from milk produced from valley pastures (850–1,100 meters). It was possible to partly attribute these differences in flavor to the presence of protein-based volatile compounds in the cheeses.

Abondance can be eaten raw at the end of the meal, or in a typical meal called *berthoud*. To make it, rub with garlic a ramekin dish; put in it thin slices of Abondance (5 ounces [150 grams] per person); add white Savoie wine and optionally Madeira, and pepper; brown it under the grill for five to ten minutes; and serve hot with bread and potatoes boiled in their skins.

See also FRANCE.

Auboiron, Bruno, and Lansard Gilles. *La France des fromages A.O.C.* Aix en Provence, France: Edisud, 1997.

Bugaud, Christophe, et al. "Relationship between Flavour and Chemical Composition of Abondance Cheese Derived from Different Types of Pasture." *Lait* 81 (2001): 757–773.

Froc, Jean. *Balade au pays des fromages. Les traditions fromagères en France.* Versailles, France: Editions Quae, Inra, 2006.

Rance, Patrick. *The French Cheese Book.* London: Macmillan, 1989.

Syndicat Interprofessionnel du Fromage Abondance. http://www.fromageabondance.fr.

Eric Beuvier and Juliet Harbutt

accelerated ripening of cheese has been a subject of scientific and industrial interest for many years. Ripening of cheese represents a significant investment of time and cost of storage under specific conditions, such as controlled temperature and humidity. Ways to reduce this time and burden seem highly attractive from practical and economic perspectives.

However, in considering how to accelerate ripening, it is critical to examine exactly what is happening in ripening overall. Cheese ripening, while differing in details from cheese variety to variety, essentially always involves the combined action of a wide range of biological agents—principally bacteria (from the added starter or non-starter lactic acid bacteria [NSLAB]), molds or other microorganisms where present, enzymes coming from these microorganisms, the milk from which the cheese has been made, and the added coagulant (e.g., rennet). Development of the characteristic flavor and texture of each variety depends on all of these reactions working in concert, and sometimes in delicate sequence, to break down the proteins, fats and lipids and transform a bland and smooth fresh curd to a much more flavorsome mature cheese.

The challenge then in accelerating ripening is how to get all these reactions, which may act independently or in a coordinated manner, to take place at a uniformly accelerated rate and arrive at the same destination, that is, a balanced and appropriate set of flavors, aroma, and texture characteristics, in a shorter space of time.

Not surprisingly, strategies for accelerating cheese ripening involve either adding higher levels or more powerful versions of the agents responsible for ripening, or manipulating the cheese environment to try and uniformly ramp up the speed of all reactions.

One of the simplest approaches involves increasing the temperature at which ripening takes place, as basic scientific principles state that most reactions (enzymatic or microbiological) take place proportionately faster as temperature increases, at least within the range of temperatures likely to be applied for cheese ripening. For example, increasing the temperature of ripening of Cheddar cheese from 54°F to 61°F (12°C to 16°C) will result in more rapid development of flavor, but may have the downside of textural problems and so has not been widely adopted. In another processing-based approach, it was reported in the mid-1990s that holding fresh cheese curd at high pressures (50 MPa) for three days could dramatically accelerate flavor development; however, subsequent studies suggested that the reduction in ripening time was not sufficient to make this attractive. In fact later studies suggested that treating cheese at much higher pressures but for much shorter times could actually be an interesting approach for decelerating cheese ripening, in essence "freezing" the quality of cheese at an optimal stage of ripeness.

In terms of modifying the microbiological population of cheese, there have been a number of studies of attenuated starter cultures, which have been treated (e.g., by drying, freezing, pressure treatment) to reduce or eliminate their ability to produce acid while retaining key enzymes, which can contribute to ripening. The advantage of adding such bacteria is that ripening can be accelerated without resulting in an excessive rate of acid production during cheesemaking. While such cultures have been shown to accelerate ripening, their commercial adoption has not been widespread.

Finally, additional enzymes may be added to the milk or curd to try and speed up the ripening process, and such enzymes may be encapsulated or otherwise treated to ensure that they are not simply inefficiently lost in the whey; studies have also examined the possibility of adding such enzymes at the dry-salting stage. Adding lipases or proteases in this manner has been shown to accelerate ripening of several cheese varieties, but obviously incurs the additional cost of the enzyme preparation.

In conclusion, when it comes to cheese ripening, the exact journey can be the key to ensuring the right destination. While the objective of saving money and time by reducing the ripening time (by accelerating the rate of all the processes involved in that period) unquestionably remains attractive, successfully managing the complex process of cheese ripening to achieve this, in a way that the cost of the solution does not cancel out the benefit, remains in large part an elusive goal.

See also LIPOLYSIS; MATURING; and PROTEOLYSIS.

El Soda, M. "Acceleration of Cheese Ripening." In *Encyclopedia of Dairy Sciences*, vol. 1, edited by Hubert Roginski, John W. Fuquay, and Patrick F. Fox, pp. 327–329. Amsterdam: Academic Press, 2003.

Fox, Patrick, Paul L. H. McSweeney, Timothy Cogan, et al., eds. *Cheese: Chemistry, Physics, and Microbiology*, Vol. 1: *General Aspects*, 3d ed. London: Elsevier Academic, 2004.

Law, Barry A. "Controlled and Accelerated Cheese Ripening: The Research Base for New Technologies." *International Dairy Journal* 11, nos. 4–7 (2001) 383–398.

Alan Kelly

accreditations for cheesemongers exist in a handful of countries around the globe. These certifications demonstrate at least a minimum level of mastery of cheese knowledge, and confer prestige. Most, but not all, accreditations are available only to cheese professionals. Those who earn such credentials are expected to serve as promoters and ambassadors of quality cheese and to share their expertise with customers and fellow enthusiasts. Being accredited can enhance job prospects as credential holders may also serve as judges in cheese competitions.

The French have probably the most comprehensive progression of certifications for cheese professionals other than cheesemakers, beginning with the Certificat de Qualification Professionelle (CQP). This certification is available to young people under age twenty-six or to unemployed persons of any age wishing to follow a job retraining scheme. The requirements for obtaining CQP status involve completing a training program over a school year (September–June) that alternates between classroom work and a hands-on internship. The candidate,

school, and employer all sign a contract outlining rights, terms, and expectations that is also signed by the French agency that oversees the training programs. Candidates are guaranteed a minimum salary and worker's rights during their training. Upon completion of the training program, candidates must pass a written exam and several practical exams demonstrating their competence in such areas as product knowledge; sanitation, and proper handling; sales and customer advice; ordering, receiving, and case setting. The CQP is recognized by the French state.

Beyond the CQP there are at least three other titles that can be earned in France through winning competitions. The Concours National des Fromagers, organized by the national trade association la Fédération des Fromagers de France (Les Fromagers de France) has been held every second year (odd years) since the mid-1990s. Candidates must be resident and working in France (of any nationality—the first-prize winner in 2013 was Matt Feroze, an Englishman working for Mons Fromager in Lyon). There may be only sixteen candidates in any given year. The competition is held during the SIRHA trade show in Lyon, and includes live tests of creating a cheese platter, blind tasting, and accuracy in cutting cheese. In addition Les Fromagers de France organizes the Lyre d'Or (golden harp) competition in even years at the Salon du Fromage in Paris. This competition is based on the creation of

The American Cheese Society's Certified Cheese Professional exam is based firmly on practical knowledge; it is only offered to individuals with 4,000+ hours of relevant experience with cheese. © AMERICAN CHEESE SOCIETY

the best cheese platter, according to a theme. The top three winners under twenty-six years of age at either the Concours National or the Lyre d'Or earn the distinction of Laureat of Young Rabelais, awarded in Paris. Another biannual competition, the Mondial du Fromage, was established in Tours in 2013 and is structured similarly to the Concours National des Fromagers.

The highest accolade available to a cheesemonger in France is to be designated Un des Meilleurs Ouvriers de France (MOF) (one of the best crafts-man of France). Established in 1924 to encourage the development of artisanal craftspersons, there are many categories of MOF ranging from textiles to metalworkers, jewelers to farmers. The "Fromager" category was established in 2000. This prestigious competition is held every four years and consists of two stages of tests over a period of several months. Candidates are judged on such areas as the quality of their cheese selection, their competence in several aspects of setting a cheese case, creating a cheese preparation from a mystery box, blind tast-ings, cheese knowledge (AOP, legislation, history, etc.), and even discussing cheese in a foreign lan-guage (optional). Candidates must attain minimum marks to pass to the final level, and also in order to achieve the designation of Un des Meilleurs Ouvriers de France. This accreditation is recognized by the French national education system as the equiva-lent of a Bac +2, or a third-level degree. MOFs earn this title for life, and are exclusively permitted to use the designation professionally, and allowed to wear the signature red, white, and blue collar on their chef coat.

Since the 1950s the French have established con-fréries (brotherhoods) around cheese, whose mis-sion is to share a passion for and promote cheese. Inductions are conducted by high-ranking mem-bers in elaborate costumes, and inductees are often awarded medals of office and certificates suitable for framing. Meetings of confréries often include sumptuous dinners (including a cheese course), in-ductions of new members, and general conviviality among confrères. Principal among the confréries is the Confrérie de Chevaliers de Taste Fromage de France (Brotherhood of Knights of Cheese Tasters of France); individual cheeses have also established their own, including the Confrérie des Compagnons du Fromage Neufchâtel, Commanderie du Fromage de Sainte Maure, Confrérie des Taste Fromages de Langres, and Confrérie du Brie de Meaux.

Originally created in France, but now truly global, is the Guilde Internationale des Fromagers. The Guilde is similar to a French confrérie and was created in 1969 and now counts more than six thou-sand members from all domains of the cheese in-dustry: dairy farmers, cheesemakers, affineurs, whole-salers, and retailers. Its sister organization, La Confrérie de St. Uguzon is reserved for cheese lovers who do not work directly with cheese: pure aficionados, chefs, food scientists, journalists, and the like. The Guilde confers several ranks on its members; candi-dates must be proposed by two current members of the Guilde. See GUILDE INTERNATIONALE DES FROMAGERS.

In Italy the Organizzazione Nazionale Assagiatori Formaggi (ONAF; National Cheese Taster's Organ-ization) was founded in 1989 with the intention of creating a national registry of qualified professional cheese tasters, and to work toward establishing legal recognition of the title of taster. The ONAF pro-vides training and two levels of diplomas, based on mastering an understanding of cheese and profi-ciency in sensory analysis of cheese. The ONAF offers two levels of recognition: Neoassaggiatore (new taster) and Maestro Assagiatore (master taster).

In Japan the Japanese Cheese Professional Asso-ciation, founded in 2000, offers certification. As of 2015 some 2,679 people, both cheese professionals and passionate amateurs, have earned certification through sitting a two-hour written exam that com-bines open-response and fill-in-the-blank type ques-tions. Successful candidates earn the title of Comrade of Cheese. The association supports candidates by providing training sessions, and in 2016 published a textbook for study.

The American Cheese Society (ACS) created its Certified Cheese Professional (CCP) exam in 2012. In the United States the cheese industry had grown rapidly in recent decades, and the impetus behind the certification program was to ensure that cheese professionals were held to the highest stan-dards and followed industry best practices. The program provides a greater level of professionaliza-tion for individuals working in the cheese industry, and it has enhanced career opportunities and em-ployee retention rates across the industry. The exam is offered to cheese professionals demonstrating four thousand-plus hours of relevant experience with cheese. The multiple choice exam covers all domains of the cheese industry, and it is based firmly on practical knowledge. See AMERICAN CHEESE SOCIETY.

As of 2016 more than six hundred individuals in the United States, Canada, and Europe have received their certification via the American Cheese Society. Certification is valid for three years, at which time ACS CCPs must recertify by demonstrating continued professional development in the field. This qualification has proven to be highly attractive to employers, who often begin their talent search by checking the American Cheese Society's online directory of ACS CCPs.

With the consistent growth of cheese as part of the specialty food market worldwide, it is likely that additional accreditations will be developed in other countries.

See also CHEESE TASTINGS; COMPETITIONS; GUILDS; and SENSORY ANALYSIS.

American Cheese Society (United States). http://www.certifiedcheeseprofessional.org.
Certificat de Qualification Professionnelle (France). http://www.ifopca.fr/cqp-cremier-fromager-_r_18.html.
Commanderie du Fromage de Sainte Maure (France). http://www.fromage-saintemaure.confreries.org.
Concours Lyre d'Or (France). http://www.fromagersdefrance.com/content/download/3611/42499/version/1/file/2015_12_04+R%C3%A9glement+Lyre+d'Or+2016.pdf.
Concours National des Fromagers (France). http://www.sirha.com/concours-national-des-fromagers.
Confrérie de Chevaliers de Taste Fromage de France (France). http://www.confreriedutastefromagedefrance.com.
Confrérie des Compagnons du Fromage Neufchâtel (France). http://www.neufchatel-aoc.org/conf.
Confrérie des Taste Fromages de Langres (France). http://www.federation-grand-est.fr/langres/index.html.
Confrérie du Brie de Meaux (France). http://www.confreriedubriedemeaux.fr.
Guilde International des Fromagers (France). http://guildedesfromagers.com.
Japanese Cheese Professional Association (Japan). http://www.cheese-professional.com/2016/01.
Meilleur Ouvrier de France (France). http://www.meilleursouvriersdefrance.org/page/index/p/historique-des-mof/id/14; http://www.meilleursouvriersdefrance.org/page/referentiels-sujets/m/fromager/g/02/c/07.
Mondial du Fromage (France). http://www.cheese-tours.com/concours-fromager.html.
Organizzazione Nazionale Assaggiatori Formaggi (Italy). http://www.onaf.it.

Susan Page Sturman

acetic acid is a volatile two-carbon organic acid that is the main acid constituent of vinegar. In cheese, acetic acid along with carbon dioxide and diacetyl may be produced through the fermentation of citrate by *Leuconostoc* species and citrate-utilizing strains of *Lactococcus lactis* ssp. *lactis*. Acetic acid and diacetyl produced in this way contribute to the background aroma of ripened rennet-coagulated washed-curd cheeses such as Gouda, Edam, and Havarti, and fresh acid-coagulated cheeses such as quark, fromage frais, and cottage cheese. Acetic acid may also be produced in blue cheeses when citrate-fermenting starters are used to promote open texture in the ripening cheese through CO_2 production. In Alpine-style cheeses such as Emmentaler, the fermentation of lactate by *Propionibacterium freudenreichii* results in the production of acetic acid along with propionic acid and carbon dioxide.

The total concentrations and relative proportions of acetic and propionic acids are influenced by the metabolism of the specific propionibacteria strains present in the ripening cheese, which in turn affect flavor and aroma. For example, strains that possess strong aspartase activity generally grow to higher populations, ferment lactate more intensively to acetic and propionic acids, and produce more intense flavor in the cheese during ripening than strains with weak aspartase activity. Also, when aspartic acid accumulates in the cheese during ripening as a result of proteolysis, the fermentation of lactate becomes coupled to the fermentation of aspartic acid, which causes a shift in lactate fermentation toward the production of more acetic acid and CO_2 and less propionic acid. For acid-heat coagulated cheeses, acetic acid is also often used at the beginning of the fabrication as an acid source to trigger coagulation, and specifically has been shown to strongly affect the quality of some Latin American cheeses like queso blanco.

See also CARBON DIOXIDE and PROPIONIC ACID.

Farkye, Nana Y., et al. "Sensory and Textural Properties of Queso Blanco-Type Cheese Influenced by Acid Type." *Journal of Dairy Science* 78, no. 8 (1995): 1649–1656.

Fox, P. F., et al. *Fundamentals of Cheese Science.* Gaithersburg, Md.: Aspen, 2000.

McSweeney, P. L. H., ed. *Cheese Problems Solved.* Cambridge, U.K.: Woodhead, 2007.

Siapantas, L. G., and F. V. Kosikowski. "Properties of Latin-American White Cheese as Influenced by Glacial Acetic Acid." *Journal of Dairy Science* 50, no. 10 (1967): 1589–1591.

Paul Kindstedt

acidification refers to the drop in pH of milk, or cheese, as the result of the fermentation of lactose to lactic acid, or by the direct addition of acid to milk. Traditionally lactic acid bacteria present in raw milk were responsible for fermentation of lactose and the formation of lactic acid (microbial acidification). Warming raw milk facilitated the rapid growth of these bacteria. Industrial cheesemaking involves the addition of "defined" or selected strains of lactic acid bacteria called starter cultures; "starter" means to initiate the fermentation process. These bacteria have been selected based on important cheesemaking characteristics including: rapid growth in milk, resistance to phage (virus attack), and the production of desirable cheese flavor. Use of added starter cultures has the benefit of providing a consistent rate of acidification compared to the undefined microbiota present in raw milk. See STARTER CULTURES.

Starter growth is closely related to acid production, and the acidification rate during cheesemaking is influenced by parameters, such as the quantity of starter added to the cheese vat, strain of starter culture, temperature profile (with higher temperatures favoring faster acidification), washing or whey dilution of the curd (which removes some lactose and acid), and the total solids content of the milk (which influences buffering or the resistance to the change in pH, but may also increase the lactose content). Once the target pH (level of acidification) has been attained, the cheesemaker tries to limit further acidification by applying dry salt directly to the curd (usually chopped into small pieces to allow for faster uptake of salt), cooling the curd (e.g., by placing cheese in cold water or brine) or heating the curd to high temperature (a form of pasteurization) as in pasta filata type cheeses. See SALT; PASTEURIZATION; and PASTA FILATA.

The rate and extent of acidification is a critical quality parameter in cheesemaking and it must be closely monitored by the cheesemaker. Acidification is usually monitored by measuring titratable acidity (TA) and pH values at specific steps of the cheesemaking process. Both TA and pH measurements are complementary tools to efficiently monitor acidification during the process. See TITRATABLE ACIDITY MEASUREMENT and PH MEASUREMENT. Acidification impacts many essential cheese quality characteristics. The level of acidification of the milk strongly affects coagulation and moisture loss properties. Lower milk pH values (higher acidification) before adding coagulant result in faster coagulation times and a direct effect on the curd mineralization and ultimate moisture loss. The more acidification that occurs after cutting the coagulum the greater the syneresis (moisture loss) of the curd. Acidification also greatly impacts flavor and texture, with more acid cheeses tasting more acidic and tending to be crumbly and brittle while less acid (higher pH) cheese tends to be sweeter (milder) in taste and curdy and rubbery in texture. More acid production prior to whey drainage also causes considerable demineralization of calcium and phosphate from the caseins. See DEMINERALIZATION and CALCIUM PHOSPHATE. At the end of the acidification phase, the final pH of most cheese varieties ranges from 5.0 to 5.3, but some cheeses are much more acidic (e.g., cream, cottage, feta).

Cheeses can also be made by direct acidification, that is, no starter cultures are used, for example, in fresh mozzarella. Acids like acetic (vinegar) or citric acid (lemon juice) are the most common acids used for direct acidification. This approach has the benefit of a faster acidification process than waiting for starter cultures to ferment milk, and this technique also eliminates the risk of slow acidification during cheesemaking due to phage attack. However this approach is only used for cheese varieties that can be consumed fresh, such as string cheese. The finish pH values of these types of cheeses are often in the range of 5.4–5.9. See ACETIC ACID; FRESH CHEESES; and MOZZARELLA.

Acidification of milk can also be achieved by the addition of carbon dioxide (pressurized) gas, which dissolves in milk and forms carbonic acid. Carbon dioxide addition is mostly used to pre-acidify (cause a small reduction in pH) cheese milk prior to renneting. Glucono-delta-lactone powder has also been used to pre-acidify cheese milk; in an aqueous solution this powder dissolves to form gluconic acid.

See CARBON DIOXIDE and GLUCONO DELTA LACTONE.

Some fresh cheeses are coagulated by rennet addition but with minimal acidification, so that the finish pH values are often in the range of 6.0–6.4 (e.g., queso fresco, Panela). Acidification impacts the safety of cheese as pathogen growth is much slower at pH values less than 5.5. Lactic acid is inhibitory to most pathogens. Cheeses without significant acidification can be a food safety concern because if there is contamination then pathogens may grow (especially if the cheese is kept at temperatures higher than 41°F [5°C]).

Cheeses can also be made by adding acid to hot milk (e.g., queso blanco, ricotta, paneer). Some types of fresh cheeses, like cottage or cream, can be made without any rennet addition. At pH values close to 4.6 the caseins become attractive and sticky and coagulation occurs (due to the approach of the isoelectric point of the caseins).

Key steps on the process to control acidification and ultimately cheese quality are:

- Acidity of the milk, both as a raw ingredient and also before setting (coagulant addition)
- Acidity before draining
- Acidity of the green cheese or pH of the cheese after un-hooping.

See also LACTIC ACID and LACTIC ACID BACTERIA.

Fox, P. F., et al. *Fundamentals of Cheese Science.* Gaithersburg, Md.: Aspen, 2000.
Kosikowski, F. V., and V. V. Mistry. *Cheese and Fermented Milk Foods.* 3d ed. Westport, Conn.: F. V. Kosikowski, 1997.

John A. Lucey

Ackawi

See MIDDLE EAST.

adjunct cultures are cultures used in cheesemaking along with the main starter and ripening cultures to perform additional functions. For example, they can be used to accelerate milk acidification and cheese ripening, to improve cheese quality, to modulate or intensify cheese flavor, to reduce the development of undesirable microflora, and to provide health benefits. Many species of lactic acid

bacteria can be used as adjunct cultures. The adjunct cultures, which are expected to grow during the ripening process, are chosen from among the lactic acid bacteria species that spontaneously grow during cheese ripening, referred to as non-starter lactic acid bacteria. See NON-STARTER LACTIC ACID BACTERIA. This group includes, in particular, some *Lactobacillus* strains that are able to use alternative carbon sources to grow in cheese in the absence of residual lactose, and thus to reach populations above 10 million cells per gram of cheese.

Adjunct lactic acid bacteria have diverse enzymatic activities, such as amino acid conversion and esterase activity, among others, which can accelerate cheese ripening or affect the resulting flavor of the cheese. Some acidifying species of lactic acid bacteria can also be used as adjuncts. *Streptococcus thermophilus* and *Lactobacillus helveticus*, two thermophilic species of lactic acid bacteria used as starters in hard cheeses, can be used in addition to *Lactococcus lactis* as adjuncts in other cheese varieties. As adjunct cultures, *S. thermophilus* increases the rate of acidification of milk, and *L. helveticus* increases cheese proteolysis. *L. helveticus* grows during the first steps of manufacture, then dies and lyses, which leads to the release of its cellular content, including the enzymes. Some of these enzymes, such as peptidases, remain active in the cheese paste, where they accelerate the hydrolysis of large peptides into smaller peptides and free amino acids, thus enhancing flavor formation. In addition to lactic acid bacteria, other microbial species can be used as adjunct cultures to modulate or intensify cheese flavor, such as *Brevibacterium linens*, yeasts, and propionibacteria. See BREVIBACTERIUM LINENS and DAIRY PROPIONIBACTERIA.

Adjunct cultures also serve other purposes. For example, *Lactobacillus rhamnosus* and *Lactobacillus casei* are used as adjunct cultures by Swiss Emmentaler cheesemakers to control the activity of *Propionibacterium freudenreichii* and to prevent the "late fermentation" that produces opening defects (the formation of slits and cracks). Some adjunct strains are used to inhibit food-borne pathogens and food spoilage microorganisms. In particular, cultures of bacteria able to produce antifungal compounds in cheese are currently being investigated to inhibit or limit the growth of undesirable fungi on cheese. Adjunct cultures can also be used to bring specific health benefits to cheese, through the production of biologically active molecules such as bioactive peptides, gamma-aminobutyric acid, and vitamins. Adjuncts can also be probiotic microorganisms themselves, that is, "live microorganisms which when administered in adequate amounts confer a health benefit on the host," as defined by the Food and Agriculture Organization of the United Nations. Cheese has been shown to be a good carrier product to deliver living probiotic microorganisms, because it protects microorganisms during intestinal transit.

Thus, despite their name, "adjunct" cultures play an important role in the process of cheesemaking, producing a wide variety of effects that range from enhancing the flavor of cheese to increasing the health benefits of eating it.

See also RIPENING CULTURES and STARTER CULTURES.

Chamba, Jean-François, and Françoise Irlinger. "Secondary and Adjunct Cultures." In *Cheese: Chemistry, Physics, and Microbiology*, edited by Patrick F. Fox et al. Vol. 1: *General Aspects*, pp. 191–206. London: Elsevier, 2004.
Johnson, Mark E. "Mesophilic and Thermophilic Cultures Used in Traditional Cheesemaking." In *Cheese and Microbes*, edited by Catherine W. Donnelly, pp. 73–94. Washington, D.C.: ASM, 2014.
Ross, R. Paul, et al. "Novel Cultures for Cheese Improvement." *Trends in Food Science and Technology* 11 (2000): 96–104.

Anne Thierry

adulteration of cheese can and has taken many forms, although the incentive is always the same: to make greater profits by cheapening the product being sold.

Most commonly the milk with which the cheese is made is not what it seems. It may come from an animal different from the one advertised; or some of the milk may be replaced with water or various starches and fats (pizza "cheese" sometimes turns out to be cheese analogue made from vegetable oil and additives), or it may be dyed with toxic colorings (there was at least one nineteenth-century case of Double Gloucester dyed with red lead instead of annatto), or blatantly contaminated (in 2011 US Marshals seized rat-infested cheese from a Wisconsin dairy). See ANNATTO. One of the most flagrant forms of cheese adulteration was that perpetrated in the working-class food markets of the north of England in the mid-nineteenth century. In the dull light of Saturday night trade, consumers might be taken in by a "polished" cheese: a rotten old cheese made to look fresh by covering the cut surface with a layer of fresh cheese. Such a deception is easily revealed on closer inspection, whereas other cheese frauds may be harder to detect. *The Times of India* advises checking whether paneer is adulterated with starches by adding a drop of iodine solution: "if it changes color to blue-black, it is adulterated." The same test was advised for counterfeit cream by the German chemist Frederick Accum in 1820, which indicates that dairy fraud has remained depressingly constant in some respects for two centuries or more. Some of the methods of detection have become markedly more sophisticated in recent years, however. The unlawful addition of cheaper cow's milk to buffalo, sheep, and goat cheeses is a widespread fraud in Europe, particularly affecting the buffalo mozzarella industry of Italy and the feta of Greece. Food analysts have developed new techniques to uncover the presence of bovine milk involving the analysis of proteins and DNA.

Our concept of what counts as adulterated cheese is not fixed, but changes with alterations to the surrounding food culture and food laws. In the 1880s and 1890s consumers in both the United States and United Kingdom were outraged by the sale of a kind of "factitious" cheese variously known as "lard cheese" or "margarine cheese." These white hard cheeses were manufactured—apparently on a large scale—from skimmed milk with added lard or other fats to disguise the absence of cream. In 1890 a Liverpool trader called Wood was fined the modest sum of twenty shillings for selling lard cheese to a food inspector. Had he been alive today, Mr. Wood could have sold something similar openly and legally, calling it "processed cheese."

Accum, Frederick. *A Treatise on Adulterations of Food and Culinary Poisons*. Philadelphia: Abraham Small, 1820.
"Adulterated Cheese." *British Medical Journal* 1, no. 1528 (12 April 1890): 853.
Feligini, Maria, et al. "Detection of Adulteration in Italian Mozzarella Cheese Using Mitochondrial DNA Templates as Biomarkers." *Food Technology and Biotechnology* 43 (2005): 91–95.
Olmstead, Larry. "Most Parmesan Cheeses in America are Fake, Here's Why." *Forbes*, 19 December 2012.
Wilson, Bee. *Swindled: From Poison Sweets to Counterfeit Coffee, the Dark History of the Food Cheats*. London: John Murray, 2008.

Bee Wilson

advertising and promotion is not a standardized affair in the cheese world, but there are a number of different ways that cheesemakers and retailers may operate. A large chain grocery with hundreds of stores and a centralized marketing department may handle promotion differently than a single store with only cut-to-order cheese. In addition, stores tend to buy cheeses through a number of different sources—some direct, some through distributors, some from a centralized cheese warehouse—so the same store may have different promotional or advertising needs for cheeses that sit next to each other in the same cooler. Some of the terms and concepts common in promoting and advertising cheese in the United States follow.

Distributor Sales

A cheese distributor buys cheese from producers and then resells it wholesale to retailers and restaurants. Most cheese in the United States is sold through a distributor, and distributors tend to work regionally. Most distributors offer a weekly or monthly sale flyer to their wholesale customers with specified pricing for a given period of time. These are often produced far ahead of time to enable retail stores to create signs and displays in anticipation of lower prices and bigger sales. These lower prices are usually borne by the producer themselves though sometimes the distributor also lowers their margin.

Distributors use a variety of strategies to sell and promote cheese besides their monthly sales. Another way distributors do this is by facilitating cooperative advertising. Commonly referred to as "co-op dollars," this is an amount of money a producer offers to be included in a regularly produced newspaper ad or in-store promotional flyer. Usually specifications are required such as a photo of the product, company logo, certain sale price, etc. Although often not a lot of money individually, these co-op dollars add up to cover the cost of the flyer's publication, if not also contributing to the sale price of a product. Another part of a distributor's contract with a producer is the bill-back section. "Bill-backs" are used by distributors to promote cheese by giving away samples to retailers to entice them into buying cheese. Sometimes controversial if a distributor bills back more than the producer expects, this practice underlines that much of the cheese selling business is still a hands-on process. Most retailers want to taste cheese before bringing in a new product line.

Bill-backs are not to be confused with sample allowance, which is cheese specifically designated by producers for sampling to customers, either actively from a cheesemonger behind the counter or passively at a space set up for that purpose. This is cheese that is not expected to be sold, but instead to be given out to consumers as a means of advertising.

Brokers

Cheese companies will sometimes contract with a brokerage to employ an outside party to sell their cheese. Usually this is done when a company is located outside a region where they want to sell cheese (e.g., a New York company trying to sell cheese in the San Francisco Bay Area) or because that brokerage is seen as having a close relationship with a chain (e.g., Whole Foods) and hiring that brokerage is a way to get sales where they could not otherwise.

Brokers meet regularly with buyers to describe their whole line of products but are also available to act as go-betweens to gather information for retailers that they might need from a company. Often brokers create "sell-sheets" for their clients, a list of all pertinent facts that a retailer may use to decide whether to carry the cheese as well as how to promote it.

Milk Marketing Boards

Milk marketing boards (e.g., Wisconsin Milk Marketing Board) can also help organize and fund events promoting cheese made within their state lines. Milk marketing boards collect money from milk or cheese producers in order to help support all the dairy farmers of the state. They often fund television and radio ads including, for example, the "Got Milk?" series. See MILK MARKETING BOARDS.

In-Store Demos

Often a retailer will invite a producer to come into their store to promote their cheese directly to store customers. Depending on the size of the cheesemaker, this is usually done by a representative of the company itself or by a demo person whom they contract with for this purpose. Many feel that this kind of personal touch, especially when coming from a local cheesemaker, creates a bond between the consumer and producer. This relationship, once formed, is hard to break. One might think of an in-store demo as a minifarmers' market in terms of personal contact. It also helps a cheesemaker build or further a relationship with the store buyer or cheesemonger.

Trust Relationships

Many promotions and sales rely on personal contacts. Retailers will buy cheeses they cannot sample beforehand if they know they can trust their sales representative or cheese producer. In turn, some cheese promotion, especially in smaller shops and independent stores, is done simply because there is a personal contact between cheesemonger and cheese producer, or because a cheesemonger wants to promote something he or she values, such as a struggling local producer. In this case cheese may be promoted even though the retailer's profit margin suffers in the short-term. Contacts like this are often made at annual events like the American Cheese Society Conference or local events like farmers' markets. See AMERICAN CHEESE SOCIETY.

Social Media

As with the rest of society, cheesemakers and retail outlets increasingly use social media to promote cheese. Hand in hand with this, and almost nonexistent around 2005, many cheese companies now ship directly to consumers, which means that a social media presence can bring intangible return in the form of cheese sold at retail, instead of wholesale, price. Additionally, cheesemakers and retailers have also used social media to draw in consumers in ways previously unheard of, including sending out samples of experimental cheese and asking for feedback.

Dahl, Gary. "Boosting Your Budget with Co-op Programs." In *Advertising for Dummies*. 2d ed., pp. 33–40. Hoboken, N.J.: Wiley, 2007.
Sowerwine, Alyssa. "E-commerce Boosts Customer Reach and Holiday Promotions." *Cheese Market News*, 14 December 2012.

Gordon Edgar

affinage

See MATURING.

Afuega'l Pitu is a soft cheese made in Asturias (northern Spain) that is considered to be one of the oldest Spanish cheeses. The name "Afuega'l Pitu" means "choking cake" in the Asturian dialect, because its unusual texture makes the cheese stick to the palate. The cheese is made from whole cow's milk through a lactic coagulation, having a variable degree of ripening from fresh to mid-ripened.

Afuega'l Pitu has been protected with a Denomination of Origin since 2004 (Commission Regulation (EC) No. 723/2008). Nowadays the PDO designation protects a production of 280,550 gallons (1.062 million liters) of milk per year that are transformed into approximately 302,033 pounds (137,000 kilograms) of cheese. Milk is coagulated at 72–90°F (22–32°C) over fifteen to twenty hours using very small amounts of calf rennet (2–5 milliliters per 220 pounds [100 kilograms] milk). Ripening takes place at 39–59°F (4–15°C) and 75–85 percent relative humidity.

There are different varieties recognized by their form and shape, the ingredients added, and the aging period. The cheese called "de trapu" or "de trapo" has a piriform shape with folds marked on its surface due to the cloth used for whey draining and molding and weighs approximately 1 pound (500 grams). The variety called "atroncau" or "atroncado" has a characteristic shape similar to an inverted flowerpot and weighs approximately half a pound (250 grams). If paprika is added during the cheesemaking process the cheese may be called "roxu" or "rojo" (red) versus the plain variety of the product called "blancu" or "blanco" (white). In addition to these types, the length of time for which the cheese has been aged also defines its varieties such as cured, semi-cured, or soft.

The briefly ripened cheeses have a white, soft, and rough rind; in those ripened, the rind is moist, yellowish brown in color and with moldy blue or white areas. The taste is lactic, slightly sour and salted in the fresh or hardly ripened cheeses, and becomes strong and spicy as the ripening progresses.

See also SPAIN.

Cuesta, Paloma, et al. "Evolution of the Microbiological and Biochemical Characteristics of Afuega'l Pitu Cheese During Ripening." *Journal of Dairy Science* 79, no. 10 (October 1996): 1693–1698.
Martínez, Sidonia, et al. "The Spanish Traditional Cheeses: Characteristics and Scientific Knowledge." In *Handbook of Cheese, Production, Chemistry and*

Sensory Properties, edited by Enrique Castelli and Luiz du Vale, pp. 123–167. New York: Nova Science, 2013.

Javier Carballo

aging

See MATURING.

ago

See NEEDLES.

An **alcohol** is an organic compound in which an oxygen atom is bonded to a hydrogen atom and a carbon atom; the carbon atom, in turn, is bonded to other hydrogen and/or carbon atoms. Alcohols are considered the most important aroma compounds in mold-ripened cheeses along with methyl ketones, which are metabolized by microorganisms into secondary alcohols (where the oxygen is bonded to a carbon atom that has two other carbons attached to it). See METHYL KETONES. Alcohols in cheese originate from microbial metabolism of amino acids, fatty acids, and lactose. The most common alcohols in cheese include 3-methylbutanol, which imparts alcoholic and floral notes; 2-heptanol and 2-nonanol, which are responsible for a herbaceous odor; 2-phenylethanol, a product of metabolism of the amino acid phenylalanine and having a rosy aroma; and 1-octen-3-ol, whose mushroom aroma can be detected at a concentration of ten parts per billion. The concentration of secondary alcohols in a cheese might be influenced by the amount of yeast growth on the cheese, since the yeasts appear to actively reduce methyl ketones to secondary alcohols.

Camembert and similar varieties are especially noted for containing the secondary alcohols 2-heptanol, 2-nonanol, and 2-phenylethanol, which are produced by *Penicillium* spp. The alcohol 1-octen-3-ol, which results from the breakdown of 18-carbon fatty acids, has also been identified as important in Brie and Camembert as well as in Grana Padano, Gorgonzola, and mozzarella. Water buffalo's milk contains 55 parts per billion of volatile alcohols, about as much as milk from cows, goats, and sheep combined. See WATER BUFFALO. Mozzarella di bufala therefore has higher levels of alcohols than mozzarella made from bovine milk. In the blue cheese

category, yeasts are capable of reducing methyl ketones to secondary alcohols. Yeasts also may play a role in blue cheese flavor by producing ethanol and other alcohols as well as certain esters, a class of compounds that impart fruity aromas. The two simplest alcohols, methanol and ethanol, are also degradation products present in small amounts in aged cheese. A few varieties of cheese are washed in beer or wine and therefore contain much more ethanol.

See also FUNGI.

Anderson, Dale Fredrick. "Flavor Chemistry of Blue Cheese." PhD Diss., Oregon State University, 1965. http://hdl.handle.net/1957/26788.
Molimard, P., and H. E. Spinnler. "Review: Compounds Involved in the Flavor of Surface Mold-Ripened Cheeses: Origins and Properties." *Journal of Dairy Science* 79 (February 1996): 169–184.

Michael Tunick

aligot is a peasant dish from Auvergne, a region of mountains, steep river valleys, and pastureland in central France. It is a dish of mashed potatoes, cheese, and usually garlic. Cattle graze the high pastures, which are dotted with *burons*, stone huts where, until some decades ago, the herdsmen lived during the summer months, milking the cows twice a day and making cheese. See BURON.

The cheese, now made in creameries, is Cantal (which is also the name of the département). The young cheese, tomme fraîche de Cantal, which is not unlike mozzarella in texture, is the cheese used in aligot and other local dishes. Most of the cheese is matured longer to produce Cantal doux (young and creamy), entre deux (between the two, a cheese with a light bite), and vieux (old, a fine, tangy cheese).

The classic recipe for aligot uses floury potatoes mashed with milk, butter, garlic, and pepper. The cheese is thinly sliced and beaten into the potatoes over heat. The amount of cheese varies; it may be half the amount of potato, or as much cheese as potato for a very rich aligot. Some versions include butter and cream. Salt is added and the mixture is beaten vigorously until the cheese runs. When pulled on a spatula, it can form strands up to 7 feet (2 meters) or longer. When it reaches this stage the aligot must be eaten at once, on its own or to accompany the local sausages or bacon.

It is often the men who make aligot because of the muscle power needed to beat it well, particularly if it is made in the large quantities needed to serve it at traditional weddings or village festivals. Aligot is also the name sometimes given to the tomme fraîche.

See also AUVERGNE and CANTAL.

Couffignal, Huguette. *La cuisine Paysanne*. Paris: Solar, 1976.
Graham, Peter. *Classic Cheese Cookery*. Harmondsworth, U.K.: Penguin, 1988.

Jill Norman

alkaline phosphatase (ALP) is an enzyme

that is present in the milk of all mammals at levels that vary considerably among species and among animals. Generally, ALP activity in milk is in the following order: (1) sheep, (2) cow, and (3) goat.

The occurrence of ALP in milk was first discovered in the early to mid-1900s when it was shown that the time–temperature combinations required for its thermal inactivation were slightly more severe than those required to kill *Mycobacterium tuberculosis*, then the target microorganism and subsequently *Coxiella burnetii*, the current target organism for adequate pasteurization of milk. The enzyme is readily assayed, and a test procedure based on ALP inactivation was developed as a routine quality control test for the confirmation of (continuous high temperature short time (HTST)—162°F [72°C] × 16 seconds or batch low temperature long time (LTLT)—145°F [63°C] × 30 minutes) pasteurization of milk. The significance of ALP activity in milk is due to its universal use as an index for adequate and correct HTST pasteurization.

Fluid milk and milk products that have ALP activity below the legal limit (i.e., <1 milligram phenol per milliliter in pasteurized milk by the Schaar rapid method, <350 mU of ALP per liter of fluid milk products, and <500 mU for other products by the fluorometric or equivalent method) are considered to be adequately pasteurized and safe for consumption. The US Food and Drug Administration's guidelines for screening cheese for residual ALP activity stipulates a negative test to ensure adequate pasteurization of milk used for the manufacture of cheese. However, the ability of the ALP assay to effectively discriminate the presence of microbial versus bovine ALP in cheeses has been questioned because certain cheeses made from pasteurized milk using certain starter cultures were shown to test positive for ALP.

See also ENZYMES; MILK; and PASTEURIZATION.

Rankin, S. A., A. Christiansen, W. Lee, et al. "Invited Review: The Application of Alkaline Phosphatase Assay for Validation of Milk Product Pasteurization." *Journal of Dairy Science* 93, no. 12 (2010): 5538–5551.
Shakeel-ur-Rehman and N. Y. Farkye. "Enzymes Indigenous to Milk Phosphatases." In *Encyclopedia of Dairy Sciences*, 2d ed., Vol. 1, edited by Hubert Roginsky, John W. Fuquay, and Patrick F. Fox, et al., pp. 314–318. Amsterdam: Academic Press, 2003.

Nana Y. Farkye

The **Alkmaar auction** is the most famous of the five traditional cheese markets that flourished in the Holland countryside from the late Middle Ages, the others being Edam, Gouda, Hoorn, and Woerden. From its humble beginnings in 1365 when the rural market center of Alkmaar owned one pair of cheese scales only, to the official opening of the market as a weekly event in 1593, to the expansion of the scales to four pairs in 1612, to the establishment of the cheese carriers guild in 1619, and the repeated enlargement of the weigh house square across the sixteenth and seventeenth centuries, Alkmaar grew to be a vital participant in the commercial expansion that undergirded the so-called Dutch "golden age." Re-enactments of the market continue to the present on Friday mornings in the summer season in the square occupied by the beautiful weigh house and its late medieval mechanical clock. The summer market attracts thousands of visitors annually who come to taste the renowned local cheese and enjoy the early modern costumes and the carrying of the traditional wooden cheese barrows, each weighing up to about 287 pounds (130 kilograms) when loaded with eight full cheeses.

The first archival mention of the weigh house structure dates from 1408, by which time Alkmaar already served as the central distribution point for cheese from across the whole northern quarter of Holland (the *Noorderkwartier*) including the islands of Texel and Wieringen. Although it only had a population of just over ten thousand inhabitants (one-tenth the size of contemporary Amsterdam), in recognition of its economic importance Alkmaar secured for itself formal town privileges at the time of the Reformation and the liberation of northern

Holland from Spanish rule in the 1580s. It was also admitted to membership in the States General during this brief moment of political openness when twelve more towns were able to join the original six that had constituted the national governing body prior to the revolt against Spain.

The period of steepest growth of the total volume of cheese produced in the North Holland countryside was during the sixteenth and early seventeenth centuries, consistent with the extensive polderization (land reclamation) of the surrounding countryside in the same period. Alkmaar was adamant that the newly built roads and major drainage canals of the reclaimed areas be constructed so as to maximize the ease of transport to their market. Nevertheless, the total geographic scope of the Alkmaar market actually shrunk over this same period as a network of additional rural markets emerged to process the huge increases in total Holland dairy production. Even without the monopoly privileges hoped for by the town burghers, the total volume of cheese sold in the Alkmaar auction amounted to between 6 and 7 million pounds annually over the course of the eighteenth century. One notable exception is the difficult period from 1744 to about 1750 in the wake of a major epizootic that devastated the dairy herds. Such periods of steep declines in production could be particularly devastating for the national economy as approximately 20 percent of Dutch milk production was exported and dairy products accounted for half of total agricultural exports. As an indication of the importance of this trade it is worth noting that even during the difficult war years of 1803–1809 butter and cheese exports continued to bring in more than 6 million guilders in annual revenue. Dairy production remains to this day the largest sector of the national agricultural economy, with the cheese sold at Alkmaar a major contributor to Dutch tourism as well.

See also NETHERLANDS.

deVries, Jan. *The Dutch Rural Economy in the Golden Age, 1500–1700*. New Haven, Conn.: Yale University Press, 1974.

deVries, Jan, and Ad van der Woude. *The First Modern Economy: Success, Failure, and Perseverance of the Dutch Economy, 1500–1815*. Cambridge, U.K.: Cambridge University Press, 1997.

Price, J. L. *Holland and the Dutch Republic in the Seventeenth Century: The Politics of Particularism*. Oxford: Clarendon, 1994.

Anne McCants

Alléosse is a cheese shop that has been located in the heart of the rue Poncelet food market, in the 17th arrondissement of Paris, since it first opened its doors for business in 1984. Today husband and wife team Philippe and Rachel Alléosse pride themselves on having one of the city's most extensive affinage sites, with four cheese caves at over 300 square meters. For customers this translates into an array of over two hundred different cheeses from all over France, about three-quarters of which are skillfully aged by Phillippe Alléosse, the owner and master fromager. Alléosse's craftsmanship comes across in his aged Comté, Brie aged with truffles, and Camembert with Calvados.

Alléosse specializes in washed-rind cheeses, which are brushed or sprayed with a solution, usually salt, as they mature. Alléosse uses the renowned salt from Guérande, which, when added to butter, delivers a slight taste of caramel. This technique produces a cheese with a richer flavor profile. In addition to the classics of this cheese genre such as Époisse, Munster, and Livarot, Alléosse carries some harder to find ones: the pungent and lusciously oozy Welsche is an Alsatian cow's milk cheese aged from four to six weeks, and rubbed with a potent eau de vie from Gewurztraminer. See WASHED-RIND CHEESES.

The shop makes its own variation of the blue cheese Fourme d'Ambert that it calls Mystère d'Ambert. It is layered with grapes and walnuts from Quercy, a region in southwestern France just north of Toulouse. Its balance of sweet and savory makes it an ideal choice for those looking for a softer introduction to blues. See FOURME D'AMBERT.

See also CHEESEMONGER; FRANCE; and MATURING.

Alléosse. http://fromage-alleosse.com.

Coffe, Jean-Pierre. "Fromage ou pas Fromages." *Paris Match*, 1 February 2015.

Pytel, Gilbert. "Les dix meilleurs fromagers de Paris." *L'Express*, 22 October 2015. http://www.lexpress.fr/styles/saveurs/les-dix-meilleurs-fromagers-de-paris_1719820.html.

Max Shrem

Allgäuer Bergkäse

See BERGKÄSE and GERMANY.

Allgäuer Emmentaler

See EMMENTALER and GERMANY.

alpage is a significant aspect of the dairy world, particularly for cheesemakers in the lofty terrain of the Alps, Pyrenees, and Jura mountain ranges. A French word meaning "mountain pasture," *alpage* can refer to both a place—high alpine grazing meadows—as well as the range of wild grasses, flowers, and brush that ruminants feed on in such high-altitude meadows. (In German, the corresponding word is *alpwirtschaft*; in Italian it's *alpeggio*.)

Alpage includes a vast family of botanicals growing in pastures as high as 9,200 feet. Beyond that, the terrain is generally not suitable for the seasonal migration (a.k.a. the transhumance) of domestic ruminants and their keepers to the alpage, from their homesteads in the valley. See TRANSHUMANCE. Each summer, as the alpine snow line retreats, shepherds typically move their animals to successively higher locations up the mountainside to feed on the new green fodder. Their eating requires

transience; some pastures are good for only a few days although others provide months of grazing. Meanwhile, the animals themselves influence the alpage composition by favoring certain plants and avoiding others. As a result, over time these high mountain meadows have developed a local flavor that shows up in dairy products, especially cheese and butter.

A cheesemaker who follows this age-old pattern of seasonal mountain dairying, turning the daily supply of alpine milk into wheels of handmade cheese in a remote creamery, is called an *alpagiste*. They're a rare and diminishing breed as modern transportation increasingly favors the delivery of alpine milk to a central co-op for processing.

Alpage began as a strategy for land use by early farmers; by default the rocky, steep terrain, and short growing season of mountain pastures became dairy zones. Moving animals to alpine meadows in the summer also allowed the farmers to use their fields in the valley to grow hay for winter feed. But the advantages of alpage feeding are not only agricultural. They're also gastronomic. With higher elevation, the intensity of sunshine increases, causing alpine plants to process a greater amount of energy.

Cows grazing on alpage in the Allgäu region of southwestern Germany. These high-altitude meadows have a range of wild grasses, flowers, and brush that ruminants feed on. © KATE ARDING

As a result, their protein and fat content is higher. Animals adapt in a similar way. Alpine living requires more of their energy for grazing, which results in less milk output—but of a higher quality. Milk from the alpage is richer and creamier with 15 to 30 percent more fat and solids than milk from the same cow fed in the valley. Alpine plants also have a greater percentage of essential oils, which can improve animal digestion and boost the aroma and flavor in milk products. All combined, these unique characteristics of milk from the alpage have given rise to some of the world's first and most beloved alpine cheeses, such as Gruyère, Comté, and Emmentaler.

More recently, the subject of alpage has become one of concern, related to global warming. As plants native to southern regions are being driven by unprecedented heat to take root in higher, cooler terrain, farmers are now seeing a gradual shift in alpine flora. As the alpage changes, experts contend, traditional cheese flavors will be affected.

Davies, Sasha, and David Bleckmann. *The Cheesemaker's Apprentice: An Insider's Guide to the Art and Craft of Homemade Artisan Cheese.* Beverly, Mass.: Quarry, 2012.
Orland, Barbara. "Alpine Milk: Dairy Farming as a Pre-modern Strategy of Land Use." *Environment and History* 10, no. 3 (August 2004): 327–364.

Elaine Khosrova

Alp cheesemaking has been undertaken in the Alps, a mountain chain meandering through eight middle European countries, for many centuries, undergoing modifications influenced by wider social changes and disasters such as the Great Plague.

Historically, even before the Roman invasion in the first century B.C.E., sour cheeses, produced without rennet and simply by letting the goat's or sheep's milk sour in its specific environment, were a food staple of the Alps. See SOUR SKIMMED-MILK CHEESES. After the plague killed about one-third of the Swiss population during the fourteenth century, many labor-intensive fields that had been cultivated to grow grain were converted into pastures and dairy operations. The steep mountain regions that had traditionally been grazed by sheep and goats saw an influx of dairy cattle. The consequent surplus of milk was used for cheesemaking, which, due to the earlier Roman influence, now happened by using rennet as a coagulant.

The Catholic Church supported the trend toward more and better cheese production by loosening its strict rules regarding dairy and allowing cheese and butter to be consumed in the regions north of the Alps during Lent. The Reformation led to further relaxation of dairy rules, making cheese even more popular. Cheese made using rennet had more and apparently better flavor than sour cheeses, leading to greater demand. It could also be stored for much longer and was easy to transport; during the sixteenth century Alpine cheese became a lucrative export product. Owing to its durability Alpine cheeses became staples on large ships that crossed the oceans over several weeks, becoming one of Switzerland's first and most important exports. See SWITZERLAND.

Defining "Alp" and "Alp Cheese"

An Alp is a high mountain pasture onto which farmers move their animals up to graze for a period of three to four months over the summer. During this time the farmers stay with and care for their animals (or hire workers to do this). This switching of places in accordance with the seasons is called transhumance. See TRANSHUMANCE. One-third of Switzerland's agricultural lands are located in the Alps, although Alpine cheesemaking occurs as well in the mountainous regions of eastern France, northern Italy, Bavaria, and parts of Austria.

Only cheeses produced during the limited time up on the Alp, and on the same soil the animals are grazing on, can be designated Alp cheeses, alpage, or alpeggio. Despite fewer and fewer farmers committing to the demanding tasks and circumstances of transhumance there were still about 15,000 people working on roughly 7,200 Swiss Alps in 2013.

Legal Structure of the Alps

In Switzerland Alp meadows are legally organized in one of three ways, and—with small variations—this is handled more or less the same way in the surrounding Alpine countries:

- Privately owned. The farmer owns the piece(s) of land on which he (transhumance is traditionally practiced by men) is summering. He is the sole proprietor of all produced goods. Fifty-four percent of the 7,200 Swiss Alps belonged to this category in 2013.

- Community owned. A political entity (village, canton, historic precedent by named citizens of a town, etc.) owns the seasonally used meadows. Each meadow is assigned a certain number of grazing rights and each co-owner receives a percentage of this total number (based on wealth, historical rights, and such). The entity decides who is in charge of moving up with the animals, tending to them and the land, cheesemaking, etc. The profits are divided according to the amount of milk the specific animals have produced. About 33 percent of all Alps in Switzerland are structured this way.
- Cooperative. Farmers choose to work together as a group. Only about 13 percent of all Swiss Alps are operated cooperatively, and they are the ones that function with the most self-established rules. The land might belong to one or more farmers, the group members might take equal turns in taking care of business or simply send their animals up for the summer with another group member. The revenue is split depending on who contributed or used services and products to what extent.

Production Place

Just like the houses in which the farmers (and sometimes their families and helpers) live on their Alp, the production areas in which the cheeses are made vary from case to case, and sometimes drastically. There are Alps with modern, rebuilt chalets and separate dairy buildings with state of the art equipment. There are houses that consist of a single room in which the people make cheese over a wood fire, eat, sleep, and age their cheese. And there is everything in between. Depending on the size of the herd a farmer brings up on the Alp, and on the person-power and the efficiency of the production and aging area, some teams produce thousands of wheels each summer while others make a single wheel per day.

Not all farmers stay on the same Alp and work in the same production place throughout the whole duration of their Alp season. Many move their herd to one Alp first and, once late spring turns to summer, switch to another Alp located at a higher altitude. The cheeses are always produced where the animals live and graze.

The animals not only deliver the base material for Alp cheeses, the milk, they also play an important role in maintaining the health of the soil and the rich variety of flora and soil as they graze the steep pastures. Having a herd on a steep pasture guarantees the maintenance of a healthy, variety-rich flora and soil.

Alp Cheeses

Some of the very first Alp cheeses produced with the help of rennet were Sbrinz and Gruyère. See SBRINZ and GRUYÈRE. Even today these two distinguish themselves from most other Alp cheeses by their significantly larger size and weight. Alp cheeses, because they have to be easy to transport and somewhat sturdy, usually weigh between 9 and 18 pounds (4 and 8 kilograms). They are semihard and hard cheeses with firm, protecting natural rinds that have the capacity to age gracefully and become more flavorful over time. Any type of rennet can be used, as well as any kind of milk, although cow's milk cheeses are by far the most common.

Alp pastures are composed of more than one hundred different grasses, herbs, and flowers, whereas grazing areas in the lower land contain fewer than two dozen. The composition of the flora also changes throughout the three to four months the animals feed on it. Thus the flavor, and even the color, of Alp cheeses can vary between batches. Different weather conditions such as heavy rains or unusual cold or heat also influence the outcome of Alp cheeses.

In Switzerland, Alp cheeses are marked with a special logo. The following alpages also are AOP (appellation d'origine protégée, or name-protected) cheeses and therefore have to be crafted according to their specific requirements: Alpensbrinz AOP, Berner Alp- und Hobelkäse AOP, Formaggio d'Alpe Ticinese AOP, L'Etivaz Alpage AOP, Le Gruyère d'Alpage AOP, and Vacherin Fribourgeois d'Alpage AOP, Bloder- und Sauerkaese Alpage AOP, Raclette Alpage AOP, Glarner Alpkaese AOP.

At the beginning of 2016 the Schweizerischer Alpwirtschaftlicher Verband (SAV)—a national organization that controls and supports the tradition, profitability, and marketing of Alpine products and thus transhumance as a whole—published new guidelines for the production of Swiss Alp cheeses. They include HACCP plans, regular testing, log keeping, etc. and are regarded as the new expected standards according to which Alp production places and goods are inspected and rated.

See also ALPAGE and ALP-STYLE CHEESES.

Felten, Beate, and Birgit Lamerz-Beckschäfer. *Käse*. Cologne: DuMont-Buchverlag, 1994.

Flammer, Dominik, and Fabian Scheffold. *Schweizer Käse*. Munich: AT-Verlag, 2010.

Grimm, Hans-Ulrich. "Kühe auf Diät." *Der Stern*, 17 October 2009.

Jakob, E., et al. "Käse, ein wertvolles Lebensmittel." *ALP forum* 66 (2008): 1–20.

Knecht, Andreas, and Armando Pipitone. *Käse & Wein*. Lenzburg, Switzerland: Fona Verlag, 2011.

Walther, B., et al. "Cheese in Nutrition and Health." *Dairy Science & Technology* 88 (2008): 389–405.

Westermair, Thomas. "Omega-3-Fettsäuren und konjugierte Linolsäure—Fakten und Möglichkeiten." *Deutsche Molkereizeitung* 17 (2006): 29–31.

Caroline Hostettler

boned animals, with dairy character that do not tend toward excess body weight. Alpines are a natural breed choice for cheese production since they give large volumes of milk with moderate butterfat and milk solids. Production volumes are excellent, with an outstanding and even lactation curve. Alpines are such good milk producers that many of them can be milked for multiple years after a single birth.

See also GOAT.

Considine, Stephen. "Dr. Charles Petit DeLangle, M.D." *United Caprine News*, May 2010.

Crepin, Joseph. *La Chèvre*. Philo, Calif.: Mountain House, 1990. English translation from French, originally published Paris: Librairie Hachette et Cie, 1918.

Jennifer Bice

The **Alpine** dairy goat comes from France, and in the United States it is also called the French Alpine. Charles Petit DeLangle was born in France and, after coming to live in the United States in 1922, imported the large group of French Alpines that would go on to provide the genetics of the Alpines of today. The Alpine dairy goat has upright ears and a straight nose. They come in a variety of recognized color patterns with French name descriptions, and their hair is fine and short.

Alpines are a good choice for the commercial producer since they are hardy, robust, and thrive in all climates. They are medium to large in size, flat-

Alpine goats are a French breed known for their excellent milk production, long lactation period, and the relatively low fat content of their milk. © REDWOOD HILL FARM

Alp-style cheeses originated in Switzerland and eastern France in remote village valleys extending high into the mountains as early as the first century C.E. Winters were long and harsh, making it difficult for people to produce enough food during summer to carry them through the colder months. Difficult terrain and a short growing season made Alpine meadows unsuitable for crop production. But they did support lush grasses and abundant water sources, making them ideal for mountainside grazing and cheesemaking. Initially, grazing and cheesemaking were restricted to lower, easily accessible meadows. Then the practice of pastoral transhumance allowed animals to follow the lush meadows up the mountainside as the snow receded. This provided access to lush, terpene-rich grasses and wild flowers. It also created a need for cooperative farming and cheesemaking. Since cows now spent the summer in remote Alpine meadows, small farmers combined their animals into a single herd. In addition, cheesemaking chalets needed to be built at different altitudes. See TRANSHUMANCE.

Today cheeses made in these chalets are called alpage. See ALPAGE. Alpage cheeses are made in the summertime, while the cows are in transhumance grazing on the Alpine pastures. Originally, all the equipment and supplies for cheesemaking, including salt, had to be hauled up the mountain (creating an incentive to use salt sparingly, which explains the characteristic low salt content of Alpine cheese). Once the cheeses were made, they had to be hard and somewhat elastic so that they would not break as they were transported down to market. They also had to be large, because it was more efficient to carry a few large cheeses down the mountain than it was to carry several smaller cheeses. And finally, they had to have a long shelf life so that they could provide nourishment through the long, harsh winters, and later, make it through long journeys to distant export markets. See SHELF LIFE.

Large size, durability, and long shelf life meant that Alpine cheese had to be low in moisture. But the fresh cow's milk with which it was made did not have the time to undergo extensive microbial growth, and thus produced little lactic acid, which aids in the expulsion of whey. Salt also promotes the expulsion of whey, but the necessity to use it sparingly only made the problem worse. Cheesemakers have taken several steps to overcome this problem. First, the curds are cut into tiny rice-size pieces, which vastly increases the surface area for whey expulsion. Then the curds are cooked at very high temperatures (around 125°F [52°C]) for an extended period of time while constantly being stirred. This also causes curd shrinkage and whey expulsion. Finally, after the curd is in a mold, external pressure is applied to the cheese, causing even more whey removal, as well as creating a tight-knit structure and a closed rind.

Slow acid production creates a cheese with high mineral content, specifically, calcium phosphate, and contributes to its firm and elastic texture. The low acidity (or high pH) also contributes to the characteristic elastic texture, as well as to the distinctive sweet notes of Alpine cheese. This, along with a sparing use of salt, has the potential to support the growth of *Propionibacterium shermanii*. This bacterium affects flavor and produces carbon dioxide, causing round holes, or eyes. See DAIRY PROPIONIBACTERIA and EYES. Low acidity also supports aerobic bacteria, such as *Brevibacterium linens*, which also distinctly affects flavor. *B. linens*, along with other microorganisms and surface-ripening bacteria, plus a brine solution, make up what French affineurs call "morge"—a salty slurry used to wash the cheeses during ripening to create the characteristic rind and flavor of Alpine cheeses. See BREVIBACTERIUM LINENS and MORGE. The extent to which these organisms flourish during aging and influence the final character of the cheese depends on the conditions during aging and the actions of the cheesemaker or affineur. Examples of Alpine cheese are Emmentaler, Gruyère, Comté, Beaufort, Fontina, and Appenzeller.

See also ALP CHEESEMAKING; APPENZELLER; BEAUFORT; COMTÉ; EMMENTALER; FONTINA VAL D'AOSTA; and GRUYÈRE.

Kindstedt, Paul. "The Rhyme and Reason of Cheese Diversity: The Old World Origins." In *American Farmstead Cheese*, edited by Paul Kindstedt and the Vermont Cheese Council, pp. 1–16. White River Junction, Vt.: Chelsea Green, 2005.
Kinstedt, Paul. "The Manor, the Monastery, and the Age of Cheese Diversification." In *Cheese and Culture*, pp. 116–157. White River Junction, Vt.: Chelsea Green, 2012.
McCalman, Max, and David Gibbons. "A Taste of Cheese History." In *Mastering Cheese: Lessons for Connoisseurship from a Maître Fromager*, pp. 28–51. New York: Clarkson Potter, 2009.

Adam Moskowitz

Altenburger Ziegenkäse

See GERMANY.

ambient storage of cheese, meaning cheese stored without refrigeration, has been an aspiration of retailers for many years. The quality, safety, and legality of ambient storage are largely determined by compositional characteristics (salt and moisture content, pH value). As these vary considerably between hard and soft cheeses, ambient storage is only feasible for hard cheese. Parmesan is probably the most robust of cheeses, so retailers can cut and wrap this cheese at the counter from displays outside the refrigerated display unit. To extend this service to varieties such as traditional farmhouse Cheddar or Gruyère, a retailer must understand how the cheese deteriorates at the higher display temperatures, and can gain this knowledge from a shelf life trial that investigates quality characteristics and confirms product safety.

How to Conduct a Shelf Life Trial

Cheese wedges are cut and wrapped according to the intended retail procedure, then stored. A regime that might provide useful information might be five to ten days, either at a continuous 39°F (4°C) or 68°F (20°C) or in a cycling profile of 39°F (4°C)/10 hours plus 68°F (20°C)/14 hours. Wedges are examined for organoleptic quality (appearance, aroma, flavor, texture) and any abnormalities at the start of the trial. They are then examined daily throughout storage for organoleptic quality and overt spoilage by yeasts and molds. For microbiological safety, cheeses are sampled at two-day intervals and tested for the major bacterial pathogens.

Likely Outcomes

Ambient storage is only appropriate for hard cheese. During ambient storage, well-made farmhouse hard cheese is likely to show deterioration of organoleptic quality before it becomes microbiologically hazardous. Combinations of defects, such as darkening in color, oil on the cheese surface, moisture beneath the wrapping, and mold growth might be expected. Although ambient storage during retail display is commercial practice in some countries, it can accelerate deterioration of organoleptic quality and reduce shelf life.

See also SHELF LIFE.

Alabdulkarim, Badriah, Shaista Arzoo, and Fadia Youssef Abdel Megeid. "Quality Characteristics of Traditional Hard Cheese (Oggtt) Packaged in Different Packaging Materials and Stored at Ambient and Refrigeration Temperature." *World Applied Sciences Journal* 21, no. 4 (2013): 593–598.
Bishop, Jay Russell, and Marianne Smukowski. "Storage Temperatures Necessary to Maintain Cheese Safety." *Food Protection Trends* 26, no. 10 (2006): 714–724.

Paul Neaves

American cheese

See PASTEURIZED PROCESS CHEESES.

The **American Cheese Society** (ACS) is

the leading organization promoting and supporting American cheeses. The society provides educational and networking opportunities, and engages with consumers, media, and regulatory authorities on behalf of specialty and artisan cheesemakers and the wider cheese community.

The society was founded in 1983, when Cornell University food science professor Frank Kosikowski proposed a "new, national grass-roots organization for cheese appreciation...(with) membership open to those with an interest in natural cheese...making cheese as a hobby or small enterprise and maintaining quality and traditional values of cheese." From the outset the society held social and technical gatherings and an annual conference. Early conferences attracted a core group of committed cheesemakers and food scientists, academics and ex-hippies, establishing a structure allowing the organization to grow. The first judging and competition was introduced at the third annual conference in 1985. Thirty cheesemakers from across the United States entered eighty-nine cheeses.

The early years involved slow growth, with limited resources and a market disinterested in quality cheese. In the 1980s and 1990s the American cheese market was focused on commodity-style products and processed sliced singles, which defined American cheese in the public mind. Small cheesemakers who wanted to create more traditional cheeses struggled to find the technical expertise to produce the kinds of products they wanted to produce, often looking to traditional European cheesemaking regions for inspiration and education. Over time ACS leadership helped bring together cheesemakers and the wider cheese community of retailers, academics, distributors, and educators.

In 2000 the ACS helped coordinate the response to increased regulatory scrutiny, joining with Oldways Preservation and the Cheese Importers Association to form the Cheese of Choice Coalition. The goal was to defend the right of cheesemakers to use traditional methods, including raw milk, for cheesemaking. The successful defense resulted in a decrease in regulatory pressure for almost a decade. See OLDWAYS PRESERVATION AND EXCHANGE TRUST and CHEESE IMPORTERS ASSOCIATION OF AMERICA.

In the mid-2000s the industry saw huge growth in the number of cheesemakers and the quantity and quality of cheeses being produced. Entries in the ACS Judging and Competition soared from 367 entries in 2000 to 1,201 entries in 2007. Today the judging regularly attracts more than 1,700 entries each year.

Over time awareness of and demand for American cheeses grew steadily with increased media interest and emerging new markets for specialty products at farmers' markets and local specialty shops.

In 2010 the ACS board opted to pursue self-management, hiring a full-time staff to support and advocate on behalf of the industry. This brought enhanced professionalism, more robust services for members, and a dedicated team committed to the organization mission and vision.

Soon thereafter the society took the lead in coordinating a response to increased regulatory scrutiny as authorities began review of the 60-day aging rule and other topics of import. See 60-DAY AGING RULE. Through educational opportunities focused on good manufacturing processes and through interfacing with regulators on behalf of specialty cheesemakers, the ACS Regulatory and Academic committee supports members in achieving the highest standards of cheesemaking at all points along the supply chain.

In 2011 ACS spearheaded the grassroots celebration, American Cheese Month, geared toward raising public awareness of American-made cheese every October through retail promotions, special events, and classes. In 2012 the first ACS Certified Cheese Professional exam was offered. This comprehensive exam is carefully constructed to confirm a candidate's understanding of all aspects of cheese production on through to the consumer. After the 2014 exam 406 people had passed.

See also ACCREDITATIONS; COMPETITIONS; and KOSIKOWSKI, FRANK.

"American Cheese Society at 25: Looking Forward, Looking Back" (Part 1), 2008.
"American Cheese Society at 25: Looking Forward, Looking Back" (Part 2), 2008.
American Cheese Society History Spreadsheet, supporting information compiled from ACS newsletters (author's personal archive).

Christine Hyatt

The **American Dairy Goat Association**

(ADGA), based in Spindale, North Carolina, and legally named and incorporated in 1964, is the current torchbearer for registered dairy goat breeds in the United States. It descended from a Civil War–era effort to transform the unregistered goats populating the early American countryside with origins from sixteenth-century Spanish and English settlers to the New World. Selections of American-born goats and importation of European and Mediterranean breeds formed the basis of the registry American Milch Goat Record Association in the 1890s to the early 1900s, with a fixed founding date

of 31 May 1905, though the association claims formation in 1904. Later, major membership bylaw changes were enacted in 1942 and it became a domestic nonprofit organization.

The association is governed by a president and four regional directors and bylaws indicate at least eight district directors are required for the association, elected by membership in each regional district. In 2016 the association boasts official genotype and milk recording of the Alpine, LaMancha, Nigerian Dwarf, Nubian, Oberhasli, Saanen, Sable, Toggenburg, and "Experimental" breeds with registrations totaling 44,288 individual goats (representing a membership of 11,590 adults plus 3,628 youth). The ADGA offers milk production testing, linear appraisal, ADGA PLUS, young sire development program, superior genetics, and DNA type testing that creates a genetic profile for identification and parentage verification.

Since 2008 a juried cheese competition takes place at the annual convention with categories for commercial and amateur cheesemakers for 100 percent goat milk cheeses from Canada and the United States. There are thirty-two categories of cheeses, fermented milk, and confections.

See also GOAT.

American Dairy Goat Association. *2014 Annual Report.* http://adga.org/wp-content/uploads/2015/05/ANNREP14.pdf.
American Dairy Goat Products. "Goat Milk Products Competition Rules." http://www.americandairygoatproducts.org/rules.htm.
Considine, Steven. "The American Milch Goat Record Association (AMGRA) Was Established in 1904." American Dairy Goat Association. https://adga.org/about-us/history.

Carol Delaney

The **American "goat ladies"** are a small but mighty collective of pioneering cheesemakers who transformed the palate of America in the early 1980s. At the time goat cheese was not being sold commercially in the United States. These entrepreneurs came to commercial production within a few years of each other in different areas of the country, introducing distinctively tangy goat cheeses to an American public increasingly reliant on convenience and commodity food.

A breakthrough moment for American goat cheese occurred when industry matriarch Laura Chenel famously began selling her fresh goat cheese medallions to noted chef Alice Waters of Chez Panisse in Berkeley, California. The breaded and baked rounds of goat cheese, served alongside simply dressed homegrown mesclun greens, became a classic salad of the era after being featured in the *Chez Panisse Menu Cookbook* (1982). Goat cheese popularity rose, helped along by tasting events and the support of chefs and food publications. See LAURA CHENEL'S CHÈVRE.

Each of the first-wave entrepreneurs had her own unique path to cheesemaking but all were influenced by two distinct philosophies: the more homespun track of back-to-the-landers of the 1970s, seeking local, healthful food sources, and those worldly cheesemakers inspired by trips abroad to traditional cheesemaking cultures, like France and Italy.

For some, including Mary Keehn, founder of Cypress Grove in northern California and Judy Schad at Capriole Goat Cheese in Indiana, the impetus came from the back-to-the-land ethos of growing their own healthy foods to feed their families. When a milk goat or two became four or eight, something had to be done with the milk. Cheese was a logical extension. Still others got their start through farming and 4H projects. Jennifer Bice, founder of Redwood Hill Cheese in Sonoma, California, was an early producer of fluid goat's milk, yogurt, and kefir for the local health food market and later developed her herd for cheesemaking. See CYPRESS GROVE CHEVRE; CAPRIOLE; and REDWOOD HILL FARM AND CREAMERY.

For a third group, travel to Europe's great goat cheese regions sparked a desire to bring those flavors back home. Laura Chenel, founder of the eponymous creamery based in Petaluma, California, Allison Hooper of Vermont Butter & Cheese, and Paula Lambert of the Mozzarella Company in Dallas, who also produced fine goat cheese early on, were all inspired by travel and tasting. Still another group of goat ladies were part of the larger cheese picture but their businesses were on a small-by-design scale. Anne Topham of Fantome Farm (Wisconsin), Barbara Backus of Goat's Leap (California), Lettie Kilmoyer of Westfield Farm (Massachusetts), and Sally Jackson (Washington State) were among the first on the scene, leading the way in their local regions. See VERMONT CREAMERY and MOZZARELLA COMPANY.

It is worth noting that though this group is affectionately known as the "goat ladies" and the most prominent names in the story are female, many men were out there promoting the goat as well, often as business partners and dairymen integral to the growth of the industry. Their contributions are legion and critical, as the grande dames of goat are quick to point out.

Most first-wave goat cheese producers made pilgrimages to Europe to learn from the masters at some point in their cheesemaking evolution, since the know-how and science of goat breeding and cheesemaking was simply not available in the United States. Consequently, there was also a distinct lack of dairy goats. Herds had to be developed to support commercial-level production over time. Further complicating growth, goat-size agricultural equipment for milking and feeding was not produced in the United States and had to be imported. At the time the entire dairy system was set up for more productive and larger bovines. Goats offered an opportunity for a smaller scale, more sustainable dairy model that allowed small farms to take root. Previously goat products in the United States were sold as an alternative to cow's milk for those with dietary restrictions or allergies, not for the flavor, so artisan goat cheese truly was a new market.

Developing the genetics for increased and consistent milk production suitable for cheese, and sourcing feed and farm and cheese equipment suitable for the smaller breed were hurdles to be cleared alongside developing recipes and building businesses. Without the infrastructure in place and the critical mass of producers needed to go mainstream, it was a herculean effort that paid off for those dedicated and determined enough to forge ahead. Boosted by the love of the intelligent and productive breed and a desire to change the American palate toward a new dairy trend, early producers banded together to "Promote the Goat" through organizations like the American Dairy Goat Association, the American Cheese Society, and 4H, all of which helped support goat dairies through improved genetics, cheesemaking technique, and consumer appreciation. See AMERICAN DAIRY GOAT ASSOCIATION.

In 1991 the American Dairy Goat Products Association was created to support industry growth through "information, promotion, research and regulatory action" (Jacobs-Welch, p. 3). Marketing efforts like National Goat Cheese Month, launched in

1998 by the American Cheese Society, and Bongrain, a French producer of goat cheese, further helped raise awareness of the health, flavor, and sustainable advantages of goat products. As more aged and specialty cheeses made their way to market in the early 1990s, classics like Humboldt Fog, Wabash Cannonball, O'Banon, and Hoja Santa introduced ripened and leaf-wrapped cheeses and further expanded the idea of what goat cheese could be in America. See HUMBOLDT FOG.

Collectively the American "goat ladies" exemplify the gumption needed to transform a national palate unfamiliar with goat cheese and hooked on sliced singles. They deserve particular credit for developing flavorful cheeses at a time when the knowledge of how to do that was remarkably hard to attain. It didn't happen overnight, but with sustained effort over fifteen or twenty years these women blazed a trail for future generations of goat cheese producers. Many of them continue to make award-winning cheeses, and to earn acclaim for their sustainable and ethical business models.

See also COUNTERCULTURE and GOAT.

"The Goat Cheese Divas." *Los Angeles Times*, 10 July 2002.
Jacobs-Welch, Laura. "The US Commercial Dairy Goat Industry: A Brief Historical Account." http://www.ansci.wisc.edu/extension-new%20copy/sheep/Publications_and_Proceedings/Pdf/Dairy/U.S.%20Dairy%20goat%20industry.pdf.
"National Goat Cheese Month" press kit and archival materials from the American Dairy Goat Products Association (author's personal archive).
Original newspaper clipping on "National Goat Cheese Month" (author's personal archive).

Christine Hyatt

The **Amish community** is a sectarian Anabaptist society with settlements predominantly in the United States and Canada. Amish communities are known for their limited use of technology and history of subsistence farming. The community was established in Switzerland in 1693 as an offshoot from the Mennonite order, and both religious cultural groups share historical practices in cheesemaking.

Cheesemaking was a craft the Amish brought with them to North America in their eighteenth-century and nineteenth-century migrations from Switzerland and Germany. No particular fabrication method or type of cheese can be designated as distinctively Amish, and today "Amish cheese" is a title granted to any cheese variety made by community members. However, some consider Limburger cheese, known as "stink cheese" in the community, to be a traditional Amish cheese. See LIMBURGER.

As befits the community's history of subsistence farming, a great deal of Amish cheese was crafted by women in their home kitchens. Ball cheese, cup cheese, and *Schmier Kase* (cottage cheese) were the three main types of Pennsylvania Dutch cheeses made in Amish and Mennonite communities. Cookbooks provide artful descriptions of making these cheeses, instructing women to heat milk on the stove "long enough so it sings" and to add coloring matter "the size of an apple kernel" (Hutchison, 1948, p. 78). See ANNATTO. Ball cheese was to be made in the fall and "stand" (i.e., ripen) throughout the winter for use in the spring, while cup cheese and *Schmier Kase* could be enjoyed within a week of being made.

The Amish have contributed to cheesemaking in the United States in various ways. When the Department of Agriculture formalized fluid milk regulations in the twentieth century, conservative settlements relied on Amish and non-Amish cheese factories to purchase and process cans of their Grade B milk. These commercial relationships allowed many Amish farmers to maintain their hand milking traditions and to refrain from using electric refrigerated cooling tanks. Other Amish farmers adopted milking machines and cooling tanks around the same time as non-Amish neighbors, some affiliations by the 1970s. Additionally, Amish cheesemakers have made both pasteurized and raw-milk cheese products, using many of the same practices and technologies as were popularized throughout the United States in the twentieth and twenty-first centuries. One significant difference between Amish and non-Amish communities in cheesemaking is in the use of pipeline systems to transfer milk directly from cows, goats, or sheep to cheese vats. The Amish continue to refrain from using pipelines whenever possible in order to maintain the manual labor of carrying milk cans to and from cooling tanks and cheese vats.

Today, Amish cheesemaking and cheese is just as diverse in method and characterization as is non-Amish cheese. Some Amish farmers make cheese out of personal interest in the art, seeking consultation from non-Amish artisans in Vermont and Wisconsin. Other Amish farmers boast of multigenerational familial traditions, often reminiscing about mothers and grandmothers making kitchen cheeses. Low-tech artisanal methods and collaboration with high-tech industrial cheese factories are both found in the Amish community, dependent on families' religious ideology, economic status, and access to resources.

Hostetler, John A. *Amish Society*, 4th ed. Baltimore: Johns Hopkins University Press, 1993.
Hutchison, Ruth. *The Pennsylvania Dutch Cook Book.* New York: Harper & Brothers, 1948.
Kraybill, Donald B., and Steven M. Nolt. *Amish Enterprise: From Plows to Profits,* 2d ed. Baltimore: Johns Hopkins University Press, 2004.
Weaver, William Woys. *Sauerkraut Yankees: Pennsylvania Dutch Foods and Foodways,* 2d ed. Mechanicsburg, Pa.: Stackpole, 2002.

Nicole Welk-Joerger

ammonia (NH_3) is a pungent colorless gas that is produced during the ripening of certain types of cheese primarily through the deamination of free amino acids that are formed as the end products of proteolysis. Depending on the cheese variety, ammonia may be produced by yeasts, molds, bacteria, or combinations thereof. The microflora of surface-ripened cheeses, such as the washed-rind (smear-ripened) and bloomy-rind (white mold-ripened) types, as well as the microflora of blue mold cheeses, tend to produce copious amounts of ammonia, which may accumulate to high enough levels in the atmosphere of the ripening room to selectively inhibit microbial growth at the cheese surface and alter the ecological balance of the surface flora. Gaseous ammonia, whether produced by microflora at the cheese surface, or by microflora internally in the cheese in the case of blue mold types, or whether simply present in the ripening atmosphere, readily dissolves into the water phase of cheese to form ammonium hydroxide, which is strongly basic and thus causes the pH of the cheese to rise.

When present at high concentrations, ammonia directly affects the flavor of cheese, imparting a characteristic pungent flavor and aroma note. Furthermore, through its effect on raising the pH of the cheese, ammonia may profoundly influence the course of ripening by (1) influencing the rate and specificity of protein breakdown, which in turn may affect both texture and flavor development; (2) reducing the volatility and therefore flavor and aroma impact of short chain free fatty acids that are produced by lipolysis during ripening; (3) acting as an important driver of zonal softening in the cheese body as aging progresses. With respect to the latter, the development of higher pH at the surface of washed-rind cheeses due to the absorption of gaseous ammonia from the atmosphere into to water phase at the cheese surface, triggers the crystallization of calcium and phosphate in the form of species such as calcium carbonate, calcium phosphate, and ammonium magnesium phosphate. The crystallization of calcium and phosphate species, in combination with the pH increase at the surface, likely contributes to localized increases in casein-water interactions and the onset of zonal softening during the ripening of smear-ripened cheeses. Similarly the zonal softening of texture in bloomy-rind cheeses, and the internal softening of blue mold cheeses, is likely partly mediated by the crystallization of calcium and phosphate species at high pH, induced by ammonia production. Therefore the rate and extent of ammonia production during ripening appear to be critical factors in determining the rate of softening and, thus, the shelf life of the soft surface-ripened cheeses such as the smear-ripened and bloomy-rind types.

See also DEAMINATION; LIPOLYSIS; MATURING; PH MEASUREMENT; and PROTEOLYSIS.

Fox, P. F., et al. *Fundamentals of Cheese Science.* Gaithersburg, Md.: Aspen, 2000.
Fox, P. F., et al. *Cheese: Chemistry, Physics and Mircobiology.* 3d ed., vol. 1: *General Aspects.* London: Elsevier Academic Press, 2004.

Paul S. Kindstedt

anari is a whey cheese that is considered a by-product during the manufacture of Halloumi cheese; as such, anari's long history of production closely tracks that of Halloumi, the major cheese of Cyprus. See HALLOUMI. Fresh anari is soft, high in moisture, and fragile, with a very mild, nutty flavor. It can be sold in vacuum packs either slightly salted or not. Salted anari cheese is usually dried, under cold air streams, in specially designed drying rooms until it becomes hard and easy to grate.

The whey derived from Halloumi cheese production is gradually heated to 149–158°F (65–70°C), and a quantity of milk (sheep, goat, cow, or a mixture) is added (10 percent of total whey) at these temperatures. The heating continues until the temperature reaches 194°F (90°C). The whey is cooked for about thirty minutes until the crumbly curds of anari (mainly denatured whey protein and fat) rise on the surface of the whey, which is ladled in molds and left to drain overnight under refrigeration temperatures. Some dairies add a quantity of citric acid in order to reduce the pH of the whey, demineralizing the whey proteins to assist their denaturation.

Fresh unsalted anari is a highly perishable product that has a very short shelf life (two to three days once the packaging is opened), although the hard, salted counterpart can be microbiologically safe for much longer periods (i.e., six months). Anari is similar to Italian ricotta, Greek mizithra, and lor peyniri of Turkey, which are also made from whey. Anari can be served fresh, used as an ingredient in confectionery, or grated over hot dishes.

See also LOR and RICOTTA.

Papademas, P. "Halloumi Cheese." In *Brined Cheeses*, edited by A. Y. Tamime, pp. 117–138. Oxford: Blackwell, 2006.

Photis Papademas

ancient civilizations are those up to and including the classical cultures of Greece and Rome. Cheese was already an important food in the early civilizations of western Asia and southern Europe, known from archaeology and frequently mentioned in literature, although no specialist writings on cheese survive from this early period. Unluckily, older texts give minimal detail on specific types of cheese. The challenge for the food historian is to reimagine the flavor of ancient cheeses on the basis of tantalizingly incomplete information.

Cheese was already valued at the dawn of civilization, in early Egypt and Sumer, although the evidence takes entirely different forms in the two cases. In Sumer we find cheese as a central feature in mythology and in the urban economy. In Egypt, thanks to the remarkable possibilities for the preservation of archaeological remains offered by the Egyptian climate, we find cheese itself, five thousand years old.

Archaic Egypt, ca. 3100 to 2900 B.C.E.

One archaeological find of ancient cheese was made by W. B. Emery in 1937 in one of the second dynasty tombs (soon after 3000 B.C.E.) in the necropolis of Saqqāra near the ancient Egyptian capital city, Memphis. This tomb, fortunately undisturbed by grave robbers, contained the body of an unnamed woman in her sixties and the goods buried with her for her use in the next life, including, astonishingly, a generous meal of fourteen dishes, neatly set out in plates and bowls, and so well preserved that all the main ingredients could be identified. Alongside soup, meat, fish, fowl, cakes, and cooked fruit—all accompanied by a large jar of wine—there was a loaf of emmer bread and three small pots containing what were soon identified as little cheeses. Examination of the woman's remains showed that in real life she would not have been able to enjoy much of this food: in her youth she had suffered some serious trauma that had almost destroyed the left side of her mouth. Soup, soft cheese, and cooked fruit, therefore, might well have represented her usual daily fare. Her mourners, confident that in the afterlife she would be healed, had provided much more.

Another comparable find is of slightly earlier date. In a tomb connected with the pharaoh Hor-Aha, usually listed as the second king of the First Dynasty (about 3100 B.C.E.), were two jars containing a fatty substance that the first excavators could not identify, with inscriptions that were read as "rwt of

This painted terracotta statue of a man grating cheese dates to the Archaic period in Greece, sixth century B.C.E. DE AGOSTINI PICTURE LIBRARY / G. DAGLI ORTI / BRIDGEMAN IMAGES

the north" and "rwt of the south." Soon afterward scientists set to work on it and pronounced it to be cheese. The monarchs of the First Dynasty, and Hor-Aha in particular, are credited with having united Egypt (the "two lands," as the country was called for some time afterward). Presenting cheese from both north and south to a deceased dignitary of this exact period would make perfect political sense. Setting the political history aside, we have a hint that there were at least two kinds of cheese worth distinguishing by their geographical origin in Egypt in 3100 B.C.E. We have not only the earliest surviving cheese, but also, perhaps, the earliest recorded appellations.

The practice of cattle herding may perhaps have reached Egypt from the west, from the Sahara, which had until about this time been much less arid than it later became. Rock paintings of the central Sahara, two thousand years earlier than the Egyptian First Dynasty, already depict cattle keeping and milking, but in these paintings there is no sign of cheese-making.

Identifying these objects as cheeses was all the more difficult because "rwt" is a doubtful reading; in any case it is an unknown word, the ancient Egyptian term for cheese being otherwise unrecorded. It is quite different with the Sumerian civilization, which flourished in southern Iraq during the third millennium B.C.E. Sumerian literature, written in a language unrelated to any modern tongue, has been gradually deciphered in recent years with the help of bilingual texts and glossaries in Akkadian, the Semitic language spoken at a later period in northern and central Iraq. The Sumerian word for cheese, *ga-har*, is found in literature from the late third millennium B.C.E.

Sumer, ca. 3000 to 2500 B.C.E.

In Sumer, cheese from cow's, goat's, and sheep's milk was known. A distinction, important to shepherds ever since, was already being made between small cheeses, likely to be eaten when fresh; and large cheeses carefully made for longer maturing. Sumerian-Akkadian glossaries contain lists of foods, including "white cheese," "fresh cheese," "rich cheese," "sharp cheese," and various flavors making up a total of twenty distinct cheeses, which presumably had a real identity in the food supply of Sumerian cities in the late third millennium.

Cheese is especially linked with the love goddess Inanna in Sumerian records because cheese was received as tribute and was redistributed by Inanna's great temple in Uruk. However, we find cheese in varied contexts in Sumerian literature. Milk and cheese were the produce of the shepherd god Dumuzi. He was to be Inanna's consort, but even in his boyhood he had been a shepherd and cheesemaker, according to the mythological poem translated by Thorkild Jacobsen under the title "Lad in the Desert." Milk and cheese were his wealth, with which he defeated his rival, the farmer god Enkimdu. Milk, cream, and cheese are metaphors for sexual pleasures in the erotic poetry that describes the lovemaking of Dumuzi and Inanna. Cheese is the rich food that the sick Lugalbanda is too weak to digest in the "Epic of Lugalbanda." See INANNA and SEXUAL IMAGERY.

Later Near Eastern Civilizations, ca. 2500 to 1250 B.C.E.

Sumerian culture is the basis of much that is written in Akkadian, the language of Babylon and Assyria. In Akkadian the basic word for cheese was *eqīdum*, and there were several more names for cheeses in addition to the eighteen or twenty identified from the Sumerian glossary; some of the names were borrowed from neighboring languages both west and east. *Nagahu* was maybe the name for a smelly cheese, because the word was also used as an insult; *kabu*, literally "dung," when used as a cheese name might (like French *crottin*) allude to the shape rather than the smell. It appears from glossaries that there were cheeses flavored with wine, dates, and various herbs: how the flavor was added is not known. A few cookery recipes survive in Akkadian, and they confirm that cheese was used as a culinary ingredient. We even know the Akkadian word for rennet, *emsu*.

In Hittite writings, from central Anatolia in the mid-second millennium B.C.E., we find that a cheese could be large or small; it could be *huelpi* (fresh), *damaššanzi* (pressed), *paršān* (broken, crumbled), *iškallan* (torn), *hašhaššan* (perhaps "scraped"). It could be "dry" and "old"; it could be "incised" (perhaps marked to show its origin); there was even "aged soldier cheese," which might or might not have been better than it sounds. See MILITARY RATIONING. Such adjectives are interesting less for what they say than for the oppositions they imply: cheese was, by this time, evaluated on several scales. It was doled out in *purpurruš* (balls) or in "loaves" (presumably a difference between small and large whole cheeses) that might be broken into *paršulli* (chunks) like those from a wheel of Parmesan. A fight with cheeses formed part of the dramatic or athletic entertainment at a certain Hittite religious festival. As H. A. Hoffner writes, "since the cheeses could hardly be the opponents, we must understand that [they] were wielded like weapons." Finally, the records of the Hittite empire's Mediterranean emporium, Ugarit, tell us that cheese, among other supplies, was exported southward from there to the Canaanite city of Ashdod: the first historical record of long distance trade in cheese.

Westward, beyond Hittite borders, the Minoan civilization was flourishing in Crete and the Greek islands. In the 1860s a French geologist, Ferdinand Fouqué, while investigating the Santorini volcano, happened on the remains of two ancient Minoan settlements buried under ash by the catastrophic eruption of 1627 B.C.E.: one at Akrotiri, now famous; the other on the tiny island of Therasia, now forgotten. Among the stored foods buried when this little town was overwhelmed, Fouqué's helpers found in a storage jar "une matière pâteuse" (a paste-like substance), which they decided must have been cheese. Not far away were the skeletons of three goats, trapped in their shed by the volcanic ash.

Weakened by this and other disasters, Minoan civilization gave way to Mycenaean, based on the Greek mainland. Although there is no known Mycenaean literature, an ancient form of Greek was employed in Linear B cuneiform tablets to record food and other stores in the Mycenaean palaces at Knossos and elsewhere. In these laconic accounts cheese is measured in units—whole cheeses—and the standard Mycenaean cheese was not so very small if we reflect that on one such tablet, a list of requisites for feasting from "Nestor's palace" at Pylos, in southeastern Greece, ten cheeses are listed alongside an amount calculated at 23 gallons (86 liters) of wine.

Classical Greece and Rome, ca. 750 B.C.E. to 450 C.E.

From Greek and Roman sources we have plentiful and varied information on the place of cheese among foods. Cheese with bread and green vegetables,

alongside wine or water, constituted an adequate simple meal for poorer people, travelers, and huntsmen. Cheese on its own was a snack—and cheese and nuts were served by winemakers at tastings to mask the poor quality of their wine. In more elaborate meals cheese could be a dessert, to be eaten with honey and bread while one was drinking wine after dinner. One might guess that the most suitable to eat with honey would be a fresh cheese, though any cheese kept in brine (as ancient cheeses often were), and washed before serving, is likely to be good with honey. At some meals goat's milk or sheep's milk cheese was fried in slices to be served as a starter. Cheese was sometimes added to bread dough before baking. It was also a culinary ingredient. Ancient chefs disputed whether cheese should or should not be used as a topping when grilling fish; the answer, predictably, was that it depended on the fish, but cheese is certainly included in the very oldest surviving Greek recipe, dated to ca. 400 B.C.E., for preparing the ribbon-like fish cépole, and was specially recommended with ray or skate. Cheese is listed as a constituent of some famous ancient dishes, such as *kandaulos*, typical of the rich cuisine of ancient Lydia in western Asia Minor (Turkey), and *tyrotarichus*, a Roman specialty with a Greek name.

In ancient Greece (ca. 750–150 B.C.E.) goat's and sheep's milk cheeses were best known: Greece was poor cattle-raising country and the few cattle that were kept were mostly working animals. However, Greek scientists such as Aristotle knew that cheese could be made from the milk of other animals including cows, mares, and donkeys. Pyetia (animal rennet) was commonly used to curdle the milk; the best variety was thought to come from the stomach of a young deer. Alternatively opos, the milky sap of the fig tree, was used as a vegetable rennet. "The fig sap is first squeezed out into wool," Aristotle explains. "The wool is rinsed, and the rinsing is put into a little milk. This, mixed with other milk, curdles it" (Aristotle, *History of Animals* 522b3-5). Young cheeses were placed in a *talaros* or cheese basket to allow the whey to run off.

Cheese is likely to have been a major food for country people, including the nomadic shepherds who kept goats in the mountain pastures of northern Greece, but most of the evidence for classical Greek life comes from city contexts. In classical Athens there was a cheese fair on the last day of every lunar month, called simply "the Green Cheese." We know this because in a recorded legal case a speaker observes that an inhabitant of the hill town of Plataiai, north of Athens, was sure to be found at this fair. Other producers named in surviving texts are the cities of Tromileia (in the Peloponnesos, southern Greece), Chersonesos (now in European Turkey), and the Aegean island of Kythnos, whose fine sheep's milk cheeses, called trophalis, fetched a high price. Sicily, partly settled by Greeks at this period, was famous as the source of fine cheese made from a mixture of sheep's and goat's milk. This fame can be traced back to the early Greek epic, the *Odyssey*, in which the gigantic one-eyed Cyclops (fated to be blinded by Odysseus) is described as a keeper of sheep and a maker of cheese; later readers believed that this evocative scene was set in Sicily, though the island is not named in the poem. See HOMER.

Turning to classical Rome and its empire (ca. 150 B.C.E. to 450 C.E.) instructions for cheesemaking are given by the farming author Columella, a native of Spain. See COLUMELLA, LUCIUS JUNIUS MODERATUS. Cow's milk cheese was familiar to classical Romans but goat's and sheep's milk cheeses were more common. The poet Virgil describes how a mountain shepherd would make cheese, from morning and evening milkings, and sell it himself at the nearest market (Virgil, *Georgics*, book 3, lines 400–403). See VIRGIL. Cheeses might be shaped in a mold, Latin *forma* (this word is the origin of French *fromage*). Salt and brine assisted in the making of cheese for long distance trade. Rome was perhaps the first culture to develop smoked cheese, using the smoke from apple wood: the best smoked cheese was matured in the Velabrum district of the city of Rome. See SMOKED CHEESES. Other flavorings, including pine nuts, thyme, and black pepper, were used in specialized cheeses.

Some cheeses became famous, including the meta (pyramid) of Sassina in northern Umbria and the smooth, round, white cheeses of Mount Sila, southeast of Naples. The cheese of Luna, in northwestern Tuscany, was stamped with a crescent moon ("luna") as an easily read designation of origin. See LUNA CHEESE. Excellent mountain cheeses were brought to Rome from the nearby territory of the Vestini. As Roman power spread around the Mediterranean, cheeses from distant provinces became known in Roman Italy. Among these were the quadra of Toulouse and the Vatusicus cheese from the same Alpine valley in which modern Reblochon is made.

Apuleius, in the fictional *Metamorphoses*, depicts an agent traveling through northern Greece to buy cheese and honey. There were also cheeses from Crete.

Cheese played a special role in the literary ideal of traditional Italian farm produce. Cheese is a principal ingredient in the peasant farmer's midday meal described in the poem "Moretum." Fine fresh local cheeses, drying on rush mats, are among the delicacies offered at an imaginary country tavern in "Copa." Both these poems have sometimes been attributed to Virgil but they are probably by contemporary poets of the first century B.C.E.

Compiled during the fifth century C.E., the farming manual by Palladius gives brief instructions for the cheesemaker. Lamb's or goat's rennet may be used, or the flowers of wild thistle or fig sap. As the milk curdles it is gradually pressed to expel the whey. The solidifying cheese is placed in a dark, cool room, pressed again using weights, and sprinkled with salt. After several days the firm fresh cheeses are placed on reed mats to mature in a draught-free room. Some makers combine fresh pine nuts, or chopped thyme, with the cheese as it begins to solidify; the cheese may be rolled in black pepper or other spices for added flavor.

Elsewhere

A single large geographical region embraces the whole story told earlier, stretching from Mesopotamia (Iraq) to Egypt, Turkey, Greece, Italy, France, and Spain.

Beyond that region evidence at this early period is slight or absent. Evidence is vanishingly scarce, and cheese was generally not an important food in early India and early China. In all of ancient Sanskrit literature there are, at most, two uninformative mentions of cheese. The archaic Rigveda poems, possibly of about 1000 B.C.E., name two kinds of *dadhanvata*, with and without holes, and the word "dadhanvata" may mean "cheese." The extensive legal treatise, Arthaśastra, attributed to Kautilya and dated conventionally to the rule of Candragupta Maurya in the third century B.C., gives an instruction, in a list of subsidiary products of animal herds that "*kurcika* is to be delivered to the armed forces," and the word "kurcika" may mean "cheese." Chinese literature offers even less: cheese was a minor food from the southern provinces that was not noticed by any authors before the medieval period. Evidence for cheese is entirely absent from the pre-Columbian New World civilizations of Mexico and Peru, where animal milk was not used as human food and cheese was unknown. It is absent, too, from the information available to us about early peoples of the Eurasian steppes. Greek and Latin sources, in fact, say specifically that among those peoples milk was an important food and was converted into butter but not into cheese.

See also ARISTAIOS; DIOCLETIAN EDICT; HYPATA; LATIFUNDIA; MESOPOTAMIA; ORIGIN OF CHEESE; PLAKOUS; and TRADE (HISTORICAL).

Bottéro, Jean. "The Cuisine of Ancient Mesopotamia." *Biblical Archaeologist* 48, no. 1 (1985): 36–47.

Dalby, Andrew. *Food in the Ancient World from A to Z.* London: Routledge, 2003.

Gouin, Philippe. "Ancient Oriental Dairy Techniques Derived from Archaeological Evidence." *Food and Foodways: Explorations in the History and Culture of Human Nourishment* 7, no. 3 (1997): 157–188.

Hoffner, Harry A. *Alimenta Hethaeorum: Food Production in Hittite Asia Minor.* New Haven, Conn.: American Oriental Society, 1974. See pp. 122–123.

Kaufman, Cathy K. *Cooking in Ancient Civilizations.* Westport, Conn.: Greenwood, 2006.

Kindstedt, Paul. *Cheese and Culture: A History of Cheese and Its Place in Western Civilization.* White River Junction, Vt.: Chelsea Green, 2012.

Simoons, Frederick J. "The Antiquity of Dairying in Asia and Africa." *Geographical Review* 61, no. 3 (1971): 431–439.

Stol, Marten. "Milk, Butter, and Cheese." *Bulletin on Sumerian Agriculture* 7 (1993): 99–113.

Zaky, A., and Z. Iskander. "Ancient Egyptian Cheese." *Annales du Service des Antiquités de l'Egypte* 41 (1942): 295–313.

Andrew Dalby

Androuët,

Androuët, a Paris shrine for connoisseurs of cheese, was opened as a cheese shop in 1909. The store on the rue d'Amsterdam in the eighth arrondissement was unusual in featuring French regional cheeses at a time when these were mostly unknown or unappreciated outside their immediate localities. Parisians then generally limited their tastes to Brie, Camembert, and other cheeses with wide circulation. After World War I and with the gradual construction of automobile routes, Henri Androuët explored France and bought directly from cheese producers. By 1925 the store was renowned for offering at least one hundred varieties of cheeses, all from France.

In 1934 a restaurant was opened above the retail establishment and it attracted an enthusiastic clientele with a menu completely focused on cheese. Orson Welles, Ernest Hemingway, and Maria Callas were among the celebrated regulars. Different from what one might now expect, the restaurant emphasized not so much the variety of cheese available or rare or exotic cheeses but featured rather standard dishes. A menu from about 1960 (undated, but with prices in "new francs") offered specials such as onion soup "au fromage," quiche Lorraine, Parmesan soufflé, croque monsieur, and Welsh rarebit.

The restaurant closed in 2007, but the shop remains in business. The name "Androuët" was licensed in the 1980s and so there are other unrelated establishments in Paris and elsewhere with the name.

See also ANDROUËT, PIERRE.

Androuët. http://androuet.com.

Menus in the collection of the Culinary Institute of America, Hilton Library, Hyde Park, New York.

Paul Freedman

Androuët, Pierre

Androuët, Pierre (1915–2005) was a legendary French fromager, affineur, and author of the *Guide du Fromage* (1973, translated in English as *The Complete Encyclopedia of French Cheese*), one of the most comprehensive and personal books ever published on cheese. He was also the owner, with his father Henri, of Androuët, a veritable mecca for cheese lovers that Henri opened in Paris in 1909. Located at 41 rue d'Amsterdam in the eighth arrondissement, Androuët quickly became Paris's best known address for cheese. By the mid-1920s the store had over one hundred kinds of cheese on offer. Chez Androuët, it wasn't just the variety but the quality of the cheeses that was so impressive. When Henri opened his shop the cheeses available to Parisians were frequently overripe or in poor condition. Arriving by rail from distant parts of France, and without adequate refrigeration, the cheeses were rarely at their peak when they reached a customer's table.

From the age of 15 on Pierre joined his parents in the running of the store. He gave up his architectural studies and soon accompanied his father on his long trips across France, to seek out new producers and solidify relationships with existing ones. Key to the Androuëts' success was the fact that they were not only sellers of cheese, they were also affi-neurs, taking in young cheeses and aging them in the shop's caves. The Androuëts understood that only by bringing in cheeses at an early stage could they guarantee consumption at exactly the right moment. In 1948 Pierre took over the running of the cheese shop and a small restaurant and tasting room above the shop, and, with the advent of air travel, established an early mail-order business for clients around the world. In 1989 Androuet was sold for the first time; a succession of owners would follow. Pierre Androuët passed away in 2005, and was eulo-gized by another well-known French cheesemonger, Hervé Mons, who wrote that "he opened the way, showed the path...he was one of those visionary men like Edouard Michelin, who wasn't content merely to sell tires, but thought about everything that went along with that: road maps, good restau-rants, the necessity of customer service."

See also ANDROUËT and MATURING.

Androuët, Pierre. *The Complete Encyclopedia of French Cheese, and Other Continental Varieties.* New York: Harper's Magazine Press, 1973.
"Androuet: Fromager Affineur." ParisGourmand.com. http://www.parisgourmand.com/boutiques_gourmandes/androuet_fromager_affineur.html.
"Androuët Pierre (75)." Camembert-Museum.com. http://www.camembert-museum.com/pages/historiques-ile-de-france/androuet-pierre-75.html.

Alexandra Leaf

Anevato is a traditional protected designation of origin (PDO) Greek cheese made from ewe's or goat's milk, or mixtures of both, at creameries in the mountain region of western Macedonia. It is a soft, spreadable cheese, with a grainy texture, lightly salted, and a pleasant sourish and refreshing flavor.

Traditionally, Anevato cheese was produced by shepherds with large flocks of goats and sheep. They made the raw milk obtained in the morning into rennet just before taking the cattle out for feeding. During the day, the curd was "raised" on the top of the whey ("anevato" means a cheese that is raised) and was ready to be drained on their return late in the afternoon. The shepherds used to visit their vil-lages once a week to see their families and sell their cheese. Following that traditional way, whole milk from local herds is left at 64°–68°F (18–20°C) to sour and curdle within twelve hours, by the activity of

the natural lactic microflora, *Lactococcus lactis* ssp. *lactis.* The addition of rennet is optional. After drain-ing in cheesecloths, salt is added (1–2 percent w/w) and the curd is thoroughly mixed. The cheese is finally transferred to cold rooms until it is sold. According to legislation, maximum moisture of 60 percent and fat in dry matter of at least 45 percent are permitted. The pH in the final product is about 4.0–4.3. Today Anevato is produced in limited quan-tities by local dairies and is sold in bulk or in plastic containers. It is consumed as a table cheese, or as a snack spread on a slice of bread.

See also GREECE.

Hatzikamari, M., E. Litopoulou-Tzanetaki, and N. Tzanetakis. "Microbiological Characteristics of Anevato: A Traditional Greek Cheese." *Journal of Applied Microbiology* 87, no. 4 (1999): 595–601.

Magdalini Hatzikamari

annatto is a natural pigment and is extracted from the dried seeds of the achiote (Spanish) or urucum (Portuguese) tree (*Bixa orellana*). It is indigenous to South America and the Caribbean but is now naturalized in other tropical areas of the world in-cluding Asia and Africa. The main producing coun-tries are Peru and Kenya. Annatto is added to milk to give Cheddar and Colby cheeses an orange color. This is for visual appeal and does not impart flavor at the concentrations used. Most Munster cheese made in the United States is dipped in annatto to give it a dark reddish orange color reminiscent of the washed-rind or smear-ripened version of the cheese produced in Europe.

The fat-soluble extract in annatto is called bixen but during processing it is exposed to sodium hy-droxide and saponified to form water soluble nor-bixin. The two are blended to give different colors from yellow to orange. The more bixen in the blend the more orange the color and the more norbixin the more yellow the color.

Although bixen and norbixin are carotenoids they are not precursors to vitamin A as is beta-carotene, the natural yellow to red pigment found in grass, vege-tables, and fruits. The yellowish color of cheeses produced from milk procured from grass-fed cows is due to beta-carotene. All carotenoids including an-natto are light sensitive and cheeses with annatto added can turn reddish pink to white depending on the intensity and duration of exposure. Even those cheeses that are yellowish in color due to naturally occurring beta-carotene will turn white after exposure to light.

Use of annatto during cheese production results in whey powders that are slightly orange but unacceptable for certain markets. See WHEY POWDER. Bleaching agents have been used to destroy the color. However, due to their oxidative chemistry they also oxidize fat and phospholipids and impart oxidized flavors to products made with whey based powders. Due to the increased use of whey derived products and a prohibition of using bleaching agents to whiten whey, alternatives to annatto (especially beta-carotene) are being used to color cheese. However, many major importing countries of whey products will not accept any whey products derived from whey if annatto or beta-carotene is used.

See also COLOR.

Campbell, R. E., R. E. Miracle, and M. A. Drake. "The Effect of Starter and Annatto on the Flavor and Functionality of Whey Protein Concentrate." *Journal of Dairy Science* 94 (2011): 1185–1193.

Kang, E. J., R. E. Campbell, E. Bastian, and M.A. Drake. "Invited Review: Annatto Usage and Bleaching in Dairy Foods." *Journal of Dairy Science* 93 (2010): 3891–3901.

Smith, Karen. *Annatto and Color Removal*. Madison: Wisconsin Center for Dairy Research, 2014.

Mark E. Johnson

Anthotyros

See GREECE.

anthropomorphism

See MAGICAL THINKING.

aphorisms and sayings

aphorisms and sayings concerning cheese abound, occurring in many languages. Examples taken from English demonstrate what varied origins such expressions may have. The sound of the word is itself expressive, as in "cheese!" (euphemism for "Jesus!"), and "cheese it!," which may have originated as "cease it!" The speaker's facial expression has provoked many a photographer to beg, "say cheese." The British usage of "the cheese" to refer to "the best thing" comes apparently from the similarly sounding Urdu, *chiz* ("thing"). The consonant sound of the words as well as something in the color and texture (and taste) of the substances gave rise to the English phrase, "chalk and cheese," used for more than six centuries as a metaphor for things that are wholly unlike one another. We perhaps know why "hard cheese" means "bad luck," but why people are "cheesed off" (bored, fed up), why the person in charge is "the big cheese," and why erotic photographs depict "cheesecake" are questions that have no easy answer: guesses at the origin of such phrases are often wrong.

As for "the moon is made of a green cheese" (a green cheese was a fresh, half-pressed, or cottage cheese), this expression has existed for 450 years in English. The implication is that no sensible person would believe such a statement, hence its inclusion in 1562 in John Heywood's verses on the lies that men and women tell one another. The basic idea has a still longer history: it is found in a twelfth century collection of animal fables, the *Disciplina clericalis* of Petrus Alfonsi, in the story of the fox that shows a wolf the reflection of the moon in water at the bottom of a well, explains that it is a cheese, and persuades the hapless wolf to go down and get it.

Cheese can be dangerously attractive, a deceptive prize. In Portuguese one may "dársela con queso a alguien" ("give it to someone with cheese"), lead him into a trap; in Spanish "me la dio con queso" ("he gave it to me with cheese"), he tricked me. In Hindi you can "panīr catānā" ("give someone a lick of the cheese") to flatter him, or you can "panīri jamānā" ("set it in the cheese"), slip something into the conversation. In Romanian cheese is food for an unwary novice, "cu caş la gură" ("with the cheese still in his mouth"). In ancient Greek "The beggar had no bread and yet bought cheese" was a proverbial comment on the wasting of limited resources, although in Italian "Fare del cacio barca e del pan Bartolommeo" ("make the cheese into a boat and the bread into Bartholomew") means eating wastefully, leaving the rinds and crusts (of Saint Bartholomew, flayed alive according to legend, nothing was left but the skin).

Sayings often focus on the place of cheese among other foods. Is it an everyday item? A German proverb answers this question: "Zwiebeln und Käse sind nicht zu verachten, man gebraucht ihn viel zum essen" ("Onions and cheese are not to be sneered at: people often have them to lunch"). Is it perhaps the only food one can afford? Then a French rhyme reassures the eater: "Qui a fromage pour tous mets peut bien tailler bien épais" ("If cheese is your only food, you can cut a thick slice"). This contradicts a medieval Latin rule, composed with diet in mind, "Caseus est sanus si data avara manus" ("Cheese is healthy if given with a sparing hand"). Another Latin verse, "Caseus et panis sunt optima fercula sanis" ("Cheese and bread are excellent foods for the healthy"), was quoted for hundreds of years. Note the implications in these learned aphorisms. Cheese is to be approached carefully; it is too strong a food for invalids. A further implication is that cheese is to be eaten with bread. Alongside that last Latin verse goes the Italian "esser pane e cacio" ("to be bread-and-cheese"), meaning, to be hand-in-glove, and the English phrase, common until the nineteenth century, "bread and cheese" as the basic and boring diet. But then "bread and cheese" found a new lease of life in the wildly popular phrase "bread and cheese and kisses." It had already been used by Jonathan Swift in the 1730s ("bachelors' fare: bread and cheese and kisses"), but it suddenly came into common use 140 years later. It was the title and refrain of a popular song of 1871. It was the title of an 1873 novel by B. L. Farjeon. It was quoted ("I never could understand the theory of bread and cheese and kisses") in H. J. Byron's successful play *Our Boys* of 1875; it was used again in the finale of Gilbert and Sullivan's *Ruddigore* in 1887. The theory was that a marriage without money (hence the bread and cheese) would succeed if it were a love-match (hence the kisses). Gilbert rhymed "kisses" with "missis"; with his help the phrase eventually gave birth to the twentieth-century Australian rhyming slang term "cheese" for "missis," that is, "wife."

Assuming that there is enough money for more than bread and cheese, proverbs can tell us what place cheese should have in a full meal. Some grate it over their pasta, giving rise to the Italian expression "cascare come il cacio sui maccheroni" ("to fall like cheese on macaroni"), that is, to make the finishing touch. But the typical place of cheese is later in the meal. Among Brillat-Savarin's "Aphorismes du professeur," set out as a preface to his classic *Physiologie du goût* (1826), this is number 14: "Un dessert sans fromage est une belle à qui il manque un oeil," ("dessert without cheese is a beautiful woman with only one eye"). "Dessert" means "the

foods that follow the main course," among which, we are told, there should be both cheese and other things.

Among those other things one name recurs. "Onques Deus ne fist tel mariage comme de poires et de fromage" ("God never made a better match than the one between pears and cheese"), according to a French proverb recorded in the fifteenth century and repeated almost in the same words in François Rabelais's *Le quart livre* on the comic adventures of Pantagruel. Others, too, think highly of the combination, whatever exactly is meant by the Italian saying "Al contadino non far sapere quanto è buono il formaggio con le pere" ("Don't tell the peasant how good cheese is with pears"): this puzzling proverb is the starting point for Massimo Montanari's 2008 historical investigation. But cheese and pears need not be in the same mouthful. Another French phrase, originally "entre la poire et le fromage" ("between pear and cheese")—nowadays sometimes reversed because in modern French meals cheese arrives before the sweets—is used of a discussion or a decision easily concluded because, by the time the desserts are being served, everyone is in a good humor.

See also ART; CHILDREN'S LITERATURE; LITERATURE; MOON; and NAMING CHEESE.

Dalby, Andrew. *Cheese: A Global History*. London: Reaktion, 2009. See pp. 114–117.

Farmer, J. S., ed. *The Proverbs, Epigrams, and Miscellanies of John Heywood, Comprising a Dialogue of the Effectual Proverbs in the English Tongue Concerning Marriages—First Hundred Epigrams—Three Hundred Epigrams on Three Hundred Proverbs—The Fifth Hundred Epigrams—A Sixth Hundred Epigrams—Miscellanies—Ballads*. London: Early English Drama Society, 1906.

Montanari, Massimo. *Il formaggio con le pere: la storia in un proverbio* [Cheese, Pears, and History in a Proverb]. Rome: Laterza, 2008. English translation, New York: Columbia University Press, 2013.

Andrew Dalby

The **appellation d'origine contrôlée** (AOC) is the French national designation of origin system. See DESIGNATION OF ORIGIN. This French creation, initially issued from the wine sector, inspired the actual European Union legislation for protection of origins. AOC translates to "controlled origin names," meaning that they are product names based in a specific geographical area whose use is reserved for a particular group of producers. They are overseen by a state agency, the Institut National de l'Origine et de la Qualité (abbreviated INAO from a previous version of the name), a branch of the agricultural ministry. French law defines an appellation of origin as "the denomination of a country, region, or locality serving to designate a product that originates there and whose quality or characteristics are due to the geographical setting, including natural and human factors."

To obtain an AOC for a dairy product (like any other product type), people from the production chain (i.e., dairy farmers, cheesemakers, and affineurs, or cheese agers) must form a union and collectively define their product and relevant production criteria in conjunction with INAO advisors, academic experts, and people from other dairy AOCs. This process can take years to complete not only because of the number of issues to be resolved but also because of the tensions that exist between dairy farmers and cheesemakers, and between industrial cheesemakers and farmstead cheesemakers. The producers' union must develop a proposal defining the acceptable cow breed(s) and feed systems, milk treatments (raw, thermized, etc.), geographical perimeter for production, cheesemaking and affinage (aging) procedures, and equipment dimensions and materials. Their proposal is studied by an INAO commission of civil servants and other AOC cheese professionals, which either accepts it or sends it back for more work on certain points. When it passes, it is voted into law. From this time on, anyone wishing to participate in producing that cheese by that name must conform to all criteria or face punitive action. The laws are enforced within the production chain by private audit companies working in agreement with the INAO, and following production, by the French antifraud agency.

The term "appellation d'origine contrôlée" was first legally defined in a 1919 law, but the groundwork for such protection had been laid at the end of the previous century in efforts to prevent winemaking fraud. A series of laws against watering down, mixing, and otherwise cheating led to a law in 1905 that included misleading food labeling among the crimes—labeling a wine as a "Burgundy" when it was made from grapes grown elsewhere, for example. This quickly led to the prickly details of determining just what was so special about grapes

from one place compared to those from another, and appellations of origin were born. See TERROIR. Modeled on a proposed 1913 law derailed by World War I, the 1919 law details that an appellation is to be defined by the delimitation of a geographical production area and the definition of the product's "qualities or character" on the basis of "local, loyal, and constant" practices—that is to say, practices that are limited to a given area, have changed little over time, and have been in use for a long time.

With this law, the tenor of regulation began to shift from consumer protection to protecting producers in terms of fair market competition and their rights to be the sole beneficiaries of a reputation for quality they and their predecessors had worked to create. Winemakers were very invested in the project, and it is not by chance that one of its main political champions was a senator from the Bordeaux region, Joseph Capus. In 1935 he was a central figure in establishing two organizations, a national agency overseeing appellations of origin (the CNAO, or Comité National des Appellations d'Origine, which became the INAO in 1947) and the national registry of recognized wine and spirit appellations and definitions, of which he became the director.

Cheeses could and did benefit from the 1919 false labeling law: Roquefort was the first to make a legally binding name for itself in 1925, and after World War II a group of cheesemakers lobbied hard for inclusion in the INAO and for a more organized national system. But they had to wait until 1955 before they got any special attention. The "Law of 28 November 1955 Relative to Appellations of Origin of Cheeses" formally extended the 1919 protections to cheese and specified what their appellations should include, namely: "come from a milk produced, delivered, and processed in a traditional geographical area, by virtue of local, loyal, and constant usage" and "present their own originality and a clear renown."

But cheeses (along with all other nonalcoholic AOCs) would be kept institutionally separate from wines and spirits until 1990, when they were integrated into the INAO. This meant that, unlike alcohol, other AOCs were rather left to fend for themselves, lacking the agency's organizational and legal support and the benefits (and drawbacks) of working in a coherent system. The ensuing years were challenging, as an institution conceived for one kind of product had to adapt its ideas to fit entirely different kinds of products, while the newcomers had to adapt to much greater oversight and new demands from both peers and bureaucrats.

This turbulence was not helped by the fact that the European Union created an EU-wide geographical indication (GI) system in 1992. Although generally seen as a positive step because it gave much greater strength to GIs internationally, this development added another layer of work for everyone involved with French products under appellation. They had to bring the national system into agreement with the European Union's, which, though heavily influenced by the French system, was still the product of compromise with other member-states. Ever since, under normal circumstances, any product that is accorded an AOC in France is passed up to the European Union for European-level recognition as an AOP (Protected Appellation of Origin). A product having (French) AOC status bears the AOC seal, but once it gets European recognition, it is required to use the European Union's AOP seal.

As of 2014, there were more than 550 AOC products in France, including 45 cheeses, 3 butters, and 2 crèmes fraîches. Approximately 20,000 dairy farms contribute to AOC dairy production, accounting for roughly 10 percent of all cow's and goat's milk and 40 percent of sheep's milk (these figures and those that follow are from 2012, the most recent available). Twenty percent of farmstead cheesemakers (1,350 of them) make an AOC cheese, adding up to about 8 percent of total AOC volume. Legal production criteria of 27 AOC cheeses require that they be made with raw milk (75 percent in terms of volume), and six others specify that farmstead versions must be raw milk while allowing milk treatments for dairy-made cheeses (one, brocciu, cannot be "raw" because its process requires heating the milk). Comté is the king, its tonnage representing a quarter of all AOC cheese production. AOC cheeses represent about 17 percent of cheeses sold on the domestic market, and the export market is worth around 2.8 billion euros—primarily sold to neighboring European countries, but the United States and Japan rank fairly high as customers, as well.

See also LABEL OF ORIGIN.

"Cheeses." Maison du Lait. http://www.maison-du-lait .com/en/milk-products/cheeses.

"Le Cnaol, au service des AOP." Infos Cniel. http:// infos.cniel.com/actualite/le-cnaol-au-service-des-aop.html.

Institut National de l'Origine et de la Qualité (website). http://www.inao.gouv.fr.

Laferté, Gilles. La Bourgogne et ses vins: image d'origine contrôlée. Paris: Belin, 2006.

Juliette Rogers

Appenzeller is a hard cow's milk Swiss cheese that enjoys a rich history. Over seven hundred years ago it was made in the Alps by herdsmen who delivered the cheese as a tithe payment to the St. Gallen monastery, and cheesemaking remains a tradition in the region today.

While Appenzeller does not belong to the AOP cheeses of Switzerland, requirements for its production are very clear: it must be made of cow's milk, in a full fat version that contains 48 percent fat, and in a low-fat version that contains 18 percent fat. The wheels measure 12 to 13 inches (30 to 33 centimeters), and they weigh around 15 pounds (7 kilograms) (full-fat) and 12 to 13 pounds (5.5 to 6 kilograms) (low-fat). During its three to seven months of maturation the cheese is treated with a smear (Sulz) that contains twenty-five herbs, an alcoholic spirit, and other undisclosed ingredients. Originally each maker would alter the composition of his smear by a small amount and thus give the cheeses a specific character. These days the Appenzeller Käse GmbH, an organization that markets and controls the sales of the cheese, wants all makers to use the Sulz produced by the Ebneter distillery in Appenzell, also the producer of the Alpenbitter brandy (*hint*). There are fifty-eight dairies that produce Appenzeller, spread between the Appenzell Aussherrhoden, St. Gallen, and Thurgau canton.

One thing though has become very unclear: How the milk used to make Appenzeller has to—or should—be treated. While the cheese was historically crafted of raw milk and the official website states that it still is, the Appenzeller organization allows the producers to make Appenzeller with thermized milk. While this results in less risk for the dairies—with its high water content, Appenzeller is very delicate and this process results in more uniformity—it also results in less flavor in the cheese.

A very small number of makers still work with raw milk exclusively. The big majority now adds a splash of raw milk to a vat full of thermized milk and calls the finished product raw-milk Appenzeller.

See also SWITZERLAND.

SO Appenzeller Käse GmbH. http://www
.appenzeller.ch.
Nantet, Bernard, Jean-Pierre Dieterlen, and Beate Felten
Patrick Rance, and Françoise Botkine. *Käse: Die 200
besten Sorten der Welt.* Cologne: DuMont, 1994.

Caroline Hostettler

Modern **apprenticeships** exist in the cheesemaking business in a wide variety of forms. Most continental European countries have formalized apprenticeship systems including the dairy industry. The most strictly formalized is found in the German-speaking countries. In Austria and Germany apprenticeships are regularly used to qualify for most nonacademic professions. They follow the completion of a secondary degree. Under the Duales system apprentices divide their time between gaining practical experience with their employer and receiving theoretical instruction at a vocational school (*Berufsschule*) dedicated to the industry. Apprentices receive wages during their training at levels agreed upon by employers and unions throughout each industry. Cheesemaking apprenticeships are geared toward industrial production and apprentices are trained in large dairy-processing businesses. The three-year apprenticeship ends with an exam conveying a state-recognized qualification (AT: Molkerei- und Käsereifacharbeiter/in, D: Milchtechnologe/-in) and a grade. This is equivalent to the journeyman's certificate (*Gesellenbrief*) in traditional manual trades and allows access to some courses in technical colleges. There are also options for further qualification on the vocational track up to mastership (*Molkereimeister/in*) and the right to train apprentices. This level is considered equivalent to a bachelor's degree. Artisanal cheesemakers do not need to complete an apprenticeship.

France is an example of a more scholastic system. Here part-time apprenticeships for many vocational occupations are integrated with an upper secondary two-year curriculum tailored to the qualification offered at dedicated schools. In the cheese industry the Certificat d'Aptitude Professionelle (CAP) of an opérateur de production en fromagerie can be obtained this way. Apprentices are paid at a fraction of the national minimum wage while acquiring their qualifications. The higher levels of the industry are regarded as an academic subject and experts acquire their qualification in the tertiary sector through curricula ranging between two and five years. Some of these are open to holders of a related CAP and can be taken alongside work.

In the English-speaking world, apprenticeships tend to be less formal. The British government has been investing heavily in developing a dual-track apprenticeship system, and some dairy businesses are now offering apprenticeships. They convey qualifications that are portable, but not standardized. Further qualification happens at the tertiary level. Apprentices are selected by their employers and do not need any specific degrees or qualifications. Employers set the length of instruction and cooperate with outside institutions to cover the formal schooling required. In the United States apprenticeships are traditionally contracts between the employer and apprentice, though they are regulated by the Department of Labor. Employers are required to provide external classroom instruction alongside in-house training. Cheesemaking is a recognized apprenticeship, but the number of places offered nationwide is small. Apprentices are paid a minimum wage, and their places can be assisted with public grants. Completing an apprenticeship is not a requirement to enter the dairy industry in either country—with the exception of the state of Wisconsin, which requires licensing for cheesemakers—and higher-level positions in industrial production tend to be filled by university graduates. Unlike in continental Europe, where apprenticeships are the rule in industrial production, in Britain and the United States, it is the artisanal cheese companies that tend to take in apprentices.

See also WISCONSIN'S CHEESEMAKER LICENSING PROGRAM.

Data on German apprenticeship for Milchtechnologe/
-in: http://www.landwirtschaftskammer.de/bildung/
milchtechnologe/einsteiger.
Data on UK apprenticeship program in general: https://
www.gov.uk/topic/further-education-skills/
apprenticeships.
DOL data on US apprenticeship program in general:
https://doleta.gov/oa/data_statistics.cfm.
Johnson, Kristina. "Want to Be an Artisan Cheesemaker?
Here's Where to Start." *Civil Eats*, 15 September 2014.
http://civileats.com/2014/09/15/want-to-be-an-
artisan-cheesemaker-heres-where-to-start.

Volker Bach

The **archaeological detection** of cheese enables an understanding of cheesemaking and dairying practices throughout antiquity. This is particularly useful both prior to and in the absence of iconographic and textual evidence. Cheesemaking can be detected in the archaeological record by a variety of approaches, such as by traditional methods like the identification of ruminant animal bones, but also novel biochemical approaches. Collectively these can be used to understand not only the innovative technological developments behind cheesemaking but also the cultural and dietary diversity of this foodstuff. In addition the human ability to digest milk sugars in adulthood, lactase persistence, represents one of the clearest examples of gene-culture coevolution. Hence the detection of dairy consumption in the archaeological record is of particular interest for understanding how behavioral practices may impact the human genome. See LACTOSE INTOLERANCE.

The study of animal bones in the archaeological record, zooarchaeology, provides information on past patterns of herd use and management. Meat and animal products often represent a significant contribution to past human diets; subsequently, the archaeological record is littered with such evidence. Careful demographic analysis of these remains (kill-off patterns) can be used to identify dairying practices. Dairying can be inferred if an overabundance of older female animals and younger male animals are found, which suggests that female animals were kept until they were old, presumably for milk production and breeding stock, while males were killed off at a younger age, presumably for meat. Much of the earliest evidence of dairying suggests that sheep, goats, and cows were milked. Unfortunately many sheep and goat bone elements are often morphologically indistinguishable, making the identification of the milk's source challenging.

Often used in combination with zooarchaeological evidence, the detection of milk residues in pottery, as well as characteristic pottery forms, has informed much of our understanding about ancient cheesemaking. See EARTHENWARE POTTERY. Such detection is most often achieved through the isotopic analysis of milk lipids (fats), which can become embedded in the walls of ceramic vessels during processing. Milk lipids constitute one of the main nutrient components of milk and are often retained for thousands of years within the porous walls of ceramic vessels. Analysis using gas chromatography mass spectrometry of lipids extracted from archaeological artifacts, such as pottery, can reveal the original foodstuffs placed in vessels during antiquity. Fats from particular food sources have characteristic lipid residues, and the isotopic analysis of these lipids is often able to distinguish between ruminant meat and ruminant milk products. In addition the identification of ketone products in the same analysis can indicate heating. Using this approach it has been possible to identify the oldest evidence of cheesemaking, in vessels dating to approximately nine thousand years ago in northwest Anatolia (present-day Turkey) and eastern Europe.

In addition the shape of pottery itself may indicate evidence of dairying. Perforated "sieves," which are thought to have been used to separate curds from whey (essential for the removal of lactose), appear in European and South Asian archaeological sites in the Neolithic (about seven thousand years ago). Analyses of lipids extracted from these vessels often indicate the presence of dairy products, supporting this hypothesis. While dairying processes and cheesemaking may have been carried out in other vessels prior to the invention of pottery, such as vessels made of perishable organic materials, these do not usually survive in the archaeological record.

While the use of lipid analysis has been instrumental in identifying ancient patterns of dairying, this method is unable to identify which animals were utilized. However the analysis of preserved milk proteins has gone some way to remedy this. Bovine-specific casein has been identified in ancient pottery using immunological methods. Analysis of protein sequences extracted from dental calculus (tartar) from human teeth has also uncovered evidence of proteins from dairy products, creating a direct link between the dairy products and the individuals who consumed them. Using this technique makes it possible to recover dairy proteins that are specific to individual ruminant species, such as cows, sheep, and goats.

Under the right conditions, such as very dry or waterlogged environments, whole fragments of dairy products may survive. For example, the oldest definitive example of a preserved ancient cheese comes from the early Bronze Age cemetery of Xiaohe (1980–1450 B.C.E.) in Xinjiang, China, where food residues were found surrounding a mummy. Analysis of proteins identified the residue as cheese, but also identified the specific bacteria involved in fermentation. Similarly in the United Kingdom a bog-preserved residue found inside a bark vessel dated to the Early Bronze Age also contained casein proteins, suggesting that the vessel contained dairy products. See BOG BUTTER.

A driving question in the archaeological detection of dairying is to pinpoint when humans evolved the genetic ability to consume lactose in adulthood. Analysis of DNA extracted from the remains of past individuals, as well as genetic modeling using genomic information from modern populations, can be used to explore when and where this occurred. Although models suggest that lactase persistence may have developed in eastern Europe, recent data from ancient DNA suggests that lactase persistence developed in the Eurasian steppes, and became incorporated into European populations during the Bronze Age. Looking to more recent time periods, the prevalence of lactase persistence in a medieval German population is similar to present-day levels in northern Europe (about 70 percent), which suggests that the selection pressure for this gene was extremely strong and individuals who carried this allele had a key advantage.

See also ORIGIN OF CHEESE.

Craig, Oliver E., et al. 2000. "Detecting Milk Proteins in Ancient Pots." *Nature* 408, no. 6810 (2000): 312.

Curry, Andrew. "Archaeology: The Milk Revolution." *Nature* 500, no. 7460 (2013): 20–22.

Evershed, Richard P., et al. "Earliest Date for Milk Use in the Near East and Southeastern Europe Linked to Cattle Herding." *Nature* 455, no. 7212 (2008): 528–531.

Warinner, Christina, et al. "Direct Evidence of Milk Consumption from Ancient Human Dental Calculus." *Scientific Reports* 4 (2014): 7104.

Yang, Yimin, et al. "Proteomics Evidence for Kefir Dairy in Early Bronze Age China." *Journal of Archaeological Science* 45 (2014): 178–186.

Jessica Hendy

Archestratus of Gela was an Ancient Greek poet active in the mid-fourth century B.C.E. No complete work remains, but sixty-two fragments of writing have been preserved via Athenaeus in his work *Deipnosophistae*. Most of the surviving fragments focus on piscine cuisine, but cheese is referenced as being particularly antithetical to the merits of high-quality fish. Cooks from Sicily, who frequently used cheese in fish dishes, come up for particular scorn. Fragment 31 suggests "plenty of cheese and oil" as a way to dress up a smaller fish, "for it takes pleasure in big spenders and is unchecked in extravagance," a sarcastic comment on the gourmet elites who would enjoy an inferior fish enhanced by cheese. From the surviving fragments, anyway, it would seem that Archestratus was no cheese fancier, dismissing the culinary significance of cheese as a cheap means of masking off flavors or inferior quality in fish.

See also ANCIENT CIVILIZATIONS.

Wilkins, John, and Shaun Hill, eds. *Archestratus: Fragments from the Life of Luxury*. Rev. ed. Totnes, U.K.: Prospect Books, 2011.

Vince Razionale

Ardrahan Farmhouse Cheese

See COUNTY CORK.

Ardsallagh Goat Farm

See COUNTY CORK.

Argentina, known worldwide for its high-quality meat and dairy products, also boasts a large number of cheeses made in various parts of the country. Roberto Castañeda, in his collaboration for the book *Quesos de América del Sur*, documents over a hundred styles, many of them based on European varieties, particularly those from Italy and Switzerland.

Cheesemaking in Argentina began as a secondary activity to meat and leather ranching. However, the vast plains used for cattle proved to be an ideal location for dairy cows and thus allowed for a strong cheesemaking industry to grow as well. The provinces of Buenos Aires, adjacent to the country's capital, and La Pampa in the central part of the country are the country's most productive cheesemaking regions. The mountainous Tandil region is known for banquete cheese, as well as the Tandil cheese, both similar to creamy young Gouda. The city of Suipacha started designating a "cheese route," to develop agricultural tourism. Visitors can tour different cheesemaking facilities and try some of the regional cheeses.

Perhaps the most popular cheese in Argentina is queso cremoso, a semi-soft, creamy, white rindless cheese. Along with the local version of the Italian mozzarella, a variant is "muzzarella," cremoso used to top pizzas that also can be eaten by itself. Similarly, cheeses like Criollo, goya, Mar de Plata, Tafí, and Taluhet are served as a snack, to stuff empanadas with corn or ham, to melt on top of milanesas, or, simply, to make sandwiches.

Outside of the country, three cheeses are recognized as distinctly Argentinean. Provoleta is a pulled curd cheese, sometimes smoked. The cheese is popular as a side dish during *asados*—the Sunday pastime of grilling on an open fire, when the cheese is melted in a ceramic container on top of the grill. This cow's milk cheese is traditionally made with goat rennet, which imparts its distinctive gamey flavor to the cheese. In Argentinean grills around the world Provoleta is served as an appetizer with a drizzle of olive oil, salt, and pepper. Two other distinct styles are Argentina's Sardo, developed using the recipe for Pecorino Sardo from the island of Sardinia in Italy and Reggianito, developed from the recipe for Parmigiano Reggiano. See PECORINO SARDO and PARMIGIANO REGGIANO. What makes these distinctly Argentinean cheeses, rather than derivatives or imitations of the European versions is not only a difference of terroir, but also different aging conditions and techniques that give these cheeses a tougher and drier texture, even though they are typically aged for a shorter period of time than Italian cheeses. Sardo is made with cow's milk instead of sheep's milk as the original Pecorino from Sardinia.

After World War II, Reggianito was popularized throughout the Americas as a cheaper alternative to the Italian original. Despite their high quality and ability to stand alone in the development of cheese-making traditions of Latin America, these Argentinean cheeses still tend to be commercialized and marketed as derivative, inexpensive alternatives to European products.

See also LATIN AMERICA.

Battro, Pablo. *Quesos Artesanales: Historia, Descripción y Elaboración*. Buenos Aires: Editorial Albatros, 2010.
Castañeda, R., S. Borbonet, A. Ibarra, et al. *Quesos de América del Sur*. Buenos Aires: Editorial Albatros, 2010.

Carlos Yescas

Aristaios (Latin spelling Aristaeus), though not one of the Olympians, was honored as a god in several regions of the ancient Greek world. Early sources agree that he was the son of Apollo and Kyrene and that he married Autonoe, sister of Semele: this makes him the uncle of Dionysos, the Greek god of wine. He is among the figures in Greek mythology who were born mortals and became immortal. His worship in Sparta, as consort of the local goddess Ortheia, and his widespread reputation as a shepherd, seem to place him in the category of pastoral gods who die and are reborn, like Dumuzi, Adonis, and Osiris, and are married to powerful goddesses. See INANNA.

Aristaios taught human beings how to keep bees (many authors agree on this) and how to press olives for oil (as several writers confirm). One source alone, the historical compiler Diodoros of Sicily (first century B.C.E.), asserts that it was also Aristaios who taught cheesemaking. This fits a pattern: Aristaios's specialties, although ancient and important to humanity, are neither plant foods brought into cultivation in the Neolithic Revolution, nor the meat of animals that were Neolithic domesticates. Thus it is possible that Diodoros is reporting a real belief, one that happens to have passed unnoticed by other surviving authors on Greek mythology.

See also ANCIENT CIVILIZATIONS.

Carter, Jane Burr. "The Masks of Ortheia." *American Journal of Archaeology* 91, no. 3 (1987): 355–383.
Diodoros. *Diodorus of Sicily*. Vol. 3: Historical Library 4.81–4.82. Translated by C. H. Oldfather. Cambridge, Mass.: Harvard University Press, 1939. See pp. 73–79.

Andrew Dalby

Arla is a dairy cooperative that had its beginnings in the small Scandinavian cooperatives that formed in the 1880s to maximize efficiency and produce better-quality products. Formed in 2000 from the largest cooperatives in Sweden and Denmark, Arla has grown enormously since 2005 and now owns businesses in Germany, Holland, and the United Kingdom. Today it is the third largest dairy cooperative in the world.

Running a business owned by more than thirteen thousand dairy farmers across five countries presents logistical challenges. The business has responded to this situation by creating an equally diverse set of services. Much of its activity is focused on research and development, with labs based in Denmark, where it has been a leading innovator of new products such as lactose-free foods and micro-filtered long-life milk. Arla also has an ingredients division that seeks to impart the goodness of milk to many value-added products and ingredients, such as milk powder, milk-based beverages, spreadable cheese, and value-added whey, to name a few. Major brands include Lurpak butter, as well as other spreads, and a new range of butters designed specifically for cooking, such as clarified butter, cooking mist, and cooking liquid. The cooperative has also invested heavily in state-of-the-art processing equipment and has recently opened the largest milk-bottling plant in the United Kingdom.

The decade from 2005 to 2015 saw a significant increase in cheese production by Arla, much of it due to acquisitions of cheese-producing businesses such as Tholstrup and Milk Link. "Castello" (originally a Danish blue cheese made by Tholstrup) is now the umbrella brand for more than forty cheeses, including industrial Brie, goat's milk Camembert, cream cheeses, and Gouda. This strategy of acquisition and expansion into a broader range of milk products is likely to continue for the foreseeable future.

See also DENMARK; NORWAY; and SWEDEN.

Arla. http://www.arla.com.

John Pearson

aroma is perceived when chemical receptors in the human nose are activated by volatile chemical compounds. Hundreds of aroma compounds have been identified in cheeses, and the diversity of cheese aromas derives from the nearly limitless combinations of these compounds in different ratios.

Although humans are often thought to have relatively weak olfactory capabilities, we are still able to detect and distinguish tens of thousands of compounds, some of them in concentrations as dilute as parts per trillion. The aroma of a specific food product is the result of specific ratios of certain chemical compounds, often mediated by the particular non-volatile matrix that makes up the rest of the food. Because of this, the range of aromas (and, therefore, flavors) in foods is effectively limitless. Aroma makes up the lion's share of flavor; to prove this, it is only necessary to recall the dulling effects of the tempo-

rary anosmia (loss of the sense of smell) characteristic of the common cold, or, more concretely, to try a bite of a flavorful Époisses or Taleggio with the nose pinched closed.

All human aroma perception takes place in the nose; the organ at which volatile aroma compounds are detected is called the "nasal epithelium," and sits in the roof of the sinus cavity. Human perception of aroma is through two distinct routes: "orthonasal" and "retronasal." The orthonasal route is what we normally think of as smelling: volatile compounds in the environment near the head are sniffed up through the nostrils. In fact, however, the retronasal route is more important for foods and flavors: aroma compounds escaping from food in the mouth travel up through the back of the throat into the sinus cavity during chewing and even after swallowing. Due to the intensity of taste sensations and the physical presence of the food, this retronasal aroma is integrated into "flavor" in the brain's sensory centers and misunderstood as occurring in the mouth. Even those who are aware of aroma's true dominance cannot, in general, separate flavor into its component sensations.

The near-synonyms of "aroma" reveal some of the ambivalence with which this critical sense is considered: "smell" and "odor" both have negative associations. This ambivalence can be traced to Platonic philosophies of the senses, in which taste and smell were both relegated to second-class status; in the modern era, fears of contamination and social anxiety are often associated with aroma, in particular the aroma of the body or food in public spaces. In this sense, cheeses are often considered archetypical "smelly" foods: Limburger or other washed-rind cheeses are frequent punch lines in popular culture for their strong aromas, and even cheeses that are not as aromatically intense but have strong in-the-mouth flavors, like blue cheeses, are synesthetically mislabeled as "stinky." Nevertheless, as we have seen above, the aroma of cheeses is a key part of their sensory profiles and appeal.

A comprehensive list of cheese aromas would run to hundreds of impressions and compounds, exhausting even the most avid researcher or enthusiast. Almost all cheeses share a set of basic, dairy-associated aromas. Among the most typical are buttery/caramel notes from diacetyl; cheesy, sharp, and sweaty notes from organic acids, most typically butyric; coconut and milk fat notes from lactones;

cooked-milk aromas that seem to derive from various sulfur-containing compounds; fruity aromas from methyl and ethyl esters; and sour/fermented aromas from lactic and acetic acids and other small, volatile products of fermentation. Beyond this basic profile, a number of types of cheese present characteristic aromas.

Cheeses made from ovine (sheep's) or caprine (goat's) milk tend to present distinctive aromas derived from their distinct fatty-acid compositions. See FAT. In particular, the "goaty" aroma associated with the eponymous cheeses is strongly related to the presence of caproic, caprylic, and capric acids (6-, 8-, and 10-carbon), as well as some isomers, not typically found in cow's milk fat, in combination with a relative paucity of butyric acid; sheep's milk contains both capric and butyric acids, as well as the typically "muttony" 4-methyloctanoic acid.

Hard cheeses can manifest a broad range of aromas. Some of the more interesting aromas include "barnyardy" or "animal-like" smells related to phenolic compounds, and pineapple or caramel aromas, which arise from highly substituted lactones, including the strawberry/pineapple/caramel accord of furaneol and the maple/fenugreek aroma of sotolon, typical of Comté, Parmigiano Reggiano, and other long-aged, hard cheeses. See COMTÉ and PARMIGIANO REGGIANO.

The characteristic sharp/sweet aroma of blue cheeses appears to derive primarily from so-called methyl ketones: carbon chains substituted with an oxygen at the second carbon, most typically 2-heptanone and 2-nonanone. See BLUE CHEESES and METHYL KETONES.

Perhaps the most famously aromatic cheeses are the washed-rind group. These cheeses are often described as "pungent." The colonies of *Brevibacterium linens* and related microflora on their brine-washed rinds produce a characteristic orange color and an initially off-putting, strong aroma reminiscent of "gym socks," "armpits," or even protein decay. This makes sense, given that the compounds identified in their aromas so far include decay products containing nitrogen and sulfur, such as sulfides, indole, and volatile phenolic compounds. Interestingly, despite their intense aromas, these cheeses tend to taste comparatively mild, although usually quite savory—further evidence of the complex relationship between aroma and flavor. See *BREVIBACTERIUM LINENS* and WASHED-RIND CHEESES.

See also FAMILIES OF CHEESE; FLAVOR; ODOR-ACTIVE COMPOUNDS; and TASTE.

Drake, M. A. "Invited Review: Sensory Analysis of Dairy Foods." *Journal of Dairy Science* 90 (2007): 4925–4937.
Koppel, K., and D. H. Chambers. "Flavor Comparison of Natural Cheeses Manufactured in Different Countries." *Journal of Food Science* 77 (2012): S177–S187.
Sablé, S., and G. Cottenceau. "Current Knowledge of Soft Cheeses Flavor and Related Compounds." *Journal of Agricultural and Food Chemistry* 47 (1999): 4825–4836.
Shepherd, Gordon M. *Neurogastronomy.* New York: Columbia University Press, 2012.

Jake Lahne

aroma wheel

See FLAVOR WHEEL.

Cheese in and as **art**—visual and sculptural—has a long genealogy, from its early depictions in medieval primers on food and health, to representations in still life paintings, to the use of cheese itself as a material in "bioart" today.

Start in the late Middle Ages: the fourteenth-century *Tacuinum Sanitatis*, a Latin adaptation of an eleventh-century Arabic manual on well-being by physician Ibn Butlan, presented cheese, a food

Vincenzo Campi's oil painting *The Ricotta Eaters* (ca. 1585) posed a thick gobbet of ricotta as a symbol of lusty indulgence. COURTESY OF MUSÉE DES BEAUX-ARTS DE LYON

crafted by feudal farmers, as part of a healthy diet for nobles. By the sixteenth century, cheese—or, better, *some* kinds of cheeses—came to suggest less salutary associations. Vincenzo Campi's *The Ricotta Eaters* (ca. 1585) posed a thick gobbet of ricotta as a symbol of lusty indulgence. Three debauched male peasants, joined by a rouged lady of the evening, dig into a mound of ricotta, a cheese that in its allegorical association with semen had by the time of this painting's production come to be linked with sex (cheese and cheesemaking long providing a repertoire of analogies for sex and procreation, as Sandra Ott [1993] has shown). Three of the characters in this painting clutch ladles, suggesting that an illicit sexual mixing is in progress (Simons, 2011, pp. 267–269). See CURDLING, CULTURAL THEORIES OF.

Later portrayals of cheese shift the moral valence of cheese back toward the positive, even toward the chaste (Janaczewska, 2013). In her 1625 *Still Life with Cheeses, Artichoke, and Cherries,* Dutch artist Clara Peeters "painted cheese and butter to represent motherhood and purity" (Dangler, 2014). It may be no accident that the cheese in Peetes's painting is Dutch, while the artichoke and cherries, representing unwholesome desire, hail from the southern, less temperate, lands of the Mediterranean. American painter Raphaelle Peale's 1813 *Cheese with Three Crackers* offers a later, less charged cheese portrait. Peale sought not to enlist cheese as an emblem of wrong or right morals (nor as a vehicle for communicating regionalist prejudices), but rather hoped, as in his other still lifes of food, to show the ordinariness of this food (Frederick, 2006). Later cheese

Synthetic biologist Christina Agapakis (left, facing) and smell artist Sissel Tolaas (right) pose with the cheese they made from starter cultures isolated from the human body. The project, called *Selfmade,* suggests how humans—individually and collectively—are tied to the microbial worlds they consume and embody. © SCIENCE GALLERY, DUBLIN

still lifes—of the sort created in the early twenty-first century by Mike Geno—turn cheeses into charismatic subjects, worthy of celebratory portraiture.

One of the stranger evocations of cheese in painting comes with Salvador Dalí's 1931 *Persistence of Memory*, an oil painting famous for its melting pocket watches, which Dalí claimed were inspired by watching rounds of Camembert deliquesce.

Cheese moves from the documented to the symbolically freighted, from the domain of sensible portraiture to that of the phantasmagorical and inspiring. In today's art world, cheese manifests as all of these—and more. Contemporary artists have lately turned their attention to the materiality of media, and cheese has arrived as a potent substance with which to work through the politics of bodies, food, farming, and much else. Such art goes beyond folk traditions of cheese sculpture (usually done in Cheddar), which have fixed on the *form* of cheese (Wisconsin Milk Marketing Board, 2012), such as the work of cheese sculptor Sarah Kaufmann. This art has delved instead into cheese's *substance*, which, artists suggest, evocatively materializes politics of relations among humans, animals, and microbes.

For example, *Selfmade*, by synthetic biologist Christina Agapakis and smell artist Sissel Tolaas asks what it is about bacterially produced smells that repel or attract people. Agapakis and Tolaas set out "to make cheeses with starter cultures isolated from the human body." After "swabs from hands, feet, noses, and armpits were inoculated into fresh, pasteurized, organic whole milk and incubated overnight" (Agapakis, 2011, pp. 141–142), Agapakis and Tolaas pressed the resulting curds into cheese. Giving their cheeses the names of the individual people whose microbes served as starter cultures, they hoped to prompt thinking about how humans—individually and collectively—are tied to the microbial worlds we consume and embody.

Bio artist Miriam Simun, undertaking a related project, in 2011 made cheese with human breast milk. Deadpanning in her description of this art project, she wrote,

Human Cheese is a socio-technical and economic system for sourcing, making and distributing human cheese, positioned as a real commodity. Sourcing human milk via the internet, making cheese in my kitchen, and adopting the storytelling practices of small-scale artisanal food brands, Human Cheese

culminates in The Lady Cheese Shop: an installation that presents ethically sourced, locally made cheeses made from "the original natural food"—human milk. (Simun, 2011)

Simun invited people to taste the cheese as a way of confronting questions about the commoditization of bodies—human and nonhuman.

In all of these art works, cheese is a symbolic substance, inviting rumination on what will count as proper moral relations among bodies and foods, whether in the realm of the sacred or the secular, or in the domain of the Christian-cosmological, or the contemporary capitalist. The long history of cheese in and as art tells the story of shifting sensibilities about the relations between food and morality, and between the material and the political world.

See also CHILDREN'S LITERATURE and LITERATURE.

Agapakis, Christina. "Biological Design Principles for Synthetic Biology," PhD diss., Division of Medical Sciences, Harvard University, 2011.

Dangler, Emily. "Picture Perfect Cheese Art." *Culture: The Word on Cheese*, 3 October 2014. http://culturecheesemag.com/cheese-bites/picture-perfect-cheese-art.

Frederick, Jason. "Painterly Struggle: Conflict and Resolution with Raphaelle Peale's Still Life Paintings." M.A. thesis, University of Florida, 2006.

Janaczewska, Noëlle. "Cheese in Art." Eat the Table, 10 October 2013. http://eatthetable.com/2013/10/10/cheese-in-art.

Miriam Simun/Human Cheese. http://www.miriamsimun.com/human-cheese.

Ott, Sandra. *The Circle of Mountains: A Basque Shepherding Community*. Reno: University of Nevada Press, 1993.

Simons, Patricia. *The Sex of Men in Premodern Europe: A Cultural History*. Cambridge, U.K.: Cambridge University Press, 2011.

Wisconsin Milk Marketing Board. "The ABCs of Carving Cheese: How to Create Dynamic Cheese Displays to Attract Customers and Increase Profits." 2012. http://training.wmmb.com/live/downloads/ABCs_of_Carving_Cheese.pdf.

Stefan Helmreich

artisanal is a term used to describe production systems that are relatively small-scale and where handworking and the skilled, intuitive judgment of the maker takes precedence over mechanized and automated methods. Common synonyms include "craft," "handmade," and "traditional." Artisanal cheese is often made on the farm with milk from the farmer's own herd (in North America, these varieties are usually known as farmstead cheese). See FARMSTEAD. However, there are also many independent cheesemakers, including a growing number of urban microdairies based in the heart of major cities such as London and New York. Although it is relatively easy to distinguish modern artisanal cheesemakers from their high-volume industrial counterparts, there is still scope for ambiguity and confusion. For example, specialty cheese, a term that is sometimes applied to artisanal products, is also used to describe exotic or novel varieties produced at an industrial scale. See SPECIALTY CHEESE.

Artisanal cheeses tend to display greater variability in comparison with their factory-produced counterparts and are characterized by distinctive organoleptic properties of taste, smell, and texture. Whereas industrial-scale cheesemakers prioritize consistency by standardizing key ingredients, artisanal makers accommodate and control for seasonal and other naturally occurring variations and nuances in more sensitive and intuitive ways. Their working practices are based on long-established bodies of knowledge, practical skills, and associated values, which can be applied to every stage, from the milking of livestock through to maturation and ripening. See MATURING. In Europe, artisanal cheeses are generally associated with a particular terroir or locality, and draw on its unique combination of environmental variables (e.g., microclimate, soil type, flora, fauna, mold, bacteria) and cultural heritage. See TERROIR. Over the centuries, many of the traditional European cheese varieties have been relocated, and to some degree reinvented, in other parts of the world. The rise of "new world" artisanal cheesemaking represents a further refinement of this process that is, like its wine industry counterpart, generating novel insights and approaches. The individual cheesemaker faces a similar set of challenges, irrespective of location. As recent anthropological studies suggest, it is precisely the capacity to think "with" and "through" these complex ecologies that gives artisanal cheeses their distinctive qualities.

In the preindustrial era, cheese was mainly produced on farms and much of it would have been of indifferent quality. Modern artisanal cheesemaking emerged largely as a reaction to the standardization imposed by industrialization. See INDUSTRIALIZATION. The movement has enrolled a varied cast of actors and has played itself out from the mid-nineteenth century up to the present day. Gastronomes and social commentators have railed against the loss of regional varieties and expressed their dissatisfaction when confronted by poor-quality cheese; small farmers and development organizations have mounted vociferous and often effective campaigns to preserve the livelihoods of rural communities in the face of industrial competition; cheesemaking enthusiasts including Juliet Harbutt, Randolph Hodgson, Jean-Claude Le Jaouen, Mary Keehn, and Patrick Rance, have been instrumental in promoting and developing new markets. Trade organizations such as the Specialist Cheesemakers Association (United Kingdom) and the Vermont Institute for Artisan Cheese (United States) have provided cheesemakers with valuable information and technical support. See HODGSON, RANDOLPH; LE JAOUEN, JEAN-CLAUDE; RANCE, PATRICK; and SPECIALIST CHEESEMAKERS ASSOCIATION. Government policies have also played an important, yet more ambivalent role. Some initiatives, such as protected designation of origin (PDO) and appellation d'origine contrôlée (AOC), have had a largely (though not entirely) beneficial impact on artisanal practice. See DESIGNATION OF ORIGIN and APPELLATION D'ORIGINE CONTRÔLÉE. Other interventions, including those designed to accelerate agricultural modernization and industry concentration, have tended to undermine smaller farm-based cheesemakers. Regulatory restrictions placed on raw-milk cheeses have proved particularly challenging for artisanal makers as far afield as Scotland, where Humphrey Errington fought successfully for his Lanark Blue sheep's milk cheese, and Brazil, where small farmers in the Campos de Cima da Serra region are defending an unpasteurized Serrano cheese that has been produced there for more than two hundred years. See RAW-MILK CHEESES.

By the mid-twentieth century, the prospect for artisanal cheesemaking was looking fairly bleak—particularly in countries like Britain and the United States, where the political consensus around "big business" was at its height. However, in retrospect, this period marked a turning point for smaller-scale producers as a new generation of artisans has made its presence felt—a trend that has been replicated in many industrialized countries. These cheesemakers are more self-consciously "artisanal" than their predecessors. They study traditional practices and seek inspiration from the past, while also making selective use of modern production technologies. There is also a growing interest in the ways that science—and microbiology in particular—can be applied to artisanal production processes in order to address food quality issues. Though many are closely connected to their local community, today's artisans also form part of a much larger community of practice that can interact via the Internet and modern transportation systems. Similarly, while many small producers are actively focusing their attention on local food markets, artisanal cheeses often travel much farther afield courtesy of global food retail and food service supply chains, as well as "alternative" channels such as online delicatessens.

There has been a rapid growth in artisanal cheesemaking in many parts of the world. For example, when the American Cheese Society awards began in 1985, there were just 89 entries from 30 cheesemakers; by 2014, the event was attracting 1,685 entries and the number of makers had increased to 289. See AMERICAN CHEESE SOCIETY. Despite this, artisanal cheese remains a niche product. Modern artisanal production processes are also something of a hybrid creation, subject to powerful competitive and regulatory pressures of a food industry that has become dominated by transnational corporations. However, there is good cause to celebrate the vision of both established and "new generation" artisanal cheesemakers who continue to thrive in a highly industrialized global food system. Working in tandem with similarly minded wholesalers, retailers, and restaurateurs, they are championing more sustainable food production methods and contributing to broader changes in the way we think about food.

See also INDUSTRIAL and INDUSTRIEL.

Cruz, Fabiana Thomé da, and Renata Menascheb. "Tradition and Diversity Jeopardised by Food Safety Regulations? The Serrano Cheese Case, Campos de Cima da Serra Region, Brazil." *Food Policy* 45 (2014): 116–124.

Paxson, Heather. *The Life of Cheese: Crafting Food and Value in America.* California Studies in Food and Culture, vol. 41. Berkeley: University of California Press, 2013.

Tregear, Angela. "From Stilton to Vimto: Using Food History to Rethink Typical Products in Rural Development." *Sociologia Ruralis* 43, no. 2, (2003): 91–107.

West, Harry G. "Thinking Like a Cheese: Towards an Ecological Understanding of the Reproduction of Knowledge in Contemporary Artisan Cheesemaking." In *Understanding Cultural Transmission in Anthropology: A Critical Synthesis,* edited by Roy Ellen, Stephen J. Lycett, and Sarah E. Johns, pp. 320–345. New York: Berghahn, 2013.

Richard K. Blundel

Artisan Dairy Program

See ONTARIO.

Arzúa-Ulloa is a soft cheese from Galicia (Northwest Spain), a region with a strong cheesemaking tradition and yielding approximately 40 percent of the cow's milk produced in Spain. The cheese is made from cow's milk (raw or pasteurized), exclusively in a specific geographic area on the banks of the Ulla River, in the central area of Galicia. The cheese, formerly known as Ulloa cheese (until 1989) and Arzúa cheese (1989–1995), has been protected since 1995 with the designation of origin (DO) "Arzúa-Ulloa" (Commission Regulation (EC) No. 20/2010). Since 2011 Arzúa-Ulloa represents the highest production among all Spanish cow's milk cheeses, at approximately 7 million pounds (3.2 million kilograms) in 2014.

The PDO designation includes three varieties of Arzúa-Ulloa: farmstead, industrial, and mature. The farmstead variety (Arzúa-Ulloa de Granxa) is usually only sold at local markets. Industrial Arzúa-Ulloa cheeses are generally made with pasteurized milk with commercial nonspecific starters added, usually *lactococci* and *leuconostocs* (mesophilic DL-starters). Milk is curdled with calf rennet (about 0.25 milliliter/liter, 1:10,000–15,000 strength) at 86–90°F (30–32°C) for thirty to forty minutes. The curd is then cut into 5 to 10 millimeter pieces and washed with pasteurized water at 93–97°F (34–36°C). The cheeses are molded and horizontally pressed (approximately 4 kilograms/centimeter^2) for at least two hours. Salting may be made performed in three different ways: directly on the milk before coagulation (a more traditional method but less popular nowadays), in the cheese vat over the curd, or at the end

Traditional Arzúa-Ulloa, a Galician pressed cow's milk cheese. © JUAN A. CENTENO

of the process by introducing the cheeses in brine for a maximum of twenty-four hours. The cheeses are ripened for at least six days at 32–50°F (4–10°C) and 80–90 percent relative humidity. They have a lenticular shape, or cylindrical with rounded edges, and the final weight ranges between 1 and 8 pounds (0.5 and 4 kilograms). The taste is slightly salty and pleasantly acidic, and the texture unctuous and creamy. The flavor is buttery and milky with nutty notes rather different from the yeasty, farmyard and slightly rancid notes of the traditional raw-milk starter-free products. The "mature" Arzúa-Ulloa variety must be ripened for at least four months, and presents a stronger flavor, more salty, and slightly spicy with delicate nutty and vanilla notes. Ripening for up to a year was a traditional practice for cheeses manufactured from the middle of autumn to the middle of winter, using milk from animals feed with a plant variety from the *Brassicaceae* family locally known as "nabiza."

See also SPAIN.

Almena M., Y. Noel, and A. Cepeda. "Rheological Characterisation of Arzúa-Ulloa Cheese by Compression." *Milchwissenschaft* 53 (1998): 319.

Almena M., Y. Noel, and A. Cepeda. "Effect of "Cheese Making Conditions on Texture of Arzúa-Ulloa Cheese during Ripening Time." *Journal of Dairy Science* 83, Suppl. 1 (2000): 100–101.

Rodríguez-Alonso P., J. A. Centeno, and J. I. Garabal. "Comparison of the Volatile Profiles of Arzúa-Ulloa and Tetilla Cheeses Manufactured from Raw and Pasteurized Milk." *LWT—Food Science and Technology* 42 (2009): 1722–1728.

Juan A. Centeno

asexual reproduction is the multiplication of cells without any sexual processes. In this way large numbers of cells can be obtained during cheesemaking and ripening (such as the surface rind that develops on bloomy cheeses). While asexual reproduction leads to genetically identical daughter cells, sexual reproduction results in genetically unique individuals. There are a number of types of asexual reproduction, such as fission, budding (like yeast on bloomy-rind cheeses), vegetative propagation, spore formation (fungi such as *Penicillium*) and fragmentation (fungi). In eukaryotic (higher) organisms, cell division (fission) is accomplished by mitosis, a multistage process that distributes the duplicated genetic material equally between two daughter cells. In prokaryotic organisms (bacteria), cell division occurs by binary fission during the exponential phase of growth. In both cases the chromosomes are doubled before separation into each cell.

There are three main phases in binary fission: elongation of the mother cell, formation of the transverse wall, and finally separation of the two daughter cells. Each cell is able to continue the cell cycle just like the mother cell. During the first phase the mother cell increases in size by synthesizing cell components, including the circular DNA molecules, the chromosomes. When the equator of the cell constricts and the transverse wall forms in the mother cell, there are two copies of each chromosome, or even four when the growth rate is very high. Once the wall is completely formed, the two daughter cells separate and become independent. With asexual reproduction, all the daughter cells have the same genetic material, unless spontaneous mutations occur.

Escherichia coli is a bacterial species that has a generation or doubling time of fifteen to twenty minutes, depending on temperature as well as readily available nutrients, so in just a few hours, millions of daughter cells can be formed. Other species multiply much more slowly, such as the pathogen *Mycobacterium tuberculosis* (doubling time of fifteen to twenty hours). See PATHOGENS. In milk *Lactococcus lactis* has a doubling time of twenty-six minutes. See *LACTOCOCCUS LACTIS*. This growth rate determines the production of acid by the starter culture, which defines the acidification profile and thus the resulting cheese. If asexual reproduction is not properly controlled from the beginning, acidification can digress extremely quickly. Rapid growth of molds can contribute positively to cheese surfaces, or negatively when contamination occurs because sanitation is not optimal. Thus managing asexual reproduction is crucial during cheesemaking.

See also ACIDIFICATION; FILAMENTOUS FUNGI; and FUNGI.

de Meeûs, T., et al. "Asexual Reproduction: Genetics and Evolutionary Aspects." *Cellular and Molecular Life Sciences* 64 (2007): 1355–1372.

Narra, H. P., and H. Ochman. "Of What Use Is Sex to Bacteria?" *Current Biology* 16, no. 17 (2006): R705–R710.

Gisèle LaPointe

ash from burnt vegetable sources has long been used for both practical and aesthetic reasons in the production of certain kinds of cheese. Perhaps the best-known use of ash is in the manufacture of the semi-soft cow's milk cheese Morbier, produced in the region of Franche-Comté. Morbier originated in the nineteenth century when producers of Comté cheese combined curds remaining in the evening with curds from the next day's milking. The leftover evening curds were pressed into the bottom of a mold, and the exposed surface was sprinkled with spruce ash to protect it from microbial growth, insects, and other contaminants. The following day, the mold would be filled with curds from that morning's milking, resulting in a distinctive black line horizontally bisecting the final cheese. Today Morbier is made

Tymsboro, a goat's milk cheese made by Mary Holbrook of Sleight Farm in Somerset, England. The cheese is coated in a mixture of ash (charcoal) and salt, which reduces the surface acidity, draws moisture out of the cheese, and promotes rind formation. © KATE ARDING

from a single milking, with the ash line included for aesthetic reasons. See MORBIER.

Aside from Morbier, ash is used in the manufacture of a variety of cow's, goat's, and sheep's milk cheeses. Many well-known goat cheeses from the Loire Valley—including Selles-sur-Cher, Valençay, and Sainte-Maure de Touraine—are coated with ash, which is often mixed with salt, to help protect and develop their rinds. See LOIRE VALLEY. The practice of coating goat cheese with ash has also been adopted by several artisanal cheesemakers in the United States. Some varieties have a striking black line in the curd that comes from ash layered in during the molding process.

The ash itself may be derived from various sources, from grapevine clippings to wood, with the more recent adoption of activated charcoal. Dye is also used by some cheesemakers to give a similar appearance.

Ash is assumed to serve a variety of functions in cheesemaking. Ash is alkaline, and so reduces surface acidity and promotes the early stages of rind formation. Alkalinity from the ash also contributes to a softer curd. With its water-absorbing properties, ash is thought to help dry the rind and aid in preserving the surface during ripening. Finally, the striking black or gray appearance of ash-coated cheeses provides them with a distinctive visual appeal.

See also SAINTE-MAURE DE TOURAINE; SELLES-SUR-CHER; and VALENÇAY.

Medina, M., and M. Nuñez. "Cheeses Made from Ewes' and Goats' Milk." In *Cheese: Chemistry, Physics, and Microbiology*, edited by Patrick F. Fox et al. Vol. 2: *Major Cheese Groups*, pp. 279–299. New York: Elsevier, 2004.

New England Cheesemaking Supply Co. "Goat Cheese with Ash." http://www.cheesemaking.com/GoatWithAsh.html.

Sister Noella Marcellino and David R. Benson

Asiago is a cow's milk cheese made only in the northeastern part of Italy, in an area strictly defined by the PDO (protected designation of origin) recognition that includes the provinces of Vicenza and Trento and part of Padua and Treviso; both the milk and the cattle must come from that limited area to meet production specifications. The town of Asiago, 1,000 meters above sea level in the province of Vicenza, gave historical and etymological origins to this cheese. Asiago is surrounded by the Plateau of the Seven Municipalities, a wide-ranging area varying in height from 229 to 2,336 meters above sea level, where splendid mountains and wildflowers abound.

Asiago cheese is one of the oldest Italian cheeses: Greek and Latin texts mention dairy production in Veneto, part of the Roman Empire until the fifth century C.E. when, following a feudal period, it became part of the Republic of Venice. Around the year 1000, there was already news of the Asiago Plateau's cheese. Those were the times of domination by bishops and feudal lords of Padua, who required duty and rent to be paid in cheese. In those periods the cheese from Asiago was made with ewe's milk, but later, under the control of the Republic of Venice, sheep were replaced with cows. In more recent decades, with the expansion of trade, identifying the product with its place of origin became a necessity: hence, the appellation "Asiago cheese."

The first Italian law to protect a food sector was passed in 1955, and Asiago cheese was awarded the Denominazione Tipica, which turned into the Denominazione di Origine Controllata (DOC) in 1978, and finally, into PDO in 1992. In 2006 Asiago PDO was awarded the European designation of Prodotto della Montagna (Mountain Product) for those cheeses produced and aged more than 600 meters above sea level.

Asiago PDO can be identified by its brand protection markings: a casein plate indicating the production date, processing date, and milk producers; an identification number linking to a unique dairy farm; "Consorzio Tutela Formaggio Asiago" (Consortium for the Protection of Asiago Cheese) stamped across the wheel; the denomination logo (the letter "A" as a wedge cut from the wheel) and the word "ASIAGO" stenciled along the rind. Two types of Asiago cheese coexist under the same "Asiago PDO" denomination: Asiago *fresco* (fresh, also referred to as sweet or pressed) and Asiago *stagionato* (aged, also referred to as *di allevo*/thoroughbred), in the varieties of *mezzano* (medium), *vecchio* (old), and *stravecchio* (very old).

Asiago Fresco

Asiago PDO fresco (fresh) is made with whole cow's milk. Its curd is broken into medium-size lumps, approximately the size of walnut shells, to limit the amount of whey drainage. After partial cooking at about 111°F (44°C), it is taken out of the boiler and, after a brief ripening and salting, poured into molds and pressed to eliminate any excess whey. The cheese, which remains soft and wet, is placed into stenciling bands to imprint its name on it. After about three weeks of ripening, the cheese becomes Asiago PDO fresco, reaching its peak at around fifty days. Asiago fresco is not suitable for aging and must therefore be enjoyed within two months. It has a soft, slightly elastic texture, a light straw color, and irregular eyes. It smells like butter and cream, with a slight hint of yogurt. Its taste confirms its lightness, with tactile creamy sensations, and its sweet, yet acidulated finish is delightfully fresh and pleasing.

Asiago Stagionato

Asiago PDO stagionato (aged/thoroughbred) involves an entirely different method of production from the very beginning. Cow's milk is left to rest for a few hours before the top cream is removed, leaving semi-skimmed milk to be processed. Following coagulation with rennet, the curd is broken into small, hazelnut-size pieces, immediately eliminating most of the whey and leaving curd of a drier texture that will not require pressing. It is then cooked to about 117°F (47°C), left to rest in the stenciling bands, and salted. After a couple of days' more rest, the cheese must be aged in the area of production. The length of time the cheese is aged—from a minimum of three months up to two years or more—determines the variety of Asiago stagionato: Asiago mezzano (medium, aged up to six months), which has a compact, still-soft texture, straw color with well-spread eyes, and smells of milk and grass with a full, but still sweet, taste; Asiago vecchio (old, aged up to fifteen months), which has a firm texture, deep straw color, and small, well-spread eyes, while smelling of grass and fruit, with a rich flavor containing hints of dried fruit that alternate with slightly pungent sensations; and "aged" Asiago stravecchio (very old, more than fifteen months), which is hard in texture, gold in color when made in the summer, with well-spread very small eyes and a powerful, complex smell that includes hints of dried fruit, pasture, and, remarkably, spices. Its flavor confirms its great personality, finishing in light "pin pricks" at the edge of the tongue, and a pleasant aftertaste of hay that alternates with dried fruit, making it both persistent and thrilling.

Production of Asiago PDO cheese, which is now well known in over fifty countries, surpasses 1.7 million wheels for a total weight of 49 million pounds (22,000 tonnes) annually, while its exports from 2009 to 2015 have more than doubled. This dramatic increase in exports was possible because the Consortium of Protection widened the production area to the plains. The Consortium of Protection coordinates the collection of milk from about 1,500 farms and supervises the production of around 40 dairies. In addition, the consortium works to carefully protect what is a great cultural legacy as well as a productive asset in the mountain area, where in the summer, many active farmsteads are still committed to making aged Asiago PDO, the most ancient product that today represents the highest quality of a mere 20 percent of the total Asiago PDO production.

See also ITALY.

Asiago Formaggio D.O.P. http://www
.asiagocheese.it/it.
Famiglia Gastaldello. http://www.famigliagastaldello.it/
en/prodotti/cheese/cheese.
"Italy: Asiago Cheese Production." CLAL.it. http://
www.clal.it/en/?section=produzioni_asiago.

Erasmo Gastaldello

The **Association of Quebec Cheesemakers** (Association des Fromagers Artisans du Québec) was founded in 2008 by a group of small-scale cheese producers. Together the twenty-one members (as of 2015) crafted over one hundred different types of cheese, turning out close to 1,102 short tons (1,000 metric tons) each year. Many are made from raw milk, and some are certified as organic. The Association filed for a farmstead appellation in the summer of 2015 to certify that cheeses produced by its members are made exclusively with milk from their own cows, goats, or sheep and are free from modified milk substances. Many of the members' cheeses, such as the Louis d'Or, the Baluchon, Alfred le Fermier, or the Zacharie Cloutier, have won a number of prizes in provincial and national competitions. The Association was established to defend Quebec's farmstead cheese producers and develop economically sustainable practices for the artisanal cheese segment. It is perhaps best known

for its itinerant cheesemakers' festival, held every summer since 2010. Each year, members gather at one of the artisans' farms to reach out to the public and offer free samples of their cheeses. The stated objectives of the festival, which generally draws between fifteen thousand and twenty thousand visitors, include democratizing fine cheeses and sensitizing festivalgoers to the amount of work involved in crafting artisanal products. In 2014, particular emphasis was placed on the importance of supporting local producers in the context of free-trade accords with the European Union, which aim to double quotas for Canadian importation of cheeses from the European Union and generates significant concerns within Quebec's artisan cheesemaking community.

See also ARTISANAL; CANADA; QUEBEC; and RAW-MILK CHEESES.

Association des Fromagers Artisans du Québec. http://
fromagersartisans.com.

Laura Shine

Australia and New Zealand are both ranked among the top ten cheese-producing countries in the world. Most of the cheese made and exported is industrially produced, with Cheddar as the mainstay, but artisan and specialty cheesemaking has flourished in the region since the 1980s.

Much of Australia is desert or semi-arid land, so most cheese production takes place along the fertile southeastern coastal zones between Brisbane and Adelaide, and in a small region south of Perth on the western coast. New Zealand's temperate climate, combined with consistent rainfall, sunshine, and fertile soils, create conditions ideal for dairy farming throughout both the North and South islands.

Dairy farming began in Australia with the arrival of the British in 1788. Commercial cheesemaking started in the 1820s, south of Sydney, and by the mid-nineteenth century bulk production of mostly Cheddar cheese was widespread. See CHEDDAR.

Italian-style cheeses were made commercially in Melbourne in the 1930s, but it wasn't until the influx of Italian, Greek, and other European migrants after World War II that continental-style cheeses became widespread within migrant communities. For most Australians during the twentieth century, cheese meant mass-produced Cheddar, such as Bega "Tasty" and Coon brands.

In the 1980s a new generation of cheesemakers, inspired by their European travels, began making specialty cheeses on small farms. In Victoria, Milawa, Tarago River, and Jindi created some of the first bloomy-rind, washed-rind, and blue cheeses, and Meredith became the first farmhouse producer of sheep's milk cheese. Many of these early pioneers were assisted by visionary cheesemaker Richard Thomas, who had traveled to Italy in the late 1970s to learn the art of making Gorgonzola. In Western Australia, Gabrielle Kervella pioneered the production of farmhouse goat's milk cheese, and her legacy is continued by producers such as Holy Goat in Victoria and Jannei in New South Wales. In Tasmania, Swiss-cheese maker Frank Marchand set up Heidi Farm, and the renewal of King Island Dairy put a tiny island in the Bass Strait on the Australian cheese map. Both are now owned by industry giant Lion, and they continue to set benchmarks for quality and innovation under head cheesemaker Ueli Berger.

Specialty production continued to flourish in the 1990s, with the revival of traditional, cloth-bound Cheddar by Pyengana, Ashgrove, and Maffra, and the introduction of buffalo milk cheeses by Shaw River. Others, such as Woodside, Yarra Valley, Red Hill, Grandvewe, and Bruny Island, created original styles that are uniquely Australian. There has been an increase from twenty cheese varieties in 1960 to more than one hundred today, with widespread use of sheep's, goat's, and buffalo's milk, as well as cow's milk.

While more than half of all cheese sold in Australia is through supermarkets, most specialty cheese is sold by smaller, independent retailers, where individuals such as distributor/retailer Simon Johnson and importer Will Studd have had a significant influence on consumer trends. A proliferation of farmers' markets throughout the country in the last decade has provided new opportunities for artisan producers to market and sell their products.

Industry associations include Dairy Australia, the Dairy Industry Association of Australia (DIAA), and the Australian Specialist Cheesemakers' Association (ASCA). Annual cheese competitions, such as the Sydney Royal, are hosted by agricultural societies in most state capital cities.

New Zealand's dairy industry began with a small herd brought to the new British colony from Australia in 1814. The first cheesemaking factory was estab-lished in 1871, and by the 1920s cooperative dairies were commonplace throughout rural New Zealand.

Prior to the 1980s, sporadic attempts were made to produce cheeses other than Cheddar. The Saxelby family made blue cheeses under the Antler brand in the early twentieth century. From 1951, Galaxy Blue was produced commercially, and it is still exported widely as New Zealand Blue Vein. Most New Zealanders, however, were brought up on the ubiquitous 1 kg "family" block of factory-produced Cheddar.

Dutch migrants to New Zealand in the 1980s signaled the revival of small-scale, artisan cheese making. Producers such as Mahoe, Mercer, Meyer, and Karikaas led the way, and are renowned for their excellent Dutch styles. In 1985, cheesemaker Ross McCallum opened Kapiti Cheese and introduced New Zealanders to white-mold Aorangi, blue Kikorangi, Hipi Iti (sheep's milk), Mt. Hector (goat's milk), and Trappist-style Brick.

From industry giant Fonterra and big players like Whitestone and Barry's Bay to boutique producers such as Over the Moon, Aroha, Crescent Dairy, Blue River, and Clevedon Valley, a vibrant cheese culture has developed, with local interpretations of European styles alongside cheeses that celebrate New Zealand's distinct heritage and character. The use of sheep's, goat's, and buffalo's milk is now widespread, but cow's milk dominates, accounting for more than 99 percent of total cheese production.

The main industry group is the New Zealand Specialist Cheesemakers Association (NZSCA), which hosts the annual NZ Champions of Cheese Awards.

Australia and New Zealand share a joint food standards code governed by Food Standards Australia New Zealand (FSANZ), but they have different regulations concerning raw-milk cheese. While the New Zealand Ministry for Primary Industries allows the production and import of all raw-milk cheeses, Australian regulations until recently allowed only cooked-curd cheeses and Roquefort to be made from raw milk. Recent changes in the Food Standards Code have been made to govern the production and sale of raw-milk cheeses in Australia. Regulations in both countries are so strict, however, that very few producers have been licensed to make raw-milk cheese. See FOOD STANDARDS AUSTRALIA NEW ZEALAND.

Australian Specialist Cheesemakers' Association. http://www.australiancheese.org.

New Zealand Specialist Cheesemakers Association. http://www.nzsca.org.nz.

Philpott, H. G. *A History of the New Zealand Dairy Industry, 1840–1935.* Wellington, New Zealand: Government Printer, 1937.

Rewi, A., and J. Nicholas. *Fine Cheese: Gourmet Cheesemaking in New Zealand.* Christchurch, New Zealand: Hazard Press, 1995.

Studd, W. *Cheese Slices.* Prahran, Australia: Hardie Grant, 2007.

Vondra, J. *A Guide to Australian Cheese.* 2d ed. Melbourne, Australia: Nelson, 1978.

Sonia Cousins

Austria is a small country (80,000 square kilometers) situated in the Alps and their foothills. This has long influenced Austria's milk and cheese production, and encouraged the survival of small scale agriculture. Austria has about nine thousand "Alpen" or "Almen," Alpine summer dairies. (Note that Alp/ Alpen is used in Switzerland and Vorarlberg, the western-most part of Austria, and Alm/Almen is used in the other parts of Austria). Traditionally dairy farmers have taken their cows, goats, and sheep to higher pastures during the summer months and produced milk and cheese. The typical altitude of such an Alp is between 1,000 to 2,000 meters above sea level. Today around 2,500 of these Alpine dairies are still active and produce milk in the summer. Some of the Almen are used for non-dairy cattle and some are used for other purposes such as tourism. However, most of the Alpine dairy farmers either sell their milk to larger dairies or make cheese or butter down in the valley. Vorarlberg (2,600 square kilometers), a small province in the utmost western part of Austria adjacent to Switzerland has 600 Alpen, of which approximately 120 to 140 still produce cheese directly at the Alp. Vorarlberg might be considered as the only part of Austria with a real culture of cheese production ranging from small artisan productions at farms or Alpen up to medium-size dairies.

Dairy farmers in the mountains practice a so-called "three-step-agriculture" (German: *Drei Stufen Landwirtschaft*). In the winter they are at their main estate in the valley, with the cows on pasture in the spring and late summer into early autumn. In late spring and early summer they move to another farmstead called *Maisäss*, referring to the month of May, or sometimes called *Vorsäss*. The *Maisäss/*

Vorsäss are situated at a medium altitude, and for the summer months they move up one step farther, to their "Alps," the true Alpine dairies. Therefore the cows moving with the farmer from location to location can be on pasture for approximately five to six months while hay can be produced for the winter months at the lower locations. Some of the farmers still produce cheese at all three locations. Bregenzerwald, a high mountain valley in Vorarlberg with a population of 30,000, is the most active cheese-producing area in the whole of Austria and its three-step-agriculture was submitted as a world heritage site to UNESCO.

Until the seventeenth century cheese in Austria was produced as sour cheese (German: *Sauerkäse*). The product was a cheese with an extremely low fat content (less than 1 percent) which could be conserved for several months. Sauerkäse made it possible to produce the maximum amount of butter from the available milk, which was used to pay taxes to the landlords. From the west to the east of Austria different types of Sauerkäse are produced, starting with Sura Kees (Vorarlberg), Graukäse (Tirol and South Tirol [Alto Adige, the Italian part of Tirol]), Steirerkäse (Styria), and Glundener Käse (Carinthia). In recent years some of these cheeses have seen a revival in their respective regions and efforts have been made to secure production and their use in local gastronomy. This was for example successful for the Sura Kees and Graukäse in the Italian part of Tirol. However these cheeses can become very intense with aging. Therefore they are sold almost exclusively in the regions in which they are produced. In fact there is no—or very little—export to other regions in Austria. See SOUR SKIMMED-MILK CHEESES.

From the seventeenth century the fat-containing cheeses were produced using rennet. This was initiated by Swiss cheesemakers who left Switzerland after the Thirty Years' War (1618–1648) and brought their cheesemaking skills to Austria, France, and other countries. Therefore cheeses similar to Swiss Gruyère were the first fatty cheeses produced in the Austrian Alpine regions. In Austria these cheeses are called mountain cheeses (German: *Bergkäse*) or—if produced at an Alp—Alpkäse/Almkäse, Alpine cheese. The designation "mountain cheese" is not protected and can be used for many different cheeses. Vorarlberger Bergkäse, the most popular of them, since 1997 has been protected by a PDO. In general

Austrian mountain cheese can be considered the nation's most important cheese. The wheels weigh 20–30 kilograms, with 45 percent fat in the dry mass, resulting from a light skimming of the evening milk, while the morning milk is used as it is. As in the past these cheeses are still produced from raw, untreated milk and are aged up to two years. It is one of the rare cases in which a type of cheese is produced on many different levels from artisan to medium-size dairies, comparable in quality to international cheeses like Swiss Gruyère and French Comté. Mountain cheeses are important for the Austrian export market, with Germany its most important destination.

Recently a small number of artisan producers have appeared on the Austrian cheese scene. These farmers produce small amounts of different types of cheeses, which are sold at small farmers' markets or to restaurants. Despite the small amounts produced—these cheeses are not available at supermarkets or any other larger distributors—the producers receive a lot of attention from the media and thus have been pushing consumers to ask for artisan cheeses. Most of those producers use raw milk or thermized milk for production. See ARTISANAL.

There are no Austrian dairies to be counted among the big European players. However, there are several dairies producing cheese and other dairy products processing 40,000–60,000 liters of milk per day. Most of them produce cheeses like Emmentaler, Gouda, and several semihard cheeses. Economically it is difficult for them to compete with the big dairies. However Germany is still an important export market for Austrian agriculture products and this is also true for cheese. Alpine and mountain cheeses are the only type of cheese from Austria with an individual and unique taste and look. This could be considered either due to a lack of other traditional cheeses or as a lack of innovation. During the last few years the use of *Heumilch* (literally "hay milk") has been strongly promoted. For this the feeding of silage, that is fermented, high-moisture stored fodder from grass or corn is not allowed. This state-initiated campaign has been quite successfully linked to higher cheese quality. See SILAGE.

In summary, when compared to Switzerland or France, Austria only has a real scene of cheese-producing farmers and dairies in the western-most part of the country, in Vorarlberg, with some small structures still left in the other parts of Austria. These areas, however, remain open for innovation and have been developing diverse new cheeses of high quality.

See also ALP CHEESEMAKING; ALP-STYLE CHEESES; GERMANY; and SWITZERLAND.

"Bregenzerwälder Mountain Cheese." Slow Food Foundation for Biodiversity. http://www .fondazioneslowfood.com/en/ark-of-taste-slow-food/bregenzerwalder-mountain-cheese.
"Intangible Cultural Heritage in Austria." UNESCO. http://immaterielleskulturerbe.unesco.at/cgi-bin/ unesco/element.pl?eid=48&lang=en.
"Traditional Montafoner Sura Kees." Slow Food Foundation for Biodiversity. http://www .fondazioneslowfood.com/en/ark-of-taste-slow-food/traditional-montafoner-sura-kees.

Stephan Gruber

Auvergne is a rugged, mountainous, volcanic region in the center of France where five major cheeses are produced.

Cantal is often called the precursor to Cheddar cheese. Legend has it that stone masons from Auvergne went to build walls in northern Britain and, on their way back home, some settled in southern England, in and around the town of Cheddar. Once there, they did what they'd always done, made large, pressed cows' milk cheese, which came to be called Cheddar. See CHEDDAR.

To make Cantal, which carries the appellation d'origine protéger (AOP) designation, cows' milk is curdled with rennet, which is then cut into cubes, mixed, salted, and finally drained and packed into large molds, where it is pressed for a period of days. When turned out of its mold, the cheese is transferred to an aging cellar to sit on wooden shelves, and regularly brushed and turned so that it ripens evenly. As it ripens, the rind initially turns a bluish gray that becomes fawn brown. The longer the cheese is aged, the thicker the rind, the sharper the flavor, and more crumbly the texture. It takes 423 quarts (400 liters) of milk to make one Cantal cheese. There are three categories of Cantal: *jeune* or mild, aged from one to two months; *entre-deux*, or medium, aged from three to seven months; and *vieux* or mature, aged more than eight months. There is no specific variety of cows' milk required for the making of Cantal. See CANTAL.

Salers resembles Cantal but has a more barn-like, ripe flavor. It has an AOP, or pedigree, which denotes where and how it must be made, but doesn't specify the type of cows' milk that must be used for production. Meanwhile, another AOP cheese is Salers Tradition, which is made exclusively with the milk from the Salers breed of cow. There is another Cantal-like, AOP cheese called Laguiole, which must be made only with milk from the Aubrac or Simmental cows, and is produced in and around the town of Laguiole. See LAGUIOLE and SALERS.

Saint-Nectaire is called a woman's cheese, because until recently women on the farm were the only ones to make it. The first cows' milk cheese in Europe to get an AOP, it reputedly gets its name from the Marechal de la Ferte-Sennectaire, who introduced it into Louis XVI's court, at Versailles. A cows' milk cheese, Saint-Nectaire is flat and round, weighing just under 2 pounds (1 kilogram). It can be either artisanal or industrial, and according to its AOP labeling, must be made only with the milk from the Salers cow. See SAINT-NECTAIRE.

The Saint-Nectaire is aged on rye straw, which gives its rind a mouse-gray bloom, often tinged with red, orange, or yellow marks. The rye, as well as the richness of the Salers milk that goes into it, accounts for its creamy texture and pungent flavor, which is accentuated after the typical six to eight weeks' aging.

Bleu d'Auvergne is a blue cheese made with cows' milk and, like its cousin Roquefort is among France's stellar blue cheeses. Bleu d'Auvergne is made in similar fashion to Roquefort, though instead of being made with sheep's milk, it is made with cows' milk. *Penicillium roqueforti*, the same bacteria responsible for the blue veins in Roquefort cheese, is blended into the cows' milk. Rennet is added, the curds are cut, drained, and pressed by hand into molds. After the cheese is drained it is pierced with metal skewers, to allow the air to penetrate the cheese, where it reacts with the enzymes and bacteria, causing the development of blue veins in the cheese's interior. Bleu d'Auvergne is aged for at least four weeks; it has a soft, tender paste with typical blue cheese flavors but without the salty tang. Bleu d'Auvergne's AOP requires that it be made and aged in the departments of the Puy-du-Dome and Cantal. See BLEU D'AUVERGNE and ROQUEFORT.

Fourme d'Ambert is a cows' milk blue cheese made in the Auvergne around the Puy-de-Dome, in several communities of Cantal, and of the Loire Valley. Historically, Fourme d'Ambert was made by the Druids, and later it was used as a form of currency by farmers who made the cheeses in the mountains and who had no money. See FOURME D'AMBERT.

The cow's milk used to make Fourme d'Ambert must come from a specific geographical region. After milking, the milk sits overnight to ripen. Then, *Penicillium roqueforti* is added, the milk is curdled, and the curds are stirred until they are the size of small peas. They are collected and pressed into a mold, which is flipped several times during a period of forty-eight hours, until the cheese is solid enough to stand on its own. It is then salted, and set on wooden shelves to age for at least twenty-eight days. During that time, the cheeses are turned regularly, so they age evenly.

Androuet, Pierre. *The Complete Encyclopedia of French Cheese.* New York: Harper's Magazine, 1973.
Rance, Patrick. *The French Cheese Book.* London: Macmillan, 1989.

Susan Herrmann Loomis

Ayrshire is a dairy cattle breed, apparently developed from a local Scottish Lowlands landrace in the County of Ayr with admixtures of Dutch, Channel Islands, and other stock. The strong-framed, red-and-white spotted animals are thought to have been bred to their present form in the eighteenth century.

Ayrshire milk became the sole basis of an aged full-fat cheese variety reported to have been introduced in the village of Dunlop around 1700 by the cheesemaker Barbara Gilmour using techniques she had learned in Ireland. Dunlop was considered one of the finest Cheddar-type British cheeses until the late twentieth century, when production nearly ceased. A few farmhouse operations survive today.

Local farmers prize Ayrshire cows for their hardiness in long, cold winters and ability to produce copious amounts of well-flavored milk on coarse forage. These qualities also made the breed successful in New England (where it arrived before 1850) as well as Finland and other parts of Scandinavia. The milk has a somewhat lean protein to fat ratio and small milk fat globules, qualities especially suited to hard cheeses. It is also rich enough to produce excellent cheeses of younger, softer types.

The Ayrshire was Scotland's only important dairy breed for several centuries, and was also considered a major American dairy breed. Its popularity sharply declined in both the United Kingdom and the United States after the 1970s, as Holsteins (British Friesians)

This photo of an Ayrshire cow was taken at Jasper Hill Farm in Greensboro, Vermont, in 2003. Farmers prize Ayrshire's hardiness in long, cold winters and ability to produce copious amounts of well-flavored milk on coarse forage. © KATE ARDING

came to dominate all cow's milk production. However it has recently acquired some prominent advocates. HRH Charles, Prince of Wales, maintains an Ayrshire herd at Duchy Home Farm in Gloucestershire. Since 2003 the brothers Andy and Mateo Kehler have called attention to the breed by using Ayrshire milk as the foundation of the small, highly regarded Jasper Hill Farm cheese operation in Vermont. See CELLARS AT JASPER HILL.

Both farmhouse cheesemakers and suppliers of milk to other artisanal cheese producers often find Ayrshires valuable in mixed-breed herds. It is possible that the breed may make a comeback in the fluid milk market along with the return of a few small dairies selling milk processed by low technology methods. But its most promising future certainly lies in artisanal cheesemaking.

See also COW.

Becker, Raymond B. *Dairy Cattle Breeds: Origin and Development*. Gainesville: University of Florida Press, 1973.
Porter, Valerie. *Cattle: A Handbook to the Breeds of the World*. London: Christopher Helm, 1991.

Anne Mendelson

Azeitão is a Portuguese protected designation of origin (PDO) cheese named after the village of Azeitão, in the foothills of the Arrábida mountains, in the southwest of the country. Azeitão is produced only in the municipalities of Palmela, Sesimbra, and Setúbal.

Azeitão cheese is made with raw ewe's milk that is coagulated using vegetable rennet made from the stamens of thistle flower (*Cynara cardunculus L.*). Fresh ewe's milk is salted (ca. 2 percent w/v), and the vegetable coagulant is then added to form a stable curd within forty minutes at 86–90°F (30–32°C). The curd is cut and molded afterward, hand pressed, and left to ripen for about twenty days in the summer or forty days in winter—with frequent turning and washing of rind with milk whey. The final product has a cylindrical shape and weighs 4–9 ounces (100–250 grams). Azeitão cheeses are molded with fine white cloth that gives them a unique rustic appearance.

Azeitão cheese has been frequently described as rich and unique in flavor. The semihard paste is yellow, with few small eyes, and possesses a sticky, almost pudding-like look. The intensity of taste ranges from medium to strong—and classical notes include acidic, salty, slightly bitter, spicy, and pungent flavor, coupled with grassy, herbaceous, and nutty aromas. As happens with most artisanal raw-milk cheeses, the microflora of Azeitão cheese is quite diverse and somewhat ill-defined—yet dominated *by Lactococcus lactis*, and lactobacilli such as *Lactobacillus casei* ssp. *casei*.

Azeitão cheese can be enjoyed either as an appetizer, or as part of a dessert along with artisanal bread and red wine.

See also PORTUGAL.

Freitas, A. C., and F. X. Malcata. "Microbiology and Biochemistry of Cheeses with Appélation d'Origine Protegeé and Manufactured in the Iberian Peninsula from Ovine and Caprine Milks." *Journal of Dairy Science* 83, no. 3 (March 2000): 584–602.

J. Marcelino Kongo and F. Xavier Malcata

Babybel

See BEL GROUP.

bacteriocins are a group of antimicrobial peptides, produced by some species of bacteria, that help to suppress pathogen growth during the cheesemaking process. Bacteriocins are distinguished from antibiotics by their narrow spectrum of activity, specifically targeting a few species or even different strains of the same species as the producer organism. Bacteriocin production has been observed in lactic acid bacteria (LAB), including *Lactobacillus, Lactococcus, Leuconostoc, Pediococcus,* and *Enterococcus.* They form one part of a complement of antimicrobial systems present in cheese. See LACTIC ACID BACTERIA.

Colicin, the first bacteriocin to be identified, was described by André Gratia in 1925 as a protein produced by strains of *Escherichia coli* to inhibit different strains of the same species. See STRAINS. Nisin was identified in 1928 during a study of the inhibitory effect of *Lactococcus lactis* on other lactic acid bacteria in yogurt, and five years later it was shown to be responsible for slow acid development in Cheddar cheese.

Nisin is used both in cheesemaking and in food production in general. It is applied directly as an additive or introduced by the incorporation of nisin-producing strains of *Lactococcus.* It is effective against *Bacillus, Streptococcus, Staphylococcus, Listeria,* and *Clostridium,* and it may inhibit late-blowing defect in hard cheeses caused by *C. tyrobutyricum.* Some strains of *Pediococcus* produce pediocin, which has

activity against *Listeria.* These strains are sometimes inoculated deliberately as part of a cheese starter culture. See STARTER CULTURES.

Studies of nisin, pediocin, and enterocin show that bacteriocins operate synergistically and are more effective when used in combination. The presence of a diverse range of lactic acid bacteria in raw milk may therefore increase the range of different bacteriocins produced, conferring enhanced resistance to pathogen growth in raw-milk cheeses. This effect may also explain the protective effects of biofilms on the surface of wooden equipment used in traditional cheesemaking. See BIOFILMS.

Production of bacteriocins is not limited to LAB, and some less desirable species also produce bacteriocins. Nonpathogenic *Listeria innocua* produces a peptide that inhibits the growth of other *Listeria* species and can mask the detection of *L. monocytogenes* in foods by outcompeting it during analysis.

Bacteriocins are produced by bacteria using a process called quorum sensing. This is a signaling system that ensures that gene expression occurs only when the producer-bacteria is present in sufficient numbers to justify the energy expense of production. A healthy culture of LAB, either added as a commercially produced starter or naturally present in raw milk, is therefore essential to ensure the control of low levels of pathogens by bacteriocins. Milk produced under hygienic conditions is also essential so that the pathogen load of the milk is sufficiently low for control to be effective. Bacteriocins cannot be relied upon to reduce pathogen levels to acceptable levels if the milk is not relatively clean to begin with or if the growth of the lactic acid bacteria is inhibited or slow. See PATHOGENS AND HYGIENE.

BACTIBASE. http://bactibase.pfba-lab-tun.org.
European Food Safety Authority. "Opinion of the Scientific Panel on Food Additives, Flavourings, Processing Aids and Materials in Contact with Food on a Request from the Commission Related to the Use of Nisin (E 234) as a Food Additive." *EFSA Journal* 314 (2006): 1–16.
Kaur, G., T. P. Singh, and R. K. Malik. "Antibacterial Efficacy of Nisin, Pediocin 34, and Enterocin FH99 against *Listeria monocytogenes* and Cross Resistance of Its Bacteriocin Resistant Variants to Common Food Preservatives." *Brazilian Journal of Microbiology* 44 (2013): 63–71.
Zacharof, M. P., and R. W. Lovitt. "Bacteriocins Produced by Lactic Acid Bacteria: A Review Article." *APCBEE Procedia* 2 (2015): 50–56.

Paul Thomas

bacteriophages

bacteriophages (also called phages), whose name means "devourer of bacteria," are viruses that specifically kill bacteria. They may be one of the most predominant organisms on earth, with a single drop of seawater containing 10^8 phages. Ranging from simple four-gene protein shells to sophisticated models with hundreds of genes, bacteriophages are obligate parasites that can only replicate after injecting their genome into the cellular fluid of a bacterial cell. Such replication, whether immediate (lytic) or after integrating into the host's own genome (lysogenic), ultimately ends with the bacterial cell lysing and releasing many new phages into the environment. Bacteriophages have long played a driving role in bacterial evolution, as a dominant force of population control and predatory pressure. However, phages also pose significant challenges for processes dependent on bacterial action, including food, chemical, pharmaceutical, pesticide, and—of course—dairy fermentations.

Milk becomes cheese through the growth and metabolic activity of specific bacterial starter cultures. If bacteriophages are present, they can kill these bacterial starters, thereby halting the fermentation. Phage proliferation, and the resulting failure of the cheesemaking process, can cause significant economic loss to the cheesemaker.

Whitehead and Cox first described phages affecting a dairy starter culture in 1935. Since then, numerous studies have examined phages of lactic acid bacteria, outlining the common sources of phage contamination and the methods through which such contamination and its impacts can be mitigated.

Given the widespread and diverse nature of phages, elimination is unlikely to be achievable; rather, the goal should be control. See LACTIC ACID BACTERIA.

One of the most common sources of phages is raw milk itself. Different sources of milk can carry different phages, which are then amplified in milk silos as the milks are combined and the phages find susceptible bacterial hosts. Because phages can be very specific, recognizing only certain strains of the starter cultures, an effective way to manage this risk is to test raw materials for concentration and type of phages and select a starter culture that is not susceptible to the present phages. See STARTER CULTURE.

Another source of phage contamination is the cheesemaking environment. Because cheesemaking is usually done in open vats, phages can be found on surfaces, in the air, in drains, and on employees. Cheesemaking ingredients derived from the cheesemaking process can also be a source of phages. Due to their minuscule size, phages can easily be retained in whey, whey protein concentrate, and other fermentation-based cheese ingredients. Inactivation processes, such as heat treatment, are a critical step in reducing phage populations in such materials. However, lysogenic phages can also be retained in starter cultures, as these phages incorporate into the main genetic material of the bacteria. Such "prophages," as they are called, can then be activated when the host bacteria are exposed to stresses, such as heat. Genetic sequencing and testing can help identify the presence of prophages in a specific starter culture, as well as the average rate of induction to the lytic phase. Interestingly, some prophages actually impart some benefit to their host; if the fermentation process can run without inducing the phages' lytic cycle, such benefits could potentially aid the process instead of hinder it. Strains with low induction rates could be used in such cases. Careful and specific attention would be needed to develop and manage such processes. See STRAINS.

Overall, there are several key components to managing phages in the dairy industry. The earlier in the process that phage contamination occurs, the more devastating the results; therefore steps to prevent inoculation of whole vats with phage is vital. The most destructive point of phage contamination is during the scale-up stage of the bacterial starter culture. Phages present at this point have the opportunity to build to damaging populations in the cheese vat. One phage control method is to avoid the scale-up process altogether and use frozen or dried concentrated starter cultures that are added directly to the vat. This is typically an expensive option, however. A comprehensive approach to sterilization is a must to control phages, using sanitizers effective against phages. Good plant design can help reduce the occurrence of phage contamination as well as limit its effects—the direction of traffic flow and airflow should not go from the plant floor back into the starter preparation room. A careful starter rotation system is also an effective control measure. Instead of reusing the same strains, rotate among a limited number of carefully chosen strains that testing has shown react to different spectra of phages. This prevents buildup of phages against the current strain. Good strain selection also includes avoiding lysogenic strains, as lysogenic phages can mutate to become lytic, as well as choosing strains with inherent phage resistance mechanisms. Many phages require divalent cations to infect bacteria, so the use of phage-inhibitory media now commercially available to chelate cations can also limit phage growth during the starter culture scale up process. A cross-section of phage-management techniques, suited for the particular process, plant and product, will likely be necessary to control the devastating effects phages can have.

Although bacteriophages pose significant challenges for the dairy industry, these pests can turn into resources when they are used to control unwanted bacteria. For example, specific phages could control bacterial contamination or early spoilage of food. Phages could also someday be used to fight antibiotic-resistant bacteria like methicillin-resistant *Staphylococcus aureus* (MRSA).

Elsser-Gravesen, D., and A. Elsser-Gravesen. "Biopreservatives." *Advances in Biochemical Engineering/Biotechnology* 143 (2014): 29–49.

Garneau, J. E., and S. Moineau. "Bacteriophages of Lactic Acid Bacteria and Their Impact on Milk Fermentations." *Microbial Cell Factories* 10, no. suppl. 1 (August 2011): S1–S20.

Mahony, J., and D. van Sinderen. "Structural Aspects of the Interaction of Dairy Phages with Their Host Bacteria. *Viruses* 4, no. 9 (2012): 1410–1424.

Whitehead, H. R., and G. A. Cox. "The Occurrence of Bacteriophage in Cultures of Lactic Streptococci." *New Zealand Journal of Dairy Science Technology* 16 (1935): 319–320.

Alexandra O.K. Mannerings and Mary Ellen Sanders

The **Baltics,** consisting of Estonia, Latvia, and Lithuania, are located on the northeastern coast of the Baltic Sea. As in other regions with short growing seasons, cheese production in the Baltics was historically dominated by acid-set cheese made from sour cow's milk. Despite the existence of variations adding fresh milk, salt, butter, eggs, caraway seeds, or herbs, fresh white curd cheese remains popular in the Baltic states today. Fresh curd cheeses are usually available in round or teardrop shapes, such as *varškės sūris* in Lithuania, *biezpiena siers* or *mājas siers* in Latvia, and *kohupiimajuust* in Estonia. Although these cheeses bear similarities to fresh curd cheeses made in neighboring countries, in the Baltics they have become strongly linked to Latvian, Lithuanian, and Estonian ethnic cuisine. See FRESH CHEESES. Recognizing their importance for local and national traditions, *Lietuviškas varškės sūris* (Lithuanian curd cheese) achieved PGI (protected geographical indication) status in 2013 and remains one of two cheeses from Lithuania with this designation. The second is a semihard fermented cheese from the village of Belvederis called Liliputas. Latvia's *Jāņu siers*, a curd cheese mixed with caraway seeds and produced for midsummer-night celebrations (St. John's Day), received TSG (Traditional Specialty Guaranteed) status in 2014.

The association of Baltic ethnic cuisine with peasant foodstuffs stems from the ethnic and linguistic differences between Baltic peasants and their ruling classes that emerged during the feudal Middle Ages. Following victorious crusades, the German-speaking elite established itself in the regions of present-day Latvia and Estonia. Subsequently, a Baltic German ruling minority coalesced and maintained local political and economic control as well as cultural hegemony until the twentieth century. In Lithuania, the Polish language became dominant among nobility, especially after the establishment of the Polish-Lithuanian Commonwealth in 1569. The coronation of the Milanese noblewoman Bona Sforza as the Grand Duchess consort of Lithuania brought important cultural influences, including cheesemaking, from northern Italy. Local cheese traditions were shaped by extensive cultural and economic exchanges that followed the geopolitical integration of the Baltics with other emerging European states. Historical cookbooks testify that various aged cheeses popular in southern and western Europe were also widely consumed in the Baltics by wealthy urbanites, by landlords, and in courts; however, a lack of abundant milk precluded their production by peasants.

In peasant households, the production of acid-set curd cheese was limited to the summer months, when milk supplies were more plentiful. However, this cheese was by no means similar throughout the Baltic states; largely unwritten recipes developed by women peasants varied by region and even between households, and the production process was itself influenced by local ecologies.

The late-nineteenth and twentieth centuries brought greater social mobility for Baltic peasants and significant transformations in cheese production and consumption that paralleled industrialization more broadly. Baltic German influence made its presence felt in the emerging cuisines of ethnic Latvians and Estonians. For instance, one local cheese in Latvia was inspired by the German Backstein variety. See GERMANY. Under Soviet rule, generic semisoft cheeses (locally known as "fermented" or "Dutch" cheeses), spreadable cheeses, and a sweet cheese curd snack (*varškės sūrelis* [Lithuania], *biezpiena sieriņš* [Latvia], and *kohuke* [Estonia]) started to be more widely produced and consumed.

Today, major industrial dairy processors have developed lines of rennet-based cheeses such as Lacey Swiss produced by Valio Eesti (Estonia), *Džiugas* from Žemaitijos Pienas (Lithuania), and several made by the Trikāta dairy (Latvia). Artisanal cheese production is also thriving in all three Baltic states, where one can taste not only cheeses made using techniques and cultures imported from France, Italy, and Spain, but also reinterpretations of local traditions using soft-ripened, washed-rind, and hard cheeses that merge local know-how and sources to produce unique cheeses (e.g., *Žan-Žakas* and *Bliuzas*, crafted by farmers from the cheesemakers' collective Sūrininkų Namai). It is also becoming increasingly common to find cheeses made from sheep's milk and goat's milk.

This diversity has not diminished the popularity of curd cheese, whether it is fresh, baked, cooked, dried, or smoked, eaten plain, or covered with herbs and spices. Consumed with breads (often rye), fresh honey, or accompanied with beer, this cheese represents historical ties to peasant traditions as well as the numerous small-scale dairy farms where cheese is made fresh and sold directly to consumers and in local markets every day.

Dumpe, Linda. *Latviešu tautas ēdieni* [Latvian National Cuisine]. Rīga, Latvia: Zinātne, 2009.
Laužikas, Rimvydas. *Istorinė Lietuvos virtuvė* [Lithuania's Historical Cuisine]. Vilnius, Lithuania: Briedis, 2014.

Renata Blumberg and Diana Mincyte

bandaging

See CLOTHBOUND CHEESES.

Bandal (ban-DAHL), also spelled "Bandel," is an unripened, salted, or unsalted, soft cheese made from cow's milk, whose name comes from a town located 25 miles (40 kilometers) north of Calcutta, India, one of several ports settled by the Portuguese in the seventeenth century. According to Indian food historian K. T. Achaya, in the seventeenth century about 20,000 Portuguese lived in Bandal and other towns in Bengal, where they introduced the separation of milk with acids to produce curds that became the basis of Bengali sweets and two cheeses—Bandal and Dacca—according to contemporary sources. The Portuguese word "bandar," in fact, means port. When making the cheese, the curd is salted and drained in perforated pots and then soaked for several days in whey or water. The cheeses are small disks that are about 1 inch (3 centimeters) wide and 1 inch (2 centimeters) thick. Both smoked and unsmoked versions are made and the smoked cheese has a pale brown coating. The texture of the cheese is smooth and creamy, similar to that of Camembert, and the flavor is mild and slightly salty. See CAMEMBERT DE NORMANDIE. The cheese is spread on bread as a snack or as part of afternoon tea. Today this cheese is available only in two stalls in Calcutta's New Market.

See also INDIA; PORTUGAL; and SMOKED CHEESES.

Banerji, Chitrita. "How the Bengalis Discovered Chhana and Its Delightful Offspring." In *Milk: Beyond the Dairy, Proceedings of the Oxford Symposium on Food and Cookery 1999*, edited by Harlan Walker, pp. 48–59. Blackawton, U.K.: Prospect, 2000.
Sen, Colleen Taylor. "The Portuguese Influence on Bengali Cuisine." In *Food on the Move, Proceedings of the Oxford Symposium on Food and Cookery 1996*, edited by Harlan Walker, pp. 288–298. Blackawton, U.K.: Prospect, 1997.

Colleen Taylor Sen

Banon is a tidy little goat cheese wrapped in a chestnut leaf, then tied with a piece of raffia. Its origins are ancient, and it was first noted at festivals and fairs in the Middle Ages under its name, "fromage de Banon," Banon cheese. According to legend, the Roman emperor Romain Antonin Le Pieux ate so much Banon he was afraid he would die of overconsumption.

Banon is from the mountainous region generally referred to as Provence. It is an appellation d'origine protégée (AOP) fromage, which requires it be made within a delineated geographic area, with milk from a specific species of goat, using certain cheesemaking techniques. Its zone of production includes four departments or regions—the Alpes-de-Haute Provence, the Hautes-Alpes, the Vaucluse, and the Drome. These areas include mountains, plateaus, and rocky hillsides—ideal terrain for goats.

The first step in the production of Banon is the collection of chestnut leaves, which is done in the woods of Provence. Only the brown leaves are collected, for these have the least tannin content. They are carefully dried and stored, then used to wrap the cheeses.

The Banon has a near-unique production process. Because it is made in a dry region with little humidity, the goat's milk must be coagulated quickly. This means that a large amount of rennet must be added to the milk, which is either kept or reheated to the temperature it was when it came from the goat—between 84.2 and 95°F (29–35°C). Within two hours after the rennet is added, the milk is curdled, and the curds are scooped by ladles into flat, round molds.

The curds stay in the molds, which are turned regularly, for twenty-four to forty-eight hours in a room that has a temperature of 68°F (20°C). The cheese is turned out of the mold and salted, and at this stage it is called a fresh tomme. See TOMME. The tomme is aged between five and ten days before it is wrapped in chestnut leaves. Before being used to wrap the cheeses, the leaves are softened in either boiling or vinegar water, then patted dry. Five to eight leaves are folded around each cheese to completely enclose it, then the cheese is tied with raffia. Tannins in the leaves contribute to the flavor and texture of the cheese which, as it ages, becomes creamy, soft, and tender. Its flavor is both mild and intense, with notes of mushrooms and forest floor after a soft rain.

Fifteen days after being wrapped, a Banon is ready to eat. It should be tender to runny, and is best eaten with a light, whole wheat bread.

Banon can be made only with the milk from the chèvre commune provençale. This small, rustic, hearty animal thrives in a landscape that produces white oaks and "aphyllantes," an asparagus relative, as well as the wild herbs of the region. Their milk is noted for its richness in both flavor and texture. The chèvre commune provençale is currently in danger of extinction, leaving the future of the Banon in question.

Androuet, Pierre. *The Complete Encyclopedia of French Cheese.* New York: Harper's Magazine Press, 1973.
Rance, Patrick. *The French Cheese Book.* London: Macmillan, 1989.

Susan Herrmann Loomis

bark-wrapped cheeses. The practice of encircling soft-ripened cheeses in "girdles" of tree bark is believed to have evolved in the Alps from a very specific set of circumstances. In the fall and winter, cheeses were made from the milk of cows that had switched to their cold-weather diet of hay and were no longer producing enough milk to make the traditional large-format cheeses such as Gruyère, Comté, and Beaufort. This fall and winter milk, which was higher in protein and fat, yielded smaller cheeses that would ripen readily and ooze easily into a gooey, amorphous state. Clearly, wrapping such cheeses in thin strips of tree bark helped shape and contain them. It also afforded the added benefit of extra flavor potential, since the milk from which they were made—although very rich—contained fewer of the flavor compounds that were found in summer milk.

During an aging period lasting from about four to as many as twelve weeks, bark-wrapped cheeses are ripened by encouraging the development of different classes of bacteria, including the so-called washed-rind *Brevibacterium linens* and the bloomy-rind *Penicillium candidum* and *Geotrichum candidum.* The chemical breakdown actions of these microorganisms and their enzymes yield cheeses with luscious, creamy pastes and complex yet subtle flavor profiles. Most modern bark-wrapped cheeses are made from cow's milk, but a handful of scarcer delicacies are made from sheep's or goat's milk.

The material for the bark strips—called *sangles* (belts or straps) in French—is most often cambium (the underlayer of bark) from spruce trees. Connoisseurs detect resulting "rustic" flavor notes of sap, resin, tannins, pine needles, forest floor, pitch, smokiness, and various herbs in the cheeses. Labor-intensive and often only available seasonally, they tend to be highly sought after and expensive. The prototypical bark-wrapped cheeses are the French and Swiss versions of Vacherin Mont d'Or, also known in France as Vacherin du Haut-Doubs. Other notables in the category are le Claousou, l'Edel de Cleron, Pechegos, Petit Sapin, and Vacherin d'Abondance (France); Bergfichte, Försterkäse, Hoelzerne Geiss (a.k.a. Hölzige Geiss), and Petit Vaccarinus (Switzerland); and Harbison, Rush Creek Reserve, and Winnimere (United States).

See also ABONDANCE; MONT D'OR; and WINNIMERE.

Herbst, Robbie. "Style Highlight: Leaf and Bark Wrapped Cheeses." *Culture: The Word on Cheese,* 11 August 2015.
Jasper Hill Farm. "Winnimere." http://www.jasperhillfarm .com/winnimere.
Mont d'Or. http://www.mont-dor.com.

David Gibbons

Barthélémy is a celebrated cheese shop on rue de Grenelle in central Paris that was founded in 1973 by Roland Barthélémy. The driving force behind its success, however, has been Nicole Barthélémy, Roland's first wife and a former fishmonger, who took over the shop after the couple's divorce in 2006.

A vocal advocate of on-the-job training, Nicole Barthélémy is completely self-taught and believes that cheese, as a live and protean foodstuff, can be observed and understood only "in the doorway," and not through textbooks. She claims never to have lost her fishwife's voice and is very demanding with suppliers who don't meet her exact requirements for quality and affinage (maturing). Barthélémy swears "on the heads of her grandchildren" that she has no clue how many cheeses her shop carries at any one time, although she concedes that it might be around two hundred. All business with her suppliers is transacted via fax, and the shop has no website.

In fact, the shop is so tiny that only the very slender can stand two abreast. Barthélémy presides over the crowded shop floor, perched on a stool behind the till. Her devoted staff, many of whom have been there for decades, do not suffer much hesitation from clients, although any appeal to their encyclopedic knowledge can cause them to soften. Cheese-selling at Barthélémy is a tactile enterprise; Camembert boxes will be opened and the cheeses squeezed vigorously to determine their ripeness.

Since 1971, the Barthélémy shop has supplied cheese to the nearby Hôtel Matignon, the official residence of the French prime minister, and since 1974, to the Élysée Palace, the official residence of the president of the French Republic.

See also CHEESEMONGER and FRANCE.

"Barthelemy: As Fluffy as a Cloud." *Mad About Paris,* 30 October 2011. http://madaboutparis.com/ shopping/barthelemy.html.

Anastasia Edwards

baskets

See CANESTRATO PUGLIESE and FORMS OR MOLDS.

The **Basque Country** is located on both sides of the western foothills of the Pyrenees along and near the Atlantic's Bay of Biscay and limited by the eastern part of the Cantabrian Mountains. The Basque Country is split between Spain and France, with the major part on the Spanish side. The region is renowned for its semihard pressed sheep's milk cheeses. The landscape of the cheesemaking area involves steep, narrow valleys and mountain streams of moderate altitude. The abrupt land characteristics challenge communication but contribute to the survival of a pastoral community. The areas of cheese production include multiple towns in the valleys close to industrial areas of Gipuzkoa and Bizkaia, as well as deep hills with the characteristic *caserios*, or typical Basque farms, and large prairies and pine forests. The area where livestock resides is dominated by an ocean climate, with recurrent rain and mild temperatures. The interior of the country, including southern Araba and the Rioja Alavesa, is governed by a Mediterranean climate mainly associated with wine production and recently also olive oil, but very limited livestock production.

The Basque Country has been and still is largely an industrial country, but over the last decades the service sector has grown and small scale food

A market visit in Saint-Jean-de-Luz, a commune in the Basque Country of northern Spain, reveals a vibrant cheesemaking tradition. Many of the cheeses are made from local Latxa sheep's milk. © NICOLAS FOIT

production businesses are highly valued. Tracing the beginnings of the movement and promotion of cheesemaking traditions in the Basque Country requires travel back in time to the 1980s, and it is synonymous with sheep's milk cheese from the Latxa breed and from enzymatic coagulation (enzymes mainly from farmstead lamb coagulant) and a pressed uncooked cheese named after a town in the interior of Gipuzkoa related to its production: Idiazabal. According to the specifications of Idiazabal cheese applicable to the PDO (protected designation of origin) for Idiazabal, the archeological remains found inside the caves of Husos and Arenzana demonstrate pastoral activity for Idiazabal cheesemaking dating back to 2200 B.C.E. Sheep farming was then conducted by shepherds who had been practicing pastoral transhumance and transferring the flocks from winter shelters on the coast and valley locations to summer prairies up on the mountains (e.g., Aralar, Urbía, Urbasa). This traditional animal husbandry of the Latxa flocks still exists; in addition to having cultural value, it also plays a very important environmental role in preserving the mountain areas. While the flocks grazed on fresh mountain grasses, the shepherds milked the sheep and made Idiazabal cheese in the *bordas* (rudimentary housing used while living in the mountains) and sold the cheeses at markets in the valley. The traditional cheesemaking process started directly after milking, with filtering done with a special strainer made from nettles. Because the *borda* did not have a fireplace, the cheeses were naturally smoked and this explained the association

between sheep's milk and smoked cheeses. Currently Idiazabal cheese is produced all over the Basque Country and Navarra in two versions, plain and smoked, the second now smoked under traditional but controlled conditions. See IDIAZABAL and LATXA.

Another local cheese, Roncal, is made from milk of both the Latxa and Rasa breeds in the Roncal Valley on Navarra. Ossau-iraty is made in the French Basque Country with milk from Latxa sheep, which is called Manech in France. Idiazabal, Roncal, and Ossau-Iraty share similar organoleptic characteristics but are still very different due to differences in the raw milk, differences in coagulant, and different production techniques. The main differences that exist among Ossau-iraty and the two Spanish varieties, which can be considered as its "cousins," are in terms of sensory characteristics. Ossau-iraty presents a more elastic paste due to higher cooking temperature and lower acidification resulting in less mineral loss on the whey. The differences among Idiazabal, Roncal, and other Spanish PDO cheeses from the interior of the country, such as Manchego and Zamorano, would be mainly associated with the characteristics of the breed as well as the climate and animal husbandry practices as the technologies are very similar. See RONCAL; OSSAU-IRATY; MANCHEGO; and ZAMORANO.

Currently the production of cheeses in the Basque Country made from milk other than sheep or deviating from pressed uncooked cheeses is negligible. After more than thirty years of dedication to the study, defense, and promotion of cheeses from Latxa sheep from the Basque Country, there is still work required to realize and understand the potential of other local breeds and traditional cheeses of multiple interests (cultural, economic, social, and environmental).

The cheeses produced in the Basque Country are mainly consumed locally. Farmers' market celebrations and agricultural fairs are part of the Basque Country's deep traditions (for instance the Fair of Ordizia in GuipuzKoa is more than five hundred years old). Often these agricultural fairs involve organoleptic cheese contests where different producers compete. To compete cheese producers must adhere to strict rules and their cheeses must meet rigorous technical norms. See FAIRS AND FESTIVALS.

Foreigners visiting the Basque Country and getting to know the world of cheeses derived from Latxa sheep's milk may be surprised by the large number of entities (organizations, associations, universities) and people that contribute to the defense and promotion of these traditional cheeses. Currently the profession of shepherd has changed from being poor, unrecognized work to a socially highly valued enterprise attractive to new generations. It is one of the agrifood sectors with promising potential within the Basque Country. See SHEPHERD.

The Basque Country is especially well known for its gastronomy, with many famous chefs. They also represent a group of professionals dedicated to the defense and dissemination of agricultural products from the Basque Country in general and the cheese in particular. There are multiple recipes involving the use of the sensorial diversity of Basque cheeses made from sheep's milk, mainly due to the differences in ripening times, different rennet use during the fabrication, and use of smoke. One of the simplest and most popular ways to enjoy the Basque cheeses is with *membrillo* (quince jelly) and walnuts. This is the typical dish served at restaurants and sidrerias or local cider houses, especially in Gipuzkoa.

See also FRANCE; SHEEP; and SPAIN.

McCalman, Max, and David Gibbons. *The Cheese Plate.* New York: Clarkson Potter, 2002.

Ministerio de Agricultura, Alimentación y Medio Ambiente (MAGRAMA). "Pliego de condiciones de la Denominación de Origen protegida (DOP) Queso Idiazábal." http://www.magrama.gob.es/es/alimentacion/temas/calidad-agroalimentaria/pliego_incluidas_modif_idi_v6-5-14_tcm7-326642_tcm7-309359.pdf.

Pérez Elortondo, F. J. "Origin and Quality of Idiazabal Cheese." *Proceedings of the Sheep Veterinary Society Meeting* 23 (2000): 13–16.

Slow Food Foundation for Biodiversity. "Basque Pyrenees Mountain Cheeses." http://www.fondazioneslowfood.com/en/slow-food-presidia/basque-pyrenees-mountain-cheeses.

Spain.info. "Idiazábal Cheese." http://www.spain.info/en/que-quieres/gastronomia/productos/queso_idiazabal.html.

Francisco José Perez Elortondo

batzos is a low-fat, semihard, white-brined protected designation of origin (PDO) cheese with a sourish and slightly piquant taste and a large number of eyes (holes) in the body, produced mainly in Western Macedonia, in northwest Greece. The real intention of batzos cheesemaking is to obtain a fat-rich whey in order to make high quality manouri cheese from caprine milk or butter from ovine milk. See MANOURI.

For this purpose, raw milk is coagulated within fifty minutes at 82–86°F (28–30°C), during which it is "hit" to exclude the fat. When the milk just begins to gel, the manufacturer hits the milk with a thick wooden stick about 150–200 times; the milk is then left to curdle for thirty-five to forty minutes before being hit again for 300–350 times, so that most of the fat is transferred to the whey. The curd is usually mildly cooked, and then left to settle, cut in appropriate pieces, put in cheesecloths, hung to drain, and ripened for twenty-four hours. The next day, the curd is cut into slices, salted with coarse salt, placed in tins, and covered with brine. Cheese is either consumed fresh, baked or fried, or stored in cool rooms.

Lactic acid bacteria (LAB) and *Enterobacteriaceae* are the major components of the cheese microflora from both milk types. See LACTIC ACID BACTERIA. It seems possible that curd acidification to pH 5.30 to 5.20 for the product from goat's milk and to pH 5.65 to 5.25 for the product from ewe's milk in spring and summer, respectively, is driven, mainly, by LAB proliferating at high levels (10^8–10^9 cfu/gram) in the ripened curd.

See also GREECE.

Psoni, L., N. Tzanetakis, and E. Litopoulou-Tzanetaki. "Microbiological Characteristics of Batzos, a Traditional Greek Cheese from Raw Goat's Milk." *Food Microbiology* 20, no. 5 (2003): 575–582.

Evanthia Litopoulou-Tzanetaki

Beacon Fell Traditional Lancashire

See LANCASHIRE.

Beaufort is a hard cooked cheese made with raw cow's milk in the mountains of the Savoie region, in eastern France. The milk used is from Tarine (also called Tarentaise) and Abondance cows. See ABON-DANCE. Beaufort cheese is produced in wheels 14–30 inches (35–75 centimeters) in diameter and 4–6 inches (11–16 centimeters) high, which weigh 44–154 pounds (20–70 kilograms) and have a typically concave shape. It has an ivory or slightly yellow color, with occasional small eyes and thin slits; the rind has an even yellow color. Beaufort cheese has been an AOC (appellation d'origine contrôlée) since 1968 and has a PDO (protected designation of origin) label since 2009. Today around 127,000 wheels are made each year, which represents around 4,500 tons of Beaufort.

During the nineteenth century a Gruyère-type cheese called grovire weighing around 88 pounds (40 kilograms) was made in the Beaufortin Valley of Savoie as well as in the nearby valleys of Tarentaise and Maurienne. It was so popular that during the French Revolution over 1,000 tons of grovire were used to feed Paris. In 1865 grovire's name was changed to Beaufort, after the Beaufortin Valley where it was made.

Beaufort's concave shape meant it was easy to transport on the backs of mules, and helped prevent sagging during ripening. Beaufort is also still made in a copper vat or cauldron. Unlike stainless steel vats, copper vats allow the control of propionic acid fermentation, which causes openness (not desired in Beaufort cheese), and prevents the development of off-flavors. See COPPER VATS and PROPIONIC ACID.

Beaufort is produced in cooperative dairies only from whole raw milk. It is usually made either twice a day, immediately after each milking, or from a mixture of morning and the previous evening's milk. No refrigerated milk can be used and milk must be processed within twenty-four hours after milking. One typical trait in Beaufort manufacturing is the use of dried calves' abomasum, macerated in deproteinized acid whey, called recuite. This unique starter contains thermophilic lactobacilli, which ensures a complete degradation of sugars at the beginning of ripening. Recuite also brings rennet to coagulate the milk.

After cutting of the curd, the mixture of curd particles and whey is heated to 127–129°F (53–54°C) within thirty-five to forty-five minutes and held at this temperature for thirty to sixty minutes. The curd is scooped out from the vat using a cheesecloth and pressed into a wooden mold. The ripening period varies from five months to more than twelve months. The wheels are salted, rubbed, and turned once or twice a week. During ripening thermophilic lactobacilli coming from recuite and natural microflora of raw milk, such as mesophilic lactobacilli, will play an important role in the aroma formation.

Production of Beaufort was initially designed to meet the needs of rural populations facing long cold winters by ensuring optimal use of vegetation at each elevation. Therefore three types of Beaufort are distinguished by the season and altitude at which they were made. Beaufort is made from November to May when cows are in the valley, including a cowshed period. Its paste is an ivory color because cows are mainly fed with hay. The last two types of Beaufort have a yellow paste because the cows grazed in pastures. Beaufort d'été is made from milk produced between June and October. Beaufort chalet d'alpage is made in the mountains from milk of cows grazing between 1,500 and 2,500 meters; only the milk from one herd of cows is used for this type of Beaufort.

Beaufort plays a part in the local gastronomy in *fondue savoyarde* and *gratin aux crozets*; it can replace cheese in any recipes with melted cheeses as well as in salads.

See also COW and HAUTE-SAVOIE.

Conseil National des Appellations d'Origine Laitières. *Prenez la route des fromages d'appellation d'origine— Des fromages faits ici et pas autrement!* Paris: CNAOL, 2010.
Le Fromage Beaufort. http://www.fromage-beaufort .com/fr/index.aspx.

Eric Beuvier

Bedford Cheese Shop first opened in 2003 at 218 Bedford Avenue, Williamsburg, Brooklyn. Its original owners were two local men, Jason Jeffries and Jason Scher, who chose to stay in the neighborhood, open businesses, and raise their families there. Throughout the 2000s the business evolved from more of an all-purpose cheese-centric grocery store to one of New York's foremost gourmet cheese specialty shops, also carrying charcuterie, antipasti, bread, and other accompaniments.

The catalyst of the shop's transformation and success is Charlotte Kamin. A food retailing prodigy and self-described "punk kid who knew how to handle cheese," Kamin is a native of the San Francisco Bay Area who grew up in and around Berkeley and Marin County, California. By the age of sixteen, she was working full-time at the Whole Foods Market in Mill Valley, and shortly thereafter managing its cheese and baked goods counter. After a year of solo travel in Europe, she settled in New York City in 1999 and four years later went to work as Bedford's first employee. She worked to alter the shop's focus from industrial cheeses to handmade farmstead and artisanal ones. By 2005, at twenty-five, Kamin became a co-owner of Bedford and added "head cheesemonger" to her title. The following year the shop moved across the street to 229 Bedford Avenue.

At Kamin's behest, a second Bedford shop was opened in 2013, at 67 Irving Place, in the Gramercy Park neighborhood of lower Manhattan. It includes a fifteen-foot cheese case, which is large enough to stock up to two hundred cheeses—all told, the shops stock three to four hundred cheeses at a time—three aging facilities and an event space for classes and seminars called The Homestead. Kamin works the counter at the Manhattan shop four days a week, in Williamsburg on Wednesdays, and travels frequently to source cheeses around the United States and Europe. She is a founding board member of the Daphne Zepos Teaching Award—named after her friend and late colleague, who inspired Bedford's emphasis on cheese education, both for its own staff members and for customers attending classes. Kamin and Bedford General Manager Nathan McElroy authored a book, *A First Course in Cheese* (New York: Race Point Publishing, 2015).

See also NEW YORK.

Bedford Cheese Shop. http://www
    .bedfordcheeseshop.com.
"Bedford Cheese Shop." *Cutting the Curd*. Heritage
    Radio Network podcast, episode 183, 14 July 2014.

David Gibbons

Beecher's Handmade Cheese is an

American artisan cheesemaking company and retailer founded by food entrepreneur Kurt Beecher Dammeier. The first Beecher's opened in 2003 on a busy corner of Seattle's Pike Place Market, one of the city's prime tourist attractions. Along with its own cheeses, Beecher's sells a range of cheese-centric prepared foods and highlights other artisan producers of the region. A unique aspect of Beecher's business is that all the cheesemaking is done within full view of the public. A modern 1,400-square-foot "cheese kitchen," encircled with windows, allows shoppers to see milk transformed into cheese. This fishbowl type atmosphere often gathers a crowd of captivated onlookers, many of whom enjoy spoonfuls of Beecher's "World's Best" macaroni and cheese, as they observe the crew making the curd. Four 10,000-pound (4,550-kilogram) vats process milk daily at the Pike Place location. Beecher's purchases its milk directly from local farms that offer a product free from antibiotics and growth hormones. Dammeier makes "pure" food a priority and does not allow artificial colors, flavors, or preservatives within the company's offerings. Along with two smaller locations around Seattle, Beecher's is now a bicoastal business. A larger retail facility, in the Flatiron District of New York City, opened in 2011. This Manhattan outpost includes a cheese kitchen, café, and restaurant and sources its milk directly from New York State herds that adhere to the same criteria as the Pacific Northwest original. Beecher's signature cheese is the award-winning Flagship, a semihard cow's milk cheese with a robust and nutty flavor, made from pasteurized milk and aged 15 months.

Peterson, Erick. "Seattle Cheese-Makers Grow Business
    in Public." *Capital Press*, 4 June 2015. http://www
    .capitalpress.com/SpecialSections/Dairy/20150604/
    seattle-cheese-makers-grow-business-in-public.

Allison Radecki

beer pairing. Beer is, it can be said without too much of a stretch, cheese's closest companion in the world of beverages. The ingredients themselves are related, if distantly, because grasses make up the bulk of the diet for cows, sheep, and goats, and the seed heads of certain grasses (usually barley and/or wheat) are the basis for traditional beer. Beer and cheese, along with the other fermented partner in the classic farmhouse triumvirate, bread, suffered the same fate during the twentieth century, as industrialization paved over the food culture of much of the Western world. Worst affected, perhaps, was the United States, where both beer and cheese were made into nearly unrecognizable facsimiles of their former selves, shorn of all variety, subtlety, and life.

Today, with craft beer and traditional cheese resurgent in the world, the stage is well set for the rekindling of a formerly tight love affair. While wine springs more quickly to mind as a partner for cheese, even many sommeliers will argue that beer enjoys several natural advantages in cheese pairing.

Almost undeniably the flavors of beer are far more various than the flavors of wine, due to beer's essential culinary nature. Malts can be roasted, smoked, or caramelized, aromatic hops are available in over one hundred distinctively flavored varieties, hundreds of yeast strains can be used to affect flavors, and beer happily embraces all manner of spices. As it ranges from 3 percent to 16 percent alcohol by volume, beer can taste like almost anything—smoke, flowers, chocolate, bananas, cannabis, bread, lemons, or coffee.

Any beverage that hopes to pair successfully with cheese needs elements that can cut through tongue-coating fats and proteins. In the case of wine, these elements are usually acid and tannin. While beer is rarely as acidic as wine, and tannin shows up only occasionally, beer employs the bitterness imparted by the hop plant, the flowers of which have been used in beer for millennia. Hop bitterness in beer ranges from very mild to bold and piercing. Another important element in beer's affinity for cheese is carbonation. Whether it is the faint tickle in cask bitter or the fresh, scouring roar of carbonation in a saison, "scrubbing bubbles" physically lift fat and protein from the palate, allowing the beer and cheese to truly combine in the senses. With the notable exception of sparkling wines, this is an advantage that beer usually enjoys and one that ought not to be underestimated by those seeking truly harmonious matches.

Beer, like cheese, is a highly complex subject, and here we can touch on it only briefly. Beer style is the main organizing principle of beer taxonomy. Fortunately cheese essentially uses "style" or "type" as well. Just as "Cheddar" suggests a relatively hard cow's milk cheese made in a particular way, "doppelbock" denotes a strong dark lager beer with mild residual sweetness and a distinctly malty flavor. The following are groupings of beer styles and some of the cheese types with which they are often nicely paired.

Pilsners, Pale Ales, and India Pale Ales (IPAs)

When made traditionally, these beer styles share notable sharp bitterness, often supported by a dry bready malt core. Together they represent a large proportion of the craft beer world and are therefore likely to be popular at the table. Although pilsner is golden and the pale ales range into caramelized copper colors, similar pairings can be used. Many cheeses can work, but semihard cow's milk cheeses are perhaps most suitable. Cheddars are at home here, with their acidity and grassiness playing off similar elements in the beer, while malt sweetness acts as a counterpoint to the salt in the cheese.

Tripels, Belgian Strong Golden Ales, and French Biéres de Garde

Dry, strong, spritzy and gently complex, these beers tend to work well with bloomy-rind cheeses such as Brie, Camembert, and triple crème, especially when the cheeses are young and the rinds have not become too sharp in flavor (at which point one might decamp for softer German weissbiers). The French beers lend their own mushroomy qualities to pair with the rind flavors, and tripels sit particularly well at the end of a meal, where their strength gives them a digestif quality. You can also look to these beers to go with aged crottins and aged goat cheeses in general.

Wheat Beers and Saisons

Wheat beers, of either the Belgian or German variety, are slightly acidic, fruity, spritzy, and refreshing as well as low in bitterness. In contrast, the Belgian farmhouse saison style tends to add sharper bitterness, often alongside peppery notes. These beers make great matches for tangy fresh goat cheeses, and can be a great way to start off a cheese and beer tasting.

"Wild" Beers

These "funky" beers contain wild yeast and bacterial strains, particularly the *Brettanomyces* family of yeasts. The yeasts give beers earthy qualities, often reminiscent of forest floor or even barnyard. Once common, they are again increasingly in vogue, especially among dedicated beer enthusiasts. Fans of "natural wine" are likely to enjoy these beers too.

The bacterial strain *B. linens* induces a funkiness in cheese similar to that produced by *Brettanomyces* in beers, and this gives "brett beers" a great affinity for washed-rind cheeses, particularly Taleggio and Époisses. *Brettanomyces* is now introduced into a wide variety of beers, and when lactic bacteria are also used, these beers exhibit notable acidity, which can be the key to pairings. These beers can also pair well with milder blue cheeses, such as young Stilton, though more piquant blues, such as Roquefort, may run into difficulty.

Brown Ales, Porters, Scotch Ales, and Doppelbocks

While these beers have disparate backgrounds, they share some flavor attributes, particularly a strong caramel element. They are also excellent with aged Gruyère, and especially the brown ales almost always show well with Pyrenees sheep's milk cheeses, such as Ossau-Iraty, and its descendants, such as Vermont Shepherd. The caramelized malts can work wonders with the lanolin nuttiness of sheep's milk. These pairings are almost always successful and can be transcendent.

Barley Wines, Old Ales, Imperial Stouts

These are the big guns of the beer world, often stronger than 10 percent ABV, and cheeses brought to pair with them should be suitably robust. All these beers show caramel and some residual sweetness, with imperial stouts adding the coffee and chocolate flavors of roasted malts. Stilton shows particularly well with them, especially with imperial stout, which brings out a latent and surprising chocolate note in the cheese. Barley wines, especially British examples, show that Stilton's true home is with strong ales as much as with sweet wines. Stilton may be the best option, but it is surely not the only one. Gorgonzola dolce also does well, as do intense Gruyères and hard cow's milk cheeses such as Parmigiano, Mimolette, and aged Gouda.

See also BREAD PAIRING; CHEESE ACCOMPANIMENTS; and WINE PAIRING.

Oliver, Garrett. *The Brewmaster's Table*. New York: Ecco, 2005.
Oliver, Garrett, ed. *The Oxford Companion to Beer*. New York: Oxford University Press, 2011.

Garrett Oliver

The **Bel Group** (Fromageries Bel) is a French multinational company owned by the successors of the founder, the Bel-Fiévret family. The company was established in 1865 by Jules Bel, an affineur and trader of Comté cheese in the Jura region. See COMTÉ. His son Léon successfully expanded the family business by specializing in processed cheese after World War I. The processed cheese industry provided an outlet for the producers of Comté and Emmentaler when they were confronted with depressed selling prices. The "process," originally developed by Walter Gerber in Switzerland in 1911, begins by milling or shredding Gruyère-type cheeses and mixing them with butter, melting salts, and other ingredients in a kneading machine. The resulting paste is then heated in a sterilizer, resulting in a stable and spreadable creamy cheese that can be kept at room temperature.

Bel has outdone its competitors through remarkable innovations in marketing: in 1921 La Vache qui Rit (The Laughing Cow) was the first processed cheese packaged in single-serving portions (triangular wedges forming a circle), wrapped in aluminum foil, and sold under a trademark. Bel was also a pioneer in its strategy for international expansion, initiated as early as 1929, by establishing subsidiaries or buying out local dairies in Europe and, more recently, in the Middle East, in the United States, and in Asia.

Branding, portioning, and adaptation to local conditions are the backbone of a business model that Bel has consistently applied to a wider range of industrial specialties: the square-shaped fresh cheese Kiri, first produced in 1966; the pressed, pasteurized, and miniaturized cheese Mini Babybel, introduced in 1977; and flavored versions of Laughing Cow cheese, called Apéricube, packaged in small cubes. These four international brands now account for the bulk of the company's sales worldwide, amounting to about 3 billion euros annually.

See also FRANCE and PASTEURIZED PROCESS CHEESES.

Bel Group annual financial report. http://www .bel-group.com/en/finance/regulatory-information/ annual-financiel-report.
Conseil National des Arts Culinaires. *Franche-Comté: produits du terroir et recettes traditionnelles*. Paris: Albin Michel, 1993. See esp. pp. 153–154.

Christine de Sainte Marie

Benedictines

See MONASTIC CHEESEMAKING and SAINT BENEDICT.

Bergkäse, literally translated as mountain cheese, is an umbrella term for Alpine style hard cheeses, produced across the borders of Switzerland, Austria, and Germany. Just like local dialects, cheese culture does not stop at the national borders; however some confusion occurs because of the varying regulations of the term itself, as well as the related Alpkäse.

Originally this family of cheeses was defined by transhumance, the practice of shifting animals to different altitudes depending on the season, permitting animals to feed on hay in colder months and to graze the famously lush grasslands in the summer. See TRANSHUMANCE. As the milk has to be transformed into something that lasts long enough to reach the markets in the valley, traditionally large wheels of hard cheese are made in big copper cauldrons over open fire—although this practice is quite rare today.

While milking happens morning and evening, cheesemaking takes place only in the morning. The evening milk is stored overnight in shallow containers to ripen as well as to allow some of the cream to rise—this is then combined with the morning milk. (Cream from the morning milk is skimmed off before cheesemaking and processed to butter.) The curd is cut very fine and cooked at a high temperature, to expel moisture, then scooped from the hot whey with a cheesecloth and shaped in large adjustable hoops. See HOOP.

The young wheels spend a night under the press to extract as much whey as possible. After salting in brine the cheeses are regularly turned and the natural rind is washed with brine over a period of weeks or months. In combination with the special composition of the high altitude pastures (the higher the pastures, the more omega-3 fatty acids the milk contains and the tastier and more complex the cheese), this typically makes for the fine nutty aromas.

However, just as the term "Swiss cheese" is in common use in the United States, the term "Bergkäse" in Germany and Austria (as well as in bilingual northern Italy) is not protected. By general agreement it stands for hard cheeses made with thermophilic (high-temperature) cultures, resulting in a sweet nutty taste. (It should be noted, however, that this group does not include Emmentaler.)

Some producers offer mountain cheese made from goat's or sheep milk, and there are quite a few cheeses under the name of "mountain cheese" made in the flatlands of the north. In contrast, since 1997 Allgäuer Bergkäse (from the Allgäu region around Kempten in southeast Bavaria) has been protected by a protected designation of origin (PDO), as are Tiroler Bergkäse and Vorarlberger Bergkäse, both from their respective regions in Austria. With weights slightly varying from a minimum of 18 pounds (8 kilograms) in Vorarlberg to at least 33 pounds (15 kilograms) in Allgäu, the regulations agree on using raw milk from cows fed with fresh grass or hay (no silage), the use of natural calf's rennet, few eyes (maximum size of a pea), and a minimum fat content of 45 to 50 percent. The minimum required age of the cheeses at time of release into the market is four months, and unfortunately this is a sign of how weak these regulations are: due to their large format the best mountain cheeses need to age much longer to develop their full flavor.

In Switzerland, regulations are much stricter concerning Bergkäse as well as Alpkäse—both cheeses produced during transhumance, Sömmerung in Swiss German, at alpine dairies. Switzerland's mountain areas are defined by law (and based not only on altitude but other factors such as the sociotopographical situation) and the milk has to be produced and processed within these borders, although the finished cheese can be matured elsewhere. Swiss law also defines that 70 percent of the cows' feed has to come from that same region. However this still allows (as in Germany and Austria) additional grain feeding to prevent high yielding breeds from starving on their summer diet of mountain grass. The use of freeze-dried starter cultures as well as industrially produced rennet is now quite widespread.

Another tendency seen today in all three countries is the production of smaller wheels in the Appenzeller style with the curd heated to a lower temperature than previously used, making for easier handling, faster maturing cheese, which also facilitates easier marketing and export—an important aspect for all cheeses in this family.

See also ALP CHEESEMAKING and ALP-STYLE CHEESES.

Heinzelmann, Ursula. "High & Mighty: Bergkäse from the Allgäu and Bregenzerwald." *Culture, the Word on Cheese* (Spring 2009): 80–87.

Ursula Heinzelmann

biblical references to milk are numerous, describing a food especially suited to young children as well as one of the products that made Israel so attractive for its fertility, as a "land of milk and honey." Cheese, however, is only rarely mentioned. Moreover, as the various English translations show, there is some indeterminacy among ancient words for cheese, butter, and curds.

One of the two most likely references to cheese is in the story of David (1 Samuel 17:18). Still a boy, David acts as a messenger between his family and his elder brothers, who are fighting the Philistines. In addition to supplies for his brothers, David's father entrusts to him a gift for the army commander. The phrase *haritzei halav* seems literally to mean "cuts of milk," for which the most likely interpretation is "cheeses." The ancient Aramaic source *Targum Jonathan* translates it as "cheeses of milk," *govnin dehalva*. Following his delivery of the cheeses, David kills the giant Goliath and cuts off his head.

The other reference is clearer and more significant. The book of Job contains a description of how God makes human beings, starting with dust and clay. Job continues: "Did you not pour me out like milk and curdle me like cheese, (*gevinah*) clothe me with skin and flesh and knit me together with bones and sinews?" (Job 10:10–11). Medieval commentators saw the "milk" in this sequence as a metaphor for semen. The text is important not simply as evidence of the familiarity of cheesemaking, but more so because it illustrates parallel images that are found elsewhere. In the book of Wisdom, a canonical text for the Roman Catholic Church but an apocryphal book for the Protestant churches, man is made when seed or semen curdles blood in the womb (Wisdom 7:1–2). In three passages in the Qur'an (22:5, 23:14, 40:67), the making of man similarly begins with dust, and continues with seed planted in the womb, the clotting of blood, and the formation of flesh. No one passage is identical to any other, but all are related, and all involve the process of clotting or

curdling. Job has the most fully developed imagery, however. In that text, not only is the seed represented metaphorically by milk, but as a consequence, the curdling is specifically likened to that of cheese.

In contrast to the canonical books of the Bible, there appears to be no mention of cheese (as opposed to curdling) in the extant Hebrew, Greek, and Latin versions of the books of the Apocrypha. However, a Syriac version of the book of Judith has the heroine taking her own supplies of cheese (*gavta*) with her when she goes to meet the enemy general, Holophernes, in his tent. The tradition about Judith's cheese is later mentioned by medieval rabbis, who wrote that Jews should "eat cheese on the Hanukkah festival because of the miracle where Judith fed milk to the enemy" (*Shulhan Arukh* OH570,2). The only source linking cheese, milk, and Judith is an anonymous Hebrew manuscript, *Megillat Yehudit*, the Scroll of Judith (subtitled "to be read on Hanukkah"), copied in 1402, probably in Provence, and now in the Bodleian Library (MSNeubauer 2746). In this account, Judith comes to Holophernes's tent with her maid, whom she instructs to make salty cheese pancakes. Judith then feeds these to the general to make him thirsty, so that he will drink a great deal of wine. Eventually Holophernes gets drunk, and Judith chops off his head with his own sword.

The term used for Judith's cheese is the same *haritzei halav*, which incorporates the word for milk, *halav,* as is used in the book of Samuel to describe David's cheeses, just before he chops off Goliath's head with Goliath's own sword. Thus, the use of cheese highlights the parallels between the boy David, who saves the Israelites from the enemy with the help of God, and later becomes king of his people, and the woman Judith, who saves the Jews from the enemy with the help of God, and, in this version at least, becomes queen. Use of the term *haritzei halav* for cheese in this description of a woman killing the enemy general in his tent also links Judith to the biblical Jael, another woman who defeated a general in a tent (Judges 4:19–21; 5:24–26). The enemy general Sisera asked her for water, but she gave him milk and butter, which put him to sleep, whereupon she killed him by hammering a tent peg into his temples and then smote off his head. The custom of eating cheese on Hanukkah in memory of Judith is rarely observed today.

See also CURDLING, CULTURAL THEORIES OF and DIETARY LAWS (RELIGIOUS).

Seow, C. L. *Job 1–21: Interpretation and Commentary*. Grand Rapids, Mich.: Eerdmans, 2013. See pp. 580–581.
Tsumura, D. T. *The First Book of Samuel*. Grand Rapids, Mich.: Eerdmans, 2007. See pp. 449–451.
Weingarten, S. "Food, Sex, and Redemption in *Megillat Yehudit* (the 'Scroll of Judith')." In *The Sword of Judith: Judith Studies across the Disciplines*, edited by K. Brine, E. Ciletti, and H. Lähnemann, pp. 97–125. Cambridge, U.K.: OpenBook, 2010.

Andrew Dalby and Susan Weingarten

biodiversity is the diversity among and within living species in a specific environment, including all types of life (i.e., bacteria, archae, and eukaria). Microbial diversity is responsible for the huge diversity of cheeses enjoyed throughout the world. There is recognition that biological diversity is a global asset of tremendous value and its sustainment is now legally supervised by the Nagoya protocol, which is a supplementary agreement to the Convention of Biological Diversity (CBD). Biodiversity is globally considered endangered. Therefore conservatory structures, including the Biological Resources Center (BRC), are dedicated to the preservation of biodiversity. Their primary mission is to be a repository of the biodiversity, to preserve it and make it accessible. Microorganisms that have both a patrimonial value and a potential for innovation, in particular for cheese technology, can be preserved in microbial BRCs, which continuously enlarge their collections of microbial resources and are major actors for innovation in the dairy industry when dedicated to bacteria or fungi of dairy interest.

Indeed bacterial as well as fungal diversity can impact acidification, ripening (as the source of ripening enzymes), safety (presence or not of pathogens), organoleptic and rheological properties of cheeses. It is thus a key factor to assess and control. As the milk in the upper part of a healthy lactating female udder is considered sterile, the origin of the microbial diversity in milk and in subsequent cheese can come from the environment of the lactating female, that is, the farm (milking machines, milk lines and tanks, feed, litter, stables), but also from the dairy plant environment. Its level (number of species but also the type of species), including both beneficial and undesirable or pathogenic microorganisms, is influenced by the environmental constraints (farmer, seasons, herd's condition, milk management, dairy plant management).

There are many ways to control the microbial diversity in milk before and during its transformation. Considering that the environment is the major source of the presence of microorganisms in milk, all the hygiene practices during its collection will considerably reduce the level of diversity of microorganisms. Likewise the different treatments of milk, performed during cheesemaking in order to eliminate undesirable and pathogenic microorganisms, such as bactofugation, microfiltration, or thermal treatment (UHT, pasteurization), drastically reduce the diversity of microorganisms in milk and in the resulting cheese. Yet these treatments are not selective and if they ensure the safety of the milk, they also eliminate beneficial microorganisms. See ECOSYSTEM and HYGIENE.

For cheesemakers the microbial diversity of beneficial microorganisms (e.g., acting positively on the flavor, texture, preservation, and visual aspect of the cheese) is a key element to consider. Indeed a high level of microbial diversity, associated with specific manufacturing methods, is correlated with high diversity of products in terms of specificity and sensory characteristics. Numerous studies describe the microbial diversity encountered in cheese. Most of them focus on traditional cheeses, and they are based on culture-dependent methods, using different media with the isolation of the dominant microbial flora. In the last decade with the use of molecular methods associated with high throughput analysis of the data, the knowledge of the microbial diversity allowed a major step forward. In its review on traditional cheeses, Montel et al. (2014) listed more than one hundred genera and four hundred microbial species detected in raw milk, including more than ninety species of Gram-negative bacteria, more than ninety species of Gram-positive bacteria, more than seventy species of yeasts and forty species of molds. A single milk sample can contain as many as thirty-six dominant microbial species. In a review dedicated to the microbial diversity of cheese rinds, Irlinger et al. (2015) underlined the extreme diversity of non-inoculated microorganisms and its unsuspected importance for the characteristics of the final products.

Given the fact that the microbial diversity, even if not inoculated, strongly affects the final characteristics of the cheeses and knowing that microbial diversity has dramatically decreased in milk during the last few decades, this diversity must be collected and preserved in dedicated BRCs in order to remain accessible and to maintain, in the future, the huge diversity of cheeses from which we have profited so far.

See also MICROBIAL COMMUNITIES; MICROBIAL FLUX AND SUCCESSION; and TAXONOMY.

Irlinger, F., et al. "Cheese Rind Microbial Communities: Diversity, Composition and Origin." *FEMS Microbiology Letters* 362 (2015): 1–11.
Montel, M-C., et al. "Traditional Cheeses: Rich and Diverse Microbiota with Associated Benefits." *International Journal of Food Microbiology* 177 (2014): 136–154.
Mora C., et al. "How Many Species Are There on Earth and in the Ocean?" *PLOS Biology* 9, no. 8 (2011): 1–8.
Woese, Carl R., et al. "Towards a Natural System of Organisms: Proposal for the Domains Archaea, Bacteria, and Eucarya." *Proceedings of the National Academy of Science USA* 87, no. 12 (1990): 4576–4579.

Florence Valence

as *Listeria*. See LISTERIA. Members of the genus *Pseudomonas* are adapted to the formation of biofilms, can grow at cold temperatures, and have high lipolytic and proteolytic activity, making them particularly common and problematic dairy spoilage bacteria. While only small numbers of bacteria may be shed from the biofilm into the milk as it passes through the system, their proliferation during subsequent cheesemaking and maturation can lead to perceptible flavor defects or unacceptable presence of pathogens in finished products.

Research into novel cleaning strategies capable of defeating biofilms is in its early phases, and includes the development of enzymes that can break down exopolysaccharides, use of bacteriophages, ultrasonic cleaning methods, and development of protective coatings for surfaces that can prevent bacterial attachment. See BACTERIOPHAGES.

Madigan, Michael T., John M. Martinko, Kelly S. Bender, et al. *Brock Biology of Microorganisms*, 15th ed. Boston: Pearson, 2015.
Marchand, S., J. De Block, V. De Jonghe, et al. "Biofilm Formation in Milk Production and Processing Environments: Influence on Milk Quality and Safety." *Comprehensive Reviews in Food Science and Food Safety* 11, no. 2 (2012): 133–147.

Bronwen Percival

biofilms are complex surface-bound networks containing many millions of microorganisms. Although bacteria may be found living in a planktonic state, floating freely in a medium such as milk, they often affix themselves to surfaces and create a stable community containing one or several species glued together with an exopolysaccharide "paste." See EXOPOLYSACCHARIDES. This mode of bacterial growth confers several advantages to its practitioners: it forms a protective barrier against cleaning chemicals and disinfectants, it resists desiccation, and it can anchor microorganisms in places where they have a rich supply of nutrients.

Biofilms may form within dairy pipelines and on bulk tank surfaces if they are not cleaned properly; indeed, the buildup of organic milk components and milk stone on stainless steel surfaces often promotes the initial attachment of biofilm-forming bacteria. If left unchecked, biofilms can cause persistent problems with the contamination of milk, either with spoilage bacteria or with pathogens, such

Bitto is a protected designation of origin (PDO) cheese produced between the months of June and September in the province of Sondrio, a mountainous district north of Milan in northern Italy, and in neighboring upland pastures of the provinces of Lecco and Bergamo. See LOMBARDY. Its production protocol is published on the website of the Italian Ministry for Agriculture and is defined as a cow's milk cheese from "traditional breeds of the area of production" fed with "grass of the upland pastures" of the production area with a daily allowance of 7 pounds (3 kilograms) of dry fodder exclusively made of maize, wheat, soy, or barley. It is to be made of milk with a "non-mandatory addition of raw goat's milk for no more than 10 percent" and is curdled on location with calf rennet within an hour from milking. Starter cultures are allowed if derived from "autochthonous ferments." Cooked at a temperature of 118–126°F (48–52°C), the curd is finely cut to rice-grain size over about half an hour's duration of time. Bitto is traditionally shaped in concave cylindrical molds, either dry-salted or immersed in salty solutions. It is matured for seventy days in upland stations or lower-altitude dairies within the production area, each wheel weighing between 17 and 55 pounds (8–25 kilograms). See TRANSHUMANCE.

Most producers of the Bitto River valleys left the Bitto PDO consortium in 2006 in disagreement with its production protocol and with its definition of production area boundaries. With persevering and vocal protection from Slow Food, the Presidium of the "Bitto valleys" has safeguarded a niche for highly priced, sought-after traditional Bitto cheese that is considered by some connoisseurs as more "authentic" than its homonymous PDO cheese (see Corti, 2012).

Corti, Michele. *I ribelli del bitto: Quando una tradizionecasearia diventa eversiva.* Bra, Italy: Slow Food, 2012.
Italian Ministry for Agriculture. "Disciplinari di produzione prodotti DOP e IGP riconosciuti: Formaggi." http://www.politicheagricole.it/flex/cm/pages/ServeBLOB.php/L/IT/IDPagina/3340.

Cristina Grasseni

Bleu d'Auvergne is a French cow's milk, blue-veined protected designation of origin (PDO) cheese. Its origins date back to 1845, when Antoine Roussel, a cheesemaker in the Puy-de-Dôme, noted that certain cheeses turned blue in the cellars and developed a pleasant and scented flavor. Roussel then set out to reproduce this development. After several unsuccessful attempts, he noted that rye bread placed near the *fourmes* turned blue in the same way. Further experiments led to the perfecting of his discovery by artificially creating holes in the cheese. A definition of Bleu d'Auvergne was approved in 1934 by the ministry of agriculture and the product received appellation d'origine contrôlée (AOC) status in 1975 and PDO in 2009. The production area includes mainly the Cantal and Puy de Dôme départements, and to a lesser extent parts of the Lot, Corrèze, Aveyron, Lozère, and Haute Loire départements.

To obtain Bleu d'Auvergne, raw, thermized, or pasteurized milk is heated to 86–93°F (30–34°C) and then inoculated with lactic ferments and *Penicillium roqueforti* (blue mold). Next rennet is added. After a sufficient time for the curds to harden, they are cut into small cubes between a corn kernel and a hazelnut in size and stirred. Stirring the cubes will develop a thin film around them, preventing them from sticking together by keeping air between them. This step is known as *coiffage* in French, and is crucial for the subsequent *Penicillium* growth. See PENICILLIUM and STIRRING.

After molding the cheese is drained. During this process the molds are turned over several times to ensure even drainage of the whey. The cheese is then manually rubbed with salt and left for two days before being pierced with needles in order to aerate the cheese and enable the blue mold to develop. The cheese then spends a minimum of four weeks in the cellars at 45–48°F (7–9°C) to mature and is then packaged in a sheet of foil and kept in cold storage. See DRAINING; DRY SALTING; NEEDLES; and MATURING.

Twenty-one to 26 quarts (20 to 25 liters) of milk are necessary to obtain a flat cylinder shape of about 8 inches (20 centimeters) in diameter, 3–4 inches (8–10 centimeters) high, and weighing between 4–7 pounds (2–3 kilograms). The rind is clean, with no wetting or exudation and is slightly gray. The product is sold in aluminum foil at cheese counters. The cheese is white to ivory in color, regularly marbled with blue to green mold. It has a firm and creamy texture. The marbling ranges from the size of a grain of wheat to a kernel of sweet corn. It has an intense and distinctive blue taste with aromas of undergrowth and even mushrooms. It can have a touch of salt and be tangy.

As of 2015 seven enterprises and four farmstead producers make Bleu d'Auvergne PDO from the milk of about 3,500 dairy farmers, with an annual production of 5,100 tons of cheese, with 29 percent being exported. The largest importer is Spain while other importers include eastern European countries, Great Britain, Italy, Belgium, the United States, Canada, Australia, Switzerland, the Emirates, and Egypt.

A cheese to be served at the end of a meal, Bleu d'Auvergne is also used in local recipes, in salads or sauces, and on toast with an aperitif. It goes well with sweet wines such as Jurançon, Saint Croix du Mont, Monbazillac, etc. The fête du Bleu d'Auvergne at Riom-es-Montagnes (Cantal) is an annual celebration of this product.

See also AUVERGNE and BLUE CHEESES.

Brosse, Anne-Line, et al. *Fromages d'Auvergne, une histoire d'hommes et de femmes.* Aurillac, France: Editions Quelque part sur Terre, 2014.

Metz Noblat, Marie de. *Fromages & Cie: Une livre qui a goût, des recettes bien du chez nous!* Paris: DL, 2008.

Jean-Louis Galvaing

Bleu de Gex (also called Bleu du Haut-Jura or Bleu de Septmoncel) is a raw-milk blue-veined cheese that has long been made in the Jura Mountains. It is a very ancient cheese, dating to cheese manufacturing techniques developed by monks at the Abbaye de St. Claude in the thirteenth century, and was cited as the favorite of Holy Roman Emperor Charles V in 1530. While it may not be the best known of blue cheeses, Bleu de Gex was the first raw cow's milk cheese to attain, through special circumstances, official protection in 1935 (exclusive area of production). It obtained appellation d'origine contrôlée (AOC) status in 1977 and appellation d'origine protéger (AOP) status in 1996. Bleu de Gex is an integral part of the heritage of this territory, adapting its production to the natural constraints.

Today some fifty farmsteads in the Haut-Jura Mountains supply their milk daily to the four dairies making Bleu de Gex (550 tons). The milk comes exclusively from Montbéliarde or Simmental cows, with grass forming a dominant part of their feed. The richness and harmony of the pastures in the region provide this cheese with aromatic diversity. See MONTBÉLIARDE.

Although the dairy machinery has been adapted over the last few years, the making of the cheese remains very traditional. The cheese is molded by hand into a round shape with a diameter of approximately 14–15 inches (36–38 centimeters) and a weight between 13 and 20 pounds (6–9 kilograms). The use of a cloth in the mold enables the whey to drain. Dry-salting is done using dry coarse salt in small tubs over several days. Maturation happens for a minimum of twenty-one days after renneting, including at least eighteeen days in a cellar. Piercing the cheese during maturing helps the blue to develop. Piercing has to be done between the seventh and fifteenth day after renneting. See NEEDLES.

Bleu de Gex is primarily consumed locally. Unadorned on a cheese platter, it often accompanies its "big brothers" from the region, namely Comté and Morbier. It is a very mild blue cheese with aromas of hazelnut and mushroom and a slight tang. It is eaten cold or warm in sauces and other preparations. A Bleu de Gex raclette is both simple to make and delicious.

See also BLUE CHEESES; COMTÉ; and MORBIER.

Bleu de Gex. http://www.bleu-de-gex.com.
Vernus, Michel, and Theirry Petit. *Le Morbier, le Bleu de Gex: une histoire.* Fleurier, France: Presses du Belvédère, 2010.

Florence Arnaud

Bleu des Causses is a semisoft French blue cheese. It strikes a skillful balance between whole cow's milk and *Penicillium roqueforti,* developing its full organoleptic qualities during the seventy days (minimum) it spends aging in the caves of the Gorges du Tarn in the Languedoc region of southern France.

While this cheese first gained appellation d'origine contrôlée (AOC) status in 1953, in 1986 the geographic production region was modified. Today ripening can take place only in natural caves occurring in the limestone plateau in a limited geographical area: the five cantons of Aveyron (Campagnac, Cornus, Millau, Peyreleau, and Saint Affrique), along with the municipalities of Trier (Gard) and Pégairolles of Escalette (Hérault). Nestled in cavities dug into cracks in the limestone, the Bleu des Causses flower in contact with the cool, damp air that blows gently through the cracks thanks to the naturally occurring fleurines. See FLEURINES.

After the "bloom" of the cheese, the master affineurs wrap the cheese in foil so that it can gently continue to ripen and release its highly specific aromas. In total Bleu des Causses takes at least 70 days (and not more than 190 days) to ripen or mature. When it does this ivory, blue-veined cheese offers a sophisticated bouquet of aromas. It is a very creamy cheese, with a high fat content of 45 percent. Sweet yet spicy, Bleu des Causses bursts with flavor, not too salty or bitter, melting powerfully in the mouth and pairing well with sweet whites and dessert wines. It is considered a close cousin of Roquefort, and its history is closely linked.

See also BLEU D'AUVERGNE; BLUE CHEESES; and ROQUEFORT.

AOP Bleu de Causses. http://www.bleu-des-causses.com.
Labbé, Marc, and Jean-Pierre Serres. *L'épopée des caves bâtardes: Du roquefort au bleu des Causses.* 1999.

Paul Zindy

Bleu du Vercors-Sassenage, one of the smallest French cow's milk protected designation of origins (PDOs), is a creamy cheese interspersed with blue veins that give the cheese a taste of hazelnut, undergrowth, and mushroom. The first traces of this blue cheese date from the Middle Ages. In June 1338 a charter by Baron Albert de Sassenage granted the inhabitants of the Vercors Massif the right to sell their cheese freely. Subsequent numerous writings attest this special status, such as *Great Universal Dictionary* of the nineteenth century by Pierre Larousse, citing King François I as being a great connaisseur of this cheese. While its reputation has crossed the centuries, the cheese almost disappeared after World War II with the decline of farmhouse production throughout France. In the early 1990s the milk producers of the Vercors Massif in eastern France joined forces to preserve their cheese and agriculture and in 1998 obtained PDO status for the Bleu du Vercors-Sassenage.

The geographic region of the Bleu du Vercors-Sassenage is tucked away in the heart of the Parc Naturel Régional du Vercors in the Auvergne-Rhône-Alpes region of France. This explains the extreme homogeneity of the production system as 95 to 100 percent of the effective surface area is given over to grassland, with specific flora and exceptional nutritional values that offer the herds rich and varied grass which forms the main part of their feed. No fodder is purchased outside the area. Bleu du Vercors-Sassenage is a flat cylindrical blue-veined cheese, 11–12 inches (27–30 centimeters) in diameter and 2½–3 inches (7–9 centimers) tall, weighing between 9–10 pounds (4–4.5 kilograms). Made exclusively from whole or partially skimmed milk of Montbeliarde, Abondance and Villard cows, this cheese has the feature of being made on a mixture of heatead milk of the day before and raw milk of the morning milking. It is aged for twenty-one days at least after renneting, in order to develop an harmonious blue, with a typical soft, smooth, subtle taste.

Bleu du Vercors-Sassenage is a perfect choice for a cheese platter but can also be used in numerous cooking recipes. It is used in the raclette called Vercouline, and in a number of sauces. It can also be enjoyed in quiches and soufflés to which it will give added flavor, in salads or with an aperitif, or served in small cubes accompanied by a Clairette de Die.

See also BLUE CHEESES and HAUTE-SAVOIE.

Fromages du Dauphiné: Saint-Marcellin, Picodon, Bleu Du Vercors-Sassenage, Saint-Félicien. General Books LLC, 2010.

Chrystelle Hustache

block-forming towers represent the final step in a modern, automated Cheddar cheese manufacturing system. Traditional methods of Cheddar manufacture begin by making salted curds, a process that takes six to seven hours. The salted curds are then loaded into appropriately sized and shaped hoops and pressed for another eight to twenty hours. See HOOP; FORMS OR MOLDS; and PRESS. During the pressing time, the hoops are often opened, the cheesecloth is redressed, and the weight is adjusted by trimming. See CHEESECLOTH. The most common hoop style yields a block of cheese measuring 11 × 14 × 7 inches (28 × 35.5 × 17 centimeters) and weighing approximately 40 pounds (18 kilograms). After pressing, each hoop must then be cleaned and sanitized before it can be refilled. All together, these steps result in a labor intensive, two-day process to manufacture Cheddar cheese.

Automated cheesemaking systems can produce a continuous supply of salted curds twenty-four hours a day. The use of block-forming towers can make the process of pressing the curds continuous as well, simplify the cleaning process, and produce a more consistent, better quality cheese. A vacuum-driven air conveyor transports the curds to the top of a tower ranging in height from 20 to 26 feet (6 to 8 meters). The curds fall into a central column that tapers down to the 11 × 14 inch (28 × 35.5 centimeter) cross-section of the traditional 40-pound (18-kilogram) block. The central column is perforated to allow the removal of gases and whey from the curds as they are compacted by the weight of the curds above them. See WHEY. The constant vacuum in the central column results in a close-knit texture with very few internal or external mechanical openings. At the bottom of the tower, a guillotine-style knife cuts blocks off the pressed curd at regular intervals to give the final cheese blocks a consistent weight in the range of 22 to 44 pounds (10–20 kilograms). The towers may also be configured to produce a round form. The towers are operated in pairs, allowing one to be cleaned while the other is still operating. Depending on the particular model, each tower can produce 700–1,600 kilograms every hour. Block-forming towers enable the efficient production of high quality cheese twenty-four hours a day, seven days a week. Cheeses produced in block-forming towers are close-textured, rindless block Cheddars that are primarily used in the commodity market.

See also CHEDDAR and COMMODITY CHEESE.

Bylund, Gösta, et al. "Cheese." In *Dairy Processing Handbook*, 3d rev. ed. Lund, Sweden: Tetra Pak, 2016.
Scott, R., R. K. Robinson, and R. A. Wilbey. *Cheesemaking Practice*. 3d ed. Gaithersburg, Md.: Aspen, 1998.

John A. Partridge

bloomy-rind cheeses

bloomy-rind cheeses are characterized by a white, edible rind consisting of a more or less complex community of molds and/or yeasts that "blooms" on their exterior as the cheeses ripen. Traditionally these molds were naturally present in the cellars where cheese was stored. These days, molds and yeasts are inoculated directly into the milk during the cheesemaking process or sprayed onto the cheese during aging to ensure a faster and homogenous development and a more consistent quality. Bloomy-rind cheeses include a vast spectrum of varieties, produced from many types of milk but most commonly from cow's, goat's, or sheep's milk and even from a mixture of milks. Bloomy-rind cheeses may also be referred to as surface-ripened, mold-ripened, or soft-ripened cheeses.

Brie and Camembert are classic examples as well as the most popular varieties in this group, but there are many delightful cheeses that fit the style. A sampling of the wide range of bloomy-rind cheeses produced throughout the world is provided below:

- **Pouligny-Saint-Pierre**: a goat's milk cheese with a pyramidal shape; produced in central France.
- **Saint-Maure**: a small goat's milk cheese with a log shape; from the western Loire area of France. See SAINTE-MAURE DE TOURAINE.
- **Robiola**: a cheese often made with a mixture of milks in a cylindrical shape; from Italy's Piedmont region. See ROBIOLA DI ROCCAVERANO.
- **Bresse Blue**: a cylindrical cow's milk cheese that is blue on the inside but has a bloomy rind outside; from the Rhone Alps of France.

- **Crottin**: a dominant lactic-style cylindrical goat cheese with either a bloomy rind or a wild mixed rind; from various areas of France. See CROTTIN DE CHAVIGNOL.
- **Humboldt Fog**: a goat's milk cheese distinguished by its centerline of ash; from the coast of California. See HUMBOLDT FOG.

During ripening, the bloomy rind style of cheese undergoes a dramatic evolution in texture, flavor, and aroma from the outside in, because of the activity of the live rind. The process usually starts out with a fresh cheese that has limited surface growth, a slightly acidic taste, and a firm, chalky body. The cheese then begins evolving, over a period of several weeks, to one covered fully with a complex of white molds. It eventually develops a very different character throughout, with more aromatics (cream/earth), more flavor (mushroom-like), and a much softer and unctuous, flowing body. The body of the cheese gradually changes from chalky white to translucent, beginning near the surface and then progressing to the center of the cheese as it ages. Depending on the degree of ripening, the paste can range from soft to quite runny when brought to room temperature.

For this style, the specific cheesemaking process may be either primarily lactic or enzymatic in nature:

- The *lactic* profile is one in which little to no rennet enzyme is used, and the milk undergoes a very long process of coagulation that is primarily a result of the production of high levels of lactic acid. This process produces cheeses with a loosely organized texture. Examples include Saint-Marcellin, Picodon, Crottin de Chavignol, and Chaource.
- The *enzymatic* profile is very different, in that a rennet enzyme is primarily used to alter the essential milk proteins (casein) and thus cause coagulation of the proteins in a much shorter period of time. This process creates a more organized and stronger cheese body. Examples include Moses Sleeper (Cellars at Jasper Hill) and Mt. Alice (von Trapp Farmstead).

The living white rind found on all members of this group is actually a complex community of yeasts and molds that determines the eventual ripening character of these cheeses. The live mold and other surface microorganisms break down the proteins, causing an increase in pH and consequent creaminess over time from the outside toward the interior of the cheese. Along with the texture, the flavors also change, developing the characteristic mushroomy and ammonia-like notes. The higher the moisture content of the paste, the faster this breakdown occurs.

A cheese produced without the proper amount of moisture is not likely to ripen effectively. On the contrary, a cheese that is produced with too much residual moisture may experience an excessively rapid rate of protein breakdown near the surface, which in turn can result in an unstable cheese body with a runny paste near the surface or in excessive amounts of ammonia.

In looking at many examples of bloomy-rind cheese, it quickly becomes evident that there is a great deal of diversity within this group. This can be seen simply by comparing the smooth surface of a mild, snow-white Camembert and the streaks of rose and yellow of the more pungent, traditional Brie found in regional markets to the east of Paris. Both of these cheeses are also very different from Robiola, with its thin, dusty layer of *Geotrichum*, and from the small logs of Saint-Maure, with their wrinkled rinds created by differences in the profiles of their surface molds. It is the range of surface microorganisms, production profiles, and ripening periods in the bloomy-rind group that results in cheeses with such diverse aromas, flavors, and textures.

One of the more interesting developments in the study of what grows on a bloomy-rind cheese surface has resulted from the work of two microbiologists, Rachel Dutton and Benjamin Wolfe. They are beginning to discover through DNA studies that cheesemakers have an important role to play in determining the final communities on the cheese surfaces. As Dutton puts it, "The environment that they create on the surface of the cheese really determines what types of microbes actually grow" (Callaway, 2014).

Using DNA sequencing, Dutton and Wolfe analyzed the microbial communities of 137 types of cheeses from around the world. They found that the pH, the moisture content, and the aging process of a cheese have a greater influence on the microbial makeup of the rind than does the cheese's place of origin. This is good news for many bloomy-rind

cheesemakers because it gives them the ability to experiment with production methods to produce ever more interesting cheeses. Nevertheless, it is bad news for many European cheesemakers, who want their cheeses to have a microbial terroir unique to their location. Measures taken around the turn of the twenty-first century to remove pathogens such as *Salmonella* and *Listeria* have had the concomitant effect of reducing microbial diversity on European dairy farms, including eliminating many specific microbes that gave regional cheeses their unique organoleptic qualities. The microbiologist Nathalie Desmasures has been working to identify factors such as cattle breeds and particular milking machines that increase microbial diversity and to isolate strains that produce desirable properties. Dutton finds these projects intriguing but warns that microbes are unpredictable—adding them to the cheesemaking process will not necessarily result in their presence on the rind.

See also BRIE DE MEAUX; CAMEMBERT DE NORMANDIE; and SOFT-RIPENED CHEESES.

Callaway, Ewen. "Scientists and Cheesemakers Gather for (Microbial) Culture." *Nature*, 27 August 2014.
Dutton, Rachel, and Benjamin Wolfe. "Microbiology of Cheese Rinds." Presentation at the American Cheese Society Conference. Sacramento, California, 30 July 2014.
Fox, Patrick F., et al. *Fundamentals of Cheese Science.* Gaithersburg, Md.: Aspen, 2000.
Mallet, A., et al. "Quantitative and Qualitative Microbial Analysis of Raw Milk Reveals Substantial Diversity Influenced by Herd Management Practices." *International Dairy Journal* 27 (2012): 13–21.
Wolfe, B. E., et al. "Cheese Rind Communities Provide Tractable Systems for In Situ and In Vitro Studies of Microbial Diversity." *Cell* 158 (2014): 422–433.

Jim Wallace

blue cheeses (or blue-veined cheeses) are a group of soft and semisoft cheeses, from crumbly to creamy in texture, characterized by white or light yellow paste with bluish to greenish veins on the interior that are caused by the growth of *Penicillium roqueforti* or with a rind made of blue mold. Different methods can be used to classify cheeses as belonging to the category "blue."

In Ottogalli's (2000) classification, blue cheeses belong to the *formatica* (meaning shaped; includes all cheeses coagulated by rennet) group (Class E) and include (E1) smear-ripened cheeses, such as Stilton from Great Britain, Gorgonzola from Italy, Danablu from Denmark, and Bleu des Causses and Saingorlon from France; (E2) cheeses with a white bloomy rind similar to that of Camembert, such as Bleu de Bresse from France and Cambozola from Germany; and (E3) ewe's or goat's milk cheeses like Roquefort from France. A limitation of Ottogalli's classification is that it considers all blue cheeses to be rennet coagulated. This excludes some cheeses like the traditional Blue Log, a semisoft, tangy, clean, and creamy log of goat cheese covered in a bluish-grayish soft rind of *P. roqueforti*. See BLEU DES CAUSSES and CLASSIC BLUE LOG.

In contrast with Ottogalli's classification, the American Cheese Society differentiates three subcategories within its "Blue Mold Cheeses" (F) category: (i) rindless blue-veined cheeses like Roquefort style or Danish style; (ii) blue-veined cheeses with a rind or coating; and (iii) external blue molded or rinded cheeses that do not contain internal blue veins but that do have a rind, cover, or crust made of blue mold, like Selles-sur-Cher. See SELLES-SUR-CHER. This classification complements Ottogalli's categories, because it considers the microbiota in blue cheese to be complex and, in addition to *Penicillium roqueforti*, includes yeasts, bacteria, and other molds, which contribute to the diverse sensory attributes of these cheeses, including their rind development.

Blue-veined cheeses could also be distinguished from one another by their source of milk. Although some blue cheeses, like Danablu and Gorgonzola, are made with cow's milk, others, such as Gamonedo and Roquefort, reflect the sweet caramel taste of goat's and ewe's milk. See GAMONEDO.

Manufacturing of blue cheese is aimed to produce an acid curd with high moisture retention and incompletely fused curd pieces within the cheese (open structure), which will favor the growth of *Penicillium roqueforti*. In most cases, the curd is only slightly cut, so that some whey can be drained. This allows for the formation of a strong-enough texture without too much moisture reduction. Curd is usually not cooked and most of the time not pressed, in order to keep an open structure that will eventually allow the mold to grow. Only a few blue cheeses are slightly pressed, including the French Bleu du Vercors-Sassenage. See BLEU DU VERCORS-SASSENAGE. Within a few days or weeks of hooping

the curd, most blue cheeses will be pierced in order to allow air in, which will start the mold development. Different strains of *Penicillium roqueforti* will develop different-colored veins that go from green to blue, including shades of gray and brown. Green veins in the interior, where the oxygen concentration is low, may revert to blue when the cheese is cut. Blue cheeses are generally classified as soft and semisoft considering their total solids content, which ranges from 45 to 55 percent.

Although most European blue cheeses develop a wet, sticky rind (most frequently preserved in foil), most British blue cheeses develop a dry rind such as the characteristic rind of the famous Stilton. See STILTON. Differences in manufacturing account for the distribution of blue molds within the internal structure of blue cheeses. In general, the internal moisture of wet-rind blues allows for the development of pockets and wider streaks of blue molds, typical of Roquefort, probably the most famous blue cheese in the world. See ROQUEFORT. On the other hand, drier and denser blue cheeses usually develop thinner and longer streaks of blue veins, imitating the appearance of marble. A great example would be Stilton. This particular 7.5 kg cylindrical blue cheese is carefully pierced on its vertical sides, allowing air to enter the body of the cheese. With its high density, air pockets, and open curd structure, Stilton develops the typical long veins that radiate from the center to the outside of the cheese within a beautiful buttery and straw-yellow dry paste.

In the European Union, many blue-veined cheeses carry a protected designation of origin (PDO), which means that the cheese can only bear the name if it has been produced in a certain region and under certain conditions. Many blue-veined cheeses without a PDO are sometimes just labeled "blue cheese." France's appellation d'origine contrôlée (AOC) list contains eight different blue-veined cheeses. Among them, Bleu de Gex is one of the most unique blue cheeses, both from a technological point of view as well as from a sensory perspective. See BLEU DE GEX. In contrast to other blues, the cheese has low acidity with dominant enzymatic character, the paste is dense and creamy with a pale ivory color and a marbling of very dark greenish-blue veins. The aroma and flavor are relatively mild with bitter notes.

See also NEEDLES and *PENICILLIUM*.

American Cheese Society. "Judging & Competition 2016 Categories." http://cheesejudging.org/wp-content/uploads/2016/03/2016-Categories-Final.pdf.

Cantor, M. D., et al. "Blue Cheese." In *Cheese: Chemistry and Microbiology*, edited by Patrick F. Fox et al. Vol. 2: *Major Cheese Groups*, 3d ed., pp. 175–198. London: Elsevier, 2004.

Ottogalli, G. "A Global Comparative Method for the Classification of World Cheeses (with Special Reference to Microbiological Criteria)." Rev. ed. *Annals of Microbiology* 50 (2000): 151–155.

Arthur Hill and Mary Ann Ferrer

Boeren-Leidse met sleutels,

is one of a few protected designation of origin (PDO) cheeses from the Netherlands and also one of its most ancient cheeses. The cheeses are imprinted with the symbol of crossed keys (*sleutels* in Dutch), the coat of arms of the city of Leiden. Above the keys is written "Boeren" (farmhouse), and underneath "Leidse" (from Leiden). Cumin seeds bring some sweetness to the hard and salty paste of the cheese.

Production of the cheese began on farms in the Western Netherlands, one of the wealthiest parts of the country. In the Middle Ages, the Dutch prized expensive butter. Cheeses made from skim milk were a mere byproduct. However, skim milk cheeses could be kept longer than full-fat cheeses, and were more resilient at warm temperatures, so the Dutch East India Company ships took Boeren Liedse met sleutels with them on their long journeys to the Far East.

The cheese was granted PDO status in 1997. Cheeses may only be produced in the area around the Old Rhine River, which is near the city of Leiden, and must use the milk from breeds including Friesian Holstein, Meuse-Rhine-Issel, or Blaarkop cattle. It is a washed-curd cheese, made using skim raw milk, animal rennet, and cumin seeds. The cheeses are pressed in molds containing a plate with the pattern of the keys, so that the figure is embossed into their surface. After pressing they are brined for four to six days, and then the rind is painted with annatto or colored coatings for protection. The cheeses are considered at their best when aged over six months. They may weigh anywhere from 6 to 24 pounds (3–11 kilograms).

By 2013 there were only eighteen producers left, in part because of the diminishing demand for low fat farmhouse cheeses.

See also ANNATTO; HOLSTEIN; and NETHERLANDS.

Boerderijzuivel oer van de Boer. http://www.boerderijzuivel.nl/kaas/boeren-leidsekaas.nl.

Boeren-Leidse. http://www.boerenleidsekaas-met-sleutels.nl.

Betty Koster

bog butter

bog butter connotes an ancient custom as well as a primitive dairy food. Historically, it refers to old world butter that was purposely buried in the depths of a peat bog, particularly in Ireland, but also in Scotland, Finland, and Iceland. More than four hundred discoveries of sunken bog butter have been unearthed from these regions, some dating from as early as the Middle Iron Age and as recently as the early 1800s. Many of the butters have been found accidentally, pulled to the surface by men who dug up the soggy peat to dry and sell for fuel. Of the surviving bog butters, most are contained in handmade wooden vessels (firkins, bowls, kegs, troughs, and boxes). But others have been wrapped in a combination of tree bark, wool, moss, or baskets, as well as animal skins and bladders.

Regardless of the packaging, none of these artifacts would have survived to the present if not for the unique conditions of the primordial peat bog. Almost completely devoid of oxygen that typically causes rot, the wet bog is also highly acidic, which prevents bacterial decay. What's more, the boggy depths are cold year round. Given these qualities, it's long been assumed that our dairy ancestors buried butter in the bog to preserve it, especially during the spring and summer months when butter making was most abundant. Storing it for leaner times made sense. But recent studies seem to indicate that there were other, more complex reasons why early dairy families chose to bury their butter—a valued commodity—and why it was sometimes never retrieved.

For centuries, butter was frequently used as a means of paying rent or taxes, with overlords often taking a percentage of the amount of butter produced. Clearly the tenant farmer would benefit from hiding some of his butter wealth. Similarly, butter was hidden from marauding thieves. More than just a valued food in preindustrial civilizations, butter was also prized for waterproofing tents and clothing; mixing with sand to make a building mortar; and for making candles.

Another theory contends that butter was submerged in the bog for gastronomic reasons. That its

More than four hundred discoveries of butter sunk in peat bogs have been unearthed in Ireland, Scotland, Finland, and Iceland. This photo shows the in-progress re-creation of bog butter undertaken by Ben Reade, the Head of Culinary Research and Development at Nordic Food Lab, in 2012. © BENEDICT READE

flavor matured there, instead of simply spoiled. The Irish are said to have buried their butter "to sweeten" it. Indeed, testimonies from those who have tasted long-buried bog butters, generally don't characterize it as being rancid; typically they describe it as having a cheese-like flavor.

So there are multiple answers to why butter might have been buried in the peaty wetlands over the centuries. But the question remains: Why were so many bog butters left in the earth, given their apparent value? The standard answer is that these sunken butters were merely lost, forgotten, or that their owners fell victim to violence or disease. But recently another theory has emerged, based on mapping the location of salvaged bog butters. Many of the ancient butters found in Ireland were discovered at geographical locations that held potent meaning for the early pagans, leading some experts to propose that these butters were never meant to be retrieved; they were deposited as votive offerings to the elemental beings.

Downey, Liam, Chris Synnott, Eamonn P. Kelly, et al. "Bog Butter: Dating Profile and Location." *Archaeology Ireland* 20, no. 1 (Spring 2006): 32–34.
Reade, Benedict. "Bog Butter: A Gastronomic Perspective." *Nordic Food Lab*, 30 October 2013. http://nordicfoodlab.org/blog/2013/10/bog-butter-a-gastronomic-perspective.
Synnott, Chris. "Records of Bog Butter Finds in the Memoirs of the Irish Ordnance Survey, 1830 to 1839." *Ulster Journal of Archaeology*, 3d ser., 62 (2003): 143–160.

Elaine Khosrova

Bohinjski sir (Bohinj cheese) is a hard cow's milk cheese produced in the Bohinj region located in the heart of the Slovenian Alps. Bohinj cheese production began in 1873 when Swiss master cheesemaker Hitz started educating shepherds in the basics of classic Swiss cheese technology. See EMMENTALER. A few years later several small dairies were established under Hitz's supervision, including the dairy in Stara Fužina where today the Alpine Dairy Farming Museum presents the history of cheesemaking in the Bohinj region, and the dairy in the village Srednja vas, which is the only dairy that still produces Bohinj cheese. In the past Bohinj cheese was produced in all Bohinj Alpine pastures and in the dairies in Bohinj valleys.

Bohinj cheese is traditionally made from raw or thermized cow's milk originating from the Bohinj region. Warm milk is inoculated with a thermophilic starter culture, along with a culture of propionic bacteria. Rennet is added to give a firm coagulum, which is gradually cut into small pieces. The curd is heated to around 120°F (50°C) and then filled into the round molds. After pressing and brine salting, the ripening starts with a short period of cold storage (60–64°F [15–18°C]). Subsequently a longer ripening period at high temperature (72–74°F [22–24°C]) allows the formation of the characteristic large eyes. See EYES. Historically the first ripening stage took place on highland farms and then the cheeses were transported to one of the dairies in the valley for further ripening at higher temperatures. The final maturation that encourages flavor development again takes place in a cold place.

Bohinj cheese is a large wheel-shaped cheese with numerous large eyes. A whole cheese weighs 99 to 121 pounds (45–55 kilograms), around 23 inches (60 centimeters) in diameter and 3 to 6 inches (8–15 centimeters) in height. The rind is firm, dry, and yellow, while the cheese body is ivory to yellow. The flavor is mild, aromatic with a nut-like taste, and with prolonged maturation it can become more aromatic and slightly piquant.

Perko, Bogdan. *Slovenski avtohtoni siri—siri z geografskim poreklom (zgodovina, področje, tehnološki postopki)* (Slovenian Autochthonous Cheeses—Cheeses with Geographical Origin [History, Region, Technological Processes]). Rodica, Slovenia: Biotechnical Faculty, 2003.

Petra Mohar Lorbeg and
Andreja Čanžek Majhenič

Bongrain

See SAVENCIA FROMAGE & DAIRY.

The **Boston Public Market,** at 100 Hanover Street in downtown Boston, Massachusetts, opened its doors in 2015. It combines fresh-food vendors and prepared-food stalls in a year-round indoor market, with a focus on products made in New England.

The project to establish the market started in 2001 with the ambition of creating a permanent food market near Faneuil Hall and Quincy Market. Both of those locations had previously housed food markets, but now they have been turned into food courts and feature prepared-food vendors, restaurants, and other retail stores. The Boston Public Market joins the Haymarket open-air fruit and vegetable market and the historic commercial Blackstone Block as part of an effort to revitalize the area between Government Center and the North End, now called the Market District.

Four permanent food stalls in the Boston Public Market sell cheese, focusing on cheeses made in Massachusetts or New England. Harlow's Vermont Farmstead sells a selection of Vermont and other New England artisanal cheeses. The Cellars sells cheeses produced in Vermont by Jasper Hill Farms and other producers, but aged at their caves located in Greensboro, Vermont. The Trustees of Reservations' Appleton Farms stall functions as the official store of the Massachusetts Cheese Guild, with dairy products made by cheesemakers in the state. Wolf Meadow Farm sells southern Italian cheeses, including fresh mozzarella and scamorza, made with milk from their Amesbury, Massachusetts, farm.

Boston Public Market. http://www .bostonpublicmarket.org.
Geller, Jessica. "Boston Public Market Opens amid Crowds." *Boston Globe*, 30 July 2015.

Carlos Yescas

bovine somatotropin (bST) was one of the first proteins produced by recombinant (r-) DNA technology in the 1970s. Somatotropin (growth hormone) is a protein produced by and secreted from the anterior pituitary of mammals. Somatotropin is species-specific in that bovine is not active in other species, such as humans and swine. The hormone affects metabolism of somatic cells in mammals either directly or by secondary messengers, for example, insulin-like growth factor-1. Somatotropin is not active orally and is degraded in the digestive tract by protein digesting enzymes, such as pepsin and trypsin.

Researchers reported a 41 percent increase in milk production by cows given daily injections of r-bST in a 188-day study. Four companies conducted extensive research with r-bST in a sustained delivery formulation in many countries during the 1980s. Milk production was increased 12 to 15 percent. Fat, protein, and lactose percentages in milk derived from cows that received r-bST were not different from that of control cows. Similarly, manufacturing properties of milk from cows that received r-bST were similar to that of control cows. Monsanto received approval for commercialization of its r-bST

(Posilac) from the United States Food and Drug Administration (FDA) in 1994.

The FDA, World Health Organization, and United States National Institutes of Health have independently asserted the safety for humans of milk and meat derived from cows treated with Posilac. Health Canada and the European Union did not approve r-bST for use in dairy cattle. Monsanto sold Posilac to Elanco in 2008.

Bauman, Dale E. "Bovine Somatropin: Review of an Emerging Animal Technology." *Journal of Dairy Science* 75 (1992): 3432–3451.

R. K. McGuffey

Bovški sir (Bovec cheese) is a hard Slovenian protected designation of origin (PDO) cheese, about 6–10 pounds (2.5–4.5 kilograms) in weight, 3–5 inches (8–12 centimeters) high, and 8–10 inches (20–26 centimeters) in diameter. First mentioned in 1756 on a price list in the Italian town of Udine, Bovec cheese was historically valued much higher than other cheeses due to its excellent quality, and was used as a means of payment. It has retained its special status as a symbol of the rich farming and cheesemaking heritage of the town of Bovec, in northwestern Slovenia, close to the border with Italy. Today Bovec cheese is produced on farms and on two highland Alpine dairies in the municipality of Bovec and its surroundings, representing the area of protection.

Bovec cheese is made from raw sheep's milk of the Bovška Ovca breed, although varieties made with up to 20 percent cow's and/or goat's milk are allowed. Traditionally ripened evening milk is mixed with freshly drawn morning milk, warmed up to 95–97°F (35–36°C) and renneted. Cutting the coagulum with stirring during the subsequent scalding results in a firm wheat-size grain. The curd is settled to the bottom of the vat and gently pressed by hand. After cutting the curd mass with a copper wire into coarse lumps, each lump is removed from the whey and placed into a mold. Alternatively the entire curd mass may be scooped into the cloth drawn across the bottom of the vat by a stainless steel rod and, by pulling together the corners of the cloth, lifted out. Drained curd is cut into portions of appropriate dimension and transferred to molds that are often cloth-lined. After a few hours pressing and frequent turning, the cheeses are brined or dry-salted. During maturation, which lasts for at least two months (57–66°F [14–19°C], 75–80 percent humidity), cheeses are frequently turned and, if necessary, wiped with brine-soaked cloth.

At this point the cheese develops a compact and homogenous texture with typical "shell" break that is liable to fracture but not crumble. Widely scattered eyes the size of lentils or peas are evident, with a few natural fissures allowed. The flavor becomes aromatic, intensive to mild-piquant, and the interior will be gray to pale yellow. The taste and smell are well rounded and pleasantly harmonized with slightly spicy notes. The rind is smooth and gray-brown in color, with a flat upper side and slightly convex peripheral side. The maturation period can be extended to two years.

Specification for Bovec cheese. Društvo rejcev drobnice Bovške, 2014. http://www.mkgp.gov.si/fileadmin/ mkgp.gov.si/pageuploads/podrocja/Varna_in_ kakovostna_hrana_in_krma/zasciteni_kmetijski_ pridelki/Specifikacije/Bovski_sir_specifikacija.pdf.

Andreja Čanžek Majhenič and
Petra Mohar Lorbeg

Bra is a pressed, semi-fat protected designation of origin (PDO) cheese that bears the name of a small town, the capital of Roero, situated on the boundary between the Langhe and the plains of Cuneo in northwestern Italy. Bra PDO cheese is produced throughout the territory of the province of Cuneo as well as in the municipality of Villafranca Piemonte, in the province of Turin. Together, these areas produce about 730 tons of Bra PDO each year. The cheese produced in the mountain municipalities listed in the PDO can be labeled with the word "d'Alpeggio"; the background of the paper label is also colored a distinctive green.

Bra PDO cheese is made from pasteurized or raw cow's milk, but when necessary, a small amount of sheep's or goat's milk may be added. The milk (from one or two milkings) is often partially skimmed. After a double curd cutting, the cheese is pressed, put into molds, and salted. Bra PDO is made in two types, semisoft and hard. The semisoft cheese must be ripened for at least forty-five days, while hard must be ripened for at least six months. Both varieties have a cylindrical form with a diameter of 11.8–15.7 inches (30–40 centimeters), a rounded edge of 2.7–3.5 inches (7–9 centimeters), and a weight of about 13–17.6 pounds (6–8 kilograms). Although both types have small, sparse eyes (holes), the interior paste of semisoft Bra is white or ivory but turns slightly yellow-ochre in the hard cheese. The soft type has a pleasant odor with milk, cream, and butter characteristics and a less intense taste that is mainly sweet. The hard type has a very aromatic odor with almond and spicy characteristics and a very savory taste. The hard type can also be grated.

See also ITALY.

Assopiemonte DOP & IGP. http://www .assopiemonte.com.

Maffeis, Piero. *I formaggi italiani. Storia, tecniche di preparazione, abbinamenti e degustazione*. Milan: Hoepli, 2010.

Ministero Agricoltura e Foreste. *DOC Cheeses of Italy: A Great Heritage*. Milan: Angeli, 1992.

Sardo, Piero, Gigi Piumatti, and Roberto Rubino eds. *Formaggi d'Italia: Guida alla scoperta e alla conoscenza*. Bra, Italy: Slow Foods Editore, 2005.

Giuseppe Zeppa

Brânză de Burduf is arguably Romania's most esteemed cheese, with a Slow Food Presidium working to protect and promote it. It is traditionally made in the Bucegi Mountains, a range of high peaks in the Southern Carpathians, where shepherds still move flocks of Turcana and Tiggae sheep, local heritage breeds, into the higher, cooler altitudes for the summer, and use their milk to make a range of *brânză* (cheese), from the Ricotta-like Urdă to the feta-like Telemea. See TRANSHUMANCE and URDĂ. As with both of these cheeses, Brânză de Burduf starts out as Caş, a fresh cheese made by curdling sheep's milk with rennet and draining the whey. It becomes Brânză de Burduf after the curds are broken into small bits, mixed with salt, and then packed into a "bellows" (*burduf*) traditionally made from a cleaned sheep's skin or stomach.

The most esteemed variation is aged in fir-tree bark that is stripped from the tree in spring and early summer, when it is most resinous, softened in whey, and then formed into cylinders. Packed with the curd and sealed at both ends with more bark, these logs of cheese are aged anywhere from three

Brânză de Burduf, one of Romania's best-loved sheep's milk cheeses, is aged in fir tree bark. Packed with the curd and sealed at both ends with more bark, these logs of cheese are aged anywhere from three weeks to three months. © OLIVIERO TOSCANI

weeks to three months. The yellowish-white paste takes on pine-like notes to complement the cheese's already spicy, sharp flavor. It melts beautifully, which may be why it is best known for adding a bright, creamy tang to the cornmeal porridge mămăliga. It can also be crumbled over fresh tomatoes or other vegetables to add a salty, spicy kick. While the bark-wrapped version is hard to find outside Transylvania, it is possible to find plastic-wrapped versions on the US market today.

FermaBucegi. http://www.ferma-bucegi.ro.

Slow Food Foundation for Biodiversity. "Bucegi Mountains Branza de Burduf." http://www .fondazioneslowfood.com/en/slow-food-presidia/ bucegi-mountains-branza-de-burduf.

Tara Q. Thomas

Brazil, as with elsewhere in Latin America, has a cheese and cheesemaking tradition that began with the arrival of European colonizers. First Portuguese and later Italian settlers brought with them cattle and milking animals. The southeastern state of Minas Gerais is the foremost producing region in the country, with smaller dairy production in the states of São Paulo, Goiás, Paraná, and Rio Grande do Sul.

Minas cheese (Queijo Minas), a popular Brazilian cow's milk cheese traditionally produced in the Minas Gerais state, may be eaten fresh (*frescal*) or aged up to thirty days (*padrão*). Pictured here is fresh Minas cheese.
© ROSANA MCPHEE

The three most popular cheeses in Brazil are coalho, requeijão, and lastly, Queijo Minas, which may be *frescal* (fresh) or *padrão* (aged). Minas cheese was developed using the recipe of Serra da Estrela, but instead of using the cardoon thistle of the Portuguese recipe, Brazilian cheesemakers use animal rennet. See SERRA DA ESTRELA. As a result, Brazilian Minas cheese has a firmer paste, less lactic flavor and a more assertive profile. Fresh Minas, sold within ten days of its production, is traditionally accompanied by fruit paste for breakfast. It is also the basic ingredient in the traditional *pao de queijo*, a savory pastry made with manioc flour. Minas cheese can be also aged up to thirty days, which allows the cheese to develop a firmer texture and drier paste, at which time it is known as Queijo Minas Padrão.

Coalho is normally cooked on a grill until it has a crispy rind and soft center. This cheese is produced in the northeastern part of Brazil. It is a common appetizer in *churrascarias*—grills that sell meat on skewers also known as *rodizio*. Coalho is also a popular snack at the beach, grilled to order on small charcoal stoves hand carried by vendors, and sometimes paired with sugarcane molasses. The name translates as rennet, and the cheese has a squeaky texture when chewed.

Requeijão can be seen in many breakfast tables kept in glass or plastic jars. Unlike Italian ricotta or Spanish requesón, this cream cheese is almost liquid because extra fresh cream or sometimes water is added to the warm curd. The most widespread brand is Catupiry, developed by Mario Silvestrini, an Italian who immigrated to Brazil in 1911. Now

made in the state of São Paulo, the cheese was originally created in Minas Gerais. Requeijao is also used as an ingredient in *coxinhas*, pastries stuffed with shredded chicken, as well as in the *camarão ao catupiry* dish popular in the Espírito Santo state.

Other cheeses produced by artisans and consumed locally include capitra from Mato Grosso; cabacinha from the Jequitinhonha Valley in Minas Gerais; queijo d'alagoa, also known as Parmesão from the Mantiqueira mountains in Minas Gerais; serrano from Rio Grande do Sul, and Santa Catarina; and manteiga or also known as requeijão do sertão, made in Bahia, Paraiba, Pernambuco, and Rio Grande do Norte.

Other cheeses made in the country by dairy conglomerates following European recipes are also popular such as mussarela, Reino, Mascarpone, and Gorgonzola.

Though the main influence has been the colonial southern European techniques, Brazilian cheesemaking culture also has taken up production of Danish cheese styles, a notable example of which is queijo prato, which resembles danbo with its yellow color. This rindless, mildly salted cheese is normally paired with fruits and cold cuts.

See also LATIN AMERICA.

Castañeda, R., S. Borbonet, A. Ibarra, et al. *Quesos de América del Sur*. Buenos Aires, Argentina: Editorial Albatros, 2010.

Carlos Yescas

bread pairing, or at least bread, is fundamental to the enjoyment of cheese. The combination is timeless; bread is *the* complement to cheese, with only a nod to crackers in Anglophone countries. The flavor and textures of fresh bread, with its crisp crust and the tender pull of the crumb, make an especially gratifying combination with cheese textures and flavors. And bread moderates the intensity of strong cheeses, making them more approachable and facilitating combinations of cheese with wine. Bread appears also with cooked cheese, as the medium for raclette and fondue, as the base for Welsh rabbit, as the support for the gratinéed cheese on onion soup, and even as crumbs on macaroni and cheese. See RACLETTE; FONDUE; WELSH RABBIT; SOUPS; and MAC AND CHEESE. Specific bread-and-cheese pairings don't exist in the way that wine-and-cheese pairings do, with the important exception of walnut bread with soft goat's-milk cheeses. Apart from that, only generalities exist, and with any sort of cheese they depend on the particular example at hand—its saltiness, acidity, moisture or dryness, maturity and intensity.

For contrast, a mild fresh cheese goes with a strong, dark bread, including one with seeds, such as sunflower. Rather than look for contrast, however, it's usually easier to match like with like. The classic baguette, made with white flour and commercial yeast, suits milder cheeses, although a fresh baguette goes reasonably well with any cheese; the same might be said about most fresh loaves. (In the countryside of Europe, where often, historically, baking took place only every two weeks, the frequent complement to cheese was stale bread. But today there may be no one who, given a choice, would prefer the taste of old bread to fresh.) Still putting like with like, a more acidic young goat cheese goes with sourdough, although the acidity of sourdough can distract from the taste of a cheese. And stronger cheeses suit stronger, often darker breads with darker crusts. Whole wheat, for instance, is an option with blue cheeses or aged cheddar. But sour all-rye may be too strong for any cheese.

Raymond Calvel (1913–2005), who taught at the École Nationale Supérieure de Meunerie et des Industries Céréalières in Paris, and during his life was France's greatest bread expert, offered his personal bread with cheese advice in his major book, *The Taste of Bread*, while noting that other people would have their own tastes. His examples unsurprisingly were wholly French, but you can easily extrapolate from them to other cheeses. He suggested baguettes with Camembert, Brie, slightly aged goat's-milk cheeses, Cantal, Emmentaler, Comté, and fromage blanc (fresh white cow's milk cheese). He suggested well-baked loaves having a high proportion of crust with Cantal, Salers, Laguiole, Bleu de Bresse, Livarot, and Fourme d'Ambert. He linked sourdough loaves with Roquefort, Bleu des Causses, Bleu d'Auvergne, the washed-rind cheeses Époisses and Munster, and (it seems) Pyrenees ewe's milk cheeses.

Fresh bread has a very different effect from that of toast, which some North American chefs began to serve with cheese early in the twenty-first century. Toast makes economical use of stale bread, but the chefs have tended to toast the bread dark—creating hard textures, aggressive flavors, and a degree of bitterness—so the toast competes with the cheese,

and wins. Sometimes a chef has even sent out buttered toast, giving an unflattering oily contrast to the flavors of the cheese.

Many people mash soft cheese into bread, which destroys the delicate texture of a hand-ladled, relatively young and not yet creamy cheese. Out of respect for texture, some tyrophiles (cheese connoisseurs) eat cheese with a knife and fork, as well as with bread. See TYROPHILE.

See also BEER PAIRING and WINE PAIRING.

Calvel, Raymond, Ronald L. Wirtz, and James J. MacGuire. "Bread and Gastronomy." In *The Taste of Bread*, pp. 193–194. Gaithersburg, Md.: Aspen, 2001. Originally published as *Le Goût du Pain* (Paris: Jérôme Villette, 1990).

Edward Behr

brebis, pronounced *breh-bee,* is a French word that refers to a female sheep, also known as a ewe. The term is an iteration of the Latin *vervex,* which means wether (a castrated ram), and the Vulgar Latin *berbex,* or *berbecis.* The phrase "fromage du brebis" refers to a cheese made from ewe's milk, though brebis is commonly used without the modifier, in a manner similar to chèvre. See CHÈVRE. Brebis refers to French cheese made from ewe's milk, or cheese made with ewe's milk in the French or Basque style. In Spanish the comparable term is *oveja,* and in Italian, *pecorino.*

Brebis can be applied to fresh cheese or aged cheese. More often than not, if a cheese has the term *brebis* in its name, one can infer that it is made in the Pyrenees, or made in the style of the Pyrenees mountain cheeses, where the shepherds practice transhumance. See TRANSHUMANCE. The region is also home to the Basque people, whose ancestral territory transverses the political border between Spain and France. Cheesemaking in the Pays Basque has an ancient history, and in Basque dialect, the term for sheep's milk cheese is *ardi gazna* (*ardi* = sheep, *gazna* = cheese). See BASQUE COUNTRY.

Ossau-Iraty-Brebis-Pyrenees, with appellation d'origine contrôlée (AOC) status granted in 1980, is a classic brebis. Ossau refers to cheeses made in the Val d'Ossau, in the French style, and Iraty refers to the cheeses of the Pays Basque. Examples of Ossau-Iraty include Tomme Brulee, Abbaye de Belloc, P'tit

Basque, and cheeses made by both Fromageries, Etorki, Agour, and Istara. See OSSAU-IRATY. Roquefort can also be considered a brebis, as can Brebisrousse d'Argental and Saveur du Maquis, but the term is more commonly used to refer to aged, mountain-style cheeses. Battenkill Brebis, made by 3-Corner-Field Farm in Shushan, New York, and Verano, made by Vermont Shepherd in Putney, Vermont, are examples of American sheep's milk cheeses modeled after the Pyrenees Brebis.

See also SHEEP.

Jenkins, Steven. *Cheese Primer.* New York: Workman, 1996.

Masui, Kazuko, and Tomoko Yamado. *French Cheeses: The Visual Guide to More Than 350 Cheeses from Every Region of France.* New York: DK Publishing, 2000.

Michelson, Patricia. *Cheese: Exploring Taste and Tradition.* Layton, Utah: Gibbs Smith, 2010.

Rance, Patrick. *The French Cheese Book.* London: Macmillan, 1989.

Weinzweig, Ari. *Zingerman's Guide to Good Eating: How to Choose the Best Bread, Cheeses, Olive Oil, Pasta, Chocolate, and Much More.* Boston: Rux Martin/ Houghton Mifflin Harcourt, 2003.

Sarah Spira

breeding and genetics are significant factors for any producer raising dairy cattle for milk intended for cheese production. Decisions on both are driven primarily by a quest for increased levels of milk solids—butterfat and especially protein—in order to maximize the yield of cheese achievable from milk. As a general rule, if a cow is bred to produce a large volume of milk for the liquid milk market,

then its milk will have a smaller percentage of milk solids. In contrast, a cow bred for cheese production is generally one which yields a lower quantity of milk, but with a higher percentage of milk solids. As an example, much of the effort in the breeding of the familiar black and white-colored Holstein and Friesian cows has been directed toward the capability of producing high volumes of milk, reflecting the breed's use in liquid milk production, where overall quantity is of paramount concern. See HOLSTEIN and EAST FRIESIAN (COW). In contrast, the Ayrshire, a breed popular with cheesemakers, has an average milk yield that is around two-thirds of that of the Holstein, but its milk quality is such that it produces 5 percent more butterfat and 4 percent more protein. See AYRSHIRE. What this means in practical terms for the small-scale cheesemaker is that using the milk of the lower yielding Ayrshire will result in an improved cheese yield, with a smaller volume of whey to dispose. For the large-scale producer, because of the increasing uses for whey in further food processing or industrial applications, the milk of a higher yielding cow may still be of interest.

While breed does have a large role to play in the quantity versus quality of milk produced, there can be large variations within breeds. The majority of cows in the Netherlands—a country whose dairy production is largely focused on the production of cheese—are Holstein. When comparing Dutch milk production averages to those of Germany—another country with a predominantly Holstein herd, but with a dairy industry that has a greater focus on milk production for the liquid market—the Dutch

Comparison of prominent dairy cattle breeds—average milk yields and compositions

	Milk yield (kg) per lactation (305 days/yr)	Butterfat	Protein
Ayrshire	6,944	4.1	3.32
Brown Swiss	7,380	4.1	3.41
Dairy Shorthorn	5,728	3.9	3.3
Friesian	6,822	4.1	3.33
Guernsey	5,927	4.71	3.54
Holstein	8,868	3.92	3.18
Jersey	5,721	5.4	3.84
Montbéliarde	6,943	3.88	3.34

Sources: CDI (2014), Nix (2013)

national herd produces lower volumes of milk but with higher levels of milk solids. The Dutch farmers have bred their Holstein cows with cheesemaking in mind, while the majority of German farmers have bred their Holstein cows to produce high yields of milk for the liquid milk market.

The concept of the angular-bodied dairy cow—a type bred purely for milk production—is one that came about as recently as the twentieth century. The interwar and postwar periods saw more farms, particularly in North America and Northern Europe, beginning to specialize production, either for milk or beef. Before this period of specialization, cattle were generally either dual purpose in nature, bred for producing both milk and meat, or triple purpose, with an additional role as draft animals. Today, some of these multipurpose cattle breeds still play a very important part in cheesemaking; indeed, some of Europe's protected designation of origin (PDO) cheeses are required to be made using the milk of specific cattle breeds that also happen to be dual-purpose types. See PROTECTED DESIGNATION OF ORIGIN. This is especially the case in France, where Comté can only be made with the milk of Montbéliarde or French Simmental cows, and Salers de Buron Traditional cheese can only be made from the milk of Salers cows. See MONTBELLIARDE and SALERS (COW). In Normandy, from 2017, Camembert de Normandie will be required to be made with at least 50 percent of milk from the Normande cow; Livarot will be required to be made with 100 percent Normande milk. See NORMANDE. Cattle breeding is also used in the marketing of differing brands of cheese within a certain type, such as can be found with some producers of Italy's Parmigiano Reggiano where there are brands that extoll the virtues of a particular indigenous Italian cow of choice, including the Reggiana, the Italian Brown, and the Vacca Bianca Modenese.

There is little evidence to suggest that the cattle breed has a direct influence on the taste, texture, or aroma of cheese, with much research suggesting it is the cows' diet that has the greater influence on these sensory properties. However, breed has been shown to affect other cheesemaking qualities. An important property is the variant of Kappa-casein protein present in the milk. BB genotype Kappa-casein has been shown to increase the quantity of cheese obtainable from milk, as well as reducing the coagulation time and improving the firmness of the curd. Breeds that have been found to have a higher incidence of BB genotype Kappa-casein include Brown Swiss, Jersey, Montbéliarde, and Normande. See BROWN SWISS and JERSEY.

The concept of breed came about in eighteenth-century Britain, when livestock breeding pioneer Robert Bakewell (1725–1795) developed the English Longhorn cattle. Before this time, cattle developed within their particular region and there may have been great variability even between the cows of neighboring valleys. Breeding methods have continued to evolve alongside scientific and technological breakthroughs, perhaps most important of which was the development of artificial insemination (AI) in the twentieth century, which has opened up dairy herds across the world to a greater variety and quality of cattle genetics for much less than the price of buying or rearing a bull. Because of AI, some farmers have been led to experiment with crossbreeding cattle of two or more breeds, a breeding practice that is very common in beef, lamb, and pork production, but had not been as popular within the dairy sector. Crossbreeding brings about the occurrence of heterosis, which means the hybrid progeny of two different breeds is expected to have improved production traits (higher milk solids yield, reduced incidence of lameness, longevity, etc.) than the two parent breeds alone would have achieved. Crossbreeding usually is carried out between two breeds, or with the addition of a third breed, crossed with the hybrid progeny of the first cross. A popular two-way cross practiced in New Zealand in order to improve milk solids and yield is the Friesian X Jersey, gaining improvements in milk solids from the Jersey and improvements in overall milk yield from the Friesian. A three-way cross growing in popularity with some American and British farmers producing milk for cheesemaking (from farmhouse to industrial-scale production) is the Montbéliarde X Swedish Red X Holstein—with higher milk yields due to the Holstein, and milk solids increases and hardiness from the Swedish Red and Montbéliarde.

See also COW.

Becker, R. B. *Dairy Cattle Breeds—Origin and Development.* Gainesville: University of Florida Press, 1973.
Porter, V. *Cattle—A Handbook to the Breeds of the World.* Marlborough, U.K.: Crowood, 2007.

Wendorff, Bill, and Karen Paulus. "Impact of Breed on the Cheesemaking Potential of Milk: Volume vs Content." *Dairy Pipeline* 23, no. 1 (2011): 1–7.

Nicholas Millard

Brevibacterium linens

Brevibacterium linens (*B. linens*), a Gram-positive bacterium that is commonly found on human skin, is typically associated with washed-rind cheeses. It is valued for its attractive creamy-white to yellow-orange pigmentation and its characteristic earthy aroma, which comes from its production of sulfur compounds. *B. linens* does, however, have a reputation that is sometimes larger than its reality.

The smeared rinds of certain cheeses (such as Limburger and Munster) might not in fact have as much *B. linens* as is generally assumed, particularly in artisan and raw-milk cheese dairies where local yeasts and other microbes provide similar effects. In farms without strict limitation of local microorganisms in the curing rooms, the conditions that *B. linens* enjoy also promote the presence of yeasts and micrococci, which increase the surface pH of the rinds. They all enjoy a very high humidity of at least 95 percent, salty rind conditions, still air, and temperatures of 57–66°F (14–19°C). Even if it is not solely responsible for giving cheese its characteristic soft rind and pungent flavor, *B. linens* does seem to have importance as a barrier against fungi and is believed to produce bacteriocins, antibacterial proteins that can inhibit pathogens like *Listeria monocytogenes*. See BACTERIOCINS.

If commercially prepared cultures of *B. linens* are introduced during cheese production in the vat, washed onto the rinds after brining in a salt solution, or mixed with wines or other liquors used for rind washing, then the bacterium should flourish. However, it will often find itself competing with the local microbes from the air, brine, human handling, or the boards that support the cheese. These local organisms may ultimately dominate without apparent loss of the scents and flavors that are associated so often only with *B. linens*.

At the Gubbeen cheese dairy in Ireland, a study was undertaken to identify the predominant rind microorganisms. Despite the introduction of commercial *B. linens* cultures and *Geotrichum*, the rinds proved to support a mixture of yeasts and a newly identified bacterium, *Microbacterium gubbeenese*.

Under the right conditions, it seems, local strains dominate.

See also INDIGENOUS MICROORGANISMS; RIPENING CULTURES; and WASHED-RIND CHEESES.

Brennan, N., et al. "*Microbacterium gubbeenense* sp. nov., from the Surface of a Smear-Ripened Cheese." *International Journal of Systematic and Evolutionary Microbiology* 51 (2001): 1969–1976.
Wolfe, B., et al. "Cheese Rind Communities Provide Tractable Systems for In Situ and In Vitro Studies of Microbial Diversity." *Cell* 158 (2014): 422–433.

Giana Ferguson and Brian Schlatter

Brick

Brick cheese is a Wisconsin original cheese made in a brick-shaped form with a sweet and mild flavor when young that matures into a strong, ripe cheese with age.

The Swiss-born American cheesemaker John Jossi developed Brick in 1877 after immigrating to Wisconsin and marrying the daughter of a local cheesemaker. He patterned the cheese after Limburger, but aimed for a milder, firmer cheese with less orange-brown mold on the rind. See JOSSI, JOHN and LIMBURGER. The key to his recipe was using bricks to press the cheese as well as to form it into a brick shape. Over time, he shared the recipe with a dozen other Wisconsin cheese factories, and the cheese became quite popular. In 1883 he gave his cheese factory to his brother, who later sold it to Kraft. See KRAFT FOODS.

Brick cheese derives its name both from its shape and from the bricks used to press the curds. WISCONSIN HISTORICAL SOCIETY

Brick is still primarily produced in Wisconsin, but like many cheeses, it has evolved into several styles. Today, many cheesemakers make mild and young versions of Brick that are not smear-ripened, because the US Code of Federal Regulations under the Food and Drug Administration requires that Brick contain a minimum of fat and a maximum of moisture content. In contrast, true Brick fashioned in Jossi's intended style is now commonly known as aged Brick, with only a handful of cheesemakers continuing to make the original recipe.

One of the last remaining cheesemakers in Wisconsin to make Brick in the Old World style, using his grandfather's bricks to press whey from the cheese, is Joe Widmer, of Widmer's Cheese Cellars in Theresa. This third-generation cheesemaker is adamant about sticking to the traditional method of brining the cheese, the key to traditional Brick. The curd is manually transferred from vat to cheese forms, with each form hand turned three times the first day. The cheese is then pressed by bricks and placed in a brine solution to absorb salt and bacterial cultures. Next, it is moved to a warmer room to encourage bacterial growth that produces a stronger flavor and a tan-red color on the surface. Each piece of cheese is washed by hand with a bacteria-infused brine to continue the bacterial growth and to encourage the cheese body to soften during ripening.

Authentic Brick cheese is best enjoyed at between ten and twelve weeks of age and is often served similar to Limburger—on dark bread with a slice of sweet onion and brown mustard. Many taverns in Wisconsin still serve Brick cheese sandwiches with beer and liverwurst.

See also WISCONSIN.

New England Cheesemaking Supply Co. "Brick Cheese." http://www.cheesemaking.com/Brick.html.
Widmer's Cheese Cellars. http://www.widmers cheese.com.

Jeanne Carpenter

Brie de Coulommiers

See COULOMMIERS.

Brie de Meaux

Brie de Meaux is a French soft cheese with a white mold made from raw cow's milk. The Union Syndicale Interprofessionnelle de Défense du Brie de Meaux was created in February 1980 and Brie de Meaux obtained appellation d'origine contrôlée (AOC) status in August 1980 and appellation d'origine protéger (AOP) status in 1996. Some 5,785 tons of this cheese are produced annually.

Brie de Meaux's origins are thought to date to the seventh century with the founding of the Abbaye de Jouarre and the discovery and appreciation of this cheese, made by monks at the abbey, by Charlemagne in 774. The proximity of the Brie terroir to the capital—and the royal court—favored its development. Brie de Meaux was made in the farmsteads and the size of the molds corresponded to the quantity of milk available on the farm.

At the end of the seventeenth century the use of rennet, until then not widespread, was better understood and the technology became specialized, leading to a large format Brie de Meaux with coagulation using rennet. The French Revolution saw it become the people's cheese and the revolutionary Lavallée wrote the following during that period: "Brie cheese, loved by rich and poor, was preaching equality before this was thought possible." In 1815, during the banquet concluding the Congress of Vienna, the Prince of Metternich and French negotiator Charles Maurice de Talleyrand, prince of Bénévent, organized a competition featuring sixty cheeses. The Brie de Meaux from the Villeroy farm (10 kilometers west of Meaux) was declared "the king of cheeses and top of the desserts." See CONGRESS OF VIENNA. In 1991 the "Brie de Meaux Companions Brotherhood" was created on the initiative of the city of Meaux. It is led by a Grand Council of the Order, consisting of farmers, cheesemakers, affineurs, and local cheese merchants who all love and promote this cheese.

It takes some 26 quarts (25 liters) of milk to make a flat cheese 14 inches (35 centimeters) in diameter; only 1 inch (3 centimeters) in height that will weigh just over 7 pounds (3 kilograms) after four weeks maturing (the minimum maturing period in order to be sold). The milk curdling takes place at a temperature never exceeding 99°F (37°C). Renneting is exclusively with bovine rennet. Molding is manual using a pelle à brie (traditional perforated ladle) and ripening takes eight to ten weeks. See PELLE À BRIE. Fully matured, its texture is supple and the cheese has delicate aromas of cream, butter, and hazelnuts.

See also FRANCE.

Confrérie du Brie de Meaux. http//:www
.confreriedubriedemeaux.fr.
Delfosse, Claire. *Histoires de bries.* Saint-Cyr-sur-Morin,
France: Musée Départément des Pays de Seine-et-
Marne, 2008.

Agnès Meilhac

Brillat-Savarin

Brillat-Savarin cheese was developed in the 1930s by Pierre and Henri Androuët, a father and son team of well-known cheese producers and sellers. The recipe is based on a cheese called Excelsior, a precursor (1890s) of the triple-cream style. Brillat-Savarin was designed to be even more decadent, in honor of its namesake Jean Anthelme Brillat-Savarin (*b* Belley, France, 1 April 1755, *d* Paris, 2 February 1826). A politician, lawyer, judge, and famed writer, he was known for such aphorisms as "A dinner which ends without cheese is like a beautiful woman with only one eye," and "Tell me what you eat, and I shall tell you what you are." Brillat-Savarin is credited with inventing the subject of gastronomy with his 1825 book, *La Physiologie du goût* (English trans., *The Physiology of Taste*), a collection of aphorisms, anecdotes, and reflections on food that reflect a lifetime of consideration and nearly a quarter century of writing.

Brillat-Savarin cheese is now widely available and the rights to the name have passed through several hands. The cheese is currently made by several fromageries in Ile-de-France and Normandy. Made from pasteurized milk, it is a triple-cream cow's milk cheese, with 75 percent dry fat matter. Brillat-Savarin has a white and fluffy *P. candidum* rind and is aged four weeks before being sold. The cheese comes in a small round, weighing just over a pound. It is about 1.5–2 inches (4–5 centimeters) high with a diameter of 5 inches (13 centimeters). The texture is semisoft, with luxurious mouthfeel reminiscent of tangy, sour, and mushroomy softened butter. It pairs exceptionally well with sparkling wines and lighter beers.

See also ANDROUËT, PIERRE.

Brillat-Savarin, Jean Anthelme. 1949. *The Physiology of
Taste: Or Meditations on Transcendental Gastronomy.*
New York: Heritage. Translated by M.F.K. Fisher.
Jenkins, Steven. *Cheese Primer.* New York: Workman, 1996.
Michelson, Patricia. *Cheese: Exploring Taste and
Tradition.* Layton, Utah: Gibbs Smith, 2010.
Rance, Patrick. *The French Cheese Book.* London:
Macmillan, 1989.
Weinzweig, Ari. 2003. *Zingerman's Guide to Good Eating:
How to Choose the Best Bread, Cheeses, Olive Oil, Pasta,
Chocolate, and Much More.* Boston: Houghton Mifflin,
2003.
Yamada, Kazuko Masui, and Tomoko Yamada. *French
Cheeses: The Visual Guide to More Than 350 Cheeses
from Every Region of France.* London: Dorling
Kindersley, 2000.

Sarah Spira

Brin d'Amour

Brin d'Amour translates in English to "bit of love." Brin also means "sprig" referring to the sprigs of herbs applied to the outside of the cheese. This small artisanal herb-encrusted squatty square or nest-shaped natural rind cheese is native to the Mediterranean island of Corsica. It is primarily produced in the more mountainous regions of the island, and occasionally produced in nearby regions of France. Weighing 1¼ to 2 pounds (½ to 1 kilograms), the cheese is typically made from raw sheep's milk or sometimes raw goat's milk, from animals which have fed on the wild herbs, flowers, and brush of the rugged landscape. Once the drained curds are shaped, the surface of the cheese is completely encased in a thick coating of a mixture of bay, rosemary, savory, and thyme; the native wild herbs of the high altitude, rocky countryside of Corsica known as the *maquis*. These aromatic wild shrubs are the same varieties of plants the milked sheep or goats have fed on. The top of the encrusted cheese is further embellished with leaves of rosemary, a few coriander seeds, peppercorns, juniper berries, small red bird's eye chili peppers, or a combination of these. It is then ripened for at least one month, and up to three months. When young (a few weeks old), the interior (paste) is soft, with a pronounced flavor of the milk and little influence from the herb crust. As the cheese ages, the interior turns firm and slightly flaky, carrying an intensified earthy flavor, and aroma of the herbs. This specialty cheese is made and consumed locally. Brin d'Amour is sometimes also known as *fleur du maquis*, or "flower of the maquis," though cheesemakers of the region consider these to be two different yet almost identical cheeses.

Masui, Kazuko, and Tomoko Yamada, *French Cheeses,*
First American ed. New York: DK Publishing, 1996.

Mary Karlin

brined cheeses

brined cheeses are traditionally made in the Balkans and Eastern Mediterranean region. They are preserved in brine (up to ¾ ounce [20 grams] sodium chloride [NaCl] per 3 ounces [100 milliliters]), which confers on them a characteristic salty taste. Salting of the cheese is achieved by immersion of the pressed curd in brine for up to a few months, but for some varieties dry-salting is used in addition to brining. Examples of brined cheeses and their origin are feta (Greece), Bulgarian White (Bulgaria), Beynaz-Peynir (Turkey), and Akkawi, Stambuli, Nabulsi, Mujaddal (braided cheese), Domiati, Halloumi, and Brinza (Lebanon, Syria, Egypt, Cyprus, and Israel). In general these cheeses are classified as semihard to semisoft. See FETA; DOMIATI; and HALLOUMI.

Methods of Manufacture

Traditional methods of manufacture of brined cheeses are broadly similar. The main factors influencing the ultimate character of the cheese are as follows:

- Type of milk—Brined cheeses are made from cow's (bovine), goat's (caprine), sheep's (ovine), or buffalo (bubalus) milk, or from some mixture thereof. For example, feta cheese is made from sheep's or goat's milk, or from a mixture of both. Beyond species variation, milk composition— hence cheese character—is influenced by diet, breed, stage of lactation, lactation number, milking strategy, and udder health. The milk for cheesemaking may be used raw or pasteurized. The type of milk used and the method of manufacture employed can affect the chemical composition of brined cheeses. See MILK.
- Starter culture—Lactic acid bacteria known as starter cultures are used to acidify the milk and to aid coagulation by chymosin (also known as rennet). Both mesophilic cultures (*Lactococcus* spp. and *Leuconostoc* spp.) and thermophilic (*Streptococcus* spp. and *Lactobacillus* spp.) cultures are used. See STARTER CULTURES.
- Curd handling—The combined effect of starter cultures and chymosin results in coagulation of milk. After a suitable time the curd is cut, allowed to rest in the whey, and gradually transferred to molds. The curd shrinks expressing whey, and this process is enhanced by pressing overnight. On the following day the molded curd is cut into retail portions, packed in bulk, and brined. However, in the

manufacture of Halloumi cheese, the molded curd is cut into retail portions and cooked in hot whey (194°F [°90°C] for thirty minutes) to plasticize the curd. When the curd blocks float, cooking is complete and the cheese is removed from the whey. The warm curd is then dry-salted, sprinkled with dried crushed mint for added flavor, and then folded. After cooling the cheese portions are stacked in metal containers and filled with salted whey (½ ounce [12 grams] NaCL per 3 ounces [100 milliliters]). See COAGULATION OR CURDLING.

- Adventitious contaminants in brine—Brine is usually reused from one batch to another, topping up the salt content as required. In some traditionally made brined cheeses, the brine is contaminated with yeast, such as *Saccharomyces* spp., *Debaryomyces* spp., *Pichia* spp., and *Hansenula* spp., which can contribute to a distinctive flavor during ripening of the product.

New Trends in Feta-Type Cheese Manufacture

In traditional methods of manufacture of brined cheeses, the whey is expressed from the curd and valuable whey protein is lost from the product. However, when milk is pre-concentrated before curd formation, some or all of the whey constituents may be incorporated in the curd. These systems were mainly developed for the manufacture of feta-type cheese made from cow's milk. Concentration is achieved by ultrafiltration (UF) using semipermeable membranes. See ULTRAFILTRATION. Two methods are available for the production of "structured" and "cast" feta-type cheeses.

For "structured" feta-type a pre-cheese is made by standardizing the fat of the milk, heating and concentrating the milk by UF to a concentration factor (CF) of 3.3. The pre-cheese is homogenized and mixed with starter culture, chymosin and Patent Blue (E 131), then pumped through a coagulator. The coagulum so formed is passed through a dicing machine before filling the molds. Whey drainage, albeit to a reduced extent, proceeds in the molds, which are turned. The last of the whey is removed by pressing. Blocks of cheese are cut into retail portions, placed into large metal containers, brined (⅛ ounce [4 grams] per 3 ounces [100 milliliters]), and transferred to the cold store.

"Cast" feta-type cheese is made from pre-cheese in which the standardized milk is concentrated by a CF of 5. To this pre-cheese, salt and the same ingredients are added similar to those used for the production of "structured" feta-type cheese. Coagulation takes in retail containers in warm rooms. When the desired pH is reached, the staked containers are transferred to the cold store.

See also BALTICS; BRINING; and SERBIAN WHITE BRINED CHEESES.

Robinson, Richard K., and Adnan Y. Tamime, eds. *Feta and Related Cheeses*. Chichester, U.K.: Ellis Horwood Ltd., 1991.
Tamime, Adnan Y., ed. *Brined Cheeses*. Oxford: Blackwell Publishing Ltd., 2006.

A. Y. Tamime

brining is a means of salting cheese, whereby the molded cheese curd is immersed in brine, which is a pH-adjusted sodium chloride solution (~18–25 percent) containing added calcium. The brining time depends on the target salt content, the size and composition of the cheese, salt content of brine, brining conditions (temperature, degree of brine agitation), and ratio of cheese to brine. Typically, the brining time can vary from less than twelve hours for small cheeses (e.g., 4–18 ounces [100–500 grams]) such as Camembert to about 15 days for a wheel of Parmesan (~ 99 pounds [~ 45 kilograms]). The brine is prepared by dissolving the appropriate quantities of sodium chloride and calcium chloride in clean water that has ideally been pasteurized or sterilized by UV radiation. The final levels of NaCl and Ca in the brine should typically be about 18–23 percent (w/w) and ~ 0.3 to 0.5 percent (w/w), respectively, even though the exact levels depend on the type of cheese. The pH is adjusted with food grade acid (e.g., lactic) to a pH value of ~ 5.1 to 5.3, and cooled to ~ 54°F (~ 12°C). Maintaining the concentrations of NaCl and Ca, pH, and temperature at the above values minimizes the incidence of defects such as rind rot or soft rind that are associated principally with excessive casein hydration at the cheese surface. Despite the brine being an unfavorable environment, some salt tolerant *Lactobacillus*, yeasts, and molds, can survive and grow. These microorganisms can contaminate the surface of the cheese during brining and lead to patches of mold growth postbrining and softening of the cheese surface due to proteolysis. Consequently, preservatives such as chlorine, potassium sorbate, hydroperoxide, ozone, and/or natamycin may also be added, subject to legislation, to enhance the microbiological keeping quality of the brine. In practice cheese brine is retained for long periods, sometimes for many years. Maintenance of the brine quality requires: (1) routine replenishment of the sodium chloride content, (2) frequent monitoring of calcium content and pH, (3) routine coarse filtration to remove fragments of curd and extraneous materials that could serve as nutrient sources for microorganisms, and (4) microfiltration; or nanofiltration to remove microorganisms.

Mechanism of Salt Uptake by Cheese in Brine

The uptake of salt by cheese placed in brine occurs by diffusion, with the salt and water (H_2O) moving in response to their respective concentration gradients from regions of high concentration to lower concentration. Therefore, when a molded cheese is placed in brine there is a net movement of salt molecules from the brine into the cheese moisture (and hence into the cheese) and a simultaneous migration of moisture through the cheese to the brine. Model studies have shown that the movement of salt into cheese and the concomitant outward migration of water during brining is an impeded diffusion process, with NaCl and H_2O moving in response to their respective concentration gradients, but at diffusion rates that are much lower than those in pure solution owing to a variety of impeding factors. The lower diffusion rate of NaCl in cheese moisture compared to water is due to the structure of the cheese matrix, which is essentially a network of casein aggregates that entraps the cheese moisture and encases the fat, which occurs in the form of globules. The movement of the salt molecules diffusing through the cheese is obstructed principally by fat globules and casein aggregates around which they must proceed and by the sieve effect exerted by the pores of the casein network.

The quantity of water lost during brining of cheese is about twice the weight of salt absorbed. A suggested explanation for the higher water loss is that the effective diffusion radius of the H_2O molecule is only half that of the NaCl molecule and its diffusion is less restricted by the sieve effect of the casein network. See CASEIN.

Factors Affecting Salt Uptake during Brining

The quantity of salt absorbed by the cheese during brining is affected by numerous factors, major ones including concentration of NaCl in the brine, brining time, brine temperature, shape of cheese, and cheese composition. The following increase salt uptake:

- salt content of the brine in the range 5–25 percent (w/w), though at a diminishing rate as the concentration of salt in the brine increases
- temperature of the brine from 41°F to 68°F (5°C to 20 °C)
- brining time
- surface area to volume ratio of the cheese
- moisture content of the cheese

Conversely, for cheeses with similar moisture content, salt uptake has been found to decrease as the pH of the cheese is increased from pH 4.7 to 5.7 in Gouda and other cheeses. These factors exert their effect on salt uptake by their influence on the concentration gradient, number of directions of salt penetration into cheese, degree of protein hydration, pore size of the casein network, and kinetic energy of the diffusing molecules.

The quantity of salt absorbed by cheese after a given time may be approximated by the following equation:

$$Q_t = 100 \, Mt \, {}^A\!/_G$$

where, Q_t is the quantity of salt absorbed (g NaCl/cm^2 cheese surface area) in time t, A = cheese surface area (cm^2), G = weight of cheese (g), where the effect of curvature is negligible.

Distribution of Salt in Cheese Following Brining

When the cheese is removed from the brine, there is a large decreasing salt gradient from the surface to the center of the cheese and a decreasing moisture gradient in the opposite direction. However, the salt continues to diffuse slowly from the surface

inward during ripening and these gradients gradually decrease as salt concentration becomes uniform throughout the cheese. The time required for equilibration of salt throughout the cheese depends on cheese type, composition, size and shape of cheese, curing conditions (temperature and relative humidity), and packaging material (which determines whether moisture is lost). Typical times required for salt uniformity throughout the cheese are seven to ten days for Camembert (9 ounces [0.25 kilograms], flat disk), four to six weeks for Edam (5.5 pounds [2.5 kilograms], sphere), seven to nine weeks for Gouda (22 pounds [10 kilograms], wheel), and greater than four months for Emmentaler (132–287 pounds [60–130 kilograms], wheel).

See also BRINED CHEESES; DRY SALTING; and SALT.

Guinee, T. P., and P. F. Fox. "Salt in Cheese: Physical, Chemical, and Biological Aspects." In *Cheese: Chemistry, Physics, and Microbiology*, vol. 1: *General Aspects*. 3d ed., edited by Patrick F. Fox, Paul L. H. McSweeney, Timothy M. Cogan, and T. P. Guinee, eds., pp. 207–259. London: Elsevier Academic, 2004.

Guinee, T. P., and B. J. Sutherland. "Salting of Cheese." In *Encyclopedia of Dairy Sciences*, vol. 1, 2d ed., edited by John W. Fuquay, Paul F. Fox, and P. L. H. McSweeney, pp. 595–606. London: Academic, 2011.

International Dairy Federation. *The Importance of Salt in the Manufacture and Ripening of Cheese*. Special Issue 1401. Brussels: International Dairy Federation, 2014.

Kurlansky, Mark. *Salt: A World History*. London: Penguin, 2003.

Timothy P. Guinee

brocciu is a cylindrical cheese with a soft, creamy texture, which is made exclusively in Corsica from the whey of ewe's or goat's milk. The brocciu cheesemaking process has a mythical origin: the recipe supposedly was passed to Corsican shepherds by King Solomon himself. Currently the only milk product to have appellation d'origine contrôlée (AOC, 1998) and protected designation of origin (PDO, 2003) status on the island, brocciu is the cheese that identifies Corsica and is certainly the delicacy of Corsican cuisine, with its meltingly creamy taste and delicious aroma. About 485 tons of this cheese are produced per year, in sizes that vary from half a pound to nearly 7 pounds (250 grams to 3 kilograms).

Brocciu's raw material, milk whey, comes from prior cheesemaking. This milk whey is traditionally poured into a copper cauldron and heated over a wood fire. When the whey temperature reaches about 104°F (40°C), a certain quantity of fresh whole milk is added (ideally 15 percent; a maximum of 25 percent), along with a small amount of water and salt. The mixture obtained is stirred and heated slowly to between 176 and 194°F (80 and 90°C), which is when the curds start to float on the surface. A few moments later, the heating is stopped. The resulting mass is then carefully scooped out and layered in the cylindrical molds called *fattoghje*, which were traditionally made of woven bulrush. Today, the materials have adapted in keeping with modern practices. Although the process (temperature, water or whole milk addition, etc.) is still the same, woven-bulrush molds have been replaced by plastic molds, and copper cauldrons are no longer mandatory. See COPPER VATS.

When brocciu is fresh, the best way to eat it is just after it has been made, while it is still warm, perhaps with a touch of sugar, or else, when it has matured, like a cheese, in which case it is called brocciu passu. When matured, brocciu becomes more like a ripened cheese and develops a saltier and more intense flavor. Numerous traditional recipes are based on brocciu: added to an omelet alongside mint, in stuffed zucchini, and fiadone (pastries, etc.).

See also CONCENTRATED WHEY CHEESE and RICOTTA.

Biancarelli, Marie-Claire. *La cuisine au brocciu: 56 recettes*. Ajaccio, France: Albiana, 2009.
Ravis-Giordani, Georges. *Bergers corses: Les communautés villageoises du Niolu*. Aix-en-Provence, France: EdiSUD, 1983.

Matteu Filidori

Brown Swiss (also called Swiss Brown, Braunvieh, or Schwyzer) is a light brown dairy cattle breed that originated in the Swiss Alps. In marked contrast to "improved" British cattle, whose physique was shaped from the outset by specialized breeding for milk production, the original Schwyzer or Braunvieh was a large, rugged mountain animal equally suitable for draft, milking, and meat purposes. It has a longer history of its own in connection with cheesemaking than any British counterpart. Before modern times it had spread beyond Switzerland to neighboring cheese-producing countries such as Italy, where it is known by the name *Bruna Alpina*.

Brown Swiss cattle arrived in the United States around 1870, later than the other major dairy breeds. They are larger, and give more milk, than any dairy cows except Holsteins. Both breeds were developed into a more spare, thin-fleshed physique to conform better to nineteenth- and twentieth-century breeders' images of ideal dairy conformation. The Brown Swiss, however, was less aggressively manipulated than the Holstein for volume of production during the era when most dairy farmers turned to single-minded pursuit of the twentieth-century fluid milk market. Consequently, the traits that had helped the animals create Swiss cheeses on their home ground did not get bred out of them in new homes (Canada and other English-speaking countries as well as the United States). See HOLSTEIN.

Practical advantages of Brown Swiss include hardiness in harsh climates or steep terrain, strong insect resistance, low incidence of pink-eye infections, and an ability to produce well-flavored milk on poor pasturage. The milk is not buttery or creamy compared with that from Jerseys or Guernseys. But like Ayrshire milk it has a fat and protein content attractive to cheesemakers, with small fat globules and a protein-to-fat ratio that make it particularly good for hard cheese varieties. See JERSEY; GUERNSEY; and AYRSHIRE. Today Brown Swiss even play a role in some production of Grana Padano or Parmigiano Reggiano.

Numbers of registered Brown Swiss in the United States have declined in the last half century, but the lineage certainly has a future in the cross-breeding programs that are coming into favor as leaders of the milk industry rethink production priorities. The breed is also positioned to become a natural choice

A Brown Swiss cow grazing on the land adjacent to Consider Bardwell Farm, in Vermont. The dairy that owns the land supplies milk to Consider Bardwell. © KATE ARDING

for artisanal cheesemakers in the United States, the United Kingdom, and elsewhere seeking to produce versions of Emmentaler, Gruyère, Appenzeller, and other Swiss originals.

See also COW and SWITZERLAND.

Becker, Raymond B. *Dairy Cattle Breeds: Origin and Development.* Gainesville: University of Florida Press, 1973.
Porter, Valerie. *Cattle: A Handbook to the Breeds of the World.* 2d ed. Illustrated by Jake Tebbit. Ramsbury, U.K.: Crowood, 2007.

Anne Mendelson

brunost

See CONCENTRATED WHEY CHEESE.

brushing

brushing is part of the affinage (maturing) process, used particularly for cheeses with washed rinds, such as soft-ripened (*pâtes molles*) cheeses like Époisses, Langres, Livarot, Pont-l'Évêque, Maroilles, Mont-d'Or, Vacherin du Haut-Doubs, and Munster. Some pressed cheeses like Morbier and Raclette or hard cheeses like Comté also have rinds that are washed and brushed. See WASHED-RIND CHEESES; SOFT-RIPENED CHEESES; PRESSED CHEESES; and COMTÉ.

The technique originated in monasteries in the Middle Ages. Morge, the solution brushed onto the cheese surface, is made of saltwater (usually about a 5 percent concentration), with the addition, principally, of *Brevibacterium* and *Micrococcus* species, although yeasts and molds can also be added. See MORGE and *BREVIBACTERIUM LINENS*.

Brushing (or rubbing) cheese promotes fermentation by preserving moisture levels on the surface, providing a controlled application of proteolytic ripening enzymes, and more evenly distributing surface flora. This technique aims to prolong the development of cheeses and to create their distinctive flavors. Washing and brushing are accomplished first by immersion and then by hand, with a sponge or brush. The rind gains a supple quality, moist and more or less sticky. Its color ranges from yellow-orange to brown, passing through shades of ochre and reds.

Some clothbound and natural-rind cheeses are also brushed during maturation to control mold growth and discourage incursion by mites. Marcel Petite has automated the brushing process, utilizing robots at Fort St. Antoine to turn and brush the large wheels of Comté during affinage. See CLOTH-BOUND CHEESES; CHEESE MITES; and FORT SAINT ANTOINE.

See also MATURING.

Kindstedt, Paul. *American Farmstead Cheese: The Complete Guide to Making and Selling Artisan Cheese.* White River Junction, Vt.: Chelsea Green, 2005. See p. 257.
Paxson, Heather. "The Art of the Monger." *Limn,* 21 January 2014.

Sylvie Lortal

Bulgaria

Bulgaria, a country in southeastern Europe, continues to struggle to meet European Union production standards for the export of Bulgarian cow's milk, based on conditions persisting from the fall of the Soviet Union. At the same time efforts are being made to revive sheep populations that will result in the recovery of treasured Bulgarian cheeses.

Bordered by Romania (north), Macedonia and Serbia (west), Turkey and Greece (south), and the Black Sea (east), Bulgaria's landscape is diverse, from the Thracian plain centered on the city of Plovdiv to the south, to the Ludogorsko plateau in the north. More than half the country is hilly or covered by mountains.

Bulgaria aligned with Germany in both world wars, and then came under the control of the Soviet Union, gaining its independence in 1991. For Bulgaria's dairy industry, the end of the communist era meant extraordinary, if not catastrophic, changes. Former employees of dairy factories were often given one or two of the cows they had been tending, many of whom sold the cows for their meat. To date there are huge numbers of very small farms, and just 2 percent of farms nationwide have as many as fifty cows. Ensuring that small farms that wish to be part of milk exports meet the proper standards is a monumental task, and the number producing non-compliant milk is substantial, as much as one-third of all small farms.

Bulgaria has always relied on its sheep population to provide milk for yogurt and its two most characteristic cheeses, Sirene (a white cheese similar to feta) and Kashkaval (a semihard yellow cheese that can be made from sheep's milk, cow's milk, or both). See FETA and KASHKAVAL. Historically a nomadic system for sheep farming was employed. Under

Soviet era collectivization, large cooperative flocks were gathered, and the population declined substantially. Since 1989 those flocks have been dispersed, and government-owned grazing land is being used without adequate control.

Today nonprofit organizations are working to preserve the sheep populations and create artisanal cheese products whose sales will undergird these efforts. Semperviva, a non-governmental conservation group, has been working since 2001 to breed not only the coarse wool Karakachan sheep, but also the Karakachan dog and Karakachan horse, support animals that protect the sheep and make herding possible. Karakachan milk is used in making an artisanal Sirene white cheese.

A third variety of cheese unique to Bulgaria is Cherni Vit Green Cheese. This is a mold cheese named for the village where it is produced. In 2007 The Slow Food Foundation established a Bulgarian Presidia to ensure the mold cheese's continued production. When they undertook this effort, the cheese was in danger of becoming extinct, the last man who knew the technique being nearly eighty years old and unable to create the cheese any longer. See SLOW FOOD.

Sirene and Kashkaval cheeses are featured in some of the country's popular dishes. For example, Sirene po shopski, a clay-pot dish featuring Sirene and tomatoes, is typical of the cuisine of Sofia, Bulgaria's capital. A popular Bulgarian street food is Kashkaval pane, made by breading and frying Kashkaval. Finally two dishes that involve baking Sirene into bread are tutmanik and banitsa.

See also GREECE and TURKEY.

Dimitrova, Dessislava. "Slow Food—the Guardians of Food Treasures of the World." Novinite.com, 2 June 2011. http://www.novinite.com/articles/128875/Slow+Food+-+the+Guardians+of+Food+Treasures+of+the+World.

Dohne, Janet Vorwald. *Livestock Guardians: Using Dogs, Donkeys, and Llamas to Protect Your Herd*. North Adams, Mass.: Storey, 2007.

Hamnett, R. "Country Pasture/Forage Resource Profiles—BULGARIA." FAO, 2006. http://www.fao.org/ag/agp/agpc/doc/counprof/Bulgaria/bulgaria.htm.

Karl Peterson

A **buron** is a small, low stone structure with slate or stone roof tiles in the mountains of Central-Southern France, built as a shelter and cheese-

Early twentieth-century photo of a cheesemaking barn, or buron, of mortared stonework under a four-sided thatched roof in the Le Mont-Dore, a commune in the Puy-de-Dôme department of France. Burons were made of wood until farmers' increasing wealth in the nineteenth century allowed them to hire masons to build sturdier (and more temperature-stable) stone structures. Later examples had slate or stone tiled roofs.

making workshop for the summer grazing season. Burons are found in higher-altitude pastures in the French administrative departments of Aveyron, Cantal, Lozère, and Puy-le-Dôme, where they were made of wood until farmers' increasing wealth in the nineteenth century allowed them to hire masons to build sturdier (and more temperature-stable) stone structures. Practicing transhumance, farmers sent their cows to graze the high pastures from late May to mid-October, accompanied by a small team of cowherds who milked twice-daily and made large-format cheeses. Cowherds set the cheeses to age in the cool interior until they all descended at the end of the season. Cantal, Laguiole, fourme d'Aubrac, and sometimes even the smaller St. Nectaire cheeses were traditionally made in this way. None of the hundreds of burons dotting the landscape are used exactly like this today, although at least a handful of them still house part of the cheese-making process (albeit with interiors updated to meet regulatory standards); some contain restaurants or museums while others have been restored by associations cherishing the region's dairying heritage and now occasionally serve as hiking shelters.

See also PASTORALISM and TRANSHUMANCE.

Association pour la Sauvegarde des Burons du Cantal (ASBC). http://www.burons-du-cantal.fr. A buron protection association in the Cantal department; its website (in French) is well-illustrated, including slide shows of the reconstruction of burons fallen into ruin and old photos of their use back in the day.

Juliette Rogers

burrata, meaning "buttery" or "buttered," originated in the commune of Andria, in the region of Apulia (Puglia), the heel of the Italian boot, during the 1920s. It is an offshoot of fresh mozzarella production, made using the same *pasta filata* (stretched curd) technique. A portion of the stretched curds are shredded, yielding *straciatella* ("little rag" or "shred"). Cream is extracted from the whey that has been drained from the curds, and the *straciatella* is added to it. The remaining stretched curds are cut and formed into rectangles that are then folded into pouch shapes; these pouches are in turn filled with the *straciatella*-cream mixture and secured with a top knot.

Part of the charm of burrata is how its rich, yet delicate, filling oozes out luxuriously when it is cut.

More often than not, burrata is made from *fior di latte* ("flower of milk"), mozzarella made from cow's milk as opposed to water buffalo's milk. Like fresh mozzarella, burrata has a short shelf life—it should be consumed within 48 hours of production—which poses logistical challenges to its exportation and at the same time makes it a highly prized delicacy. A burrata is typically about 4 to 5 inches (10 to 12 centimeters) in diameter, weighs 10.5 to 17.5 ounces (a third to a half a kilogram), and contains 60 percent fat in dry matter. Traditionally, burrata was wrapped in the green leaves of the asphodel plant (*vizzo* in Italian) to protect its thin (1 centimeter) exterior and also indicate freshness; in modern times the leaves are often replaced by plastic.

Specialty stores, cheese shops, and restaurants can make burrata in-house, buy it from local producers, or if not in Italy (and on rare occasions), obtain Italian exports. Burrata became fashionable in high-end gourmet restaurants in the United States starting in the early to mid-1990s and has remained in demand ever since. In recipes, its mild, lactic, creamy flavors benefit from simple pairings with fresh vegetables and fruits, and it works well on gourmet pizzas and in light pasta dishes.

See also ITALY; MOZZARELLA; and PASTA FILATA.

Culinary Institute of America. "Burrata: Puglia's Molten Mozzarella." YouTube video, 3:13. Posted 8 March 2011. https://www.youtube.com/watch?v=7llIboOGBrk.
Di Palo, Lou, with Rachel Wharton. "Mozzarella (Burrata)." In *Di Palo's Guide to the Essential Foods of Italy*, pp. 34–35. New York: Ballantine, 2014.
Luigi Guffanti. http://www.guffantiformaggi.com.

David Gibbons

burrini (buh-REE-nee; singular *burrino*) are small pear-shaped cheeses composed of an outer layer of soft, springy cow's milk cheese surrounding an inner layer of butter (*burro* in Italian) made from the whey. The outer straw-colored cheese sac, a pulled curd derivative of Caciocavallo, is drawn up around the butter and tied at the neck, protecting the butter from the air. Historically this process provided a way to preserve butter in warm southern climates.

Pairs of burrini are often strung together and hung over rods to age (hence colloquial references to them as *palle di mulo*, or mule's testicles). The cheeses are typically matured for at least six to eight days. Burrini have a mild, buttery flavor, yet a distinctive, some say pungent, aroma. They are primarily eaten as a table cheese, served with bread and accompanied by fresh raw vegetables such as fennel, celery, and tomatoes. Burrini are produced in southern Italy, in the regions of Campania, Puglia (where it is called manteca), Basilicata, Sicily, and Calabria (where it is known as butirro). It is the Calabrese who are generally credited with first creating this cheese. Burrini produced in Sila, a plateau region in Calabria known for its rich, fragrant pastures, are particularly prized.

See also CACIOCAVALLO; PROVOLA DEI NEBRODI; PROVOLONE DEL MONACO; and PROVOLONE VAL-PADANA

Davidson, Alan. *The Oxford Companion to Food.* New York: Oxford University Press, 1999.

Jenkins, Steven. *Cheese Primer.* New York: Workman Publishing, 1996.

Sacchi, Luisa, ed. *Formaggi Italiani dalla A alla Z.* Milan: Fabbri Editore, 2002.

Sardo, Piero, et al., eds. *Italian Cheese: Two Hundred Traditional Types: A Guide to Their Discovery and Appreciation.* Translation edited by Giles Watson. Bra, Italy: Slow Food Arcigola Editore, 2000.

U.S. Department of Agriculture. *Cheeses of the World.* New York: Dover, 1972.

Meryl S. Rosofsky

butter, a yellowish substance produced from the fatty portion of milk, is used as a spread and employed in varied ways in cooking. After the centrifugal force of a separator divides the buttercream from the rest of the milk, butter is produced by agitating the cream in a batch churn or a continuous churn. The fatty elements agglomerate into grain-size clumps that, after the serum is drained, are mixed well to form an extremely smooth emulsion. At this stage, salt is often added. Before milk was commonly pasteurized, the cream would first undergo a spontaneous crème fraiche–like fermentation, imparting a lactic, nutty finish to the butter. Today for cultured butter, the same effect is achieved by inoculating the cream with lactic cultures and allowing it to ferment for nine to fifteen hours before churning. Butter is solid at room temperature, but like no other substance, it disappears on the tongue as if by magic.

Butter texture, like cheese texture, changes by region and by season. In France, the butter of Normandy is known for its spreadability, while the firmness of Poitou-Charentes butter makes it suitable for croissants and other laminated doughs. Winter butters are firmer than summer butters, because the milk of cows on pasture contains fat that is softer and less saturated. Summer butters are also more yellow. In addition, regions that systematically use higher proportions of dry feed produce the firmest butters.

By nature, butter is subtle in flavor; the huge quantities produced industrially blur the notion of terroir. See TERROIR. It has always been the pasture, rather than the breed of cattle that has given the butter its distinctive flavors. But now that the industrial feeding regimen has become uniform, cows are often not sent out to pasture. For purists, the biggest change in butter production occurred in the 1970s, when the injection of lactic concentrates at the very end of butter making, for flavor and longer shelf life, replaced the natural maturation of the cream. Some naturally cultured butters from grass-fed cows are still made, however, and tasting them can be quite a treat.

The texture of butter is key to the production of croissants, puff pastry (*pâte feuilletée*), and other laminated doughs. Professionals tend to focus solely on high butterfat content, which in butter can range from 80 percent (the US minimum) to 82 percent (the European minimum) up to 86 percent. But for texture, more important than the percentage of fat, in the view of researchers, is the controlled

Caseificio Perrusio cheese in Sorrento, Italy. About the size of a fist, this cheese—a variety of southern Italy's caciocavallo—is filled with butter. Before refrigeration came to Italy, this was one technique for preserving butter. © VINCENZO SPIONE

cooling of the cream after pasteurization to create the ideal crystalline structure of the fats, very similar to the tempering of chocolate. The right crystallization can impart ideal firmness and spreadability to butter, but the understanding of these principles varies greatly from manufacturer to manufacturer, so that for many pâtissiers (pastry chefs) winter butter from Poitou-Charentes remains a benchmark.

Butter was sometimes eaten with cheese in the past, when cheesemaking was less controlled and a blue cheese, for example, might be very strong, salty, or sharp. In addition to the cream from cows, butter is also made from the cream of other animals, including water buffalo, goats, and sheep.

See also BOG BUTTER and MILK.

Bradley, Robert L. *Better Butter*. Madison: Wisconsin Center for Dairy Research, 2012.

MacGuire, James. "The Culture of Butter: Is Cultured Butter Better?" *The Art of Eating*, October 2014.

Meyer, Hanne-Lys. "Programme Anaxagor: Quels beurres pour satisfaire l'industrie des pates feuilletées?" *Revue laitière française*, April 2013.

Sobolewski, Franck, et al. "Modulation de l'aptitude des beurres industriels au feuilletage: Influence de la cristallisation des matières grasses." *Projet Anaxagor* (technologies des équipments agroalimentaires), 2011–2013.

James MacGuire

butyric acid is a volatile four-carbon organic acid that elicits powerful aroma and flavor responses in cheese. The effects of butyric acid may be pleasant when it is present at low or moderate concentrations that are well balanced by other volatile organic acids (e.g., in aged Cheddar and hard pecorino cheeses), or at higher concentrations when rendered less volatile by higher pH levels (e.g., in blue mold cheeses). However, its effects may be very unpleasant (e.g., soapy, rancid defects) if it is present at high concentrations when in the volatile state.

Butyric acid may be formed in cheese through the action of lipase enzymes that hydrolyze triglycerides in milkfat to release free fatty acids. Active lipases in cheese may include lipoprotein lipase (which is naturally present in raw milk), lipases secreted by contaminating psychrotrophic bacteria, such as the *Pseudomonas* species, intracellular lipases in lactic acid starter bacteria that are released when the cells lyse (burst), and pregastricesterases (lipases) present in rennet when traditional rennet paste is used to coagulate the milk. Free butyric acid may also originate through the lipolytic activity of secondary microbes that participate in the ripening process, such as *Penicillium camemberti* mold in white mold cheeses, *Penicillium roqueforti* mold in blue mold cheeses, and *Propionibacterium freudenreichii* in Alp-style cheeses such as Emmentaler. The presence of butyric acid in cheese is always undesirable when it occurs through the fermentation of lactate by contaminating *Clostridium butyricum* and *Clostridium tyrobutyricum*. The result is the formation not only of butyric acid but of carbon dioxide and hydrogen gas, as well, which are responsible for late blowing defects in many cheeses. Since *Clostridium* species are salt and pH sensitive, their growth is favored by the low-salt, high-pH environments found in the interiors of large, sweet brined cheeses such as Gouda, Emmentaler, and Parmigiano Reggiano.

See also AROMA; DEFECTS; and FLAVOR.

Fox, P. F., et al. *Fundamentals of Cheese Science*. Gaithersburg, Md.: Aspen, 2000.

McSweeney, P. L. H., ed. *Cheese Problems Solved*. Cambridge, U.K.: Woodhead, 2007.

Paul S. Kindstedt

C

Cabot Creamery's history began in 1893, when F. A. Messer built a creamery in Cabot, Vermont, to make butter, which at that time was a profitable dairy product. In 1919 ninety-four local farmers established a new dairy cooperative, Cabot Farmers Creamery, and bought Messer's plant. During the 1920s, as consumer demand for butter and milk increased, better refrigeration and transportation enabled the company to grow. In 1930 it hired a cheesemaker to make Cheddar, after which Cabot's name became synonymous with Vermont Cheddar.

In 1992 the company merged with a larger regional cooperative, Agri-Mark Inc., founded in 1918. As of 2015 more than 1,200 family farms supply milk to make a variety of products—aged and flavored Cheddar cheese in Cabot, as well as butter, yogurt, and other items at other New England plants. For decades the Creamery, now a sizable company, handcrafted forty-two-pound Cheddar wheels with a cheesecloth exterior coated with several wax layers. The company was the last producer of traditional wheels found in New York and New England country stores.

Beginning in 2003, the Creamery and the Cellars at Jasper Hill, in Greensboro, Vermont, collaborated to produce thirty-two-pound cloth-wrapped Cheddar wheels with milk from one Holstein herd in Peacham, Vermont. Cabot ships the new cloth-wrapped cheeses to Jasper Hill, where they are coated with lard and placed in an underground cave. After maturing for ten to fifteen months, the cheese develops a firm, creamy texture with flavors of nuts, butter, and caramel.

Among its many accolades, the partnership won a World Cheese Gold Award in 2004 recognizing the clothbound Cheddar as the best in the world. In 2006 the American Cheese Society awarded "Best in Show" to the cheese, a testimony to its outstanding milk and skilled cheesemakers. Equally important, the cheese contributed to a renaissance of great domestically produced artisan Cheddar.

See also CELLARS AT JASPER HILL; CHEDDAR; CLOTHBOUND CHEESES; and VERMONT.

Chenel, Laura, and Linda Siegfried. *American Country Cheese*. Berkeley, Calif.: Aris, 1989, pp. 77–81.
Roberts, Jeffrey. *The Atlas of American Artisan Cheese*. White River Junction, Vt.: Chelsea Green, 2007, pp. 60–61.
Tewksbury, Henry. *The Cheeses of Vermont*. Woodstock, Vt.: Countryman, 2002, pp. 80–83.

Jeffrey P. Roberts

Cabrales (queso de Cabrales) is a famous Spanish blue cheese produced in the eastern principality of Asturias. Beneath the towering limestone peaks, known as the Picos de Europa, are lush alpine meadows and a labyrinth of natural caves. Since around the tenth century cheesemakers have taken advantage of their cool temperature, high moisture levels, constant airflow from the natural "chimneys," and the presence of blue molds to ripen Cabrales cheese.

Protected by its PDO (protected designation of origin) status since 1981, Cabrales is made from cow's milk, with seasonal additions of goat's and sheep's milk. Those made in late spring, using cow's milk for acidity, goat's milk for piquancy, and ewe's milk for sweetness and a smoother texture, are favored by the judges at the competition and festival, held in August. The traditional manufacture of Cabrales

The view from the entrance of the limestone mountain caves in Sotres, Spain, that are used to mature Cabrales cheese.
© BALTASAR MAYO

involves curdling mixtures of evening and morning milk using farm-made kid rennet. During coagulation, the milk temperature is kept lower than other blues at 71–73°F (22–23°C), to slow the process and produce an intensely acid curd. This in turn creates a crumbly curd that ultimately will create an open paste allowing the natural blue mold to penetrate inside the cheese without using needles. The curd is then cut into hazelnut-size cubes and placed in cylindrical molds (*arnios*) for whey drainage (without pressing), and to continue the acidification process. After forty-eight hours at room temperature, the young cheese ends its acidification (about pH 4.85) and is covered with coarse salt and kept at room temperature for another ten to fifteen days.

After about two weeks the cheeses (cylindrical and weighing about 7 pounds [3 kilograms]) are taken to nearby natural caves for ripening, where, over two to three months, they are turned, cleaned, rubbed, and kept moist. Under these conditions, *Penicillium roqueforti* gradually works its way into the cheese forming the irregular fine streaks of blue that give Cabrales its intense, piquant, outspoken character with hints of hazelnuts, dark cocoa, and its sharp, metallic finish. Traditionally wrapped in Sycamore leaves but now health and safety dictates it must be green tinfoil, fortunately the custom of drinking it with a local eau-de-vie, *orujo*, still continues.

See also BLUE CHEESES and SPAIN.

Belen Florez, Ana, et al. "Microbial, Chemical and Sensorial Variables of the Spanish Traditional Blue-Veined Cabrales Cheese, as Affected by Inoculation with Commercial *Penicillium roqueforti* Spores." *European Food Research and Technology* 222, no. 3 (February 2006): 250–257.
Canut, Enric. *In Spain: Cheese & Landscape*. Somoslibros, 2010.
Yubero, Ismael Diaz. "The Birth of the Blues." Foods & Wines from Spain. http://www.foodswinesfromspain .com/spanishfoodwine/global/products-recipes/ products/more-about-products/4446000.html.

Juliet Harbutt

caciocavallo, like mozzarella and provolone, is a pasta filata or spun paste cheese, meaning the paste or curd is spun or stretched and kneaded and then sculpted, in the case of caciocavallo, into a distinctive teardrop or gourd-like shape. The name literally means "horse cheese." Some maintain the cheese was given this name because of the traditional method of hanging and curing it, where two cheeses are tied to a rope and slung over a beam, not unlike saddlebags

Various types of caciocavallo, southern Italy's beloved "cheese on horseback," a stretched-curd cousin of mozzarella and provolone. © VINCENZO SPIONE

over a horse's back. Another possible etymology suggests the original meaning is "bell cheese," for the shape.

Typically made with cow's or sheep's milk or a combination of the two, caciocavallo is also occasionally made with goat's milk and, rarely, with buffalo milk. The cheese is sometimes eaten fresh, but usually it is ripened from two to twelve months, although some producers prefer to age it for as long as two to five years. When caciocavallo is young, its color is white, its flavor is slightly sweet, and its texture is firm and sometimes chewy. As the cheese ages, it takes on a rich yellow color, its flavor intensifies, becoming sharp, piquant, and complex, and its texture becomes semihard and crumbly, dotted with small crystals throughout the paste. Caciocavallo has a smooth rind that thickens as the cheese matures. Occasionally cheesemakers will wash the rind with wine or flavor the paste with truffles. Often caciocavallo is smoked and the curd is occasionally stretched and formed around another substance such as butter or lemons.

Caciocavallo's flavor, color, and texture can vary widely from producer to producer and region to region. This variation is caused by a number of factors, including the type of milk used, the temperature to which the milk is heated, the fodder the animals have eaten, the length of time the cheese has aged, and the specific breed of animal that produced the milk.

Caciocavallo is produced by both farmstead and factory cheese producers, mostly along Italy's Apen-

nine mountain range. Several varieties of caciocavallo are recognized by the Italian Ministero delle Politiche Agricole Alimentare e Forestali (Ministry of Agriculture, Food, and Forestry Policies) as Prodotto Agroalimentare Tradizionale (traditional regional food products). One of these is Caciocavallo Podolico, which is produced using milk from the Podolica cow, a hardy breed known for its aromatic, high-fat milk and its ability to adapt to harsh mountainous conditions. See CACIOCAVALLO PODOLICO. Just one type of caciocavallo, Caciocavallo Silano, has received PDO status from the European Union. Made entirely of cow's milk, it is produced in the southern Italian regions of Basilicata, Calabria, Campania, Molise, and Puglia.

Caciocavallo is a common ingredient in the cooking of southern Italy, where it is sometimes used to stuff gnocchi, ravioli and tortellini or it is layered in casserole-style dishes, such as Parmigiana. It is popular grilled or fried and it is commonly served as a table cheese. Although caciocavallo is largely considered to be a product of southern Italian food culture, today the cheese is sold throughout Italy, is exported globally, and is even produced by cheesemakers abroad. Outside of Italy caciocavallo can be found in specialty cheese shops, Italian food markets, and online.

See also ITALY; MOZZARELLA; and PASTA FILATA.

Adams, Alexis Marie. "Curious Caciocavallo." *Culture Magazine: The Word on Cheese*, Summer 2014.
Davidson, Alan, and Tom Jaine. *The Oxford Companion to Food*. 3d ed. Oxford: Oxford University Press, 2014.

Alexis Marie Adams

Caciocavallo Palermitano is a typical Italian stretched-curd cheese produced from cow's milk within the Palermo province of western Sicily. Its history is tied to its production area, with documentation of its presence in the markets of Palermo and of its appreciation in the diet of noble families and local religious communities dating back to the 1400s.

Caciocavallo Palermitano is historically linked to the small farms of hills and semi-arid areas where cows of autochthonous breeds, especially the Cinisara, are fed mainly on natural pasture. In such farming systems, this cheese is manufactured with whole raw milk according to a two-day artisanal procedure based on the use of wooden tools, typical of the Sicilian dairy tradition. It is processed without the addition of a starter, since the native lactic microflora, nested as a biofilm on the surface of the wooden vats used for milk coagulation, inoculates the milk and persists during the production line, contributing strongly to the character of the cheese. See BIOFILM and WOODEN VATS.

Caciocavallo Palermitano has a firm paste, a characteristic parallelepiped shape acquired by placing and turning the curd in a wooden form called a *tavuleri*, a straw color that tends to turn ochre during aging, and a weight between 17.6 and 33 pounds (8–15 kilograms). It is consumed fresh or ripened for periods from two to more than twelve months. Since this cheese is not protected by a quality certification, it is also produced in intensive farms rearing cows of milking-specialized breeds fed indoor on dry diets. These farms adopt a more advanced cheesemaking procedure based on the use of modern stainless steel equipment and commercial lactic ferments. However, the traditional manufacturing process better maintains the typical sensory properties of this cheese, such as the spicy notes that result from the presence of the native microflora.

See also CACIOCAVALLO and PASTA FILATA.

Bonanno, A., et al. "Effect of Farming System and Cheesemaking Technology on the Physicochemical Characteristics, Fatty Acid Profile, and Sensory Properties of Caciocavallo Palermitano Cheese." *Journal of Dairy Science* 96 (January 2013): 710–724.

Adriana Bonanno

Caciocavallo Podolico is a pasta filata (stretched-curd) cheese made exclusively from the raw milk of Podolica cows, raised on pasture vegetation throughout the year without any additional feed. The Podolico breed, with a population of about 30,000 milked heads, is indigenous to southern Italy. The production area includes four regions: Calabria, Basilicata, Campania, and Puglia. The name probably derives from the aging process of the Provola cheeses (*cacio*), which were tied in pairs with the ends of the rope wound around the top of each cheese to make a "neck," and the rope placed astride (in Italian, *a cavallo*) a horizontal pole. In the nineteenth century, the "Caciocavalli" of Picerno in Basilicata became famous, and along with the Canestrato di Moliterno cheese (made with mixed milk and aged in typical caves, today a PGI, or protected geographical indication, cheese) even reached the United States, introduced by immigrants from the Basilicata region.

The particular characteristics of Caciocavallo Podolico—its golden color, strong animal flavor, herbaceous and flowering scent, and high content of omega-3 fatty acids—are due to a combination of the cows, the pasture feeding, and the use of traditional cheesemaking tools, such as the wooden tub called *tina*, the wooden rod called *rotula*, and the tinned copper cauldron. See TINA and COPPER VATS. The cheese is round in shape with a firm, basically fibrous texture, breaking into flakes when ripened for a long time, a savory taste, and a herbaceous and intense flavor. The cheese is aged in ventilated natural limestone caves at temperatures of 54–61°F (12–16°C) in a relative humidity of 70–80 percent. After three months of aging, it is already excellent to eat, and with more time the structure becomes firmer and the color turns ochre or golden. The cheese reaches its peak after two to three years.

For the most part, Caciocavallo Podolico is sold directly from the farms on which it is made. This cheese has been declared part of Slow Food's presidium in Basilicata and other regions of southern Italy. See SLOW FOOD. As a result of the production system and promotional activities, the selling price in the early years of the twenty-first century has increased significantly, up to 38–44 dollars/kg (35–40 euros/kg).

See also CACIOCAVALLO and PASTA FILATA.

Claps, Salvatore. "Un mondo di aromi." In *Il caciocavallo podolico e la Manteca: un grande formaggio del Sud*, pp. 77–100. Potenza, Italy: Ars Grafica, 2001.
Istituto Nazionale di Sociologia Rurale. *Atlante dei prodotti tipici: i formaggi*. Milan: Angeli, 1990.

Salvatore Claps

cacio e pepe is one of the sacrosanct pastas of Rome and is considered one of its canonical dishes. Traditionally cacio e pepe is made with only three ingredients: pasta, *pepe nero*, and Pecorino Romano. *Cacio* is the common word for cheese and is used mainly in central and southern Italy. Derived from the Latin word *caseus*, cacio has firm roots in the Roman countryside, *campagna Romana*, and most often refers to a cheese made from pressed sheep's milk curds. *Pepe* is *pepe nero*—black pepper, which entered the Italian diet during the expansion campaigns and early trade routes of the Roman Empire. Pecorino Romano is a salted, grating sheep's milk cheese to which some cheesemakers apply a *cappatura nero*, a thin black coating originally made of ochre, grape seed oil, and charcoal. The coating prevented the cheese from drying out as it matured and distinguished it from wheels of Grana Padano and Parmigiano Reggiano. Production of Pecorino Romano has its roots in the province of Lazio, but the cheese is now mainly produced in Sardinia and Tuscany. Since Pecorino Romano doesn't spoil, the Roman legionnaires of antiquity carried it in their pockets to snack on as they marched over long distances.

Cacio e pepe can be made with any kind of pasta—short or long, fresh or dried. The most traditional cacao e pepe is made with *tonnarelli*, a fresh egg noodle that looks like square-cut (rather than round) spaghetti. It is essential that cacio e pepe be made with freshly grated, sharp Pecorino Romano aged six to twelve months and fresh, coarsely ground black pepper. The pasta should be boiled in a large volume of salted water until it is cooked al dente. Then it is placed on top of the grated cheese and pepper, and a ladle of pasta cooking water is poured on top. The whole mixture is now energetically tossed, as the hot, starchy water emulsifies the cheese into a creamy, velvety sauce.

There is ongoing debate about the best method for making cacio e pepe, a pasta that belies its simplicity. Some cooks, for example, sneak in a plop of butter or a drizzle of olive oil to the cheese and pasta water to help the process along. Nevertheless, all agree that with practice and vigorous tossing, one can achieve sublime results.

See also ITALY and PECORINO ROMANO.

Grescoe, Taras. "When in Rome, Learn to Cook Italian." *New York Times*, 11 September 2015.

Mona Talbott

Cacioricotta is an Italian goat cheese that can be consumed both fresh and aged. It is produced throughout Southern Italy in the regions of Basilicata, Calabria, Puglia, and Campania. In the Campania region, the most notable cheese is the Cacioricotta of the Cilento and Vallo di Diano National Park. According to tradition, Cacioricotta production occurs from June to August, when sheep's milk is scarce but goats are still lactating. In some areas Cacioricotta can also be produced by mixing sheep's milk and cow's milk.

The name Cacioriocotta derives from "cacio" (cheese) and "ricotta" because it contains both casein (specific of cheese) and whey protein (specific of ricotta cheese) since it is made using a particular, very old practice: the milk is heated to 185–194°F (85–90°C), which causes the precipitation of both caseins and whey proteins of the milk. The wheels of white cheese that are produced weigh between 0.5 and 1.3 pounds (200–600 grams), have no rind when they are fresh, but develop a straw-color surface once they have been aged (usually for three to six months).

Fresh Cacioricotta is used as a table cheese, in salads, or on a cheese board. At this point, it has aromas of cooked milk and a delicate sweet flavor of ricotta. Aged Cacioricotta is grated on pasta dishes (the most famous is the typical dish of the Puglia region, *orecchiette* with tomatoes and Cacioricotta). Once aged, it has a stronger taste, with salty, spicy, and good animal (goat) hints. Very often, when it is produced at the artisan level, Cacioricotta is made for self-consumption, but since 2005 many medium-size dairies have begun to produce and market Cacioricotta for the general public.

See also ITALY and RICOTTA.

Pizzillo, Michele, et al. "T-cheese.Med Basilicata Cheeses." In *New Technologies Supporting the Traditional and Historical Dairy in the Archimed Zone*", pp. 146–231. Ragusa, Italy: Grafiche Cosentino, 2008.

Rubino, Roberto, Pierre Morand-Fehr, and Lucia Sepe. *Atlas of Goat Products: A Wide International Inventory of Whatever Things the Goat Can Give Us.* Potenza, Italy: Caseus, 2004.

Salvatore Claps

Cacique is a cheese company located in City of Industry, an industrial suburb of Los Angeles, California. It is the largest fresh cheesemaker and the largest Hispanic cheese brand in the United States. This family-owned company was founded in 1973 by Cuban-born immigrants Gilbert and Jennie de Cardenas. At that time high-quality fresh cheese was not available in the Los Angeles marketplace. Gilbert Sr. took his $1,500 life savings, his old world knowledge of cheesemaking, and his prowess in science and chemistry and built a company committed to authenticity, tradition, and innovation. The name "Cacique," meaning chief of a tribe, expresses experience and authority, and the company's four-pillared logo (family, quality, integrity, and authenticity) visually represents these values.

Since its founding Cacique has consistently focused on production of traditional products of the highest quality. Each day Cacique processes 1.2 million pounds (2.6 million kilograms) of hormone-free, Kosher-certified milk, taking pride from the fact that its queso fresco is created in a process that takes only two to four days from cow to store. In addition to queso fresco, the company produces a wide variety of other cheeses including panela, queso blanco, asadero, queso Oaxaca, cotija, and Enchilado. Cacique is still owned and run by the de Cardenas family's four children: Gilbert B. de Cardenas, Ana de Cardenas-Raptis, Maria de Cardenas-Krakovic, and Antonio de Cardenas.

See also FRESH CHEESES.

Cacique. http://www.caciqueinc.com.

Reinhold, Dorothy. "Learning about Mexican Cheese with Cacique." *Shockingly Delicious*, 3 March 2015. http://www.shockinglydelicious.com/learning-about-mexican-cheese.

Catherine Donnelly

Caerphilly is a semifirm cow's milk cheese from Wales. It dates to the early nineteenth century, and is named after the town in which it was first produced, about 8 miles (13 kilometers) north of Cardiff.

Caerphilly is a striking cheese visually and on the palate. Produced in approximately 10-pound (4.5-kilogram) wheels, its mottled gray-white rind conceals a beautiful tri-layered cross section. Each of the layers yields complex flavors that meld together perfectly. The rind itself is earthy and mineral, and beneath that is a supple, Brie-like texture that tastes of barnyard and mushrooms. This envelops a dense white core that is bright, lemony, and clean.

As with many cheeses Caerphilly's inception was the result of excess milk on the dairy farm. But demand for Caerphilly quickly escalated, and by 1830 farmers were allocating milk for its production, instead of simply using what was left over. Within a few decades cheesemakers in Somerset were producing it as an alternative to Cheddar. While it would never achieve the same level of acclaim as Cheddar, Caerphilly could be produced quicker due to it being approximately one-fifth the weight. This appealed to farmers, who could turn over inventory faster, and consumers, who would pay a lower price.

Caerphilly was particularly popular among miners, who would take a wedge of the nutrient-dense cheese underground with them, wrapped up in a cabbage leaf for safe travel. The thick rind was likely one of the draws for the miners, who would have been eating with coal-covered hands. They also believed that Caerphilly was capable of negating the toxins they inhaled underground.

Unfortunately Caerphilly was not immune to the maelstrom of malevolent forces that converged on cheesemaking in the United Kingdom in the early twentieth century. With the advent of industrialization, cheese production began its transition from the farm to the factory. As these facilities sprouted up domestically and in the United States, the expertise of British farmhouse producers was in high demand. Steadily cheesemakers abandoned the farm for facilities on both sides of the Atlantic.

Steadfast producers who upheld the farmhouse tradition were left to market their cheese against substantially cheaper factory-produced cheeses of the same name. By around 1910 most Caerphilly producers had either transitioned to factory jobs or capitulated to the competition. A few years later many were sent off to fight in World War I. Caerphilly's final death knell came in 1939, when the newly established Ministry of Food mandated that only hard cheese could be made. Producers of Caerphilly were ordered to produce "National Cheese," a hard, easily transportable product that was shipped to the troops in mainland Europe. See WORLD WAR I and WORLD WAR II.

By the 1950s only one farm was producing authentic Caerphilly: Duckett's farm in Wedmore. Through the remainder of the twentieth century, Chris Duckett single-handedly kept the spirit of Caerphilly alive. Before he passed away in 2009, he moved to Westcombe farm, where Duckett's Caerphilly continues to be produced today.

Duckett also bestowed his knowledge on Todd Trethowan, who established Gorwydd Caerphilly in Ceredigion, Wales, in 1996. In July 2014 the Trethowan family moved the farm to Somerset, mirroring the historical migration of the cheese, and continues to produce what is now considered to be the standard-bearer for Caerphilly.

See also INDUSTRIALIZATION and UNITED KINGDOM.

"Caerphilly." *Culture: The Word on Cheese.* http://culturecheesemag.com/cheese-library/Caerphilly-.
Hinds, Jason. "A History of British Cheese." London: Neal's Yard Dairy, 2013. http://www.nealsyarddairy.co.uk/wp-content/uploads/2015/10/A_History_of_British_Cheese.pdf.

Hunter Fike

caillé doux and caillé acide, "sweet curd"

and "acid curd," are French names for two very different ways of setting milk into curd. Caillé acide, when it isn't being compared with caillé doux, is in French almost invariably known as caillé lactique, or in English as lactic curd or acid-coagulated curd, in reference to the role of lactic acid in creating the curd structure. It's the near-universal way to make goat's milk cheeses, and it suits cooler temperatures, which favor development of the desired mesophilic lactic bacteria. Whey, full of those bacteria, is added to the cool milk, and the slowly increasing acidity over a period of up to twenty-four hours and even more, will set a delicate curd without any rennet at all, although today a small addition of rennet is usual. See CONTINUOUS WHEY STARTERS. But in the warmth of the south of France, cheesemakers have historically set their goat's milk by adding a large amount of rennet—no whey—to milk still warm from the animal, so the curd formed quickly, in as little as one hour. During that time only a small amount of acidity develops, coming from the few acid-producing bacteria in the milk itself. The two different sorts of cheese have very different qualities.

The divergent methods and cheeses represent, in dairy form, the cultural conflict between North and South in France, lost by the South notably in language. The survival of the southern caillé doux is even more limited than that of the Occitan language, but the two cheeses still being made are well-recorded and perhaps more likely to endure. Both are small, round, and made of raw goat's milk on a very limited scale.

The leaf-wrapped AOP Banon is made in the highlands of Haute Provence on about fifteen farms and in two small dairies. See BANON. The non-appellation Caillé Doux de Saint-Félicien (not to be confused with the more common, acid-curd Saint-Félicien from the same area, which can be all cow's milk) is made to the northwest, in the similarly high, hilly area of the Haut Vivarais in the Ardèche department; today this cheese is produced on just seven farms. The zones for Banon and Caillé Doux de Saint-Félicien are separated by the one for AOP Picodon, an acid-curd cheese whose area partly overlaps that for Caillé Doux de Saint-Félicien. The name Picodon means "piquant" or "spicy," which suggests it was always an acid-curd cheese, a type that can develop peppery heat, and it suggests that Picodon was a contrast to other, perhaps previously dominant sweet-curd cheeses. Among the current producers of Picodon are eighty farms, a small number of which also make sweet-curd cheeses to diversify their offerings.

An acid-curd cheese is ripened primarily by surface microbes that require oxygen. As they work from the outside in, they somewhat reduce the cheese's acidity, and their enzymes turn the cheese creamy. In contrast the sweet-curd Banon inside its leaves is deprived of air and has fewer surface microbes; after about six weeks it turns creamy almost simultaneously throughout, with much of the work done by the enzymes from the rennet. (Banon, like many and perhaps all of the southern cheeses, used to be eaten in widely varying states. Traditionally, for winter keeping, it was dried completely, and then soaked to soften it, before it was wrapped in leaves and aged further in ceramic pots. It became strong, but never sharp or peppery.) Even a relatively young leaf-wrapped

Banon, however, develops a flavor that is somewhat animal, combined with vegetal and woody notes from the leaves, giving an earthy effect.

In contrast the Caillé Doux de Saint-Félicien may be typical of the young sweet-curd cheeses that once existed over a wide area and were called simply *tommes*. This cheese, considered ripe after about fifteen days, is sold for prompt consumption, before it becomes creamy all the way to the center. Where a new acid-curd cheese is chalky and crumbly, even a new sweet-curd cheese is flexible, homogeneous, and slightly elastic. Little has been written to describe the flavor of the Caillé Doux de Saint-Félicien, and the farmers themselves aren't in the habit of applying adjectives to it. But where an acid-curd cheese has a definite acidity and typically a moderate but clear goat flavor, with sometimes a piquancy, the briefly ripened Caillé Doux de Saint-Félicien is mild with only a subtle goat flavor, tender, sweet, and fresh-tasting.

France's small goat's milk cheeses were made by peasants with just a few goats, mainly for consumption by the family. The goat was the cow of the poor. Unlike cheeses such as Comté or Roquefort, the small goat's milk cheeses were not highly regarded, and old descriptions of the techniques and taste are scarce or nonexistent. One piece of evidence of the historic extent of sweet-curd cheeses is the presence of old ceramic cheese molds with large holes that could hold the relatively firm sweet curds. Too much of the fragile acid curd would run through and be lost; it required molds with smaller holes.

It is impossible to know just how widespread the sweet-curd cheese was at any particular period. Especially during the 1950s and 1960s, many farms ceased making cheese as agriculture became more mechanized, polyculture declined, and an important part of the rural population migrated to cities. The sweet-curd had been used only on farms, and almost all those who continued to make and sell cheese switched to acid curd, partly to be more modern. When the *néo-ruraux*, the back-to-the-landers, arrived in the 1970s and 1980s and began to raise goats and make and sell cheese, they too adopted the acid-curd method, because it was more familiar to them, easier to master, and offered a higher yield. Sweet-curd Banon, however, compensated with a higher price.

Only in the late twentieth century did the small, sweet-curd goat's milk cheeses finally begin to be documented, in part, too late for complete under-standing. What is certain about the sweet curd is that before World War II it was the dominant way to make cheese in a wide swath of southern France.

See also FRANCE.

"Étude Caillé Doux: Type Saint-Félicien." Privas, France: Chambre d'Agriculture de l'Ardèche, 1980.

Lepage, Michel. *Banon: Un fromage de Haute-Provence.* Mallemoisson, France: Editions de Haute-Provence, 1996.

Mariotini, Jean-Marc. *A la recherche d'un fromage, le banon: Éléments d'histoire et d'ethnologie: Rapport d'étude.* Forcalquier, France: Alpes de Lumière, 1992.

P.E.P. Caprin. "Fromage de Chèvre: Caillé Doux." http://91.121.55.183/pepra/mydms/pep_caprins/file_4e5f9d733401f.pdf.

Edward Behr

Calandra's Cheese is an old-fashioned neighborhood cheese store located on Arthur Avenue in the Bronx, a street which, because of its many Italian shops and restaurants, has been likened to Manhattan's Little Italy. It was founded by Sicilian-born Salvatore Calandra in 1949, along with another Calandra's cheese store in Harlem, Manhattan, and a Calandra's cheese store/production facility in Nazareth, Pennsylvania. The Harlem store closed in 1968. After Salvatore died, his sons, Sal and Charlie, sold the Bronx store in 2000 to Diego Faracchio, an Argentine. The family still runs the Pennsylvania factory, which produces many of the cheeses, as well as the curds used in making ricotta, sold in the Bronx store.

Calandra's specializes in pasta filata ("spun paste"), or cheeses made by pulling and stretching fresh cow's or water buffalo milk curds. See PASTA FILATA. Selections include freshly made plain and smoked mozzarella, provola (aged mozzarella), burrata (mozzarella filled with imported Italian heavy cream and curds), burrino (aged mozzarella stuffed with butter), scamorza (a pear-shaped aged mozzarella), caciocavallo (duos of gourd-shaped cheese rounds that are bound together by twine), and provolone. Calandra's also makes ricotta daily, as well as ricotta salata, a variation of ricotta, which has been pressed, salted, and dried.

The store also sells a range of imported cheeses including several types of Parmigiano Reggiano, a Sicilian canestrato, and a selection of Pecorino Romano including an irresistible Sardinian pecorino moliterno al tartufo, marbled with black truffles. Calandra's also carries sheep's and goat's milk cheeses primarily from Spain, *salume*, and Italian pantry staples.

Alperson, Myra. *Nosh New York: The Food Lover's Guide to New York City's Most Delicious Neighborhoods*. New York: St. Martin's, 2003.

Crowley, Chris. "Arthur Avenue's Calandra Cheese Sells Burrata's More Flavorful Cousin." *Serious Eats*, 2 April 2014. http://newyork.seriouseats.com/2014/04/calandra-cheese-the-bronx.html.

Elizabeth Field

calcium phosphate is the insoluble salt complex found in milk. Milk is supersaturated with minerals like calcium and phosphate, that is, they are present at concentrations higher than their solubility in milk. To avoid unwanted precipitation of calcium phosphate during milk secretion, mammals designed an ingenious solution. The majority of the calcium phosphate is associated with the caseins (the main milk protein) and it becomes an important structural (cross-linking) component of the large casein aggregates in milk that are called casein micelles. This insoluble fraction is often called colloidal calcium phosphate (CCP). Formation of CCP allows mammals to safely (free from the risk of unwanted precipitation) deliver large concentrations of calcium and phosphate to their young, who require these minerals for bone development. CCP is readily soluble under acidic conditions and is therefore highly bioavailable during digestion.

The exact structure of CCP in milk remains unclear with conflicting reports that it may be either amorphous (non-crystalline) or some acidic or basic crystalline forms. It is known that CCP is present within micelles as small (~2.5 nm) granules, which have a molecular weight of around 7,000g/mol. Many cheese varieties are excellent sources of the essential nutrients calcium and phosphorus, especially the hard and semihard cheese varieties. In processed cheese manufacture, "emulsifying salts," actually calcium chelating salts like citrates and phosphates, are added to disrupt the indigenous CCP, which helps to hydrate the insoluble natural cheese curd. The acidification schedule during the cheesemaking process controls the final amount of calcium phosphate in the cheese and ultimately affects final texture and flavor properties.

See also ACIDIFICATION; CASEIN; HEALTH PROPERTIES; MILK; and SALT.

Fox, P. F., and P. L. H. McSweeney. *Dairy Chemistry and Biochemistry*. London: Blackie Academic and Professional, 1998.

Lucey, J. A., and D. S. Horne. "Milk Salts: Technological Significance." In *Advanced Dairy Chemistry*, vol. 3: *Lactose, Water, Salts and Minor Constituents*, 3d ed. Edited by P. L. H. McSweeney and P. F. Fox, pp. 351–389. New York: Springer, 2009.

John A. Lucey

California, stretching across much of the West Coast of the United States, enjoys a temperate climate and vast tracts of available land, both of which make the state particularly well suited to dairying. It is the most populous state in the United States and the third largest state by area. First settled by Native Americans, it came under Spanish rule in the sixteenth century and was annexed for a short time in the early nineteenth century by Mexico.

California was ratified as a state in 1850 on the gilded heels of the Gold Rush. This era catalyzed significant economic, social, and demographic change as California saw waves of immigration from within the continental United States and afterwards, from China and Italy as well. The history of cheese and cheesemaking in California is linked closely with its legacy of immigration and its rich agricultural heritage.

Unlike the on-the-farm, self-provisioning origins of most cheesemaking in Europe and New England, California cheese was strictly commercial almost from the start. The first cheese factory in California, and one of the very earliest in the country, Steele Brothers, opened north of San Francisco in 1857 and supplied the urban market and its burgeoning population. Farmer-owned cooperatives dominated the commercial cheesemaking industry in California until World War II when, as elsewhere, the combination of technological advancements, rampant urbanization, and the need to provision military troops abroad led to greater centralization of production and the development of larger farms and factories.

California is the birthplace of a number of cheeses that can rightfully be called American originals. Monterey Jack dates its origins back to 1882 and, as a vestige of Spanish rule in the early nineteenth century, derives from a Franciscan monastic style of farmer's cheese. Dry Jack was born by accident in San Francisco from desiccated Monterey Jack that was allowed to age for an extended period of time. It rose to prominence when World War I disrupted European imports and the large Italian immigrant population gravitated toward its grana-style flavor profile. See VELLA CHEESE COMPANY and JACK. Teleme, with its distinctive rice flour rind, claims Californian origins dating to the 1920s.

Since the mid-twentieth century, the California cheese industry has grown at a near exponential rate. The volume of cheese being produced annually grew from 17.5 million pounds in 1970, to 500 million in 1985, to 1 billion in 1996, and the figure was up to 2.2 billion pounds in 2006. Some dairy farms now have nearly 20,000 cows. With great economies of scale, a favorable political climate for commercial dairying, and the success of trade groups such as the Milk Advisory Board and the Real California seal, as of 2014 California is the largest dairy-producing US state and the second largest producer of cheese, behind only Wisconsin.

In parallel to this prevailing trajectory of industrial production, California has seen large growth in its specialty and artisan cheese industry since the 1980s. This is owed largely to the emergence of three distinct but interrelated factors: the countercultural ethos embraced in northern regions of the state, the rise of the wine industry centered in the Napa and Sonoma valleys, and the birth of nouvelle "California cuisine" with its emphasis on freshness, local sourcing, and Francophilic tastes. See COUNTERCULTURE and AMERICAN "GOAT LADIES." Prominent among the "back-to-the-lander" pioneering farmstead producers in California were Cypress Grove Chevre, Laura Chenel's Chèvre, Redwood Hills, and Goat's Leap Dairy. In the early 1990s, Straus Family Creamery became the first organic dairy west of the Mississippi; in addition to making a number of fresh dairy products themselves, Straus supplies milk for cheesemaking to Cowgirl Creamery. As of 2014, California is home to nearly forty artisan cheesemakers and a prominent artisan cheese trade group, the California Artisan Cheese Guild.

See also UNITED STATES.

California Milk Advisory Board. "Milestones in California Dairy History: 200-Plus Years of Dairying and Cheesemaking in the Golden State." http://www .californiadairypressroom.com/Press_Kit/Milestones.

Davies, Sasha. *The Guide to West Coast Cheese*. Portland, Ore.: Timber Press, 2010.
Paxson, Heather. *The Life of Cheese: Crafting Food and Value in America*. Berkeley: University of California Press, 2013.

Bradley M. Jones

The **camel,** or dromedary camel (*Camelus dromedarius*), is a large one-hump domesticated tylopod living mainly in arid zones from India to Mauritania in western Africa. Its anatomy and physiology are particularly well adapted to hot, dry environments with sparse vegetation. A camel's lifespan is thirty to forty years, pregnancy lasts twelve to thirteen months, and lactation also can continue for more than a year. As a result, females usually have a single calf once every two years. Camels are intelligent, temperamental, and fastidious animals.

Milk yield depends partly on genetics but more essentially on the camel's diet, ranging from 20 liters per day reported in Pakistan to an average of a little more than 3 liters per day in Mauritania. Because the udder has no storage, milk is let down on demand and well-fed camels can be milked several times a day. Camel's milk has long been considered unsuitable for making cheese, because its particular composition— lacking the kappa-casein that forms curds—does not allow the milk to curdle naturally. Other factors keeping camel breeders from making cheese include the arid climate in camel habitats, where humidity drops below 5 percent in searing heat, and the nomadic—or at least mobile—lifestyle adapted to making the most of sparse desert pastures. In these

Caravane is a brand of pasteurized camel's milk cheese made by Tiviski, a dairy plant in Mauritania. It was originally made to be exported to Europe, but regulatory hurdles blocked that plan, and sales are mainly limited to Mauritania and neighboring Senegal.

conditions cheese cannot be made without cooling and humidification—that is to say, without modern technology.

At the end of the 1980s, Tiviski, a private dairy plant in Nouakchott, Mauritania, started selling fresh camel milk in cartons. The company purchases raw milk from nomadic herders, whose camels roam over the scrubby landscape and are milked by hand. The African monsoon season dramatically increases milk supply, however, and looking for a way to use the seasonal surplus, Tiviski developed a method to produce cheese from camel's milk.

Considering the rustic conditions as well as the long distances between the herds and the delivery points where milk is chilled and enters a modern environment, all the milk has to be pasteurized. Since 1995 Tiviski has designed and made two cheeses from fresh, pasteurized camel milk: Caravane and Sahara. Originally the cheese was to be exported to Europe, because consumers in Mauritania and in neighboring countries hadn't yet developed a taste for cheese. In addition, the high price paid for raw milk and the poor yield made the cheese expensive. However, a barrage of trade barriers imposed by the European Union blocked exports, even though the cheese itself complied with exacting standards. Attempts to sell it in the United States ran into some logistical hurdles as well, which would be solved in the future. Caravane is still in production, to the great enjoyment of aficionados in Nouakchott—and by people elsewhere who get to taste it thanks to travelers' suitcases.

Camel curds tend to squeeze out water, making hard cheese yield very low; therefore, soft cheeses are preferred (specifically a modified bloomy-rind type), using various strategies for preservation, ripening, and flavor. With camel's milk being as idiosyncratic as its provider, cheesemaking is tricky and demanding, but the result is well worth it: camel cheese is white and smooth, with a fresh taste—even when very ripe and creamy. Besides, breaded and lightly fried, it is delicious on salads.

"Caravane." Cheese.com. http://www.cheese.com/caravane.

Jones Abeiderrahmane, Nancy. *Camel Cheese—Seemed Like a Good Idea*. Amazon, 2013.

Ramet, Jean-Paul. *La technologie des fromages au lait de dromadaire*. Rome: FAO, 1993.

Nancy Jones Abeiderrahmane

Camembert de Normandie is a semisoft, mold-ripened, cow's milk cheese, formed in a 4-inch (11-centimeter) -diameter disk that is 1 inch (3 centimeters) thick, weighing at least 9 ounces (250 grams). After repeated attempts since 1909 to protect its name, Camembert de Normandie became a protected designation of origin (PDO) cheese in 1983. To bear the name "Camembert de Normandie" and associated seals of authenticity, a cheese must be made following legally defined criteria; otherwise, "camembert" alone is generic and internationally defined by the *Codex Alimentarius* only by its paste texture and bloomy white rind. See DESIGNATION OF ORIGIN and *CODEX ALIMENTARIUS*.

Legend holds that Camembert was invented by a Norman farm woman, Marie Harel, during the French Revolution, although the historical record offers little proof. See HAREL, MARIE. The first known reference to cheese from the village of Camembert is from 1706, and in 1760 a nearby mayor wrote that Camembert's cheeses were reputedly even better than the local ones at Livarot's market, although cheeses from Livarot and Camembert were still richer and better than those from Pont l'Evêque. Over the nineteenth century, Camembert cheese took on many of today's features—its form, whiteness, protective wooden box, and large-scale manufacturing—and went from being a microlocal to nationwide cheese. Camembert's success was due in large part to the marketing efforts of Harel's progeny, which reached their apotheosis in 1863 when Victor Paynel, Harel's grandchild, reportedly presented his Camembert to Emperor Napoleon III, who had taken the new railway to see horse races in Normandy; Paynel subsequently became imperial supplier.

As farmstead production waned, many family-owned cheese factories opened in the latter nineteenth and early twentieth centuries, each struggling to make its name and reach new consumers. Export was hindered by the challenge of transporting delicate, ripening cheeses in hay-lined crates until 1890, when an exporter started putting them in wooden pillboxes that quickly became the norm. Boxes enhanced manufacturers' ability to "brand" their products by providing a place to stick a label, leading to abundant ephemera of Camembert labels adored by collectors (tyrosemiophiles) for their marketing kitsch. See TYROSEMIOPHILE. By this time, production was concentrating in the hands of dynastic families who formed a producers' association in 1909 to fight copycat manufacturers across France. World War I turned Camembert into a "national" cheese, according to sociologist Pierre Boissard, since it was a standard ration for soldiers from across France. Those who made it home supposedly remembered the fragile cheese fondly despite the challenging conditions of the initial encounter. See WORLD WAR I. By the 1920s Camembert was widely manufactured (and eaten) across France and Europe, a situation that long hindered requests for PDO status.

Today, appellation d'origine protégée (AOP) Camembert de Normandie's production criteria start on a map: its milk can only legally be produced and made into cheese in designated towns in the administrative departments of Calvados, Orne, Manche, and Eure in the regions of Basse and Haute Normandie, France. By 2020, at least 50 percent of milking cows on farms supplying manufacturers must come from pure-bred Normande cows, one of several criteria added to AOP regulations in 2008. This criteria was included to fight against the policy-pushed trend followed since the mid-twentieth century to "modernize" farms by using highly productive Holstein-type cattle and intensive feed systems. Although Normandes produce less milk than Holsteins, Normande milk is very high in casein (protein) and rich in fat, making it preferable for cheesemaking. A grass-based diet, ensured by the mild, damp Norman climate, enhances these qualities, so farmers must allow cows at least six months at pasture and access to hay the rest of the year, alongside a limited ration of corn silage and other allowed feeds. See NORMANDE.

Cheese must be made from raw milk (not heated over 104°F [40°C], not undergoing microfiltration or comparable processes). The only additives permitted are rennet, "inoffensive" bacterial ferments, yeast, molds, salt, and calcium chloride. Milk is coagulated in basins and may be cut before immediately proceeding to molding (although many smaller-scale producers do not follow this procedure). Curd is molded in at least five successive layers, scooped into cylindrical molds at intervals of at least forty minutes; the manual method uses a ladle to fill a table full of molds, while the industrial method uses robotic cutting scoops that feed molds on a conveyor belt. Whey is left to drain naturally and slowly—this slowness, including an avoidance of cutting or disturbing the curd, contributes to the cheese's texture. Cheeses may be turned once before placing a metal disk in the mold to gently encourage draining. Fresh cheeses are dry salted then moved to aging rooms (hâloirs) and kept at 50–64°F (10–18°C) until packaged, which is allowed thirteen days after renneting. The AOP regulation stipulates that the whole cheese must be wrapped in paper and packed in an individual wooden box. The cheeses may leave the dairy on day 17, but may not be sold until the 22nd day after renneting.

According to the standing regulation, a Camembert de Normandie's "bloomy" rind should be white with surface molds (Penicillium candidum) and may have traces of reddish-orange from Brevibacterium linens. This reflects a refinement on the pre-Pasteurian days, when the most widespread strain of penicillia in Normandy, P. album, dominated rinds and turned them a grayish blue as they aged; scientists and cheesemakers were delighted to isolate the "pure" white P. candidum and learn to control mold development in a more aesthetically appealing way. The interior should be ivory to light yellow, and its texture depends on its age. A younger cheese—as Normans commonly prefer to eat it—will have a narrow unripe white core with horizontal striations that is somewhat crumbly and dissolves in the mouth. This core will disappear as it ages into the paste preferred elsewhere in France and the world: homogeneous, bulgy but not truly runny, satisfyingly sticky and chewy in the mouth. The aromas and flavor also evolve, from more lactic, tangy, and "sweet" to more pungent, with elements of mushroom and garlic. The full process takes about thirty days, after which time flavors and aromas (such as ammonia) will take over.

In 2014, nine dairies made AOP Camembert de Normandie, including one farmstead and a range of dairies spanning manual to heavily mechanized methods. Annual production from 2009 to 2011 averaged 4,466 metric tons. This represents a dramatic drop from the preceding three-year average of 12,902 metric tons, because from 2007 to 2008 three major factories (one cooperative and two belonging to the world's largest multinational dairy) dropped the AOP to use treated milk. This came as stricter production criteria were becoming law, and was widely interpreted as an attempt to strong-arm the law toward embracing hygienic heat treatment. If so, it failed, as the raw-milk requirement was upheld and the cooperative resumed making raw-milk AOP cheese. The multinational dairy closed one factory and uses the other one to manufacture generic Camembert sold under several formerly AOP brand names collected from old regional dairies the group bought up and closed since the 1980s, relying on brand loyalty to outweigh the PDO label. The multinational dairy retains two artisanal-scale dairies for production of its upmarket brands, still in AOP. Since this "Camembert War," AOP Camembert de Normandie accounts for only about 5 percent of French Camembert production, the other 95 percent being generic or the hybrid "Camembert fabriqué en Normandie" ("made in Normandy"). In 2011 the union of AOP Camembert de Normandie producers took three "fabriqué" manufacturers to court claiming this wording misled consumers and demanding it be outlawed.

The major AOP brands (and their dairies and/or parent group) are Isigny Sainte-Mère (Cooperative Isigny Sainte-Mère); Jort, Moulin de Carel (Lactalis group); La Petite Normande, Graindorge, La Perelle (Domaine de Saint Loup, Graindorge group); Gillot, Marie Harel, St-Hilaire (Laiterie de Saint-Hilaire de Briouze, Fléchard group); Réaux, Réo, Le Gaslonde, Val d'Ay (Fromagerie du Val d'Ay); and Pré St Jean (Fromagerie du Val de Sienne). Some brands also sell under grocery chain labels. The farmstead producers are the Merciers la Ferme de la Novère in Champsecret, which is also certified as organic.

Boissard, Pierre. *Camembert: A National Myth*. Berkeley: University of California Press, 2003.

Branlard, Jean-Paul. "Le droit du camembert: Aspect juridique d'un fromage mythique du patrimoine nationale" [Camembert Law: Legal Aspects of a Mythic Cheese of National Heritage]. In *La Gastronomie. Une approche juridique*. Paris: ESKA, 2009. The top (only) source on all Camembert's legal issues, in exacting detail.

INAO. "Cahier des charges de l'Appellation d'Origine Protégée (AOP) 'Camembert de Normandie.'" [Rulebook for the Protected Appellation of Origin "Camembert de Normandie"]. http://www.inao .gouv.fr/repository/editeur/pdf/CDC-AOP/ CDCCamembertdeNormandieversion040608.pdf.

Juliette Rogers

Cheesemaking in **Canada** dates back to the early 1600s when French explorer Samuel de Champlain brought cows from Normandy. The current day Vache Canadienne, making a comeback in Quebec, is believed to be a descendant of these early bovine immigrants. The French settlers would have made soft-ripened style cheeses. Then came the English, and the Loyalists fleeing the American Revolution—and with them, the beginnings of the Cheddar revolution. See SOFT-RIPENED CHEESES and CHEDDAR.

In the 1830s a pair of Vermont farmers, Lydia and Hiram Ranney, moved to Oxford County in the British colony of Upper Canada. Lydia was the cheesemaker—a skill that brought her together with another enterprising woman, Elizabeth Elliott. Together they improved the handling of cheese and the mechanics of making it. It was Lydia Ranney who introduced the concept of cheddaring. See CHEDDARING.

While Canadian cheese continued to be made in small handmade batches, it was finding favor and even became an export by the middle of the nineteenth century. And so it was that another American immigrant, Harvey Farrington, took the next step toward commercial production. Farrington had the technology to set up cheesemaking on a larger scale, but he needed milk—lots of it. Mobilizing his persuasive Yankee ways, Farrington convinced local farmwomen to bring him their milk instead of making their own cheese. Thus was created the first Canadian cheese factory. The Pioneer opened in the town of Norwich in 1864.

By the time Canada became a country in 1867, Ontario had at least 200 cheese factories. Cheese factories had proliferated quickly, reaching a peak of 2,900 factories by the turn of the century. Aged Canadian Cheddar gained a reputation for top quality and fine flavor, which it retains today. Exports of cheese played a major part in Canada's early economy. At its height (1891–1930), annual exports averaged 70,000 tons with a peak of 106,000 tons in 1904.

Mammoth (extra large) cheeses were used for promotion and in 1893, twelve cheesemakers working in their respective facilities combined to make a giant cheese dubbed "The Canadian Mite." The 10-ton cheese gained even more attention when it crashed through the floor of an exhibit hall at the World's Fair in Chicago in 1893. The Mite eventually made its way to England, where it was cut up and sold. In the early 1900s Canada's export of cheese reached 16,000 tons annually, and most of that sailed for Great Britain.

Formal cheesemaking education contributed to this boom. In southern Ontario a mobile classroom

CANADA'S CHEESE EXPORTS HAVE INCREASED NEARLY TWENTY-FOLD IN THE LAST 60 YEARS. IN 1926 HER CHEESE AND BACON EXPORTS WERE VALUED AT OVER 47 MILLION DOLLARS.

This late-1920s color lithograph poster boasting of Canada's cheese exports was printed by Waterlow and Sons Ltd. for the Empire Marketing Board. The board was set up in 1926 to promote trade of goods within the British Empire. MANCHESTER ART GALLERY, UK / BRIDGEMAN IMAGES

twentieth century before other types of cheese became more widely produced.

That said, Canada has had a strong underground cheese culture for centuries—existing outside the traditional distribution systems. Often bartered rather than sold, or simply made at home, these are the cheeses that helped raise families in the tradition of Italians, Scots, Portuguese, German Mennonites, and, more recently, South Asians. It is from these somewhat anarchistic roots that the current cheese revolution began. Today the growing interest in fine cheese and the availability of training, on-campus and online, is fostering a new generation of excellent amateur and professional small-scale cheesemakers from coast to coast. Many are inspired by the bold Quebec cheesemakers of the 1980s and 1990s who were models of activism and skill.

Canada's modern commercial cheese renaissance began in Quebec. As a province ("a nation within a united Canada," Stephen Harper, 2006), it has encouraged this aspect of its culture more actively than other jurisdictions. The monks at the Abbaye Saint-Benoit du Lac have been making cheese since 1943, when their landmark blue, Bleu Ermite, was conceived. The recipe for Oka, dating back to 1893, was sold to the giant Agropur Corporation in 1981. It did not transfer well to mass production. However, an authentic version was reborn in Charlevoix, Quebec, in the late 1990s, in the form of Le Migneron de Charlevoix.

The other major Canadian cheese center, Ontario, did not fare so well in modern times. By the 1960s little was left of its thriving Cheddar industry of the late 1800s. Corporate buyouts of small factories often led to their closure altogether.

Today most Canadian cheese is made in large, automated factories. Opened in 1973 the factory at Notre-Dame-du-Bon-Conseil in Quebec had the distinction of being the largest in the world, making about 100 tons of cheese daily from 500,000 quarts (1 million liters) of milk. There are now five factories of that size in Canada. In 1997 there were only about 225 cheese plants, about one-half the total of five years before. Trade in cheese is less important now than it was at the turn of the century. In 1997, 18,600 tons were exported and 19,400 tons imported, 88 percent of which were specialty varieties.

Mass production aside, artisan cheese producers are active across Canada. See ARTISANAL. Many compete on the world stage. There are sheep and goat

for new cheesemakers brought teachers from what is now the University of Guelph, farm to farm. Canada's first cheesemaking school was founded in Saint-Denis-de-Kamouraska, Quebec, in 1881. And in Saint-Hyacinthe, Quebec, a dairy school opened in 1892, which even today remains one of the chief centers for research, innovation, and experimentation in Canadian cheesemaking.

While Cheddar dominated on both sides of the Canadian language divide, the flourishing cheese culture of Quebec brought forth one notable exception in the late 1800s. Following the traditions of their French forefathers, Trappist monks made their first rendition of Brittany's Port Salut and named it Oka (in 1893) after the site of their abbey. And so began commercial specialty cheese production in Canada— that is: not Cheddar. It was, however, well into the

cheesemakers in British Columbia, producers of Gouda, pecorinos, and Mozzarella di Bufala in Alberta, and variations on many wonderful Dutch cheeses and Swiss Alp styles in Ontario. Atlantic Canada hosts a range of artisan producers of sheep cheeses, Goudas, English farmhouse styles, and the ever-so-unique Dragon's Breath Blue, a pungent blue cheese from Nova Scotia sold in a black wax casing.

Quebec prides itself on a list of some 350 cheeses, a nod to its heritage in France with its prolific and impassioned cheese production. In fact those cows brought over by Samuel de Champlain four hundred years ago have regained a modern influence. One of the jewels in the Quebec cheese crown is called Le 1608. This washed-rind wonder was created to commemorate the four-hundredth anniversary of Quebec City. The milk used? That of the Vache Canadienne, recently rescued from the brink of extinction.

Also completing an historic circle was the first annual all-milk Canadian Cheese Awards competition (2014), facilitated in part by the Food Sciences faculty of Ontario's University of Guelph. Top cheese: Le Baluchon from Sainte-Anne-de-la-Pérade, Quebec.

Arguably, no discussion of Canadian cheese and its influence on the world is complete without mention of what some call non-cheese. The impact has been, for better or worse, enormous. James Lewis Kraft grew up on a dairy farm in Ontario, but the enterprising young man headed off to Illinois a decade after the Chicago World's Fair of 1893, fascinated by the promise of innovation. He resolved to find a modern, more profitable way to distribute cheese. To say the least, he succeeded. Though he was not the first to develop a processed cheese, he was the first to win a patent (1916) and eventually to capitalize on it. This patent set the course for the invention of Velveeta, Kraft Dinner, Cheez Whiz, Kraft Singles and more. Like it or not, J. L. Kraft made cheese products a staple in the diets of millions. See CHEEZ WHIZ; KRAFT, JAMES L.; and VELVEETA.

See also QUEBEC.

Menzies, Heather. *By the Labour of Their Hands: The Story of Ontario Cheddar Cheese*. Kingston, Ont.: Quarry, 1994.
Stewart, Anita. *Anita Stewart's Canada*. Toronto: HarperCollins, 2008.

Janice Beaton

cancoillotte is a smooth, creamy-textured cheese made in the Franche-Comte region of Eastern France. Some suggest that a cheese like cancoillotte was made in this area as long ago as the Roman occupation. Others believe it to be of more recent origin. Whatever the truth, cancoillotte, like many other dairy products, originates as a byproduct and attests to the frugality and resourcefulness of the farmer for whom all produce of the land must find a use. The chief ingredient of cancoillotte is a cheese called metton.

Metton is made from skim milk. Rennet is added and the curd that is produced is then thinly cut and heated to 140°F (60°C). The curd is then drained and pressed in a cloth, pounded or crumbled, and left to dry in a warm environment. In *The French Cheese Book*, Patrick Rance writes that this used to be done in "a wooden bowl under the eiderdown next to the bedwarmer in the bed." The result is a hard, protein-rich granular substance golden yellow in color. The 26 gallons (100 liters) of milk is said to give 13 pounds (6 kilograms) of metton. To make cancoillotte the metton is melted in a pot over a low heat. A third of its weight of saltwater is added and the entire liquid stirred. After it is blended, a third of its weight of butter is also added and the entire contents stirred until a smooth, elastic paste is achieved. Cancoillotte is generally eaten warm, on bread or potatoes, and can be flavored with pepper, wine, or garlic.

Traditionally, cancoillotte would have been made on the farm with the metton produced from the skim milk left over after butter making. As it had mostly regional appeal and as most people in the region made it themselves there was little need to market it beyond the Franche-Comte. During World War I, to satisfy the desire for cancoillotte by fighting Comtois, an industrialized version appeared, sterilized and packed in tins. Today, cancoillotte is made mainly in large creameries, with about 5,000 tons produced each year. However consumption remains largely a regional affair, with an estimated 90 percent consumed in the Franche-Comte alone.

Rance, Patrick. *The French Cheese Book*. London: Macmillan, 1989.

Dominic Coyte

Canestrato di Moliterno is an Italian PGI (protected geographical indication) hard cheese made from a combination of 70–90 percent goat's milk and 10–30 percent sheep's milk, in the pecorino style. It is protected and promoted by a cheese consortium located in Moliterno, in the province of Potenza. Its production area, however, is very large, including many districts in the provinces of Matera and Potenza in the Basilicata region of southern Italy, and dates back to the eighteenth century in Moliterno. Since its inception, Canestrato has been appreciated not only in national markets but also abroad, especially in the United States.

The cheese's name is derived from two sources, the first of which is the typical mark left on the rind from the *canestri* (reed baskets) in which the cheese is dried. The second is the village, Moliterno, in which the cheese is aged. The name "Moliterno" probably comes from the Latin *mulcternum*, meaning "the place where milk is produced, namely where the herd is milked and milk is curdled."

Canestrato can be eaten fresh or aged. It begins its aging process on the farm, but after about thirty to forty days, it is transferred to *fondaci* (well-aerated and underground storage rooms in large mansions or palaces) to complete the process. Specific names indicate three different stages of aging: "Primitivo," cheese aged for a maximum of six months; "Stagionato," cheese aged from six to twelve months; and "Extra," cheese aged for more than twelve months. Canestrato's taste is sweet and delicate at the beginning, and evolves to accentuate more complex aromas with longer aging. The Canestrato aged in a *fondaco* (underground storage room) can be treated with olive oil, which may be mixed with wine vinegar, or with water boiled for twenty-five to thirty minutes with soot from wood-burning fireplaces, that is added and brought to room temperature.

See also ITALY.

Acconci, Donatella, and Istituto Nazionale di Sociologia Rurale. *Atlante dei prodotti tipici: i formaggi*. Milan: Angeli, 1990.
Pizzillo, Michele, et al. "T-cheese.Med Basilicata Cheeses." In *New Technologies Supporting the Traditional and Historical Dairy in the Archimed Zone*, pp. 146–231. Ragusa, Italy: Grafiche Cosentino, 2008.

Salvatore Claps

Canestrato Pugliese is a hard, uncooked PDO (protected designation of origin) cheese produced

throughout the province of Foggia and in some municipalities of the Bari province in the Apulia region of southern Italy. Canestrato owes its name to the baskets (*canestri*) in which it is set to mold. Baskets of all shapes and sizes are among the most typical handicrafts produced in Apulia. Local craftspeople make baskets using a variety of materials, such as reed, willow, cane, wicker, and straw. However reed baskets are the most widely used for cheese production, because of the sweet taste that Apulia's reeds contribute to the cheese.

The cheese is cylindrical in shape with slightly convex sides, a brownish-yellow color, and a wrinkled rind. It is 4–5.5 inches (10–14 centimeters) high, about 10–13 inches (25–34 centimeters) in diameter, and weighs about 15–31 pounds (7–14 kilograms). The interior paste is straw-colored, compact, and friable, with a spicy taste.

Canestrato Pugliese is made with raw whole ewe's milk from one or two milkings, and is coagulated within fifteen to twenty-five minutes at 100–113°F (38–45°C) using lamb rennet. After the coagulum is cut, the curd is transferred to the baskets and pressed. Two to four days following production, the cheese—still inside the canestri—can be dry-salted or brined. Ripening lasts from 2 to 10 months in ventilated rooms kept at 50–59°F (10–15°C), during which time the rind is rubbed with olive oil and eventually vinegar to reduce mold growth.

Although this production protocol was the basis for the PDO denomination, awarded in 1996, in the twenty-first century a number of variables can be found in the scientific literature, such as the use of pasteurized milk inoculated with starter cultures (*Streptococcus thermophilus* and *Lactobacillus delbrueckii* ssp. *bulgaricus*), the use of calf rennet, and the partial cooking of the curd at 108°F (42°C) for five to fifteen minutes. Cheeses prepared with any of these variations cannot receive the PDO mark.

See also CANESTRATO DI MOLITERNO and ITALY.

Albenzio, M., et al. "Microbiological and Biochemical Characteristics of Canestrato Pugliese Cheese Made from Raw Milk, Pasteurized Milk, or by Heating the Curd in Hot Whey." *International Journal of Food Microbiology* 67 (July 2001): 35–48.
Ministero delle Politiche Agricole. "Disciplinari di produzione prodotti DOP e IGP riconosciuti." https://www.politicheagricole.it/flex/cm/pages/ServeBLOB.php/L/IT/IDPagina/3340.

Marta Bertolino

Cantal is a large firm, uncooked French cheese made from raw cow's milk, with a thin gray-white rind tending toward golden when aged. Cantal is one of the oldest French cheeses with records mentioning it going back over two thousand years; it was cited by Pliny the Elder in his work *Natural History*. Cantal received its AOC in 1956 and its PDO in 2007.

Cantal is first of all a unique cheese by its name, as it is the only French cheese to bear the name of a département, located in south-central France. A mountainous region, with its summit at an altitude of 6,096 feet (1,858 meters), Cantal is also known as the green country because of the grasslands that cover virtually its entire surface, which is mainly volcanic soil. Grassland represents an asset for pasture and fodder, enabling cows to graze in summer and reserves of fodder to be set aside for the winter. The diversity of the grasslands is considerable with over sixty types of flora recorded, and each of the thirteen hundred producers of Cantal is fully aware of this wealth and biodiversity. Daily grazing for cows is mandatory as soon as the weather permits it, with a minimum of 120 grazing days per year. Grass, either fresh or dried, needs to represent a minimum of 50 percent dry matter of the daily feed of the herd.

Whether in farmsteads or in dairies, the process of manufacturing Cantal has remained the same for centuries. Rennet is added to the milk so that it forms a gel that is cut using a wire frame to obtain small grains. After drawing off the whey, the curds are pressed in the vat using a *presse tome* (cheese press). The tome or slab obtained is left to rest for at least ten hours. The curds are then churned, salted, then molded and pressed again. The next stage is specific to Cantal cheese: the curds are again churned, salted, molded, and pressed. The molds are 14–17 inches (36–42 centimeters) in diameter. The cheese will weigh between 77–99 pounds (35–45 kilograms) in all, and require about 422 quarts (400 liters) of milk.

Once unmolded the cheeses are moved to maturing cellars for at least one month. There are three types of Cantal cheese. Cantal Vieux is aged for more than eight months and it is appreciated for its powerful and spicy aspect. Cantal Entre-Deux is aged 90 to 210 days and the taste is balanced between intense and aroma diversity. Cantal Jeune is the youngest and is only aged between thirty to sixty days; it is recognized by its softness on the palate and a milk-and-butter taste. Cantal is a great cheese on its own, and it is also used in a famous local Auvergene dish, aligot, which is made from Cantal Jeune and mashed potatoes.

See also ALIGOT; AUVERGNE; LAGUIOLE; and SALERS.

Brosse, Anne-Line, et al. *Fromages d'Auvergne, une histoire d'hommes et de femmes.* Aurillac, France: Editions Quelque part sur Terre, 2014.
De Freitas, Isabelle, et al. Microstructure, Physicochemistry, Microbial Populations and Aroma Compounds of Ripened Cantal Cheeses. *Le Lait* 85 (2005): 453–468.
De Freitas, Isabelle, et al. "In Depth Dynamic Characterisation of French PDO Cantal Cheese Made from Raw Milk." *Le Lait* 87 (2007): 97–117.

Yves Laubert

Canut, Enric. Born in Barcelona on 19 May 1956 to a family with roots in the salt-making area of the Catalan Pyrenees, Canut's professional activities have included cheesemaking and dairy-farming consultant, wholesale buyer and marketer, and print and television journalist. A 2005 article in *Food & Wine*, under the heading "Cheese Guru," called Canut "a tireless ambassador of Spanish cheeses" and suggested that he deserved "major credit" for their modern "explosion."

In 1978, shortly after he graduated from the University of Barcelona with a degree in agricultural engineering, Canut was hired by the Barcelona-based professional food fair Alimentaria to survey and promote Catalan cheeses, many of which had gone nearly extinct under the rule of Francisco Franco (1939–1975). For the next Alimentaria (1980), Canut surveyed all of Spain and identified about eighty traditional cheeses.

As part of his university studies, Canut had apprenticed in Holland, eventually becoming an accomplished cheesemaker and an adept instructor. Beginning in the early 1980s, he had a major hand in reviving and improving a near-extinct type of traditional Catalan goat cheese that was eventually given the place name Garrotxa. He also created a new cheese called Murcia al Vino. See GARROTXA and MURCIA.

Beginning in June 1980, Canut worked as a buyer for Vinoselección, a wine and gastronomy club; in 2015 he marked thirty-five years of service with that organization. In 2013 Canut became a partner in Ardai, a distributor of cheeses and other gastronomic products. Canut is the author or co-author of nine books about cheese, including *Los 100 quesos españoles* (2000) and *Quesos & paisajes: Cheese & Landscape* (2008).

Ardai. http://www.ardai.com.

Canut, Enric. *Los 100 quesos españoles*. Barcelona: Salvat, 2000.

Canut, Enric. *Quesos & paisajes: Cheese & Landscape*. Barcelona: Udyat, 2008.

Jenkins, Nancy Harmon. "Cheese Guru." *Food & Wine*, February 2005. http://www.foodandwine.com/articles/cheese-guru.

Vinoselección. http://www.vinoseleccion.com.

David Gibbons

Capriole is a goat cheese creamery in Greenville, Indiana, founded and led by Judy Schad. Schad moved her family to a farm in the mid-1970s and began to produce cheese on a commercial scale by 1988. Capriole is considered to be one of the first American artisanal goat's milk cheese operations built in the 1970s and 1980s by pioneering women cheesemakers, including Letty Kilmoyer of Westfield Farm, Laura Chenel of Laura Chenel's Chèvre, Mary Keehn of Cypress Grove Chevre, Jennifer Bice of Redwood Hill Farm, Allison Hooper of Vermont Creamery, and Anne Topham of Fantôme Farm. These women-led creameries are frequently credited with bringing an appreciation of fresh goat's milk cheese to the United States, and have inspired many other goat's milk cheese producers across the United States in the decades since. See LAURA CHENEL'S CHÈVRE; CYPRESS GROVE CHEVRE; REDWOOD HILL FARM AND CREAMERY; and VERMONT CREAMERY.

Capriole began as a farmstead operation, but Schad sold her goats to a nearby farmer in 2013 and now buys the milk back from that farmer, who manages about six hundred dairy goats. See FARMSTEAD. Her cheeses are inspired by traditional French chèvre, and every piece is still hand-ladled, distinguishing her cheese from that of many other goat cheese producers. Schad's cheeses are also distinctive in the American artisanal cheese marketplace because of their unusual shapes (such as Wabash Cannonball, a small sphere, and Crocodile Tear, in a teardrop shape) and flavor accents (such as the paprika on Piper's Pyramide, O'Banon's wrapping of bourbon-soaked chestnut leaves, and the fresh herbs on Julianna).

Capriole currently produces nine cheeses: four surface-ripened, two fresh, and three aged. A pioneer in goat cheese production, Capriole has received close to thirty awards from the American Cheese Society's annual judging competition, including Best in Show for Wabash Cannonball in 1995.

See also AMERICAN "GOAT LADIES" and CHÈVRE.

Jenkins, Steven. *Cheese Primer*. New York: Workman, 1996.

Paxson, Heather. *The Life of Cheese: Crafting Food and Value in America*. Berkeley: University of California Press, 2013.

Jessica A. B. Galen

carbon dioxide is an odorless gas that is metabolically produced by plants, animals, and microbes. In cheese the accumulation of carbon dioxide in the water phase to beyond saturation concentration causes gas bubbles to form that may exert internal pressure on the structural matrix to form cracks and slits, or eyes, or open texture, which may be considered desirable features or defects depending on the cheese variety.

Carbon dioxide formation in cheese may occur through multiple pathways. In washed-curd cheeses such as Gouda, Edam, and Havarti, carbon dioxide along with acetic acid and diacetyl is produced through the fermentation of citrate by *Leuconostoc* species and citrate-utilizing strains of *Lactococcus lactis* ssp. *Lactis*. See ACETIC ACID and *LACTOCOCCUS LACTIS*. The resulting carbon dioxide is responsible for desirable eye formation in Gouda and Edam and open texture in Havarti. In Alp-style cheeses such as Emmentaler, carbon dioxide along with propionic acid and acetic acid are produced through the fermentation of lactate by *Propionibacterium freudenreichii*. See PROPIONIC ACID; ACETIC ACID; and DAIRY PROPIONIBACTERIA. The resulting carbon dioxide is responsible for desirable eye formation, but may also cause defective slits and cracks if excessive carbon dioxide is produced or if the cheese body is weak and fails to expand elastically under the pressure of the gas bubbles due to excessive proteolysis or excessive demineralization during cheesemaking. See PROTEOLYSIS and DEMINERALIZATION.

Slits and cracks may also form in Cheddar cheese during ripening, considered a defect, due to excessive carbon dioxide production by gas-producing species of indigenous non-starter lactic acid bacteria, particularly heterofermentative lactobacilli. Excessive carbon dioxide gas production may also occur in Cheddar, as well as in soft and semisoft cheeses, during the first few days of production when high yeast populations, associated with poor sanitation and hygiene, aggressively ferment lactose to carbon dioxide and lactic acid, producing porous open texture, pinholes, and slits, considered severe defects. See CHEDDAR.

Much carbon dioxide is produced during the ripening of soft surface-ripened cheeses of the white mold (e.g., bloomy rind) and bacterial smear-ripened varieties due to the metabolism of lactate by yeasts and, in the case of white mold types, *Penicillium camemberti*. See FUNGI and PENICILLIUM. Atmospheric levels of carbon dioxide in the ripening room may reach high enough levels to selectively inhibit microbial growth at the cheese surface and alter the ecological balance of the surface flora. The accumulation of carbon dioxide may also be an important driver of zonal softening in the cheese body as aging progresses due to the formation of calcium carbonate crystals such as calcite and ikaite (calcium carbonate hexahydrate) at the cheese surface. See CRYSTAL. The development of higher pH at the surface due to microbial fermentation of lactate and the production of ammonia, combined with calcium sequestration, such as in the form of calcium carbonate crystals, likely contributes to increased casein-water interactions and the onset of zonal softening.

See also DEFECTS and EYES.

Fox, P. F., et al. *Fundamentals of Cheese Science.* Gaithersburg, Md.: Aspen, 2000.

McSweeney, P. L. H., ed. *Cheese Problems Solved.* Cambridge, U.K.: Woodhead, 2007.

Tansman, G. F., et al. "Crystal Fingerprinting: Elucidating the Crystals of Cheddar, Parmigiano-Reggiano, Gouda and Soft Washed-rind Cheeses Using Powder X-ray Diffractometry." *Dairy Science Technology* 95, no. 5 (2015): 651–664.

Paul Kindstedt

Carr Valley Cheese

Carr Valley Cheese is a Wisconsin cheese company owned by the fourth-generation cheesemaker Sid Cook. Carr Valley crafts traditional cheeses, such as Cheddar and Blue, but specializes in creating American original and mixed-milk cheeses. The company has won more awards for its cheeses than any other cheese factory in North America, garnering more than four hundred medals and ribbons at national and international competitions.

Cook earned his Wisconsin cheesemaking license at the age of sixteen and by 2015 owned and operated three cheese plants and seven retail cheese stores in Wisconsin. See WISCONSIN'S CHEESEMAKER LICENSING PROGRAM. Since its start in 1902, Carr Valley Cheese has become known across the United States both for producing high-quality aged Cheddars and for using cow's, goat's, and sheep's milk to create more than fifty original varieties. Original cheeses include Black Sheep Truffle, Cave Aged Marisa, Chevre au Lait, Cocoa Cardona, and Shepherd's Blend. Several Carr Valley original cheeses, such as Snow White Goat Cheddar, are American Cheese Society Best in Show winners.

Carr Valley Cheese is home to multiple certified master cheesemakers, a distinction bestowed on veteran Wisconsin craftsmen and women who complete a rigorous thirteen-year advanced training course. Administered by the Wisconsin Center for Dairy Research, the Wisconsin Master Cheesemaker Program is the only accreditation of its kind outside Europe. Cook is a master cheesemaker certified in Cheddar, Fontina, and Gran Canaria, an original cheese made from cow's, goat's, and sheep's milk. Gran Canaria is rubbed with olive oil and aged for two years, resulting in a fruity, nutty, and sweet flavor with a crumbly texture.

See also WISCONSIN.

"Wisconsin Cheeses from Carr Valley Cheese." Carr Valley Cheese. http://www.carrvalleycheese.com.

Jeanne Carpenter

Casatella Trevigiana

Casatella Trevigiana is a fresh raw cow's milk cheese produced in the province of Treviso, in Italy's Veneto region. The name derives from *casada*, which means "home" in the Veneto dialect. Casatella Trevigiana obtained protected designation of origin (PDO) status in 2008. The cheese is now produced commercially year-round and sold prepackaged.

Historically this cheese was made daily by farm wives as part of the ancient tradition of Veneto household dairy production. Produced alongside cheeses designated to mature, Casatella Trevigiana was made from what leftover milk was on hand from the family cow and was for household consumption. The recipe for this uncooked, quick-ripening cheese was handed down orally from generation to generation. Production had its best results in winter when milk from fodder-fed cows was richer. The nutrient-dense cheese sustained families of modest means and was consumed almost immediately. According to Venetian Republic history, sometime around 1789 *formagiele* (cylinders) of Casatella Trevigiana were included in donations made by the doge, or duke, to the guild of greengrocers.

Milk used for Casatella Trevigiana is exclusively from Frisona, Pezzata Rossa, Bruna, and Burlina breeds and crossbreeds. Liquid or powdered bovine rennet is used in an amount that must guarantee a coagulation time between fifteen and forty minutes. The cheese is dry-salted in a sea-salt solution at 39–54°F (4–12°C) for 40–50 minutes for small forms (9–25 ounces [250–700 grams]) and 80–120 minutes for large forms (4–5 pounds [1.8–2.2 kilograms]). The salting process, which is longer than that for other fresh cheeses, helps Casatella Trevigiana achieve its signature flavor. See DRY SALTING.

Sweetness is the predominant flavor of this mild and milky-tasting cheese, but pops of gently acidic notes give it distinction. The aroma is mild, the crust is thin, and the porcelain- to pale-straw-hued paste is soft. Casatella Trevigiana doesn't travel well, so it's not as widely known as other Italian cheeses.

See also FRESH CHEESES and ITALY.

Casatella Trevigiana PDO. http://www.foodinitaly .com/en-GB/prodotti/CASATELLA_ TREVIGIANA_PDO-17577.html.
Casatella Trevigiana D.O.P. http://www .casatella.it.
Centro Veneti Formaggi. "Casatella Trevigiana D.O.P." http://www.venetoformaggi.it/en/cheeses/casatella-trevigiana-dop.php.
Centro Veneti Formaggi. "Veneto: Territory and Cheeses." http://www.venetoformaggi.it/en/ territory.php.
Sandri, Amedeo, et al. *Mangiare Veneto—Veneto Cookbook: Sette Province in Cucina.* Vicenza, Italy: Edizioni Massimo Vicentini, 2009.

Robin Watson

Casciotta d'Urbino

Casciotta d'Urbino is a semisoft, semicooked cheese produced across the entire province of Pesaro-Urbino, Italy. It received the European recognition of protected designation of origin (PDO) in 1996. The most well-known consumer of Casciotta d'Urbino was the Italian Renaissance artist Michelangelo Buonarroti, who—appreciating the cheese—leased enough land to sheep and goat herders that they could pay their rent to him in cheese.

Casciotta d'Urbino is cylindrical in shape, with slightly rounded sides, a straw-yellow color, and a thin rind (1 milimeter). It is about 2–3 inches (5–7 centimeters) high, 5–6 inches (12–16 centimeters) in diameter, and weighs 1.7–2.6 pounds (0.8–1.2 kilograms). The interior paste is straw-white in color, soft, and friable, with small holes and a sweet taste. Its largest component (70–80 percent) is whole ewe's milk, mixed with a smaller amount (20–30 percent) of whole cow's milk, coming from two milkings.

The raw milk is coagulated at 95°F (35°C) using liquid and/or powdered calf rennet within 20–30 minutes. After the coagulum is cut into pieces the size of hazelnuts, the curd is cooked at 109–111°F (43–44°C) and then manually pressed in a special mold. In the past, pressing had to be performed manually because the traditional terracotta or ceramic molds had only two to four holes at the bottom, making natural drainage of the whey quite difficult. The cheese can be dry-salted or brine-salted. Ripening takes 20 to 30 days at 50–57°F (10–14°C) and 80–90 percent humidity. Some producers wrap the cheese with a clear wax to prevent mold growth during ripening.

At the market it is also possible to find this cheese made with pasteurized milk inoculated with natural starters. Such cheese cannot receive the PDO designation, however, because the production discipline approved by the European Union allows only raw milk without the use of any starter culture.

Casciotta d'Urbina. http://www.casciottadiurbino.it.
Ministero delle Politiche Agricole. "Disciplinari di produzione prodotti DOP e IGP riconosciuti." https://www.politicheagricole.it/flex/cm/pages/ ServeBLOB.php/L/IT/IDPagina/3340.
Pirisi, A., et al. "Sheep's and Goat's Dairy Products in Italy: Technological, Chemical, Microbiological, and Sensory Aspects." *Small Ruminant Research* 101 (November 2011): 102–112.

Marta Bertolino

casein

casein is a group of proteins secreted by mammary glands that were originally defined by their insolubility at 68°F (20°C) when milk was acidified to pH 4.6. All the remaining proteins were classified as whey proteins because they were found in cheese whey. See PH MEASUREMENT; PROTEINS; and WHEY. In bovine milk the casein component consists of four proteins named alpha$_{s1}$-casein (α_{s1}), alpha$_{s2}$-casein (α_{s2}), beta-casein (β-casein), and kappa-casein (κ-casein). The same or similar proteins that perform the same function are present in milk of other species. The caseins are present in milk as various genetic variants. See BREEDING AND GENETICS. Of the caseins, α_{s1}-, α_{s2}-, and β-casein are highly phosphorylated with phosphate groups covalently bound to clusters of serine amino acids. This imparts a sensitivity to calcium such that these casein proteins will precipitate in the presence of calcium. In contrast, κ-casein is insensitive to calcium. It contains only one phosphoserine but in contrast to the other caseins a portion of the protein is glycosylated. The extent of glycosylation of κ-casein and phosphorylation of the other caseins varies. See CALCIUM.

Another feature of the caseins is that they have large blocks of polar and hydrophobic amino acids so they are amphiphilic with hydrophobic-rich (water-hating) and hydrophilic-rich (water-liking) regions. This allows the caseins to interact with each other and other molecules through both entropy-driven hydrophobic interactions and calcium-mediated interactions via the clusters of phosphoserine groups as well as the general ionic, dipole, and hydrogen-bonding interactions of proteins. The caseins rarely exist in monomeric form and readily form homo- and hetero-polymers through self-association and association with each other.

The caseins are intrinsically unstructured proteins with extended coil-like structures that have considerable conformational flexibility. They can be considered as being rheomorphic or having a molten globule structure. Because of this lack of a rigid three-dimensional tertiary conformation, caseins can react very rapidly to environmental changes and function in the mammary cells by sequestering small nanoclusters (~5 nanometers in diameter) of calcium and phosphate ions. This prevents precipitation of insoluble calcium phosphate and calcification of the mammary milk synthesis and transport system. Both the polymerization tendencies of the caseins and their calcium phosphate binding ability play key roles during casein micelle synthesis, their observed properties, and their function during cheese manufacture. See COAGULATION OR CURDLING.

Casein micelles are particles of colloidal size that can be described as supramolecules, or a system consisting of multiple molecular entities held together and organized by means of noncovalent intermolecular binding interactions. In the presence of calcium phosphate the caseins interact with each other to aggregates ranging in size from about 50 to 600 nanometers with an average diameter of ~150 nanometers. The casein micelles are not large enough to separate from milk under the force of gravity but they do contribute to light scattering and the white color of milk. Casein micelles are highly hydrated holding ~4 grams of water per gram of protein and on a dry basis, consist of ~92 percent casein and ~8 percent calcium phosphate. The average ratio of α_{s1}-, α_{s2}-, β-, and κ-caseins in the bovine casein micelles is 3:1:3:1 with κ-casein tending to accumulate on the periphery of these colloidal-size supramolecules.

Within casein micelles, α_{s1}-, α_{s2}- and β-caseins can have phosphoserine-mediated interactions with calcium phosphate nanoclusters as well as hydrophobic and ionic interactions with other proteins. Four or more phosphoserine clusters stabilize calcium phosphate nanoclusters and together form aggregates ~10 nanometers in diameter. Simultaneously other interactions among the caseins produce linear and branched protein chains forming a lattice network that is interlocked together about every five proteins (~18 nanometers) by the calcium phosphate nanoclusters. More protein chains of α_{s1}-, α_{s1}- β-caseins radiate until chain formation is stopped by binding of κ-casein that acts as a terminator. The supramolecular nature of casein micelles allows for a large diversity of linkages within these colloidal particles and on the periphery where chains of proteins extending outward form protuberances up to ~30 nanometers in length. Casein micelles comprise tens of thousands of protein molecules and hundreds of calcium phosphate nanoclusters. Having a preponderance of hydrophilic and glycosolated regions on the casein micelle periphery stabilizes the colloidal particles and prevents their aggregation unless the hydrophilic portion of κ-casein is removed by renneting or the milk is acidified. See ACIDIFICATION; CHYMOSIN; RENNET; and CLOTTING.

On average, caseins in bovine species make up about 83 percent of the proteins in milk although this can vary between animals as well as varying through the lactation cycle. See LACTATION. The caseins are the major structural component providing body and texture to most solid and semisolid dairy foods such as yogurt and cheese. It is the characteristics of the casein micelles along with their interaction with the whey protein beta-lactoglobulin that determines the behavior of milk and milk products during processing such as pasteurization, concentration, acidification, and cheesemaking. Renneted cheeses and acid-set cheeses all rely on the coagulating properties of casein micelles for their manufacture. The components of casein micelles are in equilibria with the serum phase of milk. Cooling milk causes some β-casein and calcium phosphate to be lost from the casein micelles and this can subsequently interfere with coagulation upon renneting but this is reversible upon heating and coagulability is restored when milk is pasteurized prior to cheesemaking. See PASTEURIZATION.

See also MILK.

de Kruif, C. G., and Carl Holt. "Casein Micelle Structure, Functions, and Interactions." In *Advanced Dairy Chemistry*, vol. 1: *Proteins Part A*, edited by P. F. Fox and P. L. H. McSweeney, 3d ed., pp. 233–270. London and New York: Kluwer Academic/Plenum, 2003.

Horne, David S. "Casein Structure, Self Assembly and Gelation." *Current Opinion Colloid Interface Science* 7 (2002): 456–461.

McMahon, Donald, and Bonney Oommen. "Supramolecular Structure of the Casein Micelle." *Journal of Dairy Science* 91 (2008): 1709–1721.

McMahon, Donald J., and Bonney S. Oommen. "Casein Micelle Structure, Functions and Interactions." In *Advanced Dairy Chemistry*, vol. 1: *Proteins Part A*, edited by P. F. Fox and P. L. H. McSweeney, 3d ed., pp. 185–209. London and New York: Kluwer Academic/Plenum, 2003.

Donald J. McMahon

The *Caseologia* is a seventeenth-century German book providing humorous commentary on cheese varieties in a mock-learned style poking fun at contemporary academics. Its authorship is ascribed to a fictitious Fritz Käsefaix (roughly, "cheese-fool"), official assayer of cheese at Buxtehude, a town in northern Germany. The first edition appeared undated, with no printer or location, around 1650. A second printing in Hamburg in 1690 was published in a seven-part series of similar works dedicated to coffee and tea, beer, tobacco, sausages, and geese.

The text lists cheeses that would have been available for sale in northern Germany, finding them either justified or condemned based on their supposed qualities. This judgment appears as much social as culinary, praising high-status imports like Parmesan or rich Dutch full-milk cheeses while condemning the lean, hard, and preserved cheeses the lower classes enjoyed. The author struggles to develop an adequate vocabulary for the sensory qualities of the various cheeses. Descriptions of the social expectations and culinary uses for the various types are more clearly phrased and can serve as a valuable source for the culture of cheese connoisseurship in early modern north Germany. The book also provides an early reference to Mimolette-like Milbenkäse, here referred to as *madicht* (maggoty), being imported and enjoyed as a delicacy.

See also LITERATURE and LITERATURE OF CHEESE.

Käsefaix, F., et al. *Caseologia und andere Merkwürdigkeiten zu Käse und Butter im 17. Jahrhundert*, edited by C. L. Riedel and D. Hansen. Cologne: Milch & Kultur Rheinland und Westfalen, 2010.

Volker Bach

Cashel Blue is one of only a handful of Irish blue cheeses, and a consistent award winner, made on the farm of Jane and Louis Grubb in Tipperary.

Louis Grubb grew up on his parents' traditional mixed farm in County Tipperary, Ireland. After finishing an agricultural degree at Trinity College Dublin and gaining experience elsewhere, he returned with his young family in 1978 to take over the family farm and establish a dairy herd. His wife, Jane, started experimenting with cheesemaking, and by 1984 Cashel Blue was established as Ireland's first farmhouse blue. It is made not far from the Rock of Cashel, a medieval castle overlooking the Tipperary plains, which was once the seat of the kings of Munster and where lore has it that St. Patrick commenced the conversion of the pagan Irish to Christianity.

The curd of Cashel Blue is cut by hand using a "cheese harp" and then stirred using a shovel-shaped paddle, creating a soft-textured blue. See CHEESE KNIFE. It has an ivory interior when young, which gradually deepens to a warm buttery yellow as it matures. Its thin, uneven streaks of blue give it a marbled appearance. Beneath the tinfoil wrapping is an edible, sticky, blue-gray rind with some white mold, which is intrinsic to the cheese, contributing to the breakdown of the curd and adding flavor and complexity.

Cashel Blue is smaller than most blues, and so it ripens more quickly. At around six to ten weeks old, it is firm yet moist and creamy edged. By twelve weeks, its true character starts to emerge; the flavor becomes rounder and spicy, and the texture softens. By six months, the curd will have broken down completely and starts to collapse.

See also IRELAND and STEELE, VERONICA.

Cashel Farmhouse Cheesemakers. http://www .cashelblue.com.

Juliet Harbutt

Casieddu is an Italian spherical goat cheese with a diameter of 3–4 inches (8–10 centimeters). An artisanal seasonal product, it is made only between the months of July and September, when sheep's milk is unavailable but goat's milk is still plentiful. The cheese is produced in the four districts of Castelsaraceno, Grumento Nova, Lauria, and Moliterno, in the southern Italian region of Basilicata. The production technology is the same as for Cacioricotta: raw goat's milk is coagulated by kid or lamb rennet and heated to 185–194°F (85–90°C). The only differences are that the milk is filtered through a layer of intertwined ferns, and then a handful of an herb called nepeta (*Calamintha nepeta savi*) is mixed with the milk as it is heated. It is the addition of this aromatic plant belonging to the Labiates family, rich in antioxidant substances, that gives the cheese its extremely delicate taste.

Casieddu is a complementary product to Canestrato di Moliterno cheese (mixed sheep and goat cheese). It is wrapped in fern leaves, which are intertwined at the bottom and tied with a reed or a broom branch at the top. Typically, Casieddu cheese is sold directly from the farm or small dairy. But it is also sold at local markets, especially to people from the production area who return to visit for summer vacation.

In general, Casieddu, eaten fresh, is characterized by a high quantity of water (about 60 percent). It has two prevailing aromas, cooking and mint, which result respectively from heating the milk at a high temperature and from the addition of nepeta. The ferns used to filter the milk give the cheese a slightly bitter taste. The estimated annual production of Casieddu, which has decreased in the early twenty-first century, is about 1.5 to 2 tons.

See also CACIORICOTTA and CANESTRATO DI MOLITERNO.

Acconci, Donatella, and Istituto Nazionale di Sociologia Rurale. *Atlante dei prodotti tipici: i formaggi.* Milan: Angeli, 1990.
Pizzillo, Michele, et al. "T-cheese. Med Basilicata Cheeses." In *New Technologies Supporting the Traditional and Historical Dairy in the Archimed Zone,* pp. 146–231. Ragusa, Italy: Grafiche Cosentino, 2008.
Rubino, Roberto, Pierre Morand-Fehr, and Lucia Sepe. *Atlas of Goat Products: A Wide International Inventory of Whatever Things the Goat Can Give Us.* Potenza, Italy: Caseus, 2004.

Salvatore Claps

Castelmagno is a semihard cheese from the Piedmont region of Italy that has an unusual crumbly texture and sometimes shows blue veining with age. Castelmagno PDO is produced in only three towns of Cuneo province (Castelmagno, Pradleves, and Monterosso Grana) with partially skimmed raw cow's milk from the Piedmont breed, sometimes with added ewe's or goat's milk (maximum 20 percent). Each year about 250 tons are produced.

Evidence that Castelmagno cheese was already known in medieval times can be found in a text dated 1277, where it is reported that a quantity of Castelmagno was paid to the Marquis of Saluzzo for the use of pastures in the Castelmagno and Celle di Macra area. Castelmagno PDO can boast the mention "Prodotto della Montagna" (mountain product) and can be named "di Alpeggio" when it is produced over 1,000 meters above sea level. The Castelmagno DOP Prodotto della Montagna has a blue label, while the Castelmagno PDO di Alpeggio has a green label.

After milk coagulation, the curd is broken down to the size of a hazelnut, then extracted and left to drain for about twenty-four hours. At the end of draining the curd is cut into slices and immersed in tanks with serum for three to seven days, then finely chopped. The chopped curd is salted, put in molds, and pressed for twenty-four to forty-eight hours. The cheese is dry-salted and left to ripen for a minimum of sixty days, but can be ripened for six months and beyond in natural caves. Castelmagno PDO has a cylindrical form with flat faces, a diameter of 6–10 inches (15–25 centimeters), an edge of 6–10 inches (15–25 centimeters) and a weight of 4–15 pounds (2–7 kilograms). The crust is wrinkled, hard, and reddish-gray. The dough is white or ivory-white without holes.

In aged traditional cheeses, greenish-blue veins can be present when air has entered and facilitated mold growth. Some producers intentionally pierce the wheels to ensure some development of blue veining. The texture is hard, compact, and typically very friable (easily crumbled). The odor is fine and delicate or somewhat acidic in fresher cheese, strong and persistent in aged cheese. Especially in older cheeses the taste is very savory and salty. It is both a table cheese, suitable on its own or paired with honey or chutney, and a grating cheese that goes well with many traditional Italian dishes, such as over gnocchi or Piedmontese egg noodles, or in the filling of ravioli.

See also ITALY.

Assopiemonte DOP & IGP. http://www.assopiemonte.com.
Ferrari, Maurizio, et al. *Alla corte di re Castelmagno*. Cuneo, Italy: Primalpe Costanzo Martini, 2013.
Fox, P. F., et al. *Cheese: Chemistry, Physics and Microbiology*. Vol. 2: *Major Cheese Groups*. London: Elsevier, 2004.
Italian Ministry of Agriculture. *DOC Cheeses of Italy*. Milan: Franco Angeli, 1992.
Ottogalli, G. *Atlante dei formaggi*. Milan: Hoepli, 2001.
Surrusca, Angelo, et al. *Formaggi d'Italia: Guida alla scoperta et alla conoscenza*. 4th ed. Bra, Italy: Slow Food Editore, 2005.

Giuseppe Zeppa

Castelo Branco is a round Portuguese cheese ranging from semisoft to hard, if cured for at least ninety days, and made with raw sheep's milk coagulated by a milk-clotting enzyme found in the artichoke thistle, *Cynara cardunculus*. (The same plant is used in the production of Serra da Estrela PDO cheese from the Iberian Peninsula. See PLANT-DERIVED COAGULANTS and SERRA DA ESTRELA.) Castelo Branco is one of three Portuguese PDO cheeses produced in Beira Baixa province in the central part of the country. It varies from 28–45 ounces (794–1,276 grams); smaller samples of the same cheese, called Merendeiras, vary from 12–19 ounces (340–539 grams). Its color is from light yellow to orange, with small holes inside. As it warms to room temperatures it becomes spreadable.

The Castelo Branco municipality, together with Idanha-a-Nova, Fundão, Covilha, Belmonte and Penamacor, belongs to a region between Serra da Estrela and Alentejo, where the mountains thin to become the plains that characterize the landscape of southern Portugal. Traditionally these vast lands were divided into large farms, sparsely populated, with holm and cork oaks dominating the scenery, along with Bordaleira and Merino breeds of sheep. In the early twentieth century, cheese production was focused on the domestic consumption and cheese was rarely exported. By that time, producing and maturing processes followed different patterns from each place, so the quality was heterogeneous. When Portugal entered the European Union, the process for making Castelo Branco was standardized in order to obtain the PDO. Artisan producers are scarce nowadays, with most of the production concentrated in factories, such as Damar, and co-op farms.

Other cheeses from the same region are the semihard-to-hard Queijo Amarelo de Beira Baixa (yellow cheese of Beira Baixa), made with a mixture of sheep's and goat's milk and coagulated with animal rennet, and gray-white colored Picante de Beira Baixa (Spicy of Beira Baixa), also produced with mixed milk (more goat's than sheep's), and animal rennet.

See also PORTUGAL.

Barbosa, M. *ABC dos Queijos Portugueses*. Sintra, Portugal: Feitoria dos Livros, 2013.
European Commission Agriculture and Rural Development. DOOR: "Queijos da Beira Baixa." http://ec.europa.eu/agriculture/quality/door/registeredName.html?denominationId=593&locale=en.
Fox, P. F. *Cheese: Chemistry, Physics and Microbiology*. Vol. 1: *General Aspects*. Amsterdam: Elsevier, 2004.
Harbutt, J. *World Cheese Book*. London: Dorling Kindersley, 2015.
Tunick, Michael. *The Science of Cheese*. New York: Oxford University Press, 2014.

Olívia Fraga

Cato, Marcus Porcius (234 B.C.E.–149 B.C.E.) was a Roman statesman, historian, and landowner who authored a farming handbook, *De Agricultura*, translated as *On Farming*. The handbook is considered the oldest surviving book of Latin prose, and contained the first recipes for cheesecakes written in Latin. His recipe for *placenta*, which in Latin means a kind of baked cheesecake, is thought to have been derived from previous Greek recipes. The book also contains eight other cake recipes such as *libum*, with cheese as an ingredient. Some of these were thought to have been made not to eat, but more for sacrificial purposes to the gods. "There is also evidence that these cakes were served as part of the *mensa secunda* (sweet course) and that they would necessarily be delicate, and appetizing as part of a fashionable Roman" meal, according to Sally Grainger, who did extensive research and authentic re-creation of the recipes. Grainger adds that the recipe is "totally inedible when cold and in that state may well have been used simply as a sacrificial offering." See PLAKOUS.

The recipes use sheep's milk cheese and were generally baked using a *testum*, a Roman clay vessel cover with a central hole at the top used to regulate the cooking temperature. The vessel, described by Cato in *On Farming*, is covered by coals and ashes from a fire cooling down from cooking the main part of the meal. The cakes were then removed from the hearth and taken to diners almost immediately, soaked in honey. The original cheesecakes were cooked directly on a clean, heated hearth with bay leaves beneath. The cover (*testum*) was placed over the cake and a makeshift lid or stopper, possibly made from dough, was used to regulate the temperature. The actual recipes are considered to be "confusing," and at times "virtually unintelligible," Grainger adds and notes, "It is extremely unlikely that (Cato) had any conception of what he was writing about and certainly no experience of cooking or handling dough."

Cato's original cheesecake recipe is an enormous pastry measuring around 1 foot (30 centimeters) wide by 2 feet (60 centimeters) long by 2 inches (5 centimeters) high and included 14 pounds (6.4 kilograms) of cheese and 4.5 pounds (2 kilograms) of honey among its ingredients. The cheese was first soaked repeatedly in water since apparently the pastry could only be made during the cheesemaking season and was often kept in a brine to preserve it.

Cato wrote *On Farming* as an instructional and business manual on how to run an estate-type farm from the point of view of an absentee landowner—

since he spent much of his time in Rome—to train a farm manager and to make income. While his farms concentrated mostly on the production of produce, grapes, and olives, Cato also offered advice on maximizing dairy production from sheep herds. He advocated leasing out winter pasture to tenant flocks when milk and cheese production occurred with terms of the rental agreement that included payment in a percentage of the cheese production. The movement of livestock between fixed summer and winter pastures, or seasonal transhumance, was a relatively new practice in the newly emptied Italian countryside after the war with Hannibal, notes Andrew Dalby, a classical scholar and author of a translation of Cato's work. Cato also stipulated that half the cheese should be "dry"—referring apparently to early-seasonal production that was dried and hardened for several months. The dry cheese or *caseus aridus*, as opposed to the soft, fresh cheese, or *caseus molli*, was prized in Rome and could generate a handsome profit for the estate.

The question often comes up as to why a farming handbook would contain recipes. "Possibly Cato included them so that the owner and guests might be entertained when visiting the farm; possibly so that proper offerings might be made to the gods; more likely, I believe, so that profitable sales might be made at the neighboring market," notes Dalby. Another theory is that Cato understood the role good food played in elevating worker morale, loyalty, and basic quality of life amid the boredom and toils of farming.

Cato, also a respected orator and guardian of Rome's moral compass as censor, is often referred to as "the Elder," to distinguish him from his grandson, who also rose to prominence in Roman history and is known as "the Younger." In addition to *On Farming*, Cato also wrote the first Roman encyclopedia and a history of Rome and produced a work on medicine.

See also ANCIENT CIVILIZATIONS; PLAKOUS; and TRANSHUMANCE.

Cato, Marcus Porcius. *Cato on Farming: De Agricultura.* Translated with commentary by Andrew Dalby. Blackawton, U.K.: Prospect, 2010.
Cato, Marcus Porcius. *Cato the Censor on Farming.* Translated by Ernest Brehaut. New York: Columbia University Press, 1933.
Dalby, Andrew. *Cato in Culinary Biographies.* Edited by Alice Arndt. Houston, Tex.: Yes Press, 2006.
Dalby, Andrew, and Sally Grainger. *The Classical Cookbook.* 2d rev. ed. London: British Museum Press, 2012.

Grainger, Sally. "Cato's Cheesecakes: The Baking Techniques, Milk Beyond the Dairy." In *Milk—Beyond the Dairy: Proceedings of the Oxford Symposium on Food and Cookery 1999*, edited by Harlan Walker, Blackawton, U.K.: Prospect, 2000.

Kindstedt, Paul. *Cheese and Culture: A History of Cheese and Its Place in Western Civilization*. White River Junction, Vt.: Chelsea Green, 2012.

Dan Macey

A **cave** is a cool, humid environment that is used for preserving and aging cheese. Traditionally, both natural and manmade caves have been used to prolong the shelf life of cheese, long before the advent of refrigeration. A cave is slightly warmer in temperature than the average refrigerator, ranging between 45° and 70°F (7–21°C). This temperature range helps cultivate a healthy bacterial, mold, yeast, and enzymatic ripening of fresh cheese wheels into aged varieties. The cave environment controls the rate of cheese ripening so that the cheese does not get too cold or too hot.

A classic example of a natural cave climate for cheese is the Roquefort caves in Roquefort-sur-Soulzon, France. These caves are a repository for a distinctive blue mold called *Penicillium roqueforti*. Roquefort cheese's blue flavor profile is contingent upon this mold and other thriving, symbiotic bacteria, molds, and yeasts in the cave environment. The porous, cool, humid stones of the caves help promote the development of this mold. See PENICILLIUM; ROQUEFORT; and FUNGI.

Caves can also be seen as collective storage systems all over Europe, the Middle East, and now the United States. Jasper Hill Cellars in Greensboro, Vermont, is one example of this cooperative model. Jasper Hill purchases freshly made wheels of cheese from neighboring farms and then proceeds to age them in their seven underground vaults. See CELLARS AT JASPER HILL.

According to Halé Sofia Schatz, an ethnographic researcher and the director of the documentary *Daughters of Anatolia*, Turkish nomadic tribes created a cool environment for their freshly made cheeses on their journeys even when a natural cave was not present. First they would line a shaded tree area with a foundation of rocks. They would then proceed to wrap the tree trunks with camel wool blankets, completely enclosing the area so that no sunlight could filter in. Because the area was out of the sunlight, the enclosure did not radiate heat, and thus stayed much cooler than the ambient average summer temperature of 90–95°F (32 to 35°C).

Cheese caves have often been built underground to take advantage of natural temperature regulation away from any sunlight. This concept is similar to a

Wheels of Havarti-style cheeses aging in the caves of Ludwig Farmstead Creamery, a fifth-generation family creamery in Fithian, Illinois. The cheeses are made from the milk of Ludwig's purebred Holstein herd. © KATE ARDING

root cellar or wine cellar, although the cheese cave has necessary added controls for yielding the best cheese results.

An important factor in addition to temperature is the humidity of the cave. Cave humidity is described as relative humidity by modern commercial cheesemakers. The relative humidity (RH) is the ratio of the actual amount of water vapor in the air (absolute humidity) to the maximum amount of water vapor that could be in that air at the same temperature. Cheese caves range from 75 to 99 percent relative humidity. A cheese stored at lower humidity is likely to crack, harden, and become brittle, except in the case of fresh cheeses that have been encased with wax, animal hides, or vacuum sealing. The encasement preserves the cheese's internal moisture level while it ages in cave-like temperatures. See RELATIVE HUMIDITY.

Before a freshly made cheese is ready for a cave, the rind moisture and salt level must be taken into account. Cheese curds and rinds are salted through either dry-salting or brining (salt and water). Salting controls the rate of fermentation. If the rind is too wet before being placed in the cave, it is likely that the rind development will be overly moist, causing both interior and exterior textural issues. If the rind is too dry, the rate of the maturing process will be slowed down considerably, and will prematurely harden the cheese. The art of sealing the rind of the fresh wheels before aging is called curing. See PREMATURATION and MOISTURE.

Cave Maintenance

There is a certain amount of cave maintenance necessary in order to benefit from a cave's storage conditions. Maintenance of air exchange and shelving is critical to creating consistent cheeses. Flipping the cheese from twice a day to once a week is also necessary, depending on the original moisture level of the cheese. If the cheese is a higher-moisture bloomy rind, for example, it must be flipped twice a day. A low-moisture, hard natural-rind cheese must be flipped once a week. Flipping guarantees that no excess moisture builds up underneath the cheese, and it promotes even ripening.

The cleanliness required in a cheese cave is also relative to the style of cheese that is being ripened. If, for example, the cheesemaker is interested in aging a natural-rind aerobic cheese with a variety of molds on the rind, then it is not as necessary to be vigilant about cleaning the boards and the floor. In some caves in France, the ground and walls of the cave are purposefully cultivated or inoculated with molds, bacteria, and fungi in order to stimulate and promote growth. Excess cleaning in this type of cave will result in a cheese that loses its distinguishing characteristics, by not having access to ambient cultures. Risk assessments conducted by Food Standards Australia New Zealand have concluded that microbiological controls and monitoring of caves used by French Roquefort producers are adequate to provide assurances of food safety. See FOOD STANDARDS AUSTRALIA NEW ZEALAND.

Wood has historically been seen as the ideal cheese aging shelf for several reasons. It was the only material available for centuries. Wood's porous nature helps maintain humidity without condensation and also helps cultivate the particular ambient cultures necessary for different styles of cheeses. Like a cast iron skillet, the wood becomes seasoned. This type of shelving can be maintained with ritual hot water and vinegar cleanings. Commercial operations often sanitize wooden boards with the heat of an oven or kiln. Cheesemakers can afterward wash the wooden shelving with a solution of dissolved culture in order to ward off any invasive bacteria strains from gaining a stronghold in the cave. See WOODEN SHELVES.

In more modern times, plastic and metal shelving has become available. Although these options do not provide the same methods of cave microclimate cultivation as wood, they are easier to clean and sanitize according to international food safety regulations. The vast majority of artisanal cheesemakers, at 75 percent, still use wood shelving to age their cheese. Larger factory-made cheeses are more likely to be aged on plastic or metal shelving with cheese mats inserted underneath to protect the developing rind.

In any natural-rind cheese cave, cheese mites will eventually appear. Mites in small quantities are not a detriment to the cheese, and can usually be controlled by consistent cave maintenance practices. These microscopic small creatures resemble dust and can travel into the cave via hair, clothes, and skin. They can be most successfully controlled in the cave through brushing and vacuuming. Some Comté caves in Europe use robots to perform this task. See CHEESE MITES and VACUUMING.

Cave Mechanics

The stone walls of a cave provide natural insulation as well as regulating temperature and air circulation inside the cave. For most commercial cheesemaking operations, other types of insulation are used, including blankets, concrete blocks, foam boards, rigid foam, reflective systems, fiber installations, and sprayed foam.

Within a cave, air circulates at a low, gentle rate from the top and bottom, while ammoniated air is expelled in exchange for fresh air from the outside. The different air renewal and air movement rates required by particular cheeses can be provided by installing a simple piping or ventilation system. The system can be passive, composed of one high and low pipe. The system can also run passively by using thermostats to control the opening and closing of louvers in the pipes, allowing cooler air to enter the cave, while releasing the warmer air. A fan can be added to these models to help circulate the air and increase the air movement rate. If the cave is larger, it will require a more intensive air exchange system. An "air exchanger" is a more expensive option that controls the amount of warm air allowed into the cave. This last option is best used for larger operations where electricity usage will be considerable.

The concave form of a natural cave's ceiling can help direct any condensation buildup to the sides and walls. This helps prevent any extra moisture from dropping directly onto the cheeses' surfaces, which could cause another moisture issue. The vaulted design is a more expensive initial investment for building a commercial cheese cave from scratch, but it will eventually pay off because of its effectiveness. If the ceiling is flat, it will need to be layered with insulation to help control any condensation buildup.

There are variations in ideal storage conditions, depending on the particular cheese being stored. Certain cheeses require high humidity, such as bloomy-rind and washed-rind cheeses. Other cheeses, such as Swiss styles with large eye formation, need a warmer temperature, from 60° to 68°F (16–20°C), for the first two-to-four-week period of aging. In addition, lower-temperature cheeses such as blues should be aged in a separate area so as to not promote the proliferation of undesired blue mold on other types of cheeses in the cave.

See also MATURING.

Betancourt, Jennifer, and Amanda DesRoberts. *Current Options in Cheese Aging Caves: An Evaluation, Comparison, and Feasibility Study.* Westbrook, Maine: Silvery Moon Creamery, 2011. http://www.silverymooncheese.com/docs/FinalCheeseCaveReport.pdf.
Caldwell, Gianaclis. "Aging Cheese Gracefully—The Art of Affinage." In *Mastering Artisan Cheesemaking: The Ultimate Guide for Home-Scale and Market Producers*, pp. 75–100. White River Junction, Vt.: Chelsea Green, 2012.
Long, J., and J. Benson. *Cheese and Cheese-Making, Butter and Milk.* London: Chapman and Hall, 1896, pp. 18–19.

Jessica Sennett

Cebreiro is a Spanish fresh or soft cheese that has been protected with a designation of origin (DO) since 2008. The cheese is made in a picturesque mountainous area located in the eastern part of the province of Lugo, in the Galician region (northwest Spain), generally using pasteurized cow's milk. The history of this cheese goes back centuries and, based on records from 1742, it was the most expensive cheese in the country and the fourth most expensive in Europe. Currently, the PDO designation includes nine dairy farms producing approximately 250,000 liters of milk per year that are transformed into approximately 30,000 kilograms of cheese. Milk used for the manufacture of industrial fresh or soft Cebreiro cheese is curdled by a predominantly acidic coagu-

Cebreiro, a Spanish PDO soft cheese, is shaped like a mushroom or chef's hat. © JUAN A. CENTENO

lation, with the addition of (nonspecific) mesophilic DL-starters and small quantities of calf rennet (about 0.05 milliliters/liter, 1:10,000–15,000 strength) at 78–86°F (26–30°C) for at least sixty minutes (usually six to twelve hours). The curd is cut into 10–20-millimeter pieces, which are then placed in cloth (cotton) bags that are hung for five to ten hours to allow the whey to drain off. After draining, the curds are worked to give a uniform paste with a claylike texture, and salt is added.

The cheeses are molded and pressed at approximately 4 kilograms/square centimeter, and then stored in cold-storage chambers at 35–43°F (2–6°C) for at least one hour. Occasionally, ripening could take place at 50–59°F (10–15°C) and 70–80 percent of relative humidity for at least forty-five days, although the "mature Cebreiro cheese" type is not industrially manufactured at the present time. The cheese is shaped like a mushroom or a chef's hat, and ranges in weight from 0.3 to 2.0 kilograms. The product is whitish in color, soft, spreadable, and friable, with a slightly grainy texture. The taste is milky and slightly acidic, and the aroma is buttery and yogurt-like, rather different from the yeasty, slightly bitter, and slightly spicy flavor characteristic of the traditional raw-milk starter-free products. Cebreiro can be consumed by itself or as a cooking ingredient, as part of salads, sauces, seafood dishes, and creamy desserts.

See also SPAIN.

Centeno J. A., P. Rodríguez-Alonso, J. Carballo, and J. I. Garabal. "A Comparative Biochemical Study of Two Industrially Produced Short-Ripened Cow's Milk Cheeses with PDO Status: Rennet-Curd Tetilla Cheese and Acid-Curd Cebreiro Cheese." *International Journal of Dairy Technology* 68 (2015): 291–298.

Juan A. Centeno

Cedar Grove Cheese

Cedar Grove Cheese is located in Plain, Wisconsin. Owner Bob Wills and his cheesemakers craft a variety of organic, artisan, and traditional cheeses from cow, goat, sheep, and water buffalo milk. The factory is known for serving as an incubator for new artisan cheeses by allowing guest cheesemakers to use the factory during off-production hours. For example, before building his own farmstead creamery, Pleasant Ridge Reserve founder Mike Gingrich crafted what would become the three-time American Cheese Society Best in Show champion at Cedar Grove Cheese in 2000.

In 1993, Cedar Grove Cheese was the first cheese factory in the United States to craft and label its cheese as free of recombinant bovine growth hormone (rBGH), asking farmers to sign pledges to not use artificial hormones to increase milk production. In 2007, it was certified by Midwest Food Alliance as the first food processor in America for using "green" technology. The factory installed a "Living Machine"—a complex system of 10 tanks—to dispose of 7,000 gallons (26,498 liters) of daily wastewater through an elaborate filtration system using natural microbes and plants, resulting in discharging clean water to nearby Honey Creek, in the Wisconsin River basin.

A cheese-aging facility built in 2007 uses energy from the plant's nearby whey chilling unit. Inside, several varieties of specialty cheeses are custom aged for cheesemakers and dairy farmers, adding value to their operations by marketing cheese made from each farm's milk. Cedar Grove's own cheeses are specialty and organic varieties, such as Cheddar, Colby, and butterkäse. The company is also a leader in creating unique artisan cheeses made from mixed milk.

See also PLEASANT RIDGE RESERVE and WISCONSIN.

Cedar Grove Cheese. http://www.cedargrovecheese.com.

Hurt, Jeanette. *The Cheeses of Wisconsin*. Woodstock, Vt.: Countryman, 2008.

Jeanne Carpenter

Cellars at Jasper Hill

The **Cellars at Jasper Hill** are a series of seven vaulted and climate controlled aging caves, totaling 22,000 square feet (2,044 square meters), built into the rocky terrain of Greensboro, Vermont. The Cellars were opened by Jasper Hill Farm owners Andy and Mateo Kehler in 2008 with an initial investment of $2.3 million. The Cellars represent a regional model of cooperative food production, distribution, and marketing inspired by historical provisioning schemes of the French and Swiss Alps, but that also reflects the more independent, entrepreneurial spirit of Vermont's Northeast Kingdom (the region that includes the three northernmost counties of Vermont). While Jasper Hill Farm's own farmstead cheeses are aged in the Cellars, the majority of the operation is built around a cooperative dairying and cheesemaking concept. Local cheesemakers, approximately ten at any given time, sell young or "green" cheeses to the Cellars. The Cellars team of two dozen employees then cares for, markets, distributes, and sells the cheeses under a co-branded label. The model is meant, in the Kehlers' words, to lower the "barriers of entry" to value-added dairying, which the brothers envision as a cornerstone to the rural economy of the Green Mountain State. The commercial and competition success of their Cloth-bound Cheddar, a collaboration between the Cellars and the Agri-Mark-owned Cabot Cooperative, has provided much of the Cellars' sales volume. See CABOT CREAMERY.

See also UNITED STATES and VERMONT.

Paxson, Heather. *The Life of Cheese: Crafting Food and Value in America.* Berkeley: University of California Press, 2013.

Bradley M. Jones

Celtic Blue Reserve is a rich, semifirm blue cheese with a unique limestone-colored brushed rind developed with specific ripening cultures. The cheese is made by Glengarry Fine Cheese in Ontario, Canada. Owner and cheesemaker Margaret Morris Peters and cheesemaker Wilma Klein-Swormink tweaked their two-year-old, prize-winning Celtic Blue recipe to create a Celtic Blue Reserve, which is modeled on French Fourme d'Ambert and English Stilton. See FOURME D'AMBERT and STILTON. Celtic Blue Reserve placed Best of Show at the 2015 ACS (American Cheese Society) Cheese Competition out of 1,779 cheeses.

Celtic Blue Reserve is made using whole pasteurized Brown Swiss cow's milk from a neighbor's family farm. See BROWN SWISS. A bit of cream and *Penicillium roqueforti* culture is added to the cheese milk to make 4.5-pound (2-kilogram) wheels that are aged for three to four months. The Celtic Blue Reserve has a piquant but not aggressive taste. It is more mellow and complex than the original Celtic Blue, which is only aged two to three months and has a sharp and savory flavor typical of a younger, lower-fat blue. The cream and extended aging make the Reserve richer than the original recipe, similar to a French blue cheese. The silken cheese melts on the palate with lingering piquant notes, butter and sea salt, finished with fruity sweetness.

See also BLUE CHEESES; BRUSHING; LANKAASTER AGED; and ONTARIO.

Glengarry Fine Cheese. http://www.glengarryfinecheese .com.

Kathy Guidi

Chabichou du Poitou made from pure goat's milk, is a French cheese that comes in the shape of a truncated cylinder called a "bonde," by analogy with the bunghole on a barrel. Legend dates the origin of the word "Chabichou" (originally "cheblis," or "goat" in Arabic) to the eighth century following the defeat of the Arab armies by Charles Martel at Poitiers. While the Saracens may have retreated in 732, the goats that came with the troops held their ground and stayed. This small cheese (about 5 ounces [150 grams]), with its white rind dotted with occasional blue-gray patches and a slightly salty taste, encompasses all the taste of the savoir-faire of the Poitevin terroir, in western France.

The Chabichou du Poitou was granted an AOC in 1990 and PDO status in 1996 and milk production and cheese manufacturing and maturing must be carried out within the PDO geographic area, which corresponds to the limestone Haut Poitou and has long been a land for goat farming. About 400 tons are produced per year, including 33 percent from raw milk.

With farmers committed to achieving self-sufficiency in feeding stuffs, the goats are treated to fodder, cereals, grass, red clover, alfalfa, and other leguminous plants that come mostly from the PDO area and contribute to Chabichou du Poitou's distinctive taste. The goats are Alpine, Saanen, Poitou, and crossbreeds thereof. See ALPINE and SAANEN. The cheese is molded in a specific cheese-stamped sieve. It demands special care and attention and needs to be turned over several times to obtain its characteristic shape and must be matured for at least ten days. Soft and creamy when young, Chabichou du Poitou can develop strong flavor and brittle texture with aging. Chabichou du Poitou is usually consumed on its own, as a table cheese, but will also be very suitable as an appetizer, accompanied by a Pineau des Charentes, or served hot on a toasted slice of bread.

See also FRANCE.

Froc, Jean. *Balade au pays des fromages: Les traditions fromagères en France.* Versailles, France: Editions Quae, 2006.

Géraldine Verdier

Chalet Cheese

Chalet Cheese a rural factory near Monroe, Wisconsin, was founded in 1885. The factory functions as a cooperative, owned and operated by twenty-one dairy farm families who supply a blend of Holstein and Brown Swiss milk cows to make brick, baby Swiss, Swiss, German brick, and Limburger. Chalet Cheese is best known as the sole maker of Limburger in the United States, producing about 500,000 pounds (226,000 kilograms) annually for American consumption under several retail brand names, including Country Castle.

Located in Green County, the epicenter of Swiss cheesemaking in Wisconsin, Chalet Cheese is one of thirteen cheese factories within a 626–square mile area. Cheesemaker Myron Olson is the company's general manager, a role he has held since 1980, in the tradition of long-tenured cheesemakers at Chalet Cheese. In fact, Olson is only the third general manager to run the rural cheese factory since the 1930s. He succeeded the renowned Albert Deppeler, considered among many in Green County to be the "king of kings" of cheesemakers. Today, in addition to Limburger, the makers at Chalet Cheese continue to craft and market the factory's award-winning Deppeler line of Swiss cheese.

At Chalet, each batch of cheese is made in the Old World tradition in open air vats, with cheesemakers cutting curd by hand with long knives and hand scooping curd into forms. Every block and wheel of Swiss cheese is packaged by hand, and every piece of Limburger is washed by hand with a bacteria-brine solution, giving the cheese its unique orange-brown rind and pungent aroma.

See also LIMBURGER; SWISS CHEESE; and WISCONSIN.

Roberts, Jeffrey. *Atlas of American Artisan Cheese.* White River Junction, Vt. Chelsea Green, 2007.

Wisconsin Specialty Cheese Institute. http://www.wispecialtycheese.org.

Jeanne Carpenter

Chaource

Chaource is a French cheese that is appreciated for its soft and creamy texture, which bears the name of a small town in the Aube, in northeastern France. It is produced in the wet Champagne region, where the variety of soils in the region has led to the generalization of a mixed crop and livestock farming system. Through its livestock activity, Chaource has allowed traditional farming activities to continue in this sector, and this is still the case today. Chaource has been recognized as an AOC since 1970 and PDO since 1996. About 2,500 tons per year are produced. The main part of the production is sold in France but approximately 20 percent of the production is exported, mainly to four countries: Germany, the United Kingdom, Japan and the United States.

Chaource was known in the Middle Ages since around the fourteenth century, and was first produced in the abbeys in Champagne and Burgundy. The women in the region adopted this savoir-faire in the seventeenth and eighteenth centuries to produce cheeses intended for domestic consumption. The making of the cheese had to fit in with their daily chores, which meant they had little time available. This system of production is what has given Chaource its lactic character and determined the main stages of its manufacture.

Made exclusively with whole cow's milk (either raw, thermized, or pasteurized), the cheese (48 percent of fat on dry matter) is obtained by slow coagulation, before being molded and then drained naturally. It is salted with dry salt, then set to dry before being placed in the maturing cellars. After fourteen days the Chaource forms a smooth rind with the presence of white mold and an aroma reminiscent of cream and fresh mushrooms. Two sizes of Chaource are produced, the more common being the big one (16–25 ounces [450–700 grams]) and a smaller one (9–11 ounces [250–300 grams]), which can be ripened longer. Chaource is usually consumed on its own, as a table cheese or as an appetizer. It can also easily be used in various recipes such as gougères au Chaource (Chaource cheese puffs) or tarte au Chaource (Chaource tart).

Couche, René. "Le fromage à Chaource." *La Vie en Champagne* 204, special edition, October 1971.

Didier Lincet

Charles VI (1368–1422) of the Valois dynasty, king of France 1380–1422, known as "the Well-Beloved" early in his reign and "the Mad" later, is familiar in English-speaking countries as the losing party of the Battle of Agincourt (1415). Crowned as a child, he struggled with mental illness later in life. Dominated by warring noble factions and a continuing struggle against English claims to the French throne, his reign saw tax revolts, urban unrest, and the outbreak of the Armagnac-Burgundian civil war. It ended with a military defeat that led to extensive English lands in France and the claim to the French throne by the House of Lancaster being conceded in the 1420 Treaty of Troyes.

The king's significance for the history of cheese rests on a letter patent that Charles, mired in civil war and in need of allies, issued to the southern French town of Roquefort-sur-Soulzon on 4 June 1411. In it he conveyed the sole right to sell cheeses with the designation "Roquefort," as well as the exclusive use of nearby caves to age them, to the inhabitants of that town. This is considered the earliest instance of a legally protected designation of origin and was reconfirmed by numerous governments, continuing in effect to this day. It should be noted, though, that the name "Roquefort" was already valuable property at the time that the royal monopoly was obtained by the townspeople.

See also CAVE; DESIGNATION OF ORIGIN; and ROQUEFORT.

Guenée, Bernard. *Un roi et son historien: Vingt études sur le règne de Charles VI et le chronique du religieux de Saint-Denis*. Paris: Académie des Inscriptions et Belles-Lettres, 1999.
Whittaker, D., and J. Goody. "Rural Manufacturing in the Rouerque from Antiquity to the Present: The Examples of Pottery and Cheese." *Comparative Studies in Society and History* 43, no. 2 (2001): 225–245.

Volker Bach

Charolais is a raw goat's milk cheese that comes from the region surrounding the town of Charolles, between the Auvergne mountains and the Morvan Massif, centered in Burgundy, France. The area has long been known for its Charolais breed of beef cattle; cheesemaking developed as a side enterprise, the domain of women who kept dairy goats that grazed the pastures alongside cattle. In the 1970s professional affineurs and consolidators brought the cheese to Paris markets, effectively turning a local agricultural product into a national commodity. In 2010 Charolais was awarded AOC status; in 2014 the European Union approved it for PDO status.

PDO Charolais cheese is made from raw (unpasteurized) full-fat goat's milk (Alpine or Saanen breeds). See ALPINE and SAANEN. (In the past cow's milk was sometimes added.) The goats graze on pasture with supplemental fodder of hay sourced from within the delimited geographical area. The milk is slightly renneted and traditionally inoculated with lactic bacteria contained in the whey left from a previous batch of cheese. After a slow-set period, curd is ladled into cylindrical molds that give the small cheeses a slightly convex or barrel-shape form. The cheeses are salted and turned by hand as they age, for a minimum of sixteen days, to develop a bloomy, slightly wrinkled rind of mostly *Geotrichum* mold, with occasional streaks of *Penicillium*. Geographic indication stipulations require the cheeses to be between 2½–3½ inches (7–8.5 centimeters) high with a diameter of 2½ inches (6–7 centimeters). They are to weigh between 9–11 ounces (250–310 grams).

Syndicat de Défense du Fromage Charolais. PDO application to the EU no. 1151/2012. http://eur-lex .europa.eu/legal-content/EN/TXT/PDF/?uri= CELEX:52014XC0131%2803%29&rid=2.

Heather Paxson

Chäs Vreneli AG is a retailer, distributor, and caterer of fine Swiss cheeses, established in 1915 by Otto Wartmann in Zurich. Located in downtown Zurich, the store has a large selection of cheeses and other European specialties, and unique cheeses aged to their own specification for their own catering service. Chäs Vreneli also sells butters and cheeses produced by smaller village diaries.

Through a catering operation, Jürg Wartmann, the grandson of the founder, specializes in supplying small-portioned prepackaged natural cheese "delicacies" and trays for airlines, as well as cheese for hotels and restaurants around Europe. According to some reports, almost 52 percent of Chäs Vreneli AG business comes from exports of Swiss cheeses, including Tilsiter from northern Zurich, Appenzeller, Gruyère AOP, and Vacherin Fribourgeois.

A unique service offered in their catering service is the production in large scale of Tête de Moine florettes. The florettes are small (1-inch [2.5-centimeter]) shavings of cheese historically made using a sharp spoon and later produced with a girolle. This tool consists of a blade mounted on a pole that is inserted in the middle of the cheese round and goes around the top of the cheese making thin layers that bunch like small flowers. At Chäs Vreneli AG they have developed a technology to mechanically produce florettes on a large scale, with minimal waste, and package them for service and use in cheese trays.

See also SWITZERLAND.

Chäs Vreneli AG. http://www.chaes-vreneli.ch.

Carlos Yescas

Cheddar, one of the world's most famous cheeses, was originally developed in the southwest of England. Its production spread around the world over the course of the nineteenth century and since then has continued to flourish. "Cheddar" has become a generic term encompassing a vast range of hard cheeses; according to the US Code of Federal Regulations, any cheese with a moisture content of up to 39 percent and at least 50 percent fat in dry matter can legally bear the name.

Montgomery's Cheddar, a classic rendition of the Cheddar style, aging in the Neal's Yard Dairy caves in London. © NEAL'S YARD DAIRY

Cheddar is all things to all people. It is made in formats ranging from tiny truckles to 650-pound blocks. It can be dyed bright orange or left with its natural color. Some Cheddars are allowed to develop a natural rind, while others are bound in cloth or aged in plastic or wax. Cheddar can be sold when it is just a few months old or kept for several years, and its texture varies from rubbery and pliant to friable and crystalline. Flavors range from mild and buttery to brothy and savory, and often feature distinctive acidity or "sharpness." Some cheeses may be sulfurous and eggy, others winey or fruity. Although Cheddar was originally made with cow's milk, it is now sometimes made with the milk of goats, sheep, or buffalo. Particularly in its young and mild form, Cheddar is a popular choice as a base for blended and flavor-added cheeses. It is also immensely popular: more than 3 billion pounds of it are produced every year in the United States alone. It is, for many, the essential hard cheese.

Making Cheddar

Within the United States, the legal definition of Cheddar does not specify a particular method necessary to achieve the required composition, so there are potentially as many different ways to make Cheddar as there are variations on the style. However, the original process that helped it achieve world dominance differentiates Cheddar from other styles of hard cheese.

Pre-ripening the Milk

In order to achieve proper drainage and texture, it is imperative that acidification take place primarily during the initial stages of the cheesemaking process, rather than after the cheeses have been molded, in contrast with many Continental-style cheeses such as Comté and Parmigiano Reggiano. Originally, milk from the evening milking was slowly cooled to room temperature in the dairy overnight, where the native bacteria would start the process of gently acidifying the milk. Warm fresh milk would be added to the vat from the morning milking and the cheesemaking would commence; with the influx of extra heat, the latent acidification would kick into higher gear. Given the variable microbial load of raw milk extracted by hand and the lack of temperature control within the cheese dairies, it is not surprising that the speed of the make—and the results—varied substantially from day to day. The most expert and prized dairymaids could read the curd, knowing from sight, taste, and smell when it was ready for the next step. A perfectly orchestrated make, in which acidification was harmonized with all the steps in the process, yielded a cheese like no other, described by Joseph Harding in 1864 as "close and firm in texture, yet mellow in character or quality; it is rich, with a tendency to melt in the mouth; the flavor full and fine, approaching to that of a hazelnut" (Willard 1865, p. 232). See HARDING, JOSEPH.

Scalding the Curd

One of the aspects that ensures the longevity of a cheese is low moisture, and in order to make a large cheese that will keep well, the curds must be adequately dry before they can be molded. If curds that are too wet are pressed into a large mold, the moisture is locked in and the cheese rots as it ages. The cheesemakers of Somerset devised a method that allowed them to remove the moisture from their cheeses more easily than did their colleagues to the north: heating the slurry of curds in the vat to cause them to shrink and expel moisture. This way, they were able to remove moisture efficiently at an early stage, making it easier to produce larger cheeses and contributing to a smoother final texture at the same time.

Cheddaring

Cheddar is a verb as well as a noun, and "cheddaring" was developed and popularized during the mid-nineteenth century as a way of keeping the curds warm while encouraging them to expel their excess moisture before molding. Blocks of matted curd were stacked on top of one another in the vat, interlaced with cloth scrims, and often weighted down with wooden racks to promote drainage. See CHEDDARING.

Curd-salting

In many British cheeses, blocks of curd are ground to pieces ("milled") before they are put into molds and pressed. Originally the surfaces of these pressed cheeses were then rubbed with salt or the cheeses were immersed in brine ("pickled"). However, salt permeated the larger cheeses slowly, contributing to problems of spoilage and inflation ("blowing") during ripening. Mixing dry salt evenly through the milled curd before molding solved this problem, with the result that large cheeses could be made more consistently and successfully. See DRY SALTING.

The Rise of Cheddar

The combination of practices described above arose over the course of many years in the southwest corner of England, in the counties of Somerset, Gloucester, and Wiltshire. Early-modern British cheesemaking was characterized by a high level of diversity, with cheeses from a single region often made using different methods and displaying a regional style only in the broadest sense. By all accounts there was a lot of bad cheese: technical problems such as "off" flavors, poor texture, and cracked rinds filled with mites and maggots represented an important source of economic loss.

Despite these challenges, by the mid-seventeenth century Cheddar had become a famous and desirable cheese, in such demand that cheeses were often spoken for before they were even made. The best-quality Cheddar became a luxury enjoyed by the wealthy. Against this backdrop, Cheddar made its great leap from regional specialty to international hegemon. Much of the credit is due to the work of a progressive cheesemaker and educator named Joseph Harding. He came from a family of cheesemakers, and during his career became convinced that in order to secure their success for the future, Cheddar producers needed to standardize their methods according to the most recent scientific and technical developments. He promoted the development of dairy schools to disseminate knowledge, traveled far and wide to deliver lectures, and hosted visitors from around Britain, Scandinavia and, importantly, the United States.

Cheesemaking in the United States was also well established by the mid-nineteenth century, and since many of the first immigrants to colonize America had come from the United Kingdom, the template for most early cheese was British. The world's first cheese factory opened in the State of New York in 1851, processing milk from several local dairy farms. The cheese made at that factory was Cheddar. See NEW YORK.

The American cheesemakers were proactive in their efforts to acquire the latest knowledge and competitive advantage. They sent an emissary, Xerxes A. Willard, to visit Harding and learn details that could be adapted to improve factory production back in the States. Harding was happy to share his knowledge freely, particularly since his efforts to spread that information closer to home were not always as gratefully received. See WILLARD, XERXES ADDISON.

Back in America, the factory model proved to be efficient and immensely successful, and Cheddar was the ideal cheese for this method of operation. Production in North America boomed, and cheap Cheddar produced by thousands of factories soon flooded back across the Atlantic and into the British market, where its low price and consistency made it a great success, to the chagrin of the British farmhouse cheese industry. The British moved to build factories as well, the first constructed in 1870 in Derby under the guidance of an American cheesemaker from New York. But by then, the British industry was already far behind the curve, and by 1913, more than 80 percent of the cheese consumed within the United Kingdom was imported.

Many assume that the practice of binding cheeses in cloth was a facet of the original method of Cheddar production that spread with it to the New World, but there is evidence that binding hard cheeses in cloth was widely adopted within the United Kingdom only during the nineteenth century. Although cloth was often employed to bolster the sides of softer, blue British cheeses such as Stilton and Wensleydale as they matured, there is less evidence to suggest that hard cheeses were clothbound from an early date. Writing in 1784, the cheese factor (seller) Josiah Twamley described how "most people wash their cheese, putting it in a little warm water or whey to soften the swarthy coat occasioned by the cheese-cloth, ... then they rub it off with a brush, and afterwards lay it to dry, or sweat.... I think washing is preferable, care being taken not to send it off too soft, as that exposes it to crack; then the fly takes it, and maggots breeding in it damages your cheese" (pp. 100–101). He also referred to cheeses made from over-scalded curds becoming "horny-coated," a reference to their knobby external surfaces. See CHEESE FACTOR. An article published in 1842 in the *Penny Magazine of the Society for the Diffusion of Useful Knowledge,* a London weekly, noted that the characteristics of the American cheeses then beginning to arrive in British urban centers of trade consisted "in their greater diameter of breadth, ... in their being full of holes or eyes, in possessing a pungent or rather bitter taste, and in a bandage of linen or cotton cloth being passed round their outward rim" (p. 98). Although the article concluded that American

cheeses were "decidedly inferior to our own," the practice of cloth binding was gradually adopted in the United Kingdom, so that by the end of the nineteenth century almost all British hard cheeses were clothbound as well. See CLOTHBOUND CHEESES.

Factory production continued to evolve over the course of the twentieth century on both sides of the Atlantic. Experiments sponsored by the US Department of Agriculture in 1902–1903 showed that maturing Cheddar in cold conditions significantly reduced weight loss, as did enveloping the cheeses in wax. Cold-matured cheese was also less likely to develop "off" flavors. The economic incentive to adopt these practices was clear and they spread quickly. During the subsequent decades, wax was largely supplanted by plastic films, and today, the vast majority of Cheddar is aged in this way, protected from contact with the air and without the influence of the molds that play a role in the development of natural-rind Cheddar. See WAXING AND COATING.

Battles for Identity

With such a broad range of cheeses bearing the name of Cheddar, efforts have been made to define certain types more strictly in order to differentiate them from the crowd. In 1994, Cheddar producers from the southwest of England applied for and were granted protected designation of origin (PDO) status for "West Country Farmhouse Cheddar Cheese." To qualify for the PDO label, the cheese must be made in Dorset, Somerset, Devon, or Cornwall. However, members are allowed to buy milk from other parts of England to cover any shortfalls in availability, to use either raw or pasteurized milk, and to age the cheese in either cloth or plastic. See DESIGNATION OF ORIGIN.

A stricter quality mark was defined in 2003, when three Somerset Cheddar makers secured a Slow Food Presidium for "Artisan Somerset Cheddar." Their description stipulated a number of further requirements, among them that the cheese must be made from raw milk produced exclusively on the farm where the cheese is made, that bulk "pint" starters and animal rennet must be used, that the cheese must be aged with a cloth-and-lard binding, and that the cheese must have a minimum age of eleven months at sale. See SLOW FOOD.

The distinction between "cheddared" Cheddar and the alternative, "stirred-curd" Cheddar, is a matter of contention among cheesemakers, although there is nothing on the label to tell consumers which is which. One camp argues that genuine Cheddar must be made from curds that have undergone the stacking-and-restacking process of cheddaring. The other submits that equally Cheddar-like results can be achieved by stirring the milled curds before molding and pressing. See STIRRING. It is easy to conflate the process of cheddaring with labor-intensive and small-scale methods. However, tools can be developed to mechanize any process, and cheddaring is no exception; today many large factories employ Cheddar-Masters, automated systems that can cheddar up to fifteen tons of curd per hour.

Perhaps the most contentious debate in the Cheddar community today is over the subject of sweetness. In the early 1990s, experiments with various adjunct strains of lactic acid bacteria showed that they had the capacity to decrease bitterness and speed flavor development during ripening, attributes which equate to significant cost savings in a market producing billions of pounds of cheese per year. Furthermore, these adjunct strains have the capacity to deliver sweet caramel flavors and catalyze the production of crunchy crystals within the paste of the cheese, features that sensory panels rewarded with high scores and customers received enthusiastically. The use of adjunct cultures to boost cheese flavor has since spread rapidly and to a wider selection of Cheddars, including some premium and farm-made cheeses. In effect, adjunct cultures have become a new and discreet form of flavor-added cheese. In some cases, the sweetness has been dialed up to heroic levels using proprietary culture cocktails originally designed for the manufacture of Alp-style cheeses. There are some within the industry who believe that these sweet flavors, which could never have been achieved using the raw materials and methods of the early Cheddar makers, reflect the evolution of a truly American style of Cheddar, while others contend that they are no more than flavor from a packet. See ADJUNCT CULTURES.

Notable Producers

A comprehensive catalogue of notable Cheddar producers would fill an encyclopedia. Any list must start with the members of the Slow Food Artisan Somerset Cheddar Presidium—Montgomery's,

Keen's, and Westcombe—who make what is arguably the most classic rendition of the style currently on the market. Quicke's in Devon has also been making Cheddar for many years. In the United States, Bleu Mont (Wisconsin), Fiscalini (California), and Cabot Clothbound (Vermont) are benchmark examples, while Beecher's Flagship (Washington) and Prairie Breeze (Iowa) are notable for their intense sweetness. Further afield, Avonlea cheese from Prince Edward Island in Canada and Pyengana Cheddar from Tasmania in Australia are also classic examples of the genre. Large cooperatives such as Cabot Creamery in Vermont and Tillamook County Creamery Association in Oregon are synonymous with high-quality Cheddar cheese produced on a larger scale.

See also CHESHIRE CHEESE (U.K.); INDUSTRIALIZATION; MILLING; SCALDING; TERRITORIAL; and UNITED KINGDOM.

"American Cheese." *Penny Magazine of the Society for the Diffusion of Useful Knowledge,* 12 March 1842.
Babcock, S. M. *The Cold Curing of Cheese.* Washington, D.C.: U.S. Dept. of Agriculture, Bureau of Animal Industry, 1903.
Cheke, Val. *The Story of Cheese-Making in Britain.* London: Routledge & Kegan Paul, 1959.
El Soda, M., S. A. Madkor, and P. S. Tong. "Adjunct Cultures: Recent Developments and Potential Significance to the Cheese Industry." *Journal of Dairy Science* 83 (2000): 609–619.
Kindstedt, Paul. *Cheese and Culture: A History of Cheese and Its Place in Western Civilization.* White River Junction, Vt.: Chelsea Green, 2012.
Twamley, Josiah. *Dairying Exemplified, or the Business of Cheese-Making.* Warwick, U.K.: J. Sharp, 1784.
United Kingdom Dept. for Environment, Food, and Rural Affairs. "Product Specification: West Country Farmhouse Cheddar Cheese (PDO)." https://www.gov.uk/government/uploads/system/uploads/attachment_data/file/271260/pfn-west-country-farmhouse-cheddar.pdf.
United States Food and Drug Administration. *Code of Federal Regulations* Title 21, Part 133, Section 113: "Cheddar Cheese." http://www.accessdata.fda.gov/scripts/cdrh/cfdocs/cfcfr/CFRSearch.cfm?fr=133.113.
Willard, Xerxes. "Address Before the Cheese Makers Association." In *Documents of the Assembly of the State of New York, Transactions of the New York State Agricultural Society,* 1864, Vol. 24, pp. 226–311. Albany, N.Y.: Wendell, 1865.

Bronwen Percival

cheddaring, or "texturizing the curd," is the handling of the curd in the vat or cooler from the point at which the liquid whey is removed (also known as "whey-off") to milling, the objectives of which are to control the moisture content by the removal of whey and to develop the body and texture of the curd. This method of handling significantly influences the final texture of the cheese. See PITCHING; DRAINING; and MILLING.

During the process, the curd mat left behind after the whey has been removed has a central channel cut in it, and the curd removed from this channel is piled on to the curd on either side of the vat in equal quantities. This curd is then cut, within five to ten minutes, into evenly-sized blocks on each side of the vat. At this stage the curd is very fragile and the first turn must be carried out carefully. Subsequently, the blocks are turned and piled every ten to fifteen minutes depending on the rate of acidity development. The cheddaring process entails turning and piling these slices of curd. As they relax and stretch, the large blocks may be cut again for ease of handling and to assist the expulsion of whey. During this entire process the pH falls as the starter bacteria continue to multiply, and to this end the curd must be kept warm; the outside end blocks should be

turned to the inside of the vat and the top pieces to the bottom of the pile. Failure to do this during long cheddaring periods may cause some parts of the curd to become cool or discolored. During the whole process whey drains from the curd, and its texture changes from fragile and crumbly to smooth, with characteristic striations similar to cooked chicken breast.

If the acidity develops too rapidly during cheddaring, the blocks are turned more frequently to aid syneresis and not piled high to encourage cooling. See SYNERESIS. If the acidity development is slow, the curd is left for longer intervals and piled high to keep warm. A common target for milling is a pH of 5.4–5.2 and a titratable acidity of 0.45–0.50 percent lactic acid. If the curd is still wet when it is milled, then more salt may be added and the curd stirred for longer before molding to aid the release of excess moisture.

In modern day Cheddars, the whole process normally takes forty-five to sixty minutes, during which time the titratable acidity increases approximately 0.05 percent every ten to fifteen minutes. If the cheddaring period is extended beyond the normal duration, the total time from rennet to milling is also extended. Many producers refer to this scenario as a "slow vat" and adopt procedures including curd

After the liquid whey has been removed from the curd, a central channel is cut in the curd mat and the curd removed from this channel is piled on either side of the vat in equal quantities. This is called channeling. © VAL BINES

testing for organisms such as coagulase positive *Staphylococcus aureus* to ensure the cheese's safety. However, at the turn of the twentieth century, when Cheddar was often made without the addition of starter cultures, the cheddaring process often took five hours or more.

See also CHEDDAR.

Lloyd, F. J. *Observations on Cheddar Cheese-Making.* London: William Clowes and Sons, 1892.

Scott, R., R. K. Robinson, and R. A. Wilbey. *Cheesemaking Practice.* 3d ed. Gaithersburg, Md.: Aspen, 1998.

Van Slyke, Lucius. L., and Walter V. Price. *Cheese: A Treatise on the Manufacture of American Cheddar Cheese.* Rev. and enl. ed. Atascadero, Calif.: Ridgeview, 1992.

Val Bines

cheese accompaniments include any food or beverage that complements, enhances, or harmonizes with a specific cheese or style of cheese.

Complementary pairings have been part of the culinary experience for as long as cheese has been presented at the table. Only a few decades ago common pairings were limited to a few simple regional combinations of cheese and wine, cheese and bread, cheese and crackers, cheese and cured meat, or cheese and fresh fruit. Much of this narrow selection was limited to regional ingredient availability and cultural or traditional pairing preferences. Since the 1990s there has been an expanded availability of multicultural foods and beverages crisscrossing many borders, broadening the cheese options to include hundreds if not thousands from all of the traditional cheesemaking regions around the world. Complementary foods and beverages from those same regions joined the cheeses on their journey to many foreign shores. Traditional and not-so-traditional small batch artisanal cheeses, quality production cheeses, and cheese-friendly foods and beverages have made their way into regional restaurants, cheese shops, specialty cheese and deli departments, and finally into home kitchens worldwide. Due to increased exposure to diverse cuisines, consumers have become more adventurous in their food and beverage choices. Palates have expanded to explore, accept, and enjoy not only traditional but oftentimes unfamiliar cross-cultural combinations of flavors and textures when choosing cheeses and their complementary partners.

Beyond the commonly accepted combinations, the possibilities are infinite; determined by product accessibility, the planner's imagination, and personal taste.

When choosing a complement, the style and flavor profile of the featured cheese or cheeses is paramount. The accompaniments should complement, not overshadow, the cheese. After considering the profile of the cheese, next consider how the cheese is going to be presented. The cheese's profile plus how it will be presented will determine *what* it is best accompanied by. The cheese may be part of a cheese plate; presented on a cracker as embellished hors d'oeuvres; tucked inside a plain or grilled sandwich; melted onto toasted bread or flatbread; tossed or layered in a salad; or simply served in wedges with a favorite chilled beverage. The cheese can be served at room temperature sliced, wedged, or spread; while some can be baked, grilled, or broiled. Decide whether one or more items will accompany the cheese. Next decide which flavor profiles are the most interesting with the specific styles of cheeses being served. Also decide whether the accompaniment will be similar in texture or consistency as the cheese or in contrast.

The texture can be crispy, crunchy, chewy, soft, smooth, oily, or syrupy. Breads can be baked, toasted, or grilled; fruits and vegetables can be raw, pickled, fermented, or cooked; served chilled, at room temperature, warm, or hot. Beverages are preferably served at cellar temperature or chilled.

An accompaniment can be dolloped, drizzled, or sprinkled on top of the cheese; positioned underneath the cheese; mixed into the cheese; set next to the cheese; or if a beverage, drunk with a cheese. Some accompaniments can be wrapped around the cheese, or dusted, rubbed, or rolled onto the cheese. Accompaniments can include:

Condiments and Foods

- **Bread:** Plain rustic sour country or sweet baguette, seeded wheat, olive bread, herb bread, whole grain (nuts or dried fruit optional), panforte. In general sweet or frosted fortified breads are not good partners for cheese.
- **Crackers:** Plain (water crackers), salty, savory, or lightly sweetened biscuits. Biscotti with dried herbs, dried fruit, or nuts, can work when not too sweet.

- **Fruit:** Seasonal fresh fruits (apples, pears, grapes, figs, melon, berries, stone fruit, persimmons, citrus), dried fruits (raisins, cherries, plums, cranberries, dates, apricots, prunes, figs), cooked fruits (chutneys, compotes, mostarda; honey, balsamic, or spirit-glazed fruit, poached fruit, grilled tropical and stone fruit), fruits soaked in cider, wine, or spirits; or fruit syrups and molasses.
- **Olives**
- **Honey**
- **Jam, jellies, marmalades:** Savory and sweet
- **Chocolate and cocoa**
- **Salads and vegetables:** Raw vegetables (tomatoes, radishes, celery, cucumbers, scallions, jicama, fresh green salads); cooked vegetables (beets, carrots, peas, fava beans, mushrooms, asparagus, peppers, eggplant, and potato).
- **Herbs:** Fresh or dried herbs (rosemary, savory, mint, basil, oregano, tarragon, dill, chervil, chives, fennel seeds, fennel pollen, lavender); dried herb blends (herbs de Provence, fine herbs, za'tar)
- **Spices:** Peppercorns, mustard seeds; sweet, smoked, and hot paprika
- **Nuts and seeds:** Nuts (walnuts, hazelnuts, almonds, pecans; sprouted, toasted, salted, candied, spiced, butters); seeds (pumpkin, sunflower; sprouted, toasted, salted, candied, spiced, butters)
- **Oils:** Olive oil (plain extra-virgin, or flavored [citrus, smoked, truffle]); seed and nut oils (pumpkin, sunflower, sesame, pistachio, walnut, hazelnut)
- **Vinegars:** Aged wine vinegar (balsamic), Saba, fruit vinegars, shrubs; vinaigrettes and marinades
- **Pickles:** Oil-packed, marinated, brined, or fermented vegetables; tapenades
- **Mustards**
- **Meat:** Charcuterie (cured meats, confits and rillets, pâtés)
- **Cured fish and shellfish:** Gravlax; tuna, sardines, anchovies in olive oil; pickled herring; smoked fish and shellfish (oysters, mussels), caviar

Beverages

- **Beer (ales and lagers):** General matchups: delicate beers (wheat beers, pilsners, blondes, kolsch, saisons), or fruity lambics with young, fresh cheeses; malty beers (bocks, brown ales, stouts, porters) with nutty or buttery cheeses; hoppy beers (pale ales, IPAs) with tangy cheeses; sour beer (sour ales and wild yeast beers) with washed-rind "stinky" cheeses; strong beers (imperial stouts, barley wines) with blues and hard aged cheeses.
- **Wine:** Any with residual sugar (supplying sweetness or fruitiness to counteract a salty cheese) works best whether red, white, or pink; still or bubbly. The saltier the cheese, the sweeter the wine needs to be; looking for a balance of sweet and savory or salty, compatibility and harmony. Consider the cheese's origin when choosing a wine; regional matchups are a good starting point.
- **Fortified wines:** Dry or sweet sherry, port, vermouth, Marsala
- **Cordials, liqueurs, aperitifs**
- **Spirits:** Brandy, whiskey, bourbon
- **Spirit or shrub cocktails**
- **Hard cider and mead**
- **Chilled tea** (green and black)
- **Chilled coffee**
- **Kombucha**
- **Agua frescas**
- **Natural sodas**

See also BEER PAIRING; BREAD PAIRING; CHEESE TASTINGS; and WINE PAIRING.

193 Perfect Pairings. Culture Magazine, special edition, Spring 2014–Spring 2015.

Fletcher, Janet. *Cheese & Beer*. Kansas City, Mo.: Andrews McMeel, 2013.

McCalman, Max, and David Gibbons. *Mastering Cheese*. New York: Clarkson Potter, 2009.

Mary Karlin

cheese addiction. Cheese is often ranked as one of a number of foods challenging to resist. Scientific studies on food addiction and the possibility of cheese addiction more specifically, have focused on two potential causes.

First there are studies investigating the role of fat, sugar, and carbohydrate levels on the potential of a food to be addictive. Studies focusing on glycemic load (GL)—a measure of how quickly carbohydrates present in a food are available for absorption into the body, with the potential to spike blood sugar—

have found correlations between food addiction and highly processed foods, which tend to have high GL. GL, sugar content, and fat content have been identified as indicators of foods people find most challenging to avoid. However, since cheese has a GL of zero and is not typically considered processed or high in sugars, it is cheese's high fat and salt content that may be one indicator of its desirability.

A second focus of food addiction studies is specific to the unique properties of milk products including cheese. Milk contains compounds that can activate and impact the body as they are digested. As the casein protein in milk is digested it breaks down into certain types of peptides (small groups of amino acids including beta-casomorphins). These beta-casomorphins are more prevalent in fermented milk and in cheese, as compared with fresh milk. Cheese following digestion contains significantly higher levels of beta-casomorphins than unprocessed milk, although this also varies by cheese type.

Many types of food peptides, including beta-casomorphins, are actually opioid peptides that can bind to the opioid receptors in the human brain. Opioid peptides are also naturally produced in the human body—for example, endorphins, which are released during exercise. Opioid peptides are important in human brains because they influence aspects of behavior, including emotions. Opioids can influence the brain's "reward circuit" since high levels of these opioids release dopamine, a chemical that can signal feelings of satisfaction or reward.

Cheese's link, via beta-casomorphins, to the brain's reward system is one reason why scientists are studying the effect of milk and cheese consumption on the body and its potential for addiction through the opioid connection. Although these products may contain opioid peptides this does not necessarily mean they are addictive. Studies to understand these connections have not found conclusive results. At least one study suggests that the human body does not go through the same opioid-like withdrawal symptoms following large intakes of fat as occurs after large intakes of sugar. In other words, high-fat foods such as cheese, when consumed in large quantities, do not result in the same kind of withdrawal associated with sugar addiction or opioid drug addiction, for that matter. A recent review by the European Food Safety Authority found that bovine-derived opioid peptides appear to be much less potent than medically derived opioids and are not con-

clusively linked with negative effects, including increased risk for cardiovascular disease.

See also CHEESE AVERSION and HEALTH PROPERTIES.

Avena, N. M., et al. "Sugar and Fat Bingeing Have Notable Differences in Addictive-like Behavior." *Journal of Nutrition* 139 (2009): 623–628.

Corwin, R. L., and P. S. Grigson. "Symposium Overview—Food Addiction: Fact or Fiction?" *Journal of Nutrition* 139 (2009): 617–619.

De Noni, I., and S. Cattaneo. "Occurrence of β-casomorphins 5 and 7 in Commercial Dairy Products and in Their Digests Following In Vitro Simulated Gastro-intestinal Digestion." *Food Chemistry* 119, no. 2 (2010): 560–566.

European Food Safety Authority. "Review of the Potential Health Impact of β-caseomorphins and Related Peptides." *EFSA Scientific Report* 231 (2009): 1–107.

Pelchat, M. L. "Food Addiction in Humans." *Journal of Nutrition* 139, no. 3 (2009): 620–622.

Reid, L. D., and C. L. Hubbell. "An Assessment of the Addiction Potential of the Opioid Associated with Milk. *Journal of Dairy Science* 77 (1994): 672–675.

Schulte, E. M., et al. "Which Foods May Be Addictive? The Roles of Processing, Fat Content, and Glycemic Load." *PLoS One* 10 (2015): 1–18.

Meredith T. Niles

cheese aversion is a sensation of unease or discomfort with cheese, which has been observed and hotly debated since ancient times. On the one hand, cheese has been considered a highly nutritious food. It was a common food in the Western world that was consumed in many varieties. But on the other hand, cheese has at times been considered unhealthy or dangerous to certain individuals and has been known to provoke responses of revulsion and even fear. A number of theories have been advanced to account for cheese aversion, and although the basis of the arguments has changed over the centuries, research to explain why a food such as cheese produces delight in some people and disgust others is likely to persist.

In his 1658 *De aversatione casei* (On the Dislike of Cheese), the polyhistor Martinus Schoock summed up the many opposing opinions about cheese that existed in medical and dietary thought at the time. Like most of his contemporaries, he was convinced that antipathy and sympathy were the most ubiquitously secret instincts of nature. According to natural philosophy, these principles could be found in many different forms, among them the pleasurable appetite or disgust. The phenomenon that some people liked or disliked certain foods was therefore not really surprising. What was exciting to Schoock was the question of which type of individuals had a particular aversion to cheese, and why some even believed in the pathogenic properties of cheese.

In the early modern period (roughly, late fifteenth to late eighteenth centuries), physicians as well as diners became preoccupied with the question of who could safely consume cheese and who could not. Cheese consumption was also associated with living conditions and social status, but primarily it was an issue of a person's physiology. Since at least the time of the Hippocratic Corpus (fifth century B.C.E. to second century C.E.), physiological theory had taught that cheese was "the fleshy part of milk." Although the "solids" were supposed to be the main nutriments (sources of nutrition) of food, only a healthy body could manage to digest them in good order and produce a sufficient *chyle* (the milky fluid formed in the small intestine during digestion) as the raw material of new blood. Partially assimilated nutritive materials could penetrate the body, it was maintained, affecting and altering the bodily humors and the constitution and temperament of the individual. Old theories of digestion, therefore, knew a range of disagreeable and sometimes even fatal effects of foods that were difficult to digest.

On Schoock's view, the more "liquid" and warm a person was, the more life force and digestive capacity he or she would have. Blood was at its strongest in young people and in spring. By this reasoning, growing older made a person become colder, harder, and weaker, with the result that old people might have difficulty eating cheese. Thus, the last stage of life resembled its beginning. Fluid, soft milk could prolong life and was considered the perfect food for babies. But neither babies nor older people should eat cheese because of their weak digestive organs. In contrast, strong working people should find cheese easier to digest than would tender people with delicate bodies, and so on. The harder a cheese, the longer it would keep, but the refined and delicate constitutions of noble people, Schoock reflected, would not agree with the hardness of some cheeses. Digestibility remained the salient characteristic of a healthy food for centuries, and cheese belonged to that class of foods that by nature were not easy to digest.

Schoock also made arguments about a kind of hereditary, or acquired, aversion to cheese. If either the mother or the father were unwilling to eat cheese, then the child might display a similar reluctance. Most often, however, the dislike of cheese was attributed to the consumption of bad, or "cheesy," mother's milk. For instance, if a woman got pregnant while she was still nursing a child, her milk was thought to become inferior in quality (bulky or cheesy) and diminished in quantity, because now it was needed to feed the growing fetus as well. For a child who was nursed with inferior milk, then, even the flavor of cheese could provoke disgust later in life.

Today, the explanations of food likes and dislikes are no less ambiguous than they were in the seventeenth century. The primary difference is that most researchers would argue psychologically instead of physiologically. A variety of factors—including flavor perception, eating behavior, conditioning, and social learning—are taken into consideration to explain why a specific food is not perceived as positive in its appearance, smell, texture, or taste. In addition, some people avoid cheese because they have lactose intolerance and fear the physical consequences of eating it. Still, today, in a globalized world, some will avoid it because it is not part of their cultures; while others, as vegans, consider its consumption unethical.

See also CURDLING, CULTURAL THEORIES OF.

Albala, Ken. "Milk: Nutritious and Dangerous." In *Milk— Beyond the Dairy: Proceedings of the Oxford Symposium on Food and Cookery 1999*, edited by Harlan Walker, pp. 19–30. Oxford: Prospect, 2000.
Schoock, Martin. *Von der Butter; Von der Abneigung gegen den Käse.* Translated by Siegfried Kratzsch. Cologne: Verein Milch & Kultur Rheinland, und Westfalen, 2008. Originally published as *Exercitatio academica de aversatione casei,* .... (Groningen, Netherlands: n.p., 1658).

Barbara Orland

A **cheese ball** is an hors d'oeuvre made of soft cheese that is mixed or coated with other ingredients, such as nuts, fruits, herbs, spices, sauces, and meat, then shaped into a large ball. Cheese balls are usually served with another food, such as crackers, pretzels, or vegetables, on which the cheese mixture is spread. A versatile dish, the cheese ball can be savory or sweet, and, despite its name, it isn't always round. The cheese "log"—an oblong soft cheese made in the same way—is considered a cheese ball, as are soft cheeses molded into festive shapes, such as American footballs (covered in bacon bits, with Swiss cheese for laces) or snowmen (covered in shredded mozzarella, with peppercorns for eyes and a small carrot for a nose). Although many countries have round cheeses, the cheese ball is characteristically American, often served at national holidays and celebrations.

The contemporary cheese ball has its origins in the "cheese ball" salads that appeared in American cuisine at the turn of the twentieth century and grew in popularity throughout the 1920s and 1930s. These green salads featured small balls of cheese as their centerpieces. By the 1940s the mini-balls had become their own party tidbit, rolled in such ingredients as parsley or chipped beef and served at ladies luncheons. The first mention of a cheese ball large enough to feed multiple eaters appears in Virginia Stafford's *Food of My Friends* (1944) in a recipe attributed to Marie Ellertson of Minneapolis, Minnesota. The cheese ball grew in popularity throughout the 1970s and early 1980s, even becoming a slang term, meaning "goofy" or "silly." Today the cheese ball has achieved iconic status.

Lovegren, Sylvia. *Fashionable Food: Seven Decades of Food Fads*. Chicago: University of Chicago Press, 2005.

Eric LeMay

The **Cheese Board Collective** is one of the San Francisco Bay area's premier cheesemongers, and a paradigm of worker-owned retailing. Founded in 1967 as a small mom-and-pop store in north Berkeley, the Cheese Board Collective's original owner-operators were Elizabeth and Sahag Avedisian (1930–2007), who shunned the spotlight and never envisioned it as more than a part-time job to support other vocational endeavors. Now located at 1504 Shattuck Avenue, it became a thriving business and was among anchors of an area that came to be known as the Gourmet Ghetto.

At the close of the Cheese Board's opening day, Alfred Peet, founder of Peet's Coffee two doors down, asked, "How was business?" When told receipts were $75, Peet answered, "You'll do fine." In 1971, inspired by Sahag's experiences working on a kibbutz in Israel, the Avedisians converted their business, which employed six other people at the time, to a worker-

owned collective. The Cheese Board began baking bread in 1975 and was responsible for pioneering French-style baguettes in America as well as supplying them to Chez Panisse, across the street. By the late 1980s staff pizza lunches spawned another expansion: a pizzeria at 1512 Shattuck Avenue. The Collective subsequently spun off several other independent worker-owned businesses, including the bakeries of the Arizmendi Association.

In 2003 the members collaborated on a cookbook entitled *The Cheese Board: Collective Works* (New York, Ten Speed Press). In its foreword Alice Waters wrote, "The Cheese Board was there … before Chez Panisse was so much as a gleam in my eye. When the restaurant was conceived, I wanted it to be in North Berkeley so the Cheese Board would be nearby, because I knew I would be among friends."

By 2015 the Collective's members numbered about 50 and cheese was estimated to contribute 20 percent of revenues. The cheese shop carries 350 to 400 selections at peak season in November and December, with equal emphasis on local producers (California and the Northwest) and those across the United States and in Europe.

The Collective began at the height of the counterculture revolution and at its epicenter. Guided by a democratic, all-inclusive business ethic, members strive to keep its original spirit alive in a modern context. Cheese-purchasing decisions are based not only on criteria of quality, aesthetics, and traditional artisanal production but also on values such as sustainability, affordability, and eco-friendliness.

See also CALIFORNIA and COUNTERCULTURE.

Cheese Board Collective. http://cheeseboardcollective. coop.
Fletcher, Janet. "A Cheese Shop Grows in Berkeley: After 36 Years, a Venerable Workers' Collective Is Still Going Strong." *SF Gate*, 8 October 2003. http://www.sfgate .com/bayarea/article/A-cheese-shop-grows-in-Berkeley-After-36-years-2572000.php.

David Gibbons

cheese boxes, developed to protect fragile goods for trade and travel are still in use today. Historical examples have become coveted, strictly as decorative collectibles. Nearly since cheese has been made, the question of how to get it from one place to another has emerged. Cheese was carried wrapped in cloth, in earthenware pottery, or often in boxes.

But keeping it fresh, let alone unspoiled, for any amount of time on a journey posed quite a challenge. See EARTHENWARE POTTERY.

During the industrial revolution in the late 1800s, with the advent of railway and steamboat travel, cheeses were at first merely wrapped in sheets of paper and spread out on beds of straw; jostling and (mis)handling along the way led to the poor condition in which many of them arrived. One man who loved one particular cheese changed all that: an engineer and a native of Normandy, France, Eugène Ridel, invented the distinctly circular, stapled, poplar wood box into which Camembert fits so snugly and which has become beloved for its ingenuity as well as its quaintness. See CAMEMBERT DE NORMANDIE and TYROSEMIOPHILE. Ridel's development coincided perfectly with the progress of the industrial revolution, and as railways and steamboats spread across Europe, Camembert could travel without damage and even ripen slowly along the way. Thus packaged and protected, the cheese won the hearts and stomachs of a global market. The wooden box also inspired cheesemakers around the world, including in America: when pasteurized process cheese was patented by James L. Kraft in 1916, it was sent around the world in five-pound foil-wrapped "loaves" fitted into wooden boxes. The Kraft cheese box became a nifty storage container for families around the country. See KRAFT FOODS.

Today artisanal cheesemakers have revived the tradition by packaging even the smallest handmade cheeses in boxes that may remain open or come fitted with lids. To be sure, eBay keeps the tradition alive as well: an antique dealer sold a nineteenth-century Blum Bros. cheese box from a dairy in Marshfield, Wisconsin, for $540.

See also INDUSTRIALIZATION.

Boisard, Pierre. *Camembert: A National Myth*. Translated by Richard Miller. Berkeley: University of California Press, 2003. English translation of *Le Camembert: Mythe National* (Paris: Calmann-Lévy, 1992).
Ehlers, Steve, and Jeanette Hurt. *The Complete Idiot's Guide to Cheeses of the World*. Indianapolis, Ind.: Alpha, 2008.
Kraft. "The History of Kraft Foods Inc." http://web.mit.edu/allanmc/www/kraftfoods.pdf.
Schweikart, Larry, and Lynne Pierson Doti. *American Entrepreneur: The Fascinating Stories of the People Who Defined Business in the United States*. New York: American Management, 2010.

Kelly Alexander

cheesecakes date back at least two thousand years, and were originally luxury foods. For over a thousand years, young white cheeses, such as quark in Germany, Poland, and the Netherlands, tvorog in Russia, Anari in Cyprus, Lor in Turkey, manouri in Greece, ricotta in Italy, brocciu in Corsica, and Urdă in Romania, have been used in cheesecakes. See FRESH CHEESES and PLAKOUS.

The first cheesecake recipe in England appeared in the first English cookery book *Forme of Cury* (*cury* was the Old English word for cooking) in 1390. Cheesecakes were ideal for utilizing the curds produced by sour milk and every region in England developed its own distinct type of cheesecake.

The types of English cheeses used were nessh (soft fresh curd cheese), ruayn or rewain (soft, rich cream cheese), green cheese (moist, soft cheese named for its newness), and Brie imported from France. The cheese was mixed with egg yolks, sugar, and spices and sometimes finely chopped meat and dried fruits, then baked in a pastry case. Another type was made with hard cheese, sliced and covered with milk or water for several hours to soften it, before it was pulverized with sugar and butter and baked in a pastry case.

The cheese tarts of the Middle Ages continued almost unchanged into the Tudor (1485–1603) and Elizabethan (1533–1603) periods. Soft cheeses and curds were also used to make boiled and baked puddings, omitting the pastry case altogether, and by the seventeenth century these were commonly known as cheesecakes. Wine, rosewater, dried fruits, spices, and sugar were frequently included in the filling. Yet cheese tarts continued to be popular in some English regions, particularly in Yorkshire, where creamy curd tarts are still sold in bakers' shops throughout the county.

Today the world has an endless variety of cheesecakes made with indigenous soft cheeses, which are especially popular at Easter. The traditional Easter tart of Naples, *La pastiera*, for instance is made with ricotta, spices, and candied fruit baked in a pastry case. Russian *pashka* (the name actually means Easter) is a rich, creamy dessert made from curd cheese, sugar, butter, and eggs. More elaborate versions include cream, spices, dried and candied fruits, and liqueurs. The mixture is molded in a four-sided wooden mold, which gives the dessert its unique truncated pyramid shape.

Modern cheesecakes, especially in the United States and Canada, are sometimes unbaked; they have a cookie-crumb base (almost invariably graham cracker) and an uncooked velvety filling of rich cream cheese, sometimes set with gelatin. New York–style cheesecake uses cream cheese and double (heavy) or sour cream for a smooth, dense texture; Chicago-style cheesecakes are firm outside and creamy inside; Philadelphia-style cheesecake is creamy but somewhat light in texture; and Pennsylvania Dutch cheesecake uses soft pot cheese or cup cheese with large curds, similar to cottage cheese. Other contemporary cheesecakes include those from Japan, which are made with cream cheese and are a cross between a custard and a soufflé, with a very light soft texture.

Artusi, Pellegrino. *The Science of Cooking and the Art of Eating Well*. Venice: Marsilio, 1997.

Bradley, R. *The Country Housewife and Lady's Director*. London: Bradley, 1728.

Craig, Elizabeth. *Court Favourites*. London: Andre Deutsch, 1953, pp. 109–110.

Giacosa, Ilaria Gozzini. *A Taste of Ancient Rome*. Chicago: University of Chicago Press, 1992.

Maher, Barbara. *Cakes*. New York: DK Publishing, 1997.

Pettigrew, Jane. *The Festive Table*. London: Pavilion, 1990.

Roden, Claudia. *The Book of Jewish Food: An Odyssey from Samarkand to New York*. New York: Knopf, 1996.

Carol Wilson

cheesecloth, though also a broad term describing a light fabric for various cooking and cleaning applications, owes its name, first and foremost, to its use in making cheese. Traditionally, this low-thread count woven fabric has been made of cotton or linen, but synthetic material alternatives are also common in cheese production. Cotton cheesecloth is available in a variety of thread counts, ranging from coarser weaves in the range of 60 threads per inch (2.5 centimeters) to finer fabrics at 90 threads per inch (2.5 centimeters). Muslin or butter muslin, a similar fabric, has a dense weave of finer threads and is best for cheeses with a small particle size. Precut pieces of cheesecloth are available in a range of sizes that fit the intended application, and are usually stitched at the edge to prevent fraying. Cheesecloth is also available unfinished by the foot (or meter). Most cheesecloth for cheesemaking purposes is an unbleached light-beige color. Synthetic cheesecloth is typically made of nylon, which is often blue or white.

Fresh chèvre draining in cheesecloth at Rawson Brook Dairy in Monterey, Massachusetts. © KATE ARDING

Cheesecloth provides a porous channel that facilitates the drainage of whey from new curd. Cheesecloth is appropriate in the production of most styles of cheese, but works best when the weave matches the particle size of the curd. Coarser cloth is appropriate for harder cheeses that are lower in moisture at hooping, while finer cloth is best for draining soft-ripened and fresh cheeses. Cheesecloth is usually sized to fit cheese hoops. Before hooping, cheesemakers drape the wet cloth on the interior of the mold, leaving additional material at the top of the mold to fold over the surface of the new cheese before placing the follower, which is the removable top of the mold. When pulled tightly around the cheese in the hoop, cheesecloth creates a smooth and uniform rind surface. Cheesecloth may also be stitched into draining bags, which are commonly used for draining fresh spreadable cheeses. In some cases, cheesecloth is used to form a cheese wheel by binding the curd into a cohesive mass within the fabric without the aid of a hoop. See HOOP.

Cheesemaking traditions that employ a vat with no bottom outlet typically use cheesecloth to remove the curd mass from the vessel. The cloth is passed under the curd mass, which is then hoisted to drain the whey and move the curd into a hoop. During pressing, cheesecloth aids in draining excess moisture by providing a space between the cheese and interior hoop surface to wick whey from the wheel. Bandaged-wrapped cheeses are swathed in cheesecloth traditionally adhered and were sealed with lard.

Because they are made from fine organic material, cheesemakers must maintain a high level of sanitation with cheesecloth. Producers often dedicate a washing machine to cheesecloth and sterilize the fabric by boiling before use.

Caldwell, Gianaclis. *Mastering Artisan Cheesemaking: The Ultimate Guide for Home-Scale and Market Producer.* White River Junction, Vt.: Chelsea Green, 2012. See pp. 112–114.
Kindstedt, Paul. *American Farmstead Cheese: The Complete Guide to Making and Selling Artisan Cheeses.* White River Junction, Vt.: Chelsea Green, 2005. See pp. 104–107, 213.

Brent A. Wasser

A **cheese course** is an assemblage of cheeses served, usually with accompaniments, as a course in a restaurant. A cheese plate may be offered as an appetizer or, in the European tradition, after the main courses. At increasingly popular "cheese bars," cheese is often served as the meal itself, with inventive accompaniments and pairings with appropriate beverages. In more formal restaurants, and those that specialize in cheese, a cheese plate is often served from an elaborately appointed wheeled cart, with cheeses cut to order for patrons tableside, by the maitre d' or a server specifically trained for the task. Some restaurants serve a "composed" cheese course: a savory or sweet dish featuring a particular cheese served toward the end of the meal. Cheese plates are also increasingly popular in the home.

In Europe, notably in France, cheese is typically served after the main meal, before a sweet dessert. The origins of this practice are obscure but certainly old. Jean Anthelme Brillat-Savarin, the famed eighteenth-century French gastronome called cheese "the foremost among desserts," even declaring famously, "A meal without cheese is like a beautiful woman with only one eye." The late English cheesemonger and author Patrick Rance wrote, "the constant miracle of a French meal…is the pleasurable reawakening of hunger at the sight and smell of cheese." See BRILLAT-SAVARIN and RANCE, PATRICK.

No rules govern the number of cheeses on a cheese plate. Some restaurants offer just a single cheese, served with an accompaniment. Some provide patrons a cheese menu, allowing them to choose the number and types of cheeses they prefer. Restaurants with well-stocked cheese carts might serve a dozen cheeses or more to a large table.

The types of cheeses on a cheese plate vary widely, of course, but there are some generally held guidelines. Restaurants will often choose, or guide their patrons to consider in their selection, cheeses of complementary or contrasting flavors and textures, sizes and shapes, milks and styles. Some restaurants may offer an exclusively local or regional selection of cheeses, or cheeses that are available only, or are at their best, in a particular season. Patrons are often advised to eat their selection of cheeses in a particular order, progressing from milder to stronger, what the French cheesemonger Pierre Androuët called the "sacrosanct rule of the crescendo." See ANDROUËT, PIERRE.

See also CHEESE ACCOMPANIMENTS and RESTAURANT DINING.

Androuët, Pierre. *Guide de Fromage*. Paris: Stock, 1971.
Brillat-Savarin, Jean-Anthelme. *The Physiology of Taste*. Berkeley, Calif.: Counterpoint, 1994.
McCalman, Max, and David Gibbons. *The Cheese Plate*. New York: Clarkson Potter, 2002.
Rance, Patrick. *The French Cheese Book*. London: Macmillan, 1989.

Matthew Rubiner

Copeland, Robert. *Ceramic Bygones*. Princes Risborough, U.K.: Shire, 2000.
Opus Antiques. "Why Have a Cheese Coaster?" 30 September 2011. http://www.opusantiques.co.uk/#!Why-Have-A-Cheese-Coaster/hptjl/56a77cc50cf22a80b02771cb.
Woolliscroft, Pam. "Spode and Cheese Dishes." *Spode History*, 28 December 2013. http://spodehistory.blogspot.com/2013/12/spode-and-cheese-dishes.html.

Robin Watson

cheese cradles, or cheese coasters, have long provided secure yet mobile resting places for single wheels of cheese, used from cave to table. For aging dry cheeses slatted natural-wood cradles provide a secure resting space as well as good air circulation and drainage. In the eighteenth and nineteenth centuries, when cheese consumption was an important part of farm families' daily life, a cheese cradle was an essential piece for carrying and serving cheese. One example from a nineteenth-century Montgomery County, Pennsylvania, estate was crafted as a basket with long handles from which it could be suspended.

For the wealthy cheese cradles produced in precious woods or fine porcelain conveyed status. Durable and colorful toleware cheese cradles, likely used mostly in shops, showcased cheese and made portioning easy for merchants. Crescent-shape cheese cradles designed for the home could hold half or whole wheels of farmhouse cheeses that measured 18–24 inches (45–60 centimeters) in diameter. Nestled upright on their side, the cheese was cut from the top into wedges.

In the Georgian era (1714–1830) "cheese coasters" were large wooden dishes shaped to hold whole Double and or Single Gloucester cheeses on their side. See GLOUCESTER. Mounted on tiny, often leather-covered brass casters, these dishes would be passed up and down the table, and chunks of the cheese could be cut off as the coaster passed by, making them, in effect, the lazy Susans of their day. A bit of baize on the bottom of casterless cradles helped to facilitate movement and protected tabletops from scratching. Some featured an offset divider that allowed for side-by-side serving of cheese and hunks of bread.

Cheese cradles are rare today, but in 2002 Spode released a worldwide limited-edition reproduction of an elegant Georgian cheese cradle produced in its Rome pattern from 1811.

cheese curds are bite-sized pieces of fresh cheese intended for consumption within a few hours, or at most, a few days after production. They are primarily a regional food, made only where Cheddar cheese is made daily, and are most common in Wisconsin, home to more than 120 cheese factories. The hallmark of fresh cheese curds is both their springy texture and their squeak, caused by the curd's long, elastic protein strands that rub against tooth enamel. After cheese curds are made, they only maintain their squeak for about twelve hours.

Cheese curds are often purchased directly from cheesemakers at cheese factories and farmer's markets. They are eaten as a snack, right out of the bag, and may be flavored with garlic and dill, jalapeno peppers, and spice blends. In the Midwestern United States, cheese curds are often coated in batter and deep-fried. This local delicacy is popular at carnivals and fairs, as well as in restaurants and taverns. They are commonly served with a side of ranch dressing. Frozen prebattered cheese curds ready to be deep-fried are also found in Midwestern grocery stores.

One of the largest producers of cheese curds in the United States is Ellsworth Dairy Cooperative in Ellsworth, Wisconsin. More than 450 dairy farm owners ship milk to the factory, where it is made into 160,000 pounds (73,000 kilograms) of cheese curds daily. The factory is so well known for its curd production that in 1984, Wisconsin Governor Anthony S. Earl proclaimed Ellsworth the "Cheese Curd Capital of Wisconsin."

In rural Quebec, Canada, cheese curds are a main ingredient in poutine, a dish made with French fries topped with fresh cheese curds and covered with brown gravy. The dish is served at pubs and diners, and was once considered "fast food." Today, it is enjoying a gourmet renaissance and is found in restaurants across Montreal and New England. See POUTINE.

See also WISCONSIN.

Ellsworth Cooperative Creamery. http://www
.ellsworthcheesecurds.com.

Jeanne Carpenter

cheese factor is the name given to a middleman who connects producers of cheese to large scale purchasers. As a highly portable form of food, cheese for sale traveled great distances as early as the fourteenth century. Because of the need for mercantile agents who could requisition and transport products, cheese factors established a role in European trade in medieval times. The term appears in advertisements in periodical literature, according to the *Oxford English Dictionary*, in 1707, suggesting that factors were successful as experienced negotiators of rural commodities. Considerable numbers based their warehouses in regional provincial towns and shipped their supplies (sometimes including bacon and other pork products) to major cities and across oceans. Increasing demand for cheese by the navy, charitable bodies, and urban institutions with refectories catapulted cheese factors into positions of relative power and authority by the end of the eighteenth century.

The cheese factor influenced the production of cheese by bridging the distance between consumer and producer, claiming (like merchants in the textile trade) to have superior knowledge of the latest trends in products and buyer preferences. The desire for colored cheeses, for example, led factors to provide rural dairywomen with high-quality coloring materials (usually yellow and green). Cheese factors wished for predictable and uniform products, difficult to for typical dairywomen to achieve, given the many circumstances dependent upon region, weather, and customary practices. At the high end of production, greater authority rested in the cheesemaker, but in the case of more ordinary supplies, factors with commercial clout introduced recommendations and encouraged experimentation in bringing about desired results. In modernizing economies, factories eliminated the need for all but the specialty purveyor by the mid-nineteenth century. Today's artisanal farmsteads sometimes rely on affineurs and cheesemongers who fulfill the role of factor and may be referred to as such; examples of this include Neal's Yard, Hervé Mons, and Guffanti. See GUFFANTI and NEAL'S YARD DAIRY.

See also CHEESEMONGER.

Blundel, Richard, and Angela Tregear. "From Artisans to 'Factories': The Interpenetration of Craft and Industry in English Cheese-Making, 1650–1950." *Enterprise and Society* 7, no. 4 (December 2006): 705–739.

Paxson, Heather. *The Life of Cheese: Crafting Food and Value in America*. Berkeley: University of California Press, 2013.

Valenze, Deborah. *Milk: A Local and Global History*. New Haven, Conn.: Yale University Press, 2011.

Deborah Valenze

cheese fly

See *PIOPHILA CASEI*.

Designing a **cheese grading** program is an important step required to ensure consistently high-quality cheese. A thorough cheese grading program will help cheesemakers to understand and track the sensory quality of their finished product and the evolution of cheese during the aging process. A successful system should include a way to record, track, and organize both cheese manufacturing and grading data. The following steps can help build an effective grading program.

Defining the Cheese Profile

An effective grading program contains a system for measuring the degree of a defect or characteristic. While it is recommended to rely on industry accepted grading terminology (e.g., short or long texture, nutty, fruity, acid, bitter flavor), in order to communicate to other dairy professionals, in-house terms can be effective as long as they are well defined and consistent. A system for measuring the severity of a defect or characteristic is commonly accomplished through use of a numerical scale or adjectives. Examples include use of a scale from one to five or terms such as "very slight," "slight," and "definite." Once the terms and scale are defined, the cheesemaker or affineur uses these to define the ideal profile for their cheese at the end of the aging process. Two products may contain the same qualitative descriptors, but they may differ markedly in the intensity of each, thus resulting in quite different and easily distinctive sensory profiles or pictures of each product (Meilgaard et al., 2000). This is your chance to determine how intense you want your blue cheese, the degree of sulfide flavor in your Cheddar, or the balance of sweet and nutty notes in your Gouda.

Determining the Grading Schedule and Evaluation Data

A successful grading program requires a consistent evaluation schedule. At each step in the grading process, the cheesemaker or affineur needs to set the ideal degree of defects and characteristics to determine if the cheese is on track. Over time, this will help determine if a cheese needs to exit the inventory early or remain longer than typical (Bodyfelt and Tobias, 1988). Setting ideal profile benchmarks at each step in the grading will alert the grader to issues and allow for immediate corrective actions in either the make or aging process, as shown in the following example:

> A cheesemaker schedules a Cheddar grading at the start of every two months of aging. By the start of the fourth grading month, numerous make dates are grading out with higher levels of sour flavor and short body than the ideal defined profile at four months. After evaluating the make records, the cheesemaker notices the pH at salting has not been on target. The appropriate changes are made and the current aggressive cheese is slated for earlier release from the inventory.

The program should also include a list of pertinent information easily available during the evaluation. This often includes past grading information, cheesemaker notes from the make day, ingredient list, and green cheese compositional analytics. While the analytics will not always determine the outcome of cheese aging, they can trigger flags suggesting that a cheese may require special attention. During the grading, it is important to not only document your evaluation notes but also record data about the aging environment. Documenting temperature, humidity, and proximity to other cheeses can help explain aging issues. For best results, cheese ripening requires carefully controlled temperature and humidity (Clark, 2009).

Improving Cheese Quality

Inconsistent cheese quality throughout the cheesemaking or aging process can be expensive to fix and detrimental to building a customer base. Attempting to correct issues in-house, through an ingredient supplier, or hiring a consultant is much less time-consuming and less expensive when detailed grading results document the issues at different stages during the aging process. A good quality practice is to earmark cheese make dates that are of ideal quality. Not only will this make selecting customer and contest samples easier but can serve as a fast, accurate reference when discussing your ideal profile at a specific age. This is illustrated in the following example:

> A cheesemaker explains to a culture supplier that the Camembert rind thickness is five out of five at three weeks and is more effective when he can show them the earmarked sample of three out of five rind thickness at three weeks, which is ideal for their cheese.

Assembling a Grading Team

Depending on the size of an organization, it may not be possible to have all important quality stakeholders available for each evaluation. Grading sessions should occasionally be planned with all stakeholders in order to review cheese quality and affirm that all members are experiencing the same defects and degree of severity. Recommended stakeholders can include the following:

- *Cheesemakers*: need to know how to correct the make in order to get the best grading results.
- *Affineurs*: need to know how to monitor aging environment.
- *Sales*: should know how to evaluate and communicate cheese issues found at the retail level.
- *Quality control*: must learn to communicate quality issues to all stakeholders involved.

There are different grading tools or approaches that can be used. However, independently of the final approach used, a consistent component to always consider in your grading program is the training part. Sensory and grading training help to understand the sensory descriptors to evaluate and ensure that the grading team is "calibrated" and consistent. This is illustrated in the following sample grading sheet:

Cheddar Grading Sheet   Grade date: 3/17/2015

Grading Descriptors

Manufacturing Date	Vat	Profile	1	2	3	4	Notes
6/1/2013	One	Two-year super aged	Slight acid	Pronounced sweet	Slight short	Acid spots	
1/5/2015	Two	Medium	Very slight weak	Very slight lacks			Age additional one month

Room Temperature	44
Room Humidity	80%

See also CHEESE TASTINGS; FLAVOR; SENSORY ANALYSIS; and TEXTURE.

Bodyfelt, F. W., J. Tobias, and G. Malcolm Trout. *The Sensory Evaluation of Dairy Products.* New York: Van Nostrand Reinhold, 1988. See p. 347.

Clark, S. *The Sensory Evaluation of Dairy Products.* 2d ed. New York: Springer, 2008.

Meilgaard, Morton, Gail Vance Civille, and B. Thomas Carr. "Descriptive Analysis Techniques." In *Sensory Evaluation Techniques*, 3d ed., Boca Raton, Fla.: CRC, 1999. See p. 161.

Craig Gile

A **cheese grater** is a device used to pulverize cheese into small particles. Hand graters typically consist of a metal plate containing perforations with sharp elevated edges on one side, across which the cheese is scraped. When cheese is forced through the perforations particles are created with size distributions that are determined by the perforation dimensions and the force applied to the cheese during scraping. When elongated cheese particles with cylindrical or irregular cross sections are produced they are often referred to as shreds. Variants of the hand grater include a perforated metal drum that is rotated with hand crank as cheese is forced through the perforations by hand. At the industrial scale, mechanized graters that use pneumatic pistons to force cheese through rotating perforated plates, or high-speed centrifugation to force cheese through networks of knives, are common.

The development of the first cheese graters in antiquity represented a culinary milestone because graters greatly expanded the versatility of cheese in daily life. In surface area and particle number, grating enabled cheese to be distributed uniformly throughout prepared foods in controlled portions, and to heat up and melt uniformly in cooked dishes. Grating thus opened new doors to using cheese as an ingredient in cooking and as a condiment. See FUNCTIONAL PROPERTIES and MELTING.

The earliest plausible evidence of cheese graters derives from southern Mesopotamia around the third millennium B.C.E. Small, shallow perforated ceramic bowls containing very rough inside surfaces around the perforations may have been used for grating hard sun-dried cheese (a practice that is still common in some regions of the Near East and Africa), though it is impossible to say for certain. Other early evidence includes the discovery of a Hittite term on cuneiform clay tablets that date from the second millennium B.C.E. that can be translated "crumbled" or "grated" cheese.

However the first definitive evidence for cheese graters occurs in the Greek-dominated Aegean region, where graters have been recovered from ninth-century-B.C.E. tombs of aristocratic warriors. Indeed, cheese graters seemed to have occupied a special place in Greek aristocratic culture in the form of a drinking custom that may have resembled the Homeric account in *The Iliad* referred to as "Nestor's Cup." In this passage Nestor's beautiful slave girl grates goat cheese into a large ornate cup containing Pramnian wine. See HOMER. The Greek aristocratic veneration of cheese graters and their apparent use in drinking rituals spread to the Italian peninsula by the seventh century B.C.E.; bronze graters have been recovered from numerous aristocratic Italian tombs from around his time. By the classical Greek period grated sheep's and goat's milk cheeses were widely popular throughout the northern Mediterranean, and by the time of the Roman Empire, the bronze or iron cheese grater was a standard kitchen utensil. See ANCIENT CIVILIZATIONS.

During the medieval period a new type of cow's milk cheese, exquisitely suitable for grating, arose near the region of Parma in the Po River valley of northern Italy. The large hard, extremely durable grana cheeses that became known as Parmigiano by the fourteenth century C.E. were exported far and wide from the Renaissance on, achieving remarkable notoriety that has continued to this day. See PARMIGIANO REGGIANO.

See also SHREDDING.

Kindstedt, Paul. *Cheese and Culture: A History of Cheese and Its Place in Western Civilization*. White River Junction, Vt.: Chelsea Green, 2012.
Ridgway, David. "Nestor's Cup and the Etruscans." *Oxford Journal of Archaeology* 16 (1997): 325–344.

Paul S. Kindstedt

cheese harp

See CHEESE KNIFE.

A **cheesehead** hat is a bright yellow foam hat shaped as a cheese wedge, worn by Wisconsin sporting fans to show state pride, as well as an overall nickname referring to a person from Wisconsin. The "Cheesehead" trademark is owned by Foamation Inc. of St. Francis, Wisconsin. The first Cheesehead hats were manufactured in 1987, and today are sold in all fifty states and in more than thirty nations.

Since its humble beginnings as just a triangular cheese wedge, Cheesehead hats are now found in a variety of shapes, including cowboy hats, sombreros, crowns, baseball hats, and even graduation caps. Classic Cheeseheads are often worn at Green Bay Packer games, where proud Wisconsinites show their solidarity with their National Football League (NFL) home team by attending football games in the autumn and early winter and sitting on hard benches in freezing temperatures. In football season, foam Cheesehead hats both keep Packer fans warm and show faith in the home team. Cheeseheads are also often given by Wisconsinites to visiting dignitaries as fun gifts.

The classic Cheesehead hat weighs about 1 pound (one-half of a kilogram), sports 25 holes, and measures about 14 inches (36 centimeters) on each side.

See also WISCONSIN.

Foamation Inc. http://www.cheesehead.com.

Jeanne Carpenter

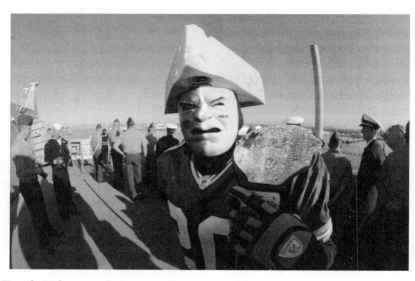

Navy ensign Timothy Mahoney on the USS *Green Bay* as it departs from Naval Base San Diego in 2011. Mahoney, a native of Green Bay, Wisconsin, showed his solidarity with the 2011 Super Bowl–winning football team and the ship named after the city he hails from by donning a cheesehead. © SGT. CHRISTOPHER O'QUIN

The Cheese Importers Association of America (CIAA) is a nonprofit trade association formed in 1945 whose membership comprises the vast majority of the firms engaged in the business of importing, selling, promoting, and distributing cheese and cheese products in the United States.

When key leaders got together in 1945 their goal was to help secure cheese supplies from Europe and South America to the United States, thus reopening trading after years of shortages and restrictions due to the war. Today CIAA serves its members, the world dairy community, and—ultimately—the end consumer by helping to facilitate the efficient import of dairy products from around the world into the United States. The CIAA endeavors to support dairy trade within the context of compliance with international trade agreements and all applicable US regulations. Through advocacy, seminars, and regular bulletins, CIAA keeps its members and interested parties informed of ongoing developments that affect the dairy trade community and maintains active contacts with government officials worldwide. Every other year the organization hosts a trip to Paris for the SIAL show, the world's largest food exhibition, to educate its members and their customers about new food products and innovative packaging from around the world.

See also WORLD WAR II.

Cheese Importers Association of America. http://www.theciaa.org.

Dominique Delugeau

A **cheese iron,** alternatively called a cheese trier, tester, or borer, is a traditional tool used to extract

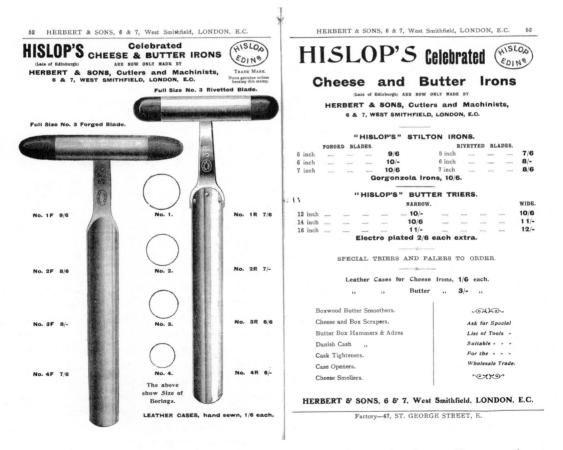

A 1905 catalogue for the London-based equipment company Herbert & Sons lists their cheese and butter irons for sale. Cheese irons, also called tryers, allow the wielder to extract a core sample from a wheel or block of cheese to help determine its degree of ripeness. COURTESY OF HERBERT & SONS

a core sample from a wheel or block of cheese during maturation, selection, judging, or grading. Made today of stainless steel, a cheese iron consists of a semicircular, sometimes tapered, blade with a crossbar handle at one end and is typically 5–8 inches (12–20 centimeters) long. The width, or "bore," can vary depending on the type of cheese sampled, with one nineteenth-century London manufacturer advertising more than thirty different irons for cheeses as varied as Stilton, Gorgonzola, Parmesan, and Gouda. Cutting open whole, large format cheeses in order to gain a sample was both wasteful and expensive, but the alternatives weren't much better when one considers tales of buyers who would "stand, or jump from one [cheese] to another…and obtained its 'feel' by the relative firmness and springiness with which it resisted the live weight" (Cheke 1959, p. 264). In light of such practices the introduction of the cheese iron offered an effective, and less destructive, means of assessment for cheesemakers, merchants and mongers alike.

In some instances, such as Parmigiano Reggiano or Comté, the handle end of a cheese iron can be employed as a hammer that, if tapped at various points on a cheese's exterior, can reveal, to an experienced ear, cracks, fissures, or holes within the body of a cheese. See MARTELLETTO. To extract a sample, the iron is first sanitized to prevent contamination and then pushed carefully into the cheese (sometimes, prior to ironing, it is necessary to score the rind with a knife, particularly with clothbound varieties), twisted through one full turn, and slowly extracted revealing the cheese in cross section from the tip of the iron to the base of the handle. The cheese is initially assessed by its resistance to the iron, with softer, high-moisture cheeses being less resistant than their harder, low-moisture counterparts. The sample is then judged by its aroma, any obvious visual defects, and the back of the iron examined for residue—further indication of the cheese's moisture content. A piece of cheese is taken from the tip of the iron and often rolled between thumb and forefinger to give a sense of its body and to release more aromatic compounds. Once tasted, the iron and remaining sample can be reinserted and the "plug" smeared with a small amount of residual cheese to limit any subsequent air penetration and bluing. Despite being one of the most important tools a cheese

professional may have, ironing is generally kept to a minimum to avoid unnecessary damage to cheeses.

See also CHEESE GRADING and MATURING.

Cheke, Val. *The Story of Cheese-Making in Britain.* London: Routledge & Kegan, 1959.
Kindstedt, Paul, and the Vermont Cheese Council. *American Farmstead Cheese: The Complete Guide to Making and Selling Artisan Cheese.* White River Junction, Vt.: Chelsea Green, 2005.

Chris George

cheese knife dimensions conform to vat shapes and to curd handling practices to achieve the most uniform cutting of the curd. The contemporary counterpart to early tools fashioned from debarked branches, now sometimes referred to as a curd knife, consists of wires stretched on a metal or wooden frame, much like those on a musical instrument. As the wires pass through the curd, they slice it into uniform pieces. Cheese knives are used almost exclusively in the production of enzymatically set cheeses. Cheese knife design is specific to cheese styles and to other equipment, such as the vats. See VATS. The spacing of the wires determines the size of the resulting curd, although the horizontal or vertical orientation of the wires determines how the curd will be cut. The wire spacing for soft-ripened cheeses is typically wider than that of hard cheeses. Wire spacing ranges from approximately 0.3–0.6 inches (8–15 millimeters).

Most cheese knives are made of stainless steel. The Italian *spino*, a voluminous wire sphere mounted on a long handle, acts as a kind of whisk as it passes through the curd repeatedly to yield very small curd pieces. The Alpine or Swiss harp design involves a series of vertical wires strung on cross pieces mounted on the end of a long pole. The pole extends the cheesemaker's reach to the bottom of the deep copper vat traditionally used in Alp cheesemaking. Cheesemakers change the orientation of the harp while slowly yet deftly passing it through the curd, resulting in uniform curd pieces.

Cheese knives designed for flat-bottomed Cheddar vats are often square, with a handle perpendicular to the wires that facilitates pulling the tool through the shallow curd. Cheesemakers often have two cheese knives, one strung vertically and one strung horizontally. To cut the curd into evenly sized pieces, they first draw the horizontal cheese harp through the curd, then follow with the vertical cheese harp to create long strands, and finally cut across the vat with the vertical wires to yield uniformly sized cubes. Some cheese knife designs combine vertical and horizontal wires into one large knife that is reversed during cutting. Cheesemakers using round Dutch vats will cut in arcs and segments of the circular vat from one side to the other. This motion causes the cut curd to well up as the harp circulates in the vat. Curd knives in automated production replace the thin wires of the cheese knife with sturdy blades. One side of the blade is sharp, while the other side is blunt. When run in reverse, the blunt end agitates the curd without cutting it further.

Kammerlehner, Josef. *Cheese Technology*. Freising, Germany: self-published, 2009. See pp. 257–259.
Scott, R., R. K. Robinson, and R. A. Wilbey. *Cheesemaking Practice*. Gaithersburg, Md.: Aspen, 1998. See pp. 171–173.

Brent A. Wasser

cheesemaker's lung is a form of hypersensitivity pneumonitis (HP), also known as extrinsic allergic alveolitis (EAA). A complex pulmonary syndrome mediated by the immune system, HP is caused by the inhalation of a wide variety of organic antigens (bacteria, fungi, or animal proteins) to which the individual has been previously sensitized. The most frequent type of HP or EAA, and the best known in rural environments, is farmer's lung disease. Another, rarer form, also associated with rural environments, is cheese-worker's disease or cheese-washer's disease. The atmosphere in the cheese-maturing cellars is thought to be an important trigger.

Despite the lack of both occupational-exposure limit values and standardized measuring methods, Simon and Duquenne (2014) suggest that the most exposed workers in the factory, cheese brushers, cheese washers, and cheese packagers, may face an immunoallergic or even toxinic risk. *Penicillium casei* usually the responsible antigen, and precipitating antibodies against this and other molds can be detected in the patients' serum. See PENICILLIUM.

Cheesemaker's lung can be categorized as acute, subacute, or chronic based on the duration of the illness, which can manifest with tightness of the chest, cough, and malaise. Acute forms of the disease usually resolve easily, but chronic forms, which are caused by persistent low-grade exposure, have a poor prognosis.

Reducing fungal concentrations in the cellar is a challenge, since the presence of airborne fungi is essential to the cheese-maturation process. Preventive measures include supplying and improving ventilation and implementing a respiratory protection program.

See also FUNGI and HYGIENE.

Crawford, Michael, and Sheilagh Crawford. *What We Eat Today*. London: Spearman, 1972.
Galland, C., et al. "Cheese-washer's Disease: A Current Stable Form of Extrinsic Allergic Alveolitis in a Rural Setting." *Revue des Maladies Respiratoires* 8 (1991): 381–386.
Martinet, Y., H. Anthoine, and G. Petiet. "Les maladies respiratoires d'origine professionnelle." In *Collection médecine du travail*, 2d ed., edited by Elsevier Masson, pp. 93–103. Paris: Elsevier Masson, 1999.
Simon, X., and P. Duquenne. "Assessment of Workers' Exposure to Bioaerosols in a French Cheese Factory." *Annals of Occupational Hygiene* 58 (2014): 677–692.
UCSF Medical Center. "Hypersensitivity Signs and Symptoms." http://www.ucsfhealth.org/conditions/hypersensitivity_pneumonitis/signs_and_symptoms.html.

Janvier Gasana

cheese mites are small arthropods that can be found living on the surfaces of naturally aged cheese where fungi are also present. They are generally only seen in aged cheeses that develop a natural rind. Two different genera of mites are most commonly found in cheese: *Tyrophagus* and *Acarus*. These mites are naturally found in soils where they feed on fungi and can also be found in other stored foods where proteins and fats are abundant. In some cheeses, such as Mimolette, the activities of cheese mites are encouraged because they are thought to impart particular flavor properties to the cheeses as well as to promote drying. See MIMOLETTE. But for most cheese producers, mites are a microscopic nuisance that requires substantial labor to control. If mites are present in large numbers and begin to dig into the cheese paste, they can allow molds to enter the paste, leading to undesirable discoloration and changes in flavor.

A scanning electron microscope image of a cheese mite (*Tyrophagus casei*) at 170× resolution. Cheese mites are small arthropods that can be found on the surface of naturally aged cheeses. These creatures are generally considered to be a pest and are regularly blown or vacuumed away, but for a few cheeses, including Mimolette and Milbenkäse ("mite cheese"), they are essential to the flavor. NATURAL HISTORY MUSEUM, LONDON, UK / BRIDGEMAN IMAGES

The patina of dust and pitted, moon-like appearance of the rind on this cheese is characteristic of cheese mite damage. © KATE ARDING

Mites are particularly problematic for long-aged cheeses, such as clothbound Cheddars, that grow sizable populations of mold on their rinds. See CLOTHBOUND CHEESES. As these cheeses age on a shelf, a dusty layer begins to form on and around the cheese. This telltale dust is a combination of the actual mites and their feces. Cheesemakers use a variety of approaches such as high-powered vacuums or air blowers to continually remove the mites and keep their populations low. Some cheesemakers use diatomaceous earth as an anti-mite treatment. As the mites eat the diatomaceous earth, which consists of fossilized hard-shelled diatoms, it shreds their digestive tracts and kills them. But because these mites are widespread in the environment, once a new cheese plant is established and mold begins to grow on aging cheeses, mites will appear despite the best efforts to keep an aging facility immaculately clean. See VACUUMING.

Cheese mites have documented negative health impacts for human beings, including allergic reactions such as atopic dermatitis or asthma and more chronic conditions such as "cheesemaker's lung." But these relatively rare mite sensitivities are generally restricted to cheese producers and affineurs who spend large amounts of time in cheese facilities where mites are in abundance. Because small portions of cheeses generally only contain small numbers of cheese mites, the currently documented health risk for cheese consumers is very low. See CHEESE-MAKER'S LUNG.

Despite their abundance in some types of cheese and their potential negative economic impact, scientists still have many questions about the biology of these mites in the cheese environment. Do they prefer specific types of molds over others? Have cheese mites become especially adapted to the cheese environment relative to their wild soil ancestors, making them even more difficult to control? We can only hope that future acarologists (scientists who study mites) will provide us with the answers.

See also DEFECTS and NATURAL-RIND CHEESES.

Anderson, Nelson Paul, and Harold C. Fishman. "Cheese Mite Dermatitis Occurring in the United States." *Archives of Dermatology and Syphilology* 57 (1948): 227–234.

Eales, Nellie B. "The Life History and Economy of the Cheese Mites." *Annals of Applied Biology* 4 (1917): 28–35.

Melnyk, J. P., et al. "Identification of Cheese Mite Species Inoculated on Mimolette and Milbenkase Cheese through Cryogenic Scanning Electron Microscopy." *Journal of Dairy Science* 93 (2010): 3461–3468.

Benjamin E. Wolfe

A **cheesemonger** is anyone who specializes in the sale of cheese. Although the earliest sellers of cheese are likely to have been the producers—farmers selling their cheese at market, for example—specialization would have come once the selling of cheese had reached a certain level of organization and scale.

Formalization, Regulation, and Market Changes

In England, large towns and cities—London in particular—acted as catalysts by providing concentrated sites of demand for all manner of goods. With such demand came commercial opportunity and a merchant class to exploit it. Gradually, those concentrating on particular trades would have formed their own associations or guilds to formalize their businesses. By 1377, the cheesemongers of London were significant enough to be charged by the Lord Mayor" to "amend" the price of cheese and butter. They presented their strategy in a list of ordinances. In essence, these precluded the sale of cheese outside designated market areas, these being "Ledenhalle [sic], or the market between St Nicholas Shambles and Neugate [sic], and nowhere else." The sale of cheese could thus be monitored, and illicit trade punished by fines or even imprisonment. Policing the sale of cheese in this way ruled out the detrimental practices of "forestalling" and "regrating," both of which involved the sale of cheese to middlemen, thus forcing the eventual market price up. Today we would see this as "normal" business practice and the interventions of the cheesemongers as decidedly self-motivated and protectionist. However, the wording of the ordinance reveals a more civic-minded attitude prevalent in trade in this period.

The fear of social unrest haunted the governments of this time. In a predominantly agricultural economy, the threat of harvest failure could easily lead to social upheaval. By stressing the needs of the "commonality," or more specifically in this instance, "the working-men in London," the cheesemongers' ordinance sought to balance the exigencies of trade with the notion of a "just price" for the consumer. However, the ordinance ends with the recommendation that two members of the cheesemongers' trade be charged each year at the feast of St. Michael with overseeing the fines collected by the ordinance. Although the penalties for misuse of office were severe, such self-regulation was open to abuse and could never allay the suspicion that the ideal of a "just price" for the consumer must never compromise the right price for the cheesemonger.

With the rise in population during the Tudor period (1485–1603)—London's population quadrupled in the seventy years before 1605—pressure to feed the populace required new mechanisms of procurement, distribution, and sale. Although the open market system provided transparent transaction and effective policing, it was logistically cumbersome. Private marketing, on the other hand, liberated an entrepreneurial spirit and dynamism that transformed the way agricultural goods were bought and sold. There was no revolution from one to the other, however; rather, private marketing experienced a gradual evolution running parallel with the open market system. Adherents of the latter viewed proponents of the former with much suspicion; the private marketeers could be accused of "forestalling" and "ingrating," after all, which the cheesemongers had sought ordinances to prevent. The private marketeers were viewed with suspicion for their "secrecy of dealing," and much moral ire was directed toward their selfishness and lack of civic responsibility. However, then as now, private marketeers were defined by their willingness to accept risk. It could be argued that groups like the London cheesemongers built up capital resources to mitigate such risk on the back of the open market system, which they controlled. Be that as it may, they still had much to lose.

Increasing Power and Conflicts

During the time of the Stuarts (1603–1714), the London cheesemongers employed an extensive network of "factors" (distributors) to procure cheese. By and large the cheese factors were local people, often itinerant buyers and sellers themselves, with extensive knowledge of the goods produced in their own area. On behalf of their employers in London, they would agree to the purchase of cheese and butter from the farmer and organize subsequent storage and transport. Such was the effectiveness of this system that in 1640 Charles I entrusted the supply of cheese and butter for the whole of his northern armies—hitherto organized in-house by the royal purveyor—to a group of five London cheesemongers.

Toward the end of the seventeenth century, the London cheesemongers owned a fleet of sixteen ships and had established warehouses on the banks of the river Dee near Chester and on the river Thames at Buscot in Oxfordshire, from where two thousand to three thousand tons of Single Gloucester cheese was shipped to London annually. They also had storage facilities near the great market of Uttoxeter in Staffordshire. Increasingly, they were able to transport cheese to other regions, in addition to London, and they developed an export trade—Welsh butter to La Rochelle, Suffolk cheese to French and Flemish ports along the English Channel. But the relationship between cheesemonger and farmer was not always cordial. On 19 November 1690, a petition of "Gentlemen, Land Owners, and Farmers of the County of Suffolke [sic]" was presented before the House of Commons. It stated that whereas an act had been passed to safeguard the trade in butter during the reign of Charles II, nothing comparable had been done to safeguard the trade in cheese. Moreover, the London cheesemongers, in a move to increase butter production in Suffolk, had encouraged the production of flett (skimmed) cheese. The petitioners noted that the quantity of butter sold with such cheese is increased to "four firkins in a load; but the cheese thereby becomes only fit for slaves." Cheese of such quality, stated the petition, would only result in a general prejudice against the entire industry. More damaging still was the practice of employing a "weigher" in most of the seaports to reweigh cheese already bought and approved at the "seller's house." Invariably, faults were found with the result that the final price paid to the seller was less than what had been originally agreed. In 1692, the main grievance of the petition was met by a law guaranteeing that the price agreed between seller and buyer would not later be altered. The London cheesemongers also clashed with the port authorities of Liverpool. The port claimed shipper's dues and the cheesemongers disputed this, claiming they were exempt under charter. Other disputes broke out with the city of Chester over maintaining the navigability of the river Dee and with the port of Dover seeking exemption from dues paid for the upkeep of the pier and harbor wall. What all these disputes reveal is how powerful the London cheesemongers had become in the seventeenth and eighteenth centuries. They might not have been an affiliated body, but they could come together both to establish an elaborate trading network and to fight for their collective interest when threatened.

In the late sixteenth and early seventeenth centuries, most cheese would still have been bought at a market. The number of London markets grew rapidly in this period. Although the London cheesemongers would have had a prominent presence, they would not have had a monopoly. Primary producers, independent factors, and even other trades would also have supplied cheese (two London fishmongers in the early 1600s employed factors in Suffolk for the supply of cheese and butter—two of whom were beaten and robbed of £40 at a farm in South Elmham). By the eighteenth century, some cheesemongers wanted to move beyond the market. In the *Calendar of State Papers* in the time of William III, mention is given of a case put forward by a cheesemonger for the right to have his own "distinctive shop." This implies that cheese was sold in shops already, but as part of a range of goods much like a modern grocery store. Increasingly, records of this period refer to cheesemongers plying their trade from fixed residences—some rented for the duration of trade, but most domicile dwellings. Whether these shopworking cheesemongers specialized solely in cheese

The two-handed cheese knife allows cheesemongers better leverage when cutting cheese. © KATE ARDING

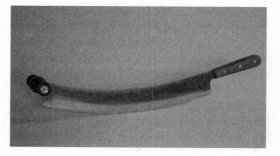

The Gouda knife, designed to cut through large, hard-textured wheels of cheese, adds a curved blade for a gentle rocking action. © KATE ARDING

is debatable. Certainly, in the nineteenth century there is mention of some doubling as tea dealers and grocers. Indeed, as late as 1851, the most common trade on the south side of Kensington High Street was the joint "grocer and cheesemonger." But, whether they diversified their wares or not, in the Victorian era the cheesemonger was a familiar sight on the streets of London. So, where did they all go? Why is it that the familiar trades on the high street—butcher, baker, greengrocer—do not include the cheesemonger?

The Cheesemongers' Decline and Resurgence

A Combination of Causes

A number of factors have likely contributed to the decline in numbers of independent retail cheesemongers. On the supply side, the growing reliance on cheese produced in factories led to standardization of the product and less need for the specialized knowledge of the cheesemonger. The tendency in the farmhouse sector to sell younger and younger cheese to compete with cheap foreign imports equally reduced the consumer's need for the specialist. Both tendencies would have driven down prices, making profitability harder except by increasing volume. The growth of the grocery trade, where grocers like the ones on Kensington High Street increased the range of goods on offer to include cheese, would have offered unwanted competition. (The first branch of Sainsbury's, a well-known British supermarket, replaced a cheesemonger's shop in the Islington borough of London). Equally, the growth in sales of liquid milk would have reduced the amount of overall cheese produced, entailed greater reliance on imports, and weakened the relationship with the traditional cheese factor.

The privations of war in the twentieth century led to greater control of the food sector by the government. Standardized grading, storage, and manufacture were seen as essential to ensure that the population got an appropriate supply of nutrients. Once introduced, these requirements were not repealed. Although some have argued that the public's taste for cheese changed in this period, it seems more plausible that it reflected a general decline in the availability of interesting cheeses.

The growth in convenience shopping after World War II dealt the final blow for the traditional cheese shop and undermined the cheesemongering talents of the local grocer. But the predictable fare served

up in the 1950s and 1960s was not to everyone's liking. In his indefatigable classic *The Great British Cheese Book*, Patrick Rance ends with a message to shopkeepers. In it he says, "Good cheese has been almost killed by lack of understanding and care among politicians, bureaucrats, dairymen and retailers. It can only be raised back to health by a professional, indeed a vocational, attitude in those who wish to put things right and make their living by doing so." One retailer who wanted to put things right was Neal's Yard Dairy.

The Road to Recovery

In the late 1970s, the small company had been making yogurt and soft cheese at their shop in Covent Garden. They bought cheese from wholesalers too—the range typical of what was expected of a "cheese shop." The soft cheese and yogurt invariably differed from batch to batch. Far from being a problem, it allowed the staff to explain why this might be, to discuss the differences, and to mull over preferences. The transaction, as a consequence, was far more dynamic than selling the wholesale cheese of which so little was known. It helped build customer loyalty and solid sales as well. What if the same could be done for all the cheese they sold? Eventually, a cheesemaker from Devon by the name of Hilary Charnley sent a Caerphilly-style cheese called Devon Garland to Neal's Yard Dairy. When Randolph Hodgson, then the owner of Neal's, tasted it, he was pleasantly surprised by its flavor and character. Hodgson decided to pay Charnley a visit. What he found was an independent cheesemaker, operating on a small scale much like he was back in London. She was not alone, either. Charnley put Hodgson in contact with other small cheesemakers in the area. Soon he was making regular visits to small-scale and traditional cheesemakers around the country. He would taste the cheese on the farm or warehouse and select the ones he wanted to buy. And in doing so, he reinvented the role of the cheese factor. Unlike his forebears in the seventeenth and eighteenth centuries, though, he was also the one who transported, stored, and ripened the cheese, and finally sold it to the customer. The knowledge built up from meeting the producers, tasting the cheese, and working out why one batch tasted different than another was brought back with him to London.

The resurgence of the cheesemonger mirrors the increased demand for artisanal cheese. This is most evident in places like the United Kingdom and the

United States, where the cheese market is dominated by large-scale production and multiple retailing, through brick-and-mortar stores as well as through the Internet. In places like France, however, where a greater proportion of cheese is artisanal in origin, the craft of the cheesemonger has remained reasonably intact. Nevertheless, the growing influence of multiple retailers on cheese production in France has led to the formation of La Fédération des Fromagers de France, an organization representing more than three thousand cheesemongers throughout the country. There is also an annual competition, the Concours National des Fromagers, designed to instill greater levels of pride and proficiency in the profession. In the United States, the American Cheese Society has developed a Certified Cheese Professional Exam to help establish greater levels of professionalism among cheesemongers. The effectiveness of these initiatives is ultimately gauged over the counter when the cheesemonger hands a sample of cheese to a customer and enacts the vocational imperative suggested by Patrick Rance.

See also CHEESE FACTOR; GUILDS; HODGSON, RANDOLPH; NEAL'S YARD DAIRY; RANCE, PATRICK; and TRADE (HISTORICAL).

British History Online. http://www.british-history.ac.uk.
Cheke, Val. *The Story of Cheese-Making in Britain.* London: Routledge & Kegan Paul, 1959.
Fussell, G. E. *The English Dairy Farmer, 1500–1900.* London: Frank Cass, 1966.
The Journals of the House of Commons. Vol. 10: *From December the 26th, 1688, to October the 26th, 1693.* London: House of Commons, 1803, p. 475.
Rance, Patrick. *The Great British Cheese Book.* London: Macmillan, 1982.
Thirsk, Joan. *The Agrarian History of England and Wales.* Vol. 4: *1500–1640.* Cambridge, U.K.: Cambridge University Press, 1967.

Dominic Coyte

The **Cheesemonger Invitational** (CMI) is a competition that tests the knowledge and skills of the nation's top cheesemongers. Twice a year, participants battle to take home the highest honor in cheese retailing through an epic multiround event dubbed "the Burning Man of cheese." The mission of CMI is to elevate best practices across the specialty cheese industry and bring the cheese community at large together under one roof.

In a short time, CMI has become a mainstay, unprecedented in its ability to highlight the innumerable acts of art and self-expression that emanate from behind a cheese counter. First debuting in 2009, CMI is the brainchild of third-generation cheese importer and distributor, Adam Moskowitz. As of 2014, CMI is a bicoastal affair, taking place in San Francisco in the winter and Queens, New York, every summer. Moskowitz hosts the East Coast competition in Larkin Cold Storage, his family's 40,000–square foot (3,716–square meter) storage and logistics facility. He's also the master of ceremonies for the event in both locales, drawing larger crowds each time—both a testament to his contagious passion for cheese and the increasing respect for cheesemongering as a profession.

A mere nine contestants competed at the inaugural CMI and in its current iteration fifty plus cheesemongers demonstrate their cutting, wrapping, pairing, and selling talents to a team of seasoned judges. The final rounds are open to the public and deliver an inordinately raucous crowd of cheese professionals and enthusiasts whose smiles only widen as they celebrate amidst drool inducing all-you-can-eat towers of the world's most revered cheeses.

Moskowitz, together with dedicated cohosts, aspires to host CMI more frequently in an effort to build awareness and shine a spotlight on the role of cheesemongers as the final, crucial link in caring for and communicating the story of cheese. Typically a sold out event, CMI stands as an integral moment fostering heritage among the specialty cheese community.

See also COMPETITIONS.

Lipinski, Jed. "New York's Prince of Cheese." *Capital,* 22 June 2012, http://www.politico.com/states/new-york/albany/story/2012/06/new-yorks-prince-of-cheese-067223.

Tess McNamara

cheese powder is a product obtained by spray-drying a liquid made from ground cheese, water, and additional ingredients to form a dispersed solid. In the first step of production, bulk cheese is cut into smaller pieces, and the rind, if present, is removed. These pieces are deposited in a cheese grinder along with water. Emulsifying salts are also added to improve the stability of the product. Additional ingredients such as flavors, colors, preservatives, starch, salt, and milkfat may also be added. The resulting mixture has an average solids content of approximately 35 percent.

The mixture is blended and pasteurized at approximately 176°F (80°C), then homogenized to form a stable emulsion. The homogenized mixture is pumped to a spray-dryer inlet, where it is immediately atomized into a stream of rapidly flowing hot air. The liquid droplets quickly dry to a powder, which is then collected, cooled, and packaged. An anticaking agent may be added at this point. The final moisture content of the powder is approximately 4–5 percent.

The process of spray-drying causes volatilization (evaporation) of a portion of the cheese flavor. Older, more flavorful cheese is often used to partially compensate for this. Cheese powder has several advantages over natural cheese. It can oxidize over time but has a longer shelf life—approximately one year under cool, dry storage conditions. In addition, its decreased shipping weight and versatility of use make cheese powder a common way to introduce cheese flavor into other food products such as soups, sauces, dips, and snack crackers.

See also INDUSTRIAL; KRAFT FOODS; and SHELF LIFE.

Fox, P. F., et al. *Fundamentals of Cheese Science.* Gaithersburg, Md.: Aspen, 2000.
Gehrig, M. "Wisconsin Process Cheese Seminar." Short course presented through the Wisconsin Center for Dairy Research, Madison, Wisconsin, 23–24 February 2015.

Dana D. Wolle

The **Cheese School of San Francisco** grew out of a series of cheese appreciation classes run by a San Francisco gourmet shop, Cheese Plus. Responding to the growing demand for classes, a store employee, Sara Vivenzio, launched the Cheese School in 2006 in a nearby office space, later moving to a historic building in the North Beach neighborhood. One guest teacher during the early years was a world-renowned cheese advocate and educator, Daphne Zepos. In time, Zepos became a regular instructor at the school.

In 2011 Zepos and Kiri Fisher, a fellow cheese devotee, purchased the school and expanded its offerings. Driven by her passion for professional cheese education, Zepos determined to provide a program that went beyond consumer-focused tasting classes and proceeded to develop curricula for cheesemongers, buyers, affineurs, and aspiring professionals. Although Zepos died the following year, Fisher continued building the business into the country's only independent cheese school of its scope and caliber.

In 2013 Fisher moved operations to a refurbished carriage house in the Mission District of San Francisco, where the Cheese School offers an array of classes for consumers and professionals alike. Fisher, her staff, and visiting experts present a full schedule of tasting and pairing classes, hands-on cheesemaking workshops, and 3- and 4-day intensive programs. They even run a catering operation that highlights their culinary achievements as well as furthering their educational objective.

See also CALIFORNIA.

The Cheese School of San Francisco. http://www.thecheeseschool.com.

Molly Stevens

The **cheese slicer** in classic modern form, in which a thin handle gives way to a wide shovel-shaped base in which a slit with a knife's edge rests on the bottom, is so taken for granted, sitting as it does in the pages of our gourmet catalogs and kitchenware emporiums and at the bottom of our knife drawers and shelves of serving implements, that it takes effort to see it as the ingenious object of technology that it is. It was invented in 1925 by the Norwegian cabinetmaker Thor Bjørklund, who was frustrated by how difficult it was to uniformly slice hard cheeses with a knife. Inspired by the plane he had been using to shape wood, Bjørklund created the "ostehøvel" as a rudimentary tool that nevertheless became a kitchen sensation. They are so indispensible that more than 50 million have been sold worldwide.

Bjørklund registered his patent as consisting of four pieces: a blade with a cutting edge, a neck, a spike, and a handle. The slicer, sometimes called a "plane," is the little serving tool that could: although the inventor himself passed away in 1975, his eponymous factory in Lillehammer continues to produce cheese slicers (along with cake and fish servers and salad sets) into the twenty-first century. Bjørklund's cheese slicer has been the inspiration for most of the cheese slicers on the market today, including the so-called "cheese wire" type that has a thin handle with two tines at the top that are the poles for a firm wire stretched between them. There is even a website called cheeseslicing.com, the online marketplace of a cheese shop in Sheboygan, Wisconsin; its best-selling cheese slicer design is one in which a wire handle and arm is attached to a marble slab on which the cheese rests.

See also CHEESE GRATER and CHEESE WIRE.

Baugh, Ingeborg Hydle, et al. *Gudrun's Kitchen*. Madison: Wisconsin Historical Society, 2011.

Bjørklund. "History." http://www.bjorklund-1925.no/index.php/en/about-us/51-history.

CheeseSlicing.com. http://www.cheeseslicing.com.

Kipfer, Barbara Ann. *The Culinarian: A Kitchen Desk Reference*. Hoboken, N.J.: Wiley, 2011.

"Thor Bjørklund: Cheese Slicer." *Tasteful Inventions*, 11 February 2010. http://tasteful-inventions.blogspot.com/2010/02/thor-bjrklund-cheese-slicer.html.

Kelly Alexander

cheese tastings breed cheese lovers. Tastings tend to attract chefs; caterers; foodies; friends with shared food or travel interests; and growing numbers of young professionals eager to learn more about pairing cheese with wine, beer, and spirits.

Establishing a Tasting Series

Tastings are often tailored around a specific theme. A regional tasting might highlight the cheeses of, for example, Switzerland or Spain or—more specifically—cheeses of the Jura region of France. Seasonal tastings can highlight a fall flight of Alp-style cheeses or create awareness around spring goat cheeses, giving tasters a chance to learn about the qualities of spring milk from pasture-raised animals. Vertical tastings offer participants a chance to sample the milk of an animal, followed by a series of cheeses from that species' milk as it expresses itself at different points during the aging process. There are also comparative tastings that concentrate on a single style (e.g., Cheddar) and explore how different makers use the same basic recipe to create variations. Finally, tastings can be pairing-focused to illustrate how cheeses respond to particular flavors, like smoky Scotches or hoppy beers. Home enthusiasts can also explore suggested tasting flights, such as those listed in *Mastering Cheese* (2009), by Max McCalman and David Gibbons.

Elements of a Cheese Tasting

Increasingly, tasting events contextualize cheese by offering a guided experience. A presenter may share stories about the producers, show illustrative photos from farms or cheese caves, discuss the steps of cheese production, and demystify terminology (e.g., terroir, raw milk, bloomy rind, artisan vs. farmstead) or debunk erroneous assumptions. The guide should also lead tasters by the tongue. Below are some helpful questions to explore while leading a tasting.

What Do You Notice about the Appearance of the Cheese?

What color is the rind? What texture is it? Is the rind formed naturally, bound by cloth or bark, or wrapped in foil or wax? Taking a moment to read the rind visually can lead into discussing bacterial cultures or offering tips on selecting cheeses for optimal ripeness. Juxtaposing a young downy-white wheel of Brie next to a ripe Brie with beige striations can be very illuminating. By noting the difference in appearance—and perhaps even feel the difference by giving both wheels a gentle squeeze—tasters can gain new appreciation for the care that cheesemakers and mongers (and *affineurs*) put into their work.

How Does the Cheese Smell? Does the Smell Remind You of Other Foods?

Since much of what we taste begins in the nose, it's instructive to take a big whiff before biting down. "Sensory bridges" reminiscent of typical smells in cheese may be offered to familiar foods: butter, yogurt, fresh mushrooms, hay or freshly mown grass, yeast, roasted peanuts, wet stone, bacon, toffee, just to name a few. These items can be passed around in covered bowls or simply named to reinforce sensory connections. Once tasters link the smell of Camembert to the scent of mushrooms, for example, it's unlikely that they will forget the association. Such visual cues can also be used to introduce basic pairing theory, for example, a mushroomy Camembert will likely pair well with other mild flavors that complement mushrooms, such as caramelized onions or green vegetables. A cheese that is evocative of wet stone will likely pair well with wines that reinforce that flavor through minerality.

How Does It Taste?

Professional tasters use a multistep process to judge cheeses that can be helpful to impart, even at a tasting among novices. Here are some steps for tasting a cheese: (1) hold the cheese, inspect it visually, tactilely, and by smelling it; (2) take a bite of cheese and warm it on the tongue for a moment; (3) inhale through the mouth to pull air in over the surface of the cheese, then close the mouth and exhale through the nose to bring the scent of the cheese into the upper palate; (4) begin to chew, working the cheese around in the mouth from front to back and side to side; (5) try to identify a "flavor journey," an initial flavor, followed by secondary and tertiary flavors, capped off by an aftertaste. Like a fine wine, a great cheese releases layers of flavor, so distinguishing between a multilayered wedge of cheese and a one-note hunk can tell you a lot about the quality of what you're eating. Not all cheeses take you on a journey, but the best ones do.

Building a Tasting Vocabulary

Becoming a skilled taster hinges on identifying flavors and textures and then being able to communicate those observations to others. A number of sources offer lexicons, including Laura Werlin's *The New American Cheese: Profiles of America's Great Cheesemakers and Recipes for Cooking with Cheese* (2000), which has an exceptional two-page list of "favorable" and "unfavorable" cheese terms. The Internet also offers myriad cheese tasting charts and flavor wheels. See FLAVOR WHEEL.

Best Practices for Setting up a Cheese Tasting

Start with fresh-cut wedges of cheese, avoiding slices that have been sitting in plastic wrap. When using wrapped cheese, scrape away the portion of the cheese in contact with plastic to avoid off tastes. Serve cheese at room temperature, at which time it is most flavorful. Serve each guest 1–2 ounces (28–57 grams) of each cheese, depending on the number of cheeses at the tasting. It is most effective to serve no more than four to six cheeses at a tasting. Slice the cheese in such a way that tasters experience both the rind and the center of the wheel (usually this means cutting slender wedge-shaped slices); even rindless cheeses have a different taste along the edge than they do at their core since the edges are exposed to air. In addition to any drinks that are provided as part of the pairing, serve filtered water to cleanse the palate between bites. Slices of plain baguette or melon are good for this, too. Avoid serving herbed crackers or anything spicy that will overpower subtle flavors. Finally, have fun! Developing one's palate takes time and should be pleasurable, not arduous or overwhelming.

See also BEER PAIRING and WINE PAIRING.

McCalman, Max, and David Gibbons. *Mastering Cheese: Lessons for Connoisseurship from a Maître Fromager.* New York: Clarkson Potter, 2009.
Werlin, Laura. *The New American Cheese: Profiles of America's Greatest Cheesemakers and Recipes for Cooking with Cheese.* New York: Stewart, Tabori & Chang, 2000.

Tenaya Darlington

cheese wire is a thin length of stainless or carbon steel attached to a wooden, marble, or stainless steel device that is intended for cutting the perfect wedge of cheese without it adhering to a cutting apparatus. Cheese wires belong in all cheesemongers' and cheese graders' tool bags.

Cheese wires are used to cut evenly and cleanly semisoft to hard pieces of cheese, through the outside rind to the inside base of the cheese. Cheese wires slice without crushing the cheese's exterior or interior. It is best to temper cheese by bringing it to room temperature before cutting, as the cheese will become more flexible. This allows the cheese body to give to slight pressure, which prevents crushing.

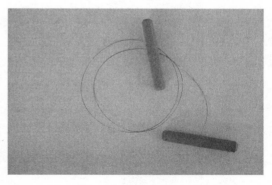

Cheese wires cut through cheese with much less drag than a knife blade, similar to a potter cutting through clay. Cheese wires are ideal for densely textured cheeses, like Cheddar, but are also good for soft cheeses where the cheesemonger does not wish to crush the cheese body by dragging a large knife through it. © KATE ARDING

What are key points to cutting the perfect slice? Always cut with a smooth motion and clean the wires between uses. Cleaning the cheese wire between cutting different types of cheese will prevent unwanted contamination of indigenous mold spores, flavorings, and colors from one cheese to another. Remember: presentation is key to a beautiful cheese board. Cutting boards that come affixed with a cheese wire can be found in a variety of exotic woods, stainless steel, or glass.

Occasionally cheese wires will need to be replaced, as they may stretch and break. When purchasing and replacing cheese wires, know the length of wire required and the type of handle apparatus the wire will be affixed to.

Industrial cheese cutting wires, such as the high carbon steel alloy spring-tempered music wire, make an art form of reducing trim waste, and enable a monger to cut cheese into various lengths, sizes, and dimensions at full scale. Industrial cheese cutting wires absorb different stress levels from different cheese densities and block sizes. Cheese wires attached to a harp that aligns numerous cheese wires on one cutting device cut cheese into sticks, wedges, cubes, and blocks. Typical manufacturing cheese cutting equipment will adjust the cutting wires to block widths and lengths for customization.

See also CHEESE GRATER and CHEESE SLICER.

CheeseSlicing.com. http://www.cheeseslicing.com.

Jill E. Allen

Cheez Whiz is a cheese-based dip invented, produced, and sold by Kraft Foods and traditionally presented in a shelf-stable glass jar. It was developed in the 1950s to provide an easy, no-work alternative to the labor-intensive sauce used in Welsh rarebit, a then-popular dish consisting of cheese sauce on toast. Cheez Whiz's mild, approachable flavor was designed to appeal to a broad audience. Cheez Whiz has lost prominence in Kraft's family of cheese-related products as the company innovated to meet market demands for more modern products. Nevertheless, it continues to represent an early example of Kraft's approach to bringing cheese products to the masses and earns the company more than $100 million in annual revenues. Cheez Whiz is popularly associated with Philadelphia ("Philly") cheesesteak sandwiches, and many famous purveyors and devotees of the sandwich insist that the proper cheesesteak preparation is "whiz wit," or with Cheez Whiz and onions. In 2015 Kraft released two spray-can Cheez Whiz flavors, Sharp Cheddar and Buffalo Cheddar.

See also KRAFT FOODS; KRAFT, JAMES L.; and WELSH RABBIT.

A tactical quantity of Cheez Whiz ready to deploy at a Yankee Stadium food truck in 2013. © PETER BURKA

Kraft Foods. "Cheez Whiz." http://www
    .kraftfoodsgroup.com/Brands/largest-brands/
    brands-C/Pages/cheez-whiz.aspx.
Moss, Michael. *Salt, Sugar, Fat: How the Food Giants
    Hooked Us*. New York: Random House, 2013.

Jessica A. B. Galen

Cheshire cheese (U.K.) is a hard cow's milk cheese made originally in the northwest of England in the county of Cheshire and surrounding areas. Known as an "acid" cheese, a traditional Cheshire has a tangy flavor with savory background notes and an open, flaky texture. Today, most Cheshire is made in creameries specializing in the manufacture of a number of English territorial cheeses. See TERRI-TORIAL. Production efficiencies tend to highlight similarities rather than differences between cheeses. As a result, most of today's creamery Cheshire is broadly similar to other "acid" cheeses like Wensleydale and Lancashire: crumbly texture, acid flavor. Though increasingly few, there are still a number of farmhouse Cheshire makers producing more distinct, traditional cheese from the milk of their own animals, but only the Appleby family of Hawkstone, Shropshire, still uses raw milk.

Cheshire's Age of Glory

Today's meager farmhouse Cheshire sector belies a glorious past. The Cheshire Plain—an area extending to Shropshire, Staffordshire, Warwickshire, and parts of Clwyd in northeastern Wales—has long been a fertile dairy region. A mix of marls, salt beds, and boulder clay deposits have enriched the soil with what many believe to be the main source of the cheese's unique flavor. Indeed, Thomas Fuller in his *History of the Worthies*, 1662, noted that anyone attempting to make Cheshire elsewhere "should fetch their ground too." Fuller also observed that Cheshire was "best for quality and quantity." Indeed, by the mid-seventeenth century, trade in Cheshire cheese had expanded beyond the local towns and markets of the northwest, most notably to London. Hitherto, London had received the bulk of its dairy produce from Suffolk. In the early years of the seventeenth century, the Suffolk dairy producers increased butter production to meet demand at the expense of their whole milk cheese. When cattle disease and floods in the late 1640s further reduced the supply of whole

milk for cheese, thereby leading to higher prices, the capital's cheese merchants began to look elsewhere. In 1650 the first cheese ship arrived in London from Chester with 20 tons of cheese on board; by the 1670s, the trade in cheese shipped from Chester had reached 1,000 tons a year. This figure doubled in a decade, and according to William Maitland in his 1756 *History of London*, 5,760 tons of Cheshire cheese were shipped to London in 1729.

Trade of this magnitude required organization. By the 1730s the London Cheesemongers (thought by some contemporaries to be a price-fixing cartel) owned their own ships for cargoing cheese. Warehouses were set up in and around Chester, and a network of factors, or buyers(descendants from itinerant sellers), were employed to buy the best quality cheese to fill them. See CHEESE FACTORS. The cheese was transported by barge from the warehouse to the ships anchored at Parkgate at the mouth of the river Dee. From there, the ships sailed south, around Cornwall, and then up the English Channel to London.

Cheshire's Remarkable Decline

The Cheshire cheese industry grew from the late seventeenth century well into the nineteenth. But its preeminence as the country's finest cheesemaking

A traditional Cheshire cheese made by the Appleby family of Hawkstone, Shropshire, the only farmhouse Cheshire maker to use raw milk. © KATE ARDING

region was coming under threat. One Cheshire maker reported in the *Farmer's Magazine* of 1862 that demand for fine old Cheshire had dropped dramatically since the late 1830s. This complaint was common throughout the Cheshire-making region. The London Cheesemongers were quick to point out that the percentage of the finest Cheshire selling in the West End had now been replaced by Cheddar. This squeeze on the quality end of the market reduced the Cheshire makers' margin to such an extent that the effort to mature cheeses for as long as a year was not financially viable. Many producers switched from making long-maturing cheese to versions that ripened for only around four to five months. Though of fine quality, these cheeses invariably came into competition with cheap American imports, which had been increasing their market share since embracing the factory system in the 1850s. In many respects, the adaptability of the Cheshire recipe, which allowed it to change to meet the needs of the market, also led to its destruction.

During the nineteenth century, advances in the dairy industry were also having a marked effect on how cheeses were made. The wider use of thermometers, jacketed vats, and cheese harps as well as a growing understanding of the role that acidity played in cheesemaking increased the cheesemakers' level of control. In the Cheshire region it allowed for three styles of cheese: early, medium, and late ripening. The principle differentiating the three was whey retention: the more whey that was retained, the quicker the cheese ripened. In essence, this was all a matter of acidity, for the retention of whey increases the potential acid development in the curd. In flavor terms, sharper, more acidic, and lactic flavors predominated in the early ripening cheese; mellow, rich, and more complex flavors, in the late. When the market for late-ripening Cheshire dropped in favor of Cheddar, the Cheshire cheesemakers' switch to medium or even early ripening cheese provoked the downward spiral of Cheshire's popularity.

In 1900 there were more than two thousand farms making Cheshire cheese. Although trains now carried the cheese to London, the bulk of it was consumed in the industrial conurbations of the North. Small farms amalgamated, and milk processing fell into fewer and fewer hands. By 1939 just over four hundred farms produced roughly 38 percent of Cheshire cheese; the rest was made in creameries. World War II and government control of food production reduced the number of farms further to

around forty. See MILK MARKETING BOARDS. As the century wore on, more cheese was made in creameries, and what came out of the farm was liable to be waxed (to prevent bluing), further restricting its maturing potential. This decline was mirrored throughout the British farmhouse sector in the twentieth century. What was unique to Cheshire was the height from which it fell. In many respects Cheshire's decline is a story played out in many industries, where the remedy for falling demand is to reduce costs (the switch from late to early ripening). Others, over the years, have pointed out that quality established demand in the first place. There is no reason why it could not do so again in the future.

See also CHEDDAR and UNITED KINGDOM.

Cheke, Val. *The Story of Cheese-Making in Britain.* London: Routledge & Kegan Paul, 1959.
Fussell, G. E. *The English Dairy Farmer, 1500–1900.* London: Frank Cass, 1966.
Long, James, and John Benson. *Cheese and Cheese-Making, Butter and Milk.* London: Chapman and Hall, 1896. Facsimile reprinted by Applewood Books (Bedford, Mass.: 2007).

Dominic Coyte

Cheshire cheese (U.S.)

Cheshire cheese (U.S.) refers to a single cheese collectively fashioned in 1801, by the townspeople of Cheshire, Massachusetts. The final product, a 14-foot (4.3 meters), 1,235-pound (560 kilograms) wheel, was presented to President Thomas Jefferson on 1 January 1802. The cheese, created by the dairywomen of the town under the leadership of Elder John Leland, was crafted to represent three things. First, it was a way for the townspeople to show their support of Jefferson. Second, it highlighted a traditional craft that was starting to lose favor in the Washington area. Third, it reaffirmed the northern citizens' antislavery position.

Community members in Cheshire, Massachusetts, were part of a religious minority of Republican Baptists; Federalists held the party majority in New England at the time, and the Congregationalist church was the larger, legally established faith. Cheshire residents were subject to legal discrimination under this system. So, one aim of the cheesemaking demonstration was to support President Jefferson and his promise to protect religious freedoms.

The cheese also marked an economic shift. Local dairies surrounding the nation's capital were now supplying the White House with cheese, replacing products that were traditionally brought in from Connecticut and Massachusetts. The success of these new southern dairies was owed to their utilization of enslaved labor. Cheshire residents spotlighted this by noting in the letter presented to Jefferson that their namesake cheese was produced without enslaved labor.

A monument commemorating the historic Cheshire cheese was erected in the Massachusetts town in 1940. The concrete replica of a cheese press honors John Leland, the pastor who coordinated the cheesemaking and who presented the final cheese to Jefferson.

Russell, Howard S. *A Long, Deep Furrow: Three Centuries of Farming in New England.* Hanover, N.H.: University Press of New England, 1976.

Kristina Nies

chèvre, pronounced "shev," is a French word that is derived from the Latin *capra*, the feminine version of *caper*, or goat. Comparable terms in Italian would be *caprino* or in Spanish, *cabra*. Chèvre is used to refer to cheese made from goat's milk in France, especially the Loire Valley and Poitou, or elsewhere when made in a French style. Chèvre comes in a range of ages, textures, shapes, and flavors. It can be soft, young, and spreadable, or aged with more rind development and concentration of flavor. Often the name of the cheese gives an indication of its shape, and also where it is from, for example, Crottin de Chavignol or Boule de Quercy. Some other common shapes, in French, include *buche, pave, coeur, brique, lingot, cloche, rond, pyramide,* and *tomme.*

Classic examples of aged chèvre include Chabichou de Poitou, bucheron, Valencay, Pouligny St. Pierre, and Selles sur Cher. Tomme de chèvre, a larger format aged chèvre, is made all around France and is often named to denote origin: Tomme de Chèvre de Pyrénées, for example, or Tomme de Chèvre de Savoie. Also considered chèvre is fresh goat cheese, such as that made in the United States by Laura Chenel or Vermont Creamery.

See also GOAT.

Jenkins, Steven. *Cheese Primer.* New York: Workman, 1996.
Michelson, Patricia. *Cheese: Exploring Taste and Tradition.* Layton, Utah: Gibbs Smith, 2010.
Masui, Kazuko, and Tomoko Yamada. *French Cheeses: The Visual Guide to More Than 350 Cheeses from Every Region of France.* London: Dorling Kindersley, 2000.

Weinzweig, Ari. *Zingerman's Guide to Good Eating: How to Choose the Best Bread, Cheeses, Olive Oil, Pasta, Chocolate, and Much More.* Boston: Rux Martin/Houghton Mifflin Harcourt, 2003.

Sarah Spira

Chevrotin is an unpasteurized, washed-rind goat's milk cheese made in the Savoie and Haute-Savoie region of France. It is exclusively produced at a farmstead level and entirely made by hand.

Chevrotin was first mentioned during the seventeenth century, coexisting with its cousin Reblochon. See REBLOCHON. Inhabitants of the Savoie Mountains would own a few goats to provide meat and milk for family use. The excess milk would be used for the production of Chevrotin for their own consumption, later developing into larger production levels.

There are twenty-two producers and four affineurs of Chevrotin in the region as of 2015 and an AOC for Chevrotin des Aravis was created in 2002 and its European equivalent AOP in 2005. Each producer has on average a herd of 60 goats but can have up to 120. The AOC states that the predominant breed must be the Alpine Chamoisée at a minimum of 80 percent of the herd, however they can also use Noire de Savoie. The goats graze on lush pastures at an altitude of 6,100 feet (2,000 meters) and they must be out on pasture for five to six months of the year. They must graze in the zone of the appellation, which is limited to the Massif du Mont Blanc, Aravis, Chablais, and Bauges. Approximately 70 tons of Chevrotin are produced annually.

The cheese is based on a Reblochon recipe, comprising slightly smaller rounds weighing 9–12 ounces (250–350 grams) with a diameter of 4–5 inches (9–12 centimeters) and a height of 1–2 inches (3–4.5 centimeters). Chevrotin uses rennet coagulation, taking thirty to forty minutes. The curds are cut to the size of rice grains in the vat while being stirred vigorously. The curd is placed into cloth-lined molds, and as soon as each mold is full, the cheeses are flipped immediately.

The cheeses are pressed for twelve hours, and after they are removed from their molds, they are placed on spruce shelves, turned every day for seven days, and washed by hand. They are matured in caves, and turned every day for twenty-one days. All these procedures must happen on the farm on which they are made. As with Reblochon, the process is extremely quick, which means that the cheeses can be made twice a day in tune with milking. The production of Chevrotin is also in tune with the natural milking cycles of the goats. The kids are born in the winter when the goats give the largest quantity of milk; however this is also the time when the cheeses are limited and most difficult to find. The cheese is most abundant throughout the summer and autumn months.

The cheeses have a pinkish exterior with a dusting of fine white mold. They have a gentle Caprine aroma, with woody and farmyard notes. The paste is a brilliant ivory color, with a soft, unctuous paste, slight elasticity when younger, and small holes present. On the palate, the cheese is mild; however there is still a gentle goatiness to it with a fine balance of salt, some vegetal notes, and alpine flowers. Chevrotin pairs well with Cotes du Rhone, Bandol, and Saint-Joseph; however it is best eaten with light Savoie wines.

See also FRANCE and HAUTE-SAVOIE.

Harbutt, Juliet. *World Cheese Book*. London: Dorling Kindersley, 2009, p. 51.
Masui, Kazuko, and Tomoko Yamada. *French Cheeses*. London: Dorling Kindersley, 1996, pp. 109–111.
Chevrotin AOP. http://www.chevrotin-aop.fr.

Emma Young

Chez Virginie is a fromagerie in Montmartre, Paris, run by Virginie, a third-generation cheesemonger. Virginie originally studied as a translator as her cheesemonger parents initially dissuaded her from following their trade because they thought it was too much work. Her roots were too strong though, and she decided to purchase her cheese shop on Rue Damrémont in 1995, in a building that had been used as a cheese shop from the early 1900s. Unusually Chez Virginie boasts its own maturing cellar. When cheeses arrive they are matured anywhere from fifteen days to several months, depending on the style of cheese. See MATURING.

Chez Virginie is small, yet every corner is packed with cheese, and merchandised impeccably. The decor changes depending on the season. The house specialties include Brillat Savarin with truffles, Brie with fresh truffles, and a Raclette meal that is a premade package including Camembert with Calvados and a Raclette ball. See BRILLAT-SAVARIN; BRIE DE MEAUX; and RACLETTE. In the summer season they also make cheese "bento"-style boxes.

Three employees work in the shop, which hosts around 120 cheeses at any time. Virginie sources them all and sells only unpasteurized cheeses that are mostly seasonal. She has a close relationship with her suppliers and makes a point of visiting them, familiarizing herself with the terroir, and learning about the origins of each product. In addition to cheese, Chez Virginie also sells excellent wines from small producers, as well as sausages and other products for aperitifs. Virginie is in the process of opening a second shop on Rue Caulaincourt close to the first.

See also CHEESEMONGER and FRANCE.

Chez Virginie. http://www.chezvirginie.com.

Emma Young

chhana

See INDIA and PANEER.

chhurpi

See INDIA.

children's literature presumes that children naturally desire sweets; not so, cheese. A taste for cheese suggests maturity—associated with ripened cheeses, but even more so with inner maturation and the body; disgust for cheese reflects youthful taste buds and bodily anxieties. Hence, the most sensational quality of cheese in children's stories is its smelliness. Its stink offers a permitted alternative to scatological humor, license to wallow in animal odors that parallel, but do not transgress, the line into "poo poo talk." The best known example of this is Jon Scieszka's *The Stinky Cheese Man and Other Fairly Stupid Tales* (1992), with the titillating, almost-forbidden language of "stinky" and "stupid" in its very title. In Scieszka's parody of the traditional *Gingerbread Man*, the cheese man disgusts everyone: "Phew! What's that terrible smell?" one asks, while others remark on his "awful," "gross," "nasty," or "funky" aura until to everyone's relief, he falls into the river and disintegrates. Similarly, the antisocial bodily aspects of cheese make up a sole, extended joke in Garrison Keillor's *The Old Man Who Loved*

Cheese (1996): the old man stinks because he eats cheese that smells "like socks from a marathon race" or dead fish, cheese that is "yellow lumps of rotten gunk," variously "sour," "vile," "fetid," or "rank," gurgling, squishing, bubbling, and burbling. The plenitude of cheeses Keillor lists—Cheddar, Limburger, Emmentaler, Cheshire, Parmesan, Velveeta, Swiss, Romano, Roquefort, and more—emphasizes cheese's varied bouquet as putrid and comic.

Stink may explain how cheese comes to be associated with isolation, as it is in Robert Cormier's novel, *I Am the Cheese,* the title itself an allusion to the nursery song *The Farmer in the Dell,* with its final line, "the cheese stands alone." And perhaps, too, stink offers a rationale for the insult implied in Lewis Carroll's *The Hunting of the Snark,* in which the baker's "intimate friends call him 'Candle-ends,' and his enemies 'Toasted-cheese.'" The sociologist Christie Davies suggests that this is an epithet mocking the baker as an eater of Welsh rarebit, a food that the English found ridiculous.

But despite the easy laughs of comic smelliness, in children's literature cheese figures most often in positive, complex ways. The nuances of flavor, texture, scent, and provenance implied in Keillor's list point to the abundance of figurative possibilities cheese affords, from its function as a nourishing food to its potential to satisfy existential longing. In its most basic role, cheese is a wholesome sustainer of life. In *Heidi,* by Johanna Spyri (1880), Heidi thrives on goat's milk and her Alm-Uncle's golden-yellow toasted cheese; her sickly friend Clara's hunger for a "second piece of cheese" is evidence of the healing qualities of mountain air and goat cheese. In "Baltzli" (in *The Three Sneezes and Other Swiss Tales,* told by Roger Duvoisin, 1941), fairies reward a boy with an ever-replenishing chamois cheese. "With this cheese in your pocket you will never again be hungry," the Bergmännlein tells the boy, suggesting that one can live on cheese alone. In Edward Lear's *The Jumblies* (1871), "no end of Stilton Cheese" figures in provisions for the Jumblies' sea voyage. Indeed, Lear, who was also a landscape painter, recounts that he began to draw "for bread and cheese" (preface to *Nonsense Songs,* 1900). In *The Witch of Clatteringshaws,* by Joan Aiken (2005), an army subsists on "hard, round blue-veined cheeses the size of golf balls." Bread and cheese are the default travelers' food in so many epic fantasies that Diana Wynne Jones, in her parodic *Tough Guide*

to Fantasyland (1996), considers them to be standard fare; while in Terry Pratchett's *A Hat Full of Sky* (2004), Tiffany Aching knows that "the typical food for taking on an adventure [is] bread and cheese."

For humans, cheese is basic sustenance; in rodent stories, there is nothing meager about it. Cheese is to mice what sweets are to children, the desirable object of glorious indulgence—as it is in Jean Van Leeuwen's *The Great Cheese Conspiracy* (1969), in which gangster mice arrange a heist on a cheese shop. But rodents' desire for cheese is not always a matter of sheer greed: often, a rodent's interest implies discernment, the ability to appreciate cheese's flavorful subtleties. In *The Wind in the Willows,* by Kenneth Grahame (1908), Ratty respects a visiting rat's "origins and preferences" by providing not the usual fare of British bread and cheese, but "a yard of long French bread … [and] some cheese which lay down and cried." In Eve Titus's *Anatole* (1956), Anatole the mouse's nuanced awareness of flavor results in a professional career as a taster and advisor at a cheese factory. In *Anatole and the Robot* (1960), the cheese-tasting robot's clumsy machinery can't compare to Anatole's intelligence and skill: "I sniff, I taste, I think, and then I use the magic of my imagination!" he explains, restoring the flagging business. Both stories recognize and celebrate the diversity of cheese as well as the skills that are essential to both its making and its appreciation.

Perhaps because cheesemaking is a delicate matter, children's literature uses the role of cheesemaker to convey a clever, nurturing nature. In *Heidi,* the Alm-Uncle's misanthropic ways are belied by the golden cheeses he makes so carefully, and with which he physically nurtures the child who in turn nurtures him emotionally. In *A Hat Full of Sky,* the apprentice witch Tiffany is known for her "excellent prowess with cheese": adolescent rebellion and the subsequent return to her wiser, compassionate self plays out, in part, when she makes a cheese by magic, rather than making it the "right way." The "foul cheese on the slab, sweating and stinking" becomes an emblem of the moral rot of arrogant egotism, in contrast to the proper care one should show toward both cheeses and humans. In Frances Hardinge's *A Face Like Glass* (2012), cheeses are cheesemaker Grandible's "only friends and family, their scents and textures taking the place of conversation. They [are] his children, waiting moon-faced on their shelves for him to bathe them, turn them and tend to them." In making the cheese Stackfalter Sturton, Grandible nurtures it as he would a sensitive pet or baby: "Every day the Stackfalter Sturton's dappled white-and-apricot hide had to be painted with a mixture of primrose oil and musk, and its long, fine mosses groomed with a careful brush; . . . the great cheese had to be turned over every 141 minutes." In all cases, cheesemaking implies an attentiveness to others' needs that extends beyond cheese to human relationships.

Cheese is a matter of nurture, but like a half-wild creature, it is dangerous: in *A Face Like Glass*, "open the wrong door and you might find yourself faced with . . . some great mossy round of Croakspeckle, the very fumes of which could melt a man's brain like so much butter"; Stackfalter Sturton, if not treated properly, will explode. In Joan Aiken's *Dido and Pa* (1986), cheese in combination with apple-punch is fatal. With such dire possibilities, children's authors acknowledge the complexity of cheese chemistry. Cheese is not just a big stink: it is exciting, hazardous, and unpredictable, its animal nature enfolded in its qualities and effects.

Like a good analyst, Stackfalter Sturton can "tell you things you know but still need to be told, because you won't face up to them, or you've forgotten them"; while "Whispermole Mumblecheddar [is] famous for revealing flashes of the future." Cheese's complex of rot, animal sources, and good flavor is probably part of what leads Hardinge to associate it with cognitive perceptions; but the metaphysical, psychological, and moral insights cheese offers are most often rooted in the time-honored mistaking of cheese for the moon, or the moon for cheese. In works that pivot on the cheese-moon confusion, either the moon or cheese can carry the same weight of disappointment, emphasizing illusory ambitions. In Aesop's fable "The Fox, the Moon, and the River" (from as early as the fifth century B.C.E.), a fox mistakes the reflection of the moon for a cheese. She drinks the river in her greed to get it, ultimately choking to death on the water. For Anne Page in the 1920s, the nature of the deceptive goal is inverted: "Many there are who cry for the moon, down here on the kind, old earth," she moralizes in "Green Cheese" (in *The Boy's Own Paper*, January 1924), but "they find at last, when they hold her fast, they've nothing but plain green cheese!" Green cheese is humdrum, undesirable, Page implies; but, in Edward Abbott Parry's *Gamble Gold* (1907), the cheese moon signifies the unattainable dream not because of its

composition, but because it belongs elsewhere: "But the green cheese is clever, / the green cheese is sly, / you will capture it if ever in the sweet by-and-by. / You've sighed for it, and sobbed for it, / 'tis hanging there to tease: / the heavens won't be robbed of it, / the Good Green Cheese." Unsatisfied longing, unattainable desire, and false ambition are at the heart of these and other tales in which moon and cheese are mistaken. See MOON and GREEN CHEESE.

"Green cheese is sly," Parry writes, personifying cheese in a way that would be recognized by the foolish characters of the Grimms' *Frederick and His Katelizabeth* (1823–1825) or of Joseph Jacobs's "Of Sending Cheeses" (*More English Fairy Tales*, 1894), who roll one cheese after another in the hope that the second will retrieve the first. But cheese's real slyness lies in its deceptive appearance, which extends beyond its famous look-alike, the moon. Cheese looks like things it is not, and many things that are not cheese look like cheese—or so children's literature tells us. In folktales, more than one hero challenged to squeeze water from a stone tricks his opponent by squeezing whey from cheese that looks like a stone, as the tailor does in the Grimms' *The Brave Little Tailor*. In *Winnie-the-Pooh* (1926), Pooh scrutinizes his honey, suspicious that it may not be honey: "It *looked* just like honey," Pooh thinks, "but you never can tell. I remember my uncle saying once that he had seen cheese just this color." In *Memory*, by Margaret Mahy (1987), Jonny is "rather disconcerted to find that what looked like a cake of cracked yellow soap was actually a small block of cheese set squarely in the soap dish." The cheese in the soap dish becomes a haunting sign for him, its incongruence and deceptive appearance a hint that he might have "cut through the defenses people put up against natural anarchy to the true disintegrating center of things." Even in a simpler story, cheese's capacity to trick by appearance implies a complex nature: in "The Story of a Cheese" and "King Cheese" (in *St. Nicholas Magazine*, 1878–1879), a vast Gruyère proves to be nothing but a hollow rind, its insides eaten away by rodents. These and other such deceptions acknowledge and play off cheese's manifold possibilities of texture, aroma, flavor, and appearance, and indeed, the mystery of the very life of the cheese as it curdles, ferments, and grows into its ripened self.

The role cheese plays in children's literature is not a simple matter of repugnance or desire; instead, cheese's complexities figure as a means of revealing contradictions in perception, illusive longing, isolation, or the glorious or dangerous results brought about by craft. As an animal product, it conveys nurture, home, and the smells of home, whether of Hardinge's "ordinary, homely pungent air of the cheese tunnels"; of the not-so-attractive quality of the man known as "Toasted-cheese"; or of *The Farmer in the Dell*'s lonely cheese. The bodily aspects of cheese may provoke laughter, but those same aspects compound and enrich its weightier meanings in works for children.

The author gratefully acknowledges the staff of the Osborne Collection of Early Children's Books, Toronto Public Library.

See also LITERATURE and MAGICAL THINKING.

De la Mare, Walter. *The Dutch Cheese*. New York: Knopf, 1931.
Gardner, Martin, ed. *The Annotated Hunting of the Snark: The Definitive Edition*. New York: Norton, 2006, p. 21.
Jones, Diana Wynne. *Enchanted Glass*. London: Harper Collins, 2010.
Opie, Iona, ed. *Ditties for the Nursery*. London: Oxford University Press, 1954.
Stevenson, Robert Louis. *Treasure Island*. London: Cassell, 1883.
Stilton, Geronimo (pseudonym of Dami, Elisabetta). *The Curse of the Cheese Pyramid*. New York: Scholastic, 2004.

Deirdre Baker

In **China** cheese has always been a food on the extreme fringes of the national diet, and the consumption of dairy products in general has long been associated with the nomadic cultures to the north of the country rather than the mainstream. During the Northern and Southern dynasties (420–589 C.E.), *lao* (酪), a beverage made from soured cow's or sheep's milk, was well known in the north of China, and Jia Sixie's sixth-century agricultural treatise, *Qimin Yaoshu*, outlines methods for making dried lao (干酪) and strained lao (漉酪), both of which are rudimentary lactic cheeses. By the time of the Tang dynasty (618–907 C.E.), an era of widespread trade and cultural interaction across central Asia, the Chinese upper classes enjoyed the dairy product *ru fu*, also known as *ru bing* (乳腐; 乳饼), described in a recipe of the much-later Yuan dynasty (1271–1368 C.E.) as made by coagulating hot, filtered cow's milk with vinegar, "just like the making of tofu,"

before straining out and pressing the curds, and then storing them in a jar with salt. (For a fascinating discussion of the relationship between the techniques used to make simple lactic cheeses and tofu, see Huang 2001, pp. 302–330.) By the time of the Qing dynasty, dairy products in general had largely disappeared from the Chinese diet, with soy and its derivatives, including tofu, occupying a similar nutritional position in the Chinese diet to dairy foods in the West.

Cheese made with rennet has never been a feature of Chinese food culture, or the food cultures of neighboring nomadic tribes. In much of modern China, cheese is regarded as an unsavory aberration. When faced with their first taste of cheese in 2010, a group of culinary professionals in the eastern city of Shaoxing, notorious for its own "stinking and moldy" (*chou mei* 臭霉) delicacies, were generally of the opinion that the cheeses they sampled were offensively smelly, greasy, sour, and bitter. One person

A specialty of Lunan County in southwestern Yunnan Province is "milk cake" (*ru bing* 乳饼), a fresh white cheese made by coagulating goat's milk with vinegar or another souring agent, straining the curds, and then pressing them overnight under a heavy stone. The pressed cheese is cut (pictured here), cooked, and then served with rice as part of a meal. © FUCHSIA DUNLOP

interviewed by the anthropologist E. N. Anderson described cheese as "the mucous discharge of some old cow's guts, allowed to putrefy." Nonetheless, there are some interesting local exceptions.

In southwestern Yunnan Province, a specialty of Lunan County is a fresh white cheese made by co-agulating goat's milk with vinegar or another souring agent, straining the curds, and then pressing them overnight under a heavy stone—this is known as "milk cake" (*ru bing* 乳饼). In this region, the warm, unpressed curds may be eaten immediately after coagulation, in a manner reminiscent of fresh, unpressed tofu curds. More commonly, the pressed cheese is cut, cooked, and then served with rice as part of a meal. Common cooking techniques include frying the sliced cheese until it is golden on both sides and eating it with a dip of white sugar or salt mixed with Sichuan pepper, and steaming it with slices of the famous Yunnan ham. The cheese may also be cut into pieces and stir-fried with other ingredients.

In Dali in the northwestern part of Yunnan, the Bai nationality have an extraordinary specialty called "cheese fans" (*ru shan* 乳扇). They use soured but-termilk or a sour liquid made from Chinese quinces to coagulate fresh cow's milk over a gentle heat. As the curds form, they are manipulated with a pair of sticks to form an elastic white mass. The cheese is then gently massaged by hand, stretched into sheets, wound around bamboo poles, and hung up to dry. (The whey may be left to sour and used as the following day's coagulant.) The leather-dry, yellowed cheese sheets may be deep-fried to form puffy shapes that are often sprinkled with sugar and eaten as an appetizer: they are crisp, soft, and fragile, with a distinctly cheesy taste. "Milk fans" are also a favorite street snack: vendors toast them gently over a grill, spread them with rose-petal jam, and then roll them up around a stick so they can be eaten like lollipops. Both of these Yunnan cheeses are thought to have developed through contacts with either Mongolian or Tibetan food traditions.

Cheese also has a role in the diets of some of the northwestern minority nationalities of China. Tibetans, while favoring butter, occasionally eat lactic yak cheeses made from buttermilk or yogurt. These cheeses may be eaten fresh or sun-dried into rock-hard lumps that must be sucked for a long time before they are soft enough to be nibbled, layer by layer. Similar cheeses are eaten in the far western region of Xinjiang.

Since China began its "Reform and Opening Up" (*gai ge kai fang*) in the 1990s, cheese has made some new inroads into the country, as well. Bland, pro-cessed cheese is widely consumed on pizzas, partic-ularly by young people, while the growing expatriate communities in larger cities are driving an expan-sion in the range of imported cheeses sold in the local market. One enterprising, French-trained cheesemaker, Liu Yang ("Le Fromager de Pekin") is hoping that his artisanal cheeses, including Beijing Grey, a local version of Camembert, will eventually be as popular with Chinese customers as it is with Western expatriates.

See also TIBET.

Anderson, E. N. *The Food of China*. New Haven, Conn.: Yale University Press, 1988.
Chang, K. C. *Food in Chinese Culture: Anthropological and Historical Perspectives*. New Haven, Conn.: Yale University Press, 1997.
Huang, H. T. *Science and Civilisation in China*. Vol. 6: *Biology and Biological Technology*, Part 5: *Fermentations and Food Science*. Edited by Joseph Needham. Cambridge, U.K.: Cambridge University Press, 2001.

Fuchsia Dunlop

chura

See TIBET.

chymosin is the primary milk-clotting enzyme with its origin from the fourth true stomach, abo-masum of ruminants. It is secreted as an inactive precursor (zymogen), prochymosin, from the glands of the abomasal mucosa together with pepsinogen, another proteolytic and milk-clotting enzyme. When prochymosin and pepsinogen come in contact with the acid environment in the abomasum, they are ac-tivated to chymosin and pepsin, respectively. In the young suckled or milk-fed calf, chymosin dominates (up to 90 percent of the milk-clotting activity ratio) compared to the amount of pepsin. When the calf (e.g., lamb, kid) grows older and is weaned, the pro-duction/secretion of chymosin decreases and finally stops in favor of pepsin. This is the reason why the feeding regime and the age of calves and cattle in-fluences the composition of milk-clotting enzymes in rennet, which is an extract from the abomasum used to clot the milk since time immemorial. See

RENNET. Evolutionary chymosin was developed in ruminants because it has a very high milk-clotting activity, but a low general proteolytic activity per mole. The latter is important because ruminants have a postnatal transfer of the immunoglobulins to the offspring in the very first milk, colostrum. Because chymosin only clots the milk, the immunoglobulins will remain intact and could be absorbed in the intestine for later protection against illness of the offspring. Pepsin, with its high proteolytic activity, would have been detrimental for the immunoglobulins in the colostrum.

Chymosin is classified as an acid proteinase (EC 3.4.23) and has 323 amino acids in its primary structure and the molecular mass is about 35,600 Da. The active site of chymosin is within an extended cleft of the tertiary structure in which at least seven amino acid residues of its substrate, kappa-casein, could be accommodated during the hydrolysis action, that is, the first step of the milk-clotting reaction where the Phe_{105}–Met_{106} bond of kappa-casein is split. See COAGULATION OR CURDLING. The pH optimum of chymosin is around pH 4, but it has still very high milk-clotting activity at pH 6.5, the pH of cheese milk. In addition, it has to be remembered that the calcium content and temperature of the milk highly influence the milk-clotting activity of chymosin. Normally chymosin from a certain species has the highest milk-clotting activity on the milk of its own species, that is, bovine chymosin for cow's milk, ovine chymosin for ewe's milk, etc. However, camel chymosin has been shown to have a higher specific activity on cow's milk than bovine chymosin.

Chymosin is correlated with a high yield of cheese, the very best of the coagulants known. It is the dominant enzyme in calf rennet, which was used in the development of most different varieties of cheeses around the world. Therefore, there has been considerable interest in a new recombinant deoxyribonucleic acid (DNA) technique, where chymosin is produced by a fermentation process of the fungi *Aspergillus niger* or the yeast *Kluyveromyces lactis*, which have the DNA sequence of the bovine chymosin genome incorporated. The product is named fermentation-produced chymosin (FPC) and the properties are in principal identical to bovine chymosin. The market share of FPC is now about 50 percent in the world. The latest development is fermentation-produced camel chymosin, which has a higher specific milk-clotting activity and a lower general proteolytic activity on cow's milk compared to bovine chymosin.

See also ENZYMES; FERMENTATION-PRODUCED CHYMOSIN; and RUMINANTS.

Andrén, Anders. "Milk-Clotting Activity of Various Rennets and Coagulants: Background and Information Regarding the IDF Standards." *Bulletin of the International Dairy Federation* 332 (1998): 9–14.
Andrén, Anders. "CHEESE: Rennets and Coagulants." In *Encyclopedia of Dairy Sciences*, 2d ed., edited by J. W. Fuquay, P. F. Fox, and P. McSweeney, pp. 574–578. Amsterdam: Elsevier, 2011.

Anders Andrén

Classic Blue Log is the flagship cheese of Westfield Farm, in Hubbardston, Massachusetts. Made of high-quality goat's milk from several farms within a twenty-mile radius, Classic Blue's charms are due to its rare, if not unique, recipe: it is a young chèvre-style cheese inoculated with *Penicillium roqueforti*, the same mold responsible for famous blues including Roquefort, Stilton, and Cabrales. See PENICILLIUM. An American original at the cutting edge of the late twentieth-century US artisanal cheese boom, Classic Blue was created in the early 1990s by Westfield's proprietors Bob and Lettie Kilmoyer under their Capri brand. When the Kilmoyers retired in 1996, they sold the farm to Bob and Debby Stetson.

Classic Blue begins as an 8-pound bundle of curds, drained in a bag, to which salt and *P. roqueforti* are added. The curds are wrapped in cheese paper and left to sit for four to seven days. Next they are extruded into logs about 4.5 inches long and 1.5 inches in diameter (10 × 4 centimeters), weighing approximately 4.5 ounces (128 grams), and placed in specially designed curing cabinets. (A larger-format 7-ounce Classic Blue is also made, as is a 1-ounce version called Bluebonnet.) The cheeses spend five days in the cabinets, where they develop their powdery blue rinds. Finally, the logs are wrapped in breathable cellophane and spend several more days under refrigeration to dry out and stabilize before shipping. The cheeses ripen from the outside in, gradually turning softer and more liquefied, beginning just under the surface. They are generally considered to be at their peak within two to three weeks of wrapping, when the tang of the fresh chèvre is well balanced with the emerging bite of the blue. As they continue to age, the blue flavors become stronger and more Roquefort-like, while the consistency continues to liquefy, potentially throughout the entire log.

Westfield produces approximately two thousand Classic Blue Logs per month. Classic Blue has been a perennial prizewinner: from 2000 to 2015, it won seven first-place ribbons, three seconds, and one third at the annual American Cheese Society (ACS) judging. Its "baby sister," Bluebonnet, won Best in Show at the 1996 ACS.

See also BLUE CHEESES.

Westfield Farm. http://westfield-farm.myshopify.com.

David Gibbons

clean break is when the condition of a milk coagulum is tested for readiness for the cutting stage, and the curd is judged firm enough to be cut into evenly sized particles.

There are several methods of assessing the curd. The easiest method is to place the heel of the hand against the side of the vat and gently press down and pull the curd away from the side of the vat. The whey should be clear and free from any curd particles, which would cause a reduction in yield. Another test is to use a sanitized stainless steel knife (or finger) to make a slight cut in the surface of the curd and then slide the knife in at right angles to the cut and at an angle of 45° to the surface, slowly lift the knife and observe the curd as it splits open. The sides should be smooth and the whey clear. Milky whey and free curd particles indicate that the curd is not ready to cut. On the other hand, grainy edges indicate that the optimum cutting point has been missed.

Another method to determine the proper point for cutting the curd is to observe the flocculation time. Each type of cheese requires a different hardness of curd, which equates with a different multiple of the point at which the milk begins to flocculate. It is important to keep the temperature of the cheese room warm as chilling of the surface of an open vat will give false readings to the clean break and flocculation tests.

With all of these tests the cheesemaker's skill in interpreting the signs is also of great importance.

See also COAGULATION OR CURDLIN and FLOCCULATION.

Kindstedt, Paul, with the Vermont Cheese Council. *American Farmstead Cheese: The Complete Guide to Making and Selling Artisan Cheeses.* White River Junction, Vt.: Chelsea Green, 2005.
Maddever, K. D., Bath and West and Southern Counties Society, and Milk Marketing Board. *Farmhouse Cheddarmakers' Manual.* Thames Ditton, U.K.: Milk Marketing Board, 1988. Out of print.
Van Slyke, Lucius. L., and Walter V. Price. *Cheese: A Treatise on the Manufacture of American Cheddar Cheese and Some Other Varieties.* Atascadero, Calif.: Ridgeview, 1992.

Val Bines

Clonmore

See COUNTY CORK.

clothbound cheeses are bandaged in cheesecloth or muslin to protect the rind. Evidence suggests that the practice was born in the Mendip Hills of Somerset, England, where the pastures and climate offered perfect conditions for maintaining large herds that provided the opportunity to produce substantial (up to 90-pound [45-kilogram]) wheels of Cheddar that required two to three years to mature. Binding the Cheddar wheels with cheesecloth reduces moisture loss and mold growth better than brushing alone. Cloth bandaging is also superior to plastic wrapping because it produces a firmer cheese (by allowing some moisture loss) with more complex and earthy flavors. See CHEESECLOTH.

Clothbound cheeses are wrapped in cheesecloth and covered with lard, butter, vegetable oil, or a paste made from flour and water to seal the cloth and reduce the access of air to the rind. A single or double layer of cheesecloth is applied to the top of the cheese first, after which the softened fat is brushed on. The same procedure is repeated on the bottom of the cheese, and then the sides are bandaged and greased. Additional layers of fat may be added to some varieties during ripening, but traditional British clothbound cheeses are generally greased only once, followed by regular turning and brushing (or rubbing with a dry cloth) to minimize mold growth and the incursion of cheese mites. Although some cheeses are bandaged before pressing, others are pressed first and then bandaged and pressed again to fuse the cloth to the cheese.

In addition to giving the cheese a firmer texture and a more complex flavor, bandaging also prevents the cheese sides from bulging and imprints a fine texture on the rind. The trade-off relative to aging in plastic is reduced yield due to moisture loss and trim loss. To avoid these losses, some cheesemakers use wax or plastic coatings, which depending on specific formulations, may allow the cheese to breathe, while also resulting in less yield loss and minimizing surface defects.

Great Britain still produces the largest variety of clothbound cheese in the world. Cheshire is a cylindrical cheese whose cloth was traditionally tied with calico lace, a cheap and rustic fabric derived from cotton that was produced in India. Calico lace trade caused concerns in England in the eighteenth century because it competed with home-produced cotton and wool. Therefore, the lace was replaced by cheesecloth that was stuck to the surface with a flour-and-water paste. Lancashire, a close and generally less aged relative of Cheshire, is bandaged and covered in butter. Other clothbound British cheeses include Double Gloucester, Red Leicester, and Wensleydale. See CHESHIRE CHEESE (U.K.); GLOUCESTER; RED LEICESTER; and WENSLEYDALE.

Only a few clothbound cheeses, mostly Cheddar, are well known outside the United Kingdom. Avonlea Clothbound Cheddar is produced by Cows Dairy in the Canadian province of Prince Edward Island. According to promotional literature from Cows Dairy, Avonlea was inspired by similar Cheddars produced in the Scottish Orkney Islands, although Orkney Cheddar is film wrapped for ripening rather than clothbound. The common characteristic is that both Avonlea and Orkney Cheddar are made from stirred curd rather than cheddared curd. American examples of clothbound Cheddar include Cabot Clothbound, Fiscalini Bandaged Cheddar, and Bleu Mont Bandaged Cheddar. See CABOT CREAMERY; FISCALINI FARMSTEAD CHEESE; and ORKNEY CHEESE.

Although all of these varieties are hard cheeses, a small number of semisoft and younger cheeses may also be lightly bandaged to provide support during ripening, including the Portuguese Serra da Estrela (PDO) and Queso de la Serena in Spain. See SERRA DA ESTRELA and LA SERENA.

See also CHEDDAR; CHEESE MITES; LARDING; and UNITED KINGDOM.

Cheesemaking Gourmet Cheese Simply & Easily. "Bandaging Cheese, What Does That Mean?" http://www.cheesemaking.com.au/bandaging-cheese-what-does-that-mean.

Council Regulation (EC) No 510/2006 on protected geographical indications and protected designations of origin "Orkney Scottish Island Cheddar." https://www.gov.uk/government/uploads/system/uploads/attachment_data/file/271289/pfn-orkney-scottish-island-cheddar-pgi.pdf.

Eekhof-Stork, Nancy. The World Atlas of Cheese. New York: Paddington, 1976.

Smith, Robert. The Great Cheeses of Britain and Ireland: A Gourmet's Guide. London: Aurum, 1995.

Arthur Hill and Mary Ann Ferrer

clotting

See COAGULATION OR CURDLING.

coagulant

See COAGULATION OR CURDLING; CHYMOSIN; FERMENTATION-PRODUCED CHYMOSIN; PLANT-DERIVED COAGULANTS; and RENNET.

coagulation or curdling refers to the essential first step in the production of all cheeses, whereby liquid milk is transformed into a three-dimensional gel or coagulum. The resulting coagulum can then be manipulated in various ways during the subsequent steps of cheesemaking to separate the whey (that is, water plus dissolved solid components such as lactose and soluble minerals) from the curds, which consist primarily of casein, fat, and casein-associated minerals that become concentrated as the whey is separated off. Curdling during cheesemaking can be accomplished by four different mechanisms, which give rise to four distinct families of cheeses: namely, rennet-coagulated, acid-coagulated, acid-rennet coagulated, and acid-heat coagulated cheeses. The vast majority of ripened or aged cheeses are rennet-coagulated or acid-rennet coagulated types. In contrast, cheeses produced by acid and acid-heat coagulation are mostly fresh types that are consumed immediately after manufacture.

Rennet Coagulation

"Rennet" refers to a group of enzymes, classified as aspartic proteinases, that are used in cheesemaking to coagulate milk. See RENNET. Technically, the term "rennet" is restricted to enzymes that are derived from the stomachs of mammals, most commonly milk-fed calves, kids, or lambs, although adult animals may also serve as the source of rennet enzymes. Animal rennets consist of a mixture of the enzymes chymosin and pepsin, with chymosin dominating when the source is young milk-fed animals, and pepsin dominating when the rennet is derived from the stomachs of adult animals. However, in common usage the term "rennet" may also include milk-coagulating enzymes that originate from plant sources, such as fig sap or the flowers of the thistle *Cynara cardunculus*, which are used in very traditional artisanal cheesemaking. In modern practice, rennets can come from microbial sources such as cultures of the molds *Rhizomucor miehei* or *Cryphonectria parasitica*, as well as cultures of genetically modified organisms such as yeasts that have acquired the gene for chymosin through recombinant DNA technology. See CHYMOSIN and PLANT-DERIVED COAGULANTS.

Rennet coagulation occurs when the cheesemaker deliberately adds a source of rennet enzymes to warm milk at temperatures ranging from around 86–95°F (30–35°C). These enzymes rapidly attack and enzymatically clip off the polar negatively charged ends of the kappa-casein "hairs" that line the surfaces of casein micelles and that enable the micelles to remain dispersed in the water phase of the milk. Consequently, the micelles undergo reductions in net negative charge and in diameter, and they are rendered unstable in water in the presence of calcium ions, which are usually abundantly present in milk. This causes the micelles to aggregate in the form of chains that increase in both length and thickness to form a three-dimensional casein matrix. The resulting net-like casein matrix constitutes the structural skeleton of the coagulum, which entraps fat globules, bacteria, and, initially, all the water in the milk. Rennet coagulation generally takes place at a high pH (e.g., around pH 6.6 to 6.3), before the lactic acid bacteria in the milk have had time to extensively ferment lactose to lactic acid. This results in a casein matrix that is rich in calcium phosphate. The entire coagulation process occurs rapidly, typically reaching completion within thirty to sixty minutes after the rennet is added. See LACTIC ACID; LACTIC ACID BACTERIA; CASEIN; and CALCIUM PHOSPHATE.

The coagulum produced by rennet enzymes possesses two key features that are central to explaining the enormous diversity of ripened cheeses that make up the rennet-coagulated family. First, the gel possesses a strong capacity to contract and expel whey in response to a variety of conditions that cheesemakers have learned to manipulate during the subsequent steps of cheesemaking. Depending on those manipu-

lations, it is possible to produce rennet-coagulated cheeses that vary widely in moisture content, ranging from over 60 percent to as low as 30 percent moisture. Second, because the casein matrix is initially rich in calcium phosphate, it is possible to produce rennet-coagulated cheeses that vary widely in calcium phosphate content by modulating the fermentation rate of lactose to lactic acid by lactic acid bacteria during the subsequent steps in cheesemaking. For example, rapid acidification causes more calcium phosphate to dissolve from the casein matrix into the whey than does slow acidification, resulting in a newly made cheese with lower mineral content. This is important because calcium phosphate content directly influences the initial cheese pH; high calcium phosphate content favors a higher initial pH; low calcium phosphate, the opposite. The bottom line is that rennet coagulation affords the cheesemaker great latitude to produce cheeses that may vary in both moisture content and acidity (pH) over wide ranges, depending on the conditions employed during the various steps of cheesemaking. When combined with the cheesemaker's capacity to vary the cheese salt content over wide ranges, such versatility in the chemical composition of the newly made cheese opens the door to an astonishing array of potential ripening outcomes because collectively the pH, moisture, and salt contents profoundly shape the microbiological, enzymatic, and physicochemical processes that transform a newly made cheese into its fully ripened state.

Acid Coagulation

Acid coagulation occurs solely through the action of lactic acid bacteria that are present in the milk either as a result of uncontrolled natural inoculation from the environment, as in the case of very traditional artisanal cheesemaking, or, more commonly, as a result of the deliberate addition of a starter culture by the cheesemaker. These bacteria ferment lactose to lactic acid over an extended period that may range from around five to twenty-four hours, depending on the bacterial population and incubation temperature of the milk. Lactose fermentation results in the steady accumulation of lactic acid and thus a steady decline in milk pH, which causes casein micelles to become progressively demineralized as calcium phosphate contained within the micelles dissolves into the water phase of the milk.

During the early stages of lactose fermentation, casein micelles remain dispersed in the water phase of the milk because the polar, negatively charged "hairy" kappa-casein layer at the micelle surface stabilizes the dispersion. However, when the pH eventually falls below pH 5.0 to 4.6, the net negative charge of the casein micelles decreases considerably because of the high acidity, and the "hairy" outer layer apparently collapses. This renders the micelles unstable in water and causes them to aggregate in the form of chains that eventually form a three-dimensional casein matrix, much like the process that occurs during rennet coagulation.

However, the casein matrix that forms at low pH during acid coagulation is radically different from that produced by rennet coagulation because it is completely depleted of calcium phosphate and has very limited capacity to contract and expel whey. Therefore, in addition to being characteristically low in pH, acid-coagulated cheeses are also high in water content, which generally translates cheeses that are soft and spreadable as well as very prone to undesirable microbial changes and spoilage during extended storage. Not surprisingly, therefore, most cheeses in the acid-coagulated family are consumed fresh. Well-known examples include quarg (quark), cream cheese, cottage cheese, and fromage frais. See FRESH CHEESES.

Acid-Rennet Coagulation

Acid-rennet coagulation is sometimes referred to as lactic coagulation, and is used in the production of a family of cheeses that is predominantly composed of soft surface-ripened goat's milk cheeses, especially from France. Similar to acid coagulation, acid-rennet coagulation occurs slowly over the course of around twenty-four hours, at temperatures maintained at around 68°F (20°C). Coagulation occurs when lactic acid bacteria progressively ferment lactose to lactic acid, causing the milk pH to fall to around pH 4.6 (the isoelectric point of casein), which triggers the coagulation process. The process differs from that of acid coagulation, however, in that a reduced amount of rennet, for example around one-third of the level used in rennet-coagulated cheesemaking, is added to the milk before coagulation. The rennet enzymes act on the casein micelles while acidification proceeds, but the low enzyme concentration and low setting temperature (around 68°F [20°C]) prevent the rennet-altered micelles from aggregating quickly. When coagulation finally does occur at around pH 4.6, the renneted casein micelles form a casein matrix that is completely depleted of calcium phosphate but that has a greater capacity to contract and expel whey than the coagulum produced by acid coagulation alone. The end result is a newly made cheese that is similar to acid-coagulated cheese in its acidity but differs by virtue of its lower moisture content. The lower moisture content, in turn, opens the door to a variety of ripening possibilities involving the surface growth of yeasts and molds that are not feasible in acid-coagulated cheeses because of their higher moisture contents. Examples of soft surface-ripened acid-rennet coagulated (or lactic) goat's milk cheeses include Sainte-Maure and Crottin de Chavignol. See CROTTIN DE CHAVIGNOL and SAINTE-MAURE DE TOURAINE.

Acid-Heat Coagulation

The term acid-heat is used for this form of coagulation because the milk must be both acidified to around pH 6.0 to 5.4 and heated to around 176–185°F (80–85°C) to induce coagulation; neither acidification nor heating alone, to the same levels, is sufficient to cause coagulation. Acidification may take place before heating, as in the making of whole milk ricotta cheese, by fermenting the milk using lactic acid bacteria to attain the target pH, or by adding a food-grade acidulant such as vinegar, citric acid, or a yogurt-like starter culture to the milk before heating. The acidified milk is then heated to the target temperature, which induces coagulation in the form of curd flakes, or flocs, that spontaneously separate from the whey. Alternatively, fresh milk may be first heated to the target temperature, as in the making of queso blanco cheese, and then the hot milk acidified to the target pH by the addition of a food-grade acidulant, which also induces coagulation to form curd flocs that spontaneously separate from the whey. Either way, the curd flocs can be readily recovered from the whey using a sieve or a perforated ladle.

The mechanism of acid-heat coagulation is not completely understood. It involves both whey proteins, which are denatured and which adsorb onto the surfaces of the casein micelles, and the casein micelles themselves, which become unstable and aggregate into networks that entrap fat globules. The resulting curd flocs are high in moisture content, about 70 percent, which imparts a soft and spreadable texture and renders them very prone to undesirable microbial changes and spoilage during extended storage. Like the acid-coagulated cheeses, most cheeses in the acid-heat coagulated family are consumed fresh. However, a major difference between the two families is that, unlike acid-coagulated curds, the curds produced through acid-heat coagulation can withstand high pressure that may be applied to press out whey, enabling the production of cheeses with moisture contents down to around 50 percent, as in the case of queso blanco.

A variation of acid-heat coagulation is also used in the making of whey ricotta, which is produced from whey that is generated as a byproduct of rennet-coagulated cheesemaking, or from blends of milk and whey. Like whole milk ricotta, whey ricotta is produced through coagulation that is mediated by the combined action of acid and heat; however, the coagulation process is dominated by the denaturation and aggregation of whey proteins that spontaneously separate as curd flakes or flocs from the remaining deproteinated liquid phase of the whey.

See also ACIDIFICATION; PH MEASUREMENT; and WHEY.

Fox, Patrick F., et al. *Fundamentals of Cheese Science.* Gaithersburg, Md.: Aspen, 2000.
Kosikowski, Frank V., and Vikram V. Mistry. *Cheese and Fermented Milk Foods.* Vol. 1: *Origins and Principles.* 3d ed. Westport, Conn.: F. V. Kosikowski, 1997.

Paul S. Kindstedt

The **Codex Alimentarius** provides a definition and general standard for cheese as well as standards for individual varieties of cheese and groups of varieties of cheeses. It serves as the global reference point for consumers, food producers and processors, national food control agencies, and the international food trade. *Codex Alimentarius* is a Latin term that means "code" and "food," translated as "food code." With the goal of protecting the health of consumers by enhancing the safety and quality of food while ensuring fair practices in the international food trade, the Codex Alimentarius Commission (CAC) is responsible for compiling the standards, codes of practice, guidelines, and recommendations that constitute the *Codex Alimentarius.* The single-volume compilation "Milk And Milk Products" contains all

Codex standards and related texts for milk and milk products adopted by the CAC. This text also includes the general standard for the use of dairy terms, the code of hygienic practice for milk and milk products, guidelines for the preservation of raw milk by use of the lactoperoxidase system, and the model export certificate for milk and milk products.

The CAC is an intergovernmental body within the framework of the Joint Standards Program established in the early 1960s by the Food and Agriculture Organization (FAO) of the United Nations and the World Health Organization (WHO). With 186 member countries, the *Codex Alimentarius* system is in a unique position to develop food safety standards for global implementation. The *Codex Alimentarius* is a science-based activity assisted by independent experts and specialists including independent international risk-assessment bodies and ad-hoc consultants from a wide range of disciplines. Most of the work is the result of collaborative studies among individual scientists, laboratories, institutes, universities, and joint FAO/WHO expert committees and consultations. The resulting texts are therefore based on the work of scientific experts and organizations and serve as a focal point for food science research, thereby establishing the importance of the commission as an international forum for the exchange of such information.

Codex standards, guidelines, codes of practice, and advisory texts (standards) cover the operation and management of production processes, as well as the operation of government regulatory systems, for food safety. Codex texts are based on the principle of sound scientific analysis of the best available independent scientific advice to ensure that they withstand the most rigorous scrutiny and are subject to revision when necessary to ensure consistency with current scientific knowledge. In addition to more than two hundred standards and more than forty hygienic and technological codes of practice, the CAC has developed several general standards and codes of practice that are specific to dairy products, including a general standard for the use of dairy terms and codes of hygienic practice, among others.

Codex standards are intended as recommendations for voluntary application by members, yet they serve in many cases as a basis for national legislation. Governments are advised to support and, when possible, adopt standards from the Codex when establishing national food policies. Codex food safety standards are considered by the World Trade Organization (WTO) as the international reference point for the resolution of disputes concerning food safety and consumer protection. Reference to the Codex standards in the WTO's Agreement on the Application of Sanitary and Phytosanitary Measures (SPS Agreement) and the Agreement on Technical Barriers to Trade (TBT Agreement) highlights their significance for resolving trade disputes. As such, Codex standards have become the benchmarks against which national food measures and regulations are evaluated within the legal parameters of the WTO agreements; WTO members that wish to apply stricter food safety measures than those set by the Codex may be required to justify those measures scientifically.

See also HYGIENE and WORLD TRADE ORGANIZATION.

World Health Organization, and the Food and Agriculture Organization of the United Nations. *Understanding the Codex Alimentarius.* 3d ed. Rome: FAO/WHO Food Standards Program, 2006. ftp://ftp.fao.org/codex/Publications/understanding/Understanding_EN.pdf.

Dennis D'Amico

Colby cheese was originally called Colby Cheddar due to its origins in Colby, Wisconsin, and its similarity in manufacture to Cheddar cheese. Colby cheese was developed by Joseph Steinwald in 1885 in response to consumers who preferred less acidic tasting cheeses. Colby has a US Standard of Identity (Code of Federal Regulations Chapter 21 part 133.118) similar to Cheddar cheese. Both require that the solids content of the cheese be at least 50 percent fat and because both are produced from whole milk the fat on a solids basis is usually between 52 and 53 percent. The fat content of Colby on a total weight basis is around 31–32 percent. Cheddar has the maximum allowed moisture content of 39 percent while that of Colby is 40 percent. The salt content of both cheeses generally ranges from 1.5 to 1.8 percent.

Colby is characterized by its mild, milky flavor, and lack of acidity as compared to Cheddar, and has a slightly curdy and softer mouthfeel than Cheddar but is always colored orange. It is best when consumed within three months of age. Older cheeses tend to develop an excessively soft body and lose their milky taste over time. Very young Colby will string like mozzarella when heated and is used in cheese blends on pizza. Its mild flavor lends itself to be consumed as a table cheese, on salads, or sandwiches including toasted cheese sandwiches rather than being used as a condiment to add cheesy flavor to other foods. It is most often sold as longhorn pieces (described later), minihorn (half-circle) pieces, rectangular blocks, and as a shred in blends with other cheeses. A variant of Colby called Colby Jack is actually a mix of colored and noncolored curds (e.g., Monterey Jack curds). There are also many other private names and variations of this blend.

Colby is usually made from pasteurized whole milk but is not aged purposefully to develop flavor. It is always made using a stirred curd method and the salt is applied directly to the curd. Stirred curd method means that the curd is continuously stirred as whey is removed. The curd is not allowed to mat as is done with milled curd Cheddar. When most of the whey has been drained, cold water is added, and the curd and water are continuously stirred for a time. The cold water dilutes any remaining whey and also pulls some lactose and lactic acid out of the curd. The cold water addition results in a less acid tasting cheese and firms the curd. The firm curd does not fuse together into a solid block but rather leaves small irregularly shaped holes in the cheese, called an open texture. Until recently the standard of identity for Colby in Wisconsin demanded the open texture. With the advent of vacuum packaging that requirement has been lifted as the packaging pulls the curd tight and results in loss of the holes.

The water /whey is eventually fully drained but stirring continues. Once the whey is fully removed salt is added to the curd and the salted curd is then put into a form and pressed. The traditional form is called a "longhorn." It is a long cylinder that is 13 inches (33 centimeters) high and 4 inches (10 centimeters) or 6 inches (15 centimeters) in diameter. Because of its cylindrical form, Colby has also been called longhorn or longhorn Colby.

Colby can also be pressed in a rectangle block form and smaller retail size rectangular blocks are cut from it. Some suppliers cut a roundish, half-moon shape out of the blocks to emulate the traditional round cuts obtained from Colby pressed in the longhorn forms.

See also CHEDDAR.

City of Colby. http://www.ci.colby.wi.us.
Kosikowski, Frank V., and Vikram V. Mistry. "Cheddar Cheese and Related Types." In *Cheese and Fermented*

Milk Foods, Vol. 2: *Procedures and Analysis,* 3d ed. edited by F. V. Kosikowski and V. V. Mistry, p. 103. Westport, Conn.: F. V. Kosikowski, 1997.

Wison, Harry L., and George W. Reinbold. *American Cheese Varieties.* New York: Chas. Pfizer, 1965. See pp. 42–43.

Mark E. Johnson

colony-forming unit

colony-forming unit (CFU) is the means by which the number of viable microbes in a sample is evaluated. Due to their tiny size it is not possible to use the naked eye to count individual microbes (e.g., bacteria, yeast, mold) in a sample such as a starter culture or raw milk. Even if we could observe the cells, there is no way of telling if the cell is actually viable (i.e., alive). However, if a viable microbe is placed on a solid medium that supplies all of the nutrients the cell needs to grow, it can reproduce to form a colony. Colonies are large enough that they can be counted with the naked eye. Although it is not true all of the time, in the vast majority of cases, each colony-forming unit began as a single cell. In this regard, counting colony-forming units is an indirect measure by which we can tell how many viable cells were present in the original sample. Knowing the number of colony-forming units in a starter culture is important to the cheesemaker as it will aid in knowing that there is an active starter culture of sufficient number to convert the cheese milk into curds. The CFUs are also used to establish safety and quality parameters for pathogens and indicator organisms in milk and cheese, which is of importance to cheese safety and quality.

See also STARTER CULTURES.

Weir, H. Michael, and Joseph H. Frank, eds. *Standard Methods for the Examination of Dairy Products.* 17th ed. Washington, D.C.: APHA, 2012.

Todd Pritchard

color

color is used to market cheeses, to differentiate cheeses from one another, and in particular to enhance the color of pale cheeses. The color of cheese varies depending on different factors, among them, the origin of the animal source (i.e., water buffalo, goat, and sheep milks are completely white due to the lack of beta-carotene), the length of the ripening time (longer aged cheeses are darker due to moisture loss and oxidation during the ripening period), the acidity of the cheese (acidic cheeses are whiter), the use of specific technological factors like milk homogenization or type of mold or bacterial strain, and more specially the change with the seasons and the feeding of the animals producing the cheesemaking milk.

There is a noticeable difference between the color of winter and summer milks. The fresh summer grasses offer a much higher concentration of the carotenoids. To offset this difference and to offer a more consistent product the cheesemaker has a few coloring agents to choose from, the most popular of which is derived from the South American shrub *Bixa orellana,* commonly known as annatto. The color is extracted from the plant seeds with hydrogen peroxide. The pigment in annatto is bixin, which in its alkaline extract form becomes norbixin. On cheese, annatto becomes a protein dye, which attaches to the casein. It is susceptible to oxidation from hydrogen peroxide released by bacterial reactions and from the air. Some cheeses traditionally colored by the action of coryneform bacteria now have annatto added to the brine solutions in which they are bathed. The annatto gives a similar hue to what is derived from the bacterial effects. When annatto is extracted by oil, it can be used to color butter and cheeses with higher fat contents. Carotene itself has been added as a colorant but has had only limited success. See ANNATTO.

The FAO/WHO Committee makes recommendations regarding use of food color additives for the international arena but individual countries have final control over their usage. A food color additive is legally defined in Title 21, Part 70 of the US Code of Federal Regulations as any ingredient with the sole purpose of adding color to a food or beverage, all requiring approval by the FDA. In the United States synthetic food colors are subject to testing for certification and approval for use in foods, drugs and cosmetics. Colors exempt from this certification are derived from plants, minerals, insects, and fermentation, sources considered to be "natural." However "all-natural" labeling is permitted only in cases where the color is natural to the food itself. Color derived from the above-mentioned exempt colors would be considered to be artificial, though they are resources considered to be "natural."

Synthetic colors are derived with chemical alterations, having a source not found in nature, and are further classified as dyes or lakes. Dyes are water soluble and oil insoluble. Lakes are made by combining dyes with salts to make them water insoluble thus making them more stable and suitable for foods that contain fat.

The two primary colors in milk itself are a greenish color derived from riboflavin and a yellow color derived from carotene. Most of the riboflavin is concentrated in the whey so most of this color is lost in cheesemaking. A vat full of curds and whey has a green fluorescence. Most of the carotene is concentrated in the milk fat, so, when present, this yellow color is retained.

Saffron has also been used to yield a yellowish color, as well as a distinct flavor, but is expensive so it is used rarely. Lüneberg is an Alp-style of cow's milk cheese from western Austria that adds saffron to the milk. Saffron is sometimes added after production for coloring and flavoring of an ancient vegetarian rennet sheep cheese from southern Italy, the Cacio-Fiore.

Marzolino is a traditional and seasonal cheese from Tuscany made with the spring milk (Marzo = March). It has a natural rind and is soaked in tomato and olive oil for forty-five to sixty days. The tomato imparts a reddish color to the cheese but it is primarily applied for the slight tangy flavor it provides.

Another colorant that has been used in cheese is carmine, derived from the South American insect, cochineal. A cheese colored by carmine would not be considered suitable for vegetarians however and some cases of allergic reactions have been reported.

Green colors are added to cheeses too, not just the green-blue striations in Gorgonzola and Roquefort. The natural green colors are derived from the chlorophylls, the chlorophyllins, and their copper complexes. These are extracted from wheat, kale, and other curly leaves. Interestingly, the green used to color the curds in Sage Derby is not sage, as those leaves turn an unappetizing brown. Synthetic green coloring has proven to be unsuccessful, yielding an unnatural color, aroma, and flavor.

Sapsago (a.k.a. Schabsiger) is a cheese from Canton Glarus in Switzerland, flavored and colored with the sap of aromatic blue fenugreek (a.k.a. blue melilot). It is a low-fat cheese with a strong flavor.

Another coloring treatment some cheeses receive is bleaching—used to highlight the veining in certain blue cheeses. The milk is homogenized and the beta-carotene in the cream is bleached using benzoyl peroxide, then added back to the skim milk. This step makes the blue-green veining stand out. Some cheeses receive added colorations by bathing in wines, beers, and spirits. One of the most distinctive of these is the Queso Murcia al Vino, a Spanish goat cheese washed in red wine. The traditional wine used to bathe this cheese is Jumilla, a wine dominated by the Monastrell varietal. The color of the rind offers a stark contrast to the white paste within. In this example the signature inky purple color seems to be as important as the juicy flavoring added by the wine. Wine, beer, and spirits have been used in cheesemaking for centuries; in most cases the goal is to enhance flavor but the rind color is also altered, and in some cases the paste color is as well.

Colors are considered additives and their use and tolerated levels are regulated by individual countries. There are colors added for the coloring itself and colors arising from treatments cheeses receive, either for flavor enhancements or for their preservation. Cheeses in the "color added for color alone" category include Mimolette, Edam, Leicester, Cheshire, and Double Gloucester. Some cheeses appearing to have orange or amber color added, such as aged Gouda, gain enhanced hues from oxidation and caramelization of residual sugars.

Some cheeses acquire their color from the darkening effects of rind applications such as food-grade oils and herbs or spices. Generally these are not considered to be additives.

See also AROMA; FLAVOR; TASTE; TEXTURE; and YELLOW VS. WHITE.

Fox, P. F., et al. *Fundamentals of Cheese Science.* Gaithersburg, Md.: Aspen, 2000, p. 13.
Wadhwani, R., and D. J. McMahon. "Color of Low-fat Cheese Influences Flavor Perception and Consumer Liking." *Journal of Dairy Science* 95 (2012): 2336–2346.

Max McCalman

colostrum is a pre-milk fluid produced by the mammary gland of female mammals during the first two to four days after the birth of their young. Colostrum differs from milk in its quality and composition. It is relatively high in protein and nutrients and, above all, is full of antibodies that confer passive immunity to the newborn.

In many cultures colostrum from cows or sheep or goats was heated and then consumed, salted or more usually sweetened. Due to the high protein content, colostrum coagulates when heated, at about 158°F (70°C). The appearance is that of a pudding.

In antiquity colostrum was considered a delicacy in Greece, known as *pyriate*, and in Rome, mentioned by some authors, for example Martial (III, 38):

Colustrum. Subripuit pastor quae nondum stantibus haedis/de primo matrum lacte colustra damus.

Colostrum. I offer the colostrum that the pastor stole to kids who do not yet stand, the first mother's milk.

Today this food is typical to and traditional in many countries: in India (known as *junnu, posu, bari,* etc.), in Sweden (*kalvdans*), in Iceland (*broddur*), in Finland (*uunijuusto*), in Turkey (*ağiz*), and in Italy, especially in Sardinia, where the production and consumption of *casada* (from Latin *caseus*, cheese) is still alive. Sardinian *casada* is made from ovine colostrum, with the addition of sugar and lemon peel, and sometimes thin slices of almonds, and coagulated in a bain-marie on the stove. When the casada thickens, it is placed in a bowl and eaten warm. It is mostly made for domestic consumption. Recently manufactured colostrum, in powder or capsules, is sold as a functional food in pharmacies and e-commerce stores.

See also MILK.

Perry, Charles. "Medieval Arab Dairy Products." In *Milk— Beyond the Dairy: Proceedings of the Oxford Symposium on Food and Cookery, 1999,* edited by Harlan Walker, pp. 275–277. London: Prospect, 2000.

Alessandra Guigoni

Columella, Lucius Junius Moderatus

(4 C.E.–ca.70 C.E.), was a first-century Roman agricultural writer from southern Spain who produced a detailed farming manual, *Res Rustica*, around 60 C.E. *Res Rustica* was written as a series of twelve books that contained practical guidelines for the efficient management of the latifundia, the large landed estates that arose in Italy following the Punic Wars, which transformed Roman agriculture and the Italian countryside. The latifundia typically specialized in the production of high-value cash crops, with olive oil, wine, and sheep products (wool and cheese) as major enterprises. Columella was not the first Roman writer to address the management of latifundia; Varro had written an agricultural manual in the first century B.C.E., and Cato had done so a century before

that. However, Columella's instructions in section eight of book seven, which pertain to the cheesemaking operation that complemented the raising of sheep for wool on the latifundia, constitute by far the most detailed and insightful analysis of cheesemaking produced in antiquity. See LATIFUNDIA.

Columella was the first writer to describe cheesemaking from start to finish. He stressed the importance of beginning with high-quality milk, of adding the correct amount of rennet, and of maintaining the proper temperature during coagulation. He described the different sources for rennet that were in use at the time, including lamb and kid rennet, as well as rennet derived from the flower of the wild thistle, the seed of the safflower, and fig sap. He stressed the importance of the richness of the milk, foreshadowing the current understanding of the importance of milk's casein to fat ratio, and he was keenly aware of the need to control curd drainage in order to attain the proper moisture content in the final cheese. Thus, Columella stressed the steps of draining, pressing, and salting as means to accomplish this. He also recognized the need to control temperature and humidity during aging in order to produce durable, hard-rind cheese "that can even be exported beyond the sea." He even offered a troubleshooting guide for common cheese defects.

Columella also demonstrated considerable marketing savvy, suggesting that fresh, unaged cheese can be transformed into flavored products by adding "any seasoning you choose," such as pine nuts and thyme, or by apple-wood smoking. Finally, Columella was the first to write about the addition of hot water during cheesemaking, which may have been an early form of cooking, or an early form of pasta filata cheesemaking; either way, the application of heat represented a giant step forward in the history of cheese technology. As a written source of cheesemaking knowledge, *Res Rustica* remained unsurpassed during the Middle Ages. Copies of the work were preserved in monasteries throughout Europe until the end of that period, raising the possibility that Columella's influence on cheesemaking extended far beyond the confines of the Roman latifundia on the Italian peninsula to the great monastic and manorial cheesemaking enterprises of medieval Europe. A statue of Columella can be seen at the Plaza de los Flores, in Cadiz, Spain.

See also ANCIENT CIVILIZATIONS.

Columella, Lucius Junius Moderatus. *On Agriculture.* Edited by E. S. Forster and E. H. Heffner. Translated by Harrison Boyd Ash. Cambridge, Mass.: Harvard University Press, 1941–1955.

Kindstedt, Paul. *Cheese and Culture: A History of Cheese and Its Place in Western Civilization.* White River Junction, Vt.: Chelsea Green, 2012.

Paul S. Kindstedt

commodity cheese names cheese that is affected by public trading at the CME Group (formerly Chicago Mercantile Exchange), but also refers to USDA requirements and dairy procurement by the US government. In the case of the latter, commodity cheese consists of (legally): mozzarella cheese, natural American cheese (Cheddar) and pasteurized process American cheese. In the case of the former, public trading of Cheddar in both 40-pound (18-kilogram) blocks and 500-pound (227-kilogram) barrels, along with various federal and state regulations, sets the price at which block cheese, including natural American cheese (Cheddar), mozzarella cheese, and pasteurized process American cheese, is sold throughout the United States.

The Cheddar wholesale market is a "spot market" meaning that, unlike a "futures" commodity market, purchased cheese must actually be exchanged within two working days. Cheddar has been publicly traded in Chicago since 1997, when the National Cheese Exchange in Green Bay, Wisconsin, was closed down. In addition to Cheddar, the CME Group also exchanges butter (since 1898) and nonfat dry milk. Cheddar purchases are made in "carload" quantities of 40,000–44,000 pounds (18,144–20,412 kilograms).

Because of the quantity of cheese involved in these transactions, very few bidders and sellers are involved. This "thin" trading has been criticized by dairy industry watchdogs as ripe for manipulation. The CME's predecessor group, the National Cheese Exchange, was ended partially due to this criticism. While the CME does not represent itself as a forum to determine fluid milk prices, state agencies often use it to determine fluid milk prices; therefore what happens at the CME can affect every non-organic cow dairy farmer.

This exchange has also influenced the parlance of the cheesemaking world, creating a means of dividing cheese into two groups: commodity cheese, which is influenced by the public trading prices of Cheddar

and milk, and specialty cheese, which, owing to greater costs derived from manufacturing, is not.

See also CHEDDAR; INDUSTRIAL; PASTEURIZED PROCESS CHEESES; and SPECIALTY CHEESE.

Yale, Ben. "Why Dairymen Absorb the CME's Rough Price Ride." *Progressive Dairyman,* 21 May 2010. http://www.progressivedairy.com/topics/management/why-dairymen-absorb-the-cmes-rough-price-ride.

Gordon Edgar

Cheese **competitions** serve to distinguish high-quality products within a crowded market. They provide objective feedback to cheesemakers, a tool for sourcing product for retailers and distributors, and they highlight interesting quality cheeses to consumers.

Competitions range from very local (e.g., competitions among a single style of cheese such as Sainte-Maure de Touraine, or the Concorso Caseario Premio Pienza, dedicated to the sheep's milk cheeses of the provinces of Siena, Arezzo, and Grosseto in Italy), to national competitions such as the Swiss Cheese Awards, to international competitions such as the World Cheese Awards (Birmingham, UK), the International Cheese Awards (Nantwich, UK), and the World Championship Cheese Awards (Madison, Wisconsin), to name the top three. Competitions frequently take place as part of a larger cheese or food fair, whether it be a local fair celebrating local agricultural products as in the case of state fairs in the United States, or larger public gatherings such as the Salon des Gourmets in Madrid, or the World Cheese Awards, held during the BBC Good Food Show. The American Cheese Society's Judging & Competition has traditionally been held in conjunction with the society's annual conference. See AMERICAN CHEESE SOCIETY.

As a general rule cheesemakers choose which cheeses to enter, and must enter their cheese in the appropriate category, corresponding to a style of cheese, make process, type(s) of milk, and/or region. Cheeses can usually be submitted only under a single category, even if they may conform to more than one. Cheesemakers must pay an entry fee, provide paperwork relative to the production of the cheese, and must ship the cheese to the designated location at their own cost. Cheeses are judged blindly, all packaging, labeling, and other identifying factors removed prior to entering the judging room.

Judging Categories

Judging categories can vary enormously from competition to competition, making comparisons of the value of awards difficult. The International Cheese Awards (Nantwich, UK) is an annual competition with 458 awards classes, and an additional 107 sponsored trophies awarded to cheeses from around the world. Some examples of judging categories from various competitions include staples such as fresh curd; pasta filata (stretched curd); sheep's milk; Cheddar; and washed-rind. More narrowly defined categories include "Raclette and toasting cheese," "Cheese innovations," "Low-fat/low-salt cheese," "Flavored Semi-Soft (Semi-hard) Goat's Milk Cheeses" and "Cheese any variety produced by small producers who are producing 2 tonnes or less per week." Winning a competition with nearly two thousand entries may indicate a higher level of quality than a winner from among fewer than two hundred entries; however large competitions with hundreds of categories will inevitably produce hundreds of winners.

Juries

Juries may consist of technical judges: academicians who teach technical cheesemaking, generally from a university or research institute, or master cheesemakers, who have competence to judge a variety of cheeses from a technical standpoint. In addition sensory analysis specialists may be included, drawn from retail, distribution, affinage, or the restaurant world; these judges may not have deep technical expertise but do have significant experience with cheese and are competent to discern organoleptic qualities in cheese products. Finally some competitions include cheese consumers, either incorporated into the tasting panels (as at the Concours Général de l'Agriculture, Produits Laitiers, France's General Agriculture Competition, Dairy Products sector) or voting a "People's Choice" award. Such is the case of Quebec's Sélection Caseus wherein members of the public vote at various public places. Those votes are tallied and awards are announced during the Victoria Fine Cheese Festival. Judges either work on a volunteer basis or are paid a portion of their expenses (e.g., hotel nights during the two days of judging at the American Cheese Society) and/or a small stipend. Some competitions, such as the Australian Grand Dairy Awards, draw exclusively from

within the judging country, while other competitions invite judges from around the world, either for their expertise judging products for export or in order to have a broader point of view included.

Sensory analysis training for judges is sometimes offered: Italy's Organizzazione Nazionale Assaggiatori Formaggi (ONAF, National Cheese Taster's Organization) was formed in 1989 to train cheese tasters and to promote the appreciation and production of artisanal cheese. The Concours Général in Paris offers training sessions for judges on two separate dates prior to the competition. The American Cheese Society conducts a training webinar for judges, and the first morning of the two-day judging begins with an in-depth training session on how the competition works and what is expected of judges. In the case of large categories that require multiple teams of judges a "norming" session is held to ensure that the judging teams are evaluating on a similar basis.

Judging teams may be structured in various ways. At the Concours Général in Paris, over 160 categories are judged in teams of three to six jurors, of whom two-thirds must be considered expert. Each judging team is responsible for six to eight cheeses, generally all from the same category. Each team has a moderator, who is responsible for obtaining a consensus among the team of jurors on each product, and who provides a written summary of their sensory analyses. Thus there are approximately one thousand judges involved. Near the other end of the spectrum is the American Cheese Society, which organizes judges into some twenty teams of two: a technical judge and an aesthetic judge. The technical judge is tasked with finding defects in the cheese: starting with a maximum score of fifty points, the technical judge may only deduct points. See DEFECTS. The aesthetic judge may only add points from a minimum score of fifty for positive organoleptic elements. Judges are not expected to compare notes or be influenced by their partners' observations, thus this system is not based on consensus but on individual scores. Minimum scores for first, second, and third place must be met; the highest three scores within each category are then awarded medals. Thus it is possible for a category to only have a second place winner (whose score was within the range required) but no first or third. Some competitions add an extra level of recognition in the form of best in show, super gold, or trophies that are selected in a second round of judging from among the category winners.

Benefits to Cheesemakers

Cheesemakers, even if they do not win recognition for their cheese, benefit from the judges' tasting notes, which in many competitions are forwarded to the cheesemaker. These notes offer a fresh view of how their cheese is perceived, and can sometimes be one of the few sources of professional feedback to which they have access. When a cheese does win an award its market value increases, at least theoretically, and may open the doors to distribution contracts and new markets, if not to increased asking price. Some producers have had to increase production dramatically upon receiving a major award, due to instant market demand—a good problem to have. Many competitions offer official labeling for winning cheeses, some with strict rules around how that labeling may be applied and how long the product may bear the label.

New cheese competitions are being created each year, as appreciation for cheese as both a basic, healthy foodstuff and a source of gustatory pleasure seems to be growing worldwide since the late twentieth century. In 1997 Japan's Cheese Professional Association launched its own national cheese competition, which is held biannually. However one of the most venerable cheese competitions, the Global Cheese Awards (Frome, UK) was established in 1861.

See also CHEESEMONGER INVITATIONAL; FAIRS AND FESTIVALS; and SENSORY ANALYSIS.

American Cheese Society Judging & Competition. http://cheesejudging.org.

Concours Général Agricole regulations. http://www .concours-agricole.com/documents/cga_reglement .pdf.

Global Cheese Awards. http://www.globalcheeseawards .com.

International Cheese Awards. http://www .internationalcheeseawards.co.uk.

Japan Cheese Awards. http://www.cheese-professional .com.

Organizzazione Nazionale Assaggiatori Formaggi. http://www.onaf.it.

World Championship Cheese Awards. http://www .worldchampioncheese.org.

World Cheese Awards. https://gff.co.uk/awards/ world-cheese-awards.

Susan Page Sturman

Comté is a cooked-curd, pressed cheese made from raw cow's milk in the Massif du Jura region of eastern France. It has a smooth texture and a range of flavors from nutty, creamy, and sweet through more meaty and roasted. It is sold as young as four months (the minimum age) and in some instances as old as three years, with an average of eight months. Comté received its AOC designation in 1958 and its PDO in 1996. See APPELLATION D'ORIGINE CONTRÔLÉE and DESIGNATION OF ORIGIN.

Comté is produced in wide, flat wheels up to around 28 inches (70 centimeters) diameter and 4 inches (10 centimeters) high and weighing anywhere from 71 to 99 pounds (32 to 45 kilograms). An average of 423 quarts (400 liters) of milk is required to make each wheel. The vast majority of Comté are produced in cooperative dairies called fruitières, which gather milk from surrounding farms. Then the cheeses are transferred to one of twenty maturing companies, or affineurs.

In accordance with its PDO regulations, Comté must be made from the milk of the Montbéliarde or French Simmental cow. See MONTBÉLIARDE. The cows have a grass-based diet (pasture in the summer, hay in the winter) with a limited daily allowance of cereal-based supplements (strictly non-GMO). According to the PDO requirements, each cow when at pasture must be allowed at least two acres (one hectare) of grazing land and half her daily food must come through foraging. The Comité Interprofessionnel de Gestion du Comté is responsible for the maintenance and evolution of the PDO guidelines, and it plays a role in marketing, export strategy, R&D, and quality monitoring.

There are approximately 150 fruitières in the Jura, Doubs, and Ain departments that constitute the Comté cheesemaking region. Most are situated in the heart of a village and owned by the surrounding farmers. The distance from where the cows are milked to where cheese is made can be no farther than 16 miles (25 kilometers) as the crow flies. This ensures the quick delivery of milk to the dairy necessary to preserve the microflora of the milk and a strong connection between the characteristics of the cheese and its terroir. The cows are milked twice a day. First thing in the morning the milk is delivered to the fruitière by the farmer, though increasingly it is collected by tanker. At the fruitière it is poured into copper-lined vats and warmed slightly (the PDO forbids a temperature higher than 104°F [40°C]).

Comté cheesemakers rely largely on whey for preparing the starters. The cheesemaker takes two

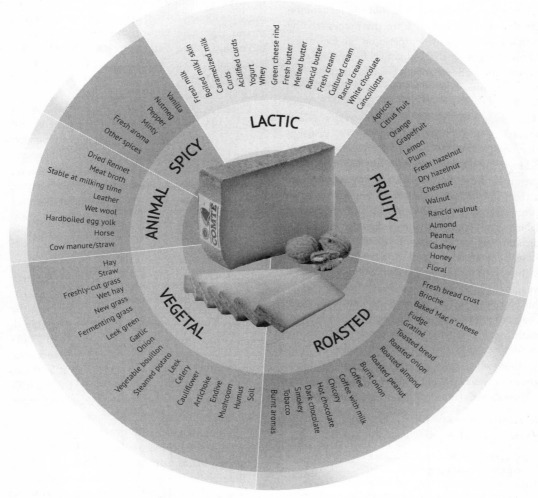

LACTIC
Fresh milk/ skin
Boiled milk/ milk
Caramelized milk
Curds
Acidified curds
Yogurt
Whey
Green cheese rind
Fresh butter
Melted butter
Rancid butter
Fresh cream
Cultured cream
Rancid cream
White chocolate
Cancoillotte

SPICY
Vanilla
Nutmeg
Pepper
Minty
Fresh aroma
Other spices

FRUITY
Apricot
Citrus fruit
Orange
Grapefruit
Lemon
Plum
Fresh hazelnut
Dry hazelnut
Chestnut
Walnut
Rancid walnut
Almond
Peanut
Cashew
Honey
Floral

ANIMAL
Dried Rennet
Meat broth
Stable at milking time
Leather
Wet wool
Hardboiled egg yolk
Horse
Cow manure/straw

VEGETAL
Hay
Straw
Freshly-cut grass
Wet hay
New grass
Fermenting grass
Leek green
Garlic
Onion
Vegetable bouillon
Steamed potato
Leek
Celery
Cauliflower
Artichoke
Endive
Mushroom
Humus
Soil
Burnt aromas

ROASTED
Fresh bread crust
Brioche
Baked Mac n' cheese
Fudge
Gratiné
Toasted bread
Roasted onion
Roasted almond
Roasted peanut
Burnt onion
Coffee
Chicory
Coffee with milk
Hot chocolate
Dark chocolate
Smokey
Tobacco

The Comté Aroma Wheel showcases the eighty-three terms or descriptors that correspond to the most frequently found aromas in Comté, grouped within six families: lactic, fruity, roasted, vegetal, animal, and spicy. COURTESY OF COMTÉ CHEESE ASSOCIATION

buckets of whey from a day's make and incubates them overnight in preparation for the following day. One bucket is held at 86–90°F (30–32°C), and a commercial mesophilic starter added. These starters are usually based on local strains. The other bucket will be held at 104–113°F (40–45°C) to encourage the growth of naturally occurring thermophilic bacteria. If a cheesemaker uses the traditional vell (salted calf's stomach) for the source of rennet, this will be added to the thermophile bucket as well. Both buckets of whey, usually along with local strains of *Streptococcus* and *Lactobacillus*, to assure proper acidification and add to the microflora

and aromatic development, are added to the vat before the milk reaches its ripening temperature of around 86–90°F (30–32°C). See CONTINUOUS WHEY STARTERS.

Then the cultures are added and the milk is allowed to ripen for around an hour before renneting; half an hour later the subsequent curd is ready to cut. Cutting is done by mechanical rotating "harps" (*lyre* in French) composed of vertical wires. To begin with the motion is gentle so as not to release too much fat. Soon the rate increases and the gel is cut to small pea-size particles. While this is happening the curd is heated gradually to around 131°F (55°C).

See CUTTING and SCALDING. About a quarter of an hour later the curd is tested by hand to see if it is ready to go into the molds. It should have the consistency of rice grains. At this point a giant snaking pipe is put into the vat and the contents are siphoned off into a number of molds. The whey drains into a trough beneath the cheese. The cheeses are labeled using casein tags, which are slipped between the mold and the side of the curd. Each tag indicates the vat, date, and identity of the fruitière where the cheese has been crafted. The cheeses are then pressed until the following day when they are removed to the fruitière's ripening cellar. There they sit on wooden boards and are turned and salted each day. They're also washed periodically with a broth-like substance called morge to encourage the development of the correct rind microflora. See MORGE.

Affinage

Generally, fruitières work with partner affineurs who collect the young cheeses after about two to three weeks. Twenty affineurs mature Comté cheese in the Massif du Jura region and of these, just five handle 75 percent of the 64,000 tons of Comté made each year. The role of the affineur is fourfold: to supply the conditions to mature the cheese successfully, to supply the labor to care for the cheese, to select and sell the cheese when it has reached the peak of its maturity, and to provide cash flow to the fruitière. See MATURING.

The conditions for maturing Comté are very specific: The cheeses must be aged on wooden boards, and the humidity in the cellars should be between 94–97 percent. See WOODEN SHELVES and RELATIVE HUMIDITY. The temperature depends on the stage of the affinage (often warmer to begin with, then cooler) and the rate of maturation desired: 46–50°F (8–10°C) for slow and uniform ripening or 59–64°F (15–18°C) for three to six weeks before final maturation at 41–43°F (5–6°C) for several months. The affineur must carefully control the propionic fermentation so it can contribute to the aromatic diversity of the cheeses, without causing any cracks. See DAIRY PROPIONIBACTERIA. Adequate ventilation is also key.

By far the most time-consuming job is turning and washing the cheese. Until relatively recently this was done entirely by hand. Today, however, the large affineurs employ laser-guided robots to do the heavy lifting. These work twenty-four hours a day, seven days a week.

To know when a cheese is ready to sell requires a keen olfactory sense and a lot of experience. Thanks to research in sensory analysis carried out by the CIGC, six broad categories of flavor have been identified and subdivided into eighty-three different aromas. See FLAVOR WHEEL. Recognition of these flavors will supply the affineur with the rudimentary knowledge to gauge how long a cheese will take to reach full maturity. A more accurate evaluation comes when the affineur takes a bore sample of the cheese and tastes it. At this point experience comes to bear and the affineur must decide when the cheese will reach its peak, what flavor it will have, and who, of all their customers, is likely to appreciate it.

See also FORT SAINT ANTOINE; FRANCE; and GRUY-ÈRE.

Comité Interprofessionel de Gestion du Comté. "Cahier des charges consolidé de l'Appellation d'Origine Protégée 'Comte.'" http://www.inao.gouv.fr.
Comté official website. http://www.comte.com.
Rance, Patrick. The French Cheese Book. London: Macmillan, 1989.

Dominic Coyte

concentrated whey cheese is the technical English term for Norwegian brunost. See CONCENTRATED WHEY CHEESE. As the Norwegian name implies, it comes in shades of brown, and it has a fudge-like consistency and taste. To make brunost whey is boiled for hours until it darkens and most of the water has evaporated. Up to 40 percent whole milk and cream is added to improve the taste and consistency. Shortly after it has been cooled and molded into blocks, it is ready to eat, although it keeps well for a long time. Brunost is usually eaten, thinly sliced, on sandwiches.

Its history, connected with mountain farming, goes back hundreds of years. The mountain farms were the domain of women, the *budeier* (dairymaids). They ran a frugal household where everything, including all parts of the milk, was utilized, often being conserved for use throughout the year. Concentrating the whey made it easy to store and to transport down from the mountains. Lots of firewood made it possible. Some products, usually the fattier ones, like sour cream, butter, or full-fat cheese, were sold, and those remaining were eaten by the family. During the nineteenth century, when demand for full-fat cheese fell, people started adding cream to the concentrated whey to make a smoother, tastier, and more valuable brunost. This was the beginning of the cheese later known as Gudbrandsdalsost ("cheese from the Gudbrandsdal"), often said to have been invented by Anne Hov in 1863. It is made from cow's milk whey and cream with roughly 10 percent goat's milk. Gudbrandsdalsost is sold in the USA as Ski Queen® gjetost. The latter is a now obsolete spelling for geitost (goat cheese), which in Norway is legally reserved for pure goat's milk cheeses, ekte geitost.

Brunost (brown cheese) is the general name for any concentrated whey cheese. Mysost (whey cheese) could also mean any kind, but is usually understood as the cow's milk varieties, especially fløtemysost, to which cream has been added. Brunost contains around 20 percent water, and has a fat content of 25–30 percent (30–35 percent FDM). Lighter varieties have a fat content of 16 percent (20 percent FDM). Most are made from nothing but whey, milk, and cream. A few have added sugar, and some have added spices like cardamom.

Shorter cooking time yields a softer, spreadable product known as prim, with around 30 percent water and a fat content of around 8 percent (11 percent FDM). Industrial prim has more ingredients, such as sugar, powdered milk, flavoring, and preservatives (sorbic acid).

Most brown cheese is made from the whey left after the making of renneted cheeses. Whey from skimmed sour milk cheeses has also been used, but it resulted in a sour, less valuable product.

The annual sale of brown cheese in Norway is around 12,000 tons. Most is industrial, but a growing number of farmhouse cheesemakers are adding to the diversity and quality of brunost. Production in Sweden is smaller. There the most popular kind is the soft messmör (whey butter), but you also find the solid mesost (whey cheese). Iceland too has a small production of mysuostur and soft, spreadable mysingur. In Iceland hot springs replaced firewood in the development of whey cheese production.

The Alps have a history of transhumance and mountain farming similar to that in Scandinavia, and they also developed condensed whey cheeses, but not much of the tradition remains. Sig, Gsig, and Wälderschokolade (forest chocolate) are names for the elusive product now almost only made in the Bregenz forest of western Austria. See TRANSHUMANCE and ALP CHEESEMAKING.

See also NORWAY and SOGNEFJORD ARTISAN GEITOST.

Abrahamsen, Roger K., et al. *Brunosten: En norsk historie.* Oslo: Tun Forlag, 2008.
Gudheim, Helge. *Kinning, bresting og ysting i Valdres.* Ulnes, Norway: Mat og Kultur AS, 2013, pp. 303–316, 405–449.
Selgin, Peter. "Gjetost." *Alimentum: The Literature of Food* 9 (Winter 2010): 18–23.

Ove Fosså

cone-shaped cheeses are a group of fresh, acidic dried cheeses which are traditionally produced on family farms in northwest Croatia. They are typically flavored with dried red pepper and salt. Three cheeses that belong to this category are Turoš, Prgica, and Kvargl.

Turoš cheese is produced in the Međimurje region of Croatia near the Hungarian border and, according to Kerecsényi (1982), in Hungary by Croats from Pomurje. Prgica, from the Podravina region of Croatia, and Kvargl, from the Bjelovar region, are similar cheeses to Turoš. These cheeses are traditionally produced on family farms from fresh cow's milk without added starter cultures. Clay or glass jars with a volume of 2–3 quarts (2.5–5 liters) filled with milk are left in a warm place for acidification. When the milk becomes sour, the cream that is separated on the surface is skimmed. Skimmed sour milk is poured into the pot that is heated to 105°F (42°C) for a period of up to three hours (without stirring) until the cheese curd appears on the surface. The cheese curd is poured into a cheesecloth and it is left to drain for one day. Obtained fresh, drained cheese is flavored with salt and dried red pepper, mixed, and shaped into cones, which are sun dried or dried above the oven for about seven days. For every 2 pounds (1,000 grams) of fresh cheese up to 1 ounce (20 grams) of salt and a half ounce (10 grams) of dried red pepper is added. The newest investigation determined differences among these three cheeses considering different making procedures, consumer's preferences, and textural characteristics, distinguishing them as regional-specific products.

See also CROATIA and SOUR SKIMMED-MILK CHEESES.

Kerecsényi, E. *History and Material Culture of Croats from Pomurje.* Budapest: Company for Textbooks, 1982.
Valkaj, Kristijan, et al. "Chemical and Microbiological Characterization of Turoš Cheese." *Agriculturae Conspectus Scientificus* 79 (2014): 201–207.

Samir Kalit

In **confocal microscopy** of cheese, proteins and fats (lipids) are stained with fluorescent dyes so that thin sample sections can be scanned sequentially with a microscope to obtain a three-dimensional image. Typically, stained proteins appear green or blue and stained lipids appear red. Features as small as one micrometer can be observed, and bacterial colonies can also be seen within the cheese.

Confocal microscopy was invented in the 1950s and now employs a laser beam to cause the dye to fluoresce; the full name of the technique is therefore confocal laser scanning microscopy, abbreviated CLSM. An advantage of CLSM is the relatively short sample preparation time: the specimen is placed on a glass slide, the dyes are added, and the scanning is performed, a procedure that takes twenty to thirty minutes. Higher magnification is available through electron microscopy (EM), but this technique requires several hours to dehydrate the specimen and prepare it before inserting it into the equipment, and it can generate artifacts.

CLSM provides the researcher with an overview of the distribution of fats and proteins in the cheese as it develops during manufacture and aging. CLSM of Mozzarella di Bufala reveals the lengthening of casein fibers and fat globules as a result of the stretching process, while micrographs of Cheddar or Swiss cheese show curd grain junctions and the coalescence of irregularly shaped globules of various sizes. Products made from homogenized milk, such as processed cheese and some Mexican cheeses, have been shown to contain spherical globules within a narrow range of diameters. CLSM is not used as a routine tool in cheesemaking, but it is useful for observing cheese microstructure. When coupled with photobleaching (fluorescence recovery after photobleaching, or FRAP), confocal laser microscopy allows the researcher to determine the diffusion coefficient of large molecules within the cheese.

See also FAT; MICROSTRUCTURE; and PROTEINS.

Floury, J., et al. "First Assessment of Diffusion Coefficients in Model Cheese by Fluorescence Recovery after Photobleaching (FRAP)." *Food Chemistry* 133 (July 2012): 551–556.

Jeanson, S., et al. "Spatial Distribution of Bacterial Colonies in a Model Cheese." *Applied Environmental Microbiology* 77 (February 2011): 1493–1500.

Tamime, A. Y. *Structure of Dairy Products.* New York: Wiley, 2008, pp. 18–22.

Michael Tunick

The **Congress of Vienna** was an attempt to forge a lasting peace in Europe following the Napoleonic Wars by redrawing state borders and thus balancing power in the region. Europe had seen more than twenty-five years of war, beginning with the French Revolution in 1792 and continuing to Napoleon's march across Europe during the Napoleonic Wars, his short-lived exile to the island of Elba in 1815, his unthinkable escape (which occurred during the Congress), and his final defeat at the Battle of Waterloo on 18 June 1815. From September 1814 to June 1815 ambassadors representing virtually every European state met in Vienna to formulate treaties and to engage in border negotiations. All of France's conquests were reversed, while Prussia, Austria, and Russia saw their territories expanded considerably.

France did come out ahead in one respect though: Brie de Meaux was crowned "le roi des fromages" (king of cheeses) in a contest organized by the French diplomat Charles Maurice de Talleyrand-Périgord. At the Congress—which was a monumental social event as much as it was an interminable series of meetings—Talleyrand quickly became known as an unsurpassed host and a gastronome who deeply valued the role cuisine can play in politics. His personal chef Antonin Carême, credited with developing the high art of French cooking, traveled with him to Vienna; when Louis XVIII sent Talleyrand overbearing letters with advice for negotiations, Talleyrand responded, "Sire, I need casseroles more than written instructions." How better to make the argument that France itself had been betrayed by Napoleon, and should yet emerge as a strong nation, than to demonstrate the strength of French culture and cuisine—particularly French cheese?

Journals and memoirs from ambassadors record that in 1815 a debate broke out about which nation had the finest cheese, and Talleyrand proposed hosting a competition to decide the matter. Other sources suggest Talleyrand simply proposed the competition as an amusing diversion. Regardless, a competition was held, and sixty cheeses entered. Among them, England was represented by Stilton, Switzerland by Emmentaler, Holland by Edam, and Italy by Strachino. The Brie de Meaux, from the Villeroy farm (10 kilometers west of Meaux), was the last cheese presented to the fifty-two judges. Though the negotiators had consistently rated their own national cheese highest, they were unanimous in voting Brie de Meaux "le roi des fromages." The French historian Jean Orieux wrote that "the brie rendered its cream to the knife. It was a feast, and no one further argued the point." The Congress of Vienna reestablished France's status as a key power in Europe, offering extraordinarily lenient terms to the defeated nation, and Talleyrand's shrewd culinary diplomacy seems at least partly responsible for that.

See also BRIE DE MEAUX.

Chapple-Sokol, Sam. "Culinary Diplomacy: Breaking Bread to Win Hearts and Minds." *The Hague Journal of Diplomacy* 8 (2013).
Orieux, Jean. *Talleyrand—The Art of Survival*. New York: Knopf, 1974.
Pitte, Jean-Robert. *French Gastronomy: The History and Geography of a Passion*. New York: Columbia University Press, 2002.

Max P. Sinsheimer

conjugated linoleic acid (CLA) is a naturally occurring fatty acid produced in the rumen of dairy animals by a process of biohydrogenation. It's often called the healthy trans-fat because the type and placement of its double bonds differ from the unhealthy double (trans) bonds created during hydrogenation of fat in industrial food production. CLA exists in at least twenty-eight different forms, but the most common type is called cis-9, trans-11, which represents about 75 percent of all CLA in the diet. Ongoing research into CLA's positive health effects indicates that it can have potent anti-cancer and anti-atherogenic properties as well as drive healthy insulin regulation. Scientists are still teasing apart the mechanisms by which the compound exerts these beneficial effects, but there is almost no doubt that CLA supports good health in various ways. The diet of dairy animals significantly affects the amount of CLA in the foods they provide. Grass-fed dairy products and meats are the richest sources of CLA, with three to five times the amount compared to products from grain-fed animals.

CLA dietary supplements have been popularized as a weight loss treatment, based on animal trials that showed an increased breakdown of body fat with synthetic CLA. These results, however, have not been replicated in human studies. In fact, manmade supplements of the fatty acid—which generally contain 50 percent of CLA in a different chemical structure (trans-10, cis-12) than the kind found in food—have been shown to cause fatty liver, inflammation, and insulin resistance. Natural sources of CLA—meaning all ruminant meats, cheese, and butter, but especially those that are grass-fed—remain the healthiest way of boosting CLA consumption.

See also HEALTH PROPERTIES.

Banni, S. "Conjugated Linoleic Acid Metabolism." *Current Opinion in Lipidology* 13, no.3 (June 2002): 261–266.
Brody, Jane E. "What You Think You Know (But Don't) About Wise Eating." *Well* blog, *New York Times*, 31 December 2012. http://well.blogs.nytimes.com/2012/12/31/what-you-think-you-know-but-dont-about-wise-eating.
Kresser, Chris. "Can Some Trans Fats Be Healthy?" http://chriskresser.com/can-some-trans-fats-be-healthy.
O'Connor, Anahad. "Ask Well: Is Grass-Fed Beef Better for You?" *Well* blog, *New York Times*, 23 October 2013. http://well.blogs.nytimes.com/2015/10/23/ask-well-is-grass-fed-beef-better-for-you.
"Perspectives on Conjugated Linoleic Acid Research: Current Status and Future Directions." https://ods.od.nih.gov/pubs/conferences/cla/cla.pdf.

Elaine Khosrova

Consorzio del Formaggio Parmigiano-Reggiano is an organization founded in 1934 as Consorzio Interprovinciale Grana Tipico, changing its name in 1938. It was established to regulate the production, control the quality, and coordinate the marketing of Parmigiano Reggiano cheese. In 1955 the entire provinces of Parma, Reggio Emilia, and Modena, and portions of the provinces of Bologna to the west of the Reno River and Mantua to the east of the Po River were designated by Italian law as a controlled cheesemaking district, legally linking Parmigiano Reggiano to its geographic place of origin. In 1996 the European Union awarded protected designation of origin (PDO) status to Parmigiano Reggiano, further enhancing its global geographical indication (GI).

Because of stringent Italian and European Union laws governing Parmigiano Reggiano and the fact that the consorzio also holds several certification mark registrations granted by the US Patent and Trademark Office, the consorzio serves to legally defend its certification marks. The consorzio will take legal action to safeguard the use of the Parmigiano Reggiano marks, to increase consumer awareness of the cheese, and to eliminate potential marketplace confusion for importers, distributors, retailers, restaurateurs, and consumers between Parmigiano Reggiano and other very hard grating cheeses that do not meet the consorzio's stringent requirements for certification.

Parmigiano means "of or from Parma," and Reggiano means "of or from Reggio." Parma and Reggio [Emilia] are two cities in north-central Italy at the geographic heart of the production of Parmigiano Reggiano cheese, and these two names identify for consumers worldwide the origin of this famous Italian product. There are four thousand farms where the cattle are fed on locally grown forage. From this protected environment come the qualities that characterize the "king of cheeses." The use of silage and fermented feeds are banned. Regular controls are carried out on the milk used in the manufacturing process to ensure high quality and the presence of special characteristics that allow Parmigiano Reggiano to continue to be a purely natural product, without additives or preservatives.

The consortium identifies the product by fixing symbols and marks; protects and defends Parmigiano Reggiano PDO through supervision of sales and the use of designations and marks; promotes product knowledge to help sales and exports; protects the product's typicality and characteristics; and implements initiatives for the qualitative improvement of the product by conducting research and providing technical support. In compliance with the legislation, managing the PDO has two distinct phases, controlled by two different bodies:

Consortium of Producers

The Protection Consortium is a voluntary, not-for-profit association providing oversight for all the producers of Parmigiano Reggiano cheese. The consortium has been recognized by the Ministry for Agriculture, Food and Forestry Policies (MiPAAF). It submits any changes to be made in the production regulations to the MiPAAF for approval by the European Commission. Its tasks are supervision and protection.

Control Bodies

Control and certification of Parmigiano Reggiano PDO is carried out by an independent control body appointed by the consortium. The Organismo Controllo Qualità Produzioni Regolamentate Soc. Coop. is a private body recognized and authorized by the MiPAAF as the exclusive control body for Parmigiano Reggiano PDO. It ensures the correct implementation of the production regulations throughout the production chain.

Marks

The marking of Parmigiano Reggiano helps identification of the product, improving traceability and providing more information for the protection and benefit of consumers. The mark of origin is engraved on the first day of the wheel and consists of a casein plate applied to the surface of the cheese with a unique identification code for identification and traceability. This is made from casein, that is, cheese protein; when it comes into contact with the hot, moist cheese (immediately after extracting it from the vat) it blends with the surface leaving the identification code legible.

By the evening of the first day the cheese in the molds has taken on a cylindrical shape. While the cheese is moist and plastic a stenciling band is inserted between the mold and the cheese; in one night the band engraves on the vertical side the characteristic wording "Parmigiano Reggiano" in pin dots, the dairy identification number, the month and year of production, and the health code given to every dairy.

Experts within the consortium examine each cheese individually. Following the control body's inspection, a mark is fire-branded onto the individual cheeses that meet the requirements of the protected designation of origin. Cheeses that do not meet PDO requirements will have their identifying marks and dotted inscriptions removed. This is one of the most crucial moments for cheesemakers and consumers alike—the moment of selection and the granting of a certificate that guarantees the authenticity of the product.

The cheeses that are sent for sale to the consumer as "fresh," designating a cheese that has been maturing for a year, will have parallel lines engraved on them, indicating the second class of Parmigiano Reggiano called "mezzano." When the cheese has matured for eighteen months, the "extra" or "export" mark can be added. A system of colored seals assists the consumer with identification of the level of maturation of the prepackaged products available to retailers.

See PARMIGIANO REGGIANO.

Boccaccio, Giovanni. *Decamerone* VIII 3. Translated by J. M. Rigg. New York: E. P. Dutton, 1930.
Pepys, Samuel, diary entry for 4 September 1666.
"Production Standard." Parmigiano Reggiano website. http://www.parmigianoreggiano.com/consortium/ disciplinare_produzione_vigente_sino_agosto_ 2011/production_standard.aspx.

Cherry Haigh

Consorzio Ricerca Filiera Lattiero-Casearia

(CoRFiLaC) is a publicly governed regional entity in Italy, located in Ragusa, Sicily. Founded in 1991, CoRFiLaC was established as an applied research center to support the development of the dairy sector in Ragusa. The main focus of the research center is the evaluation of food safety and quality in producing traditional cheeses made with raw milk, the characterization of aromatic and sensorial properties derived from the specificity of territory investigated, and the nutritional value in the traditional cheeses.

CoRFiLaC has established relations with several internationally renowned researchers, with which bilateral research projects and exchange training programs even at their institutions are ongoing. CoRFiLaC also provides an extension service for herdsman and cheese producers, assisting them throughout the whole chain of production, starting from forage analysis and diet formulation to milk and cheese analysis, implementation of the best practice for milking, improvement of herd management and animal welfare to optimize milk yield and quality. Furthermore, CoRFiLaC works on the supervision of correct cheesemaking and aging procedures, and the definition of experimental marketing activities to strategically position in the market all the dairy products belonging to the territory of origin.

CoRFiLaC offers a wide training program for students, technicians, veterinarians, farmers, cheesemakers, operators in the dairy sector, and consumers. CoRFiLaC is appointed by the Italian Ministry of Agricultural, Food and Forestry Policies (MiPAAF) for the public protected denomination of origin (PDO) recognition applied to Ragusano and Pecorino Siciliano cheese. Within CoRFiLaC, people can experience the Mediterranean Institute of Culinary Art of Sicily (MICAS), whose activities are targeted to valorize the food and wine heritage of the Mediterranean area. Primarily MICAS brings out the art of using raw materials in the kitchen, introducing it to national and international consumers, opinion leaders, gourmets, reporters, and gastronomy lovers.

See also SICILY.

CoRFiLaC. http://www.corfilac.it.

Margherita Caccamo

constant ration technique

See TOTAL MIXED RATION.

continuous whey starters

are commonly used in a variety of cheeses as alternatives to factory-produced starter and ripening cultures. They involve the use of whey from one batch of cheese as a starter for the following batch. As such, they represent diverse and site-specific communities of microorganisms that possess the capacity to acidify milk for cheesemaking at an appropriate rate and under the right conditions (whatever they may be) for a successful outcome. See MICROBIAL COMMUNITIES. Two types of continuous whey starters are thermophilic and mesophilic.

Thermophilic starter cultures are most famously used for hard European cheeses such as Comté and Parmigiano Reggiano. See COMTÉ and PARMIGIANO REGGIANO. Depending upon the cheese, the whey may or may not be incubated in conjunction with the rennet extract. Thermophilic whey starters often reach a very low pH (high acidity) during their incubation period, and are prepared on a daily basis by reserving a portion of the sweet whey from the day's cheese production and keeping it at a controlled temperature overnight.

Mesophilic whey starters are used by more than 80 percent of the farmhouse lactic goat's cheese producers in France. The principle is similar to that of the thermophilic cultures, though the process is less complex, because the long, slow process of lactic cheesemaking means that the whey has fully acidified within the coagulum and is ready to use as an inoculant when the following morning's milk comes into the dairy. Mesophilic whey starters are not combined with rennet, since lactic cheese-making requires a pre-ripening step (limited acidification to take place) before a small amount of rennet is added.

Although continuous whey starters are now integral to the production of a number of continental cheeses, at one time their use was even more widespread. In the early 1890s, F. J. Lloyd, a scientist working for the Somerset County Council, reported the use of "stale whey" as an inoculant by Cheddar makers whose milk was not ripening quickly enough under the influence of its native lactic acid bacteria. Writing in 1896, Long and Benson advised Cheshire cheesemakers to "keep the milk in the vat at a temperature of 94°F until it is ripe enough, or add sour whey, which latter is the more common method" (p. 96). Of course, this method was not foolproof, and spoilage microbes or "taint" could be propagated from day to day if the milk for cheesemaking was impure or the whey was carelessly handled.

As with many processes reliant upon undefined mixtures of microbes whose workings are not fully understood, concerns have been expressed over the use of continuous whey starters, including the potential to transfer pathogenic microorganisms across successive batches of cheese. Pejorative terms such as "backslopping" reinforce this aura of threat and uncleanliness. Although any process that is not properly controlled can present risks, this viewpoint fails to recognize the benefits of the use of these natural starter communities, whose complexity provides them with a degree of bacteriophage resistance still yet to be achieved by manufactured starter cultures, with cost-effectiveness for the cheesemaker, and with the typicity of a farmhouse product.

See also RIPENING CULTURES and STARTER CULTURES.

Cogan, T., and J. -P. Accolas. *Dairy Starter Cultures.* New York: VCH, 1996.

Institut de l'Elevage. "Pérennité de l'utilisation du lactosérum en technologielactiquefermière."*Le cahier fermier*, November 2011. http://idele.fr/recherche/publication/idelesolr/recommends/le-cahier-fermier-n-20.html.

Lloyd, F. J. *Observations on Cheddar Cheese-Making.* London: William Clowes, 1892.

Long, J., and J. Benson. *Cheese and Cheese-Making, Butter and Milk.* London: Chapman and Hall, 1896. Facsimile reprinted by Applewood Books (Bedford, Mass.: 2007).

Bronwen Percival

cooking with rinds is generally done with hard, flinty cheeses such as Parmesan, Romano, aged Gouda, pecorino, and others that have a natural rind (no wax or cloth covering). The technique is simple: save the tough ends of cheese in an airtight bag in the freezer and the next time a pot of soup, sauce, stews, or broth is simmering on the stove, stir in the rinds (about 1 ounce [30 milliliters] for every 1 cup [237 milliliters] of liquid); leave them to cook for at least an hour. Generally the longer the rind braises, the greater the depth of flavor it contributes to the liquid. (The rind itself will become a soggy wad; it can be minced into little pieces and stirred back into the pot if desired.) The equivalent of nose-to-tail eating for turophiles, cooking with cheese rinds is both frugal and effective, as anybody who has ever simmered the bony rind of a chunk of Parmigiano Reggiano will attest to. The hard husk of the cheese is a potent flavor enhancer in cooking because it's particularly rich in umami, the savory, satisfying "fifth taste" that is neither salty, sweet, sour, or bitter. Umami richness is the result of an amino acid, glutamate, converting to L-glutamate, which our palate detects as delicious; Parmigiano Reggiano contains more glutamate than any other natural food on earth. In addition to simmering cheese rinds, it's also possible to lightly grill them until slightly softened and chewy. They can be eaten warm; if cooled, the grilled rinds will resume their tough texture.

See also FLAVOR and RINDS.

Andrews, Colman. "The Perfect Cheese." In *The Country Cooking of Italy*, p. 92. San Francisco: Chronicle, 2011.

Spieler, Marlena. "Parmesan Rind Adds Flavor." *SFGate*, September 2010. http://www.sfgate.com/food/rovingfeast/article/Parmesan-rind-adds-flavor-rich.

Elaine Khosrova

Coolea

See COUNTY CORK.

copper vats have been used in cheesemaking for centuries but are less common today given the prevalence of stainless steel. The sanitary, conductive, and chemical properties of copper make it a preferred vat material in the production of cheeses as geographically diverse as Emmentaler PDO, Parmigiano Reggiano PDO, and Spring Brook Farm Tarentaise. Copper vats are used in certain geographic regions and by particular cheesemakers in observance of tradition and for the metal's unique influence on milk in cheese production. Although copper is historically significant in cheesemaking and remains a preferred vat material for some cheeses, its cost and oxidizing influence make it less than ideal for other cheesemaking applications.

Copper oxidizes rapidly. Vats made from the metal react with their contents as well as with the atmosphere, as is evident in the blue-green patina copper surfaces develop when they are not continually cleaned. This reactivity is responsible for oxidative chemical processes in cheese milk that influence proteolysis and the creation of aroma compounds characteristic of some cheeses. But copper's influence is not always desirable in dairy processing. The corrosive pits that oxidation creates in the vats lead sanitation officials to worry that they could harbor pathogens, and the metal's oxidative properties can lend fluid milk products a metallic flavor. Yet, these same oxidative reactions are so important to the flavor and aroma of some cheeses that, in the absence of copper vats, copper supplements may be added to the milk to produce the desired effect.

Copper vats are valued in the production of certain styles of hard cheeses. A 2009 study of Parmigiano Reggiano DOP by Pecorari et al. concluded that cheeses made in copper vats were superior in structure and sensory qualities to cheeses made in steel vats. A 1996 publication by the Comité Interprofessionnel du Gruyère de Comté references a study showing that Comté PDO contained 3 milligrams of copper per kilogram when it was made in steel vats, as opposed to 12.7 milligrams of copper per kilogram in cheese processed in copper vats. The report attributed the absence of aromas and flavors typical of Comté PDO to this chemical difference. Comparisons of cheeses made in copper vats with those made in stainless steel vats have shown differences not only in copper concentrations but also in eye formation, acid development, elasticity, and microbiological viability. In Austria, regulations require

Vorarlberger Alpkäse PDO to be made in *Sennkesseln*, the name of the traditional copper kettles there, in accordance with this understanding of the importance of copper exposure in the production of Alp-style cheeses. Swiss regulations require cheesemaking dairies (*fruitières*) to employ copper vats in the production of Sbrinz AOP. Most Swiss-style cheese made outside of the Alpine regions of Switzerland, Germany, and Austria is made in stainless steel vats. This could be one reason why Swiss-style cheeses made in New World countries often do not achieve the complexity in aroma and flavor of their Alpine models.

Some cheesemakers in Canada and the United States have found ways to use copper vats where the government otherwise forbids the use of the oxidative metal. Health Canada and the United States Food and Drug Administration generally do not allow the use of copper vessels in domestic cheese production; but, in several provinces and states, older copper kettles have been "grandfathered" in, and permissions have been offered to producers who have been able to demonstrate that copper is a safe and sanitary metal in cheese production.

See also VATS and WOODEN VATS.

Maurer, L., G. W. Reinbold, and E. G. Hammond. "Influence of Copper on the Characteristics of Swiss-Type Cheeses." *Journal of Dairy Science* 58 (1975): 645–650.
Pecorari, M., et al. "The Use of Copper or Steel Vats in Parmigiano-Reggiano Cheese-Making: Effects on Qualitative Characteristics of the Cheese." *Scienza e Tecnica Lattiero-Casearia* 60 (2009): 97–118.

Brent A. Wasser

Cornish Yag

See LEAF-WRAPPED CHEESES and NETTLE.

Cotija

See MEXICAN CHEESES.

cottage cheese, at first glance, is a humble, fresh cheese—a mid-twentieth century American staple. However, when made in the traditional way, using a slow lactic acid fermentation, it is one of the most complex cheeses produced in this category.

During World War I the United States produced posters that asked the citizenry to make food conservation a priority. This poster encouraged civilians to eat cottage cheese as a source of protein in order to save meat for soldiers.
STATE ARCHIVES OF NORTH CAROLINA

Cottage cheese was developed on farms as a way to use the low-fat milk that remained after cream was skimmed from the evening milking for the purpose of making butter. The process was simple. Whole milk was poured into shallow pans in the evening, usually by the farm wife, and by morning the cream floated to the top. Overnight, naturally occurring lactic acid bacteria had also begun to ferment both the cream and the skim milk. The cream was then churned into butter, and the skim milk was set aside in a warm place until a curd with the consistency of firm yogurt formed. Curd formation could take anywhere from eight to fifteen hours.

The fragile curd was then cut with a knife into small cubes and cooked and stirred in a pot on the stove at a low temperature for an hour or more. This process firmed up the curds and released most of the whey. The curds were then given a cold water bath, which helped to wash away any trace of acidity, and were poured into a colander to drain. When the curds were dry, they were salted and "dressed" with a little cream.

Because cottage cheese is made with skim milk, it is a natural alternative for people on a low-fat diet. The butterfat in the dressing can easily be modified, which makes it possible to control the caloric and fat components in the cheese.

Today, most commercially produced cottage cheese is made using a short four-to-six-hour set time. Quick curd development is accomplished by increasing the dose of lactic acid starter culture and adding rennet. Cooking is speeded by heating the curd to a higher temperature and decreasing the stirring time. This fast method was developed after World War II, when the industrialization of food production was in full swing. The shortening of production time and the addition of rennet meant that fermentation time was reduced, and the sweet, lemony flavors that develop in long-set cottage cheese were eliminated entirely. Machine stirring replaced hand stirring, and the natural cream dressing was replaced with a dressing of sweet milk or cream, stabilized with cornstarch. Flavors such as pineapple, apple, or cherry were sometimes added.

Massive amounts of cottage cheese were produced in large dairy plants, starting in the 1950s, as a source of protein-rich food to satisfy the needs of a postwar society experiencing a population explosion. This was the "baby boom" decade, and low-cost cottage cheese was an inexpensive way to feed growing families. Dairy farms responded to the growing demand for fluid milk by adding more cows to their herds. Cheese plants became larger and more efficient, and small processors could not compete with the larger plants.

By the 1990s just a few cottage cheese plants were left in the country. Demand has declined, and because of advances in food technology, refrigeration, and transportation, cottage cheese production has become centralized. Now would be a good time to bring back small-scale cottage cheese making to every region in the United States.

See also FRESH CHEESES and INDUSTRIALIZATION.

Caldwell, Gianaclis. *Mastering Artisan Cheesemaking: The Ultimate Guide for Home-Scale and Market Producers.* White River Junction, Vt.: Chelsea Green, 2012.
Kosikowski, Frank V., and Vikram V. Mistry. *Cheese and Fermented Milk Foods.* 3d ed. 2 vols. Westport, Conn.: F. V. Kosikowski, 1997.
Mollison, Bill. *Permaculture Book of Ferment and Human Nutrition.* Tyalgum, Australia: Tagari, 1993.

Sue Conley

Cougar Gold is a Cheddar-style cow's milk cheese produced by the Washington State University (WSU) Creamery in Pullman, Washington. Cougar Gold is perhaps best known as one of the only cheeses in the United States that is packaged and sold in steel cans.

While canned cheese is something of a novelty today, during the early twentieth century, canning was a cutting edge packaging technology in the United States. Industry researchers struggled, however, to solve a significant problem: aging cheese caused cans to burst due to a buildup of carbon dioxide. During the 1940s Dr. Norman S. Golding of what was then Washington State College, working in conjunction with the American Can Company, developed a combination of cultures that produced a cheese that remained stable in a vacuum-sealed can. The result was dubbed "Cougar Gold" after the school's mascot, a cougar, and Dr. Golding. Cougar Gold continues to be produced with the same cultures developed by Dr. Golding and his team.

Cougar Gold is produced on the WSU campus by students enrolled in the School of Food Science. The cheese is made by hand at the university's creamery, pressed and sealed into 30-ounce (850-gram) cans, then aged for one year. The milk comes

Cougar Gold, produced by the Washington State University Creamery, is perhaps best known as one of the only cheeses in the United States that is packaged and sold in steel cans. The man depicted here is Dr. Norman S. Golding, who developed the recipe for Cougar Gold. © WASHINGTON STATE UNIVERSITY

from a herd of Holstein cattle maintained by faculty and students of the WSU Department of Animal Sciences. While Cougar Gold currently makes up approximately 80 percent of the WSU Creamery's overall production (to the tune of approximately 250,000 cans per year), the facility makes several other styles of cheese as well as ice cream.

See also CHEDDAR.

Parr, Tami. "Expansion and Innovation." In *Pacific Northwest Cheese: A History*, pp. 83–107. Corvallis: Oregon State University Press, 2013.

Tami Parr

Coulommiers is a soft ripened, disk-shaped French cheese made from cow's milk, with a white *Penicillium candidum* rind. It is named after the small town of Coulommiers in the historic county of Brie, the modern département of Seine-et-Marne, east of Paris. It has no appellation and no geographical delimitation.

Historically Coulommiers is one of the same group of cheeses as Brie (the alternate name "Brie de Coulommiers" can be found). Before refrigeration it was the easiest of these cheeses to handle in local and regional trade. The outward point of distinction is diameter: Brie de Meaux is the largest of all; Coulommiers is the smallest, slightly thicker than the others. Tortes were traditionally made with a pastry incorporating fresh Coulommiers. It even had its share of royal favor, like the more expensive Brie cheeses. Marie Leczinska, Louis XV's queen, not only a gourmet but a careful housekeeper, instructed that Coulommiers be used in her Bouchées à la Reine.

In modern times most of the Coulommiers that is widely sold in other parts of France and internationally is factory-made from pasteurized milk in

Normandy or other regions. For that Coulommiers the period of ripening is about four to six weeks. The fat content is 40 percent. The exterior is pure white and smooth, the interior butter-colored. It tastes fresh and creamy and is firm rather than runny. There is nothing not to like about it. It fits into the market between Camembert, which ripens and sours steadily, and Brie, which is classier and less predictable. It is claimed to be the third highest-selling cheese in France, after so-called Emmentaler and pasteurized Camembert. See EMMENTALER and CAMEMBERT DE NORMANDIE.

The artisanal or farmhouse Coulommiers that is made near Coulommiers is much more distinctive. This Coulommiers, usually but not always made from unpasteurized milk, is well worth finding. Matured for five to eight weeks, it will have some reddish blush in parts of the rind, a finer and stronger flavor, and a readiness to run. The majority of it is sold to local and Parisian markets.

See also BRIE DE MEAUX and FRANCE.

Bazin, Alexandre. *Notice sur le fromage de Coulommiers.* Rebais, France: Ménard, 1910.
Chesnaye, Eric de la. "Le camembert chahuté…" *Le Figaro: Economie,* 4 February 2010.

Andrew Dalby

The **counterculture** of the late 1960s and 1970s, with its anti-establishment sentiment and ethos of self-sufficiency, played a key role in the rise and popularity of "natural" foods and the revival of farmstead cheesemaking in the United States. Belonging to the baby-boomer generation, the generally young, white, and educated members of the counterculture rebelled against the postwar consumerism and conservative family values that characterized their upbringing. Opposed to the Vietnam War and distrustful of corporations and politicians, countercultural "hippies" sought to develop a more harmonious relationship with nature and experimented with collaborative living arrangements. According to Warren Belasco, the counterculture developed a "countercuisine" with its own supply lines, food staples, and provisioning schemes. Elements of this provisioning system emphasized whole foods, agrarian self-sufficiency, ethnic multiculturalism, and craftsmanship. For many, food was a vehicle to broader change.

From the outset, counterculturalists rebelled against the plasticity, conformity, and blandness of prominent commercial cheeses such Velveeta, Kraft, and Cheez Whiz, which they viewed as metonyms for the synthetic nature of society at large: owned by large corporations, produced in automated factories, and shelf-stable for an eternity. Instead, hippies turned to handmade cheeses that were alive with bacteria and full of flavor and aroma. Out of the counterculture emerged the roots of the farmstead cheese movement in America. See FARMSTEAD.

The movement started with hippie "goat ladies" (as they're affectionately known in the cheese world). Adhering to the countercultural ethos, a handful of self-empowered women moved "back to the land" and started homesteads. Largely in an effort to be more self-reliant and at one with nature, these women (sometimes in collaboration with men) grew vegetables, kept chickens, and raised small livestock. When the livestock, mostly goats, started producing more milk than could be consumed in liquid form, the women started making cheese in their own kitchens. As their craft improved, and as countercultural compatriots and the development of "California cuisine" created a market for unconventional cheeses, these hobbyist cheesemakers expanded into larger commercial operations and began selling their cheese at farmers' markets and food co-ops. Prominent among them were Judy Schad of Capriole Farms in Indiana, Anne Topham of Fantôme Farm in Wisconsin, Allison Hooper of Vermont Creamery in Vermont, and in California, Mary Keehn of Cypress Grove, Barbara Backus of Goat's Leap, and Laura Chenel of Laura Chenel's Chèvre. The early efforts and slow successes of these cheesemaking counterculturalists has given rise to a veritable renaissance of specialty and artisanal cheese production in America.

Today, the countercultural culinary ethic informs consumers who, like those a half century ago, seek the vitality, flavor, and nutritional value of natural foods. Whether they buy locally made or organic cheeses or seek out raw-milk varieties, environmentally conscious consumers are seeking to realize values that extend beyond the plate and palate. Moreover, the same self-reliant sensibilities of the counterculture are manifest in a burgeoning do-it-yourself ethic of home cheesemaking as well as in a desire for living foods. Both form the foundation of a growing interest in fermentation that is enthusiastically supported by the contemporary counterculturalist Sandor Katz and his followers.

See also AMERICAN "GOAT LADIES" and HOME CHEESEMAKING.

Belasco, Warren. *Appetite for Change: How the Counterculture Took on the Food Industry.* New York: Pantheon, 1989.

Katz, Sandor Ellix. *Wild Fermentation: The Flavor, Nutrition, and Craft of Live-Culture Foods.* White River Junction, Vt.: Chelsea Green, 2003.

Katz, Sandor Ellix. *The Art of Fermentation: An In-Depth Exploration of Essential Concepts and Processes from Around the World.* White River Junction, Vt.: Chelsea Green, 2012.

Paxson, Heather. *The Life of Cheese: Crafting Food and Value in America.* Berkeley: University of California Press, 2013.

Bradley M. Jones

County Cork. Ireland's modern farmhouse cheese movement began in the 1970s on the Beara Peninsula in West Cork. Veronica Steele, the charismatic woman now referred to as the matriarch of the Irish farmhouse cheese industry, launched a generation of cheesemakers from a farm she and her husband, Norman, had purchased near Allihies. Within a short time, Declan Ryan and Myrtle Allen had tasted her cheese and enthusiastically featured their discovery on the cheese boards of two of Ireland's most renowned restaurants, Arbutus Lodge and Ballymaloe House. The response from the delighted guests to her washed-rind cheese was overwhelmingly positive. Steele shared her knowledge with local farmers' wives, many of whom are now well-known cheesemakers in their own right. See STEELE, VERONICA.

Around fifteen farmhouse cheeses are now made in County Cork, and many use the milk of their own herds. Each cheese reflects the place where it is made—its character, the breed of the animal, the biodiversity of the pasture, the unique microflora on the farm, and the personality of the cheesemakers. Some of the most famous County Cork cheese are washed-rind cheeses.

Washed-Rind Cheeses

The West Cork washed-rind cheeses Milleens, Durrus, Gubbeen, and Ardrahan, each of which has an international reputation, were all created by remarkable, spirited women. The semisoft Milleens farmhouse cheese was created by Steele. Its flavor, reminiscent of Munster, helps to support Steele's theory that it was possibly the Irish who taught the Swiss and French how to make cheese. She credits the monks who left Ireland to establish monasteries on the continent after the Dark Ages with also spreading their knowledge of cheesemaking. Veronica and Norman Steele's son Quinlan now carries on their proud tradition of making Milleens.

Jeffa Gill started to make her semisoft, washed-rind Durrus cheese on her hillside farm in Coomkeen on the Sheep's Head Peninsula in 1979. She too was one of the first generation of Irish farmhouse cheesemakers. She now makes a smaller cheese called Durrus Óg as well as Dunmanus, a mature Durrus weighing about 6.6 pounds (3 kilograms).

Gubbeen farmhouse cheese is made from the milk of Tom and Giana Ferguson's herd of Friesian, Jersey, Simmental, and Kerry cows. One of the distinguishing characteristics of Gubbeen cheese is the unique type of microflora on the rind, which has now been identified and given the name *Microbacterium gubbeenense*. When smoked Gubbeen was introduced in 1978, it was the first smoked farmhouse cheese produced in modern Ireland.

Ardrahan, made by Mary Burns near Kanturk in North Cork since 1983, is possibly the feistiest and most pungent of all the washed-rind cheeses of County Cork. The cheeses are beautiful, wrinkly 3.3-pound (1.5-kilogram) rounds made with the milk of the Burns family's own Friesian herd.

Although the washed-rind cow's milk cheeses have the highest profile they are by no means the whole cheese story of County Cork. Other fine cheeses, made from both cow's milk and goat's milk, round out Cork's contribution to cheesemaking.

County Cork's Other Cheeses

Cow's Milk Cheeses

Dick and Helene Willems started making cheese in 1979 as a way to use up excess raw milk from their own herd of cattle and to provide the Gouda cheese that they were craving from their native Netherlands. Their son Dicky continues to make superb cheese according to a Dutch Gouda recipe using milk from two local herds. The Willems farm makes cheese from February to October and has added a mature Coolea to its offerings in recent years.

Frank Shinnick and his German wife, Gudrun, began making raw-milk cheese in 1996 from their own dairy herd outside Fermoy, in North Cork. The cheeses are made in a 396-gallon (1,500-liter) copper vat procured at considerable effort from Switzerland. The Fermoy Natural Cheese Company produces a washed-rind St. Gall, a smear ripened St. Brigid, and more recently, a Ballyhooly Blue. Fermoy cheeses are part of the Slow Food raw-milk cheese presidium. See SLOW FOOD.

Goat's Milk Cheeses

Jane Murphy, a microbiologist by profession, started to make cheese on the Ardsallagh farm in 1980. She and her family produce a wide range of cheeses from a mixed herd of Anglo-Nubians, Saanens, and Alpine goats raised by a neighboring farmer in East Cork. In 2015 Ardsallagh cheeses were awarded McKenna's Guides Best in Ireland Award as well as the Cáis Gold Irish Cheese Award. See NUBIAN; SAANEN; and ALPINE.

Tom and Lena Biggane, along with their son William, make Clonmore goat's milk cheese and Shandrum cow's milk cheese on their farm in the midst of the Golden Vale. All the milk for their cheeses comes from their Saanen and Toggenburg goats, as well as from their own herd of dairy cows.

On Cape Clear Island off West Cork, the remarkable blind cheesemaker Ed Harper makes small quantities of cheese from the milk of British Alpine goats that graze on his beautiful rocky farmland. The cheese resembles a Coulommiers and is named Cléire Goats Cheese, after the island. See COULOMMIERS.

Other notable cheeses of County Cork include clothbound Hegarty's Cheddar, Havarti-like Carrigaline Farmhouse Cheese, soft goat's cheese from Orchard Cottage Dairy, and Glenilen cream cheese. Desmond and Gabriel, two beautiful thermophilic Alp-style cheeses made by Bill Hogan and Sean Ferry, are sadly no longer being produced.

See also IRELAND.

Anderson, Glynn, and John McLaughlin. *Farmhouse Cheeses of Ireland: A Celebration*. Cork, Ireland: Collins, 2011.

Darina Allen

The **Courtyard Dairy** was established in 2012 by Andy and Kathy Swinscoe in North Yorkshire, England. It has earned accolades practically since opening day, in 2013 winning the Best Cheese Counter during the World Cheese Awards competition. A focus on raw-milk cheeses and direct relationships with cheese producers (the Swinscoes visit many producers to learn their methods and practices) are key to the success of this small cheese shop.

The Courtyard Dairy specializes in cheeses from the British Isles, with Andy overseeing maturation in the store. The cheeses are aged for sale directly in the shop, and for distribution to restaurants in the area. Andy received training in cheese affinage at the Hervé Mons caves in France, and later worked selecting and maturing cheeses for market at Bath's Fine Cheese Company. He received a grant from the Queen Elizabeth Scholarship Trust to learn about affinage in France, and has used that knowledge, as well as retail experience in Paxton and Whitfield, to set up their operation and to firmly advocate for British cheese made with raw milk. See FINE CHEESE COMPANY, THE and PAXTON AND WHITFIELD.

Among the cheeses aged to specific criteria and available at The Courtyard Dairy is Kirkham's Lancashire, which due to its size (44 pounds [20 kilograms]) requires a longer maturation time to gain its characteristic flavor and light texture than smaller wheels sold by other retailers. In the store, rounds of Dale End Cheddar and Hafod Cheddar are available directly from the producers and chosen specifically for the Swinscoes. They are continually tended on traditional spruce wood boards that allow them to breathe and maintain their rich flavor. See WOODEN SHELVES.

See also RAW-MILK CHEESES and UNITED KINGDOM.

The Courtyard Dairy. http://www.thecourtyarddairy.co.uk.
McGuigan, Patrick. "The Only Whey Is British: The Great Cheese Revolution." *Telegraph*, 11 July 2015.

Carlos Yescas

The **COW** is the female of the domestic cattle species *Bos bovis;* other names used are *Bos taurus* for Western-type cattle and *Bos indicus* for the humped

The first milking of the day in the Sicilian countryside with local shepherds Filipo and his son, Enzo. © HALEY POLINSKY

Montana cheesemaker Margaret Adams makes a feta-style cheese with milk from her two LaMancha goats. © VINCENZO SPIONE

Colonies of molds isolated from the Cellars at Jasper Hill in Greensboro, Vermont. © BENJAMIN E. WOLFE

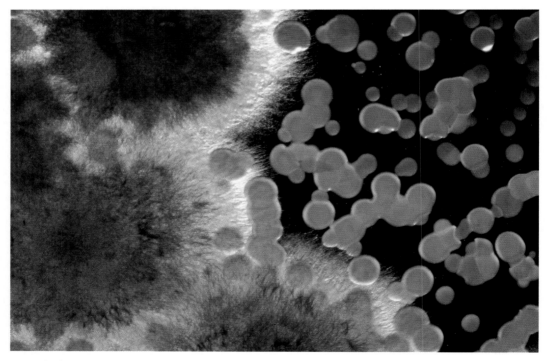

Molds (left) and Proteobacteria (right) isolated from the rind of Robiola di San Lorenzo, a lightly aged goat cheese mainly produced in the Province of Alessandria, Italy. © BENJAMIN E. WOLFE

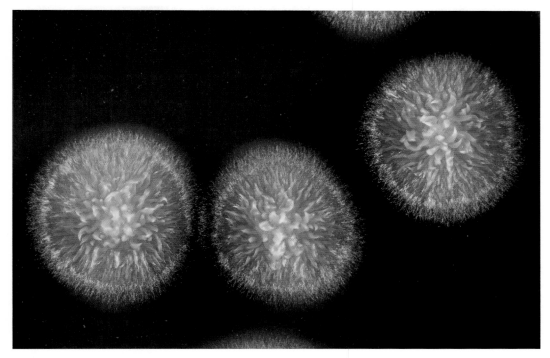

Colonies of the yeast *Geotrichum candidum*, commonly used in the production of surface-ripened cheeses. While *Geotrichum candidum* is a yeast, its appearance on cheese and when grown in the laboratory is mold-like. This particular strain was grown in a petri dish. © BENJAMIN E. WOLFE

Colonies of bacteria (orange and white) and fungi (fuzzy white) clustered on the relatively dry surface of Bayley Hazen Blue, a natural-rind cheese made by Jasper Hill Farm in Greensboro, Vermont. © BENJAMIN E. WOLFE

Antonio Rodeghiero, the owner of Malga Manazzo, making Asiago. Asiago is a cow's milk cheese produced only in the northeastern part of Italy, in an area strictly defined by the PDO recognition that includes the provinces of Vicenza and Trento and part of Padua and Treviso. COURTESY OF CONSORZIO DI TUTELA DEL FORMAGGIO ASIAGO

A worker at one of the temperature- and humidity-controlled warehouses that mature Asiago cheese brands the wheels with the phrase "Prodotto della Montagna," meaning "made on the mountain." This asserts that all phases of production—including pasturing and milk collection—took place at an altitude between 600 and 2,300 meters above sea level. COURTESY OF CONSORZIO DI TUTELA DEL FORMAGGIO ASIAGO

In the Spring Brook Farm caves in Reading, Vermont, an employee washes Redding cheese with a brine solution.
© KATE ARDING

A panel from the fourteenth-century text *Tacuinum Sanitatis* (1474), a Latin adaptation of an eleventh-century Arabic manual on well-being. The text presented cheese, a food crafted by feudal farmers, as part of a healthy diet for nobles.
PHOTO © TALLANDIER / BRIDGEMAN IMAGES

Bog butter, or butter that has been buried in a peat bog to preserve it, is a well-known (but mysterious) archaeological phenomenon, with hundreds of discoveries in Ireland and Scotland dating back as far as the Middle Iron Age (400–350 B.C.E.). Ben Reade, of the Nordic Food Lab, attempted to re-create bog butter to gain insight into how and why ancient peoples buried their butter. Here he is filtering milk cream through a grass "nest" to remove insects and dirt, which has the added benefit of supplying the cream with ample lactic acid bacteria for souring. © BENEDICT READE

Roquefort cheese is aged in the natural Combalou caves under the village of Roquefort-sur-Soulzon. These caves are naturally ventilated with cool, humid air from faults in the rocks, called "fleurines." © MANUEL HUYNH, ROQUEFORT SOCIETY

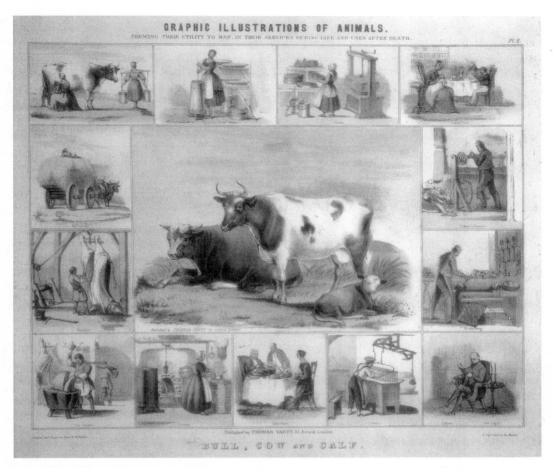

A hand-colored lithograph from *Graphic Illustrations of Animals, Showing Their Utility to Man*, published in London in 1850. Drawn by Benjamin Waterhouse Hawkins (1807–1894), an artist and sculptor of natural history subjects, the vignettes surrounding the central image showcase some of the ways cows benefit man, from the milk and meat they give to the vellum, or calfskin, that is used to bind books. UNIVERSAL HISTORY ARCHIVE/ UIG / BRIDGEMAN IMAGES

cattle of India and some African regions. They have been raised for meat, dairy, and draft purposes for the last 10,500 years. The chief differences between cow's milk and that of sheep and goats (the other major European and western Asian dairy animals) are greater volume per animal, smaller percentages of some short-chain fatty acids responsible for "goatiness," and larger milk fat globules that easily form a cream layer on the top, an advantage in butter making. By the Middle Ages cattle were the most important draft, meat, and milk animals in the British Isles and much of northwestern Europe. They accompanied Dutch and British settlers to North American colonies, where cow's milk dairying predominated for more than three and a half centuries.

The Start of Intensive Breeding

During the eighteenth century the so-called British agricultural revolution triggered huge increases in the cattle population and a lengthening of the breeding season through new winter crops and "improved" pasture and hay management. Specialized breeds for meat and milking purposes did not yet exist. Eurasian cattle had evolved into many landraces adapted to distinctive ecological niches (e.g., humped cattle's unusual ability to thrive in tropical heat) without systematic human control of the process. British and European cheeses from small rural districts always bore the individual stamp of milk from local cows grazing on unimproved local pasturage.

Jersey cows grazing at Cedar Mountain Farm in Vermont, which supplies milk to its sister cheesemaking business, Cobb Hill Cheese. © KATE ARDING

In the United Kingdom further nineteenth-century advances in progressive farming brought rapid change. Influential livestock raisers developed systems of intensive artificial selection for specific traits such as rapid weight gain or large milk yield that could be transmitted to offspring within a few generations and at least theoretically perpetuated as long as "purity" of blood was maintained. These intensive livestock breeding programs based on matings between near relatives had reverberations in major cattle-raising regions of Europe.

With no knowledge of actual genetics, early breeders tended to confuse signs of an animal's fitness for desired purposes with particular phenotypes, or sets of external features like coloring and body conformation. Vastly popular agricultural fairs featuring competitions among show animals accelerated the development of individual breeds with sharply differentiated appearance.

The first cattle breed deliberately promoted for dairying purposes was the Shorthorn, advertised as equally fit for meat and milking. See SHORTHORN. But as the British and American urban market for various dairy products became more clearly divided into particular sectors, butter makers and cheesemakers soon found that Shorthorns gave thinner (though more) milk than other rising breeds. Advocates of the newly popular Ayrshires, "Alderneys," and "Dutch cattle" pointed to their leaner, bonier

conformation as evidence of correct "dairy type" associated with high milk yield. See AYRSHIRE; GUERNSEY; JERSEY; and HOLSTEIN.

Implications for Cheesemaking

Dairy products made from cow's milk soon emerged as an important sector of expanding agricultural economies in industrialized nations, but during the nineteenth century the fluid milk and butter markets became especially dominant forces in the United States, United Kingdom, and several northwestern European nations. Qualities important to cheesemakers dwindled accordingly. The trend was less pronounced in France, where both rural and metropolitan consumers long remained loyal to regional cheeses reflecting the character of local soil, pasturage, and dairy landraces including sheep and goats.

By 1900 the United States stood at the forefront of world cow dairying, including dairy science and manufacturing technology. This progress, however, had come at a great cost to cheesemaking. For most dairy farmers the priority was a large milk output to supply the fluid milk market. For others it was butter, which was usually produced by centrifuge either on the farm or at "creameries" (small butter-manufacturing plants). Agriculture schools' research on increasing total milk or butter output, through work with a few breeds, benefited both camps. The

1900 USDA census records a dairy cow population of roughly 17,140,000 and total milk production of more than 7.2 billion gallons (33 billion liters), with annual output per cow at an all-time high average of 424 gallons (1,928 liters). According to the same source, between 1850 and 1900 the amount of butter produced on US farms had risen from about 313.3 million pounds (142.1 million kilograms) to more than 1 billion pounds (453.6 million kilograms) between 1850 and 1900. Meanwhile the corresponding amounts of cheese made from cow's milk had shrunk from about 105 million pounds (48 million kilograms) to 16 million pounds (7.2 million kilograms).

Nearly all US cheeses now came from small factories, which began replacing farmhouse operations after 1850. Like earlier North American farmhouse cheeses, all factory cheese was of a general English Cheddar type. Cheese milk qualities crucial to its manufacture mattered little in advanced modern cow breeding and feeding programs.

The gap between cheesemaking and other priorities grew exponentially with every cost-effective twentieth-century dairying innovation. One reason was that amounts of milk produced by dairy animals, measured by either weight or volume, chiefly depend on percentages of water, which vary inversely with all other factors. The milk of cows bred for extremely high yield often has too little casein (thus too little calcium phosphate) for optimal curd-setting. Milk fat and casein percentages, on the other hand, almost always vary together; it is difficult to increase or decrease one independently of the other. The rich, creamy milk of cows bred for butter making is also excellent for many unaged, bloomy-rind, and semisoft cheeses. But in hard cheeses like Cheddar high milk fat content can be a liability, impeding the natural loss of moisture from curd during aging. It thus became difficult for cheesemakers to find milk that produced good results without readjusting casein and/or fat levels.

A general shift to pasteurized milk in all dairy manufacturing early in the twentieth century soon dictated complex readjustments of starter and rennet amounts as well as aging schedules to approximate the older factory cheeses. However the pasteurization revolution allowed commercial versions of simple unaged cottage cheese, pot cheese, and cream cheese from cow's milk to become permanent fixtures of the American table. See PASTEURIZATION.

Cows Pushed to the Limits

In roughly a century of developments beginning with the first pasteurization experiments of the 1880s and 1890s, cows and their milk underwent not just changes but transformations beyond any previous imagining, all driven by the fluid milk market. For progressive dairy farmers it was axiomatic that getting more milk from fewer cows automatically lowers labor/production costs per unit of milk produced. Already more responsive than other dairy animals to human interventions like out of season breeding or prolonged lactation, cows were now manipulated into unprecedented performance. Between 1950 and 2000 the US dairy cow population shrank from about 24 million to about 9.2 million, while total milk production per year increased from about 127.2 billion pounds (57.6 billion kilograms) to more than 200 billion pounds (90.7 billion kilograms).

Contributing factors to this change include methods of scientifically calculating rations for higher milk yield, a knowledge of cattle genetics not available to the first breeding pioneers, and an overwhelming focus on raising Holsteins ("Friesians" in Europe). All these have affected not only commercial dairying worldwide, but also the production of milk for such cheeses as Parmigiano Reggiano and Cheshire.

The more-milk-fewer-animals equation has backfired to such an extent that some leaders of the milk industry are rethinking its premises. The success of small goat's milk and a few sheep's milk cheese operations since the early 1980s has inspired some dairyists to turn away from the single-minded focus on quantity promoted by the fluid milk market and to concentrate on other quality factors such as the solids non-fat components, including casein, other proteins, and dissolved minerals—all indicators of suitability for cheesemaking.

Holstein breeding, dramatically transformed by artificial insemination with frozen semen from a comparative handful of sought-after sires, has caused genetic bottlenecks affecting dairy herds around the world. The crisis has encouraged programs of outcrossing with previously obscure breeds including the French Montbéliarde and Normandy, sacrificing something in milk volume for the sake of the animals' health and sounder genetic future as well as improved milk quality. Meanwhile the Jersey breed has staged an extraordinary comeback following aggressive promotion campaigns by the American

Jersey Cattle Association. Among its arguments are that somewhat larger herds of smaller cows giving less but richer milk can be more energy-efficient, environmentally advantageous, and suitable for cheesemakers' needs than smaller herds of bigger high producers. The same case can be made for other once-disregarded dairy cow breeds.

In the future many cow farmers are likely to rethink their relationship with the huge but deeply troubled US fluid milk market—now hit by frequent surpluses, and generally offering either razor-thin profit margins or actual losses to operations under the size of several thousand cows. Both factory-scale and artisanal cheesemaking stand to benefit. Representatives of all dairy breed organizations are aware of the sizable premiums paid by cheesemakers for milk that meets their standards. For small and midsize farms, cheese-focused priorities offer every advantage over selling to the fluid market. Minor breeds of cow, including some recently threatened with extinction, are likely to become more visible in this sector of dairying.

See also GOAT and SHEEP.

Derry, Margaret. *Masterminding Nature: The Breeding of Animals, 1750–2010*. Toronto: University of Toronto Press, 2015.
Hall, Stephen J. G., and Juliet Clutton-Brock. *Two Hundred Years of British Farm Livestock*. London: Natural History Museum, 1989.
Mendelson, Anne. *Milk: The Surprising Story of Milk Through the Ages*. New York: Knopf, 2008.

Anne Mendelson

Cowgirl Creamery

Cowgirl Creamery is a company on a mission to showcase California's west Marin regional identity around dairy farming and cheese. Operated by Sue Conley and Peg Smith, Cowgirl Creamery produces six cheeses year-round: Mt. Tam, Red Hawk, Inverness, Wagon Wheel, Fromage Blanc, and Crème Fraîche. The creamery also produces four seasonal cheeses: St Pat (spring), Pierce Pt (summer), Chimney Rock (fall), and Devil's Gulch (winter). Cumulatively, Cowgirl Creamery cheeses have won more than twenty-five awards.

Conley and Smith met at the University of Tennessee, where they were both liberal arts students, avid music fans, and—most telling—protesters against the Vietnam War and supporters of equal rights. After college, they visited the Bay Area in California on a cross-country road trip, fell in love with the culture, and decided to move there permanently.

For almost two decades, they worked in the restaurant scene—most notably, Conley at Obrero Hotel and Bette's Diner, and Smith at Chez Panisse. In the early 1990s, Conley met Ellen Straus, learned about the struggles of dairy farmers, and committed herself to the Straus Family Creamery. Cowgirl Creamery was started in 1994 when Conley and Smith purchased an old hay barn in Point Reyes Station to make cheese from Straus Creamery milk.

Today Eric Patterson is the lead cheesemaker, assisted by cheesemakers Miguel Martinez, and Matt Brown. Cowgirl Creamery purchases milk from the Straus Family Dairy. Milk from the Chileno Valley Dairy is used for the seasonal cheese, as well as the Inverness, and milk from Bivalve Dairy is used for the Red Hawk. Cowgirl Creamery is now headquartered in Petaluma, California, the production site of all their cheeses except Red Hawk, which is made exclusively at the creamery's original location in Point Reyes Station. In 2016 Cowgirl Creamery was purchased by the Swiss dairy company Emmi, along with the company's distribution business, Tomales Bay Foods. Sue Conley and Peg Smith will continue to oversee Cowgirl Creamery as president and vice president. See EMMI.

See also RED HAWK.

Conley, Sue, and Peggy Smith. *Cowgirl Creamery Cooks*. San Francisco: Chronicle, 2013, pp. 10–26.
Roberts, Jeffrey. *The Atlas of American Artisan Cheese*. White River Junction, Vt.: Chelsea Green, 2007, pp. 344–345.
Thorpe, Liz. "Fighting the French: Conquering America's Chefs." In *The Cheese Chronicles*, pp. 236–239. New York: HarperCollins, 2009.

Adam Moskowitz

cream cheese

The term **cream cheese** can be a bit confusing, as it is applied to two very different products: (1) the American industrialized product sold in a brick or tub, and (2) European high-fat spreadable cheeses that are usually eaten young.

American Cream Cheese

In the United States cream cheese refers to a specific product: an industrialized pasteurized cow's milk cheese. It is (perhaps ironically) categorized as a "fresh, soft cheese," because it does not require ripening or aging. Typically cheeses are made by curdling the protein in milk, or mixtures of milk and cream, through the use of rennet or other coagulating substance. American cream cheese is usually curdled with lactobacillus cultures, then pasteurized.

In preindustrial America "cream cheese" was a generic name for any fresh cheese made by skimming ripened cream off the top of milk and allowing it to sit and ferment. It wasn't until the late 1920s, with the invention of hot pack stabilization, which liquefied cheese curd above boiling, mechanically separated it, and added locust bean, carob bean, or guar gum stabilizers, that the term referred to the standard, foil-wrapped block that comes to mind today.

The history of its creation goes as follows: In 1872 a Chester, New York, dairyman, named William Lawrence began to make what he called "Neufchâtel cheese"—which bore no similarity to the Neufchâtel made in Normandy, France, since at least the sixteenth century (and neither does the Neufchâtel available for sale in the United States today). Three years later, at the request of the Park & Tilford grocery company, he began manufacturing a richer cheese, using the same method, and called it "Cream Cheese." In 1880 a savvy New York distributor started carrying Lawrence's cheese under the name "Philadelphia Cream Cheese," named for the city then known for good cheese. Two years later the same distributor, Alvah Reynolds, bought the Empire Cheese Factory to produce his own Philadelphia Cream Cheese, and in 1903 sold the brand to the Phenix Cheese Company, which in 1928 merged with Kraft Foods, making Kraft the premier producer of what we today call Philadelphia Cream Cheese. See KRAFT FOODS.

Today the FDA defines cream cheese as a soft, uncured (i.e., fresh) cheese made from pasteurized milk and cream, with the final product having a minimum milk fat content of 33 percent and a maximum moisture content of 55 percent. The high fat and moisture content can lead to issues like whey separation and excess moisture, since fats repel water. Thus the addition of stabilizers such as guar and carob gums to improve shelf life. American Neufchâtel is sold as a lower-fat version of cream cheese, with about a third less fat (23 percent milk fat). Cream cheese maintains its connection to New York as an essential component of two Big Apple classics: bagels, atop which cream cheese is "shmeared," and cheesecakes, where it forms the filling. See CHEESECAKES.

European Cream Cheeses

In Europe cream cheese is a broader category of high fat, young, soft cheeses. The French in particular have more soft rich cheeses than the rest of the world combined, and many of them are modern inventions.

In France "crème" indicates cheeses with higher than normal butterfat content (minimum 55 percent fat), regardless of the style of the cheese. "Double-crème" cheeses (factory-made, such as Boursin and Caprice des Dieux) have at least 60 percent fat. Fontaineblau, softened with whipped cream, is often served sweetened (like Italy's mascarpone) with fruit. Gratte-Paille is another cream-enriched cheese.

"Triple-crème" must be at least 75 percent butterfat. Examples are Champagne's Brillat-Savarin (and imitators, such as Brillador, Brivarin, Saulieu, and Vatel), Explorateur (invented in 1950 in Seine-et-Marne), and Saint-André. Saint-André and the similar Saint-Gildas are still made in dairies, but, like American cream cheese, Explorateur is a factory-made cheese. Croupet and sometimes Grand Mogul are artisanal cheeses made with unpasteurized milk. Jean-Grogne is Gratte-Paille, with added crème-fraiche. See BRILLAT-SAVARIN.

With just 45 percent fat, Normandy's Neufchâtel, the model for American cream cheese, is neither double-nor triple-crème. However, adding cream to Neufchâtel yields Petit-Suisse (both double- and triple-crème varieties). Soft, high-fat cheeses, like Brie and Camembert, are usually eaten well ripened. While sometimes labeled "double-" or "triple-crème" they are not really cream cheeses, and are better discussed elsewhere. See NEUFCHÂTEL; BRIE DE MEAUX; and CAMEMBERT DE NORMANDIE.

Outside of France a few cream cheese–like products exist. England's cream cheese and Scotland's Caboc have 60–75 percent butterfat. Liptauer, from Hungarian "liptói," or Slovakian "liptovska," is a soft, often flavored cheese that comes in a small tub (like commercial cheese spreads). German Doppelrahmfrischkäse, a double-crème cheese, is sold in foil-wrapped cubes, as is Holland's Mon Chou. Italy's mascarpone, at 80 percent butterfat, is the richest cream cheese of all. See MASCARPONE.

See also FAT and TRIPLE-CREAM CHEESE.

Jaine, Tom, ed. "Cream Cheese." In *The Oxford Companion to Food*, 3d ed. Oxford and New York: Oxford University Press, 2014.

Marks, Jeffrey. "'The Days Had Come of Curds and Cream': The Origins and Development of Cream Cheese in America." *Food, Culture, & Society* 15, no. 2 (June 2012).

Mendelson, Anne. *Milk: The Surprising Story of Milk Through the Ages*. New York: Knopf, 2008.

United States Food and Drug Administration. *Code of Federal Regulations* Title 21, Part 133, Section 133: "Cream Cheese." http://www.accessdata.fda.gov/scripts/cdrh/cfdocs/cfcfr/CFRSearch.cfm?fr=133.133.

Tamar Adler and Gary Allen

critical control points (CCP) are part of a properly prepared Hazard Analysis Critical Control Point (HACCP) plan. Critical control points are identified after a flow diagram, as well as a complete hazard analysis, of the cheesemaking process have been prepared. These are the points in the process in which a recognized hazard of sufficient concern to health and safety can be prevented, reduced, or eliminated. Critical control points are based both on the likelihood that a particular hazard will occur and on the severity of the resulting harm if it were to occur. A properly designed critical control point is based on scientific data that show what the hazard is, how it can properly be monitored, and what corrective actions may be taken that will bring the hazard back under control.

Critical control points must be both quantifiable and observable in real time. Examples of quantifiable measurements include the use of a pH meter to evaluate the amount of acid that has been produced; the use of recording charts for a vat pasteurizer to indicate how much time the milk spends at each temperature during the heating step; as well as tests of the water activity of the cheese or the presence or absence of antibiotic residues in the milk. On the contrary, a test of viable microbes such as a standard plate count, although quantifiable, is not observable in real time and therefore does not lend itself to being a critical control point.

Although control may occur during any step in the cheesemaking process, it is important to note that critical control points are distinct in that they address specific hazards that may result in harm at a specific place and time. A cheesemaker typically employs sanitation practices to control the possibility of microbial cross-contamination of the entire facility. In contrast, the cheesemaker may use pasteurization as a critical control point to eliminate the specific pathogenic bacteria that may be present in the cheese milk. See PASTEURIZATION.

Inherent in their nature is that critical control points must be the final step in the process of preventing a specific hazard from ultimately damaging the product. There should be no step further along in the process that can address the hazard. For example, in the case of antibiotic residues, testing the milk at the time of receipt is a critical control point. There is no other step in the cheesemaking process that will test for, or eliminate the presence of, antibiotic residues. Failure to identify antibiotic residues at the receiving step could result in cheese that could cause harm to consumers with allergies to antibiotics.

Properly designed and implemented critical control points are essential to the production of a safe, unadulterated product. They can aid in identifying issues before they get out of control, and if addressed in real time, they can bring the system back into control.

See also HAZARD ANALYSIS AND CRITICAL CONTROL POINT.

Pritchard, T. "Ensuring Safety and Quality I: Hazard Analysis Critical Control Point and the Cheesemaking Process." Chap. 7 in *American Farmstead Cheese*, edited by Paul S. Kindstedt. White River Junction, Vt.: Chelsea Green, 2005.

Todd Pritchard

Croatia is known for culinary diversity so extensive that its signature products have been called "the food of the regions." More specifically the geographical and cultural localism of Croatian cheeses reflects the influence of explorers, conquerors, and neighboring countries to convey a vivid sense of place.

Historians believe the Romans taught cheesemaking to Croatians on the Adriatic island of Pag in 1 B.C.E. The Republic of Venice's rule of Dalmatia from the sixteenth to the eighteenth centuries also laid down an Italianate influence on Croatian cheese. Specific Croatian identity can be ascribed to a cheese as far back as 1749 in a market listing of items that referred to Croatian or Hungarian cheese; it's assumed the cheese was produced in both regions and was named for the place of origin. Cheese remains an important part of the Croatian diet and is often served sliced into triangles.

Climatic and cultural influences account for significant differences between coastal and continental Croatian cheeses. Arguably the most celebrated coastal Croatian cheese is produced on Pag. Until the twentieth century Pag shepherds milked sheep and processed cheese in stone huts above pastures on common land. Once pastures became privately owned the huts were made into private homes, so shepherds commuted to care for the sheep and women became cheesemakers. Pag cheeses, along with sea salt, have played an important role in the Croatian economy.

Pag cheese is made from the ultra-rich and fatty milk of the indigenous Pag sheep. Living outdoors year-round in the island's harsh climate, they graze on wild aromatic herbs that grow in the rocky soil and are seasoned with sea salt dust dried and deposited by the fierce *bura* (wind). The diet infuses the ewe's milk with a distinctively salty, piquant flavor. Aged two to eighteen months, Pag cheese ranges from pale yellow, soft, easily sliceable, and pleasantly sharp (young) to harder, muted yellow, and sharper in taste (mature) to tough and brown (old).

Paški sir DOP, soaked in olive oil and aged in stone, is considered the best Pag. Dinarski sir iz maslinove komine, a hard and somewhat crystalline cheese from the island of Skradin, is made with pasteurized mixed cow's and goat's milk and aged for at least six months in pressed olive skins. Paški sir iz komine maraske, Pag cheese from Zadar, is made with marasca cherries from Komin.

Continental Croatian cheeses are produced in a hotter, drier climate and are influenced by farmland food practices, as well as the people and foodways of other cultures, particularly Austro-Hungarians, Slavs, and Turks. Infusions—paprika, nettles, black truffles, herbs, etc.—are introduced to sheep's, cow's, goat's, or mixed-milk cheeses. Shapes may be more elaborate, and preservation approaches such as smoking are put into play for some cheeses. See SMOKED CHEESES.

Notable continental examples include Turoš, orangey, cone-shaped, cow's-milk, paprika-spiced cheese dried for days in smoke or sunlight from Međimurje in northernmost Croatia; Prgica, cone-shaped and air-dried, with dried red pepper, produced in northwestern Croatia; and Škripavac, a soft, full-fat, low-protein, raw, squeaky cow's milk cheese. Croatian cheeses have scored important wins at the World Cheese Awards and are gaining public awareness as tourism in the region grows.

Evenden, Karen. *A Taste of Croatia*. Ojai, Calif.: New Oak, 2007.

Fine, John V. A. *When Ethnicity Did Not Matter in the Balkans: A Study of Identity in Pre-Nationalist Croatia, Dalmatia, and Slavonia in the Medieval and Early-Modern Periods*. Ann Arbor: University of Michigan Press, 2006.
"Pag Cheese—Paški sir." http://www.pagcheese.com.
"Sheep Milk Cheese: Recognized Top Quality." http://www.pagcheese.com/sheep-milk-cheese-recognized-top-quality.

Robin Watson

cross-contamination is what happens when microorganisms or chemicals are transferred between foods and food contact surfaces. In the dairy industry, the risk of cross-contamination increases as one moves from large, highly mechanized, state-of-the-art dairies to the small, farmstead cheesemakers who pride themselves on hands-on production of certain specialty cheeses from raw milk. However, the likelihood of tracing an outbreak to such farmstead cheese is far lower due to the smaller quantities produced. The potential routes for cross-contamination are many, ranging from inadvertent commingling of raw and pasteurized milk through pinholes in the pasteurizer to the direct contact of milk or cheese curds with potentially contaminated vats, cheese knives, stirrers, cheese hoops, cheese presses, brine solutions, or packaging materials. The surrounding manufacturing environment also poses a risk for cross-contamination if microorganisms living on the floor or in floor drains become aerosolized from the use of high-pressure hoses during cleaning operations.

Raw milk is a known source of foodborne pathogens including *Listeria monocytogenes*, *Salmonella*, *Campylobacter*, and *Escherichia coli* O157:H7 among others. Since these same bacterial pathogens will periodically enter dairy facilities with the raw milk supply, all cheesemakers must remain vigilant and make every attempt to separate the raw and pasteurized areas of the facility, assuming that the cheese in question is to be prepared from only pasteurized milk. Many areas in cheesemaking facilities that are difficult to clean, such as cracked floor tiles, floor drains, door seals and gaskets, walk-in coolers, and rough welds on equipment, can serve as potential harborage sites for bacterial pathogens as well as for spoilage organisms that negatively impact product shelf life. If these sites are not properly cleaned and sanitized on a daily basis, bacteria can attach to them and grow in the presence of water and dairy-product residues to produce biofilms. Once formed, the complex communities of microorganisms that make up these biofilms are embedded within sticky polysaccharide matrices that afford protection from chemical sanitizers. Under these conditions, bacterial pathogens such as *Listeria monocytogenes* may become permanent residents, with these colonized environmental niches serving as sources of cross-contamination for many years. Since these biofilms are akin to tartar on teeth, physical scrubbing using brushes or other means is necessary before detergents and chemical sanitizers can eliminate these sites as potential sources of contamination.

Failure to prevent cross-contamination during cheesemaking has led to dire consequences, including numerous recalls involving *Salmonella, E. coli* O157:H7, and *Listeria monocytogenes*, as well as scores of notable foodborne outbreaks. In one of the largest outbreaks on record, a valve in a state-of-the-art dairy facility that was inadvertently turned to allow raw milk to contaminate pasteurized milk led to more than 16,000 confirmed cases of salmonellosis in the Chicago area in 1985. However, *Listeria monocytogenes* has continued to be the most problematic foodborne pathogen for cheesemakers following a 1985 landmark outbreak of listeriosis in California from soft, Mexican-style cheese. That outbreak was attributed not only to cross-contamination in the cheesemaking facility but also to the intentional addition of raw milk to previously pasteurized milk in order to increase the amount of cheese produced. Several years earlier, the use of wooden shelves to transport wheels of soft-ripened Vacherin Mont d' Or cheese between various caves in the Swiss Alps for ripening led to an outbreak of listeriosis that killed 34 people and infected 122 others. Given the hands-on nature of the production of many cheeses, particularly the more exotic varieties, due diligence to effective cleaning and sanitizing is of paramount importance in minimizing the risks associated with cross-contamination during cheesemaking.

See also BIOFILMS; HYGIENE; *LISTERIA*; OUTBREAK; PATHOGENS; and *SALMONELLA*.

Byrne, R. D., and J. R. Bishop. "Control of Microorganisms in Dairy Processing: Dairy Product Safety Systems." In *Applied Dairy Microbiology*, 2d ed., edited by Elmer H. Marth and James Steele. New York: Dekker, 2001.

Kornacki, J. L., and J. B. Gurtler. "Incidence and Control of Listeria in Food Processing Facilities." In *Listeria,*

Listeriosis, and Food Safety, 3d ed., edited by Elliot T. Ryser and Elmer H. Marth. Boca Raton, Fla.: Taylor & Francis, 2007.

Robinson, R. K., and A. Y. Tamime. "Maintaining a Clean Working Environment." In *Dairy Microbiology Handbook: The Microbiology of Milk and Dairy Products*, 3d ed., edited by Richard K. Robinson. New York: Wiley, 2002.

Elliot Ryser

Crottin de Chavignol is a small tasty cheese (2 ounces [60 grams]) made exclusively from the whole goat's milk of the Alpine breed in the Sancerre region of France. See ALPINE. The well-being of goats, the care that breeders bring to them, and the availability of local forage are the guarantees of quality milk. Crottin de Chavignol has been recognized as an AOC cheese since 1976 and PDO since 1996. About 1,000 tons are produced annually, including 30 percent directly by farmers.

In the Sancerre area, goat breeding is a tradition that dates back to the sixteenth century. At that time most farms that had vineyards also raised goats. Goats, also called the "poor man's cow" because they are not hard to please and accept several sorts of food, produced milk (and from it, cheese) daily, which represented extra income. At the end of the nineteenth century the European phylloxera infestation forced the removal of the diseased vines, providing plots of land perfectly suited for grazing, as the pastures were excellent. Goat milk production then spread to the Champagne Berrichonne, Pays Fort, and Val de Loire.

Around 1900 the first refiners set up their business and with the arrival of the newly created railway line between Paris and Nevers, they could sell cheese at the markets of the capital city. It is difficult to know exactly when the words "Crottin de Chavignol" first appeared. It was first seen in 1829, when a tax and land register inspector in the Cher département wrote in the column "goat" that "their milk is not good for making butter, but with it, delicious cheese is made." in the Sancerrois region, it is known under the name "Crottins de Chavignolles." The origin of that name comes from the word *crot*, used in the Berry area for a small oil lamp (made from clay) that winemakers used to light their cellar and the goatherds used to light their barn at milking time.

Crottin de Chavignol is covered with a natural rind, white or blue. Its white or ivory texture is firm and smooth. The Chavignol goat cheese PDO must be aged for at least ten days. It offers a range of varying flavors depending on its maturing stage. When young, it gives off a light goat flavor with a slightly floral and perfectly balanced taste. When a bit older, the Crottin de Chavignol is covered with blue *Penicillium* and has aromas of mushroom and forest undergrowth. Mature, the Chavignol reveals walnut and hazelnut flavors. When even more mature, and kept in stoneware pots, the Chavignol called "repassé" will surprise with its strength and its creamy texture. It is best appreciated with a wine from the central Loire, particularly a Sancerre.

See also FRANCE; GOAT; and LOIRE VALLEY.

Chavignol. http://www.crottindechavignol.fr.
Lavaud, Bernadette. *Le Crottin de Chavignol*. Paris: Edition Les Quatre Chemins, 2008.
Léry, Jean de. "L'histoire mémorable de Sancerre." 1573.

Mireille Faguet

Crowley Cheese is a semifirm raw-milk cheese, with a distinctive smooth, creamy texture, and sweet buttery flavor. Although similar to a Wisconsin Colby, it predates that cheese and retains its reputation as an America original. See COLBY.

From seventeenth-century colonial Dutch and English cheesemaking until the mid-nineteenth century in the United States, small farms produced cheese for private use or sale to local customers. In 1824, John Crowley started to make a mild, washed-curd raw cow's milk cheese in his farmhouse in Healdville Vermont. For sixty years, the family made cheese by hand for themselves and neighboring farmers. In 1881, these farmers established a cheese cooperative with Nellie and Winfield Crowley (John's grandson) as the cheesemakers. In 1882, with demand exceeding the scope of their farm kitchen, they built the Crowley Cheese Factory; with expanded capacity and railroad access, they shipped cheese to many East Coast cities.

After 1882, the company changed hands several times and in 2009, Jill and Galen Jones purchased it. In 2016, using milk from one local farm and still following the original recipe, they make cloth-wrapped, waxed wheels and waxed blocks. They produce only a few hundred pounds of handmade cheese a day. Crowley uses animal rennet for coagulation and washes the small granular curds with warm water to create the cheese's signature creamy

texture. Aged for a minimum of four months, the soft to semihard cheeses range in flavor from mild to extra sharp. In 1979, the factory was placed on the National Register of Historic Places.

Jenkins, Steven. *Cheese Primer*. New York: Workman, 1996. See pp. 423–425.
Roberts, Jeffrey. *The Atlas of American Artisan Cheese*. White River Junction, Vt.: Chelsea Green, 2007. See pp. 66.
Wolf, Clark. *American Cheeses: The Best Regional, Artisan, and Farmhouse Cheeses, Who Makes Them, and Where to Find Them*. New York: Simon & Schuster, 2008. See pp. 77.

Jeffrey P. Roberts

A **crystal** is defined as any solid that is formed of elements, compounds, or a combination of elements and compounds that has an ordered and repetitive three-dimensional arrangement. In cheese, crystals may form from a variety of building blocks and may

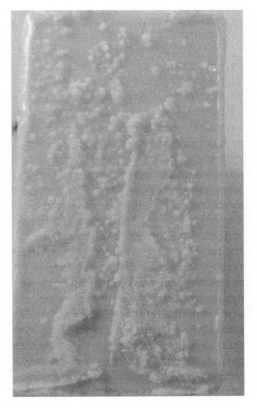

Cheddar cheese displaying extensive calcium lactate crystallization on an exposed surface. © GILS FILS TANSMAN

be imperceptibly small or large enough to see or feel. Cheese crystals may be composed of inorganic or organic material. Crystals that form from inorganic material are composed exclusively of minerals and resemble crystals in rocks and soil. Inorganic crystals may appear in process cheese from emulsifying salts that are used in the manufacturing process. Inorganic crystals of calcium phosphate are frequently observed under the rind of white mold-ripened (bloomy-rind) cheese.

In contrast to inorganic crystals, organic crystals are formed from biological compounds that contain carbon and may or may not contain minerals as well. These crystals may be composed of amino acids, such as tyrosine, cysteine, and leucine, or lactate, which is the byproduct of lactose fermentation. Crystals in cheese that form from lactate also contain calcium.

Whether crystals are inorganic, organic, or a combination, the same chemical dynamics can be used to describe their growth. Crystals form when compounds from cheese manufacturing or aging dissolve in the water phase of cheese and saturate it. This process may be very slow (for instance, the accumulation of amino acids in Parmigiano Reggiano), or may be very rapid (as in the accumulation of calcium phosphate in bloomy-rind cheese). After saturation crystals arise at nucleation sites within a cheese or on exposed cheese surfaces. A nucleation site provides a favorable environment for the initial formation of a crystal nucleus. Irregularities in the cheese matrix may provide nucleation sites, and some evidence suggests that dead bacteria and microcrystals of other compounds may provide suitable nucleation sites. Currently very little is known about the nucleation of crystals in cheese.

Once a crystal nucleus has formed, the crystal begins to grow by adding building blocks in a very specific three-dimensional configuration around the nucleus. As the crystal grows, the building blocks of that crystal diffuse toward the growing crystal from the surrounding area. The crystal will continue to grow until the surrounding area is depleted of the compounds that are needed to grow the crystal. Crystals may grow to the visible threshold either on the cheese surface or as embedded deposits. These visible crystals are composed of many fused crystallites that grow in a manner that is still poorly understood.

When crystal aggregates become perceptible, they can affect the visual and sensory properties of cheese.

Often crystals may be considered unsightly or unappetizing; in rindless Cheddar cheese, calcium lactate crystals form as a white haze or white deposit on exposed surfaces of blocks. The crystalline precipitate may be mistaken for white mold, which often causes the product to be rejected, discarded, or trimmed. In other cheeses crystal precipitates may be distinctive features that do not diminish marketability, but may affect sensory properties. For example, aged Gouda sometimes forms crystals of tyrosine on the internal surfaces of eyes, as well as granular clusters of crystalline tyrosine embedded within the cheese body. Such crystals are often desirable because they contribute to the visual splendor of these cheeses and may be perceived as crunchiness when eaten. Under certain manufacturing conditions, calcium lactate my form as granular crystals within Cheddar cheese, instead of on the surface. In this form, the deposits resemble tyrosine crystals and are thus more desirable. Occasionally large, hard, unpalatable calcium lactate crystals develop in Cheddar cheese, and these may diminish a cheese's quality. See CHEDDAR.

A variety of crystals also form at or just beneath the rind of surface-ripened cheeses, such as bloomy-rind cheeses (Camembert, Brie, and St. Andre). Crystals in bloomy-rind cheeses are often too small to be perceived. In contrast washed-rind cheeses are frequently characterized by surface grittiness or sandiness that may be caused by surface crystallization. The formation of calcium phosphate on the surface of bloomy-rind cheeses also impacts cheese softening; acidity gradients cause calcium phosphate to crystallize at the cheese surface, which then triggers the outward diffusion of calcium phosphate from the cheese interior to the surface; this causes calcium to dissociate from the cheese proteins and contributes to softening of these cheese varieties. Thus the formation of calcium phosphate crystals under the rinds of these cheeses is a critical process in the development of soft texture. See BLOOMY-RIND CHEESES and WASHED-RIND CHEESES.

Although crystals occupy a very small volume in mature cheese, the formation of crystals is central to the ripening process in some cheeses. Microscopic crystals, such as those in bloomy-rind cheeses, are as important to the overall sensory qualities of cheese as large crystals, such as tyrosine granules in grana cheeses that directly impact texture. As consumers demand more unique cheeses, the predictable and controlled formation of crystals may become a useful tool for cheesemakers to differentiate their offerings.

See also CALCIUM PHOSPHATE.

Bianchi, A., et al. "Amino Acid Composition of Granules and Spots in Grana Padano Cheeses." *Journal of Dairy Science* 57, no. 12 (1974): 1504–1508.
Brooker, B. E. "The Crystallization of Calcium Phosphate at the Surface of Mould-Ripened Cheeses." *Food Microstructure* 6 (1987): 25–33.
Dybing, S. T., et al. "Effect of Processing Variables on the Formation of Calcium Lactate Crystals on Cheddar Cheese." *Journal of Dairy Science* 71, no. 7 (1988): 1701–1710.

Gil Fils Tansman

culture houses are companies that develop, produce, and market starter and ripening cultures for use in cheesemaking. See STARTER CULTURES and RIPENING CULTURES. Culture houses generally produce multiple lines of products, including starter cultures consisting of single and multiple strains of both mesophilic and thermophilic bacteria; so-called specialty cultures, a.k.a. premixes or blends, designed for specific types of cheeses; and ripening cultures tailored for aroma and flavor development as well as eye formation and resistance to contaminating microorganisms. Most companies offer their cultures in freeze-dried granular, frozen pellet, or liquid form, both in bulk starter and DVI (direct vat inoculation) forms.

Many culture houses were founded by microbiologists and dairy scientists, and indeed most engage in significant research and development. According to US industry veteran Mike Comotto, "The amount of effort and research that goes into developing even one successful culture strain from isolation, characterization, field testing, commercialization, manufacturing to the final market is a real deal to the cheese maker."

The larger culture houses have order minimums, often in the range of US$100,000, and employ separate agents for sales to smaller and medium-size cheesemakers and to the general public. Orchard Valley Dairy Supplies, for example, is the UK distributor for DuPont Danisco, which by most accounts has the industry's largest market share. In the United States companies such as Dairy Connection and Artisan Geek sell Danisco products along with those from other culture houses such as ABIASA, Chr. Hansen, Mofin Alce, and Sacco. In France and also Switzerland the industry has tended toward smaller laboratories that develop different strains and in turn license or sell their products to bigger manufacturing or sales firms.

Culture houses and their sales agents—whether small, medium, or large—frequently offer detailed technical advice and tailored solutions to their customers via dedicated phone lines and their websites. Most houses also pride themselves on supplying customized blends of defined or undefined strains.

History

For all of cheese history until the late nineteenth century, cheesemakers relied on naturally occurring lactic acid bacteria, captured from the byproducts of previous batches or simply allowed to enter the milk from the surrounding environment. The groundwork for the modern starter culture industry was laid in 1878 when Joseph Lister isolated lactic acid bacteria (LAB) and published his results in the *Transactions of the Pathological Society of London*. Another major advance occurred in 1893, when Christian Hansen (1843–1916), who had already done much to popularize his rennet products since the mid-1870s, began manufacturing and selling the first powdered starter cultures in Copenhagen. See LACTIC ACID BACTERIA and HANSEN, CHRISTIAN D. A.

In 1906 Robert Marschall founded his eponymous culture house, Marschall Dairy Laboratory, in Madison, Wisconsin, a US milestone. According to Ralph Early, in his book *The Technology of Dairy Products* (1998), "the first commercial starters were likely to have been mixtures of strains of unknown composition—commercial undefined mixtures—obtained from raw milk. For the first half of this century such commercial mixtures were supplied in dried or liquid form to cheese creameries where they usually required several subcultures to be fully activated. Two major principles are apparent in the development of commercial starter cultures: firstly describing the culture itself, its composition and characteristics, and secondly establishing the form in which it can be offered to the creamery."

S. Orla-Jensen (1870–1949) laid more crucial groundwork, studying LAB and publishing the results in his seminal work *The Lactic Acid Bacteria*

(1919). Starting in the early 1930s Hugh Whitehead (1899–1983), an English-born biochemist who made his career in New Zealand, demonstrated the deleterious effects of bacteriophages on cheesemaking. See BACTERIOPHAGES. He also introduced selected single-strain cultures and the notion that they had flavor-giving potential. Meanwhile, similar work—applying pure strains to cheesemaking—had been done by A. B. Shelton at the Hawkesbury Agricultural College (now University of Western Sydney) and was soon implemented in Australian cheese factories as well as exported to New Zealand. The practice of blending between two and six single strains became the industry standard for starter cultures until the end of the twentieth century.

Despite these earlier innovations from Australia and New Zealand, throughout the 1960s and into the 1970s, many US dairies and factories continued to use the traditional method of maintaining a mother culture and preparing bulk starters for daily cheesemaking. Eventually economic pressures to expand forced them to seek greater efficiencies. Research and innovation in bulk starter technology proceeded at Utah State and Oregon State universities: starters could be concentrated using centrifuges and frozen or freeze-dried so they could be added directly to the bulk starter vat. On the for-profit side, into the 1990s, both Hansen and Marschall developed highly concentrated, efficient DVI cultures. The principles of genetic discovery and manipulation began to be applied to starter-culture development, and advances were made in selection for phage resistance.

The mid-1970s through mid-1980s was a period of innovation aimed at offering increased efficiency and cost savings for large commercial manufacturers. "The cheese industry was growing rapidly from the small local factories, many independently owned, to huge corporate facilities," writes Comotto. "As factories grew, demands on the ingredient business had to meet these new challenges." Several firms (Hansen, Marschall, and Dederich) began developing proprietary cultures designed to create enzymes that would maximize flavor while minimizing aging time, thus offering attractive shortcut options for factory customers.

Throughout the twentieth century, particularly toward the latter half, and into the twenty-first, the history of cheese culture houses is one of consolidations, mergers, and acquisitions. The Danisco factory, which has remained in Madison, Wisconsin since its beginnings as the Marschall Lab, is a prime example. In 1966 Miles, Inc. bought Marschall and subsequently became a unit of the German company Bayer AG. In 1989 Bayer sold Marschall to the French conglomerate Rhône-Poulenc SA, which in turn spun it off as part of its Rhodia Food division divestiture. In 2004 Danisco acquired Rhodia, then in 2009 DuPont acquired Danisco, and the Madison factory was officially renamed the DuPont Nutrition & Health Danisco Cultures Plant.

Chr. Hansen: A Leading Role

Founded eponymously by the young Danish biochemist in 1873, Chr. Hansen has been a perennial industry leader since its inception. It remained family owned for its first 115 years while continuing to expand and become one of the largest culture houses, with subsidiaries in the United States, Europe, Latin America, and India with about 2,600 employees worldwide. Beyond initiating commercial rennet and starter culture production, the company's history claims numerous other innovations: in 1974 it introduced DVS (direct vat set) cultures for sale and in 1980 built a culture factory that incorporated up-to-date technologies, including freeze-drying.

In 1985 Hansen introduced phage-resistant cultures; it continued to expand its culture-production facilities and by 1989 had factories in Roskilde, Denmark; Milwaukee, Wisconsin; and Arpajon, France. In the early 1990s Hansen began developing cheese ripening- and flavor-control cultures. In 2000 the company introduced Easy-Set, a line of cultures in frozen pellet form designed for large dairies as an alternative to in-house bulk starters. In 2004 it began applying genome-sequencing to culture strains and in 2008 opened what it claims is the world's largest culture factory.

Products

Products offered by culture houses include the mesophilic acid-producing starter *Lactococcus lactis* (particularly *L. lactis* ssp. *lactis* and *L. lactis* ssp. *cremoris*), the mesophilic aroma producers *L. lactis* ssp. *lactis biovar diacetylactis* and *Leuconostoc mesenteroides* ssp. *cremoris*, the thermophilic starter cultures *Streptococcus thermophilus* and *Lactobacillus* (several species), and the eye-producing *Propionibacterium freudenreichii* ssp. *shermanii*. Ripening cultures include *Brevibacterium linens*, corynebacteria, *Geotrichum candidum*, *Penicillium camemberti*, and *Penicillium roqueforti*. See LACTOCOCCUS LACTIS; LACTOBACILLUS; BREVIBACTERIUM LINENS; GEOTRICHUM CANDIDUM; and PENICILLIUM.

Chr. Hansen, for example, offers starter packages for a number of cheese types including Cheddar, continental, cottage cheese, Grana Padano, pasta filata, propionic, soft cheese, and white cheese. DuPont Danisco typically sells a wide range of cheese culture products under its Choozit brand, including simple acid-producing lactic cultures; simple mesophilic acid-producing cultures that are defined blends of pure strains and others that are undefined, multi-species mesophilic cultures for eye formation and diacetyl flavor production; thermophilic cultures for production of acid as well as flavor components such as acetaldehyde; thermophilic-mesophilic blends; adjunct cultures for additional flavor and texture development; and ripening cultures, including yeasts and molds. Danisco also sells ready to use Choozit blends for various types of cheeses as well as bulk set starters and cultures media.

Roughly 80 percent of culture houses' products are quite similar, without great differentiation from one company to the next. Basic lactic acid starter cultures, for example, provide specific functionality: they deliver certain levels of acidification within certain periods of time under specific conditions. Where fundamental product differentiation and claims for a competitive edge may become relevant is in ripening cultures and in the advancing field of phage resistance, also known as "phage hardening." Another area of potential differentiation is identification of single strains and particular "recipes" for them. While the individual strains themselves may not be unique or proprietary, a company's knowledge of their combinations and respective applications may well be. Additionally traditional undefined strains, if obtained from unique sources—for example, specific provenances of raw cheesemaking milk from grass-fed animals, and carefully preserved as so-called heirloom cultures—can be valuable for perpetuating fine cheesemaking traditions.

Artisan and farmstead cheesemakers; smaller, more traditional creameries; and other companies seeking to produce distinct fine table cheeses often employ heirloom cultures, which are generally slower-acting and tend to yield more complex, authentic, or traditional flavor profiles. AJ & RG Barber Ltd., a family firm founded in 1833 and located in Somerset, England, is exemplary, having identified and maintained heirloom cultures for West Country Farmhouse Cheddar, which was awarded its European PDO in 1996.

Cutting-edge Research

While sequencing the genome of *Streptococcus thermophilus* in the early 2000s, scientists at Danisco noticed a particular pattern called CRISPR (clustered regularly interspersed short palindromic repeats) that had apparently evolved as bacteria's way of becoming phage-resistant. They were able to harness this discovery and in 2007 began "vaccinating" cultures to enhance their resistance. For opponents of GMO (genetically modified organisms), the appeal of this technology is that it avoids recombinant DNA techniques such as electrophoresis. It is simply a way of using gene-mapping, the argument goes, to manipulate and select existing strains for such traits as phage resistance without creating new "artificial" strains that would not otherwise have occurred in nature. See GENETICALLY MODIFIED ORGANISM.

Another notable locus of research and development was the not-for-profit Dairy Innovation Australia Ltd. (DIAL), which was founded in 2007 as the merger of the Australian Starter Culture Research Centre with four other technical centers. Like other similar organizations—both academic and commercial—DIAL practiced bacterial genome-sequencing. It amassed an archive of about three thousand culture strains, called the Australian Starter Culture Collection (ASCC). Entries were extracted from various sources—dairy companies, cheeses, other collections, and variants produced in DIAL's lab—stored frozen, purified, and assessed for potential applications. In 2012 DIAL opened a purpose-built facility for this work in Werribee, on the outskirts of Melbourne; in 2015 the collection was sold to Chr. Hansen and the facility began operating as part of Hansen's Australian subsidiary.

Prominent Culture Houses

Prominent culture houses today include:

- ABIASA (Avances Bioquímicos Alimentación S.L.)—The commercial offshoot of the Instituto Rosell, founded by Spanish dairy chemist and pioneering researcher on lactic acid bacteria José María Rosell (1886–1963), first in Canada and then in Spain. ABIASA is located in Tui, Galicia, northwestern Spain, on the border with Portugal.

- CSK Food Enrichment—A large Dutch multinational, with divisions in Poland, Hungary, France, and the United States, CSK offers numerous product lines in mesophilic, thermophilic, and mixed starters, single- and multiple-strain, for both bulk and DVI inoculation as well as its trademarked ripening and specialty culture brands Flavour Wheel, Dairy Safe, Opti Strain, and Health Plus, all with specific industrial applications.
- DSM Food Specialties—A division of the larger Dutch parent company DSM, which employs nearly 22,000 people worldwide and had net sales of close to 9.3 billion euros in 2014. DSM's cultures product line is DelvoCheese. In 2012 the company acquired Cargill's cultures and enzymes division, cementing its place as a dominant player in the industry.
- Mofin Alce Group—Founded in 1950 by microbiologist Mario Mogna, this family firm located in Novara, Italy, specializes in lactic starter cultures, blue molds, and other dairy manufacturing ingredients, including so-called "autochthonous natural starters," particularly for Italian PDO and other traditional, artisanal cheeses that require slow development of complex flavor profiles.
- Sacco SRL—Italy's largest producer and exporter of thermophilic starter cultures. Sacco began as a culture house in Milan in 1948 and in 1984 merged with Caglificio Clerici, a family firm founded in 1872 whose principal products were liquid and powdered rennet. Located in Cadorago, between Milan and Como, its product lines are Lyofast (freeze-dried starter cultures), Cryofast (frozen pellet starter cultures), and Lyoto (bulk starters). Sacco offers single-strain thermophilic and mesophilic starters; multi-strain blends; ripening cultures for various acidification and ripening schedules as well as for numerous types of cheeses, including blues, soft mold-ripened, and traditional Italian varieties. They have also isolated and developed gas- and aroma-producing and protective (mold- and spoilage-resistant) cultures from mountain raw-milk sources.

Among other notable houses are Laboratoires Abia, in Meursault, France; Laboratorios Arroyo, in Santander, Spain; and Biena, in Hyacinthe, Quebec, Canada.

See also LABORATORIES.

Barber's Farmhouse Cheesemakers (AJ and RG Barber Ltd.). http://www.barbers.co.uk.
Chr. Hansen. http://www.chr-hansen.com.
Comotto, Mike. "Starter Culture Technology and Application: Initial Thoughts on Past and Present Culture Use." *Cheese Reporter* 132, no. 15 (12 October 2007).
Comotto, Mike: "Starter Culture Technology and Application: Advances in Flavor-Enzyme Modified Cheese (EMC) and Flavor." *Cheese Reporter* 134, no. 39 (26 March 2010).
CSK Food Enrichment. http://www.cskfood.com.
DSM. http://www.dsm.com
DuPont Danisco. http://www.danisco.com.
Early, Ralph. "Microbiology of Fermented Milk Products." In *The Technology of Dairy Products*, pp. 51–65. Glasgow: Blackie Academic and Professional, 1998.
Gruppo Mofin Alce. http://www.mofinalce.it.
Laboratorios Arroyo. http://www.laboratoriosarroyo.com.
Powell, Ian. "Cheese Starter Cultures: A Thousand Years of Tradition Wrapped in a Century of Microbiological Science." A webinar presented via the National Centre for Dairy Education, Australia, 4 April 2013.
Powell, Ian. "Your Cheese Is Alive." DIAL blog, 15 December 2014. http://www.dairyinnovation.com.au/di-blog/your-cheese-is-alive.
Sacco SRL. www.saccosrl.it.

David Gibbons

curdling, cultural theories of.

The notion that human conception is analogous to the curdling of milk into cheese has appeared in a wide range of texts in different parts of the world and across the centuries. In *De Generatione Animalium*, Aristotle proposed that the material secreted by the female in the uterus is fixed by the semen of the male to form a fetus in the same way as rennet coagulates milk to form a cheese. Several classical and medieval scholars drew upon the Aristotelian cheese analogy of conception. The early Greek theologian, Clement of Alexandria, argued that conception resulted from the commingling of semen and menstrual blood and used the Aristotelian cheese analogy to illustrate his point. St. Hildegard of Bingen (1098–1180) employed the analogy when describing a vision concerning the human embryo. See HILDEGARD OF BINGEN. The same cheese analogy of conception appears in Job 10:9–11 "Remember, I beseech thee, that thou hast fashioned me as clay; and wilt thou bring me into the dust again? Hast thou not poured me out as milk, and curdled me like cheese? Thou hast clothed me with skin and flesh, and knit me together with bones and sinews." See BIBLICAL REFERENCES. The French historian, Emmanuel Le Roy Ladurie, provides a fourteenth-century example of the rennet/semen analogy from the Occitan village of Montaillou. The concubine of the village priest once asked her lover how to prevent a pregnancy. The priest recommended a particular herb. His concubine asked if local shepherds used the same herb to prevent milk from curdling.

These examples of the cheese analogy of conception mirror the folk theory of conception once found in a remote French Basque community, Sainte-Engrâce. Until recently, cheesemaking syndicates of shepherds combined their flocks during the period of summer transhumance in alpine pastures along the Franco-Spanish border. See BASQUE COUNTRY and OLHA. Shepherds took turns tending the flocks and making prized "mountain cheeses" for home consumption. They rotated in pairs and stayed in rustic huts owned by their houses in the valley.

As exclusively male domains, the huts gave the shepherds a strong, collective social identity. Mountain cheeses not only formed an important staple in the local diet; they also served as a standard for judging a shepherd's artisanal skill and his sexual prowess. A shepherd who made a first-rate mountain cheese knew exactly when and how much rennet to put into his kettle of heated milk. Until the 1970s, people reckoned that such knowledge also made a man skilled at both causing and preventing (through *coitus interruptus*) the pregnancy of his wife. Mountain cheeses traditionally generated as much competition among shepherds as newborn infants did among the women in that society.

Until the 1990s, elderly Basques in Sainte-Engrâce still explained human conception in terms of cheesemaking. People made not only linguistic connections between the two processes but also conceptual, sociological, and symbolic ones. In the local Basque dialect, the verb *gatzatü* means both "to curdle" and "to conceive in the womb of a woman." When a woman became pregnant, it was said that she had been "curdled."

According to traditional local ideas about the human body, a man's semen had the same properties as rennet; it curdled a woman's hot red blood in the womb to create a fetus in the same manner as rennet curdles ewe's milk to form a cheese. Rennet was also the substance that gave a cheese "bone" (its hard, dense interior), in the same way that human semen contributed to the substance of bones. Shepherds sometimes referred to their mountain cheeses as their "little babies." They reasoned that rennet gave life to their cheeses and that a newly made cheese was as fragile as a newborn infant. Shepherds salted and rotated each cheese in order to develop a rind and "bone" essential to maturation and preservation. Until the 1950s, childbirth took place in the farmhouse kitchen. The midwife or husband rotated the newborn infant in front of the open fire in order to harden the baby's bones.

In traditional Sainte-Engrâce society, men and women had separate social domains: the male domain of the hut in the mountains and the female domain of the house in the valley. When a shepherd took his turn to make a mountain cheese in the hut, he became the "woman of the house" (*etxekandere*), a role that entailed cooking and other domestic chores in the hut—work that no man would ever perform in his house, where the elder female "woman of the house" (his mother or mother-in-law) reigned supreme. People associated male procreativity with the mountain hut, where shepherds curdled ewe's milk to make cheese. Female procreativity was traditionally associated with the house, where (it was said in Basque) "children are curdled."

The Basques of Sainte-Engrâce were the only ones in their province to articulate an understanding of human conception in terms of cheesemaking. They provided an intriguing modern example of an Aristotelian notion that found its way into disparate cultures and into a variety of religious, philosophical, and scientific discourses.

Aristotle. *De Generatione Animalium.* In *The Works of Aristotle,* translated by Arthur Platt. Oxford: Clarendon, 1972.

Le Roy Ladurie, Emmanuel. *Montaillou, village Occitan de 1294 à 1324.* Paris: Gallimard, 1995.

Needham, Joseph. *A History of Embryology.* New York: Abelard-Schuman, 1959.

Ott, Sandra. *The Circle of Mountains: A Basque Shepherding Community.* Reno: University of Nevada Press, 1993.

Sandra Ott

A **curd mill** is a piece of cheesemaking equipment that converts matted slabs of curd into small pieces known as cheese curds. Mills were first used in England to produce iconic cheeses such as Cheddar, Cheshire, and Stilton. They came into general use in many parts of the United States in the 1870s. The mills at that time were mainly peg style — named for the pegs protruding from a rotating roller that tears the slab into irregularly shaped pieces. These mills were operated manually and constructed of iron and wood. Steam was used to power some of the first mechanized curd mills in the early 1900s.

There are three types of curd mill in use today: peg; rotary or chip; and plunger or drawer style. Peg mills are used to make more traditional or artisan cheeses and are still available in a manual form for home cheesemakers. The tearing and squeezing motion of the peg mill causes high fat losses, which resulted in the development of knife mills that slice the slab rather than tear it and produce more uniform pieces. Further innovation led to the rotary or chip mill and safety considerations necessitated the more common use of the plunger or drawer style mill.

While curd mills are most commonly associated with the production of Cheddar cheese, they are also used to improve the early machinability of mozzarella and to create unique artisan and specialty cheeses. An estimated 20 percent of Cheddar and less than 10 percent of mozzarella in the United States is made using a curd mill.

See CHEDDAR; CHEESE CURDS; MILLING; MOZZARELLA; and SHREDDING.

Decker, John W. *Cheddar Cheese Making*. Madison, Wisc.: Published by the author, 1893.
Tillamook Co-Op. "A Slice of History: First Power Curd Mill." http://www.tillamook.com/community/blog/a-slice-of-history-first-power-curd-mill.
Willard, Xerxes Addison. *Willard's Practical Dairy Husbandry*. 3d ed. New York: D. D. T. Moore, 1872.

Gina L. Mode

Customs of Corbie, The, refer to an administrative ordinance written in 822 C.E. by Adalhard, the ninth abbot of Corbie, to guide the day-to-day operations of the abbey of Corbie in Northern France. The Customs were a series of managerial directives for the oversight of the abbey's various economic activities that provided for an adequate flow of food supplies and other material necessities to the monastery. Today, this document serves as an informative window into the economic operations of a large medieval Benedictine monastery, including the place that cheese and cheesemaking played in the monastic community.

Balthilde, widow of the English King Clovis II, founded Corbie during the seventh century. By the time of Adalhard, Corbie had acquired extensive manorial holdings through aristocratic endowments that presented the abbey with complex managerial challenges. The Customs specify twenty-seven villas, seven of which were adjacent to the abbey and twenty that were farther away at distances of up to 60 kilometers. However, it is also known from other documents that Corbie held many other villas even farther afield. A monk, or "mayor," who was appointed by the abbot, administered each villa.

Many of the directives had to do with the oversight of the tithes that each villa owed annually to the abbey, consisting of one-tenth of all agricultural production, including all milk from cows, sheep, and goats. For the seven villas adjacent to the abbey, milk could be delivered fresh to the gate to satisfy the tithe, but the more distant villas had to convert the milk into cheese and tithe in the form of cheese. The directives do not describe the cheeses that were produced by the villas; however, with respect to cheeses that were produced from goat's milk, the Customs specifically directed that they be delivered to the abbey on a monthly basis in order to prevent the cheeses from spoiling through over-aging. This suggests that the goat's milk cheeses were neither fresh cheeses that would spoil very quickly, nor dry aged cheeses that would last for months, but perhaps soft surface ripened types with shelf lives of several weeks.

In addition to the cheeses received from their manorial holdings, the brothers of Corbie also produced their own cheeses during the summer from ten flocks of sheep that the monastery maintained on site. The Customs do not indicate the size of the flocks, but a typical flock at that time was around one hundred ewes, which would mean that the milk from up to one thousand sheep was made into cheese. This in-house cheesemaking capacity was maintained specifically to provide for the needs of the many pilgrims and other travelers that would regularly seek overnight refuge in monastic houses. Providing hospitality to travelers was a central expectation of the Benedictine monastery, and the abbey of Corbie did not want to be dependent on cheeses transported from distant villas to fulfill this essential service. In addition, one-fifth of the cheeses from the ten flocks went to the monastic poor house to feed the poor (another core social function of Benedictine houses), some of whom would appear at the gate and then leave after receiving alms, others who were given overnight lodging andinfirm and being cared for by the monastery.

See also MONASTIC CHEESEMAKING.

Adalard, Saint, and Charles William Jones. "Appendix II: The Customs of Corbie." In *The Plan of St. Gall*, Vol. 3 by Walter Horn and Ernest Born, pp. 91–128. Berkeley: University of California Press, 1979.
Kindstedt, Paul S. *Cheese and Culture: A History of Cheese and Its Place in Western Civilization*. White River Junction, Vt.: Chelsea Green, 2012.

Paul S. Kindstedt

cutting is the process of breaking up the continuous milk gel (coagulum) that forms during coagulation into smaller particles. See COAGULATION OR CURDLING. Cutting initiates the process of selective concentration whereby casein, fat, and the casein-associated minerals in milk become concentrated in the form of cheese curd. Water, lactose, soluble minerals, and other minor soluble milk components separate out in the form of whey. The primary function of cutting is to control the initial stages of syneresis, the process by which the coagulum contracts and expels whey from the curd. The free whey that forms through syneresis is ultimately removed from the curd permanently during draining. See SYNERESIS and DRAINING.

Cutting the coagulum into small particles with a high surface area relative to their volume encourages syneresis because small particles contract more readily than large particles, and there is less distance for the whey to travel in order to exit through the particle surfaces. Therefore, cheesemakers vary the cut size (particle size distribution) to control the final moisture content of their cheese, with larger cut sizes used for higher-moisture cheeses and smaller cut sizes for drier cheeses. Thus, it is not surprising that a wide range of cutting utensils, such as metal and wire knives, harps, and spinos, and elaborate cutting techniques were developed by cheesemakers of old to assist in making diverse cheeses with widely varying moisture contents. See CHEESE KNIFE; CHEESE WIRE; and MOISTURE.

For cheeses that are cooked, a secondary but important function of cutting is to promote uniform heating throughout the curd mass. During cooking, the interiors of large curd particles heat up more slowly than do those of smaller curd particles. Such size-dependent differences in the rate of temperature increase may influence both the syneresis and acidification rates among curd particles. Therefore it is important to minimize variation in the size of the particles produced by cutting in order to limit the formation of pockets of variable moisture and acidity within the final cheese.

In the making of rennet-coagulated cheeses, cheesemakers must be mindful of two important parame-

This image shows the mechanized (automated) cutting of a dense, high-fat curd performed in the cheese vat.
© KATE ARDING

Stichelton cheese curds are cut by hand into sugar cube–size pieces before gently hand-ladling them onto a draining table. © KATE ARDING

ters during cutting. The first is curd firmness, because firmness at the time of cutting affects syneresis rate and ultimately the moisture content of the final cheese. During the early stages of coagulation and gel formation, the chains of fused casein micelles that make up the curd casein matrix are thin and closely spaced around small pores filled with fat globules and the water phase of the milk, forming a fine coagulum. The coagulum at this point is very soft, but soon the thin strands of casein will aggregate into thicker strands that will produce a coarser, stronger casein matrix containing larger pores and possessing greater firmness. This coarsening of the casein matrix creates syneretic pressure that promotes whey expulsion, but the amount of whey that is actually released from the curd will be a function of whether the curd is cut soft (before coarsening of the casein matrix has proceeded very far) or firm (after matrix coarsening has progressed to near completion). If cutting occurs when the coagulum is soft, the subsequent rearrangement and coarsening of the casein matrix will be accompanied by a surge of syneresis as the small curd particles contract and whey exits en masse through the abundantly available surface area. Thus, cutting when the curd is soft ultimately translates to a lower-moisture cheese. In contrast, if the uncut curd is allowed to become very firm, the syneretic pressure caused by matrix coarsening induces little release of whey, because the surface area of the uncut coagulum is minuscule relative to the volume. When the firm coagulum is finally cut, the process of matrix coarsening is already nearly complete, and so there is much less syneretic pressure within the particles immediately after cutting, despite the creation of abundant new surface area. Thus, cutting when the curd is firm ultimately translates to a higher-moisture cheese.

A second parameter that has great practical importance is the cutting time; that is, the time it takes to attain the optimum firmness. Variation in the cutting time from vat to vat, or from one day to the next, is undesirable because the amount of time that elapses from one step to the next in cheesemaking affects the population growth of the starter culture lactic acid bacteria, and thus the rate of acidification during subsequent steps of cheesemaking. See ACIDIFICATION. For example, if the time from adding rennet to attaining proper cutting firmness takes thirty minutes one day and sixty minutes the next day, the additional thirty minutes on the second day could result in up to a doubling of the starter culture population during the lapse, which in turn could accelerate acidification during the subsequent steps of cheesemaking, to the detriment of final cheese quality. The bottom line is that both cutting firmness and cutting time need to be optimized and held constant in order to produce cheese with consistent moisture content, acidity, and ultimately, quality.

Johnson, M. E., and B. A. Law. "The Origins, Development, and Basic Operations of Cheesemaking Technology." In *Technology of Cheesemaking*, 2d ed., edited by Barry A. Law and Adnan Y. Tamime. Oxford: Wiley-Blackwell, 2010.

Paul S. Kindstedt

Cyclops Polyphemos

See HOMER.

Cypress Grove Chevre is one of America's best-known goat cheese operations and the producer of one of America's most popular cheeses, Humboldt Fog. See HUMBOLDT FOG. Mary Keehn, the company's founder, was a self-avowed hippie, who in 1970 made the decision to feed her first child goat's milk instead of cow's milk. The source of that milk was two goats that she caught, quite literally, as they foraged next door to the Sonoma, California, farm where she was living. Keehn had been told by that neighbor, who used the goats for weed control, "If you can catch them, you can have them."

A move to California's northernmost county of Humboldt, followed by a stint living off the grid, the birth of her twin girls and a fourth daughter, and the need to make a living, ultimately led Keehn to turn her kitchen hobby of making goat cheese into a business. So, too, did the desire of a local restaurateur to buy her cheese.

So Keehn converted a nearby abandoned chicken coop into a creamery in McKinleyville, California, and opened for business in 1983. Her first cheeses were fresh chèvre disks and logs and fromage blanc. Although the company bought some of the milk needed to make their cheeses, they also used milk from their own fifty goats. Eventually, though, Keehn, who had won four national Alpine goat championships, sold the goats so she could concentrate exclusively on making cheese. Nearby goat farmers, held to high milk standards, became the source of Cypress Grove Chevre's milk.

It can be said without overstatement that Keehn's creation of Humboldt Fog in 1992 changed not only the course of Cypress Grove Chevre but possibly American goat cheese consumption itself. Distinguished by its midline of edible vegetable ash, this relatively mild but flavorful and aesthetically beautiful cheese caught on quickly with American cheese consumers. Little did Keehn know that that cheese would become synonymous with the company itself. Indeed, many people still think that the name of the company is Humboldt Fog.

After outgrowing the McKinleyville facility, Cypress Grove Chevre built a new creamery in nearby Arcata, California, in 2004. Six years later the global cheese company Emmi purchased Cypress Grove Chevre. Keehn was given the title of founder and continues working with the company on a daily basis. See EMMI.

In 2014 a new, larger creamery was constructed next to the one in Arcata. The former creamery is now used for research and development. In addition, the company returned to its roots and acquired several hundred goats, half of which are used for milking. The company may have come full circle, but it is a long way from its early days when fifty goats were nearly enough.

See AMERICAN "GOAT LADIES" and GOAT.

Cypress Grove Chevre. http://www.cypressgrovechevre .com.

Laura Werlin

Daani

See EGYPT.

dairy allergy refers to an immunological response that occurs after consumption of dairy products. The typical response involves release of large amounts of the antibody class Immunoglobulin E (IgE) and is characterized by a range of symptoms from skin rashes, itchiness, or hives, to swelling of the lips, tongue, and throat, difficulty breathing, and a drop in blood pressure, which can be life-threatening (anaphylaxis). There are also non-IgE mediated reactions to dairy that are most often associated with gastrointestinal symptoms such as nausea, vomiting, diarrhea, and bloating. Importantly, these responses are to the proteins in milk and stem from immune system stimulation, which differentiates dairy allergies from the more common lactose intolerance, the inability to digest the milk sugar lactose. See LACTOSE INTOLERANCE.

Dairy allergies affect about 2–5 percent of children in the United States and Europe, with uncertain prevalence in other parts of the world. They are among the top eight food allergies, which collectively account for about 90 percent of all such reactions. The majority of children outgrow dairy allergies by adolescence. There is some controversy about whether early life exposure to dairy products increases or decreases the risk of developing allergies in general, or whether raw milk has protective effects compared to commercially processed milk.

Milk contains a wide variety of proteins that serve a number of important purposes for nursing infants, and no specific protein has been identified as the unique trigger of dairy allergies. The main protein groups are the caseins, which comprise about 80 percent of all cow milk proteins, and the whey proteins, α-lactalbumin and β-lactoglobulin. See CASEIN and WHEY. Sensitivity to the caseins appears to be the most common, but can co-occur with allergy to the whey proteins, especially β-lactoglobulin. Cow milk allergies have been the most extensively documented and studied, given the ubiquity of cow milk in the commercial dairy industry, but there is substantial cross-reactivity among different mammalian milk proteins (especially those from other bovine species) such that sensitivity to cow milk frequently co-occurs with sensitivity to goat, sheep, or water buffalo milk. Human milk contains relatively little casein compared to cow milk and contains no β-lactoglobulin; camel milk similarly has little casein and has been proposed as an alternative milk source for those with a cow milk allergy. See CAMEL.

Most cheeses are formed by coagulation of casein, which occurs when milk is acidified by bacterial fermentation and then treated with the proteolytic enzymes in rennet. Thus caseins are found in high concentration in cheese, and the processing does not substantially alter their allergenicity. However, prolonged aging, as in the production of Parmigiano Reggiano, can result in substantial breakdown of caseins to the point that they do not trigger a reaction in some allergic individuals. Whey proteins can also be found in cheese, especially those with high fluid content, and may trigger allergic symptoms, although some studies suggest that fermentation by lactic acid bacteria may ameliorate their allergenicity. Caseins are resistant to heat processing, but high heat may reduce the allergenicity of whey proteins.

While dairy allergies are the major cause of immunological reactions to cheese, it is also important to keep in mind that other components introduced during the ripening or processing may also contribute to these reactions. Molds such as *Penicillium* may trigger respiratory symptoms, especially among cheese producers. Individuals may also be allergic to coloring agents such as annatto or preservatives used in commercial cheese production.

Downs, Melanie L., Jamie L. Kabourek, Joseph L. Baumert, et al. "Milk Protein Allergy." In *Milk and Dairy Products in Human Nutrition*, edited by Young W. Park and George F. W. Haenlein, pp. 111–128. New York: Wiley, 2013.

Restani, Patrizia, Cinzia Ballabio, Chiara Di Lorenzo, et al. "Molecular Aspects of Milk Allergens and Their Role in Clinical Events." *Analytical and Bioanalytical Chemistry* 395 (2009): 47–56.

Andrea S. Wiley

Dairy Business Innovation Center, a

not-for-profit organization in Wisconsin, worked in partnership with industry and trade groups from 2004 to 2012 to grow and launch new specialty, farmstead, and artisan dairy processing businesses. With a team of twenty part-time consultants, each an expert in his or her field, the Dairy Business Innovation Center (DBIC) provided an array of technical services for farm and cheesemaking clients, such as business planning, product and label development, facility and equipment expertise, and increased recognition of the quality of Wisconsin artisan cheese.

The Center built a unique operating model by offering forty hours of free consultation to dairy business clients, offset by federal funds secured with the help of U.S. Senator Herb Kohl. The Center welcomed repeat clients with new projects by offering a low fee structure for an additional twenty hours of work. In addition, a host of fee-based services, including business audits and consumer focus groups, ensured vital services were available to clients at industry-reduced rates.

During its tenure, the DBIC helped two hundred Wisconsin dairy farmers and cheesemaking companies launch more than seventy new dairy products to market. In all, forty-three new dairy processing plants opened and ninety-two more modernized and expanded into more profitable specialty and artisan products with the help of the DBIC team. This period of significant growth in Wisconsin's dairy industry was in steep contrast to a trend in declining dairy plant numbers before 2004. Today in Wisconsin, more than 75 percent of all cheese factories craft at least one type of specialty or artisan cheese.

See also WISCONSIN.

Wisconsin Department of Agriculture, Trade and Consumer Protection. http://datcp.wi.gov.

Jeanne Carpenter

dairymaids, also known as milkmaids, were responsible for milking cows and for making cheese in much of Europe and the United States before the nineteenth-century industrialization of agriculture and centralization of cheesemaking. The word "dairy" is derived from the Old English word for "female servant," linking the domestic practice of dairying to woman's work in Anglo-European culture. Skills and knowledge of dairying and cheese- and butter-making were passed down through generations of women and, in the case of upper-class farming homes, from female supervisor to female servant. These women often closely guarded their family-based recipes and techniques, preserving their authority over this essential economic driver of farm sustainability. Throughout Europe during the Middle Ages cheeses were used as payment by peasant families to the manor lords, for family sustenance, and for additional family income when surplus permitted. In large manor-based communities, dairywomen directed the manor's cheesemaking operations in service of the manor.

An aura of mystery surrounded the curdling of milk and the maturation of cheese, leading to both awe-inspired reverence for a dairywoman's skills and fear of poorly understood or possibly occult forces at work. In some instances the appreciation of the special skills of female cheesemakers provided women with superior social status in a community, along with outsize authority over the cheesemaking domain. Careful dairymaid selection was considered essential to a dairying enterprise, and women were often the ones making these critical hiring choices. But despite appreciation for dairywomen's talents and the market value of the fruits of

A woman dressed in traditional Dutch dairymaid garb in Eckles, Virginia, in 1919. HARRIS & EWING COLLECTION, LIBRARY OF CONGRESS

their labor, cheesemaking was also sometimes feared or reviled because of its feminine mystery. Dairymaids' close association with livestock suggested sensuality and reproduction. As a highly feminized product, cheese likewise came to represent sex and original sin in common imagery and mythologies during the Middle Ages. In some European cultural theories, human conception—the product of sin and mystery—was understood on analogy to the apparently magical process of coagulation. Coagulation, whether of humans or cheese, was so troublingly mysterious that it—or, rather, its absence—was sometimes associated with or attributed to witchcraft. Some feared that an evil power derived from coagulation lurked within cheese, and such powers were sometimes connected with the stereotype of cheese as a contributor to indigestion. See CURDLING, CULTURAL THEORIES OF and MAGICAL THINKING.

By the latter half of the eighteenth century scientifically minded men began a campaign to rein in the unruly, unpredictable nature of cheesemaking and constrain it through newly developed systems of agricultural science and technology. These men of enlightenment were confounded when dairywomen did not heed their advice, adding to the notion that dairywomen were not only profoundly and offensively unscientific in their pursuits, but also dim-witted. The men could not fathom any other explanation for the women's rejection of scientific reason.

In spite of efforts to systematize cheesemaking, in England dairying remained the purview of women through the eighteenth century. American colonists continued this gendered division of labor to some extent. Because men sometimes participated in cheesemaking in the American colonies, however, early American dairywomen did not necessarily enjoy the same prestige as their English predecessors had. Cheesemaking nevertheless remained largely feminized in the early United States, including in the highly regarded cheese enterprises of Rhode Island, where during the eighteenth century much of the cheesemaking was carried out by enslaved dairymaids.

In both England and the United States, beginning in the mid-nineteenth century, the majority of cheese production moved off the farm and into factories, shifting cheesemaking to the purview of men. Even as cheese became ever more standardized, however, the image of the strong, hardy dairymaid continued to represent authenticity of origin and purity of product in American dairy advertisements, as she had throughout the centuries in Europe.

Dairymaids also hold a prominent place in public health history. The first vaccination was administered by Edward Jenner, an English country doctor.

He extracted pus from a milkmaid's cowpox lesion—it was well known by the late eighteenth century that dairymaids' exposure to cowpox protected them against smallpox—and used it to inoculate a small boy, who became immune to subsequent smallpox exposures. The stereotype of milkmaids with soft, rosy skin is rooted in this history: while smallpox survivors often sported significant pockmarking from the healing of lesions, milkmaids did not suffer those physical consequences because they were immune to smallpox.

See also GENDER.

Bruyn, Josua. "Dutch Cheese: A Problem of Interpretation." *Simiolus: Netherlands Quarterly for the History of Art* 24, nos. 2–3 (1996): 201–208.

Kinstedt, Paul. *Cheese and Culture: A History of Cheese and Its Place in Western Civilization.* White River Junction, Vt.: Chelsea Green, 2012.

McMurry, Sally A. "Women's Work in Agriculture: Divergent Trends in England and America, 1800 to 1930." *Comparative Studies in Society and History* 34, no. 2 (April 1992): 248–270.

Oates, Caroline. "Cheese Gives You Nightmares: Old Hags and Heartburn." *Folklore* 114, no. 2 (August 2003): 205–225.

Paxson, Heather. *The Life of Cheese: Crafting Food and Value in America.* Berkeley: University of California Press, 2013.

Stern, Alexandra Minna, and Howard Markel. "The History of Vaccines and Immunization: Familiar Patterns, New Challenges." *Health Affairs* 24, no. 3 (May–June 2005): 611–621.

Valenze, Deborah. "The Art of Women and the Business of Men: Women's Work and the Dairy Industry c. 1740–1840." *Past & Present*, no. 130 (February 1991): 142–169.

Valenze, Deborah. *Milk: A Local and Global History.* New Haven, Conn.: Yale University Press, 2011.

Jessica A. B. Galen

dairy propionibacteria

dairy propionibacteria are used as ripening cultures in Swiss cheese (Emmentaler cheese) and other cheeses with "eyes," or holes. See EMMENTALER and EYES. Propionibacteria were isolated from this cheese more than a century ago, and their presence was soon associated with the formation of eyes. They have a peculiar metabolism: they ferment lactic acid, which is produced in cheese by lactic starters, into acetic acid, propionic acid, and carbon dioxide (CO_2) as their primary end products. See LACTIC ACID; ACETIC ACID; PROPIONIC ACID; and CARBON DIOXIDE. The CO_2 saturates the cheese and generates small holes that further increase in size, forming the typical eyes observed in Swiss-type cheeses.

Four species of dairy propionibacteria have been described: *Propionibacterium freudenreichii*, *P. jensenii*, *P. thoenii*, and *P. acidipropionici*. The main species used as a ripening culture in cheese is *P. freudenreichii*, because it is capable of withstanding the "cooking" step applied during the manufacture of Swiss cheese better than the other propionibacteria species. Besides its role in eye formation, *P. freudenreichii* has other effects related to cheese quality, most of which are strain dependent. *P. freudenreichii* produces a range of flavor compounds associated with the typical flavor of Swiss-type cheeses: propionic acids from the fermentation of lactic acid; branched-chain volatile acids from the conversion of some amino acids, which impart the typical "old cheese," "feet" flavors; and free fatty acids from the hydrolysis of milk fat, associated with "pungent" flavors. Propionibacteria also impart healthful qualities to cheese. They produce vitamin B9 (folate) and vitamin B12 (cobalamin), the most complex vitamin synthesized by bacteria. Propionibacteria also promote in vivo the growth of bifidobacteria, a group of bacteria associated with gut health.

Propionibacteria have mainly been isolated from milk but can be found in cattle environments (straw, hay, soil, rumen, etc.). Therefore, their presence in milk as "natural" contaminants is not surprising. They grow in cheese when conditions are appropriate, typically at ripening temperatures above 59–68°F (15–20°C) and at salt concentrations below 3 percent. In the case of Swiss cheese, which is ripened at 75°F (24°C) with 1 percent salt, propionibacteria have reached populations above one billion cells per gram of cheese. They can also grow in cheeses such as Grana and Gruyère, where they can be responsible for defects. *P. freudenreichii* is a hardy bacterium compared to most species of lactic acid bacteria. It has few nutritional requirements and wide biosynthetic abilities, enabling it to synthetize amino acids and many vitamins. It also displays features allowing its long-term survival, by accumulating energy and carbon-storage compounds, such as glycogen.

Dairy propionibacteria are known to remain active in various environments, including cheese. In two-year-old Swiss Emmentaler cheese, for example, very high populations of viable propionibacteria have been enumerated. The hardiness of that species was recently explained by several genomic features. *P. freudenreichii* has been granted Generally Recognized As Safe (GRAS) status for its use as a cheese culture from the US Food and Drug Administration and belongs to the list of agents recommended for Qualified Presumption of Safety (QPS) by the European Food Safety Authority (EFSA). See GENERALLY RECOGNIZED AS SAFE.

See also RIPENING CULTURES.

Falentin, Hélène, et al. "The Complete Genome of *Propionibacterium freudenreichii* CIRM-BIA1, a Hardy Actinobacterium with Food and Probiotic Applications." *PLoS One* 5 (July 2010): e11748.
Fröhlich-Wyder, Marie-Thérèse, and Hans-Peter Bachmann. "Cheeses with Propionic Acid Fermentation." In *Cheese: Chemistry, Physics, and Microbiology*, edited by Patrick F. Fox et al. Vol. 1: *General Aspects*, pp. 141–156. London: Elsevier, 2004.
Thierry, Anne, et al. "New Insights into Physiology and Metabolism of *Propionibacterium freudenreichii*." *International Journal of Food Microbiology* 149 (September 2011): 19–27.

Anne Thierry

deacidification typically refers to a process in surface ripened cheeses when yeasts colonize the cheese surface and utilize lactate to form metabolites, such as ammonia, that lead to deacidification of the cheese surface. Various processes can also be used in the manufacture of cheese to decrease the lactose content of the milk or the cheese, thereby preventing the potential formation of excessive levels of lactic acid in the cheese.

• Whey dilution: Part of the whey is removed after the coagulum is cut, and warm water is added back. Depending upon the desired pH of the cheese, about 10 to 30 percent of the original milk volume is removed as whey and replaced with water, which will dilute the lactose content of the remaining whey. Consequently, the lactose in the curd will diffuse into the whey. With less lactose in the curd, there will be less lactic acid produced by the starters, resulting in a cheese with a higher pH (5.2–5.4). Whey dilution is used in the manufacture of Swiss varieties, Gouda, Edam, Havarti, Brick, and similar cheeses in which a mild and less acidic taste is desired. See WHEY and PH MEASUREMENT.

• Curd washing or rinsing: in the manufacture of Colby and Monterey cheeses, the curd is soaked, washed, or rinsed with water. This curd-washing step is traditionally performed with the stirred-curd manufacturing process and after most of the whey has been drained. Generally, cool water is used, and it removes residual whey from the curd. The water can be drained directly or it can be allowed to sit in contact with the curd. The latter process is then identical to whey dilution. Cold water clings to the curd and slows syneresis (release of moisture from the curd). Consequently, curd washing helps increase the moisture of cheeses. Typically curd washing is less effective at removing lactose from the curd than is whey dilution, resulting in cheeses with a lower pH (pH 5.1–5.3). See WASHED-CURD CHEESES.

With either whey dilution or curd washing, the proportion of whey removed and water added along with the length of time the water will be in contact with the curds determines the level of residual lactose and thus the final pH of the cheese. The temperature of the water that is added is also very important because it affects the moisture content of the cheese. Generally, the rule is that cooling the curd below 88°F (30°C) will increase the moisture content of the curd, but will also result in cheese with an open texture.

See also ACIDIFICATION and LACTIC ACID.

Fox, P. F., and P. L. H. McSweeney. "Cheese: Chemistry, Physics, and Microbiology." In *Cheese: Chemistry, Physics, and Microbiology*, edited by Patrick F. Fox et al. Vol. 2: *Major Cheese Groups*, 3d ed., pp. 95–96, 103–105. London: Elsevier, 2004.
Kindstedt, P., and the Vermont Cheese Council, eds. *American Farmstead Cheese*. White River Junction, Vt.: Chelsea Green, 2005.
Lee, M. R., et al. "Effect of Different Curd-Washing Methods on the Insoluble Ca Content and Rheological Properties of Colby Cheese During Ripening." *Journal of Dairy Science* 94 (2011): 2692–2700.

Bénédicte Coudé

deamination in cheese involves the catabolism of amino acids, whereby the amine group is removed from the amino acid to produce ammonia.

Deamination occurs by two different enzymatic pathways in cheese, one involving dehydrogenases that produce ammonia plus an α-keto acid, and the other involving oxidases that produce ammonia plus an aldehyde and hydrogen peroxide. Depending on the cheese variety, deamination may occur through the metabolic activities of yeasts, molds, bacteria, or combinations thereof. The production of ammonia through deamination is particularly important to the ripening of washed-rind (smear-ripened), bloomy-rind (white mold ripened) and blue mold cheeses, influencing both their flavor and texture development.

See also AMMONIA; BLOOMY-RIND CHEESES; BLUE CHEESES; and WASHED-RIND CHEESES.

Fox, P. F., et al. *Cheese: Chemistry, Physics and Microbiology*, 3d ed., vol. 1 *General Aspects*. London: Elsevier Academic, 2004.

Paul S. Kindstedt

Debaryomyces is a genus of yeast that includes the species *Debaryomyces hansenii*, the most widespread yeast in surface-ripened cheeses. It is widely used as a starter culture, but also commonly colonizes cheeses from environmental sources such as raw milk or from the brines used to salt cheeses. *Debaryomyces hansenii* is among the most salt-tolerant yeasts studied to date, and can be grown in the lab in media with up to 25 percent salt (the ocean is on average about 3 percent salt). See SALT.

Debaryomyces hansenii is known to play key roles in rind development by reducing the acidity of the rind and allowing acid-sensitive bacteria, such as *Brevibacterium* species, to grow. It also plays a role in cheese flavor and aroma by producing a variety of volatile compounds, including aldehydes, which produce nutty or malty aromas; sulfur compounds, which contribute to cheddar or cooked vegetable aromas; and 2-phenylethanol, which smells like a faded rose. Some strains have been identified as inhibiting the growth of contaminant molds, suggesting that this yeast can serve as a natural antifungal agent.

See also BREVIBACTERIUM LINENS and FUNGI.

Gori, Klaus, et al. "*Debaryomyces hansenii* Strains Differ in Their Production of Flavor Compounds in a Cheese-Surface Model." *MicrobiologyOpen* 1 (2012): 161–168.

Jacques, Noémie, and Serge Casaregola. "Safety Assessment of Dairy Microorganisms: The Hemiascomycetous Yeasts." *International Journal of Food Microbiology* 126 (2008): 321–326.

Benjamin Wolfe

defects are undesirable or imperfect characteristics of the attributes related to cheese flavor, body, texture, and appearance. The defects in cheese may be due to multiple causes associated with milk quality, cheesemaking process, packaging, storage, aging, or retailing of finished products. There are specific conditions that affect the quality of cheese, such as use of poor quality milk and ingredients, unsanitary milking and cheese manufacturing conditions, presence of undesirable microorganisms, the feeding and health of the animals, and incorrect chemical composition of the cheese in terms of pH, moisture, fat or salt content as well as improper protein and lipid degradation during ripening. Both lactose fermentation and ripening are fundamental factors for causing defects if they are not controlled properly. Acid development, cooking temperature and time, and vat agitation are critical factors shaping the characteristics of cheese curd in terms of chemical composition and enzymatic activity, and thus the quality of the finished product.

There are multiple criteria to classify the different defects of cheese: (1) based on the origin of the cause of defect (microbial defects such as coliform or *Pseudomonas* contamination; enzymatic defects such as rancidity or bitterness associated with high plasmin activity; and chemical defects such as butyric acid flavor); (2) based on the type of critical step on the process (acidification defects such as "hard heart" or cheese with a white hard interior due to improper acidification and consequently improper moisture loss, and ripening defects such as "cat-hair" or "toad-skin" defects, associated with contamination by *Mucor* or *Geotricum*, respectively); (3) based on the specific property of the cheese that is directly affected (flavor, body, texture, and external defects). It is this last criterion of classification that may be the most suitable for discussion, because most typical defects that can be found in cheese fall into the following categories: flavor, body, and texture. Further this kind of categorization of cheese defects is usually applied to evaluate the quality of the product when grading cheese or for judging purposes. See CHEESE GRADING and SENSORY ANALYSIS.

The flavor of cheese is the result of complex chemical, enzymatic, and physical changes that start with the milk and the action of the lactic starter cultures or non-starter microorganisms during the cheesemaking process. Due to the wide diversity of products, there is not a single ideal cheese flavor because some expected or desirable flavors in certain types of cheese may be undesirable in others. However there are some common flavors that can be considered defects and normally referred to as off flavors.

Acid flavor can be the single most important factor in most cheese products that develops from the activity of lactic acid bacteria, and regulates the pH and the structure of the product. If the lactic acid bacteria activity is out of control, a high acid defect flavor may be produced. To avoid acid cheese it is very important to control acidification during the cheesemaking process. See LACTIC ACID BACTERIA and ACIDIFICATION. Acid cheeses present a whiter color than the regular product and normally are also associated with some kind of textural defects too, due to an inadequate amount of moisture and demineralization level resulting from the pH effect (higher residual moisture in the fresh cheese, translating into higher residual sugar and consequently post-acidification during ripening that affects the textural properties and flavor or the final cheese). Bitter flavor is in most cases the result of high acid that enhances the action of proteolytic enzymes causing excess proteolysis. Additional causes of bitterness in cheese can be associated with the quality of the milk (due to high plasmin levels at the end of lactation, or microbial contamination with *Pseudomonas* due to long milk storage periods), as well as excess of residual rennet activity associated with the use of a large dose of coagulant or low pH levels (especially at setting and draining) that increases residual rennet and ultimately increases bitter peptide formation. Bacterial fermentation and enzyme activity on proteins results in the production of sulfide off flavor, a characteristic especially important to the quality of Cheddar cheeses. See PH MEASUREMENT and CHEDDAR.

Inadequate acid development also produces a sweet fruity fermented flavor, associated with high moisture content of cheeses and indirectly an increase in microbial activity and also sometimes yeast activity, resulting in characteristic fruity notes. Fruity cheeses often are associated with low levels of salt. See FRUITY. The activity of lipase enzymes produces

butyric acid that is characteristic of rancid flavor. See BUTYRIC ACID. Rancid flavor is also frequent when milk is not handled properly, like freezing during storage, rapid pumping of milk into the vat, or fast stirring of curd inside the cheese vat. All these conditions increase degradation of the fat globule membrane, increasing exposure of the triglycerides to the lipase action and consequently formation of free fatty acids. See FAT and LIPOLYSIS. Other common off-flavors result from what the animals eat, which imparts tastes like silage, alfalfa, fishy notes (if feeding soy bean meal), or garlicky or oniony flavors. This last flavor defect results when cows graze on fields infested with those products.

In addition to the above off-flavor collection, another type of flavor defect corresponds to the lack of flavor, also called "flat" cheeses, normally due to a short ripening period or improper chemical composition.

Defects in body and texture of cheese products are related to the physical characteristics such as cohesiveness, firmness, plasticity, and elasticity. The compositional changes continue to take place during the draining and ripening processes of cheesemaking. The sources of texture and body defects can also result from fat, protein, and moisture content levels, inadequate acid development, overheating during the cooking operation, and salt content. Curd cutting pH values can produce different defects such as fragile, firm, or high-in-solids curds when cooked. After coagulation, curd is drained and the milk components are concentrated influencing the moisture of the product. The pressing methods, entrapped air and production of CO_2 by non-starter microorganisms can produce mechanical and slit openings in the body. The presence of undesirable microorganisms from contamination also produces small gas holes about the size of a pinhead or larger. Cheese with low pH (<5.0) is high in moisture after ripening. This condition can make the curd too dry and brittle in dry hard cheese or result in pasty body in soft cheese. Weak body defect is due to high moisture or high fat content in some cheeses. At low pH, cheese loses serum, which results in crystal formation of calcium lactate on the surface. See CRYSTALLIZATION. Low pH also may promote microbial growth and the formation of rind rot on the surface in packaged cheese.

Moisture and salt content also play a critical role in the prevention of defects in cheese. See MOISTURE and DRY SALTING. Using high-quality raw milk plus controlling the chemical composition of the fresh cheese before ripening, in terms of moisture and salt content along with pH and acidification process, greatly decrease the chances of defects during ripening and ultimately the quality of cheese as a finished product.

Table 1 summarizes major defects in Cheddar cheese. Similar defects apply to most of the hard and semihard cheeses. Readers interested in specific cheese defects are referred to the references.

See also AROMA; COLOR; FLAVOR; TASTE; and TEXTURE.

Chandan, R. C., et al. *Dairy Processing and Quality Assurance*. 2d. ed. New York: Wiley-Blackwell, 2015.
Fox, P. F. *Cheese: Chemistry, Physics and Microbiology*, vol. 2. 2d ed. Gathersburg, Md.: Aspen, 1999.
Montgomery, P. L. H. *Cheese Problems Solved*. Sawston, U.K.: Woodhead, 2007.
Partridge, J. A. "Cheddar and Cheddar-Type Cheese." In *The Sensory Evaluation of Dairy Products*, 2d ed., edited by S. M. Clark, et al., pp. 225–270. New York: Springer, 2008.
Smukowski, M., and Ping Y. "Cheese Defects in U.S Graded Cheeses." *Dairy Pipeline* 15, no. 3 (2003): 1–7. https://www.cdr.wisc.edu/sites/default/files/pipelines/2003/pipeline_2003_vol15_03.pdf.

Valente B. Alvarez and Montserrat Almena-Aliste

Table 1. Description of major defects in Cheddar cheese by category (appearance, body, texture, and flavor)

Type of Defect	Defect Category/Description	Possible Cause (s)
Appearance	**Shape**	
	- Ends not parallel	- *Uneven pressing*
	- Uneven edges	- *Uneven pressing*
	- Bloating/puffing	- *Microbiological contamination*
	Exterior Surface	
	- Cracked cheese surface	- *Excessive drying between pressing and waxing*
		- *Temperature too cold at pressing*
	- Cracked or loose wax (scaly)	- *Waxing temperature to low or too high, respectively*
	- Mites (natural-rind Cheddar)	- *Contaminated cheese*
		- *Poor hygiene of shelves*
	- Open cheese surface	- *Pressing temperature too low (<85°F/<30°C)*
		- *Pressing pressure too low*
		- *Acid development too slow or too fast*
	Color	
	- Acid-cut, bleached	- *Fast acidification*
		- *Low pH at salting/pressing*
		- *High moisture/low salt*
	- Mottled	- *Non-uniform moisture/uneven salting*
		- *Combining curds from different vats*
	- Seamy	- *Uneven salting*
		- *Excessive drying before pressing*
	- White specks	- *Cheese surface*: primarily calcium lactate*
		- *Interior: tyrosine and/or calcium lactate*
		*Favored by:
		- loose wrapping, low temperature,
		- dehydration of surface
		- low initial pH (< 5.0)

(*continued*)

Table 1 Continued

Type of Defect	Defect Category/Description	Possible Cause (s)
Body	- Corky, dry	- *Incorrect composition (low fat, low moisture, high salt)* - *Slow acid development*

	- Crumbly, friable (curd fractures easily)	- *Over-acidification*
		  Excess wet acid (low draining pH)
		  Excess dry acid (low pH at salting/pressing)

	Note: Usually associated with acid flavor defect	*Note: May occur naturally after long aging (not a defect)*
Texture	- Fish eyes, slits, yeast holes	- *Yeast contamination (poor sanitation)* - *Favored by slow starter* - *Favored by high moisture/low salt* - *Accompanied by fermented off flavors*
	- Pinholes	- *Caused by coliform (sometime yeasts) contamination* - *Favored by slow starter* - *Favored by high moisture/low salt* - *Accompanied by fermented, unclean off flavors*
	- Fissures/fine slits	- *Caused by heterofermentative* Lactobacilli - *Flavor often not affected* - *Sulfur notes may be more prominent*
	- Blowing (massive cracks, cavities)	- *Caused by* Clostridium *species* - *Associated with fermented grass silage* - *Associated with very low salt*
	- Greasy (free fat at cut surface, mechanical openings)	- *Temperature too high at salting/pressing (often accompanied by seaminess)* - *Exposure to high temp (>60°F/>15°C) during aging*
	- Mealy (roughness, lack of waxiness)	- *Low moisture combined with low pH (low salting pH)* - *Exposure to high temperature (>60°F/>15°C) during aging*
	- Pasty/sticky (smears, clings to the fingers)	- *Caused by high moisture* - *Often associated with low salt* - *Associated with weak body*
	Note: Often associated with acid-cut color and/or acid, fruity and fermented flavor defects	
	- Weak	- *Caused by high moisture (precursor to pasty)*
	- Curdy, rubbery (firm, elastic)	- *Lack of aging*
Flavor	- Acid/sour	- *Cheese pH abnormally low (over-acidification)* - *Associated with acid-cut color* - *Associated with weak and pasty body when high moisture is the cause* - *Associated with crumbly body when high moisture is not the cause*
	- Bitter	- *Caused by protein breakdown* - *Low pH draining (high residual rennet)* - *High moisture content* - *Low salt (increase bacteria activity)*

(continued)

Table 1 Continued

Type of Defect	Defect Category/Description	Possible Cause (s)
	- Fermented, fruity	- *Milk late lactation (high plasmin dose)* - Pseudomonas *activity (poor quality milk or long storage periods)* - *Microbiological origin (yeast, coliforms)* - *Caused by lapse in sanitation* - *Favored by high moisture* - *Favored by low salt*
	- Sulfide	- *Microbial origin* - *Associated with high moisture, high temperature during storage* - *May occur naturally after long aging (not a defect)*
	- Rancid, lipase	- *Caused by enzymatic breakdown of fat* - *Mastitic or late lactation milk* - *Long storage periods/high psychotrophic bacteria* - *Poor quality milk/bacterial contamination* - *Freezing, temperature cycling*
	- Unclean, barnyardy	- *Microbial origin* - *Associated with poor quality milk/microbiological contamination*
	- Yeasty	- *Yeast contamination* - *Caused by lapse in sanitation* - *Favored by slow starter* - *Favored by high moisture/low salt* - *Associated with fish eyes/yeast holes*
	- Flat, insipid, lacking flavor	- *Associated with poor starter activity* - *Associated with low moisture, high salt* - *Associated with corky, dry body*

De Kaaskamer van Amsterdam is Amsterdam's most famous cheese emporium, located in the "Negen Straatjes" (nine streets) area in the Jordaan district close to the city center. De Kaaskamer has been operating since the late 1990s, and owner and cheesemonger Tim van Laar bought the store from the previous owners in 2014.

Today De Kaaskamer sells over four hundred styles of cheeses from all over Europe. Mr. van Laar personally selects Goudas and other Dutch cheeses and maintains a close relationship with producers. De Kaaskamer carries Dutch staples such as Gouda and Edam, as well as cheeses with caraway seeds and other spices, and a well-curated selection of goat's and sheep's milk cheeses made all over the Netherlands. Alongside cheese the store sells a selection of meats and wines, and serves a small lunch menu.

See also NETHERLANDS.

De Kaaskamer van Amsterdam. https://www.kaaskamer.nl.

Carlos Yescas

demineralization is the partial release of protein-bound minerals such as colloidal calcium phosphate (CCP) into the whey in response to acidification of milk or cheese. A certain level of demineralization is necessary in order for curds to knit to form a solid block of cheese, for cheese to melt and stretch, to prevent excessive hardness or chewiness, and for curd to absorb serum as it cools. Losses of CCP during cheesemaking promote protein mobility, which is reflected in the melt and stretch characteristics of cheeses like mozzarella. Although cheesemakers do not directly measure the levels of residual CCP required to make their cheese melt and stretch, they carefully control the rate and extent of acidification (pH drop) to control the extent of the solubilization of CCP. Traditional cultured mozzarella usually requires the cheese to reach a pH value of 5.2–5.3 before it is suitable for stretching. At this pH value sufficient demineralization occurs to facilitate the proteins becoming fluid enough to stretch when heated. If too little demineralization occurs before heating, then the curd will be tough, whereas excessive demineralization (e.g., promoted by direct acidification techniques, or an excessively low pH, e.g., < 5.1 for cultured mozzarella) can result in a very soft and excessively fluid curd. Acidification that occurs in milk before coagulation causes greater demineralization than acid development that takes place later in the cheesemaking process (i.e., within curd particles). See ACIDIFICATION; MOZZARELLA; PH MEASUREMENT; and STRETCHING.

Immediately after cheese manufacture, a significant amount (e.g., ≥ 70 percent) of the CCP originally associated with casein in milk is still retained in most cheeses (e.g., Cheddar, mozzarella). During the first few weeks of ripening further demineralization occurs, with the solubilized calcium and phosphate released into the serum of cheese. Demineralization makes the caseins more susceptible to degradation during ripening. In cheeses with low pH (< 5.0) extensive demineralization takes place and these cheeses tend to have a white color, brittle texture, and can readily lose serum (i.e., the cheese sweats). See CASEIN.

CCP is an important buffering component in cheese. The release of phosphate helps to buffer or hinder further pH drop even when there is significant fermentation of residual lactose post cheese manufacture. Excessive demineralization prior to coagulant addition can negatively impact cheese quality by reducing the potential amount of CCP buffering available, which in turn can result in an acidic cheese (brittle, short body). Acid production during ripening, also called post-acidification, can increase the risk of calcium lactate crystal development. Post-acidification is usually associated with a high moisture content on the young cheese, containing high residual levels of lactose ultimately transformed into high levels of acid during ripening. High acid levels in cheese promote demineralization, and the increased calcium concentration in the serum phase of cheese may form complexes with lactic acid (calcium lactate crystals).

In acid-coagulated cheeses, like cottage, the low pH value of the whey at drainage results in extensive demineralization. The acid whey produced from acid-coagulated cheeses is also rich in minerals (ash).

See also CALCIUM PHOSPHATE and WHEY.

Lucey, J. A., and P. F. Fox. "Importance of Calcium and Phosphate in Cheese Manufacture: A Review." *Journal of Dairy Science* 76 (1993): 1714–1724.

John A. Lucey

In **Denmark** the first written evidence of cheese is found in medieval sources as part of the yearly tithe to the church, a practice that continued up to the nineteenth century. The best known of these tithe cheeses is Thybo, a cheese made by the parsonages in Thy in northern Jutland. Danish artisanal cheesemakers have recently tried to re-create it using local milk and traditional methods.

Danish cheesemaking as a full-scale industry had a very slow start in the nineteenth century. The Danish dairy industry was first and foremost directed toward the making of butter. Cheeses made by the dairies were a secondary product made from skimmed milk. As a result the cheeses were very low in fat and, according to contemporaries, not of a very good quality. The establishment of cooperative dairies in the late 1800s and the development of better centrifuges resulted in an even more marginalized cheese production.

At the same time Danish dairymen, primarily from the manorial dairies, had been studying cheesemaking abroad. They returned to Denmark and began to establish a more specialized artisanal cheese industry. One of the first of these cheesemaking experiments was undertaken by Constantin Bruun on Antvorskov Manor, where he started production of Gruyère-style cheeses in 1801. The best known of these Danish cheese pioneers is Hanne Nielsen. Beginning in the 1860s she made the Havarthi farm famous for its production of different styles of foreign cheeses, such as Cheddar, Camembert, and Gorgonzola. These experiments prompted a new scientific interest in further developing cheesemaking in Denmark; as a result several experimental dairies and a governmental research institute for dairy industry were established in the early twentieth century.

Danish cheese became a successful export during the twentieth century with the rise of cheeses such as Danbo, Havarti, Danablu, and Castello. See HAVARTI. In recent years there has also been considerable success exporting a type of feta made from cow's milk to the Middle East. As of 2016 the entire Danish export of cheese amounts to about 300,000 tons a year. Danish cheese is sold all over the world and the oldest and now also international cooperative dairy company, Arla Foods, is among the biggest dairy companies in the world. See ARLA.

Since the Danish cheese industry began by developing Danish versions of European cheese varieties, it is hard to find original Danish cheeses. But there is one completely original Danish cheese, Rygeost, or Røgeost as it is sometimes called, a specialty of the island of Funen. It is a round, unripened cheese made of curdled milk. It is then drained, salted, and finally smoked using straw. Preferably oats but sometimes nettles are added. It is usually eaten on rye bread but can also be used in dressings.

There has been established quite a scene for artisanal cheesemaking in Denmark in the last few decades. Some of these artisan cheesemakers, inspired by the locavore philosophy of the New Nordic Cuisine, add flavors unique to the Scandinavian region and experiment with using unpasteurized milk or traditional methods, such as storing cheeses in grain piles.

See also NORWAY and SWEDEN.

Burchard, Jørgen. *Da ost blev for alle: 100 års udvikling set fra Brørup Mejeri* [When Cheese Became for Everyone: 100 Years' Development Seen from Brørup Dairy]. Ringe, Denmark: Forlaget Kulturbøger, 2005.
Jensen, H. M. *Bidrag til den danske osteproduktions og de danske ostesorters historie* [Contributions to the History of the Danish Cheese Industry and the Danish Cheeses]. Copenhagen: De Danske Mejeriers Fællesorganisation, 1974.

Nina Bauer

designation of origin

designation of origin (DO) is a term for a specific product that is entirely produced in a specific place, according to long-standing production methods, whose use is protected by law. It is a subset of geographical indication (GI), subject to the same international debate, but DOs up the ante by requiring, in addition to delimited geographical zones, stricter standards for more "traditional" production techniques. See GEOGRAPHICAL INDICATION. Countries that have instituted a DO system establish a governmental office (usually part of the agricultural ministry or the national trademark and patent agency) to manage the application and registration process and implement all relative regulation (such as ensuring that producers respect the regulated criteria and pursuing impingements on the domestic market and abroad in countries that have reciprocal GI agreements).

The earliest such formal, nationwide systems were developed in France and its southern neighbors, with a distinctive label to guarantee against fraud. As part of its expanding responsibilities for the European economy and trade, the European Union (EU) passed regulation standardizing member-state DOs in 1992, making various preexisting systems in member states compatible and extending the system to countries where it had not previously existed.

The EU system has three related labels—PDO (protected denomination of origin), PGI (protected geographical indication), and TSG (traditional specialty guaranteed, which does not have a geographical component)—and has developed an EU-wide logo for each. In 2011 the EU label superseded various member-state logos, and the names are translated into local languages—*appellation d'origine contrôlée* or *protégée* (AOC/AOP in France, Belgium), *Geschützte Ursprungsbezeichnung* (Germany, Austria), *Denominazione di origine controllata* (Italy), *Denominação de Origem Protegida* (Portugal), *Denominación d'Origen* (Spain)—and the EU logo is legitimate in English or any other member-state language. Some non-EU countries have developed comparable systems, especially Switzerland, where the same terminology and criteria types are used (in French and German).

DOs need to have specific geographical and production criteria. In their legally binding defining texts, EU food producer associations must declare a precisely delimited production zone whose boundaries are based mostly on geological analysis and historical research into where the product was produced in the past, but inevitably the zone is also influenced by where active producers are located at the time of application. In this respect DOs resemble any GI. But they must additionally provide detailed descriptions of how the product is produced, referred to as "human factors," "know-how," or "savoir-faire." For cheeses these criteria may include the species and breed of dairy animal used; what and how they are fed, housed, and milked; how milk may be stored, transported, treated (pasteurized, microfiltered, raw, chilled, reheated, inoculated); its physical description (dimensions, acceptable and unacceptable molds, colors, or other components like leaves, bark, smoking, or alcohol); the steps of the fabrication and aging process (including vat and other equipment sizes, shapes, and materials; the degree of mechanization permissible; aging cave materials and conditions), scale of production (farmer-cheesemaker, collective systems like fruitières, etc.); and how the cheese can be put on the market (packaging, possibility of selling cut or whole).

To reach appropriate definitions, the producer association works with employees of the government oversight agency and, depending on the country, with a team of expert consultants (geographers, anthropologists, sociologists, historians, agronomists) to arrive at a proposal that is mutually acceptable and legally admissible. Negotiations can be very long and divisive, and ultimately only producers located within the chosen zone that are willing to adhere to all selected criteria will be able to continue to use the resulting DO; all others must change their product name or cease commercial production.

Many misconceptions surround which words are protected and which words are generic, resulting from the evolving history of DO systems (since in some cases the name that is protected has been changed to fit newer requirements) and from some agri-food industry alarmism that influences how DOs are presented in the media and political contexts. Camembert, for example, is a generic name. Anyone in the world can make a bloomy-ripened semi-soft cow's milk cheese about five inches around and one inch thick and call it Camembert and not run into trouble. "Camembert de Normandie," however, is a designation of origin, highly protected under French and EU law and international trade agreements. See CAMEMBERT DE NORMANDIE. Other DOs and their generic versions include Brie de Meaux and Brie de Melun (brie); Yorkshire Wensleydale (Wensleydale); Orkney Scottish Island Cheddar and West Country Farmhouse Cheddar (Cheddar); Provolone del Monaco and Valpadana (provolone); several pecorino varieties, such as Pecorino Romano (pecorino); Allgäuer Emmenthaler (Germany) and Emmenthaler AOP (Switzerland) (Emmentaler); Crottin de Chavignol (crottin); Noord-Hollandse Gouda (Gouda); and Mozzarella di Bufala Campana (mozzarella). For an up-to-date list of all EU-recognized PDOs, the DOOR registry is available online in all official EU languages.

Generic names acknowledge that some cheese names have become too widespread to expect cheesemakers to change the name to something else. DO producers fight for sole rights to the name (that is,

against the persistence of generics), while DO-ineligible manufacturers protest the possibility of making a suddenly nameless product. The case of feta exemplifies how controversial this issue is, even among countries fully invested in a DO system: Greece's efforts to claim feta were heatedly resisted by France, Denmark, and Germany, countries with significant industrial "feta" production. The Greek victory forced them to rebrand their versions, which are now sold under proprietary names alongside their PDO role model.

DOOR list. European Commission. http://ec.europa.eu/agriculture/quality/door/list.html.

Gangjee, Dev. *Relocating the Law of Geographical Indications.* Cambridge, U.K.: Cambridge University Press, 2012.

Juliette Rogers

Di Bruno Bros. is the premier cheese shop of Philadelphia, Pennsylvania. The original store opened as a small grocery in 1939 by a pair of Italian immigrants, Danny and Joe Di Bruno. By carrying cheeses from the Old Country, such as Pecorino, they served the needs of the vibrant neighborhood around them, known as the Italian Market. Gradually, they expanded their line to include cheeses from around the world. Third-generation owners Emilio, Billy Jr., and Bill Mignucci have grown the business to five locations and developed an import arm that services hundreds of retailers and restaurants along the East Coast. Di Bruno Bros. strives to introduce customers to high-quality artisan products, fulfilling their motto as "culinary pioneers."

Darlington, Tenaya. *Di Bruno Bros. House of Cheese: A Guide to Wedges, Recipes, and Pairings.* Philadelphia: Running Press, 2013.

Tenaya Darlington

dietary laws (religious) refer to restrictions or prescriptions imposed by a community on what its members consume. Regulations around cheese in Jewish, Islamic, Hindu, Ayurvedic, and Rastafarian communities variously reflect concerns about individual ingredients in cheese; how ingredients are combined; circumstances under which cheese is produced and consumed; and effects of cheese on body and mind. Though secular observers have tended to interpret such dietary practices in

A line forms during the busy Christmas season at Di Bruno Bros., a cheese shop in the Italian Market in Philadelphia.
PHOTO BY BRIAN DUNAWAY

terms of either symbolic or rationalist arguments, focusing on psychological or material outcomes, adherents in these communities often have little interest in why guidelines are articulated as they are, concerning themselves instead with how to enact guidelines correctly. One thing is certain: religious dietary guidelines are never static, self-evident, or irreproachable, and the prescriptions relating to cheese are no exception. As production shifts among homemakers, villagers, hobbyists, artisans, and multinational corporations, religious authorities, practitioners, and adherents continually make determinations about the status of cheese as a category of food, as well as the suitability of individual cheeses given how they are produced and the circumstances under which they are consumed.

Judaism

Jewish food regulations are known as *kashruth*. The fundamental textual source for this is the Torah, the first five books of the Hebrew Bible. Karaite Jews, a minority group, look uniquely to the Torah for guidance about how G-d wants them to eat. Karaite readings of the Torah have led them to prohibit the consumption of cheese during the Jewish holiday of Passover, when they eat only foods actually mentioned in the Torah and refrain from anything fer-

mented or with the potential to ferment. During the rest of the year, Karaites consider themselves free to consume all cheeses (provided they do not include forbidden products such as pork).

Rabbinic Certification

The majority of today's world Jewry comes from communities that have looked to the Talmud, the central text of Rabbinic Judaism, to interpret how to enact the commandments set forth in the Torah. To discern which foods, including cheeses, fulfill the standards established in the Talmud, they rely on *hechsherim* (sing. *hechsher*), seals or stamps attesting that the product is kosher. A number of different certifying agencies (e.g., OK, OU, and Star K) send *mashgichim* (supervisors; sing. *mashgiach*) around the world to ensure that foods are produced according to their label's particular standards. Food producers pay for such certification, presumably because it expands their market. Some Jews who observe the dietary laws are content with any *hechsher*, but others rely on their rabbi or other authorities to tell them which are trustworthy. Jewish approaches to cheese cover a spectrum of practices characterized by varying degrees of restriction, and *hechsherim* signal to concerned consumers how such restrictions have been met. Nevertheless, predominant rabbinic concerns about whether or not the cheese is kosher are in regards to the consumption of nonkosher animals and their products, including dairy (as well as the products and meat of kosher animals not properly slaughtered); the mixing of milk and meat products; and the manufacture of cheese by non-Jews.

Kosher Animals

Whether a cheese can be kosher depends in part on whether the milk from which it is made comes from a kosher animal. Cheese made from the milk of goats, sheep, or cows has the potential to be kosher; cheese made from the milk of camels does not. More complexly, *chalav Yisrael* (also transliterated as *halab Yisrael* or *cholov Yisroel*) refers to milk that has been obtained under constant rabbinical supervision to ensure that it has not been contaminated with the milk of nonkosher animals. Many highly observant Jews will not consume milk or any milk product that does not demonstrate such supervision; however, some respected nonliberal authorities (e.g., Rav. Moshe Feinstein) have argued that such supervision is unnecessary in the United States where government regulators ensure that the milk of nonkosher species is excluded from the milk supply.

Meat and Dairy

Mixing dairy and meat is a further concern for Jews guided by interpretations of the dietary standards in the Talmud. Here, two questions are raised: first, can cheese be consumed alongside meat and, if not, how long must one wait after having consumed one to consume the other? Second, does the introduction of rennet, the enzyme traditionally derived from the lining of calves' stomachs used in the production of hard cheese, itself entail the mixing of meat and dairy? Regarding the former question, kosher Jews will not consume cheese and meat at the same meal. Most will wait one hour to consume meat after having consumed soft cheese, and between three to six hours to consume meat after having consumed hard cheese. Many observant Jews also wait six hours to consume cheese after having consumed meat. These guidelines are based on assessments of how long it takes to clear the palate of any tastes or residues.

Rennet

Regarding rennet, two issues are raised: one is the mixing of meat and milk; the other is the consumption of products made from animals that have not undergone kosher slaughter (*shechitah*). Authorities have long debated these topics, and although there

is no consensus, general conclusions can be drawn. The first is that if animal-derived rennet is an ingredient, it must come from a properly slaughtered and inspected kosher animal. See RENNET. The second relates to *batel b'shishim*, the principle that a problematic ingredient is acceptable so long as it constitutes less than one-sixtieth of the whole (by weight), and does not convey its taste. Animal-derived rennet in cheese normally meets these criteria, so even though its inclusion in cheese may be construed as mixing meat and milk, its insignificant quantity overrides such concerns. It is worth noting that *batel b'shishim* could be interpreted to mean that the rennet could even come from a nonkosher animal, because its portion in the food is so small, but authorities have argued that because rennet gives hard cheese its shape, it must come from a properly slaughtered and inspected kosher animal regardless of how minute a quantity it constitutes in the final product.

Manufacture by Non-Jews

A final concern is the Talmudic ban on consuming cheese manufactured by non-Jews. Most authorities today argue that this restriction arose from concerns about the potential use of rennet derived from an animal that had not been properly slaughtered and inspected. But some authorities maintain that the ban applies even to soft, or acid-set, cheese, not only to hard cheeses made with rennet. Thus, on the strictest end of the spectrum lie Jews who only consider kosher a cheese that was manufactured by Jews under proper religious supervision. However, many Jews who are also concerned with consuming kosher food will not only eat soft cheese manufactured by non-Jews, but hard cheese as well, so long as its production was supervised by a rabbinical authority and, in the case of hard cheese, a Jewish person either added the rennet personally or activated the rennet feeder (in sites of automated food production).

Islam

Halal, or Islamic dietary prescriptions, reflect similar concerns about consuming the products of forbidden animals (e.g., pig) and the products of permissible animals that were not slaughtered according to the laws of *zabiha* (Islamic ritual slaughter). Thus, the sourcing of rennet is also a concern for Muslims. Halal certification is a growing industry, and, along with kosher certification, is becoming increasingly scrupulous as laboratory techniques for detecting ingredients in food improve, awareness of what others around the world are eating heightens, and markets grow.

Hinduism

Hinduism considers cows sacred, and use of animal rennet is forbidden by law. Coagulation of dairy products such as paneer is achieved through acid or thermic coagulation. Sweet milk products such as Mawa and Penda are obtained through heating and the addition of sugar.

Ayurveda

Ayurveda, a system of healing associated with Hinduism but also followed by some non-Hindus today, categorizes cheese as a tamasic food (one of three categories, the other two being sattvic and rajasic). As a tamasic food, cheese is considered heavy and dulling. However, if consumed in moderation, it can be a grounding force.

Rastafarianism

Rastafarians, who eschew the consumption of mammals and birds and value the consumption of fresh plants, have not historically prohibited the consumption of cheese; however, Rastafari discussion boards and blogs reveal an increasing concern about the use of any animal products and a turn among some toward veganism. Casual observers today can note the mushrooming of specialized diets to which people in industrialized and industrializing societies prescribe. Increasing scrutiny and concern among religious authorities, believers, and adherents may be part of this broader movement to ask where food comes from, and under what circumstances.

Forst, Binyomin. *The Laws of Kashrus: A Comprehensive Exposition of Their Underlying Concepts and Applications.* 2d ed. Brooklyn, N.Y.: Mesorah, 2000.
Kashrut.com. http://www.kashrut.com.
Riaz, Mian N., and Muhammad M. Chaudry. *Halal Food Production.* Boca Raton, Fla.: CRC, 2004.

Shari Jacobson

The **Diocletian Edict,** *De pretiis rerum venalium,* was commissioned by the Roman emperor Diocletian and published in 301 C.E. This edict established price limits for wages and commodities, including two different types of cheese—soft and dry. The soft cheese was listed with other farm produce (eggs, fruit, etc.), whereas the dry cheese (aged for longer preservation) was included in a section dedicated mostly to fish. This categorization of dry cheese would seem to imply that it was prepared with fish (perhaps in a sauce), eaten alongside fish (perhaps with bread), or consumed in a similar fashion to preserved fish, as a source of protein. That cheese was important enough to the Roman cuisine and economy to be mentioned in the edict is notable, as is the differentiation in classification between fresh and aged cheese.

See also ANCIENT CIVILIZATIONS.

Kindstedt, Paul. *Cheese and Culture: A History of Cheese and Its Place in Western Civilization.* White River Junction, Vt.: Chelsea Green, 2012.
Leake, William M. *An Edict of Diocletian: Fixing a Maximum of Prices Throughout the Roman Empire, A.D. 303.* London: John Murray, 1826.

Vince Razionale

Domiati, also called *Gebnah bēḍa* ("white cheese") or *Gebnah tariyah* ("soft cheese"), is a soft fresh cheese made primarily in Egypt, but found throughout the Arabic nations of the Middle East. It is named after the port city of Damietta in Egypt. The first recorded making of Domiati in Egypt was around 332 B.C.E. Domiati is usually made from buffalo milk, but other types of milk such as cow's, goat's, sheep's, camel's or a mixture of milks may be used. Domiati is unique in that salt is added to the milk before renneting, essentially pickling the cheese.

To make Domiati the milk is pasteurized at 140–176°F (60–80°C) for fifteen to sixty seconds. Salt is then added to a part (one-third) of the pasteurized milk at 6–14 percent by volume. The more salt that is added to the milk, the sharper the taste of the final cheese. The salted pasteurized milk is mixed with two parts unsalted pasteurized milk and then the rennet is added to the mix. It takes two to three hours for the milk to coagulate. The curds are scooped into molds that are lined with cheesecloth. The molds can be made of wood or steel and can be lined with cloth or netting. They can vary in size depending on the size of the manufacturer. The cheesecloth is fully wrapped around the cheese and then pressed in a mold for twelve to twenty-four hours at 100°F (38°C). Small molds have to be turned frequently. For large industrial-scale molds, the curd is put under pressure by a built-in vise. After the cheese has been pressed the block is cut into (typically rectangular) pieces. Domiati may be eaten fresh or tinned and covered with brine (with a 14–18 percent salt content). The tins are welded shut and the cheese is pickled for three to four months at room temperature before serving.

Fresh Domiati is characterized by high levels of moisture and salt. It is considered similar to feta, with the main difference being that salting occurs before renneting in Domiati. Domiati cheese tastes salty and has been described as being chewy in a way that is almost squeaky on the teeth. Egyptians in particular enjoy eating fresh Domiati as a daily snack.

See also EGYPT and FETA.

Abd El-Salam, M. H., et al. "Domiati and Feta Type Cheeses." In *Cheese: Chemistry, Physics, and Microbiology*, vol. 2: *Major Cheese Groups*, 2d. ed., edited by P. F. Fox, et al. pp. 301–335. Gaithersburg, Md.: Aspen, 1999.
Food and Agriculture Organization of the United Nations. "4. Near East: 4.7 Domiati." *The Technology of Traditional Milk Products in Developing Countries*. http://www.fao.org/docrep/003/t0251e/t0251e13.htm.
Fox, P. F., et al., eds. *Cheese: Chemistry, Physics, and Microbiology*, vol. 2: *Major Cheese Groups*. 3d ed. London: Elsevier, 2004.
Harris, Emily. "Making Cheese in the Land of the Bible: Add Myrrh and a Leap of Faith." Radio segment. NPR, 28 March 2015. http://www.npr.org/sections/thesalt/2015/03/28/395796557/making-cheese-in-the-land-of-the-bible-add-myrrh-and-a-leap-of-faith.
Robinson, R. K., and A. Y. Tamime, eds. *Feta and Related Cheeses*. Cambridge, U.K.: Woodhead Elsevier, 1991.
"What Is Domiati?" Wise Geek. http://www.wisegeek.com/what-is-domiati.htm.

Sara Rodgers

The **donkey** (*Equus africanus asinus*) or ass is a domesticated member of the horse family. They were first domesticated in either Egypt or Mesopotamia before spreading around the world. Today there are two main strains of wild donkeys, Asiatic and African. The Asiatic's habitat ranges from the Red Sea to northern India and Tibet. The African donkey's habitat ranges from North Africa between the Mediterranean coast and the Sahara desert to the south of the Red Sea. A male donkey is called a "jack" and a female donkey is a "jenny."

Pliny, Hippocrates, Cleopatra, Ovid, and the Scythians all believed that jenny or ass milk effaces wrinkles in the face, renders the skin more delicate, and preserves whiteness (Pliny, 1855). All were prescient in advocating for jenny milk as a healing or cosmetic remedy. Jenny milk uniquely has natural antimicrobial factors, an epidermal growth factor, and an extended shelf life causing it to be considered a "functional food." It has been particularly beneficial to infants, the elderly, and convalescents with fragile or diminished immune systems. Raw jenny milk has virtually no food-borne pathogens. These characteristics have fostered a desire to make cheese from the milk, but that has proven a challenge, as the average jenny's milk supply is quite limited. Jenny's have twelve-month pregnancies and then can be milked for only twenty to ninety days after foaling. They produce only about a quart (liter) of milk per day during that milking period.

Scientific experiments have successfully produced jenny milk cheese by substituting the standard bovine stomach cell enzymes that aid in coagulating milk into cheese for those derived from camel's milk. Unfortunately the average daily volume of milk produced by donkeys is approximately 3–4 pints (1.5–2 liters). With an approximate retail value of six hundred dollars per pound, Serbia's donkey cheese, called Pule, is Pule is a pale yellow semihard cheese that is produced at the Zasavica Special Nature Reserve in Serbia.

Barlowska, J., et al. "Nutritional Value and Technological Suitability of Milk from Various Animal Species Used for Dairy Production." *Comprehensive Reviews in Food Science and Food Safety* 10 (2011): 291–302.
Brumini, Diana, et al. "Whey Proteins and Their Antimicrobial Properties in Donkey Milk: A Brief Review." *Dairy Science & Technology* 96 (2016): 1–14.
Cosentino, Carlo, et al. "Innovative Use of Jenny Milk from Sustainable Rearing." In *The Sustainability of Agro-Food and Natural Resource Systems in the Mediterranean Basin*, edited by Antonella Vastola, pp. 113–132. New York: Springer, 2015.
Pliny the Elder. *The Natural History of Pliny*, vol. 1, translated by John Bostock and Henry T. Riley. London: H. G. Bohn, 1855.
Vincenzetti, Silvia, et al. "Nutritional Characteristics of Donkey's Milk Protein Fraction." In *Dietary Protein Research Trends*, edited by Janet R. Ling, pp. 207–225. New York: Nova Science, 2007.

Scott Alves Barton

Double Gloucester

See GLOUCESTER.

draining is a necessary and important step in cheesemaking that separates the formed curd from the free whey.

Before the draining process can commence, both syneresis and curd demineralization will occur during coagulation. Syneresis is the separation of the whey from the forming coagulum (curd body) in the vat. The rate of acidification during syneresis largely affects the final mineral content of the curd. The casein micelles in the curd act as a sponge for acid, and they absorb hydrogen ions while releasing calcium phosphate into the whey. This process is called demineralization. See SYNERESIS; DEMINERALIZATION; and COAGULATION OR CURDLING.

The final texture of the curds is directly affected by the draining processes that are associated with different styles of cheeses. Curds are ladled into bags and forms to drain or into forms that allow the curd particles to coalesce into one large mass. When choosing a form for a cheese, there are ideal diameter-to-height ratios for the best curd formation results. See FORMS OR MOLDS.

Lactic and soft-ripened curds, which form predominantly through acidifying and culturing the milk, lose a large proportion of their calcium phosphate during coagulation. This results in a more delicately structured curd, as the calcium phosphate is a key component of strong curd structure. Often these cheeses are ladled into smaller format forms so that they hold a good texture and do not sink under their own weight. Some lactic curds are predrained before being ladled into forms. The newly formed curds fuse together more compactly when initially ladled into cotton or nylon bags and hung or pressed over a draining table. Using a fine weaved draining cloth ensures that no butterfat is lost to the whey, leaving the whey clear. Lactic and soft-ripened styles commence draining almost immediately after syneresis begins, such that draining occurs concurrently with syneresis and proceeds slowly over long periods of time. See SOFT-RIPENED CHEESES.

Rennet curds are more prone to syneresis and able to develop firm characteristics, as these larger format cheeses need to be more heavily renneted in order to maintain the necessary level of structural integrity during aging. For the most part, rennet curds allow syneresis to proceed nearly to completion, thereby creating a massive volume of free whey, before commencing draining. There are a few techniques employed that facilitate a contraction in the curd, and the expulsion of a larger quantity of serum from the curd during the syneresis phase. The rennet curds are mechanically cut in order to multiply the number of whey-exuding surfaces. The curds are stirred while still sitting in the whey, which prevents clumping and increases the rate of expulsion. Heating the curds at varying temperatures will aid in a more rapid expulsion of whey. The more the curds sit in the whey, the more they acidify and lose calcium phosphate. After rennet curds have reached the correct moisture level, they are ladled into forms and the draining process begins. See RENNET.

Some recipes remove a large portion of the whey (whey off) from the vat before ladling the curd. Other recipes ladle both curds and whey into the forms (dipping) so that draining happens more gradually over time. The presence of whey during drain-

Torta cheese draining at Finca Pascualete, a creamery in Trujillo, Spain. © KATE ARDING

ing within forms allows the curd to fuse while preventing pockets from forming among curd particles, giving a closer knit texture. After draining, pressing low moisture cheeses serves to expel more whey and to knit the curd grains together to create a homogenous body. See PRESS.

Draining time for cheeses takes between two to thirty-six hours depending on the cheese being produced. In order for the draining to be thorough, the curds must reach a proper acidity (pH) before being ladled into forms during syneresis and demineralization. A consistent acidity level of the curd right before draining is critical to creating a consistent cheese product, both in flavor and texture. Washed-rind cheeses, for example, require a lower acidity/high pH level both before and during draining in order to ripen properly and attract the desired bacteria for rind development. In contrast bloomy-rind cheeses need an increasingly high acidity/low pH. See WASHED-RIND CHEESES and BLOOMY-RIND CHEESES. These desired acidity levels are contingent upon a starter culture and rennet that produces acid on a consistent schedule from milk to curd to ladling. The whey produced at the end of the draining cycle also has a specific acidity level that can help indicate when the draining time has come to an end. It is important for most cheeses midway during the draining process to be flipped in their forms. This promotes even draining on both sides of the cheese body being formed.

The temperature of the cheese make room, where the draining of cheese in forms and cloth bags is taking place, is crucial to maintaining a healthy draining rate. The temperature should be maintained between 68–72°F (20–22°C). If the curd itself is over 75°F (24°C) it must be handled with care, as the butterfat becomes liquid and can seep through the cheesecloth or form. If the room is too cold, whey expulsion will be insufficient, resulting in a higher moisture curd. If the room is too hot, whey expulsion will happen too rapidly and could give way to the development of coliform bacteria, resulting in bloated cheese curd, or the curd will become too dry. Regulating the water content in the cheese during draining is crucial, as deficient draining can never be corrected during the drying or curing process. Excessive draining can cause ripening issues, or lack of desired ripening results. See MOISTURE.

After the majority of whey expulsion and curd formation has taken place, it is time to remove the knitted curd from the forms and place the cheese on draining mats on a draining table for salting. Salting can also be done during draining when turning the cheese in the form. This salting is the final aid in whey expulsion and prepares the curd for the curing or aging in a cave. Salt dissolves into the water phase at the surface of the curd and moisture is drawn, by means of osmosis, to the surface where it accumulates as salt diffuses into the curd. See SALT.

See also CHEESE CURDS; DRAINING TABLE; and WHEY.

Caldwell, Gianaclis. "Draining and Pressing." In *Mastering Artisan Cheesemaking*, pp. 53–57. White River Junction, Vt.: Chelsea Green Publishing, 2012.
Kindstedt, Paul. "The Eight Basic Steps of Cheesemaking." In *American Farmstead Cheese*, edited by Paul Kindstedt and the Vermont Cheese Council, pp. 109–111. White River Junction, Vt.: Chelsea Green, 2005.
Le Joauen, Jean-Claude. "Basic Principles of Cheesemaking" and "A Practical Guide to Making Farmstead Goat Cheeses." In *The Fabrication of Farmstead Goat Cheese*, pp. 52–56 and 103–108. Ashfield, Mass.: Cheesemaker's Journal, 1987.

Jessica Sennett

A **draining table** is a specialized piece of equipment designed to rapidly drain the whey from the curd. It is used in cheesemaking procedures that allow syneresis to proceed nearly to completion before draining begins, so that a massive volume of free whey can be released at the start of draining. Draining tables can be used to prepress the curd, drain the whey, and cut blocks that fit into a particular size of cheese mold. The table is designed to promote even draining of the cheese curd. See DRAINING; SYNERESIS; and WHEY.

Draining technique is important for efficient preservation of the cheese curd. When draining tables began to be used consistently in cheesemaking operations in the mid-1800s, certain components were engineered and standardized. Commercial draining tables lay down plastic draining mats atop sloped stainless steel tables to facilitate whey drainage. The sloped design directs all free whey from beneath the cheese molds to a hole, spout, or valve on one side of the table. This valve can be connected to a pipe that redirects the free excess whey down the cheese make room drain or to a whey tank. Both the plastic mats and the stainless steel tables are the most efficient to clean, and do not rust easily. Mats can also be made of straw and rubber. See STRAW MATS.

Draining for Cheddar cheese, for example, is completed within the cheese vat itself. After the curds have been formed and are floating in the whey, the vat's valve is slowly opened to allow all free whey to drain. The banked curds, left at the bottom of the vat, fuse together by gentle force of consolidating all curd particles on the bottom sides of the vat. The heat from the whey allows the curd particles to fuse effectively, and then these larger slabs of fused curd are cut and turned regularly in the process known as "cheddaring." See CHEDDARING.

Higher-moisture cheeses, such as Brie or Camembert, are ladled and drain gradually in the molds or forms resting on elevated cheese mats on a separate draining table. Slowly over time, the curd fuses. In cases such as this, the curds knit together purely via the force of gravity, without the need of any extra weight on top of the cheese curd.

The pressing table for larger wheels of low-moisture cheeses that have been settled into a form will also require a certain level of directed drainage. As cheese wheels and forms are being pressed, excess whey will continue to expel at varying rates of expulsion. Because of this the opening at the side, bottom, or corner of the table are necessary. The difference between a draining and pressing table is that the surface of the table must be flat for pressing, whereas it is sloped for draining. See PRESS.

Large-scale cheesemaking requires specially designed draining tables, such as the prepressing vat and tower systems, and the horizontal perforated conveyor system. In general prepressing vats are square ended and the bottom and sides are made of stainless steel, and provide uniform whey draining that can be programed via a control panel. The bottom is a wide slat conveyor which is moved forward at the end of the prepressing stage, so that the matted curd is cut into sections that fit into molds. The prepressed tower is a vertical draining table that drains and compacts the curd at the top of the tower, before releasing it into a form. The horizontal drainage conveyor consists of a series of perforated plates mounted on an endless chain, the adjacent side edges of each plate being unperforated, bent through an acute angle, and connected to the adjacent plates so as to prevent the cheese from passing through.

See also BLOCK-FORMING TOWERS; FORMS OR MOLDS; VATS; and WHEY.

C. van 't Riet/Dairy Technology USA. "Manual Drainage-Finishing Table." http://www.schuller.us/products/manual-drainage-finishing-table.

Kindstedt, Paul. "The Eight Basic Steps of Cheesemaking." In *American Farmstead Cheese*, edited by Paul Kindstedt and the Vermont Cheese Council, pp. 109–111. White River Junction, Vt.: Chelsea Green, 2005.

Robinson, R. K. *Modern Dairy Technology*, vol. 2: *Advances in Milk Products*. 2d ed. New York: Springer, 1993. See pp. 119–120.

Jessica Sennett

dry salting refers to the application of salt either directly on the surface of a formed cheese or by mixing it into milled curds before pressing. See SALT.

Surface salting is commonly employed in the production of soft and semisoft cheeses, where the high surface area to volume ratio will allow sufficient salt to penetrate into the paste of the high-moisture cheese. Salt is sprinkled or rubbed on to each side of the cheese, drawing moisture to the surface while salt diffuses into the paste.

In larger, harder, and therefore lower-moisture cheeses, it is difficult to get sufficient salt into the core of the cheese before the high salt concentration on the surface makes the rind less permeable to further salt diffusion. In the production of large, flat, Alp-style cheeses, such as Gruyère, Comté, and Emmentaler, small quantities of dry salt are rubbed on to the rind repeatedly during early ripening. Where appellation d'origine contrôlée (AOC) rules permit, this may follow brining. Salt may also be present and dissolved in the smear solution. The time taken for salt to build up in the core of the cheeses allows *Propionibacterium* to grow within them, resulting in flavors characteristic to these cheeses and, sometimes, the formation of large, spherical eyes. High salt levels have been shown to contribute to undesirable splits in the paste—a texture defect sometimes seen in these cheeses.

In the production of British territorial cheeses, such as Cheddar, Cheshire, Lancashire, Stilton and Wensleydale, blocks of curd that have reached their target acidity are put through a mill and a percentage of salt (usually around 1.7–2.0 percent) is mixed in before molding and pressing. See TERRITORIAL. The curd pieces become coated in salt, drawing out more moisture and enabling faster distribution of salt than would be possible with surface salting. Salt has a well-documented ability to inhibit starter lactic acid bacteria with starter-manufacturers sometimes reporting salt-inhibition levels in their product specifications. Salt-reduction has been shown to lead to higher acidity and delayed dominance of more salt-tolerant non-starter lactic acid bacteria (NSLAB), which are crucial to correct ripening. As territorial cheeses tend to have a relatively low surface-area-to-volume ratio, surface-salting alone would result in over-acidification at the core, retained moisture and poor salt distribution.

The manner in which milled curds are salted has a significant impact on the quality of the finished cheese. It is good practice to add the salt in a few successive applications rather than all at once to minimize the extent to which dissolved salt runs off in the whey that is drawn out. It is important that the salt is both well mixed in and that the curd particles are roughly the same size to ensure even uptake and a consistent end-product. Giving salted curds sufficient time to mellow, a process in which excess whey drains from the curd chips before molding, can improve the moisture loss and salt uptake of the cheese.

With the exception of Cantal, Salers, and Termignon, surface-salting and brining remain the most common technique used in Continental cheeses, while traditional British cheese varieties are all milled and dry-salted.

Fox, P. F., P. L. H. McSweeney, T. M. Cogan, et al. *The Fundamentals of Cheese Science*. Gaithersburg, Md.: Aspen, 2000.

Fox, P. F., P. L. H. McSweeney, T. M. Cogan, et al., eds.: *Cheese Chemistry, Physics, and Microbiology*. Vol. 1: *General Aspects*. 3d ed. London: Elsevier Academic, 2004.

Grappin, R., D. Lefier, A. Dasen, and S. Pochet. "Characterizing Ripening of Gruyère de Comté: Influence of Time × Temperature and Salting Conditions on Eye and Slit Formation." *International Dairy Journal* 3 (1993): 313–328.

McMahon, D. J., C. J. Oberg, M. A. Drake, et al. "Effect of Sodium, Potassium, Magnesium, and Calcium Salt Cations on pH, Proteolysis, Organic Acids, and Microbial Populations during Storage of Full-Fat Cheddar Cheese." *Journal of Dairy Science* 97 (2014): 4780–4798.

Paul Thomas

Durrus

See COUNTY CORK.

earthenware pottery. Before considering the role of pottery in cheesemaking in past human societies it is useful to make a number of general observations. First, cheesemaking forms part of a larger domain of human practice involving the processing of primary animal or plant products (e.g., meat, wool, milk, cereals) to create secondary products (e.g., bread, wine, oil, textiles) that bring added advantage and value to human existence. Second, the archaeological visibility of the technologies employed in the creation of secondary products in pre-modern human societies is contextually variable and typically limited: many of these technologies relied partially or entirely on the use of tools or containers in organic materials that typically do not survive archaeologically except in exceptional conditions. Consequently to trace these technologies, particularly their early history, it is necessary to adopt an interdisciplinary approach that takes into account an array of direct and indirect indicators. In the case of cheesemaking this includes not just textual and iconographic sources, where available, but also information from the study of animal management practices, container technologies and typologies, organic residues, and genetic lactase-persistence in past human populations.

Pottery can only ever provide some of the pieces of this jigsaw. Indeed it is arguable whether ceramic technology would have conferred any distinct improvement in performance over non-ceramic containers in early cheesemaking. In the best circumstances, the presence of a specialized type of ceramic container (e.g., strainer) and of dairy product residues in archaeological pottery may provide direct indications that cheesemaking, or at least dairying, was practiced and made use of ceramic containers.

Pottery may also take on the form of containers more usually produced in other materials, which may sometimes provide indirect testimony to organic containers, whose form suggests an association with cheesemaking. However, such crossovers into the ceramic realm are typically too infrequent to challenge the general rule that early cheesemaking was normally achieved without recourse to the use of specialized ceramic containers. As a result, where the testimony of pottery is mute or equivocal, it is as well to pay heed to the dictum that absence of evidence is not necessarily evidence of absence.

It would be logical to suppose that the practice of cheesemaking began as soon as human populations entered into managerial relationships with animals in which milk exploitation played a role. Cheesemaking offered distinct adaptive advantages: it created a product that not only extended the normal use-life of milk from days to weeks or months, but also, more crucially, was more easily digestible for populations that had yet to develop tolerance of the far higher lactose concentrations that occur in raw milk. This should mean that the origins of cheesemaking go back to the beginnings of animal domestication in the Near East at the beginning of the Neolithic (ca. 9–11,000 B.C.E.). Unfortunately, however, the fact that these earliest farming groups only used organic containers means that we cannot use pottery to test this hypothesis. It is nevertheless suggestive that as soon as pottery first appears in the farming societies of the Near East and southeastern Europe (ca. 7300–6000 B.C.E.) it provides direct evidence, in the form of milk residues, for dairying practices, which in all probability means cheesemaking. In addition the presence of milk lipids in early

This reconstructed Neolithic cooking pot from Ireland showed traces of milkfat, evidence that the prehistoric Irish incorporated dairy products, possibly including cheese, into their diets. DEPARTMENT OF ARCHAEOLOGY, UNIVERSITY COLLEGE CORK

Neolithic pottery from Central Europe and England suggests that dairying accompanied the spread of agriculture into northwestern Europe. Similar work suggests a fifth millennium B.C.E. date for the inception of dairying practices in Saharan Africa.

Interestingly this picture shows notable regional variation, with residues from dairying most clearly attested in northwestern Turkey but absent or more equivocal in the areas farther east where animal domestication first took place. Viewed in narrow ceramic terms such variation (if not a function of sample size and distribution) has been interpreted as indicating that emphasis on dairying varied between regions. However, while regional variation is to be expected, it cannot be excluded that meaningful variation in the presence or absence of dairying residues in pottery could result from variation in cultural preferences for the use of ceramic or organic containers in dairy processing or consumption. And so while the ceramic evidence broadly supports a close connection between the development of cheesemaking and early farming, it is not always a consistent guide to its chronology, nature, or distribution in time and space.

That said, pottery can, in favorable circumstances, provide glimpses of some of the techniques used in early cheesemaking—and thereby hints of what types of cheese were produced—and possibly also of how dairy products may have played a role in ritual practice. For instance, the identification of milk lipids in Early Neolithic ceramic perforated bowls from Poland implies a solid fermented milk method where curd required straining using a cloth, or in this case a strainer. In contrast a liquid fermented milk technique is implied by a class of closed barrel or bag-like pottery vessels that occur in the Levant, the north Aegean, and the Balkans between the late fifth and third millennia B.C.E. The positioning of handles or lugs on these vessels indicate that they were intended to be suspended, which would have allowed milk to be periodically agitated, after being soured, fermented, or cultured. Although no residue analysis has yet been performed, their form and likely function closely resemble suspended containers of skin or wood that are still used by traditional herding communities across the same region to produce a dry crumbly cheese or buttermilk. These ceramic versions enjoy a wide distribution but are never common and would have been heavier and less shock-resistant than the original skin or wood containers that provided their inspiration. It seems likely, therefore, that these ceramic versions represent rare crossovers into the visible ceramic realm, possibly for reasons of prestige or ritual, of an otherwise invisible organic vessel type that formed the mainstay of dairying over a large area and for a very long period of time. Occasional ceramic miniatures of these vessels provide further support for the idea that the ceramic versions were specially made for ritual purposes. A connection between smaller or thinner-walled ceramic vessels and the ritual deployment of dairy products has also been suggested by residue analysis of Neolithic pottery from Britain and Germany.

See also ARCHAEOLOGICAL DETECTION and ORIGIN OF CHEESE.

Copley, M. S., et al. "Processing of Milk Products in Pottery Vessels through British Prehistory." *Antiquity* 79 (2005): 895–908.

Craig, O. E., et al. "Did the First Farmers of Central and Eastern Europe Produce Dairy Food?" *Antiquity* 79 (2005): 882–894.

Craig, O. E., et al. "Feeding Stonehenge: Cuisine and Consumption at the Late Neolithic Site of Durrington Walls." *Antiquity* 89 (2015): 1096–1109.

Curry, A. "The Milk Revolution." *Nature* 500 (2013): 20–22.

Dunne, J., et al. "First Dairying in Green Saharan Africa in the Fifth Millennium BC." *Nature* 486 (2012): 390–394.

Evershed, R. P., et al. "Earliest Date for Milk Use in the Near East and Southeastern Europe Linked to Cattle Herding." *Nature* 455 (2008): 528–531.

Morris, S. "Dairy Queen: Churns and Milk Products in the Aegean Bronze Age." *Opuscula* 7 (2014): 205–222.

Salque, M., et al. "Earliest Evidence for Cheese Making in the Sixth Millennium BC in Northern Europe." *Nature* 493 (2013): 522–525.

Peter Tomkins

East Africa is home to a developing dairy sector that remains deeply rooted in traditional practices. Even as the region is embracing a wave of agricultural investment, particularly in dairy, most dairy products are consumed in the form of raw fluid milk that is boiled before consumption. Traditional cheesemaking is often found in rural areas, and interest from a growing middle class is increasing demand for new varieties of cheese. Most governments recognize the nutritional and economic benefits dairy can bring to rural economies, making the continued growth of dairy a priority. However, many challenges exist for the region, as transforming a largely informal, local dairy model into one that includes value-added products, such as cheese, requires significant investment in education and infrastructure.

Kenya is the leading dairy processor in East Africa and home to a variety of cheeses. A rising middle class, expatriate population, and many nonprofit internationals drive demand for specialty cheese. Further, as imported cheeses from Europe are subject to a high tariff, domestic production is especially attractive. Kenyan dairy processors produce a variety of cheeses, including blue, Brie, Camembert, Cheddar, cottage cheese, feta, Halloumi, Gouda, mozzarella, and paneer. The milk supply has been supported by the government for some time, which began an artificial insemination program to improve the genetics of dairy herds over forty years ago.

Although many cheese brands can be found across Kenyan markets, the bellwether for the country and East Africa is Brown's Cheese. Founded in 1979 by David and Sue Brown, Brown's Cheese has been passed on to the second generation and remains dedicated to crafting natural cheeses with the utmost passion and care. Located in the small town of Tigoni, about an hour north of Nairobi, the factory produces an astonishing seventeen dairy products.

Their product line ranges from more traditional Brie, Cheddar, and Gouda cheeses; to delicate, mold-ripened goat cheeses; to a balanced, creamy blue cheese; and even a washed-rind cow's milk cheese reminiscent of reblochon. The farm is open to the public for tours as well, hosting factory tours, cheese tastings, and lunches complete with ingredients sourced from the farm's own biodynamic garden. Milk for Brown's Cheeses is sourced from some three thousand small farmers, many of whom own only two to three dairy cows.

Although cheese companies have found success across Kenya and East Africa, many challenges to their growth remain. Only a few regions contain fertile land and adequate rainfall; most suffer from drought lasting three or more months each year. Even with appropriate climate, dairy farmers lack adequate education on basic disease management, breeding, animal nutrition, and milking hygiene. This presents additional challenges for milk collection and distribution—owing to poor milking hygiene the quality of milk is not able to withstand transportation over long distances. Thus, what limited milk is available must be supplied to processors within local territories. And, although dairy equipment and supplies are beginning to become more widely accessible, the technical training for cheesemakers is lacking. Despite this challenge, there is much hope that East Africa can increase its dairy production by making simple improvements in cow productivity and transportation.

Although the focus is often on commercial cheese production, many villages within East Africa continue to make traditional cheeses. Ayib is traditional acid-set soft cheese in Ethiopia, and is often an accompaniment for spicy meals. The process begins with naturally culturing milk at room temperature. The soured milk is churned, and the resulting buttermilk is slowly heated to 104°F (40°C) until the coagulation of protein occurs; the product is then allowed to cool, and the whey is strained from the curd. Ayib often has a smoky flavor, imparted from the smoking of dairy tools used to make the cheese.

The traditional cheese of Kenya is mboreki ya iria, which is a fresh, soft cheese. Milk is boiled, then cooled to room temperature before adding a fermented milk starter. Once a coagulum is formed, the curd is placed in cheesecloth and left to hang for a day.

The most popular cheese in Sudan is Karish, but it is also known for two pasta filata cheeses—braided and mudafera. Karish is prepared by culturing fresh, whole milk. After the cream rises to the top it is skimmed, and the sour skim milk is poured into cheese molds. After a few hours the molds are pressed gently to remove whey; multiple presses are applied to expel whey until the desired texture is achieved. The finished product is cut into pieces and salted. Braided cheeses are made from cow's, goat's or sheep's milk. After a rennet set, whey is separated from the curd, then salted heavily (10–15 percent), and seasoned with black cumin. Next the curd is heated, cut into strips, and then braided. The finished braids are stored in a large tin with brine. Mudafera is made in a similar fashion to braided cheese, but only from cow's milk. The finished curd is heated in hot water, then braided in large hanks. These too are stored in tins filled with brine.

Rural communities in East Africa continue to depend on dairy for their livelihoods. With continued investment in the dairy sector, hopefully these communities can keep their traditions, while increasing the milk supply through improved herd management. As most own only a few animals, this will require extensive training and resource distribution to small stakeholders.

Brown's Cheese. http://www.brownscheese.com.
Food and Agriculture Organization of the United Nations. "White Gold: Opportunities for Dairy Sector Development Collaboration in East Africa." http://edepot.wur.nl/307878.
Fox, P. F. *Cheese: Chemistry Physics, and Microbiology*, Vol. 2, *Major Cheese Groups*. 2d ed. London: Chapman and Hall, 1993.

Matt Ranieri

The **East Friesian (cow),** Ostfriesenrind, is a historic breed from Ostfriesland, a coastal area in Germany bordered by the Weser, the Netherlands, and Westphalia. It is thought to have emerged as a distinct breed in the eighteenth century, when cattle from Denmark and western Germany were imported to replenish stocks depleted by an epizootic disease outbreak in 1744–1756. It is then that the characteristic black-and-white (*schwarzbunt*) coloring associated with Friesian cattle today first shows up in the region. Systematic breeding records begin

in the mid-nineteenth century and a breeders' association was formed in 1883. Friesian cows were known to achieve high milk yields if fed well, with over 2,900 kilograms per animal recorded in a test as early as 1833. By 1899 average yields of 3,366 kilograms per animal with a fat content of 3.1 percent were recorded, with individual cows giving over 9,000 kilograms. Accordingly East Friesian cows were used for intensive dairy farming in many parts of Germany and beyond.

East Friesian breeds were important in founding both the American Holstein breed optimized for milk yields and the German dual-purpose Schwarzbuntes Niederungsrind that is frequently called "Friesian" in English-language literature. Following World War II West German cattle were extensively crossbred with imported Holstein cattle, producing the currently dominant Holstein-Friesian breed.

See also COW and HOLSTEIN.

Brade, W., and E. Brade. "Zuchtgeschichte der deutschen Holsteinrinder." *Bericht über Landwirtschaft* 91, no. 2 (2013).
Lydtin, A., and H. Werner. *Das deutsche Rind*. Berlin: G. Unger, 1899.

Volker Bach

The **East Friesian (sheep)** is the most prolific dairy breed on record, producing about 450–500 liters of milk per 220–240 day lactation. Reports of significantly higher quantities, as high as 951 quarts (900 liters) in the same period, are not uncommon. As such the East Friesian sheep is analogous to the Holstein cow, the cattle breed with the highest milk production, which also originated in the Friesland area of Germany and Holland.

There are actually several related Friesian sheep breeds that are similar in appearance. These include the Dutch Friesian from West Friesland in the Netherlands, the Zeeland Milk Sheep from the island of Walcheren in the Netherlands, and the East Friesian from, unsurprisingly, East Friesland, a coastal region bordering the North Sea in northwest Germany. Of them, the East Friesian is by far the most widespread and popular due to their astonishingly high milk production and prolific breeding.

East Friesians are medium to large wide-bodied sheep, with rams weighing 200–265 pounds (91–120 kilograms) and ewes weighing 145–165 pounds (66–75 kilograms). Classic coloration is white wool with a sleek white face and pink nose. The legs, face, and ears are all free of wool. There is also a dark brown variation. East Friesians are naturally polled, meaning that both sexes lack horns. A distinctive physical trait is this breed's thin wool-less "rat-tail," which farmers typically leave intact rather than removing. East Friesians are known for being docile and relatively easy to manage. They are fairly good wool producers, with fleeces that average 9–11 pounds (4–5 kg) of wool. They are also very fertile, with a 230 percent prolificacy rate, meaning that ewes tend to produce twins or triplets.

But purebred East Friesians do have some drawbacks, including the fact that they are not well suited to hot climates or intensive husbandry practices. Their history in Friesland was as specialized household milk producers. And East Friesian milk, while voluminous, is not very high in the solid matter that determines cheese yield, flavor, and texture. East Friesian milk averages 5.5–6.5 percent fat content, where other breeds can exceed 7 percent. The protein content is also somewhat lower than average, at 5 percent. For richer styles of cheese that require high butterfat, East Friesian milk may therefore be unsuitable. For all these reasons, East Friesians are some of the most crossbred animals in the world. By crossbreeding East Friesians with local breeds better adapted to the environment, such as Awassi sheep in the Middle East, dairies raise the lambing and milk production of their ewes while ensuring the health of the herd.

Today the East Friesian is one of only two dairy sheep breeds widely found in the United States (the other being the French Lacaune). See LACAUNE. This is a relatively recent phenomenon; in fact, East Friesians were only introduced to North America in the early 1990s. From the mid-1980s to the mid-1990s demand for sheep's milk cheeses in North America soared. In the United States, imports rose from 37 million pounds (16.7 million kilograms) in 1987 to 66 million pounds (30.1 million kilograms) in 1997, and the United States became the world's largest importer of sheep's milk cheese. This in turn supported the rapid emergence of a domestic sheep's milk cheese industry. At first non-dairy sheep were used, since dairy breeds were not available. But in 1992 Canada imported the first East Friesian sheep for commercial dairying and in 1993 the University of

Wisconsin-Madison, the University of Minnesota, and private breeders followed suit, purchasing East Friesian crosses from Canadian dairies. Research conducted by the University of Wisconsin-Madison showed that the East Friesian ewe crosses produced nearly twice as much milk as non-dairy ewes. Commercial sheep dairies quickly took note, and the East Friesian's popularity was assured.

See also SHEEP.

Berger, Yves, et al. *Principles of Sheep Dairying in North America*. Madison: University of Wisconsin Extension Service, 2005.
National Research Council. *Changes in the Sheep Industry in the United States: Making the Transition from Tradition*. Washington, D.C.: National Academies Press, 2008.
Thomas, David, et al. "Milk and Lamb Production of East Friesian-Cross Ewes in Northwestern Wisconsin." Department of Animal Sciences, Spooner Agricultural Research Station, University of Wisconsin–Madison, 1999. http://www.ansci.wisc.edu/extension-new copy/sheep/Publications_and_Proceedings/Pdf/Dairy/Reproduction and Genetics/East Fries-cross ewes-milk and lamb production.pdf.

Max P. Sinsheimer

École Nationale d'Industrie Laitière

(ENIL)—the (French) National Dairy School—sprang from two major late nineteenth-century developments: increasing international competition from Swiss imported cheeses; and discoveries in the science of bacteriology. Agricultural reformers in the Jura mountains hoped to improve the quality and market value of local Gruyère (Comté) through dissemination of the latest technical innovations to peasant producers. Reformers founded the first advanced dairy schools, the Écoles Pratique d'Industrie Laitière, at Mamirolle (Doubs department, 1888) and Poligny (Jura department, 1889), directed by Charles Martin and Hippolyte Friant, respectively. Both men studied under Émile Duclaux, himself a student of Louis Pasteur. See PASTEUR, LOUIS.

Duclaux's research led to numerous advances in dairy science that his students built on and popularized. Mamirolle, named an *école nationale* in 1893, also housed a research laboratory. Both schools hoped to revolutionize cheesemaking by teaching the chemistry of cheese, use of strict hygiene, careful temperature control, the centrifuge and other forms of mechanization, as well as ready-made rennet.

They trained specialists in making Gruyère and Emmentaler as a means to modernize the traditional village dairy cooperative (*fruitière*) common in the Franche-Comté region. New statutes for cooperatives written by Friant (among others) excluded use of goat's milk and increased control over the quality of milk farmers could bring to the co-op, leading to a more standard product. Similar schools soon developed elsewhere in France. The impact of the programs offered by these schools expanded as agricultural education and modernization gained ground in France, especially after World War II.

Today six establishments offer technical dairy education under the aegis of the Ministry of Agriculture. ENIL Besançon Mamirolle and ENILBIO Poligny are the linked national flagship schools, with four agricultural high schools (*lycées agricoles*) also offering post-secondary degrees such as the brevet de technicien supérieur agricole (BTSA). None of these technical schools offers a master's or doctorate. Students wishing to pursue these degrees attend SupAgro (Montpellier) or Agro Paris Tech.

See also COMTÉ and FRANCE.

Charmasson, Thérèse, and Anne-Marie Lelorrain. *L'Enseignement Agricole et Vétérinaire de la Révolution à la Libération: Textes Officiels avec Introduction, Notes et Annexes.* Paris: Institut National de Recherche Pédagogique, Publications de la Sorbonne, 1992.
Vatin, François. *L'industrie du lait: Essai d'histoire économique.* Paris: L'Harmattan, 1990.

Lynn L. Sharp

An **ecological niche** is the specific environment in which an organism has adapted to grow and includes how that organism responds within the environment to both resources and competing organisms. Whether or not an organism flourishes within a given environment includes what mechanisms it has to respond to and the intrinsic qualities of the environment (e.g., temperature, pH, water activity) as well as what mechanisms it has developed in order to compete with other organisms (e.g., bacteriocins, growth rate, nutrient utilization). For example, an osmophilic yeast is adapted to grow in high osmotic pressure, usually due to sugars present, and it may become an issue for a person making chocolate truffles. Likewise, organisms such as *Listeria monocytogenes* or *Yersinia enterocolitica* have the ability to grow

under refrigeration conditions and this would provide these two pathogenic organisms with a growth advantage during cold storage of a product.

O'Sullivan, O., J. O'Callaghan, A. Sangrador-Vegas, et al. "Comparative Genomics of Lactic Acid Bacteria Reveals a Niche-Specific Gene Set." *BMC Microbiology* 9, no. 1 (2009): 1–9.

Todd Pritchard

An **ecosystem** consists of all the living things (plants, animals, and microorganisms) in a given area, interacting with each other, and with their non-living environment (weather, earth, sun, soil, climate, atmosphere). Ecosystems work by exchanging energy and matter between biotic (living) and abiotic (non-living) components that impact their distribution and abundance. Each organism has its own niche, or role to play. See ECOLOGICAL NICHE.

The biotic component of the cheese ecosystem is called the microbiota, consisting of introduced starter and ripening cultures, as well as strains from the environment. As conditions during milk fermentation and cheese ripening change over time, and microbial species interact, the total microbiota also undergoes modifications. See MICROBIAL FLUX AND SUCCESSION. The abiotic factors (temperature, water, salt, and other elements) determine which microbial populations will become the biggest in size, depending on the characteristic requirements of individual species. Thus cheese ecology is intimately linked with microbial physiology, as the ecophysiological parameters determine the activities within individual cells and the sum of these activities defines the response of microbial populations to environmental influences.

In cheese internal factors influencing microbial growth are pH, water activity (amount of available free water), oxygen (redox potential), nutrients, antimicrobial substances (bacteriocins produced by lactic acid bacteria), and the food matrix itself. See PH MEASUREMENT; MOISTURE; and BACTERIOCINS. Externally applied (temperature, relative humidity) and cheesemaking factors (heat treatment of cheese milk, inoculation rate of starters, acidification, coagulation, drainage, salt concentration) will also influence the conditions in the cheese and impact the microbial populations. See RELATIVE HUMIDITY;

ACIDIFICATION; COAGULATION OR CURDLING; DRAINING; and SALT. The three main factors affecting the final cheese are the level of fat present in the milk, the cooking temperature of the curd, and the extent and the rate of acid production in the cheese. The main factors controlling the growth of microorganisms in cheese are: water content, salt concentration, and pH. Most lactic acid bacteria (LAB) need available water to grow. A water activity of less than 0.96 does not allow the development of such bacteria. See LACTIC ACID BACTERIA. Yeasts and molds are less sensitive to salt and can continue to grow at water activity values between 0.86 and 0.94. A reduction of the water content by addition of salt is very effective in controlling bacterial growth. In a cheese it is the ratio of salt to moisture (% S/M), rather than the concentration of added salt, that determines the inhibitory effect of salt. Activity of cheese starters will be inhibited at S/M of 6 percent in dry-salted cheese. See DRY SALTING.

Multispecies microbial communities help develop the flavor and texture of many foods of vegetable (wine, bread, pickles, coffee, chocolate) and animal origin (fermented fish, meats, cheese). The diversity of microorganisms contributes to the wide variety of tastes, smells, and textures of cheese. See TASTE; AROMA; and TEXTURE. The interactions between the cheese, the microbial community, and its environment determine the ripening processes that will be typical of a producer, a process style, a cheese type, or a region. These microorganisms may come from the raw milk, from production and transport facilities, from personnel, or from the ripening environment. See TINA; WOODEN VATS; and WOODEN SHELVES.

In order to better control the cheesemaking process, selected microbial strains are added as starter or ripening cultures during manufacturing. See STARTER CULTURES and RIPENING CULTURES. Cheese starters are mesophilic (*Lactococcus lactis*) or thermophilic (*Streptococcus thermophilus, Lactobacillus helveticus,* and *Lb. delbrueckii*) bacteria with optimum growth temperatures around 86°F (30°C) or 108°F (42°C), respectively. Non-starter lactic acid bacteria (NSLAB) are mesophilic lactobacilli (*Lactobacillus casei, Lb. plantarum, Lb. rhamnosus,* and *Lb. curvatus*) or pediococci (*Pediococcus acidilactici* and *Pe. pentosaceus*), which represent a significant portion of the microbiota of several varieties of cheese during ripening. For Cheddar cheese LAB are the only agents responsible for ripening. Propionibacteria are mesophilic

bacteria characteristic of Swiss-type cheese. For soft cheese other microorganisms (yeasts, molds, and bacteria) are typical of ripening. Molds such as *Penicillium camemberti* will grow on the surfaces of soft cheeses when oxygen is present. Halophilic microorganisms such as the yeast *Debaryomyces hansenii* out-compete other species in high salt environments, while thermophilic microorganisms thrive at higher temperatures. Low pH values, low moisture levels, low temperatures, and high salt levels promote the growth of yeasts. Lowering the ripening temperature can thus have a significant impact on the abundance of certain species of the cheese microbiota, slowing down many microbial activities such as glycolysis. Psychrotrophic species such as *Listeria* and some spore-forming bacteria survive at refrigeration temperatures and can flourish in the absence of competition with other microbial species. Chilling can also promote the growth of spoilage microorganisms such as *Pseudomonas*, yeasts, and molds, while some spore-forming bacteria and lactic acid bacteria grow at higher temperatures. See LISTERIA and SPORES.

The combined metabolic activity and metabiosis of the microbial community on milk fat, proteins, and carbohydrates is the result of microbial competition as well as cooperation. See SYNERGISTIC EFFECTS and SYMBIOTIC RELATIONSHIP. Microbe-microbe interactions can be positive, negative, or neutral for each species, giving rise to a number of possible configurations where one or all members benefit or are adversely affected. For example, yeast and bacteria can show mutualism, where both benefit. In commensalism some species benefit while others are not affected. In smear cheeses, for example, yeasts can produce stimulatory compounds for the growth of *Brevibacterium linens*. For amensalism one microbe adversely affects another generally without harming itself (as with bacteriocin production, or yeasts producing ethanol, for example). Among the strategies that microbes have to compete for nutrients are higher metabolic activities, scavenging specific elements such as iron, changing the environment by producing acid to lower the pH, or consuming acid to raise the pH. Ammonia production raises the pH, allowing yeasts and molds to become abundant in the microbiota on surface-ripened cheeses. This shows how the cheese matrix consists of microenvironments where conditions may differ with respect to oxygen, pH, water activity, and nutrients, leading to specific localized microbial associations. Some microbes even cheat by prospering from the work of others, without putting in the effort of contributing to the community. Finally microbes can communicate within and between species by producing signaling molecules that can diffuse in the food matrix. These molecules can have an impact on growth and specific activities of the microbiota, such as DNA transfer and biofilm formation, which are layers of microbe communities attached to surfaces and embedded in a polysaccharide matrix. See BIOFILMS. Whole microbial community analysis is now possible through new technologies of DNA sequencing, with the potential to help us understand the interactions within the microbial ecosystem of cheese.

See also MICROBIAL COMMUNITIES.

Ndoye, Bassirou, et al. "A Review of the Molecular Approaches to Investigate the Diversity and Activity of Cheese Microbiota." *Dairy Science & Technology* 91 (2011): 495–524.

Wolfe, Benjamin E., and Rachel J. Dutton. "Towards an Ecosystem Approach to Cheese Microbiology." *Microbiology Spectrum* 1 (2013): 1–2.

Gisèle LaPointe and Denis Roy

Edam. As with the other enormously popular Dutch cheese—Gouda—this sweet, slightly rubbery cow's milk product—though crystalline in texture and Parmigiano-like when aged—shares its name with a long-running cheese market in the north of Holland. Currently it is found in two iterations—the round raw-milk cheese from traditional farmhouse dairies in Holland, and the rubbery-textured industrial imitation, which can be found in countries all over the world in various forms as it is not name protected. Edam has been mentioned as far back as 1439, when it shipped out from the port of Edam, and was made largely with skimmed milk. It was, for the most part, a cheese designated for export.

Edam production is characterized by washed curds, rennet coagulation, and only slight pressing, in round wooden presses that were developed by the Dutch in a way that they revealed neither corners nor edges. This allowed for an extended life and greater protection against rot in shipping or mishandling and bruising in the process of unloading or unpacking, whether from seventeenth-century ships or contemporary containers at port. Like its cousin to the south, Edam showcases Dutch innovation in the cheese production and manufacturing process. A step introduced sometime around or before the seventeenth century demanded scalding the pressed and salted cheese, immersing it in hot whey. This accounts for the signature texture as well as the extended shelf life and durability. Who developed this scalding step and when is a debated issue when it comes to Edam and Gouda in Holland and their procedural counterparts in England, Gloucester and Cheddar. There is the possibility that these ideas did germinate with the English first and then spread to the Dutch. That said there seems to be general agreement that in the Netherlands these methods were widely in place decades, if not centuries, before 1700, which is substantially before it was recorded in English texts. See CHEDDAR; GLOUCESTER; and SCALDING.

The final innovation which Edam represents is in relation to its exterior, a smooth rind that has for centuries been known for its striking red hue. This was historically achieved with a dye of turnsole, whose other use was to illustrate manuscripts. Turnsole seeds were pressed and ground to make a juice that was then mixed with urine; the alkaline ammonia compounds reacted together to create a shade of intense light purple. This thin coating of red is now achieved through a wax-dipping process, similar to how wine and bourbon bottles are sealed. See TURNSOLE and WAXING AND COATING.

Edam cheese in the warehouse of Gestam Cheese Export, on the Voorhaven canal in the town of Edam, the Netherlands. The exterior of the cheese is not wax—which will be applied later—but a coating brushed onto the cheese in order to prevent mold while aging. © KATE ARDING

Edam has long had a global reputation, due not just to its mellow flavor and widely appealing mouthfeel, but also because of the prodigious Dutch trading capabilities. Its name can actually can be traced back to what traders from the German Rhineland called it, due to its geographical root in the city of Edam, with which the merchants had strong connections. From cheese markets and ports to spice trading networks and a global trade presence, cheeses like Edam took their place alongside spice in making their way around the world. See TRADE (HISTORICAL).

A pressed and semihard cheese, Edam should weigh between 2–3 pounds (1–1.5 kilograms) and comes in a round shape. It is made with mostly pasteurized milk, one more trait that enhances its mass-market appeal globally. It is normally aged three months, but if aged longer changes markedly in flavor, hardening and displaying caramel and roasted nut qualities. Classically it is eaten young, and in recent times has become a mainstay on breakfast tables. In the Netherlands it is also served with chocolate and eggs. When young it makes for an excellent melting or grating cheese. Typical flavors include sweet milky-ness, light Brazil nut and almond tones, and a gentle buttery-ness. Its popularity is also reflected in the many imitations made by industrial dairies from Europe and the Americas to Australia and New Zealand. There are also many artisanal expressions now being made by farmhouse cheesemakers, including Mahoe Vintage Edam, a Kiwi product, and Tulare Cannonball, made with Jersey cow's milk in California.

See also GOUDA and NETHERLANDS.

Androuet, Pierre, et al. *Guide to Cheeses*. Rev. English ed. Henley-on-Thames, U.K.: Aidan Ellis, 1993.
Dalby, Andrew. *Cheese: A Global History*. London: Reaktion, 2009.
"Edam Holland I.G.P." Formaggio.it. http://www.formaggio.it/formaggio-estero/edam-holland-i-g-p.
Harbutt, Juliet, and Martin Aspinwall. *World Cheese Book*. New ed. London: Dorling Kindersley, 2015.
Kindstedt, Paul. *Cheese and Culture: A History of Cheese and Its Place in Western Civilization*. White River Junction, Vt.: Chelsea Green, 2012.
McCalman, Max, and David Gibbons. *Cheese: A Connoisseur's Guide to the World's Best*. New York: Clarkson Potter, 2005.

Robert McKeown

"**Egypt** is the gift of the Nile," according to the Greek historian Herodotus (484–425 B.C.E.). The Nile flows down from Ethiopia, with its heavy rains and floods, passes through Sudan bearing silt, and reaches Egypt, where it forms the Nile Delta. The fertile river-fed soil and ideal climate—mildly hot and dry in summer, and warm and rainy in winter—supported a thriving agriculture going all the way back to the days of the pharaohs. The tombs connected with the pharaoh Hor-aha, who lived around 3100 B.C.E., contained two jars with a fatty residue and inscriptions that read "*rwt* of the north" and "*rwt* of the south." Chemical analysis determined the residue was cheese, suggesting that the jars contained two cheeses, one from Upper Egypt and the other from Lower Egypt.

Papyrus documents show that cheese was a major food in Ptolemaic and Roman Egypt (third century B.C.E. to fourth century C.E.). Local manufacture was supplemented by imports from Greece, just as it would be in later periods. On the other hand the Greek historian Diodorus Siculus (first century B.C.E.) was the first to report that some Egyptians would not eat cheese at all.

Several Arabic writers confirm that cheese remained important in medieval Egypt.

The local cheesemaking tradition of Damietta, relying on cow's and buffalo milk, can be traced with certainty to the eleventh century and is claimed to go back much earlier still. The khaysi cheese of medieval Damietta was made from the milk of khaysiyya cows, a breed apparently native to Egypt. A fifteenth-century mention of washing khaysi cheese implies that it was stored in brine, like modern Domiati, then washed to reduce the saltiness before eating. It was fried and sold at street stalls. The thirteenth-century Mamluk sultan al-Nasir Muhammad liked it so much that he took cheese fryers with him when he made the pilgrimage to Mecca. It was still popular in the seventeenth century, and fried khaysi cheese from Damietta (Paulina Lewicka suggests) was what was in the mind of the poor Cairene fisherman Judar, of the *Arabian Nights*, when he was asked what food he would most like to eat and at once replied "bread and cheese."

Egyptians today still consume large quantities of cheese at breakfast (typically with eggs), and at dinner (with milk or yogurt). On hot summer days Egyptians eat cheese for lunch, with watermelon, grapes, tomatoes, and cucumbers.

Egypt's main milk producers today are cows, buffalo (introduced in the early medieval period), and sheep. Bovine milk has a yellowish-white color and is used extensively in large-scale production of cheese due to its cheapness. Buffalo milk is characterized by its bright white color and is used for drinking and in the manufacturing of yogurt, while the surplus is used in cheesemaking to give a creamy taste while raising the lipid content. Sheep's milk is not used in abundance in cities or villages, but rather in desert regions.

There are many types of Egyptian cheese, but the most popular are Domiati, roomy, daani, karish, kishk, and mish.

- **Domiati** (also called Gebnah bēda, Damiati, or Damieta) is named after the city of Damietta where the Nile Delta splits into two branches. It is a firm fresh white cheese with a distinctive salty taste. It is considered to be similar to feta, the main difference being that salting occurs before the renneting. Domiati, a very popular cheese, is made by artisanal producers and also mass-produced. Factory-made versions contain less buffalo milk and may include vegetable oils to eke out the milk. It is packaged in 44-pound (20-kilogram) metal containers (tins) and sold by the pound (kilogram) in supermarkets. See DOMIATI.
- **Roomy** (rumi, romy, or ras) is a very popular hard yellow cheese. It is similar to Kashkaval, although Kashkaval is a pasta filata type. See KASHKAVAL and PASTA FILATA. Roomy is made from cow's milk or a mixture of cow's and buffalo milk. The curds are cooked at a moderate temperature until the beginning of ripening, poured into circular molds, and pressed under high pressure for thirty-six hours. The next step is to store them for three months with continuous salting and turning until ripening is complete. Roomy may be kept in a refrigerator and used over the course of a year. It is sold in wheel-shaped discs weighing 31 pounds (14 kilograms).
- **Daani** is a soft fresh cheese that is made from sheep's milk or a mix of sheep's and goat's milk. The unheated milk is allowed to acidify until it reaches 68–77°F (20–25°C) for up to thirty minutes. Rennet is added and the mixture sits for up to two hours. The curd is molded in cheesecloth and drained for two days. The curd is then cut and dry-salted. Fresh daani can be served immediately. It can be cured in brine for three to four months before being eaten.

The following cheeses are all made from a base of *laban rayeb*, a curdled skim milk. *Laban rayeb* is traditionally made in shallow earthenware pots where milk is left for a day in a warm place until it is naturally fermented by the milk flora. The top layer is removed for butter making while the bottom layer (*laban rayeb*) is used as a base for cheesemaking.

- **Karish** (or kareish) is a soft acid white cheese made from sour skimmed cow's milk, fermented buffalo milk, or buttermilk from sour cream. It has a cylindrical shape 3–4 inches (8–10 centimeters) long and 6 inches (15 centimeters) in diameter with a ridged surface. No starters are used and acidification develops from the natural flora of milks after one to three days. The curd is spooned onto a "shanda" mat and left to settle and drain. A small amount of salt is sprinkled on it and the salted curd is rolled in the shanda mat. The cheese is not pressed and it can be kept for one to two weeks. Karish is only made on farmsteads and is typically sold at local markets by women.
- **Kishk** is made from two to three parts fermented milk (*laban rayeb*) and one part wheat flour. The mixture of milk and flour is boiled then sun dried. It can be stored in open jars for one to two years without deteriorating.
- **Mish** (also called mesh or old cheese) is a soft pickled cheese without a rind. It is a product with a long history: a seventeenth-century author already describes it as "karish cheese kept for so long that it cut off the mouse's tail with its burning sharpness and the power of its saltiness." Today's mish cheese has a yellowish to brown color and a sharp salty taste. It is karish cheese that is ripened by pickling. Karish is left out for several days to dry, then the cheese is rinsed with water and layered in earthenware jars called *zalaa*. Salt is sprinkled over each layer of cheese and then the *zalaa* is filled with brine. The brine consists of buttermilk laban rayeb, whey, morta, red and green peppers as well as old mish (as a natural starter). The *zalaa* is sealed and the mish is fermented for a year at ambient temperature. Mish is an unregulated cheese mainly made for family consumption, and is a fundamental food

for Egyptian farmers, but similar products are now made commercially from roomy and Domiati cheeses.

Many Egyptian cheeses are made at home or by small producers, particularly farmers, before being sold at market. The vegetable oil feta cheese trade accounts for more than 6 billion Egyptian pounds a year.

See also ANCIENT CIVILIZATIONS.

Abd El-Salam, M. H., et al. "Domiati and Feta Type Cheeses." In *Cheese: Chemistry, Physics, and Microbiology*, vol. 2: *Major Cheese Groups*, 2d ed., edited by P. F. Fox, et al., pp. 301–335. Gaithersburg, Md.: Apsen, 1999.
Darby, William J., et al. *Food: Gift of Osiris*. London: Academic Press, 1977.
Food and Agriculture Organization of the United Nations. "4. Near East: 4.5 Daani, 4.7 Domiati, 4.15 Karish, 4.20 Mish, 4.22 Rahssr." *Technology of Traditional Milk Products in Developing Countries*. http://www.fao.org/docrep/003/t0251e/t0251e13.htm.
Goitein, S. D. *A Mediterranean Society: The Jewish Communities of the Arab World as Portrayed in the Documents of the Cairo Geniza*, vol. 4: *Daily Life*. Berkeley: University of California Press, 1983.
Kindstedt, Paul. *Cheese and Culture: A History of Cheese and Its Place in Western Civilization*. White River Junction, Vt.: Chelsea Green, 2012.
Lewicka, Paulina. *Food and Foodways of Medieval Cairenes*. Leiden, The Netherlands: Brill, 2011.
Robinson, R. K., and A. Y. Tamime, eds. *Feta and Related Cheeses*. Cambridge, U.K.: Woodhead Elsevier, 1991.

Amr Daoud

Emmentaler is a hard or medium-hard cheese (depending on age) made from raw milk. The round loaves have a diameter of 28–39 inches (80–100 centimeters) and weigh between 150–240 pounds (70–120 kilograms). A 220-pound (100-kilogram) wheel of cheese requires about 3,000 pounds (1,361 kilograms) of whole milk. The fat content of the cheese, measured in dry matter, must be a minimum of 45 percent. The most typical feature of the Emmentaler is its holes, which develop during the maturation. Their number and size varies according to the microflora of the manufacturing process, but usually should be between the size of a cherry and a walnut. See EYES.

The name "Emmentaler" originally designated a cheese from the Emmental, the valley of the small river Emme, in the canton of Bern, Switzerland. Yet, since the eighteenth century, business with fatty

Emmentaler cheese, which was increasingly being marketed under the collective trade name "Swiss Cheese," went so well that other parts of Switzerland, like the Zurich region or Grisons, entered the dairy business. Since the turn of the twentieth century the method of Emmentaler cheesemaking was copied in Germany, France, Italy, and even in Finland and Russia. Today countless Emmentaler cheeses of different types are produced in many regions worldwide, and "Swiss" and "Emmentaler" cheese are often interchangeable. Swiss cheesemakers missed the chance to protect the name at the right time. It was not until 2004 that Emmentaler cheese of Swiss origin was given a protected denomination of origin (PDO).

The earliest records mentioning cheesemaking in the Emmental date from the thirteenth century, but the cheese was first called by its name in 1542. That was about the time when commercial cheesemaking emerged, because the herders of the canton of Bern began with the production of fatty cheese, a product that was easier to transport and export. This shift in the method of production had some operational implications. In general dairy farming relied on the number of cows that could be fed throughout the year and the amount of milk produced at one time. A pre-modern farm seldom got enough milk to process butter and cheese simultaneously. To be able to manufacture 22 pounds (10 kilograms) of cheese even in the best months— May to July—the milk of ten to fifteen cows was necessary. The production of extraordinary dairy products in great quantities therefore could only be the outcome of the summer Alpine pastures. In the valley one family might manage two or three cows without the help of farm laborers; on the Alpine meadows three or four laborers could take care of fifty, sixty, or even more cows together.

But even under these privileged circumstances self-sufficiency and trade could obstruct each other. If the amount of available milk is restricted and one wants to receive butter and cheese, then one produces only a low-fat cheese from the skimmed milk. This cheese will have a considerably reduced durability. In the Bernese Oberland butter was the main milk product and commodity traded up to and into the sixteenth century. After 1481, however, city councils of the canton of Bern repeatedly fixed butter prices and banned exports in order to guarantee the domestic supply of butter. But instead of increasing the butter production, the herders switched to fat cheeses that were sold at a good price at home and abroad. In contrast to earlier cheesemaking traditions, from now on, all elements of milk were used to make cheese—the cream was not skimmed off, nor was it churned into butter. The improvement involved the hardness of the cheese. By subjecting the curd to greater heat, cutting it into smaller pieces in the cauldron, and storing the loaves in the pantry for a longer time, the cheese became considerably harder and thus more durable. To use the herdsmen's terminology, the cheese was "burned."

The fact that the loaves of cheese became smaller through this method, though, was not in the merchants' interest. Duties on the cheese were determined by quantity and not by weight. Therefore larger loaves of cheese were easier to sell than smaller loaves. The large Alpine pastures, having large cattle populations and thus being able to produce large quantities of milk, were especially suited to meeting this customer demand, limited only by the volume of the cauldrons. This explains the success of certain types of cheese such as the Emmentaler. As huge summer cheeses they sold well abroad; the soft and smaller autumn cheeses remained in Switzerland.

Between the sixteenth and eighteenth centuries many who could not subsist through farming entered the prosperous fatty cheese business. Laborers, milkers, cheese farmers trained by Alpine cooperatives, and the so-called kuher (the sons of farmers who did not inherit enough land to live on) reacted to the rising demand. In the canton of Bern these kuher jointly leased cow herds or bought pregnant cows and went from farm to farm with their animals through the farmstead meadows and Alpine meadows of their region in order to buy stall space and hay from farmers. Until the beginning of the nineteenth century this system went quite well. But then, around 1820, the first commercial cheeseries were established in the valleys, not by farmers but by cheese traders, agricultural reformers, or dairymen with business acumen. In the aftermath the Alpine cheese farming was headed downhill. Valley farmers started to form cooperatives and the Emmental cow herders' foray into the world of free enterprise came to a quick end. Many of them left their country and exported the know-how of Emmentaler cheesemaking to other regions of Europe and the United States. By the 1860s the former capital of cheesemaking in the Bernese Oberland had been degraded to a cattle-supplying area for the lowlands.

Between 1870 and the beginning of World War I cow's milk became a mass consumer good that was increasingly being sold fresh, especially as a drink. Even Emmentaler cheeses, despite being traded as a Swiss specialty, were soon no longer the exclusive preserve of Switzerland. Starting in 1914 fake Emmentaler cheese was produced in Germany, France, Italy, and even in Finland and Russia. However, due to protective tariffs, a fiercely run competition, and the outbreak of World War I, when cheese exports were stopped completely in favor of the country's supply, caused the Emmental sector to face a serious crisis. To prevent a possible collapse, the Swiss Cheese Union AG was founded and became responsible for the marketing of the three hard cheese varieties, Emmentaler, Gruyère, and Sbrinz, until the end of the 1990s. Since the 1950s the export of Emmentaler benefited greatly from federal aid. The annual production continuously increased until 1985 and then reached its peak of about 58,000 tons.

See also SWISS CHEESE UNION and SWITZERLAND.

Orland, Barbara. "Alpine Milk: Dairy Farming as a Pre-modern Strategy of Land Use." *Environment and History* 3 (2004): 327–364.
Schneider, Ida. *Die schweizerische Milchwirtschaft mit besonderer Berücksichtigung der Emmentaler-Käserei.* Zurich: Rascher, 1916.

Barbara Orland

Emmi AG, headquartered in Lucerne, Switzerland, is a large cheese manufacturer founded in 1907 by a group of local dairy farmers who formed a cooperative, the Central Switzerland Milk Association (Zentralschweizerischer Milchverband, MVL). The Emmi brand name was first used in 1947 to sell yogurt, which the company continues to produce and sell along with other dairy products. The name refers to the municipality of Emmen, a suburb of Lucerne, according to the company.

Through a series of acquisitions, including the purchase of Roth Kase USA in 2009, Emmi has grown to $3.2 billion in net sales in 2015, with twenty-five production sites in Switzerland and another seven in thirteen other countries employing 5,300 personnel worldwide. Emmi sells its own cheese production plus over 30,000 tons of cheese bought from other commercial dairies, which is then "matured, refined and packaged by Emmi," the company says. As of 2016 it is the largest Swiss milk processor.

In 2010 the firm repositioned 150 products under the Emmi brand in uniform packaging including its shelf-stable, ready-made fondue kits, using a Swiss flag symbol and the silhouette of a mountain peak in red and white. In 2012 Emmi agreed to discontinue labeling its US-made pasteurized-milk cheese as "Grand Cru Gruyère," instead just calling it "Grand Cru," when traditional Gruyère producers began seeking global recognition that the Gruyère appellation could only apply to Gruyère cheese made in certain parts of Switzerland. See GRUYÈRE.

With a history of selling traditional Swiss cheeses such as Gruyère and Emmentaler, Emmi is branching out to more niche markets such as goat cheese, recently acquiring stakes in several European and US artisan goat cheese producers, including the makers of Humboldt Fog and Cowgirl Creamery. See EMMENTALER and HUMBOLDT FOG. With the end of European milk quotas that restricted milk production, Emmi, like other Swiss cheese producers, is seeing increased competition by non-Swiss companies producing their own versions of Swiss-type of cheeses, forcing Emmi to concentrate on increasing sales outside of its home country.

See also SWISS CHEESE and SWITZERLAND.

"Emmi Acquires Redwood Hill Farm & Creamery to Expand in Goat Milk Product Market." Food Ingredients First, 4 December 2015. http://www .foodingredientsfirst.com/news/Emmi-Acquires -Redwood-Hill-Farm-Creamery-to-Expand-in-Goat -Milk-Product-Market?type=article.
"Emmi Surrenders 'Gruyère' Label in US." SWI: Swissinfo.ch, 4 May 2012. http://www.swissinfo.ch/ eng/business/cheese-dispute_emmi-surrenders --gruy%C3%A8re--label-in-us/32628886.
Gretler, Corrine. "End of Milk Quotas, Strong Franc are Bad Recipe for Swiss." Bloomberg.com, 6 April 2015. http://www.bloomberg.com/news/articles/ 2015-04-06/end-of-milk-quotas-strong-franc-are -bad-recipe-for-swiss-cheese.
"History of Emmi." Emmi Group. https://group .emmi.com/en/about-emmi/history-of-emmi.

Dan Macey

The **environmental impact** of cheesemaking derives principally from energy consumption, waste generation (whey), eutrophication (nutrient runoff), and the emission of greenhouse gases. Its severity depends on the type, scale, and location of the cheese-making facility.

By far the most impactful stage is milk production. Nitrous oxide from fertilizers and pesticides used in the cultivation of fodder crops, as well as the carbon emissions that are a direct result of the transportation of crops to the farm, and then of milk from the farm to the creamery, are significant pollutants of air, land, and water, along with the methane produced by ruminant animals and their manure. Sheep are thought to produce the most methane, cows and goats slightly less. Some larger facilities invest in digesters that convert manure's methane into biogas that can reduce reliance on other types of fuel.

Small, cyclical, and closed farming systems do not contribute greenhouse gases to such an extent. Although milking animals will always produce methane, grass feeding on open pastureland, and rotating crops in order to maintain soil fertility, reduces reliance on chemical fertilizers (and the transportation of fertilizers and of fodder). Further, the need to transport refrigerated milk is eliminated for those creameries that produce milk on their own farms.

At the processing stage, pasteurization, heating, stirring milk and curds, and maintaining temperature and humidity in the production space all consume energy. Producers who use raw milk and make their cheese by hand create less impact. Whey is a significant by-product of cheesemaking, and its nutritional content means that in small amounts it can be spread back on to the land or fed to pigs and other animals. In greater quantities, however, whey can be toxic to soil, and to fish if it leaches into rivers. Many industrial-scale producers sell their whey to companies that convert it into whey protein concentrate, used for emulsifiers, baby powders, and sports drinks, while others have introduced equipment that enables them to do this themselves. It is the medium-sized creameries for whom whey poses most of a problem, as they have too much to spread back on to the land but not enough to warrant an investment in the technology needed to convert it. Some plants have systems in place to create biogas from their wash water and their whey. Others have created wet beds, or reed beds, which naturally filter waste water and make it reusable on site.

The impact of processing also depends on the type of cheese being made. Hard cheeses that are aged use more energy, for heating the milk and curds (necessary for the whey expulsion required in these types of cheeses) and for controlling temperature and humidity during ageing. In some regions natural environments such as caves provide sufficient cooling and humidity and so no refrigeration is required.

Distribution generates direct carbon emissions during transportation and cooling. Energy and materials used for packaging, particularly if this process is mechanized and if slices of cheese are individually cut and wrapped, can be significant. These environmental costs are reduced if the cheese is sold locally and cut to order, and wrapped in compostable material (such as waxed paper) rather than plastic.

Conflicting information and consumer anxieties contribute to the environmental impact of cheese when it reaches the household. As a perishable foodstuff cheese requires refrigeration, although in some climates cheese could be safely stored in a box in a shed or garage. Cheese is often discarded if it has accrued certain molds, many of which are harmless, and is consigned to landfill because of questions about whether it is compostable. Buying cheese in small quantities and leaving it in a cool spot for immediate consumption reduces its energy demands at this final stage.

Traditionally cheesemaking was a small-scale endeavor developed by dairy farmers to make use of their surplus milk. On such a scale, and in the context of cyclical farming systems, no chemical fertilizers were required for soil or fodder, as whey was spread back on to the land and fed to pigs, and no emissions were accrued through transportation. As demand for cheese has increased, and farming of livestock and crops has intensified and become specialized, synthetic fertilizers have been introduced, and more energy is consumed by large-scale mechanized production, including pasteurization. Some countries or states have regulations in place that require manufacturers to reduce their impact. However, these tend to overlook the small and medium-sized creameries, which are often ignored and therefore denied opportunities for grants and funding, or treated the same as larger producers, which can be costly and inappropriate for their particular output. With the proliferation of good, small-scale and medium-scale production, consumers are increasingly likely to buy a local, or at least national product, where once they may have valued the foreign import. However, more still needs to be done to reduce the reliance on industrial-scale manufacture and the intensive farming on which it depends.

Aguirre-Villegas, H., S. Kraatz, F. Milani, et al. *Sustainable Cheese Production: Understand the Carbon Footprint of Cheese.* Madison: University of Wisconsin–Madison College of Agricultural and Life Sciences, 2011.

Daesoo, Kim, Thoma Greg, Darin Nutte, et al. "Life Cycle Assessment of Cheese and Whey Production in the USA." *International Journal of Life Cycle Assessment* 18, no. 5 (2013): 1019–1035.

Environment Protection Authority, State Government of Victoria. "Environmental Guidelines for the Dairy Processing Industry." 1997. http://www.epa.vic .gov.au/~/media/Publications/570.pdf.

Foster, C., K. Green, M. Bleda, P. Dewick, et al. *Environmental Impacts of Food Production and Consumption: A Report to the Department for Environment, Food and Rural Affairs.* Manchester Business School. London: Defra, 2006.

Hamershlag, K. *Meat Eater's Guide to Climate Change and Health.* Washington, D.C.: Environmental Working Group, 2011.

Joby Williams

enzymes are, without doubt, a critical contributor to the manufacture and ultimate characteristics of cheese. They have been described as biological catalysts, and are proteins that have the ability to act on other molecules to exert specific changes or effects.

In the case of cheese, enzymes play a role in influencing the suitability of milk for cheesemaking, are critical to the actual manufacture (as the coagulation of milk is an enzymatic process), and ultimately determine properties such as texture and flavor, due to their action during ripening in breaking down components such as proteins, lipids, and carbohydrates in the curd.

Milk itself is a complex biological fluid, and contains a number of enzymes that originate from the mammal's blood and mammary cells or pass into milk through the process of secretion. Perhaps the best known is alkaline phosphatase, which has the very useful property of being almost exactly as resistant to heat as the most heat-resistant vegetative pathogen that might be found in raw milk, *Mycobacterium tuberculosis*; thus, the effectiveness of pasteurization of milk is routinely evaluated by rapid tests for residual activity of this enzyme, and its absence used as an indication that the milk has been heated under conditions that would be sufficient to kill this pathogen, were it to be present. See MILK; PASTEURIZATION; and ALKALINE PHOSPHATASE.

In addition, milk contains a protease called plasmin (the same enzyme that plays a key role in dissolution of blood clots) that acts readily on many milk proteins, particularly beta-casein. Plasmin may influence the formation of the rennet gel, the yield of casein converted into cheese, and losses of protein fragments in the whey. Notably, the activity of plasmin is not constant in milk and can increase, for example, during late lactation and with increasing somatic cell count. In addition, quite a lot of the plasmin in milk is incorporated into cheese, and is acknowledged to play a key role in the early breakdown of proteins during cheese ripening, feeding large protein fragments into pathways that ultimately contribute to flavor and texture, and so the action of this enzyme is not necessarily a negative factor.

Milk also contains a lipoprotein lipase that can act on milk lipids, enzymes that can inhibit bacteria in milk, and probably several dozen other enzymes, the activity and significance of which are comparatively less well studied and understood. Thus it must be recognized that the raw material from which the cheese is made is a complex and variable starting point, and that many of the key agents that can influence the quality of the cheese, positively or negatively, are present right from the start.

In terms of cheese manufacture, the coagulation of milk by rennet or its substitutes is a purely enzymatic phenomenon. The key active agent in calf stomach extracts is an enzyme called chymosin, which has been used in cheesemaking for centuries, long before the idea of an enzyme being the key agent responsible was understood. The key function of chymosin is to initiate milk coagulation by a very specific hydrolysis of the kappa-casein that stabilizes casein micelles in milk; removal of part of this protein (the glycomacropeptide) critically destabilizes the micelle such that, at the right temperature and in the presence of sufficient calcium, the milk transforms almost magically from a liquid to a semi-solid gel. After cutting, much of the chymosin is lost in the whey but the remainder plays a key role, alongside plasmin, in the initial breakdown of the intact protein during cheese ripening. Calf stomachs do contain other enzymes as well, and for this reason and also ethical and economic reasons relating to its use as a milk coagulant, biotechnology has been applied to take the gene for chymosin and insert it into a range of safe microorganisms that produce a purer form of the enzyme, that is, fermentation-produced chymosin (FPC), which is widely used industrially today. See CHYMOSIN and FERMENTATION-PRODUCED CHYMOSIN.

Over the years, numerous substitutes or alternatives to rennet or chymosin have been investigated, from sources such as fungi or plants; the key consideration for any of these possible replacements is that their activity is focused very much on the specific hydrolysis of kappa-casein when added to milk rather than hydrolyzing other bonds in the milk proteins non-specifically at that time; if the balance between these reactions is not right, the milk might clot but collateral damage to the proteins will lead to losses of protein fragments in the whey and perhaps impairment of gel or cheese texture. In addition, some coagulant preparations deliberately include other enzymes, for example lipases to break down fats and thereby yield strong and piquant flavor notes desirable for some cheeses. See COAGULANT and PLANT-DERIVED COAGULANTS.

The final family of enzymes of critical importance to cheese play their roles during ripening and originate from the microorganisms present, such as starter lactic acid bacteria, adventitious non-starter lactic acid bacteria, and added molds in varieties such as bloomy and blue cheeses. This complex cheese microbial community includes a huge range of possible enzymes, some of which are released gradually as cells die and burst open, spilling their internal enzymatic complement into the curd, and these act through a multitude of pathways to break down the raw materials present in the cheese curd to the vast array of compounds that give each cheese variety its particular flavor and aroma. See LACTIC ACID BACTERIA; NON-STARTER LACTIC ACID BACTERIA; and MICROBIAL COMMUNITIES. Slight variations in the range of enzymes, and hence reactions taking place, are responsible for huge differences in ultimate cheese flavor and character, explaining why choice of cultures, and encouraging or controlling their growth by altering the conditions within (e.g., pH and salt) and outside (e.g., temperature and humidity) the cheese, are so critical.

In conclusion, enzymes are in every sense agents of change, and without these diverse and powerful products cheese would not exist. Every cheese is a complex ecosystem of biology, rich in a huge list of these catalysts, from the milk, the coagulant and the microbiome, and their concerted action during cheesemaking and ripening is the secret to obtaining the cheese desired.

See also LIPOLYSIS and PROTEOLYSIS.

Jacob, M., et al. "Recent Advances in Milk Clotting Enzymes." *International Journal of Dairy Technology* 64 (2011): 14–33.

Kelly, A. L., and P. F. Fox. "Indigenous Enzymes in Milk: A Synopsis of Future Research Requirements." *International Dairy Journal* 16 (2006): 707–715.

Kelly, A. L., et al. "Indigenous Proteolytic Enzymes in Milk: A Brief Overview of the Present State of Knowledge." *International Dairy Journal* 16 (2006): 563–572.

Wilkinson, M. G., and K. N. Kilcawley. "Mechanisms of Incorporation and Release of Enzymes into Cheese During Ripening." *International Dairy Journal* 15 (2005): 817–830.

Alan Kelly

Époisses is a soft washed-rind cheese made from cow's milk with both peasant and monastic origins dating back to the fourteenth century in the Auxois and Terre Plaine regions of Burgundy, France. It has been recognized as AOC since 1991 and PDO since 1996. About 1,400 tons of Époisses are produced annually as of 2015, including 8 percent from raw milk. Époisses is available in both a small size (9–12 ounces [250–350 grams]) and a large size (25–39 ounces [700–1,100 grams]).

The highly original principles for manufacturing Époisses were transmitted orally from mother to daughter up to the middle of the twentieth century; all testify to a singularity founded on the slow coagulation of whole milk, spontaneous draining, dry-salting, drying, and then ripening in cool, humid cellars associated with frequent cheese washings using marc de Bourgogne. The mastery of this process was such that Époisses was crowned "king of cheeses" by Brillat-Savarin himself at the beginning of the nineteenth century. See BRILLAT-SAVARIN.

After the high point of farm manufacturing at the start of the twentieth century, Époisses cheese almost disappeared in the wake of the two World Wars, when the women, left alone to tend to the farms, had no time to make cheeses. It was revived around 1960 by two passionate farmers, Robert and Simone Berthaut, eager for this unique heritage not to die out completely. They found out from old women in the vicinity the original recipe and slowly expanded their production.

Today Époisses is made from whole milk from authorized farms in the west of the Côte d'Or and south of the Haute-Marne départements, which comply with a specifications document founded on a strong link with the terroir and extensive feed autonomy. Local cow breeds (Brunes, Montbéliardes, or French Simmentals), fed with coarse non-GM fodder coming exclusively from the designated area, produce a protein-rich milk that is well suited to lactic manufacture. Époisses is the only lactic curd washed-rind PDO cheese. In the ripening rooms, modern techniques for temperature and humidity control and air circulation reproduce the original conditions prevailing in the cool cellars of the northeast-facing farms in the Auxois, where the cheeses quietly matured in winter.

The natural color of Époisses, resulting from the maturing ferments and bacteria, varies from orange ivory to brick red depending on the maturing stage. This lasts for a minimum of twenty-eight days, during which time the cheeses are hand washed several times a week with water to which quantities of marc de Bourgogne are added progressively. The cheese is a uniform butter yellow, soft and creamy. It has a penetrating odor with aromas of undergrowth. On the palette it is soft and melting, with a central part slightly crumbly if the cheese has not been long in maturing. Its taste is subtle, fruity, distinctive, and balanced with a delightful creamy sensation on the palette.

See also FRANCE and WASHED-RIND CHEESES.

Behr, Edward. *Burgundy I: The Art of Eating*, no. 59, 2001.

Boulenger, Florence. "Époisses, la clef des champs." *Profession Fromager*, September–October 2004, pp. 35–42.

Risoud, Georges. *Histoire du fromage d'Époisses: Chronique agitée d'un fromage peu banal*. Paris: Armançon, 2000.

Georges Risoud

equivalence of pasteurization is the recognition that alternative non-thermal processes and combinations of processes and treatments for pathogen reduction can be equally effective in protecting public health. In international public health circles, "equivalence" is the concept that the same level of public health protection can be achieved through various hazard control measures as well as inspection and certification systems. Equivalence can also be applied to specific requirements in regard to premises and equipment, processes such as Hazard Analysis Critical Control Point (HACCP) programs, and end-product microbiological limits. Under the World Trade Organization (WTO) Agreement on Sanitary and Phytosanitary Measures (SPS), member countries are compelled to ensure that their public health and safety measures are consistent, to focus on outcomes rather than processes, and to recognize the "equivalence" of measures to ensure safe food where the level of public health protection is the same. See HAZARD ANALYSIS AND CRITICAL CONTROL POINT and WORLD TRADE ORGANIZATION.

In the United States, Title 21 of the Code of Federal Regulations, Section 1240.61, mandates pasteurization for all milk and milk products in final package form intended for direct human consumption, except where alternative procedures are provided for by regulation, such as the curing of certain cheese varieties. For example, the standard of identity for Cheddar cheese (21 CFR 133.113) allows for the use of dairy ingredients that are not pasteurized, as long as the cheese is cured at a temperature of not less than 35°F for at least sixty days. See STANDARDS OF IDENTITY. The Food and Drug Regulations (FDR) of Canada also provide an alternative to pasteurization by requiring that cheese made from an unpasteurized source be stored at 35.6°F (2°C) or more for at least sixty days. Inconsistent with its domestic policy, Canada determined that the French regulations and control systems concerning soft and semi-soft raw-milk cheese manufacturing provided an appropriate level of protection to allow the importation of these products without requiring the sixty-day storage period. Similarly, in contrast with domestic policy, Australia and New Zealand have permitted the import from France of selected raw-milk cheeses such as Roquefort, based on equivalence determinations achieved through comprehensive risk assessments. These permissions reflect the capacity of regulatory systems and processing conditions to produce cheeses of equivalent food safety to those made from pasteurized milk.

See also HYGIENE; PASTEURIZATION; and 60-DAY AGING RULE.

Food Standards: Australia New Zealand. *Final Assessment Report: Application A499, To Permit the Sale of Roquefort Cheese.* 3 August 2005. http://www .foodstandards.gov.au/code/applications/documents/ A499_Roquefort_FAR_FINALv2.pdf.

United States Food and Drug Administration. "Cheeses and Related Cheese Products." *Code of Federal Regulations.* Title 21, Part 133. http://www .accessdata.fda.gov/scripts/cdrh/cfdocs/cfcfr/ CFRSearch.cfm?CFRPart=133.

World Trade Organization. "Decision on the Implementation of Article 4 of the Agreement on the Application of Sanitary and Phytosanitary Measures (G/SPS/19)." 4 October 2001. http://www.wto.org/ english/tratop_e/sps_e/equivalence2001_e.htm.

Dennis D'Amico

The **etymology** of words for cheese reflects human migration and advancement. The origins of the English word "cheese" are but a small part of a larger picture that also includes early Greek, Sanskrit, Chinese, and Arabic words.

While no one can be sure when the first word for cheese was uttered, hieroglyphics for cheese have been observed on murals and alabaster burial jars in Egyptian tombs from 3000–2000 B.C.E. How the pronunciation of those hieroglyphics is related to more recent words for cheese is unknown. In ancient Egyptian Coptic however, an Afro-Asiatic language written in the Greek alphabet, the word *halum* was used for cheese eaten in medieval Egypt. This word then became the origin of both an Egyptian Arabic loanword for the Cypriot *halloumi* (حلوم *ḥallūm* in Arabic), and the Turkish *hellim*, and for the modern Egyptian cheese *hâlûmi*, although these are essentially distinct cheeses.

The early Greeks used both *tyros* and *formos* for cheese. Although these words have no direct English descendants meaning cheese, *tyros* is still present in words such as *tyrogenous* (originating in or produced in or by cheese), *turophile* (a lover of cheese), and *tyrosine* (an amino acid named by the German chemist Baron von Justus Liebig in the nineteenth century because it was easily extracted from cheese).

The French and Italian words for cheese, from the Latin *forma* (mold), can therefore be taken one step farther back in history to the Ancient Greek *formos*. Thus the Latin *caseus formaticus* (cheese made in a mold) was partially derived from the Greek *formos* and developed into the words *fromage* in French and *formaggio* in Italian. The initial connection is considered to be related to the wicker baskets (*formos*) that held the curd while the whey drained away.

The evolution of the French *fromage* from the Greek *formos*, via the old French word *fourmage*, gave rise to the term *fourme* that is now applied to French cheeses of a cylindrical shape including *Fourme d'Ambert*, made in the Auvergne.

The English word "cheese" has had an equally convoluted journey from the Latin *caseus* (cheese) via the Middle English *chese*, the Old English Anglian form *cēse* (but not the late West Saxon *cÿse*) which is of West Germanic origin and is related to the Dutch *kaas* and the modern German *Käse*. That, in turn, was one of the earliest words borrowed from Latin into a Germanic language via the reconstructed West Germanic **kasjus* and the Old Low German **kasi*. There is also a close connection to the West Frisian *tsiis*.

Cheese in a number of other European languages can also be traced back to the Latin *caseum* including the Spanish *queso*, the Portuguese *queijo*, and the Italian *cacio* (colloquial for cheese, initially as *caxo*, then becoming *casio*, *cascio*, and finally evolving into *càcio*).

The Latin *caseus* also gave us the word "casein," the predominant protein group in cheese. The relationship of cheese with the Latin *caseus* may also have had an earlier beginning from the Old Church Slavonic *kvasu*, "leaven, fermentation, fermenting agent," the Proto-Indo-European root **kwat-*, "to ferment, become sour," and the related Prakrit (a Middle Indo-Aryan language that was the common man's Sanskrit) word *chasi* "buttermilk."

The world's oldest cheese was discovered in a northwestern Chinese desert around the neck of mummies and has been dated to approximately 1615 B.C.E. This may have been a precursor of the cheese traditionally made by the Bai people, called *nvxseiz* or *yenx seinp*. While the etymology is unclear, *yenx* may be from the words *ye* (to eat) and *nox* (able), and *seinp* (thread), from the stretching process during the production of cheese. The current Chinese name *rushan* (乳扇, milk fan) comes from the phonetic translation of *seinp* to *shan* and *ru* (dairy). Also the early Chinese name of *rushan* is *ruxian*, literally dairy thread.

Other languages have made their contributions to the current usage of cheese terms. The South Asian *paneer*, modern Hindi *panīr*, Armenian *panir/banir*, Turkish *peynir*, and Bengali *ponir* are all borrowed from the Persian and Middle Persian *panīr* (رينپ, made from milk), the Avesta (Zend) word *payah*, and initially from the Sanskrit word *páyas* (पयस्, milk).

As with any tracing of words over millennia, one comes across blind alleys. Cheese has been linked back to the Urdu word *chiz*, although the Persian translation, "a thing," suggests that it is more likely to be linked to the expression "big cheese" meaning "important person." Also, there is the record of cheese being exported in the third century B.C.E. from the Greek island of Chios to ancient Egypt. The name of the island just begs to be taken as the origin of the word "cheese." There is, unfortunately, no evidence of a linkage.

See also NAMING CHEESE.

Bishai, W. B. "Coptic Lexical Influence on Egyptian Arabic." *Journal of Near Eastern Studies* 23, no. 1 (1964): 39–47.

Durkin, P. *Borrowed Words: A History of Loanwords in English.* New York: Oxford University Press, 2014.

Kindstedt, P. S. *Cheese and Culture: A History of Cheese and Its Place in Western Civilization.* White River Junction, Vt.: Chelsea Green Publishing, 2012.

Partridge, E. *Origins: A Short Etymology Dictionary of Modern English.* 2d ed. London: Macmillan, 1959.

Don Otter

The remit of the **European Court of Justice** (ECJ) is to ensure that European Union (EU) law is uniformly administered throughout the twenty-eight EU member states. The ECJ was founded in 1952 and is based in Luxembourg. EU law is created by the European Commission. Member states can appeal to the ECJ if they disagree with Commission laws. In 1992, the Commission passed Regulation 2081/92 on "the protection of geographical indications and designations of origin for agricultural products and foodstuffs." This created an EU-wide scheme of geographical indications (GI). The names of food and drink GIs cannot be used by producers located outside the defined boundaries of production. *See* GEOGRAPHICAL INDICATION.

The conflict over the feta GI is the best-known cheese case to have been decided by the ECJ. The European Commission awarded Greek feta protected designation of origin (PDO) status in 1996. However, there existed numerous Danish, French, and German "feta" producers. These manufacturers wanted to retain the legal right to invoke the valuable "feta" nomenclature. They claimed that the decades-long production of "feta" outside Greece proved that the cheese had no geographical specificity. Instead, they asserted that "feta" was simply a generic term for a white salty cheese in brine. Regulation 2081/92 prohibits generic names like "Cheddar" from becoming GIs. In 1996, the Danish, French, and German governments asked the ECJ to nullify the PDO. In 1999, the ECJ annulled the PDO on the grounds that the European Commission had failed to conduct sufficient research to determine whether "feta" was generic.

Greece appealed to the European Commission which, in 2002, reregistered feta as a PDO. The Commission's decision derived from the revelation that non-Greek "feta" producers utilized Greek iconography on their products, which denoted a clear Greek connection. This led to the ECJ case *Federal Republic of Germany and Kingdom of Denmark v Commission of the European Communities*. The ECJ decided that the European Commission had correctly ascertained that "feta" was not generic. The ECJ ruling meant that, in 2005, feta was confirmed as a PDO.

The ECJ noted that,

> the geographical area defined by the Greek legislation covers only the territory of mainland Greece and the department of Lesbos. Extensive grazing and transhumance, central to the method of keeping the ewes and goats used to provide the raw material for making feta cheese, are the result of an ancestral tradition allowing adaptation to climate changes and their impact on the available vegetation…thus giving the finished product its own specific aroma and flavor. The interplay between the natural factors and the specific human factors, in particular the traditional production method, which requires straining without pressure, has thus given feta cheese its remarkable international reputation.

The ECJ decided that the unique terroir, defined boundaries, and specific methods of production proved that feta was geographically specific, which justified PDO status.

See also FETA.

Gangjee, Dev. "Say Cheese! A Sharper Image of Generic Use through the Lens of Feta." *European Intellectual Property Review* 29, no. 5 (2007): 172–179.

Matthew J. Rippon

exopolysaccharides are a broad class of viscous carbohydrate polymers produced by bacteria and some algae. Microbes have evolved a vast array of characteristic exopolysaccharides, many of which have important applications in dairy and other industries.

Exopolysaccharides are secreted by microbes and released into their immediate environment as a sort of loose slime. They are highly soluble and may have a significant effect on the texture of liquids and gels even at very low concentrations. Exopolysaccharides secreted by lactic acid bacteria such as *Streptococcus thermophilus* and *Lactobacillus delbrueckii* spp. *bulgaricus* have the capacity to contribute to a creamy mouthfeel and inhibit syneresis (whey separation) in yogurts and fermented milk drinks. These and other functional adjunct starters have generated interest as a means of improving the texture and consistency of reduced-fat dairy products and stirred-style yogurts without the need for added stabilizers or emulsifiers.

A typical example is kefiran, produced by *Lactobacillus kefiranofaciens*, a member of the community of lactic acid bacteria and yeasts that ferment milk into kefir. Its presence in kefir contributes to the fermented milk drink's smoothness and viscosity. Lactic cultures with vigorous exopolysaccharide production are used to make traditional Scandinavian ropey milk products including Finnish *viili* (a viscous mesophilic fermented milk similar to yogurt).

The residual lactose in whey, which is produced in large quantities as a by-product of large-scale cheesemaking, may be repurposed as an energy source for bacterial synthesis of commercially significant microbial exopolysaccharides including xanthan gum, dextran, and gellan. These are used as texturing agents and thickeners in a wide variety of industrial foods and cosmetics, as well as laboratory and medical applications.

Exopolysaccharides are also implicated in the formation of biofilms. See BIOFILMS.

De Vuyst, L., and Bart Degeest. "Heteropolysaccharides from Lactic Acid Bacteria." *FEMS Microbiology Reviews* 23, no. 2 (April 1999): 153–177.

Fu, Jen-Fen, and Yi-Hsiung Tseng. "Construction of Lactose-Utilizing *Xanthomonas campestris* and Production of Xanthan Gum from Whey." *Applied Environmental Microbiology* 56, no. 4 (April 1990): 919–923.

Bronwen Percival

eyes are the round holes that form within the body of certain varieties of cheese such as the Dutch types (e.g., Edam and Gouda) and the Alpine types (e.g., Emmentaler). Eyes are formed when internally produced carbon dioxide that is dissolved in the water phase of cheese production exceeds the saturation concentration and forms bubbles at suitable nucleation sites. Nucleation sites are thought to occur at extremely fine irregularities within the cheese body, such as around microscopic entrapped air bubbles. Carbon dioxide in Dutch-type cheeses is produced mainly through the fermentation of citrate by *Leuconostoc* species and citrate-utilizing strains of *Lactococcus lactis* ssp. *lactis*, whereas carbon dioxide in Alpine cheeses is produced through the fermentation of lactate by *Propionibacterium* species. In order for the carbon dioxide to accumulate sufficiently to supersaturate the water phase, the cheese must possess a suitable barrier to gas diffusion at the surface, either in the form of a dense dehydrated natural rind or an exogenous coating or film applied to the cheese surface. An essential prerequisite to eye formation is a very tight, close-knit, and elastic cheese texture, free of mechanical openings, that expands without fracturing under the internal pressure applied on the curd matrix by the growing gas bubble. Excessive demineralization during manufacture, which results in abnormally low calcium content and low pH, and extensive proteolysis during ripening may weaken the body to the extent that it cannot withstand the pressure of the expanding gas bubbles, causing the body to fracture into cracks and slits instead of forming eyes.

See also CARBON DIOXIDE.

McSweeney, P. L. H., ed. *Cheese Problems Solved.* Cambridge, U.K.: Woodhead, 2007.

Fox, P. F., et al. *Fundamentals of Cheese Science.* Gaithersburg, Md.: Aspen, 2000.

Paul S. Kindstedt

The **Fairfield and Greenwich Cheese Company** is an American business that operates two small, independent retail stores in the state of Connecticut. The Fairfield store opened in 2009 with a second location in Greenwich launched in 2014. Co-owners Laura Downey and Chris Palumbo maintain an approachable, well-curated selection of American artisan and farmstead cheeses and other gourmet provisions. With the help of a welcoming staff, the company earned a coveted place in *Food & Wine* magazine's "Top Five Cheese Shops in the U.S." as selected by cheese expert Laura Werlin. The company sources approximately 50 percent of its cheeses regionally, from small farms in New England, and the rest from European producers of traditional varieties. Their commitment to education led to the founding of The Cheese School of Connecticut, which holds a variety of classes at their two locations.

See also ARTISANAL and FARMSTEAD.

Heins, Barbara. "Retailer Profile: Greenwich Cheese Co." American Cheese Society. http://www.cheesesociety.org/retailer-profile-greenwich-cheese-co/.
Thelin, Emily Kaiser. "Laura Werlin's Top 5 Cheese Shops in the U.S." *Food & Wine*. http://www.foodandwine.com/articles/top-5-cheese-shops-in-the-us.

Allison Radecki

fairs and festivals centered on cheese are numerous. From local feasts and national festivals to international fairs, the events have a variety of aims, and cheese plays different roles within them.

Local cheese feasts and festivals often center on a particular cheese or a category of cheeses. The celebrated cheese could already be protected by a designation of origin or producers may be seeking to obtain it. In either case, the festival affirms or creates a visible connection between a product, local skills (savoir-faire), a place of production and a particular terroir. See DESIGNATION OF ORIGIN and TERROIR.

The event is also the occasion to affirm or to reinvent a production tradition, and to demonstrate its embeddedness within a cultural context. For example, the Picodon Feast (La Fête du Picodon), organized each summer in the village of Saoû in the South of France, celebrates a specific cheese, produced using raw goat's milk and protected by an AOP label, as well as a production area and the history of this specific cheese production, transforming the event into a tourist attraction. Cheese becomes an occasion for creating a performance, drawing attention to a local production and more generally to a specific locality as the cheese's place of production. In this way, cheese contributes to the existence of the locality—the municipality, but also the larger area of production, the Drôme and the Ardèche regions in the case of Picodon cheese—and of its history.

The ritual dimension that characterizes local cheese festivals allows people living in the production area to create a sense of community and belonging. Cheese becomes a point of connection as well as a means of communication, linking producers and consumers and creating a sort of imagined community. The collective performances and the exhibitions of a common good—that is, the local cheese that is celebrated—may nonetheless hide deeper social conflict. As happens in other rituals, the event marks a temporary

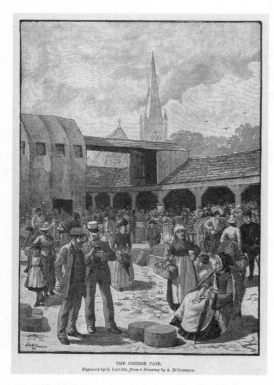

THE CHEESE FAIR.
Engraved by O. Lacour, from a Drawing by A. M'Cormick.

This illustration of a London cheese fair was produced by Arthur David McCormick (1860–1943) for *The English Illustrated Magazine* in 1885. PRIVATE COLLECTION / © LOOK AND LEARN / BRIDGEMAN IMAGES

social equilibrium among various groups having different interests or divergent positions; or it can become a time and a place to express frictions.

More generally such festivals help to define economic spaces and market positions. Festivals not only create links between people, products, and places: they also establish a connection with the market. Spaces for showing, selling, and buying cheeses organized within festivals are also often marketplaces. This market dimension is well developed in cheese fairs, which are not only selling places but also places where connections between producers and distributors or sellers are created and sustained.

Commercial cheese fairs—such as the biennial Cheese and Milk Products Fair (Salon du Fromage et des Produits Laitiers) in Paris, one of the international meetings for cheese professionals in the production sector—are the occasion to show "new" goods, whereas artisanal fairs, such as the annual California Artisan Cheese Festival, emphasize the importance of handicraft and the history of local

cheeses. Either way, such festivals help to shape the national image of the place where they are organized. This is especially the case for the host country of an international event, by affirming "national" prominence in an international arena.

The most prominent of international festivals is Cheese, the open-air exhibition fair showcasing high quality artisanal cheese organized by Slow Food. Cheese, is organized every two years in the center of Bra, in the northwest of Italy, where the Slow Food headquarters have been located since the creation of the association in the 1980s. Almost 250,000 visitors attend the event each year. Slow Food is an international association with more than 100,000 members in different countries around the world. During the four days of the exposition, around 350 exhibitors occupy the streets of the town. Cheese has an important commercial dimension, having become a well-known cheese fair where visitors buy and taste products from the different regions of Italy, and from other European, American, and African countries as well. As with other cheese fairs, it is also a cultural event: conferences, taste workshops, children's activities, and cultural meetings fill the program and the places of the town. Conferences and workshops allow the organizers and Slow Food members and visitors to discuss food politics, sustainable breeding, or the future of local economies through cheese and cheese production, thereby also making Cheese a political event. Cheeses allow the Slow Food leaders to speak about the movement (its projects, its campaigns, its philosophy), but—as at other ritualized fairs and festivals—also to speak to public powers and politicians who attend or observe the media coverage of this event. The aim of Cheese is to introduce people to knowledge about handmade cheese, to "good, clean and fair" (the Slow Food key words) cheeses, but also to the challenges of cheese production. During the workshops people are invited to taste and to compare artisanal cheeses with industrial ones and to take a position, in favor of the small producers, to join the movement. These two dimensions—the political and the commercial—exist side by side inside Cheese as well as in other smaller fairs. See SLOW FOOD.

Finally fairs are places where regulations, prices, and cultural values surrounding cheese are created, negotiated, or contested. They are places where "good" quality is defined, where the "correct" ways to produce cheese are demonstrated and affirmed, and where "alternative" means of production and distribution are expressed. In these events the cultivation of taste for "good" cheese (through tasting sessions) can become a political instrument in artisan producers' struggles to be recognized against state regulations (e.g., in countries where there are restrictions on selling cheese made from raw milk), or against labeling schemes deemed overly restrictive or, alternatively, too loose. In this sense fairs also perform a regulatory function, becoming communications hubs where the regulation, circulation, and marketing of cheeses as a global good take place.

See also COMPETITIONS.

Paxson, Heather. "Locating Value in Artisanal Cheese: Reverse Engineering Terroir for New-World Landscapes." *American Anthropologist* 12, no. 3 (2010): 444–457.
Siniscalchi, Valeria. "Slow Food Activism between Politics and Economy." In *Food Activism: Agency, Democracy and Economy*, edited by C. Counihan and V. Siniscalchi, pp. 225–241. London: Bloomsbury, 2014.
Wilk, Richard. "From Wild Weeds to Artisanal Cheese." In *Fast Food/Slow Food: The Cultural Economy of the Global Food System*, edited by Richard Wilk, pp. 13–27. New York and Toronto: Altamira Press, 2006.

Valeria Siniscalchi

faiscre grotha is the Irish name for curds that have been pressed in a mold of some kind to provide shape and solidity. According to historical record, this was probably a relatively small cheese; medieval manuscripts speak of women able to carry several of them in the folds of their cloaks. As a curd cheese, it was likely to have been consumed when fairly fresh, which seems to have been a feature of the native Irish diet centered upon the consumption of *bàn bídh* (white meats). Dairy produce was prevalent in the diet for at least half the year (between May and November) in Gaelic Ireland, and an abundant supply of milk from upland pastures was turned into curds, cheese, salted butter, and above all, sour milk drinks. Although unpressed curds were a summer subsistence dish, the whey was also a popular drink. Consequently, *faiscre grotha* was simply one of many varieties of dairy products that were once a staple part of the Irish diet.

Unfortunately, *faiscre grotha* disappeared during the seventeenth century, when the subjugation of Ireland by the English resulted in the development of a provision trade, particularly of salted butter (as well as salt beef), that absorbed much of the country's milk and cream stocks. The displacement of white meats (*bàn bídh*) eventually paved the way for the potato to become the country's dietary staple, which of course resulted in the tragedy of the Irish Potato Famine of 1845–1849.

See also IRELAND.

Ó Sé, Micheál. "Old Irish Cheeses and Other Milk Products." *Journal of the Cork Historical and Archaeological Society* 53 (1948): 82–87.

Colin Sage

families of cheese form a classification system that groups together similar cheeses. Cheese families are useful because they provide practical guidelines to understand the vast world of cheese. Also, by understanding the characteristics of each family, people can better explore new cheeses; if they like one they are more likely to enjoy others in the same family. Cheese families are helpful when shopping, as this is how cheesemongers often organize their display cases. In addition serving cheeses from different families assures variety, one mark of a successful cheese plate.

There is no single system of cheese classification that is universally accepted or able to perfectly classify the staggering number of cheeses in production worldwide. Some systems are based on the source of milk, the length of aging, the moisture content and firmness of the cheese, or the country of origin.

The families discussed here are mainly based on the technological steps of the cheese making and aging process that most contributes to a cheese's characteristics. Some of the larger cheese families can be divided into subfamilies. The main technological factors that determine a cheese's family include the method of coagulation used to transform the milk into a gel, processes used to control the moisture levels of the young cheese (such as the acidification, cooking temperature, and pressing of the curds), and ripening characteristics (such as the aging time and the secondary bacteria or mold cultures that are used). One of the first systems of classifying cheese based on the cheesemaking and aging process was suggested by Jean Lenoir in 1985, and has since been refined and recognized as an important integrative classification system (Almena and Mietton, 2014).

Fresh Cheeses

Fresh cheeses are defined by the lack of aging. They are consumed without ripening, and do not have a rind. Most of the cheeses in this family are coagulated with acid or heat rather than coagulant enzymes (rennet). Examples include ricotta, mascarpone, Galotyri, quark, chèvre, paneer, cream cheese, and queso blanco. Their flavors are mild and milky, with dominant lactic notes, and their textures are moist and soft, ranging from creamy to crumbly, depending on the intensity of acidification and fat content. Some fresh cheeses are stored for long periods in saltwater (brine). These cheeses, such as feta and Domiati, are firm and salty as a result. See FRESH CHEESES.

Surface-Ripened Cheeses

Surface-ripened cheeses have a thin coating of mold, yeast, or bacteria on their rinds. During the ripening period the microflora from the surface transform the taste and texture of the cheese, progressing inward during aging. These are small, medium-to-high moisture cheeses that were first made at monasteries and farms in northwestern Europe during the Middle Ages. There are two major subfamilies of surface-ripened cheeses: bloomy rind and washed rind.

Bloomy-Rind Cheeses

Bloomy-rind cheeses are ripened with the molds *Penicillium camemberti* and/or *Geotrichum candidum*. The surface can be felt-like and snowy white, such as with Brie and Camembert, or it can be ash gray and wrinkly, such as with Selles-sur-Cher, Saint-Maure, and Valencay. During aging the paste (interior of the cheese) turns creamy, and the flavor becomes earthy and mushroomy. The strength of the flavor depends on the specific cheese, mold strain, and length of ripening. See BLOOMY-RIND CHEESES.

Washed-Rind Cheeses

Washed-rind cheeses are also ripened from the outside in, but with bacteria rather than mold. The dominant bacteria are coryneforms and micrococci. Historically *Brevibacterium linens* was considered the dominant bacterium, but more recent studies suggest it comprises less than 20 percent of the microflora. The growth of the bacteria is mainly fostered by periodically washing the rind with a brine solution. During aging the rind becomes orange or pink, and the cheese gains its notoriously pungent aroma and develops bacony, barnyardy, gamey, and meaty flavors. The paste of the ripened cheeses may range from soft and semisoft, such as with Taleggio and Morbier cheeses, to gooey and almost liquid, such as with Époisses, Vacherin Mont-D'Or and Torta del Casar. See WASHED-RIND CHEESES.

Blue Cheeses

Blue cheeses are so called due to the color of the mold *Penicillium roqueforti*, the main microorganism in these cheeses. However, depending on the specific mold strain and the acidity of the cheese, gray and green colors may also be present. At the start of the aging process, a thin spike is used to create holes through the cheese, and veins of mold grow where there is access to air. These cheeses taste salty and spicy and have a moist, crumbly texture. Examples include Gorgonzola, Maytag, Roquefort, and Stilton. Some distinctive types of blue cheese have mold only on the rind (e.g., Classic Blue Log and Monte Enebro), are unpierced (e.g., Castelmagno and Bleu Termigon), or have unique bitter notes (e.g., Bleu de Gex). See BLUE CHEESES.

Uncooked, Pressed Cheeses

Uncooked, pressed cheeses use a mechanical press to force whey from the curds, resulting in a cheese that is drier and firmer than the previously discussed families. Despite the name the curds actually are heated to up to 104°F (40°C) while still in the whey, but this is a lower temperature than the cooked cheese family reaches. After the heating process, the curds are placed into perforated molds and pressed, which expels the whey and knits the curds together. The paste of these cheeses is moderately firm yet moist and pliable. Examples include the Tomme-style cheeses (e.g., Tomme de Savoie), Raclette, and Manchego. Some of the members of this family are made by washing the curds, a technique used to reduce acidity, resulting in a sweet flavor and firm, elastic paste when the cheese is young. Examples include Gouda, Edam, Monterey Jack, Colby, and Havarti. See TOMME; RACLETTE; MANCHEGO; GOUDA; EDAM; JACK; COLBY; HAVARTI; and PRESSED CHEESES.

Milled-Curd Cheeses

Milled-curd cheeses are a subfamily of the uncooked, pressed family made by draining the whey and then breaking the curds into small pieces. The milled curds are salted, and their high surface area makes the process of whey extraction through osmosis highly effective. The result is dry, firm, durable cheeses. This technique was developed in the Middle Ages to make cheeses suitable to be stored or transported for trade. Examples include Cheddar, Cheshire, and Cantal. See MILLING; CHEDDAR; CHESHIRE CHEESE (U.K.); and CANTAL.

Cooked, Pressed Cheeses

Cooked, pressed cheeses are made by heating the curds above 118°F (48°C) while in the whey. Cooking the curds helps to expel moisture because the curds' protein matrices contract, resulting in a drier paste and cheeses suitable for long aging and transport. These are large cheeses with textures ranging from semihard to very hard, depending on the heating, salting, and aging conditions. The cooking of the curds in Alp-style cheeses like Gruyère or Comté and Appenzeller cheeses results in a pliable and elastic paste with sweet and fruity flavors. Some Alp-style cheeses such as Emmentaler and Swiss have holes or "eyes," due to the CO_2 gas produced during ripening by propionic bacteria. Some Alp cheeses are washed during aging, but this is done to form a rind and has a minor effect on the characteristics of the cheese compared with the washed-rind family. See ALP-STYLE CHEESES. Higher cooking temperatures and extensive brining of the wheels, like Parmigiano Reggiano, Grana Padano, Sbrinz, and the multiple varieties of pecorinos (made from *pecora*, or sheep's milk) result in a concentrated flavor and drier, granular paste, which is especially suitable for grating. See GRANA PADANO; PARMIGIANO REGGIANO; PECORINO ROMANO; and SBRINZ.

Pasta Filata Cheeses

Pasta filata cheeses are made by heating the curds in hot water and then stretching them. When the curds are stretched, the protein molecules are broken from their interconnected matrix into long fibers. As a result the fresh cheese is smooth and stringy and has desirable melting characteristics. This family includes a range of textures, from the delicate and luxuriously creamy burrata, to the elastic and stringy fresh mozzarella and pizza-style cheeses, to the firm and more structured paste of provolone and caciocavallo, to the extra firm Ragusano. See PASTA FILATA.

Processed Cheese

Processed cheese is a "cheese product" made by mixing multiple cheeses with dairy byproducts, emulsifiers, oils, food coloring, and/or sugar. Examples include American Cheese, Velveeta, Cheez Whiz, and Government Cheese. Processed cheese is not recommended as a table cheese but is sometimes used as a cooking ingredient. See PASTEURIZED PROCESS CHEESES.

Categorizing cheeses based on the cheesemaking step that leads to the most distinctive characteristic of the cheese results in the greatest distinction among families (compared to, say, grouping cheeses by texture). However it does have drawbacks. In some cases a cheese can straddle two families or not fit into any. Also this system may give the impression that one cheesemaking step completely determines the characteristics of a cheese. Frank Kosikowski, a father of the American artisan cheese movement and founder of the American Cheese Society, wrote that "cheesemaking can be likened to playing a viola. The viola has four strings, but the degree of strength with which the violist applies the bow, and the knowledge of when and how to apply it, leads to either a concerto or a lullaby." The families of cheese discussed here are based on how the cheesemaker plays the "strings" of coagulation, moisture control (including acidification, cooking, milling, pressing, and salting), and aging techniques.

See also NAMING CHEESE.

Almena-Aliste, Montserrat, and Bernard Mietton. "Cheese Classification, Characterization, and Categorization: A Global Perspective." In *Cheese and Microbes*, edited by Catherine W. Donnelly, pp. 39–72. Washington, D.C.: ASM Press, 2014.

Cogan, Timothy, et al. "Biodiversity of the Surface Microbial Consortia from Limburger, Reblochon, Livarot, Tilsit, and Gubbeen Cheeses." In *Cheese and Microbes*, edited by Catherine W. Donnelly, pp. 219–250. Washington, D.C.: ASM Press, 2014.

Jenkins, Steven. *Cheese Primer*. New York: Workman, 1996.

Kindstedt, Paul S. *Cheese and Culture: A History of Cheese and Its Place in Western Civilization*. White River Junction, Vt.: Chelsea Green, 2012.

Kosikowski, Frank V., and Vikram V. Mistry. *Cheese and Fermented Milk Foods*, vol. 1: *Origins and Principles*, 3d ed. Westport, Conn.: F. V. Kosikowski, 1997.

Lenoir, J., et al. "La maîtrise du bioréacteur fromage" [Control of Cheese Bioreactor]. *Biofutur*. 41 (1985): 23–50.

Jeremy Snyder and Montserrat Almena-Aliste

farmer cheese (also known as farmer's cheese or farmers' cheese) is a form of cottage cheese that was developed in America. Cottage cheese has origins in central and eastern Europe and, as with many cheeses, was brought to America by immigrants. In the early part of the twentieth century, in the northeastern region of the United States, a new form of the European cottage cheese was developed. This variation on the soft, unripened, cooked-curd cheese known as cottage cheese was a lightly pressed, acid-curd version made from cow's milk and without rennet.

In the early household kitchens, the cheese curds were developed by keeping unpasteurized milk warm on a corner of the stove, allowing the milk's bacteria to naturally develop lactic acid to a high enough acidity that the milk's protein would form into soft curds. The curds were lightly pressed and then formed into loaves, logs, or round basket shapes.

This cheese went by the names "New York cheese" or "country-style cottage cheese" and then became more widely known as farmer cheese. In its original form, the nonrennet cheese had a sharp aroma and an acidic flavor. The flavor and aroma of today's commercially produced (using commercial lactic starter cultures and small amounts of rennet) farmer cheese is mild and only slightly acidic.

The name "farmer cheese" was generic, keeping the cheese somewhat undefined, having different meanings to different people, and often just referring to any simple, unripened, white cheese made from raw or pasteurized cow's milk. In the early years of this cheese's growing popularity, it became apparent that the name needed to be more distinctive to set it apart from the plump-curd cottage cheese. Because the curds of farmer cheese were lightly pressed and those of cottage cheese were not, the cheese was renamed "farmer's pressed cheese." The name and popularity remained strong through the 1940s and then waned, only to regain popularity in the early 1980s. Still popular today, we now know this cheese as farmer('s) cheese.

An American creation, this style of lightly pressed cheese can be found in nearly every dairy-producing region of the world. It is the universal cheese that often goes by the loving description "the cheese I remember my grandmother making." In the home kitchen of days past, it probably didn't have a specific name other than "cheese" in English or the equivalent name in the native region.

Farmer cheese can be found in specialty cheese departments. It can be eaten within a week of being freshly pressed or dried to a crumbly texture and stored for a month or more. It can be plain or flavored with a wide variety of seasonings such as dried herbs, spices, and even preserved jalapenos—the seasonings typically reflecting a given cuisine or region. When fresh, it can be used as a spread or filling (as one would use ricotta), or when pressed it can be served sliced with bread and fresh fruit or fermented vegetables.

See also COTTAGE CHEESE.

Herbst, Sharon Tyler, and Ron Herbst. *The Cheese Lover's Companion.* New York: Morrow, 2007.
Kosikowski, Frank V., and Vikram V. Mistry. *Cheese and Fermented Milk Foods.* 2 vols. 3d ed. Westport, Conn.: F. V. Kosikowski, 1997.

Mary Karlin

The **Farmhouse and Artisan Cheese & Dairy Producers European Network** (FACEnetwork) is a consortium of European cheesemakers. Started in 2006 by cheesemakers in France and Germany, the network has grown to represent more than three thousand dairies in fourteen countries. Its stated goal is to protect the wealth of knowledge of the indigenous milk and cheese producers throughout Europe.

Membership is open to all cheesemakers through their national cheesemakers organizations, and associated members include educational bodies, individuals, and service industries. The constitution and council structure were ratified at the FACE annual meeting in Cork, Ireland, in 2013. Members of the council meet regularly to discuss shared problems, meet with EU officials to discuss legislative issues, and plan for the future. Each year a three-day congress is held in a different country, where members explore local cheesemaking and discuss cheese-related topics.

The organization is working on several initiatives, including preparing a common "Guide to Good Hygiene Practices" for dairies. This guide will disseminate knowledge of best practices in making traditional products, making this information available to a wider audience and gaining the support of EU authorities. The network is also active in providing support for cheesemakers with technical queries and marketing cheese and dairy products.

Farmhouse and Artisan Cheese & Dairy Producers European Network. http://www.face-network.eu.

George Keen

farmstead is an informal classification used in the United States and much of Canada to designate cheese made on a dairy farm from the milk of that farm's animals. In Great Britain and Australia, the preferred term is "farmhouse." In England, farm-based cheesemaking predominated until the 1930s, and farmhouse production continued to coexist alongside industrial cheesemaking. In the United States, however, "farmstead" is a relatively recent appellation. Before the introduction of the factory system of associated dairying fully displaced cheesemaking from the American farm in the mid-1800s, there was no need to call attention to a cheese made on-farm—*all* cheese was farmmade. But then, for more than one hundred years, on-farm commercial cheesemaking in the United States was for the most part limited to the Amish community. See AMISH COMMUNITY. Only in the 1980s, when a few former hippies began to commercialize cheeses they had learned to make as part of a self-sufficient homesteading practice, did it become meaningful to designate some American cheeses as "farmstead," in opposition to the norm of centralized factory production. See AMERICAN "GOAT LADIES" and COUNTERCULTURE.

Today in the United States, farmstead cheese production is undertaken by a number of urban transplants, newcomers to both cheesemaking and dairy farming, who are seeking a meaningful alternative to office jobs and professional careers. At the same time, increasing numbers of farmstead cheeses are made by third- or fourth-generation dairy farmers, seeking in cheese a value-added alternative to shipping fluid milk for pennies a pound. The economic viability of farmstead cheese has been bolstered by the rise of rural and urban farmers' markets since the 1980s, as well as by specialty shops that trade in local and artisanal products.

One commonly cited benefit of on-farm production is that the cheesemaker—since she or he works on the farm and also often owns and cares for the animals that provide the milk—enjoys a higher degree of oversight over milk quality than is otherwise possible. Indeed, as a commercial designation, "farmstead" has successfully come to connote a wide range of desired qualities, including the complex flavors associated with artisanal production, the environmental and ethical virtues of craft farming and humane husbandry, and the social benefits of supporting small family-run farms. However, since "farmstead" is not a legal designation, there is considerable variation in how farmstead producers operate, as well as some controversy within the industry over how the term should appropriately be applied.

According to the American Cheese Society, "Milk used in the production of farmstead cheeses may not be obtained from any outside source." Note that scale of production is not here stipulated. Moreover, although the American Cheese Society insists that a farmstead cheese must not contain milk sourced beyond the farm in question, it does not require that all milk from a farm's animals be used to make cheese. By this understanding, a tiny cheesemaking operation with a dozen goats would jeopardize its farmstead status if it were to supplement its own milk with that of a neighboring farm, while a ten-thousand-head dairy farm could make and legitimately market farmstead cheese while also selling thousands of pounds of milk to commodity-processing plants. This logical outcome does not sit well with some who believe that "farmstead" is—and should be—understood by the consuming public as an indicator of humane husbandry and high-quality milk and cheese.

As consumer interest in farmstead cheeses has grown, many farm-based cheesemakers face the challenge of expanding their inventory without compromising the ideal of the farmstead label. The volume of cheese a farmstead operation can produce is limited by the number of livestock that the land, and those who farm it, can handle. To increase salable product without increasing herd size (which might overstretch the land or the farmers' labor capacity), some farmstead producers buy milk from nearby farms to augment their own. Many endeavor to preserve the meaning of their own farmstead cheeses (i.e., made from their own animals' milk) by buying cow's milk, say, if they raise dairy goats; the resulting cow's milk or mixed-milk cheeses need not be labeled "farmstead," although in marketing them the producer may yet trade on her own status as a farmstead cheesemaker. Some of the imprecision in the term's meaning, then, has to do with the fact that it is commonly used to describe not only cheeses, but also cheesemakers.

See also ARTISANAL; INDUSTRIAL; and INDUSTRIALIZATION.

American Cheese Society. "Cheese Glossary." http://www.cheesesociety.org/i-heart-cheese/cheese-glossary/.
Blundel, Richard, and Angela Tregear. "From Artisans to 'Factories': The Interpenetration of Craft and Industry in English Cheese-Making, 1650–1950." *Enterprise & Society* 7 (2006): 705–739.

Paxson, Heather. *The Life of Cheese: Crafting Food and Value in America*. Berkeley: University of California Press, 2013.

Heather Paxson

Farrington, Harvey

See CANADA.

The **fascèra** (plural, fascère) is an Italian cheese mold, made of wood or metal and circular in form. The etymology of fascèra shows that it derives from *fascia*, a band, Latin *fascĭa*. Sometimes it can be written as fasciera, but this is incorrect. The fascèra or cheese ring can be either fixed or adjustable. When it is adjustable, the ring is tightened and secured by a clamp (Italian *gattello*) and cord (Italian *tirante*), in the fashion of a springform pan.

The function of the fascèra is threefold: to press the curd and expel the whey, to shape the cheese into a round wheel, and to impress the maker's logo, mark, or other information onto the cheese wheel.

The fascèra is one type of cheese mold used in Italian cheesemaking, to be distinguished from *fascella* (or *fustella*). Fascelle are cheese strainers in the shape of a cylinder, truncated cone, or rectangular parallelepiped, which are perforated at the bottom and/or at the edges, so that the whey can run off. The holes are more or less numerous and have different diameters, depending on the type of cheese one plans to produce. An example of a cheese formed in a parallelepipedal fascella is Taleggio DOP. The main difference between fascelle and fascère is that the latter are rarely square and generally do not have a bottom or holes; only the side ring. These cheese rings can have different diameters and heights.

Centuries ago the traditional fascèra was fashioned from a strip of wood, usually poplar or willow or other flexible wood. Today the preferred material for the fascèra is metal (such as aluminum), plastic (e.g., polypropylene), or Teflon.

The fascèra can be decorated with marks to be impressed across the heel (Italian *scalzo*) of the cheese. This particular type of fascèra is called *fascera marchiante*; it is often made of plastic and it conveys the logo and other product information, such as the province of origin, the code of the cheesemaker, the month and year of production, and any other desired labeling information.

The duration of time that the cheese remains in the fascèra depends on the production regulations

An antique fascèra, or Italian cheese mold traditionally used in the production of Fontina Val d'Aosta. It is composed of a ring of beech wood with notches inside to make it flexible and a wooden locking system. The mold holds the curd and presses it to expel the whey, while also shaping the cheese. COURTESY OF PETIT-MONDE MUSEUM

for the particular cheese being made: it spans from a few hours to a few days. When the cheese ring or fascèra is removed, the cheeses are put in brine or dry-salted, and then placed on boards in preparation for the maturing or refinement process. These are usually hard cheeses, ripened and aged for several months, such as Italian Parmigiano Reggiano DOP and Grana Padano DOP. See MATURING; PARMIGIANO REGGIANO; and GRANA PADANO.

Epistola de caseis et operibus lactariis et modo quo in Rhæticis regionibus et alpibus parantur by Jachiam Bifrun (in Latin Jacobus Bifrons) is one of the first sources on fascèra. It was written in Latin in 1556, and deals with the subject of Alpine cheesemaking:

> Caseus…deinde cum subsederit excipitur, & in formas ligneas, quas à similitudine fasciæ, fasceras appellant, transfertur, easque fune circumligant. (1556, p. 224)

Freely translated, it states: "Cheese…when it has settled is removed and put into molds of wood, which because they are similar to bands, are called *fasceras*, and these are bandaged with a rope."

See also FORMS OR MOLDS.

Bifrun, Jachiam. *Epistola de caseis et operibus lactariis et modo quo in Rhæticis regionibus et alpibus parantur* (1556). In *Ars magirica hoc est, coquinaria, de cibariis, ferculis opsonijs, alimentis & potibus diversis parandis, eorumque facultatibus*, by Willich Iodocus, pp. 220–227. Zurich: Gesnerus, 1563.
"Jacobus Bifrons." http://www.staff.uni-giessen.de/gloning/bifrun/bifrun.htm.
Pellegrino Luisa, Resmini Pierpaolo. "Cheesemaking Conditions and Compositional Characteristics Supporting the Safety of Raw Milk Cheese Italian Grana." *Scienza e Tecnica Lattiero-Casearia* 52 (2001): 105–114.

Alessandra Guigoni

fat, also referred to as "milk fat" or "butter fat," is a major constituent of many different cheeses. Fat content can have dramatic effects on cheese yield, texture, cooking properties, flavor, and aroma. Scientifically fat specifically refers to lipids that are solid at room temperature, called triglycerides, which make up about 98 percent of the lipid (fat) content of cow's milk. The remaining 2 percent of the lipid content includes diglycerides, monoglycerides, fatty acids, phospholipids, cholesterols, and fat-soluble vitamins (A, D, E, K).

The amount of fat in cheese is often discussed in terms of the solids content, not taking moisture into account. This is known as fat in the dry matter (FDM) or fat in the dry basis (FDB). The highly variable intra/inter-variety moisture content differences can lead to large variations in the overall fat content of cheeses with similar FDM content. For example, Tilsit and Comté usually have similar percentages of FDM (~45 percent), but often have dramatic differences in percent of fat (Tilsit: 26 percent, Comté: 30 percent) due to moisture content differences (Tilsit: 42 percent, Comté: 33 percent). The cheesemaking process concentrates the fat that was present in the initial milk (whole milk: ~29 percent FDM). Most rennet-coagulated cheeses have FDM between 42 percent and 56 percent, but can reach high levels (~70 percent) in triple-cream cheeses and low levels (~33 percent) in certain cheeses such as low-moisture part-skim mozzarella. Acid-coagulated cheeses usually have lower FDM (<45 percent), except in certain cases (e.g., mascarpone: ~90 percent FDM). Fat content is used as a parameter for many standards of identity and protected designation of origin regulations. For example, the Code of Federal Regulations (CFR) in the United States indicates that low-moisture part-skim mozzarella must contain between 30 percent and 45 percent FDM. The European Union's protected designation of origin for feta indicates a minimum of 43 percent FDM.

Milk fat occurs as globular structures. These milk fat globules are less dense than the surrounding watery portion of milk and, left to their own devices, will cluster and rise forming a "cream line" or "cream top." Milk is often homogenized to reduce globule size and form a more stable emulsion preventing the separation of cream. Milk fat globules have a core of triglycerides that are enveloped in a protective membrane, referred to as the milk fat globule membrane. This membrane protects the fatty core from various reactions that can have detrimental effects on milk, and, furthermore, cheese quality. Excessive disruption of this membrane by processes such as homogenization and vigorous handling or pumping can expose more of the fat to air and enzymes allowing oxidation and lipolysis reactions to occur more readily. In cheese homogenized milk often confers a higher moisture content, whiter color, less free oil, and smoother body (often noticed in blue cheese). See HOMOGENIZATION.

During the cheesemaking process, casein micelles aggregate and cluster, forming a protein matrix that serves as the primary structure for the coagulum and resulting cheese. See CASEIN; PROTEINS; and COAGULATION OR CURDLING. This matrix has fat globules included in its porous structure. Increased presence of fat globules in the voids of the casein network can restrict the continued aggregation and contraction of the protein matrix, resulting in less whey expulsion, often times leading to higher moisture content. Fat globules are also thought to bind to the casein matrix to some degree, further disturbing the protein structure. These alterations to the casein matrix lead to a softening of the cheese coagulum. For these reasons, cheeses higher in fat usually have a weaker, softer body. When the coagulum is cut, small amounts of fat are lost from curd and are drained with the whey. Additional fat can be lost during further processing steps such as the pasta filata process, where the stretching action and presence of hot water allows fat to leak and escape from the protein matrix. See PASTA FILATA.

Fat content has pronounced effects on the texture of cheese. Lowering the level of fat often yields a firmer cheese, and in extreme cases a more springy or corky body. This can be explained by the effect of fat on cheese microstructure as discussed above and the changes to the protein-to-fat ratio of the cheese; lowering the amount of fat shifts this ratio to higher amounts of protein, conferring a firmer structure. In cooking applications cheese functionality plays a critical role. The ability of a cheese to stretch, brown, and melt plays an important part in overall acceptability. Reduced-fat cheeses such as low-fat mozzarella (~22 percent FDM) often don't melt completely and have restricted stretch profiles when shredded and baked on a pizza. The reduction in fat content leads to a more intact casein network and a larger volume fraction of protein in the cheese. Whole milk mozzarella with higher levels of fat (>48 percent FDM) can produce a lot of free oil when melted. The increased oil film can insulate the surface of a pizza and lead to less browning and fewer blisters during baking. See FUNCTIONAL PROPERTIES.

The flavor of cheese is affected directly and indirectly by the fat content. Many flavor and aroma compounds are lipid soluble, meaning they are heavily partitioned in the fat portion of cheese. Reduced-fat cheeses are often described as lacking in overall flavor or having disagreeable flavors due to the ab-sence of pleasing flavors that are usually present in full-fat varieties. The intact triglycerides of milk fat do not elicit any flavor/aroma directly on their own. Fatty acids liberated from triglycerides provide a wide range of flavors and secondary reactions involving fatty acids create a plethora of volatile flavor compounds during cheese ripening and aging. See FLAVOR.

See also LIPOLYSIS and MILK.

Everett, D. W. "Microstructure of Natural Cheese." In *Structure of Dairy Products,* edited by Adnan Tamime, pp. 170–209. Oxford: Blackwell, 2007.

Fox, Patrick F., et al. *Fundamentals of Cheese Science.* Gaithersburg, Md.: Aspen, 2000.

Guinee, T. P., and P. L. H. McSweeney. "Significance of Milk Fat in Cheese." In *Advanced Dairy Chemistry*, Vol. 2: *Lipids*, 3d ed., edited by P. F. Fox and P. L. H. McSweeney, pp. 377–440. New York: Springer, 2006.

Martini, S., and A. G. Marangoni. "Microstructure of Dairy Fat Products." In *Structure of Dairy Products*, edited by Adnan Tamime, pp. 72–103. Oxford: Blackwell, 2007.

Tunick, Michael H. "Lipids in Cheese." *Lipid Technology* 27, no. 4 (2015): 83–85.

Pat Polowsky

fermentation-produced chymosin

(FPC). The first critical step in cheese manufacture is the coagulation of milk by rennet or an enzyme that shares the ability of rennet to coagulate milk, and can do so in a way that very specifically favors the critical destabilizing bond in kappa-casein, without causing significant additional proteolysis in the cheese vat. In recent years, for ethical and other reasons, there has been significant interest in finding alternatives to traditional calf rennet, and coagulants from many microbial, plant, and other sources have been studied. However perhaps the most intuitively direct way of obtaining the same key enzyme without the disadvantages of using the traditional calf extracts was to apply biotechnology and take the gene for chymosin and insert it into a range of safe microorganisms that produce a purer form of the enzyme. The enzyme produced in this way, fermentation-produced chymosin (FPC), is widely used industrially today in the production of a significant majority of the commercial cheese made in the United Kingdom, the United States, and internationally.

FPC is produced by fermentation of engineered strains of *Aspergillis niger* or *Kluyveromyces lactis*, followed by cell inactivation, lysis, and purification of the enzyme. Key brands available are Chy-Max (from Chr. Hansen) and Maxiren (DSM). The gene for chymosin from species other than the bovine (e.g., camel chymosin) has also been used for production of FPC. While FPC is produced by genetically modified microorganisms, the product is identical to the purified bovine enzyme, and FPC was the first artificially produced enzyme to be permitted for use by the US Food and Drug Administration. It has been reported that FPC results in higher cheese yields and better quality cheese than any alternative coagulant, including traditional rennet, due to its enzymatic purity.

See also CHYMOSIN; COAGULATION OR CURDLING; ENZYMES; PLANT-DERIVED COAGULANTS; and RENNET.

Barbano, D. M., and R. R. Rasmussen. 1992. "Cheese Yield Performance of Fermentation-Produced Chymosin and Other Milk Coagulants." *Journal of Dairy Science* 75 (1992): 1–12.
"What Is Fermentation-produced Chymosin?" CheeseScience.net, July 2008. http://www .cheesescience.net/2008/07/what-is-fermentation-produced-chymosin.html.

Alan Kelly

fermier is a French descriptor that indicates that a cheese has been made on a farm (farmhouse production). To use the term *fermier* in France, the cheese must be made on one farm with milk from only that farm's herd of animals. The same regulations apply to the phrase *fabriqué à la ferme*. In nations such as the United Kingdom and the United States, the term "farmhouse" is not so strictly defined, and can refer to a cheese that could be made in a creamery with milk pooled from many farms.

Although fermier denotes farmhouse production, which is still relatively common in France, use of the term does not mandate the size of the farm (which could vary from a handful of animals to a couple of thousand), the way the animals are fed, the pasteurization status of the milk, the conditions of production, the feeding of the animals, etc. Therefore, though fermier does stipulate that the cheese is made from the milk of a single herd, it should not necessarily be viewed as an indicator of quality or that production is small-scale.

As well as applying the term fermier to a product, certain French AOC (appellation d'origine contrôlée) cheeses have specific markings to denote when they are also fermier. See APPELLATION D'ORIGINE CONTRÔLÉE. Examples of this include Reblochon (with a green oval label for fermier and a red label for non-fermier), St. Nectaire (with an oval label for fermier and a square one for non-fermier), and Pouligny St. Pierre (with a green label for fermier and red for non-fermier).

See also FARMSTEAD and FRANCE.

Institut National de l'Origine et de la Qualité. French appellation product specification for Pouligny St. Pierre, Reblochon, and St. Nectaire Cheeses. http:// www.inao.gouv.fr/public/produits.
Ministère de l'Économie et des Finances. "Décret n° 2013-1010 du 12 novembre 2013 modifiant le décret n° 2007-628 du 27 avril 2007 relatif aux fromages et spécialités fromagères." *Journal Officiel de la République Française* 2064, 12 November 2013. [French Government Change to Decree 628 on Cheese and Dairy Products.]
Rance, Patrick. *The French Cheese Book.* London: Macmillan, 1989.

Andy Swinscoe

feta is a soft, white cheese that is commonly aged in brine and has no rind or skin. It is traditionally made from sheep's milk or a blend of sheep's and goat's milk.

Feta is produced throughout Greece by industrial and artisanal cheesemakers as well as home cheesemakers. From producer to producer, season to season, and region to region, feta's flavor and texture can vary considerably. It can range from sharp, dry, and hard to mild, rich, and creamy with aromas of sheep's milk, grass, and clover. These varieties depend on production methods, the breed of the animals that are milked, the time of year the cheese is produced, and whether the milk came from animals eating grains or wild grasses. The high fat content of sheep's milk imparts creaminess; goat's milk imparts tang. Therefore, the type of milk used in feta's production plays a significant role as well.

Although commercial dairies typically pasteurize the milk they use to produce feta, the practice of pasteurization varies for home and small-scale cheesemakers, some choosing to leave the milk raw and others choosing to pasteurize it. Feta is usually produced using compacted and drained curds that are sliced into blocks, dry-salted for several days, and then submerged in brine and allowed to ripen. However, not all feta is brined. Instead, it is sprinkled with

Feta is usually produced using compacted and drained curds that are sliced into blocks, dry-salted for several days, and then submerged in brine and allowed to ripen. While historically feta was aged in birch wood barrels, today cheese-makers more often choose the convenience of metal tins or plastic tubs. © VINCENZO SPIONE

coarse sea salt, turned for two to four days, and then packed into wooden barrels with more sea salt and allowed to mature in its own liquid. Although commercially produced feta must be aged for at least two months before going to market, many of Greece's artisanal producers age their cheeses for six months or longer. Historically, feta cheese was aged in birch-wood barrels and occasionally it still is aged in this manner. Barrel-aged feta is widely considered to possess superior characteristics as the barrels are said to aid fermentation and impart a distinctive flavor to the cheese. However, use of the wooden barrel has decreased significantly as cheesemakers choose the convenience of metal tins or plastic tubs, which are easier to maintain and less expensive to ship than barrels. Once feta has aged sufficiently, producers usually ship it within the container in which it was aged to market where the cheese is cut and sold directly from the container. Today, feta is also sold in slices and blocks submerged in a small amount of brine in plastic containers.

Greece initially applied in 1994 for protected designation of origin (PDO) status for feta cheese from the European Union (EU). The European Commission adopted measures to grant the status in 1996; however, because of challenges mounted by Denmark, Germany, and France, which also produced cheeses sold as "feta," the European Commission's decision was overturned in 1999. The Commission conducted an investigation into the cultural origins of feta, accepting information from both sides, and in 2002 declared that PDO status would be given to Greece.

Other countries have continued to protest the ruling. See DESIGNATION OF ORIGIN.

As a result of the European Commission's ruling, only those cheeses produced from sheep's milk or from a mixture of sheep's milk and up to 30 percent goat's milk using traditional methods in specific regions of Greece may bear the name "feta." There are seven PDO regions for feta production: Thessaly, Epirus, central mainland Greece, Macedonia, Thrace, the Peloponnese Peninsula, and the northeastern Aegean island of Lesbos. Because similar brined cheeses produced outside the EU are often made of cow's milk and are sometimes sold as "feta," unless one purchases feta that is produced in Greece, one cannot be sure one is purchasing authentic, PDO feta cheese. Similar white-brined cheeses (often called "white cheese" in various languages) are also found around the Black Sea and in the Eastern Mediterranean.

Feta is by far the most popular cheese in Greece where it is commonly used as a table cheese and as an ingredient in Greek cookery. In cafes across the country, it is often sprinkled with dried oregano, drizzled with olive oil, and served as an appetizer with an aperitif. It is used in salads, most typically to top the iconic Greek "village" salad made with tomatoes, cucumbers, bell peppers, and olives. And it is crumbled into gratins and stuffings, melted into sauces, blended with olive oil and fresh herbs to create dips. Feta is fried, grilled, and baked into savory pies, such as the ubiquitous cheese and phyllo dough pie called tiropita, which is sold in bakeries and food stalls in cities, towns, and villages throughout Greece.

Cheese made from sheep's or goat's milk, or a combination of the two, was a common food in ancient Greece. Feta cheese, specifically, was first recorded during the Byzantine Empire in the *Poem on Medicine* where it was referred to as a fresh cheese kept in brine and called "prosphatos," which can be translated as "recent" or "fresh." The Greek word "feta" (φέτα) became a widespread term for the cheese much later, in the nineteenth century. It is said to come from the Italian word "fetta" or "slice" and likely refers to the practice of slicing the cheese in order to pack it into barrels.

Although 85 percent of Greek feta is consumed in Greece, feta and feta-style cheeses are highly consumed abroad as well. The feta industry in Greece accounts for more than 70 percent of the country's cheese exports. In 2012, 35,000 tons (31,751 metric tons) of commercial feta was exported from Greece (12,000 tons [10,886 metric tons] of this went to Germany, the first market in Greek feta cheese exports). Major producers of PDO feta cheese include Dodonis, Fage, and Mevgal, all of which both export their product and sell it nationally. Mt. Vikos, which also exports the cheese, produces a birch barrel-matured feta that is aged for four months before being sold. In 2012, feta production in the United States totaled 108,500,000 pounds (49.2 million kilograms), according to the United States National Agricultural Statistics Service. Major US producers of feta-style cheeses, some of which are made from cow's milk, are President, Nikos, and Athenos.

See also GREECE.

Dalby, Andrew. *Tastes of Byzantium: The Cuisine of a Legendary Empire*. London: I. B. Tauris, 2010.

Gooch, Ellen. "Truth, Lies, and Feta: The Cheese that Launched a (Trade) War." *Epikouria: Fine Foods and Drinks of Greece*, Spring–Summer 2006. http://web.archive.org/web/20090705120910/ http://www.epikouria.com/issue2/truth-lies-and -feta.php.

Kochilas, Diane. "Feta Unbound: Greek Cheese Triumphs in Court." *New York Times*, 8 March 2006.

Martin, Aaron. "Feta Market Shows Steady Growth, Holds More Potential." *Cheese Market News* 33, no. 19 (31 May 2013). http://www.cheesemarket news.com/articlearch/2013/05_31_13.pdf.

Robinson, R.K., and A. Y. Tamime. *Feta and Related Cheeses*. Cambridge, U.K.: Woodhead, 1996.

Alexis Marie Adams

filamentous fungi are molds, that is, microscopic fungi that form hyphae. See HYPHAE and MYCELIA. They are often distinguished from yeasts, which are unicellular and do not form hyphae. However, it is noteworthy that "filamentous fungi" and "yeasts" are morphological rather than taxonomic groups (grouped by appearance rather than relatedness). Indeed some species, for example *Mucor circinelloides* and *Geotrichum candidum*, are dimorphic, meaning that they can occur either in a filamentous or a unicellular yeast form. See MUCOR; GEOTRICHUM CANDIDUM; and TAXONOMY.

Filamentous fungi play a major role in the production of surface-ripened and blue cheeses. Their hyphae can spread on the surface and penetrate the cheese, and through the action of secreted enzymes degrade the milk fats and proteins into breakdown products that can directly contribute to the cheese flavor. See ENZYMES; PROTEINS; and MATURING. *Penicillium roqueforti* and *P. camemberti*, *Mucor fuscus* and *M. lanceolatus*, *Fusarium domesticum*, and *Sporendonema casei* are among the most common filamentous fungal species used as adjunct cultures. For example, the emblematic *Penicillium roqueforti* species colors blue cheese veins and gives these cheeses their typical flavor by producing, among other things, methyl-ketones. Another example is *Penicillium camemberti* that forms the characteristic white coat observed on mold surface-ripened cheeses like Camembert and also imparts their typical mushroom-like flavor by synthesizing 1-octen-3-ol. Nevertheless, many filamentous fungi are also cheese contaminants and can cause off-flavors and other defects or potentially pose safety concerns (mycotoxin production). The most frequent contaminants belong to the *Penicillium* and *Mucor* genera. See PENICILLIUM.

See also FUNGI.

Chamba, J. F., and F. Irlinger. "Secondary and Adjunct Cultures." In *Cheese: Chemistry, Physics and Microbiology*, edited by P. F. Fox, et al., pp. 191–206. London and New York: Elsevier Academic, 2004.

Gow, N. A. R., and G. M. Gadd. *Growing Fungus*. New York: Springer Science & Business Media, 1995.

Jean-Luc Jany

Fine Cheese Company, The, was founded by Ann-Marie Dyas in 1988 as a retail shop, with local distribution in Bath, England, one of two World

Heritage cities in Europe. It has become one of the United Kingdom's largest artisan cheese distributors. It now also encompasses a cheese café, cheese club, mail order business, and annual artisan Cheese Festival. They introduced cheese celebration cakes to the broader retail market in 1998.

Inspired by Patrick Rance's *The Great British Cheese Book*, Dyas is committed to the survival of traditional cheesemaking, and to introducing distinctive and unique farmstead cheeses to as wide a public as possible. The company's mottoes are: "I love cheese" and "People should have what they enjoy."

The Fine Cheese Company has carefully curated around 150 largely raw-milk traditionally made cheeses from Britain, and directly imported from Europe, preferring cheese sold whole. Their range now includes crackers for cheese and cheese condiments. They export to distributors and stores across four continents, also acting as a judge and ambassador of British cheeses.

The Fine Cheese Company has been a critical friend and champion of traditional artisan cheese in the United Kingdom, collecting cheese from farms, maintaining direct links with terroir, and unofficially partnering with cheesemakers to hone flavors. They have been an influential part of the renaissance of British cheese, championing originals, new, and those inspired by European models. And they have won awards for their exclusive products, retail offering, website, mail order service, and contribution to the artisan cheese ecosystem.

Harbutt, Juliet. *Cheese: A Complete Guide to 300 Cheeses of Distinction*. Minocqua, Wis.: Willow Creek, 1999.
Rance, Patrick. *The Great British Cheese Book*. 2d ed. London: Macmillan, 1988.

Mary Quicke

Finlandia is the US subsidiary of the Finnish dairy giant Valio Ltd., which was founded as that country's first milk-producing co-op by seventeen farmers in 1905. Valio has grown into an international conglomerate that processes 85 percent of Finland's milk. As of 2015 its revenues exceeded 2 billion euros per year; all profits are returned to its member farmers.

With the explosion of Swiss-style cheese sales in America during the 1950s, Valio began exporting its product in this category to the United States. See SWISS CHEESE. Valio's American importer, New Jersey–based Atalanta Corp., branded its Swiss cheese as Finlandia and began marketing it to delicatessens in the New York City metropolitan area. Valio acquired the brand and it subsequently penetrated the entire US retail market. Finlandia's US Swiss cheese imports account for between 48 and 53 million pounds (22–24 million kilograms) per year or 15–16 percent of the category import total, approximately equal to Germany and second only to Norway. See JARLSBERG. Valio cheeses bound for the international market are sold under the coop's eponymous brand; in Mexico and parts of Asia, they are sold as Finlandia.

Finlandia's headquarters is located in Parsippany, New Jersey. Most of its cheeses are still imported from Finland, though some are made in partnership with US manufacturers. Finlandia's principle varieties are Swiss, Lacey Swiss, and Light Swiss. They are marketed as having full, robust, authentic Swiss cheese flavors and featuring the highest quality milk and all-natural production. In the early 2000s Finlandia introduced other varieties popular in the US market, including Cheddar, Gouda, Gruyére, Havarti, and provolone. The Swiss varieties still account for nearly 50 percent of sales.

Finlandia. http://www.finlandiacheese.com.
United States Department of Agriculture (USDA), Foreign Agricultural Service. Licensed Cheese Imports: January–December 2014–2015. *Dairy Monthly Imports*, pp. 14–17.
Valio. http://www.valio.com.

David Gibbons

Fiore Sardo, translated as the "Sardinian Flower," is a cheese that comes from the island of Sardinia in the Mediterranean Sea. The provenance of the name either refers to the previous use of wooden molds to shape the cheese that were made from chestnut and had a flower carved on the bottom (along with the initials of the manufacturer), or it may be an acknowledgment of the fact that cheesemakers once used cardoom flowers as rennet. Fiore Sardo is a sheep's milk hard cheese, coagulated with lamb's rennet, molded, brined, lightly smoked, and then aged to maturity in the cool air of Sardinian cellars.

Historically Fiore Sardo was the premier cheese for Sardianian shepherds, but industrial development resulted in dairy manufacturing refocusing from Fiore Sardo made by herders to large-scale dairies driven by

Fiore Sardo, a sub-style of Pecorino Sardo, is a Sardinian sheep's milk hard cheese. © FORMAGGIO.IT

Pecorino Romano production. The island is known for its sheepherding culture and for its many long and unbroken attachments to local traditions and style. Certain accounts trace the origins of Fiore Sardo back to the Bronze Age, while similar pecorino cheeses were consumed by the Greeks in the eighth century B.C.E. on another Italian island, Sicily.

Fiore Sardo is a subcategory of the more common Pecorino Sardo and has had a DOP (Denominazione di Origine Protetta) designation since 1996. This mandates that those who produce Fiore Sardo use milk from the local and indigenous Sardinian breed of sheep (Sarda), which must also come from a single flock; such flocks can be traced directly back to the mufflons still found in remote corners of the island of Sardinia today. See SARDA. True Fiore Sardo must also be air-dried by a brazier for two weeks, a process that imparts a smoky aroma. The sheep that produce milk for the best Fiore Sardo are grazed in the mountainous Sardinian interior, and their diet is full of wild herbs, brush, and vegetation, and these rich and earthen tastes come through in the final product.

The cheese once was produced by heating raw milk with hot rocks—an ancient dairy technique—but today the curd is kneaded and pressed by the cheesemaker into molds by hand. At certain points in the aging process, the rind may be rubbed with a blend of olive oil, wine vinegar, and salt, while the cheeses are also turned frequently. The production period is from December to June and aging begins at four months and can go much longer for mature cheeses. The weight is 8 pounds (3.5 kilograms) and size is approximately 7–9 inches (18–22 centimeters) tall. Fiore Sardo develops a crust that can range from straw yellow to dark, earthen brown. Depending on its age, it can be used as a grating cheese for pasta and vegetables or a table cheese—growing spicier, more herbaceous, and sheepier as it ages—a fine match for southern Italian reds.

See also PECORINO SARDO; SARDINIA; and SMOKED CHEESES.

Androuët, Pierre, et al. *Guide to Cheese*. Rev. English ed. Henley-on-Thames, U.K.: Aidan Ellis, 1993.
Dalby, Andrew. *Cheese: A Global History*. London: Reaktion, 2009.
Harbutt, Juliet, and Martin Aspinwall. *World Cheese Book*. New ed. New York: Dorling Kindersley, 2015.
"Il Fiore Sardo, formaggio dei pastori che fa bene anche allo spirito." Formaggio.it. http://www.formaggio.it/senza-categoria/il-fiore-sardo-formaggio-dei-pastori-che-fa-bene-anche-allo-spirito.
Kindstedt, Paul. *Cheese and Culture: A History of Cheese and Its Place in Western Civilization*. White River Junction, Vt.: Chelsea Green, 2012.
McCalman, Max, and David Gibbons. *Cheese: A Connoisseur's Guide to the World's Best*. New York: Clarkson Potter, 2005.

Robert McKeown

Fiore Sicano is a traditional raw cow's milk cheese produced in various townships of the Sicani Mountains in the western part of Sicily, Italy. The original name is "Fior di Garofalo," from the name of the farm countryside where the cheese is produced, but regional bureaucracy decided to use the name of the mountain area of production.

Fiore Sicano is still produced using traditional techniques and equipment. The milk from two milkings is curdled in a wooden container, called *ciscuni*, at 99–102°F (37–39°C) with rennet paste of lamb or kid, for approximately sixty minutes. A wooden tool called a *rutula* is used to break the curd. This step takes place in two different modes and stages. The first breaking is rough and less vigorous. After three minutes a more vigorous second breaking commences, until the curd becomes the size of corn kernels. The curd is separated from the whey and placed on a wooden board where it is held for about four hours and rotated five or six times.

Fiore Sicano is a dry-salted cheese. See DRY SALTING. The aging process occurs in natural environments, at a temperature of 46–54°F (8–12°C), with 80–90 percent humidity, from a minimum of sixty days to over one year. The natural microclimate allows the creation, on the surface of the cheese, of indigenous molds that belong to the *Penicillium* type. See PENICILLIUM. Since 2010 more producers have decided to make Fiore Sicano–type cheese, introducing new technology to the cheesemaking, and obtaining a product with less specificity.

The traditional Fiore Sicano has a soft and compact texture, and a color that is yellowish white. The rind is thin and has a gray-green color due to the settling of molds. This cheese is characterized by a buttery and floral flavor and a finishing hint of mushroom taste, with a slightly acidic and bitter aftertaste. The shape is cylindrical with flat sides, a diameter of 7–8 inches (18–20 centimeters) and height of 2–2½ inches (4–6 centimeters). The weight is approximately 3–4 pounds (1.5–1.8 kilograms). The best time for consumption is within four to six months of aging.

See also SICILY.

Campo, Patrizia, and Giuseppe Licitra. *Historical Sicilian Cheeses*. Ragusa, Italy: CoRFiLaC Press, 2006.
Consiglio Nazionale delle Ricerche. "I prodotti caseari del Mezzogiorno." Edizioni Tecnos, 1992
Istituto Nazionale di Sociologia Rurale: *Atlante dei prodotti tipici: I formaggi*. Milan: Franco Angeli, 1991.
Vizzardi, Mario, and Piero Maffeis. *Formaggi italiani*. Bologna: Edizioni Agricole, 1990.

Ivana Piccitto

Fiscalini Farmstead Cheese produces award-winning handmade farmstead cow's milk cheeses at their dairy facility in Modesto, a town in California's San Joaquin Valley. The farm has been owned and operated by the Fiscalini family for over one hundred years. Founded in 1912 by John Baptiste Fiscalini, the original 160-acre farm has grown to over 500 acres with more than 3,000 contented, ethically raised Holstein and Brown Jersey cows. Though the dairy operation is considered large compared to many artisanal cheesemaking companies, half of the milk production of more than three thousand cows is dedicated to making handcrafted, small batch cheeses.

Inspired by a trip in 1999 to Lionza, Switzerland, where his family's dairy roots originated in the 1700s, third-generation owner John Fiscalini's vision was to continue the traditions of his family's cheesemaking operation. His dream was fulfilled in the year 2000 when the facility was established.

Lead cheesemaker Jorge "Mariano" Gonzalez had years of cheesemaking experience at England's Montgomery Farms, and the notable Shelburne Farms in Vermont, before joining Fiscalini. Since 2000, Mariano has developed raw-milk English-style Cheddars showcasing Fiscalini's farmstead milk. San Joaquin Gold is the company's award-winning original. The natural-rind, firm cheese is mildly sweet with flavors of browned butter and toasted nuts. Aged for sixteen months, crunchy protein crystals dot the cheese. Bandage Wrapped Cheddar is made in the tradition of British clothbound Cheddars and is firm, smooth, and crumbly. Aged eighteen months or thirty months, it was the first non-British Cheddar to win Best Cheddar in the 2007 World Cheese Awards competition and in 2012 was voted one of the top sixteen cheeses in the world. Lionza is a traditional Alp-style natural-rind hard cheese, aged six to seven months, and made in the same style as cheese made by the Fiscalini family in Switzerland for over three hundred years. Fiscalini Cheddar (plain or in multiple flavors) is milled and shaped into blocks and aged for twelve months. Scamorza (plain and smoked) is a hand-shaped, stretched-curd cheese made from pasteurized milk.

See also CALIFORNIA.

Cowgirl Creamery. http://www.cowgirlcreamery .com/library.
Fiscalini Farmstead Cheese Company. http://www .fiscalinicheese.com.
Roberts, Jeffrey P. *The Atlas of American Artisan Cheese*. White River Junction, Vt.: Chelsea Green, 2007.

Mary Karlin

flavor is awarded the greatest proportion in scoring at cheese competitions. Cheese flavor is also one of the most important criteria determining consumers' choice and acceptance. Flavor can be defined as the complex effect of basic taste sensations, olfactory sensations (aromatics), and chemical feeling sensations stimulated by a substance in the mouth.

Salt, sweet, umami, sour, and bitter notes are taste components but also key factors influencing the final flavor profile of cheese. The first four of these are attractive. Bitter notes are generally perceived to be flaws, or are recognized in a cheese not fully aged. Through ongoing protein metabolism bitter peptides may dominate the flavors of relatively young cheeses before the confluence of the various organoleptic profiles reach their aggregate optimal levels. Main aromatic compounds include acids, alcohols, aldehydes, esters, ketones, terpenes, lactone, pyrazine, and sulfurous; while trigeminal factors involve pungency, piquant, and sharp notes. The different ingredients shaped by terroir and the various cheesemaking and affinage practices direct flavor components into a balance appropriate for a cheese type. A particular cheesemaking region may have higher concentrations of certain volatile esters than other regions. Esters such as 1-hexanol and acetic propyl, which are associated with the pleasant aromas found in perfumes and pears are dominant in cheeses from southern Germany's Allgäu, while in most other dairy lands of Europe their presence is negligible.

Development of cheese flavor is a complex and elaborate process involving multiple factors affecting the degradation of milk proteins, fats, and carbohydrates. Some of these factors involve the characteristics of the milk, rennet, processing conditions, the starter cultures, and secondary flora.

The flavor of cheese is heavily dependent on the vegetation in the animal's diet: the grasses, trees, shrubs, bushes, fruits, grains, and legumes (either fresh, fermented, or dried). Fresh vegetation transmits far greater diversity of terpenes than the same vegetation in a fermented or dried state. The terpenes offer fingerprints of the milk sources and are major identifiers of a cheese type. The antimicrobial capacity of terpenes has the consequence of interfering with the production of molecules via protein metabolism, thereby reducing aroma potential. So terpenes yield aromas on their own yet they also reduce others.

The components in the milk itself are not the only sources of cheese flavors. Milk picks up bacteria, yeasts, and molds as it exits the udder. These enzymes contribute to flavor development in the breakdown of the lactose, fats, and proteins in milk. The glycolysis of lactose by lactic acid bacteria lowers the pH of the milk. This process continues well into the cheesemaking practice and is slowed down with the addition of salt. The acidity created helps produce a pleasing flavor in the cheese.

Native lipase, which may be present in raw milk or the lipase that may be added in the cheesemaking process, metabolize the milk fat to release short-chain fatty acids, contributing both flavor and aroma. The lipase found in some natural animal rennets is stronger than native lipase. Lamb rennet is strongest

and calf rennet is the mildest. However, all of the commercial calf rennet is lipase free. An excess dose of any coagulant, especially if used at lower pH can yield bitter flavors.

Typical cheese flavor can be attributed to milk's high distribution of the short-chain fatty acids within the triglycerides. When released from the triglyceride structure through lipolysis, the short-chain fatty acids (four to twelve carbons in length) are volatile with the potential for assertive flavors. See LIPOLYSIS. The relative concentrations of fatty acids vary from species to species and among breeds as well. Goat's and sheep's milk have a higher proportion of the short-chain fatty acids than cow's milk. This gives the cheeses produced from the small ruminants' milks the potential for more assertive aromas. Sheep's milk has a high concentration of butyric acid, a fatty acid that can yield the aroma of dirty socks or decayed meat. This quality is appropriate for some cheese styles although other aromas can be lost or overwhelmed by its strength. The short-chain fatty acids: caproic, caprylic, and capric acids, are associated with goat, having the ancient root word for goat—capr(a)—in their names. The flavors and aromas arising from the free fatty acids may be pleasing or not, depending on the relative concentrations of the free fatty acids and personal preference. Goat cheeses can smell "goaty"—which can be pleasing to a degree—but if the goat (not the doe) gets too close to the milking parlor its musky goaty scent, an aphrodisiac to the does, is conveyed into the milk and then can be detected later in the cheese.

There are flavors expected from a cheese category. That being said, the cheesemaker and affineur have ingredients and processes at their disposal to yield those typical organoleptic profiles. These distinctive flavors are important to the consumer. They are what is expected in a cheese style. For instance, the flavor of Cheddar cheese varies strongly with source, aging, moisture, and fat content. However, Cheddar is expected to taste like Cheddar.

The flavors of cheeses can vary depending on a number of factors: the influences of soil, water, pasturage, the breed, the individual animal, the weather, the varieties and amounts of cultures, adjunct cultures, the coagulant type and coagulant dose, the make processes, whether or not the milk is pasteurized and/or homogenized, acid development and temperature, the salt, and affinage treatments. Two wheels produced by the same cheesemaker using the milk of the same animal, on the same day, with the same recipe, can taste different. This is part of the beauty as well as the challenge of artisan cheesemaking. In many cheesemaking plants the goal is to make a standardized and consistent product each and every time. Variations in cheeses can be reduced through bulking of milk and pasteurization. Sanitary cheesemaking is important, though normal cheesemaking conditions and practices may allow contamination by adventitious microbes, some of which may yield desirable flavor attributes, others which may yield undesirable or hazardous qualities.

Ripening cultures add their own flavor profiles to a ripe cheese. These adjunct cultures include bacteria, yeasts, and molds. The native milk bacteria also influence flavor and aroma characteristics, and these can work in combination with the added cultures to yield the desired qualities. Once their tasks are completed the deceased bacteria cell walls contribute additional flavors. See ADJUNCT CULTURES.

Adventitious bacteria, yeasts, and molds, whether intentionally added or not in the make process, serve as sources of lipase, capable of releasing free fatty acids from milk fat. Mold species then contribute their various volatile sensory notes via the free fatty acids. Molds that grow on or within cheeses such as *Penicillium*, *Geotrichum candidum*, and *Mucor*, can produce their own lipases and proteases, which can yield unusual flavors and aromas, some of these pleasing, others less so. *Propionibacterium freudenreichii* subsp. *shermanii* is a bacterium that yields the sweet nutty flavors in Alp-style cheeses, in addition to CO_2 which is responsible for the characteristic holes in some Alp-style cheeses. See PENICILLIUM; GEOTRICHUM CANDIDUM; MUCOR; and DAIRY PROPIONIBACTERIA.

The most significant vehicles for carrying the aromas are the milk fats—the primary source of flavors and aromas in cheese. A reduced fat cheese has less flavor, whereas a nonfat cheese has virtually no flavor and aroma. The aromatic qualities can be traced to aromatic esters in the animal's diet and to minerals in the soil. The elements are released by proteolysis and lipolysis, beginning when the milk leaves the teat canal and on through the aging process. Trace minerals influence aromas with their linkages to the casein and fatty acids. See FAT; PROTEOLYSIS; and LIPOLYSIS.

Heat treatment has a neutralizing effect on the ester aromas so that cheeses crafted from pasteurized milks have little or no aroma. These esters are composed of fatty acids, which with the minerals are carried through into the milk. Heat treatments can denature proteins, reducing their capacity for chelation of flavor-giving minerals. Pasteurization destroys most of the native lipase and retards or arrests the development of flavor and aroma in a ripening cheese. Non-starter lactic acid bacteria (NSLAB) contain enzymes that influence flavor development rate in an aging cheese. See PASTEURIZATION and NON-STARTER LACTIC ACID BACTERIA.

Homogenization breaks the fat globules, releasing short-chain fatty acids, which can yield unbalanced or unpleasant flavors. Homogenization also changes the protein network with consequences to flavor development. Salt's primary role in cheesemaking is to slow down acidification but it also helps draw out flavor and inhibits competing molds and bacteria that can yield undesirable aromas or alter the desired flavor. See HOMOGENIZATION and SALT.

Rennet enzymes assist in proteolysis with influences over flavor development in an aging cheese. Too much coagulant can lead to bitter flavors in a ripened cheese. The most widely used vegetable coagulant is *Cynara cardunculus*, commonly known as cardoon—more suitable for high-fat and high-protein milks such as sheep's milk, with a strong proteolytic capacity that can lead to an accumulation of bitter peptides to the point a bitter flavor is detected. See PLANT-DERIVED COAGULANTS.

Citrate is present in milk in minute quantities. Its metabolism by bacteria occurs separately but concurrently with the fermentation of lactose. Flavor and aroma byproducts of citrate breakdown include acetoin, acetate, and diacetyl.

See also FLAVOR WHEEL; SENSORY ANALYSIS; and TASTE.

Caldwell, Gianaclis. *Mastering Artisan Cheesemaking: The Ultimate Guide for the Home-Scale and Market Producers*. White River Junction, Vt.: Chelsea Green, 2012.

Donnelly, Catherine W. *Cheese and Microbes*. Washington, D.C.: ASM, 2014.

Hassan, Fatma A. M., Mona A. M. Abd El-Gawad, and A. K. Enab. "Flavour Compounds in Cheese (Review)." *Research on Precision Instrument and Machinery* 2, no. 3 (June 2013): 15–29.

McCalman, Max, and David Gibbons. *Mastering Cheese: Lessons for Connoisseurship from a Maitre Fromager*. New York: Clarkson Potter, 2009.

Rance, Patrick. *The Great British Cheese Book*. 2d ed. London: Macmillan, 1988.

Scott, R., R. K. Robinson, and R. A. Wilbey. *Cheesemaking Practice*. 3d ed. Gaithersburg, Md.: Aspen, 1998.

Max McCalman

flavored cheeses are created by adding flavor topically to the rind, or processed into the curd in many forms, in order to enhance the aroma, texture, flavor, and appearance. Herbs, beer, wine, fruit, chocolate, coffee, and peppers are ingredients that can be added to the making and curing of cheese to create flavored cheese. In addition flavored cheeses can be created environmentally by aging in a smoker, ripening near an open cauldron of Sauterne wine or spirits such as brandy, and affected by humidity-enriching bacteria like *Brevibacillus brevis*. Other methods include marinating the curd in oil, essential oils, beer, wine, and spirits, and smearing or washing the surface with a diluted brine solution of bacteria and spirits.

The American Cheese Society (ACS) has created the most extensive category for flavored cheeses. This is attributed to the innovation of American cheesemakers building this category. The category identifying these cheeses by the American Cheese Society's Judging and Competition committee is K and includes numerous subcategories identified by cheese type, flavor, and milk. This category among others listed below was created by a panel of international cheese judges and volunteers with both technical and aesthetic expertise to identify and judge the vast and growing number of cheeses equitably. This also allows cheesemakers to more appropriately and accurately define cheeses, for example, category "KK: Rubbed-Rind Cheese with added flavor ingredients rubbed or applied on the exterior surface of the cheese only (Washed-Rind cheeses, please refer to Category T) – all milks" (American Cheese Society, 2016). There are more categories beyond category K; category L identifies smoked, category P marinated, and T identifies washed-rind cheeses.

The core of cheese flavor is controlled by the characteristics of the raw milk ingredient, especially milk type and quality, as well as the chemical composition of the cheese, in terms of pH, moisture, and salt levels. Raw-milk cheeses are particularly influenced by what animals are foraging and grazing. Cheese flavors are more pronounced while animals are grazing, but this can also be the cause of off flavors. In addition to the natural flavors from the milk, cheese-makers may add flavors from other sources. Today cheesemakers are especially innovative in their approach to ripening cheese by enhancing or altering flavors with adjunct cultures and flavors from beer, truffles, chocolate, peppers, spices, and other flavorful products. The correct proportions of flavorings are essential in creating an ideal experience.

In creating and evaluating flavored cheeses "ACS judges look for a balance between body and flavoring" (American Cheese Society, 2014). It is also implied when making cheese using flavors that strict standards are in place to control purity and document possible allergens. The safety of any cheese "can only be achieved through strict adherence to high standards of hygiene and sanitization" (Kindstedt, 2005).

Flavored cheeses have been made for decades, and in the last decade this category has grown exponentially. A few examples follow:

- Barely Buzzed, Beehive Cheese Co., Utah, USA is a 16-pound (7.26-kilogram) wheel Jersey milk semihard Cheddar-style cheese. The set is vegetarian with microbial enzymes and the surface is rubbed with freshly roasted ground coffee and French lavender in vegetable oil. The flavor of the paste is toasty, nutty, and caramel. The paste is cream to yellow and the rind a dark rich chocolate color, granular in texture. The wheels are aged four to eight months.
- Vermont Creamery Cranberry, Orange, and Cinnamon Chevre, Websterville, Vermont, USA is a fresh goat cheese log made with fresh milk sourced from seventeen small family farms stretching from Vermont to New Hampshire to Ontario. The chèvre is a lactic set and after a twenty-four-hour fermentation the set is extruded into 4-ounce (113-gram) logs; dried cranberries, orange zest, and cinnamon are then hand rolled over the surface.
- Brin d'Amour ("breath of love") from the island of Corsica is a semisoft sheep's milk cheese made from the milk of Lacuane ewes. The milk is set with traditional rennet and the curd is formed into wheels 4 inches (10.16-centimeter) in diameter, 2 inches (5.08 centimeters) high, and weighing 1 pound (440 grams). As it develops its gray-blue mold it is wrapped in herbs from the land on which the ewes forage, including rosemary, juniper berries, and fennel seeds. The

flavor is citrusy, sour, and tangy when young and when it achieves the age of three months the flavor of the paste becomes balanced and is reminiscent of the Corsican landscape, with savory flavors enhanced by the herbs.

There are hundreds of flavored cheeses. The above provides just three examples of outstanding flavored cheeses from cow's, goat's, and sheep's milk.

See also LEAF-WRAPPED CHEESES; OIL-MARINATED CHEESES; and SMOKED CHEESES.

Almena-Aliste, Montserrat, and Bernard Mietton. "Cheese Classification, Characterization, and Categorization: A Global Perspective." In *Cheese and Microbes*, edited by Catherine W. Donnelly. Washington, DC: ASM Press, 2014.
American Cheese Society. "Judging & Competition 2015 Categories." http://www.cheesejudging.org/wp-content/uploads/2015/03/2015-Categories-FINAL-Revised-2015-03-03.pdf.
Kindstedt, Paul. *American Farmstead Cheese: The Complete Guide to Making and Selling Artisan Cheeses*. White River Junction, Vt.: Chelsea Green, 2005.
Kindstedt, Paul. "The Basics of Cheesemaking." In *Cheese and Microbes*, edited by Catherine W. Donnelly. Washington, DC: ASM Press, 2014.

David Gremmels

A **flavor wheel** is a pictorial diagram, generally consisting of two or three concentric circles, that identifies and categorizes the flavors found in a particular food product. Flavor wheels exist for a variety of products, including beer, whiskey, and wine, but also maple syrup, coffee, and of course, cheese. Since they often focus on the identification of aromatic descriptors, they are also referred to as aroma wheels. Generally, the inner circle of the wheel consists of class terms (e.g., fruity); the second circle, of sub-class terms (e.g., citrus fruits); and the third circle, of specific descriptors (e.g., lemon). The terminology is not evaluative or hedonic, but descriptive and aimed at facilitating communication within a taste community, which may include food producers, marketing personnel, researchers, writers, and consumers. As a classification system that relates terms to one another, such wheels help communities establish shared references and vocabularies, but also further detail product descriptions.

Flavor wheels also serve as memory aids during tastings, thus helping novice tasters in particular build a taste vocabulary and competency. The Comté Aroma Wheel is an early and well-known example in the realm of cheese. First published in 1997, the Comté Aroma Wheel contains the eighty-three aromatic descriptors, classified into six aromatic classes, most frequently found in Comté cheese by a panel of trained tasters from the Comté supply chain and the region. See COMTÉ. Another example is the Aroma Wheel for Hard and Semi-Hard Cheeses, which includes three concentric circles, with a sub-class level in between the class terms and specific descriptors. Both wheels have been adapted and published for use by the general public as well.

See also FLAVOR.

Bérodier, F., C. Stèvenot, and P. Schlich. "Description of the Flavour of Comté Cheese." *LWT-Food Science and Technology* 30 (1997): 298–304.
Bérodier, F., et al. "Guide to the Smell, Aroma, and Taste Evaluation of Hard and Semi-Hard Cheeses." *LWT-Food Science and Technology* 30 (1997): 653–664.

Christy Shields

fleurines are natural faults occurring in the rock walls of underground caves in south-central France. When it comes to cheesemaking, the fleurines are among the most fortuitous of natural occurrences, the site of a remarkable confluence of Earth's geological evolution and human ingenuity in the pursuit of gastronomy.

France's Massif Central features a series of vast limestone karst plateaus, called *causses* in the local Occitan tongue. Due to the relatively soft, breakable nature of this rock, as the Earth's crust formed and shifted via earthquakes, volcanic activity, and erosion over millions of years, sections of these plateaus collapsed, creating underground caves with interconnected faults. These internal cracks, called fleurines, from the Occitan word *flarina*, meaning to "breathe" or "blow," allow the movement of steady, gentle air currents that moderate and stabilize both temperature and humidity within the caves year-round.

The most famous fleurines run through Mont Combalou, above and behind the town of Roquefort-sir-Soulzon, and facilitate the aging of France's original blue cheese, the eponymous Roquefort. This small mountain crumbled sometime more than a million years ago, leaving a cliff fronting a network of caverns with chimneys that extend vertically about

328 feet (100 meters) and exit near its top. In addition to Roquefort, another regional blue cheese, Bleu des Causses, is ripened under similar conditions but with less-stringent geographical limitations. See ROQUEFORT and BLEU DES CAUSSES.

Beginning in the seventeenth century, the caves of Combalou were enlarged and reinforced into modern cheese-aging facilities. Passageways were carved out and doors installed to provide ready access to the fleurines, enhancing this natural air-conditioning system. As the cool outside air currents flow down through the mountain, they pick up moisture from its internal aquifer. To make adjustments and thereby maintain constant conditions of about 46–50°F (8–10°C) and 95–98 percent humidity necessary to propagate the blue-cheese ripening molds, affineurs (ripeners) need simply to open and close those doors.

See also FRANCE.

Bardou, Nicolas. *Société Roquefort: A Legendary Pleasure.* Toulouse, France: Éditions Privat, 2013.

David Gibbons

flocculation is a term used in cheesemaking to describe the precise moment when the protein structures (micelles) in milk lose their ability to repel each other and begin to visibly cluster. Flocculation occurs thanks to the enzymatic activity of the added coagulant (rennet), which cuts the negatively charged and water-binding exterior tips (both of which keep the micelles suspended in the milk) of the protein micelles. See COAGULANT; PROTEINS; and RENNET. Once rennet is added to the warmed and cultured milk, the enzyme activity begins. At the point when approximately 80 percent of the protein strands have been cleaved, the micelles will begin to link up with other micelles with the help of calcium phosphate to form connections. See CALCIUM PHOSPHATE. If a milk sample is kept in motion, such as swirled in a clear jar, the moment that the enzymatic phase is complete and flocculation begins is visible as small, white clumps, or flocs, form in the fluid. When observed in the vat, however, flocculation is noted by the perceptible increase in surface tension of the milk, which is now becoming curd. Cheesemakers tend to prefer a specific method for observing this change, including observing how a floating cup will

spin and touching the top of the milk with their hand or a utensil.

Flocculation is an important indicator for the cheesemaker. It can help assess the quality of the rennet, the readiness of the milk to coagulate (including temperature, acidity, and protein quality), and the amount of time that should elapse before the curd mass is ready to be cut into smaller pieces. Formulas, using what is called flocculation factors, can be applied to calculate the exact time when the curd is to be cut. One method takes the amount of time that has elapsed from when the rennet was added to when flocculation is observed and multiplies it by a factor to determine the total amount of time from adding the rennet to cutting the curd. For example, a semihard cheese might use a factor of 3 or 3.5 while a surface-ripened white mold cheese might use a factor of 5 or 6.

See also COAGULATION OR CURDLING.

Fox, Patrick, et al. *Fundamentals of Cheese Science.* Gathersburg, Md.: Aspen, 2000, p. 112.
Kindstedt, Paul. *American Farmstead Cheese: The Complete Guide to Making and Selling Artisan Cheese.* White River Junction, Vt.: Chelsea Green, 2005, pp. 97, 207, 208.

Gianaclis Caldwell

flower of the molds is a term that refers to the fungus *Trichothecium roseum* and describes the pinkish or bluish color its growth lends to the appearance of cheese rinds, a characteristic valued by French cheesemakers. *Trichothecium roseum* has a world-wide distribution and is often isolated from decaying plant substrates, soil, seeds of corn and food-stuffs (especially flour products). In cheese the fungus is especially associated with the production of Saint-Nectaire cheese (an uncooked semihard surface mold-ripened cheese) because cheesemakers in the Auvergne region of France have traditionally placed rye straw under the ripening cheese to encourage the growth of *T. roseum*.

T. roseum is known for its lypolitic activity; however its direct contribution to the flavor of cheeses like Saint-Nectaire has not been studied. Cheesemakers have observed that using rye straw seems to produce the best cheeses because of its role in the fungal succession on the rind. Some cheesemakers have continued slipping the straw between the shelves of aging cheeses despite the fact that this may be seen as out of compliance with more recent regulations of the European Union that call for the cheeses to be aged on plastic mats on shelves as opposed to resting directly on top of the straw. *T. roseum* grows well under conditions of high humidity, such as those found in a cheese aging cave. The compounds cis- and trans-octa-1,5-dien-3-ols produced by *T. roseum* have been also found to be strong attractants for mites. See CHEESE MITES.

See also FUNGI and SAINT-NECTAIRE.

Marcellino, Noella, and David R. Benson. "The Good, the Bad and Ugly: Tales of Mold-Ripened Cheese." *Microbiology Spectrum* 1, no. 1 (2013): 1–27.
"*Trichothecium roseum*." Mycology Online. http://www .mycology.adelaide.edu.au/Fungal_Descriptions/ Hyphomycetes_(hyaline)/Trichothecium.

Carly Cody

fondue traditionally refers to a communal dish of melted cheese and wine served in a pot (*caquelon*) set over an open flame (*réchaud*); it is eaten by dipping bite-size pieces of bread, speared on long-stemmed forks, into the soupy cheesy mixture. While the name fondue, which derives from the French word *fondre* ("to melt"), has been generalized to mean almost anything (chocolate, broth, olive oil, etc.) heated for dipping, classic fondue is a quintessential Swiss cheese dish (though there are variations found in the French Alps). It originated in the eighteenth century among poor town dwellers as a way to make stale bread and hard cheese palatable. Today, Gruyère is *de rigueur* in Swiss fondue, but many cooks also add a second cheese—Fribourg Vacherin, Emmentaler, or Appenzeller—depending on local tastes.

To prepare Swiss fondue, the inside of the *caquelon* is first rubbed with a cut garlic clove. White wine and cornstarch are added and heated until simmering on the stovetop, whereupon the grated cheese is stirred in. As it blends, the mixture is often topped off with a dash of *kirschwasser,* cherry brandy. The *caquelon* is transferred to its stand over the *réchaud* where the fondue is served warm enough to stay smooth and molten, but not so hot that it burns. Ideally, a thin crust of toasted cheese will line the bottom of the pot after the fondue is all eaten. This cracker-like cheese wafer, nicknamed *la religieuse* ("the nun"), is lifted out and shared as the finale of the meal. Other than bread for dipping, fondue also includes side dishes of pickles, olives, raw garlic, cured meat, and pearl onions.

"History of Fondue." Everything Fondue. http:// everythingfondue.wordpress.com/history/.
"A Proper Swiss Cheese Fondue." Just Hungry, 7 November 2013. http://justhungry.com/proper -swiss-cheese-fondue.

Elaine Khosrova

Fontina Val d'Aosta, the original protected, guaranteed version of Italy's quintessential mountain cheese, is an often sublime expression of its spectacular terroir in the Western Alps. Fontina is the pride of the smallest and northwestern-most of Italy's twenty regions, whose steep, narrow valley extends past some of Europe's most famous mountains—the Gran Paradiso, Monte Rosa, and the Matterhorn—and culminates at its highest peak, Mont Blanc.

There are several hypotheses for the etymology of Fontina. It might come from two local place names, Fontin (a hamlet) and Fontinaz (a village), or from a family name from the thirteenth century, de Funtina, or it might descend from the archaic French term "fontis" or "fondis," for melting. A similar word, "fondente," has the same meaning in modern Italian, and the cheese has long been prized for its property of melting while retaining its cohesion and flavor.

Fontina-style cheese was first mentioned by name in a Latin document dated 1270; cheeses clearly identifiable as Fontina appear in a fifteenth-century fresco in the Castello di Issogne. Fontina is the featured ingredient in the traditional local version of fondue (Fonduta Valdostana), which is made by soaking sliced strips of the cheese in milk, adding eggs and butter, and melting the mixture.

The Italian government awarded Fontina its DOC (denominazione di origine controllata, or controlled designation of origin) in 1955, and the European Union its PDO (protected designation of origin) in 1995. The Fontina consortium (Consorzio Produttori e Tutela della DOP Fontina), founded in 1957, is charged with enforcing PDO rules, and protecting and promoting the brand.

Fontina's zone encompasses the entire Valle d'Aosta region. PDO rules dictate that the cheese be made from the raw whole milk of the local Valdostana breed of cattle, each batch from a single milking. The curds are gently cooked and stirred at a temperature not to exceed 118°F (48°C). They are pressed in molds for up to twelve hours and then turned daily and brine-washed every other day. Aging lasts a minimum of eighty days at 41–54°F (5–12°C) and 90 percent humidity; some affineurs age the cheeses for six to nine months.

A majority of producers belong to the Cooperativa Produttori Latte e Fontina, a coop founded in 1958 that has grown from forty-six members to about two hundred. Overall approximately 400,000 wheels of Fontina PDO are produced each year, of which about 10 percent is exported. The PDO cheese is identified by a label featuring a circular logo centering the Fontina brand lettering with a stylized line drawing of the Matterhorn on top.

Producers are divided into two main categories: caseificio (dairy) and alpeggio (mountain pasture), with about eighty of the former and more than two hundred of the latter. The smaller alpeggi (alpine producers) operate only during the summer months, when the cows benefit from the ancient practice of transhumance, grazing at successively higher elevations, up to about 8,200 feet (2,500 meters), and enjoying a rich diet of Alpine flowers, plants, and herbs. See ALPAGE and TRANSHUMANCE. Alpeggio cheeses are slightly more concentrated, meaning they have less water content, and are more dense and slightly higher in fat than their off-season counterparts while offering significant increases in such potentially beneficial nutrients as omega-3 and omega-6 essential fatty acids, oleic acid, and conjugated linoleic acid (CLA).

Fontina comes in flat wheels with concave sides, 12–18 inches (30–45 centimeters) in diameter and 3–4 inches (7–10 centimeters) high, weighing 17–26 pounds (7.5–12 kilograms). The thin rind is an orange-tinged chestnut brown that grows darker as it ages. The paste is ivory to straw yellow in color; the texture smooth, compact, and dense, with occasional air pockets; and the consistency supple and somewhat elastic yet toothsome. Semisoft when young, Fontina grows firmer with age.

Many generic Fontina-style cheeses are made elsewhere, but they are essentially commercial imitations; by comparison, the flavors and aromas of genuine Fontina Val d'Aosta are much more distinct and assertive. In fact its aroma has often been characterized as pungent, funky—even "stinky." When young its flavors are subtle and complex, yet never very strong. Guffanti, the northern Italian affineur, touts

its highly selected PDO Fontinas as "floral, nutty, barnyardy and sweet…with a bit of lactic zing on the finish." Among other notes frequently detected are fruity, grassy, nutty, and with hints of truffle.

See also ITALY.

Disciplinare di Produzione della DOP "Fontina" (official product specification). http://www .fontina-dop.it/pdf/disciplinare-fontina_49.
Fontina consortium. http://www.fontina-dop.it.
Fontina coop. http://www.fontinacoop.it.

David Gibbons

The **Food and Drug Administration**

(FDA) is the US federal agency that regulates the safety of cheeses that are produced in or imported to the United States. The FDA was originally established by the Department of Agriculture in 1848 to perform chemical analyses of agricultural products. In 1906 the US Congress passed the Pure Food and Drug Act to prevent adulteration and misbranding of foods, drinks, and drugs. Harvey Wiley, chief chemist with the US Department of Agriculture, led the enforcement to protect food and drugs for consumers that had not been done prior to this time.

Today the FDA is a part of the US Department of Health and Human Services. There are four core areas of the FDA: Medical Products and Tobacco; Foods and Veterinary Medicine; Global Regulatory Operations; and Policy and Operations. The FDA is responsible for protecting the safety and security of the US food supply. The FDA regulates a number of foods such as dietary supplements, bottled water, food additives, infant formula, and other food products. They also have jurisdiction over 80 percent of the US food supply that enters interstate commerce including seafood, dairy, and produce. The FDA enforces the US Code of Federal Regulations (21 CFR, Part 133), which provides specific requirements for cheeses by category. The US Department of Agriculture (USDA-FSIS) has federal regulatory authority over meat, poultry, and egg products. USDA-Dairy (another branch) performs plant inspections, grading, export certification programs, standards, and equipment review. Plants that work with the USDA-Dairy do so on a voluntary basis. Plants can request the USDA-Dairy to perform a plant inspection, grade products, or execute an equipment review. They are then charged a fee for this service.

There are several areas that the FDA is involved in regarding regulation of food and food production. Information about recent recalls, outbreaks, food-borne illnesses, contaminants, or emergencies can be found on the FDA website (http://www.fda.gov). The website is also a good resource for information about pathogens, contaminants, and chemicals that might cause a food-borne illness and how to prevent that from occurring. Discussions about ways to diminish acts of criminal or terrorist actions on the US food supply provide a good forum for food defense. Lists of ingredients, packaging, and labeling (to help identify allergens, GRAS, or nutritional information) can also be found on the FDA website.

Guidance and regulations are also covered on the website. This section includes guidance documents, Food Safety and Modernization Act (FSMA), cGMPs, HACCP, facility registration, and import/export information. In addition there is an area on compliance and enforcement that covers reportable food registry, warning letters, and inspection programs.

Both new and current cheese manufacturers must comply with FDA requirements. In addition, depending on what state cheese manufacturing takes place in, there may be local and state regulations as well. According to the FDA, "Each facility that manufactures, processes, packs or holds food that is intended for human consumption in the United States, must register with the FDA before beginning these activities. All registered manufacturers must report if any food [cheese] could cause adverse health concerns or death to humans and animals."

Records are required for all cheese manufacturers. This includes records from ingredient suppliers, production records, temperature logs, shipping and receiving logs, sanitation records, etc. Good Manufacturing Practice (GMP) regulations are required to ensure that a safe and wholesome product was manufactured each and every day. Nutritional labeling is also necessary for all FDA-regulated food products. The name of the food, net quantity of contents, claims, and allergens are all required to be listed on the label.

The FDA is now focusing on preventing food safety problems as opposed to reacting to a problem after it occurs. These are known as preventive controls. A cheese manufacturer will be required to have the following in place:

- Evaluation of all hazards within the facility;
- Implementation of preventive controls to minimize or prevent hazards from occurring;
- Ensure no adulteration has occurred with the manufactured product;
- Monitor controls;
- Records must be in place

All FDA facilities will be inspected on a routine basis depending on the risk of the product, time since last inspection, and previous history of the facility.

FDA Code of Federal Regulations , Title 21, Chapter 1, Part 133: "Cheeses and Related Cheese Products." http://www.accessdata.fda.gov/scripts/cdrh/cfdocs/cfCFR/CFRSearch.cfm?CFRPart=133.
US Food and Drug Administration website. http://www.fda.gov.

Marianne Smukowski

Food Standards Australia New Zealand

(FSANZ) is a bi-national government agency that develops and administers the Australia New Zealand Food Standards Code. Enforcement and interpretation of the code is the responsibility of state and territory government agencies within Australia, and the Ministry for Primary Industries, public health units, and local governments in New Zealand.

Following the creation of the National Food Authority in Australia in 1991, a treaty between Australia and New Zealand—aiming to reduce compliance costs, harmonize food standards, and remove regulatory barriers to trade in food between the two countries—came into force in 1996. The joint code was introduced in 2000 under the former Australia New Zealand Food Authority, and FSANZ was established on 1 July 2002.

Food standards in the code are developed with advice from other government agencies and input from stakeholders. A risk analysis framework ensures food regulatory measures are based on the best available scientific evidence, and public input is an important part of the decision-making process. When FSANZ develops standards, the Australia and New Zealand Ministerial Forum on Food Regulation has the capacity to adopt, amend, or reject them, and to ask FSANZ to review them, or create new ones.

One significant area of the code where the two countries differ is in Primary Production and Processing

(PPP) Standards, which only apply in Australia. The PPP standard for dairy includes amendments made in 2012 to allow the production and sale of hard to very hard cooked-curd cheeses made from raw milk. Significant further changes, encompassing provisions for a wider range of raw-milk cheeses, became law in Australia in February 2015. In New Zealand, the Ministry for Primary Industries allows the local production of specific styles of raw-milk cheeses, and import of raw-milk cheeses from the European Community only.

See also AUSTRALIA AND NEW ZEALAND and RAW-MILK CHEESES.

Food Standards Australia New Zealand: Australia. http://www.foodstandards.gov.au.
Food Standards Australia New Zealand: New Zealand. http://www.foodstandards.govt.nz.

Sonia Cousins

Formaella Arahovas Parnassou is a PDO (protected designation of origin) semihard cheese traditionally produced in the mountain town of Arahova, on the slopes of Mt. Parnassus in the Viotia prefecture of Greece. Milk used for its production comes exclusively from herds of sheep and goats traditionally raised and adapted to this region, and whose diet is based on wild plants, which gives this pale yellow to white cheese its unique peppery or spicy and rich flavors. It is produced mainly in small dairy plants, and today most of the cheese is sold fresh to tourists visiting the nearby ski resort at Mt. Parnassus. See FRESH CHEESES.

To produce Formaella Arahovas Parnassou, the milk is heated and coagulated at 90°F (32°C) within the first two hours. Next the curds are brought up to 104°F (40°C) for ten minutes. The developing cheese is then divided into large pieces that will go into special molds (*kofinaki*). These molds with the curd are submerged into whey at 140°F (60°C) for one hour. At this time the cheese will be removed from the molds, turned over, and replaced in the molds. The molds again are immersed into warm whey at 167–176°F (75–80°C) for an hour. Finally the cheese is pulled out of the whey, salted, and left to dry for twenty-four hours. After this drying period cheeses are either delivered to the market for fresh consumption or transferred to cool rooms for ripening for at least three months.

The final cheese has a 50 percent maximum humidity and 40 percent minimum dry fat content. It has a compact texture and a yellowish color, and is commonly available in the market as small cylindrical pieces weighing 14–18 ounces (400–500 grams). Most often the cheese will be sold after three months of aging. When ripened, Formaella Arahovas Parnassou presents a semihard structure, piquant taste, and rich aroma, and is consumed as a table cheese or used for grating. With its long cylindrical shape and ridged texture, the cheese can be eaten fresh, roasted, grilled, or fried. It is often consumed fried as saganaki: round slices of cheese are dredged lightly in flour and then pan-fried. Typically the saganaki-cheese will be covered with drops of lemon juice. See SAGANAKI.

See also GREECE and MOZZARELLA.

Anyfantakis E. M. *Greek Cheeses, a Tradition of Centuries.* Athens: National Dairy Committee of Greece, 1991.
"Formaella Arahovas." Cheesenet.gr. http://www .cheesenet.gr/english/cheeses/formaella.htm.
Kochilas, Diane. "From Villages and Caves, the Glorious Cheeses That Are Greek." *New York Times*, 2 October 1991.

Anastasios Aktypis and Megan A. Schraedley

Formaggella del Luinese is a semihard Italian cheese made with raw, whole goat's milk from the Camosciata delle Alpi, Nera di Verzasca, and Saanen breeds (and their crosses). See SAANEN. The cheese is produced in the valley of Luinese in the Province of Varese in Lombardy and has had protected designation of origin (PDO) status since 16 April 2011. Treaties and essays from the seventeenth century demonstrate that Formaggella del Luinese has long been part of the area's cheesemaking and gastronomic tradition.

Formagella del Luinese is cylindrical in shape: 5–6 inches (13–15 centimeters) in diameter, 2–2½ inches (4–6 centimeters) high, and weighing 25–31 ounces (700–900 grams). The rind is natural, not hard, and presents characteristic white molds. The paste is compact, white, and soft with the possible presence of small eyes.

The milk used for the production of Formagella del Luinese may be stored for a maximum of thirty hours at a temperature not higher than 39°F (4°C). Heating the milk can be done only using a wood fire, gas, or steam. Only a natural or prepared inoculum, made of thermophilic lactic bacteria, may be used, with the possible addition of small doses of mesophilic strains. The coagulation takes place at 90–93°F (32–34°C) in thirty to forty minutes using natural calf rennet only. The coagulum is cut into corn kernel–size particles. The cheese is then drained for a maximum of forty-eight hours at room temperature, salted (brine or dry-salt), dried, and ripened in controlled aging room (85 percent humidity, 59°F [15°C]) for at least twenty days. The cheese should have a minimum of 41 percent fat, 45 percent dry matter.

Formagella del Luinese has a pleasant sweet flavor and a delicate aroma that intensifies with time. The cheese is supple, moist, and soft. It is consumed locally as a table cheese but is also used to prepare risotto and antipasti.

See also LOMBARDY.

European Union. "Publication of an application pursuant to Article 6(2) of Council Regulation (EC) No 510/2006 on the protection of geographical indications and designations of origin for agricultural products and foodstuffs: Formaggella del Luinese." *Official Journal of the European Union* 220 (2010): 18–21. http://eur-lex.europa.eu/legal-content/EN/TXT/?uri=CELEX%3A52010XC0814%2805%29.
"Formaggella del Luinese DOP." Regione Lombardia. http://www.agricoltura.regione.lombardia.it.

Bénédicte Coudé

Formaggi Ocello

was opened by Carmelo and Sogna Ocello in 2009, and is one of the only specialty cheese shops in Sydney, Australia. While other shops in Sydney feature cheese counters within delicatessens or large food stores, Formaggi Ocello exists exclusively as a cheese emporium, selling more than two hundred artisan cheeses from Australia and Europe, cheese accompaniments from Italy, and cheese accessories and equipment. The store includes an immaculate cheese counter, a café/bar for enjoying cheese and wine on the premises, and a viewing area for the large maturation room where hard cheeses are aged prior to sale.

Before the store opened in 2009, the Ocello brand was already well established on the Sydney food scene. In 2001 a chance meeting with a goat farmer from Queensland led Carmelo to open his first stall at one of Sydney's weekly produce markets, selling a small range of locally made cheeses. On a trip to Italy in 2004 Carmelo and Sogna discovered many artisan cheeses that were not available in Australia, which inspired them to expand their range at the markets when they returned. By 2006 they had set up their own import company, which now sources cheeses directly from Italy, Spain, France, Switzerland, the United Kingdom, and the Netherlands. Today the store also features a selection of cheeses from Australian artisan producers. Other aspects of the business include a wholesale division (supplying cheese to restaurants and other retailers in Sydney and elsewhere), an online shop servicing cheese lovers Australia-wide, and regular cheese and wine appreciation events.

See also AUSTRALIA AND NEW ZEALAND.

Formaggi Ocello. http://ocello.com.au.

Sonia Cousins

formaggio di fossa, officially called Formaggio di Fossa di Sogliano, is a semihard PDO (protected designation of origin) cheese produced in the Emilia-Romagna and Marche Apennines foothills and hills of central northern Italy. It received the European recognition of protected designation of origin in 2009.

Formaggio di Fossa owes its name to "fossa," the pits dug into tuffaceous rock where the cheese is ripened. Before welcoming cheeses the pits are disinfected with fire, raised wooden platforms are placed at the bottom of the pits, and the walls are lined with a 4-inch (10-centimeter) layer of wheat straw supported by vertical reed fencing. Then the pits are filled to the top with cheeses placed in cloth bags. When the pits are full they are closed by wooden plank and covered using rocks, sandstone powder, and sand. The cheese stays in the pit from 1 March to 20 June or from 21 June to 21 September of each year.

The cheese is irregular in shape with a wet surface that sometimes may be covered by butterfat or mold; small cracks and ocher stains can be present. There is no or minimal rind and the cheese weighs 1–4 pounds (500 grams–1.9 kilograms). The interior paste is ivory or straw colored, compact, and friable. The cheese is characterized by a strong odor of brush and truffle and a taste from bitter to spicy in relation to the milk used, which has a fat content of at least 40.5 percent on a dry matter basis, and a sweet, buttery aroma.

Formaggio di Fossa is made with whole cow's or ewe's milk or a mixture of both with a ratio of 4:1 respectively coming from two milkings. The raw or pasteurized milk is coagulated at 86–100°F (30–38°C) using natural rennet. After coagulum cutting the curd is transferred into molds 2–4 inches (6–10 centimeters) high, 5–8 inches (12–20 centimeters) in diameter, and manually pressed. The cheese can be dry- or brine-salted.

See also FOSSA.

"Disciplinari di produzione prodotti DOP e IGP riconosciuti: Formaggi." Ministero delle Politiche Agricole. https://www.politicheagricole.it/flex/cm/pages/ServeBLOB .php/L/IT/IDPagina/3340.
Pirisi, A., et al. "Sheep's and Goat's Dairy Products in Italy: Technological, Chemical, Microbiological, and Sensory Aspects." *Small Ruminant Research* 101 (2011): 102–112.

Marta Bertolino

Formaggio Kitchen is one of New England's finest cheese shops and gourmet grocers. Founded in the 1970s as a neighborhood grocery in Cambridge, Massachusetts, since 1992 it has risen to prominence under the ownership of Ihsan and Valerie Gurdal. Two characteristics mark the store as particularly distinctive: a commitment to direct importation, and an underground aging cellar for ripening cheese. Ihsan and Valerie travel regularly throughout Europe in search of the best small producers of cheese and other artisan products. As a testament to their relationships with small producers forged since the late 1990s, the shop features cheeses rarely found elsewhere in the United States, and some found rarely beyond their places of production.

During their frequent buying trips, Ihsan and Valerie realized that fromageries in France maintain climate-controlled aging cellars beneath their retail stores designed to keep cheeses in optimum condition. Coupled with a need to store the larger quantities necessitated by cost-effective import, in 1996 the Gurdals converted an old office beneath their store into an affinage cave. Wood boards line each of the walls and the concrete floors are regularly dampened to maintain high humidity. Formaggio Kitchen was the first retail store in the United States to install their own aging cellar, and a number of prominent cheese shops have since followed suit. In addition to cheese, the store features a wide array of gourmet food items sourced with a similar commitment to quality, including cured meats, produce, spices, chocolate, baked goods, preserves, and other accompaniments. In the 2000s, the Gurdals opened additional locations in Boston's historic South End and in Manhattan's Essex Market.

Formaggio Kitchen. http://www.formaggiokitchen .com/about.

Bradley M. Jones

Formatgeria La Seu is a small but successful specialty cheese shop in Barcelona, Spain, owned and managed by Scotswoman Katherine McLaughlin. The shop, opened in a former butter factory in January 2000, is located in Carrer de la Dagueria, a street in the charming Barri Gòtic (Gothic neighborhood). Formateria La Seu sells only small-scale production Spanish and Catalan farmhouse cheeses, carrying a range of twenty to twenty-five types of regional cheeses each season.

The store sources a distinctive ensemble of cow's milk, goat's milk, and sheep's milk artisan cheeses, such as San Simon da Costa PDO, a Galician smoked cheese made with cow's milk which has a pyramid shape; Pasiego de Las Garmillas, a pancake-shaped cow's milk cheese from Cantabria; Manchego DOP aged for six months minimum; and Torta de La Serena, made of unpasteurized sheep's milk, with a semihard rind and soft and creamy paste, from Estremadura. See MANCHEGO and LA SERENA.

McLaughlin, who once owned a restaurant in Scotland, houses the products in a tailor-made cave, a cold room where the temperature varies between 46–54°F (8–12°C), in order to keep the cheeses developing and aging in a controlled climate. Customers can sample before buying and the cheeses are presented on a flat, portable taste plate specially designed to accommodate a glass of wine and be held like a palette. The stand-up tasting consists of three cheeses and a small glass of wine. Cheese tastings are available but due to space constraints can only accommodate a maximum of fourteen people. McLaughlin also produces and sells Formatgelats, a small-batch artisanal ice cream in three flavors, each one with a different variety of cheese: goat, cow, and blue cheese. In 2009 Katherine and her sister, Mary, opened Bar Zim next door to the shop, serving tapas along with Spanish wines and charcuterie.

Harbutt, J. *World Cheese Book*. London: Dorling Kindersley, 2015.

"Katherine McLaughlin: Formatgeria La Seu." Kiss from the World. https://www.kissfromtheworld.com/i-people-travel-video/spain/barcelona/katherine-mclaughlin-formatgeria-la-seu-27.html.

Winkle-Bryan, R., and A. B. Martos. *Eat Guides: Barcelona* (ebook). Barcelona: Eat-Guides.com. http://www.eat-guides.com.

Olívia Fraga

forms or molds are among the most important and fundamental pieces of equipment necessary for executing the basic recipes for most cheeses. They are the receptacles into which the acidified or coagulated curds are placed so they may complete the final stages of taking shape and becoming a cheese. In the cheesemaking process, forming or molding generally takes place after the curds are separated from their whey and before the cheeses are placed in drying or aging rooms to begin ripening.

Solidifying a fresh cheese via forming or molding goes hand in hand with drainage. Cheesemaking is largely a process of dehydration and controlling acidification, which is determined by the moisture levels at which bacteria can function; ergo, the amount and speed of drainage occurring not only prior to molding or forming but within the molds or forms themselves is crucial to success. The rates and levels of drainage and acidification of a forming cheese are, in turn, largely determined by how—and how much—the mold or form is perforated. See DRAINING and ACIDIFICATION.

History

Shards of sieve-like ceramic pots found in Anatolia and the Levant area of the Fertile Crescent and dating from approximately 6500 B.C.E. have been established as the earliest evidence of cheesemaking. Similar shards from about a century later were discovered in northern Europe and confirmed to carry traces of milk fat. In his book *Cheese and Culture*, Paul Kinstedt writes that "the very strong association between the appearance of perforated sieves in the archeological record and the arrival of dairying in the Near East and Europe, along with the strong ethnographic record of the continued use of ceramic sieves in cheese making into the modern era" leaves little doubt these were forms or molds for cheesemaking. Kinstedt further notes that woven baskets were probably also used for the same purpose but naturally they decayed and did not survive.

From an etymological standpoint, the notion of forming an agglomeration of coagulated curds into a definite shape is the very basis for the word "cheese" in several Indo-European languages, including French (*fromage*), Italian (*formaggio*), and Catalan (*formatge*), whereas others derive theirs from the Latin root *caseum*: *Käse* (German), *queijo* (Portuguese), and *queso* (Spanish). See ETYMOLOGY.

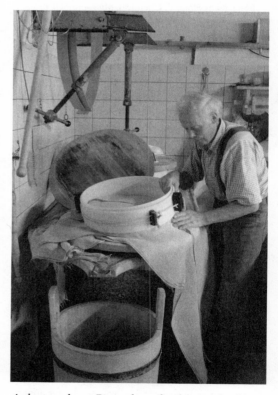

A cheesemaker at Piesenalpe, a family-owned and -operated Alp dairy in the Allgäu region, setting the hoop. Wooden hoops with adjustable sides—featuring straps that can be tightened to exert additional lateral pressure—are traditionally employed for large Alp-style cheeses. © KATE ARDING

Tradition and Geography

Traditionally there is a distinct correlation between geography and climate, and the types of molds employed and cheeses produced. In northern, colder, and higher elevation regions, where the curds are subjected to more cutting, cooking, and washing, and the cheeses undergo more extensive pressing, the molds must be thicker and stronger. In lower-lying, more temperate regions—for example, much of France—the molds are thinner, with more perforations and flexibility. Farther south, in the warmer Mediterranean climates, where milk acidifies more quickly and the whey therefore must be extracted faster, highly perforated basket-type molds are the norm. It's generally a more rudimentary style of cheesemaking that can nevertheless yield large, hard cheeses from curds that are cooked, cut, and drained in quicker succession.

For large Alp-style cheeses, for example, Beaufort, Abondance, Comté, Gruyère, Fontina, and Bitto, wooden hoops with adjustable sides—featuring straps that could be tightened to exert additional lateral pressure—were traditionally employed. See HOOP. In France's Loire Valley, another entrenched cheese-making region, the ancient clay molds used for traditional chèvres, were converted to tin in the eighteenth and nineteenth centuries. Among traditional materials—clay; wood; woven wicker, reed or straw—perhaps the most distinctive is the Spanish *pleita* (plaited raw esparto grass), which gives Manchego and similar types their easily recognizable external "rope-tied" pattern. The *pleita* is flexible, low in perforation, and allows for slow draining of the whey while hard-pressing a cheese.

Materials

The majority of modern cheese molds are made from food-grade synthetic polymers, mostly polypropylene and HDPE (high-density polyethylene). These plastics can be fashioned in various thicknesses for greater or lesser flexibility and are convenient for cleaning, sterilizing, or autoclaving.

In general molds made of softer, more flexible materials are used to produce the smaller, lighter, more delicate cheeses, while those with less perforation yield soft-ripened cheeses with more moisture retention, for example, the Camembert, Brie, and triple-cream types. Larger, harder, denser cheeses that require more moisture extraction, such as Cheddar, Gouda, Parmesan, and the Alp types, are formed in stronger, more rigid molds; paradoxically, however, since their curds are subjected to more heat and pressure, the molds for these types may require less perforation. Forms or molds for such larger format cheeses are more often than not made of stainless steel.

Shapes and Sizes

One major subcategory of forms or molds is the hoop, which is hollow at each end. Placed in a hoop on a mesh-like mat, a forming cheese can drain its whey through the bottom of the hoop; in addition, it can be pressed, for further consolidation and drainage, by placing weights on the top. Indeed many cheese molds have an additional part called a "follower," which is usually some type of hollow lid that fits into the top of the mold and allows for placement of a weight and/or stacking, so the cheeses may be pressed under their own weight. Another accessory often used with molds or hoops is a cloth liner (cheesecloth) for ease of insertion and extraction. See CHEESECLOTH.

The basket mold is another important subcategory. And while they are not hollow, baskets often have very open sides and bottoms to facilitate gravity draining. Traditional cheeses such as the Italian canestrato types exhibit distinctive patterns on their rinds; so as not to lose these distinguishing "brand features," modern plastic or metal molds retain these patterns. In addition other distinctively branded cheeses display their names or logos on their rinds, imprinted via a pattern on a matrix placed inside the molds. Genuine Parmigiano Reggiano PDO—with its famous pin-dot lettering—is a prime example of this.

Among prominent manufacturers of cheese molds are Anelli Luigi in Italy; Busqui in Catalonia, Spain; Kadova in the Netherlands; and Mino Gaillard in France. These companies make individual forms for just about every major type and category of cheese. In addition they often produce so-called "multi-forms" for molding many small cheeses at once.

See also EARTHENWARE POTTERY; FASCÈRA; MOLDING; and TRADITIONAL EQUIPMENT.

Anelli. http://www.anelliluigi.it.
Busqui. http://www.moldes-queso.com.

"Cheese Moulds." Artisan Geek. http://www.artisangeek
.com/cheese-moulds.

Fromagex. http://www.fromagex.com.

Kadova Cheese Mould Shop. http://www
.kadovacheesemouldshop.com/index.php?action=
home&lang=EN.

Kinstedt, Paul S. "Southwest Asia and the Ancient Origins
of Cheese." In *Cheese and Culture: A History of Cheese
and Its Place in Western Civilization*, pp. 10–12. White
River Junction, Vt.: Chelsea Green, 2012.

"Wiki: Hoops & Molds." CheeseForum.org, 23 October
2011. http://www.cheeseforum.org/articles/
wiki-hoops-molds.

David Gibbons

Fort Saint Antoine is an old French military
fort later used to mature cheese by the affineur
Marcel Petite. See PETITE, MARCEL. The structure is
part of a grand fortification system designed by
Gen. Raymond-Adolphe Séré de Rivières, director
of the Military Engineers Service at the French
Ministry of Defense. Following the humiliation of
the Franco-Prussian war of 1870–1871, a review of
France's eastern defenses was undertaken. The fortification system had not been upgraded since its
creation by the brilliant military engineer Vauban in
the seventeenth century, and the recent war revealed its shortcomings. Nothing short of a wholesale transformation was now needed, and in 1874
Gen. Rivières was given carte blanche to realize such
an aim.

What became known as the Séré de Rivières
System was a line of forts originally intended to
stretch from Dunkirk to Nice. They were designed to
have both defensive and offensive capabilities and
were situated in such a way as to channel attacking
forces through a first layer of forts onto a second. One
of the forts built in the earlier phases of construction
stood in a woodland area above the town of Saint-
Antoine, near Pontarlier in the Franche-Comté
region of eastern France.

Work on the fort at Saint-Antoine was started in
1879 and completed in 1882. It is built entirely of
masonry. Its construction involved the work of 600
masons and an equal number of stone cutters, as
well as the labor of 3,000 troops. The completed
fort had barracks for 420 men, a parade ground, and
its own kitchen. Rainwater was collected and filtered
through sand, gravel, and activated carbon before it
was pumped up from huge, underground stone tanks,
giving the fort its own water supply. The powder room,
which stored 38 tons of gunpowder, was illuminated
by "lamp rooms"—small niches behind thickened
glass—to guard against accidental explosions.

In 1887 the fort was renamed Fort Lucotte after
the general of the French Revolutionary wars. By this
time, however, advances in artillery ordnance—in
particular, the use of picric acid as a high explosive—
rendered defensive structures made of masonry obsolete. Fort Lucotte served its time as a store and
training ground, but strategically it was of little importance. After World War II, it drifted toward obso-
lescence until finally being abandoned by the military
in the 1960s. Then, in 1966, Marcel Petite negotiated
with local government to rent Fort Lucotte.

Around this time, the tendency among the affineurs of Comté was to mature the cheese at warmer
temperatures than had been done in the past. The
result was a quicker ripening cheese. But Marcel
Petite wanted to do things differently. He felt that
quick ripening brought to the fore a limited range
of flavors at the expense of broader, more complex
ones that could only be expressed if slower maturation were adopted. In the fort, he found what he had
been looking for: a place of even, cool temperatures
and high humidity. One of the key factors of cool
maturation is its effect on propionic bacteria. The
metabolites of propionic acid fermentation play an
important role in the flavor of Comté and other Swiss-
style cheeses. They grow rapidly at warm temperatures such as $64.5°F$ ($18°C$) or above, and produce
carbon dioxide gas, which creates the holes in Emmentaler and Swiss cheese. At lower temperatures the propionic fermentation takes place more slowly, and the
gas produced diffuses through the cheese and beyond.
See DAIRY PROPIONIBACTERIA.

Initially, Petite stored 2,500 cheeses at Fort Lucotte.
By the turn of the millennium, this had risen to
65,000. Following the completion of an extension
in September 2011, the capacity is approximately
100,000 wheels. As each cheese matures, the degradation of its structure produces a small amount of
heat. Multiply this by 100,000, and enough heat is
generated to offset the natural temperature afforded by
the fort's structural fabric. The temperature, therefore,
has to be regulated. This is done following the Canadian Well principle. In short, the fort takes in air from
old tunnels deep underground, which helps maintain a constant cool temperature throughout the year.

As of 2015, about fifteen people tend the cheese
at Fort Lucotte de Saint Antoine. Whereas in the

1960s, much of the labor spent was in turning and washing the cheese, now all this is done automatically. Special robots, built in Switzerland, patrol the aisles lifting cheeses from their shelves with laser-guided forks. The cheeses are then turned and scrubbed in a saltwater solution by rotating brushes. Each cheese is turned and washed once a week. To maintain this level of activity, the robots run continuously and have their own maintenance team. With this time-consuming work taken care of, the cheese workers have more time to concentrate on assessing the quality of Comté. Each batch of cheese is tasted at between six to eight months of age to see how it is maturing. Between ten and twenty-four months, each cheese will be assessed to ascertain when it is ready to be sold. Although far from its original purpose, Fort Saint Antoine is gallantly defending the culture that it was originally designed to protect.

See COMTÉ and FRANCE.

Fortiff'Séré: L'association Séré de Rivières. http://www.fortiffsere.fr.

Dominic Coyte

A **fossa** is a cylindrically shaped hole, built as a barrel, with a diameter (in its widest part) and depth of about 11 feet (3 meters). It is dug in tuff (a porous volcanic rock) in Sogliano al Rubicone and in the stone in Talamello, two adjacent places located in different regions of Italy: Emilia Romagna and Marche, respectively. The cheese technology, still applied today through a complicated ritual, was born by chance. In order to preserve food provisions from an army raid by French king Charles VIII, during their passage in 1495, the inhabitants of these places hid the cheese in the tuff and stone trenches. It was discovered that cheeses coming from the trenches obtained a particular flavor and aroma profile. The months spent in the closed and heated subsoil, under the weight of tens of pounds (kilograms), changes the cheeses considerably. They undergo a new fermentation process and take on unusual flavors, unobtainable by any other means, that reflect the tuff and subsoil they are buried in. The different composition of a tuff trench versus the stone one is considered a diversity factor yielding a specific flavor profile. In Sogliano the cheese is classified as "fossa" cheese, whereas in Talamello it is classified as an "amber" cheese.

The accidental discovery of this phenomenon has since given way to a standardized production process. It begins in mid-August when the small sheep's milk or pecorino cheeses, produced in Montefeltro and Tuscany, are enclosed in canvas (jute) sacks (mainly white), and signed by producers with two numbers: the first corresponds with the owner, the second specifies the weight in pounds (kilograms). The cheeses are then put into the fossas, which have been disinfected and dehumidified with fire and subsequently draped, as an isolated wall, with a layer of straw supported by a framework of vertical rods, tied horizontally by circles of wood. The sacks are placed in the fossa and compressed in layers, each separated by axes and sand. The opening of the fossa is closed hermetically. The lot is aged in these subterranean environmental conditions. Anyone walking past the trench would notice nothing except for the presence of the cobblestones placed to cover the opening of the well.

On 25 November, the feast of St. Catherine, everything is revived amid great excitement: the cobblestones are removed, the fossas are opened, the sacks are drawn from the subsoil and cheeses are freed from the compression that joined them during the aging. A strong, entangling, and enchanting aroma of cheese spreads in the air. This means that fossa cheese is ready to be sold and eaten. The fossa opening is celebrated as a big feast; on this day people look back to the past when farmers came to the town to collect the cheeses stored in subsoil during summer to face the difficulties during the wintertime.

Production was limited in the past, due to the supply of fossas and the short period in summer and autumn for production, but has now improved due to increased demand for this product, thus requiring a production outside traditional areas and periods of the year. These cheeses produced during other seasons offer to consumers a product with different characteristics in comparison to the traditional production.

Fossa cheese received the protected designation of origin (PDO) certification in 2009 with the denomination of Formaggio di Fossa di Sogliano DOP. Today the strict discipline of production requires that the cheese, already partially aged, be made using high-quality milk only from sheep, cows, or mixed, produced on farms situated in the hills and mountains of Marche and Romagna territory.

See also CAVE and FORMAGGIO DI FOSSA.

Androuët, Pierre. *Le dictionnaire des fromages du monde.* Paris: Le Cherche Midi Editeur, 2002, p. 141.

Angeli, Franco. *L'Italia dei formaggi DOC; Un Grande Patrimonio.* Italy: UNALAT con INSOR, 1992, p. 127.

Cremona, Luigi, and Francesco Soletti. *L'Italia dei formaggi.* Milan: Touring Club Italiano, 2002, p. 85.

Fiori, Giacomo, et al. *Formaggi italiani.* Novara, Italy: EOS Editrice, 1999, p. 71.

Fiori, Giovanni Guffanti, and Carlo Vischi. *Formaggi italiani* Savigliano, Italy: Gribaudo, 2004, p. 179.

Guatteri, Fabiano. *Formaggi.* Novara, Italy: Istituto Geografico De Agostini, 2005, p. 142.

Sardo, Piero, et al. *Formaggi d'Italia.* Bra, Italy: Slow Food Editore, 1999, pp. 91, 154.

Carlo Fiori

Fourme d'Ambert is a blue-veined cheese produced in the French Auvergne region at altitudes between 1,968 and 5,249 feet (600 and 1,600 meters), in the mountain zone of the Puy-de-Dôme, five cantons in the Cantal, and eight communes in the Loire. The richness and biodiversity of this terroir gives the cheese its subtle and delicate aroma. Fourme d'Ambert was granted appellation d'origine contrôlée (AOC) status in 1972, and protected designation of origin (PDO) status in 1996. It is made from the milk of cows fed on grass coming exclusively from the designated area in wheels weighing 4–6 pounds (1.9–2.5 kilograms). About 5,000 tons of Fourme d'Ambert are produced every year.

In Gallo-Roman times druids were already using Fourme d'Ambert in celebrations of their cult at Pierre-sur-Haute, the highest point in the massif du Forez, in Auvergne. Later in the eighteenth century Fourme d'Ambert was used as a currency for renting jasseries, the thatched summer farm huts that are found on the Monts du Forez. From the twentieth century small dairies gradually replaced the jasseries and the production techniques were improved to guarantee better product quality.

Fourme d'Ambert comes upright and cylindrical, with a light gray-blue rind similar to stone. This protective rind proves soft to the touch and gives off a delicate aroma of the underwood. Fourme d'Ambert has a soft and creamy texture with a bright ivory color, the result of a long alchemy between the blue and white that is enacted in it during maturing. This balance is naturally released on the palate with scented and delicate aromas and a soft round taste that makes it one of the mildest of the blue cheeses.

To obtain the marbling of Fourme d'Ambert, the milk is inoculated with *Penicillium roqueforti*, which needs space and oxygen to develop. This is why the manufacturing includes specific stages such as curd graining and piercing of the cheeses using large needles to create aeration chimneys. There are hundreds of strains of *Penicillium*; for Fourme d'Ambert, specific strains are selected to produce a soft and creamy cheese. See PENICILLIUM and NEEDLES.

After inoculating the milk with *Penicillium roqueforti*, renneting takes place to cause coagulation. The curd is then cut and stirred for an hour, resulting in bead-size curds that are then drained and put into molds using a conveyor belt. See MOLDING. After twenty-four to forty-eight hours of further draining, during which time the cheeses are turned regularly, the cheese is dry-salted or brined. See DRAINING; DRY SALTING; and BRINING. On the fourth day after renneting, piercing takes place; this is when holes are made using large needles in order to convey air to the heart of the cheese and enable the blue to develop. Finally the fourmes are transferred to the cellars for maturing. The cheese can only be called Fourme d'Ambert from the twenty-eighth day after the date of renneting. See MATURING.

See also AUVERGNE; BLUE CHEESES; and FOURME DE MONTBRISON.

AOP Fourme d'Ambert. http://www.fourme-ambert.com.

Brosse, Anne-Linne, et al. *Fromages d'Auvergne—une histoire d'hommes et de femmes.* Aurillac, France: Editions Quelque part sur Terre, 2014.

Aurélien Vorger

Fourme de Montbrison is a blue-veined protected designation of origin (PDO) cheese made from raw or pasteurized cow's milk and produced in thirty-three communes in the Monts du Forez (east of the Massif central in France). Similar to but different from Fourme d'Ambert—a drier texture, a less developed blue—the appellation d'origine contrôlée (AOC), which was originally common for the two cheeses, was separated in 2002 into two different AOC, one for the Fourme d'Ambert, one for the Fourme de Montbrison. See FOURME D'AMBERT.

Known to the Gauls, Fourme de Montbrison's origins date back to the Middle Ages when it was known as fromage de Roche, a commune in the PDO area. In the nineteenth and twentieth centuries it was the women and their eldest daughter who led the herds up to the jasseries (the local name for the small mountain pasture farms) where the

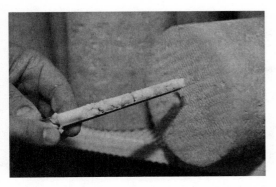

A Société Fromagère de St. Bonnet le Pont de la Pierre employee uses a cheese iron, or trier, check the development of Fourme de Montbrison cheese. © PONT PIERRE JCPARAYRE

Les jasseries et la Fourme de Montbrison. Les cahiers de Village de Forez, no. 3. Montbrison, France: Centre Social de Montbrison, 2004.

Aurélie Passel

mountain pastures were used six months of the year, while the men worked in the fields below on the other farms. Matured all summer, the fourmes were then brought down to be sold at the Montbrison market.

One Fourme de Montbrison weighs around 6 pounds (2.5 kilograms) and requires 21–26 quarts (20–25 liters) of milk. *Penicillium roqueforti* is added to the milk during renneting (calf rennet) in order to later develop blue moistures. Dry salting is done during the molding, which produces the original taste of its blue. The Fourmes de Montbrison are then laid on wooden racks made of spruce. Manually turned one quarter turn every twelve hours, it is during this period that the rind takes on its specific fine orangey color. See WOODEN SHELVES.

Matured for a long period in the heart of the mountains, the Fourme de Montbrison is unique in its expression of this mountainous terrain, the fragrance of heather and gentian flowers, the influence of the seasons and the savoir-faire of the men and women of the Forez. Dry and slightly rough, the cheese is yellow and discretely blue-veined, with a marbled aspect and a mild and refined taste. Traditionally Fourme de Montbrison is cut in two along its diameter and then into four along its length. Its delicate taste and its qualities in cooking make it an appreciated ingredient in numerous recipes. The most famous one is certainly the Montbrison fondue, served directly in the cheese, which has been hollowed inside. Fourme de Montbrison is perfectly paired with a red Côtes du Forez basaltique or a white St. Joseph.

See also BLUE CHEESES and FRANCE.

France's wide and distinguished variety of cheeses has emblematized the modern nation. It is certainly the country where the art of cheesemaking, and savoring, were brought to an extraordinary degree of refinement and inventiveness. Winston Churchill, during World War II, is said to have declared that a country able to offer 360 cheeses to the world "cannot die." Charles de Gaulle, suggesting something quite different, quipped, "How can you govern a country which has two hundred forty-six varieties of cheese?" Today there are close to fifteen hundred varieties of cheese produced from all cheese families, including a remarkable diversity of soft-type cheeses. The jewels of ancestral French savoir-faire, or know-how, are under the protection of protected denomination of origin (PDO) appellations; France has the highest number of name-protected cheeses, with forty-five, as well as three protected butters and two protected creams. The cheesemonger Pierre Androuët once said (in translation), "Delicate and alive, infused with identities and traditions, cheese exhales the soul of the land and its inhabitants." See ANDROUËT, PIERRE.

With 1.9 million tons of cheese produced every year (that's 132 pounds [60 kilograms] of cheese per second), France is the third-largest producer after the United States and Germany. However, taking into account its area, it is the "densest" country in terms of cheese production, with an average of 3.6 tons per quarter square mile (one square kilometer) versus 0.45 ton per quarter square mile (one square kilometer) in the United States. Most French cheese is made from cow's milk, but 28,000 and 93,000 tons of cheese are produced, respectively, from ewe's and goat's milks. Between 10–15 percent of cheese is still made from raw milk, although this value is decreasing, owing in large part to the European Union food safety law passed in 2012, which makes cheesemakers directly and criminally responsible in cases of food poisoning. Raw milk is required of some PDO cheeses, but not for all of them. The forty-five PDO cheeses represent in volume about 190,000 tons of cheeses or about 10 percent of the whole production. If ewe's milk and goat's milk cheeses are specifically

This vintage poster by the French illustrator Benjamin Rabier shows an advertisement in German for La Vache qui Rit (The Laughing Cow), the first processed cheese packaged in single-serving portions, wrapped in an aluminum foil, and sold under a trademark (1921).

considered, 22 percent of their production is under the protection of a PDO. The French cheese industry is a highly dynamic sector in which a few corporate giants operate alongside a large number (about three thousand) of farmstead and small artisanal producers or cooperatives. See BEL GROUP; LACTALIS; SAVENCIA FROMAGE & DAIRY; FARMSTEAD; and ARTISANAL.

The second half of the twentieth century saw the rapid industrialization of cheese production and the spread of mass-market retailing in France. Traditional terroir productions coexisted with this new massive industrial production and marketing. The industrial sector continues to develop new technologies for cheesemaking, such as ultrafiltration. See INDUSTRIALIZATION and ULTRAFILTRATION. Starting in the 1970s both artisanal and industrial sectors of the cheese industry have worked with dairy scientists. This synergy, along with a strong food safety system and transmission of customary knowledge, contributes to the generally high quality of cheeses sold in France.

France has the highest rates of cheese consumption in the world, with 57 pounds (26 kilograms) per person consumed each year. Cheese in France is most often enjoyed on its own, served on a cheese tray (64 percent of consumption), and accompanied by bread and various wines, which makes for infinite pairings. The early nineteenth-century gastronome Jean-Anthelme Brillat-Savarin famously aphorized the importance of cheese to the French meal: "Un dessert sans fromage est une belle à qui il manque un oeil" ["A dessert without cheese is like a beautiful woman with an eye missing"].

Cheese is also deeply associated with French gastronomy and features as a key ingredient, both raw and cooked, in many recipes for salads, gratins, soufflés, etc. (26 percent of cheese is consumed in this way). Androuët has assembled 1,096 French recipes involving cheese. Traditional cheese-based recipes from Savoie contribute greatly to French gastronomy and to winter meals, in particular: for example, fondue savoyarde, the famous Raclette, and tartiflette. See FONDUE; RACLETTE; and TARTIFLETTE. Another region, Aveyron, in the center of France, gave the world the unique aligot, a fabulous mixture of potatoes and young Tomme cheese melted together. See ALIGOT. The central place of cheese surely contributed to the 2010 addition of the "gastronomic meal of the French people" to UNESCO's representative list of humanity's intangible cultural heritage.

The diversity of cheese in France can be traced to a conjunction of geographic, climatic, historic, social, religious, and political factors. Ruminant breeding has occurred in the region since prehistoric times (around 8500 B.C.E.), with local breeds adapted to the diversity of its geography, geology, and climate. From oceanic coasts to inland mountainous areas, a trip from the north of France to the south, and from the east to Brittany in the west (only 621 miles [1,000 kilometers] in either case), reveals that cheeses cannot be made in the same way in these different climatic and geological settings. Cultural history is equally significant; monks, farmwomen, and kings have all played decisive roles in diversifying and reinforcing French cheese production.

Because of its Roman Catholic roots, France has been home to hundreds of abbeys run by monks. Monks, ruled by the Rules of St. Benedict, were told to avoid idleness and that manual labor was equal to prayer and study. As a way of remaining active, as well as making abbeys self-sustaining, monks began to develop cheesemaking techniques and recipes. An example of this is Munster cheese, which was

Brie de Meaux, a soft cow's milk cheese with a white mold, is one of the great French raw-milk cheeses.

created in 855 in an Alsace monastery; its name means "abbey church." It is emblematic of the role of monks during the Middle Ages in preserving and optimizing cheese varieties. See MUNSTER and MONASTIC CHEESEMAKING.

Historically cheeses were also used as tithes that local cheesemakers would pay to the abbeys. Women, the agents of milking and dairy processing at the farm level, were often very inventive in optimizing their resources and minimizing their labor. Kings, who appreciated cheeses as emblematic of the bounty of their domain, politically supported their development by edict when they felt it necessary. In 1411 King Charles VI granted a letter of patent to the inhabitants of Roquefort, who refined cheeses in their cellars and ever since have retained a monopoly over this practice. Charles VI's decree was confirmed by all successive kings and provided the basis of Roquefort's recognition in 1925 as the first AOC cheese. See CHARLES VI; ROQUEFORT; and APPELLATION D'ORIGINE CONTRÔLÉE.

Specific regions of France have developed their own types of cheese based on the environmental and historical factors. For example, in Normandy the wet and mild maritime climate ensures the presence of grass and thus milk all year long. There it is not necessary to keep (that is, to ripen) cheeses for a long time. This led to a tradition of soft cheeses such as Brie and Neufchâtel. Upon tasting Brie in 774, King Charlemagne declared it one of the most delicious foods he had ever tasted. Several centuries later, under Louis XIV, each week fifty carts left Meaux to deliver Brie to Versailles. Also in Normandy legend has it that in 1791, in the midst of the French Revolution, a farmwoman named Marie Harel devel-

oped a recipe given to her by a fleeing priest, thereby making the first Camembert; what is certain is that Harel, working with her sons, launched a cheese dynasty that secured Camembert's wider fame. When winter comes in Normandy, aging times are lengthened, creating cheeses such as Livarot, with a washed rind described as early as 1236. To supply urban Paris, such soft cheeses were delivered only partially ripened; ripening continued in the calcaire (limestone) cellar of the town, a practice that still continues beneath some of the famous cheese shops today. See BRIE DE MEAUX; NEUFCHÂTEL; HAREL, MARIE; CAMEMBERT DE NORMANDIE; and LIVAROT.

By contrast the farmers of the Alps struggled to produce milk. Under the challenging living conditions and limitations of seasonal milk production in the mountains, the first producers' cooperatives, or fruitières, were created in the Alps in the thirteenth century. The dairy farmers of Alpine villages in the Jura pool their daily collection of milk to make a large format cooked-curd cheese that is easy to transport to the valley, easy to share among the farmers, and can be kept for several years. This social innovation led to the creation of France's largest cheeses, including Beaufort, Comté, and Abondance. See ABON-DANCE; ALP CHEESEMAKING; BEAUFORT; and COMTÉ.

The Mediterranean climate of southern France, with its sparse vegetation and hot, dry weather, is more hospitable to ewes and goats than to cows. The cheeses of this region, such as Pelardon or Banon, are smaller in size and can be produced independently by isolated cheesemakers. See BANON.

French cheeses are the fruits of their terroir, emerging from the confluence of local weather, soil, geography, and human inventiveness—plus the social organization required today to protect and valorize culinary custom and local biodiversity. See TERROIR. The long history of France saw the crossing of these variables at different times and places to generate the exceptional diversity we enjoy today.

See also HAUTE-SAVOIE; LOIRE VALLEY; and NORMANDY.

Boisard, Pierre. *Camembert: A National Myth*. Translated by Richard Miller. Berkeley: University of California Press, 2003.

"Cheese Library." Fromages.com. http://www .fromages.com/en/encyclopedie.

Dalby, Andrew. *Cheese: A Global History*. London: Reaktion, 2009.

Delfosse, Claire. *La France fromagère, 1850–1990*. Paris: BH, la Boutique de l'Histoire, 2007.

Drouin, Dominique. *Une bibliographie fromagère: 1550–2009*. 4th ed. Nantes, France: D. Drouin, 2009.

Lindon, Raymond. *Le livre de l'amateur de fromages*. Paris: Editions Robert Laffont, 1961.

"1096 Recettes Androuet." Androuet.com. http://androuet.com/recettes-fromage.html.

Sylvie Lortal

fresh cheeses include a wide variety of cheeses with only one common characteristic, the fact that there is no ripening involved. Most fresh cheeses are not pressed and therefore have higher moisture and less fat than other varieties. Acid-coagulated fresh cheeses include (i) cheese made by acidification of skim milk (with cream added or not after the curd is made) such as North American cottage cheese and European quark types; (ii) cheese made out of milk or cream by acidification with starter cultures such as chèvre, cream cheese, and Neufchâtel; (iii) heat-acid precipitated types including paneer (India), some traditional versions of queso blanco (Latin American), Italian ricotta and Greek Manouri made with cheese whey as the main ingredient, and Italian mascarpone made from cream. Rennet-coagulated fresh cheeses include most Latin American white cheeses (queso fresco), many French cheeses, such as Vache Frais and fromage blanc, queijo fresco in Portugal, and Robiola d'Alba in Italy. It is important to note that according to French legislation the term "fromage frais" is reserved for lactic acid–coagulated cheese that contains living lactic acid bacteria at the time of consumption.

In general fresh cheeses are soft cheeses with high moisture content, which contributes to their short shelf life. See SHELF LIFE. Therefore, most fresh cheeses are commercialized within the region they are produced. Each country has its own varieties of fresh cheese. In Great Britain ancient varieties of fresh cheese include crowdie (similar to cottage cheese), Colwick, and the spreadable York. French cuisine includes many fresh cheeses, which are served at the end of a meal or with fresh fruit, such as fromage blanc and fromage à la crème, which is kneaded with cream and sugar before hooping.

The most famous fresh cheese in Italy is ricotta, a cheese made by heating and acidification of whey obtained during the manufacture of many cheeses.

Not less known are fresh mozzarella, bocconcini (both pasta filata types), and smooth and creamy mascarpone. In North America the American Cheese Society includes in the fresh unripened cheese category (A) cheese curds, mascarpone and cream cheese, cow's milk ricotta and fromage frais, fromage blanc, and quark, with three subcategories to include cheese made out of other species' milk, one of the best known fresh cheeses from the region See CREAM CHEESE; CHEESE CURDS; MASCARPONE; MOZZARELLA; QUARK; and RICOTTA.

In general fresh cheeses are not pressed and never ripened, but we also need to consider fresh versions of ripened cheeses. For example, from the French-speaking Canadian province of Quebec we have Cheddar cheese curds sold at the checkout counters of variety stores and gas stations and used to make poutine. Other examples are White Stilton from England and unripened Neufchâtel from France, one of the best known fresh cheeses from the region. See QUEBEC; POUTINE; STILTON; and NEUFCHÂTEL.

See also CHÈVRE; MANOURI; and PANEER.

American Cheese Society. "Judging & Competition 2015 Categories." http://www.cheesejudging.org/wp-content/uploads/2015/03/2015-Categories-FINAL-Revised-2015-03-03.pdf.

Schulz-Collins, D., and B. Senge. "Acid- and Acid/Rennet-Curd Cheeses Part A: Quark, Cream Cheese and Related Varieties." In *Cheese: Chemistry, Physics, and Microbiology*, vol. 2: *Major Cheese Groups*, edited by Patrick Fox, et al., pp. 302–328. New York: Elsevier, 2004.

Arthur Hill and Mary Ann Ferrer

frico is a pan-fried dish from Friuli-Venezia in north-eastern Italy, typically cooked with the local Alp-style cheese, montasio. Friulians make two different kinds of frico—one delicate and crispy, the other soft and thick. For crispy frico, a thin layer of grated montasio is melted in an oiled skillet and cooked until it forms a lacy, crunchy wafer of cheese that shatters delectably on the palate. The more substantial version, frico con patate, is similar to a dense omelet, made with grated cheese, potatoes, and onion. Three different ages of montasio are used, depending on the style of frico being prepared. Montasio fresco is ripened for 30 to 45 days and has a creamier texture; it produces a runny, soft frico. Montasio semistagionato, aged 90 to 120 days, has a sharper flavor and less moisture. It gives frico a crust, but with a tender and cheesy middle. Two-year-old wheels of montasio stagionato have a distinct butterscotch-like flavor and hard texture that yields the best crispy frico.

As regional Italian cuisine spread throughout Europe and North America in the late 1990s, so did frico. Particularly the wafer-like version, adored for its lacy, tuile-like texture that could be shaped, while still warm, into curls or cups. Western chefs appropriated the frico concept but substituted more available cheeses, such as aged Asiago and Parmigiano Reggiano. They also improvised an oven-baked version, heating small rounds of grated cheese on cookie sheets to produce quick bite-size batches of fricos. Today, frico are a fixture in modern cooking, served plain or spiced as a snack or used as a savory garnish.

Clark, Melissa. "How to Make Frico." *Diner's Journal*, 21 September 2012. http://dinersjournal.blogs. nytimes.com/2012/09/21/video-how-to-make-frico.
"Frico with Potatoes and Montasio." Lydia's Italy. http:// lidiasitaly.com/recipes/frico-potatoes-montasio-cheese.
"What Is Frico?" MontasioCheese.com. http:// montasiocheese.com/About%20Frico.

Elaine Khosrova

fromage fort, or "strong cheese," is a preparation of leftover cheese common throughout France and in the Catalan region of Spain, where it is known as tupi. Traditionally fromage fort is made with white wine, garlic, and herbs, then aged to encourage

Fromage fort, French for "strong cheese," is a preparation of leftover cheese common throughout France and in the Catalan region of Spain. © REGAN76

fermentation, though recipes vary widely by region. The name refers to the spread's powerful aroma and flavor, derived not only from uncooked garlic but from the combination of cheeses such as over-ripe bloomies and blues, as well as potency derived from bacterial fermentation and maturation.

Fromage fort originated as an economical way to utilize cheese scraps and ends at home and in cheese shops. Historically some French families dedicated a special vessel to its preparation, which would have been imbued with bacteria from leftover cheese for years or decades. Today fromage fort is more often enjoyed unaged, its pungency coming from the choice of cheeses and additions.

Regionally, recipes vary, depending on the local cheese types, the alcohol used (besides wine, some recipes call for cider, beer, apple brandy, marc, and more), adjuncts (garlic, oil, herbs, vinegar, broth), and how long the spread is aged, if at all. Some recipes call for an extended fermentation period, hastened by additions of whey or broth, after which a spirit or fortified wine would be added to halt any bacterial behavior. French cheese expert Pierre Androuët gives recipe variations from Lyon, Beaujolais, Lorraine, Provence, and more, all of which share a "forte odeur" and "saveur piquant."

Jacques Pépin, the noted French chef, is a devotee of fromage fort and grew up eating a version that combined a variety of cheeses, white wine, and garlic, and left to marinate for up to two weeks.

See also COOKING WITH RINDS.

Androuët, Pierre. *Guide du Fromage*. Paris: Stock, 1971.
Caldwell, Gianaclis. "Comeback Curds: Make Fromage Fort at Home." *Culture Magazine*, 3 December 2013. http://culturecheesemag.com/diy/fromage-fort.
Rance, Patrick. *The French Cheese Book*. London: Macmillan, 1989.

Sam Chapple-Sokol

Fromagerie Beaufils, a cheese shop on rue de Belleville, Paris, since 2011 has been owned by Christophe Lesoin, a true supporter of the biodiversity of cheese. Although occasionally working for Fromagerie Escudier, a cheese shop in Boulogne-Billancourt, his main career was as a consultant engineer. In 2009, while working on a project in the United States, he decided that his future lay with cheese and he set about looking for a shop to take over in

Paris. With his cheese background he had witnessed the loss of certain cheeses over the years, the trend of fewer and fewer producers using raw milk, and the loss of historical starter cultures. Lesoin set about making his shop a focal point to showcase and sell the best of traditional farmhouse cheese.

Core to Fromagerie Beaufils' values is an appreciation of the importance of microbial populations of raw milk, husbandry, bacteria and molds and their vital role in cheesemaking. Dialogue and contact with the cheesemakers and affineurs whose cheeses it sells are equally important. To better understand the cheeses selected and sold, and to ensure they are sold at their best, Lesoin and his team have constructed several maturation rooms under the shop in Paris, including one dedicated to goat's milk cheese. In 2014 Lesoin and his team opened their second Paris shop on rue Cadet, and their dedication to working with the best producers continues from strength to strength with cheeses sourced not only from France but also from the British Isles, Switzerland, Italy, Spain, the Netherlands, Greece, and the United States.

See also FARMSTEAD and FRANCE.

Fromagerie Beaufils. http://www.fromagerie-beaufils .com.
Laske, Karl, and Elsa Casalegno. "Les secrets du fromager." In *Les Cartels du lait*, edited by Elsa Casalegno, et al., pp. 333–339. Paris: Editions Don Quichotte, 2016.

Jay Butcher

Fromagerie Fermier is a Japanese specialty cheese store founded by Rumiko Honma in 1986 in the Atago district of Tokyo. Today Fromagerie Fermier specializes in selling cheeses from France, Italy, Spain, and other European countries, as well as other gourmet products.

Ms. Honma is the mastermind behind Fromagerie Fermier. She started working in cheese in the 1980s, after returning to France from a trip to Europe. She was a pioneer in bringing high quality cheeses to a country with a small dairy culture. In addition to running her company, Honma conducts tours of farms in Europe for Japanese travelers and maintains a strong working relationship with cheese producers in France. She also began a cheese specialty seasonal email magazine, *Aristeeas*, in 1991.

There are three Fromagerie Fermier branches in Tokyo and a fourth one in Sapporo. The Atago location features a small café, where customers can order cheese boards and drinks, or an espresso. Their second location in the Shibuya Department Store caters to an upscale clientele in one of the iconic food halls of the capital city. A third location in Tokyo is located in the Variety Market in the famous Shinagawa train station. Fromagerie Fermier opened its first store outside of Tokyo in Sapporo in 2007. That branch relocated in 2010 to the Maruyama area, west of the city. All the branches host tasting courses and lectures for local cheese aficionados. In addition to their retail locations, Fromagerie Fermier sells wholesale cheeses to hotels and restaurants in the city, and has a mail order service that delivers cheese to buyers in other areas of Japan.

See also CHEESEMONGER and JAPAN.

Fromagerie Fermier. https://www.fermier.co.jp.

Carlos Yescas

fruity flavor is associated with the presence of fruit-like notes on the flavor characteristics of the cheese (e.g., pineapple, grapefruit, berries, and apples). In most cases, the term fruity refers to a flavor defect, often associated with fermented fruity notes due to the presence of yeast or other unwanted microflora due to hygiene issues or high moisture content. However, in some cheeses the term fruity may describe a positive characteristic associated with a unique pleasant fruity flavor (like the characteristic pineapple flavor notes of Parmigiano Reggiano cheese, or the complex fruity notes of some alpine cheeses). For cheeses like Cheddar, Colby, or Jack, fruity notes are associated with an unpleasant flavor characteristic, often reminiscent of fresh pineapple or fermenting apples.

As Cheddar ages, the fruity characteristic will typically dominant the cheese profile, resulting in a perceived "flat" flavor. A weak body characteristic often accompanies this flavor defect, often associated with high moisture cheeses and low salt moisture cheeses.

The fruity flavor defect is associated with higher levels of ethyl hexanoate and ethyl butyrate esters than in Cheddar without the defect. These higher levels are responsible for the distinct odor present in Cheddar with the fruity defect (Bills et al., 1965).

The fruity flavor can be detected as early as thirty to sixty days of aging. In a 2002 study by the Wisconsin Center for Dairy Research, 2 percent of retail mild Cheddar evaluated displayed the fruity flavor defect (Smukowski et al., 2003). Since fruity notes become more pronounced with age, once detected, a savvy manufacturer or grader will formulate plans to remove the cheese from long aging programs. Assigning the cheese to programs such as mild or medium is a way to utilize the Cheddar in a profile where the consumer will only notice the defect under critical evaluation.

See also FLAVOR and FLAVOR WHEEL.

Bills, D. D., M. E. Morgan, L. M. Libbey, et al. "Identification of Compounds Responsible for Fruity Flavor Defects of Experimental Cheddar Cheeses." *Journal of Dairy Science* 48, no. 9 (1965): 1168–1173.
Smukowski, M., Y. Ping, and W. L. Wendorff. "Cheese Defects in U.S. Graded Cheese." *Dairy Pipeline* 15, no. 3 (2003), 1–6.

Craig Gile

The **Fulbe** (as they call themselves) are a traditionally caste-stratified, Muslim pastoral people living across a wide area of sub-Saharan West Africa, from Mauritania to Cameroon, numbering as many as 20 million. Speaking Fulfude as their primary language, they are also known as Fulani (in English, borrowed from the Hausa) and Peul (in French, borrowed from the Wolof).

Many Fulbe groups are semi-sedentary, practicing a mixed economy of agriculture and transhumant cattle herding, while others practice nomadic pastoralism, moving with their herds of cattle following patterns of rainfall, in search of resulting natural pastures. See TRANSHUMANCE and PASTORALISM. The pastoralist economy is based on cattle breeding, trade, and the production and sale of dairy products. For the Fulbe, cattle represent wealth, both as a primary mechanism of savings and as a source of prestige. Dairying—milking cows and processing milk for subsistence and trade—provides an important source of income. As is common under pastoralism, a gendered division of labor organizes the economic activities of the Fulbe. Cattle herding and trading fall to men and boys, while women and girls are directly engaged in processing milk into fermented foods, including cheese. Milking generally falls under the domain of women and girls (although increased sedentarism has, in some instances, led to the masculinization of milking). Although women and men work in distinct spheres of operation, their productive labor is complementary. Even when men own the cattle, the milking rights bestowed to wives grants women the ability to earn a cash income through direct marketing of their dairy products in the cities of West Africa. Fulbe women control the income earned by selling dairy products. In the early 1990s an estimated 90 percent of the milk processed in Nigeria (Africa's most populous nation) was "handled by several hundred thousand Fulani women in the informal sector" (Waters-Bayer 1994, p. 87). See GENDER.

The Fulbe breed and graze cows in large herds, without feeding supplemental grains or stored forages. Milking occurs in the open, in the mornings only. Milk is generally collected in a calabash (fashioned from an emptied and dried gourd) and may be consumed fresh or fermented. A fermented skimmed milk product, *nono*, is made into a nutritious drink served with boiled millet or sorghum (*fura*). Some 70 percent of milk is fermented and consumed as *nono*. Less common but more lucrative products include butter and cheese. Butter, produced in wooden churns, is sold both as a food and a hair-care product. In some regions Fulbe women make a fresh cheese, Wagashi or wara. See WAGASHI.

Under pressure by West African governments and the World Bank, and amid drought and competition for resources with other pastoral groups in the region, since the mid-twentieth century the Fulbe have become increasingly sedentary. By the mid-1990s only about one-third of the Fulbe lived a nomadic or semi-nomadic lifestyle, practicing transhumance from a base settlement. See TRANSHUMANCE.

Ndambi, O. A., et al. "Milk Production amongst Fulani Grazers in the Western Highlands of Cameroon: Constraints and Development Perspectives." *Livestock Research for Rural Development* 20 (2008): article 13. http://www.lrrd.org/lrrd20/1/ndam20013.htm.
Shehu, D. J., and W. A. Hassan. "Women in Dairying in the African Savanna: Their Contribution to Agro-Pastoral Household Income in the Dry Northwest of Nigeria." *Nomadic Peoples* 36–37 (1995): 53–64.
Waters-Bayer, Ann. "Studying Pastoral Women's Knowledge in Milk Processing and Marketing—For Whose Empowerment?" *Agriculture and Human Values* 11 (1994): 85–95.

Heather Paxson

functional properties of cheese are demonstrated by how it is used extensively in the home and catering sector as an ingredient in culinary dishes such as quiche, lasagna, cheesecake, toasted sandwiches, omelets, sauces, or gratins. Cheese is also used as an ingredient in the industrial sector in the manufacture of various assembled food products (e.g., frozen pizza, frozen cheeseburgers, frozen quiche), co-extruded foods (e.g., cheese-filled meatballs and sausages), formulated foods (e.g., gratins, prepared meals, dried soups), and cheese ingredients (e.g., cheese powders, dried cheese). In these applications, the cheese is required to perform one or more functions, such as the ability of unheated cream cheese to spread on crackers, molten mozzarella to form strings, or paneer to retain its shape when heated in casserole dishes.

The functional properties refer to those attributes that enable the cheese to serve certain functions, while the functionality denotes the suitability of the cheese in performing the composite of functions required in different usage applications. The functional properties contribute both to the preparation of these cheese-containing foods (e.g., uncooked pizza) and to the sensory properties of the final products (cooked pizza). The combination of functional properties and their intensities (e.g., low or high flow or fluidity when heated) depend on the usage application.

The functional properties may be categorized into size-reduction and cooking properties. Size-reduction properties refer to how the cheese reacts when subjected to stresses and strains, for example, in commercial operations involving portioning, slicing,

Table 1. Functional properties of cheese

Functional property	Description
Unheated cheese	
-Shreddability	Ability to cut cleanly into shreds of uniform dimensions (typically cylindrically shaped; 2.5 centimeters long) that are resistant to fracture (forming curd dust), sticking, matting or clumping when stored in bins or retail packs
- Sliceability	Ability to be cut cleanly into thin slices without fracturing or crumbling or sticking to cutting implement, and of cheese slices to resist breakage or fracture at edges, undergo a high level of bending before breaking, resist drying-out and curling at ends on moderate exposure to atmosphere, and to exhibit a high degree of peelability (e.g., from stacks of slice-on-slice in food service)
- Grate-ability	Ability to fracture easily into small hard particles, that flow freely and resist matting during shearing, crushing, fluidization, or piling
- Spreadability	Ability to spread easily when sheared
- Crumbliness	Ability of cheese to fracture (break) easily into small irregularly shaped pieces, for example when rubbed between fingers
Heated Cheese	
- Meltability	Ability to soften on heating
- Flowability	Ability of cheese (shredded, grated, or sliced) to spread or flow on heating
- Flow resistance	Ability of cheese to resist flow or spread, and to retain original shape and dimensions on heating
- Stretchability or stringiness	Ability of heated cheese to form strings and/or sheets when extended
- Oiling-off (surface sheen)	Ability of cheese to express a moderate level of free oil on heating, to impart gloss and succulence to the molten cheese mass
- Fluidity	Ability of cheese to attain desired fluidity on heating, and not to congeal too rapidly on cooling.
- Blistering	Ability of cheese to display a moderate to low level of blistering in some applications

shredding, dicing, grating, or crumbling. These properties are critical in the primary stages of preparation of various dishes (e.g., the ability of mozzarella to form clean, nonsticky shreds that can be uniformly distributed over the pizza base, the ability of feta to crumble easily into salads or Parmesan to grate for lasagna). The cooking properties (also referred to as melt properties) characterize how the cheese reacts when heated, as in baking, grilling, or frying. The heated cheese may be required to melt, flow, stretch, brown, blister, oil-off, or stretch to varying degrees depending on the application.

Affecting the Functionality of Cheese

The functionality of cheese is affected by many factors including the following:

- Macrostructure and microstructure, which represent the arrangement of, and attractions between curd particles comprising the molded cheese loaf.
- The microstructure within individual curd particles that represents the spatial distribution of, and the types and levels of intramolecular and intermolecular attractions between the compositional components (e.g., casein, minerals, fat, serum) that make up the cheese.
- The composition of the cheese, which affects:
  - The concentration of the casein network, the structural fabric
  - The levels of calcium and calcium phosphate, which are major components in cross-linking the casein molecules into a network where they essentially behave as glue
  - The levels of fat and moisture, which act as lubricants on fracture surfaces of the casein matrix during size reduction operations and heating
- The level of acidity of the cheese, as measured by pH, which affects the degree of solubility of the calcium phosphate, and its effectiveness as a glue.
- The properties of the serum phase (e.g., pH, salt, temperature), which affects the degree of hydration and solubility of the casein and its ability to form an intact coherent network.
- The extent of cheese maturation, which influences the degree of hydrolysis or degradation of casein into peptides (by proteolytic enzymes within

the cheese) and thus, the strength of the casein network and its ability to withstand stresses inflicted during size reduction operations and cooking.

Both the type and intensity of functional properties differ markedly with respect to cheese variety, owing to differences in manufacturing procedure, composition, and degree of proteolysis. Likewise, intravariety variation in the functional properties can be notable because of differences in composition, pH, and level of maturation.

Guinee, T. P. "Protein in Cheese and Cheese Products: Structure-Function Relationships." In *Advanced Dairy Chemistry*, Vol. 1: *Protein*, Part B. 4th ed. edited by P. L. H. McSweeney and S. A. O'Mahony. New York: Kluwer Academic/Plenum Publishers, 2015.
Guinee, T. P., and K. N. Kilcawley. "Cheese as an Ingredient." In *Cheese Chemistry, Physics, and Microbiology*, Vol. 2: *Major Cheese Groups*, 3d ed., edited by P. F. Fox, P. L. H. McSweeney, T. M. Cogan, et al., pp. 395–428. Oxford: Elsevier Academic, 2004.
Kindstedt, P. S. "Effect of Manufacturing Factors, Composition and Proteolysis on the Functional Characteristics of Mozzarella Cheese." *Critical Reviews in Food Science and Nutrition* 33, no. 2 (1993): 167–187.

Timothy P. Guinee

fungi, including both single-celled yeasts and multicellular molds, are eukaryotic microbes that are commonly found on surface-ripened cheeses and can also grow internally in the paste of cheeses. Unlike plants that use photosynthesis, fungi cannot produce their own food and most fungi rely on decomposition of materials in their environment to provide food. In cheesemaking, fungi use the fats, proteins, and sugars in cheese as their primary food source. One of the key defining characteristics of fungi is the presence of the compound chitin in their cell walls. Filamentous fungi (commonly called molds) produce networks of hyphae (collectively called a mycelium). See FILAMENTOUS FUNGI; HYPHAE; and MYCELIA. Yeasts produce individual cells and most cheese yeasts reproduce asexually by budding off new cells. Some fungi can form complex fruiting structures such as mushrooms, but these fungi are not found in the cheese production environment. Most cheese fungi reproduce asexually, with the rapid production of mycelium followed by spore production in filamentous fungi and budding to form a parent and daughter cell in yeasts.

Mycologists have divided the fungi into a handful of taxonomic groups, called phyla, and the main cheese-associated fungi are found in the phyla Ascomycota, the Basidiomycota, and the Zygomycota. Most fungi that are used in cheesemaking come from the Ascomycota, including yeasts (*Geotrichum* or *Galactomyces, Kluyveromyces, Debaryomyces, Yarrowia,* and *Candida*) as well as quintessential cheese molds such as *Penicillium*. Other important groups of cheese fungi in the Ascomycota include molds that colonize the rinds of cheeses, including *Lecanicillium, Fusarium, Scopulariopsis, Acremonium, Sporendonema,* and *Chrysosporium*. See GEOTRICHUM CANDIDUM; DEBARYOMYCES; PENICILLIUM; and SCOPULARIOPSIS.

A few important cheese-associated fungi fall outside of the Ascomycota. In the Zygomycota, several species of *Mucor* are commonly found in the dairy environment with a typical gray-brown cat fur appearance ("poil de chat" in France) on the surface of cheeses. In some parts of Europe (especially France) these *Mucor* species are actually inoculated onto the surface of natural-rind cheeses, but most commonly *Mucor* species are considered spoilage molds. See MUCOR. In the Basidiomycota, a group of fungi that includes most of the iconic mushrooms, pink or red yeasts are the most important cheese-associated fungi. *Rhodosporidium* is a pink yeast that is sometimes used as a starter culture in washed-rind cheeses (often sold with the name R2R).

Fungi play diverse functions in the production of cheese, ranging from development of characteristic flavors and textures, as well as producing enzymes necessary for cheese production. One function is the protection of cheeses from undesired contaminants. Desirable molds can quickly colonize the cheese surface and can provide a thick layer that protects the cheese from unwanted molds. These surface colonizing molds can also contribute flavors and aromas through lipolysis (fat breakdown) and proteolysis (protein breakdown). See LIPOLYSIS and PROTEOLYSIS. Fungi can also grow on the inside of cheeses, such as *Penicillium roqueforti*, which creates the blue veins in blue cheese. Yeasts play important roles in rind development of surface-ripened cheeses. Yeasts rapidly colonize the surface of these cheeses in early stages of development and decrease the acidity of the cheese surface. As the acidity decreases, acid-sensitive bacteria that play important roles in flavor

production, such as *Brevibacterium*, can proliferate. Some molds are used to produce microbial rennet, proteases with a similar function to those in rennet isolated from calf stomachs. These microbial rennets are often produced using *Rhizomucor miehei* (formerly known as *Mucor miehei*). See BREVIBACTERIUM LINENS and RENNET.

Despite their many beneficial roles, fungi can be the cause of some of the most economically devastating and difficult to control defects in cheesemaking. *Penicillium* species with blue or green spores are common contaminants of cheeses. The mold *Scopulariopsis* can bore into the paste of many long-aged natural-rind cheeses, such as clothbound Cheddars, leading to brown discoloration in the paste. *Cladosporium* species can cause black discoloration on natural-rind cheeses and cause so-called "thread mold defect" in plastic-wrapped Cheddar cheeses. The pink yeast *Rhodotorula mucilaginosa* commonly colonizes the surfaces of bloomy-rind cheeses, leading to discoloration of the white rind.

Fungi in cheesemaking come from a variety of sources including industrial starter cultures that are added to the milk during cheese production, raw milk, and the aging environment. A variety of fungal ripening cultures are available, usually in a freeze-dried form. These cultures are added to the milk used for cheesemaking, sprayed onto the cheese surface, or added to wash solutions used during the aging process. In raw-milk cheeses, the milk can serve as a source of the fungal cultures that colonize the cheese, particularly for yeasts, which can be abundant in raw milk. If the cheese is aged in an environment that mimics a cave environment (high humidity and cool), the cave will quickly accumulate a high concentration of molds that can colonize the cheese surface. See CAVE.

To control the growth of fungi in the cheese production environment, cheese producers can use chemical, environmental, and biological controls. Natamycin is a widespread antifungal that is commonly added to large-scale and some artisan cheese to prevent growth of spoilage molds. This antifungal is produced by the bacterium *Streptomyces* and it inhibits fungal growth by binding to a compound only found in fungi (ergosterol). One of the best ways to prevent fungal spoilage of cheese is to produce and age cheese in a highly controlled and very clean environment, where the migration of fungal spores is limited. Cheese producers can also use the actions of other fungi to fight off undesirable species. Some strains of white *Penicillium camemberti* have been developed that decrease the growth of contaminating molds such as *Mucor*.

The health impacts of cheese fungi have been fairly well characterized, in large part due to concerns about mycotoxin production by some fungi. Reports of confirmed fungal allergies or mycotoxin-associated food poisoning from cheese products are rare. While many individuals may be allergic to penicillin, starter cultures of *Penicillium* used for the production of cheeses are generally screened for the production of secondary metabolites such as penicillin. Some molds, such as the ripening culture *Penicillium nalgiovense*, and some contaminant species have been shown to produce penicillin. Production of mycotoxins, such as cyclopiazonic acid, is also carefully screened in mold starter cultures, although some contaminant molds, such as *Penicillium commune*, have been shown to produce significant quantities of these mycotoxins. Some individuals may experience allergies to fungi in general and several reports in the scientific literature describe hypersensitivity to fungi developed in cheese workers. See CHEESEMAKER'S LUNG; MYCOTOXINS; and PATHOGENS.

Ropars, Jeanne, et al. "A Taxonomic and Ecological Overview of Cheese Fungi." *International Journal of Food Microbiology* 155, no. 3 (2012): 199–210.

Webster, John, and Roland Weber. *Introduction to Fungi.* Cambridge, U.K.: Cambridge University Press, 2007.

Benjamin Wolfe

G

Galotyri, widely considered to be one of Greece's oldest varieties of cheese, is a soft curd cheese produced on mainland Greece in the northern regions of Epirus and Thessaly. Although it is now also manufactured industrially, Galotyri is a simple cheese, one that is moderately easy to produce. It was historically, and remains today, a handmade affair typically produced by shepherds and home cheesemakers.

Until recently, Galotyri was typically available to purchase only in or near the communities in which it was crafted; recently, however, industrial production of the cheese has made it more widely available throughout much of Greece. Galotyri is produced from sheep's milk, or from a combination of sheep's and goat's milk, from animals that are free ranging and that feed on the wild grasses and herbs of the regions' mountain pastures. The cheese is made both with and without rennet and often with the addition of yogurt culture. It is lightly salted and it is aged in wooden barrels or cloth sacks for at least two months before going to market. There, it is typically sold in round ceramic or plastic containers. Creamy, pungent, and with a slightly sour flavor reminiscent of yogurt, Galotyri is easily spreadable and is commonly served with bread as a table cheese. Galotyri was named a protected designation of origin (PDO) cheese by the European Commission in 1996.

See also GREECE.

DOOR list. European Commission. http://ec.europa.eu/agriculture/quality/door/list.html.

Alexis Marie Adams

gamalost

See SOUR SKIMMED-MILK CHEESES.

Gamonedo is a rustic, Spanish protected designation of origin (PDO) cheese from the Asturian region, in the northwest of the country. Gamonedo cheese is made in two villages, Cangas de Onís and the nearby village of Onís bordering the mountain range "Picos de Europa." Most of the cheese is made using raw cow's, sheep's, and goat's milk, or any combination. The cows are Friesian, Asturiana de los Valles, and Pardo Alpina breeds or crossbreeds of these; the sheep are Lacha, Carranzana, and Milschalfe breeds or crossbreeds of these; and the goats are Alpine-Pyrenean, Picos de Europa, Murciano-Granadina, and Saanen breeds or crossbreeds of these. The cheese is made all year in the valley called "Gamoneu del Valle" or "Gamonedo del Valle"; however, 10 percent of the production is made by a few producers in huts located in mountain passes between June and September. This variety is called "Gamonedo del Puerto" or "Gamoneu del Puerto." The different flora of the two regions ("Puerto" and "Valley") give a different flavor for each cheese. Examples of Gamonedo cheese producers are Covadonga making del Puerto, and L'Arbyal creating Gracelia and Rucuesto the Natalia.

The make process begins with the milk being heated between 75 °F and 86 °F (24 °C and 30°C), rennet and enzymes are then added, and allowed to set for an hour. The vat is then cut into curds between 0.2 to 0.6 inches (5 to 15 millimeters), the curd drains for ninety minutes and then is dipped, packed into hoops, and in some instances pressed. The cheese is removed from hoops, salted on top and bottom surfaces, and smoked over heather, ash, beech wood, chestnut, or oak for ten to twelve days before ripening. The sizes of the wheels vary in size from 3 to 6 inches (8 to 15 centimeters) high, 4 to 12 inches (10 to 30 centimeters) in diameter, and weigh between 18 ounces and 16 pounds (0.5 and 7 kilograms).

The cheese is ripened for a minimum of sixty days up to five months in limestone caves, cellars, or ripening chambers at temperatures of 46–53°F (8–12°C) with a relative humidity of 85–95 percent. The rind is inedible and varied in color from linen to reddish brown hues created during the smoking and maturation. The paste is white toward yellow in color, with small caves with sporadic blooms of *Penicillium roqueforti*, although heavier streaks exist at the rind. The rinds are cleaned to balance its flavor, which is buttery and slightly nutty with a hint of hazelnut, smokiness, and pungency.

See also SPAIN.

Cheese from Spain. http://www.cheesefromspain.com/spanish-cheese-guide/do-gamonedo.
Consejo Regulador de la DOP Gamonedo. http://www.quesogamonedo.com.
Cook's Info. http://www.cooksinfo.com/gamonedo-cheese.
McCalman, Max, and David Gibbons. *Mastering Cheese: Lessons for Connoisseurship from a Maître Fromager.* New York: Clarkson Potter, 2009.

David Gremmels

gaperon, from the Auvergne region, is noticeable among French cow's milk cheeses for its fat, round base that ends in a point at the top. Said to have been formed to resemble Puy du Dome, the cinder cone deep in the heart of the Auvergne, its base is buttermilk, or what the French call "babeurre." In the Auvergne dialect, babeurre is called "gape," thus the name of the cheese.

Like so many cheeses, gaperon was invented as a result of hunger. The peasants, who sold their butter and cream, were left with the babeurre, mixed in some whey, and perhaps some curdled milk, and let the mixture sit. They strained it through a cloth, tied up the curds tightly, and hung the bundle from the ceiling near the kitchen fireplace. After several weeks,

the cheese was ready to eat. A peasant family's wealth was judged by the number of gaperon hanging from the rafters.

The first cheeses must have been insipid to the Auvergnat palate, and they were soon seasoned with minced garlic, salt, and black pepper that are mixed directly into the buttermilk. To test the ripeness of the cheese, it was unwrapped and set on the floor, between the farmer's feet. He would take his knife and drop it into the cheese from eye level. If the knife stood up straight, the cheese was unripe; if it fell to the side, the gaperon was ready to eat.

Today, gaperon can be made with raw or pasteurized milk. Its flavor is sharp, its texture soft.

See also AUVERGNE.

Rance, Patrick. *The French Cheese Book.* London: Macmillan, 1989.

Susan Herrmann Loomis

Garrotxa. Among the many laudable results of the creative renaissance in post-Franco Spain is the revival—and improvement—of a Catalan cheese that had all but disappeared. It was brought back in the early 1980s by a movement of idealistic young city-dwellers, self-described as urban hippies or "neorurals," who moved to the country seeking a closer and more productive connection to the land. The Franco regime had for years enforced large production quotas that virtually outlawed small artisan operators. The neorurals established cooperative or communal living arrangements, and sought to earn their livings from traditional practices, among them cheesemaking. Several of these new arrivals collaborated with local cheesemakers, and the result was a cheese that was eventually built into a brand with worldwide recognition.

Garrotxa hails from the *comarca* (county) of the same name in the province of Girona, in northeastern Catalonia. It is manufactured in ten creameries—all family firms—by traditional, artisanal methods. Altogether they produce approximately 363,000 pounds (165,000 kilograms) per year in two sizes of small wheels, 1 pound (500 grams) and 2½ pounds (1,100 grams). About 108,000 of the former and 102,000 of the latter are made annually, with roughly 80 percent consumed domestically, mostly within Catalonia, and the remaining 20 percent exported.

Garrotxa is made from pasteurized goat's milk and aged from four weeks to three months.

Among the neorurals were Toni Chueca and his wife, Rosa Heras, who took up residence in a local *bauma* (Catalan for "den" or "shelter") in 1979, and Llorenç Muguruza. Chueca named his operation Formatge Bauma and Muguruza called his Blancafort; they were established in 1980 and 1984, respectively. Other top producers are Sant Gil d'Albió, founded by Salvador Martí and Nati Ninot, in the mid-1980s, and subsequently run by their son, Josep Martí, and Formatges Mont-Bru, headed by Oriol Antunez.

In the humid climate of the area, strains of *Penicillium* mold, particularly *Penicillium glaucum*, readily grow on the ripening cheese's rind; thus it was originally referred to in Catalan as *pell florida* ("bloomy rind"), distinguishing it from its antecedents, most of which were simple, fresh goat cheeses sold young. Modern-day cheesemakers "surrendered" to the mold, recognizing it as a beneficial ripening agent with a neutralizing effect on the cheese's natural acidity, lending some sweetness and subtle flavors—part of what helped it grab attention as a novelty in the marketplace. Early on Garrotxa was billed as the region's first mold-ripened goat cheese that was creamy and mild, as opposed to acidic and earthy. See PEN-ICILLIUM.

A young cheese entrepreneur and consultant, Enric Canut, along with his colleague Ramón Badía, spearheaded the revival of goat cheesemaking in Garrotxa and the emergence of its modern-day eponymous cheese. Between 1982 and 1985 they offered classes, consultation, and technical assistance to local cheesemakers. Canut presented a cheese made by Formatgeria Mogent to colleagues at the Consorcio de Quesos Tradicionales de España (Consortium of Traditional Spanish Cheeses)—its introduction as "Queso de La Garrotxa" and first exposure outside local markets. In 2014, having legally branded Garrotxa several years before, Canut, Martí, and their colleagues launched an effort to obtain its European PGI (protected geographical indication).

Garrotxa's exterior is an attractive blue-gray color. With proper aging, the cheese offers delectable textures and a complex flavor profile. Its paste is bright white, turning slightly darker toward the outside, with a semisoft, moist, and creamy consistency that nevertheless borders on flaky, and smooth, unctuous, melting texture on the palate. Its flavors are mildly goaty, buttery, and tangy (lightly acidic) with notes of citrus, mountain herbs, damp earth, and an aftertaste of dried fruits or hazelnuts.

See also CANUT, ENRIC and SPAIN.

Canut, Enric. *Quesos y Paisajes—Cheeses & Landscape.* Barcelona: Udyat D.L., 2008 (text in Spanish and English).
Canut, Enric, et al. *Quesos: Alimentos de Espana.* Madrid: El Pais Aguilar, 1992.

David Gibbons

Ġbejna

Ġbejna (plural "ġbejniet") is a homemade cheese produced with whole raw milk from the Maltese breed of sheep and its crosses. Earliest reports on cheesemaking date back to the fifteenth century and again in the seventeenth century. The arid terrain typical of the Maltese islands favors the grazing of sheep, as these animals can use marginal agricultural areas unsuitable for other agricultural purposes. Moreover cheesemaking was a logical way to preserve the milk for longer periods of time.

To make Ġbejna, the milk is coagulated adding natural animal rennet in a vat at 95–99°F (35–37°C). The curd is transferred to baskets and a small quantity of locally sourced sea salt scattered on the surface. The Ġbejniet are turned over inside the mold once or twice, after which they are usually sprinkled with other salt and then placed in a refrigerator to allow them to set in the traditional shape. Fresh Ġbejna (friska) is normally sold within twenty-four hours of production. The color is white and glossy, with a soft core that is the same color as the surface. It has a savory taste typical for sheep cheeses. The Ġbejna can be dried in a *qanniċ*, a wooden frame cupboard covered in wire or nylon mesh with a mesh size ≤2 mm. The *qanniċ* is placed outside in a ventilated area, normally on a rooftop, to air dry the Ġbejna in a natural environment. Ġbejna may be consumed fresh (*friski* or *tal-ilma*), air-dried (*moxxa*, *bajda* or *t'Ghawdex*), salt cured (*maħsula*), or peppered (*tal-bżar*).

Attard, Everaldo, et al. "New Technologies Supporting the Traditional Cheeses in Sicily and Malta Islands—From Farm to Fork."
Fiorini, Stanley. *Documentary Sources of Maltese History / Part I, No. 1 Notarial Documents; No 1, Notary Giacomo Zabara R 494/1 (I): 1487–1488.* Msida: Malta University Press, 2006, pp. 249–250, 291–292, 330.

Stefania Carpino

gender roles and norms have shaped the making of cheese like any other form of labor. The eighteenth and nineteenth centuries saw a major shift of dairy production from a feminine realm to a masculine one. Location and modes of production factored most importantly in determining who took charge of cheesemaking and who profited from it.

Historically and across many cultures, most cheese has been the province of women. Women reigned over the farmyard animals; milking and dairy production were women's work. Through the mid-nineteenth century, European and North American dairymaids carried their stools to the muddy pastures to milk cows and goats and carried full milk pails back to the farm where farmwives or paid dairywomen made the cheese.

High mountain cheeses—Gruyère, Comté, Cantal, some of the Pyrenees cheeses—are the exception; these were made by men. Male shepherds took cows and sheep to the richer mountain pastures for the summer, usually June–October. The cheeses they made had to last long and travel well. The bigger and heavier cheeses that resulted, some scholars have assumed, could only be moved by men. However, men held no monopoly on strength. In England, dairywomen made and turned Cheddars weighing 140 pounds (63 kilograms) until wealthy farmers

acquired a status that meant their wives were considered too delicate for such work. Cultural standards determined who followed the cows to the mountains; married women *could* not be separated from the family for that long; single women *should* not be.

Dairying in any century meant long, hard labor. Dairywomen, managers of production, saw the dairymaids out to milk in the predawn and finished supervising the cheesemaking long after sundown. A good dairywoman could make or break a farm, and for smaller farms, the farm wife's cheese sales often more than paid the annual rent. Thus the art of dairying garnered respect and a talented dairywoman earned a significant income (Valenze 1995). See DAIRYMAIDS.

The European Enlightenment created a new faith in scientific observation as a means to improve agriculture. Wealthy, educated, rural elite men set out to observe and standardize best practices for cheesemaking. These amateur scientists resented the secrecy many dairywomen wove around the art of cheesemaking. They looked to find measurable factors that dictated the quality of a cheese (excluding womanly talent). Although these men gained their knowledge of cheese through observing and talking to women, they categorized it and publicized it and claimed it as their own. Their access to publishing in the scientific world persuaded others of their claims. In France,

A plate from *Dairy Farming: Being the Theory, Practice, and Methods of Dairying*, by John Prince Sheldon (1880). By this point the nineteenth-century shift from farm to factory was already well underway, and with it a swing in the gender balance of cheesemaking from women to men.

England, and the United States, scientific discourse consistently accused women of clinging to outmoded, unscientific ways, whether this was true or not.

Perhaps the most famous product of these investigations was the "Harding method." In the 1850s Joseph and Rachel Harding introduced, and Joseph publicized, a method based on strict control of temperature and hygiene along with a new way of cutting curds to make Cheddar. It depended less on expertise learned by experience and could easily be replicated, facilitating truly large-scale production of cheese. See HARDING, JOSEPH.

This shift from farm to "factory" most affected women's control over dairy. Mass production developed rapidly in the United States beginning in the 1850s, followed by France and Great Britain in the 1890s. Factories and cooperatives moved milk off the farm for processing and thus out of women's traditional purview. Women lost control over the making of cheese, while still doing the hard labor of milking. Cultural norms continued to envision "women's place" as on the farm, even when dairy production moved off-site. What farm women thought of this transition is difficult to know. Historian Sally McMurry has shown that American women promoted this change because it lightened their load, making it more equal to their husbands'. See INDUSTRIALIZATION.

Professionalization of dairying did not necessarily exclude women. In France, women ran large dairies up through the 1930s, especially in the Nord region. Records of Camembert syndicates show women participating as full members. However, in much of France modernization meant marginalization for women. Cooperatives that privileged scientific education and practices brought more men into the business of dairying and moved more cheesemaking off the farm. Greater demand encouraged market-oriented, male-dominated cheesemaking in new areas, such as the Haute Saône in the Franche Comté. Local women lost control of their cows' milk, could not make butter for sale, and thus lost their "butter money," their independent earnings. This loss shifted decision-making power in the household to men. In England, for this exact reason, farmers' wives vocally resisted the factory system, often successfully.

In Europe, from Germany to Sweden, state-sponsored education played a key role in promoting "scientific" cheesemaking and bringing men into the business of cheesemaking. Not only did dairy schools

educate more men than women (though this varied by country), but the state also moved, no later than the 1920s, into the business of regulating milk. Scientific standards for the quality of milk required measuring and recording production off-site. Promoted as consumer protection measures, new laws and standards nonetheless further alienated women, who were viewed as less educated and seen as less scientifically inclined, from dairy management.

The nineteenth century saw a great swing in the gender balance of cheesemakers, but it was never absolute. Where women participated in mass production, their role shifted to that of single women working as unskilled labor. Thus women moved from having complete charge to having no control over the end product. Despite massive changes, women continued to make cheese on the farm, quietly adopting scientific methods into their small-scale production. With the return of a market for high-quality farm-made cheese, women are reasserting their prominence in the making of excellent cheeses.

Blundel, Richard, and Angela Tregear. "From Artisans to 'Factories': The Interpenetration of Craft and Industry in English Cheese-making, 1650–1950." *Enterprise and Society* 7, no. 4 (2006): 705–739.

Boisard, Pierre. *Camembert: A National Myth*. Translated by Richard Miller. Berkeley, 2003. English translation of *Le Camembert: Mythe National*. First published in 1992.

Boulet, Michel, ed. *Les Enjeux de la Formation Des Acteurs de l'Agriculture: 1760–1945*. Dijon, France: Educagri, 2000. [*The Challenges of Educating Agriculturalists: 1760–1945*. Chapters sum up the numerous approaches to introducing scientific knowledge to rural workers.]

McMurry, Sally. *Transforming Rural Life: Dairying Families and Agricultural Change, 1820–1885*. Baltimore: Johns Hopkins University Press, 1995.

Valenze, Deborah M. "The Art of Women and the Business of Men: Women's Work and the Dairy Industry." In *The First Industrial Woman*, pp. 48–67. New York: Oxford University Press, 1995.

Lynn L. Sharp

The **General Agreement on Tariffs and Trade** (GATT)

The **General Agreement on Tariffs and Trade** (GATT) was a multilateral agreement signed in 1947 to promote international economic cooperation. From 1948 to 1994 the GATT provided the rules for much of world trade evolving through several rounds of negotiations. The Uruguay Round (1986–1994), the last and largest, recognized that measures adopted by national governments to protect the health of their consumers, animals, and plants could be utilized as discriminatory barriers to trade and sought to improve market access for agricultural products and to harmonize standards between member countries. Consequently the Agreements on Sanitary and Phytosanitary Measures (SPS) and Technical Barriers to Trade (TBT) were included among the Multilateral Agreements on Trade in Goods, annexed to the 1994 Marrakesh Agreement, which established the World Trade Organization (WTO), which replaced the GATT as an international organization.

See also WORLD TRADE ORGANIZATION.

World Trade Organization. *Understanding the WTO.* 5th ed. Geneva, Switzerland: WTO, 2011. http://www.wto .org/english/thewto_e/whatis_e/tif_e/tif_e.htm.

Dennis D'Amico

generally recognized as safe (GRAS)

is a designation of the US Food and Drug Administration (FDA), found in sections 201 (s) and 409 of the Federal Food, Drug, and Cosmetic Act. In essence it says that any substance that is intentionally added to food is a food additive, and is subject to premarket review and approval by the FDA.

All substances added to foods or that may come in contact with food must be reviewed based on published scientific studies, information from textbooks, expert review, and any other scientific data and information. This list of GRAS substances can be found in the FDA Code of Federal Regulations (CFR) Title 21 section 182. Some examples of GRAS items are anticaking agents (calcium silicate, magnesium silicate), chemical preservatives (sorbic acid, sodium bisulfite), nutrients (ascorbic acid, zinc oxide) essential oils and natural extractives (anise, basil), spices and other natural seasonings and flavorings (celery seed, clover) and multiple-purpose food substances (caramel, sodium phosphate).

A good example of a GRAS substance is calcium chloride. This substance is an additive that is used in the cheesemaking process to restore the calcium balance of the milk, which in turn would give a firmer curd for easier cutting of the curd. An example of a non-GRAS substance would be food packaging material that contains ink. The food packaging material

might contain ink that is a non-GRAS substance that could leach into the food. That non-GRAS substance must be approved by FDA prior to its use.

See also FOOD AND DRUG ADMINISTRATION.

US Food and Drug Administration. "Generally Recognized as Safe (GRAS)." http://www.fda.gov/Food/ IngredientsPackagingLabeling/GRAS.

Marianne Smukowski

genetically modified organism (GMO)

refers to those plants, animals, and microorganisms in which the genetic material (DNA) has been altered in a way that does not occur naturally. This is accomplished by moving a desired characteristic, encoded in the genetic material or genes of one species, into a different host species. Also called "genetic engineering," this method of altering the genetic material of a plant or animal produces desired outcomes more accurately than does traditional breeding, which is limited to breeding within a species, generally transfers many genes (some potentially undesirable) to the next generation of organisms, and can take a great deal of time to generate results. See BREEDING AND GENETICS.

The genetic makeup of microbes has also been modified to produce dairy enzymes for cheesemakers. For example, the milk-clotting enzyme chymosin can be produced from a genetically engineered strain of *Aspergillus niger*, a common fungus found on fruits and vegetables. Also, known as FPC—fermentation-produced chymosin—this enzyme is extremely efficient at clotting milk protein and is lower in cost than traditional milk-clotting enzymes produced from animals. See FERMENTATION-PRODUCED CHYMOSIN.

Other important dairy enzymes include lipases and bioprotective ingredients. Lipases are critical to optimize aroma development in dairy products like provolone cheese. Bioprotective ingredients can improve both the safety and the shelf life of dairy products by preventing the growth of undesirable bacteria, yeasts, and molds. Many examples of bioprotective ingredients, such as nisin, are produced from genetically modified fungi. Often, the products of these GMO organisms offer vegetarian alternatives to those enzymes traditionally isolated from animals.

GMOs can be found throughout our food system. Animal feed crops, including corn, soybeans, and alfalfa, have been genetically engineered to improve crop yields; this is accomplished by placing genes for resistance to droughts, herbicides, or pesticides within the host (i.e., plant) genome. Globally, genetically engineered crops account for 70–90 percent of the feed used in agriculture. Since 1996, when genetically engineered crops were first introduced as animal feed, scientific research has found no differences in the nutritional profiles of animal products, including milk, derived from animals fed genetically modified crops. However, considerable controversy has surrounded, and continues to surround, GMOs and their use. Opponents to GMOs argue that long-term human impact studies are lacking and that genetically modified crops are harmful to the environment. Proponents highlight numerous risk-analysis studies that have not indicated any risk of GMO foods to human consumers. Those in favor of genetic modification also argue for the utility of GMOs in helping to feed a rapidly growing human population.

Van Eenennaam, A. L., and A. E. Young. "Prevalence and Impacts of Genetically Engineered Feedstuffs on Livestock Populations." *Journal of Animal Science* 92 (2014): 4255–4278.
World Health Organization. "Frequently Asked Questions on Genetically Modified Foods." http://www.who.int/foodsafety/publications/biotech/20questions/en.

Matt Ranieri

A **geographical indication** is a form of legal protection reserving use of a specific place name in association with a specific product name for a good that genuinely comes from that place, thereby conferring something distinctive to the product. Geographical indication (GI) is the term codified into World Trade Organization (WTO) language to refer to a variety of systems aiming to ensure accurate use of geographical place names connoting a positive reputation to a particular product—such as a cheese—in that product's name and labeling. In the European Union (EU) there are two kinds of GIs: protected geographical indication (PGI), indicating only a geographical origin, and the more strict protected designation of origin (PDO), which

adds specific processing requirements. See DESIGNATION OF ORIGIN.

The earliest European initiatives to protect a geographical name in labeling comestibles include the wine zones of Chianti (1716), Tokaj-Hegyalja (1730), and Porto (1756). Regulatory and legal frameworks ensuring foods really were from where they claimed to be developed in France (with a series of laws starting in 1905, initially aimed to prevent consumer fraud through false or misleading labeling) and comparable systems were soon pursued in nearby countries (e.g., Spain starting in the 1920s, Italy in 1963). The EU implemented EU-wide equivalency in 1992, creating an umbrella system obliging member-states to make consistent national rules and introducing GIs where they had been unknown. Initially this was to allow free and fair trade among member-states, but given the promise of GIs as a means of bringing high-value economic activity to poorer rural areas, the placement of high-value foods and drink in the export economy would soon dominate, especially as EU assumption of responsibility for GIs put it in the position of defending them in international trade negotiations.

The process of obtaining a GI varies by national rules, but generally, a group of producers files a request with the governmental agency overseeing intellectual property protections or GIs and other food labeling systems in their country. There are currently two general system types for this. Most countries have a system where products are registered after passing through a governmental approval process ensuring that the GI proposal and its language conform to national and international law. In EU member-states the registry is usually managed by a branch of the ministry responsible for agriculture, and applications can be quite demanding, requiring research and negotiations between producers, scientific experts, and governmental employees to decide the boundary of the geographical territory (and, in the case of PDOs, production guidelines). Once approved, the member-state passes the indication upward for EU recognition, allowing the product to bear the appropriate label (PDO, PGI).

Beyond Europe, however, few countries have a specific system for GIs and instead use national trademark law to protect distinctive product names, usually through collective or certification marks. As of 2009, fifty-six countries used this more general system, including the United States, where the US

Patent and Trademark Office has handled GIs since 1946. Having obtained national-level recognition, the product is accorded all protections guaranteed by any active international agreements between its country of origin and other countries.

The coexistence of these approaches—and the economic stakes involved—have made GIs a recurring theme in international trade negotiations since the 1883 Paris Convention, when deliberate false labeling was the target. The 1981 Madrid Agreement further forbade "merely" misleading labeling and made an exception for names that had become generic. In 1958 the Lisbon Agreement focused on GIs by forming a union of signatory countries that agreed to mutually respect each other's GIs and PDOs, which were defined as products whose reputation is associated with a specific geographical zone (composed of both "natural and human factors") that makes a substantive contribution to product characteristics. These treaties are all still in effect and are administered by the World Intellectual Property Organization (WIPO), but only concern the contracting parties: 175 countries for the Paris Convention as of 2014, but only 28 for the Lisbon Agreement.

Since the 1990s, WTO negotiations have dominated the fate of GIs in an effort to shift recognition from an assemblage of multilateral accords to a global system. The Uruguay Round of General Agreement on Tariffs and Trade (GATT) talks concluded in 1994 with the Trade Related Aspects of Intellectual Property Rights (TRIPS) Agreement, which established the outline of a two-tier system for GIs—and made "GI" the worldwide term of reference. Article 22(1) of the Agreement defines a GI (edible or otherwise) as "a good originating in the territory of a Member, or a region or locality in that territory, where a given quality, reputation, or other characteristic of the good is essentially attributable to its geographical origin," which have been accorded formal recognition by the appropriate government. Members must implement the legal means to prevent misleading use of all such names within their territory. Article 23 specifically concerns wines and spirits and is much more exacting, specifying that use of the name is not allowed even when there is no fraud and little risk of consumer misunderstanding—even if qualifiers like "-style" are used or if the actual place of production is specified in addition to an allusion to the protected place name.

The debates continue. If a post-TRIPS dispute ruling required the EU modify its system to give equal treatment to other GI systems (resulting in a streamlined law in 2012), the EU—at the urging of cheese producers—is committed to ratcheting up all GI protections to the same level as wines and spirits. See GENERAL AGREEMENT ON TARRIFS AND TRADE.

This difference in status is a reflection of an imbalance favoring wines and spirits (or rather, their producers) dating back to European GI systems' inception, although a few cheese producers' groups were quick to see the laws' potential. The Roquefort producers' association was famously precocious, taking measures to protect the use of its name worldwide in 1925 and pursuing imposters at home and abroad, and by the 1950s several European countries had one or more cheeses with some kind of national-level recognition. The International Convention on the Use of Designations of Origin and Names for Cheeses held in Stresa, Italy, in 1951 (ratified by Austria, Denmark, France, the Netherlands, Norway, Sweden, and Switzerland) defined "cheese" itself (as well as several generic cheese-types, from Camembert to Danablu) and signatory countries promised to crack down on fraudulent cheeses and naming practices, even those with a qualifier (a precursor to the TRIPS language). Only four cheeses, made or aged in their traditional region according to "local, loyal, and uninterrupted usages," qualified to be honored as "appellations of origin," as GIs were termed in the day (based on their French name, appellations d'origine): Gorgonzola, Parmigiano Reggiano, Pecorino Romano, and Roquefort.

Although Europe is the epicenter of GI regulation, the system has interested many countries and producers around the world. Beyond the appeal in economically strong countries of attractive domestic and export sales possibilities, many in developing countries see the system as a way to reclaim the reputation of their agricultural heritage for the benefit of smaller farmers and processors. By creating a scarcity of "the real thing," GI producers would secure a higher price for their products, allowing them to stay farming, earn a living income, and continue producing in a way that responds to norms other than those of mass-production at the lowest price (including preserving biodiversity). See BIODIVERSITY. This is why many development agencies such as the Food and Agriculture Organization of the United Nations (FAO) encourage and guide such undertakings in less developed countries worldwide and a great many producers and researcher-consultants from European countries with experience in building GI programs at home are engaged in spreading the concept around the world.

Countries may adopt a European-type system, stick to a preexisting trademark system, or conform to both to get whatever recognition they can in the most countries possible—whatever it takes to set products developed with local know-how apart from versions grown or made elsewhere. Indian Darjeeling tea, Ethiopian Fine Coffee, Thai "Hom Mali" rice, and Peruvian Pisco brandy are just a sampling of the hundreds of products with or working piecemeal toward recognition within their own countries and abroad. Although protected dairy products remain concentrated in Europe for the time being, efforts in other world dairy regions and former European colonies are beginning to mature, from Mexican Cotija cheese to Lebanese lebneh.

The websites of all the institutions cited here have detailed presentations of GIs from their perspective.

See also UNITED STATES DEPARTMENT OF AGRICULTURE and WORLD TRADE ORGANIZATION.

Blackeney, Michael, ed. *Intellectual Property Rights and Food Security*. Wallingford, U.K.: CABI, 2009.

Echols, Marsha. *Geographical Indications for Food Products: International Legal and Regulatory Perspectives*. Alphen aan den Rijn, The Netherlands: Kluwer Law International, 2008.

European Commission. "Geographical Indications and Traditional Specialties." http://ec.europa.eu/agriculture/quality/schemes.

Robinson, Jancis. *The Oxford Companion to Wine*. 4th ed. New York: Oxford University Press, 2015.

US Department of Agriculture. "Geographical Indications." http://www.usda-eu.org/topics/geographical-indications.

World Intellectual Property Organization. "Geographical Indications." http://www.wipo.int/geo_indications/en.

World Trade Organization. "TRIPS—Part II: Standards concerning the Availability, Scope and Use of Intellectual Property Rights. Section 3: Geographical Indications." http://www.wto.org/english/docs_e/legal_e/27-trips_04b_e.htm#3.

Juliette Rogers

Geotrichum candidum is one of the most widespread species of fungi used in surface-ripened cheeses because it can have major effects on both the appearance and the flavor of the cheese. Based on DNA-sequence data, fungal taxonomists have changed the name of *Geotrichum candidum* to *Galactomyces geotrichum*, but because of its long use in industry as a starter culture prior to this taxonomic shift, most in the cheese industry still refer to it as *Geotrichum candidum*. The fungus exhibits high phenotypic and genotypic diversity within and across cheesemaking regions, with variation in appearance (from oily and flat to fluffy and raised), salt tolerance, production of enzymes that break down fats and proteins, and production of volatiles such as sulfur compounds. This diversity provides cheesemakers with a microbiological toolbox to unlock flavors as their cheese ripens. See PHENOTYPIC VARIABILITY.

Based on genetic similarity with other fungi, *Geotrichum candidum* is a yeast, but its appearance on cheese and when grown in the laboratory is more like a mold. Variations in yeast-like appearance across strains is due to the relative amount of arthrospore production. Arthrospores are produced when the filaments that make up the fungus (hyphae) break into fragments that become reproductive structures. Genetic sequencing has revealed an interesting explanation for this mycological identity crisis: this is a mold in transition to becoming a yeast. All true yeasts are descendants of molds; they evolved a single-celled lifestyle from their multicellular ancestors, letting go of moldy habits such as growth using filaments. But *Geotrichum candidum* hasn't let go of all of the genetic parts associated with growing like a mold.

Geotrichum candidum has been isolated from a variety of habitats, including plants, soil, mammals, and food production facilities. The strains found in cheeses come from two main sources: industrial starter cultures, which are widely used in cheese production, and raw milk, where the fungus is considered a normal part of the raw milk microbiome. This fungus has also been isolated from the skin and digestive tracts of humans, possibly as a result of their consumption of cheeses and other fermented foods. Although *Geotrichum candidum* is not considered to be a pathogen in healthy humans, in very rare cases with patients that have extremely compromised immune systems, *Geotrichum candidum* has functioned as an opportunistic pathogen, leading to infections and, very rarely, death. See OPPORTUNISTIC PATHOGEN.

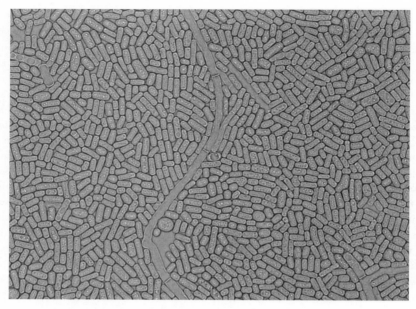

Cells of the yeast *Geotrichum candidum* under a microscope. © BENJAMIN E. WOLFE

Geotrichum candidum tolerates a wide range of conditions, including pH levels from 3 to 11 (5.5 is optimal) and temperatures from 41° to 100°F (5–38°C). Despite its pervasiveness and ability to thrive in the cheesemaking environment, *Geotrichum candidum* does have one weakness in this setting—salt. Although many surface-ripening microbes used in cheesemaking can tolerate very high levels of salt (5 percent w/v and higher), *Geotrichum candidum* grows best in the range of 1–2.5 percent salt.

The major contributions of *Geotrichum candidum* to cheese ripening are consistency in rind development, visual appearance of the rind, and development of cheese flavor. *Geotrichum candidum* aids in rind development by making the rind less acidic and thus allowing the proliferation of bacteria that are unable to grow at a low pH. As the fungus breaks down proteins and fats in the cheese, it releases a diverse bouquet of volatile compounds that can give cheeses yeasty, moldy, fruity, sulfury, and buttery flavors, among others. In the breakdown of proteins, *Geotrichum candidum* is particularly good at producing methanethiol and dimethyl sulfide, volatiles that give cheeses a cooked cabbage odor. In the breakdown of fats, *Geotrichum candidum* can produce abundant methyl ketones that provide fruity and floral notes to cheeses. See METHYL

KETONES. There is some evidence that *Geotrichum candidum* can inhibit the growth of undesirable microbes in cheese production including *Mucor* and *Listeria*, but this is highly dependent on the particular strains used as well as on environmental conditions.

The growth of *Geotrichum candidum* is considered desirable in most cheeses, though some strains can produce unpleasant flavors such as bitterness, and excessive growth can cause rind defects. When some strains of the fungus grow too quickly during ripening, they can lead to a "slippery rind," causing the rind of a cheese to fall off easily during the aging process. See DEFECTS.

Among surface-ripened cheeses, *Geotrichum candidum* produces advantageous results with bloomy-rind cheeses such as Camembert, which is almost always highly colonized by this and other fungi such as the mold *Penicillium camemberti*. The undulating surfaces of many ripened French goat cheeses such as Valençay and Chabichou du Poitou are caused by the abundance of *Geotrichum candidum*. Depending on salt concentrations, *Geotrichum candidum* can also be found in many washed-rind cheeses such as Limburger, Livarot, and Munster. *Geotrichum candidum* is also important in the early stages of ripening in some natural rind cheeses such as Saint-Nectaire and Tomme de Savoie, where it helps to increase the pH of the cheese surface and promote the growth of later-colonizing bacteria and molds.

See also BLOOMY-RIND CHEESES; FILAMENTOUS FUNGI; FUNGI; HYPHAE; and WASHED-RIND CHEESES.

Boutrou, R., and M. Guéguen. "Interests in Geotrichum Candidum for Cheese Technology." *International Journal of Food Microbiology* 102 (2005): 1–20.

Larpin, Sandra, et al. "Geotrichum Candidum Dominates in Yeast Population Dynamics in Livarot, a French Red-Smear Cheese." *FEMS Yeast Research* 6 (2006): 1243–1253.

Marcellino, Noella, et al. "Diversity of Geotrichum Candidum Strains Isolated from Traditional Cheesemaking Fabrications in France." *Applied and Environmental Microbiology* 67 (2001): 4752–4759.

Morel, Guillaume, et al. "Differential Gene Retention as an Evolutionary Mechanism to Generate Biodiversity and Adaptation in Yeasts." *Scientific Reports* 5 (2015): article no. 11571.

Benjamin E. Wolfe

Germany is the world's second-largest producer of industrial (mass-produced) cheese, manufacturing almost 2.4 million tons in 2012, behind the United States, with almost 5 million tons, and followed by France and then Italy. In contrast to what happened in rural France with its many remote corners but a common market in Paris, late nineteenth-century industrialization in decentralized Germany turned cheese into a much more standardized and more widely tradable commodity.

However, somewhat similar to what has happened in the United States, an artisanal cheese movement has sprung up since the last decade of the twentieth century, revolutionizing a market that had been based on three traditional landmarks: pungent, semi-firm, block-shaped Tilsiter on the Baltic coast going back to the mid-1800s; the much older Alpine mountain Bergkäse, the hard cheese in the south; and the historic Sauermilchkäse, the very simple, small hand-shaped cheeses made from sour skim milk, originally a byproduct of butter making. See TILSITER; BERGKÄSE; and SOUR SKIMMED-MILK CHEESES.

Early milk drinkers in what is now Germany would certainly have known of the benefits of natural curdling as a way of adding a little extra "shelf life" to a perishable source of protein. This is confirmed by recent archaeological findings of ceramic vessels riddled with holes, visually reminiscent of cheese strainers and with traces of milk fat still on

Viehscheid is an annual tradition each September in the southern Bavarian Allgäu region, when thousands of cows are led down from their summer Alp pastures into the valleys to be returned to their owners. © KATE ARDING

them. German recorded cheese history began with the Roman historian Tacitus (ca. 55–115 C.E.). In his work *Germania* he provided written evidence of the food habits of the German tribes, opposing "Barbarian" *lac concretum* (solid, curdled milk, or quark) to "civilized" (renneted, storable) *caseus*, cheese. Over the centuries most farmers stuck to quark and Sauermilchkäse, producing renneted cheese only when they had a surplus of milk, or when fresh milk and butter were not economically viable on the local market. Keeping animals was expensive, and many farmers were forced to slaughter their cows each autumn for lack of feed. See ANCIENT CIVILIZATIONS and QUARK.

The revolution of 1848 extended farmers' independence from the former feudal system, and the subsequent agrarian revolution introduced more efficient systems of farming. At the same time, urbanization, new cooling technologies, and transport systems created new markets. As workers flocked to the cities, rural labor became scarce and expensive. In general, German farmers at the time switched from labor-intensive crops to more productive and financially lucrative pastures. Cattle breeding was intensified to achieve higher yields of both meat and milk, and feeding regimes were optimized. As the agronomist and writer Josef von Schreibers predicted in 1847 for modern dairy farming, "The animal has to be turned into a machine, destined to transform the given feed in the shortest time and in the least amount of space into the maximum amount of milk."

Despite efforts by temperance movements to promote milk as a healthy alternative to beer and spirits, including its free distribution, the working classes did not develop a liking for it. Butter and cheese, however, were highly esteemed. With the economy booming after unification following the Franco-German War of 1870–71, cheese consumption in Germany rose, and sour-milk and skim-milk cheeses were abandoned in favor of cheeses with a higher fat content. From 1900 onward, consumption increased rapidly, rising from 13.2 pounds (6 kg) of dairy foods per capita per year in 1860 to 25.6 pounds (11.6 kg) in 1910. This might have been the historic moment for a true artisanal cheese movement to develop, but the lure of efficient machinery was too strong. By the end of the nineteenth century, cheesemaking in Germany had become quite industrialized, moving beyond the small, personalized, domestic (and female) realm into the anonymous (male) world of standardized commodities. See GENDER. When World War I's disastrous misplanning led to state-controlled food production and distribution, cheese, like all other food products, came under government regulations that emphasized safe supplies for everyone instead of luxury and fine taste for the few. The *Reichsmilchgesetz*, the German dairy law of 1932, further controlled both production and rationing. This trend continued after World War II through the 1950 *Bewirtschaftungsnotgesetz*, an emergency law enacted to regulate the production, distribution, and pricing of milk and fat, which remained in effect until 1969. See WORLD WAR I and WORLD WAR II.

In the 1960s, cheese was plentiful but mostly as a plain and affordable alternative to cold cuts like sausage and ham, largely eaten on buttered bread. Imported cheeses from places like France were (and still are) regarded as a luxury for connoisseurs. From the end of the 1970s until the creation of the European Union (EU), worry over short supply evolved into anxiety about overproduction. *Milchsee*, "milk lake," and *Butterberg*, "butter mountain"—the colloquial terms for stockpiled dairy products—grew. In 1984 a milk quota with severe financial sanctions for overproduction was introduced in the European Union. This system, combined with falling milk prices, created a vicious circle of ever-growing but ever-less-profitable dairy farms that had to pay high prices to obtain additional quotas in order to survive. The result was a conventional dairy market dominated by a very few international conglomerates. The EU ended the milk quota system in 2015, leaving German farmers free to increase production.

The new artisanal cheese producers attempted to break out of the vicious shortage-surplus cycle by either turning their cow's milk into cheese, thus creating added value and needing less milk to make a living, or starting new farms with goats or sheep (which were quota free). These new farmers enjoyed stylistic freedom because they had no customary role models. Distribution presented a challenge, however, because the lack of an artisanal cheese tradition also translated into a paucity of dedicated cheesemongers. Although some affineurs have sprung up since the 1980s, they mostly deal in French and Italian wares whose logistics are well established.

It is nothing short of a miracle that the spirit of independent farmers' responsibility for their own products survived at all, since it is the opposite of how most conventional farmers in the Western world work and live today. One important reason for this was the *Lebensreform*, or life reform movement that began in the 1860s. It was rooted in a new awareness of nutrition as well as in an uneasiness about Germany's rapid urbanization and industrialization. Its principles can be summarized by the slogan "back to the purity of nature," including the notion of "whole food," which gained a new dimension when the anthroposophist Rudolf Steiner set forth the precepts of biodynamic agriculture in 1924. Following anthroposophy's holistic approach to life, Steiner placed agriculture into a larger, cosmic context, emphasizing the independent, self-sufficient structure of farms. Many of Germany's new artisanal cheese producers belong to this school, following either organic or biodynamic principles. While the dairy industry's big players export mainly to Italy, the Netherlands, and France with ever-larger amounts of German cheese going to Russia and Japan, a growing number of small producers explore the notion of terroir in the form of solid milk beyond the *lac concretum* of Tacitus's times. Successful dairy farms combine production with processing and distribution, selling their own bread, cheese, meat, and other products at farm shops or farmers' markets and even taking in vacationers. Dottenfelder Hof near Frankfurt is one of the oldest and most important of Germany's biodynamic farms, home to anthroposophic research stations and instrumental in plant breeding. Its dairy was established in the early 1970s by Ebba Bauer. Many of Germany's new cheesemakers at some point worked or trained there. Of the large selection of cheeses made from its raw cow's milk and sold on the farm, *Möhrenlaibchen* (or "small carrot wheel") has been the most innovative and successful. The carrot juice that colors it a bright orange comes from the farm's own ultra-tasty Rodelika variety.

EU legislation, often accused of furthering uniformity on its citizens' plates, also offers bureaucratic structures to protect regional foodstuffs with an entire framework of geographical indications. Seven types of German cheese (Allgäuer Emmentaler, Allgäuer Bergkäse, Altenburger Ziegenkäse, Odenwälder Frühstückskäse, Sonneborner Weichkäse, Tiefländer, and Tollenser) carry the PDO (protected designation of origin) seal, under which all the ingredients and the whole production process are tied to a place and traditional methods. In spite of this, most of these cheeses have been cannibalized, their quality tumbling in a downward price spiral. But the new cheese impulses have also had their effect on the old landmarks. Once again, excellent Tilsiter, organic Sauermilchkäse, and above all, some truly exciting mountain cheeses in the south are being made. Although the quality of the latter had begun to be eroded by the large dairies, a few pioneers such as the affineur Thomas Breckle (Jamei cheese shop) and the producers Evelyn Wild (Käsküche Isny dairy), Anton Holzinger (Zurwies dairy), and Arturo Chiriboga (Obere Mühle dairy) are applying the "new" old ideas to the milk of a quality-driven group of local dairy farmers. Käsküche Isny has been a pioneer in rethinking old cooperative dairy structures and developing smaller cheese formats without losing anything in terms of taste. Zurwies's large collection of soft cheeses is based on traditional models such as Romadur and Limburger (very aromatic, small-format, washed-rind soft cheeses introduced in the 1930s by an innovative dairy entrepreneur from Belgium, Carl Hirnbein) as well as the more homemade Backsteinkäs (literally, brick stone cheese, traditionally made by Alpine dairies in addition to hard cheese, for faster consumption). Chiriboga Blue is an utterly successful take on the tradition of Bavarian blue cheeses. In shape and in size, the 5.5-pound (2.5 kg) wheels resemble Roquefort or Bleu d'Auvergne, but with a much sweeter taste and with only a few blue veins inside the dense, silky, cream-white paste. The new landscape of cheese in Germany is expanding all the time, down the valleys and up the hills.

Heinzelmann, Ursula. "Möhrenlaibchen: How the Carrot Got into the Cheese." *Gastronomica: The Journal of Food and Culture* 9 (2009): 48–52.

Heinzelmann, Ursula. *Beyond Bratwurst: A History of Food in Germany.* London: Reaktion, 2014.

Schreibers, Josef von. *Die Milchwirthschaft im Innern großer Städte und deren nächste Umgebung.* Prague: Calve, 1847, p. 3.

Studd, Will. "Germany: Artisan Cheeses of Germany." *Cheese Slices*, season 5, episode 9, aired 2011. http://www.willstudd.com/season/season-5/#germany-artisan-cheeses-of-germany.

Ursula Heinzelmann

gilomeni manoura

See GREECE.

Ginzburg, Carlo (1939–) is a historian and author of *The Cheese and the Worms*, first published in Italian in 1976 and translated into English in 1980. Based on court records left by the Inquisition, Ginzburg explores the worldview of Menocchio, a sixteenth-century miller, who believed that the world originated in putrefaction. Charged with heresy, Menocchio was questioned at length about his adherence to Catholic doctrine. He articulated a complex and heartfelt cosmogony that was rooted more in the experiences of daily life than in theology. When asked where angels came from, Menocchio replied, "They were produced by nature from the most perfect substance of the world, just as worms are produced from a cheese." Maggots appearing in rotting cheese were likely a common sight in the sixteenth century, and the idea of spontaneous generation—that life can emerge *sui generis* from inorganic material—was widely held, but the materialism of his ideas did not appease the inquisitors, and they were concerned that he had been spreading his heretical ideas to other villagers. Ginzburg wonders about the similarity of this idea to a Vedic myth of the world emerging from coagulation, then explores what these ideas suggest about the lively oral culture of peasants in early modern Italy.

See also CURDLING, CULTURAL THEORIES OF.

Ginzburg, Carlo. *The Cheese and the Worms: The Cosmos of a Sixteenth-Century Miller*. Translated by John Tedeschi and Anne Tedeschi. Baltimore: Johns Hopkins University Press, 1980. English translation of *Il Formaggio e i Vermi: Il Cosmo di un Mugnaio del'500*, first published in 1976.

Maria Trumpler

Giolito Formaggi is a family business that spans three generations in the Piedmont region of northern Italy. Its current proprietor, Fiorenzo Giolito, is the charismatic operator of a cheese business in the town of Bra, as well as stalls at various open-air markets in the province of Cuneo. Within the butter-colored walls of his family home, Fiorenzo and his staff manage a small store, complete with maturing rooms.

Founded in the 1920s by Fiorenzo Giolito's grandmother as a wholesale cheese reseller, the company's efforts shifted under his father's guidance to selling directly to the public through the region's weekly markets. The business's current incarnation, located within the same town as the headquarters of the international Slow Food movement, attracts cheese lovers from around the globe. Traveling turophiles and celebrities alike are drawn to the decades-old shop for the chance to taste and purchase the best regional and national cheeses, all refined by Fiorenzo's practiced hand. A personal collection of vintage tools, gathered from local pastures, serves as a dairy museum within the store, honoring the traditional methods of shepherds and cheesemakers.

As a co-founder of the famed biannual CHEESE festival in Bra and an external consultant to Eataly, one might imagine Fiorenzo Giolito to be a staid figure on the international cheese scene. However, after glimpsing him posed as "Mr. September" in a local fundraising calendar (confidently covered by only an apron and a few strategically placed wheels of cheese), or hearing him exuberantly sing along to the music of a local a cappella group, echoing throughout his shop in the local Piemontese dialect, one gets a sense of the joyful, playful pleasure that he brings to every aspect of his work.

Along with selecting and aging many different forms, Giolito Formaggi is the sole producer of Braciuk, a tipsy version of the town's namesake cow's milk cheese. This unique product, whose name in the Piemontese dialect translates to "drunken Bra," falls within the category of *ubriaco* (drunken) cheese. This class of cheese, very prevalent in Italy's Veneto region, includes all cheeses that are washed or soaked in wine or grape skins. Legend has it that this style resulted from northern Italian farmers' attempts at hiding their wheels from hungry soldiers who often looted cellars and pantries during World War I. In doing so, the farmers realized that not only did the cheeses keep for much longer after being immersed, a wealth of new flavors also emerged from the close contact with the grape pomace. Braciuk is created by maturing wheels of Bra Tenero DOP in the grape residue left over from the individual pressing of local Nebbiolo, Pelaverga, Barbera, and Cabernet varieties. This treatment results in a cheese with a slightly alcoholic paste and a vibrant purple rind, encrusted with the skins of dried grapes.

See also BRA; ITALY; and SLOW FOOD.

"The Drunken Cheeses." *Slow Wine Magazine*. http://www.slowwinemagazine.com/en/the-drunken-cheese.

La Terre dei Savoia Guide. http://www
.visitterredeisavoia.it/en/guide/?IDR=1686.

Prakash, Sheela. "Inside One of Italy's Best Cheese
Shops, Giolito Formaggi in Bra." *Serious Eats*, 21
January 2014. http://www.seriouseats.com/2014/01/
inside-one-of-italys-best-cheese-shops-giolit.html.

Allison Radecki

Gjetost

See CONCENTRATED WHEY CHEESE.

Gloucester cheese comprises two main varieties, Single Gloucester and Double Gloucester. Other lesser known varieties include Sage Gloucester, Cotswold, and Double Berkeley. The two main varieties are indigenous to the county of Gloucestershire in England, which bestrides the river Severn and its wide estuary. The meadows adjoining the Severn where the Old Gloucester cows grazed (a few still do) are rich and ideally suited for dairying and cheesemaking.

The farmers there typically milked herds of Old Gloucester cows. These beautiful and distinctively marked cattle are inextricably linked to the cheeses of the region. In 1796 William Marshall described the breed in detail in his *Rural Economy of Gloucestershire,* along with the Gloucester cheeses and the method of making them, which varied a little from farm to farm. This method was handed down from mother to daughter.

Double Gloucester cheese is richer and higher in fat than its Single counterpart. Wealthy urbanites would buy Double Gloucester cheese, which could withstand the rigours of travelling by horse-drawn wagon and barge. It crossed the oceans in sailing ships, reaching America and New Zealand.

Single Gloucester was very much the cheese of the poor. Often made of partly skimmed milk, it was also made during the winter when cows were fed on hay. Hence, it was sometimes known as "hay cheese." It was eaten on the farms where it was produced and in the surrounding country districts, and was particularly suited to toasting. The large thin wheels were rather delicate and so could not be transported easily. The mere act of stacking these cheeses more than three or four high could result in significant damage.

As late as the mid-twentieth century, there were people who grew up on the farms in Gloucestershire who had never eaten Double Gloucester cheese because it was too valuable. It was always sent away, they complained, to provide the farm with its income, while a farmer and his family had to make do with the "inferior" Single Gloucester cheese.

Single Gloucester is a relatively quick cheese to make, with a lower acidity than Double Gloucester and a higher moisture content. Nevertheless, it is classified as a hard cheese. It is best eaten at 4–6 weeks of age, when the texture is smooth and the flavour mild and lactic. It is made without colouring and is not suitable for ageing. Double Gloucester is a harder, drier cheese that undergoes more heating during the making process. It is also made to a higher acidity. It is coloured orange by the addition of annatto. See ANNATTO. Allegedly, the practice of colouring the cheese originated from a deception committed by the dairymaids of Gloucestershire. Wanting to make extra butter, they skimmed some of the cream from the milk that was intended for cheese. However, the resulting cheese was paler in colour than it should have been, and so to conceal their deceit they added annatto. The addition of colour came to be standard and is carried on to this day. Double Gloucester was purchased from the farms by cheese factors. They would check the quality of the cheeses by walking on them. If any gave in, they were deemed to be "hoven" (diseased) and unsuitable for purchase. See CHEESE FACTOR.

Cheesemaking in the county of Gloucestershire is now a shadow of what it was in the early nineteenth century when over a thousand tons was produce annually in the Vale of Berkeley alone. At that time, almost all dairy farmers would have been obliged to make cheese from their milk, since before refrigeration and the advent of railways, there would have been no other way of getting their produce to market. Today Single Gloucester cheese is made on six farms in Gloucestershire. Its production is covered by a protected designation of origin (PDO). This restricts its production to farms within Gloucestershire that have a herd of Old Gloucester cows. Individual producers typically make up to 250 pounds (113 kg) per week, and many make a lot less. Double Gloucester cheese is made on a similar number of farms within the county, though its production is not covered by any legislation. It is also made on an industrial scale by large dairy concerns in various parts of Britain and may be produced in block form for the budget market.

There are a number of traditions associated with cheesemaking in Gloucestershire. Cheese "coasters," large wooden dishes shaped to hold both a whole Double and a whole Single Gloucester cheese on their sides, were produced during Georgian times. This dish would be passed up and down the table, and chunks of the cheese would be cut off as required as the coaster passed by. While genuine Double and Single Gloucester cheese, like the Old Gloucester cows, are rare, they are a source of considerable pride for the people of Gloucestershire and beyond.

Low, David. *On the Domestic Animals of the British Islands.* London: Longman, Brown, Green, & Longmans, 1850.
Marshall, William. *The Rural Economy of Gloucestershire, Including Its Dairy.* London: G. Nicol, 1796. Facsimile reprinted by Alan Sutton (Gloucester, U.K.: 1979).
Stout, Adam. *The Old Gloucester: The Story of a Cattle Breed.* Gloucester, U.K.: Alan Sutton, 1980.

Charles Martell

glucono delta lactone (GDL) is a natural acidifying compound that can reduce progressively and regularly the pH of a solution. It is a fine, white crystalline powder, freely soluble in water. It is practically odorless and has a slightly sweet taste. Nontoxic, GDL is completely metabolized in the body like a carbohydrate.

GDL is obtained from natural vegetable sources, like honey or grapes, by dehydration of gluconic acid. It can be also obtained by fermentation. Highly soluble in water, the glucono-delta-lactone partially hydrolyzes itself into gluconic acid, leading to the pH reduction. The kinetic of hydrolysis depends on temperature and pH. This property led to interesting functionalities in food processing in baking, or cheesemaking, or ready-to-eat foods (soy matrix, surimi, etc.). It is classified in Europe as a food additive under the number E575 and necessarily indicated on the label. Roquette is the world leader in GDL production.

GDL is used in cheesemaking to precisely reach a desired pH for renneting, which then impacts mineralization and final dry matter. This use is forbidden in PDO cheeses. In Europe the use of additives is strictly regulated according to the principle "of positive lists." In other words: what is not expressly authorized is forbidden. A new additive can be used only after notice to the European Authority on Food Safety (EFSA). There is a special joint FAO/WHO Expert Committee on Food Additives.

See also PH MEASUREMENT.

Chen, Y. C., et al. "Proteomic Profiling of the Coagulation of Milk Proteins Induced by Glucono-delta-lactone." *Food Hydrocolloids* 52 (2016): 137–143.
Grygorczyk, A., and M. Corredig. "Acid Induced Gelation of Soymilk, Comparison Between Gels Prepared with Lactic Acid Bacteria and Glucono-delta-lactone." *Food Chemistry* 141 (2013): 1716–1721.

Sylvie Lortal

glycolysis, in its strictest sense, refers to a universal pathway used in all living cells, including microbial cells, to produce energy from a ubiquitous sugar, glucose. It is the first step in the production of energy by cells. Glycolysis consists of ten reactions catalyzed by enzymes called glycolytic enzymes, which convert glucose into pyruvic acid. The energy released by these reactions is produced in the form of ATP (adenosine triphosphate), a high-energy compound, and NADH (reduced nicotinamide adenine dinucleotide).

Glycolysis occurs in nearly all organisms, both aerobic and anaerobic. The term "glycolysis" can also be used in a broader meaning. In the field of cheese ripening, glycolysis is used along with proteolysis and lipolysis to refer to all the reactions that convert milk sugar (lactose) and, by extension, other carbon substrates into end products of metabolism by cheese microorganisms. Lactose is converted into lactic acid as a main end product by lactic acid bacteria, with a concomitant production of carbon dioxide and ethanol or acetate by heterofermentative lactic acid bacteria. The complete metabolism of cheese lactose is essential for the production of good-quality cheese because the presence of residual lactose may promote the growth of undesirable bacteria during cheese ripening. Lactic acid can be further metabolized by ripening cultures. For example, propionibacteria convert lactic acid into propionic acid, acetic acid, and carbon dioxide. Citric acid, another carbon source present in milk, is co-metabolized with lactose by some strains of lactic acid bacteria and converted to other metabolites, such as diacetyl and acetoin, two compounds associated with a butter flavor.

See also DAIRY PROPIONIBACTERIA; LACTIC ACID; LACTIC ACID BACTERIA; LIPOLYSIS; and PROTEOLYSIS.

McSweeney, Paul L. H. "Biochemistry of Cheese Ripening: Introduction and Overview." In *Cheese: Chemistry, Physics, and Microbiology*, edited by Patrick F. Fox et al. Vol. 1: *General Aspects*, pp. 347–360. London: Elsevier, 2004.

McSweeney, Paul L. H., and Patrick F. Fox. "Metabolism of Residual Lactose and of Lactate and Citrate." In *Cheese: Chemistry, Physics, and Microbiology*, edited by Patrick F. Fox et al. Vol. 1: *General Aspects*, 3d ed., pp. 361–371. London: Elsevier, 2004.

Anne Thierry

The **goat** (*Capra hircus*), in the company of sheep, was the first ungulate livestock to be domesticated, ahead of cattle and pigs. Recent interpretation of ancient artifacts strongly suggests that domestication of goats began around 9000 B.C.E and maybe even earlier. Even with this long association, the ancestry of goats is still incomplete. Three main ancestral lines have contributed to the genetic breadth of current populations persisting still as wild descendants: the Ibex (*Capra aegagrus ibex*), the Bezoar (*Capra aegagrus aegagrus*), the Markhor (*Capra aegagrus falconer*), and to a smaller extent the Tur (*Capra caucasica* spp.). Theories now point to the Bezoar as the most common wild ancestor, which was brought under human stewardship first in the eastern Iranian plateau and eastern Anatolian region of Turkey. Even with the Bezoar's grand contribution, the lineage of the modern goat is a swirl of locally selected pockets infused with animals transported in from other regions. A recent study suggests an affinity of the gene pool between the western part of the Mediterranean and the Near East thousands of miles away, giving a picture of the maritime diffusion of goats, by way of human-directed trade, across northern Africa, southern Europe, and criss-crossing through the Strait of Gibraltar. After being domesticated goats spread south throughout the continent of Africa and east to all of Indo-Asia, as well as to Spain, Portugal, France, and Great Britain. This portable animal went with colonists to South Africa, the Americas including the Caribbean, and is now found worldwide.

Domestication of goats was driven by the need for meat, fiber, and leather for the first few thousand years. After the discovery of milk storage in about 6500 B.C.E., the image of a specially bred, extra-productive dairy goat comes into view. Because goats and sheep have been subjected to more time under domestication than cattle, humans probably used goat's milk first to provide extra milk for feeding human infants, who naturally produced lactases to digest the milk sugar lactose. Since human adults universally showed lactose intolerance after infancy, the production of cheese or lactic-fermented milk products allowed consumption without digestive upset.

Why was the goat easily domesticate-able? According to one theory the animals most easily domesticated could live off the food scraps and byproducts of food processing done by humans, had a short reproductive cycle and grew at a rate for quick harvest, were able to breed in more confined areas, and took humans as their new herd leaders and followed with submission. Perhaps this closely matching description

Gunilla Andersson of Raftsjöhöjdens Farm Dairy in Sweden feeding her goats. © PAULINA RYTKÖNEN

Montana cheesemaker Margaret Adams milking one of her two LaMancha goats, whose milk she uses to make feta cheese. © VINCENZO SPIONE

explains why the goat is extremely popular in the world with a wider distribution than any other domestic herd animal, with more people drinking goat's milk than cow's milk.

Centers of Goat Cheese Production

Early and current centers of cheese production are found radiating out from the birthplace of goat domestication centers in what are now Turkey and Iran. Historically cheese production arose in Egypt (5500–4500 B.C.E.) where even the pharaoh Tutankhamen had goat cheese placed in his tomb (3300 B.C.E.). Later goat herding and cheesemaking is recorded in Greece (500 B.C.E.) and in the Roman Empire (27 B.C.E.–500 C.E.), including the Middle East. Even after this classic regime's decline, the legacy of dairying continued in what is now France and Great Britain. However recent analysis of potsherds in northern Europe now date cheesemaking to 7200 B.C.E.! Combined with sheep's milk, goat's milk in Greece is mostly made into feta but, unlike sheep's milk cheeses, no other types of goat cheese have protected designation of origin (PDO) in 2016. In Europe, Switzerland is the proud birthplace of the

development of the globally influential dairy goat breeds of Alpine, Toggenburg, Saanen, Oberhasli, and locally the Appenzeller, starting in the 1800s. The Swiss contributed to the progress of cheese production by being among the first to mechanize the process. France, a country capitalizing on these high milk volume breeds, has settled nicely into the number-two ranked and arguably best-known producer of the world's goat cheese due to its persistent support of breed selection and the creation of fourteen PDO cheeses.

In terms of a global view of goat's milk and cheese production, it is difficult to compare countries such as France, where milk recording is standard practice, with other countries where production is extrapolated by estimates of live animals, as in India. Thus, while Europe has only about 3 percent of the world's total goat population (including meat and fiber goats) made up of the most productive and large dairy breeds like the French Alpine, it produces about 15 percent or more of the world's goat cheese. Contrast this with India, which cares for 35 percent of the world's goats and has 22 percent of the world's cheese production. Worldwide estimates are 457,401 metric tons of goat cheese production

Table 1. Goat milk production rank by country with principal milk products and breeds of goat.

Country	1000 M tons[1]	Primary consumption Cheese(C), Milk (M), Fermented Noncheese (F)	Representative breed[2]
India	4,850	M/C	Jamunapari
Bangladesh	2,608	M	Black Bengal
Sudan (former)	1,532	M	Nubian
Pakistan	779	M	Beetal
Mali	715	M	Sahelian
France	624	C	French Alpine
Spain	444	C	Murcianna-Granadina
Greece	407	C	Native
Iran	225	M	Arab
Somalia	500	M	Benadir
China	292	M	Xinong Saanen
Turkey	369	C/F/M	Kilis
Algeria	267	F/C/M	Berber
Mexico	166	M/C	Mexican Criolo
Brazil	150	C	Crioulo
Netherlands	217	C	Dutch White
United States	50	C	LaMancha
Norway	21	C	Nordic

[1] FAOSTAT 2012.
[2] Hamid 2014; Porter 1996.

and there is increasing interest by producers, consumers, and governments alike to augment this.

Dairy Goat Breeds

The last 150 years has seen a tidal flux of focused breed development as compared to the previous 500. While new breeds are continually being developed and some are not even characterized, according to the Food and Agriculture Organization of the United Nations (FAO) in 2009, there are 1,153 goat breeds in the world. If the small populations of goat groups that are not well classified are removed, the number of recorded breeds drops to about 570. The vast majority of the goat population is in countries that practice extensive management, such as Africa and Asia, where there is also the most variation genetically. In Europe, where the breeds are notably large, the highest recorded milk production yields exist (along with the lowest percent of fat and protein since they are inversely related) and the lowest breed genetic variation is seen. From a 46-country survey, between 30 and 160 breeds have been listed as primarily dairy and of these, recorded goat milk production levels have identified 89 breeds. The recognized highest producing breeds in the world are the Swiss Alpine, Appenzell, Oberhasli, Saanen, and Toggenburg, the American-bred LaMancha, Nubian, and Oberhasli, the Cyprian Damascus, the Spanish Muciana-Granadina, Malagueña, Canaria, and Guardarrama, the French Poitevine, and the Norwegian Nordic (due to its almost twelve-month lactation).

Methods of Production

Current methods of dairy goat production vary widely due to the exceptionally adaptive qualities and the still present wide genetic variation of the caprine species. The goat is a ruminant animal having evolved with an anaerobic rumen (vat-like stomach) full of microorganisms in a beautiful and delicate symbiotic relationship. The protozoa, bacteria, and fungi inside are bent on turning the digested forage into more microbes, and in turn nourishing the host animal with the byproducts of microbial digestion and offering their own protein-rich microbial cells up to the goat GI tract as a nutritious offering. As long as there are enough grasses, legumes, leafy forbs, or woody plants and water, goats can survive on harsh terrain. Indeed goats originated in dry, arid regions and current desert breeds of goats like the

Bedouin (North Africa, Middle East) and Aradi (Saudi Arabian dairy goat) are able to go without water for two to four days at a time while maintaining proper blood metabolites and then can rehydrate by drinking up to 40 percent of their body weight at one time. Goats are also able to select the most nutritious parts of a plant, leaving trees and brush vulnerable. When faced with lower quality feed, they don't eat more like cows or sheep, rather they select the best parts and eat the same amount or less.

Agility, smallness of size, adaptability to environment, and ability to forage selectively allow many management systems to apply in dairy goat production. Naturally extensive systems are employed where there is much rangeland, and where goats are left to forage or a goat herder is employed to watch over and move the goats to new areas to prevent over-defoliation or killing of plants. The advantage for cheese lovers is that the aromatic compounds from plants like wild thyme, rosemary, mint, gorse, lavender, geranium, and chamomile are transported to the milk after ingestion, providing a premier and unique gustatory experience. If little or no grain is fed, the quantity of milk produced is lower but richer in fat, protein, and distinctive flavors. An example is Crottin de Chavignol PDO cheese from the French Loire region whose definition requires that the goats graze. This type of system underscores a more even and predictable level of production and high quality milk for cheesemaking.

At the other extreme, the farming system commonly employed in North America and many parts of Europe is a more intensive, confinement system where farmers bring preserved or fresh forage to dairy goats and add concentrates or grain in the milking parlor. This is for the convenience of the farmer, for labor efficiency, and in areas where inclement weather dominates the year. These systems require a high input of machinery and feed delivery systems, as well as manure and bedding management. Some farming systems go halfway and allow some grazing or "browsing" outside seasonally and then add supplemental protein and energy to balance the diet and improve production.

Milk Characteristics

Like other mammals, goat's milk is an excretion from the specialized alveolar cells of the mammary gland and is composed of an approximate proportion of the general nutrients at 5 percent lactose (sweet milk sugar), 3.5 percent protein (primarily four types of casein with some lactalbumin and lacto-globulin), 4 percent fat (mostly triglycerides with fatty acids), and 0.5 percent of minerals (calcium, phosphorus, potassium, sodium, and magnesium being the major ones), vitamins (an array including thiamine and niacin), non-protein nitrogen and minute amounts of biological proteins like antimicrobial enzymes.

Lactose, created in the alveolar cells by combining the simple sugars glucose and galactose, is the energy source for cheese culture. Protein in goat's milk is suspended in a form called a micelle with phosphorus and calcium and caprine. Goat's milk micelles are smaller than those in cow's or sheep's milk. The unique distribution of casein fractions in goat's milk affects the texture of the curd, making it less firm and difficult to make yogurt set well. The milk protein structure and components are thought to explain why infants and some adults digest it well and do not have allergic reactions. See DAIRY ALLERGY.

The fat or cream is present in goat's milk as globules that do not clump together and rise to the top of the container as they do in cow's milk. See FAT. This natural homogenization is due to the low adhesion quality of the goat's lactadherin molecule in the fat globule. Fat contains fatty acids and the distinct goat cheese flavors come from the abundance of short- and medium-chain fatty acids: butyric C4:0, caproic C6:0, caprylic C8:0, and capric C10:0 acids, lauric C12:0, and myristic C14:0. Demonstrating the importance of these in human health, the C6–C14 medium-chain fatty acids are used in established medical treatments for a range of serious digestive disorders. Goat's milk and cheese are always white because the fat-soluble pre-vitamin beta carotene of a rich yellow color is converted to a colorless vitamin A (retinol) before entering milk. Goats feeding on fresh plants have higher vitamin E content in the milk and vitamin D if they are out in the sun, both of which are fat soluble.

Due to its early domestication and then widespread global migration, a spectrum of genetic traits exists in different breeds around the world. For example, a selection for high milk production in about twenty to thirty breeds are dependent on a good forage and grain supply, while lower milk yields in over one hundred other dairy breeds work very well in extensive systems with little or no supplementation and often have higher solids in their milk and a higher cheese yield to milk ratio. With their agile bodies and prehensile lips, given the chance goats are able to select plants to eat that have more aromatic compounds that will directly influence the flavor of the cheese. This along with the unique protein and fat composition create cheeses that provide an exclusive and distinctive gustatory experience.

See also COW and SHEEP.

Cannas, A., and G. Pulina *Dairy Goats Feeding and Nutrition*. Bologna: CAB International, 2008.
Devendra, C. "Small Ruminants in Asia: Contribution to Food Security, Poverty Alleviation and Opportunities for Productivity Enhancement." Mekarn Proceedings International Workshop on Small Ruminant Production and Development in South East Asia. Hanoi, Vietnam, 2–4 March 2005.
FAOSTAT. http://faostat3.fao.org/home/E.
Hamid, M. A., and K. M. Hossain. "Role of Private Sector in the Development of Dairy Industry in Bangladesh." *Livestock Research for Rural Development* 26 (10) 2014. http://www.lrrd.org/lrrd26/10/hami26179.htm.
Hatziminaoglou, Y., and J. Boyazoglu. "The Goat in Ancient Civilisations: From the Fertile Crescent to the Aegean Sea." *Small Ruminant Research* 51 (2004): 123–129.
Naderia, S., et al. "The Goat Domestication Process Inferred from Large-scale Mitochondrial DNA Analysis of Wild and Domestic Individuals." *Proceedings of the National Academy of Science* 18, vol. 105 no. 46 (2008): 17659–17664.
Park, Y. W., et al. "Physico-chemical Characteristics of Goat and Sheep Milk." *Small Ruminant Research* 68 (2007): 88–113.
Porter, V. *Goats of the World*. Ipswich, U.K.: Farming Press, 1996.
Starbard, Ann. *The Dairy Goat Handbook*. Minneapolis: Voyageur Press, 2015.

Carol Delaney

Gorgonzola is a straw-white soft cheese, known for two different type of production: "dolce" (sweet) and "piccante" (savory). The sweet version, which represents 90 percent of the total Gorgonzola production, is creamy and soft, with a slightly spicy, delicate taste. The "piccante" version is more blue-veined, thicker, and more crumbly, with a strong taste and a firmer paste with less serum content due to a longer "baking" period. Gorgonzola received

DOC status in 1955 and PDO certification in 1996. The Gorgonzola PDO represents the third Italian cheese by quantity produced, after Grana Padano and Parmigiano Reggiano. The total production of the Italian PDO cheeses is 500,000 tons of which Gorgonzola represents 10 percent. See GRANA PADANO and PARMIGIANO REGGIANO.

Gorgonzola's origin is described by a Lombardy legend which says that one evening centuries ago a cheese producer rushed out to meet his lover, left a vat of curds open all night, returned later, and, in order to cover up his mistake, added fresh curds the following day. A few months later, at the end of aging, he discovered with disappointment that a bluish mold had invaded his cheeses. At first embarrassed, he was soon pleasantly surprised when he tasted it and realized that the cheeses had a delicious and interesting taste. This cheesemaker casually discovered the process of "erborinatura" that means the creation of molds. The name of "erborinatura" derives from the Lombardy dialectical word *erburin* that means parsley, because of the greenish streaks in the cheese structure.

The developing (growing) of molds happens because of the use of two curds. The more acid curd from the previous evening does not amalgamate perfectly with the morning's curd, creating a wealth of folds and crannies that encourage the development of molds (*Penicillium glaucum* for Gorgonzola) inside the cheese with widespread bluish-green marbling and a strong, savory taste ("piccante" in Italian). The method of working with a double paste, mixing the evening's curd with that of the morning, has been used for many years in the production of Gorgonzola.

Gorgonzola cheese production technology has been defined since the beginning of the twentieth century, along with the denomination. In fact the original Gorgonzola's name was Stracchino or Stracchino di Gorgonzola, from the town of Gorgonzola, which was the main trading center but not the production center. Gorgonzola cheese production is allowed in two provinces of Piedmont, Novara and Vercelli, and also in other provinces of Lombardy. The disciplinary rules stipulate cheeses weighing from 13 to 26 pounds (6 to 12 kilograms), with a diameter of 10–12 inches (25–30 centimeters), and a height of 6–8 inches (15–20 centimeters). Gorgonzola is made with whole pasteurized cow's milk. Gorgonzola is produced all year round. The aging, two to three months minimum (prolonged aging is for "piccante") starts with a few days of "baking" at 68°F (20°C) and consists of placing fresh cheeses in a heated room to favor the expulsion (draining) of the serum. During aging the cheeses are regularly turned and pierced with needles into both the top and bottom to encourage development of *Penicillium*. See NEEDLES. This creates a passageway for air to enter the cheese and interact with the mold to create veining. At the end of this process Gorgonzola is wrapped in aluminum foil sheets that are exclusively assigned to the producers authorized by the consortium. The aluminum foil sheets enable moisture retention and eliminate rind dehydration.

See also BLUE CHEESES; ITALY; LOMBARDY; and PENICILLIUM.

Androuët, Pierre. *Le dictionnaire des fromages du monde.* Paris: Le Cherche Midi Editeur, 2002, p. 158.

Angeli, Franco. *L'Italia dei formaggi DOC.* Unalat con INSOR edizione Franco Angeli, 1992, pp. 55–58.

Cremona, Luigi, and Francesco Soletti. *L'Italia dei formaggi.* Milan: Touring Club Italiano, 2002, pp. 29–37.

Fiori, Giacomo, et al. *Formaggi italiani.* Novara, Italy: EOS Editrice, 1999, pp. 74–75.

Fiori, Giovanni Guffanti, and Carlo Vischi. *Formaggi italiani.* Savigliano, Italy: Gribaudo, 2004, p. 194.

Guatteri, Fabiano. *Formaggi.* Novara, Italy: Istituto Geografico De Agostini, 2005, pp. 146–147.

Sardo, Piero, et al. *Formaggi d'Italia.* Bra, Italy: Slow Food Editore, 1999, pp. 174–175.

Carlo Fiori

Gouda. There are very few cheeses that have played as big a role in their country's history of trade, industry, and taste as Gouda. For many around the world it is the first cheese they will know when asked about the Netherlands. Gouda takes its name from one of Europe's largest cheese markets, Goudse Kaasmarkt, in the town of Gouda, in southern Holland. Gouda has hosted some form of the renowned cheese market since the seventeenth century, or quite likely since the end of medieval times. In fact the history of Gouda-style cheeses and markets in the Netherlands specializing in their trade may go back as far as the twelfth century, when weigh houses for cheese were already in existence in many Dutch towns. See ALKMAAR AUCTION.

But it was during the seventeenth century that the fortunes of the country and the cheese rose in concert. The first reason for this can be attributed to an innovation in cheesemaking that is the hallmark of this cheese, a method developed to achieve a balance between the large size of Gouda cheeses (most wheels are 15–16 pounds [7 kilograms]), and the need to reduce the moisture content to reduce the risk of internal rot. In response to these circumstances, the cheesemakers in the south—as opposed to the north where the smaller Edam cheeses were predominant—developed a process that first scalded and stirred the curds in hot water, then removed the whey, before molding and pressing the cheese. Pressing the cheese produces a drier, more durable cheese ideal for aging. Removing the whey also removes some of the lactose, which reduces the acidity, leaving behind a sweeter cheese. See PRESS and SCALDING.

There is some controversy over who, exactly, originated this method, for it is nearly identical to the method employed by English dairies in Gloucester and Cheddar at the end of the 1700s. While there is no definitive answer to who developed the process first, and where and when it was developed, there is agreement that there was substantial activity in cheesemaking and cheese export in southern Holland during the years 1500–1700, and the method for Gouda and its signature mark of scalding were more than likely established before the English recorded their technique in the late 1700s. See GLOUCESTER and CHEDDAR.

Another historical innovation credited to Gouda—as well as its success in export globally, then and now—is its recognizable form. Gouda is shaped into a very large wheel, pressed with round wooden molds. See FORMS OR MOLDS. This results in a very durable rind, again similar to its northern cousin Edam. Long before the era of mass food packaging, Gouda was one of the first widely distributed dairy products to have a signature look—in this case, a bright yellow coat died with saffron threads steeped in vinegar; to this day the look is distinct. Several centuries ago this telltale rind also protected against maggots during long shipping journeys and as cargo across continents. During the spice trade of the seventeenth century, other flavoring and coloring agents such as cumin and cloves also found their way into Gouda; today spiced cheeses still emerge from the Dutch market.

Gouda has an enormous range of flavors and textures, depending on when it is eaten, which deepen and evolve substantially with age. The scalding and washing of the curd and the removal of the lactose creates a subtly sweet and slightly elastic curd that forms the base for an initially supple texture. In the first few months Gouda exhibits a mellow, lightly fruity, milky-sweet taste. But as it ages—especially after eighteen months and up to three or four years—it begins to turn granular, with hard layers of mature cheese revealing flavors at once nutty and herbaceous, with notes of chocolate, Brazil nut, and butterscotch.

During the early 1900s cheese production in the Netherlands was as high as 42.1 million pounds (19 million kilograms) for export, even higher than the 41.8 million (18.9 million kilograms) for the domestic market. As of 2016 production stands at 730,000 metric tons of cheese (550,000 is exported), and 60 percent of that is Gouda. While farmhouse versions of Gouda almost disappeared during the end of the twentieth century, there are now around 250 dairies producing an artisanal version known as "goudse boerenkaas," roughly translating as "farmer cheese." Like similar cheeses such as Mimolette, it can age up to five or six years and has a rich, grainy paste that crumbles and slowly melts on the palate. The finish is emphatic, staying in the mouth for several minutes and a superb match for red and botrytized dessert wines. Currently there are three producers making aged raw-milk boerenkass, organized in a Slow Food presidio. See MIMOLETTE and SLOW FOOD.

Dutch cheesemakers moving abroad and foreign dairies looking to capitalize on the popularity of Gouda also mean variants are available worldwide. Despite the centuries-old history, massive sales, and traditional brand power of the cheese, Gouda is not name protected, which has resulted in a flood of imitators (and namesakes), and—even for farmhouse versions—a concurrently low price ceiling for the cheese. Only one style of Gouda is name protected: Noord Hollandse Gouda, which was awarded a PDO in 1996. Today Noord Hollandse Gouda is produced only by the dairy conglomerate Friesland Campina, in their Lutjewinkel, North Holland, cheesemaking facility.

See also EDAM; NETHERLANDS; and WASHED-CURD CHEESES.

Androuet, Pierre. *Guide to Cheese*. Henley-on-Thames, U.K.: Aidan Ellis Publishing, 1993.

Dalby, Andrew. *Cheese—A Global History*. London: Reaktion, 2009.

Formaggio.it. http://www.formaggio.it.

Harbutt, Julie, and Martin Aspinwall. *World Cheese Book*. New York: DK, 2015.

Kindstedt, Paul. *Cheese and Culture: A History of Cheese and Its Place in Western Civilization*. White River Junction, Vt.: Chelsea Green, 2012.

McCalman, Max. *Cheese: A Connoisseur's Guide to the World's Best*. New York: Clarkson Potter, 2005.

Robert McKeown

government cheese refers to commodity cheese that was regulated and stored by the US federal government from the conclusion of World War II until the early 1980s to protect the price of dairy. Dairy industry subsidies had artificially driven up supply and the surpluses of fluid milk were industrially processed into cheese, butter, or dehydrated powder and taken off the (supposedly free) market. These products were stored in over 150 warehouses in 35 states and the amount of cheese alone totaled over 500 million pounds (227 million kilograms).

Government cheese became national news in the early 1980s when prominent press learned that cheese was rotting in national vaults while millions of American's remained food insecure. At the same time that the conservative Reagan administration cut the budget of the national food stamp program, progressives and left-wing politicians rallied around the cause to push through legislation that would ameliorate widespread hunger. By the winter of 1981, President Reagan enacted the Special Dairy Distribution Program (SDDP), which gave away 30 million pounds (14 million kilograms) of commodity cheese. Although frequently moldy, this cheese was dispersed to nonprofit organizations, which then distributed it to long lines of hungry patrons.

The SDDP did not end that winter, however, and, because price controls continued to encourage surplus production, the federal government, now in the national spotlight, continued to give away surplus cheese. By 1983 over 300 million pounds (136 million kilograms) of the commodity had been distributed. When free cheese and butter began to cut into the dairy processing industries' profits, the National Cheese Institute rebelled, and concerns further escalated. Eventually, the federal government instituted the whole dairy herd buyout, which provided incentives for farmers to "liquidize" their dairy assets and resulted in a significant reduction of milk and cheese production and, by extension, surplus.

While the government cheese scandal dates to the early 1980s, it is clear that the contributing factors are systemic. Government cheese and other food commodities are built into a regulated economy that encourages agricultural surplus. Faced with the alternative between stockpiling excess provisions to protect profitability or the danger of empty federal food coffers as experienced during the Great Depression and again throughout Word War II, government cheese proves to be a complicated matter.

See also COMMODITY CHEESE.

Poppendieck, Janet. *Sweet Charity: Emergency Food and the End of Entitlement*. London: Penguin. 1998.

Bradley M. Jones

Grafton Village Cheese was originally started in 1892 as a cheesemaking cooperative in rural Vermont. Such cooperatives were very common at the time. In the era before refrigeration farmers needed to pool their resources to turn a surplus of fresh, highly perishable milk into cheese, butter, and other shelf-stable products. In 1912 a fire destroyed the original factory. However in the mid-1960s the Windham Foundation, a nonprofit dedicated to promoting Vermont's rural communities, restored the company, bringing cheesemaking back to Grafton Village. The Windham Foundation's mission is "to promote the vitality of Grafton and Vermont's rural communities through its philanthropic and educational programs and its subsidiaries whose operations contribute to these endeavors." Today Grafton Village Cheese continues its historic tradition of buying raw, hormone-free milk from local dairies and turning that milk into a wide array of Cheddar cheeses. Grafton now has two production facilities— the Grafton Village facility that the Windham Foundation restored, and another newer facility in nearby Brattleboro, Vermont. Grafton Village Cheese's signature cheese is Cheddar—it produces an award-winning line of Cheddar cheese that is aged for up to five years. Grafton also produces a line of flavored Cheddars, as well as a newer line of cave-aged cheeses.

See also CHEDDAR and VERMONT.

Grafton Village Cheese. http://www.graftonvillagecheese
.com.
Werlin, Laura, and Martin Jacobs. *The New American
Cheese: Profiles of America's Greatest Cheesemakers and
Recipes for Cooking with Cheese.* New York: Stewart,
Tabori & Chang, 2000.

Anne Saxelby

Grana Padano is the most produced among
cheeses covered by the protected designation of
origin (PDO) scheme within the European Union.
Nearly 4.5 million cheeses are manufactured yearly
in about 150 factories across the Po River Valley in
northern Italy, a region rich in fresh water, grass,
and dairies. About 30 percent of those cheeses are
exported.

The origin of Grana Padano cheese goes back to
the twelfth century, when local monks developed
the unique recipe to turn milk into a hard cheese
that can be aged for years, the salt being a natural
preservative and the thick dry rind a natural seal.
Since then the production method has hardly changed
in its characterizing traits. The raw milk, coming
from the production area, is partly skimmed by natural creaming, poured into a bell-shaped copper-
lined vat, inoculated with natural whey culture derived from the cheesemaking of the previous day,
and coagulated with calf rennet. The cheese curd is
manually cut into small granules while it is heated
up to 127–129°F (53–54°C) under continuous stirring. When stirring stops, the curd compacts on the
vat bottom and rests in the hot whey for around an
hour. Compacting proceeds through placement of
the cheese into a mold to cool down slowly while
the lactic acid fermentation takes place. Two days
later the cheese is placed in a brine bath for around
three weeks. The ripening period lasts for a minimum of nine months to over two years. A large variety of thermophilic lactic acid bacteria species live
and work into the cheese, coming from both the
raw milk and the whey culture, where they start
growing twenty-four hours before inoculating the
milk. These microbiota represent the fingerprint of
the Grana Padano cheese and are responsible for
the typical crumbly texture and the excellent flavor.
This process necessarily takes a long time; it cannot

be accelerated. Hundreds of enzymes slowly transform proteins, lipids, and sugars into a rich pattern
of soluble tasty molecules.

Grana Padano can be found in three different ripening stages:

- Grana Padano: 9–16 months
- Grana Padano: over 16 months
- Grana Padano Reserve: over 20 months

The more mature the cheese, the nuttier and more
intense the flavor. Furthermore, a characteristic trait
of long-ripened hard cheeses develops, that is, the
formation of crystals due to increased concentration of the less-soluble molecules. The most abundant crystals are white and crunchy, and mostly
consist of tyrosine. Other crystals, made of calcium
phosphate or calcium lactate, are less visible but still
represent a feature consumers appreciate.

Grana Padano is a highly nutritious food. Water
represents one third of the cheese, the other two-
thirds are made of nutrients. During the lengthy ripening, proteins are broken down to small peptides
and free amino acids by the cheese enzymes, thus
the cheese becomes highly digestible and its components are rapidly adsorbed. The rest of the cheese
mostly consists of fat, vitamins, and minerals, among
which calcium and phosphorous are present in a 1.7:1
ratio, considered optimal for absorption by human
body. Due to the extensive lactic acid fermentation
taking place in the first hours after the curd leaves
the vat, Grana Padano cheese is free of lactose. Glucose
and galactose are also fermented very quickly.

Grana Padano cheese is a safe food. The combined effects of the high temperature and acidity
development occurring within the molded cheese
inactivate any pathogenic bacteria that might be
present initially in the raw milk. In fact, as in cheeses
made with pasteurized milk, the alkaline phosphatase within Grana Padano cheese is inactivated. The
outermost zones of the cheese (¾–1 inch/2–3 centimeters in depth) remain phosphatase-positive,
proving that the cheese was made with raw milk.
However this part of the cheese is also safe because
the water activity is so low that no harmful bacteria
can survive.

The whole production chain is regularly inspected
by an independent official organization and guaranteed by the Italian Ministry of Agriculture, to make
sure it fulfills all of its requirements. The Consorzio

di Tutela del Formaggio Grana Padano DOP, established in 1954, is responsible for final grading of the cheeses and gives the heat-branded logo to those cheeses that pass the tests for appearance, aroma, and texture. Besides this, the Consorzio promotes the Grana Padano cheese around the world and protects it from imitation, ensuring that consumers, wherever they buy Grana Padano, even pre-cut or grated, are dealing with the authentic cheese. Scientific research has demonstrated that some analytical methods can be reliable tools for assessing the genuineness of Grana Padano cheese and for discriminating imitation cheeses. Among the Consorzio's tasks is providing technical assistance to cheese-makers in order to preserve quality and distinctive features of this cheese.

See also ITALY.

Consorzio Tutela Grana Padano. http://www.granapadano.it.

European Commission. "Geographical Indications and Traditional Specialties." http://ec.europa.eu/agriculture/quality/schemes.

Gatti, M., et al. "Invited Review: Microbial Evolution in Raw-Milk, Long-Ripened Cheeses Produced Using Natural Whey Starters." *Journal of Dairy Science* 97 (2014): 1–19.

Masotti, F., et al. "Proteolysis Indices Related to Cheese Ripening and Typicalness in PDO Grana Padano Cheese." *International Dairy Journal* 20 (2010): 352–359.

Pellegrino, L., and C. Donnelly. "Public Health Issues in Dairy Production and the Implications on the Safety of Aged Cheeses Made with Raw Milk." In *Safety Assurance during Food Processing*, edited by F. J. M. Smulders and J. D. Collins, pp. 33–55. Wageningen, The Netherlands: Wageningen, The Netherlands, 2004.

Pellegrino, L., and P. Resmini. "Cheesemaking Conditions and Compositive Characteristics Supporting the Safety of the Raw Milk Cheese Italian Grana." *Scienza e Tecnica Lattiero-Casearia* 52 (2001): 105–114.

Tansman, G. F., et al. Crystal Fingerprinting: Elucidating the Crystals of Cheddar, Parmigiano-Reggiano, Gouda, and Soft Washed-rind Cheeses Using Powder X-ray Diffractometry." *Dairy Science & Technology* 95 (2015): 651–664.

Luisa Pellegrino

grated cheese

See CHEESE GRATER and FUNCTIONAL PROPERTIES.

Graukäse

See SOUR SKIMMEDMILK CHEESES.

Graviera Agrafon is a Greek protected designation of origin (PDO) cheese produced in the mountainous regions of Agrafa (western Thessaly), specifically in Agrithea, Ithomi, Gomfous, Nevropoli, Itamo, Menelaidos, and Tamasio. The name Graviera Agrafon was recognized in 1994 as a PDO for the cheese traditionally produced from sheep's milk. Goat's milk can be also added but its percentage must not exceed 30 percent of the total weight. The origins of Graviera Agrafon date back to 1888, when Raymond Dimitriadis, a pioneer of the art of cheesemaking in Greece, produced the first improved Greek hard cheese with the name of Agrafa cheese, which was then renamed Graviera Agrafon.

Graviera Agrafon has a maximum moisture content of 38 percent and a minimum fat in dry content of 40 percent. It is hard, yellow, cylindrical cheese with a sweet taste and rich aroma. Its mass is compact and full of small round holes. During cheese manufacturing, the addition of rennet, lactic acid starter and propionic bacteria, and calcium chloride (up to 1 ounce per 220 pounds/20 grams per 100 kilograms of milk) is allowed. Coagulation of milk takes place at 93–97°F (34–36°C) and the curd separation from the whey occurs after twenty-five to thirty-five minutes. Under constant stirring the coagulum is reheated up to 118–126°F (48–52°C), poured into molds and kept under pressure for one day. The cheese is removed from the molds and it is left on wooden racks for two days. Afterward it is placed in 19–20 Be brine for another two to four days. Maturation of the cheese occurs in rooms at 54–59°F (12–15°C) with an approximate humidity of 85 percent. For three weeks the surface of the cheese is salted repeatedly, reaching around 2 percent salt in the mature product. The cheese remains at 61–64°F (16–18°C) for one month and then at 54–59°F (12–15°C) with 90–95 percent humidity until the maturation is completed (overall ripening time is three months).

Graviera Agrafon can be eaten cooked or fresh, and can also be used as a grated cheese. In 2012 the production of PDO Graviera Agrafon cheese was 4 tons.

See also GRAVIERA KRITIS and GREECE.

Anifantakis, E. *Greek Cheeses: A Tradition of Centuries.* Athens: National Dairy Committee of Greece, 1991.
"Graviera Agrafon." Cheesenet.gr. http://www.cheesenet.gr/english/cheeses/graviera_agrafwn.htm.
Greek Official Journal, Series B, No 16, 14-01-1994.

Maria Kazou and Konstantinos Papadimitriou

Graviera Kritis (in Greek, Γραβιέρα Κρήτης) is a hard cheese with a natural rind produced on the island of Crete, the largest and most populous of the Greek islands. Awarded protected designation of origin (PDO) status in 1996, the cheese is made predominantly with sheep's milk or with a combination of sheep's and goat's milk. When goat's milk is added, it cannot exceed 20 percent of the total amount of milk used in the cheesemaking process.

Graviera Kritis is produced by small-scale cheesemakers and factories across the island of Crete using milk collected from sheep and goats that are free ranging and that graze on wild grasses in the lowlands in winter and in mountain pastures during the hot summer months. Graviera Kritis is aged at least three months before going to market. When young, its flavor is mellow, nutty, and slightly sweet. As the cheese ages, its flavor sharpens and becomes slightly peppery. Typically served as a table cheese, Graviera Kritis is also grated onto pasta, used as an ingredient in pies and stews, and is one of several cheeses that is battered, fried, and served as the meze known as "saganaki." See SAGANAKI. Graviera Kritis is one of the most popular cheeses on Crete. It is widely available throughout Greece and it is exported. In Greece, it is typically sold in wheels, or as wedges cut from wheels, by butchers, cheese shops, supermarket delis, and directly from producers at roadside stalls and farmers' markets. Outside of Greece, it is sold from the wheel and also in individually packaged slices in specialty cheese shops, Greek ethnic markets, large supermarkets, and online.

See also GRAVIERA AGRAFON; GRAVIERA NAXOU; and GREECE.

"Graviera Kritis D.O.P." Formaggio.it. http://www.formaggio.it/formaggio-estero/graviera-kritis-d-o-p/.
Greek Ministry of Rural Development and Food. "List of the Greek PDO and PGI Products and Specifications."

http://www.minagric.gr/index.php/en/farmer-menu-2/pdo-pgi-tsgproducts-menu/listpdoproducts-menu.

Alexis Marie Adams

Graviera Naxou. Graviera is a hard protected designation of origin (PDO) cheese, initially manufactured in the second decade of the twentieth century, made in various areas of Greece and traded under the name of the region where it is produced (Graviera Kritis, Naxou, Agrafon, etc.). Graviera Naxou is one of the very few Greek cheeses that are produced from raw cow's milk with limited quantities (up to 20 percent) of sheep's or goat's milk added, and serves under a PDO status.

Graviera is produced traditionally on a small scale, without starter, by farmers whose animals are fed by fresh pasture. In the past every house owned a cow, the milk of which covered the daily needs of the family. With spare milk they produced cheese that was sold to the island's local market.

The milk is renneted at 91–97°F (33–36°C) with traditional rennet from lamb's stomach, with a quantity able to curdle the milk within twenty-five to thirty minutes. The curd is cut in pieces the size of rice grains, cooked at 118–122°F (48–50°C) under continuous stirring and pressed in molds for twenty-four hours. After pressing, the cheese is put on shelves in the salting rooms (57–61°F [14–16°C]) where it is dry salted thirty-five to forty or even sixty times on the surface, depending on the cheese height (3–4 inches [8–10 centimeters] or 5–6 inches [12–15 centimeters]).

The cheese ripens for at least three months, has a smear rind, and exhibits small or larger irregular holes. Its color is yellowish, with an elastic body and cylindrical shape. Graviera Naxou can be enjoyed raw, pan-fried, or grilled, but it is ideal raw, accompanying summer fruits, such as grapes, figs, and melon.

See also GRAVIERA AGRAFON; GRAVIERA KRITIS; and GREECE.

Bozoudi, D., et al. "Graviera Kritis and Graviera Naxou Greek PDO Cheeses: Differences on Microbiological and Physicochemical Characteristics." International Scientific Symposium of Bioengineering of Animal Resources, Timisoara, Romania, 29–30 May 2014, poster presentation.

Bozoudi, D., et al. "Graviera Naxou and Graviera Kritis Greek PDO Cheeses: Discrimination Based on Microbiological and Physicochemical Criteria and Volatile Organic Compounds Profile." *Small Ruminant Research* 136 (2016): 161–172.

Litopoulou-Tzanetaki, E., and N. Tzanetakis. "Microbiological Characteristics of Greek Traditional Cheeses." *Small Ruminant Research* 101 (2011): 17–32.

Litopoulou-Tzanetaki, E., et al., eds. 2007. Proceedings of the International Symposium on Historical Cheeses of Countries Around the Archipelago Mediterraneo, held 6–8 December 2007, in Thessaloniki, Greece, pp. 110–113.

Despina Bozoudi

Great Hill Blue

Great Hill Blue is a cheese made by Great Hill Dairy, located in Marion, Massachusetts, fifty miles south of Boston on Buzzard's Bay. Established in 1997, Great Hill Dairy produces only this one cheese, made from raw cow's milk in a 6-pound wheel.

In the 1990s, Vermont's growing artisanal cheese industry was inspiring producers in neighboring Massachusetts. There, Tim and Tina Stone were looking to get out of the dairy farming business, when they considered taking up cheesemaking. The Stones discovered that no American cheesemaker at that time was producing a blue cheese from raw milk. For reasons of taste and mouthfeel, the Stones decided to make a blue from milk that was neither pasteurized nor homogenized. The result, Great Hill Blue, quickly met with success, and the cheese has gone on to win a number of American Cheese Society awards. The 3,700 gallons of Jersey milk that Tim uses each week to make his cheese come from neighboring farms.

Great Hill Blue has a round, buttery flavor that derives, in part, from the fact that fat globules break down more slowly in unhomogenized milk, thus enhancing the texture. Furthermore, homogenization tends to increase the piquancy in blue cheese. Great Hill Blue, aged for at least 120 days, has a moderate amount of blue mold, minimal piquancy, and hints of sweetness. The fact that it is made with raw milk gives the cheese greater flavor notes and more complexity.

See also BLUE CHEESES.

Kaufelt, Rob, and Liz Thorpe. *Murray's Cheese Handbook: More than 300 of the World's Best Cheeses.* New York: Broadway, 2006.

Roberts, Jeffrey. *Atlas of American Cheese.* White River Junction, Vt.: Chelsea Green, 2007.

Alexandra Leaf

Greece

Greece, a country in Southern Europe, is perhaps most famous for its production of feta cheese; however, the diversity of the Greek terrain, vegetation, microclimates, local animal breeds, and traditions have influenced the evolution of a wide variety of artisanal cheeses, each with their own distinctive textures, flavors, and aromas—characteristics that clearly reflect their terroir. Throughout the country, each village has its own cheesemaking traditions and its own variety, or varieties, of cheese. Much of this cheese is still crafted seasonally, by hand, by shepherds, small-scale dairy farmers, and home cheesemakers for personal use and small-scale local sale. It is rare that these cheeses are consumed outside of the villages in which they were created and because the trade of these products is largely unaccounted for, many of them do not appear in dairy and agricultural statistics. Moreover, they remain unknown outside of Greece—and, in some cases, outside of the regions in which they are produced—due to their highly localized and inconsistent production, off-the-books trade, and nonexistent marketing. Awareness of the diversity of Greek cheeses is also partly obscured by nomenclature. The term "graviera" (derived from the Swiss Gruyère), for example, is used for many hard cheeses made in many different regions of Greece. See GRAVIERA KRITIS; GRAVIERA AGRAFON; and GRAVIERA NAXOU.

Approximately 80 percent of Greece's terrain is rocky and mountainous and is more suitable for the production of sheep and goats than cattle. Thus, the use of cow's milk is not common in Greek cheesemaking and the majority of Greek cheeses are made from ewe's and goat's milk. The small amount of cow's milk that is produced in Greece is primarily sold to dairies, which then process and distribute it for drinking or use it in the production of industrial cheeses, butters, and yogurts.

Throughout Greece, cheese production peaks in spring and early to midsummer. By midsummer, when temperatures rise and the grasses the goats and sheep graze on diminish, milk production slows; consequently, shepherds and farmers cease production of cheese and other milk products until the milking season begins again.

A scene from the home of a traditional cheesemaker in the village of Peleta on the southeastern Peloponnese peninsula in Greece, where she and her daughter craft feta from the milk of her goats and sheep. © VINCENZO SPIONE

Because goats and sheep have slightly different milking seasons, cheesemakers typically use milk from their entire herd, combining the milk of their sheep and goats to craft cheese and other dairy products. In this style of cheesemaking, the ratio of sheep's to goat's milk is never the same, and so the flavors of a type of cheese can vary considerably from batch to batch and from producer to producer. In the mountains of the Peloponnese Peninsula and Northern Greece, and on the islands, sheep and goats are often semiferal, allowed to wander the meadows and forests. Once or twice a day, the animals are gathered and milked. The flavor of the resulting cheese is closely related to the fodder the animals feed on, which, for free-range animals grazing wild grasses, changes from week to week. Again, the result is a cheese whose flavor changes, subtly, from batch to batch and producer to producer.

Evidence of cheese production in Greece dates back to the Neolithic Age. Clay cheese strainers dating from the Neolithic Age and early Bronze Age were discovered in the Palaikastro archaeological site on the eastern end of the southern Greek island of Crete. At the Minoan Palace at Knossos on Crete, tablets dating to 3000 B.C.E. depict men making cheese. Cheese was one of the main foodstuffs of Ancient Greece and references to cheese are made in Ancient Greek literature and mythology, including in the works of Herodotus and Aristotle. See ANCIENT CIVILIZATIONS and HOMER. *The Odyssey*, one of two major ancient Greek poems attributed to

Homer, describes Polyphemus, the Cyclops, as a shepherd and a cheesemaker:

> We soon reached his cave, but he was out shepherding, so we went inside and took stock of all that we could see. His cheese racks were loaded with cheeses and he had more lambs and kids then his pens could hold... The pails and bowls for milking, all solidly made, were swimming with whey. (trans. Samuel Butler).

Since the days of Homer, shepherds have been Greece's principal cheesemakers and in parts of rural Greece they still are, migrating with their flocks from lower-altitude grazing lands in winter to mountain pastures in summer, following ancient migratory trails, called *monopatia*. See SHEPHERD and TRANSHUMANCE. They remain in the high country until autumn, allowing their goats and sheep to graze on the still-green grasses, living in primitive stone huts called *kalivia*, and crafting cheese and other dairy products. From this practice, called transhumance, which is defined as the seasonal migration or movement of humans and their livestock from lower to higher pasture in spring and summer, came the practice of using the tanned and heavily salted skins of sheep or goats to store, age, and transport cheese. This cheese was commonly called "touloumotiri," from touloumi, modern vernacular Greek for the skin of the animal, and "tiri," which means cheese. Touloumotiri is widely considered to be the origin of feta cheese. See FETA. Many small-scale cheesemakers

The daughter at the same home in Peleta, scooping feta curds from the whey. © VINCENZO SPIONE

still craft a cheese they call touloumotiri, but few still use the *touloumi*, or animal skin, to produce it. See SHEEP- and GOAT-SKIN CHEESES.

Greece leads the world in annual cheese consumption at roughly 72 pounds (33 kilograms) per person. Cheese is often served for breakfast with fruit and bread; as a snack in a rustic phyllo-dough pastry called *tiropita*; as an appetizer or meze to accompany wine, ouzo, and other aperitifs; and as an ingredient in salads, stews, and savory pies for lunch and dinner. It is grated over pasta, fried and doused with a squeeze of lemon, or drizzled with honey and eaten as a dessert. The iconic Greek salad, a summertime favorite, is commonly topped with a hearty slab of feta cheese, oregano, and olive oil and served at tavernas and homes throughout the country.

As a result of the Greek fondness for cheese, the Greek dairy industry is the third most important segment of the country's commercial food and drink sector, accounting for 17 percent of total production. Despite the country's current economic crisis, the commercial cheese industry remains strong. In 2013, the total value of commercial cheese production in Greece reached 809 million euros, experiencing just a 2 percent decline in volume and value sales since the onset of the country's recession. Commercially, feta is the most popular cheese in Greece. Commercially produced kefalotyri, graviera, and manouri also experience high sales. See MANOURI.

In 1996, the European Commission awarded nineteen cheeses from Greece protected designation of origin (PDO) status, defining their areas of origin and methods of production. In 2002, feta cheese received PDO status as did Xigalo Sitias in 2008, bringing the number of Greece's PDO cheeses

to twenty-one. All Greek PDO cheeses are made from fresh milk using traditional methods. They are naturally coagulated and fermented, using rennet and native cultures. See RENNET. Most are relatively simple to produce, keep, and transport. Just two Greek cheeses containing cow's milk have PDO status: Metsovone, which also contains sheep's milk, and Graviera Naxos. Although most of Greece's PDO cheeses are still made almost exclusively for personal consumption and for small-scale and local sale, in the past decade several manufacturers have undertaken the commercial production of several PDO cheeses. Those manufacturers include Dodoni, Olympus, and Epoch as well as Mt. Vikos, which produces traditional wooden-barrel aged feta.

Greek artisanal cheeses include the following:

- Anthotiros: Produced mainly on the Ionian Islands and on Crete, in Macedonia and Thrace, anthotiros is made from the milk and whey of sheep or goats or a combination of the two. When fresh, anthotiros is fluffy, delicate, and ricotta-like. When aged, it dries, hardens, and sharpens considerably in flavor and is most often used as a grating cheese.
- Gilomeni manoura: Produced on the island of Sifnos with raw sheep's milk, gilomeni manoura is allowed to dry and then submerged and aged in wine sediment. Pungent and salty, it is commonly served as a table cheese. See MANOURA.
- Kalathaki Limnou: Produced on the northern Aegean island of Limnos using sheep's milk or a combination of sheep's milk and no more than 30 percent goat's milk, Kalathaki Limnou is a brine-matured PDO cheese similar in taste and texture to feta cheese, but unlike feta, the curd is shaped into small balls in basket-like molds. See KALATHAKI LIMNOU.
- Ladotyri Mytilinis: A sheep's milk cheese aged in olive oil and produced on the island of Mytilini. This PDO cheese is shaped into small round blocks in molds made of reeds and matured until it reaches a sharpness that is balanced by the flavor imparted by the olive oil. See LADOTYRI MYTILINIS.
- Metsovone: Like mozzarella or provolone, metsovone is a pasta-filata or "spun paste" cheese, meaning the "paste" or curd is "spun" or stretched and kneaded and then sculpted, in this case into a long sausage-like shape. Made with cow's milk, it is cellar-aged for several

months and then smoked and sealed in paraffin wax. Metsovone is named for the town in which it is produced: the Vlach community of Metsovo in the Pindus Mountains of northern Greece. Metsovone is a PDO cheese. See METSOVONE.

- Kopanisti: A salty, spicy blue cheese produced on the Cycladic islands of Mykonos, Tinos, and Syros, Kopanisti is a PDO cheese and it is often served as a meze with tsipouro, ouzo, or wine. See KOPANISTI.

Adams, Alexis Marie. "In Pursuit of the Cheese of the Skin: Shepherd Cheesemaking in Tsakonia." *The Art of Eating*, no. 89.

"Dairy Facts." Dairy Doing More. http://www.dairy doingmore.org/economicimpact/DairyFacts.aspx.

Euromonitor International. *Cheese in Greece*. 2015. http://www.euromonitor.com/cheese-in-greece/ report.

Fletcher, Janet. "Beyond Feta: The Cheeses of Greece." *Specialty Food Magazine*, 5 January 2014. http:// www.specialtyfood.com/news-trends/featured-articles/article/beyond-feta-cheeses-greece.

Greek Ministry of Rural Development and Food. "List of the Greek PDO and PGI Products and Specifications." http://www.minagric.gr/index.php/ en/farmer-menu-2/pdo-pgi-tsgproducts-menu/ listpdoproducts-menu.

Homer. *The Odyssey*. Book IX. Translated by Samuel Butler. Internet Classics Archive. http://classics.mit .edu/Homer/odyssey.9.ix.html.

Kremezi, Aglaia, and Penny de Los Santos. *Mediterranean Vegetarian Feasts*. New York: Stewart, Tabori and Chang, 2014.

USDA Foreign Agricultural Service. "Dairy Annual 2012: Greece." GAIN Report GR1214. http://gain .fas.usda.gov/Recent%20GAIN%20Publications/ Dairy%20Annual%202012_Rome_Greece_ 12-14-2012.pdf.

Alexis Marie Adams

green cheese is a term that has been used since the late fourteenth century. It refers not to cheese that is green in color, but rather cheese that is new, young, as-of-yet unaged, or underripe. It should not refer to fresh styles of cheese that are intended to be consumed without aging, such as chèvre or mozzarella, but should refer to cheeses that are early in their life cycle and have yet to undergo the aging process. The term "green" could also be used as a tasting note to indicate that the cheese is underripe. The myth that the moon is made of cheese comes from the fact that the full moon looks much like a wheel of green cheese; round, white, and luminescent.

See also MOON.

"green cheese, n." OED Online. http://www.oed.com.

Molly Browne

grilled cheese is a hot cheese sandwich with countless iterations and almost as many explanations about its origin and even its name, but the one area where there is wide consensus is in its inherent appeal. Fundamentally, the American version is a cheese sandwich that is heated in a pan with butter or oil until the cheese becomes molten and the bread is toasted.

Modern renditions of the sandwich may include ingredients such as bacon, avocado, tomato, roasted peppers, or a combination of those ingredients and more. A grilled cheese sandwich might have elaborate fixings such as short ribs, eggplant Parmesan, cooked chicken, pesto, jam, chutney, or almost anything else the cook wants to include. More than one cheese is often used as well to create a balance of flavors and textures, and in the American South, the spicy mixture called pimento cheese might be used instead of natural cheese. See PIMENTO CHEESE.

There is little consensus on the origin of the grilled cheese sandwich, partly because of semantics. Whereas the word "grilling" in the United Kingdom refers to a form of cooking in which the food is placed directly below a heat source, in the United States this is known as broiling. Consequently, a cheese sandwich, typically open-faced and cooked under a so-called griller in England might be called a grilled cheese sandwich (or sometimes a toasted cheese sandwich) in the United Kingdom. However, in the United States the sandwich is most often cooked in a pan on top of the stove. It may also be made in a panini maker, but in that case it's usually called a panini, not a grilled cheese sandwich.

The US grilled cheese sandwich can be traced back to the turn of the twentieth century, when sliced bread itself was invented. However, it wasn't until the 1940s, when J. L. Kraft introduced processed cheese slices that the American grilled cheese sandwich as we know it today took hold. See KRAFT FOODS. Before, most documented versions of the sandwich indicate it was cooked open-faced and either served the same way or "sandwiched" together just before serving. The open-faced variety was known as a "cheese dream" and was usually made with tomatoes and bacon or ham, and served with pickles and olives—it was much like today's grilled cheese except that it was eaten with a knife and fork.

Werlin, Laura. *Great Grilled Cheese: 50 Innovative Recipes for Stovetop, Grill, and Sandwich Maker.* New York: Stewart, Tabori & Chang, 2004. See pp. 9–11.

Laura Werlin

Grobnik cheese is produced in the valley of Grobnik, located near the town of Rijeka on the northern coast of Croatia. It is traditionally a Croatian sheep's milk cheese produced by small-scale farms with about one hundred head of sheep. Grobnik cheese has a cylindrical shape with a diameter of approximately 14 inches (35 centimeters), a height of approximately 6 inches (15 centimeters), and a weight of approximately 33 pounds (15 kilograms). The cheese is ripened in brine and does not have a rind. It is chalky-white in color, and typically has many circular or slightly elliptical eyes (holes) that are uniform in size with a diameter of less than a quarter of an inch. The cheese body is hard, possibly exceptionally hard, non-elastic, and granulated, but not too dry. Generally, Grobnik cheese is very salty, with a pleasant taste. Connoisseurs prefer a well-ripened cheese with a stringent taste, typical of sheep's milk cheeses.

To make Grobnik cheese, sheep's milk is filtered into a copper vat and is heated to about 88°F (31°C) for a period of one hour, using natural rennet from calves for coagulation. The coagulum is then cut into grains, usually the size of rice, and heated to a temperature of 113°F (45°C) for a period of eight minutes. After heating, the grains will settle to the bottom of the concave-shaped vat. The curd is then removed to a large pot to be formed into the characteristic cheese shape and coated with medium-size salt granules. During salting, the cheese releases the whey into the pot and is ripened in the salted whey (brine) for up to one year. Salt is applied repeatedly to the cheese until it can no longer be absorbed.

Grobnik cheese is cherished among locals and is usually consumed as an appetizer, together with local traditional ham.

Sabadoš, Dimitrije. "Grobnički sir [Grobnik Cheese]."*Mljekarstvo* 12 (1959): 265–271.

Samir Kalit

Gruyère is an appellation de contrôlée (AOP) cheese from Switzerland and a family of mountain cheeses, all made from cow's milk and all large, cooked-curd, pressed, and aged. Besides Gruyère these include, from France, AOP Comté and AOP Beaufort; from Italy, AOP Asiago and AOP Montasio; and from Switzerland, the exclusively alpage AOP L'Étivaz. Gruyère originated in the same mountainous Swiss area where the primordial, long-aged Sbrinz is made. Compared with it, the cheeses of the Gruyère family are moister, though dense in texture, with today, as a rule, only a few small holes or none. A wheel of AOP Gruyère measures 22–26 inches (55–65 centimeters) across and averages 77 pounds (35 kilograms), while it can weigh anywhere from 55 to 88 pounds (25–40 kilograms). It must be aged for at least five months, but cheeses in the family are typically sold in a range of ages, sometimes up to twenty-four months and more. The best wheels, particularly of Gruyère, Comté, and Beaufort, are widely considered among the greatest of all cheeses. See ASIAGO; BEAUFORT; COMTÉ; MONTASIO; and SBRINZ.

The two giants that combine quality and quantity come from adjacent zones, predominantly in the Jura Mountains, on either side of the French-Swiss border: AOP Gruyère in Switzerland and AOP Comté in France. More AOP Gruyère is produced than any other Swiss cheese, a stable figure of around 30,000 tons a year, about half of which is exported. Annual production of AOP Comté is more than twice that.

The name "Gruyère" comes from the Swiss town of Gruyères (with an "s"), which was for centuries the main market town for the cheese. Historically France and Switzerland have shared the name, but in 1986 Gruyère de Comté was officially simplified to Comté. Then in 2010 the EU granted the valuable AOP "Gruyère" to Switzerland. All along France has had its own plain "Gruyère," which in 2012 was granted only a less-valuable IGP (indication géographique protégée). To further reduce the possibility of confusion, the label is required to show "France" in the same size as "Gruyère," and the wheels must be filled with plenty of old-school holes "from the size of a pea to the size of a cherry." Annual production is 3,000 tons. The Swiss market their cheese as "Le Gruyère"—in effect, "*The* Gruyère."

The Milk and Method in Switzerland

The official *cahier des charges* for AOP Gruyère tends to be broader than that for Comté. It specifies no breed of cow, and in practice the cows are mostly Holstein, originally from the Netherlands. (Comté's cows are its indigenous Montbéliardes.) The feed for the Swiss appellation must be at least 70 percent "forage," which in summer may include such non-pasture items as fresh potatoes, corn, and turnips. (Comté's *cahier des charges* cites studies showing that the native plant species in a small area can convey a taste of terroir, and mandates that the milk at each cheese plant come from within a 25-kilometer circle.) For AOP Gruyère the milk must come from within 20 kilometers of the plant, making a square area two and half times that for Comté.

The cheese is made at 167 village dairies (and additionally, in summer, on farms located in alpage) The microorganisms for AOP Gruyère come primarily from an addition of levain, which is whey from the previous cheesemaking, and that may be supplemented with laboratory cultures. The raw milk is warmed to about 88°F (31°C), rennet is added, and the curd sets in thirty to fifty minutes. According to the *cahier des charges*, the choice between these two limits depends on the equipment and the consistency sought in the curd. The tactics in the vat (cutting, stirring, heating) are left to the initiative of the maker—as long as the cheese ends up with a supple, smooth texture. The cut curd is heated for an hour or a little more to 129–138°F (54–59°C), which selects more heat-tolerant organisms and shrinks and dries the curd. Once taken from the presses, the Swiss wheels are commonly brined, as opposed to being sprinkled with dry salt.

AOP Gruyère d'alpage

AOP Gruyère d'alpage is the original kind, made only when the cows are in high summer pastures, and the cheese must be made in the same alpage where the cows graze or in a neighboring one. The fifty-two huts where Gruyère d'alpage is made typically have no electricity, and the cheesemaker may produce just half a dozen wheels a day. See ALPAGE.

The milk and curd are heated in copper vats over wood fires, and the curd is gathered up from the whey, as it always was, in a great linen cloth. The cheeses, once pressed and unmolded, are brined on site, then shipped to affineurs—specialists in ripening. Production is 500 tons per year.

The Aging

Ten affineur businesses both ripen and market all the thousands of wheels of AOP Gruyère. They mature on spruce planks in the high-humidity caves, and the rules pay particular attention to the morge, which is the somewhat orangy, sticky surface of Gruyère and a number of other kinds of cheese. The morge is created by rubbing the wheels at intervals with brine, so as to protect the interior, add a little more salt, and develop ripening organisms. Nowadays the heavy wheels are lifted, turned, and rubbed by robots. See CAVES; MATURING; and MORGE.

A key to flavor is the temperature of the aging. Beaufort, from the alpine pastures of the French region of Savoie, was always aged in higher, colder caves (specified today as 43–54°F [6–12°C]), which prevented holes from forming. Until the 1980s Gruyère and Comté were aged at somewhat warmer temperatures of about 57–61°F (14–16°C). That encouraged propionic bacteria to produce carbon dioxide gas, which inflated a large number of eyes, although not as many or as large as those of Emmentaler. See DAIRY PROPIONIBACTERIA and EYES. Then in the 1990s, in search of more consistency and finer flavors, Comté began to be aged, after an initial warmer period, at temperatures as low as 43–48°F (6–9°C), through use of higher-altitude caves or refrigeration, and soon the change spread to AOP Gruyère, where the norm is now somewhat lower temperatures, averaging 55–59°F (13–15°C). Holes have all but disappeared from the cheeses.

A small portion of both AOP Gruyère and Comté excels with longer aging, becoming almost a different cheese, with a drier, more granular texture and, when all goes well, finer and more complex aromas. For AOP Gruyère the period is fifteen to twenty-four months and for Comté twenty-four to as many as forty months. This aged cheese, though scarce and expensive, has become so popular that more wheels are being aged longer to meet the demand.

The Taste of Gruyère

Younger cheese is more for eating in quantity; it melts better, and is used more for cooking. Older cheese is more intense, and one eats less of it. Rather than forming the center of a light meal or snack, it's more a cheese-course cheese, more for tasting.

The taste of Comté is less salty and more restrained and has a drier texture; its aroma develops more slowly in the mouth. You might find flavors such as walnut, coffee, brown butter, caramel, meat broth, celery, or cauliflower. AOP Gruyère is a little more tender and moist, and has more immediate impact on the palate, with flavors in the same broad range but often earthier, sometimes barnyardy, as well as fruitier from the morge. The taste of Gruyère d'alpage is more pronounced, more animal, less standard, and more often includes a bitter note.

To go with cheeses in the Gruyère family, a simple, light wine, a white or a low-tannin red is generally safe. But connoisseurs find magic in the combination of a fine Comté with the region's nutty, complex aged *vin jaune*. AOP Gruyère forms an ideal combination with an old Chasselas from the historic vineyards at Lavaux on Lac Léman, in Switzerland, whose wines can have aromas of saffron, white-fleshed fruits, and even white truffles. These combinations take you deep into the realm of the sybaritic.

See also SWITZERLAND.

"Cahier des charges: Gruyère." Bern, Switzerland: Office Fédéral de l'Agriculture.

"Cahier des charges de IGP Gruyère."

"Cahier des charges consolidé de l'appellation d'origine 'Comté.'"

"Cahier des charges de l'appellation d'origine 'Beaufort.'"

"Disciplinare di produzione DOP 'Asiago.'" Vicenza, Italy: Consorzio per la tutela del formaggio Asiago.

"Disciplinare di produzione della denominazione di origine protetta 'Montasio.'" Direzione generale per la promozione della qualità agroalimentare e dell'ippica.

Fiori, Giacomo. "Antichi formaggi d'alpeggio tra le alpi lepontine et il milanese." http://www.ruralpini.it/file/Alpeggi/Fiori_Antichi_formaggi_d'alpeggio.pdf.

Vernus, Michel. *Une saveur venue des siècles: Gruyère, Abondance, Beaufort, Comté*. Yens, Switzerland, and Saint-Gingolph, France: Éditions Cabédita, 1988.

Edward Behr

Gubbeen

See COUNTY CORK.

Guernsey is a dairy cattle breed from the Channel Islands, a near cousin to the Jersey. See JERSEY. Since cattle from several of the islands were imported to England during the eighteenth century as "Alderneys," it can be difficult to know which is meant in some early accounts. But mentions of such distinguishing Jersey qualities as small, delicate build and a doe-like appearance generally rule out the slightly heavier-framed, less picturesque Guernsey. By degrees they became established in the United States by the mid-nineteenth century.

Like Jerseys, Guernseys were admired for the richness of their milk, which was well-suited for butter making during the flowering of the urban market for farmhouse butter. Though they do not quite match the milk fat and protein averages of Jersey milk, they outperform nearly all other dairy breeds in both.

The signal Guernsey attraction has always been the golden tinge of their cream and the deep yellow color of the butter made from it. The reason is a metabolic quirk that causes Guernseys to convert more of the carotenoids in grass or hay into the vitamin A precursor beta-carotene (which imparts the characteristic color) than actual vitamin A (which is colorless).

Though Guernsey milk is well suited for the same kinds of cheesemaking as Jersey, neither breed began as a major player in cheese dairying. This was in part because cheesemakers' priorities were often for hard, relatively aged cheeses in which the larger fat globule size and higher fat content of the milk can hinder curd from knitting together. The butter market was the real focus for farmers raising Channel Islands breeds. But the color of Guernsey cream—easily visible in glass bottles when milk was sold unhomogenized—helped the milk to capture a recognized niche in the fluid milk market that dominated US dairying throughout the twentieth century. In the 1920s some dairies began bottling Guernsey milk and selling it at a premium as "Golden Guernsey," a trademark licensed to the American Guernsey Association. The "golden" selling point disappeared with the post–World War II adoption of homogenized milk in opaque cardboard containers.

Neither of the Channel Islands breeds had been more than sporadically used for cheese dairying when the late twentieth-century cheese revival opened up opportunities to various dairy breeds long overshadowed by the "Holsteinization" of the milk industry. At that point Guernseys appeared better positioned for success than Jerseys. Their seeming advantages were the higher average milk yield per cow and—at a time when health advisors strongly warned against full-fat dairy products—slightly lower milk fat content. But for some reason it was the smaller, lower-yielding Jersey that underwent a dramatic comeback. Of all the major dairy breeds, Guernseys suffered the steepest decline in the late twentieth century. At present their cheesemaking potential is underexploited. They are unlikely to overtake the very similar Jerseys in contributions to the field without serious efforts on the part of breed association leaders to develop genetic and promotional programs.

See also BREEDING; COW; and GENETICS.

Becker, Raymond B. *Dairy Cattle Breeds: Origin and Development.* Gainesville: University of Florida Press, 1973.

Porter, Valerie. *Cattle: A Handbook to the Breeds of the World.* 2d ed. Illustrated by Jake Tebbit. Ramsbury, U.K.: Crowood, 2007.

Anne Mendelson

Guffanti is a cheese maturer, wholesaler, and retailer based in Arona, Piedmont, Northern Italy. Their official company name is Luigi Guffanti Formaggi 1876.

Luigi Guffanti began maturing Gorgonzola in an abandoned silver mine in Valganna, Lombardy, in 1876. See LOMBARDY. As he learned his trade he began to mature other specialties, and passed on his expertise to his sons Carlo and Mario. By the end of World War II, this second generation had moved the maturing site to neighboring Piedmont, to caves beneath the ancient city walls of Arona's old town.

In 2016 the business was headed by fourth-generation Carlo Fiori, joined by sons Giovanni and Davide, though the maturing site moved again in the early 1990s when new legislation and planning restrictions conspired to direct them to a new home. The current site is a restored former *salumificio*, a network of underground caves previously used to mature cured meats, providing ideal conditions for the cheese maturation that remains at the heart of the business. See MATURING.

Carlo and Giovanni continue to visit some two hundred producers regularly to select the cheeses that will best mature under their care. They have earned a reputation for pushing the boundaries of maturation, with select Parmesans matured for as long as thirteen years. Their range now includes over three hundred Italian cheeses as well as a choice selection of imported cheese. Exports now form the mainstay of the business, though they continue to serve a loyal base of shops and restaurants within Italy.

See also CAVE and ITALY.

Il Latte. http://www.lattenews.it/allevatori-di-formaggio-dal-1876.

Luigi Guffanti Formaggi 1876. http://www.guffantiformaggi.com.

Katy Gunn

Guffanti, a cheese maturer and retailer in Piedmont, Italy, has earned a reputation for pushing the boundaries of maturation. Pictured here are wheels of Parmigiano Reggiano, some of which Guffanti matures for as long as thirteen years. © KATE ARDING

Guilde Internationale des Fromagers

was founded by Pierre Androuët, who himself was a Maître Fromager and Critique Gastronomique, member of the l'Institut Français du Goût and a publisher of many cheese and cooking with cheese books. In 1969 the Guilde Internationale des Fromagers was formed.

The full name of this organization is Guilde Internationale des Fromagers Confrérie Saint-Uguzon; the association between Saint Uguzon and the church of San Lucio, which borders Switzerland and Italy in a pass between Val Colla in Tocino and Val Cavergna in Italy, was made after extensive research by Pierre Androuët. Saint Uguzon was the patron of alpine industries, milk, and cheesemaking, and also a healer of eyes. His symbol is a cheese. The church and shrine are visited annually by more than a thousand pilgrims. The saint was a shepherd who discovered the importance of caseation. He offered cheese to the poorest for sustenance. It is believed that the place where Uguzon lost his life is the source of healing virtues, most notably for eye complaints. It was thus that the worship of San Lucio–Uguzon was born; celebrated on his birthday, 12 July, each year. However, the biggest celebration takes place on 16 August, the feast of Saint Roch. It is a big, popular Italian/Swiss feast and, under the loving eyes of the Italian customs, San Lucio became a free zone in honor of the patron of cheesemakers (*caseari* in Italian).

Pierre Androuët recognized the efforts of many professionals in promoting and supporting cheese and formed a council to recognize cheese professionals including makers, affineurs, cheesemongers, chefs, educators, journalists, and writers. He formed the Guilde to honor them in a ceremony and to preserve and transmit the knowledge of these professionals for generations. The organization is headquartered in France and has clubs and embassies in six European countries and in a total of thirty-three countries internationally. Most notably the New World Chapter was formed among the United States, Canada, Australia, and Mexico in 2013. There are about fifteen inductions annually throughout the world honoring cheesemakers, dairy workers, producers, affineurs, refiners, cheese and cream refiners, and, under the fraternity of Saint Uguzon, amateur gourmets, restaurateurs, scientists, artists, journalists, and generally anyone who has a well-developed palate to relish the delights of milk products.

The ranks in the Guilde International des Fromagers are Garde et Juré (guard and judge), Prud'homme (educator), Maître Fromager (cheese master), Ambassadeur (ambassador), Protecteur (protector), Maître Honoris Caseus (honoris caseus master), and in the Confrerie of Saint Uguzon are Compagnon (companion) and Compagnon d'honneur (honoris caseus companion).

As of 2015 the Guilde is led by Roland Barthelemy, who was inducted in 1973 and became its Provost in 1992. The Guilde is made up of over 6,300 members worldwide.

See also ANDROUËT, PIERRE and SAINT UGUZO.

"Androuët Pierre (Paris 75)." Camembert Museum. http://www.camembert-museum.com/pages/historiques-ile-de-france/androuet-pierre-75.html.
Guilde Internationale des Fromagers. http://www.guildedesfromagers.com.
Sturman, Susan. "The Napoleon of Cheese: Roland Barthélemy Is a Force to Be Reckoned With." *Cheese Connoisseur* (Summer 2012): 44–47.

David Gremmels and Cathy Strange

guilds are rare in the history of cheesemaking due to the rural nature of the dairy industry. Where specialization and concentration occurred, it was mainly in the hands of landlords or merchants, not producers themselves. Guilds, mainly a product of urban society, emerged in the cheese trade where it flowed through urban markets. In areas that exported cheese these became the centers of expertise and quality control, often government-imposed, though at times through self-organization of participants. In one example, the *kaasdragers* (cheese porters) in the Dutch cheese markets of Alkmaar, Edam, Hoorn, Gouda, and Woerden organized themselves into guilds in the Early Modern period, monopolizing transport services, weighing, and market management. The Alkmaar Kaasdragersgilde founded in 1593 exists to this day, now functioning as a heritage club. This was not the case everywhere. In most cities cheese was traded and sold by general merchants who were often already organized in guilds. As the example of the cheesemongers of London shows, even a flourishing cheese market in the hands of specialized professionals was possible without a permanent guild organization.

The notion that producers of cheese could form a guild as full-time professional artisans is a relatively new one. Today organizations of artisanal cheese producers called guilds exist in many countries, though the scale at which they operate can vary greatly. In the cheese business modern guilds function in the context of market economies that rarely allow them the benefit of monopolies or enforcement powers enjoyed by their historic predecessors.

Self-organized guilds consciously modeled on historic structures have been emerging throughout the United States since the early 2000s. The Maine Cheese Guild, an association of individuals and businesses involved in the cheese industry, was the first in 2003, though similar organizations also exist, for example, in California, Oregon, Ohio, Massachusetts, New Hampshire, and Wisconsin as well as across the Southern states. Founded by artisanal cheesemakers, they are designed to accommodate small businesses rather than industrial producers and seek to address their concerns. The largest business in the Maine Cheese Guild recorded an output of 75,000 pounds (34 metric tons) in 2013, compared to thousands of tons in industrial dairies.

Guild structures offer small producers an amplified political voice as well as support in professionalization and further education on administrative, technical, and business aspects of cheesemaking and trading. Workshops and guild publications aimed at members disseminate information and training while outreach activities aimed at the general public raise awareness of the artisanal cheeses and try to stimulate demand for local products. Guilds also hold internal competitions as well as supporting members entering their products in other contests. They facilitate networking, helping members to contact suppliers and raise capital. The guilds' web presence also serves as an advertising vehicle for members who would otherwise struggle to reach a wider customer base. Membership in these organizations is voluntary, and though they cooperate with regulators to disseminate knowledge on food safety and trade standards, they do not have any formal powers of certification or enforcement. Some offer a certification of voluntary adherence to a guild code of conduct.

While cheese guilds in the United States are mostly rooted in a food counterculture antagonistic to industrial production, similar organizations in other countries more readily embrace large-scale businesses. The Quebec Artisan Cheese Guild (Guilde Québécoise des Artisans Fromagers) engages in professional brand management, raising the international profile of regional cheeses. The annual output of its 21 dairies was over 2,300 tons. In the United Kingdom the Specialist Cheesemakers Association (SCA) serves a similar function for producers and vendors of artisanal cheeses. It cooperates officially with regulatory authorities, serving as a nexus between its members and the government and helping to develop authoritative guidelines for hygiene and food safety that are used by government inspectors. This kind of formal involvement by industry bodies in regulatory processes is more common in Europe than in America. See SPECIALIST CHEESEMAKERS ASSOCIATION.

Though not formally referred to as guilds, associations of cheese producers found throughout Europe are comparable to historical guilds in their function. These bodies are usually set up as cooperatives or associations under civil law whose members produce a certain type of cheese. Frequently they originated when cheesemakers organized to obtain a protected designation of origin for their cheese and were kept alive to manage the shared interest in this intellectual property. They market their product, codify quality standards and practices, and develop and defend their trademark. Such associations can range in size from clubs of part-time producers to highly professional operations with revenues in the millions of euros such as the very influential Consorzio del Parmigiano-Reggiano founded in 1934. See CONSORZIO DEL FORMAGGIO PARMIGIANO-REGGIANO.

Actual guild structures, though heavily modernized, survive in the chambers of agriculture (Landwirtschaftskammern) of Germany and Austria. These were founded in the nineteenth century, but modeled on the surviving structures that craft and trade guilds had taken following industrialization. In several North German states, they provide formal vocational training and have considerable say in regulatory matters. Membership in the chambers is mandatory for all agriculture- and forestry-related businesses, including dairies. In South and East Germany as well as Austria, government authorities carry out these functions and membership in the chambers is voluntary, but they are influential bodies everywhere. Cheese is only a small part of their remit, though. Their policies often favor the interests of industrial dairies, many of which are owned by farmers' cooperatives.

Curtis, Abigail. "Maine's Cheese Making Industry on the Rise." *Bangor Daily News*, 2 August 2013.

Stern, Walter M. "Where, Oh Where, Are the Cheesemongers of London?" *The London Journal* 5 (1979): 228–248.

Volker Bach

Halloumi is the traditional cheese of Cyprus and the major agricultural product of the island. The first references linking Halloumi with Cyprus date back to 1554, when Florio Bustron referred to the sheep and goats of Cyprus, and to a cheese named Halloumi (in Italian, *calumi*) made from a mixture of sheep's milk and goat's milk. In his historical review of 1778, Kyprianos of Cyprus described Halloumi cheese as "delicious" and noted that "quantities were sold abroad." By 2015 Cyprus was producing 19,000 tons of Halloumi each year, of which 15,000 tons were exported (mainly throughout Europe and the Middle East), with an annual market value of $72–83 million (€65–75 million).

Halloumi is traditionally made from sheep's and goat's milk mixed at undefined proportions. Pure goat's milk Halloumi cheese and pure sheep's milk Halloumi cheese are also produced. Since the end of the twentieth century, increasing demands for exports have led to the addition of a significant proportion of cow's milk to the mixture of sheep's milk and goat's milk.

Halloumi cheese production in Cyprus is regulated by CYS (Cyprus Organization for Standardization) Standard 94:1985, which specifies that it may contain sheep's milk and/or goat's milk, with or without cow's milk, but may not be made in Cyprus from cow's milk alone. Other ingredients in Halloumi include rennet, salt, and mint. Although mint was once added for its antibacterial properties, it is now considered part of the flavor of the cheese. Two aspects of the cheesemaking process also contribute to Halloumi's distinctive flavor: (1) no starter cultures are added to the milk; and (2) the curds of cheese are heat-treated in de-proteinated whey at 194°F (90°C) for 30 minutes. In addition, Halloumi cheese is left to mature in whey brine (12 percent sodium chloride) for at least 40 days. During this ripening period, Halloumi becomes harder, saltier, and more acidic in taste.

Halloumi is a white to light yellow, semihard elastic cheese with no rind and no holes that has a compact texture and is easily sliced. It has a pleasant, mild flavor and a salty, minty, milky taste. Halloumi is a very versatile cheese, an important quality for its commercial success. It is served fresh with fruit (e.g., watermelon), cooked (e.g., shallow-fried, grilled, or boiled in traditional trachanas soup), or grated over pasta.

See also ANARI.

Papademas, Photis. "Halloumi Cheese." Chap. 4 in *Brined Cheeses*, edited by A. Y. Tamime. Oxford: Blackwell, 2006.

Photis Papademas

hammer

See MARTELLETTO.

Handkäse

See SOUR SKIMMED-MILK CHEESES.

Hansen, Christian D. A. (1843–1916), was a pioneering Danish pharmacist and biochemist whose eponymous company has been an innovative

The front cover of an 1899 pamphlet produced in conjunction with the twenty-fifth anniversary of the founding of Chr. Hansen's Teknisk-Kemiske Laboratorium. It contains the company's first mention of starter culture offerings. COURTESY OF ERIC JOHANSEN / CHR. HANSEN A/S

worldwide leader in the food- and cheese-ingredients industry since he founded it in 1874. Born on 25 February 1843, and christened Christian Ditlev Ammentorp Hansen, he began his apprenticeship at Copenhagen's Royal Frederik's Hospital pharmacy in 1859, at the age of sixteen. Within three years he became an assistant pharmacist and also set up a lab to teach himself analytic chemistry. In 1864 Hansen enrolled at the University of Copenhagen, earning a master's degree in pharmacy after just seven and a half months. For the next eight years he tutored pharmacy students, founded a pharmaceutical journal, translated the *Pharmacopoea Danica* into Danish, and continued to study chemistry.

In 1869 Hansen became a lecturer at his alma mater, and in 1871 and 1872 worked as a research assistant to Professor Julius Thomsen, studying the enzyme pepsin, as extracted from pig stomachs. His thesis on the crystallization of such substances won a gold medal with a cash stipend, which he used to travel around Europe visiting pharmaceutical factories and educational institutions. Upon his return to Denmark Hansen began producing pepsin as treatment for digestive problems and also worked on other enzymatic animal extracts, including purified rennet for cheesemaking, which would soon become the industry standard, greatly enhancing the efficiency and consistency of larger-scale cheese production. See ENZYMES and RENNET.

In 1874 Hansen founded Chr. Hansen's Teknisk-Kemiske Laboratorium in Copenhagen to produce commercial rennet as well as natural cheese and butter colorings and malt extract. Over the next several years Hansen worked hard to promote his rennet products, which eventually included powders and tablets. The company remained under family control until 1989 when it was sold to the Lundbeck Foundation, which became majority shareholder.

By 1877 Hansen's customers throughout Europe were producing about 1 million pounds (about 455,000 kilograms) of cheese per day using his rennet. His eldest son, Johannes, who took over as managing director after his father's death on 30 June 1916, often told the story of how Hansen addressed certain claims at a cheese industry conference in New York in 1879: "He countered the rumors of poisonous rennet by drinking a glassful while on the speaker's podium. That shut them up." In 1878 Hansen opened a factory in Little Falls, New York, to supply the growing US market, expanding in 1891 by buying an island in the Mohawk River that became known as Hansen Island.

In 1893 Hansen introduced the first standardized commercial starter cultures for acidification of milk for cheese and other dairy products. Hansen's business success made him a wealthy man; he bought two farms in Denmark that had herds numbering 450 cows, and built a state-of-the-art dairy with milking machines and an American-style cheese factory. He also established what became the School of Pharmaceutical Sciences at the University of Copenhagen.

See also CULTURE HOUSES and STARTER CULTURES.

Chr. Hansen website. http://www.chr-hansen.com/about-us/history.

Frederiksen, J. D. "Christian D.A. Hansen: A Memorial." *New York Produce Review and American Creamery*, vol. 42, July 1916.
Funding Universe. "Chr. Hansen A/S History." http://www.fundinguniverse.com/company-histories/chr-hansen-group-a-s-history.

David Gibbons

Harding, Joseph

Harding, Joseph (1805–1876), is often considered the "father of Cheddar cheese." His greatest gift to the cheesemaking world was his promotion of the application of scientific knowledge and dairy hygiene to the cheesemaking process.

Harding was born in 1805 to a Somerset, England, family with a long tradition of farming. Harding settled into dairy farming and Cheddar-making in 1851 at Vale Court Farm,which was slightly north of the traditional Cheddar-making region of the time. Since his farm was considered an undesirable region for making Cheddar, Harding set out to learn as much as possible about the Cheddar-making process, both by experimenting with variations in procedure and by consulting the best practices of other cheesemakers.

Noticing the improvement in his own cheese, Harding spread the word to others in an article published in 1860 in the *Journal of the Royal Agricultural Society of England* about his method for making Cheddar. In that article, Harding detailed his first innovation, scalding the Cheddar curd before milling in order to produce a finer texture of cheese. See SCALDING. Harding also is often credited with improving the cheese mill, a tool used to break curds into small, fine pieces, which is essential for traditional Cheddar-making. See CURD MILL. These two contributions became central parts of the Cheddar-making process for the next century.

Harding also promoted and helped popularize other cheesemaking concepts that are taken for granted today: cooling milk that is stored before production, using litmus tests for cheese acidity, moving farm animals away from cheesemaking, or "make" rooms, using commercial rather than homemade rennet, omitting the use of sour milk in order to prevent over-acidification, and aging the cheese at higher temperatures (50–70°F [10–21°C]) than had previously been commonly done.

Harding's lasting influence was due to his desire to gather information, incorporate new science, and disseminate the best cheesemaking practices. His dedication is one of the factors that helped make Cheddar one of the most popular cheeses in the world.

See also CHEDDAR.

Cheke, Val. *The Story of Cheese-Making in Britain*. London: Routledge & Kegan Paul, 1959.
Heeley, Ann, and Mary Vidal. *Joseph Harding, Cheddar Cheese-Maker*. Glastonbury, U.K.: Friends of the Abbey Barn, 1996.

Gordon Edgar

An etching of the English cheesemaker Joseph Harding, from *Dairy Farming: Being the Theory, Practice, and Methods of Dairying* (1880), by John Prince Sheldon.

Harel, Marie

Harel, Marie (1761–1844), was the legendary inventor of Camembert cheese, heroine of a popular creation myth that is haunted by historical doubt. Lore holds that Harel, a farmwife in the tiny village of Camembert in Normandy (France), sheltered a priest fleeing the Revolutionary loyalty oath in 1791. In gratitude, he taught her the cheesemaking technique used in his former parish in Brie, and Harel cleverly married it to local cheesemaking methods to create Camembert. Her descendants carried on the tradition and her grandson, Victor Paynel, allegedly introduced it to Napoleon III, bringing it to the nation.

What is certain is that Marie Fontaine was born in Crouttes, France, in April 1761, to Jacques Fontaine

This Camembert label pays tribute to Marie Harel, the heroine of a popular Camembert creation myth of dubious historical accuracy.

and Marguerite Legendre; her father remarried Charlotte Perrier and they moved in with their in-laws, tenants of a farm called Beaumoncel in Camembert. Marie married a Beaumoncel farmhand Jacques Harel in 1785, and they moved to his home village of Roiville and had a daughter (also named Marie) in December 1787.

Although a few clergymen did pass through the area in the 1790s, the historical record contains no trace of Harel meeting one. Worse, references to distinctive cheeses from Camembert predate her birth. Such records as exist fail to describe such cheeses, so Harel may have refined local methods to help change Camembert's cheese between 1760 and 1800. Researcher Pierre Boissard credits Harel's legendary status to her founding a cheesemaking family with exceptional commercial sense. Cyrille Paynel, Harel's grandson, evoked his grandmother to lend greater authenticity to his "brand," which he defended assiduously. The entire Camembert industry revived and enhanced her legend in the 1920s, consecrating it with a statue in Vimoutiers where she would have sold "her" cheese.

See also CAMEMBERT DE NORMANDIE.

Boissard, Pierre. *Camembert: A National Myth.* Translated by Richard Miller. Berkeley: University of California Press, 2003.
Louis Le Roc'h-Morgère, Pierre Boisard; and Calvados, Archives départementales *Carnet Cyrille Paynel*

(1817–1886): Un eleveur-fromager du Pays d'Auge [Carnet Cyrille Paynel's notebook (1817–1886): A farmer cheese-maker of the Pays d'Auge]. Caen, France: Conseil Générale du Calvados, 1997; the only published source related to the Harel family.

Juliette Rogers

Harzer Käse

See SOUR SKIMMED-MILK CHEESES.

A **hastener** is a temperature-controlled room used during the production of mold-ripened cheeses such as Stilton and Camembert and washed-rind or smear-ripened cheeses such as Reblochon. Temperatures are typically in the region of 60–71°F (16–22°C) with high humidity to encourage the growth of ripening organisms that may have been introduced deliberately to the milk or are present environmentally in the dairy.

In the first few days of cheese production, curd acidity is high due to the presence of lactic acid, which can inhibit the growth of ripening molds and bacteria. The hastener creates optimum conditions for the early growth of yeasts and *Geotrichum*, which raise the pH by consuming lactic acid and pave the way for subsequent mold and bacterial growth. *Penicillium candidum*, which is present on surface mold-ripened cheeses, has an optimum pH above 5.00, while the bacteria associated with the rinds of smear-ripened cheeses, such as *Arthrobacter* and *Corynebacterium*, are even less acid-tolerant. See GEOTRICHUM CANDIDUM and PENICILLIUM.

A more complex system of yeast-ripening may be observed in Stilton, with which the word "hastener" is most often associated. The majority of yeasts present are associated with the rind, where they are involved in the neutralization of the rind, which ultimately becomes dominated by bacteria. Yeast is also implicated in the internal mold ripening of Stilton by *Penicillium roqueforti*, where they contribute lipolytic products that are involved in the formation of characteristic blue cheese flavor. See STILTON.

The normal ripening and flavor development of mold-ripened and smear-ripened cheese would not be possible without a period of hastening.

See also BLOOMY-RIND CHEESES; BLUE CHEESES; and WASHED-RIND CHEESES.

Gkatzionis, K. "The Flavour Production of Stilton Blue Cheese Microflora." PhD diss., University of Nottingham, 2009. http://etheses.nottingham.ac .uk/1395/1/K_Gkatzionis1_Thesis.pdf.

Paul Thomas

Haute-Savoie, the department in the eastern flank of central France, belongs to the Rhone-Alps region. It includes the highest mountain of Europe and covers the widest range of elevation in France, from 673 feet (205 meters) at the Rhone River to 55,780 feet (4,810 meters) at the top of Mont Blanc. The northern part of the Haute-Savoie meets mountain at Lake Geneva, and the southeastern section borders Italy. This area produces several AOP (appellation d'origine protégée) and IGP (indication géographique protégée) cheeses: Abondance AOP, Reblochon AOP, Chevrotin AOP, Tome de Bauges AOP, Tomme de Savoie IGP, Emmental de Savoie IGP, and Raclette de Savoie are the main items. All the AOP cheeses are produced from raw milk.

The Alps were formed by the collision of the African and European plates about 30 million years ago and made soaring snow-covered peaks, steep valleys with torrent streams, impossibly narrow mountain passes, countless crystal-clear Alpine lakes and surrounding wildflower-covered meadows, and numerous prominent massifs. Through the activity of many glaciers, the landscape of Haute-Savoie is still evolving. Each valley has a distinctive microclimate and flora. The harsh weather and difficult terrain made people conservative and resilient, and dairy farming in Haute-Savoie developed following the strict demands of its natural conditions. Twenty-five percent of total land is used for agricultural activity, but the soil is too poor to support large-scale farming. More than 80 percent of agriculture is livestock and dairy farming, and the other major industry is wine production. Traditionally small farms kept goats for milk and meat, but most of the modern commercial milk production is from cows, mainly of the breeds Abondance, Tarine, and Montbéliarde. Those three breeds, which produce more concentrated but a lot less milk than conventional breeds like Holstein, worked out well for a low yield and high quality production. They evolved to thrive in the Alpine pastures and the harsh weather of the high mountains. See COW; HOLSTEIN; and MONT-BÉLIARDE.

Of the current 3,120 dairy farms, more than half are located over 5,250 feet (1,600 meters) elevation. Compared to the adjoining Savoie area, Haute-Savoie farms are smaller and are still run traditionally by families. Average herd sizes are 45 for cows and 120 for goats, and most of the milk is used for farmstead or cooperative cheese production. Depending on the type, 10–30 percent of all cheese is produced at the farms, the exception being Chevrotin, which is produced only in the farmstead style. See CHEVRO-TIN; FARMSTEAD; and FERMIER.

Cheesemaking in Haute-Savoie has a long history from the Roman period, but the Catholic monks who settled in the mountain valleys in the early twelfth century to build abbeys contributed to the major development of this area's dairy farming. The monks started cutting trees to make the Alpine pastures and brought in cow breeds that could thrive in the high mountain areas. They also transferred their knowledge of good dairy farming and cheesemaking to the peasants. See MONASTIC CHEESEMAKING. The development of salt mining in the fifteenth century in the Swiss part of the Alps provided much needed salt for large cheese production. Abundant summer rain and the presence of active glaciers supply plenty of water for the thriving dairy farming, and grazing animals provide enough fertilizer for the next year's healthy pasture.

Due to the popularity of winter sports in the early 1960s, the steep mountains turned into ski slopes, and fancy ski resorts started popping up in the remote valleys. The rough terrain became the major attraction for year-round tourism and brought much needed infrastructure such as roads and power supplies to the community. People who suffered extreme poverty through the generations are no longer poor. Nonetheless the practice and pattern of dairy farming has undergone few significant changes these last several centuries, and the traditional method of transhumance is still very much alive. See TRANSHUMANCE. If you travel in this area in late spring to early fall, you will be awoken by the gentle sound of cowbells, and the air in the late afternoon is highly perfumed by wildflowers and shrubs including wild bilberries, red primulas, and yellow amiculas. The people who are defending traditional practices produce the highest quality mountain cheeses according to the rhythm of the seasons, using recipes passed down through the generations.

See also ALP-STYLE CHEESES and FRANCE.

Chambre d'Agriculture Savoie-Mont Blanc. http://rhone-alpes.synagri.com/portail/accueil7374.

Kamman, Madeleine. *Madeleine Kamman's Savoie: The Land, People and Food of the French Alps.* New York: Atheneum, 1989.

Planbol, Xavier de, and Paul Claval. *An Historical Geography of France.* New York: Cambridge University Press, 1994.

Préfet de la Haute-Savoie. http://www.haute-savoie.gouv.fr.

Soyoung Scanlan

Havarti

Havarti is a mild, buttery, slightly acidic cheese of Danish origin. It carries the name of the farm where Hanne Nielsen, a peasant woman, created the now most famous Danish cheese in the 1800s. Mrs. Nielsen had traveled around Europe to learn cheesemaking and after returning to Denmark she experimented with different recipes, creating the traditional Havarti cheese. Quality Havarti is made in the United Kingdom, Canada, and the United States, including the states of California, Wisconsin, and New York. Famous mass-production of Havarti cheese in North America is done by Arla Foods in Canada and Costello in the United States, with some artisanal cheese still being imported from Denmark. See ARLA.

Canadian composition standards for Havarti are a maximum 50 percent moisture and minimum 23 percent fat, corresponding to 46 percent fat on a dry matter basis. Codex Standard 267-1966 specifies a reference range for fat in dry matter of 45–55 percent. Typically moisture is in the range of 40–45 percent. US FDA standards of identity do not include a standard for Havarti. According to Danish cheesemaker and grader Hans Somer, creamy versions of Havarti contain up to 65 percent fat on a dry matter basis, but maximum 55 percent is recommended if the cheese is to be sliced on mechanical slicers. Holes formed by mechanical and gas holes tend to be smaller (typically the size of rice grains) in North American Havarti, relative to traditional Danish Havarti. More openness is encouraged by selection of gassy (heterofermentative) cultures and modified atmosphere packaging with sufficient nitrogen to ensure positive or slight negative pressure in the package.

A useful description of manufacturing parameters for Havarti is provided by Danlac Canada, Inc. and another in *The Cheesemaker's Manual* (Morris, 2003). Typically mesophilic starter is used at relatively low levels with minimal pre-ripening (although the Danlac procedure pre-ripens to pH 6.5), so there is minimal acid development (pH about 6.5) when part of the whey is removed and replaced with hot water to bring the temperature to 100°F (38°C). After a short cooking period (thirty to forty minutes) the curd and whey are transferred to the forms and pressed lightly or held with occasional turning at room temperature for several hours followed by brining. Pre-brining pH should be 5.3–5.4 and post-brining pH should not reach less than 5.0.

Some recipes include salt addition before draining, probably to firm the interior of the curd to help the cheese hold its shape and also to promote uniform ripening. There are also recipes that drain and dry-salt the curd before forming; this process has the advantage of labor and resource savings because it avoids the brining process. The disadvantage is that it produces a cheese with little open structure (few eyes) that tastes and appears more like Colby than Havarti. See COLBY.

Washed-rind versions of Havarti have an added pungent aroma and earthy taste. Texture is smooth and firm with many irregularly shaped small holes that create a lacy appearance. Havarti comes in various shapes but is most often formed in a rectangular shape and for many consumers is a favorite sandwich cheese. It may be complimented with herbs or jalapeño peppers.

See also DENMARK.

Canadian Food and Drugs Act and Regulations. http://laws-lois.justice.gc.ca/eng/regulations/c.r.c.,_c._870/page-43.html#docCont.

Danlac Canada. "The Manufacture of Havarti Cheese." http://www.danlac.com/news/manufacturing-havarti-cheese.

Morris, Margaret. *The Cheesemaker's Manual.* Corvallis, Ont.: Glengarry Cheese Making and Dairy Supply, 2003.

Arthur Hill and Mary Ann Ferrer

hay

See PASTURE.

Hazard Analysis and Critical Control Point

Hazard Analysis and Critical Control Point (HACCP; pronounced "has-sip") is a food safety management system developed by the US National Aeronautic and Space Administration (NASA) in the 1960s to prevent astronauts from succumbing to food poisoning in zero gravity. Today, in the European Union, the implementation of a system based upon HACCP principles is mandatory for all food businesses other than farming, while businesses in many other countries implement HACCP systems at the request of their customers to ensure the safety of their products. The internationally accepted format for HACCP is described by the Codex Alimentarius Commission, which is affiliated with the Food and Health Organization (FAO) and World Health Organization (WHO) of the United Nations. See CODEX ALIMENTARIUS.

HACCP is intended to identify and take immediate steps to control three classes of "significant" hazards, that is, hazards that are severe and/or frequent. Hazards are classified as microbiological (e.g., the presence of pathogens such as *Salmonella* spp. or *Listeria monocytogenes*), chemical (e.g., the presence of contaminant substances such as veterinary residues or allergens), or physical (e.g., the presence of "foreign bodies" such as glass shards or metallic particles). Ideally, a HACCP program should be specific for each product, but if the composition of several products is similar and the processes undertaken in their manufacture are not very different, several products may be covered by one HACCP plan. So, for example, a single HACCP system might cover different types of hard cheese, but hard and soft cheese would require different HACCP protocols.

Before conducting a HACCP study, the "HACCP team" has some preliminary work to do. The product and its intended use must be described in great detail, a process-flow diagram must be drawn up, and measures must be taken to control minor hazards. When these steps have been completed, the HACCP study can begin, following these seven principles:

1. Conduct a hazard analysis (identify significant hazards that could occur);
2. Identify critical control points (the places where hazards could be prevented or controlled);
3. Establish critical limits (the tolerances allowable for each critical control point);
4. Establish monitoring procedures (devices or methods to measure the critical control points);
5. Establish corrective actions (what immediate steps must be taken to reduce or eliminate the hazard);
6. Establish documentation and records (to keep track of monitoring and corrective actions); and
7. Establish verification procedures (such as a review of the study).

When done correctly, the HACCP study generates a control chart that provides all the information needed to identify and control the significant hazards in real time. It is a blueprint for the process that defines how to monitor critical control points in order to ensure that the critical limits are maintained and that appropriate corrective action is taken if they are not.

HACCP is a logical and effective approach to managing food safety that relies wholly on the integrity of the information used to compile it. The team that conducts a HACCP study for a food business must therefore be multidisciplinary and have the necessary expertise to identify all significant hazards and understand how to control them.

See also CRITICAL CONTROL POINTS and PATHOGENS.

Codex Alimentarius [International Food Standards]. *Milk and Milk Products.* 2d ed. Rome: World Health Organization/Food and Agricultural Organization of the United Nations, 2011. ftp://ftp.fao.org/codex/Publications/Booklets/Milk/Milk_2011_EN.pdf.
Mortimore, Sara, and Carol Wallace. *HACCP: A Practical Approach.* 3d ed. New York: Springer, 2013.

Paul Neaves

health properties

health properties of cheeses are related to their various nutrients and to the microorganisms present as a result of fermentation and ripening. Cheese comes in many varieties and thus nutritional value as well as effects on health may also vary considerably among them. The cheese microbiota may consist of just a few to hundreds of species of organisms. In raw-milk cheeses microbial biodiversity is normally greater and provided by raw-milk microbes. In cheeses made from heat-processed milk a certain degree of biodiversity is provided by the heat-resistant microbiota in raw milk that survive pasteurization, starters and non-starter organisms inoculated into pasteurized milk, as well as organisms that are transferred onto the cheese during ripening. The diversity of cheeses, so important in terms of flavor and taste, also allows consumers to choose cheeses that may best fit with their own health requirements.

Nutrition facts

Cheese diversity makes a general description of the nutritional value of cheese impossible. The amount of salt, enzymes, and acids introduced in cheese-making processes, residual water, processing method, and type and length of ripening greatly influence both the macro- and micro-nutrient content of cheeses.

Proteins

Protein content of cheese may vary between 12 grams per 100 grams of soft white cheese to 36 grams per 100 grams of Parmesan cheese with an average of 22 grams per 100 grams of Camembert, Brie, or blue cheese, according to FAO reports. Breakdown of casein produces soluble oligopeptides, amino acids, ammonia, and ammonia-derived amines. Cheese contains essential amino acids, that is, amino acids that cannot be synthesized de novo by humans, and the bioavailability of essential amino acids in cheeses is one of the highest among foods (close to 90 percent). See PROTEINS.

Lipids

Fat content of cheeses may vary between 5 grams per 100 grams of cottage cheese to 32 grams per 100 grams of Cheddar or cream cheese, with an average of 27–29 grams per 100 grams of Emmentaler, Tilsit, Gouda, or blue cheese (always lower than that of butter, i.e., 80 grams per 100 grams). Lipolysis, also important for cheese flavor through the production of volatile fatty acids, is performed by the microbial lipases. Lipolysis leads to diglycerides, monoglycerides, and saturated and unsaturated free fatty acids, which may amount up to 5–10 grams per kilogram of well-ripened cheese, and short-chain free fatty acids. See FAT and LIPOLYSIS.

Carbohydrates

Ripened cheeses no longer contain sugars, since lactose is totally transformed into lactic acid, which is of interest for diabetic and lactose-intolerant persons. Lactose may be found in fresh soft white cheeses (because of their low level of fermentation) or in processed cheeses (because of the addition of lactose during processing).

Minerals

The calcium and phosphorus content of cheeses accounts for a large part of their health benefits. Parmesan and Gruyère-type hard cheeses have the highest calcium and phosphorus content (1,000 milligrams per 100 grams and 600 milligrams per 100 grams of cheese or more, respectively), compared to cream or cottage cheese (less than 100 milligrams per 100 grams and 150 milligrams per 100 grams, respectively). Hard cheeses contain twelve times more and soft cheeses four times more calcium than milk. The high calcium-to-phosphorus ratio confers interesting nutritional properties to cheeses, since low calcium-to-phosphorus ratio contributes to osteoporosis by inducing an increase in parathyroid hormone release. Sodium content varies significantly between cheeses, from 0.4–4.6 grams per 100 grams depending on cheesemaking processes, and especially the addition or not of salt at any step of the process; as an example, Gruyère or Cheddar cheeses contain 500–600 milligrams per 100 grams of sodium compared to more than 1,000 milligrams per 100 grams for Roquefort, Camembert, Brie, or Parmesan cheeses. Trace elements also vary significantly between cheeses, and their concentration may depend on particularities in cheesemaking utensils, such as copper vats for some mountain cheeses (e.g., Comté). See COPPER VATS.

Vitamins

Fat-soluble vitamins present in milk are transferred to cheeses, so most cheeses are rich in vitamin A; conversely vitamin D, which is naturally low in milk, is consequently low in cheeses. Almost all of the US and Canadian milk supply is voluntarily fortified with respectively 100 and 35–40 international units (IU) per cup; this is usually not done in Europe, except for infant formulas. However, except for fortified yogurts, dairy products such as cheeses are generally not fortified. In 2005 the US FDA allowed cheeses to be fortified with up to 81 IU of vitamin D_3 per 30 gram serving, an increase of more than 250 percent over the previous limit, providing 20 percent of the daily value. The decision applies to most cheeses, but specifically excludes cottage cheese, ricotta cheese, and hard grating cheeses, such as Parmesan and Romano. In Europe cheeses are not fortified with vitamin D. A proportion of the water-soluble vitamins in milk is transferred to the whey and only a fraction of the total amount is found in cheese. However, taken all together, cheeses represent a significant source of vitamins, since vitamins of the B group may be synthesized by molds, especially on the rind. Propionic bacteria present in some cheeses (eyed cheeses) increase their content in vitamin B_{12}.

Influence of Cheese Consumption on Health

Numerous studies dealing with cheese influence on health have considered "consumption of dairy products" or even "consumption of milk and dairy products" as a whole, which makes conclusions on the effect of cheese consumption difficult. The type of cheese consumed is rarely considered in epidemiological studies either. Conflicting results may thus come from differences in the composition of the various dairy products consumed and their effect on specific diseases and risk factors. Among cheeses, the wide variety in their nutrient and microbial composition, and the cultural habits of the populations under study (amount and ratio in daily diet, main type of cheese, raw versus pasteurized milk, etc.) may also explain discrepancies among studies.

Cheeses and promotion of bone health

Cheeses are the best source of bioavailable calcium and as such contribute a lot to bone health at any age of life, especially childhood. There is no consensus on the optimal calcium intake to prevent osteoporosis in adults and elderly subjects but increased calcium consumption has usually been found protective against complications of osteoporosis, especially hip fractures. European subjects greater than fifty years of age who consumed more milk and cheese were shown to have fewer hip fractures than people with lower consumption; this was true for men and women. Together with calcium, vitamin D is essential for bone health and especially to prevent osteoporosis; cheese is not a natural source of vitamin D, which should be provided by sun exposure or supplementation; consumption of fortified cheese may be an alternative, as cheese taste and flavor are unaltered with the addition of vitamin D_3 even after ripening for several months.

Cheeses and prevention of dental caries

Prevention of dental caries in children and adults has been associated with cheese consumption in several studies. Saturation of the saliva in calcium and phosphorus seems to be the main mechanism, which may act both on tooth mineralization/prevention of demineralization, and on the microbes involved in dental caries by abolishing the fall in salivary pH caused by sugar consumption. Data even suggest that high cheese intake by the mothers during pregnancy may reduce the risk of childhood dental caries.

Cheeses and cancer

Allegations concerning the carcinogenic effect of milk and dairy products have increased since 2006. Several studies have been performed to support such allegations; the most convincing evidence concerns thyroid, testicular, and prostate cancer. A large cohort study showed that greater dietary intake of calcium and dairy products may be modestly associated with increased risk of prostate cancer; however, in this and other studies increased risk was observed mostly with low-fat types of dairy products, and the risk was slightly increased only for nonaggressive forms of the disease, which raises doubt about whether a significant biological effect exists. Studies on breast cancer and Hodgkin's disease are controversial. Recent systematic reviews of the published studies do not show a significant link between cheese consumption and cancer risk, at least for the cancers under study. Cheese was even found to be protective against cancer in several studies, including lung cancer in non-smokers. The high calcium content of cheese has been claimed to be both a risk and a protective factor against cancer. Taken together, the studies performed with a sound methodology do not support a carcinogenic risk from cheese consumption within a balanced diet.

Cheeses and cardiovascular diseases

The link between cheese consumption and cardiovascular diseases is also controversial. The saturated fatty acids could contribute to the increased risk of death due to cardiovascular diseases and of myocardial infarction observed in some studies. However, as mentioned above, the fat content may be very different among cheeses, which might explain opposite results found in other studies. The "protective effect" of cheeses against cardiovascular disease (for instance, compared to butter or other dairy products) could be due to their lower ability to promote hypercholesterolemia, their low content in "trans" fatty acids (which are known to raise LDL and lower HDL cholesterol), and the lower potency of the "natural" trans fatty acids, compared to those due to hydrogenation of vegetal oils, to promote hypercholesterolemia. The high calcium content of some cheeses, such as Gruyère, Comté, or

Beaufort, might be responsible for fat saponification in the intestine, thus leading to less bioavailability of cheese fat. Nevertheless, it may be appropriate to adapt daily cheese consumption to the fat content of each cheese; for example, 100 grams of 30 percent fat-cheese contains 1.7 grams of trans fatty acids, that is, less than the 2 grams per day recommended by WHO as a maximum. Protection against cardiovascular diseases by cheese consumption, compared to other sources of fat, could also be related to the specific protective effect of the cheese microbiota, especially lactic acid bacteria, and to antihypertensive properties related experimentally to specific peptides and to calcium content. This effect on blood pressure may be counterbalanced by the high salt content of some cheeses, which should thus be taken into account in the diet of subjects with hypertension.

Cheeses and the immune system

Cow's milk allergy is the most common food allergy in infants, and cheese must be avoided if it is diagnosed. Cross-reactions often exist between different species' milks, and thus cheeses of any origin may be equally responsible for allergic reactions. However, in most children milk allergy is transient and cheese may be consumed first, at the stage of milk reintroduction, since it usually contains fewer allergenic proteins than milk or even yogurt. Fully maturated hard cheese such as Parmesan is tolerated by 58 percent of patients with confirmed cow's milk allergy.

Cheese microbial content may provide additional effects on health that go far beyond the basic "nutrition facts." The cheese microbiota may actually produce beneficial metabolites (the biogenic effect) or may themselves interact with the host in a positive manner (the probiotic effect). Cheese's influence on the immune system likely operates through the intestinal microbiota, and cheese consumption has been shown to prevent emergence of antibiotic-resistant strains in the intestines of young adults after antibiotics treatment.

Observations of the protective effect against allergic/atopic diseases of raw milk consumption by mothers during pregnancy and their infants in the first year of age have been confirmed by longitudinal studies, that is, long-term follow-up of mothers and their newborns. Farm cheese consumption was also found to be associated with protection. Preliminary results from the Pasture cohort of a thousand European children suggest that early food diversification and, independently, the number of cheese types consumed before eighteen months of age are associated with significant protection against allergic diseases. Microbial biodiversity, polyunsaturated, omega-3, as well as conjugated fatty acids (CLA) (in high concentration in unprocessed Alpine milk), and presence of intact immune-modulating proteins in whey are the main candidate for protective factors in raw milk, and all but the whey proteins may play a role in cheese.

See also DAIRY ALLERGY and LACTOSE INTOLERANCE.

Alessandri, C., et al. "Tolerability of a Fully Maturated Cheese in Cow's Milk Allergic Children: Biochemical, Immunochemical, and Clinical Aspects." *PLoS One* 7 (2012): e40945.

Bertrand, X., et al. "Effect of Cheese Consumption on Emergence of Antimicrobial Resistance in the Intestinal Microflora Induced by a Short Course of Amoxicillin-clavulanic Acid." *Journal of Applied Microbiology* 102 (2007): 1052–1059.

Food and Agriculture Organization of the United Nations. "Milk and Dairy Products in Human Nutrition." *Alimentation et Nutrition* 28. Rome: FAO, 1998. http://www.fao.org/docrep/t4280f/t4280f0g.htm.

Ganmaa, D., et al. "Incidence and Mortality of Testicular and Prostatic Cancers in Relation to World Dietary Practices." *International Journal of Cancer* 98 (2002): 262–267.

Legatzki, A., et al. "Microbiome Diversity and Asthma and Allergy Risk." *Current Allergy and Asthma Reports* 14 (2014): 466.

Montel, M. C., et al. "Traditional Cheeses: Rich and Diverse Microbiota with Associated Benefits." *International Journal of Food Microbiology* 177 (2014): 136–154.

Moorman, P. G., and P. D. Terry. "Consumption of Dairy Products and the Risk of Breast Cancer: A Review of the Literature." *American Journal of Clinical Nutrition* 80 (2004): 5–14.

Norat, T., and E. Riboli. "Dairy Products and Colorectal Cancer: A Review of Possible Mechanisms and Epidemiological Evidence." *European Journal of Clinical Nutrition* 57 (2003): 1–17.

Ravishankar, T. L., et al. "Effect of Consuming Different Dairy Products on Calcium, Phosphorus and pH Levels of Human Dental Plaque: A Comparative Study." *European Archives of Paediatric Dentistry* 13 (2012): 144–148.

Saito, T., et al. "Isolation and Structural Analysis of Antihypertensive Peptides that Exist Naturally in Gouda Cheese." *Journal of Dairy Sciences* 83 (2000): 1434–1440.

Tanaka, K., et al. "Dairy Products and Calcium Intake During Pregnancy and Dental Caries in Children." *Nutrition Journal* 11 (2012): 33.

Tavani, A., et al. "Milk, Dairy Products, and Coronary Heart Disease." *Journal of Epidemiology and Community Health* 56 (2002): 471–472.

Tholstrup, T., et al. "Does Fat in Milk, Butter and Cheese Affect Blood Lipids and Cholesterol Differently?" *Journal of the American College of Nutrition* 23 (2004): 169–176.

von Mutius, E. "Maternal Farm Exposure/Ingestion of Unpasteurized Cow's Milk and Allergic Disease." *Current Opinion in Gastroenterology* 28 (2012): 570–576.

Dominique Angèle Vuitton

heritage breeds are animals that reflect the historical agricultural practices of particular regions and the environmental conditions of those places. Although all animal breeds are products of genetic selection, heritage breeds possess characteristics that make them ideally suited for certain uses and situations. These traditional breeds collectively represent a large swath of genetic variation within a domesticated species. Heritage dairy breeds offer unique qualities often sought by cheesemakers and are important repositories of genetic material for future breeders. The Livestock Conservancy, an American organization devoted to genetic conservation, first introduced the term "heritage" to describe a turkey breed in 1997. That organization and others work to save and restore heritage breeds threatened by extinction through disuse. A few industrial breeds dominate agriculture today after having usurped heritage breeds' place-specific adaptations in favor of high-input farming systems.

Heritage dairy breeds of cattle, goats, sheep, and other species tend to express traits for animal hardiness and independence. Such traits include tolerance of temperature extremes, effective grazing and browsing habits, sturdy conformation, and strong maternal instincts. Heritage breeds were developed under circumstances that required this resilience and demanded that animals could care for themselves to a significant degree. This independence predates the high-input agricultural models that have become the norm in the global dairy industry today.

Contemporary conventional agriculture favors animals that produce so effectively that their feed and water needs can only be met within the industrialized systems under which most milk is now produced. International breeds dominate national dairy herds and flocks, meaning that many heritage breeds have been reduced to small numbers. The danger of

extinction is not necessarily a characteristic of a heritage breed, yet many face the risk of disappearing from world agriculture. The loss of a breed is an omission of genetic information that cannot be recaptured.

Heritage breeds are true genetic breeds in the sense that when mated, they produce offspring of the same breed. These breeds' qualities are clearly defined, and two animals of the same breed will produce offspring with the same phenotype, or physical and behavioral traits. Heritage dairy breeds developed over many generations in regional efforts to select for traits that enhanced milk production and overall animal health and hardiness. This type of breeding is done in isolation from other stock. Such a process can be extremely localized, as was the development of Randall Cattle on one farm in southwestern Vermont in the early twentieth century. Randall Cattle are called a "landrace" breed because they are perfectly suited to the environment of the location in which they live. Selection in this and other cases was thus driven both by the environment and by humans, guiding a process in which traits favoring milk production are selected with a holistic perspective on animal health, such as the maintenance of the animal's capacity to sustain itself with a grass-based diet.

Unlike many industrial breeds, heritage dairy breeds are often multipurpose. Milk quantity and quality have been an important selection trait in heritage dairy stock, but so have other traits such as litter size and meat or fiber quality. Also, compared with international and industrial breeds, which are mostly homogenous phenotypically and genetically, the members of heritage breeds look and behave similarly but possess much greater genetic diversity among members of the same breed. The genetic makeup of each animal in the breed will vary depending on its breeding line. Over time, for example, breeders of dual-use heritage breeds may focus on one aspect of production, such as meat, and minimize other production traits.

Specific Heritage Dairy Breeds

The foundation of heritage breeds generally occurred under circumstances where limited communication and transportation left farmers with a narrow stock to begin with. Spanish settlers brought a mere three hundred head of cattle to the Americas in the fifteenth and sixteenth centuries, yet this population serves as the foundation of many distinct heritage

American cattle breeds. The Channel Islands of Jersey and Guernsey developed their sought-after dairy breeds of the same names largely by closing the islands to importation over two hundred years ago and then refining the available stock to express the traits for which those breeds are now known. The unique qualities of heritage dairy breeds are most apparent in contrast with international or industrial breeds. Heritage breeds are usually recognized as having been founded before 1950. While heritage breeds represent regional specificity and genetic diversity, industrial or international breeds often exhibit genetic uniformity, which is made possible by a worldwide market in semen. Nevertheless, international breed genetics may sometimes be introduced into heritage breed herds or flocks to increase milk production, such as in sheep flocks when governments or individual farmers seek to improve local sheep breeds with traits for producing greater milk volume.

Cattle

Heritage dairy cattle breeds distinguish themselves from the Friesian Holstein, the dominant international high-production dairy cow breed, with their strong grazing instinct, high milk solids production, and robust build suited to varied terrains such as mountain pastures. See HOLSTEIN. Dutch Belted, for example, perform exceptionally well in pasture-based agriculture. Whereas the Holstein breed yields milk with an annual average of 3.64 percent butterfat and 3.19 percent protein, the Scottish Ayrshire breed produces milk with 3.92 percent fat and 3.39 percent protein. Guernsey cows' milk boasts 4.55 percent fat and 3.56 percent protein. See AYRSHIRE and GUERNSEY. Heritage dairy cattle that give higher milk solids reward cheesemakers with higher yields. Heritage breeds also support regional cultural practices among people. In Québec, the campaign to restore the native Canadienne breed, which developed from stock imported from France in the seventeenth century, asserts that the environmentally adapted breed is not only best suited for sustainable agricultural practices in eastern Canada, but is also part of the cultural preservation of that area's francophone culture.

Sheep

Of cattle, sheep, and goats, heritage sheep breeds are the most likely to be multipurpose, meaning that they are valued for a combination of their meat, milk, and fiber attributes. These breeds developed in the context of local or regional-based subsistence agriculture or simple trade, when all three products were valued on the farm or within the community. The combination of high-quality fiber and meat production is most common in sheep; but certain breeds, such as the Icelandic or Finnsheep breeds, excel in all three categories. The East Friesian, Lacaune, and Awassi breeds are the most common internationally. See EAST FRIESIAN and LACAUNE. Shepherds often start with or introduce genetics from one or more of these breeds to increase milk production, but other nondairy breeds such as the heritage Tunis may be introduced into dairy flocks to increase hardiness. Prolificacy is an especially important trait among dairy sheep because of the financial dependence many sheep dairy farmers have on lamb production. Finnsheep can have unusually large litters of three or more.

Goats

The French Alpine breed dominates much of commercial goat dairying, while a handful of common central European and African breeds such as the Anglo-Nubian, Saanen, and Toggenburg frequently round out diversified goat herds. See ALPINE; NUBIAN; and SAANEN. Heritage goat breeds are rare in commercial dairying. The Golden Guernsey from the Channel Islands, the German Frankenziege, and the Arapawa from New Zealand, for example, do not appear in many commercial herds. Heritage goat breeds with dairying capacity in the United States, such as the Spanish goat, are threatened by small populations and interbreeding with more common breeds. Interbreeding reduces the purebred genetic stock over the long term and threatens the continuation of the breed.

Breed-Specific Cheese and Breed Availability

Heritage breeds are particularly suited to the production of cheeses with geographical indications that specify milk from traditional stock. Cheese made from native breeds' milks maintains the place-specific identities of cheeses in cooperation with the influence of the local environment and particular feed. Examples of cheeses requiring breed-specific milk include Manchego DOP, which is made from the milk of Manchega sheep; Robiola di Roccaverano DOP, made from the milk of the northern Italian

Roccaverano goat breed; and Abondance AOP, which may be made from the milk of the local Tarentaise, Montbéliarde, or Abondance cattle breeds in the Haute-Savoie region of France. See MANCHEGO; ROBIOLA DI ROCCAVERANO; ABONDANCE; MONTBÉLIARDE; and HAUTE-SAVOIE. These and other geographical indications recognize that not all milks are equal and consider heritage breeds a vital part of the ecosystem that supports a cheese's unique identity.

The diversity of available heritage dairy breeds varies by species and by location. Whereas European localities often possess historic regional breeds, farmers in the New World might rely on imported breeds that have acquired different traits during the maintenance of the breed in its new setting. An example of this process is the American Milking Devon: a cattle breed that finds its source genetics in the English Devon (now used primarily for beef) but was brought to North America in the seventeenth century and subsequently bred in the United States for its milk production. Cheesemakers and dairy farmers desiring milk with higher solids may prefer heritage breeds to their international counterparts, but will have access to them only if their country allows their importation.

Preserving Agrobiodiversity

The global transition from localized breeds to international breeds has greatly altered genetic diversity. International breeds have been developed for high production, while heritage breeds have been allowed to decline. Artificial insemination and the global trade in semen has made it possible for a single Holstein bull to produce 50,000 heifers according to the Holstein Association USA. Such intensive breeding possibilities contribute to the loss of genetic diversity and the creation of phenotypically and genomically similar individuals. The annual milk production average for Danish Holsteins more than doubled from 1950 to 2013, but those animals' productive milking years are now only a fraction of those of heritage breeds. The Food and Agriculture Organization (FAO) of the United Nations reports that the vast majority of Holsteins in the United States' herd are related to fewer than twenty animals. In contrast with this trend toward genetic uniformity, few breeding programs support the propagation and development of indigenous breeds. Landrace and heritage breeds outnumber international breeds in their genetic variety but are nevertheless threatened by the dominating genetics of the largest populations.

A renewed interest in heritage breeds has grown with the realization that it is important to maintain diversity in herds and flocks in order to preserve genetic information for future breed adaptations. The FAO hosts the Domestic Animal Diversity Information System, which includes a searchable database of worldwide breeds. FAO programs seek to stem the global decline in genetic diversity. The Slow Food Foundation for Biodiversity links culturally specific food products with the animals that traditionally produce them, arguing for the necessity of genetic diversity by recognizing the importance of traditional and landrace breeds worldwide. The Livestock Conservancy studies endangered heritage breeds and implements breeding plans to restore traditional breeds in the United States. Much like a seed bank keeps seeds for preserving biodiversity, the SVF Foundation in Rhode Island cryogenically preserves the semen and embryos of rare and endangered breeds. The SVF Foundation works under the premise that even if the last living animal of a breed dies, the germplasm in its freezer banks will facilitate its reintroduction. See BIODIVERSITY.

Many support the preservation of heritage breeds but argue that if these breeds are to be saved, then they must be eaten. This leading theory suggests that if heritage breeds were to meet more consumers' dairy, milk, and fiber needs, then these animals could look forward to a more secure future.

See also BREEDING AND GENETICS; COW; GOAT; and SHEEP.

Sponenberg, D. Phillip, and Donald E. Bixby. *Managing Breeds for a Secure Future: Strategies for Breeders and Breed Associations*. Pittsboro, N.C.: American Livestock Breeds Conservancy, 2007.
Thrupp, Lori Ann. "Linking Agricultural Biodiversity and Food Security: The Valuable Role of Agrobiodiversity for Sustainable Agriculture." *International Affairs* 76 (2000): 283–297.

Brent A. Wasser

Herzegovina sack cheese is a Bosnian semi-hard cheese ripened and stored in sheep- or goat-skin sacks. One tax document referring to this cheese from the Ottoman period dates back to 1487, so it is rightfully considered the oldest documented Bosnian cheese. It is made of raw cow's, sheep's, or goat's milk, and mixtures of these milks in various ratios. In addition to good milk quality, this cheese requires proper preparation of the animal skin forming the sack. After slaughter the skin is thoroughly washed, shaved, salted, dried, and stored in a cool place until its use. For practical reasons Herzegovina sack cheese cannot be made industrially and is slowly entering the international Slow Food scene as an important traditional product in the Nevesinje area. See SLOW FOOD.

After milking, the raw milk is filtered and heated to 88–95°F (31–35°C). Animal rennet is added so as to make the milk coagulate, which takes between twenty and sixty minutes. The curd is then cut by mixing, the whey is allowed to run off, and the curds are strained in a cheesecloth. To improve the drainage, the curd is pressed in the cloth. Before placing it in the sack, the dry curd is broken or cut into 3–4-inch (8–10-centimeter) cubes, and salted to about 3 percent. While filling the sack, it is important to pack it tightly because any remaining air in the sack may cause spoilage. After filling, the sack is closed and left for ripening for a minimum of sixty days at a temperature between 59–64°F (15–18°C) and a humidity of 60–80 percent.

When ripened and taken out of the sack, the cheese should be dry and crumbly. Its taste is moderately salty and piquant, typical for the type of milk used in the production. The cheese body ranges from white to yellowish.

See also SHEEP- AND GOAT-SKIN CHEESES.

Bijeljac, Sonja, and Zlatan Sarić. "Autochthonous Dairy Products with the Basics of Cheesemaking." Sarajevo: Faculty of Agriculture, University of Sarajevo, 2005.
Sanders, George. Cheese Varieties and Descriptions. Washington, D.C.: U.S. Department of Agriculture, 1954.
Zdanovski, Nikola. Dairy Science. Sarajevo: Faculty of Agriculture, University of Sarajevo, 1962.

Svijetlana Sakić, Tarik Dizdarević, and Zlatan Sarić

Hildegard of Bingen (1098–1179), the Benedictine polymath, drawing from Aristotle and the Hebrew Scriptures (Job 10:10), compares human reproduction with cheesemaking. Her scientific book *Cause et cure* (ca. 1151–1158) describes conception as analogous to the early stages of making cheese. Semen coagulates and becomes flesh in the woman's womb just like milk curdles in a vessel and turns

into cheese; and if a woman, shortly after she has conceived with one man, has intercourse with another, the semen within her is contaminated—as milk would be were someone to add another liquid just as it was about to curdle. After birth the analogy still holds, because infants and children continue to need food much like freshly pressed cheese needs the continued addition of curdled milk. In her theological book *Scivias* (ca. 1151), Hildegard argues that having sexual relations with relatives produces bad offspring just like cooking and curdling milk multiple times produces bad cheese. In a vision, in this same book, of men and women carrying milk and making cheese with it, Hildegard realizes that people born of strong semen are gifted physically and spiritually, like ripe cheeses made of thick milk; those born of weak semen are like bland cheeses made of thin milk, imperfectly matured and useless; those born of corrupted semen are like bitter cheeses, misshapen and unable to mature. For Hildegard as for thinkers before and after her, the mystery of how semen becomes a body had much in common with the mystery of how milk turns into cheese: both are transformations of liquids into solids and of ephemeral substances into long lasting ones.

See also CURDLING, CULTURAL THEORIES OF and SEXUAL IMAGERY.

Hildegard of Bingen. On Natural Philosophy and Medicine: Selections from Cause et Cure. Translated and edited by Margret Berger. Cambridge, U.K.: D.S. Brewer, 1999.
Hildegard, Saint. Scivias. Translated by Mother Columba Hart and Jane Bishop. New York: Paulist, 1990.

Cristina Mazzoni

Hodgson, Randolph (1956–), the cheesemonger and cheesemaker credited with saving British farmhouse cheeses, was born in Norwich. He spent much of his childhood in colonial Hong Kong until attending Downside school. He then moved on to further education in London, briefly studied philosophy of science, and then earned a degree in food science.

After graduating in 1979 Randolph was introduced to Nicolas Saunders, who was creating a network of food businesses at Neal's Yard, Covent Garden. Randolph helped build the dairy and began creating yogurts and fresh cheeses. As the retail business grew, his own love of cheese led him to source

A young Randolph Hodgson from the early days of Neal's Yard Dairy, when he began visiting cheesemakers and bringing whatever cheese he could lay his hands on back to London. © NEAL'S YARD DAIRY

artisan cheeses being made around the country. He noticed that raw-milk cheeses were most interesting as they varied by batch, some of which needed further aging to make them truly superb. Neal's Yard Dairy became known for the highest quality British cheeses.

In February 1989 an outbreak of *Listeria* caused by thermized Vacherin prompted British agriculture minister John MacGregor to announce a plan to ban the sale of unpasteurized milk and cheese. Randolph used his knowledge of the microbiology of *Listeria* to challenge the need for legislation on cheese, becoming a representative of the artisan cheese industry. He then organized leading cheesemakers into creating the Specialist Cheesemakers Association. The SCA grew to build a working relationship with government agencies, and brought makers together to support one another.

In recognition of his role in saving small scale cheeses Randolph was honored with an OBE in 2007. In semi-retirement he is examining old cheese recipes on a kitchen scale.

See also NEAL'S YARD DAIRY and SPECIALIST CHEESE-MAKERS ASSOCIATION.

Dillon, Sheila. "How Randolph Hodgson and Neals Yard Dairy Gave Cheese a Chance." *The Guardian*, 1 May 2015. http://www.theguardian.com/lifeandstyle/2015/may/01/how-randolph-hodgson-and-neals -yard-dairy-gave-cheese-a-chance.

James Montgomery

Holstein cattle have their origins in the black and white dual-purpose cattle of the Netherlands and northern Germany. These cattle were exported in large numbers to the United States starting in the 1860s, where according to a chronicler of the breed, writing in 1897, "Dairying had become an important industry in the Northern States and was extending to the prairie land of the West, where especially large cattle were demanded. No breed ever spread with such rapidity.... It has become one of the largest and most popular breeds in our country" (Houghton, p. 17). The cows were referred to by some American breeders as Dutch Friesians and by others as Holsteins (after the region in northern Germany), and in 1885 the two American breed associations settled on the name Holstein-Friesian to encompass all of their animals. Over the following years, selective breeding in the United States focused exclusively on milk production, while in Europe the Friesian breed remained multipurpose, valued for both milk and meat. Today, the American breed is generally referred to as Holstein; with the advent of artificial insemination, these "improved" Holstein genetics have been widely introduced back into the European Friesian gene pool, where the Holstein breed is gaining ground.

The Holstein is the largest dairy breed, with an average cow weighing approximately 1,500 pounds (680 kg). Their black and white coats have become emblematic of dairy cows in general, although red and white cows also are found within the breed. In the United States, Holsteins are by far the most popular dairy breed, making up more than 90 percent of the nine million cattle in the national herd. Their wide adoption by liquid-milk producers throughout the United States and Europe is due to their impressive production levels, with cows giving an average of 23,000 pounds (10,400 l) of milk per lactation in 2012, over 40 percent more than Jerseys.

Holsteins can be successfully raised in a variety of systems, though their high production levels require large amounts of feed, often in the form of concentrates, to maintain their body condition. The same intensive breeding programs that successfully increased milk yields over the second half of the twentieth century have also resulted in unintended negative effects on overall health, including decreased fertility and difficulties with calving. These issues have begun to be addressed through breeding strategies that emphasize health indicators alongside total production, as well as through new technologies such as genomic analysis and selection.

With milk containing relatively low levels of fat and protein (the building blocks of cheese) and requiring high inputs of energy, the Holstein is a cow that has been honed for the liquid milk industry rather than for cheesemaking. Although genetics companies have begun to offer cheesemakers the option of sires chosen for attributes such as higher milk solids, the breed as a whole remains geared towards intensive, high-input farming systems.

See also BREEDING AND GENETICS; COW; and EAST FRIESIAN (COW).

Holstein Association USA. "Facts About Holstein Cattle." http://www.holsteinusa.com/pdf/fact_sheet_cattle .pdf.

Houghton, Frederick L. *Holstein-Friesian Cattle: A History of the Breed and Its Development in America*. Brattleboro, Vt.: Holstein-Friesian Register, 1897.

Bronwen Percival

home cheese care

home cheese care has a rich and diverse history that employs different techniques for varying styles and ages of cheese. The main criteria for storing cheese efficiently in the home is finding a cool, dark, clean, and aerated environment that maintains a desired moisture level of the cheese. Some storing methods dry the cheese out over time. Certain styles, such as French Crottin, fare well and retain flavor at an increased, drier stage. Before the advent of refrigeration, there were many different methods of storage.

Clean goat hides were traditionally used as natural preservation encasements for aged cheese varietals of the Turkish nomadic tribes who traveled with goats. Some of these traditions are still practiced today. Initially during butchering the hides are removed in such a way as to have minimal sewing of the entire hide. The nomads salt, pack, and pound the cheese tightly with a stick, and make sure it is

airtight with additional sewing of the neck. In order to ensure consistent flavor development of the cheeses, the goat hides are washed and prepared with home-made yogurt. The yogurt bacteria maintain the hide when stored in a natural or manmade cave for six months. See SHEEP- and GOAT-SKIN CHEESES.

Clay and terracotta have also been used by many civilizations for home cheese care. The porous nature of unglazed clay and terracotta helps cultivate an environment for cheese that is both cool in temperature and thriving with the cheese's necessary microclimate and microflora. One traditional Greek island cheese, Lathotyri, is preserved in a clay pot full of olive oil. This cheese can be eaten after three weeks, but can also be stored this way for up to a year. As the cheese ages, the flavor profile becomes more piquant. See EARTHENWARE POTTERY.

Various cloths such as muslin and linen have a certain level of breathability that allows cheese to be stored in the open air, without exposing wedges and wheels to sunlight or vermin. A more advanced version of these cloths is called Bee's Wrap, a piece of muslin cloth that has been encased in beeswax, jojoba oil, and tree resin. The beeswax and resin retain the moisture level of the cheese, but do not inhibit breathability. The antibacterial properties of the jojoba and beeswax keep the cheese fresh for longer. See CHEESE-CLOTH.

Finding natural cool climates in a household, such as a basement, was important for long-term cheese storage before refrigeration was available for domestic use. One of the quintessential pantry cheese storage devices in Europe and early America are cheese safes, as part of the broader category of food safes. The cheese safe can be freestanding, can be found outside under shade, or can be attached to the outside of the house. The safe is made from local untreated wood such as pine or birch and the sides are aerated with tiny perforated holes or fine grade wire mesh. This allows for necessary ventilation. The safes also include wooden shelving. Fluctuations in humidity and temperature can drastically affect the cheese body over a few days' time in this environment, depending on the ambient environmental conditions.

When refrigeration entered domestic kitchens in the late 1800s, cheese could then be consistently stored at a cold temperature. The average temperature of a fridge, between 34–39°F (1–4°C), is intended to halt all forms of fermentation in food so that it is more shelf stable. In fact, if cheese is not

A 1946 advertisement for DuPont Cellophane extolls the protection cellophane wrap offers cheese. Plastic wrap is actually not an ideal breathable material, due to its tendency to suffocate the cheese and promote plastic off flavors on the cheese's surface. HAGLEY MUSEUM & LIBRARY, WILMINGTON, DELAWARE, USA / BRIDGEMAN IMAGES

properly packaged, the refrigerator can be too cold for some aged styles. If not properly packaged, cheese can drastically alter in texture within a few days in the fridge.

The most popular packaging for cheese storage in modern life is plastic wrap. Plastic wrap is unfor-tunately not an ideal breathable material, due to its ability to suffocate the cheese and promote plastic off flavors on the cheese's surface. An alternative plastic vacuum seal is a better application, as the lack of any oxygen within the packaging can halt any unwanted growths. It is plastic wrap's incapacity to completely prevent oxygen from entering the cheese body that expedites the cheese's capacity to become ammoniated and trap moisture, producing excessive amounts of CO_2.

Plastic storage containers are seen as an alternative solution. For fresh varietals such as mozzarella and feta, storing the cheese in a light saltwater/ solution (brine) in Tupperware is very effective. The salt level of the brine holds the acidity of the fresh cheese so that it does not become too alkaline and decompose too quickly. For more aged styles, however, a plastic container with no air ventilation can trap all excess moisture and leave the cheese overly moist, causing excessive bacterial development.

One modern solution is to wrap aged styles of cheese in wax paper and store the cheese in the vegetable drawer. The humidity in the vegetable drawer indirectly permeates the breathable wax paper. There also exists a dual-ply paper that helps promote a cave-like environment. See CAVE. The outer layer is wax paper and the inner layer is plastic. The two work together to control condensation buildup while allowing the cheese to breathe.

Other advancements, such as an improved cheese safe with humidity, air exchange, and temperature controls, would also be promising for increased home cheese care efficiencies. These types of environments would require no extra packaging for the wedges and wheels of cheese to preserve well. One makeshift example of this is a wine cooler that has adjustable temperature and humidity controls.

Cheese will naturally develop mold and bacteria on its surfaces and rinds over time. Blue mold development is part of the natural evolution of aerobic cheeses, and can easily be scraped off the surface of cheese with a knife, leaving the rest of the cheese edible. Depending on an individual's preference, blue molds on rinds can be eaten, or the rind can be discarded. Certain bloomy rinds such as Brie styles, develop a "smear," or orange hue, due to salt-loving bacteria. This transformation in the home is a sign of the cheese reaching its peak in flavor. The cheese in this state is fully aromatic and is usually more creamy and unctuous in its texture. It should be eaten within a few days to one week, as it can begin to develop ammoniated, bitter flavors if left too long.

Black and pink molds are a sign of cheese degradation, and fuzzy brown or gray molds, called "poil de chat" (cat's fur), develop when the cheese is excessively humid. If the black and pink colors are seen on the surface and rinds of the cheese, it is best if the cheese is disposed of. If the brown fuzzy mold is seen in small quantities, it can be patted down with a paper towel or cloth. If it is excessive, it is best to claim it as inedible. Allergic reactions to molds are seen in some individuals, so caution should be taken.

See also PACKAGING.

Daughters of Anatolia, interview with its director Hale Sofia Schatz, 4 August 2015.

Epicure Trading. "French cheese safes." http://www .epicuretrading.co.nz.

Franklin, Linda Campbell. "Cupboards and Food Safes." In *The Oxford Encyclopedia of Food and Drink*, 2d ed, edited by Andrew F. Smith, p. 591. New York: Oxford University Press, 2013.

Le Jaouen, Jean-Claude. "Rind Defects." *The Fabrication of Farmstead Goat Cheese*, p. 124. Ashford, Mass.: The Cheesemaker's Journal, 1987.

Walker, Harlan, ed. "Fat as a Preservative: Cheese in Oil." In *The Fat of the Land: Proceedings of the Oxford Symposium on Food and Cooking*, pp. 40–41. Oxford: Oxford Symposium. 2002.

Jessica Sennett

home cheesemaking is a household means of storing liquid milk in solid form. "Home" cheesemaking has occurred throughout much of human dairying history. In many cultures, cheesemaking for domestic consumption has been the purview of women. The Puritans, who brought cheesemaking and dairy cows with them to the New World from England in the 1600s, were no exception. In the nineteenth century, when cheesemaking moved out of the North American household and into the factory, tradesmen displaced farm women as skilled cheesemakers. See GENDER; DAIRYMAIDS; PURITANS; and INDUSTRIALIZATION.

Although hard-aged, English-style cheeses were fully industrialized in the nineteenth century, immigrants from Italy continued to pass down the custom and practical skill of making fresh mozzarella and other cheeses in their home kitchens, and fresh farmers' cheeses were similarly produced in the kitchens of dairy farms across the country. See MOZZARELLA; AMISH COMMUNITY; and FARMER CHEESE.

Home cheesemaking underwent a symbolic and practical revival in the United States during the "Back to the Land" movement of the 1960s and early 1970s. Hippie homesteaders, committed to self-sufficiency and wary of industrially manufactured foods, learned to make cheese for domestic consumption not from their grandmothers, but from books and fellow travelers. At that time in the United States, only a few how-to books were in circulation, including *Making Your Own Cheese and Yogurt* by Max Alth and *Kitchen Cheesemaking* by Lue Dean Flake. Although both books provided a measure of practical information, aspiring home cheesemakers were challenged by limited access to ingredients and equipment. At the same time, technical knowledge was almost unheard of for home cheesemakers, and so a few people in the United States started looking to Europe to satisfy their cheesemaking needs. Bob and Ricki Carroll, who helped to raise fifteen backyard goats on a communal property in western Massachusetts, started the New England Cheesemaking Supply Company in 1978. They bought bulk quantities of starter cultures and rennet, broke these down into small quantities, and offered domestic-scale supplies to home cheesemakers along with technical cheesemaking classes. Most of the home cheesemakers at that time were living in rural areas, close to the land, often with a goat of their own in the backyard. See COUNTERCULTURE and AMERICAN "GOAT LADIES."

In the 1990s, with the arrival of the Internet and the World Wide Web, city dwellers became newly interested in home cheesemaking. These were professionals who had developed a taste for artisanal cheeses while traveling in Europe and wanted to reproduce that experience at home. Even people who lived in city apartments started coming to workshops with the desire to try their hand at the art of cheesemaking. This changed the profile of home cheesemaking yet again. Newcomers to cheesemaking began by mastering simpler cheeses to be eaten fresh (such as mozzarella), before moving on to the techniques required to mature aged cheeses.

When higher pasteurization temperatures were introduced for many brands of store-bought milk, home cheesemaking became more difficult. Pasteurization at higher temperatures damages the proteins in milk and impedes the stretching required in making cheeses such as mozzarella. Recent support for "local" food includes local milks, which do not have to travel far and can be pasteurized at gentler temperatures, thus, in turn, helping the home cheesemaker. See PASTEURIZATION.

In hard times, people are likely to turn to home cheesemaking as a means of saving money; in prosperous times, they want to try their hand at a new hobby. Today, both the recipes and the bacterial cultures are available to enable enthusiasts to make and mature small quantities of quite sophisticated cheeses. Making cheese by hand, in one's own kitchen, brings awareness, just as does making bread, wine, or beer. It brings cognizance of and appreciation for the farmers who produce the milk as well as for the artisans who handcraft cheese for commercial sale. Enthusiasm for home cheesemaking should also engender support for craft farming and artisanal food production.

Recipe for Queso Blanco

If you would like to try turning a gallon of liquid milk into a pound of solid cheese yourself, open your kitchen cabinet and take out some vinegar. You can make this simple white cheese in about twenty minutes.

Ingredients:
1. 2 ice cubes
2. 1 gallon of milk
3. ¼ cup of apple cider vinegar (or any other vinegar with 5 percent acidity)

Utensils Needed:
4. a one-gallon nonreactive pot (stainless steel is best; do not use aluminum or cast iron)
5. 2 square yards of butter muslin cheesecloth
6. a one-cup measuring cup
7. a large spoon for stirring
8. a dairy thermometer; or any thermometer that will read from 185–220°F (85–104°C)

Cheesemaking Process:
1. Take the 2 ice cubes and place them in your pot. Roll them around the pot until the bottom is cold to the touch from the outside. This creates a steam barrier that will prevent scorching as your milk heats.

2. Add the gallon of milk and heat it to 185°F (85°C). When the milk reaches this temperature, gently stir in the ¼ cup of vinegar, being careful not to stir the bottom of the pot (this would break the steam barrier and cause the milk to scorch). Continue heating (do not boil) until you see a clear separation of curds (solid) and whey (clear yellowish liquid). If you do not see this by 200°F (93°C), add a little more vinegar.

3. When the separation has occurred, turn off the heat, ladle out the curds into a butter muslin cloth, and hang the cloth to drain over a bowl or inside a colander in the sink. The cheese will be ready to remove from the cloth in about an hour.

Now you have succeeded at your own home cheese-making. This cheese is bland and can be used like tofu. Cut it into chunks, brown it in some oil, add a little bit of tamari and Herbs de Provence, and enjoy!

Alth, Max. *Making Your Own Cheese and Yogurt.* New York: Funk and Wagnalls, 1973.

Caldwell, Gianaclis. *Mastering Artisan Cheesemaking: The Ultimate Guide for Home-Scale and Market Producers.* White River Junction, Vt.: Chelsea Green, 2012.

Carroll, Ricki. *Home Cheese Making: Recipes for 75 Homemade Cheeses.* 3d ed. North Adams, Mass.: Storey, 2002.

Flake, Lue Dean. *Kitchen Cheesemaking.* Harrisburg, Pa.: Stackpole, 1976.

Karlin, Mary. *Artisan Cheese Making at Home: Techniques and Recipes for Mastering World-Class Cheeses.* Berkeley, Calif.: Ten Speed, 2011.

Morris, Margaret. *The Cheesemaker's Manual.* Alexandria, Ontario: Glengarry Cheesemaking, 2003.

Ricki Carroll

Homer (b. unknown) was a Greek poet most famous for creating the epics the *Iliad* and the *Odyssey*. Although the time and place of authorship have long been disputed, most scholars agree on the ninth century B.C.E. as the likely time when Homer was active. Both epics reference cheese in ways that help us understand the beginnings of cheesemaking in classical society.

In the *Odyssey*, the Cyclops Polyphemus is said to have produced aged goat's and sheep's milk cheeses. Wheels of cheese, presumably being ripened to develop a natural rind, were discovered by Odysseus and his men on aging racks in Polyphemus's cave. In addition, the Cyclops's pens outside the cave were described as overflowing with lambs and kids. Upon returning home, Polyphemus milks his animals one at a time, setting aside half of the milk to curdle in wicker strainers, and consuming the other half as a drink with his supper. Although no reference is made to a salting step during production, the fact that Polyphemus's cheese was lightly pressed in wicker baskets and put up to age indicates at least a rudimentary technology for cheesemaking beyond fresh, high-moisture cheeses. And because the coagulation step was described as occurring rather quickly, scholars believe that this may be an indirect reference to a rennet-set cheese, which would be one of the first mentions of rennet coagulation in literature.

It is unlikely that animal rennet would have been used at this point in history, but the fig sap referenced in Homer's other work, the *Iliad*, may be a candidate. In a scene in which the physician-god Paieon tends to Ares's wounds, the speed with which Paieon's ointments work is compared to the rate at which a particular sort of fig juice (ὀπός) can curdle milk (V.902–904). Another reference to cheese in the *Iliad* comes in the form of a restorative use for grated goat cheese—mixed with barley and added to wine as an invigorating beverage for the wounded physician Machaon (XI.638). This use of cheese as an additive to wine (often alongside other ingredients) was known as early as the ninth century, when bronze cheese graters were buried alongside warriors, suggesting their connection to the concepts of strength, health, and virility.

See also ANCIENT CIVILIZATIONS and LITERATURE.

Kindstedt, Paul. *Cheese and Culture: A History of Cheese and Its Place in Western Civilization.* White River Junction, Vt.: Chelsea Green, 2012.

Oldfather, W. A. "Homerica: I. akrhton gala, i 297." *Classical Philology* 8 (1913): 195–212.

Vince Razionale

homogenization is the process of pumping milk or cream under high pressure through a homogenizer valve that is designed to break up milk fat globules into much smaller sizes. The principal function of homogenization is to prevent creaming in cow's milk. Milk fat globules in unhomogenized cow's milk readily separate to form a cream layer because of their large size, their lower density relative to the serum phase of milk, and because they adsorb cryoglobulins onto their surface, which cause globules to cluster. Sheep's and goat's milk lack cryoglobulins and therefore are much less prone to creaming. Homogenization creates numerous smaller fat globules with increased surface area, which causes micellar casein to adsorb onto the globule surface and form a casein membrane. Consequently homogenized milk fat globules behave much like casein micelles during coagulation and become incorporated into the casein matrix. This alters the rheological properties of the

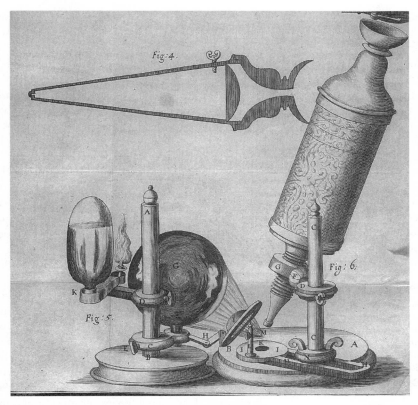

A drawing of the compound microscope Robert Hooke built from his groundbreaking book *Micrographia* (1665), in which he includes extensive descriptions of blue and white cheese molds.

coagulated milk, producing a weaker gel with greater water-holding capacity, which often leads to defects in cheese associated with greater moisture retention, altered texture, and excessive lipolysis. However homogenization of cream is sometimes employed in the making of blue mold cheeses to produce a whiter cheese with enhanced lipolysis and flavor. Homogenization is also employed in the making of hot-pack cream cheese, and it is used to produce recombined milk by emulsifying butter oil in reconstituted skim milk from skim milk powder. Recombined milk is used for cheesemaking in some regions of the world where fresh milk is unavailable.

See also FAT and MILK.

Law, B. A., and A. Y. Tamime, eds. *Technology of Cheesemaking*. 2d ed. Chichester, U.K.: John Wiley & Sons, 2010.
Walstra, P., et al. *Dairy Science and Technology*. Boca Raton, Fla.: CRC Press, 2006.

Paul S. Kindstedt

Hooke, Robert (1635–1703) can be best described as a genius, brilliant scientist, and maverick. After entering Oxford University in 1653, Hooke studied with the also legendary chemist, physicist, and inventor Robert Boyle (1627–1691) who is best known for Boyle's Law: at a constant temperature, the volume of a gas varies inversely with pressure. Having a mind of extraordinary fertility, Hooke joined the Royal Society of London in 1662 where he remained as a professor. He is credited with inventing the first spiral spring balance watch based on Hooke's Law, which states that the force needed to compress a spring by some distance is proportional to that distance, fixing the freezing point of water at 32°F (0°C), and developing the wheel barometer. Hooke was also active in astronomy, discovering the dark red spot on Jupiter and calculating the rotation rate of Mars to within thirty-seven minutes of the currently accepted value. Hooke, who was also one of the seventeenth-century pioneers of microscopy with Antonie van Leeuwenhoek (1632–1723), built a compound microscope with an illumination system that led to his groundbreaking book *Micrographia*, published in 1665. This work contains a series of exceptional copperplate engravings of the miniature world, including the structure of various insects (including cheese mites), sponges, and bird feathers as well as leaves, seeds, fish scales, and other objects from nature. After observing minute boxlike structures in a piece of cork, Hooke coined the term "cell" for what he had seen. Most importantly for cheesemakers, Hooke provided the first detailed descriptions of several blue and white moldy spots on green cheese, including that from a hairy mold subsequently identified as *Mucor*. This has proven to be important both in the ripening of certain cheeses and as a source for enzymes similar to rennet, which is required for coagulation of milk.

See also COAGULANT; MUCOR; and RENNET.

Espinasse, Margaret. *Robert Hooke.* 2d ed. Berkeley: University of California Press, 1962.

Hooke, Robert. *Micrographia: Or Some Physiological Descriptions of Minute Bodies Made by Magnifying Glasses with Observations and Inquiries Thereupon.* London: Royal Society of London, 1665. http://www .gutenberg.org/files/15491/15491-h/15491-h.htmy.

Elliot Ryser

hoop describes both the verb of placing cheese curd in a mold and the mold itself. The word "hoop" suggests a bottomless open cylinder, but cheese forms may or may not have fixed bottoms and can result in various shapes. The hoop is the form that contributes to a cheese's characteristic shape and qualities. In addition to the common circular shape that produces round wheels of cheese, hoops may be square, rectangular, or conical. Hoop construction reflects the style of the cheese for which the design is intended. The traditional wooden ring cinched with a rope contributes to AOP Beaufort's convex wheel edge, while DOP Queso tetilla receives its conical shape from a uniquely dedicated hoop, specific to that cheese. See BEAUFORT. Cheesemakers line the hoop with cheesecloth before hooping to facilitate drainage and a smooth rind surface, or the hoop may have an integrated cloth insert. See CHEESECLOTH.

The components of a hoop include its walls, bottom, and a follower. Simple hoops are open cylinders without a bottom or a follower, usually used over a draining mat. Hoops with followers usually have bottoms. The follower fits inside the inner diameter of the hoop to provide a moving uniform surface for pressing the cheese. Block molds combine multiple hoops into one assembly that is turned

Workers hooping the curd to make Cheddar cheese at the Plymouth Cheese factory in 1914. WISCONSIN HISTORICAL SOCIETY

at once during draining for greater efficiency. Most hoops are perforated, some more and some less, depending on the style of the cheese. Cheese hoops are commonly made of plastic, stainless steel, aluminum alloys, or hardwood. Wooden hoops, often made of teak for its water resistance, are uncommon due to sanitation concerns.

Because they are not pressed, fresh and soft-ripened cheeses take a variety of shapes and do not require hoops made of heavy materials. Plastic basket-style hoops emulate the woven-reed construction of vessels traditionally used for draining acid-set cheeses. Cheesemakers use thin-walled cylinders, pyramids, and tubes to produce the iconic shapes of aged Loire Valley lactic-set goat's milk cheeses. Cheese forms designed for receiving very wet curd, such as in soft mold-ripened cheese production, are sometimes divided into stacking segments so that they may be reduced to the level of the drained curd a short while after hooping. The traditional heart shape of AOP Neufchâtel illustrates the creative shapes afforded by unpressed cheeses. See NEUFCHÂTEL.

Pressed cheeses are almost always round or square so that pressure can be distributed equally across the hoop, as well as to ensure uniform ripening. Thick-walled hoops contain pressure and exert it evenly on the cheese. Historically pressed in strong teak molds, contemporary Gouda is hooped into heavy forms with rounded bottoms and high-rise followers that result in a tightly knit cheese wheel with rounded edges. See GOUDA. Cheesemakers hoop block Ched-

dar curds into rectangular two-piece stainless steel molds, the top and bottom portions nesting within each other at the center so that the segments telescope inward when loaded into a press. See CHEDDAR. Automated block cheese production involves cutting rectangular segments from tall vertical columns of continuously compacting curd as they exit block forming towers. Small-scale cheesemakers have been known to improvise inexpensive hoops by cutting rounds from segments of wide-diameter water pipes.

See also BLOCK-FORMING TOWERS and PRESS.

Kammerlehner, Josef. *Cheese Technology*. Freising, Germany: Printed by author, 2009. See pp. 282–285.
Scott, R., R. K. Robinson; and R. A. Wilbey. *Cheesemaking Practice*. 3d ed. Gaithersburg, Md.: Aspen, 1998. See pp. 258–262.

Brent A. Wasser

Humboldt Fog is a soft-ripened pasteurized goat's milk cheese. It is also the result of a dream. Its creator, Cypress Grove Chevre founder Mary Keehn, was on a flight back to the United States from France, where she and fellow cheesemaker Judy Schad, of Capriole Goat Cheese in Indiana, had traveled to visit cheesemakers. See CAPRIOLE and CYPRESS GROVE CHEVRE. Keehn says she fell asleep and dreamed about a cheese with a line running through it. With that, Humboldt Fog was born.

Humboldt Fog, a soft goat's milk cheese, has a distinctive gray stripe that runs through the middle, as well as under the rind. A thin layer of vegetable ash gives the cheese its aesthetically pleasing stripe, but does not flavor it. COURTESY OF CYPRESS GROVE CHEVRE

The year was 1992, nine years after Cypress Grove Chevre opened for business. The cheese, as we now know it, is a 6-pound 3-kilogram wheel made with microbial rennet and a small amount of *Geotrichum*. See RENNET and *GEOTRICHUM CANDIDUM*. To form the cheese, half the curds are ladled into molds, and that once only-dreamed-of line of vegetable ash is applied to the surface. See ASH. The second layer of nascent curds is then poured on top of the ash to form a layer of cake-like cheese. The cheese also gets an exterior coat of ash before being sprayed with *Penicillium candidum*, which grows on the surface during the aging process. See PENICILLIUM. Although the ash used to be applied by hand, it is now distributed via an airbrushlike device. This ensures a much tidier application process for the opportunistic lighter-than-air ash.

The cheese, called Humboldt Fog Grande as distinct from its 1 pound (.5 kilogram) counterpart, Humboldt Fog Mini, is named for the county in which it is made and that county's signature climactic condition. The milk to make it comes from nearby goat dairies as well as Cypress Grove Chevre's own goats. It is aged for two to three weeks before being distributed.

When it is young, the paste of the soft-ripened cheese is firm and a little chalky. As it ripens, the curds begin to break down to form a cream-like layer just under the rind. When cut, the cheese reveals a thin dark outline of the ash just under the rind, as well as its mid-stripe of ash. Although the ash does not flavor the cheese, it lends an aesthetic beauty that distinguishes the bright white goat cheese from most of its counterparts.

Early on, the ash line was new to US cheese consumers because they were not familiar with the similar-looking French cow's milk cheese Morbier. See MORBIER. Because of that, the ash was often mistaken for a line of "blue." To this day, the ash has been cause for confusion because many consumers and even food professionals occasionally mistake the cheese for a blue cheese despite the fact it has no blue molds in or around it.

Roberts, Jeffrey P. *The Atlas of American Artisan Cheese.* White River Junction, Vt.: Chelsea Green, 2007.
Werlin, Laura. *The New American Cheese: Profiles of America's Great Cheesemakers and Recipes for Cooking with Cheese.* New York: Stewart, Tabori & Chang, 2000.

Laura Werlin

humidity

See RELATIVE HUMIDITY.

Hungary, a country in Central Europe, lags behind most of its neighbors as a producer and consumer of cheese. Of what it does consume, processed cheese makes up nearly 25 percent, a much greater percentage than that of any other European country. Cheese is featured regularly in Hungarian cuisine, and is thus an oft-encountered element of the Hungarian diet.

Hungary occupies the Carpathian Basin in Central Europe, bordered on the north by Slovakia; on the east by Ukraine and Romania; on the south by Slovenia, Croatia, and Serbia; and on the west by Austria. See CROATIA and AUSTRIA. With a relatively flat landscape and controlled natural water systems going back to the nineteenth century, more than three-quarters of the land in the country is productive. The seven regions of Hungary's grasslands are all dairy-farmed, with the largest farms in the southern Transdanubia region.

Hungary was established as a country by seven unified Magyar tribes under their King Arpad in 895 C.E. It is highly likely that the nomadic Magyars brought cheese to Hungary. We know that they milked not only cows, goats, and sheep, but also horses and camels, to supply milk for kumiss, a carbonated alcoholic drink that was very popular at their feasts.

Hungary was a monarchy for more than six centuries, and then part of several empires, before finally achieving autonomy with the collapse of the Soviet Union in 1989. Agriculture, including dairy farming, experienced a huge boom in the 1960s through 1980s, but with the dissolution of the national Dairy Industry Trust and privatization of the dairy market, this period was at an end. Multinational companies entered the dairy market during a second period of privatization in 1993–1995.

Hungary produces much less cheese than, for example, Germany and France, with about 80,000 tons produced in 2014, compared to 2.3 million tons for Germany and 1.6 million for France. Cheese for the Hungarian market is mainly produced by domestic companies, such as Baranyatej, or foreign companies through domestic subsidiaries, such as Bongrain SA., with more than 99 percent made from domestic cow's milk. See SAVENCIA FROMAGE & DAIRY. Low-fat and organic varieties of dairy products are becoming popular. Artisan cheesemakers are popping up around the country, including Tekeresvölgyi Artisan Dairy on Lake Balaton and Bükki Sajt in Eger.

Imported cheeses such as Emmentaler and Edam are popular in Hungary, alongside Hungarian varieties such as Túró, Trappista, and Pannonia. See EMMENTALER and EDAM. Túró, a fresh lumpy curd cheese made from either cow's or sheep's milk (similar to farmer's cheese), may be the most popular Hungarian cheese. See QUARK. However, recent statistics suggest that semihard cheeses are gaining in popularity, such as Trappista (a cow's milk cheese, pale yellowish in color with small holes) and Pannonia (a cow's milk cheese with large holes, which tastes rather bittersweet, like walnuts).

While drizzling sour cream over gulyas may be the stereotypical dairy usage in a Hungarian dish, cheese is actually found throughout their cuisine. For example, breakfast is often Túró, cream cheese, or a cheese spread called Körözött on bread or toast. Hungary's most popular fast food is *Langos*, a deep-fried flat bread (Hungarian pizza) usually smothered with sour cream, yogurt, and grated cheese. Túró appears in a number of dishes, such as *Túrós Csusza* (hand-made noodles with sour cream and Túró) and *Túrógombóc* (dumplings made with túró, which can be savory or sweet). Another Hungarian dish that features cheese is *Rántott sajt* (cheese croquette).

Bánfalvi, Carolyn. *Food Wine Budapest*. New York: Little Bookroom, 2008.

Cheese Industry Profile: Hungary. New York: Datamonitor, 2004.

Laszlovszky, József, ed. *Tender Meat under the Saddle: Customs of Eating, Drinking and Hospitality among Conquering Hungarians and Nomadic Peoples*. Krems, Austria: Medium Aevum Quotidianum, 1998.

Karl Peterson

hygiene refers to sanitary conditions and practices that help to maintain health and prevent the spread of diseases. Food hygiene therefore encompasses all the conditions and measures necessary to ensure the safety and wholesomeness of food. Proper hygiene and hygienic practices aid in the prevention of food-borne illness by limiting the exposure of foods to hazardous agents including chemicals, toxins, and pathogenic microorganisms. From raw material production to the point of consumption, dairy products and their ingredients should be subject to a combination of control measures to ensure a safe food supply. This outline merely skims the surface of the full scope of food hygiene practices and approaches.

In general food business operators are responsible for ensuring that the necessary level of food hygiene and safety is attained from primary production to delivery. Governments are more often responsible for issuing regulations, guidance, policies, and microbiological criteria related to hygiene to adequately protect consumers, thereby verifying and providing assurance that food is suitable for consumption. This may include the examination of establishments, animals, and food, as well as food processing activities. Inspection activities can also encompass management and production systems, including documents, finished product testing, feeding practices, and the origin and destination of production inputs and outputs.

Microbiological criteria are utilized to protect consumers against pathogens in food. Because the use of microbiological examination to assess the safety of foods is limited, current hygiene programs often utilize a preventive, Hazard Analysis and Critical Control Point (HACCP)–based system wherever possible. See HAZARD ANALYSIS AND CRITICAL CONTROL POINT. The US Food and Drug Administration Food Safety Modernization Act of 2011 incorporates such an approach in its Hazard Analysis and Risk Based Preventive Controls and related rules. See FOOD AND DRUG ADMINISTRATION. A risk-based approach matches regulatory requirements to food safety outcomes providing businesses flexibility to adapt technical requirements based on the nature of the business. This flexibility allows operators to develop their own systems to ensure food safety thereby allowing for the continuity of traditional products and production methods with long-standing food safety records such as those utilized in the manufacture of various cheeses.

The full application of HACCP principles can be limited at the farm level, emphasizing the importance of other preventive controls including good hygiene, agricultural, and veterinary practices. In addition to the location, design, maintenance, and use of premises, controls at primary production of milk include the management of water and other environmental factors to minimize potential transmission of hazards (e.g., pests, chemicals, pathogens, etc.)

to feed, equipment, or milking animals that could, directly or indirectly, contaminate milk. This includes the proper procurement, manufacturing, and handling of animal feed to limit the introduction and elaboration of hazards including pathogens, pesticide residues, and mycotoxins. Care is taken with pests so as to control potential vectors of human and animal disease in the production environment while minimizing the risk of introducing chemical hazards into milk. The health status of herds or flocks and milking animals is managed in a manner to limit the spread of disease among animals and to milk via the mammary glands or from environmental contamination. Milking equipment is also designed, constructed, installed, and maintained to avoid damage to the udder and teats and to limit the spread of disease between animals. The development and implementation of standard operating procedures documents and standardizes the entire milking process, including the steps taken to minimize the exposure of milk to undesirable or pathogenic microorganisms as well as chemical and physical hazards.

The identification and control of hazards during processing relies heavily on HACCP-based principles where a combination of control measures are designed and adapted to the hygiene status of the milk and raw materials to prevent, eliminate, or reduce the identified hazards to acceptable levels to achieve the desired objectives or criteria. Microbiological criteria are often utilized in the design of control measure combinations and for verifying the efficacy of controls along the continuum. This could include microbiological criteria for incoming milk, in-process product, or finished product. The ability to trace and recall products in the case of non-conformance with established standards provides another line of defense in the prevention of food-borne illness. Effective recall requires appropriate labeling, documentation, and record keeping. Proper labeling also provides appropriate information to ensure that the next link in the food chain, including consumers, knows the proper way to handle, store, process, prepare, and display the product safely.

In support of an HACCP-based system, the proper location, design, and layout of food processing facilities permits good food hygiene practices. Structures and equipment are built of durable materials that are easy to maintain, clean, and disinfect (where appropriate), including the use of nontoxic and impervious materials. Floors are constructed to allow adequate

drainage and cleaning to prevent the accumulation of water and soil. Facility layout minimizes the risks of cross-contamination by controlling the flow of ingredients, equipment, and products in a forward progression from raw material receipt to finished product packaging. Similarly ventilation systems are designed so that air does not flow to sensitive areas of the facility from less clean zones. Where appropriate, physical barriers or sanitary breaks (e.g., sanitizing footbath) are utilized to prevent or minimize the transfer of contaminants or potential sources of contaminants by employees or equipment between areas of varying risk.

Additional key hygienic controls focus on the cleaning and sanitation of facilities and equipment. The objective of cleaning and sanitizing is to remove soils and nutrients that microorganisms need to grow, and to kill those microorganisms that are present. Cleaning and sanitation are considered two discrete steps in the overall procedure. Cleaning is the complete removal of food residues and soil from surfaces while sanitation is the process by which microorganisms are reduced to a level that is safe from a public health standpoint. Inadequate cleaning can compromise the efficacy of subsequent sanitation. Sanitation of food contact surfaces is defined as a process that reduces the contamination level by 99.999 percent (5 logs) in 30 seconds whereas sanitation of non-food contact surfaces requires a reduction of 99.9 percent (3 logs) with *Staphylococcus aureus* and *Escherichia coli* as typical test organisms. Effective programs ensure that all parts of the facility are appropriately cleaned and sanitized, including the tools used cleaning in the process. Documentation of such programs specifies areas, pieces of equipment, and utensils to be cleaned and sanitized, the detailed methods and frequency, and the means of monitoring and verifying efficacy such as audit pre-operational inspections or, where appropriate, microbiological sampling of the environment and food contact surfaces.

Ensuring food safety through the application of good hygienic practices at the source, during production and processing, through handling, distribution, storage, sale, preparation, and use is the responsibility of all involved along the food chain. All personnel engaged in food operations that come directly or indirectly into contact with food and food animals should be aware of their role and responsibility in protecting food from contamination and should have the necessary knowledge and skills to handle food and animals hygienically. This includes, at minimum, hand washing when cleanliness may affect food safety and, where appropriate, wearing suitable protective clothing, head coverings, and footwear. However, it cannot be overstated that effective hygiene and good manufacturing practices at all stages rely on training, routine supervision, and audits to ensure that procedures are being carried out effectively.

See also CRITICAL CONTROL POINTS and POST-PROCESS CONTAMINATION.

European Commission. *Food Hygiene.* http://ec.europa
.eu/food/food/biosafety/hygienelegislation/
index_en.htm.
Food and Agriculture Organization of the United Nations and International Dairy Federation. *FAO Animal Production and Health Guidelines,* no. 8: *Guide to Good Dairy Farming Practice.* Rome: FAO, 2011. http://www.fao.org/docrep/014/ba0027e/
ba0027e00.pdf.
Food and Drug Administration. *Current Good Manufacturing Practices.* Code of Federal Regulations Title 21, Part 117. 2016. http://www.ecfr.gov/
cgi-bin/text-idx?SID=a62390cdc74b6114fd08fe55a4
73ef5b&mc=true&node=pt21.2.117&rgn=div5
Food and Drug Administration. *FDA Food Safety Modernization Act (FSMA).* 2014. http://www.fda
.gov/Food/GuidanceRegulation/FSMA.
World Health Organization/Food and Agriculture Organization of the United Nations. *Food Hygiene: Basic Texts.* 4th ed. Rome: World Health Organization, 2009. http://www.fao.org/docrep/012/a1552e/
a1552e00.htm.

Dennis D'Amico

Hypata, known in modern times as Ypati, was a commercial capital of Aeniania, which was often considered part of Thessaly. Hypata was founded at the end of the fifth century B.C.E. and was at its commercial height in the first few centuries of the Common Era in the Roman Empire. In Apuleius's novel *The Golden Ass,* which takes place in the second century B.C.E., the character Aristomenes recounts having traveled to Hypata in search of a well-regarded cheese that was on sale for a good price, but finds himself a day late—just a day earlier a well-known businessman named Lupus had bought up the entire supply. This short anecdote is notable in that it demonstrates cheese's role in the commercial world as a business

opportunity, particularly in the case of Aristomenes, who makes a living traveling around the region buying and selling cooking items. Cheese is only one of two products he mentions by name—honey is the other—which could indicate the prominent role that cheese played in the cuisine and commerce at the time.

See also ANCIENT CIVILIZATIONS.

Warner, C. D., et al., eds. *Library of the World's Best Literature: Ancient and Modern.* London: International Society, 1986.

Vince Razionale

hyphae are fungal structures. Most filamentous fungi, so-called molds, consist of a macrostructure named mycelium. See FILAMENTOUS FUNGI and MYCELIA. After spore germination, the first hypha or germ tube emerges from the spore, grows, and then branches to form the mycelium. See SPORES. Hyphal growth is apical, which means that membrane and cell wall syntheses are mainly localized at each elongating hyphal tip. This apical hyphal growth leads to radial mycelium growth.

In cheeses, mold adjuncts may belong to higher fungi such as *Penicillium camemberti* and *P. roqueforti* or to lower fungi such as *Mucor lanceolatus.* See ADJUNCT CULTURES; PENICILLIUM; and MUCOR. Hyphae in higher fungi are septate, with each cell compartment containing one or two nuclei (dikaryon), depending on the life-stage cycle considered. These hyphae are about five micrometers in width and can reach incredible lengths of up to several kilometers. In lower fungi, hyphae are not septate and wider, and their growth is generally faster. Fungal hyphae are responsible for the typical characteristics of certain cheese varieties: for example, the dense white coat observed on the surface of Camembert-type cheeses results mainly from the growth of *Penicillium camemberti* mycelium. See CAMEMBERT DE NORMANDIE.

During cheese ripening, growing hyphae spread on the cheese surface, while some also penetrate the substratum. At the same time, exoenzymes are secreted to degrade milk proteins and lipids into peptides and fatty acids that can contribute to the ripening process. Aerial hyphae can differentiate into structures that will support sporogenesis. These structures correspond to conidiophores in higher fungi or to sporangiophores in lower fungi.

See also FUNGI.

Chamba, J. F., and F. Irlinger. "Secondary and Adjunct Cultures." In *Cheese: Chemistry, Physics, and Microbiology*, edited by Patrick F. Fox et al. Vol. 1: *General Aspects*, 3d ed., pp. 191–206. London: Elsevier, 2004.

Gow, Neil A. R., and Geoffrey M. Gadd. *Growing Fungus*. London: Chapman and Hall, 1995.

Jean-Luc Jany

Iceland's harsh landscape and significant meteorological activity have combined to shape both the agriculture, and more specifically, the dairy production of this small country.

Iceland was settled in the ninth century by Vikings from Norway and Britain. They brought with them both livestock and farming practices, as well as the ability to make skyr. This yogurt-like soft cheese was found across Scandinavia at that time, but for some reason the other countries stopped making it, and skyr became exclusively a product of Iceland.

The making of skyr is inextricably linked to the traditional food-preservation methods of Iceland, which themselves cannot be separated from the landscape and weather. The key consideration was how to preserve meat and dairy produce from the short growing season through the harsh, nine-month winter. A compounding problem was the shortage of timber, as forests were rapidly depleted just to keep people warm. Not only did this rule out smoking as a preservation method, but it also ruled out salt, which was obtained by boiling off seawater.

Turning cream to butter was a common way of preserving it through the winter; it would ferment, and so it would keep for months. The remaining skim milk was placed in a bucket at a favored area of the farm, where the local environmental microbes that make up the unique skyr culture would acidify the milk. This mixture was then added to heated fresh milk and rennet; once it had coagulated, it was strained through cloth, removing the whey and leaving the skyr. The same container would be used for the next batch, thereby passing on the favored culture. The remaining whey provided the answer to the preservation of meat; whey ferments to lactic acid, which lowers the pH of the food, thus preserving it in much the same way as pickling in vinegar. See WHEY; LACTIC ACID; and PH MEASUREMENT.

This practice continued more or less unchanged until the advent of urbanization in the nineteenth century. Because production of skyr was so tied up with the preservation of meat and butter, it left little room for the development of any other type of cheese. Subsistence farmers trying to keep their families alive over a long winter in an unforgiving climate were unlikely to risk precious milk on an experiment in cheesemaking.

This is not to say that there was no other cheesemaking at all. During the short summer, the sheep and goats would be taken to higher ground while the lower meadows were put into hay production for the winter feed. The (mainly) girls who stayed up in the summer quarters (*seters*) may well have made some fresh cheeses in small quantities, but this was likely to have been on a simple and limited scale.

Moving forward to the nineteenth century, the shift to urban centers in Iceland mirrored the industrialization across Europe. As men moved away from the family farm and into town, they provided a market for dairy products at the very time when a surplus was beginning to show. Farmers began to organize themselves into associations and thus benefit from the economics of scale and the stronger voice that numbers provide. The government (again in tandem with other European countries) provided generous subsidies in an attempt to grow more food and boost the farming industry. This in turn led to another wave of surplus, both of milk and of lamb, creating the perfect conditions for a new cheese industry in Iceland. The new farming cooperatives inspired farmers to create a whole new cheese-making tradition; the product was there and the market was ready.

Iceland, which produced one cheese for hundreds of years, is thus seeing a new tradition of cheesemaking emerge. This young country, with a landscape that has yet to settle down and people who are used to dealing with change, has a cheesemaking future as exciting and unpredictable as the land itself.

See also DENMARK; NORWAY; and SWEDEN.

Gísladóttir, Hallgerður. *Íslensk matarhefð* [Icelandic Food Heritage]. Reykjavik, Iceland: Mál og Menning, 1999.
Jónasson, Jónas. *Íslenzkir þjóðhættir*. Reykjavik, Iceland: Ísafoldarprentsmiðja, 2010.
Júlíusson, Árni Daníel. *Landbúnaðarsaga Íslands*. 2d ed. Reykjavik, Iceland: Skrudda, 2013.
Pétursdóttir, Hólmfríður. *Íslenzktskyr* (June 1960): 13–17.
Thorlacius, Sigríður. "Do You Know Skyr?" *Petits Propos Culinaires* 4 (1980): 34.
"Viking Farming Methods." Danishnet.com. http://www.danishnet.com/vikings/viking-farming-methods.

Eirny Sigurdardottir

Idiazabal cheese is one of the most emblematic traditional food products of the Basque country, a region in the north of Spain bordering the Atlantic Ocean and France. Named after the village of Idiazabal, the cheese has been protected since 1987 with a protected designation of origin (PDO). Today Idiazabal is the second most produced PDO ewe's milk cheese in Spain after the PDO Manchego cheese, with around 1,500 tons produced annually.

Idiazabal is made exclusively in the Basque country and Navarre, from raw ewe's milk from the Latxa breed. See LATXA. Latxa is an indigenous breed adapted to grazing in the extreme conditions of the region. Latxa sheep are particularly apt for dairy purposes, and nearly all the milk produced is destined for cheese production. Shepherds are generally the owners of the flocks, and the cheese is usually made by women in the family dairy business. Cheese-making adds value to the milk produced on the farms, ensuring the maintenance of the population in rural areas.

Historically the sheep migrated to higher pastures in summer to graze on the blossoming new grass. Under this system of summer dairying in mountain pastures, the shepherds milked the sheep, made the cheese, and aged it for a minimum of two months up in the mountains. See TRANSHUMANCE. At the end of summer, when the cheesemakers returned to the valleys with their sheep, the cheese was ready for sale. Nowadays only a few producers continue to make cheese in the mountains owing to the difficult logistics of the process, including the challenge of maintaining sanitary conditions. However, the current denomination supports a "mountain"-labeled cheese variety to promote a product that combines these traditional manufacturing conditions in the mountains with high standard sanitary conditions. Even if most of the cheeses are made from November to July at the dairy farms, taking advantage of the valley pastures, most of the animals still benefit from a grass diet on the mountain communal land, grazing from June through October. Husbandry of the Latxa flocks preserves a cultural legacy associated with the grazing areas of the mountain communal land and the socioeconomic development (associated with cheesemaking, lamb, and milk sales) of the rural areas.

Idiazabal is an enzymatic-coagulated, pressed, uncooked (temperature of the curd lower than 99°F [37°C]) cheese, aged for a minimum of sixty days. It has a cylindrical shape and weighs between 2 to 7 pounds (1 to 3 kilograms). The cheese can be smoked or not, and in both cases most of the cheeses are sold before one year of ripening. The exclusive use of raw milk from the Latxa breed maintains the natural enzymes and microflora present in the milk, and it is a determinant factor in obtaining a complex and distinctive product from a sensory point of view. The use of traditional lamb rennet paste gives the cheese an intense aroma and slightly piquant taste.

Early in the 1990s the sensory characteristics of the cheese were scientifically identified, allowing identification and recognition of the Idiazabal cheese by experts and consumers, despite the intrinsic variation associated with traditional fabrication methods. The rind of Idiazabal cheese is hard, smooth, and varying from a creamy yellow to a deep brown for the smoked variety. The paste presents small irregular openings, with a color ranging from ivory to pale yellow. The texture is firm and slightly elastic, but with aging the cheese becomes harder, less elastic, and more friable. The aroma is intense and deep, mainly characterized by lactic (fresh butter), roasted (cooked milk and toffee aromas), and animal (lamb rennet paste) notes. The aroma often has nutty and vegetable (hay) notes. However, the most characteristic note and what really differentiates Idiazabal from other cheeses are the aromatics associated with the degradation of the fat during the ripening. This lipolytic activity is mainly due to the enzymes present in the lamb rennet paste used in the traditional elaboration, and is not replicated when using commercial rennet. These enzymes are responsible for the dominant character of the "acid" aromas (like butyric acid) on the profile of the cheese. Smoking Idiazabal cheeses today presents a subtle aesthetic variation, whereas originally smoking was used to hide a defective cheese. See SMOKED CHEESES.

Idiazabal has won many different recognitions and awards. In 1992 the French Ministry of Agriculture and Rural Development and the French National Council of Culinary Art carried out a study in conjunction with the European Community of Chefs (Euro-Toques), which consisted of a survey of the products making up the European culinary heritage. Euro-Toques, an organization bringing together over three thousand chefs from all over the European Community, selected fifteen products in Europe to describe as European Culinary Heritage Products. Both Idiazabal cheese and Bellota cured ham have won such a title. In October 1993, at a meeting in Parma, Italy, the International Academy of Gastronomy awarded its Gold Medal to Idiazabal, considering it one of today's best European cheeses.

The most traditional version of the cheese is made on small farmstead dairies, and consumed mainly locally. Thus the best way to discover the uniqueness and complexity of this exciting cheese is to visit the Basque country and taste the product locally while visiting some of the more than one hundred families involved in traditional Idiazabal cheesemaking.

See also BASQUE COUNTRY.

Renobales, Mertxe de, et al. "La investigación científica en el queso Idiazabal." *Revista Internacional de los Estudios Vascos* 53, no. 2 (2008): 395–431.

Urarte, E., et al. "Idiazabal Cheese and the Production Systems Used with Native Latxa and Carranzana Breeds of Sheep." In *Basics of the Quality of Typical Mediterranean Animal Products.* EAAP–FAO–CIHEAM–Junta de Extremadura–UE International Symposium. Wageningen, Netherlands: Wageningen Press, 1998, pp. 147–152.

Francisco José Perez Elortondo

Illinois, and particularly its northwest region, was from the mid-nineteenth to the early twentieth century covered with small dairy farms, many of which produced butter and cheese. As Chicago grew, dairy farmers switched to the production of fluid milk for the city market. Illinois's most famous figure in the cheese world was the Canadian-born James L. Kraft, who moved to Chicago in 1903 and began packaging cheese under the Kraft name. He and his brothers also developed a method of processing cheese to increase its shelf life. Kraft's worldwide headquarters are in Northfield, Illinois, a suburb of Chicago, and today the company still operates one plant in Illinois that produces processed cheese (Kraft Slices and Velveeta) as well as dinners and salad dressing. See KRAFT, JAMES L.; KRAFT FOODS; and VELVEETA.

As late as the 1950s, Illinois had fifty-two cheese plants. After the introduction of commercial fertilizers in the 1950s, many farmers turned to large-scale production of corn and wheat, with the result that most of the cheese plants disappeared. However, the "locavore" (eating locally grown food) movement and the growth of farmers' markets have led to a revival of artisanal cheesemaking in the state. Some cheesemakers, like the owners of Ropp Jersey Cheese in Normal, in central Illinois, and Lime Rock Brown Swiss Cheese in Davis and Prairie Pure Cheese in Belvidere (both located near the Wisconsin border) are third-, fourth-, and even fifth-generation farmers who turned to cheesemaking in the 2000s. Ludwig Farmstead Creamery in Fithian, in western Illinois, makes handcrafted European-style aged cheese using milk from Holstein cows. Marcoot Jersey Creamery was started in 2010 in Greenville, forty miles east of St. Louis, by seventh-generation family members. It produces sixteen varieties of fresh, cave-aged, and farmstead cheeses. Many small cheesemakers have on-farm retail outlets and sell their products online.

Several manufacturers, many the descendants of Swiss and German immigrants, are located in northwestern Illinois near the Wisconsin border, where the terrain is rolling pastureland. Large-scale, industrial producers include family-owned Torkelson Cheese in Lena, which produces more than thirty thousand pounds a day of Brick, Munster, and Mexican-style cheeses and has won twelve awards at the World Champion Cheese Contest in Madison, Wisconsin. Also in Lena, Kolb Lena Cheese, owned by Bongrain Cheese USA, produces European-style cheeses, including Camembert, Brie, Swiss, and baby Swiss. Other Swiss-cheese manufacturers are Brewster Cheese in Stockton; Wenger's Springbrook Cheese in Davis; and Berner Valley Cheese in Rock City. Berner has developed a line of cholesterol-free, lactose-free dairy products called Earth's Answer, in which the butterfat is replaced with vegetable oil. In 1978 Rene and Pasquale Caputo founded Wiscon Corporation, which manufactures Parmesan, Romano, mozzarella, and other Italian cheeses at its 200,000-square-foot facility in the Chicago suburb of Melrose Park. It includes a cheese-aging room as well as the Caputo Cheese Market, which carries more than a thousand domestic and imported cheeses. The Mancuso Cheese Company in Joliet, forty miles southwest of Chicago, produces mozzarella and ricotta.

Illinois's most famous cheese is no longer produced in the state. Nauvoo, in southern Illinois, was the capital of the Church of Jesus Christ of Latter Day Saints (Mormons) between 1839 and 1846, and in the 1850s was settled by the Icarians, a French sect who planted grapes and made wine. Prohibition in 1929 ended wine production there, but the cool wine cellars—and caves—were ideal for aging cheese. In the mid-1930s Oscar Rohde, a professor at Iowa State University, developed a new blue cheese and found the abandoned winery caves in Nauvoo to be the perfect place to produce it. Nauvoo Blue, as he called his new cheese, was distinguished by its smooth, creamy texture and clean, fresh, slightly piquant flavor. Soon outgrowing its caves, the Nauvoo Blue Cheese factory became the second largest producer of blue cheese in the United States until 2002, when it was acquired by a conglomerate; the following year, the Nauvoo factory was closed. There are ongoing efforts to reopen it.

See also INDUSTRIAL and UNITED STATES.

Illinois Department of Agriculture. http://www.agr .state.il.us/.
Illinois Farm Bureau Partners. http://www.ilfbpartners .com/tag/cheese.

Colleen Taylor Sen

Inanna was the Sumerian goddess of love and war. She is identified with the Assyrian and Babylonian goddess Ishtar and the Phoenician Astarte.

Sumerian mythology of the third millennium B.C.E., as rediscovered in cuneiform tablets from south-

ern Iraq, records several stories of Inanna, who was the patron goddess of the city of Uruk. Important in this context is the courtship of Inanna and Dumuzi, mythical king of Uruk before the flood. Dumuzi was a shepherd, and Inanna at first rejected him: "No! The farmer is the man of my heart!" Dumuzi responds jealously, "If he gives you beer, I will give you milk. If he gives you bread, I will give you honey cheese!" Eventually they are united and Inanna sings, "Let the milk of the goat flow in my sheepfold. Fill my holy churn with honey cheese."

Cuneiform tablets were used not only for literature but also in account keeping. These practical texts make clear the economic reality behind the myth. Although the cheese on which the Sumerians fed was produced by shepherds and goatherds they brought it as tribute to the temple of Inanna, and it was the priests of this temple who distributed it. Thus, in religious terms, Dumuzi made the cheese but Inanna ensured its supply to the people of Uruk.

See also ANCIENT CIVILIZATIONS.

Limet, Henri. "The Cuisine of Ancient Sumer." *Biblical Archaeologist* 50 (1987): 132–147.
Wolkstein, Diane, and Samuel Noah Kramer, translators. *Inanna, Queen of Heaven and Earth: Her Stories and Hymns from Sumer.* New York: Harper & Row, 1983. See pp. 30–49.

Andrew Dalby

India's most famous cheese across the world is paneer, a fresh, pressed cheese similar to queso fresco. See PANEER. It is used in North Indian cuisines and is increasingly popular in South India as well. However, few people in India would classify paneer as "cheese." Since the 1950s, cheese in India has meant Amul cheese, the processed Cheddar made in Khatraj, Gujarat, grated and sprinkled on popular street snacks such as pavbhaji, bhelpuri, and pulao, and melted on pizza and in sandwiches. Nevertheless, beginning in the 1970s, small-scale producers have experimented with a broad range of nonprocessed cheeses. In the first two decades of the twenty-first century, growth in restaurants, international travel, and access to imported foods has significantly increased interest in cheese. A vibrant group of young cheesemakers is now experimenting in a wide range of styles, resulting in some remarkable successes despite challenging conditions.

Although India is the world's largest dairy producer, cheese has had a marginal place in its everyday cuisine. Even where paneer is widely consumed, it is slotted into the side-dish category. Despite this, there has been a long history of cheesemaking on the subcontinent. Texts from the Vedic period (1750–500 B.C.E.) refer to cheese production with the aid of barks and fruits with coagulating enzymes, as well as *dadhanvat*, a cheese-like substance made with and without eyes. Perhaps because upper-caste Hinduism contains taboos on adding souring agents to milk, the production of paneer and other dairy products was not widespread in North India until the sixteenth century and in Bengal until the Portuguese settlement in the 1700s.

Early Cheesemaking

The most important sites of indigenous cheesemaking are in the country's Himalayan regions, including (from east to west), Arunachal Pradesh, Sikkim, Ladakh, and Kashmir. Nearly all cheeses produced in these areas are manufactured domestically or in small farm-based operations. A stretched fresh buffalo's, cow's, or goat's milk cheese called Kalari (or *maishkrej*) is produced in Kashmir and Jammu. It is flattened into a thin round patty and has the consistency of firm mozzarella. In the Pehalgam valley, semi-nomadic Gujjar shephards make Qudum, a sheep's milk cheese. Dry and crumbly, with the texture of caciocavallo, this melting cheese is not aged to develop a natural rind, but meant to be stored for long periods of time. Churpi (or chhurpie, also called Sherkam and Durkha in Nepal and Durukho in Bhutan) is produced in Sikkim, Arunachal Pradesh, and Ladakh, reflecting cultural influences from Bhutan, Nepal, and Tibet. Soft churpi is made from cow's buttermilk. Hard churpi is made with yak's or chauri's (a hybrid of yak and cow) milk. It is curdled with lime, wrapped in jute, and smoked until it is extremely dry. In some high-altitude areas, one piece might be consumed for hours like chewing gum. In Arunachal Pradesh, churpi is strained in bamboo containers, slowly cooked over a fire, and then hung over a kitchen stove to dry. This cheese is eaten as is, or sprinkled on vegetable dishes for a deeper flavor. Mild, soft churpi is often cooked with wild ferns or in a soup.

Portuguese colonial incursions in the sixteenth and seventeenth centuries influenced the development of cheesemaking on the east and west coasts of India. The most important cheese product influenced by the Portuguese is chenna (or channa), a soft yellowish cow's milk cheese made by hanging curds from muslin cloth. Since the late nineteenth century, chenna has formed the basis of a genre of popular Bengali sweets called *sandesh*, such as *kachagolla*. A similar soft cheese product called *chakka* is produced in Maharashtra and used in sweet dishes such as *shrikhand*. In Varanasi, putty-like *khoya* is made by slowly reducing cow's milk. Mixed with nuts and dried fruits, it becomes *barfi*, another sweet that is widely available throughout India.

India's most well-known indigenous cheese is Bandal (or DakkaBandel), which is now only available in Kolkata's New Market. Bandal is made in Tarakeshwar and Bishnupur, however it is named after a town in West Bengal settled by the Portuguese in the seventeenth century. Small discs of Bandal cheese are either white (when fresh) or brown (when smoked). It has a crumbly texture and an intense, salty flavor. Other Portuguese-influenced cheeses include surti (or surtipaneer), which is made with buffalo's milk and curdled with rennet. Like chenna, the curds are hung in cloth or wicker baskets rather than pressed. See BANDAL and PORTUGAL.

Modern Cheesemaking

A new category of Indian cheesemakers emerged in the late 1970s making nonprocessed European-style cheeses for nationwide distribution. These pioneers included Sunil Bhu's Flanders' Dairy Products and Rohinton Aga, Adi Bhathena, and Eruch Chinoy's ABC Farms, each producing mozzarella and Cheddar styles. Other early producers included Brother Abraham, a priest in Sikkim, who made Kalimpong, a high quality Gouda-style cheese. Meanwhile, attention to cheese in India grew with the help of the importer and passionate tyrophile Jehangir Lawyer, who single-handedly advocated for artisanal and rare cheese varieties, as well as ABC Farms' popular annual cheese festival in Pune, Maharashtra.

The vast majority of India's artisanal cheese producers started operations in the 2000s. Acres Wild, India's first farmstead facility, opened in 2004 in the Nilgiri Hills in Tamil Nadu. Run by Tina Khan and Mansoor Khan, a well-known Bollywood film director, Acres Wild is known for its flavorful aged Cheddar. Milky Way Dairy, in Pune, produces buffalo's milk mozzarella from locally sourced milk. Others producing high-quality cheeses include Cinnabar Farms in Kodaikanal and Father Michael's Vallombrosa, in Bangalore, which makes a variety of Italian-style cheeses. Chris Zandee's Himalayan Dairy, located in Langanbal village, Kashmir, produces Gouda and Cheddar from milk locally sourced from 150 semi-nomadic pastoralists. A number of expatriates have also started important facilities; they include the La Ferme, in Pondicherry, which makes a blue cheese called Auroblochon; the Georgian-run Maia Cheese, in Goa; and the Italian-run Exito Gourmet, in Chandigarh, which produces high-quality mozzarella. Furthermore, a number of these new cheesemakers have experimented with adding Indian flavors to their cheese. The Mumbai-based Cheese Collective makes a fresh Cabécou-style cheese aged with whole paobhaji masala; Mango Hill makes Le Pondicheri, a cheese wrapped in curry leaves; Himalayan Dairy makes a fenugreek-flavored Gouda; and Aditya Raghavan makes a Malabar Jack, rubbed in Malabar spices and coconut oil.

Small-scale cheese producers in India face a variety of difficulties. A major challenge is securing a steady supply of unadulterated, hormone-free milk produced in hygienic conditions. Procuring milk is especially challenging because farmers are unfamiliar with cheesemaking practices. Other challenges include limited access to bacterial cultures, the purported (but rarely enforced) ban on animal rennet, the humid, subtropical climate found in much of the country, and food safety laws that implicitly assume industrial cheesemaking facilities.

A new group of artisanal producers—often urban-based professionals turned full-time cheesemakers—have worked creatively to overcome these difficulties, with impressive results. These include the Cheese Collective, started in 2013 by the public relations professional turned cheesemaker and curator Mansi Jasani. The Cheese Collective produces fresh Chèvre, one of India's first, as well as Cabécou. Eleftheria Cheese, also in Mumbai, makes a cow's milk feta and a fromage blanc. Another important new producer is the Spotted Cow Fromagerie, which is tucked inside Dahisar, a densely populated suburb on the outskirts of Mumbai. Started in 2014 by Prateeksh Mehra, a food photographer, and his brother, Agnay Mehra, a film and television producer, the creamery makes high-quality soft-ripened cheeses from locally sourced milk. They include an earthy Bombrie, a

silken Camembay, and a tart Robiola, all covered in a vibrant bloomy rind developed in a climate-controlled cave built into the basement of their family home. Making cheese inspired by, but not mimicking, existing cheese styles and marketing them as artisanal but explicitly not farmstead, the Mehra brothers exemplify the exciting new genre of "urban cheese" being developed by young producers in India.

Banerji, Chitrita. "How the Bengalis Discovered *Chhana* and its Delightful Offspring." In *Milk: Beyond Dairy,* edited by Harlan Walker, pp. 48–59. Proceedings of the Oxford Symposium on Food and Cookery 1999. Totnes, U.K.: Prospect, 2000.
Kindstedt, Paul. *Cheese and Culture: A History of Cheese and Its Place in Western Civilization.* White River Junction, Vt.: Chelsea Green, 2012.
O'Brien, Charmaine. *The Penguin Food Guide to India.* New Delhi, India: Penguin, 2013.
Raghavan, Aditya. "Meet the Cheesemakers of Kashmir." *National Geographic Traveller India,* 10 February 2015. http://www.natgeotraveller.in/meet-the-cheesemakers-of-kashmir.

Jonathan Shapiro Anjaria and Mansi Jasani

indigenous microorganisms are distinct from those that are inoculated because they occur naturally in the milk and environment rather than being added by the cheesemaker before or during the cheesemaking and ripening process. See STARTER CULTURES and RIPENING CULTURES. They include several broad groups of bacteria and fungi, including lactic acid bacteria, Gram-negative bacteria, Gram-positive "ripening" bacteria, yeasts, and molds. Under the right conditions, these microorganisms may have a significant impact on the flavor, texture, and appearance of a finished cheese.

Although the range of starter and ripening cultures produced by culture houses has become progressively more sophisticated, the availability of these strains to commercial producers has led to concern among artisanal cheesemakers that their cheeses may taste the same as cheeses made on a much larger scale. See CULTURE HOUSES. Likewise, there is evidence that inoculated strains, particularly of ripening bacteria, may not always compete with the native microbiota, and that adding them may not significantly affect the microbial community that develops on the rind. The microbes that are naturally present on an individual farm will differ at the strain level from their laboratory-derived counterparts, even if at a genus or species level the two are indistinguishable. See MICROBIAL COMMUNITIES and STRAINS.

In the mid-twentieth century, as more and more milk was processed off the farm, systems were adopted throughout Europe and America to reward the cheesemakers with the "cleanest" milk, which was measured through the total viable count (TVC), the number of colony-forming microorganisms per gram or milliliter of a sample. Cleanliness was considered to confer a combination of both safety and the ability to store the milk for long periods before it was processed. Milk-borne pathogens and spoilage microorganisms may of course be present in raw milk, and even small numbers of them can create significant problems for a cheesemaker, particularly in soft or slowly acidifying cheeses. However, their incidence is seldom correlated with high total viable counts, and evidence is accruing that it is the *balance* of organisms in a population, rather than the total number, that influences cheese safety. By successfully reducing the total viable count of their milk, farmers may inadvertently be shifting the population dynamics to favor the growth of pathogens and spoilage microorganisms.

Concerned by matters of typicity—those characteristics that make a cheese unique—as well as cheese safety and eating quality, a consortium of French scientists under the name of RMT: Fromages de Terroirs, carries out research on the practical aspects of farming and milk production that affect the diversity and type of naturally occurring milk microbes. Their aim is to define the practices that allow producers to control their milk's indigenous populations holistically, identifying the "reservoirs" of microbes at the farm level, from the animals' bedding to the skin of the teats to the inside of the milking machine. This knowledge has relevance far outside France, as the market for artisanal cheese becomes ever more sophisticated and success for artisan producers depends more on creating unique "cheeses of place."

See also FUNGI; LACTIC ACID BACTERIA; PATHOGENS; and TAXONOMY.

Brennan, Noelle M., et al. "Biodiversity of the Bacterial Flora on the Surface of a Smear Cheese." *Applied and Environmental Microbiology* 68 (2002): 820–830.

Laithier, Cécile, ed. *Microflore du lait cru*. Paris: National Council for Dairy Designations of Origin, 2011.

Bronwen Percival

industrial is an adjective commonly used to characterize the large-scale production of food in a mechanized and, today, often automated fashion. The first recognized "industrial" cheese plants were built in the early and mid-nineteenth century in Europe and North America, respectively; these plants were the first to remove cheesemaking from the farm, where milk had traditionally been transformed into dairy products. With improved transportation, the collection and delivery of raw milk to cheese factories was facilitated, as was the transportation of finished cheeses to consumers.

At the turn of the twentieth century, the availability of cheesemaking vats, tools, cultures, and rennet further supported the development of industrial cheesemaking. The shift from small-scale, local cheese production to larger, mechanized, industrial production continued through the twenty-first century. A major development in the production of industrial cheese was the application of scientific principles to cheesemaking. Defined times, temperatures, and acidity targets were implemented, which greatly improved the quality and consistency of cheeses. Another key technology that successfully increased cheesemaking capacity was the pasteurization of milk. By eliminating the majority of vegetative bacterial cells, dairy processors could transform larger volumes of milk into cheese, with much better control over the fermentation and ultimately the quality of the finished cheese. Furthermore, industrial cheese production largely advanced through the application of process engineering, with computer-operated tools and equipment for pasteurization, cutting, draining, molding curd, and packaging finished wheels.

Although most small cheesemakers process less than three thousand pounds of milk into cheese daily, a modern industrial cheese plant can easily turn over one million pounds of milk into cheese in a single day. Such a feat can only be executed with precise tools to control the transformation of milk into cheese; this process starts with standardizing milk fat and protein and using reliable bacteriophage-resistant starter cultures. The entire process of culturing, renneting, and cutting the curd often takes place in fully enclosed stainless steel equipment. Each step in the cheesemaking process is monitored, with a focus on pH, time, and temperature.

One example of the advancement of processing technology in cheesemaking can be found in Cheddar factories. In industrial processing plants, after the milk has been transformed into curd, the curd is drained and then transported along a series of conveyors, all while being gently stirred and sprayed with water to control acidity development—this is known as the stirred-curd method. In contrast, traditional cheesemakers employ the milled-curd method of Cheddar manufacturing, where curd is allowed to knit together before it is cut into blocks, laboriously stacked, and flipped for hours prior to milling the curd into small pieces. Both the milled-curd and stirred-curd Cheddar methods allow for proper acidity development prior to forming cheese blocks, but the stirred-curd method can be executed continuously, with complete automation. See BLOCK-FORMING TOWERS; CHEDDAR; CHEDDARING; and CURD MILL.

Today industrial cheesemakers operate using technologies such as pasteurization and standardization of fat and protein, with equipment that largely removes human beings from the handling of milk and curd. This allows for massive volumes of cheese to be produced, but such products are not intended to achieve the full range of flavor available through artisanal methods. There are still many cheesemakers, however, who blend traditional and industrial practices to control product quality. The result is rich, flavorful cheeses that can be enjoyed by consumers year-round, everywhere.

See also INDUSTRIALIZATION; PASTEURIZATION; and STANDARDIZATION.

Kindstedt, Paul. "The Puritans, the Factory, and the Demise of Traditional Cheese Making." In *Cheese and Culture: A History of Cheese and Its Place in Western Civilization*, pp. 185–211. White River Junction, Vt.: Chelsea Green, 2012.

Matt Ranieri

industrialization is the historical development that transformed cheesemaking from a largely craft-based or artisanal activity, often located on a dairy farm, to a production process that, for the most part, takes place in large "cheese factories" or creameries. See ARTISANAL. The principal features of modern industrialized cheesemaking that set it apart from traditional approaches include high production volumes; sourcing of milk from multiple dairy herds; pasteurization and re-balancing of milk supplies to minimize variability; use of standardized, commercial starter cultures and rennet; mechanization and automation of manual processes such as stirring

and cutting the curd; detailed "recipes" and fixed procedures; and the precise measurement and control of key variables such as temperature and acidity using specialized instruments. See PASTEURIZATION and STANDARDIZATION. This transformation of long-established cheesemaking practices was accompanied by equally radical innovations in product marketing and distribution. See ADVERTISING AND PROMOTION. Together, these changes have exerted a profound influence on the quality and variety of cheeses available and in overall patterns of cheese consumption.

From Farm to Factory

Today, most of the world's cheese is produced on an industrial scale, yet the journey from farm to factory was far from straightforward. The British pioneered commercialized cheesemaking and marketing in the preindustrial era, but it was left to others to create a full-fledged industrial model of cheesemaking. The story begins in the mid-seventeenth century, when farmers in England's more productive dairying regions began to specialize in making cheese for distribution to wider markets. These changes were driven by a combination of factors, including the drive for agricultural "improvement," which helped to generate milk surpluses, and London's rapidly growing demand for butter and cheese. In an early example of commercialization, cheesemakers in the Cheshire Plain began to pool their resources to make "greate" (i.e., large) Cheshire cheeses that were suitable for transportation by coastal routes to the capital. See CHESHIRE CHEESE (U.K.). Although cheesemaking retained much of its artisanal character, this period saw the introduction of several key prerequisites for industrial production, including the rise of market intermediaries or "cheese factors," government interventions to regulate the trade, and an increasing emphasis on a limited number of regional varieties, such as Cheshire, Cheddar, and Stilton. A similar commercialization process could be observed in parts of the Netherlands at this time, where Dutch cheese began to be exported in larger volumes, much of it destined for London. See CHEESE FACTOR; CHEDDAR; and STILTON.

Science and Cheese

The next major development was the application of scientific principles to cheesemaking. By the mid-nineteenth century, England's commercial cheese-makers were experimenting with new techniques in order to produce more reliable and consistent products. Joseph Harding and his contemporaries had started to monitor key variables such as temperature and acidity in a systematic way. See HARDING, JOSEPH. They also promoted a free flow of information by publishing their findings in specialist journals and promoting dairy education programs. This spirit of self-improvement and scientific inquiry helped to formalize their cheesemaking practices into distinctive "systems," or sets of detailed instructions, that could be accurately reproduced in other locations. These early evangelists had made a decisive first step toward industrial-scale production, but its consequences were to be realized much farther afield. The earliest cheese "factories" have been variously identified in Switzerland (1815) and in the United States (1851), but in reality these were little more than purpose-built, and somewhat larger, versions of their farm-based precursors. The American Civil War (1861–1865) provided the catalyst for rapid factory building and was accompanied by an equally dramatic increase in cheese exports from the Northern states. Key figures in this period included Xerxes Addison Willard of the American Dairymen's Association, who popularized Harding's Cheddar system as part of his effort to promote the factory system. See WILLARD, XERXES ADDISON. Competitiveness was fueled by the country's large, productive dairy herds and by technological innovations such as the "gangpress," which kept the cheese from buckling. By the mid-1870s, it is estimated that more than a quarter of the cheese consumed in England was imported from factories in the United States.

By the 1880s, New Zealand, Australia, and Canada began to challenge the United States dominance of the British market, each of them contributing to a new and thriving international trade in factory-produced cheese. Britain's own transition to the modern industrial-scale creamery was much slower and more faltering. In the end, it occurred largely as a result of direct state intervention over two decades from the early 1930s. Controls were introduced by the government's milk marketing boards and subsequently extended with the onset of World War II, when all domestic cheese production was redirected to creameries. See MILK MARKETING BOARDS and WORLD WAR II. Other countries followed their own distinctive paths to industrial-scale production. For example, Dutch cheesemaking experienced a relatively smooth transition from the late nineteenth century, with varieties such as Edam and Gouda helping to bolster export sales. See EDAM; GOUDA; and NETHERLANDS The French also introduced their first factory systems in this period. However, while retaining their familiar array of territorial varieties, France's leading dairying regions also exploited improved transport links to Paris to initiate new "national" varieties, notably Camembert. See CAMEMBERT DE NORMANDIE and FRANCE.

Industrialization Assessed

Criticism of industrialization tends to revolve around two closely related issues: the quality of cheese produced by industrial creameries and its impact on more traditional modes of production. From the earliest times, people have been complaining about the quality of factory cheese. For example, in the mid-1930s the cheese connoisseur Sir John Squire dismissed imported products as "mere generic soapy, tasteless stuff," while his compatriots mocked the "mousetrap cheese" that formed part of their wartime rations. Despite these periodic outbursts, popular tastes became accustomed to the flavor, texture, and convenience of prepackaged and often branded supermarket products, while factory-produced mozzarella has become one of the world's favorite cheeses. See MOZZARELLA.

The spread of industrial cheese production and marketing is also seen as a primary cause of declines in artisanal cheesemaking and the disappearance of regional varieties. Even in France, efforts to protect these traditional practices eventually came under pressure from agricultural modernization policies. Critics have also pointed out that the high-profile appellation d'origine contrôlée (AOC) system was not designed to resist the underlying logic of industrial-scale cheesemaking, particularly when it became coupled with a highly concentrated food retail sector. See APPELLATION D'ORIGINE CONTRÔLÉE. There is still a substantial philosophical and practical gulf between the world of the large-scale, technologically advanced industrial creamery and that of the small artisanal cheesemaker. However, the dividing lines are permeable and can sometimes blur at the margins. For example, international dairy companies such as Arla and Kraft Foods have responded to market pressures by seeking to introduce distinctive and novel organoleptic qualities into their premium cheeses. See ARLA and KRAFT FOODS. Their efforts have been rewarded in international cheese competitions, where industrial and artisanal products often share in the prizes. At the same time, some artisanal producers are making selective use of innovations in technology and practice such as Hazard Analysis and Critical Control Point (HACCP), a preventive quality control method, and microbiological analysis, both of which were first introduced by industrial creameries. See HAZARD ANALYSIS AND CRITICAL CONTROL POINT.

See also INDUSTRIAL and INDUSTRIEL.

Blundel, Richard, and Angela Tregear. "From Artisans to 'Factories': The Interpenetration of Craft and Industry in English Cheese-Making, 1650–1950." *Enterprise & Society* 7 (2006): 705–739.

Boisard, Pierre. *Camembert: A National Myth*. Translated by Richard Miller. Berkeley: University of California Press, 2003. English translation of *Le Camembert: Mythe Nationale*, Paris, 1992.

McMurry, Sally A. *Transforming Rural Life: Rural Dairying Families and Agricultural Change, 1820–1885*. Baltimore Md.: Johns Hopkins University Press, 1995.

Taylor, David. "Growth and Structural Change in the English Dairy Industry, c 1860–1930." *Agricultural History Review* 35 (1987): 47–64.

Richard K. Blundel

industriel is a French term used to signify large-scale creamery or factory production, in contrast to *artisanal* or *fermier* (on-farm) production. See ARTISANAL and FERMIER. Milk is sourced and pooled from many farms (from hundreds to thousands) and collected and transformed into cheese in factories. Milk is standardized (to ensure consistent fat and protein contents) and pasteurized (to remove ambient microorganisms) before being made into cheese by a mechanized process in which every stage is systematically controlled. While many of the higher-quality industriel cheeses may appear more similar to the fermier version than a block Cheddar does to a cloth-bound farmhouse wheel, the industriel versions' reliance on standardized input means that they do not share the unique qualities of the fermier. The cheeses produced remain consistent and standardized all year round.

Industriel production makes up the majority of cheese production in France as well as most other cheese-producing countries. The best-known French industriel producers of cheese is Lactalis, the world's leading producer by volume of dairy products, collecting 16 billion quarts (15 billion liters) of milk a year, and generating €15.7 billion in revenue. Lactalis manufactures under well-known brands such as President, Roquefort Société, and McCelland Seriously Strong Cheddar. See LACTALIS. Other industriel producers include Bongrain, which makes well-known brands such as St Agur, Chaumes, and Camembert Le Rustique, and Bel, which produces Baby Bel, Laughing Cow, and Boursin. See BEL GROUP and SAVENCIA FROMAGE & DAIRY.

As bemoaned by Patrick Rance in his 1989 book on French cheese, fermier production has given way to industriel, even in well-known appellation d'origine contrôlée (AOC) cheese regions. At the time of this writing, of only seven makers of Roquefort, six were listed as industriel. Camembert de Normandie had eight industriel and only one fermier producer, and Brie de Meaux had five industriel and only one fermier producer.

See also INDUSTRIAL; INDUSTRIALIZATION; and STANDARDIZATION.

Froc, J. *Balade au pays des fromages: Les traditions fromagères en France*. Versailles, France: Quae, 2007.

Institut National de l'Origine et de la Qualité. French appellation product specification for Brie de Meaux, Camembert, and Roquefort cheeses. http://www.inao.gouv.fr/public/produits.

"Les transformateurs: La diversité fait la force." Centre National Interprofessionnel de l'Economie Laitière. http://www.maison-du-lait.com/fr/filiere-laitiere/les-transformateurs-diversite-fait-force.

Rance, Patrick. *The French Cheese Book*. London: Macmillan, 1989.

Andy Swinscoe

inoculum refers to a biological agent such as a bacterium, yeast, mold, or virus that is deliberately introduced into a person or animal (e.g., vaccination) or a food to obtain a beneficial effect. In the production of fermented foods including sausage, pickles, sauerkraut, wine, beer, and many dairy products, an inoculum or "starter culture" must also be introduced to develop the desired aroma, taste, and texture and enhance end-product safety and shelf life. In cheese-making, the use of different types of inoculums in various combinations has led to the wide range of cheeses available today. Up until the 1890s, cheesemakers typically obtained their inoculum from a previously successful fermentation in a process known as "back slopping." However, the introduction of defined starter cultures by Christian Hansen Laboratories in 1893 revolutionized the fermentation process and removed much of the guesswork so that cheeses of consistent quality can now be produced on a regular basis. See HANSEN, CHRISTIAN D.A. Lactic acid bacteria that convert lactose to lactic acid and various flavor compounds during fermentation and subsequent aging are an essential component of any inoculum for cheese manufacture. Depending on the type of cheese to be produced, other bacteria such as propionibacteria may also be added for proper flavor and "eye" development in Swiss-like cheeses. Alternatively, other bacteria, such as *Brevibacterium linens*, may be smeared directly on the cheese surface to obtain the pungent aroma associated with Limburger cheese. In the production of other cheeses such as blue and Camembert, special mold cultures must also be added to the milk at the start of cheesemaking to achieve the desired end result.

See also *BREVIBACTERIUM LINENS*; DAIRY PROPION-IBACTERIA; LACTIC ACID BACTERIA; and STARTER CULTURES.

Hassan, A. N., and J. F. Frank. "Starter Cultures and Their Use." In: *Applied Dairy Microbiology*. 2d ed., edited by Elmer H. Marth and James L. Steele, pp. 151–206. New York: Marcel Dekker, 2001.

Elliot Ryser

inspection systems

See HYGIENE.

Institut National de la Recherche Agronomique (INRA)

is a research organization under the supervision of the French Ministry of Agriculture and the Ministry of Education and Research. In 2013 INRA had eighteen research centers across France and 8,500 researchers, technicians, and support staff conducting fundamental and applied research. INRA research covers a wide range of disciplines, from biological research and experimentation on plants, animals, and microbes, to economic study of the farm-scale up to the global food supply, to agronomic work to improve agricultural and forestry management, quality, and productivity, to sociological analysis of farmers, rural society, and behaviors all along the food chain.

INRA was founded in 1946 to guide an agricultural renaissance after World War II by applying scientific and technological research to the improvement of agricultural genetics, techniques, and productivity. It is the culmination of agricultural research development since the mid-nineteenth century, begun with a scattering of regional research stations that were variously affiliated with the Ministry of Agriculture from its creation in 1881.

By the 1960s France had regained food self-sufficiency, and INRA-guided policies were reshaping France into specialized production zones—for example, wheat and grains were top priority on plains, suitable to heavy equipment use, and milk production became concentrated in the northwest and mountain areas too steep for mechanized cultivation but accessible to ruminants. Over the years INRA's interests have expanded to include food processing, the environment, rural development, food safety, product quality, and global food security, in some cases going back on earlier recommendations (concerning agricultural source pollution or the imperative to replace small farms with "more efficient" large ones, for example).

INRA's overall effects hide diverse and even contradictory positions among its scientists reflecting the debates of our times over just what is best for the food supply, its producers, its consumers, and the economy—issues like genetically modified organisms, the tension between high productivity and "quality," or even the balance between fundamental and applied research. For example, some INRA sociologists work to get farmers to appropriate the notion of terroir and appellation d'origine contrôlée (AOC) initiatives, while others analyze the social and political construction of the AOC system and its effects with a critical eye.

As one might expect, INRA's influence on French cheeses is wide ranging. Going the farthest back, INRA researchers led the postwar charge for agricultural "modernization" and productivity that pushed farmers to convert from local animal breeds to those making more milk (like Holsteins and related breeds) and to change feed systems from extensive grazing to supposedly more efficient corn silage. The composition of the cheesemaking milk supply gradually changed, altering the process and the resulting cheeses in the most affected regions and obliging cheesemakers to adapt. But at the same time a minority of INRA researchers was studying what makes regional breeds distinctive, comparing their milk's characteristics to that of other breeds and arguing the value of minority breeds for cheese.

More recently a growing number of INRA researchers concentrated in specialized centers in Poligny, Aurillac, Grignon, Clermont-Ferrand, and Rennes have been studying cheese technology and microbiology. Some examine the effects of agricultural, procedural, and technical variations on cheese outcomes, from their influence on affinage through consequences on aromas and flavors. Others focus on microbiology to improve and refine the variety of available cultures, understand the microbial ecosystems of cheeses, and master the consequences of raw versus heated or microfiltered milk in technical, gustatory, and food safety terms. For example, the Rennes center developed ultrafiltration, patented in 1969. The procedure uses a series of very fine filters to remove small molecules from milk, concentrating it and preserving soluble proteins and minerals that are lost in traditional methods in order to facilitate industrial cheesemaking and produce a cheese richer in calcium and other nutrients.

See also CONSORZIO RICERCA FILIERA LATTIERO-CASEARIA.

Cranney, Jean. INRA: 50 ans d'un organisme de recherché. Paris: INRA, 1996.
INRA History Committee. http://www.inra.fr/comitedhistoire.

Juliette Rogers

Iran is a country in western Asia, the second-largest nation in the Middle East and the eighteenth-largest in the world, comprising a land area of 636,372 square miles (1,648,195 square kilometers). It is bordered to the west by Turkey and Iraq; to the east by Pakistan and Afghanistan; to the northwest by Azerbaijan and Armenia, with Kazakhstan and Russia across the Caspian Sea; to the northeast by Turkmenistan; and to the south by the Persian Gulf and the Gulf of Oman. Iran has a well-established and developed commercial cheese and dairy industry. According to published data, the total raw milk production of Iran reached 7,952 thousand tons in 2012, an increase of 3.5 percent from 2011. More than 84 percent of the total milk production belongs to cow's milk, 7.1 percent to sheep's milk, 5.2 percent to goat's milk, and 3.2 percent to buffalo's milk. The livestock population in the country in 2012 consisted of 46.2 million sheep and lambs, 21 million goats and kids, 7.8 million cows and calves, 199,000 buffaloes, and 158,000 camels.

The history of the modern dairy industry in Iran dates to 1940, during World War II, when the first breed of dairy cattle was purchased from the French and delivered to the Heydar Abad Institute. The first dairy company, Alfa, was built in late 1948 in Javadiyeh, Tehran. The company started with five tons of raw milk per day and introduced new equipment in Iran such as the separator, pasteurizer, bottle filler, and semi-automatic bottle-washing machine. The Miky Mast and Larak companies, in those years, started the production and distribution of packed milk and yogurt. Between 1957 and 1960 in Tehran, two new companies opened: Astara and the Pak Pasteurized Dairy Company. In subsequent decades, the development of the dairy industry was guided by a government strategic development plan that was renewed every five years, with the objective of building the industry within the major cities and regions of Iran. During the second development plan, which was in effect until 1962, units in the cities of Tabriz, Rasht, and Abadan were established. In the third plan, from 1963 to 1965, six other units in the cities of Isfahan, Shiraz, Mashhad, Sari, Kermanshah, and Ahvaz were built. In the fourth plan, which lasted from 1969 to 1973, the Iran Milk Industry Company was established, composed of the Tabriz, Tehran, and Shiraz pasteurized milk factories. Also, a private milk factory was founded in Urmia in 1974 and joined the company in 2000.

During the fifth development plan, from 1973 to 1978, milk production units were established in the Arak Agro Industrial and Madi "Mimas" dairy companies through the private sector and in the Shir Iran Dairy Company. The Moghan Agro-industrial and Animal Husbandry Company, which was established in Pars Abad, Ardebil province, in 1975, is now the largest animal husbandry complex in Iran. In early 1979, milk plants were launched in regions of Azerbaijan, Khorasan, Isfahan, and Fars. From 1982 onward, pasteurized and sterilized milk plants of the regions of Kerman, Gilan, Gorgan, Zanjan, Hamedan, Lorestan, and Khozestan were launched. As of 2012 there were 538 dairy industries with a production capacity of 506 million tons in Iran.

The emerging dairy industry, along with the complementary industries of the agricultural sector, play an important role in the sustainable development of the country. The increased investment by the government in the subsidies provided for household milk purchases, in cheese coupon distribution, and in milk supplied to schools led to the growth of the culture of dairy product consumption. Some successful dairy and cheese brands in Iran are Pak, Pegah, Kaleh, Kalber, Damdaran, Mihan, Choopan, Hamvatan, Mimas, and others. The Pegah Dairy Company, the Kalleh Dairy Company, and the Sahar Dairy Industrials Company have remained strong leaders in cheese production, accounting for respective market shares of 28 percent, 26 percent, and 14 percent in 2013.

Along with the development of commercial cheese industries in Iran, artisanal cheese production has also grown in the country. Traditional cheesemaking has a long history in Iran, with a variety of traditional cheeses produced in different regions of the country especially in Azerbaijan, Ardabil, Kordestan, Gilan, Semnan, and Khorasan provinces. However, most of them have remained unknown outside of their areas of production.

Generally two types of traditional cheeses are produced: fresh and ripened. Fresh cheeses can be categorized in three groups, based on the raw material used: raw milk, whey, or yogurt. Ripened cheeses can be divided into four different groups based on their maturation style: brined cheeses, pot cheeses, sheep-skin cheeses, and moldy cheeses.

The most famous traditional cheese of Iran is Lighvan Paniri, a white brined cheese produced in Lighvan, a verdant village located southeast of Tabriz, Iran. Many other varieties of white brined cheeses that are similar to Lighvan Paniri are produced in different regions of Iran and known as Lighvan-like cheeses. See LIGHVAN PANIRI. Kat Paniri is the general name for the other types of brined cheeses, which are known by the name of their rural producing areas, such as Ahar Paniri, Heris Paniri, and Sarab Paniri.

Other types of cheeses are distinguished for the container in which the cheeses are ripened: the use of the earthenware container called Kupa characterizes the Kupa Paniri or Panire Koozeh, Jajikhli Panir, and Zirali Panir. See KUPA PANIRI; JAJIKHLI PANIR; ZIRALY PANIR; and POT CHEESES. Containers prepared from sheep's or goat's skin bags are used for ripening Motal Paniri, Panire Khiki, Panire Assalem, and Tavalesh. See MOTAL PANIRI and SHEEP- AND GOAT-SKIN CHEESES. The last group of Iranian ripened cheeses are the moldy cheeses, represented by the Panire Ghermeze Salmas, which is produced in an artisanal cheese plant located in Salmas city, in the West Azerbaijan province of Iran.

Some traditional cheeses are fresh or have a short maturation period. These include Ghircha and Peche, which are produced from raw milk, Lor, produced from whey, and Shor, produced from yogurt after making Ayran. See LOR.

Iranian culinary style is unique to Iran, but has historically both influenced and been influenced by Iran's neighboring countries and civilizations at various stages throughout its history. There have been reciprocal influences specifically to and from Anatolian cuisine, Caucasian cuisine, and Mesopotamian cuisine, owing to geographical proximity and ethnic relations. Cheese has been a staple of Iranian cuisine, especially for breakfast, for many years. Cheese along with bread and sugary tea is considered the most popular breakfast in Iran. Sometimes vegetables, fruits, and nuts are consumed alongside cheese and bread. In the Azerbaijan region of Iran, a traditional food prepared from cheese called Doymaj (Döyməc) and served for breakfast. It is prepared by mixing ground cheese with slices of dry bread such as Usku Chorayi (Üskü Çörəyi) and a certain amount of milk and butter.

Per capita consumption of milk, which was about 265 pounds (120 kilograms) in 2008, rose to 319 pounds (145 kilograms) by the year 2012. Per capita consumption of cheese was recorded as 7.7 pounds (3.5 kilograms) for the year 2011. However, this seems to be much less than the actual amount, at least for the Azerbaijan provinces of Iran. The annual per capita cheese consumption in these regions is higher than 33–44 pounds (15–20 kilograms) according to raw data. See also TRADITIONAL EQUIPMENT.

"Take a Look at Dairy Industry in Iran." Donya-e-Eqtesad. http://www.donya-e-eqtesad.com/news/515587.

Euromonitor International. *Cheese in Iran.* http://www.euromonitor.com/cheese-in-iran/report.

Food and Agriculture Organization of the United Nations. *FAO Statistical Yearbook 2013: World Food and Agriculture.* Rome: FAO, 2013. http://www.fao.org/docrep/018/i3107e/i3107e00.htm.

Helgi Library. "Cheese Consumption per Capita." http://www.helgilibrary.com/indicators/index/cheese-consumption-per-capita.

Profile of Moghan Agro-industrial & Animal Husbandry Company. http://www.investiniran.ir/OIETA_content/media/image/2014/06/4069_orig.pdf.

Yahya Shafiei Bavil Oliaei

Ireland experiences a markedly oceanic climate with frequent rain and a relatively narrow range of annual temperature change. With autumn and winter months characterized by wind-driven Atlantic storms, and spring and summer by sunshine and showers, it is unsurprising that Irish farming over most of the past two thousand years has made extensive use of conditions favoring the abundant growth of grass. Cattle have consequently held an important place in Irish culture, with dairy herds, not beef animals, seen as a measure of wealth and social standing as well as providing the currency with which to pay rents, tributes, and gifts.

In Gaelic Ireland, cattle grazed the upland pastures between the important festivals of Beltane (May 1) and Samhain (November 1), delivering an abundant supply of milk that was turned into curds, cheese, salted butter, and sour milk drinks. A visitor in 1690 described the Irish as "generally being the greatest lovers of milk I ever saw which they eat and drink about twenty several sorts of ways and what is strangest love it best when sourest" (Sexton, 1998, p. 96). *Bainne clabhair*, a renneted milk left for two days to stand, was especially esteemed.

Despite a popular misconception abroad that cheesemaking was limited in Ireland, monastic and secular manuscripts reveal that both soft and hard cheeses were made. Legend even credits Irish monks with bringing the secrets of cheesemaking to central Europe in the sixth century. In an old Irish tale, Queen Maeve of Connaught is killed by a piece of *tanag* (a skim-milk cheese) that her nephew fired at her from a slingshot. As Ó Sé remarks, while one might not give credence to the tale, the implication is that *tanag* was a remarkably hard cheese. Another cheese, *mulchán*, was reputedly exported in large quantities but was so hard that a hatchet was required to cut it. And in a ninth-century tale, a ferocious warrior was said to possess buttocks that were each the size of a *maethal*, a large, round, soft cheese.

By the seventeenth century, decades of political and land upheavals resulting from oppressive English laws had effectively killed the Gaelic farm economy and, with it, the native cheesemaking tradition. Butter now became the means by which small farmers paid their rent as well as the object of a thriving international trade. By the early nineteenth century, Cork's Butter Exchange had become the largest trading floor of its kind in the world. Meanwhile, the potato became the main staple of the Irish diet, given that its yield enabled small parcels of land to support large numbers of people. Population grew during the eighteenth and early nineteenth centuries until blight struck the potato crop in 1845 resulting in the Great Famine, which saw a million people dead and millions more emigrating with barely their lives.

It was not until the early twentieth century that Irish cheesemaking reappeared. The foundation of the cooperative movement in the 1890s witnessed most success in the creation of local dairy societies, and several creameries in Munster began industrial-scale production of cheese that had absolutely no connection with earlier traditions. With British tariffs on Irish exports (1921–1945) and with a limited domestic market (cheese was largely unavailable in rural Ireland), production grew only slowly and was fairly undistinguished—until the late 1970s and the emergence of the farmhouse cheesemakers.

This group of pioneers, many of whom were immigrants, had little prior knowledge or experience of cheesemaking and learned through experimentation and by attending the occasional course in microbiology. Having bought small farms in remote rural locations, especially in the southwest of Ireland, these individuals began making cheese on their kitchen stoves as a way of using up surplus milk, and in turn created a livelihood for themselves. Gradually their numbers swelled, and an association of Irish farmhouse cheesemakers, Cáis, was created in 1983 to act as a forum and lobbying body. Although the cheeses were a diverse range reflecting the personalities and origins of their producers, the artisanal nature of the process, which involved a handmade element with an upper limit on the volume produced and a single or limited number of milk sources used, has been an important defining characteristic of the sector, as has the original criteria of using raw milk.

It is not the case, however, that Irish farmhouse cheese has always been given the same respect in regulatory circles that it has acquired among cheesemongers and their customers. The introduction into Irish law of European Directive 92/46/EEC in 1997 significantly increased the pressure for mandatory pasteurization and brought more rigorous monitoring and compliance standards that forced many cheesemakers out of business. One particular problem facing raw-milk cheesemakers is bovine tuberculosis, which remains a significant animal health problem. Without pasteurization as a line of defense, raw-milk cheesemakers must rely on their skills and integrity to ensure high levels of safety as well as quality. This issue formed the basis of a legal wrangle between 2002 and 2004, when a batch of thermophilic cheese (Desmond) was ordered by the authorities to be destroyed. Although a number of the cows that supplied milk for the cheese had tested positive for tuberculosis, it was argued that the cheesemaking process involving higher cooking temperatures (126°F [52°C]) and long maturation (over one year) rendered the cheese safe for human consumption. Both the District and the Circuit Court ruled in favor of the cheesemaker, although the cost of waging the appeals ultimately put the company out of business and Desmond is no longer made. It was in this context that the Irish Raw Cow's Milk Cheese Presidium was created to help promote and protect the distinctive attributes of such cheeses as Durrus, Dilliskus, and Drumlin. There are, however, some extremely fine pasteurized milk cheeses, among them Gubbeen, Milleens, and Cashel Blue, that together have reestablished Ireland's reputation as the home of exceptionally fine farmhouse cheese.

See also CASHEL BLUE and COUNTY CORK.

Cáis: Association of Irish Farmhouse Cheesemakers. http://www.caisireland.wordpress.com.
Ó Sé, Micheál. "Old Irish Cheeses and Other Milk Products." *Journal of the Cork Historical and Archaeological Society* 53 (1948): 82–87.
Sage, Colin. "'Bending Science to Match Their Convictions': Hygienist Conceptions of Food Safety as a Challenge to Alternative Food Enterprises in Ireland." In *Alternative Food Geographies: Representation and Practice*, edited by D. Maye, L. Holloway, and M. Kneafsey, pp. 203–221. Oxford: Elsevier, 2007.
Sexton, Regina. *A Little History of Irish Food*. London: Kyle Cathie, 1998.

Colin Sage

Isigny Ste-Mère is a dairy cooperative based in Isigny-sur-Mer in Normandy, France. The cooperative was founded in 1932 by forty-two dairy farmers to process and market their milk, and grew to more than eight hundred members before it merged with the cooperative Sainte-Mère-Église in 1979. By 2015 they had approximately seven hundred dairy farmer-members, six hundred employees, and an annual revenue of 288 million euros.

In addition to fresh, everyday, and food-industry products like baby formula (their specialty), canned whipping cream, powdered milk and derivatives, and generic cheeses, they make Camembert de Normandie and Pont-L'Évêque AOC, Red Label Mimolette, and AOC Isigny crème fraîche and butter. See CAMEMBERT DE NORMANDIE; PONT-L'ÉVÊQUE; MIMOLETTE; APPELLATION D'ORIGINE CONTRÔLÉE; and LABEL ROUGE. The cooperative has left its mark on the manufacture of Camembert de Normandie with its invention of the controversial "ladling robot," which allows the curd to be cut in a way comparable to the traditional handheld ladle; it was implemented by Isigny in 1985 and later adopted by some other large-scale manufacturers. In 2008 Isigny Ste-Mère joined with some Lactalis-owned brands and stopped making their Camembert according to appellation d'origine contrôlée (AOC) standards in an effort to force other appellation stakeholders to accept heat-treated milks for making AOC Camembert de Normandie. See LACTALIS. When their gambit failed, Isigny Ste-Mère resumed raw-milk Camembert production in order to resume the AOC label.

See also FRANCE and NORMANDY.

Torres, Felix, and Jérome Aumont. *Isigny: l'expression d'un terroir*. Paris: Éditions Hirlé, 2009.

Juliette Rogers

Istrian cheese is a traditional, full-fat, hard sheep cheese that has been produced for several hundred years along the Croatian peninsula of Istria. The Istrian peninsula is characterized by hilly relief rich with pasture and plenty of aromatic sub-Mediterranean herbs. Many of the local farmers still produce Istrian cheese exclusively from raw ewe's milk by milking the autochthonous Istrian Pramenka sheep breed. According to official data, only 2,314 head of Pramenka sheep still exist in Istria. Istrian sheep produce 53 gallons (200 liters) of milk per lactation, which lasts, on average, for two hundred days. Pramenka have adapted to the local ecological conditions and particularly to the flora available for grazing, therefore producing milk of exceptional quality.

Istrian cheese is characterized by a cylindrical shape, 7 to 8 inches (18 to 20 centimeters) in diameter and 2.8 to 3.5 inches (7 to 9 centimeters) in height. Only rennet is added to the milk, without using starters. Therefore, the acidification that occurs, as well as the specific flavor of the cheese, is caused by natural, non-starter lactic acid bacteria that originates in raw ewe's milk and in the wooden tools traditionally used in Istrian cheese production.

To make Istrian cheese, sheep's milk is heated to a temperature of 88 to 91°F (31–33°C) and coagulated for 30 to 60 minutes. The coagulum is cut into grains, usually the size of a pea, and heated for 20 to 30 minutes at a temperature of about 108°F (42°C), while constantly being mixed. Curd grains are allowed to settle for 10 minutes on the concave bottom of the vat. The cheese body is then cut to the size of the molds. The cheese is pressed for 4 to 5 hours until it reaches a pH of 5.2 to 5.3. The cheese is salted by rubbing the salt on the surface or by brining, after which it is ripened for at least 60 days at a temperature of 61°F (16°C) and a relative humidity of 70 to 85 percent.

See also CROATIA.

Magdić, V., et al. "A Survey on Hygienic and Physicochemical Properties of Istrian Cheese." *Mljekarstvo* 63 (2013): 55–63.

Samir Kalit

Italy is home to many of the world's great cheeses, and cheesemaking in the region may date back to as early as 2800 B.C.E. This is the date attributed to one of the most ancient dairy finds, discovered in Piadina, in the Po Valley: an earthenware strainer most likely used for draining curd.

In the ancient Greek period, Sicily was famous for its cheese, which was so common a specialty that it was exported together with wheat, wine, and honey from the Iblean Mountains. The art of cheesemaking, especially with the use of vegetable rennet, was improved by the Etruscans and handed down to the Romans. The Romans elaborated the cheesemaking of the Greeks by introducing the use of cow's milk. During the Imperial Age, cheese was served at banquets with refined culinary preparation. Archestratus of Gela (fl. fourth century B.C.E.) declared "Caci di Sicilia" to be "the best and more flavorful than caseus of Lesbo and Creta." See ARCHESTRATUS OF GELA and ANCIENT CIVILIZATIONS.

Many Roman writers, including Cato the Elder (234–149 B.C.E.), Marcus Terentius Varro (ca. 116–27 B.C.E.), and Pliny the Elder, described the process of cheesemaking as well as the quality and the culinary uses of cheese. Cheesemaking was well known among the Roman population, which spread knowledge of the process throughout the duration of the Empire period. The most complete ancient description of cheesemaking is given by Lucius Junius Moderatus Columella, a Roman soldier and author from Gades (modern Cadiz), in his twelve-book treatise on agriculture, *De re rustica* (ca. 65 C.E.). It includes many observations and practices recognizable to modern cheesemakers. That work, combined with an earlier writing of Columella's on trees, were translated into English in 1745 under the title *Of Husbandry*. See CATO, MARCUS PORCIUS; VARRO, MARCUS TERENTIUS; PLINY THE ELDER; and COLUMELLA, LUCIUS JUNIUS MODERATUS.

In the Middle Ages, the most important sites for the development of cheese technology and the evolution of cheese varieties were monasteries and feudal estates, which became oases of religious devotion, culture, and enlightenment. The Age of Enlightenment, arising from the Renaissance, was a time of tremendous creativity and entrepreneurial spirit. Cheesemakers created new and exciting varieties to augment both the traditional cheeses passed down from Roman times and the monastic ones born in the Middle Ages.

A large variety of cheeses found in Italy today have been produced for centuries, including Ragusano and the Sicilian Pecorino. See RAGUSANO and PECORINO SICILIANO. After the unity of Italy in 1861, the Italian parliament initiated a number of studies to understand the living conditions of farmers and their agricultural problems. Italy boasts an extraordinary agricultural and food heritage, including more than four hundred distinct cheeses. A strong connection to regional territory and the continuation of agrarian

A fifteenth-century Italian fresco showing peasant farmers milking cows and making cheese in the mountain pastures. Cheesemaking in the region may date back to as early as 2800 B.C.E. CASTELLO DEL BUONCONSILIO, TORRE DELL'AQUILA, ITALY / BRIDGEMAN IMAGES

traditions that are handed down from parent to child see Italy competing with France as a place with a well-rooted dairy culture. The Italian dairy sector is the country's largest food sector and alone represents more than 12 percent of the total turnover of the national food system. Production value exceeds 14.5 billion euros annually. Italy produces about 1.2 billion tons of cheese, of which, 982,000 tons are made from cow's milk, 203,000 tons are made from other types of milk, and 40,000 tons are melted (processed) cheeses.

Italy's livestock comprise 1.85 billion dairy cows and 5 million sheep and goats. The country produces about 11 million tons of cow's milk and a combined total of about 650,000 tons of sheep's and goat's milk each year. This production is insufficient to cover the needs of the nation, and so the country imports some 40–45 percent of the milk it uses, albeit while allocating a portion for the export of products with high added value. Exports from 1980 to 2008

increased exponentially in volume and in value, a trend that continues to grow, reaching volumes that in 2014 exceeded the 290,000 tons corresponding to the 23 percent of total production of cheeses (1.2 billion tons).

The Italian dairy sector is diversified into industrial and traditional products that are directed to two different markets. The industrial sector is linked to international markets and includes undifferentiated commodity products (such as milk, butter, milk spots exchanged between operators, liquid whey, cheeses, and dairy products with a strong technological innovation of industrial types). The traditional sector concerns products of quality such as PDO (protected designation of origin) and IGP (protected geographical indication) cheeses and historical territorial products. These traditional products absorb 70 percent of the national milk production and, compared to the industrial sector, are more sheltered from international economic trends, thus ensuring greater

A scene from the home of Antonio and Maria Roccia, at the edge of the Apennine Mountains in southern Italy. The couple crafts caciocavallo from the milk of their two cows. © VINCENZO SPIONE

stability. As the largest European country producing PDO cheeses (as of 2015 there are forty-nine), Italy assumes a prominent position within the worldwide dairy sector.

At 497,000 tons, Italy's PDO cheeses represent 41 percent of the country's total production. Italian PDO cheeses come from cow's milk (86.6 percent, or 430,000 tons), buffalo's milk (7.4 percent, or 37,000 tons of mozzarella), and sheep's milk (6 percent, or 30,000 tons). The diversity of Italian dairy products is strongly related to the territorial topography, with flat areas accounting for 23.2 percent (where industrial agriculture has developed), hill areas, 41.6 percent, and mountain areas, 35.2 percent. The less favored areas for agriculture contain extensive farming systems that have become the sources of traditional and quality dairy products, strongly characterized by territorial biodiversity, including indigenous breeds and native feeding pastures.

As of 2014, Grana Padano (184,964 tons) and Parmigiano Reggiano (132,684, tons) represented 63.9 percent (317,648 tons) of the total production of PDO Italian cheeses. Other cheeses with a relevant production are Gorgonzola (53.3 tons), Mozzarella di Bufala (38 tons), Pecorino Romano (24 tons), Asiago (21.5 tons), Taleggio (9 tons), Montasio (6.9 tons), Provolone Valpadana (5.3 tons), and Fontina (3.5 tons). These 10 PDO cheeses together account for 94.6 percent of the total production of PDO cheeses in the country. See GRANA PADANO; PARMIGIANO REGGIANO; GORGONZOLA; MOZZARELLA DI BUFALA CAMPANA; PECORINO ROMANO; ASIAGO; TALEGGIO; MONTASIO; PROVOLONE VALPADANA; and FONTINA VAL D'AOSTA.

Consequently, the other 39 PDO cheeses as a whole account for only 5.4 percent (26,665 tons) of national PDO output, with an average annual production of about 680 tons per cheese, although there are cheeses with production of less than 15 tons, such as the Aosta Valley Fromadzo and Murazzano. See VALLE D'AOSTA FROMADZO and MURAZZANO. Low-production PDO cheeses are destined for local markets or are sold directly from the farm, with the exception of some requests from gourmet and specialty stores, including international ones.

The average dairy consumption per person in Italy from 2010 to 2014 included approximately 51 pounds (23 kilograms) of cheese, 112 pounds (51 kilograms) of milk, 5 pounds (2.3 kilograms) of butter, and 18.5 pounds (8.4 kilograms) of fermented milk (e.g., yogurt), with the country supplying, on average, 68 percent of the raw materials for its dairy production. Italy is eighth in the world for per capita cheese consumption; moreover, its cheese brands and dairy products are highly sought after the world over. Consequently, there is some concern of a growing risk of counterfeit Italian brands and products, which could put at risk the image and sustainability of this important economic sector.

See also SICILY.

D'Alessio, Massimiliano. "Filiera lattiero-casearia: caratteri strutturali e andamenti congiunturali." *Economia della produzione* 17 (2014): 15–24.

European Union. Council Regulation (EEC) No. 2081/92 on the Protection of Geographical Indications and Designations of Origin for Agricultural Products and Foodstuffs. 14 July 1992. http://www.wipo.int/wipolex/en/details.jsp?id=1412.

European Union. Council Regulation No. 2082/92 on Certificates of Specific Character for Agricultural Products and Foodstuffs. 24 July 1992. http://publications.europa.eu/en/publication-detail/-/publication/a109261e-f10f-4710-a609-5d4a0a282252/language-en.

Fox, P. F., and P. L. H. McSweeney. "Cheese: An Overview." In *Cheese: Chemistry, Physics, and Microbiology*, Vol. 1: *General Aspects*, 3d ed., edited by Patrick F. Fox et al. Vol. 1: *General Aspects*, 3d ed., pp. 1–18. London: Elsevier, 2004.

Ministero delle Politiche Agricole. http//:www.politicheagricole.it.

"Production Volumes of the Italian PDO Cheeses." CLAL.it. http://www.clal.it/en/?section=formaggi_dop.

Salvadori del Prato, Ottavio. *Trattato di tecnologia casearia*. Bologna, Italy: Agricole, 1998.

Salvadori del Prato, Ottavio "Pecorini, formaggi di tradizione plurisecolare." *Supplemento Informatore Zootecnico*, 16 June 2004.

Ivana Piccitto

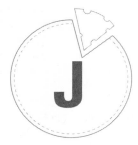

J

Jack or Monterey Jack is a mild to full flavored cheese with a cream-colored paste that becomes more golden with age. The name is associated with its early production in Monterey County, California. According to the Monterey County Historical Society, the recipe for Monterey Jack was brought to California by Franciscans monks (who called it queso del pais) from Spain via Mexico in the 1700s. Different characters have been mentioned in history records as the first to commercialize Monterey Jack during the 1850s. However it is David Jacks, an immigrant from Scotland with considerable (but maybe unethical) business skills who is mainly known as the creator of Jack's cheese. Jacks had great marketing for his "Jack's Cheese" and he expanded his business in the 1880s to include up to fourteen dairies which sold Jack's Cheese all over northern California. Today production of Monterey Jack is not limited to California as Wisconsin shares a large part of the market. US production of Monterey Jack is reported together with Colby cheese, so it is hard to obtain statistics on its individual production. However it is safe to say that Jack cheese represents more than 10 percent of all cheese produced in California and more than 5 percent of all cheese produced in Wisconsin. See CALIFORNIA and WISCONSIN.

The make-procedure for Jack is similar to Colby in that: (1) the curds are washed, meaning that water is added to the drained or partially drained curd; (2) the curd is stirred after draining until the pH reaches about 5.3; and (3) the curd is dry-salted before it is formed and pressed. This process suggests that Jack is a close cousin of Colby and is probably a derivative of Cheddar, although other origins are claimed.

According to FDA standards, Monterey Jack must be made from pasteurized milk and must contain not less than 50 percent fat on a dry basis and not more than 44 percent moisture; this corresponds to 28 percent fat wet basis. The regulation also defines "high moisture Jack" with permitted moisture between 44 and 50 percent. Similar to its cousin

The Vella Cheese Company in Sonoma, California, makes Dry Monterey Jack rubbed with a mixture of soybean or safflower oil, black pepper, and unsweetened cocoa. The rub preserves the cheese wheels for longer aging and also gives them their signature dark brown rind. © 2016 FRANKENY IMAGES

Colby, the initial pH of Jack is in the range of 5.0–5.2, and increases slowly during ripening.

Film-wrapped Monterey Jack is consumed as a mild cheese (six weeks to four months) and may include flavorings such as peppers (hence, Pepper Jack or Salsa Jack Cheese) or may be blended with Colby to make Colby-Jack, a version of marbled cheese. The film-wrapped version is most common, but does not age well because the moisture is too high. Traditional Jack is not film wrapped; rather oil is rubbed on the surface and the cheese is ripened at around 85 percent humidity to encourage rind formation. The cheese slowly dehydrates and firms with age. Older Jack in excess of ten months, referred to as Dry Jack, is quite firm and can be used as a grating cheese. Cheesemongers variously describe the flavor of old Jack as sharp, rich, fruity, and caramel.

See also CHEDDAR and COLBY.

Moss, Wendy. "The 'True' Story of Monterey Jack Cheese." Monterey County Historical Society. http://www.mchsmuseum.com/cheese.html.
US Food and Drug Administration. Code of Federal Regulations, Title 21, Chapter 1, Subchapter B, Part 133.135: "Monterey Cheese and Monterey Jack Cheese." http://www.gpo.gov/fdsys/pkg/CFR-2006-title21-vol2/pdf/CFR-2006-title21-vol2-sec133-153.pdf.

Arthur Hill and Mary Ann Ferrer

Jajikhli Panir (Cacıxli Pənir) is a type of pot cheese that has been produced for many years mainly by Turkish and Kurdish tribes in different areas of northwestern and western Iran, such as in the Ghotoor (Qotur) area, a country region of Khoy

Jajikhli Panir, a traditional Iranian pot cheese containing herbs. © YAHYA OLIAEI

city. It is also called Penjarli Panir (Pencərli Pənir). "Penjar" and "Jajikh" are regional terms meaning vegetables or mountain herbs. Jajikhli Panir is a semihard, brined or dry-salted cheese that is primarily prepared from raw ewe's milk with no heat treatment during the cheesemaking process. Vegetables and herbs are added to the curd or cheese before it is put into pots. The rest of the production process is the same as for Kupa Paniri. See KUPA PANIRI. The cheese is ripened in brine for few days and then placed in pots and matured underground for four to six months, at which point it is ready for consumption as a table cheese. It is characterized by a brittle texture, a white color flecked with green from the vegetable pieces, a slight salty, acidic taste, and a fermented aroma combined with the aroma and flavor of the added herbs.

Vegetables and herbs mixed with Jajikhli Panir are collected from the local hillsides. Most are from the genus *Allium* (local names: Ghorat [Qorat], Piyaze Vahshi, and Tareh Kohestani), *Chaerophyllum, Ferula* (local names: Məndi, Məndik or Manda, Sire Kuhi, Sire Sabze Kuhestani, and Sirik), *Thymus* (Dağ Mərzəsi or Avishan), *Mentha* (Yarpız, Pooneh), *Ocimum* (local name: Reyhan), *Anthriscus, Silene, Heracleum,* and a bitter parsley called injibir (Incibir). A similar type of cheese produced in Turkey called Otlu Peynir also contains some of the same herbs.

See also IRAN; POT CHEESES; and TURKEY.

Hayaloglu, Ali A., and Patrick F. Fox. "Cheeses of Turkey: 3. Varieties Containing Herbs or Spices." *Dairy Science and Technology* 88 (2008): 245–256.
Lame, H., M. Hekmati, and M. Moharramkhani. "Contribution à l'étude du 'fromage en pot' de l'Iran." *Le Lait* 53 (1973): 163–168.
Shafiei, Y. "Iranian Traditional Cheeses." Paper presented at the 1st Conference of Iranian Traditional Dairy Products. Khoy, Iran, 24 February 2013. In Persian.

Yahya Shafiei Bavil Oliaei

Jamei-Laibspeis is a cheese shop and affineur specializing in Alpine cheeses in Kempten, Bavaria. Since 2004 Thomas Breckle, a former professional cross-country skier, has specialized in ripening great mountain cheeses from the Allgäu, Austria, and Switzerland in an old monastery cellar in Kempten. Together with his partner Martin Rößle, a former cheesemaker in Germany's largest organic dairy, the Andechser Scheitz Dairy, he travels the mountains over sixty days per year to find the very best Alpine cheeses—usually by mountain bike.

The criteria for the selection are severe: raw milk from horned cows, dairy-made cheese cultures, artisanal, slow and careful processing of the raw materials. Every lot of cheese is tasted at its origin. The wheels are collected after six weeks of pre-ripening at the Alpine dairy. On principle, Jamei pays higher prices than the industry standard. The cheeses are then ripened very slowly, at a maximum of 50°F (10°C) and 99 percent humidity in a former ice storage cellar. As a result the cheeses do not dry out, but condense their taste and texture.

Three people work in the cellar to brush and turn the approximately five hundred 88-pound (40-kilogram) wheels one to two times per week. The cheese is sold at their own very elegant shop in Kempten, at some open air food markets in Hamburg, as well as a select few cheese shops.

See also ALP-STYLE CHEESES and MATURING.

Charis. "Genuss statt Fernweh—Jamei Laibspeis—Allgäuer Bergkäse." *Wohlgeraten Tagebuch*, 19 November 2013. http://blog.wohlgeraten.de/genuss-statt-fernweh-jamei-laibspeis-allgaeuer-bergkaese.
Jamei-Laibspeis. http://www.jamei-laibspeis.de.
Läufle, Monika. "Vom Käse, der Zeit und der Dunkelheist." *Allgäu* 4 (2012).

Theresa Malec

Japan is home to a well-established commercial cheese industry and a small but growing community of artisanal cheese producers. Between 1940, when annual per capita consumption was a mere 0.14 ounces (4 grams), and 2011, when it topped 5.5 pounds (2.5 kilograms), cheese secured a place on the table in a country whose population for many centuries eschewed dairy products almost entirely. The tastes of the average eater remain timid, however, with processed cheeses comprising nearly half of sales and mild standbys such as Gouda, Cheddar, Camembert, and mozzarella making up most of the remainder. Domestic companies meet just under a fifth of total demand. Although a number of individual producers have developed unique varieties over the past few decades, Japan has yet to produce a distinct regional cheese along the lines of Spain's Manchego or England's Stilton. Some of the most exciting developments entail the blending of Japanese flavors with classic techniques of cheese production and cookery.

The history of cheese in Japan is long but fragmented. Although ancient Japanese farmers used cows to till their fields, they did not consume their milk. In the sixth century, however, a visiting physician from the Korean peninsula instructed the Imperial Court in the health benefits of dairy products. Courtiers were soon eating a thick paste of boiled-down milk called *so*, which some scholars classify as Japan's earliest cheese. *So* remained a food for the elite over the following centuries, with farmers required to supply it as a tax-in-kind. As imperial power declined in the twelfth century and Japan fell into a long period of internal conflict, however, all traces of dairy consumption disappeared from the culture.

It did not reemerge until 1727, when shogun Yoshimune Tokugawa imported a herd of white milk cows from India. Around the same time Dutch merchants began bringing cheese to their lone trading post in Nagasaki Bay, but isolationist policies insulated the rest of the nation from foreign influence. Cheese began its true ascent only with the political and cultural opening of the Meiji era (1868–1912). The government, enamored of all things Western, encouraged dairy farming on the recently colonized northern island of Hokkaido, where pastureland was abundant, and spearheaded experiments in cheese production. In 1932, one dairy cooperative and one company began mass-producing bricks of processed cheese for the first time. They would later become two of Japan's largest cheesemakers, Snow Brand and Meiji.

Culinary westernization continued with renewed vigor following Japan's defeat in World War II. Dishes such as gratin, cheesecake, pasta, and sandwiches gained popularity, and the cheese industry grew in tandem. A market for high-quality natural cheese developed as well, with the first airplane load of imported cheese touching down in 1964 to feed athletes competing in the Tokyo Olympics. By the 1960s domestic companies were producing Camembert, blue, Parmesan, Swiss, and several other types, but it was not until the 1980s that farmstead cheesemakers began to produce unique artisanal varieties capable of competing with the best imports.

Today Japan's cheese industry is split between a handful of large companies catering to the mass market on the one hand and several hundred farmstead and artisanal producers on the other. While both groups are recognized for their excellent technical skill, the latter leads in terms of innovation.

Small producers have responded to the increasingly adventurous consumer palate with stronger flavors and varieties that incorporate traditional Japanese ingredients. Examples include Furano Cheese's Camembert-type Sepia, whose snow-white rind conceals an interior dyed black with squid ink; Kyodogakusha Shintoku Farm's Sakagura, which is both fermented with sake yeast and washed with sake; and numerous varieties wrapped in bamboo, cherry, or shiso leaves. Chefs, too, are experimenting with miso-infused Mimolettes, fresh mozzarella with wasabi-soy dressing, Roquefort sushi, and other East-West hybrids.

The industry nevertheless faces a number of challenges, foremost among them the government ban on raw milk (low-heat pasteurization is permitted). In addition, Japan's dairy herds are composed almost entirely of Holsteins, so that cheesemakers in search of richer or more flavorful milks must often begin by importing animals from abroad. Finally, due to the limited supply of arable land and the long tradition of livestock confinement, few farmers pasture their dairy cows.

A number of excellent Japanese cheeses have emerged despite these challenges. Shimizu Bokujo, a family-run business whose small herd of Brown Swiss cows and Friesland sheep grazes on natural meadow high in Nagano Prefecture's Japanese Alps, produces a range of good fresh and aged cheeses. Zao Dairy Center, also on the main island of Honshu, is known for its cream cheeses and for its leading role in educating natural cheese producers across Japan since the early 1980s. On Hokkaido, which remains the heart of Japan's dairy industry, Kyodogakusha Shintoku Farm has developed some of Japan's best unique varieties. Among them is the delicate, cherry-scented Sakura, which has won numerous international awards. Other notable Hokkaido cheesemakers include Mitomo Farm, producing nutty, semi-hard mountain cheeses, and organic Fermier Tomita, which follows the increasingly popular agrotourism model.

"Cheese." In *Chiiki Shokuzai Daihyakka* [Regional Food Encyclopedia]. Tokyo: Rural Culture Association Japan, 2011.

Honma, Rumiko. *Chizu: Shurui, erabikata, oishii tabekata* [Cheese: Varieties, Selection, and Suggestions for Eating]. Osaka, Japan: Hoikusha, 1997.

Ootani, Hajime. "Chizu no Kigen to Rekishi" [The Origins and History of Cheese]. *New Food Industry* 49 (2007): 25–36.

Tokita, Fumisaburo. *Chizu no Kita Michi* [The Road Cheese Has Traveled]. Tokyo: Kawade Shobo Shinsha, 1977.

Winifred Bird

Jarlsberg is a registered trademark for a semihard Norwegian cheese made from pasteurized cow's milk.

With the beginning of industrialization of dairies in Norway in the nineteenth century came a disdain for the old Norwegian cheeses. Foreign cheeses, especially Swiss Emmentaler, were the ideal. Many Swiss cheesemakers came to Norway to teach their craft. The history of Jarlsberg goes back to the Jarlsberg countship where in the mid-1800s a hybrid between Emmentaler and Gouda cheeses was developed. It was never very successful, and mostly forgotten. In the 1950s an improved version was developed at the Agricultural University of Norway. Eventually Jarlsberg became the biggest export of TINE Norwegian dairies.

Jarlsberg has a mild, sweet, and nutty flavor and large eyes. Propionibacteria form an important part of the culture that gives Jarlsberg both its flavor and its eyes. It is manufactured as 22-pound (10-kilogram) wheels with a plastic-covered rind, but also as rindless blocks or loaves. Regular Jarlsberg has 27 percent fat (45 percent FDM) and is usually sold at three months of age, but some is matured for twelve months or more. A low-fat version, in block form only, has 16 percent fat (30 percent FDM).

Jarlsberg and Jarlsberg Lite are also sold sliced, and, in the United States only, as mini wheels of ¾ ounce (20 grams) each. The annual production worldwide is over 27,000 tons, most of it in Norway. The export from Norway is around 11,000 tons, mostly to the US. Other important markets are the United Kingdom, Australia, and Canada. Several thousand tons are also produced in the United States for the TINE subsidiary Norseland Inc.

See also EMMENTALER; GOUDA; and NORWAY.

Abrahamsen, Roger K., et al. *Jarlsbergosten: Historie og utvikling* [Jarlsberg Cheese: History and Development]. Oslo: Tun Forlag, 2006.

Ove Fosså

Jasper Hill Farm

See CELLARS AT JASPER HILL.

Jean d'Alos is a cheese shop in the historic center of Bordeaux, in southwest France. Jean-Claude Cazalas and his wife, Pascale, who were originally from the village of D'Alos, opened the shop in 1983. Their goal was to find and affiner—age—the finest cheeses in France, taking advantage of the fifteenth-century caves beneath their shop. Their careful attention and the cheeses it produced made Maison Jean d'Alos a national reference for fine, raw-milk, artisan-produced cheeses.

At Jean d'Alos, cheeses are aged on spruce shelves, some of which are lined with rye straw depending on the needs of the cheese, in caves that are temperature and humidity controlled. For the cow's milk cheeses, the temperature ranges from 52°F to 54°F (11°C to 12° C) and the humidity is 95 percent. Goat cheeses need colder temperatures, around 46°F (8°C), and about 90 percent humidity.

In 2009, the *fromagerie* was sold to Clarence Grosdidier, a businessman with his own passion for cheese. Under his direction, the Jean d'Alos philosophy remains the same. Mr. Grosdidier continues to look for new cheeses with a preference for those produced in the southwest of France; he exports around the world, with a particular focus on Asia and Europe where the name Jean d'Alos is well known.

There are now five Jean d'Alos shops—three in Bordeaux, one in Pau, and one in Montpellier. In addition to the five caves below the original shop in Bordeaux, Jean d'Alos has six aging caves in the city of Pau.

See also FRANCE.

Susan Herrmann Loomis

Jersey is a dairy cattle breed, one of several from the Channel Islands west of Normandy that were first known in England under the catchall name "Alderney." By 1800 one Alderney type bore a distinctive reputation mirrored in George Eliot's novel *Adam Bede* (set in 1799) by a farm wife's unfavorable comparison of a Shorthorn to "that little yellow [*sic*] cow as doesn't give half the milk, and yet I've twice as much butter from her."

Cows of this kind would later be named for their place of origin, the island of Jersey. Their milk is richer than that of any other breed, as measured by such criteria as amounts of calcium, protein, milk fat, and several vitamins per volume or weight unit of milk. They became an important US dairy breed after about 1850. As in England, their success reflected a lucrative urban market for farmhouse butter. They were little used for commercial English or American cheesemaking, both then largely geared to Cheddar types that are usually based on leaner milk.

Since the mid-nineteenth century the dairy industry has been reshaped by a hugely expanded

Jersey herd at New Moor Farm in County Durham, England. New Moor is locally famous for making delicious ice cream from their Jersey cow milk. © STORYE BOOK

market for drinkable fluid milk above all other forms. At times Jersey milk's superior flavor guaranteed it a certain market niche. But an inexorable trend toward pooling milk from many farms eventually made sheer volume of yield the major yardstick. Increasing milk yield per animal tends to disproportionately boost water content in relation to everything else. Jersey milk's virtues thus became all but irrelevant for the fluid milk market, while the alternatives of cheese-making or butter making declined in importance throughout most of the twentieth century.

A further handicap was a USDA price support system for fluid milk (introduced in 1937, with many later amendments) intended to guarantee farmers in different geographical locations certain base prices per hundredweight. In fact, it has enmeshed dairy farmers in a regulatory labyrinth that frequently leaves them struggling to recoup production costs. Opting out of the USDA "milk marketing orders" system in favor of sales to businesses that value milk quality was seldom a realistic choice for Jersey farmers, until the 1980s' cheesemaking renaissance and the USDA's later introduction of "multiple component pricing." See MILK.

Artisan cow's milk cheesemakers soon found milk produced to supply the fluid milk market nearly useless for their purposes. After investigating different breeds, many opted for milk from herds of registered Jerseys or "grade" Jersey herds with cows of mixed, predominantly Jersey ancestry. Goat's milk and sheep's milk cheesemakers seeking to diversify their lines by introducing cow's milk blends also frequently chose Jersey milk.

The American Jersey Cattle Association (AJCA) seized the opportunity to begin an ambitious promotional campaign partly addressed to cheesemakers. For farmers it stressed selling points like early maturation, relative ease in calving, and highly efficient conversion of feed to nutrient-dense milk, resulting in a smaller average carbon footprint per unit of milk (or cheese) produced as compared to Holsteins. See HOLSTEIN.

The rebound has been astonishing. In the 1970s an industry joke suggested that Jersey cows soon would be found only in zoos. They are now the second most popular US dairy breed, with annual AJCA registrations climbing steeply and owners of other cattle breeds often deciding to upgrade a herd by adding a few Jerseys. It is also recognized that they tolerate hot weather better than other European-descended cattle breeds, allowing them to thrive in the tropics and suggesting that Jerseys may prove hardy under advancing climate change.

Jersey milk is particularly good for relatively soft, rich cheeses including a few fresh unripened kinds, bloomy-rind cheeses of the Brie group, washed-rind cheeses resembling Taleggio or Époisses, and some blues. When used in hard cheeses it can require careful management to prevent the high fat content from prolonging retention of moisture during the aging process, but produces excellent flavor. The words "Jersey milk" on a cheese label now carry recognized cachet for knowledgeable shoppers.

See also COW.

Becker, Raymond B. *Dairy Cattle Breeds: Origin and Development*. Gainesville: University of Florida Press, 1973.
Porter, Valerie. *Cattle: A Handbook to the Breeds of the World*. 2d ed. Illustrated by Jake Tebbit. Ramsbury, U.K.: Crowood, 2007.

Anne Mendelson

Jervaulx Abbey in Yorkshire, England, is widely believed to be the original home of Wensleydale cheese. In France monks had long been associated with cheesemaking, and a group from near Roquefort settled in Wensleydale soon after the Norman Conquest, bringing with them their skills in making ewe's milk cheese. They joined the Cistercian order in their monastery at Fors. An abbey inventory for 1150 included cheeses.

The community was granted a new site, in Lower Wensleydale, and Jervaulx Abbey was dedicated in 1156. The land was more favorable for farming, and the abbey became a center of agricultural expertise. The monks used the summer milk of the ewes and the molds found in the local stone to make a blue cheese, as they had done in France. The abbey's lands extended beyond Wensleydale as its wealth increased, and the monks taught their tenant farmers how to make cheese. They built granges to store produce, and the tenants used cheese and butter to pay rent in kind.

The cheese was most likely open-textured and susceptible to the natural molds of the humid cellars. Cheesemaking knowledge continued to be handed down from generation to generation. Even after the dissolution of the monasteries in the sixteenth century the monks' traditional methods survived. At some point after this farmers started to use a mixture

The ruins of the Jervaulx Abbey cloisters in 2011. © MATT BUCK

of cow's and ewe's milk, and by the seventeenth century cow's milk predominated.

The name "Wensleydale" has been traced back to 1840 when it was used at local cheese fairs. Thanks to the animated characters Wallace and Gromit, Wensleydale is renowned worldwide today, even if the origins of the cheese are almost forgotten.

See also MONASTIC CHEESEMAKING; WALLACE AND GROMIT; and WENSLEYDALE.

Cooper, Michael. *Discovering Farmhouse Cheese.* Aylesbury, U.K.: Shire Publications, 1978.
Rance, Patrick. *The Great British Cheese Book.* London: Macmillan, 1988.

Jill Norman

Jibneh Arabieh

See MIDDLE EAST.

jolie robe (French for pretty dress) is a vernacular term sometimes used by French cheesemakers to describe the appearance of cheese rinds, especially those belonging to the *pâte molle* (soft) class of cheeses. See SOFT-RIPENED CHEESES. The term is also applied in wine tasting to describe the color, clarity, and consistency of a wine. The *jolie robe* of surface-ripened *pâte molle* cheese consists of a uniform, white, velvety coat of filamentous fungi, in particular the yeast-like fungus *Geotrichum candidum.* Saint Marcellin is probably the best example of a cheese with a *jolie robe.* The role of *G. candidum* is to contribute to the appearance of the ripened cheese and stabilize the rind. On Brie and Camembert-type cheeses, *G. candidum* proliferates around the third day of ripening but is not visible at the end, since it is overgrown by a white layer of the fungus *Penicillium camemberti,* which appears around the sixth day of ripening.

Although the term *jolie robe* refers to the appearance of a cheese, the filamentous fungi creating the fungal coat play a significant role in the ripening process. The proteolytic and lipolytic activities of enzymes contributed by the fungi break down protein and fat respectively, and impart the aroma and creamy consistency of these cheeses. The development of a uniform layer of *G. candidum* on the cheese surface early in the ripening process also aids in the inhibition of fungal contaminants such as *Mucor.*

See also FILAMENTOUS FUNGI; *GEOTRICHUM CANDIDUM; MUCOR;* and *PENICILLIUM.*

Marcellino, Noella, and David R. Benson. "The Good, the Bad and the Ugly: Tales of Mold-Ripened Cheese." *Microbiology Spectrum* 1 (October 2013): 1–27.

David R. Benson and Sr. Noella Marcellino

Jones, Evan (1916–1996), the author of the influential book *The World of Cheese* (1976), was a freelance writer who came from a family of journalists and newspaper publishers in Minnesota. He and his wife Judith Jones (née Bailey) settled in New York in the 1950s after living in Paris from 1948 to 1952, where they had fallen in love—with each other and with French cuisine. Mr. Jones wrote on a variety of subjects, from Minnesota's history to the delights of amateur archaeology, but after moving to New York he increasingly focused his efforts on food history, cooking techniques, and recipes. This was in tandem with Judith's growing reputation in the food world as the Knopf editor who discovered and published Julia Child's enormously successful *Mastering the Art of French Cooking*. Judith went on to publish a host of other cookbooks by food luminaries such as James Beard, Jacques Pépin, and Marion Cunningham. The couple became well known for hosting dinners for their friends, including the *New York Times* critic Stanley Kauffman, who described their East 66th Street apartment as "the best restaurant in New York."

In 1976 Evan Jones wrote *The World of Cheese*, the first book on international cheese to be published in America. It represented a real departure as far as American gastronomic book publishing was concerned as it was more than just a compendium; it was a thorough cheese history and told a story that most Americans and novice cheese lovers knew nothing about. Mr. Jones had been inspired by his experiences living in Paris and his experiences purchasing cheese in New York City. *The World of Cheese* also included directions for making cheese at home, recipes for appetizers, and tips on buying and serving cheese. It was considered one of the definitive works on cheese at the time, and was reissued in 1989.

Jones, Evan. *The World of Cheese*. New York: Knopf, 1976.
Smith, Andrew F. "Jones, Judith and Evan." In *Savoring Gotham: A Food Lover's Companion to New York City*. New York: Oxford University Press, 2015.
Thomas, Robert McG., Jr. "Evan Jones, 80, a Food Writer Renowned for His Own Cooking." *New York Times*, 5 February 1996.

Bronwyn Dunne and Sara Rodgers

Jossi, John (1845–1902) was a Swiss-born cheesemaker credited with developing Brick, one of the earliest truly American cheeses. In 1857 Jossi immigrated with his parents to upstate New York at the age of twelve and two years later he was managing a small Limburger cheese factory in southwest Wisconsin. After marrying a Wisconsin cheesemaker's daughter he moved back to New York in 1873 to work at a larger Limburger plant. Jossi eventually returned to Wisconsin to run a newly built cheese factory in 1877. There he pursued his idea of developing a surface-ripened cheese with a lower moisture content.

No one knows whether leftover construction materials contributed to his inspiration, but Jossi used bricks for a double pressing and shaping method. Thus "Brick" cheese was born in 1877. Its distinctive shape, a firm, almost Cheddar-like texture, and a flavor that was smooth yet with a somewhat sharp finish, made it a hit. So too did its mild aroma, which earned the cheese its nickname of "the married man's Limburger." Jossi taught his Brick recipe to a dozen other Wisconsin dairies before giving the cheese factory in 1883 to his brother, who later sold it to Kraft. Kraft then turned Brick into a mass-produced item that, while popular, bore little resemblance to Jossi's vision. See KRAFT FOODS.

Jossi's legacy lives on at Theresa, Wisconsin–based Widmer Cheese Cellars, just twenty minutes from where, brick by brick, Jossi's vision came to life. There Joe Widmer, a third-generation cheesemaker who is also of Swiss descent, remains faithful to Jossi's method of producing distinctive Brick. The result of Widmer's efforts is an award-winning piquant aged Brick that's comparable to European washed-rind cheeses. Widmer's Brick is a restoration of a signature American artisan cheese and a product that likely would register as very familiar to Jossi himself.

See also BRICK; LIMBURGER; and WISCONSIN.

Brown, Robert Carlton. *The Complete Book of Cheese*. New York: Gramercy, 1955.
Jenkins, Steve. *Cheese Primer*. New York: Workman, 1996.
Widmer's Cheese Cellars. "The Story of Wisconsin Brick Cheese." http://www.widmerscheese.com/the-story-of-wisconsin-brick-cheese.

Robin Watson

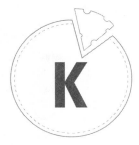

Kalathaki Limnou is a Greek PDO cheese produced on the island of Lemnos in the northern part of the Aegean Sea. Kalathaki Limnou received PDO distinction in 1994 for the cheese traditionally produced from pasteurized sheep's milk. Goat's milk can also be added, but its percentage may not exceed 30 percent of the total weight. Kalathaki Limnou has a 56 percent maximum moisture content and a 43 percent minimum fat content. It has the shape of a small wheel with no external rind and carries the marks of the willow or plastic baskets in which it is matured. A soft, white cheese, Kalathaki Limnou has a pleasant, slightly acidic taste and a rich aroma.

During the manufacturing process, the addition of rennet, starter lactic acid bacteria, and calcium chloride (up to 20 grams per 100 kilograms of milk) is allowed. Coagulation of the milk takes place at about 91–93°F (33–34°C). After coagulation, the curd is cut into particles the size of beans and left to drain for a while. For the final draining and acidification, the curd is then transferred to special cylindrical molds, which give the cheese its characteristic form. When draining is complete, the cheese is removed from the molds, salted, transferred to metal containers, and covered with brine. The cheese is matured in the containers at a temperature of about 57–64°F (14–18°C) for three weeks and then at a temperature of less than 43°F (6°C) for at least two months. Close to three hundred tons of PDO Kalathaki Limnou cheese are produced each year.

See also GREECE.

Anifantakis, E., and G. Moatsou. "Kalathaki Limnou Cheese." In *Brined Cheeses*, edited by A. Y. Tamime, p. 63. Oxford: Blackwell, 2006.

"Kalathaki Limnou." Cheesenet.gr. http://www.cheesenet.gr/english/cheeses/kalathaki.htm.

Maria Kazou, Efstathios Giaouris, and Konstantinos Papadimitriou

kashkaval is a hard cheese made in the Balkans, Bulgaria, Romania, and Turkey from sheep's, goat's, or cow's milk or a mixture of milks. The cheese dates to Roman times and derives its name from caciocavallo, a southern Italian cheese with similar production characteristics. The same style of cheese is made in the southern part of the former USSR, in Greece, and through the Levant, but may carry different names. The steps of production may differ slightly according to location, but the pulled-curd process unifies all variations.

The cheese curds must reach a pH of 5.2 to be elastic during the texturing process. Bulgarian kashkaval involves an intermediate texturing in which the initial curd is milled and then pressed for six to eight hours to develop texture, much like the cheddaring process. Cheesemakers work the curd in hot brine and later dry-salt the 13–20 pound (6–9 kg) cheeses for more than two weeks, first at a temperature of about 63°F (17°C), followed by cooler ripening at typical cellar temperatures. The production of the Romanian variety Cașcaval Dobrogen involves salting the curd directly during kneading. The European Economic Community defines kashkaval as aged for a minimum of two months and having a minimum 45 percent fat content in dry matter.

The cheese ages until the paste takes on a medium-hard to hard, yet elastic and pliable, texture that is somewhat crumbly. The cheese may possess a few mechanical holes, but gas holes are considered a fault. It has a piquant flavor that is enhanced in cheeses made from 100 percent sheep's milk, as are the Romanian versions. Kashkaval is mildly salty and acidic and melts well. The cheese has many applications in cooking, from pan-fried preparations to use as a pizza topping. In some areas where kashkaval is common, the name may be used to describe other types of slicing or hard cheeses, not just the historic type original to the Balkans. More than twenty production areas in Romania carry PDO (protected designation of origin) status for their cheeses.

See also CACIOCAVALLO and SERBIAN WHITE BRINED CHEESES.

Carić, Marijana. "Ripened Cheese Varieties Native to the Balkan Countries." In *Cheese: Chemistry, Physics, and Microbiology*, edited by P. F. Fox, et al. Vol. 2: *Major Cheese Groups*, pp. 263–279. London: Elsevier, 1999.
Mijačević, Zora, and Snežana Bulajić. "Traditional Manufacturing of Hard Cheese—Kachkaval on Stara Planina Mountain." *Acta agriculturae Slovenica* 84 (2004): 11–15.

Brent A. Wasser

kasseri is a pale yellow, semihard cheese made with sheep's milk or a combination of sheep's and a small amount of goat's or, rarely, cow's milk. It is produced in northern Greece in the regions of Thrace, Macedonia, Thessaly, and on the northeastern Aegean island of Lesbos. When made using traditional methods and ingredients—sheep's milk that is unpasteurized, a natural rennet, and aging the cheese sufficiently—kasseri develops rich, complex flavors, a buttery texture, and a flowery aroma.

Although kasseri is traditionally made entirely from sheep's milk, the inclusion of a maximum of 20 percent goat's or cow's milk is permitted in the cheese's production. The texture of kasseri made entirely from sheep's milk is firm; the addition of goat's milk leads to a harder cheese. Traditionally, kasseri is a raw-milk cheese; however, more and more cheesemakers, particularly large-scale industrial producers, are using pasteurized milk to produce the cheese. Like Italy's provolone, kasseri is a "pasta filata," or stretched-curd cheese. See PASTA FILATA. Even with industrially produced kasseri, the warmed, malleable curd must be kneaded by hand to just the right consistency. Kasseri is produced in wheels. Before being presented at market, the cheese must be aged for at least two months; however, it obtains its peak flavor when aged for ten or more months. As kasseri ages, it develops a hard rind and a coating of mold, which, at the final stage of the cheese's production, is washed off with brine.

Kasseri is among the most popular cheeses in Greece where it is commonly served as a table cheese and also used as an ingredient in cooking and baking. It is one of several Greek cheeses that are fried and served as "saganaki" and it is used as a filling in savory pies, or pittes. See SAGANAKI. Kasseri is the main ingredient in the cheese pie known as kasseropita, which is made by layering thin sheets of buttered or oiled phyllo dough with a mixture of egg and kasseri cheese. (The pie's name is a compound word derived from "kasseri" and "pita," modern vernacular Greek for "pie").

Kasseri is similar in flavor and texture to kashkaval, a pasta-filata cheese produced in Bulgaria, Romania, and other Balkan nations, and caciocavallo, also a stretched-curd cheese, which is made in southern Italy. See CACIOCAVALLO and KASHKAVAL. When aged for ten months or more, kasseri develops a flavor profile similar to that of Italy's Asiago and Parmigiano Reggiano cheeses. It is thought that production of kasseri in Greece began in the nineteenth century in the Pindus Mountains, the principal range and backbone of mainland Greece, which extends from southern Albania toward the Peloponnese Peninsula.

Although originally produced and consumed in northern Greece, kasseri is now widely available throughout the country. It is also exported; outside of Greece, it is sold in specialty cheese shops, Greek ethnic markets, and online. Commercial producers of kasseri include Olympus, Fantis, and Mt. Vikos. Kasseri was awarded protected designation of origin (PDO) status by the European Union in 1996.

See also GREECE.

Kitrilakis, Sotiris. "The Art of Making Kasseri." *Epikouria Magazine*, Fall/Winter 2006.
Kochilas, Diane. "Kasseri: The Ultimate Greek Table Cheese." http://www.dianekochilas.com/kasseri-the-ultimate-greek-table-cheese.

Alexis Marie Adams

Katiki Domokou is an unripened light, white, spreadable cheese without a rind. It is a PDO cheese, traditionally produced in the municipality of Domokos of the Fthiotida prefecture of Greece. The cheese is made using traditional technology, and has been taught from generation to generation by nomadic shepherds who live in the area. The earliest mentions of Katiki Domokou can be found in the writings of the ancient historian Thucydides, who wrote that the first inhabitants of Fthiotida were pastoralists skilled in cheesemaking.

Katiki Domokou cheese is made mainly from sheep's milk, goat's milk, or mixtures of the two. The milk comes exclusively from herds of sheep and goats raised and bred in the plateau of Mount Othris in the Domokos area. Their diet is based on locally found plants. After pasteurization the milk is cooled to 68–72°F (20–22°C) and remains in the vat until its acidic coagulation, either with or without the aid of a small quantity of rennet. The curd is then mashed and salted with 1 percent salt, mixed thoroughly, and transferred to cloth bags that are then hung from the rafters for whey drainage. The next day the cheese is packed into containers of various sizes for the market, or into barrels for longer storage at 39°F (4°C). Katiki Domokou contains 75 percent maximum moisture with little fat (10–14 percent), and is recommended for low fat diets.

Katiki Domokou has a sour refreshing taste and pleasant aroma. It can be served with a spoon and consumed in many ways; as a table cheese, on fresh or toasted bread, and added to salads, omelettes, sandwiches, and in many recipes.

See also GREECE.

Anyfantakis E. M. *Greek Cheeses, a Tradition of Centuries.* Athens, Greece: National Dairy Committee of Greece, 1991.
Greek Food and Drinks Code (FDC). Ministerial Decree No. 313048/1994 codifying the cheese "KATIKI DOMOCOU." Athens, Greece, 2011.
Thucydides. *The Peloponnesian War.* Book 1, Ch. 2. Translated by Martin Hammond. Oxford: Oxford University Press, 2009.

Anastasios Aktypis

Keen's Cheddar

See CHEDDAR.

Kefalograviera

Kefalograviera is a Greek hard cheese, which technologically stands between Kefalotyri and Graviera cheeses. In 1994 the name Kefalograviera was recognized as PDO for the cheese produced either from sheep's milk or from mixtures of sheep's and goat's milk (up to 10 percent) in western Mace-

donia, Epirus, Etoloakarnania, and Evrytania. However sometimes mixtures of cow's and sheep's milk (60:40) are also used.

Calcium chloride, starters, and rennet are added to pasteurized milk. Coagulation takes place within thirty to thirty-five minutes. The coagulum is cut into particles the size of corn kernels and cooked at 118°F (48°C) until the curd reaches the desired firmness. After scalding, the curd is transferred into molds and pressed for approximately three hours and then left for twenty-four hours at 57–61°F (14–16°C). Subsequently the cheese is salted in brine (18–20 percent, two days) and then dry-salted at 57–61°F (14–16°C) (ten saltings). Finally the cheese is left at 43°F (6°C) to ripen for three months. The final product has a maximum moisture content of 40 percent, a minimum fat in dry matter content of 40 percent, and a salt content of 3.4 percent.

Kefalograviera combines the pleasant taste of Graviera with the appearance of Kefalotyri. It has a firm, elastic body with few irregular holes (with diameter ranging from ⅛ to ⅓ inch [0.5–1 centimeter]) interspersed in its mass. Although Kefalograviera only came into production in recent decades, it has become very popular in Greece and abroad due to its good sensorial properties. In 2012 the production of PDO Kefalograviera reached 2.439 tons.

See also GRAVIERA AGRAFON; GRAVIERA KRITIS; GRAVIERA NAXOU; and GREECE.

Anifantakis E. *Greek Cheeses—A Tradition of Centuries.* Athens: National Dairy Committee of Greece, 1991, pp. 78–80.
"Kefalograviera." Cheesenet. gr. http://www.cheesenet.gr/english/cheeses/kefalograviera.htm.
Official Journal of the Hellenic Republic, Series B, no 8, 11 January 1994.

Voula Alexandraki and Effie Tsakalidou

khoya

See INDIA.

Kopanisti

Kopanisti is a traditional Greek PDO cheese exclusively produced on the Cyclades islands, the most famous being the Kopanisti produced on the islands of Mykonos and Tinos. It is a soft, spreadable cheese, with an intense salty and peppery taste and rich, zesty flavor. Its color ranges from off white to beige.

According to Greek legislation, Kopanisti should have a 56 percent maximum moisture and 43 percent minimum dry fat content (OG 16, 14-01-1994). It is manufactured from whole raw cow's, ewe's, and goat's milk or mixtures of them, derived from animals that are fully adapted to the particular region and whose diet is based on the flora of the area. The coagulation of the milk takes place at 82–86°F (28–30°C) in about two hours. The curd remains in the cheese vat for about twenty-four hours to complete clotting and develop acidity. It is then cut and put into cloth sacks to drain. After drainage, the curd is mixed by hand with salt (4–5 percent w/w) and placed in a container in a cool area with high relative humidity until a light-colored layer of molds develops on the surface. At this stage the curd is kneaded by hand in order to mix uniformly the microbial flora in the cheese mass and is left again in the cool area until the mold layer grows again. This process is repeated three to four times, until mature Kopanisti cheese is produced after thirty to forty days.

A special characteristic of Kopanisti cheese manufactured in the traditional way is the addition of 1 percent ripe Kopanisti cheese to the fresh curd in order to accelerate ripening. This ripe Kopanisti is called "Mana" (the Greek word for mother).

The piquant taste of Kopanisti accompanies ouzo, tsipouro, or wine very well, but it can also be consumed as a table cheese and in cheese pies. The locals prepare a dish called *mostra* with Mykonian rusks moistened with a little water and a little olive oil, spread with Kopanisti, and topped with chopped tomatoes. In 2012 the production of Kopanisti reached twenty-four tons.

See also GREECE.

Anifantakis, Emmanuel. *Greek Cheeses: A Tradition of Centuries*. Athens, Greece: National Dairy Committee of Greece, 1991.
Kopanisti. http://www.cheesenet.gr/english/cheeses/kopanisti.htm.

Rania Anastasiou

kosher

See DIETARY LAWS (RELIGIOUS).

Kosikowski, Frank (1916–1995), was born in Torrington, Connecticut. His association with the dairy industry originated in sixth grade when he began

working in a dairy plant. Receiving his BS from the University of Connecticut and MS and PhD degrees from Cornell University, he served as a dairy/food science faculty member at Cornell University from 1945 until his retirement in 1987 and continued his work until his passing in 1995. He was a mentor to over sixty graduate students and thirty postdoctorates from around the world. He authored or coauthored approximately 450 scientific papers, technical articles, book chapters, 12 patents, and 3 books. His book *Cheese and Fermented Milk Foods*, first published in 1966, continues to be widely used by students, researchers, and industry personnel.

Kosikowski developed and taught a wide range of courses: dairy products judging, butter making, cheesemaking, food fermentations, international food science, and high-protein-food technology. He was a pioneer on work on the origins of cheese flavors, accelerated ripening of cheese, whey utilization, low-lactose milk, pasteurization and antibiotic tests for milk, the Bactotherm process, application of ultrafiltration in cheesemaking, and removal of antibiotics from milk. The Bactotherm process is used commercially and his work on membrane processing in dairy during 1970–1990 set the stage for the wide scale use of this technology in the United States today. Kosikowski cofounded the American Cottage Cheese Institute in 1958. His broad, global view of the world came from his extensive travels that covered developing as well as developed countries. This gave him a unique appreciation of traditional cheesemaking, and the importance of preserving this diversity. This passion led him to create the American Cheese Society in 1983. This was a radical step at the time, but the Society now has 1,200 members, is vibrant, meets annually and serves a wide array of interests ranging from cheese enthusiasts to writers and cheese makers.

See also ACCELERATED RIPENING; AMERICAN CHEESE SOCIETY; MEMBRANE FILTRATION; PASTEURIZATION; TASTE; ULTRAFILTRATION; and WHEY.

Kosikowski, Frank, and Vikram V. Mistry. *Cheese and Fermented Milk Foods*. 3d ed., 2 vols. Westport, Conn.: F. V. Kosikowski. 1997.

Vikram Mistry

Kraft, James L. (1874–1953), is credited with creating American processed cheese. Founded in 1915, his company began producing pasteurized processed cheese in small tins. The production process was considered revolutionary, as the cheese did not spoil and could be shipped long distances. It was granted a patent in 1916. Kraft would go on to introduce additional products, including Velveeta in 1928, Miracle Whip at the 1933 World's Fair, and Kraft macaroni & cheese dinner in 1937. See VELVEETA and MAC AND CHEESE

From early sponsorship of television and radio shows, to the creation of simple recipes designed to lighten the modern American housewife's workload, Kraft products soon became an American household name. The company remains one of North America's leading food producers.

Born on a dairy farm in Stevensville, Ontario, Canada in 1874, Kraft was the second of eleven children. His parents were Mennonites. He later moved to the United States, where he invested in a cheese company. While working in Chicago in a management position, he was forced out of the cheese business by his partners. He then purchased a horse and wagon, bought cheese wholesale daily, and resold it to local merchants. The new venture was so successful that by 1909, four of his brothers joined the company.

Kraft was noted for his philanthropy. Before dying in 1953, he donated much of his wealth to religious organizations and religious education for young people.

See also KRAFT FOODS and PASTEURIZED PROCESS CHEESES.

Kraft Foods. http://www.kraftfoodsgroup.com.

Jeanne Carpenter

Kraft Foods (now the Kraft Heinz Company) is the world's fifth-largest food and beverage company and the largest cheese manufacturer in the United States. Cheese and cheese products make up the company's historical roots and continue to form one of its largest sales categories. Kraft has come to represent the innovation, standardization, and industrialization of cheese in the United States, a phenomenon that began in the mid-nineteenth century with the advent of cheese factories and is currently made manifest in Kraft's omnipresent, often shelf-stable cheeses and cheese-derived food products. Cheese consumption has increased dramatically in the United States over the past century thanks in large part to Kraft's success with cheese products, as well as its emphasis on cheese as an ingredient in a vast number of other food products. Kraft's most well-known cheese brands and products include Kraft Singles, Velveeta, Cheez Whiz, Kraft Macaroni and Cheese, and Philadelphia cream cheese. See CHEEZ WHIZ; CREAM CHEESE; MAC AND CHEESE; and VELVEETA.

International delivery truck with an advertisement for Kraft Cheese on its side, 1926. WISCONSIN HISTORICAL SOCIETY

The company that became Kraft Foods had its origins in the cheese business of a Wisconsin man named J. L. Kraft who, in 1903, began to distribute wholesale cheese in Chicago. The company first produced its own cheese in 1914, and received its first patent in 1916 for its innovative process cheese in tins. The tinned, shelf-stable cheese was popular with the US government, which used it to feed soldiers during World War I, and with grocers who saw the value in a cheese that did not need to be refrigerated. Kraft Singles were introduced in 1965 as the first individually wrapped cheese slices, and have become synonymous with the generic term "American cheese." In the latter half of the twentieth century, Kraft went through a series of corporate transitions, including purchase of and mergers with a number of other large food and consumer goods brands and two entrances into the public markets. The company became part of the Dow Jones Industrial Average in 2008, but was removed in 2012 after spinning off a large part of its business.

see also KRAFT, JAMES L. and PASTEURIZED PROCESS CHEESES.

Kraft Foods Group. "Kraft Foods Corporate Timeline." http://www.kraftfoodsgroup.com/SiteCollectionDocuments/pdf/CorporateTimeline_KraftGroceryCo_version.pdf.

Kraft Foods Group. "The Kraft Heinz Company Reports Second Quarter 2015 Results for Kraft Foods Group, Inc. and HJ Heinz Holding Corporation." http://newscenter.kraftfoodsgroup.com/phoenix.zhtml?c=253200&p=irol-newsArticle&ID=2078520.

Moss, Michael. Salt, Sugar, Fat: How the Food Giants Hooked Us. New York: Random House, 2013.

Paxson, Heather. The Life of Cheese. Berkeley: University of California Press, 2013.

Jessica A. B. Galen

Kraški kozji sir (Karst goat's cheese)is a semi-hard round cheese typical of the Karst region, a limestone plateau extending across southwestern Slovenia. Small ruminant breeding in the Karst region has a tradition that goes back a few hundred years, where in the past locals mostly bred sheep and poorer farmers bred goats. The wealthy class from the nearby city of Trieste was particularly interested in kids of 22–29 pounds (10–13 kilograms) of live weight, and the cheese produced from their milk. After World War II the government suppressed goat breeding due to the negative effect on afforestation efforts, but after the 1980s goat breeding was revitalized with the introduction of high-yielding dairy goat breeds. Nowadays herds are anywhere from twenty to one hundred animals, and their milk is mostly processed into cheese, with some into fresh cheese, goat butter, and herbal spreads.

The starting material for Kraški kozji sir is either raw or thermalized full-cream goat milk, mostly of the Slovenian Alpine goat breed, combined from the ripened evening and freshly milked morning milk. See ALPINE. At 90°F (32 °C) milk is renneted by the addition of chymosin and inoculated with starter culture. This is followed by cutting the curd into 2-inch (4-centimeter) pieces and the curd and whey mass is further stirred and scalded to 97–100°F (36–38°C). At this point about 30 percent of the whey is replaced by clean and warm water, heated to the temperature of the contents of the vat. Firm curd grains in the size of hazelnuts are collected in perforated or cloth-lined molds for pressing at 68–73°F (20–23°C), initially short and gentle, and later with natural drainage of whey until a pH of 5.2–5.3 is reached. Sea salt is used for dry salting that lasts for two days at 55–59°F (13–15°C). Ripening is normally finished within twenty to thirty days, and up to six months, at 80–85 percent humidity and 52–57°F (11–14°C).

The finished product weighs between 4–5 pounds (1.7–2.2 kilograms), and is 3–4 inches (7–9 centimeters) high and 7–8 inches (17–19 centimeters) in diameter. The rind is smooth and flat, with slightly convex peripheral side and round edges, from pale gray to whitish or brownish gray or to pale straw in color. The cheese body is uniform, elastic, compact to firm, with few, if any, rarely and evenly scattered eyes the size of lentils. Extending maturation to six months results in a harder and more compact texture that is liable to fracture. The taste and smell are clean and typical, with specific "goaty" notes mostly due to caprylic and capric fatty acids, but not intensive, aggressive, or even piquant. A high-quality matured goat cheese is served with Karst prosciutto that by tradition goes hand in hand with the red Karst wine called Teran. For even more enjoyable culinary delights, the Karst people offer goat cheese with an omelet, called *frtalja,* or grated on pasta.

See also KRAŠKI OVČJI SIR.

Perko, Bogdan. Slovenski avtohtoni siri—siri z geografskim poreklom (zgodovina, področje, tehnološki postopki)

(Slovenian autochthonous cheeses—cheeses with geographical origin [history, region, technological processes]). Rodica, Slovenia: Biotechnical Faculty, 2003.

*Andreja Čanžek Majhenič
and Petra Mohar Lorbeg*

Kraški ovčji sir (Karst ewe's cheese) is a hard cheese made from the milk of the autochthonous ewes breed istrska pramenka in the Karst region, extending across southwestern Slovenia. The Kraški ovčji sir denomination is recognized at the national Slovenian level.

Sheep farming in the Karst region goes back over three hundred years, a tradition that, especially in the past, has been vital for meat and milk production. Milk yield was usually the highest in May, although in the spring 11 quarts (10 liters) were required to make 2 pounds (1 kilogram) of cheese, while in August and September 6 quarts (5 liters) of milk were sufficient. Karst cheese was important merchandise for innkeepers and cheese merchants, but only if the cheese was of high quality, tested using a cheese borer. Old cheesemakers and cheese merchants were known to be able to discern where the sheep grazed simply by smelling the cheese wheel. For special customers innkeepers sought "rotten cheese" that contained live worms; by the end of the 1950s this gourmet specialty was appreciated particularly by elderly men.

Traditional production of Kraški ovčji sir is from raw sheep's milk, but the use of thermalized milk is also allowed. During the milking season cheese is made from a mix of evening and morning milk or, rarely, immediately after each milking. When warmed up to 88–91°F (31–33°C) the bulk milk is inoculated with either 0.4–0.6 percent of "kisava" (fermented secondary whey), or thermophilic starter bacteria. Addition of chymosin or of chymosin-pepsin mix results in gel formation, which is cut into wheat-size granules. Slowly scalding (100–108°F [38–42°C] for ten to fifteen minutes) and stirring produce firm pieces of curd that rapidly settle from the whey once stirring ceases. After ten minutes the curd mass is collected into cloths and placed in molds. Alternatively, immediately after scalding the entire content of the vat is transferred into perforated molds to allow the whey to drain off. Collected either way, the cheese is pressed, turned three times, and dry salted for three to six days or brined for

twenty-four hours. Cheeses are matured (59–64°F [15–18°C] at 75–85 percent humidity) for two to three months, or exceptionally for up to one year.

Between 13 to 15 pounds (5.8 to 6.6 kilograms) of sheep's milk is needed for the production of 2 pounds (1 kilogram) of Karst ewe's cheese, where the wheel is about 3–5 inches (8–12 centimeters) in height, 8–10 inches (20–26 centimeters) in diameter, and between 6–10 pounds (2.5–4.5 kilograms) in weight. The rind is smooth and flat, with slightly convex peripheral side, and yellow brownish in color. The cheese has a compact and uniform texture that is liable to fracture but not crumble. The color of the body is straw yellow to gray brownish. None or only a few scattered eyes the size of small lentils are visible on cutting, and few natural fissures are apparent. At the minimum ripening time of two months the flavor is aromatic. With the passage of time the color of the interior darkens and the flavor becomes more piquant. Nowadays Karst cheese can be enjoyed as an appetizer or as a dessert; as part of a cheese plate it can also be drizzled with olive oil.

See also KRAŠKI KOZJI SIR.

Specification for Karst ewe's cheese. Društva rejcev drobnice Krasa in Istre, 2008. http://www.mkgp.gov.si/fileadmin/mkgp.gov.si/pageuploads/podrocja/Varna_in_kakovostna_hrana_in_krma/zasciteni_kmetijski_pridelki/Specifikacije/KRASKI_OVCJI_SIR.pdf.

*Andreja Čanžek Majhenič
and Petra Mohar Lorbeg*

Krasotyri is a traditional semihard Greek cheese produced mainly on the island of Kos, among the Dodecanese islands of the Aegean. After ripening the cheese is immersed in wine sediment (*possia*) that dyes the surface of the cheese with a reddish color and gives the cheese its special appearance; the final product is covered with a red-brown rind resembling a wooden trunk. The organoleptic characteristics of Krasotyri are significantly affected by the phenolic compounds of the red wine sediment; indeed, *kraso* means "wine" and *tyri* means "cheese" in Greek. Overall the cheese has a slightly sour taste and is customarily accompanied by watermelon or bread. It is said that the origin of Krasotyri goes back 2,400 years, when due to a lack of olive oil commonly used to preserve cheese at this time (e.g., the PDO cheese

Ladotyri Mytilinis), wine was used as an alternative. As a result a cheese with new and delectable organoleptic characteristics emerged. See LADO-TYRI MYTILINIS.

Krasotyri is made from sheep or caprine milk, or mixtures of both. Traditionally the milk from the afternoon milking is heated until boiling and is then transferred into shallow clay containers. The next morning, the milk fat that has risen to the top is removed and the boiled milk is thoroughly mixed with fresh milk from the morning milking. After the addition of rennet, isolated from the stomachs (abomasum) of milk-fed yeanlings, the milk coagulates after approximately sixty minutes at about 93°F (34°C). The resulting curd is then cut into small pieces and the curd particles are stirred for about fifteen minutes without cooking (scalding). After the curd has been left to settle for a few minutes, it is then transferred into hoops (molds), which are commonly elongated molds woven from rushes, to drain for two to four hours. See HOOP. After draining the hoops are removed and the surface of the cheese is salted with coarse salt and the cheeses are immediately transferred into containers where they are submerged in brine and left to ripen in a cool place for twenty to thirty days. After brining the cheeses are removed from the vessels and placed on shelves to dry. In the last step of Krasotyri production, the dry cheeses are placed in vessels and covered with wine sediment (sometimes diluted with wine) where they remain for at least one week.

The moisture of Krasotyri is on average 45–50 percent. The non-starter lactic acid bacteria (NSLAB) are the predominant microflora of the cheese at similar levels on the cheese surface and in its interior. See NON-STARTER LACTIC ACID BACTERIA. Moreover the salt-tolerant and coliform microflora are less concentrated on the cheese surface in comparison to the interior. This is possibly due to the effect of the wine sediment rather than to the pH or salt content, which is similar at the cheese surface and the interior. The wine sediment also affects the composition of the lactic microflora; the surface lactic acid bacteria (LAB) microflora is composed mainly of lactobacilli and enterococci, with *E. faecium* predominant. The LAB microflora of the cheese interior usually consists of lactobacilli, enterococci, and lactococci, with lactobacilli predominating. *Lb. plantarum* and *E. faecium* are the most frequently isolated species.

See also GREECE.

Anifantakis, Emmanuel. *Greek Cheeses: A Tradition of Centuries.* Athens: National Dairy Committee of Greece, 1991

Litopoulou-Tzanetaki, Evanthia, and Nikolaos Tzanetakis. "Microbiological Characteristics of Greek Traditional Cheeses." *Small Ruminant Research* 101 (2011): 17–32.

Thomas Moschakis

Krk cheese is a traditional cheese produced from raw sheep's milk on the Island of Krk, which is located in the northern part of the Croatian Adriatic coast. The sheep's milk has a specific chemical composition typical of extensive farm management, which includes grazing the sheep on the Croatian islands year-round. The natural grazing land there is characterized by aromatic Mediterranean plants that give the milk its typical organoleptic features, which in turn, contributes to the cheese its unique flavor. Krk is a small, cylindrical cheese with a diameter of 4.5–6 inches (11.5–15 cm) and a height of 1.8–2.4 inches (4.5–6 cm). The color of the cheese varies between light yellow and a deep gold. On the cut surface, a small number of widely spread eyes can appear. The flavor is delicate, full, and strong, and can be quite intense depending on the length of the ripening period. Traditionally, Krk cheese is consumed with Vrbnička zlahtina, a famous white wine produced on the same island.

Raw sheep's milk is used in the manufacturing of Krk cheese. After adding the starter culture, the milk is coagulated, using natural rennet, within thirty minutes at a temperature of 86°F (30°C). The coagulum is then cut into grains the size of a pea using a cheese knife. Whey is removed during the filling of the perforated molds. The cheese is self-pressed over a period of six hours, and then it is brine-salted for twelve hours. After salting, the cheese is removed to a traditional ripening chamber typical of most Croatian coastal farms. These chambers are usually located in the cellar, where the cheese is placed on shelves made from beech wood. The temperature of the ripening room can vary between 50°F (10°C) and 64.4°F (18°C), and the relative humidity, from 70 percent to 80 percent. The ripening process can last from two to four months.

See also CROATIA.

Mikulec, Nataša, et al. "Characteristics of Traditional Croatian Ewe's Cheese from the Island of Krk." *International Journal of Dairy Technology* 61 (May 2008): 126–132.

Samir Kalit

Kumis

See MARE.

Kupa Paniri (Küpə Pəniri), also called Oghma (Oğma) or Ovma and Panireh Koozeh (in Persian), is a traditional cheese produced by the Turkish and Kurdish tribes in Khoy, Salmas, Makoo, Maraghe, Miyandoab, Mahabad, Urmia, Tabriz, Bookan, Saghez, Shahindejh, and generally Azerbaijan and Kurdestan regions of Iran. It is called Kupa Paniri because its maturation stage is accomplished inside the specific earthenware container called Kupa (Küpə). See EARTHENWARE POTTERY. In some areas other types of Kupa Paniri are produced that contain cumin seeds or vegetables, respectively called Ziraly Panir (Zirəli Pənir) and Jajikhli Panir (Cacıxli Pənir), the same as Carra Peynir of Turkey. See JAJIKHLI PANIR and ZIRALY PANIR. Kupa Paniri is a semihard cheese with a very pleasant taste and flavor. It's characterized by a dry appearance, yellowish-white color, salty taste, specific pleasant aroma, and brittle and ground texture. Organoleptic properties of Kupa Paniri are the same as Motal Paniri. See MOTAL PANIRI.

Milk of ewes, goats, cows, and buffalo, or a mixture of them, can be used for manufacturing Kupa Paniri. It is manufactured from a fresh cheese called Ghircha (Qırça) prepared by traditional methods. The greater the use of milk rich in fat (in the case of sheep's milk), the greater the final product with a delicious taste, reminiscent of the pungency of Roquefort. See ROQUEFORT. White cheese, obtained by coagulating milk with rennet, is then sprinkled with powdered salt on all sides, up to 10 percent of cheese weight (some producers keep the cheese in brine for nearly forty days to absorb salt well). This gives the salt required for the product and also removes the excessive moisture (the moisture reaches about 60 percent). About twenty-four hours after salting the cheese blocks must be rinsed and ground to small pieces, mixed with certain amounts of salt and packed in earthen pots using a metal pestle. These are sometimes coated with a lacquer layer. The use of glazed pots is also preferred because they retain the cheese moisture better. Their capacity ranges from 0.26 to 1.32 gallons (1–5 liters). The opening of the pots are finally closed by grapevine leaves and a sheet of paper or clean cloth, or both. This plug is sometimes covered with a clay layer. The prepared pots are stored underground into deep pits (about 16–20 feet [5–6 meters] below the ground surface) for four to six months. They are placed upside down in holes containing washed and wet sand, so that their bottom is barely flush.

Potting usually starts in late June to early July, when milk is abundant and white cheese is cheap. It is consumed as a table cheese after the maturation period. The mean composition of Kupa Paniri is 42.8 percent moisture, 22.3 percent fat, 43 percent protein, 0.95 percent calcium, and 0.69 percent phosphorus. The concentration of calcium, magnesium, phosphorus, and potassium in the cheese is affected by the method of salting, as dry salted cheeses show a higher level of the noted minerals than cheeses salted in brine. Microbiological studies have confirmed that Kupa Paniri is a safe product.

See also IRAN and POT CHEESES.

Karali, F., et al. "Influence of Salting Way on the Mineral Content of Ovine Halloumi Cheese." Paper presented at the IDF International Symposium on Sheep Goat and Other Non-Cow Milk, Athens, 17 May 2011.

Lame, H., et al. "Contribution à l'étude du 'fromage en pot' de l'Iran." *Le Lait* 53 (1973): 163–168.

Shafiei, Y. "Iranian Traditional Cheeses." Paper presented at the 1st Conference of Iranian Traditional Dairy Products, Khoy, Iran, 24 February 2013. In Persian.

Yahya Shafiei Bavil Oliaei

Kvargl

See CONE-SHAPED CHEESES.

A **label of origin** is an official seal that serves as a guarantee that the product bearing it was made in the geographical location named on the label. Although such labels can take many forms, the most formal and recognizable in the world of cheese are the European Union's PDO (protected designation of origin) and PGI (protected geographical indication) seals, which are described in greater detail in separate entries. See DESIGNATION OF ORIGIN and GEOGRAPHICAL INDICATION.

But alongside or instead of national PDO or PGI systems, origin labeling on food packaging or signage can also happen through truth-in-labeling and consumer protection laws. This means they can be regulated and are legally binding. National rules vary on which products can or must be labeled and how the labeling should be done. As of 2015 in the United States, for example, country-of-origin labeling is not required for dairy products, but manufacturers or vendors may label products voluntarily—on signage, on identification and pricing stickers, or on packaging. Canada, in contrast, does require that all imported dairy products, prepackaged or bulk, be labeled with their country of origin (and all cheese for export likewise must be identified as Canadian).

The global food chain being what it is today, however, the meaning of "origin" is not always as clear as it seems. In the United Kingdom, for instance, a food's origin is defined as "the place of last substantial change"—which could be a generic Cheddar made in Somerset with milk from anywhere in the world. Once again, specifying the origin of the milk in a cheese is an option open to producers who wish to put the locality of their production chain in evidence. In addition, national regulations may address potentially misleading elements on labels—the Italian flag, the Eiffel tower, a sombrero—that might lead consumers to think they are buying an imported product without actually "lying"; in the United Kingdom such products also bear a specific statement of the origin of the product to permit the consumer to distinguish between the connotation of the imagery and the actual place of production. US trademark law protects geographical place names—as well as words and symbols implying a place—as "certification marks," placing the onus of enforcement on the region that is misrepresented. Thus, it is up to the state of Idaho to file a complaint against misleading use of the outline of the state on sacks of potatoes from Montana, or up to France to defend the name "Roquefort" against an American-made "Roquefort-style" cheese.

Barham, Elizabeth, and Bertil Sylvander, eds. *Labels of Origin for Food: Local Development, Global Recognition.* Cambridge, Mass.: CABI, 2011.

Juliette Rogers

Label Rouge (Red Label) is a French seal guaranteeing that a food is grown, raised, and/or processed in a specific way, giving the food particular characteristics that are elaborated in its regulatory texts, to ensure that it is of superior quality. The types of criteria vary significantly according to product type, but for cheese they address how milk is handled in the dairy, the fabrication process, affinage, appearance, and flavor profile.

The label dates to 1960, and was first accorded to chicken raised in the Landes. Over the years, some

The Label Rouge is a French seal that guarantees that a food product is of superior quality to other similar products. For cheese, the criteria addresses how milk is handled in the dairy, the fabrication process, affinage, appearance, and flavor profile.

products, including Camembert de Normandie, have used the Label Rouge as a steppingstone on their way to subsequent appellation d'orgine contrôlée (AOC) status. See CAMEMBERT DE NORMANDIE and APPELLATION D'ORIGINE CONTRÔLÉE. Oversight of the Label Rouge is now assured by the Institut national de l'origine et de la qualité (INAO), the agency in charge of all food quality labels in France.

In 2014, the following cheese names bore the Label Rouge: mimolette vieille and extra-vieille, Brie au lait thermisé (thermized-milk Brie), fromage à raclette (raclette cheese), and emmental grand cru (which also bears a European protected geographical indication [PGI], and is the only one to be limited to a particular geographical zone).

Label Rouge. http://www.labelrouge.fr. Overview of all Label Rouges.
Produits Alimentaires de Qualité. http://www.paq.fr/galerie/filiere-laitiere-autres-produits. Specifically for dairy products.

Juliette Rogers

laboratories are used to conduct a wide variety of analytical tests that provide valuable information to the cheesemaker. Tests are performed on milk, curd, and cheese at a number of stages of production, from raw-milk intake through to testing the finished product before dispatch. Testing is used to provide verification of the safety and quality of the product, to generate data for farmer payment schemes, to monitor hygiene in the dairy, and to obtain information for on-package nutritional labeling.

Some larger dairies have their own on-site laboratories. This arrangement has a number of benefits

including being able to test the quality of the incoming raw milk before it is off-loaded from the tanker, being able to test samples and deliver results much more quickly, and having laboratory staff on hand with technical expertise and product knowledge. Smaller dairies and artisan cheesemakers, however, must enlist the services of a contract testing laboratory. These are often large food testing laboratories that offer a full range of analytical services, including microbiological, chemical, and nutritional analysis. Some offer more specialized testing including detection of histamines, pesticide residues, and allergens, as well as rapid pathogen testing methods and DNA-based identification techniques.

The design and layout of the laboratory must be carefully considered. There will be a sample receipt area, where incoming samples are logged, labeled, and stored at the necessary conditions before testing. The samples will then either be sent to the chemistry or microbiology laboratory, so it is important that the cheesemaker provides enough sample to perform all the tests required, and have some remaining in case of the need for repeat testing. The chemistry and microbiology laboratories are separated primarily because additional controls and practices are required for microbiological analysis. The majority of food microbiology laboratories should be biosafety level 2 laboratories, which means they have controls in place to handle biological agents with the potential to cause illness. These controls include restricted access, use of dedicated personal protective equipment, appropriate hand-washing facilities, decontamination procedures, the use of sterile equipment, and in some laboratories the use of microfiltered air or laminar air flow cabinets.

The modern dairy or food testing chemistry laboratory will use specialized equipment for milk compositional testing and a range of sensitive analytical instruments to test for vitamins, minerals, heavy metals, pesticides, and various other chemical agents. Some laboratories specialize in milk quality testing for farmer payment schemes. Samples of milk taken directly from the farm or milk tanker are delivered to the milk testing laboratory on a scheduled basis, and subjected to a range of analyses including bactoscan, somatic cell count, total viable count, antibiotics, percentage fat, and freezing point depression (a test for the addition of water to milk). The results from individual farms are tracked over time to give a rolling average of the milk quality, and this information is used to help determine farmer payments. The information obtained from raw milk quality testing is very useful to the cheesemaker, as raw milk quality can have a direct impact on the cheesemaking and quality of the finished product. Pathogen testing should also be included for milk that is used for raw-milk cheese manufacturing, particularly soft or mold-ripened raw-milk cheeses.

Laboratories are also used to test environmental swabs to monitor the general hygiene of the dairy or to look for specific pathogens such as *Listeria monocytogenes*. Water samples are also analyzed by laboratories for microbiological quality as well as chemical content.

It is important for the cheesemaker to be able to rely upon and trust laboratory results. A false negative result could mean a food safety issue goes unnoticed; a false positive result could lead to an unnecessary and costly product withdrawal or rejection of stock. Using a reputable, accredited laboratory helps to provide assurance that the laboratory adheres to a recognized standard and follows good laboratory practice. United Kingdom Accreditation Service (UKAS) in the UK, French Committee for Accreditation (COFRAC), and the American Association for Laboratory Accreditation (A2LA) in the United States are examples of national accreditation bodies that audit laboratories against ISO 17025, the internationally recognized laboratory accreditation standard.

Another way in which a laboratory can demonstrate competence is by taking part in proficiency testing schemes. The organizers of these schemes send the laboratories a food sample that has been contaminated with a particular microorganism or mixture of microorganisms unknown to the laboratory. The laboratory tests the sample and reports back its findings. The results from all the participating laboratories are statistically analyzed to determine the standard deviation, with each laboratory receiving a detailed report of their performance. Laboratory performance can also be checked by sending the same sample to multiple laboratories and comparing results. It is good practice for laboratories to conduct a number of quality control checks on their media and reagents, including using laboratory strains of the target organism to check the reliability of their testing methods. Competent laboratories also regularly conduct verification checks on their equipment, for example autoclaves, incubators, and pipettes.

The cheesemaker has many factors to consider when choosing a laboratory: reliability and competence, how samples are treated, whether the methods are fit for purpose (i.e., suitable for testing milk and cheese), how results are reported, the level of customer service, and of course the cost of testing. As with many things in life, it is often a case of you get what you pay for.

See also HYGIENE; *LISTERIA*; and PATHOGENS.

Chris Bell, Paul Neaves, and Anthony P. Williams. *Food Microbiology and Laboratory Practice.* Blackwell, 2005.
International Organization for Standardization. ISO/IEC 17025:2005. General requirements for the competence of testing and calibration laboratories. http://www.iso.org/iso/catalogue_detail.htm?csnumber=39883.
World Health Organization. *Laboratory Biosafety Manual.* Geneva: WHO, 2004.

Marissa Schwoch

The **Lacaune** is France's largest breed of milking sheep in sheer numbers and its most famous, thanks to Roquefort, which is made exclusively from the milk of its ewes. The Lacaune's native territory comprises the arid mountains and plateaus of the southern part of France's Massif Central. It is a hybrid of local pre-twentieth-century breeds, including Camarès, Causse, Larzac, and Lauraguaise, with infusions of such foreign breeds as Southdown, Merino, and Barbarin. Its name comes from the Lacaune canton, located about 34 miles (55 kilometers from Roquefort-sur-Soulzon, in the cheese's milk production zone, where 90 percent of the breed's population lives.

Lacaunes are hornless, 28–32 inches (70–80 centimeters) tall and covered with fine white hair; females weigh 143–165 pounds (65–75 kilograms) while the males are closer to 220 pounds (100 kilograms). The doe's lactation period lasts six to eight months between December and August. Known for their milking properties and adaptability, Lacaunes thrive in the often harsh conditions of their expansive, exposed grazing lands. Depending on the weather, they are put out to pasture daily beginning in March or April. When winter sets in again, they are kept in their sheltered pens for the duration. There are about 1.1 million head in France, around 800,000 of which are devoted to milk production and the rest to meat.

Since the 1960s Lacaune breeders have instituted artificial insemination, thorough documentation, and selective breeding to attain genetic improvements. These include increased milk production and quality (increased butterfat and protein content; decreased somatic cell count); udder morphology; and resistance to mastitis and scrapie, a fatal prion-borne illness. According to the breeding organization UPRA Lacaune (Unité pour la race Lacaune), the breed's milk yield has increased from 91 quarts (86 liters) in 150 days of milking (1965) to 278 quarts (263 liters) in 165 days (1995), and 299 quarts (283 liters) in 160 days (2004). Génétique Lacaune Export (GENELEX) has exported the breed to other European countries as well as to North Africa and Latin America. In addition to Roquefort, Lacaune milk is used to make Pérail, feta, the fresh cheese Brousse in France, Brin d'Amour and Fleur de Maquis in Corsica, and Azeitão and Serpa in Portugal. See FETA; BRIN D'AMOUR; AZEITÃO; and SERPA.

See also ROQUEFORT and SHEEP.

AgroParisTech. "UFR Genetics, Breeding and Reproduction: French Sheep Breeds." http://www.agroparistech.fr/svs/genere/especes/ovins/lacaulai.htm.
Babo, Daniel. *Races ovines et caprines françaises*. Paris: Éditions France Agricole, 2000. See pp. 39–42.
Collectif des Races des Massifs. "Ovin Lacaune." http://www.races-montagnes.com/fr/races/lacaune.php.
La Brebis Lacaune. http://brebis-lacaune.monsite-orange.fr.

David Gibbons

La Cave à Fromage

La Cave à Fromage is an innovative British cheese business offering more than two hundred British and European cheeses, mostly sourced directly from producers. Conceived in 1999 at the kitchen table of Amnon Paldi, a former consultant to Marks & Spencer, the business was soon joined by Frenchman Eric Charriaux, a former refrigerated-transport specialist. Although neither had a background in cheese, today the wholesale arm of La Cave à Fromage, Premier Cheese, supplies some 650 wholesale clients, including many household name chefs and top restaurants.

Premier Cheese's distribution is both traditional and modern. Vans are driven by knowledgeable salespeople. They effectively bring the market to the customer by transporting a selection of cheeses directly to the client's door, with no obligation to buy. There are also six depots dotted around England to assure that the cheeses are kept in optimum condition.

There are three La Cave à Fromage shops, two located in London and one in Brighton. Customers can sit and sample cheese from an extensive menu, along with bread and wine, in a convivial atmosphere akin to a bistro. The selection includes around twenty unique cheeses that owner Amnon Paldi either commissions especially from producers or else adapts in house. These include The Boxer, a creamy English cow's milk cheese matured in beer, so named because of its "punchy" flavors, and a Brillat-Savarin into whose center is inserted a delicate layer of truffles. See BRILLAT-SAVARIN.

In 2011 Paldi founded the annual Cheese Makers Market, which takes place in Beaconsfield, in England, where he lives. Some sixty producers make the trip from around the United Kingdom and continental Europe to introduce and sell their cheeses directly to the public.

See also UNITED KINGDOM.

Cheese Makers Market. http://www.cheesemakersmarket.com.
La Cave à Fromage. http://www.la-cave.co.uk.

Anastasia Edwards

Lactalis

Lactalis is the world's largest dairy group, based in Laval, France, with an annual turnover of 16 billion euros. It is owned by its founding family. As of 2014 it had two hundred manufacturing sites in thirty-seven countries worldwide, processing 15 billion quarts (14.6 billion liters) of milk annually.

The company took the name Lactalis in 1999, but was originally known as Société Laitière de Laval A. Besnier et Cie., founded in 1935 by André Besnier as a small Camembert-maker. By the time his son Michel took over in 1955, the company had fifty employees and processed 8 million quarts (7 million liters) of milk per year. Under Michel Besnier's leadership, then accelerating when his son Emmanuel took over in 2000, the company embarked upon an aggressive acquisition strategy that gradually expanded their product line to a full range of dairy products across France and then abroad—Italy and the United States at first, then moving into Eastern Europe, the Middle East, and Asia.

Lactalis is particularly known for its collection of AOC (appellation d'origine contrôlée) cheeses. These efforts were notable in their home region, with the gradual acquisition of several Camembert brands beginning in the late 1970s (including

LePetit, Vallée, Jort, Moulin de Carel, and Lanquetôt), which made them responsible for the overwhelming majority of AOC Camembert de Normandie production until they withdrew all but their upscale brands from the AOC in 2008. See CAMEMBERT DE NORMANDIE. By 1996 the company owned dairies manufacturing twenty-five different French AOC cheeses, and has since acquired significant market shares of non-French appellation d'origine protegée (AOP) cheeses, including Manchego, Gorgonzola. See MANCHEGO and GORGONZOLA. They have tried to use their weight to influence AOC regulations in favor of mass production and distribution, with mixed results: if their withdrawal from AOC Camembert was partly a failed tactic for eliminating its raw-milk requirement, they were a key player in allowing machine molding of AOC Camembert (instead of manual). At the EU level, they fought Greece's application for AOP recognition for feta, because Lactalis is a major producer of French-made feta-style cheese. When feta got the AOP, the group transitioned to using the brand name Salakis. See FETA.

In 2014 Lactalis owned the following companies or brands of cheeses (non-exhaustive) that are made or sold in the following countries (though some brands are also exported). In France: Président, Bridel, Rondélé, Société, Valmont, Pochat, Lou Perac, Beulait, and Chaussé aux Moines; in Italy: Locatelli, Invernizzi, Cardemartori, Galbani, and Parmalat (Lactalis owns a controlling share of over 80 percent); in the United States: Sorrento, Mozzarella Fresca, Precious, Istara, and Valbreso; in Great Britain: McLelland, Seriously Strong Cheddar, Galloway Cheddar, Orkney Cheddar, Lubborn Creamery, and Rachel's; and in Australia: Lemnos, Jindi, and Harvey Fresh.

Besnier, Emmanuel. *Lactalis, une histoire du lait, 1933–2008.* Lyon, France: Histoire d'entreprises, 2010.

Juliette Rogers

lactation is the collective process of secretion and removal of milk from the mammary gland. Milk is produced by specialized cells (mammary epithelial cells) that are organized within the microscopic secretory structures of the gland; these structures are called alveoli. The alveoli can be pictured as hollow balls or sacs lined by a single layer of mammary epithelial cells. Milk is secreted by the mammary epithelial cells and accumulates in the central space or lumen of the alveoli, in essence filling the sacs. Each alveolar lumen is continuous with the lumen of a single microscopic duct, and milk drains from the alveoli into these ducts (one might picture the alveolus as a globe-shaped glass bottle with a long neck). The individual ducts arising from the alveoli coalesce into increasingly larger ducts that eventually terminate at the nipple or teat. Alternatively, starting at the teat or nipple and moving into the gland, the mammary ductal structure is often described as being analogous to a tree, with a single large duct (the trunk) branching (or arborizing) into many smaller ductules, which continue to arborize and finally terminate at each alveolus. The alveoli and ducts are surrounded by the supporting tissues of the mammary gland, including an extensive network of blood vessels (mammary arteries, veins, and capillaries). Milk secreted by the mammary epithelial cells accumulates in the alveoli and passively fills the ductules and ducts.

The mammary gland is an epithelial gland, a secretory tissue derived from the same embryonic tissues that give rise to the skin. The presence of mammary glands (and thus the ability to lactate) is one of four key characteristics that distinguish mammals from other classes of vertebrate animals such as amphibians, fish, birds, and reptiles. All female mammals are able to nurse their young with mammary gland secretions. The term "mammal" is derived from the Latin *mamma*, meaning teat or udder. To lactate is to secrete or produce milk, and the word "lactate" is derived from the Latin *lac*, meaning milk. Bats lactate, seals and whales lactate, kangaroos, wallabies, and other marsupials lactate, and of course, the domestic dairy species lactate. There is significant variation among mammals in the number and location of mammary glands and in the composition of mammary secretions. For example, the udder of the cow is composed of four mammary glands and is located in the inguinal region of the body, between the hind legs. The udder of sheep and goats has two glands also located in the inguinal region, while pigs have eighteen mammary glands distributed from the chest, or thoracic region, across the abdomen and into the inguinal region. Elephants, like primates, have only two mammary glands, located in the thoracic region. Yet, the basic structure and function of the mammary gland is common to all placental mammals.

Lactation is a tightly regulated secretory process influenced by circulating hormones. Both local and systemic factors influence mammary gland development and lactation. During pregnancy, the mammary epithelial cells and the alveoli increase in number and differentiate to become capable of milk secretion, yet milk secretion is kept in check by the balance of hormones associated with pregnancy. At parturition, or delivery, this balance shifts and milk secretion is initiated. This transition of the mammary gland to the secretory state is called lactogenesis. Milk secretion and milk removal are separate processes. Milk removal is required for the continued secretion by the mammary epithelial cells; if milk is not removed from the gland, the epithelial cells will stop secreting. In other words, milk removal promotes continued mammary secretion. Increasing the frequency of milk removal in early lactation positively affects the continued increase in the number and function of the mammary epithelial cells. Milk ejection from the alveoli is an additional process. The act of nursing is the process of milk ejection, which is more commonly described as milk letdown. Milk is ejected from the alveoli and adjacent ducts by the contraction of myoepithelial cells, specialized cells that surround the alveoli and adjacent ducts. These cells respond to oxytocin by contracting and essentially squeezing milk out of the alveolus. Oxytocin is a hormone released into the blood from the posterior pituitary gland. The signal to release oxytocin originates from the nervous system. When the teat skin is stimulated by touch or pressure, nerve impulses are sent from skin receptors to the hypothalamus in the brain. These impulses stimulate the release of oxytocin into the blood. This pulse of oxytocin quickly circulates to the mammary gland to stimulate myoepithelial cell contraction. As most dairy farmers and mothers can tell you, manual stimulation of the teat or nipple is not always required for milk ejection or letdown. Oxytocin release can become a conditioned reflex, stimulated by auditory or visual clues. For example the sound of milking machines or music playing in a milking parlor can stimulate some cows to let down milk, or the sound of her crying baby can stimulate milk letdown in a nursing mother.

In dairy production systems, farmers often keep track of the lactation number as a representation of an animal's approximate age. This is especially true for cattle, and farmers will describe cows being in their first, second, or third (etc.) lactation, reflecting the number of times a cow has given birth. Dairy farmers will often describe a cow that has had its first calf, and thus is in its first lactation, as a "first-lactation heifer." This might be confusing because a

heifer is a young cow that has never had a calf, and so this first-lactation cow is not really a heifer; but farmers use the term "first-lactation heifer" to distinguish this age group from the older cows because these young mothers often have special needs compared to the older cows.

"Stage of lactation" is another bit of jargon used in the dairy industry. Stage of lactation refers to the approximate number of days an animal has been lactating. Dairy farmers will refer to animals in early, mid, or late lactation; there are no specific days since birth defining these stages; but generally, for dairy cows, early lactation can be defined as the first 100 days after calving, and late lactation as the period starting 270 to 290 days after calving. Peak lactation is the time after giving birth when milk production is highest. In dairy cattle this often occurs between 60 and 90 days after calving. The lactation curve is a graphic representation of milk production over time, often with the amount of milk produced measured in weight or volume on the y axis plotted against time in days, weeks, or months on the x axis. The same concepts (lactation number, stage of lactation, peak lactation, and lactation curve) can be applied to any mammalian species, although the length of lactation differs among species.

When studying lactation, biologists will refer to different lactation strategies. The term "lactation strategy" is often used to describe the behavioral, physiological, and ecological parameters influencing factors such as the duration of lactation, the timing of feeding, and the amount of time spent nursing the young. The lactation strategy of a particular species is intertwined with the reproductive strategy because, ultimately, lactation is the physiological process that allows mammals to invest in the continued growth and development of their young after birth.

See also BREEDING AND GENETICS; MILK; and RUMINANTS.

Akers, R. M. *Lactation and the Mammary Gland*. Ames: Iowa State University Press, 2002.
Capuco, A. V., and R. M. Akers. 2009. "The Origin and Evolution of Lactation." *Journal of Biology* 8 (2009): 37.
Hurley, Walter L. Lactation Biology website. University of Illinois, Urbana-Champaign. http://ansci.illinois.edu/static/ansc438/index.html.
Neville, Margaret C. "Milk Secretion: An Overview." Health e-Learning. https://www.health-e-learning.com/articles/Neville_MILK_SECRETION_2008.pdf.

John Barlow

lactic acid is a weak water-soluble carboxylic acid with the chemical formula $CH_3CH(OH)COOH$, molecular mass of 90.08 g mol^{-1}, and pK_a of 3.86. Lactic acid can exist as two optical isomers, $(+)$ or (S) and its mirror image $(-)$ or (R), commonly referred to as L- and D-isomers, respectively.

In the context of cheese, lactic acid is of most importance as the major metabolic end-product of lactose metabolism by lactic acid bacteria (LAB). Different species of LAB produce L, D, or DL-lactate either homofermentatively, or together with other metabolic products (heterofermentatively).

Lactic acid has a sharp, sour taste and contributes directly to the flavor of cheese and fermented milks. Together with the buffering capacity of cheese curd and other factors (e.g., production of bases during ripening), the amount of lactic acid produced by the starter determines cheese pH. Cheese pH in turn influences activity and retention of coagulant in the curd, gel strength, syneresis (and hence moisture), cheese microflora, texture, and flavor. See PH MEASUREMENT.

Lactic curds have a texture similar to firmly set yogurt, due to the action of lactic acid on the casein proteins in the milk. Lactic curds are more permeable than rennet (enzymatic) curds and therefore drain freely when scooped into molds. © BRONWEN PERCIVAL

During the ripening of hard cheeses such as Cheddar, small white crystals of calcium lactate pentahydrate form. Although connoisseurs of cheese often desire these crystals as being indicative of strong-flavored cheese, they are not desired by retailers as consumers often confuse them with mold or foreign bodies. See CRYSTAL.

Also, during ripening, L-lactate can be converted to D-lactate by oxidation to pyruvate and followed by reduction to D-lactate by D-lactate dehydrogenase, often of the nonstarter microflora. Although this has no flavor significance, DL-lactate has been associated with increased formation of calcium lactate crystals. Lactate is also metabolized during ripening of Swiss-type cheese to products including CO_2, which forms the eyes, and lactate is oxidatively metabolized during the ripening of mold-ripened cheese. See CARBON DIOXIDE and EYES.

See also LACTIC ACID BACTERIA.

McSweeney, P. L. H., and P. F. Fox. "Metabolism of Residual Lactose and of Lactate and Citrate." In *Cheese: Chemistry, Physics, and Microbiology*, 3d ed., Vol. 1: *General Aspects*, edited by P. F. Fox, P. L. H. McSweeney, T. M. Cogan, et al., pp. 361–371. Amsterdam: Elsevier Applied Science, 2004.

Parente, E., and T. M. Cogan. "Starter Cultures: General Aspects." In *Cheese: Chemistry, Physics, and Microbiology*, 3d ed., Vol. 1: *General Aspects*, edited by P. F. Fox, P. L. H. McSweeney, T. M. Cogan, et al., pp. 123–147. Amsterdam: Elsevier Applied Science, 2004.

P. L. H. McSweeney

lactic acid bacteria are a cluster of microorganisms grouped primarily on functional traits—most notably their ability to produce lactic acid as a major end product during growth from carbohydrates in food substrates. For centuries, mankind has harnessed this talent of lactic acid bacteria to transform raw foods into more stable, and often more desirable and nutritious, fermented foods. Other defining characteristics of lactic acid bacteria include a Gram-positive designation, absence of spore formation, a nonrespiring rod or coccus shape, absence of catalase, and being anaerobic but aerotolerant. The lactic acid bacteria are considered safe for use in foods, as indicated by the European Food Safety Authority and their Qualified Presumption of Safety program.

There is not full agreement on which microbes should belong to this category. Lactic acid bacteria are not the only bacteria to produce lactic acid, but in general the term lactic acid bacteria is reserved for the genera *Lactobacillus, Lactococcus, Leuconostoc, Pediococcus,* and *Streptococcus* (primarily the *thermophilus* species). *Bifidobacterium* is often considered along with lactic acid bacteria, due to its common use along with *Lactobacillus* as a probiotic, but since it is not used in food fermentations it is not strictly speaking a member of the lactic acid bacteria. Other genera represented in the lactic acid bacteria are *Carnobacterium, Enterococcus, Oenococcus,* and *Weissella.*

Two main routes of carbohydrate utilization—homolactic and heterolactic—are seen in lactic acid bacteria (Axelsson, 1998). Homolactic fermentation ultimately converts one molecule of glucose into two molecules of lactic acid. Heterolactic fermentation typically breaks down glucose into ethanol, carbon dioxide, and lactic acid; this fermentation process is also known as the phosphoketolase pathway. Different growth conditions and substrates can influence end-product formation. Lactic acid bacteria are mostly constrained to nutrient-rich environments, having few biosynthetic abilities of their own. Most lactic acid bacteria either live freely or in neutral or beneficial relationships with animal hosts. Some genera featuring lactic acid bacteria might also contain species that are pathogens or opportunistic pathogens, including, for example, some species of the *Streptococcus* genus. Since lactic acid bacteria are considered safe for use in foods, these pathogenic species are not considered lactic acid bacteria.

Lactic acid fermentations as a means of food preservation can be used efficiently and safely with little infrastructure such as cold chains and industrial-scale processing. Carried out in developing countries, such fermentations are typically conducted under non-sterile conditions, resulting in a mixed microbiological composition of the final product. Lactic acid bacterial fermentation is especially useful in these conditions, as the lactic acid and other byproducts help prevent or delay food spoilage that would normally occur rapidly without refrigeration or sterile packaging.

A diverse and wonderful array of products—across many regions of the world—owe their existence to lactic acid bacteria fermentations (e.g., fermented milks, yogurts, hundreds of varieties of cheeses, sausages, vegetables, breads). Raw materials of both plant and animal origin are used—cereals, starchy roots and stems, leafy vegetables, beans, milk, meat, and fish.

Researchers now speculate that fermented foods may in fact be an important dietary component. For example, exposure to microbes at an early age—even in utero—is likely essential for proper development of the immune system. Such studies drive home the potential value of fermented foods, especially ones where a diverse, viable microbial population is part of the food.

See also LACTIC ACID; *LACTOBACILLUS*; and *LACTOCOCCUS LACTIS*.

Axelsson, L. "Lactic Acid Bacteria: Classification and Physiology." In *Lactic Acid Bacteria: Microbiology and Functional Aspects,* 2d ed., edited by Seppo Salminen and Atte von Wright, pp. 1–72. New York: Marcel Dekker, 1998.

European Food Safety Authority. "Qualified Presumption of Safety (QPS)." http://www.efsa .europa.eu/en/topics/topic/qps.

Munyaka, P. M., E. Khafipour, and J. E. Ghia. "External Influence of Early Childhood Establishment of Gut Microbiota and Subsequent Health Implications." *Frontiers in Pediatrics* 2 (October 2014): 109.

Sanders M. E., I. Lenoir-Wijnkoop, S. Salminen, et al. "Probiotics and Prebiotics: Prospects for Public Health and Nutritional Recommendations." *Annals of the New York Academy of Sciences* 1309, no. 1 (February 2014): 19–29.

Alexandra O. K. Mannerings and Mary Ellen Sanders

Lactobacillus is a prominent genus of the group lactic acid bacteria, with over two hundred recognized species. They are Gram-positive, non-spore-forming, facultative anaerobic or microaerophilic, catalase negative, rod-shaped bacteria. Like other lactic acid bacteria, they produce lactic acid as a byproduct of carbohydrate fermentation, a trait that mankind for millennia has harnessed for food production. *Lactobacillus* species are also common colonizers of plants, as well as mammalian gastrointestinal tracts, oral cavities, and vaginal tracts.

The importance of this genus for humans is represented by the vast array of food types for which its traits have been exploited. Sauerkraut, pickles, sourdough bread, sausage, cocoa, kimchi, wine, kefir, yogurt, and of course many cheeses all rely on various species and strains of lactobacilli, and the acid they produce, for their unique fermentation processes.

While a few species of lactobacilli can cause food spoilage, the majority are harmless or even directly beneficial to their hosts or to mankind. Of the species important to cheesemaking, *Lactobacillus delbrueckii* ssp. *bulgaricus* is used in combination with *Streptococcus thermophilus* as a starter culture for mozzarella cheese manufacture. *Lactobacillus helveticus* is used as a starter culture in the manufacture of Swiss-style and Italian Grana cheeses, such as Gruyère, Emmentaler, Grana Padano, and Parmigiano Reggiano. The name *helveticus* derives from the Latin *Helvetia*, which means "Switzerland." See STARTER CULTURES.

Important non-starter lactobacilli include *Lactobacillus brevis*, *L. buchneri*, *L. casei*, *L. curvatus*, *L. farciminis*, *L. fermentum*, *L. paracasei*, *L. pentosus*, *L. plantarum*, and *L. rhamnosus*. Some non-starter lactobacilli play major roles in cheese ripening, while others cause quality problems, such as slit defect in Cheddar cheese. See NON-STARTER LACTIC ACID BACTERIA.

Lactobacilli also produce a range of bacteriocins—small antibacterial proteins—that can specifically inhibit food spoilage or pathogenic bacteria. But perhaps the best-known health benefits of *Lactobacillus* come from their role as probiotics. See BACTERIOCINS. A probiotic is a live microorganism that, when administered in adequate amounts, confers a health benefit on the host. The best studied probiotic across the different bacterial genera is a *Lactobacillus* strain: *Lactobacillus rhamnosus* GG. Other key probiotic species of *Lactobacillus* include *reuteri*, *acidophilus*, *casei*, *paracasei*, *fermentum*, and *salivarius*.

An array of healthful properties is associated with probiotic *Lactobacillus* strains. Although the concept of probiotics is decades old, well-controlled, high quality studies that test probiotic health effects are more recent. In most cases probiotic benefits are considered to be attributable only to the specific strain or strain combination that was studied. However the extent of accumulated data convinced a panel of experts that some well-studied species of *Lactobacillus* and *Bifidobacterium* can be considered healthful (primarily for digestive benefits), even without strain-specific studies.

Probiotics have been shown to improve digestion of lactose in lactose maldigesters, reduce the incidence or duration of common respiratory tract infections, reduce low density lipoproteins in hypercholesteremic subjects, reduce vaginal tract infections, and improve numerous GI conditions, such as treat acute diarrhea, prevent antibiotic-associated diarrhea, and help manage irritable bowel symptoms. Other benefits are currently under investigation, such as the impact of probiotics on brain function, metabolic syndrome (including obesity and insulin resistance), and skin.

Research focused on elucidating the role of colonizing microbiota on human health and development has provided a valuable context for understanding how exogenously applied microorganisms (including *Lactobacillus* probiotics) might benefit health. Through complicated interactions of bacteria, bacterial surface molecules and secreted bacterial products with human immune and hormonal sensing molecules and cells, bacterial colonization plays an important role in epithelial cell development and immune system development, among others. Although it is not possible to define a single "healthy microbiota" set, abnormal patterns associated with suboptimal health (obesity) or disease (diabetes, allergy) are known. Probiotics offer a strategy to manipulate the gut microbiota to improve the outcomes of bacterial-human interactions.

No other genus can claim to benefit humans in as many ways as *Lactobacillus*. In fact, Christopher Lloyd, author of *What on Earth Evolved*, considers *Lactobacillus* to be the fifth most influential species that has most changed life on Earth. Although future research on colonizing microbiota will likely uncover novel microbes with unique abilities to impact human health, the safety of lactobacilli is reinforced through centuries of consuming many *Lactobacillus* species in high numbers in delicious and nutritious fermented foods. Such is the remarkable partnership between *Lactobacillus* and humans.

See also LACTIC ACID BACTERIA.

Bäckhed, F., et al. "Defining a Healthy Human Gut Microbiome: Current Concepts, Future Directions, and Clinical Applications." *Cell Host Microbe* 12, no. 5 (13 November 2012): 611–622.

Beresford, T. P., et al. "Recent Advances in Cheese Microbiology." *International Dairy Journal* 11, nos. 4–7 (2001): 259–274.

Hill, C., et al. "Expert Consensus Document. The International Scientific Association for Probiotics and Prebiotics Consensus Statement on the Scope and Appropriate Use of the Term Probiotic." *National Review of Gastroenterological Hepatology* 8 (11 August 2014): 506–514.

International Scientific Association for Probiotics and Prebiotics. http://www.isappscience.org.

List of Prokaryotic Names with Standing in Nomenclature. http://www.bacterio.net.

Ritchie, M. L., and T. N. Romanuk. "A meta-analysis of Probiotic Efficacy for Gastrointestinal Diseases." *PLoS One* 7, no. 4 (2012): 34938.

US Probiotics. http://www.usprobiotics.org.

Mary Ellen Sanders and Alexandra O.K. Mannerings

Lactococcus lactis subsp. *cremoris*

Lactococcus lactis subsp. *cremoris* is one of the most frequently used bacteria in the manufacture of cheese. It is often referred to as a primary starter, that is, it is used to ferment lactose to lactic acid during the manufacture of cheese. In contrast a secondary starter consists of microorganisms added to produce a specific flavor component in cheese and are not added to ferment lactose although many are capable of doing so. See STARTER CULTURES and RIPENING CULTURES.

Lactococcus (Lc.) lactis subsp. *cremoris* and its sibling *Lc. lactis* subsp. *lactis* are the only two subspecies of *Lc. lactis* currently used in the dairy industry. Together they are referred to simply as mesophiles or mesophilic starters because their optimum temperature for growth and lactose fermentation is around 86–90°F (30–32°C). Consequently *Lc. lactis* subsp. *cremoris* strains are used in cheeses where the cook or scalding temperatures do not exceed 102°F (39°C). These strains are traditionally used in cheeses that require more moderate temperatures during manufacture, such as Cheddar, Colby, brick, Limburger, blue, and Gouda cheeses.

Originally isolated from fermented cream butter and later from fermented milks and cheeses, *Lc. lactis* subsp. *cremoris* was called *Streptococcus cremoris* before 1985. The name was changed to segregate it from other *Streptococcus* species that were potential human pathogens. Although strains of lactococci are isolated from plant material, which is considered the host environment, these strains are not able to grow well in milk. Strains we use today evolved from these strains and have acquired the ability to thrive in milk by being able to ferment lactose and utilize casein.

Lc. lactis subsp. *cremoris* is a Gram-positive, non-spore-forming, nonmotile, round-to-ovoid-shaped bacterium that generally grows in pairs or short chains and ferments lactose to produce L (+)-lactic acid as the principle metabolic end product. This trait is called homofermentative metabolism. It does not produce carbon dioxide and thus it is not responsible for the formation of splits in cheese. *Lc. lactis* subsp. *cremoris* is very weakly lipolytic and it will never cause rancidity nor fruity flavors in cheese. It can grow in the presence of oxygen but can be inhibited by high oxygen content as it produces hydrogen peroxide. This ability is exploited for the inhibition of spoilage bacteria during prolonged storage of refrigerated raw milk. In this technique called cold milk inoculation, raw milk is inoculated with *Lactococcus lactis*. The culture produces hydrogen peroxide in milk (there are sufficient levels of oxygen in milk to enable this reaction). Raw milk naturally contains lactoperoxidase, an enzyme that in the presence of thiocyanate, also a native substance in milk, and hydrogen peroxide (formed by the added lactococci) can produce substances that are bacteriocidal and bacteriostatic to pathogenic and spoilage bacteria, particularly the bacteria capable of growing at refrigeration temperatures (*Pseudomonas* species in particular).

Lc. lactis subsp. *cremoris* is weakly proteolytic compared to yeasts, molds, and lactobacillus starter cultures. However it has very active peptidases, which are enzymes that metabolize or break down peptides produced from the action of proteolytic enzymes such as rennet used in cheesemaking. It is this trait that is of major interest to technologists and cheesemakers as this ability is extremely important to the eventual development of flavor in cheese.

The two subspecies of *Lactococcus lactis* were often separated based on three phenotypic differences. *Lc. lactis* subsp. *cremoris* cannot produce ammonia from arginine, cannot grow if the salt in moisture content of cheese is over 4 percent, and cannot grow at 104°F (40°C). However they are now more accurately separated based on a combination of phenotypic and genotypic profiles. Genetic diversity (and phenotypic diversity) between subspecies of *Lactococcus lactis* as well as between strains of each subspecies can be so overlapping that many cheese technologists (the people who use them commercially) no longer speak in terms of what subspecies to use but rather make recommendations based on what phenotypic or metabolic characteristics of the starter is desired. See TAXONOMY and PHENOTYPIC VARIABILITY.

Lc. lactis subsp. *cremoris* appear to be more prone to bacteriophage infection than *Lc. lactis* subsp. *lactis*. Bacteriophage (commonly referred to as phage) are viruses that kill bacteria. Reduction or secession of acidification (commonly called "dead vats") is generally a sign of a phage infection. Although bacteriophage are generally thought of as species and even strain specific, bacteriophage that attack strains of *Lc. lactis* subsp. *lactis* can also infect strains of *Lc. lactis* subsp. *cremoris*. See BACTERIOPHAGES.

All bacteria have one chromosome but all strains of *Lc. lactis* subsp. *cremoris* contain at least four to six plasmids. Plasmids are self-replicating, double-stranded circular DNA molecules found in bacteria that are separate genetic material from the chromosome. They are transferred from one cell to another by conjugation. Conjugation is the transfer of plasmids between a donor bacterial cell and a recipient cell by direct cell-to-cell contact. Plasmids encode for several important characteristics including the ability to ferment lactose, breakdown protein, and even to resist phage infections. It is the natural acquisition of plasmids by *Lc. lactis* subsp. *cremoris* that has allowed this species to thrive in milk. Conjugation is used to produce strains of *Lc. lactis* subsp. *cremoris* with superior phage resistance. Because it is a natural transfer of genetic material naturally found in the donor cell the resultant new strain is not considered a genetically modified organism (GMO). See GENETICALLY MODIFIED ORGANISM.

See also LACTIC ACID BACTERIA.

Kindstedt, P. "Starter Culture: The Heart of Cheesemaking." In *American Farmstead Cheese*, edited by P. Kindstedt, pp. 57–78. White River Junction, Vt.: Chelsea Green, 2005.
Mullan, W. M. A. "Lactic Streptococci Now Classified As Lactococci." *Dairy Science and Food Technology*, 2011. http://www.dairyscience.info/index.php/cheese-starters/201-lactic-streptococci.html.

Mark E. Johnson

Lactography

Lactography is a small cheese shop co-owned by siblings Carlos Yescas and Georgina Yescas Angeles Trujano. It is located in the Mercado Roma, a gourmet food hall in the bohemian Colonia Roma Norte neighborhood of Mexico City. Lactography is the first cheese shop in Mexico City to sell only cheese produced in Mexico. It carries about sixty regional cheese varieties that fall into three categories: popular traditional farmstead style cheeses, such as panela, queso Oaxaca (or quesillo de hebra as it is known in Mexico), and queso Cotija; obscure cheeses, such as bola de Ocosingo and poro de Balancan; and new and innovative cheeses, such as Sierra Encantada al Aguacate, a fresh goat cheese wrapped in avocado leaves. In addition to selling cheese in the shop, Lactography has a robust direct wholesale business and supplies several of Mexico City's top restaurants.

The Yescas siblings have encouraged their artisanal cheesemakers to experiment with new styles and techniques. Their efforts have been rewarded at the international World Cheese Awards. In 2011 their queso de oveja semi-maduro, an Idiazabal-like raw sheep's milk cheese made by Rancho San Josemaria, won a bronze medal. In 2014 Sierra Encantada al Aguacate won Best New Cheese. In addition to submitting cheeses to competitions, Carlos has been an active judge, serving as one of the fourteen supreme judges for the World Cheese Awards, and attaining the degrees of International Supreme Judge of the Guild of Fine Foods of England and Judge and Guard (Garde et Jure) of the Guilde Internationale des Fromagers of France. Lactography is the only store in Latin America recognized by the Guilde Internationale de Fromagers.

Georgina Yescas manages the day-to-day operation of Lactography and sources new cheeses. Both Carlos and Georgina are strongly involved in educating producers, retailers, and consumers about artisan Mexican cheese. They teach classes at Lactography and lead tastings specializing in pairing traditional Mexican cheese with wine, beer, spirits, teas, and chocolate. The siblings plan to expand their selection to the United States.

See also MEXICO.

Fletcher, Janet. "Mexico's Ambassador of Cheese." *Planet Cheese*, 19 January 2016. http://www.janetfletcher.com/blog/2016/1/16/mexicos-ambassador-of-cheese.
"Quesos Artesanales Mexicanos." Lactography website. http://www.lactography.com/nosotros.
Tellez, Lesley. "Carlos Yescas on the Myths about Mexican Cheese." *The Mija Chronicles*, 24 May 2012. http://www.themijachronicles.com/2012/05/carlos-yescas-on-the-myths-about-mexican-cheese/.

Sara Rodgers

lactose intolerance

lactose intolerance occurs when individuals experience gastrointestinal symptoms following consumption of lactose, the sugar found in milk and some dairy products. Symptoms include nausea, vomiting, diarrhea, gas, and bloating, which result from bacterial fermentation of undigested lactose in the colon. These symptoms disappear when lactose is eliminated from the diet. Lactose intolerance most frequently results from the absence, or very low levels of activity of the digestive enzyme lactase in the small intestine—lactase is necessary to break down lactose into its component sugars glucose and galactose. This is referred to as primary lactose intolerance. Secondary lactose intolerance can stem from pathologies of the small intestine such as gastrointestinal infections or inflammatory bowel diseases that interfere with lactose digestion. Lactose intolerance is typically diagnosed with a breath hydrogen test after lactose ingestion. Higher concentrations of breath hydrogen are found when undigested lactose is present in the colon. A blood glucose test can also be done after a lactose challenge; if lactose is mostly undigested, blood glucose levels should not change.

Lactose intolerance is very rare in infants and young children, and then increases in prevalence among older children and adults, and correlates with changes in the expression of the lactase enzyme across the lifespan. The typical age pattern of lactase activity for mammals is illustrated by the solid line in Figure 1. Note that the decline in lactase occurs around the time of weaning, when milk ceases to be a part of the diet, and most likely represents the adaptive down regulation of lactase when its lactose substrate is no longer consumed. This down regulation is under genetic control and cannot be modified by continued milk consumption; it is referred to as "lactase impersistence." This pattern is also typical of most human populations, but among some, lactase activity remains high throughout life (Figure 1, dotted line). This is referred to as "lactase persistence."

The genetic mutations underlying lactase persistence have been identified in a regulatory area close to the lactase gene in the human genome. These are found in high frequencies (80–90 percent) in northern Europeans, pastoralists of east and west Africa, Central Asian pastoralist populations, and those living in the northwestern region of the South Asia subcontinent. All of these populations share a long history of keeping dairy animals and using their milk. Among other populations, especially East and Southeast Asians, nonpastoralist sub-Saharan Africans, and Native Americans and Australians and those in Oceania, lactase impersistence rates approach 100 percent. The reasons why lactase persistence is so common among dairying populations are undoubtedly related to extensive reliance on dairy products, but specific advantages of those mutations have not been identified. Hypotheses proposed include general nutritional advantages of milk drinking, access to a rich source of calcium, or milk's contributions to child growth. Others are specific to those living in particular regions—at high latitude the lactose in milk may be useful as a substitute for Vitamin D, which may be limited when its synthesis is reduced by lack of exposure to sufficient UVB light for much of the year. In arid regions, milk may be an important source of hydration; milk sugar may be important for pastoralist populations subsisting primarily on animal products.

It is important to note that there is considerable individual variation in lactose intolerance symptomatology among individuals who are lactase impersistent, and thus lactase impersistence and lactose intolerance rates are not perfectly correlated. Some report few or no symptoms after a lactose challenge. The reasons for this are poorly understood, but may be related to colon bacterial composition. On the other hand, some individuals who report symptoms of lactose intolerance are in fact lactase persistent, indicating that lactose intolerance stems from a secondary cause.

Lactose is only found in milk and its concentration varies across mammalian milks. Cow's, goat's, and sheep's milk contain about 12 grams of lactose/ 1 cup (5 grams/100 milliliters), while human milk is similar to that of other primates in that it is at the high end of the spectrum 17 grams/cup (7 grams/

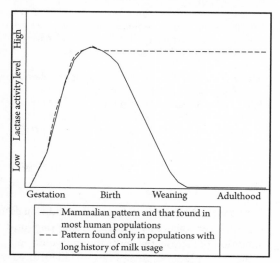

Figure 1: Lactase activity across the lifespan

100 milliliters). Some mammalian milks, such as those from many species of seals, contain no lactose, and those species also produce little to no lactase during infancy. Milk processing techniques can significantly alter the quantity of lactose in dairy products. Simply heating milk does not result in any changes, but in yogurt production, lactophilic bacteria convert lactose to lactic acid in the fermentation process. Separation of milk into solid and liquid components (curds and whey) in cheesemaking leaves lactose in the whey component, as it is water-soluble. Thus cheese contains variable amounts of lactose, with higher quantities in fresher, softer cheeses that contain more whey and only trace amounts in hard, dry cheeses such as Parmigiano Reggiano. As a result, individuals with lactose intolerance may experience fewer symptoms when they consume yogurt or cheese compared to fresh milk. Butter contains little or no lactose.

Consumption of milk or other dairy products historically was much more common among those relatively few populations that had high rates of lactase persistence, but starting in the late twentieth century this practice spread rapidly along with consumption of other animal source foods. As a result, populations that previously did not have high rates of lactose intolerance because they consumed scant dairy products are expected to report increasing incidence; fermented milk products are likely to be better tolerated.

See also DAIRY ALLERGY and MILK.

Suchy, F. J., P. M. Brannon, T. O. Carpenter, et al. "NIH Consensus Development Conference Statement: Lactose Intolerance and Health." NIH Consensus State-of-the-Science Statements 27 (2010): 1–27. http://consensus.nih.gov/2010/lactosestatement.htm.
Wiley, Andrea S. Re-imagining Milk: Cultural and Biological Perspectives. 2d ed. New York: Routledge, 2016.

Andrea S. Wiley

A ladle is used in cheesemaking to separate curds from whey or to remove curds and whey from the vat. Ladles can be made of wood, but the most commonly used ladles are made of stainless steel because it is easier to clean and sterilize. Ladles come in two forms. The first, a dipper, has a wide, deep bowl. A dipper is similar in size and shape to any large kitchen ladle one might use to serve a soup or a stew. It typically holds up to a cup of liquid and is used to transfer liquids from one container to another. For example, when making Skyr, a ladle is used to scoop the curdled milk into a cheesecloth so that the excess whey can drain. In this scenario, the ladle is used not to separate the curds and whey but instead transfers both out of the vat.

The second kind of ladle is a perforated skimmer, sometimes also called a *pelle à brie*, which has a shallower, punctured bowl. The skimmer is used in the making of some soft and mold-ripened cheeses to separate the curds from whey as the curds are transferred to the molds. When making Brie, for example, a skimmer is used after cultures have been added to the milk. When the mixture has acidified and the curds and whey have separated, the skimmer is used to move the curds to the molds, where they will be further drained and shaped. A skimmer can also be used to help distribute rennet across the surface of the milk before it is stirred in, or to stir the milk or curds while they are still in the vat, though more specialized tools are often used for those purposes.

See also PELLE À BRIE; SKIMMING; and STIRRING.

Caldwell, Gianaclis. Mastering Artisan Cheesemaking: The Ultimate Guide for Home-Scale and Market Producers. White River Junction, Vt.: Chelsea Green, 2012.
Helweg, Richard. The Complete Guide to Making Cheese, Butter, and Yogurt at Home: Everything You Need to Know Explained Simply. Ocala, Fla.: Atlantic, 2010.

Sara Harrison

Ladotyri Mytilinis is a light yellow, hard PDO (protected designation of origin) cheese produced on the island of Lesvos, Greece, with ewe's milk or mixtures of ewe's and goat's milk (maximum 30 percent). It is also referred to as kefalaki ("little head"). Its basic characteristic is that is preserved in olive oil (*ladi* = olive oil; *tyri* = cheese). It has a strong, salty taste and pleasant aroma, and is considered a hard table cheese with a dry rind.

For its production milk coagulation occurs at 90–93°F (32–34°C), with enough rennet added for the coagulation to be complete in thirty minutes. The curd is then divided, warmed up to 113°F (45°C) and poured into molds, where it stays until it obtains a constant structure and its characteristic shape. It is then salted and left to mature in rooms with a high relative humidity of approximately 85 percent and a temperature of 54–64°F (12–18°C) for at least three months. The pH is over 5, its maximum moisture

Ladotyri Mytilinis, a hard yellow Greek PDO cheese, is preserved in olive oil. © GEORGE SAMOURIS

content is 38 percent, and minimum fat in dry matter content is 40 percent. Its salt content is approximately 3 percent.

Ladotyri cheese can be consumed alone as an appetizer or incorporated into traditional island recipes such as saganaki (ladotyri prepared in a small frying pan), bread with zucchini and ladotyri, tart with ladotyri, and lamb with mint sauce and ladotyri.

See also GREECE; OIL-MARINATED CHEESES; and SAGANAKI.

Anyfantakis, E. M. *Greek Cheeses.* Athens: Greek National Dairy Committee, 1998. See pp. 105–107.
"Ladotyri." Cheesenet.gr. http://www.cheesenet.gr/ english/cheeses/ladotyri.htm.
Litopoulou-Tzanetaki, E., and N. Tzanetakis "Microbiological Characteristics of Greek Traditional Cheeses." *Small Ruminant Research* 101 (2011): 17–32.

George Samouris

La Ferme Saint-Hubert

La Ferme Saint-Hubert is a cheese shop in Paris, on Rue Rochechouard, which has been run by the husband and wife team Henry and Paulette Voy for more than thirty years. Well-known cheesemongers, the Voys have even sold cheeses to former French presidents François Mitterrand and Jacques Chirac. La Ferme Saint-Hubert's popularity can be attributed to the shop's enormous selection of cheeses coming from small producers throughout France. And unlike most French cheese shops that sell mostly dairy products, La Ferme Saint-Hubert also carries exceptional specialty foods, such as handmade jams,

olive oils, dried sausages, prosciutto, cans of boudin noir, and jars of foie gras.

Henry Voy is a native of Poitou, a region of France known for its goat's milk cheeses. As such, the first cheese display that customers will notice when entering the marble Art Deco shop is a cart of chèvres, including the classics Pouligny Saint Pierre, Sainte-Maure de Touraine, and Charolais. One of Henry and Paulette's favorites is their aged Charolais, which they call "the king of chèvres." Beyond the *chariot des chèvres* however there lies a world of cheeses, with everything from the popular Beaufort d'Alpage to the one-of-a-kind Vieux Salers. See CHAROLAIS; BEAUFORT; and SALERS.

See also CHEESEMONGER; CHÈVRE; and FRANCE.

La Ferme Saint-Hubert. http://www.la-ferme-saint-hubert-de-paris.com.
Pudlowski, Gilles. "La Ferme Saint-Hubert." Personal blog, 3 March 2012. http://www.gillespudlowski.com/47268/produits/la-ferme-des-voy-paris-9e.

Max Shrem

La Fermette

La Fermette is a traditional cheese store near Les Halles de Paris, a famous fresh food market in Paris. It opened in 1895 on the renowned Rue Montorgueil, a street known for the concentration of food stores and stalls. The street is closed to cars and attracts shoppers and tourists with charming original cobblestones and a tight footprint.

La Fermette has a wide selection of cheeses from France, Switzerland, and the Netherlands. The store itself is big in comparison to other stores in the city, and their selection of French cheeses includes products from all corners of the country. They stock around 250 types of cheese, excellent sausages, and jams. It is one of the few stores in Paris open seven days a week, selling cheese plates to go and vacuum-packed cheeses for travelers.

See also CHEESEMONGER and FRANCE.

La Fermette. http://www.la-fermette-paris.com.

Carlos Yescas

La Fromagerie

La Fromagerie is a London-based cheese seller and maturer with two locations, one in Marylebone and the other in Highbury & Islington. The shops feature climate-controlled display facilities, including walk-in "cheese rooms" that allow customers to fully immerse themselves in the experience of tasting and selecting. La Fromagerie sells cheeses from around the world, with an emphasis on the United Kingdom and France and the odd guest appearance from the United States.

The company's owner, Patricia Michelson, tells the story of her inadvertent baptism as a cheese seller. On a skiing vacation in the French Alps in the late 1980s she tasted a glorious wheel of Beaufort d'Alpage and intimated to the cheesemaker that she would like to take some back to London. When a 77-pound (35-kilogram) wheel arrived at the hotel, she had no choice but to drag it home with her, sharing it with friends and selling it on to a few restaurants. When they came back for more, she converted a shed in her garden into a small cheese store and sourced more cheese to fill it, and from those small beginnings the business grew. See BEAUFORT.

Michelson describes her shops as "a larder of ideas and of interesting foods." Today the business includes the two shops (which also sell a wide range of seasonal produce, dry goods, and wine) and a maturation facility where cheeses that need extra care are turned, washed, and refined before sale. There is also a café, called No 6, next door to the shop in Marylebone.

See also MATURING and UNITED KINGDOM.

Aubin-Parvu, Jean Paul. "Food and Me: Patricia Michelson." *Marylebone Journal*. August 2015, p. 22–23.

Francis Percival

La Fromagerie Goncourt

La Fromagerie Goncourt is a cheese shop in Paris's eleventh arrondissement that has risen to the top of the city's cheese sellers in just a few years of operation, appearing (for example) in *Conde Nast Traveler*'s April 2015 list of best cheese shops in Paris. In 2012 owner Clément Broussault left a career in banking to become a cheesemonger. He took a three-week training course with the French Federation of Cheesemongers, followed by a summer spent bicycling around the country, discovering France's regional cheeses and making personal connections with cheese producers. His adventure has been described as the "Tour de France of Cheese." He followed this tour with working for Pierre Gay in Annecy for six months, before returning to Paris to open shop on 25 October 2013.

To bolster his cheese merchant credentials, in 2013 Broussault enrolled in the three-year Meilleur Ouvrier de France (MOF) contest organized by the French Ministry of Labor. While many other culinary professions (such as pastry chefs, bartenders, and sommeliers) have been recognized by this award for nearly a century, the cheesemonger designation has only been given since 2000 (and thus only a small number of French cheesemongers have the coveted MOF title). Broussault completed the enrollment and qualification events, and competed as a finalist for the coveted MOF title in February 2015.

La Fromagerie Goncourt serves Paris's most densely populated district with a modern eco-friendly sensibility—plastic bags are eschewed and local deliveries are made on bicycle. Specialties include the regional delights that Broussault encountered on his summer trip, such as Dent du Chat, Tomes de Bauges and Persillé de Tignes from the Savoy area. In December 2014, La Fromagerie Goncourt won the Prix d'Encouragement des Commerces Alimentaires, an award given in support of young food shops and to aid in the improvement of the neighborhoods in which they reside.

See also CHEESEMONGER and FRANCE.

Bethune, Meredith. "The Best Cheese Shops in Paris." *Conde Nast Traveler*, 15 April 2015.
"Fromagerie Goncourt: Le tour de France des fromages avec Clément Broussault." 17 December 2014. http://www.commercedeparis.fr/actualites/interviews/clement-broussault-artisan-fromager-dans-le-11e-arrondissement.
Raynaud, Serge. "MOF Classe Fromager 2015: Épreuves, interviews et présentation des finalistes." Hôtellerie-Restauration, 10 May 2015. http://www.hotellerie-restauration.ac-versailles.fr/spip.php?article2418&lang=fr#Presentation-du-concours

Karl J. Peterson

Laguiole

Laguiole, a cylindrical uncooked, pressed cheese weighing as much as 110 pounds (50 kilograms) and first made as long ago as the twelfth century, nearly disappeared during the French rural exodus in the first half of the twentieth century. Fortunately a cooperative called Jeune Montagne put in a great deal of effort to ensure that this cheese didn't become a thing of the past, and obtained protected designation of origin (PDO) specification in 2015. The cheese is named for a commune in the Aveyron department of southern France, where it is made.

The PDO for Laguiole stipulates that cheesemakers use whole, raw cow's milk from the Simmental or Aubrac breeds, on the Aubrac plateau, situated in the southern part of the Massif Central. Production per cow is limited to 6,339 quarts (6,000 liters) of milk per year, and the cows are fed only with grass or hay. Fermented fodders are prohibited. The cheese is produced all year round—formerly in burons, stone-built mountain shelters—and matures for at least four months, and is even better at ten months or more. See BURON.

Young Laguiole has a dry whitish to light gray rind, which as the cheese ages can become amber-brown to granite gray. The body is ivory to straw yellow, and both firm and supple. Milky and fresh grass aromas emanate from the veined body, and dried meat scents from near the rind. The taste is medium to intense, with a lactic flavor depending on the degree of aging, balanced with a specific character featuring nuances from fresh grass through to nuts. Laguiole is usually consumed as a table cheese, after a meal, accompanied by a regional red wine, like a Marcillac. It is also prized as an appetizer, in salads, or for cooking. Tome Fraîche de l'Aubrac—the product of the first stage of the cheesemaking process—is known as an ingredient in a famous dish, aligot de l'Aubrac. See ALIGOT.

See also FRANCE and PRESSED CHEESES.

Garric, Yves, and André Molinier. *Paroles de burons.* 3d ed. Rodez, France: Fil d'Ariane Éditeur, 2004.
Samson, Catherine. *L'Aubrac: la race d'un pays de résistants.* Villefranche Rouergue, France: Éditions Terres d'Excellence, 2012, p. 144.

Paul Zindy

LaMancha a breed notable for its "pixie ears," has attracted the US dairy industry almost as much as it has charmed its loyal fanciers, less than 50 years after the breed was recognized by the American Dairy Goat Association.

Worldwide sightings of goats with similar ears to the American variant pop up as far back as the nineteenth century; however, without intensive DNA analysis, it is impossible to do more than speculate about the origin of this curious mutation. The Mediterranean is the favored theory of LaMancha's origin because the word, "LaMancha," is Spanish and short ear black goats, usually with red trim, do show up within the area's local Murcian herds, where they are called "Monadas," or monkeys, both for the facial resemblance and their amusing personalities. See MURCIANA. Stories and photos provide further evidence of the spread of this hardy animal in Cyprus, Greece, Turkey, and Kurdistan where they have found homes due to their ability to produce quality milk in respectable quantities.

Cheese factories, many of which outsource their goat milk, are increasingly using LaMancha milk in great part because the breed, while not known for racking up the fluid volumes for which the Swiss breeds are known, compensates by competing with the Nubian breed's high butterfat and protein components. See NUBIAN. High solids combined with long, level lactations make this American breed a welcome contributor to the cheese world, especially in small to medium-sized operations.

See also GOAT.

Backus, Barbara. "Tale of the Ear." Goat's Leap Cheese. http://www.goatsleap.com/info.html.
Porter, Valerie. *Goats of the World.* Ipswich, U.K.: Farming Press, 1996.

Barbara Backus

La Mancha, Spain, a region at the heart of the Iberian Peninsula, can trace its history of cheesemaking back several thousand years and is the birthplace of what is arguably Spain's most famous cheese, Manchego. Like Manchego, the majority of the region's cheeses are made from uncooked pressed curds and bear a distinctive zigzag pattern on their rind. See PRESSED CHEESES. These include "Iberico," a cheese made from a blend of cow's milk with goat's and/or sheep's milk, which, although similar to Manchego in character, is more subtle in flavor and less expensive, making it a favorite among Spaniards. Also found locally is "queso de oveja al romero," a sheep's milk cheese covered with lard and topped with a thick layer of rosemary leaves, a botanical abundant in the region.

La Mancha constitutes the southern portion of the autonomous community of Castile–La Mancha and lies south of Madrid on the Meseta plateau, a vast plain bordered and bisected by mountain ranges that dominates the Spanish interior. Castile–La

LaMancha does in pasture at Quixote Lamanchas, a dairy goat breeder in California specializing in this breed.
© BARBARA BACKUS

Mancha is made up of five provinces, each named after its major city: Toledo (the regional capital), Ciudad Real, Albacete, Guadalajara, and Cuenca. It was established in 1982 from the historic region of Castilla la Nueva ("New Castile"), which until that time had also incorporated Madrid. "Old Castile" (now part of Castile and Leon) lay to the north, and it was from there, over many centuries, that Spain's Catholic aristocracy slowly wrested the Spanish peninsula from Muslim control, peppering the landscape with the castles that gave Castile its name. La Mancha's diverse cultural heritage is testament to the centuries spent under Roman, Muslim, and Catholic rule and can be seen today in the region's classical ruins, mosques, synagogues, churches, and cathedrals.

Synonymous with La Mancha's plains are its windmills, immortalized as giants in Miguel de Cervantes's novel *Don Quixote*. They dot the landscape and reflect the region's traditional agricultural economy. This area of the Meseta, around 2,000 feet (610 meters) above sea level, is treeless and arid ("La Mancha" is commonly thought to come from the Arabic *ma-ansha*, which translates as "no water") with low hills and rolling plains; bitterly cold winters are followed by fiercely hot summers. Nevertheless the land is fertile and supports not just extensive crops but also vines, which cover an area of 637 square miles (165,000 hectares) making the La Mancha DOP the largest continuous wine region in the world. Other important commodities include olives, garlic, saffron (which, like Manchego cheese, has DOP status), and livestock, the most significant being the indigenous Manchega sheep. Originally bred for meat and wool, Manchega is now best known for milk and the associated cheese, Manchego.

Geographically Spain can be viewed as three distinct cheesemaking zones. Cow's milk cheese is found mainly to the north in the wetter and more temperate "Green Belt," which runs from Galicia in the west to the Catalan Pyrenees mountains in the east. In the south and along the rugged Mediterranean coastline (and on the Canary and Balearic Islands) goats proliferate as their agility and ability to browse on a range of scrubby flora make them well suited to those sparse and rocky landscapes. However it is sheep that dominate Spain's interior. Evidence of sheep farming can be traced back several thousand years and left a legacy that includes an extensive network of migratory paths (around 77,675 miles [125,000 kilometers] in total) known as "las canadas," which crisscross the Meseta and were used by shepherds and drovers to move vast flocks between summer and winter pastures. Known commonly as transhumance, this practice that extended from prehistory into the middle of the twentieth century. See SHEEP and TRANSHUMANCE.

Manchego, La Mancha's only DOP cheese, is one of Spain's most familiar exports. The formal protection dictates that it can be made only within the region of historic La Mancha (specifically Toledo, Cuenca, Albacete, and Ciudad Real) from the whole milk of the Manchega sheep. It is a hard cheese categorized by age: "semi-curado," which are aged for a minimum of three months, "curado" for six months, "viejo" up to twelve months, and "anejo" for one year or more. Two basic types of Manchego fall under the DOP, an industrial cheese made from either pasteurized or raw milk, and a handmade farmhouse cheese that uses only raw milk. Only a handful of farmhouse producers (labeled "Artesano") remain. Both types are distinctive in appearance due to their patterned exterior that harks back to the traditional baskets, hand woven from local esparto grass, in which they were formed. It is replicated in modern cheeses by plastic molds that have the familiar zigzag pattern imprinted on their interior.

Other cheeses also produced in the region are: Campo de Montalban, a local blend of cow's, goat's, and sheep's milk that was classified as Manchego until it lost that right in 1985 with the DOP specification that Manchego must be made from 100 percent sheep's milk. La Leyenda, similar to Manchego but rubbed in oil or lard, coated in herbs, and then

sometimes spending several days soaking in brandy. The most exceptional cheese, Mitibleu, strays significantly from tradition. In 2003 production began at a modern facility near Toledo of this raw, blue sheep's milk cheese that is aged for four months and shares a recipe more in common with French Roquefort than with La Mancha's more typical fare.

See also LAMANCHA; MANCHEGO; and SPAIN.

Clarke, Oz, and Margaret Rand. *Grapes and Wines.* Toronto: Sterling, 2010.
Denominacion de Origen, Queso Manchego. http://www.quesomanchego.es.
Phillips, William D., Jr., and Carla Rahn Phillips. *A Concise History of Spain.* New York: Cambridge University Press, 2010.

Chris George

L'Amuse is a cheese retailer, wholesaler, importer, and exporter in the Netherlands, owned and operated by Betty and Martin Koster. Founded in 1989 there are two locations, one in Amsterdam and the other in IJmuiden. Betty is a third-generation cheesemonger, and eight out of her grandfather's fourteen

L'Amuse is a well-known cheese shop in Amsterdam owned by husband-and-wife team Betty and Martin Koster.
© KATE ARDING

siblings worked in the industry. Martin Koster heads up the administrative side of the business, having come from a career in banking. L'Amuse carries over four hundred types of cheese as well as other fine foods and tea from around the world.

Over the years Betty and Martin have developed close relationships with a number of traditional and artisan cheesemakers in the Netherlands. L'Amuse specializes in selling small-production and farmstead cheeses from Dutch producers. A particularly successful item for L'Amuse is their self-titled Gouda, made at the Cono cheesemaking plant in northern Holland. The wheels are hand selected by Betty and then aged for a minimum of two years in the L'Amuse cheese shop under her specifications. The signature L'Amuse Gouda is aged in a warmer environment than is usual for the style and the region.

L'Amuse Cheesemongers frequently lead tasting and pairing classes with customers, and one particularly unique pairing combination that they have drawn attention to in recent years is the combination of Dutch cheese and different types of tea. L'Amuse is one of a handful of European sources for the Essex St. Cheese company, an importer and wholesaler with most of their operations based in the United States.

See also GOUDA and NETHERLANDS.

Essex St. Cheese Co. "L'Amuse Gouda Collection." https://essexcheese.com/about/gouda.
L'Amuse. http://www.lamuse.nl.

Vince Razionale

Lancashire is one of the classic cheeses of the British Isles, a semihard cow's milk cheese described by Osbert Burdett in his 1935 *Little Book of Cheese* as "a cheese that can be spread with the knife, and at its best it is mellow and delicious; ... its richness of flavor is superb. It has the opulence of a fine old Madeira." Originally made in and around the county of Lancashire in the northwest of England near Manchester, over the course of the twentieth century the cheese has been adapted for factory production and is now made on a range of scales, from farmhouse to industrial.

Lancashire cheese as it was made in the nineteenth and early twentieth century was every bit a farmhouse product, and the process of making it was very slow.

The milk was renneted when still very low in acidity, and the curd was subjected to a series of intensive manipulations, including cutting, draining, stacking, and a series of repeated pressings and "breaks" requiring the cheesemaker to pull the curd into small pieces by hand. These took place at intervals over the course of an entire day, allowing excess moisture to escape from the curd as it slowly acidified. The curd was then left to drain and complete its acidification under pressure overnight. The amalgamation of several days' worth of curd, which was ground together and pressed into a single cheese—which many see as definitive of Lancashire—was no affectation, but rather a reflection of the fact that most cheesemakers in the county owned small farms and did not produce sufficient milk to make even a single cheese per day. (In fact, this practice of mixing curds over several days was not limited to Lancashire, but was commonly used for a variety of other farmhouse cheeses such as Dorset Blue Vinney and Stilton as well.) See STILTON.

A few Lancashire cheesemakers continue to make cheese using these labor-intensive methods. As the older curds sit to the side in the cheese room for two or even three days, waiting to be ground, they relax and "mellow," while their aroma becomes yeasty and a little sour. These older curds are then finely ground together with the slightly rubbery, milky-tasting one-day-old curds and mixed with salt before being bound in cloth and pressed into 22- or 44-pound (10-or 20-kilogram) cylinders. After several days, the cloth bindings are rubbed with melted butter, a local alternative for the lard used on many other clothbound British cheeses. See LARDING and CLOTHBOUND CHEESES. Lancashire cheese may be eaten when it is just a few weeks old, when it is known as "Creamy" Lancashire, or it may be matured for up to a year, during which time its flavor deepens and intensifies, earning it the moniker "Tasty" Lancashire.

In the mid-twentieth century, there emerged a third kind of Lancashire cheese, "Crumbly" Lancashire, the result of attempts to adapt the cheese's long and laborious process to the requirements of factory production. Many feel that as the factory technicians succeeded in their quest to turn a twenty-four-hour process into a three-hour one, they also robbed the cheese of its charm. Nevertheless, inexpensive factory-produced "Crumbly Lancashire" has become the definitive Lancashire cheese for a

Ruth Townley turning wheels of Lancashire in 1976. She is the mother of Ruth Kirkham, who founded Mrs Kirkham's Lancashire Cheese. COURTESY OF THE KIRKHAM FAMILY

generation of Britons, many of whom have never tasted the farmhouse version.

In 1939 there were 202 farms making Lancashire cheese in the county; the ravages of World War II decreased that number to 22 farms in 1948. See WORLD WAR II. In 2007 the eleven remaining producers joined together to form the Lancashire Cheesemakers Association and made a successful application for a protected designation of origin (PDO) specification for "Beacon Fell Traditional Lancashire Cheese." Today, the Kirkham family of Beesley Farm in Goosnargh makes the only remaining raw-milk farmhouse Lancashire cheese.

See also TERRITORIAL and UNITED KINGDOM.

Burdett, Osbert. *A Little Book of Cheese*. London: G. Howe, 1935.
Cheke, Val. *The Story of Cheese-Making in Britain*. London: Routledge & Kegan Paul, 1959.
Rance, Patrick. *The Great British Cheese Book*. London: Macmillan, 1982.
Richardson, Robert. *Lancashire Cheesemaking, Including Small Cheese*. Preston, U.K.: Toulmin & Sons, 1921.
United Kingdom Department for Environment, Food, and Rural Affairs. "Protected Food Name: Beacon Fell Traditional Lancashire Cheese (PDO)." https://www.gov.uk/government/publications/protected-food-name-beacon-fell-traditional-lancashire-cheese-pdo.

Bronwen Percival

Land O'Lakes began as a small regional dairy cooperative in Saint Paul, Minnesota, and has grown into a multibillion-dollar national corporation with an international market of products that range from the cornerstone butter and cheese production to animal feed and seed manufacturing.

Land O'Lakes was originally established in 1921 as The Minnesota Cooperative Creameries Association, which was a cooperative of 320 co-op creameries. They changed their name to Land O'Lakes Creameries, Inc. in 1926. After the 1922 passage of the Capper-Volstead Act, dairy farmers could collectively organize to promote their goods. Land O'Lakes began with the mission of dairy farmers who wanted to use their bargaining power. By 1930, 470 creameries, including dairies from nearby states, were all a part of Land O'Lakes. This made Land O'Lakes the largest dairy distributing cooperative in the world at that time. They built their reputation, and a significant market share, by selling butter of a superior quality that was created using "sweet cream" rather than soured cream.

In 1934 Land O'Lakes added cheese and processed cheese products to their value-added product line. Since then they have produced and marketed a wide range of new items, from blue cheese (1940–1959) aged in a former underground speakeasy in Saint Paul to the culturally iconic Land O Lakes (no apostrophe) American processed cheese. The closing decades of the twentieth century witnessed product innovation, mergers and acquisitions, and company restructuring. Milk production shifted away from Minnesota and toward California. New products and technology were developed, including the trademarked "Extra Melt" cheese loaf, the regional brand New Yorker, and a line of low fat, low sodium cheeses after 1997 when Land O'Lakes acquired Alpine Lace.

See also BUTTER.

Abrahamsen, Martin Abraham. *The Land O'Lakes Creameries, Inc: An Historical Account and Recent Development of a Cooperative Butter Marketing Organization in the Middle West.* Madison: University of Wisconsin Press, 1933.
Bolan, Michael, et al. "Land O'Lakes." *International Food and Agribusiness Management Review* 7, no. 2 (2004).
Ruble, Kenneth Douglas. *Men to Remember: How 100,000 Neighbors Made History.* Chicago: Lakeside Press, 1947.

Beth M. Forrest

Langres is a protected designation of origin (PDO) cheese made from whole cow's milk in the Plateau de Langres, in northeastern France (Champagne region). The milk comes from Montbéliarde, Brune, and Simmental cows. See MONTBÉLIARDE. Langres is a soft-rind cheese with an orange rind, colored by annatto, and a naturally formed bowl on the top, called the "fontaine." See ANNATTO. This bowl is naturally formed during ripening as the cheese is not turned after molding.

The result of a tradition and savoir-faire dating back to the eighteenth century, the first written reference to a cheese called Langres comes from a book written in 1874 by A. F. Pauriau (*La laiterie, art de traiter le beurre, de fabriquer les beurres et les principaux fromages français et étrangers*). After a significant development of Langres at the end of the nineteenth century, notably linked to wholesalers, World War I marked the beginning of the decline of farmhouse production. It was not until 1950 that some craftsmen began making Langres again and thus revived the production of this cheese. In 1981 a general union of Langres cheesemakers was created with the objective to obtain appellation d'origine contrôlée (AOC) status in 1991. A PDO followed in 2009.

The Langres cheesemaking process is particularly characterized by two essential steps: a slow maturation of the milk to obtain a lactic type curd, and care during ripening through washing with salt water. The resulting semisoft cylindrical cheese is about 4 inches (11 centimeters) wide and 2 inches (4 centimeters) high, weighing 10 ounces (284 grams), with a unique sunken top.

Langres is excellent on its own, paired with a pinot noir or Champagne, or used in numerous cooking recipes. Its distinctive taste with creamy aromas and a taste of hazelnut make it an ideal ingredient in recipes such as fondue champenoise with melted Langres or crispy bites stuffed with Langres. It can be enhanced by adding a little marc de Champagne or marc de Bourgogne on the top in the fontaine.

See also FRANCE.

Benêt, Jérôme, and Georges Risoud. *Histoire du fromage de Langres*, Langres. Langres, France: Éditions Dominique Guéniot, 2005.

Alexandra Jacquot

Lankaaster Aged is a hard Gouda-style cheese shaped like a loaf of bread with a slightly open texture, made exclusively from local pasteurized Brown Swiss cow milk. See BROWN SWISS. It is handcrafted by Glengarry Fine Cheese in Ontario, Canada, where cheesemakers Margaret Morris Peters and Wilma Klein-Swormink are of Dutch heritage. When they began making cheese in the early 2000s, Gouda was their first choice of cheese to make. The loaf shape is traditional and convenient because Dutch farmers slice cheese directly onto bread for eating. The unique flavor profile of Lankaaster is the result of the cows' local forage, milk source, and a "cocktail" of starter cultures crafted to provide a flavor profile more typical of cheese made on Dutch farms earlier in the twentieth century.

Lankaaster Aged loaves remain in the aging room for nine to twelve months to develop complex yet balanced layers of caramel, butterscotch, pineapple, and butter flavors that linger on the palate while the body goes from semi-firm to hard without losing the overall smoothness in texture. In late 2013, after winning Best Gouda-style Cheese at the American Cheese Society, Lankaaster Aged earned a seminal award; Global Supreme Champion, at the Global Cheese Competition in Somerset, England, out of over 1,800 varieties. See COMPETITIONS.

Margaret Morris Peters is living her dream of making artisan cheese and using family milk from a farm in the county where she grew up. This reality grew out of a company she started in 1995, Glengarry Cheesemaking Supply Inc., which provides technical support in farmstead cheesemaking while selling equipment and supplies to farmstead and artisan cheesemakers. Over the years Glengarry has mentored many artisan cheese companies in the United States and Canada, while developing recipes for their own prize-winning family of cheeses, which also includes Celtic Blue and Celtic Blue Reserve.

See also CELTIC BLUE RESERVE; GOUDA; and ONTARIO.

Glengarry Fine Cheese. http://www.glengarryfinecheese .com.

Kathy Guidi

larding is a technique used by makers of traditional clothbound cheese (such as some Cheddars) to bind a muslin (calico) cloth to the outside of a cheese. Attaching the cloth is part of the process called "bandaging" that takes place immediately after the cheese is removed from the press. Melted or semi-solid lard (rendered pig fat) is applied to the cloth (and/or the cheese rind) to assist the application of the cloth dressing. The muslin cloth acts as a protective barrier and, particularly in times past, helped the cheese hold its shape. The cloth and lard allow the cheese to breathe and protect it from damage and excessive weight loss because of evaporation (drying) during aging, as a natural rind forms on the cheese under the cloth, often combining with the cloth to form a continuous layer. During the course of maturation the lard itself is eaten away by molds, leaving a dry, canvas-like surface in its wake. Correctly matured clothbound cheese should have no remaining trace of lard, either on the surface or under the cloth once it's peeled away.

Although mainly associated with farmhouse Cheddar, there are other traditional British territorial cheeses that have a muslin cloth bound onto the outside by larding. Examples include Red Leicester and Double Gloucester. In some areas the cloth is attached using alternatives to lard, such as cellulose-based paste (e.g., for Cheshire cheese), or butter (e.g., for Lancashire cheese, where the process is termed "buttering-up"). Other alternatives used to bind the cloth to the cheese in the past include using a flour and water paste, or sewing the cloth on to the cheese.

The process of larding (and cloth binding) cheese is largely the reserve of traditional farmhouse production in the United Kingdom and the United States and is still carried out by many small-scale and medium-scale producers. The majority of industrial cheese production, however, favors the use of plastic or wax coatings instead of cloth and lard, as they minimize weight loss and are impervious to molds.

See also CHEDDAR; CLOTHBOUND CHEESES; and TERRITORIAL.

Davis, J. G. *Cheese*. Vol. 1: *Basic Technology*. London: J&A Churchill, 1965.
Ministry of Agriculture Farm & Fisheries. *Bulletin No. 43: Cheese Making*. London: His Majesty's Stationery Office, 1938.
Saker, Dora G. *Practical Cheddar Cheese-Making*. St. Albans, U.K.: Camfield, 1917.

Andy Swinscoe

La Serena (also known as Torta de la La Serena) is an ancestral Spanish soft cheese made from Merino sheep's milk in the Extremaduran county of La Serena. The cheese has been protected with a designation of origin since 1993. The protected designation of origin (PDO) currently protects 136 livestock farms, which have 120,000 milking sheep (heads) that produce 226,029 gallons (855,614 liters) of milk per year that are transformed into approximately 451,947 pounds (205,000 kilograms) of cheese.

The traditional method of manufacture used by the shepherds has been maintained in an unaltered way up to the present. For production, raw milk is coagulated at 77–90°F (25–32°C) for fifty to seventy-five minutes, using vegetable (*Cynara cardunculus*) rennet as coagulant. These two circumstances, moderate temperature and the vegetable rennet having low clotting ability, result in prolonged clotting times and quite soft curds. The high moisture content and high photolytic activity of the vegetable rennet are also responsible for the characteristic runny texture of the cheese when it is fully ripened. Ripening takes place at 50–59°F (10–15°C) and 80–90 percent relative humidity for more than sixty days. See PLANT-DERIVED COAGULANTS and RELATIVE HUMIDITY.

La Serena has a lenticular shape and weighs 2–4 pounds (0.90–2 kilograms). It displays a waxy yellow to ochre rind and the imprints of esparto grass used in the molding process. The texture of the mass is smooth or semihard, with small holes. After twenty days from the beginning of the manufacture, a phenomenon called "atortado" generally takes place in the cheese, the mass becomes very smooth, quite liquid, and the handling of the cheese must be done carefully to prevent the crust from being broken and the spilling of the paste. The taste is slightly bitter, yet pleasant, often attributable to the action of the vegetable rennet, not acid, slightly salty, very oily, with spicy notes and lingering aftertaste. A fully matured La Serena cheese has a creamy consistency that can be scooped out after cutting out the circular lid.

See also SPAIN.

Martínez, Sidonia, Juan A. Centeno, Inmaculada Franco, et al. "The Spanish Traditional Cheeses: Characteristics and Scientific Knowledge." In Handbook of Cheese: Production, Chemistry, and Sensory Properties, edited by Enrique Castelli, and Luiz du Vale, pp. 123–167. New York: Nova Science, 2013.
Medina, Margarita, Buensuceso Fernandez Del Pozo, M. Asunción Rodríguez-Marin, et al. "Effect of Lactic Starter Inoculation on Chemical, Microbiological, Rheological and Sensory Characteristics of La Serena Cheese." Journal of Dairy Research 58, no. 3 (August 1991): 355–361.

Javier Carballo

latifundia were Roman landed estates that specialized in the production of high value cash crops such as wine, olive oil, and sheep products. Much of what is known about the cheesemaking conducted by latifundia comes from the Roman writers Cato, Varro, and Columella, who wrote agricultural manuals during the second and first century B.C.E., and the first century C.E., respectively. Cato advised that

an olive plantation of 160 acres (65 hectares) could support one flock of one hundred sheep for the production of wool and cheese, and that the whey from cheesemaking could feed ten swine. Varro described latifundia having one thousand sheep that were divided into flocks of eighty to one hundred. Shepherds moved the sheep from the estates in the coastal lowlands where they overwintered to pastures high in the Apennines during the summer, where cheeses were made. This transhumant migration required complex coordination to maintain order among the shepherds and their flocks. Columella described in great detail the practices used by the shepherds for making dry aged pecorino cheeses and unaged cheeses flavored with condiments such as pine nuts or thyme. See CATO, MARCUS PORCIUS; COLUMELLA, LUCIUS JUNIUS MODERATUS; and VARRO, MARCUS TERENTIUS.

The Romans eventually established villas in the provinces north of the Alps that were modeled after the latifundia. The economic strategy of raising sheep for wool and cheese, and raising pigs on the whey, was replicated on many provincial villas, especially in northwest France and England, where pecorino cheesemaking and pig raising were indispensable to feeding the Roman legions who guarded the borders. The Roman villas were taken over by invading Germanic aristocracies after the fall of the Roman Empire and contributed to the rise of the medieval manor, the birthplace of many new cheese varieties during the Middle Ages.

See also ANCIENT CIVILIZATIONS.

Kindstedt, P. S. Cheese and Culture: A History of Cheese and Its Place in Western Civilization. White River Junction, Vt.: Chelsea Green, 2012.

Paul S. Kindstedt

Latin America, as well as North and Central America, owe the development of dairy agriculture in general, and the technology of cheesemaking in particular, to the Europeans who colonized the New World. French, British, and Dutch settlers brought cheesemaking traditions and tastes to what would become Canada and the United States. Meanwhile, Spaniards brought cheesemaking to Mexico and Central America. Italian and Portuguese settlers brought their techniques to Brazil, Uruguay, and Argentina; while more recently, Swiss migrants have shared their expertise with cheesemakers in Chile and Ecuador.

Before the arrival of Europeans to the Americas, there were no large domesticated mammals, no adult consumption of milk, and consequently, no development of cheesemaking anywhere on the continent. Native populations were predominantly lactose intolerant after infancy. See LACTOSE INTOLERANCE.

The transfer of particular European techniques and traditions led to the development of parallel cheese customs throughout Latin America, replicating some aspects and styles but evolving within new conditions. The results are cheeses created with similar technical skills, but with new flavors. Most Latin American cheeses are made with cow's milk aged less than two months and are consumed as an ingredient in recipes that combine European tastes with indigenous Latin American cooking techniques and ingredients.

The cheesemaking of Central and South America tends to be focused on three primary styles: fresh, semisoft, and hard. No major innovations were made by combining milks of more than one type of animal, by washing curds or rinds, or even by adding molds. This is gradually changing, however, as immigrants continue to arrive and introduce different techniques and as nationals bring back new recipes after traveling or working abroad. Experimentation and innovation in styles is especially prevalent in Argentina, Brazil, and Chile, where cheesemaking is promoted as a value-added venture to augment earnings for small farmers in places where milk prices are depressed by international conglomerates that control the dairy industry.

Most Latin cheeses take their names from the places where they are made, such as Andino, Patagonico, or Guayanés, from the eponymous regions in Peru, Argentina, and Venezuela. Others derive their names from the names of the original European recipes or inspirations for their styles. Similarly, other cheeses use the diminutive of the original name, such as Reggianito, an Italian-style Parmesan cheese made in Argentina and Uruguay, following cheesemaking and aging techniques from Italian immigrants; or Provolandino, a copy of Italian provolone made in Brazil, Ecuador, and Uruguay.

In addition to the heavy Italian influence in cheesemaking in Argentina and Uruguay and the Portuguese influence in Brazil, there are also important Swiss influences to be found in the mountainous regions of South America. Copies of Emmentaler, also known as Gruyère or Suizo, called diminutively "Gruyerito," can be found in Argentina, Colombia, Chile, Ecuador, and Uruguay.

José Dubach arrived in Ecuador in the late 1970s and settled in the Salinas district. He participated in a diplomatic project sponsored by the Swiss Agency for Development and Cooperation to teach local peasants to make cheese. Since then, multiple producers have established a prosperous cheesemaking culture using mostly Holstein and Friesian cattle or Jersey cows and developing versions of various Alp-style cheeses sold locally by the Salinerito co-op.

Other cheesemakers in the Andean region have also adopted Swiss techniques and have developed local versions of Emmentaler and Gruyère. In recent years, many cheesemakers have added other European styles to diversify their offerings, responding to local demand for inexpensive cheeses. The most common styles sold are mozzarella, Raclette, Manchego, and more recently chèvre. Many of these cheeses are excellent and deserve to be highlighted in their own right. However, an overestimation of the quality of European styles by higher income consumers forces producers to identify their cheeses with origin-protected names despite their local variations, innovations, and singular terroir.

Mexico is known for its Spanish influence, but cheesemaking there also borrowed from the Netherlands and Denmark. Dairy production in Central America and southern Mexico is characterized by the use of a hybrid breed of cows popularly known as Criollo Tropical. These animals are a mix of Zebus and Holsteins. The females are docile and seasoned to the extremely hot climate. Commonly, cows are left without supervision to pasture on tropical, lush grasses during the rainy season and kept in communal lands or backyards during the dry season. Their milk, which is naturally low in fat, is used immediately, either to drink or to make into fresh cheeses.

Cheeses from this region tend to be made with fresh cow's milk, lightly salted, and sold to be eaten within days of their production. They are sprinkled on top of dishes or eaten as snacks. Salt is normally added as a preservative. Some versions of these cheeses are left to dry unrefrigerated to develop flavor. The milk used to produce them normally comes from animals that are kept primarily for their fresh milk and meat.

Traditionally, cheeses in Central America are unpasteurized, but common cheesemaking techniques include a demineralizing process, which ensures that the pH is inhospitable to pathogens. Recently, health ministries in the region have pushed for pasteurization of all milk as a quick fix to eliminate risks from unsanitary conditions. However, some producers in Nicaragua and Costa Rica continue to use raw milk, while implementing safeguards to ensure that the milk is safe for human consumption.

The Food and Agricultural Organization has sponsored development projects to support cheesemaking in the region as a poverty reduction mechanism. As part of this effort, Costa Rican producers organized to promote the creation of an appellation of origin for Turrialba cheese, which was registered in 2012.

Elsewhere in the region, cheesemaking has been heralded as a value-added production that can support families and small towns. Meanwhile, Latin American dairy conglomerates have depressed the value of fluid milk by flooding the local markets. The indiscriminate use of bovine growth hormones and steroids in dairy production is seldom well regulated. Consumers are therefore advised to seek traditional producers and to inquire about the diet and treatment of animals.

See also ARGENTINA; BRAZIL; and MEXICO.

Azuola, Carlos C. "Costa Rica: 'Turrialba Cheese' Registered as First Appellation of Origin." *INTA Bulletin*, 1 January 2013. http://www.inta.org/INTABulletin/Pages/COSTARICA%E2%80%9CTurrialbaCheese%E2%80%9DRegisteredasFirstAppellationofOrigin.aspx.
Blanco, Marvin, and Leonardo Granados. *Queso Turrialba Costa Rica*. San José, Costa Rica: Biblioteca Venezuela, 2007. http://www.fao.org/fileadmin/templates/olq/documents/Santiago/Documentos/Estudios%20de%20caso/Turrialba/Queso_CostaRica.pdf.
Castañeda, Roberto, et al. *Quesos de América del Sur*. Buenos Aires, Argentina: Albatros, 2010.

Carlos Yescas

La Tradizione is a specialty retailer located at Via Cipro 8 in Rome, just outside the Vatican walls. The shop was founded by Renzo Fantucci and Valentino Belli, who had both moved to Rome as young men in 1959 from their native rural Umbria and had both gained tremendous knowledge of Italian foods by working their way up the ranks in various Roman shops. A shared interest in true artisanal production, traditional processes, and utmost dedication to quality led Fantucci and Belli to join forces and take over an old Roman neighborhood salumeria, reopened as La Tradizione in 1980.

The shop is stocked with more than four hundred quality cheeses, primarily from Italy but also imported, and is especially regarded for its selection of "formaggi di fossa" ("pit-aged" cheeses), a fifteenth-century tradition from Emila Romagna; and "formaggi di botte" ("barrel-aged" cheeses), an equally venerable tradition from various Italian regions where green cheeses are ripened in sealed wooden barrels, often infused with natural aromas. See FORMAGGIO DI FOSSA and GREEN CHEESE.

Fantucci and Belli produce their own aged cheeses in caves in their native Valnerina. The shop also carries an impressive array of local, regional, national, and international delicacies as well as a selection of prepared foods. In 2015 the owners opened Secondo Tradizione, an affiliated enoteca/gastropub around the corner from the shop at Via Rialto 39.

See also CHEESEMONGER and ITALY.

Corucci, Domenico. "Da ragazzo di bottega a imprenditore." Umbri nel Mondo, 8 November 2000. http://www.umbrinelmondo.org/articoli.asp?id=28.
Formaggi a latte crudo della Valnerina. "L'Affinamento del formaggio." http://www.formaggidellavalnerina.it/l-affinamento-del-formaggio.
In Orvieto. "I formaggi nell' Orvieto." http://www.inorvieto.it/it/gusta/i_formaggi_nell_orvietano.html.
La Tradizione. http://www.latradizione.it/index.html.
Piumatti, Gigi, et al. *Il Buon Paese*. Bra, Italy: Slow Food Editore, 2000.

Robert LaValva

Latxa is an ancient breed of sheep native to Spain's Pais Vasco (Basque Country) region in the western Pyrenees and also prevalent in the northeastern part of the contiguous Navarra region. The milk of Latxa sheep is used to make two of Spain's most renowned protected designation of origin (PDO) cheeses, Idiazabal and Roncal. See IDIAZABAL and RONCAL. There are two sub-breeds of Latxa (also known as

"Lacha" in Castilian Spanish): the Cara Negra (black-faced) and the Cara Rubia (blond- or white-faced). On the French side of the Pyrenees the breed is known as Manech.

In Basque *latxa* means *basta* ("enough" or "sufficient") and refers to the breed's heavy winter coat of straight, coarse wool that was traditionally used for making mattresses and carpets. The breed is often described as rustic or primitive and, though its historical origins are obscure, it is generally believed to be the oldest in Spain. It has excellent milking properties, with large globular udders, and yields about 1 liter per day during a lactation period of 140 days (for the black-faced) and 155 (for the white-faced).

Latxa rams reach a height of 28–32 inches (70–80 centimeters) and weigh from about 120–175 pounds (55–80 kilograms); the females are 22–26 inches high (55–65 centimeters) and weigh 99–132 pounds (45–60 kilograms); the black-faced are larger on average than the white-faced. Both sexes grow horns; the males' are larger and spiraled. There are about 280,000 head of Latxa in Basque Country, 60 percent of which are black-faced; about 165,000 in Navarra, where the majority is white-faced; and roughly 34,000 in other regions of Spain.

Latxa are raised in herds of around two hundred and spend six months per year, starting in May or June, grazing in mountain pastures, a period that corresponds to their breeding season. Their agility and long coats render them well suited to the steep terrain and rainy climate of their native territory. There are three Latxa breeders' associations in Basque Country, one in each of its ancient Basque provinces of Alava, Bizkaia, and Gipizkoa; one in Navarra, the Asociación de Criadores de Ovino de Raza Latxa de Navarra (ASLANA); and an umbrella association, the Confederación de Asociaciones de Criadores de Ovino de Razas Latxa y Carranzana (CONFELAC). (The Carranzana is a similar but distinct breed whose milk is also used to make Idiazábal.)

See also BASQUE COUNTRY and SHEEP.

Confederación de Asociaciones de Criadores de Ovino de Razas Latxa y Carranzana. http://www.confelac.com.

Ubicación INTIA. "Latxa." http://www.intiasa.es/en/explotaciones-ganaderas/areas-de-interes/ganaderia-navarra/razas-autoctonas/nuestras-razas/latxa.html.

David Gibbons

Laughing Cow

See BEL GROUP.

Laura Chenel's Chèvre

Laura Chenel's Chèvre is a Sonoma, California–based goat cheese company founded by native Californian Laura Chenel in 1979. It produced the first commercial goat cheese, or chèvre, in the United States. See CHÈVRE.

Laura Chenel was born in 1949. She grew up in Sebastopol, California, the daughter of local restaurant owners. A member of the back-to-the-land generation, Chenel started raising goats—as did many of her contemporaries—out of the general (and generally correct) belief that they were a good herd for a family homestead. She began making cheese to preserve excess goat's milk. Her early cheesemaking experiments were unsuccessful. In 1979, at the direction of French dairy expert Jean-Claude Le Jaouen, Chenel traveled to France to study with four cheese producers in Charente, near Toulouse, and in Burgundy. Later that year she returned to Sebastopol and founded her chèvre company, on about five thousand dollars and a single herd of goats. See LE JAOUEN, JEAN-CLAUDE.

In 1981 restaurateur Alice Waters, whose ten-year-old Berkeley restaurant, Chez Panisse, spearheaded the local, seasonal food movement, tasted Chenel's chèvre and placed a standing order of 50 pounds (23 kilograms) a week, which remained in place until the mid-2000s. To increase production, the company moved to a plant in Santa Rosa, California. It also began producing harder-textured Laura Chenel Tome. In subsequent years Chenel added a soft-ripened Goat Brie, an aged crottin, taupiniere, and Buchette. In 1993 the company moved again, to the Stornetta Gold Medal Dairy, south of Sonoma. In 2006 Laura Chenel sold Laura Chenel Chevre to the French Rians Group, a family-owned dairy company headquartered in Rians, France. Today, Laura Chenel Chevre makes twenty-two different goat cheeses, served in restaurants nationwide, and for retail sale in Wegman's and Whole Foods supermarkets, among others.

See also AMERICAN "GOAT LADIES"; CALIFORNIA; and COUNTERCULTURE.

Severson, Kim. "For American Chèvre, an Era Ends." *New York Times*, 18 October 2006.

Wolf, Clark. *American Cheeses: The Best Regional, Artisan, and Farmhouse Cheeses: Who Makes Them and Where to Find Them.* New York: Simon and Schuster, 2008.

Tamar Adler

Laurent Dubois stores in Paris are named after their eponymous proprietor and Meilleur Ouvrier de France (MOF). Dubois opened his first cheese store in Paris in 1996; in 2000 he gained fame after winning the title of MOF in the 2000 competition. That was the first time cheesemongers were invited to participate alongside bakers, pastry chefs, and chefs. The Dubois family had been involved in farming and cheesemaking, but it was Laurent Dubois who finally opened a cheese store with his wife, Carole. He traveled around France meeting cheesemakers and carefully selecting his stock.

Apart from building a reputation for selecting cheeses at their point of origin, the cheeses at these stores are well regarded as the work of expert affineurs. As an affineur Dubois follows in the tradition of other stores in the city that have cellars under their retail premises, as well as a dedicated staff in the craft of aging cheese. This focus on maturing cheese in Paris has gained him a reputation with customers who seek out his extra-aged cheeses, including an aged Fourme d'Ambert or his one-hundred-day aged Saint-Maure de Touraine or an eight-month aged Brie Noir. See FOURME D'AMBERT and SAINTE-MAURE DE TOURAINE.

The stores are also known among Parisians for their unique combinations of traditional cheeses. In the three stores one can find Roquefort matched with quince paste presented as a delicious layered cake or Brie stuffed with walnuts, and the iconic Camembert au Calvados. Dubois's interest in unique cheeses has extended to those made outside of France. It is one of the few stores in Paris with a small, but well curated selection of Italian, British, Spanish, and even American artisan cheeses.

See also MATURING.

Durand, Jacky. "Laurent Dubois, Fromage et Disert." *Libération*, 18 October 2013.
Fromages Laurent Dubois. http://www.fromageslaurentdubois.fr.

Carlos Yescas

Lazy Lady Farm was founded by cheesemaker and farmer Laini Fondilier in 1987. Located in the remote hills of Westfield, Vermont, the farm was born from humble beginnings: an acre of vegetables, a goat named Blooper, and three sheep. With no electricity or running water, Fondilier relied on hand pumps, candles, gas lamps, and an outdoor lavatory. Remarkably, she made cheese in the kitchen sink for seven years. Finally, in 1995, a licensed cheesemaking room was built on the premises. A geothermal aging room followed the next year, and slowly the farm's offerings expanded.

Today Lazy Lady Farm continues to operate entirely off the grid through the application of solar panels and wind turbines. Fondilier milks a herd of forty Alpine goats that rotationally graze across thirty-five acres. See ALPINE. She makes an array of classic French style cheeses seasonally, which include classics such as La Petite Tomme, Bonaparte, and Les Pyramids. Fondilier's inspiration stems from the early years she spent in France traveling, eating cheese, and apprenticing on goat and sheep dairies. Occasional mixed-milk cheeses are produced using cow's milk from a nearby farm. Fondilier also has a knack for whimsically adding new products to her lineup that speak to current political figures and commentary. "Barick Obama" and "Fil-A-Buster" are among the most memorable. A second aging cellar was added in 2009 to accommodate her growing product line.

Breeding for strong genetics is also a seasoned skill of Fondilier's. She has extensive experience working with registered herds. She keeps impeccable lineage records and serves as a source of does for others in search of a healthy addition to their herd.

See also VERMONT.

Lazy Lady Farm. http://www.lazyladyfarm.com.

Tess McNamara

leaf-wrapped cheeses. A traditional way of transporting cheese or aging small pieces of cheese without a humid aging cellar was to wrap them in leaves. The leaf wrap gave the cheese a slightly creamy texture. Most of the traditional leaf-wrapped cheeses originated in Mediterranean areas where the climate is warm and dry, and the cheeses were produced mostly on a small scale from goat's and sheep's milk.

Many different types of leaves, anything big enough to be a wrapper and not toxic, were used: chestnut, grape, maple, cherry, sycamore, plane, fig, and walnut. These leaves are harvested fully grown but still green, to be pliable for wrapping. The local eau de vie was often used as a soaking liquid to enhance the flavor and as a preservative.

These leaves act as a moisture barrier for the aging of small cheeses such as Banon and Robiola di Castagna in chestnut leaves, and Robiola Incavolata in a cabbage leaf. See BANON. The traditional Spanish blue cheeses, such as Valdeon, Cabrales, and Picon Bejes-Tresviso are traditionally wrapped in sycamore leaves to encourage the growth of *Penicillium* since the leaves allow enough airflow into the cheese. These leaves also give the cheeses their distinctive herbaceous, mushroomy, and earthy flavors, and the leaves' tannins act as preservatives. See VALDEON and CABRALES. Pecorino foglie di Noci from Italy is an example of a hard cheese aged in and perfumed by walnut leaves. Traditional leaf-wrapped cheeses express their terroir in a unique way both inside and outside the cheese.

If traditional cheesemakers used this labor-intensive way of packing cheese in leaves out of necessity, modern artisan cheesemakers use the same method to express their products' seasonality and their own creativity. When specially designed cheese papers are widely available and modern dairies are equipped with the climate-controlled aging cellars to provide high humidity, the leaf-wrapped versions are developed to add flavors to the cheese and for decorative purposes. Cornish Yarg is beautifully covered with stingy nettle leaves; O'Banon from Capriole dairy in the United States is neatly wrapped in chestnut leaves but local bourbon is used as a soaking liquid instead of traditional eau de vie; Rogue River Blue cheese from Rogue creamery in the United States is wrapped in local grape leaves soaked in pear brandy. See ROGUE RIVER BLUE and CAPRIOLE.

Unfortunately the numbers of leaf-wrapped cheese are diminishing, not only because the technique is labor-intensive and no longer needed or practical, but also because of tightening sanitation regulations. The new rules consider real leaves not sanitary enough to ensure food safety; many countries have therefore banned the importation of these types of cheese. In Spain to export Cabrales PDO it must be wrapped in green-leaf printed food grade foil. The real sycamore leaf-wrapped Valdeon is disappearing even

within Spain. The cheese sold as Banon in many countries is wrapped in chestnut-leaf printed paper and tied with a plastic strip instead of raffia string. There are exceptions, however; if the leaves used for wrapping are included in a cheese's PDO disciplinary regulation as an essential component that characterizes the product, the leaves cannot be the subject of health discrimination. For these PDO cheeses authorities would need to prove that the leaves compromise food security to eliminate their use, rather than predefined discrimination.

See also BARK-WRAPPED CHEESES.

Dalby, Andrew. *Cheese: A Global History*. London: Reaktion Books, 2009.
Michelson, Patricia. *Cheese: Exploring Taste and Tradition*. Layton, Ut.: Gibbs Smith, 2010.

Soyoung Scanlan

Leeuwenhoek, Antoni van (1632–1723),

was a Dutch cloth merchant, a self-taught lens maker, and a natural philosopher who is best known for his microscopic studies of a plethora of organic objects. Although Leeuwenhoek was neither the inventor of the single-lens microscope nor the first to discover "little animals" or particles in fluid bodies, his microscopic investigations became the touchstone of the so-called theory of *animalcula*—an early theory of microorganisms and the starting point of the discipline of microbiology.

Leeuwenhoek devoted himself to the development of powerful lenses and private investigations of the microscopic world. Like his contemporaries, he took insects or parts of them and any kinds of plant materials as his first objects of study. However, Leeuwenhoek found "living atoms" in many different shapes. While examining mites in cheese ("the smallest animal that I have ever observed about our houses"), he became aware that even smaller organisms must exist. In 1675 he observed a whole colony of organisms in a drop of rain that had stood for a few days in a tub. From that time he was persuaded of the existence of a living world of microscopic creatures, and as a businessman he speculated about the practical application of such observations. One of the practical questions he wanted to resolve was the function of rennet in cheesemaking. After several experiments, however, he admitted that its mechanism remained a mystery. He could only surmise that something similar must take place in our stomachs in order to transform food into a nutritive substance.

See also CHEESE MITES and RENNET.

Fournier, Marian. *The Fabric of Life: Microscopy in the Seventeenth Century.* Baltimore, Md.: Johns Hopkins University Press, 1996.

Leeuwenhoek, Antoni van. *The Select Works of Antony van Leeuwenhoek: Containing His Microscopical Discoveries in Many of the Works of Nature.* Vol. 1. Translated by Samuel Hoole. London: G. Sidney, 1800.

Barbara Orland

Le Jaouen, Jean-Claude,

is one of the world's foremost goat cheese experts. He was born in France and completed a master of science degree in agronomy and animal sciences in France at the Institut Technique de Pratique Agricole (ITPA) in the 1960s.

As head of the goat research department at the French National Institute for Small Ruminants (Institut Technique de l'Élevage Ovin et Caprin) for more than thirty years, Le Jaouen has been a driving force behind the modernization of the goat industry in France. Beginning in the 1970s, when the industry had a negative image, Le Jaouen worked to organize dairy and cheese producers and to protect traditional French cheesemaking methods.

His impact has reached well beyond the French borders. He was the president of the International Dairy Federation for fifteen years. He headed international projects in more than twenty-five countries and organized the second international symposium on the goat industry in 1971 in cooperation with the French National Institute for Agricultural Research. He also served as editor in chief of the two goat- and sheep-industry professional magazines, *La Chèvre* and *Pâtre*.

His how-to manual, *The Fabrication of Farmstead Goat Cheese*, first published in English in 1987, is considered to be the goat-cheese-making bible. His book had a tremendous impact in the United States because it brought technical knowledge to farmstead cheese producers at a time when America did not have such expertise. In addition, Le Jaouen educated, trained, and judged professionals during contests to help America build its artisanal cheese industry.

Although he is now retired, Le Jaouen continues to share his expertise through conferences and workshops.

See also GOAT.

Le Jaouen, Jean Claude. *The Fabrication of Farmstead Goat Cheese.* Translated by Elizabeth Leete. Ashfield, Mass.: Cheesemakers' Journal, 1987.

Gersende Cazaux

Lighvan Paniri

is the most famous traditional cheese of Iran, known around the world as Iranian white cheese. Lighvan Paniri is a semisoft brined cheese with unique organoleptic properties, which is ripened in brine for three to twelve months. It is produced by artisanal cheesemakers in Lighvan, a green village located at the foothills of Mount Sahand, southeast of Tabriz, the capital city of the East Azerbaijan province. This village has a population of about 5,000 people, whose primary occupations are animal husbandry and cheesemaking, dating back hundreds of years. By some estimates there are more than 200 artisanal cheese producers in this village and adjacent villages, and approximately 65,000 sheep, mainly of the Ghizil (Qızıl) breed. The clean air and the unique flora of this region, as well as a peculiarly hygienic style of milking (with slight pulling of the udder outwards and milking in oblique position to prevent the possible entry of urine and feces into milk) used in this village and the quick delivery of fresh milk to cheese producers, lead to the production of high-quality milk and cheese.

Lighvan Paniri is a starter-free cheese characterized by its white color, salty and acidic taste, pleasant aroma, and soft and brittle texture including numerous round or tear-shaped eyes (holes). It is mainly manufactured from ewe's milk, but mixtures containing up to 20–30 percent goat's milk may occasionally be used. Microbial studies of Lighvan Paniri reveal that this cheese contains many probiotic species, such as *Lactobacillus brevis*, *L. plantarum*, and *L. paracasei*. Also, it is indicated that the typical sensorial properties of this cheese are related to the complex biochemical processes driven by the indigenous flora. Genus *Enterococcus*, *Lactobacillus*, and *Lactococcus* constituted the main LAB (lactic acid bacteria) flora during production stages, respectively. However, the microbial flora of Lighvan Paniri could be changed over the maturation period as *L. brevis* and *L. paraplantarum* strains that are replaced by *L. plantarum* and *L. paracasei* strains with the progress of ripening.

Although production is restricted to Lighvan village, many types of brined cheeses similar to Lighvan Paniri are produced in other regions of Azerbaijan and mistakenly referred to as Lighvan cheese.

Lighvan Paniri is distributed to the market in different sizes, from 3.5 ounces (100 grams) to 37 pounds (17 kilograms), in tin boxes or plastic containers, with more than twenty types of commercial packaging. Annual production capacity of Lighvan Paniri is about 4,000 tons, of which about 1,000 tons are exported annually to locations including the United States, Canada, Japan, and Malaysia. Some of the major brands of Lighvan Paniri in Iran are Kheyrollah Shahiye Lighvan, Lighvan Sabet, Taksaz Labane Sahand, Nasehe Lighvan, Panirak Sepidare Lighvan, Davtalabe Lighvan, Ali Panahiyane Lighvan, Panirak-Zaghak, Hallaj Laban, Mohammad Khoda Doost, Shadiye Lighvan, and Noori.

Lighvan Paniri is consumed as a table cheese or in Doymaj (Döyməc), a traditional food of the Azerbaijan region of Iran. Lighvan Paniri is usually served for breakfast along with bread, sugary tea, or walnuts. It is very similar to Greek feta cheese. See FETA. The mean composition of Lighvan Paniri after sixty days of ripening is: moisture 53.75 percent, fat 17.27 percent, salt 3.68 percent, acidity 2.2 percent, and pH 4.87.

See also BRINED CHEESES and IRAN.

Edaltian, M. R., et al. "Isolation and Identification [of] the Indigenous Lactic Flora from Lighvan, as an Iranian Raw Milk Cheese from Milk to Ripened Cheese." *World Academy of Science, Engineering, and Technology* 68 (2010): 1346–1351.

Kafili, T., Z. Emam-Djomeh, and B. Mayo. "Physiological Biodiversity of Lactobacillus Strains Isolated During Traditional Iranian Lighvan Cheese Manufacturing." *International Journal of Food Properties* 16 (2013): 9–17.

Mirzaei, H. "Microbiological Changes in Lighvan Cheese Throughout Its Manufacture and Ripening." *African Journal of Microbiology Research* 5 (2011): 1609–1614.

Shafiei, Y. "Iranian Traditional Cheeses." Paper presented at the 1st Conference of Iranian Traditional Dairy Products, Khoy, Iran, 2013. In Persian.

Special Products of East Azerbaijan Center. "Industrial Production of Lighvan Paniri." http://tabriz.irib.ir/tolidat/video/tabiat-sanaye-dasti/12804-1392-03-13-10-43-20. In Persian.

Yahya Shafiei Bavil Oliaei

Limburger cheese was originally created by Belgian Trappist monks in the 1800s in the Limburg region of Belgium. It became so popular, that by 1830, German cheesemakers in the Allgäu region began making Limburger, and today, Germany is the largest producer in the world. See MONASTIC CHEESEMAKING.

Limburger is typically crafted in a brick shape, wrapped and sold in foil. Known for its pungent odor, the cheese's meaty and farmyard flavors are significantly milder than its smell. At four weeks of age, Limburger is firm and crumbly. At six weeks, the straw-colored interior becomes softer along the edges, but is still firm on the inside and tastes salty and chalky. After two months, it is mostly creamy from its edges to center, and by three months, it is spreadable and exceptionally stinky, similar to smelly feet. Its sticky orange-brown rind and distinctive odor comes from washing the cheese in a brine solution containing *Brevibacterium linens*, the same type of bacteria found on human skin that is partially responsible for body odor. See *BREVIBACTERIUM LINENS*.

In the United States, all American Limburger is made at one cheese factory: Chalet Cheese Cooperative in Monroe, Wisconsin, a farmer's cooperative dating to 1885. See CHALET CHEESE. Historically, American Limburger was considered a working man's cheese, served on dark bread with brown mustard, onion slices, and enjoyed with a beer—essentially the American version of the English ploughman's lunch. Up until the 1960s, the cheese was especially popular in the Midwest with German immigrant descendants, and was once made at more than one hundred cheese factories in Wisconsin. Today, the cheese has diminished in popularity, and only about 500,000 pounds (227,000 kilograms) are made annually in the United States. In Wisconsin, where it continues production, a Limburger sandwich may often still be found on a tavern menu, served with mustard and raw onion on two pieces of rye bread, served with a local lager.

Due to its distinctive odor, Limburger has achieved a somewhat notorious reputation in American popular culture. For example, it is the only known weakness of Mighty Mouse, and has been featured in many Abbott and Costello routines, including one in which Lou uses a clothespin and gas mask to avoid the smell when serving a customer a Limburger sandwich. The Three Stooges created the famous tag line "Moe, Larry...the cheese!" after Curly eats a piece of Limburger, exhales, and causes the protagonists to faint, ending the episode. Even the author Mark

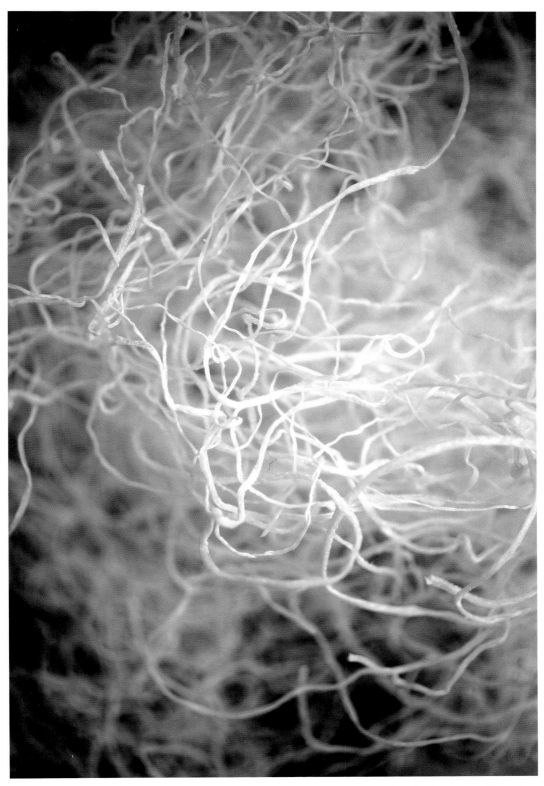

Türkmen Saçağı is an unusual Turkish cheese that looks like a mass of strings. It is produced in the cities of Kars and Ardahan in the East Anatolia region of Turkey by the Turkmen people. © HALEY POLINSKY

Brocciu, a cheese strongly identified with the Mediterranean island of Corsica, is made from ewe's or goat's milk whey taken from prior cheesemaking. Here an old shepherd and his young son use traditional methods to make brocciu, heating the whey in a copper vat over a wood fire. © UNION PDO BROCCIU

Each September herders in the Allgäu region lead their cows back down from the Alpine meadows, where they were pastured for the summer. The return of the cows is a celebration, and the men dress up in traditional garb. Each mountain has its own symbol, which is why edelweiss is pinned to the young boy's suspenders. © KATE ARDING

A portrait of Ignazio (Ig) Vella, who took over the Vella Cheese Company in 1981. Under his leadership Vella cheeses were seen as a standard for artisan cheese production, influencing the wave of artisan cheesemaking that has flourished in California and the rest of the country since the end of the twentieth century. © 2016 FRANKENY IMAGES

Sister Noella Marcellino is a Benedictine nun and cheesemaker from the Abbey of Regina Laudis in Bethlehem, Connecticut. She holds a PhD in microbiology from the University of Connecticut, and her research has provided scientific evidence for the idea that the diversity of local ripening strains reflects the diversity of the people, animals, land, and geology of a region. © ROBERT FENTON HOUSER

This Stilton, a traditional English cow's milk blue cheese, is from Colston Bassett and District Dairy, the smallest producer of farmhouse Stilton in the UK. They have been producing Stilton since 1913 and still hand-ladle their curd from the vat to the cooling trolley, much as Stilton makers would have done in the 1700s. © KATE ARDING

Wheels of Reypenaer cheese aging in their historic warehouse in the Dutch town of Woerden. This cheese obtains its inimitable flavor during a long natural ripening process (up to two and a half years) in a unique microclimate. © RENGENIER C. RITTERSMA

An employee at Finca Pascualete, a Spanish dairy, draining the curd for their sheep's milk Torta cheese. © KATE ARDING

In the remote mountain village of Babbala on the southeastern Peloponnese peninsula in Greece, cheesemakers produce touloumotiri, or "cheese of the skin," using the ancient technique of aging the cheese in the cleaned and heavily salted skin of a goat. © ALEXIS MARIE ADAMS

The Fulbe people of sub-Saharan West Africa practice nomadic pastoralism, moving their herds of cattle in search of natural pastures. Most of the milk from Fulbe cows is consumed either fresh or as a fermented skimmed milk product called *nano*. The Fulbe women also make a fresh cheese called wagashi. © PAUL VAN MELLE

Tymsboro is a pyramid-shape goat's milk cheese produced by Mary Holbrook at Sleight Farm in Somerset, England. A mixture of ash (charcoal) and salt is applied to the cheese a day or two after it is made, which acts via osmosis to draw moisture out of the cheese, promoting rind growth. © KATE ARDING

Twain used Limburger in his play, *Is He Dead?*, putting Limburger in a casket to replicate the smell of a dead body.

Despite its storied reputation, Limburger continues to be one of the most famous washed-rind cheeses made in the world. In addition to a sandwich staple, it may also be served with boiled potatoes and butter.

See also WASHED-RIND CHEESES.

Harbutt, Juliet. *World Cheese Book*. New York: DK, 2009.
"Limburger." CheeseWiki. http://www.cheesewiki.com/limburger.
United States Department of Agriculture, National Agricultural Statistics Service. *Wisconsin Ag News—Specialty Cheese Production*. 6 May 2014. https://www.nass.usda.gov/Statistics_by_State/Wisconsin/Publications/Dairy/2014/WI_SpecialtyCheese_05_14.pdf.

Jeanne Carpenter

lipolysis during cheese ripening is the liberation, by enzymes called lipases, of fatty acids from the triglycerides of milk fat. Lipases catalyze the hydrolysis of the ester linkages in triglycerides, breaking the ester bond with the addition of water. The products of lipolysis are partial glycerides (or glycerol if all three fatty acids are removed) and free fatty acids (FFA).

Lipases in cheese originate from five sources:

1. Milk contains an indigenous lipoprotein lipase (LPL), which is largely inactivated by pasteurization.
2. The coagulant, in cheeses where rennet paste is used. Rennet *paste* contains an enzyme, pregastric esterase, which is strongly lipolytic. Rennet *extracts*, which are used much more commonly, should be free from lipase activity.
3. Starter and non-starter lactic acid bacteria are weakly lipolytic but do contain intracellular enzymes that are released during ripening by cell lysis and contribute to lipolysis in varieties such as Cheddar and Edam that contain no other strongly lipolytic agent.
4. Secondary organisms (e.g., mold in mold-ripened cheeses or smear organisms) are often strongly lipolytic.
5. Exogenous lipases are sometimes used to accelerate cheese ripening.

Levels of lipolysis vary greatly between varieties. Lipolysis is often high in smear-ripened cheeses due to their surface microflora, in cheeses made using rennet paste (e.g., Italian pecorino cheeses) and in varieties ripened for a long time. Cheeses made from raw milk have higher levels of FFA than those made from pasteurized milk due to the activity of LPL. Levels of lipolysis are highest in blue cheese due to extracellular lipases produced by *Penicillium roqueforti*.

Short-chain FFA contribute directly to flavor and levels of FFA in cheese vary from very low (e.g., mozzarella) to extremely high (blue mold varieties). FFA can also be further metabolized to a range of volatile flavor compounds (e.g., methyl ketones, the characteristic flavor compounds of blue cheese).

See also FAT and MILK.

Collins, Y. F., P. L. H. McSweeney, and M. G. Wilkinson. "Lipolysis and Free Fatty Acid Catabolism in Cheese: A Review of Current Knowledge." International Dairy Journal 13, no. 11 (2003): 841–866.
Collins, Y. F., P. L. H. McSweeney, and M. G. Wilkinson. "Lipolysis and Catabolism of Fatty Acids in Cheese. In *Cheese: Chemistry, Physics, and Microbiology*, Vol. 1: *General Aspects*, 3d ed., edited by Paul F. Fox, P. L. H. McSweeney, T. M. Cogan, et al., pp. 374–389. Amsterdam: Elsevier Applied Science, 2004.

P. L. H. McSweeney

lisnati is a pasta filata cheese produced in the central and northern parts of Montenegro. Historical data indicate that nomadic Vlachs tribe brought the technology to this area. It is also known as Kolašin cheese, for the town at the center of its production area. Lisnati has a distinctive, soft, elastic, and smooth structure, mild sour aroma, and porcelain white color. The most recognizable feature is its unusual form of slices that are extremely thin, like a sheet of paper or leaf. Hence the name "lisnati," meaning "foliate" or "leafy."

The technology of this cheese is unique and hard to implement under conditions of industrial production. Raw cow's milk is heated to 113°F (45°C) and left for twelve to twenty-four hours for acidification by the activity of natural microorganisms from milk. Thereafter milk is skimmed and mixed with fresh raw milk and 10–15 percent water. Rennet is added at 95°F (35°C). After thirty to forty-five minutes, coagulation is complete and the coagulum is cut and collected in the curd. Collecting the curd is done in whey. Then the curd is removed from the whey and pressed. Pressing is done by use of a wooden plank and by putting a heavy stone on the plank to evenly distribute the weight. During pressing, the curd should be topped by warm whey (up to 131°F [55°C]) and folded very often. First it is folded in half of the total amount of curd and later to one-fourth. This is repeated several times in order to produce more sheets. Lisnati can be consumed immediately or left for ripening. Salting is optional, using dry salt. Lisnati cheese is the rare cheese that can be frozen and, after defrosting, there are slight or no changes in its sensory, nutritional, qualitative, and quantitative traits.

See also PASTA FILATA.

Dozet, N., et al. "Autohtoni mlječni proizvodi" [Autochthonous Dairy Products]. Belgrade, Serbia: Poljoprivredni institut Podgorica, SILMIR-Beograd, 1996.

Mirecki, S., et al. "Characteristics of Montenegrian Autochtonous Lisnati Cheese." *Journal of Hygienic Engineering and Design* 1 (2011): 320–325.

Rakocevic, N. "Mljekarstvo na Sinjajevini I mjere za njegovo unapredjenje." *Stočarstvo*, br. 3–4, VI, Zagreb, 1952.

Zdanovski, N. *Ovcje sirarstvo.* Zagreb: Poljoprivredni nakladni zavod, 1947.

Slavko Mirecki

The genus **Listeria** represents a group of bacteria that are widely distributed in nature. While most members, such as *L. innocua, L. welshimeri,* and *L. grayi,* are nonpathogenic and associated with soil and green plant material, included among this group is the significant human pathogen *L. monocytogenes.* Outbreaks of illness and death linked to consumption of cheese contaminated with *L. monocytogenes* have occurred throughout the world. In order to maintain the safety of cheese and prevent contamination, it is essential for cheesemakers to control the risk of this pathogen on their farm, in their cheesemaking facilities, and during affinage and distribution.

Individuals who are susceptible to infection by *L. monocytogenes* include persons with immune system compromise due to conditions such as cancer, diabetes, HIV/AIDS, kidney disease, advanced age (over age sixty-five), medications (corticosteroids/acid inhibitors), and pregnancy. There are two syndromes associated with listeriosis, the disease caused by *L. monocytogenes.* The first is diarrheal illness, characterized by rapid onset eighteen to twenty-four hours following consumption of a contaminated food. This syndrome is rarely if ever fatal. The second form, invasive illness, is representative of listeriosis in pregnancy or in immunosuppressed hosts. Invasive listeriosis has a mean incubation period prior to illness onset of thirty days, with a range of ten to seventy days. This extended incubation period makes identification of infective food vehicles challenging. Currently there are approximately 1,600 cases of listeriosis, 1,500 hospitalizations, and 260 deaths per year from all food sources reported to the US Centers of Disease Control and Prevention. Despite being a rare cause of food-borne illness, 30 percent of these cases will lead to death, making listeriosis a leading cause of death from a food-borne pathogen and an organism of major public health concern worldwide.

Listeria monocytogenes is ubiquitous in nature. It has been isolated from diverse sources including soil, sewage, water, green plant material, fresh produce, and wild and domesticated animals including ruminants, poultry, and seafood. The association between poor quality silage feeding and onset of listeriosis in ruminants is well recognized. See SILAGE. Infected animals display neurological impairments and may circle endlessly in one direction, causing listeriosis to be referred to as circling disease. *L. monocytogenes* possesses characteristics that make it very tolerant of a wide range of environmental conditions, and this confounds control of this pathogen. Most importantly *L. monocytogenes* is one of very few human pathogens that has adapted to growth at refrigeration temperatures, which is why it poses challenges to the safety of cheeses. During refrigerated storage, low initial levels of *L. monocytogenes* can grow and multiply to levels that cause human illness. This pathogen can also display resistance to salt, acid, sanitizers, and heat. *L. monocytogenes* grows best at neutral pH ranges and in high moisture environments, which is why fresh soft and soft-ripened cheeses support growth of this pathogen to high levels that can pose a risk to public health, especially for products that are stored under refrigeration for extended time periods. In contrast in hard cheeses such as Cheddar, Swiss (Emmentaler, Gruyère), and Italian Grana cheeses, factors such as low pH and low moisture interact to create a hostile environment for this pathogen, preventing growth and accelerating declines in population levels during aging. See FRESH CHEESES; PH MEASUREMENT; and MOISTURE.

A number of notable cheese-associated outbreaks of listeriosis have occurred around the world. In 1985 a large outbreak involving 142 cases of illness and 52 deaths was linked to consumption of contaminated Mexican-style soft cheese. The facility that manufactured the cheese had illegally used a combination of raw and pasteurized milk for cheese production, and the processing plant environment was heavily contaminated with *L. monocytogenes*. See MEXICAN CHEESES. An outbreak linked to Vacherin Mont d'Or soft-ripened cheese occurred in western Switzerland over the years 1983–1987, resulting in 122 cases of illness and 30 deaths. Implementation of rigorous cleaning and sanitation protocols in caves and manufacturing environments along with use of equipment that could be effectively cleaned and sanitized were extremely effective in ending the outbreak. See MONT D'OR. An outbreak linked to Brie de Meaux, a soft-ripened raw-milk cheese, occurred in France in 1995. Twenty people developed listeriosis and four fetal deaths were reported. See BRIE DE MEAUX. In 2000 illegally produced Mexican-style soft cheese (queso fresco) resulted in 13 cases of illness, 11 perinatal infections, and 5 stillbirths in North Carolina. During 2009 and 2010 a large listeriosis outbreak involving 34 cases of illness and 8 deaths was reported in Austria, Germany, and the Czech Republic. This outbreak was linked to Quargel, a traditional Austrian acid curd, red smear cheese made from pasteurized milk. An outbreak linked to imported ricotta salata cheese occurred in the United States in 2012, resulting in 22 cases of illness and 4 deaths. See RICOTTA.

While *Listeria* can be shed into raw milk by infected cows, it is well recognized that *Listeria* is an environmental pathogen and the primary route of contamination of cheese is from the processing environment. It is critical that cheesemakers engage in control of their processing environment through use of Hazard Analysis, Critical Control Point (HACCP) programs, enhanced sanitation, alteration of foot traffic, and microbiological testing to identify and eliminate niches of this pathogen. *Listeria* is inactivated by pasteurization, and contamination of processed dairy products is therefore most likely a function of post-pasteurization contamination from the dairy plant environment. See HAZARD ANAL-YSIS AND CRITICAL CONTROL POINT; PASTEURIZATION; and POST-PROCESS CONTAMINATION.

In fact numerous surveys document the presence of *Listeria* within the dairy plant environment including floors, drains, freezers, processing rooms (particularly entrances), cases and case washers, floor mats and foot baths, and brushes used to apply smear cultures/washes during affinage. Research from the author's laboratory found that processing plants located near a farm had a significantly higher incidence of *Listeria* contamination than those without an on-site dairy. Additional research demonstrated the link between on-farm sources of *Listeria* contamination (dairy cattle, raw milk, and silage) and subsequent contamination of dairy processing environments. The finding of *L. monocytogenes* common to both dairy processing and farm environments clearly implicates the farm as a natural reservoir for *Listeria* ribotypes capable of entering dairy processing facilities. These findings, which support the link between on-farm sources of *Listeria* contamination and subsequent contamination of dairy processing environments, stress the importance of farm-based HACCP programs for controlling *Listeria*. Europe and the United States differ in their regulatory approach to *Listeria* control, with the United States having a zero tolerance policy (0 *Listeria* in a 25-gram sample of cheese). In contrast, the Eurpoean Union has a food safety objective of fewer than 100 *Listeria* per gram of cheese at time of consumption. Both regulatory approaches assure low levels of contamination, which has shown to be protective to public health for the general population.

See also OUTBREAK and PATHOGENS.

Donnelly, C. W. "Growth and Survival of Microbial Pathogens in Cheese." In *Cheese: Chemistry, Physics and Microbiology*, 3d ed., Vol. 1: *General Aspects* edited by P. F. Fox, et al., pp. 541–560. New York: Elsevier, 2004.

Donnelly, C. W., ed. *Cheese and Microbes*. ASM Press, Washington, D.C.: ASM Press, 2014.

Donnelly, C. W., and F. Diez-Gonzalez. "*Listeria monocytogenes*." In *Guide to Foodborne Pathogens*, 2d ed., edited by R. G. Labbe and S. Garcia, pp. 45–74. Chichester, U.K.: Wiley Blackwell, 2013.

Ryser, Elliot T., and Elmer H. Marth, eds. *Listeria, Listeriosis, and Food Safety*. 3d ed. Boca Raton, Fla.: Taylor & Francis, 2007.

Catherine Donnelly

literature. A phrase such as "ripe Stilton" has the power to bring to mind a blue-streaked cylinder on a market stall, a well-remembered taste, a recollected occasion, a conversation with friends, and a cheesy atmosphere pervading the larder. What follows is an attempt to classify the meanings and undertones that accompany the mention of cheese in literature.

The name of a cheese can recall vignettes and literary allusions from the whole world of recorded human experience. What does the word "Angelot" evoke? Perhaps the seventeenth-century comedy by Thomas Duffet in which an old woman is said to be "as mellow as an Angelot Cheese that has been mortified fifteen months in horse-dung" (*The Amorous Old Woman*, 1674, act 1, scene 2). Dutch cheese? A quiet retirement home for a rat in one of La Fontaine's *Fables* (1678, book 7, no. 3). Parmesan? One remembers Samuel Pepys, watching with horror as the flames of the fire of London advanced toward his own house in 1666: "And in the evening Sir W. Penn and I did dig another [pit] and put our wine in it, and I my Parmazan cheese as well as my wine" (*Diary*, 4 September 1666).

In ancient and medieval texts, the mention of cheese often suggests rusticity or wildness. Thus in Homer's *Odyssey* (ca. 700 B.C.E., book 9, lines 219–225) cheese is only once mentioned, in the passage in which the making of cheese is described as the everyday activity of the savage Cyclops (though the poet seems to be as familiar with cheese terminology as any nomadic pastoralist would have been). See HOMER. In the *Idylls* of Theocritus (ca. 260 B.C.E., idylls 5, 7, 11) cheese is typically a gift by a shepherd to a lover, or else an offering on a rustic altar to one of the gods or goddesses of the countryside. In the Latin poem "*Copa*" (ca. 20 B.C.E., line 17) a hospitable country inn, somewhere in Roman Italy, offers its own homemade cheeses among other delicacies from farm and orchard. In a poor, rural society such as that of medieval Iceland, curds and cheese might well be the only food available even at a feast, as they are in the *Eyrbyggja Saga* (ca. 1250, chapter 45). In Ben Jonson's *The Sad Shepherd* (1637, act 1, scene 7), cheese and milk products abound at an imagined country festival: "Fall to your cheesecakes, curds, and clotted cream, Your fools, your flans . . . strain ewe's milk Into your cider syllabubs."

Yet cheese is a valuable food for which even city dwellers will pay highly. The anonymous compiler of the *Journal d'un Bourgeois de Paris* or *Parisian Journal*, a record of the years 1405–1449, notes repeatedly the destruction inflicted on the Brie region, close to Paris, by French and foreign armies. He rightly links these violent episodes with the fluctuating availability and price of Brie cheese on Paris markets. In Dutch paintings of the seventeenth century, cheeses frequently appear in market and household scenes, depicted with loving realism, symbolizing prosperity or overspending or wise use of a limited budget. The wealth of cheeses brought to market in Paris in the late nineteenth century for the delectation of city gourmets is memorably evoked by Emile Zola in his classic novel *Le ventre de Paris* (The Belly of Paris).

So is cheese a rustic or an urbane food? Is it traditional or fashionable? Can it somehow be both? The ambiguity may help to explain the unexpectedly low opinion of cheese expressed by most early dietary writers. The anonymous author of *Ancient Medicine* (attributed to Hippocrates, ca. 400 B.C.E.) is a good deal more sensible than most of his successors: "We must not simply say, 'Cheese is a bad food.' Cheese does not harm every person alike. Some can eat their fill of it without the slightest ill effect. Indeed those with whom it agrees are remarkably strengthened by it." The treatise *Regimen*, in the same Hippocratic collection, also gives a positive evaluation: "cheese is strong, healing, nourishing, settling." Paradoxically in traditional medicine these strong positives were sufficient to condemn cheese as an ingredient in most people's diet: such a powerful food would unbalance the constitution. Moreover most dietary writers who followed "Hippocrates" were hoping to establish simple, general rules—just the kind of rules against which *Ancient Medicine* warns us. Finally, to early scientific minds cheese seemed to demonstrate its own dangerous nature; it was well known to be the product of putrefaction. For all these reasons early medical authorities such as Galen, Oribasius, and Avicenna generally advised their readers against cheese. Sometimes they make an exception for soft, fresh cheese, because that is not heating and not putrescent. Thus, in speaking up for the dietary qualities of cheese, the Italian Renaissance writers Pantaleone da Confienza and Giulio Landi were contradicting the medical consensus of the period.

The dramatist John Heywood (ca. 1497–ca. 1580) was ahead of his time in reflecting, in his poem "On Books and Cheese," that cheese arouses as many contrasting opinions as literature does. With the gradual recognition of regional excellence in cheesemaking, it is the demand by gourmets for their favorite cheeses that eventually defeats the dietary writers. But authors and playwrights must generally rely on the mere names of cheeses, and perhaps on a well-chosen adjective or two, to suggest the presence of a luxury food, the price paid for it, and the pleasure it brings. In John Ford's comedy 'Tis Pity She's a Whore, a young rake is said to love his mistress "almost as well as he loves Parmesan" (1633, act 1, scene 4). The Roquefort sniffed and praised by the French poet Saint-Amant, in 1642, was "one of the most refined." In J. K. Huysmans's A Rebours ("Against Nature," 1884, chapter 11), a Stilton cheese is sufficiently special to attract the interest even of the sensation-hungry hero Des Esseintes. "Cheese was forthcoming," we are told in Elliott Paul's Narrow Street (1942), "a Port Salut that increased my respect for the fat cook who did the daily marketing." Wensleydale was the cheese that stood on the sideboard at a dinner of spies in Our Man in Havana: it was "perfect" (1958, part 4, chapter 2). Little is heard in early modern literature of Spanish cheese, but fresh cream cheeses can be seen in Spanish and Portuguese paintings of the seventeenth century; Luis Meléndez, in eighteenth-century Madrid, liked to depict a wider range of cheeses in his household scenes.

There is a negative side. In Monica Dickens's Man Overboard (1958, chapter 15) seasickness is amusingly suggested: "His face remained the colour of Caerphilly cheese." A recent French novel by M. Peyramaure (L'orange de Noel, 1982) uses almost the same simile: "Tu es blanche comme une caillade. Qu'est-ce que tu as?" (You're as white as cottage cheese. What's the matter with you?) These images were not chosen at random. Cheese—its smell, its taste, its appearance—can easily suggest illness and can even provoke it. No reader of Jerome K. Jerome's Three Men in a Boat (1889, chapter 4) will forget the anecdote that demonstrates the "advantages of cheese as a travelling companion." The narrator has been entrusted by an unnamed friend with two fine, unnamed mature cheeses (Cheshire? Lancashire? We are not told) to carry three hundred miles by rail from Liverpool to London. These odoriferous cheeses ensure that even on a crowded train he has always a compartment to himself: one temporary traveling companion, an undertaker, observes that the smell "puts him in mind of a dead baby," after which everyone else in the carriage tries to escape at the same

moment. As if to provide advance support for this jaundiced view of cheese, Giulio Landi, who favored the cheeses of Piacenza and Parma, had made unfavorable comparisons of Provatura with an old man's testicle, Caciocavallo with an old woman's sagging breast, and Marzolino with a cucumber.

See also ART; CHILDREN'S LITERATURE; and LITERATURE OF CHEESE.

Burdett, Osbert. "The Literature of Cheese." In A Little Book of Cheese, pp. 64–83. London: G. Howe, 1935.
Camporesi, Piero. Le officine dei sensi. Milan, Garzanti, 1985, pp. 47–77.
Camporesi, Piero. La miniera del mondo: Artieri, inventori, impostori. Milan: Il Saggiatore, 1990, pp. 89–117.
Jones, W. H. S., ed. and trans. Hippocrates. London and Cambridge, Mass.: Harvard University Press, 1923, vol. 1, p. 55; vol. 4, p. 325.
Milligan, B. A., ed. John Heywood: Works. Urbana: University of Illinois Press, 1956.
Saint-Amant, Marc-Antoine Girard de. Oeuvres. Paris, 1654. "Le Brie"; "Lettre à M. de Melay."
Shirley, Janet, trans. A Parisian Journal, 1405–1449. Oxford: Clarendon, 1968.
Zola, Emile. Le ventre de Paris. Paris: Charpentier, 1873, vol. 2, p. 106.

Andrew Dalby

The **literature of cheese** may be said to begin in the late fifteenth century. Cheese is mentioned in passing in many early texts, but no surviving work of literature in any language is devoted entirely to cheese before the landmark year of 1477.

At this date (less than thirty years after the introduction of printing to Europe) Pantaleone da Confienza, a native of northern Italy, published his wholly original survey of European cheeses and cheesemaking. He called it Summa Lacticiniorum or "Outline of Milk Products," a title that alludes to venerable works such as the vast Summa Theologiae or "Outline of Theology" by Saint Thomas Aquinas. In giving his book this deliberately grandiose title Pantaleone asserts that it, too, is definitive in its limited field. Composed in Latin, the usual language for serious writing at this period, Summa Lacticiniorum opens with a general section discussing the nature of milk and the range of products made from it, especially cheese. Pantaleone moves on to the variety of cheeses, relating these to the seasons, the climate, the origin of the milk, and the methods used in making and maturing. In part two he surveys the regional and local cheeses known to him. This impressive survey begins with Pantaleone's native Italy, focusing entirely on the north, from the marzolino of Tuscany to the cheeses of the Alpine valleys. Having evidently traveled widely in northwestern Europe, Pantaleone continues his cheese itinerary through Savoie and across France to Poitou and Brittany. He notes the importance of the cheese of Brie, before moving on to England, Flanders, and the Rhine valley. He has no high opinion of German cheese, but considers some English cheeses equal in quality to the best Italian kinds. Part three of Pantaleone's book discusses the nutritional value of different cheeses in accordance with medieval dietary theories.

Sixty years later appeared a whimsical book entitled *Formaggiata di Sere Stentato*. This "Cheesery," attributed to an imaginary Sere Stentato, was in fact written by Giulio Landi, member of a society of gastronomes in Piacenza in northern Italy. Landi takes up the defense of cheese, and in particular the wonderful hard cheeses of the Po Valley, against all kinds of detractors, using all kinds of arguments—some of them so scurrilous or indecent that they were deleted from later editions of the book by the censor.

Since the cheeses of northern Italy are among the greatest in the world, it is quite appropriate that these two short texts from Renaissance Italy set a pattern for cheese writing to come. One line of descent, beginning from Pantaleone, led to informative books about cheese and technical texts about cheesemaking. Most of these will not be listed here because, generally speaking, the more factual, the less literary. Two exceptions are to be noted for their literary quality. In the late sixteenth century Thomas Tusser wrote a didactic poem on farming, entitled in its final version "Five Hundred Points of Good Husbandry." This contains a section in which the imaginary dairymaid Cisley (Cicely) is sharply instructed about all that can go wrong in cheesemaking. In the early twentieth century Osbert Burdett wrote *A Little Book of Cheese*, very British but also very readable.

The second line of descent, beginning from Giulio Landi, led to literary appreciations and polemics for and against cheese. The first poem devoted entirely to cheese—again in Italian—is by Ercole Bentivoglio. Published in his collected poems in 1557 it firmly asserts—against the weight of medieval medical opinion—the nutritional benefits of cheese, with light-hearted attention to its claimed aphrodisiac effect. In later centuries Paris became the epicenter of gastronomy, and the next poems about cheese are to be found in the French writings of Marc-Antoine Girard de Saint-Amant, published in Paris in 1654. Saint-Amant was an enthusiastic gourmand and versifier whose works offer the earliest literary mention of Cantal and Roquefort. However, he praises Brie above all others. A long time later—around 1900—the Belgian poet Thomas Braun included a poem in praise of cheese in his *Livre des Bénédictions* (Book of Blessings). The poem was translated into English verse by Jethro Bithell in 1911, and in the same year the British poet Hilaire Belloc included an essay "On Cheeses" in his collection *First and Last*.

Although not devoted entirely to cheese, Emile Zola's novel *Le ventre de Paris* (The Belly of Paris), published in 1873, deserves mention. The events of this episode from Zola's classic Rougon-Macquart series take place in and around Les Halles, the central food market of Paris. The pages that describe the cheese market, with its powerful flavors and overpowering aromas, are a classic of cheese literature. Zola's pursuit of realism permits him to devise striking similes that conjure up the looks and smells of famous French cheeses: a Port Salut is compared to an antique discus, while a Roquefort, posing under its glass dome with a princely air, is compared to marble in its appearance.

A new development of the end of the twentieth century is the novel on a gastronomic theme. Among the many recent examples, at least one is devoted to cheese—to the imaginary Coolarney Blue, inspired by real artisan Irish cheeses, around which the New Zealand author Sarah-Kate Lynch has woven an unusual romance.

See also CHILDREN'S LITERATURE.

Belloc, Hilaire. *First and Last*. London: Methuen, 1911.
Bentivoglio, Ercole. *Le satire et altre rime piacevoli*. Venice: G. Giolito de' Ferrari, 1557.
Berno, Francesca Romana. "Cheese's Revenge: Pantaleone da Confienza and the Summa Lacticiniorum." *Petits Propos Culinaires* 69 (2002): 21–44.
Bithell, Jethro, ed. *Contemporary Belgian Poetry*. London: Walter Scott, 1911.
Burdett, Osbert. *A Little Book of Cheese*. London: G. Howe: 1935.
Landi, Giulio. *Formaggiata di Sere Stentato: Al serenissimo re della virtude*. Edited by Alberto Capatti. Milan: Grana Padano, n.d.

Lynch, Sarah-Kate. *Blessed Are the Cheesemakers.* New York: Warner, 2002.

Naso, Irma, ed. *Formaggio del Medioevo: La "Summa lacticiniorum" di Pantaleone da Confienza.* Turin, Italy: Il Segnalibro, 1990.

Pantaleone da Confienza. *Trattato dei latticini.* Edited by Emilio Faccioli. Bra, Italy: Slow Food Editore, 2001.

Saint-Amant, Marc-Antoine Girard de. *Oeuvres.* Paris: Guillaume de Luyne, 1661.

Tusser, Thomas. *Five Hundreth Pointes of Good Husbandry.* London: Richard Tottell, 1573.

Zola, Emile. *Le ventre de Paris.* Paris: Charpentier, 1873.

Andrew Dalby

Livarot is a washed-rind cow's milk cheese from Normandy, France. Its classic format is a cylinder about 4.7 inches (12 centimeters) in diameter and one inch (3 centimeters) high, with a rather sticky, orangey rind. The paste is somewhat chewy but melts in the mouth, with a pungent animalian aroma and flavors reminiscent of onion, hay, and even smoke. It is easy to identify thanks to the five or so *laîches*, wrappings of plant fiber (or paper), around the perimeter. The classic five stripes led to its nickname "the Colonel," for their resemblance to service stripes.

Historical references to cheeses from the village of Livarot go back to the dawn of the eighteenth century, though with no description of what they were like. These early sources say it was available in Paris already, but the nineteenth-century development of rail transport ushered in its golden age as Normandy's best-selling cheese, with 4.5 million sold in 1877 alone. It was apparently mostly consumed by working-class people, earning it its other nickname, "the meat of the poor." Into the twentieth century, Livarot was made with skimmed milk, resulting in a finished cheese of 5–10 percent milk fat (the cream having been reserved for more-lucrative butter making), necessitating the use of *laîches* to help the resultant tender cheese keep its shape; but the milk fat crept to 30 percent by the 1930s and is set at 40 percent today. Up through World War II, Livarot was predominantly made by farmer-cheesemakers and sold "white," that is, fresh, to affineurs who oversaw its maturation and sale. In this system's heyday, there were approximately 350 cheesemakers and 23 affineurs.

Livarot has had AOC (appellation d'origine contrôlée) status since 1975, and its production rules became stricter in the 2000s. Its production zone corresponds roughly to the Pays d'Auge, a verdant rolling area spanning the Calvados department into the Orne along the Dives and Touques rivers, centered on its namesake town Livarot. By 2017, all herds producing for Livarot must be entirely Normande breed cows that spend at least six months of the year at pasture, with hay available the rest of the year. See NORMANDE.

Milk for Livarot production may be pasteurized or thermized before being renneted, after which it is cut into medium curds and molded. It is left to drain, being turned once, for up to forty-eight hours, before being dry-salted or brined. During ripening, the cheese must be washed at least three times in brine (which may contain annatto to boost the color), and may be brushed to favor growth of the characteristic *Brevibacterium linens* on the rind. See ANNATTO; BREVIBACTERIUM LINENS and BRINED CHEESES.

Each cheese is then wrapped with *laîches*, traditionally strips of the inner core of cattail leaves that were harvested, prepared, and dried in late summer for use throughout the year. One manufacturer continues this practice, growing cattails in ponds behind the dairy, while others purchase them or substitute orange paper (to be phased out in 2017). Livarot must be aged for twenty-one days before leaving the dairy. In addition to its classic size, it may also be sold in smaller and larger formats.

As of 2014, annual production was at 1,200 metric tons per year, of which 12 percent was made with raw milk, coming from four Livarot makers: Domaine Saint Hippolyte (farmstead, made from raw milk), Fromagerie de la Houssaye (which grows and harvests its own *laîches*), Fromagerie Graindorge, and Société fromagère d'Orbec (owned by Lactalis, selling under the brand Lanquetot).

See also NORMANDY and WASHED-RIND CHEESES.

Legifrance. "Décret du 30 mars 2007 relatif à l'appellation d'origine contrôlée 'Livarot.'" https://www.legifrance.gouv.fr/affichTexte.do?cidTexte=LEGITEXT000006055826.

Mackiewicz, François. *Fromages et fromagers de Normandie.* Le Puy, France: Bonneton, 1983.

Juliette Rogers

Livno is a hard cheese produced in the area of Livno in western Bosnia and Herzegovina, which is the largest karst field in Europe. Livno cheese was originally produced from sheep's milk, but today it is mostly produced from a mixture of sheep's and cow's milk in which the share of cow's milk should not exceed 30 percent. The first production of the cheese, as was the case of mountain cheeses, is associated with the establishment of the Country Agricultural Station in Livno in 1888 by the Austro-Hungarian government. The main task of the station was the production of cheese as well as training of local manufacturers in the production of cheese. For this purpose the station brought eminent cheesemakers from France, Switzerland, and the Czech Republic.

To produce Livno cheese the evening and morning milks are mixed and heated to 88–91°F (31–33°C). Natural calf rennet powder is then added to the milk, so the milk coagulates in a period of fifty to seventy-five minutes. The resulting cheese curd is cut into about 3-inch (8-centimeter) cubes and then granulated to the size of a kernel of wheat. These kernels are cooked at a temperature between 113–118°F (45–48°C) for twenty to forty minutes. After cooking, the cheese mass is poured into molds lined with jute cheesecloth. The cheese is gradually pressed from twelve to twenty-four hours, with constant rolling over. Then it is salted in a brine concentration of 22–25 percent salt for forty-eight hours. The usual ripening lasts between six and twelve weeks (at a temperature of 54–59°F [12–15°C] and humidity of 70–85 percent).

Livno cheese is cylindrical, hay yellow in color, and weighs between 4–7 pounds (2–3 kilograms). Its cross section shows several regular small holes. The consistency is solid. The taste is mildly milky sour, moderately salty and piquant, and the smell is pleasant and characteristic for sheep's milk cheeses. Livno cheese, together with local ham fried dumplings (called "peksimeti"), represents the typical starter of Bosnian and Herzegovinan gastronomy, served with the traditional wines Blatina (red wine) and Žilavka (white wine).

Mair-Waldenburg, Heinricha. *Handbuch der kase.* Kempten, Germany: Volkswirtschaftlicher Verlag, 1974.

Sarić, Zlatan, et al. "Autochthonous Cheese Making in Bosnia and Herzegovina—Historical Aspect." *Biotechnology in Animal Husbandry* 24 (2008).

Sarić, Zlatan, et al. "Sensory Properties of Livno Cheese in Relation to Consumers Preferences." *Food Industry* 21 (2010): 35–41.

Tarik Dizdarević and Zlatan Sarić

The **Loire Valley** is a region situated in northwest France. Sometimes referenced as part of central France, it is the geographical area surrounding the Loire River. France's longest river, at 629 miles (1,012 km) in length, the Loire River flows from the Massif Central highlands to the Atlantic Ocean. The Loire Valley has a moderate, oceanic climate becoming more continental farther inland; temperatures do not vary wildly, resulting in cool winters and warm summers. The region is generally known for its viniculture as much as for its cheesemaking, especially the production of Sancerre, Vouvray, Muscadet, Chinon, and Pouilly-Fumé wines.

The Loire Valley is France's center of goat cheese production as well as the internationally recognized home of chèvre (French for goat, but also used as a term in English to refer to cheeses made from goat's milk, often in the French style). See CHÈVRE. The origins of goat cheese production in the Loire Valley date back to at least the eighth century C.E. and the Saracens (also historically called Moors, Arabs, Berbers, or Turks; in modern day, Saracens could be classified as Muslim Arabs). The proliferation of goats and of soft-ripened goat cheese is attributed to this population and their presence in France through the thirteenth century. When the Saracen army finally retreated, their animals and equipment were left behind and production continued locally by French farmers.

In the cheese industry, the Loire Valley is referenced as a broader area than in most political and geographic descriptions. AOC (appellation d'origine contrôlée) cheeses often referred to as Loire Valley goat cheeses, but actually produced in neighboring geopolitical regions along the Loire River tributaries, include Chabichou du Poitou (Poitou-Charentes region) and Pouligny-Saint-Pierre, Sainte-Maure de Touraine, Selles-sur-Cher, and Valençay (Centre region). See CHABICHOU DU POITOU; SAINT-MAURE DE TOURAINE; SELLES-SUR-CHER; and VALENÇAY. These cheeses predominantly fall under the soft-ripened goat cheese category and are generally small-format cheeses, though they vary somewhat in age, shape, and rind characteristics. Vegetable or oak ash is a feature on the rinds of many Loire Valley cheeses, as well as the brainy-looking *Geotrichum candidum* yeast and the white, bloomy *Penicillium candidum* mold. See ASH; *GEOTRICHUM CANDIDUM* and *PENICILLIUM*. Universally known for being soft, younger cheeses, they proliferate in the spring just after kidding (the goat-specific term for giving birth), when milk production is high and milk is rich with extra fat content. Traditionally thought of as cheeses made and sold in the spring, Loire Valley goat cheeses have become available year-round in modern times.

Cheeses from the Loire Valley vary in production from high-volume industrial operations to *fermier* (farmstead) producers. P. Jacquin et Fils (est. 1947) and Fromagerie d'Anjouin are well-established producers and affineurs in the region, and Rodolphe Le Meunier has emerged as a major affineur with a strong market presence in the United States. In addition, there are currently hundreds of local farmhouses, dairies, and co-ops producing and aging cheeses in the Loire Valley region.

See also FRANCE.

Androuët, Pierre. *The Complete Encyclopedia of French Cheese*. New York: Harper's Magazine, 1973.
Masui, Kazuko, and Tomoko Yamada, eds. *French Cheeses*. 3d ed. London: Dorling Kindersley, 2004.

Elena Santogade

Lombardy is an agricultural and industrial region in northern Italy, characterized by thriving dairy farming and a centuries-old cheesemaking industry. Recent decades have seen the consolidation of dairy farms, decreasing the number of enterprises while increasing herd sizes, but decreasing the overall number of cattle due to doubling milk yields since the 1980s. In the 2010 agricultural census, the number of farms with cattle was 14,718, with a total of 1,484,991 cattle (ISTAT, 2012).

A number of Lombard cheeses have their origins in the tradition of transhumant dairy-farming. As this practice straddled peaks and lowlands between summers and winters, many upland cheese productions distinguish between cheese from the milk of animals fed on fresh grass, and milk obtained from cows in lowland farms and fed on hay and fodder. This marks an important distinction between artisanal cheese (which is associated with open pasture grazing, small quantity, seasonal, upland production) and industrial cheese (which is associated with sedentary breeding, high milk yields, and all-year round production). See ARTISANAL; INDUSTRIAL; and TRANSHUMANCE.

A representative upland cheese type is the high-prestige, round-shaped, matured, yellowish wheels (of about 22 pounds [10 kilograms] and upward),

with brushed and hardened crust, from the family of Bitto, *Formai de Mut*, and Branzi (the latter is similar to Parmesan or Grana but smaller, less cooked, and less matured). Local historians of animal husbandry argue that these three upland cheeses share the same roots in longer circuits of Lombard transhumance. See BITTO.

Meanwhile, lowland dairy production is characterized by the family of Taleggio and stracchino cheeses (including Gorgonzola, originally called Stracchino di Gorgonzola). These are various types of fresh, raw, whitish, soft, flowery-crust cheeses (usually square and weighing around 4 pounds [2 kilograms]—except for the round Gorgonzola). These lowland cheeses are usually produced at competitive prices for common and everyday consumption, although niche and traditional craft production survives or has been actively revived, for instance under the protection of Slow Food Presidia (such as the Presidium of Stracchino all'Antica delle Valli Orobiche, established in 2010, preserving the technique of curdling raw milk in situ, at milking temperature—*a munta calda*). See SLOW FOOD.

The latest European hygiene regulations concerning milk and cheese production affected Lombardy through the regional decree (Decreto del Presidente della Repubblica [DPR]) No. 54 of 14 January 1997 and subsequent modifications, which established clear food safety criteria for cheese made in mountain stations. This has impacted an already marginal upland cheesemaking tradition, which is nevertheless being revived by an active policy of "patrimonialization" of cheese as an item of local heritage. See PATRIMONY.

See also ITALY.

ISTAT. *Censimento dell'Agricoltura in Breve*, 2012. http://censimentoagricoltura.istat.it/inbreve/?QueryId=675&lang=it&graph=&subtheme=5&cube=DICA_ALLEVAMENTI#.

Cristina Grasseni

Lor is an Iranian traditional cheese manufactured from whey resulting from cheese production. See WHEY. It is manufactured in rural areas of the Azerbaijan and Kurdistan Provinces of Iran, from whey derived from semihard cheeses such as Peche, which is produced in Miyandoab city. Lor is similar to Italian ricotta; Greek Mizithra, Anthotiros, and Manouri;

and Turkish Lor, which are also made from whey. See MANOURI and RICOTTA.

To manufacture this cheese, whey is heated at about 212°F (100°C) for 30 minutes. The combination of low pH and high temperature breaks down the protein and causes it to precipitate, forming a fine curd. After the solid materials (which appear as foam on the whey) rise to the surface, they are collected and strained using a cloth bag. Because of the small percentage of residual lactose, the resulting product tastes like slightly sweet cream. It has no particular smell, a relatively soft texture, and a creamy white color. Since the color-producing components are fat soluble, the color tends to become more yellow as the fat content increases. Lor is rich in serum proteins, particularly albumin and globulin, and it has a high nutritional value because of the essential amino acids it contains, including threonine, valine, leucine, isoleucine, and cysteine, which make it comparable in composition to egg albumin. The milk yield for Lor production is higher from ewes and buffalos than it is from cows. The mean value of acidity is about 1.66 percent, and the pH is 6.83. Lor is consumed fresh with other dairy products like Shor, a traditional dairy product that is produced from Ayran [churned yogurt buttermilk], after heat coagulation, or salted and consumed as a table cheese like Mizithra. Fresh Lor is highly perishable.

See also IRAN.

Alichanidis, Efstathios, and Anna Polychroniadou. "Characteristics of Major Traditional Regional Cheese Varieties of East-Mediterranean Countries: A Review." *Dairy Science and Technology* 88 (2008): 495–510.

Ghavidel, Fatemeh. "Lor or Lorak, Traditional Dairy Product of Whey." Paper presented at the 1st Conference of Iranian Traditional Dairy Product, Khoy, Iran, 2013. In Persian.

Khurana, H. K, and S. K. Kanawjia. "Recent Trends in Development of Fermented Milks." *Current Nutrition & Food Science* 3 (2007): 91–108.

Shafiei, Yahya. "Iranian Traditional Cheeses." Paper presented at the 1st Conference of Iranian Traditional Dairy Products. Khoy, Iran, 2013. In Persian.

Yahya Shafiei Bavil Oliaei

Lou Castenou is a small cheese store in the picturesque town of Vaison la Romaine in the southern Vaucluse department in the Provence-Alpes-Côte d'Azur region in France. The store is located in the main square of this Romanesque village. Lou Canesteou is run by Josiane Deal, who in 2004 was named a Meilleur Ouvrier de France (MOF), and her husband, Christian Deal, who is Maitre Fromager of the Guilde Internationale des Fromagers. Josiane Deal was only the second woman to receive the MOF recognition. See ACCREDITATIONS. Mrs. Deal started working in cheese in the 1980s, and she is known for providing her customers with recipes to cook traditional Provençal dishes.

Mrs. Deal selects seasonal cheeses for her store, while Mr. Deal selects cheeses for restaurants in the region. The store is rustic and cozy, with an ample selection of French cheeses, and some staple Italian and Spanish cheeses. On their website a useful interactive map of French cheeses can be found. They also sell fine wines, sausages, and delicatessen foods.

See also CHEESEMONGER and FRANCE.

Lou Canesteou. http://www.loucanesteou.fr.

Carlos Yescas

Luna cheese is one of the earliest documented Roman cheeses, a large, aged cheese made in the city of Luna (now Luni) in Etruria (modern-day Tuscany). In his *Natural History* (11.97), Pliny described it as being esteemed at Rome and remarkable for its large size, weighing up to a thousand pounds (454 kilograms). And in his *Epigrams* (13.30), Martial claimed that a wheel was large enough to "afford your slaves a thousand lunches." Although these claims were most likely exaggerations, the fact that Luna was large enough to elicit comments on its size indicates that it was a different style of cheese than otherwise was common at the time.

Luna's size is significant, because large cheeses have a tendency to rot unless they have a lower moisture content than smaller cheeses before they begin the aging process. Two ways the Romans could have decreased the initial moisture content of this cheese are through high-temperature cooking or high-pressure pressing, or both—pivotal methods in the history of cheesemaking, according to Paul Kindstedt, "because they opened the door to the creation of *much larger* dry or aged cheese than it had previously been possible to produce" (2012, p. 105). Another noteworthy characteristic of Luna cheese is that each wheel was stamped with an Etruscan crescent moon, an identifying mark that would have been recognizable to others outside the region, seeming to suggest the concept of a designation of origin or a local brand or trademark.

See also ANCIENT CIVILIZATIONS; DESIGNATION OF ORIGIN; and PLINY THE ELDER.

Kindstedt, Paul. *Cheese and Culture: A History of Cheese and Its Place in Western Civilization.* White River Junction, Vt.: Chelsea Green, 2012.

Rogers, Edward S. *Good Will, Trade-Marks, and Unfair Trading.* Chicago: A. W. Shaw, 1914.

Vince Razionale

mac and cheese is an American comfort food made by combining cooked pasta (usually elbow or shell macaroni) with a creamy but sharp-tasting cheese sauce (usually made with American, Cheddar, or a similar orange-colored cheese). A similar dish, called macaroni cheese, is also popular in other countries, such as Australia, Canada, and the United Kingdom.

Recipes for macaroni (once a generic term for pasta) served with cheese, particularly grated Parmesan, have appeared in cookery manuscripts, and then in cookbooks, for almost nine hundred years. The invention of extruder machines in the eighteenth century made possible tubular macaroni shapes such as penne, ziti, mostaccioli, and what Americans call "elbows."

Recipes for macaroni and cheese were published in American cookbooks beginning in the nineteenth century; they often took the form of a casserole in which the macaroni was layered with white sauce, grated cheese, and breadcrumbs. That combination, in various forms, was popularized by Italian immigrants and restaurateurs in the early twentieth century.

In 1937 Kraft Foods introduced a boxed macaroni-and-cheese product called the "Kraft Dinner." The company's earlier research into shelf-stable processed cheese made it possible to include a packet of grated sharp cheese in the box. Preparation required only Kraft Dinner, boiling water, milk, and butter, and took only nine minutes. It could be served straight from the pot or, for a browned top crust, baked in the oven. It was a cheap, simple supper dish that swept the nation in the closing years of the Depression and during World War II, when working women had less time to cook and meat and dairy products were rationed.

Always popular with children, macaroni and cheese became a favorite of the baby boom generation during the 1950s and 1960s. Kraft suggested adding other ingredients to make the dish heartier, such as tuna, hot dogs, chicken, or vegetables. Kraft subsequently introduced a "deluxe" version with a can of cheese product that melted more smoothly than the dried cheese powder provided with its "original" version, a microwavable version, and pasta in kid-friendly shapes such as dinosaurs and characters from children's movies.

Beginning in the 1990s, the shortened term "mac and cheese" appeared on restaurant menus featuring comfort food or retro cuisine. Even chefs in upscale restaurants addressed the dish, adding ingredients such as lobster or truffle oil (and upping the price accordingly). In the twenty-first century, thousands of recipes for "mac and cheese" appeared in cookbooks and on the Internet. By 2015, more than fifty cookbooks and children's books had been published with "mac and cheese" in their titles.

See also KRAFT FOODS.

Serventi, Silvano, and Françoise Sabban. *Pasta: The Story of a Universal Food*. New York: Columbia University Press, 2002.

Andrew F. Smith

magical thinking is the attribution of causal effects to actions that cannot be explained by scientific reason. Magical thinking reflects a tacit if not overt belief that humans can influence the natural or supernatural world through ritual activity. When undertaking risky or uncertain enterprises—for example, fishing, farming, recovering from illness, stepping up to the plate to bat in baseball—magical thinking can give people the confidence to carry on, or help to make sense of misfortune.

Artisanal cheesemaking is full of uncertainty and potential misfortune. Artisanal cheesemaking can itself be distinguished from industrial fabrication by virtue of allowing, even celebrating—rather than working to eliminate—elements of variation in milk composition, microbial populations, and the environmental conditions in which cheesemaking occurs. Such variability leads to uncertainty in product outcome. Milk may sour, curd may not set properly, cheeses can puff up and "blow" with gas, rinds may fail to form or crack open. See ARTISANAL.

In confronting such uncertainty, cheesemakers throughout history and across cultural traditions have adopted metaphoric language and ritual behaviors that reflect magical thinking. They have done so in conjunction with empirical observation, the practice of hygiene, and the exercise of reason.

Prior to the discovery by researchers at the Pasteur Institute in the 1870s that microbes are responsible for the coagulation of milk, the moment of transubstantiation when liquid milk suddenly becomes gel-like curd seemed magical indeed. In Early Modern Europe and Colonial New England, it was not entirely clear to witnesses why some farmwomen's cows were especially prolific milk producers, or why some women's cheese turned out better than others'. Not surprisingly, accusations of witchcraft often pointed to alleged attacks on the precarious provisioning of food and drink, especially with regard to brewing, baking, and cheesemaking—all of which rely upon the invisible agents of microbial fermentation. In England into the Victorian era accusations of witchcraft could be prompted by such domestic misfortunes as cheese not setting, or were brought upon a woman for uttering such "witch-like" expressions as "may your cheese never take." At the same time, unusually proficient dairywomen were vulnerable to suspicion ("How *is* it that she would seem to have such a touch, or knack, for cheese…?"). Throughout much of Europe, successful butter or cheese development could be thwarted by the casting of an envious "evil eye," a popular form of sympathetic magic in which characteristics inherent in an individual or object are transmitted to another. Isabella Hay, before being imprisoned in Scotland for witchcraft in 1822, was known as a healer of both humans and animals and was called on to perform "countermagic" to (among other things) "restore the curdle in milk for cheese making." Even today in the United States, some cheesemakers may avoid handling ripening cheeses when they are upset or angry, just in case their own ill-tempered moods might deleteriously affect cheese development through a sort of associative contagion.

Cheese is an object in which "human" and "natural" worlds meet. As if by some spontaneous generation, cheese shape-shifts from the time of formation until the moment it's consumed. As such, not only is cheesemaking vulnerable to sympathetic magic; cheese can be enlisted as its tool. According to Scottish folklore, some farmers would affix a bit of cheese to their plows before breaking ground in early spring. Cheese itself has been taken as a microcosm of God's creation. See HILDEGARD OF BINGEN and GINZBURG, CARLO.

A more common yet conceptually related response to cheese's perceived aliveness is a tendency to anthropomorphize cheese. Anthropomorphism attributes to nonhuman entities a human form or personality. In anthropomorphizing cheese, cheesemakers borrow developmental metaphors to describe the transformations that a cheese undergoes during the aging process. Basque shepherds who articulate a theory of coagulation that likens it to insemination and conception also describe fresh cheeses as newly born infants that require care and nurturing until they become sturdier. Acting on the analogy, anthropologist Sandra Ott documents, the Basques ritually cared for cheeses and babies in similar ways: they held both over an open fire to "strengthen its bone," and both are confined to a prescribed space for the initial three months of life. See CURDLING, CULTURAL THEORIES OF.

In the contemporary United States, cheesemakers who nurture cheeses to develop so-called natural rinds often describe such cheeses as having "a life of their own." Fresh from a brine bath, cheese wheels may be referred to as "toddlers"; when their surfaces begin to bloom with a sprinkling of fungi, the cheeses "hit puberty" and "graduate" to dryer aging boards. Others describe their cheeses as moving from "preschool" to "kindergarten" and on to "graduation," when they are ready to be marketed.

Such language, while playful, is not merely incidental. Cheese, anthropomorphized as having a developmental life of its own, would seem to demand proper care; perhaps unwittingly, producers thus legitimate the excessive labor required to ripen cheese properly—labor that helps to account for the relatively high retail prices such cheeses command on the market. Furthermore, in recognizing the limits of human control over the organic processes of fermentation, curdling, and maturation, anthropomorphizing and magical thinking expresses an artisan's humility, a recognition that complete control over the cheesemaking process remains elusive. Artisans make cheese with the aid of microorganisms, enzymes, heat, humidity, time—and a bit of luck.

Blécourt, Willem de, and Owen Davies, eds. *Witchcraft Continued: Popular Magic in Modern Europe*. Manchester, U.K.: Manchester University Press, 2004.

Cowan, Edward J., and Lizanne Henderson. "The Last of the Witches? The Survival of Scottish Witch Belief." In *The Scottish Witch-Hunt in Context*, edited by Julian Goodare, pp. 198–217. Manchester, U.K.: Manchester University Press, 2002.

Ott, Sandra. "Aristotle Among the Basques: The 'Cheese Analogy' of Conception." *Man* 14, no. 4 (1979): 699–711.

Paxson, Heather. *The Life of Cheese: Crafting Food and Value in America*. Berkeley: University of California Press, 2013.

Purkiss, Diane. *The Witch in History: Early Modern and Twentieth-century Representations*. London: Routledge, 1996.

Heather Paxson

magic tricks featuring cheese belie the vexed relationship entertainment magicians have with cheese. In popular culture magicians themselves are often depicted as "cheesy" (in the sense of kitschy). For instance, a character in the bestselling young adult novel *Bad Magic* by Pseudonymous Bosch says that a magician who does "card tricks, coin tricks, hat tricks" and the like is "somebody who acts cheesy … Magicians are masters of cheesiness. They're the ultimate cheese-wizards." Magicians today strive to overcome this "cheese factor" by finding new ways to keep their material up to date and their personae stylish, at times turning to cheese itself as a source of inspiration. Thus, despite the specter of metaphorical cheesiness, literal cheese has found a home in their repertoire of illusions.

As early as the twelfth century medieval romances described court entertainers performing the trick of turning stones into cheese. In 1912 British magician P. T. Selbit introduced a blockbuster stage illusion called "The Mighty Cheese." Selbit would invite five or six strong men from the audience to face off against a wheel of "the strongest cheese in the world," offering a cash prize to anyone who could successfully wrestle it to the ground. They could push the cheese around, but never knock it down; a powerful gyroscope hidden inside thwarted all comers. When American magicians Penn and Teller reprised the illusion for a television show in 2011, a flummoxed mixed martial arts fighter said, "I'm going to go home and cry now. I can't beat a cheese."

More recently performers have employed cheese in close-up magic, a fashionably un-cheesy subgenre emphasizing sleight-of-hand skill. In a signature routine, world champion French magician Jean-Jacques Sanvert reveals a spectator's borrowed banknote inside a waxed Babybel cheese. Spanish magician

"The Mighty Cheese" was a blockbuster stage illusion by British magician P. T. Selbit. Selbit invited audience participants to attempt to wrestle a large wheel of cheese to the ground; invariably they were thwarted by a powerful hidden gyroscope.

Luis Piedrahita has performed a similar effect, revealing a signed playing card embedded within a waxed queso de bola (Edam) cheese.

See also ART and MAGICAL THINKING.

Jones, Graham. *Trade of the Tricks: Inside the Magician's Craft.* Berkeley: University of California Press, 2011.

Roy, Bruno. "The Household Encyclopedia as Magic Kit: Medieval Popular Interest in Pranks and Illusions." *Journal of Popular Culture* 14, no. 1 (1980): 60–69.

Steinmeyer, Jim. *Hiding the Elephant: How Magicians Invented the Impossible and Learned to Disappear.* New York: Carroll & Graf, 2004.

Graham M. Jones

Mahón-Menorca is a traditional pressed, uncooked Spanish cheese presenting a distinctive parallelepiped shape, characteristic orangish rind, and salty and spice flavor. Mahón-Menorca has enjoyed protected designation of origin (PDO) status since 1985 (MAPA, 1985) and is the second most popular Spanish cheese after Manchego. See MANCHEGO. The PDO regulation stipulates that the cheese is produced and ripened exclusively in Menorca, the second largest of the Balearic Islands.

The seafarers of ancient Greece knew the livestock wealth of Menorca, which they called Meloussa or "land of cattle," showing that cow's milk was available on the island since early times. Bishop Severo's encyclical letter, now preserved in the Vatican library, reveals Mahón-Menorca cheese to have been made on the island at least as far back as the year 417. Later, in the fifteenth century, the trading company of the Datini de Lucca brothers (who were from Tuscany) had dealings with Menorca, where merchants traded in wool and local cheese. It was the British, however, who ruled Menorca in the eighteenth century, who added the name "Mahon" (to indicate the port of origin) to what until then had no name. And it was the British who stimulated the large increase in its production. Since the cheese can be legally produced anywhere on the island, it was officially named "Mahón-Menorca" in 1993.

As stated in its official technical annex, Mahón-Menorca cheese is made from Friesian, Menorcan, and/or Brown Alpine cow's milk, sometimes with the addition of a small amount of ewe's milk (maximum 5 percent). Two different varieties are contemplated: "artisanal" cheese, which is manufactured from raw milk, and "industrial" cheese which is made from milk that has been subjected to any authorized preservation technology. Production in 2013 by the twenty-nine factories associated with the PDO was estimated at 2,200 tons.

One of the most distinctive elements of Mahón-Menorca cheese is its traditional molding. After cutting and draining off the whey, the curd is pocketed in squares of cheesecloth (*fogasser*), which are then suspended by their four corners. When the whey has drained off, the corners of the cheesecloth are tied together with a fine, multi-stranded thread with a stick at the end (*lligam*). During pressing the cheesecloth leaves a characteristic mark (*mamella*) on the upper surface of the cheese. See CHEESECLOTH. Another distinguishing practice is the treatment of the rind during ripening, which is smeared in cow's butter, olive oil, or a mixture of olive oil and paprika. This step, which is repeated frequently during ripening, prevents excessive drying of the rind, repels insects, and provides the cheese with its typical color and external appearance.

The cheese matrix is firm in texture. It has an ivory-yellow color and a few unevenly distributed small eyes. Semi-matured cheeses have a lactic, clean flavor that acquires piquant notes with further ripening.

Based on the ripening time, the PDO recognized the following varieties of Mahón-Menorca cheese:

- Tender (twenty-one to sixty days). This young variety has a smooth yellowish white paste with a tender and elastic rind. The aroma is lactic and buttery.
- Semi-cured (two to five months). This is the most characteristic version of the product, presenting the orangey color, or brownish gray if it is a farmhouse cheese. It has a firmer texture and stronger flavor. It is a legal requirement that raw-milk cheeses be ripened for more than sixty days.
- Vintage or mature (more than five months). This has a firmer texture that almost flakes when sliced. Flavor is strong and complex.

A number of studies have been performed on the proteolysis occurring within Mahón-Menorca cheese during its manufacture and ripening (López-Fandino et al., 1994), as well as on its fatty acid composition (Fuente et al., 1993); free amino acid content (Polo et al., 1985; García-Palmer et al., 1997); and volatile fraction (Bosset and Gauch, 1993; Mulet et al., 1999).

Cheeses made from raw and pasteurized milk have been reported to show different free amino acid profiles (García-Palmer et al., 1997). The free amino acid content has also been found to increase with time, providing a suitable ripening index. Regardless of the ripening time, the main components of the volatile fraction are non-branched aliphatic fatty acids (Bosset and Gauch, 1993; Mulet et al., 1999). The flavor of the cheese is thought to depend not only on these particular compounds, but on the critical balance among all the cheese's components (Bosset and Gauch, 1993). Although the organoleptic properties of the cheese (flavor and aroma) depend largely on the activity of the proteolytic and lipolytic enzymes provided by its microbiota, microbial analyses of Mahón-Menorca cheese have yet to be performed.

See also SPAIN.

Bosset, J. O., and R. Gauch. "Comparison of the Volatile Flavour Compounds of Six European AOC Cheeses by Using a New Dynamic Headspace GC-MS Method." *International Dairy Journal* 3 (1993): 359–377.

Fuente, M. A., et al. "Fatty Acid Composition of the Triglyceride and Free Fatty Acid Fractions in Different Cows, Ewes and Goats Milk Cheeses." *Zeitschrift fuer Lebensmittel Untersuchung und Forschung* 196 (1993): 155–158.

García-Palmer, F. J. et al. "Free Amino Acids as Indices of Mahón Cheese Ripening." *Journal of Dairy Science* 80 (1997): 1908–1917.

López-Fandino, R., et al. "Proteolysis Assessment of Several Cheese Varieties Using Different Methods." *Milchwissenschaf* 49 (1994): 315–318.

Ministerio de Agricultura, Pesca y Alimentación. "Denominación de Origen 'Mahón.'" 1985. http://www.magrama.gob.es/es/alimentacion/temas/calidad-agroalimentaria/Registro_INDO_tcm7-206476.pdf.

Mulet, A., et al. "Changes in the Volatile Fraction during Ripening of Mahón Cheese." *Food Chemistry* 65 (1999): 219–225.

Polo, C., et al. "Free Amino Acids by High Performance Liquid Chromatography and Peptides by Gel Electrophoresis in Mahon Cheese during Ripening." *Food Chemistry* 16 (1985): 85–96.

Baltasar Mayo

Maiorchino is a traditional hard Sicilian cheese made with raw whole sheep's milk, sometimes mixed with goat's milk (at a maximum of 25 percent). The production area covers the townships on the northern side of the Peloritani Mountains in Sicily. According to Sicilian folklore, it is believed that this cheese made its first appearance in the 1600s during a "maiorchina" festival, where the cheesemakers, using very aged cheeses as wheels, participated in a race in the streets of a small town by rolling the cheese with a stick. At the end of the race many producers offered bystanders the opportunity to test the best Maiorchino cheeses. The traditional festival continues to be held every year during Carnival in February. Maiorchino is still produced with traditional techniques and the best period for the production is spring until the second week of June, during the forage season.

Milk, at a temperature of 95°F (35°C), is curdled in a tinned copper boiler called a *quarara*, with rennet paste of lamb or kid. The breaking of the curd occurs after fifty-five to sixty minutes, using a wooden tool, in a vigorous manner. After breaking, the curd is placed on heat until it reaches the temperature of 113°F (45°C). Then it is left at the bottom of the *quarara* for twenty minutes, gathered manually and given a spherical shape, and placed on a wooden band called a *garbua* to form the curd. Afterward it is placed on a wooden table called a *mastello* to continue to drain the whey with a unique technique that consists of puncturing and pressing the curd by hand, for about two hours, with a thin iron pole known as a *minacino*. One day later the cheese is taken out of the *garbua* and placed on walnut shelves. The next day the cheese is dry-salted and left for twenty to thirty days on the same wooden shelves. See COPPER VATS; DRAINING TABLE; DRY SALTING; and WOODEN SHELVES.

The aging process occurs in caves, stone structures, sometime underground, that are typical of the production area, in which the temperature and the humidity are constant and cool through the year. See CAVE. The ripening phase to obtain a good Maiorchino must be at least six to eight months, and normally over twelve months; it is possible to find cheeses older than twenty-four months. Maiorchino is the longest aged cheese in Sicily. It has a delicate taste tending toward spiciness with prolonged aging and an herbaceous, floral, and fruity aroma. The shape is cylindrical with a flat or slightly concave face, a diameter of 14 inches (35 centimeters) and a height of 5 inches (12 centimeters). The weight is approximately 22–40 pounds (10–18 kilograms).

See also SICILY.

Campisi, Carmelo. *Pecore e Pecorino della Sicilia*. Catania, Italy: Francesco Battiato Editore, 1933.

Campo, Patrizia, and Giuseppe Licitra. *Historical Sicilian Cheeses*. Ragusa, Italy: CoRFiLaC Press, 2006.
Istituto Nazionale di Sociologia Rurale. *Atlante dei prodotti tipici: I formaggi*. Milan: Franco Angeli, 1990.

Ivana Piccitto

Maître Philippe et Filles

Maître Philippe et Filles is a French cheese shop, delicatessen, and wine store in Berlin. When Philippe Causse, a wine merchant from Marseille, founded his shop in 1994 he knew nothing about artisan cheese. During a wine research trip to the Loire, he encountered a local cheese producer and tasted her excellent Crottin de Chavignol, and thus the idea of importing such specialties to Berlin was born. See CROTTIN DE CHAVIGNOL.

From the beginning the key aspect of this concept was the collaboration with his most important supplier, the affineur Janier, whose family-run business in Lyon has specialized in the ripening and trading of traditional farmhouse cheeses for four generations. On Janier's advice Philippe installed a humidifier to create the best conditions to store cheese in. Even today this system is quite unique in Germany and allows all cheeses to be displayed unpackaged. The assortment consists of over fifty different types of raw-milk cheeses, mostly French, but also from Italy, Portugal, and the United Kingdom, all delivered weekly.

For proper storage there are four refrigerated holds, in which both temperature and humidity can be adjusted according to the specific cheese types and ripening stages. Additionally damp cloths are used to cover certain cheeses and protect them from drying out. The renunciation of any plastic wrap requires a higher effort in terms of cheese care but also has a crucial impact on the product's quality. Some of Berlin's best restaurants are among Maître Philippe's customers.

Fresh dairy, charcuterie, delicatessen, wine, and an extensive selection of fish preserves complete the product range of this aromatic shop. Philippe's daughters Anaïs and Noémie have joined the family-run business, therefore renamed Maître Philippe et Filles (Master Philippe and Daughters) in 2014.

Janier. http://www.janier.fr.
Maître Philippe et Filles. http://www.maitrephilippe.de.
"Maître Philippe: Berlin's Favourite French Delicastessen." Sofitel Berlin Kurfürstendamm blog, 12 March 2014. http://blog.sofitel-berlin-kurfurstendamm.com/matre-philippe-berlins-favourite-french-delicatessen.

Theresa Malec

Manchego

Manchego is one of the most famous of the traditional Spanish cheeses. It accounts for more than one third of all traditional cheese production in Spain. It is manufactured only in the Toledo, Ciudad Real, Cuenca, and Albacete provinces of the La Mancha region, from which it takes its name. Manchego is an enzymatically coagulated, pressed, uncooked (<113°F [<45°C]), semihard, cured cheese made from raw or pasteurized Manchega ewe's milk. It has enjoyed protected designation of origin (PDO) status since 1984. Similar types of cheese are produced all over Spain, some of which (e.g., Idiazábal, Roncal, and Zamorano) have also been awarded PDO labels. See IDIAZABAL; RONCAL; and ZAMORANO.

La Mancha was given its name by the Arabs: "Al Mansha" meaning "land without water," which perfectly describes the climatic harshness of the region. La Mancha has been involved in raising sheep and in cheesemaking since ancient times. Proof of this lies in the basins, bowls, and other cheesemaking tools found at archaeological sites across the region, and which are now exhibited at local museums. La Mancha's links with cheese are apparent in many historical and literary documents, including Miguel de Cervantes's *Don Quixote*. Manchego cheese first appeared under its present name in a book entitled *Explotación y Producción de Leches, Mantequillas y Quesos de Diferentes Clases* by Balanguer and Primo (1878), in which a chapter devoted to the main Spanish cheeses refers primarily to Manchego. It further appears in the culinary treatises *Diccionario General de la Cocina* (1892) and *El Practicón* (1898), both by Ángel Muro, and in the books *Fabricación de Quesos y Mantecas de Todas Clases* by Buenaventura Aragó (1909) and *Guía del Buen Comer Español* by Dionisio Pérez (1929).

More than 58 million quarts (55 million liters) of Manchega ewe's milk were used in producing some 10,757 tons of Manchego cheese in 2013. When raw milk is used, a ripening period of sixty days is required for a cheese weighing up to 3 pounds (1.5 kilograms), a period reduced by half if pasteurized milk is used. In either case, the milk is heated to 82–90°F (28–32°C) and then coagulated with animal rennet for forty-five to sixty minutes. The curd is then cut into rice-size grains, stirred, and heated to 104°F (40°C) before molding to form cylindrical cheeses (with flat faces) some 3–5 inches (8–12 centimeters) in height and 7–9 inches (18–22 centimeters) in diameter. The rind of Manchego cheese shows the imprints of the molds, which are of the "pleita" type around the cylinder (a pleita is a belt of esparto grass that was used in ancient times to help in whey drainage) and of the "flor" type on the flat surfaces.

The cheese matrix is compact, firm in texture, and varies from white to yellowish ivory. It may contain small, irregular, unevenly distributed eyes. Its flavor is slightly acidic with a sharp background of ovine milk components; the flavor increases over ripening and develops piquant notes. Manchego may be sold at several different age gradations: *fresco* (aged for two weeks; mostly just in Spain), *semi-curado* (aged for at least three weeks and up to four months), *curado* (aged for 3–6 months), and *viejo* or *anejo* (aged for one year). In addition to the mandatory PDO label on the upper surface, each piece of Manchego cheese carries a casein plaque with a serial number on its lower face; this identifies the producer and batch number.

Manchego is by far the most studied of the traditional Spanish cheeses. In the 1970s, when pasteurization became the norm, researchers began to characterize the microbiota of the cheese with the aim of designing specific starters (Román-Piñana, 1975; Núñez, 1978; Ordóñez et al., 1978). Species of lactic acid bacteria (*Lactococcus lactis*, *Lactobacillus plantarum*, *Leuconostoc* spp., *Enterococcus* spp.) make up the predominant bacterial populations throughout manufacturing and ripening. In order to reproduce the complex flavor profiles of traditional Manchego cheese, the suitability of different strains for use in starter and adjunct cultures has been tested (Ramos et al., 1981; Gómez et al., 1999).

The proteolytic and lipolytic reactions that occur during the maturation of Manchego cheese, and which provide precursor molecules to its volatile compound fraction, have been intensely investigated. The volatile compounds that characterize the mature cheese have also been extensively studied and, in contrast to other ewe's milk cheeses, a series of alcohols—which includes a large proportion of 2-butanol—dominates the Manchego volatile profile. Attempts to enhance proteolysis aimed at shortening the ripening time while maintaining the chemical, textural, and sensorial characteristics of the cheese have also been made. These have included the use of free and encapsulated proteolytic enzymes, such as recombinant chymosin, neutral proteases from *Bacillus subtilis*, and cyprosins from the wild cardoon *Cynara cardunculus*. Other studies on Manchego cheese have focused on the inhibition of pathogens such as *Staphylococcus aureus* and *Listeria monocytogenes*. The formation of bioactive peptides and biogenic amines has also been investigated.

New technologies have recently been used to study the textural, chemical, and microbial variables of Manchego cheese. The data provided, and those now becoming available via the use of high throughput "omic" techniques (genomics, metabolomics, proteomics, etc.), could help link the diversity and development of microbial populations in Manchego cheese with its particular sensorial attributes.

See also LA MANCHA and SPAIN.

Gómez, M. J., et al. "Characteristics of Manchego Cheese Manufactured from Raw and Pasteurized Ovine Milk and with Defined-Strain or Commercial Mixed-Strain Starter Cultures." *Journal of Dairy Science* 82 (1999): 2300–2307.

Ministerio de Agricultura, Pesca y Alimentación. "Denominación de Origen 'Queso Manchego.'" 1984. http://www.magrama.gob.es/es/alimentacion/temas/calidad-agroalimentaria/registro_INDO_tcm7-206531.pdf.

Núñez, M. "Microflora of Cabrales Cheese: Changes during Maturation." *Journal of Dairy Research* 45 (1978): 501–508.

Ordóñez, J. A., et al. "Study of Manchego Cheese Ripened in Olive Oil." *Milchwissenshaft* 33(1978): 600–613.

Ramos, M., et al. "Evaluation of a Specific Starter for Manchego Cheese Production." *Milchwissenshaft* 36 (1981): 528–532.

Roman-Piñana, M. "Etude de la flore microbienne du fromage espagnol Manchego. I. Son evolution au cours de la fabrication et de l'affinage." *Lait* 55 (1975): 401–413.

Baltasar Mayo

manorial cheesemakers made important contributions to the economies of European medieval manors and to the history of cheese. The details of manorial cheesemaking varied according to region, due to regional differences in manorial organization, and social and cultural differences.

For example, the manors of England and northwest France were strongly influenced by the well-developed system of Roman villas that preceded them. They were typically organized agriculturally and socially into a peasant side and an aristocratic demesne side. The peasants, free and unfree tenants who had hereditary rights to small parcels of manorial land, served as the labor force for the manor lord's private farm or demesne, which might encompass up to half of all manorial lands. To support their families, the peasants worked their smallholdings and grazed a cow or two (or sheep or goats, depending on location) on common lands that the lord made available. Peasant manorial cheesemaking thus involved very small quantities of milk, harvested daily and made into very small cheeses in the home by peasant women who had to multitask extensively to accomplish a daunting array of daily duties. The survival of the peasant family, and thus the maintenance of a sustainable manorial labor force, depended on peasant access to common lands for grazing, milk production, and cheesemaking.

In contrast, the manor lord's demesne typically maintained a sizable herd of cows (or flock[s] of sheep, or both) that produced relatively large volumes of milk that were processed into cheese by full-time professional cheesemaking women who were recruited from the peasant side of the manor. In addition to stocking the lord's larder, demesne cheeses were used as a form of currency to compensate the professional administrative staff and artisans that labored on the lord's demesne, and to pay annual taxes due to aristocratic overlords and the king.

Interestingly, demesne cheesemaking in northwest France ended long before the end of the middle ages, as manorial demesnes began to break up into small peasant holdings starting around the tenth century c.e. This ultimately encouraged the development of a plethora of beloved local soft-ripened peasant cheeses in France. In contrast, demesne cheesemaking in England persisted and eventually became highly market oriented. Indeed, the market-driven posture of English demesne cheesemaking during the late Middle Ages set the stage for the highly capitalistic yeoman cheesemaking that subsequently arose in England during the sixteenth and seventeenth centuries, which, in turn, served as the "maternity ward" for many of the great English cheeses.

Manors in the sparsely populated mountainous regions of central Europe generally were not organized around demesnes but rather consisted of peasant villages or groups of small tenant farmers who paid the aristocratic lord of the region a share of their agricultural production in return for the lord's protection and inherited rights to their small landholdings. Common lands for grazing cows or goats in the summer were often situated in the adjacent highlands, thus the manors of central Europe assimilated the transhumant survival strategy that had been practiced there since pre-Roman times. Under manorial supervision, transhumant alpine cheesemaking evolved

beyond a subsistence strategy to, in some cases, highly successful market-driven enterprises. This was especially true for manors that were under the control of monastic houses. Monasteries such as St. Gall in the Appenzell region of Switzerland did much to encourage the development of wilderness regions into productive Alpine cheesemaking centers.

See also MONASTIC CHEESEMAKING and SAINT GALL.

Kindstedt, Paul. *Cheese and Culture: A History of Cheese and Its Place in Western Civilization*. White River Junction, Vt.: Chelsea Green, 2012.

Paul S. Kindstedt

Manoura is a traditional Greek cheese manufactured in Sifnos, a small island in the Aegean Sea, part of the Cyclades complex. Manoura Sifnou ("of Sifnos") is produced mainly from raw ovine milk, or from a mixture of raw ovine and caprine milk from small local herds in which, usually, the proportion of ewe's milk exceeds that of the goat's milk.

Manoura is a hard cheese traditionally made from raw morning milk without the addition of any starter culture. Once the coagulum has been formed by using usually homemade rennet manufactured from extracts of the fourth stomach (abomasum) of milk-fed lambs or goat kids, the curd is cut into fine pieces with dimensions of approximately ⅛ inch (0.5 centimeter) and after a thorough stirring, it is left to settle at the bottom of the vat. After removal of the whey, the curd is transferred with a cheesecloth into hoops to drain. See CHEESECLOTH and HOOP. The hoops (molds) are traditionally baskets woven with rushes, called *tyrovolia*. The cheeses in the baskets are turned and salted regularly for two to three days with coarse salt. After that the cheeses are removed from the hoops and placed on perforated shelves, traditionally made from straw or reeds, and left to dry for at least two months. During this period the cheeses are frequently (initially every day) turned over. At the end of this step the cheese has lost approximately 40 percent of its initial weight. Afterward some producers (optionally) put the cheeses into barrels with red wine to "soften," for about one day. Subsequently, the surface of the cheeses is fully covered with wine sediment. The wine sediment is typically produced from local vine grapes that had been left to dry under the sun for approximately ten to fifteen days. Some producers also add the herb savory (*Satureja thymbra*) to the wine sediment, which contributes to flavor and additionally has antimicrobial effects. The cheeses afterward ripen for at least another thirty days.

The final product has a natural reddish rind as a result of the wine sediment treatment. Moreover, this treatment preserves the cheese, which can then be stored at ambient temperature for at least six months without considerable changes in its sensory characteristics. The final cheese dimensions are approximately 3 by 5 inches (8 by 12 centimeters) (height by diameter) with a mean weight of about 17–21 ounces (500–600 grams).

During ripening various microbial groups are developed on the cheese surface. However the red wine and sediment treatment have an inhibitory effect on microorganisms especially at the cheese rind. Many pathogens (e.g., Enterobacteriaceae) and spoilage microorganisms are reduced sharply during ripening, while lactic acid bacteria prevail. *Ln. mesenteroides* subsp. *cremoris, P. pentosaceus, Lb. paracasei* subsp. *Paracasei Weissella paramesenteroides, Lb. bifermentans,* and *Lb. brevis* are the most frequently found lactic acid bacteria in matured cheeses.

An application is being submitted to register "Gilomeni Manoura Sifnou" (*gilomeni* means covered with wine sediment) as a protected designation of origin (PDO) cheese.

See also GREECE.

Gerasi, Ekaterini, et al. "Microbiological Study of Manura, a Hard Cheese Made from Raw Ovine Milk in the Greek Island Sifnos." *International Journal of Dairy Technology* 56 (2003): 117–122

Thomas Moschakis

manouri is a semisoft fresh white cheese produced on the Greek mainland in the designated appellation of origin regions of Central and Western Macedonia and Thessaly. A byproduct of feta production, it is made from the whey of sheep's or goat's milk, or from a blend of sheep's and goat's milk whey to which fresh sheep's or goat's cream, or sometimes full-fat milk, is added. The curds are collected, drained, and packaged in cylinders, which are sold whole or in segments. With a fat content ranging from 36 to 38 percent, manouri's texture is smooth, dense, and buttery, not unlike the texture of a French chèvre. See CHÈVRE. Its flavor is rich, milky, and slightly tangy and citrusy.

During its production, manouri is very lightly salted, thus it retains the sweetness of the fresh cream that is added to the whey. In Greece, manouri is a popular table cheese and it is also commonly served as a dessert cheese. In the latter case, it is often drizzled with honey and served with fruit. With its mild flavor profile, it is used as an ingredient in recipes for both savory and sweet dishes, including salads and pastries. It is typically eaten young, but can be aged to become an excellent grating cheese. Although manouri is exported to northern Europe, the United States, and Australia, it is primarily consumed in Greece.

See also GREECE.

Kitrilakis, Sotiris. "The PDO Cheeses of Greece." http://www.kerasma.gr/default.asp?entryID=407&pageID=96&tablePageID=35&langID=2.

Alexis Marie Adams

manual testing can be used to monitor the quality of raw milk, curd acidity, and aged cheese. The lacto-fermentation test and the *Clostridium tyrobutyricum* test can predict gas formation in cheese during aging. These tests are performed by taking sanitary samples of raw milk from the bulk tank or from the cheese vat prior to adding starter cultures. For the lacto-fermentation test, raw milk samples are placed in sterile test tubes and incubated at 86–98.6°F (30–37°C) for twenty-four to forty-eight hours until the milk curdles. The amount of gas produced in the samples indicates the likelihood that there will be gas formation in the cheese during the first three weeks of aging. For the *C. tyrobutyricum* test, samples of raw milk are placed in test tubes, pasteurized, sealed with wax plugs, and incubated at 100.4°F (38°C) for twelve to twenty-four hours. If gas is produced during incubation, then the plugs will move up the tubes, indicating that gas may form after three weeks of aging.

The hot iron test was developed to test the acidity of cheese curd. A piece of iron is heated until it is red-hot. A piece of curd is placed against the iron and drawn away. The length of the strand of curd that can be pulled indicates the level of acidity: the longer the strand, the more acidic the curd. This determination of acidity is important for deciding when to salt the curd, because salt uptake varies with acidity. A cheese trier, a tool resembling an apple corer but longer and narrower, is used to take a core sample of cheese from a wheel or block for sensory evaluation to determine the development of flavor and texture during aging. After testing, the plug is returned to cheese.

See also TITRATABLE ACIDITY MEASUREMENT and SENSORY ANALYSIS.

Biss, Kathy. *Practical Cheesemaking*. Ramsbury, U.K.: Crowood, 1988.

Kindstedt, Paul. *American Farmstead Cheese*. White River Junction, Vt.: Chelsea Green, 2005.

Peter H. Dixon

Marcellino, Sister Noella

Marcellino, Sister Noella (1950–), is a Benedictine nun and cheesemaker from the Abbey of Regina Laudis in Bethlehem, Connecticut. She holds MS and PhD degrees in microbiology from the University of Connecticut, where she helped establish the view that ripening cheeses can be viewed as ecosystems in which microbes are selected by the environment for their physiological attributes. Her doctoral work, supported by a Fulbright Fellowship and the French National Institute of Agricultural Research (Institut National de la Recherche Agronomique, INRA), took her on a pilgrimage of more than 18,000 miles through France, collecting milk and cheese samples from farms. She isolated hundreds of different strains of the fungus *Geotrichum candidum*, commonly found on "fungal surface-ripened" cheeses. Her work provided scientific evidence for the empirical idea that the diversity of local ripening strains reflects the diversity of the people, animals, land, and geology of a region. By extension, she showed that such diversity would be lost should government or industry impose standardized cultures and ripening conditions.

A documentary film, *The Cheese Nun: Sister Noella's Voyage of Discovery*, produced by the Paris American Television Company, has been shown in film festivals and aired on national television in the United States. Sister Noella was honored with the French Food Spirit Award in Scientific Advancement, given by the French Senate in 2003. She was a scholar-in-residence at the 2011 American Cheese Society Conference in Montreal and is a contributing author of the American Society of Microbiology book *Cheese and Microbes*, released in April 2014.

See also GEOTRICHUM CANDIDUM.

Marcellino, Noella, and David R. Benson. "The Good, the Bad, and the Ugly: Tales of Mold-Ripened Cheese." *Microbiology Spectrum* 1 (October 2013): 1–27.

Pollan, Michael. *Cooked: A Natural History of Transformation*. New York: Penguin, 2013.

David R. Benson

mare's milk, the milk of non-ruminant horses, has been traditionally fermented and consumed by peoples of Central Asia. The fermented product, kumis or koumiss (*airag* in Russian), is mentioned by Genghis Khan, and cited by Avicenna (known as Ibn Sīnā), in his *Therapeutic Book of Healing*. Persians, Russians, and Mongols throughout Eurasia have made kumis for over two millennia.

High in lactose, raw mare's milk is a laxative for adult humans. Thus for human consumption, raw mare's milk is customarily fermented, then churned for hours or days to produce kumis, a product similar to kefir. The addition of yeast carbonates the milk and renders it slightly alcoholic, while lactobacilli bacteria culture acidifies the milk. Physical agitation follows in a manner roughly analogous to butter production. Kumis has an increased nutritional value due to the combination of carbon dioxide, alcohol, and lactic acid. The acid creates productive intestinal microflora which aid digestion. In addition to kumis, mare's yogurt and a semisoft whitish cheese named *aarts* are commonly made in Mongolia.

Similar to human milk, mare's milk is low in nitrogen, has a low casein-to-whey protein ratio, and high lactose content. The added benefits achieved through the production of kumis render it into a healthful and highly nutritious food. However, the average daily milk yield produced by thoroughbred mares is just 2–3 quarts (2–3 liters) per 220 pounds (100 kilograms) of body weight.

See also DONKEY.

Avicenna. *The Physics of the Healing: A Parallel English-Arabic Text*. Edited and translated by John McGinnis. Provo, Utah: Brigham Young University Press, 2009.

Faye, B., and G. Konuspayeva. "The Sustainability Challenge to the Dairy Sector—The Growing Importance of Non-cattle Milk Production Worldwide." *International Dairy Journal* 24, no. 2 (2012): 50–56.

Kücükcetin, A., et al. "Adaptation of Bovine Milk towards Mares' Milk Composition by Means of Membrane Technology for Koumiss Manufacture." *International Dairy Journal* 13, no. 12 (2003): 945–951.

Uniacke-Lowe, Therese, et al. "Equine Milk Proteins: Chemistry, Structure and Nutritional Significance." *International Dairy Journal* 20, no. 9 (2010): 609–629.

Scott Alves Barton

Marie-Anne Cantin is a celebrated, family-run cheese shop in Paris, France, located on Rue du

Champ-du-Mars in the city's seventh arrondissement. Situated on a side street that connects to Rue Cler, one of the capital's beloved open-air market streets, this neatly organized and elegant boutique, opened in 1982, is operated with great care by its namesake owner and her husband, Antoine Dias.

Cantin has quite the pedigree and often proclaims that she was "born in cheese"; her father, Christian Cantin, opened his own landmark Paris cheese shop in 1950 and was founder of the French Cheese Merchant's Guild (la Guilde des fromagers). As a celebrated affineur, second-generation cheesemonger, and upholder of French gastronomic tradition, Cantin has achieved rock star status. This "tidy, super-aromatic cheese fantasy," as David Rosengarten descriptively put it, stocks over one hundred selections from French farms, many made from raw milk, and ages them on straw in their on-site cellars. The shop's cellars are rigorously controlled in terms of temperature and humidity. The floor of the cow's milk vault is lined with small stones, which are watered regularly to guarantee the proper humidity needed to coax its inhabitants to their perfect expression.

Along with supplying many of Paris's finest restaurants with gems to display on their cheese carts, the fromagerie also holds tasting classes and is the appointed supplier of the Élysée Palace, the official residence of the president of the French Republic. The house specialty cheese is Saint-Antoine, a super-lush triple-cream cheese made from cow's milk and named in honor of Marie-Anne's husband.

See also CHEESEMONGER and FRANCE.

Rosengarten, David. "Gettin' Cheesy in France: Why the 'Affineur' Is So Damned Important." 14 May 2013. https://davidrosengarten.com/blog/gettin-cheesy-in-france-why-the-affineur-is-so-damned-important.
Wells, Patricia. The Food Lover's Guide to Paris. New York: Workman, 1999.

Allison Radecki

The **Marin French Cheese Company** is the oldest continually operating cheese company in the United States, founded in 1865 by Jefferson Thompson. Located on the privately owned 700-acre Hicks Valley Ranch in Marin County, California, and known locally as the Cheese Factory, the Marin French Cheese Company began producing European-style, soft-ripened cheeses in the early 1900s. Marin French Cheese is best known for their Brie and Camembert cheeses, along with an Austrian-style washed-rind cheese called Schloss, and a "breakfast cheese." The company has sold their pasteurized-milk cheeses under the brand name Rouge et Noir since the 1920s.

Originally called the Thompson Brothers Dairy, in the 1930s the Thompson family ceased their dairy operation and began purchasing milk from local farmers in order to focus on cheese production and support a dependable milk market for neighboring farms in Marin and Sonoma Counties. All cheese production continues to be handcrafted and packed on site at the Hicks Valley Ranch creamery, and shipped to retailers across the United States.

In 1995, the Thompson family sold Marin French Cheese to Jim Boyce, who diversified the product line from five to forty cheeses, including a blue cheese. Marin French Cheese garnered many national and international awards, most notably at the 2005 World Cheese Awards where their French Triple Crème Brie won first place—the first time an American cheese overtook the French in Brie. When Jim Boyce passed away in 2010, French cheese company Rians, the brand of artisan food company Laiteries H. Triballa, purchased Marin French Cheese.

See also CALIFORNIA.

Marin French Cheese Company. http://www.marinfrenchcheese.com.
Paxson, Heather. The Life of Cheese: Crafting Food and Value in America. Berkeley: University of California Press, 2013.

Stephanie Maroney

Maroilles is a semisoft washed-rind cheese made from cow's milk and produced in the north of France. Its origins date to 960 when the Benedictine monks at the Abbaye de Maroilles perfected this cheese with its creamy taste and powerful aroma. See SAINT BENEDICT. It obtained AOC (appellation d'origine contrôlée) status in 1955. A PDO (protected designation of origin) cheese since 1996, its production area is limited and covers the Nord and Aisne departments. This wooded region is called the Thiérache and produces an abundance of quality grass. Only milk produced in this area may be used to make Maroilles.

The milk is heated, calf rennet is added and when it has coagulated, the curds are cut and placed in square molds that are turned over several times until the following day to aid draining. After removal from the molds, the cheeses are brined or dry-salted, or sometimes both, and placed in a dryer for several days. They are then transferred to the maturing cellars, or natural caves for traditional producers, where they are brushed with saltwater with added red ferments enabling the development of a reddish-orange color natural rind.

Five weeks are required for the ripening of a 25-ounce (720-gram) Maroilles. Three other standard smaller sizes exist: Sorbais (19 ounces [550 grams]), Mignon (12 ounces [350 grams]), and Quart (6 ounces [180 grams]). Their ripening times are shorter. Maroilles can be eaten at the end of a meal or cooked in delicious recipes such as *flamiches* and sauce au Maroilles accompanying meat and fish. Maroilles has a pungent smell of cellars, wet brick, and undergrowth, a light ammoniac smell, and a milky, slightly salty taste with acidity in the cheese and flavors of milk curd, hazelnut, and a hint of garlic.

See also FRANCE and MONASTIC CHEESEMAKING.

Auzias, Dominique, and Jean-Paul Labourdette. *La route des fromages*. Paris: Editions Petit Futé, 2012.

Elodie Herninelle

martelletto is the Italian informal word for a small stainless steel hammer that is used to test, through acoustics, a cheese's ripening stage and for the presence of defects. It is one of several traditional pieces of equipment used to control cheese quality in Parmigiano Reggiano and Grana Padano, the others being the screw-needle and probe. The hammer is an irreplaceable instrument for tapping the cheese, which can reveal the formation of irregular holes in the cheese (swelling), or reveal cracks in the paste, defects due to abnormal fermentative phenomena. It is made by only a few skilled experts. See DEFECTS.

Edmond and Jules de Goncourt, two French writers, during a journey in Italy between 1855 and 1856, wrote after a visit to a dairy farm producing Grana cheese that "in Italy cheese merchants recognize the quality of cheese tapping the cheese with their percussion hammer while listening carefully." This description recalls the image of a doctor who listens and diagnoses his patients using his stethoscope. When we talk about cheese, the best way to verify the quality and the internal structure of a cheese, before cutting it, is tapping with a hammer and listening to the cheese carefully at various points.

Usually the organoleptic characteristics of hard cheeses can be tested with the screw-needle (a long instrument similar to a screw) that allows for piercing the cheese to extract a minute sample of its content. The sample allows the expert to judge the aroma, the degree of maturation, and taste (and consequently to verify the presence of defects linked to these characteristics). However the screw-needle cannot inform us about the consistency of the texture, whether it is spongy in places, or the presence of holes and other defects and discontinuity under the rind. All these defects depend on different factors like incorrect whey draining, the quality of milk or the fat content, or in general an incorrect dairy process management. At this point it is necessary to use martelletto to test the quality of the cheese. In fact it is important that the expert taps the cheese at various points while listening carefully to the way the crust takes the blows. This tells the expert what is going on inside in much the same way a stethoscope does. If cheeses are carefully positioned to avoid resonances due to bad positioning on the table, "hammering" highlights even the smallest internal discontinuities in the structure. From the joint exam of the screw-needle and the hammer, the professional cheese testers reveal the quality level of a single wheel of cheese and determine the evaluation and qualification in terms of price.

See also GRANA PADANO; NEEDLES; and PARMIGIANO REGGIANO.

Androuet, Pierre. *Le Dictionnaire des fromages du monde.* Paris: Editions Le Cherche Midi, 2002, p. 158.
Cremona, Luigi, and Francesco Soletti. *L'Italia dei formaggi.* Milan: Touring Club Italiano Editore, 2002, pp. 29–37.
Fiori, Giacomo, et al. *Formaggi italiani.* Novara, Italy: EOS Editrice, 1999, pp. 74–75.
Fiori, Giovanni Guffanti, and Carlo Vischi. *Formaggi italiani.* Savigliano, Italy: Gribaudo, 2004, p. 194.
Guatteri, Fabiano. *Formaggi: conoscere e riconoscere le produzioni migliori d'Italia e d'Europa.* Novara, Italy: Istituto Geografico de Agostini, 2005, pp. 146–147.
Sardo, Piero, et al. *Formaggi d'Italia.* Bra, Italy: Slow Food Editore, 1999, pp. 174–175.
UNLAT, and INSOR, eds. *L'Italia dei formaggi DOC.* Milan: Edizione Franco Angeli, 1992, pp. 55–58.

Carlo Fiori

mascarpone has ridden tiramisu's coattails, as an essential ingredient for that ubiquitous Italian dessert, to enjoy the popularity it has today. A double- to triple-cream cow's milk cheese originating from the

Lombardy region of Italy, it can also be found in cannoli and cheesecakes. In savory applications, it can substitute for butter or Parmigiano Reggiano to add richness to and thicken risottos, or be served simply with anchovies, mustard, and pine nuts. The cheese's mild flavor, which ranges from buttery to slightly tangy, makes it ideal for enhancing the texture and flavor of dishes, while not overwhelming them with its own flavor.

There are many different theories to explain how mascarpone got its name. The popular etymology holds that the name "mascarpone" may come from the Spanish *mas que bueno* (better than good), from the days when the Spanish ruled Italy in the seventeenth century. Another possibility is that the name "mascarpone" comes from *mascarpa*, the name for the whey discarded in making stracchino, or perhaps from *mascarpia*, the local dialect term for ricotta, because the making of both cheeses, mascarpone and ricotta, involves similar technology. See RICOTTA INFORNATA. However, rather than ricotta, mascarpone most closely resembles clotted cream, cream cheese, and crème fraiche. See CREAM CHEESE. What distinguishes it from those other soft, spreadable cheeses is that it is the richest, with the highest percentage of milk fat (60 to 75 percent).

Mascarpone is an ideal cheese for making at home. The method can be as easy as adding cream to a double boiler; adding an acid such as lemon juice, acetic acid, or vinegar; bringing the mixture to a boil for about ten minutes at 185–195°F (85–90°C), stirring constantly; leaving it to rest for ten hours to allow the whey to separate; and then straining off the whey with a cloth. An additional step that enhances the cheese's classic richness (and high milk-fat content) is to first simmer the cream until it has reduced to about two-thirds of its original volume before adding the acid. See HOME CHEESEMAKING.

Usually made from cow's milk, Mascarpone di Bufala di Battipaglia can be found in Salerno, Italy. mascarpone is listed as a *Prodotto agroalimentare tradizionale* (traditional agricultural product), which protects it within Italy only. As a result, mascarpone is commercially produced, for example, in the United States.

See also ITALY.

Rubino, Robert, et al., eds. *Italian Cheese: A Guide to Its Discovery and Appreciation.* 2d ed. Bra, Italy: Slow Food, 2005.

Buratto, Tessa. "Mastering Mascarpone: What It Takes to Make a Perfect Batch of Mascarpone Cheese." PhD diss., California Polytechnic State University, 2010. http://digitalcommons.calpoly.edu/cgi/viewcontent.cgi?article=1044&context=dscisp.

Karl J. Peterson

matting

See STIRRING.

maturing is the management of changes in the flavor, aroma, texture, and appearance of cheese between the completion of the cheesemaking process and the point at which the cheese is ready to be eaten.

Cheese changes as it gets older. This is due to the interactions among the fats, proteins, moisture, bacteria, yeasts, molds, enzymes, and salt within the cheese. These interactions can be influenced by the conditions in which the cheese is kept and by the actions performed upon the surface of the cheese. Once the cheese is made, soft cheese changes far more quickly than hard cheese and requires more day-to-day decision making and handling. The interactions among the various constituents happen far more quickly, mainly because there is so much more moisture in soft cheese (moisture can account for up to 50 percent of the weight of soft cheese and as little as 30 percent of hard cheese).

At each stage of its life, the cheese will require different conditions and treatment. It is the work of the affineur (cheese refiner) to decide when these changes need to happen and to provide the necessary conditions. First of all the rind needs to grow. Then the cheese needs to ripen. And at the correct time, the cheese needs to be packaged and sold. Maturing ultimately ends when the cheese is eaten, so conditions still need to be managed once the cheese has left the control of the affineur.

Temperature and Humidity

Maturing conditions vary from 32 to 68°F (0–20°C) in temperature, and from 50 to 100 percent in relative humidity (RH). Low temperatures tend to slow maturation, and high temperatures accelerate it. Low relative humidity can retard rind growth and dry the cheese, while high relative humidity can encourage

Wheels of sheep's milk cheese maturing at Everona Dairy in Rapidan, Virginia. © KATE ARDING

rind growth and prevent the cheese from drying out. A supply of fresh air is important because, without it, humidity and byproducts such as ammonia can build up. These may make the cheese damp, damage the rind, taint the atmosphere to the extent that the flavor is affected, and even, in the case of ammonia, affect the speed of maturation. See RELATIVE HUMIDITY and AMMONIA.

Warm, humid conditions (as high as 68°F [20°C] and 100 percent RH) favor the early stages of rind growth. The correct yeasts, molds, and bacteria (such as *Geotrichum*, various types of *Penicillium*, and the vast array of bacteria involved in washed-rind cheeses) are favored, and undesirable microbes are outcompeted. Once the rind is established, it is likely that the temperature and humidity will be reduced (as low as 36°F [2°C] and 50 percent RH, but more likely 46–54°F [8–12°C] and 80–100 percent RH, depending on the type of cheese) to prevent the rind from developing more quickly than the cheese ripens. The combination of low temperature and high humidity is generally avoided because it discourages the growth of advantageous microbes while allowing undesirable microbes the opportunity to colonize the surface of the cheese.

The flavor, texture, appearance, and smell of the cheese will also be determined by how it is handled and treated as it ripens. It will probably need to be dried, turned, patted, and sometimes, depending on the type of cheese, washed.

The Need for Drying

Particularly in the early stages of maturation, soft cheese may need to be surface dried. If the cheese is allowed to ripen when it is too full of moisture, the rind will quickly grow out of control, becoming soggy all over or in patches. Excessive moisture will also allow too much microbial activity, causing the cheese to ripen too quickly, which may produce unpleasant flavors. Active drying can be achieved by combining the effects of heat, refrigeration, and airflow. Temperatures of 59°F (15°C) and above, along with vigorous refrigeration and exaggerated airflow, provide the most aggressive drying conditions. Cheese needs to be dried with care, though, since it is possible to remove too much moisture. See MOISTURE.

Turning the Cheese

All cheese needs to be turned throughout its life. The younger, softer, and more full of moisture it is, the more frequently it must be turned. Without turning, the moisture contained within the cheese will sink to the lower surface, which will become soft and wet. If left long enough, the moisture will accumulate, the cheese will slump and disintegrate, and finally, the cheese will rot. The rind will also form patches on exposed surfaces, and on the underside, not at all. See TURNING.

Patting and Rubbing

If left to its own devices, the mold-covered rind of some cheese will grow excessively and become very thick. As well as hardening and becoming cardboard-like and unpleasant, this will trap moisture inside the cheese, which will have a negative effect on the texture and flavor of the cheese. The rind of soft cheese needs to be patted to keep mold under control, while the rind of hard cheese needs to be rubbed. Rubbing controls not only the growth of mold on hard cheese but also the multiplication of cheese mites. Cheese mites, which are tiny arachnids that feed on the mold growing on some hard cheeses such as Cheddar, will sometimes even be vacuumed off if they are too numerous. If allowed to proliferate, they will cause damage to the rind, resulting in mold growth within the cheese and considerable waste. See CHEESE MITES.

Washing

The character of a cheese can be completely changed by washing the rind with water, saline, vinegar, beer, wine, cider, pear cider, or other alcohols in varying concentrations. Another washing solution is morge, which is a water or brine solution inoculated with particular surface flora. See MORGE. Washing the rind produces a number of effects on the cheese. First, any visible mold that is starting to grow is rinsed away. Second, the pH on the surface of the cheese is raised toward neutral, making the environment more hospitable for the required yeasts and bacteria. These, in turn, further raise the pH, a major contribution to the ripening of the cheese. With repeated washes, this effect is exaggerated. Soon the rind changes color, usually to a pinkish orange, and becomes sticky and pungent. In soft cheeses, the paste underneath breaks down and softens. Often, although the rind may be smelly, the paste remains gently flavored. Sometimes, however, fierce and powerful flavors develop. It is not just soft cheeses that are washed; some continental hard cheeses such as Comté and Beaufort also undergo this process. Since these are lower-moisture cheeses, however, they do not ripen in the same way as soft cheeses but remain firm. See BEAUFORT; COMTÉ; and WASHED-RIND CHEESES.

Different affineurs can achieve very different results with the same cheese. This is because there are so many points in the life of a cheese at which decisions need to be made. And at each of those points, there are several options available to the cheesemaker. It is often said that it is almost impossible to make a bad cheese good by maturing, but very easy to ruin a good one.

See also CAVE; DEFECTS; ENZYMES; *GEOTRICHUM CANDIDUM*; MICROBIAL FLUX AND SUCCESSION; *PENICILLIUM*; RINDS; and RIPENING CULTURES.

Anglade, P. *La fromagerie à la ferme*. Le Chaffaut-Saint-Jurson, France: Centre Fromager de Carmejane & Methodes et Communication, 1998. A very informative publication for the small-scale cheesemaker, which looks at most aspects of cheesemaking at a very practical level.

Eck, A., and J.-C. Gillis. *Cheesemaking: From Science to Quality Assurance*. 2d ed. London: Intercept, 2000.

Le Jaouen, J.-C. *The Fabrication of Farmstead Goat Cheese*. Translated by Elizabeth Leete. Ashfield, Mass.: Cheesemakers' Journal, 1987.

Scott, R. *Cheesemaking Practice*. 3d ed. Boston: Springer, 1986.

Owen Baily

Maytag Blue is produced by the family-owned Maytag Dairy Farms in Newton, Iowa. The cheese is a lasting heritage of the appliance-famous Maytag family, German Americans who tended an award-winning show herd of Holstein-Friesians in the early part of the twentieth century. See HOLSTEIN. That herd produced much more milk and cream than the family could consume, so it was often given away or sold locally. Later generations tapped the agricultural researchers at Iowa State University to create blue cheese—a twist from the French Roquefort tradition of using sheep's milk from the herd's milk. The Maytag family began selling blue cheese in October 1941, capitalizing on gift-giving time.

The blue cheese is still produced at the original location, and many of its employees have worked there for decades, if not generations. Milk comes from dairy farms in the area. The process is much the same as it was in the 1940s: heated homogenized milk is combined with rennet then, when it reaches a particular firmness level, cut into small cubes. The curd is hand-strained, mixed with *Penicillium roqueforti*, the blue mold powder, and scooped into hoops. See *PENICILLIUM* and HOOP. The curd is salted and then aged in curing caves. Six months later the rind is removed and the cheese is hand-packed into wheels or wedges, then wrapped in silver foil stamped with the dairy's logo. Each batch is individually tested by Maytag Dairy Farm employees. Although the cheese still does a brisk direct-mail business, it is also sold nationwide to restaurants and specialty food and grocery stores.

See also BLUE CHEESES.

melting refers to a substance's change from a solid or crystalline state to a liquid. The transformation from solid, sliceable cheese to an oozing Brie-en-croute or a stretchy bite of warm mozzarella begins with the chemical properties of the cheese's milk protein, or casein, network. When rennet and heat are applied to milk during the cheesemaking process, caseins coagulate, trapping fat and water molecules within their web. It is the breakdown of this web structure that allows cheese to ooze, stretch, and flow. See RENNET; CASEIN; and PROTEINS.

Around 90°F (32°C) milk fat begins to melt, at which point the cheese begins to become more pliable and you may notice beads of "sweat" appear on the cheese's surface. As more heat is applied to the cheese, bonds holding the casein proteins together begin to unravel, allowing the cheese structure to become more free-flowing and liquid-like. Protein networks begin to unravel between 130–180°F (54–82°C). Typically high moisture cheeses like mozzarella melt at 130°F (54°C), aged cheeses like Cheddar and Swiss melt at 150°F (65°C) and hard, very low moisture cheeses like Parmigiano Reggiano melt at 180°F (82°C). In part good melting cheeses are distinguished by the strength of their protein network, as well as water and fat content. See MOISTURE and FAT.

Typically younger, high-moisture cheeses like mozzarella, Brie, Gruyère, and Emmentaler are reliable melters, while low-moisture cheeses like Parmesan and pecorino are not. The proteins in low-moisture cheeses are more tightly packed with tighter protein bonds, which require higher temperatures to melt. During the aging process, older cheeses lose moisture over time through evaporation. While the moisture evaporates, milk fat remains trapped in the cheese's web of protein and therefore they have a higher concentration of fat. As a result low-moisture aged cheeses tend to become greasy when melted, as the fat releases from the casein protein bonds.

Aging also affects how cheese melts because the calcium atoms that hold the casein molecules together begin to dissolve over time. See MATURING and CALCIUM. As a result with fresh unaged cheeses, the calcium holds tight to the casein network as it is melted, resulting in a stretchy and stringy texture. Aged cheeses, on the other hand, can flow without resistance and melt more smoothly. This is why cheese like mozzarella will melt, but won't make a smooth and creamy sauce like aged Cheddar. Additionally the cheesemaker greatly impacts the grip of the calcium "glue" on the casein protein bonds through salt level, acidity, fat, and moisture content.

There are some cheeses, like ricotta, queso fresco, and paneer that will never melt. Unlike most cheeses, which are curdled with rennet, these non-melters are curdled with an acid, such as lemon juice or vinegar. Other non-melters, like fresh goat cheese, rely on naturally occurring acidity, which is created as bacteria convert the milk's lactose to lactic acid. See LACTIC ACID. Unlike rennet, the acid completely dissolves the calcium and also eliminates the protein's negative electrical charge. Therefore, when heat is applied to these cheeses, the proteins do not unravel. Instead as heat increases, water is expelled from the cheese and the proteins continue to get closer and closer together. Generally, for good melting cheeses, turn to young, moist, rennet-set cheeses that are easily sliced at room temperature.

See also FUNCTIONAL PROPERTIES.

membrane filtration, which includes reverse osmosis, nanofiltration, ultrafiltration, and microfiltration, involves pumping of milk under pressure across a membrane to achieve milk concentrates with special characteristics for cheesemaking. Possibilities include increase in the yield of cheese, modification of the quality of cheese, modified cheese functional properties, and development of new cheese varieties. Reverse osmosis functions in a way similar to thermal concentration. It removes water from milk resulting in concentrates that can be used for making cheese with an increase in yield. Nanofiltration is used for removing water and soluble minerals from milk and such milk is generally not used in cheesemaking. With ultrafiltration lactose and soluble minerals are removed and proteins are concentrated, producing milk with increased buffer capacity and modified rennet coagulation characteristics. Such concentrates can be used at low concentration (concentration factor of less than two) for manufacture of cheeses utilizing existing cheesemaking equipment. At higher concentrations (factor of three and a half and above) the concentrates can be used for increasing cheese yields and for developing new cheese varieties. With microfiltration it is possible to remove bacteria from milk and separate casein and whey proteins depending on pore size of membranes. This enables standardization of casein in cheese milk to increase cheese yield and the development of whey products with unmodified whey proteins. The technology also enables, with appropriate formulations, the use of liquid concentrates in the manufacture of process cheeses. In general, membrane processing allows for increased efficiency in cheesemaking as well as for introduction of new cheeses.

See also COAGULATION OR CURDLING; FUNCTIONAL PROPERTIES; MICROFILTRATION; ULTRAFILTRATION; and YIELD.

Kosikowski, Frank, and Vikram V. Mistry. *Cheese and Fermented Milk Foods.* 3d ed. 2 vols. Westport, Conn.: F. V. Kosikowski, 1997.
Tamime, A. Y., ed. *Membrane Processing: Dairy and Beverage Applications.* Oxford: Wiley-Blackwell, 2013.

Vikram Mistry

Mercearia Mestre Queijeiro

Mercearia Mestre Queijeiro is the first artisanal cheese store in Brazil focusing on local products. The store is located in the Pinheiros section of São Paulo city, and was opened in 2014 by Chef Bruno Cabral. After spending a couple of years in Spain, Cabral returned to his native Brazil with the mission to safeguard artisanal Brazilian cheeses. His appreciation for traditional products, raw milk, and other traditional cheeses was sparked during a short stint at a cheese store in Barcelona. There Cabral learned about careful sourcing, affinage, and retail services. He is recognized as the foremost cheese expert in his country and has served as a supreme judge at the World Cheese Awards in England.

The selection at Mercearia Mestre Queijeiro includes the famous Queijo de Minas Gerais, the newer Azul do Bosque and Azul de Ovelha blue cheeses, as well as other traditional cheeses from Brazil like the Serranos from Rio Grande do Sul. Most cheeses are finished in the store's small cellar and carefully tended by Cabral himself. He has worked closely with producers to have the best selection and support traditional producers. In 2014 he co-organized the first Brazilian Cheese Awards, bringing experts from Latin America to judge a wide variety of cheeses.

See also BRAZIL.

Orenstein, Jose. "Nova queijaria em Pinheiros." *Paladar,* 12 March 2014.

Carlos Yescas

Mesopotamia

Mesopotamia is possibly the area where the first cheese was made. According to a myth, cheese was accidentally invented some eight thousand years ago by an Arab trader who had to cross the desert and had taken some milk with him in a vessel made from a ruminant's stomach. As a result of rennet diffusion in the milk and the hot weather, the milk clotted. The trader not only ate the coagulated milk but liked it and decided to repeat its production.

From the time of the Assyrian king Sargon II, the economy of Babylonia was based greatly on animal husbandry and on agriculture. Milk was transported then in vessels made of ruminants' stomachs. Prior to the development of cheesemaking, in the period around 7000 to 6500 B.C.E., pottery for food storage, processing, and transport was developed. Surplus milk could now be collected and stored in ceramic pots. Pottery sieve-strainers were also designed and used for straining the coagulum. At that time, cheesemaking became common in Mesopotamia. Analysis of lipids on pottery from 6500 to 6000 B.C.E. confirmed that pots from this period were widely used to store dairy products. The nature of the lipids suggested that the products were cheese or other processed dairy products. It seems likely that cheeses of Neolithic ages were soft and acid coagulated, similar to traditional varieties still produced in this area. Hard cheeses may also have been manufactured. Small ceramic sieves with rough interior surfaces that have been found in this area may have served as graters of very hard, sun-dried cheeses. See EARTHENWARE POTTERY.

Archaeological evidence from southern Mesopotamia indicates that cow's, goat's, and sheep's milk were all consumed as beverages. The discovery of cheesemaking was a huge step for Neolithic man toward a vital food, appropriate for both young and old people that could be stored for later use. Cheese had been an integral element of religious practice in Mesopotamia for more than a thousand years. Offerings of cheese and butter were common in temples during the third millennium B.C.E. The Hittites not only ate cheese, but also used it with bread as an offering in religious rituals.

Cheese was well known among the Sumerians. During the Ur III dynasty (2100 to 2000 B.C.E.), Sumerian-Akkadian bilingual lexicons written in cuneiform scripts on twenty-four tablets contain more than eight hundred items of food and drink. Among them, twenty different kinds of cheese were recorded. An unusually detailed seal of the fourth millennium B.C.E. shows a kneeling woman working with both hands in a trough, while a man seated in front of her lays out ring-shaped objects, possibly cheeses, on a flat surface. In the dairy of the palace of Mari (third millennium B.C.E.) cheese molds were found.

Cheese was appreciated by the ruling elite as well as by the deities. The deities Ningal and her daughter Inanna demanded daily offerings of cheese and butter. Inanna's husband, Dumuzi, who was a shepherd, produced two cheese types: "small cheeses piled up high in heaps for him" and large cheeses that "laid on the rod for him" in reference to their measurement. See INANNA. Large and small cheeses are also mentioned in the Mesopotamian myth "The Marriage of Sud."

See also ANCIENT CIVILIZATIONS and ORIGIN OF CHEESE.

Kindstedt, Paul. *Cheese and Culture: A History of Cheese and Its Place in Western Civilization.* White River Junction, Vt.: Chelsea Green, 2012.

Evanthia Litopoulou-Tzanetaki

methyl ketones consist of a chain of at least three carbon atoms in which the first carbon is bonded to three hydrogen atoms and the second carbon is double-bonded to an oxygen atom. Methyl ketones are formed in cheese when microorganisms metabolize lipids. Lipase enzymes in bacteria, yeast, or mold break apart triglycerides to form fatty acids, which are oxidized and then converted into methyl ketones containing one fewer carbon atom than the fatty acid. Most fatty acids in milk contain an even number of carbon atoms, so methyl ketones in cheese predominantly contain an odd number of carbons. Methyl ketones are often found in concentrations exceeding one milligram per kilogram of cheese, which is above the human detection threshold. The smallest methyl ketone (containing three carbons) is 2-propanone, better known as acetone. The methyl ketones 2-butanone (four carbons) and 2-pentanone (five carbons) contribute acetone flavor notes to cheese; 2-heptanone (seven carbons) imparts a blue cheese aroma; and 2-octanone (eight carbons), 2-nonanone (nine carbons), and 2-decanone (ten carbons) are characterized by fruity aromas mixed with musty notes. The generation of methyl ketones is especially important in mold-ripened cheeses, where most of the total aroma compounds come from methyl ketones generated by *Geotrichum candidum*, *Penicillium camemberti*, and *P. roqueforti*. The most abundant methyl ketones in Gorgonzola and Roquefort are 2-heptanone and 2-nonanone, and the primary methyl ketones in Stilton are 2-heptanone, 2-butanone, and 2-pentanone. Methyl ketones are also found in other aged cheese varieties such as Cheddar, Gouda, and Parmigiano Reggiano.

See also ALCOHOL; AROMA; and RIPENING CULTURES.

Collins, Yvonne F., Paul L. H. McSweeney, and Martin G. Wilkinson. "Lipolysis and Free Fatty Acid Catabolism in Cheese: A Review of Current Knowledge." *International Dairy Journal* 13 (2003): 841–866.

Michael Tunick

Metsovone is a Greek semihard to hard smoked cheese with a PDO (protected designation of origin) since 1994; it belongs to the group of pasta filata cheeses. See PASTA FILATA. Metsovone bears the name of the town in which it is exclusively manufactured,

Metsovo, in the Epirus region of northern Greece. It is made from cow's milk, or with small amounts of ewe's or goat's milk added. Metsovone cheese is produced by the pasta filata technique, which was taught many years ago to young cheesemakers from Metsovo who were sent to Italy by the Tositsa Foundation, begun by Baron Michael Tositsa (1787–1856), to refine their skills.

Metsovone ripens for at least three months. After maturation it is smoked for one to two days by natural smoke from local plants, then coated with wax and delivered to the market. It is made in three sizes, 3.3, 5.5, and 10 pounds (1.5, 2.5, and 4.5 kilograms). Metsovone cheese resembles Italian pasta filata provolone cheese in appearance and flavor. See PROVOLONE DEL MONACO and PROVOLONE VALPADANA. It is cylindrical in shape, with a yellow-brown paste scattered with very small holes. Its flavor is slightly salty and piquant. Metsovone can be eaten as it is, grilled, or used in the preparation of salads, pies, gratin, tarts, pastas, pizzas, vegetables, meats, or appetizers, to which it contributes its special smoked perfume. It pairs well with white wines or light- to medium-body red wines. The fastest and tastiest way to eat Metsovone cheese is to roast a slice of it with lemon over charcoal.

See also GREECE.

Anifantakis, E. M. *Greek Cheeses: A Tradition of Centuries.* Athens: National Dairy Committee of Greece, 1991, pp. 84–85.
Newspaper of Government of Greek Democracy. "Metsovone Cheese." 18 January 1994.

Aikaterini Georgala

Metton

See CANCOILLOTTE.

Mexican cheeses

Mexican cheeses range from fresh, soft, firm, hard, to pulled curd, and aged cheeses—with blue cheeses as the only main category that are not currently produced in the country. While Mexico is best known for its fresh young cheeses, there are approximately sixty types of cheese currently produced in Mexico. The majority of cheeses are made from cow's milk, traditionally left raw without pasteurization. However, all commercial dairy producers now pasteurize milk. A resurgence of artisanal production has led to increasing production and consumption of goat's and sheep's milk cheeses. Some commercial fresh goat's milk cheeses also target a growing health and fat conscious consumer.

Cheesemaking in Mexico began in colonial times, starting with the first sheep's milk cheeses in the northern state of Nuevo León in 1585. After independence, fresh cow's milk cheeses became popular products in central Mexico, as well as goat's milk cheeses in the Bajío region. Today, the traditional mercados sell a range of different types and styles of cheese, mostly from small, local producers. A number of stand-alone traditional dairy stores also sell these traditional products. In contrast, most cheeses retailed at supermarkets are from corporate distribution networks, selling only the brands owned by Mexico's major dairy conglomerates. Corporate branded fresh cheeses tend to be bland, in part for the quality of their milk, and partly because dairy products are made with oils, potato starch, and other fillers that could be marketed as cheese. Since 2013, the law changed requiring those products to be labeled "formulas lácteas."

The most popular dairy products in Mexico are cow's milk fresh cheeses, butter, and sour cream. Meanwhile, yogurt, aged cheeses, and goat's and sheep's milk cheeses retail mostly at niche markets. The most sold cheese is quesillo de hebra, also known controversially as queso Oaxaca. This pulled curd cheese is originally from the town of Etla in the southern state of Oaxaca. It was traditionally made with semiskimmed milk. Now this style of cheese is made everywhere in the country using full-fat milk. It is used whenever a melting cheese is needed. Its flavor profile is lactic, creamy, and at times sour. The texture is bouncy and stringy, while the smell is normally of fresh milk and sometimes a little of milk whey. In some regions of the country this cheese is also known as asadero. However, in Aguascalientes, Chihuahua, Coahuila, Durango, Guanajuato, and Jalisco, queso asadero refers to a distinct kind of a semicooked curd cheese that most resembles an Italian provolone.

Second in popularity is queso de la panela. Originally made with goat's milk, now it is almost exclusively made from cow's milk. A fresh, lightly salted cheese, panela is high in moisture and sold fresh or oreado—left to dry. It is used to make tortas—Mexican sandwiches—or also used to stuff chiles. The flavor is lactic, sweet, and very fresh. Its texture is curdy and full, while its smell is fresh and very milky. Panela oreado is sold in some states in central Mexico. These panela cheeses are not refrigerated in order to develop a very fine rind from wild yeasts in the environment. The oreado's flavor develops a meaty note, while the smell becomes sharper but less milky. The oreado is a process found in many regions of the country and for many types of cheeses. However, the technique is falling out of fashion as consumers distrust unrefrigerated cheeses.

Another very popular cheese all over the country is queso Cotija. The original version, now referred to by the appellation mountain Cotija, or Cotija de Origen, is made from raw cow's milk, only in the Jalmich mountain range in central Mexico spanning some municipalities in the states of Jalisco and Michoacán. The cheese is made only during the rainy season in the mountains, and then brought down to the town of Cotija to be aged. According to the Collective Trademark granted by the Mexican government, the rules to make Cotija de la Region de Origen, each wheel of cheese must weigh around 49 pounds (22 kilograms), be salted with Colima salt, and aged for at least two months. Its smell is very similar to leather and wet earth; the flavor is salty, nutty, and milky; while its texture can vary from firm to crumbly, depending on the altitude in the mountain where the cheese was produced. The cheese can be aged up to twenty-four months.

Since the Collective Trademark was only granted in 2005, there are many copied versions of this cheese marketed under the name Cotija, made in other parts of the country. However, the copies tend to be inferior, and rather concentrate on the saltiness but not the creamy taste of the high quality raw milk used to make the mountain version. The two are easily distinguishable, as the mountain version has a pale yellow color, while the copies are normally white and fresh looking.

Finally, Mexico has a number of cheeses that are locally popular in different regions but that do not find national distribution or markets. Each is unique in flavor and all are central components of local dishes. Some of the most popular include: fresco, molino, de aro, de tenate, and del morral. These are fresh cheeses made with animal rennet and either ladled into forms or milled before molding. They are mostly consumed in central Mexico and the Pacific coast. In southern Mexico, doble crema and de cuadro, along with sopero and tropical are popular cheeses. Menonita, Chihuahua from northern Mexico, and

Manchego mexicano, and Chipilo, from central Mexico are semihard cheeses. Hard cheeses made in various states of Mexico include queso de añejo, de cincho, and criollo.

See also MEXICO.

Cervantes Escoto, F., A. Villegas de Gante, A. Cesín Vargas, et al. *Los quesos mexicanos genuinos: Patrimonio cultural que debe rescatarse.* Chapingo, Mexico: Universidad Autónoma de Chapingo, 2008.
Muñoz Zurita, Ricardo. *Diccionario enciclopédico de la gastronomía mexicana.* Mexico City: Larousse, 2012.
Yescas, Carlos. *Quesos mexicanos.* Mexico City: Larousse, 2013.

Carlos Yescas

In **Mexico,** cheese is a key component in cooking, a main ingredient in many regional recipes, and widely eaten as a garnish—either melted or crumbled on many traditional dishes. Although Mexico is not typically recognized abroad as a cheesemaking and eating culture, cheesemaking is in fact present in all regions of the country.

Queso (cheese) arrived in Mexico with Spanish settlers. The first record of cheese in Mexico comes from the north of the country, when in 1585 a rancher named Diego Montemayor is said to have acquired lands in present day Nuevo Leon, where ewe's milk was made into a Manchego-style cheese. During this early period, only Spanish settlers consumed cheese. Indigenous Mexican communities were lactose intolerant, meaning that when dairy animals were introduced to the Americas, most indigenous communities were not using their milk. See LACTOSE INTOLERANCE.

Based on accounts recovered from cookery books and manuals, historians suggest that cheesemaking skills were not shared with indigenous communities, thus further delaying the development of a cheese eating culture among Mexican nationals. The much warmer climate conditions in most of the country (compared to Spain) and lack of expertise prevented the perfection of aged cheese styles. The two exceptions are Cotija cheese from Michoacán and queso maduro, or añejo, from Estado de México and Tlaxcala. These areas offer drier climates more conducive for maturation and so these cheeses can be aged by rubbing the rinds with salt and leaving them to dry without refrigeration.

Cheeses consumed in central and southern Mexico tend to be fresher and made primarily from cow's milk. However, beginning in the 1820s, goat's milk cheeses have been produced and consumed in the Bajío region of central Mexico. Known for its flatlands and nestled between the two main mountain ranges that run down the length of central Mexico, the Bajío region is optimal for growing vegetables; large dairy cattle have not gained favor among ranchers. As a result, the main farm animals are goats and sheep primarily reared for their meat, and are the basis for some of the most iconic dishes in the region.

Cheese plays a part in almost all Mexican regional cuisines. It can be used as a filling in dishes such as stuffed chilies (chiles rellenos) and tortillas (quesadillas, enchiladas, tlayudas, or flautas), to stuff or garnish masa (cornmeal) dishes (sopes, tlacoyos, huaraches, and gorditas), to create sauces (nogada, made with fresh goat's cheese and walnuts), to melt (queso fundido) or fry crispy as in chicharrón de queso.

Cheeses from central and southern Mexico are most widely known abroad due to their use in many traditional dishes. They are sold everywhere within the country and in the United States, produced by both artisans and industrial dairy conglomerates. Mexico's emigrants to the United States, particularly those from the state of Oaxaca who settled in California, brought with them cheesemaking techniques and have popularized Oaxaca style cheese and queso fresco. The Oaxacan style "quesillo" is a pulled curd cheese made with cow's milk. Queso fresco is a lightly salted and pressed cheese.

The most popular cheeses in Mexico include asadero, botanero, fresco, quesillo de hebra (also known as Oaxaca), and panela—they can be found anywhere in the country. Cheeses like Chihuahua, Menonita, añejo, oreado, and Zacatecas are sold locally in their places of origin or in large markets in Mexico City and other cities. All are made using cow´s milk. Less well-known cheeses include queso de moral, de tenate, tetilla, sierra, tropical, sopero, criollo, de cincho, and Chipilo. These are often only locally distributed and consumed by a small number of farmers using milk from cows kept primarily for their fresh milk and meat.

Mexico has four cheeses that have been granted a collective trademark by the Mexican Institute for Industrial Property as a way to protect the quality and culture of their production. These are Queso Cotija de la Región de Origen (Michoacán) granted protection in 2005, Queso de Bola de Ocosingo (Chiapas) in 2005, Queso de Poro de Balancán (Tabasco) in 2012, and Queso Crema de Cuadro (Chiapas) in 2013. Despite these legal protections, lax supervision, rampant infringement, and lack of marketing and information campaigns mean that uninformed consumers do not demand original products, choosing instead the widely available knock-offs made by conglomerates.

Food conglomerates that process milk and dairy products for sale now control Mexico's milk production through their hold on distribution and retail sales in supermarkets, including where the majority of Mexico's urban lower and middle classes shop. The cheeses sold at both domestic and foreign-owned supermarkets are mostly produced with adulterations, including potato starch and vegetable fat, which have further suppressed the market price for cheese. In 2012, Mexico produced over 290,000 tons (263,084 metric tons) of cow's milk cheese. According to government figures, the consumption of cheese is increasing and in 2013 Mexicans consumed 358,000 tons (324,772 metric tons) of cheese, of which approximately 92,000 tons (83,461 metric tons) were imported into the country. Mexico produced, in 2012, approximately over 2,122,692 gallons (8,035,263 liters) of fluid cow's milk, with the largest production located in the Lagunera region in the states of Coahuila and Durango. Mexico is among the fifth largest importers of powdered milk in the world, as national production is insufficient to meet the demand of the growing urban population.

Traditionally, Mexican cheeses were made with raw cow's milk, but since 2010 the NOM-243-SSA1-2010 rules have required pasteurization of all liquid milk for human consumption, including that used for cheesemaking. However, in response to the lobby of some artisanal producers, companies can now apply for a waiver for the production of raw-milk cheeses, although health inspectors seldom approve permits for raw-milk cheese producers, claiming unsanitary conditions.

See also MEXICAN CHEESES.

Cervantes Escoto, F., A. Villegas de Gante, A. Cesín Vargas, et al. *Los quesos mexicanos genuinos: Patrimonio cultural que debe rescatarse.* Chapingo, Mexico: Universidad Autónoma de Chapingo, 2008.

SAGARPA. *Boletín de leche: Enero-marzo de 2013.* Mexico: Servicio de Información Agroalimentaria y Pesquera, 2013. http://www.siap.gob.mx/wp-content/uploads/2013/BoletinLeche/LecheMar2013.pdf.

Yescas, Carlos. *Quesos mexicanos.* Mexico City: Larousse, 2013.

Carlos Yescas

Michel Van Tricht and Son (Kaasaffineurs Van Tricht) is a third-generation affineur and cheese shop in Antwerp, Belgium. Owners Pieter and Juliette Van Tricht started the family business as a bakery and delicatessen in 1970, in Berchem, a suburb of Antwerp. Their son Michel took over the store and built a cheese aging cave behind the shop in 1978. Over the years cheese maturation and wholesale became a bigger and bigger focus for the Van Trichts, and the maturation cave was expanded a number of times. In 2001 Michel's son Frédéric joined him to help with the distribution and import end of the business.

In 2007 Michel Van Tricht and Son moved into a larger shop in Berchem, where they now also operate a wine bar. By 2012 they had outgrown their space once again, so the affinage and wholesale business moved into the De Koninck Brewery in Antwerp. Here Michel and Frédéric maintain eight rooms for cheese ripening.

Michel Van Tricht and Son has an emphasis on Belgian cheeses, and are known as the premier exporter of these cheeses throughout the world. They also import fine cheeses from all over the world for aging in their caves. They have a second shop slated to open in 2016, and also have plans to expand their operations at the brewery in the future. In 2010 *the Wall Street Journal* named Michel Van Tricht and Son one of the top ten cheese shops in Europe.

See also CHEESEMONGER and MATURING.

"Top Ten Cheese Shops: Michel van Tricht and Son." *Wall Street Journal Online.* http://online.wsj.com/public/resources/documents/info-TopTenWeekend.swf.
Verdonck, Eric. "Cheese and Beer—A Marriage Made in Heaven." Beertourism.com, 19 March 2013. http://belgium.beertourism.com/blog/cheese-and-beer-a-marriage-made-in-heaven.

Molly Browne

microbial coagulant

See COAGULATION OR CURDLING and FERMENTATION-PRODUCED CHYMOSIN.

microbial communities

microbial communities refer to cheese ecosystems that are composed of two interconnected systems: the cheese rind (an open system) and the paste (the interior, a closed system from early on in the process). The living parts of these ecosystems are the microbial communities. Cheese microbial communities are microbial populations that live in community and cooperate together to ensure the cheese ecosystem functions for building sanitary and sensorial qualities.

Claude Bernard (1813–1878), a French scientist and father of modern physiology, said "the microbe is nothing, the terrain is everything." Indeed the life of a microbial community is dynamic and governed by a network of interactions involving biotic factors but also abiotic factors. The biochemical composition of milk, microbiota composition at the species and strain levels, population counts and balances, acidification kinetics, the addition of exogenous microbial strains, pressing, salting on the surface or in the mass, heating (or not) of the curd, temperatures during manufacturing and ripening, the size of the cheeses, along with their ripening times, are all factors that together determine the dynamics of the native microbial population of raw milk and modulate their interactions and expression of their intrinsic enzymatic potential. The multiplicity of these interactions makes the control of complex fermentations by the cheesemakers therefore difficult. Faced with this complexity, and over their viewing experience and readjustments, cheesemakers have created their own repositories. They have largely contributed to the domestication of microorganisms in cheese.

The structural diversity within communities is generally evaluated by the number of species or Operational Taxonomic Units (OTU). For example, species belonging to four major groups defined on taxonomic and functional criteria including lactic acid bacteria (sixty-six species), ripening bacteria (thirty-two species), Gram-negative bacteria (twenty-six species), and fungi (consisting of yeasts [forty-nine species] and molds [twenty-seven species]) can cohabit in the microbial community in the core of raw-milk cheese. See TAXONOMY.

In the core of pasteurized milk cheeses, the number of strains or species is often less than five. Even if the cheese process reduces the microbial diversity of raw milk, the traditional raw-milk cheeses are the most complex ecosystems with over thirty species in the microbial community of the core or rind of a single cheese. They combine the great microbial diversity often produced with raw milk (more than four hundred microbial species, nearly forty species in a single raw milk) and the greatest diversity in the cheese production and ripening practices associated with human know-how. Variability in the microbial balance in milk is generated by wide inter-farm variability and intra-farm variability from season to season. Intraspecies diversity must be further explored as it is the key factor in functional diversity even if it remains difficult to assess in complex microbial communities. The functioning of these complex microbial communities is difficult to decode and still often remains a black box. Indeed complex microbial ecosystems ensure many functions that cannot be inferred from the intrinsic characteristics of each individual. Interestingly these complex microbial ecosystems are better able to continue to function if external perturbations appear. Indeed several microbial individuals can ensure the same enzymatic activity such as those leading to degradation of amino acids or fatty acids, especially important for the synthesis of aromatic compounds and phage resistance. See BIODIVERSITY and PHENOTYPIC VARIABILITY.

The synergy between microbial populations is also illustrated in their fight against *Listeria monocytogenes*. See LISTERIA. This microbial biodiversity naturally present in cheese should be preserved in situ by maintaining raw milk and diversity of traditional practices regarding milk inoculation (whey culture, wooden vats, etc.), manufacturing and ripening (old-young smearing, wooden shelves, etc.). This microbial heritage can also be preserved in public strain collections. However it will not be easy to reconstruct the complex community from isolated clones, so the preservation of microbial communities' richness requires preservation of dairy traditional practices.

See also ECOSYSTEM and MICROBIAL FLUX AND SUCCESSION.

Montel M. C., S. Buchin, A. Mallet, C. Delbes-Paus, D. Vuitton, N. Desmasures, and F. Berthier. "Traditional Cheeses: Rich and Diverse Microbiota with Associated Benefits." *International Journal of Food Microbiology* 177 (2014): 136–154.
Wolfe B. E., J. E. Button, M. Santarelli, and R. J. Dutton. "Cheese Rind Communities Provide Tractable Systems for *in situ* and *in vitro* Studies of Microbial Diversity." *Cell* 158 no. 2 (2014): 422–433.

Marie-Christine Montel

microbial flux and succession

microbial flux and succession are terms that refer to the transfer and change in the composition of the microbial community comprising the cheese microflora.

Microbial Flux

Microbial communities of milk and cheeses are extremely diverse, composed of at least 250 bacterial species identified to date. Microbial flux specifically refers to the transfer of diverse microbial populations from dairy environments (water, air, farmers, teats and teat skin, hay, pasture, silage, litter, etc.) to milk and the cheese, whereas microbial succession refers to changes within the microbial population of the cheese microflora during ripening due to selection of microbial species dependent upon the cheese technology utilized, death and lysis of starter cultures, growth of secondary flora, etc., as well as drivers of the microbial succession, which include carbon sources, salt levels, and ripening temperatures.

Early in the cheesemaking process, the selective pressure is high due to factors including addition of starter cultures, acidification, and decreases in milk temperature. These factors work to reduce the natural microbial communities of raw milk to favor lactic acid bacteria that become the predominant population. Microbial dynamics in the cheese core and on the cheese surfaces of traditional cheeses vary between cheese styles and, within a style, between dairies and time periods. The core of cheese is a closed ecosystem, much like a jail, and its microbial diversity during ripening will not benefit from external microbial enrichment, unlike the rind, which remains an open ecosystem.

Microbial Succession

But it is also interesting, especially for traditional cheese production, to take into account microbial flux and ecological diversity. At first the microbial community of raw-milk cheese is tightly associated with microbial meta-ecosystems in dairy farms. During milk production, the composition of the raw-milk microbiota depends on the composition of the microbiota of sources directly in contact with the milk: the animal's teat and dairy equipment such as milking machines, milk lines, and tanks. For example, microbial communities of teats harbor a great bacterial diversity, more than ninety genera, including ripening bacteria of importance in cheesemaking. These direct microbial reservoirs are supplied by indirect sources (feed, litter, drinking and washing water, stable and milking parlor air, and the milker). The milk microbiota is obviously strongly influenced by the overall farm management systems and farm practices.

Microbial transfers from reservoirs to farm milk remain to be established by tracking strains. The presence of the same species in different reservoirs does not provide information about circulation through the different ecosystems. Milking practices can play an important role in breaking down of microbial flux from teat to milk. An important goal is to identify the best milking practices for udder cleaning, teat-disinfecting procedures, and for washing milking machines to eliminate pathogenic bacteria while preserving useful microorganisms. Refrigeration of milk at 39°F (4°C) is also a concern for maintaining beneficial microbial diversity in milk, as refrigeration temperatures select for psychrotrophic spoilage and pathogenic bacteria. See HYGIENE and PATHOGENS.

Secondarily the milk microbiota in the vat can be enriched by microorganisms coming from the cheesemaking environment and dairy equipment. The transfer of microorganisms having beneficial applications in cheese technology from wood vats to milk is a good example. See WOODEN VATS. During ripening, microbial transfer from ripening surroundings and brines to rind also occurs. The presence of environmental bacteria on the cheese rind raises the question of their origin. For example, halophilic bacteria (*Carnobacterium, Alkalibacterium*) are directly provided by salt, brine, or indirectly by the environment that offers favorable conditions for their amplification. The microbial biofilms in all these environments should be better investigated as they undoubtedly contribute to the formation of milk and rind microbiota in cheese.

See also BIODIVERSITY; BIOFILMS; ECOSYSTEM; MICROBIAL COMMUNITIES; and RINDS.

Verdier-Metz I., G. Gagne, S. Borne, F. Monsallier, P. Veisseire, C. Delbes, M. C. Montel. "Cow Teat Skin, A Potential Source of Diverse Microbial Populations for Cheese Production." *Applied and Environmental Microbiology* 78, no. 2 (2012): 326–333.

Marie-Christine Montel

microbial identification

See TAXONOMY.

microfiltration (MF) is the use of membranes to separate milk into various components, such as somatic cells (15–6 μm), fat globules (15–2 μm), bacteria (6.0–0.2μm), or casein micelles (0.3–0.03 μm). This separation technique was restricted to laboratory use until the 1980s, when it became commercialized. Its industrial application to food liquids was made possible thanks to two main innovations: the development of highly resistant ceramic membranes (Garcera and Toujas, 1998) initially created for the separation of uranium isotopes; and a new hydraulic concept proposed by Sandblom (1974) that maintains uniform transmembrane pressure (UTP) either by a co-current recirculation of the microfiltrate in the membrane module or by membranes with a porosity gradient or a variable thickness.

In cheesemaking, microfiltration is used to remove the bacteria in milk by preventing microbes from passing through the filter. Pumping milk over a membrane with an average pore size of 1.4 μm, generally at a temperature ranging between 99 and 126°F (37–52°C), results in the concentration in the retained liquid, called the "retentate," of at least 99.99 percent of the microflora present in the raw skim milk. These contaminating microorganisms are concentrated in a volume limited to 0.05 percent of the entering milk, which is then discarded after heat treatment for animal feeding. The hygienic efficiency of microfiltration is similar to that of pasteurization for the removal of pathogens, but with two strong differences. In MF milk, there are neither spore-forming bacteria nor dead microbial cells with which thermoduric enzymes can initiate organoleptic defects in ripened cheese. MF milk has a very low bacterial count (less than 50 CFU/ml^{-1}). For making satisfactory cheese varieties, a specific microbial ecosystem must be added to realize adequate acidification, proteolysis, and lipolysis.

Microfiltration is also used to adjust the casein content of cheese milk. Indeed, using a membrane with an average pore size of 0.1 μm, at 122°F (50°C), allows specific separation of all milk particles. In MF retentate, micellar casein content increases proportionally to the volume of extracted microfiltrate. In most cheese plants, micellar casein is continually adjusted by about 20 percent to the same content—30 or 32 g/kg^{-1}. With microfiltration, daily variations in milk composition are erased, the rennet curd is firmer (resulting in a 1 percent cheese yield increase), and mechanization of the cheese process becomes very easy. In addition, the obtained microfiltrate, named by Maubois et al. (2001) "ideal whey," has a potentially high added value not only because it is sterile and completely fat-free, but also because its proteins are easily concentrated by membrane ultra-filtration while maintaining their native state. The so-obtained whey protein isolates (WPI) were shown to be superior for the nutrition of human beings (92 percent postprandial utilization), and particularly for infants, athletes, and seniors.

See also PASTEURIZATION; ULTRAFILTRATION; and WHEY.

Garcera, D., and E. Toujas. Support macroporeux à gradient de perméabilité et son procédé de fabrication. European Patent 0870534,A1, filed 31 March 1998, and issued 14 October 1998. https://docs.google.com/viewer?url=patentimages.storage.googleapis.com/pdfs/a8979daac39cf4e6f97e/EP0870534A1.pdf.

Maubois, J. L., et al. "Milk Microfiltrate, a Convenient Starting Material for Fractionation of Whey Proteins and Derivatives." In *The Importance of Whey and Whey Components in Food and Nutrition*. Proceedings of the Third International Whey Conference, Munich, 2001, pp. 59–72. Hamburg: Behr's Verlag, 2001.

Sandblom, R. M. Filtering Process. Swedish Patent 7,416,257-9, filed 23 December 1974, and issued 15 December 1977.

Jean Louis Maubois

The **microstructure** of cheese relates to the spatial distribution throughout the cheese of components such as protein, fat, insoluble salts, and microorganisms that can be observed using various types of microscopes. A study of cheese microstructure increases our understanding of the chemical and microbial changes that take place during the manufacture and ripening of cheese, and allows insight into the physical characteristics and functional properties of cheese. Using an ordinary light microscope the larger fat globules in milk can be observed and with proper staining so can bacteria. Large crystals that form during cheese ripening and become visible on the cheese surface or interior, and are part of the mouthfeel experience when eating a vintage Cheddar or Parmesan cheese can also be examined using light microscopy. See CRYSTAL. Further information can be obtained using fluorescent microscopy in which different components can be tagged so that they fluoresce when exposed to light with a specified wavelength, and increased resolution obtained using confocal laser scanning microscopy. To study the other components of milk requires use of electron microscopes with their ability to show images that have been magnified 1,000 to 100,000 times. Scanning electron microscopy can be used to view surface characteristics of cheese, or if the sample is fractured it can show arrangements of protein in cheese after coating with gold or other metal. Transmission electron microscopy provides more information on the interior organization of components in cheese.

See also CONFOCAL MICROSCOPY and LEEWENHOEK, ANTONI VAN.

Ong, L., et al. "Microstructure of Milk Gel and Cheese Curd Observed Using Cryo Scanning Electron Microscopy and Confocal Microscopy." *LWT—Food Science Technology* 44 (2011): 1291–1302.

Pastorino, A. J., et al. "Temperature Effect on Structure-opacity Relationships of Nonfat Mozzarella Cheese." *Journal of Dairy Science* 85 (2002): 2106–2113.

Donald J. McMahon and Almut H. Vollmer

Cheeses from the **Middle East** come from ancient traditions. Shards of pottery from archeological digs in the region indicate that cheese was consumed up to 4,000 years ago. Lactose tolerance among populations of humans indicates it was developed after humanity left Africa and before it reached Europe—that is, when people first populated the Middle East.

Without written record, we can only infer that cheese was invented in the Middle East when people tried to store milk from sheep or goats in pouches. Pouches, in antiquity, were commonly formed from animal stomachs and used to carry liquids such as wine or water. It is a small step of imagination to consider the likelihood that someone transported milk in a pouch made from a fresh young animal's stomach. The rennet in the lining of the stomach would have coagulated the milk into fresh curds. Imagine the surprise when this person tried to drink the milk and instead got lumps of cheese. One doubts he felt pride at having invented cheese!

We can say with some certainty, that in the time of *The Iliad*, the ancient Greeks were eating cheese. See ANCIENT CIVILIZATIONS and HOMER. We can also say the ancient Sumerians, Hebrews, and nomadic tribes consumed cheese. We can further acknowledge the similarities of these cheeses. Their preservative-oriented formulation would have been common thousands of years ago: boiled in water or whey (which would have had the effect of killing most bacteria introduced during milking or coagulation) and heavily salted by being stored in concentrated salt brine (which would have stemmed growth of most organisms introduced after the cheese was formed).

It is startling to remember that until the twentieth century, most meats and cheeses of the world were preserved in this fashion. It is likely that the sailors who explored the Mediterranean, lived through the adventures of *The Odyssey*, and brought the Middle Age Arabic Caliphate to Spain, all ate salt pork and pickled cheese in brine.

Cheesemakers who grew up in the Middle East tell that their ancestors made cheese in a simple fashion. Bedouins would bring the milk from their sheep to cheesemakers. The milk was curdled either with the dried stomach of young animals or, when there were no innards available, by using the acidic sap of freshly cut fig branches. They would boil the cheese and then salt it by immersion in brine. As salt was a valuable commodity, it was measured sparingly. The metric was that brine had sufficient salinity when a fresh egg would float. They knew it had too little salt when the egg would not float and too much salt when the egg would bob buoyantly—a flagrant waste of precious salt!

Traditionally, cheese was made from sheep's milk while kefir and yogurt were made from goat's milk. Goat's milk is more homogeneous, so drinks and spoonable yogurts made from fresh goat's milk are less liable to have the fat rise than sheep's milk. Sheep milk, on the other hand, offered cheesemakers a better yield and was more plentiful than goat's milk. The exception was roomy cheese made from the milk of gamoosas—female bovine animals similar to buffalo. Gamoos are native to Egypt and their milk makes a strongly flavored, pungent cheese.

Today, these ancient cheeses have as their descendants several families of cheese. Fresh cheeses have names such as jibneh, baladi, tuma, and Ackawi. Boiled and salted cheeses are called feta, Halloumi, naboulsi, mechalla, or majdouli. Fermented products such as kefir, yogurt and roomy cheese maintain their ancient, strongly flavored taste profile.

Cheese production in the Middle East is on the rise. The Cypatriots have trademarked "Halloumi"

and export it around the world. The Greeks, of course, are leading exporters of feta. Unfortunately, political turbulence in the Arabic portion of the region has limited its export capability.

To the positive, Arab expatriates are succeeding in popularizing their cuisine. While solid data is difficult to obtain, there are strong indications that Arabic cheese consumption is growing around the world. There is hope that cheese will become a reliable source of export for the embattled countries of the Arabic Middle East.

Fresh, Uncultured Cheeses

Paneer (panir) refers to cheese originally found in the area that today encompasses Iran, India, and Pakistan. In both the language of Urdu and Armenian, the word "paneer" means "cheese". Paneer is the largest selling variety of cheese in the world's largest milk producing country: India. It can be made from either buffalo's or cow's milk. The cheese is white; has little acidity; no salt added; smooth texture; and a fresh, clean taste. It is used in curried dishes, wrapped in dough, for dessert preparations. Since it is a high protein food, this cheese is often substituted for meat in many vegetarian entrees of Indian cuisine. Traditionally, this cheese had a five-day shelf life. See PANEER.

Ackawi is a soft, white cow's milk cheese that is native to Lebanon and Syria. The cheese is now popular throughout the Middle East among people of Arab descent. Ackawi is mild tasting but salty; white; without acidity; and has a smooth, fresh, curdy texture. Traditionally, the cheese was very salty as it was sold in brine. Today, modern storage methods allow the cheese to be more modestly salted.

Jibneh Arabieh is simple cheese found all over the Middle East. "Jibnah" in Arabic means "cheese." It refers to homemade, very fresh cheese. It is particularly popular in Egypt and the Arabian Gulf region. The cheese has an open texture, mild taste, and is widely used in cooking and snacking. The heritage of the product started with Bedouins using goat's or sheep's milk, however, current practice is to use cow's milk to make the cheese.

Basket cheese is a white, soft cheese that is formed in a basket. The traditional cheese has a circular basket shape and a salty taste. Because of the cheese's distinctive appearance it is difficult to mass-produce and the genuine product is easily recognizable.

Tuma, also known as **baladi**, is a favorite cheese from the Armenian region. It is a free-formed cheese made in baskets, open textured, a fresh product with a mild taste. It is widely used as an ingredient in cooking and for snacking. See TUMA PERSA.

Chanakh cheese is very similar to tuma and baladi but is not formed in a basket. It is one of the most popular native Armenian cheeses. It is fresh, often has small eyes, and is sold in brine so is quite salty—much akin to Ackawi cheese.

Brinza is a fresh cheese from Georgia and South Ostesia. This is a mild, salty, and open-textured cheese usually formed in round pieces.

Boiled Cheeses

Naboulsi (boiled cheese) is made by boiling fresh Ackawi cheese in a fragrant mixture of gums, spices, and seeds. The cheese is then stored in a salt brine so that it is effectively shelf stable. When taken from the brine, the cheese is very salty so common practice is to set the cheese pieces in a clear water solution for thirty-six hours or boil it for one hour in clear water. This removes enough salt so that the cheese becomes enjoyable to eat. It is flavorful, chewy, salty, firm, with a hint of the seasonings and gums in which it was originally boiled. The cheese is popular in Syria, Lebanon, and Jordan.

Halloumi is a cheese from the island of Cyprus. Originally made from sheep's or goat's milk, today the cheese is made from cow's milk as well. As with naboulsi, the milk is curdled either with acid or rennet, the resulting curds are formed, then boiled in whey. Unlike naboulsi, the whey in which Halloumi is boiled does not contain herbs or seasoning. Instead, the boiled cheese pieces are folded around mint leaves. The folded cheese is stored in salt brine so that the cheese is effectively shelf stable. The cheese is often grilled, fried, or baked. See HALLOUMI.

Lori cheese (another popular Armenian cheese) is firmer than chanakh or tuma. Like naboulsi and Halloumi, it is made by boiling fresh cheese. It is sold in brine so it is quite salty and firm.

Fresh, Cultured, Salty Cheeses

Feta is the most popular cheese in the northeastern part of the Middle East. It can be made from goat's, sheep's or cow's milk. The cheese is a cream to white color depending on the milk's origin (animal and season). When the cheese is made from higher fat milk such as sheep's or goat's milk, or when the cheese is made from cows that are eating fresh grass, the cheese is a richer, yellow tint. When it is made from lower fat milk or from cows fed from stored feed, it is whiter. The cheese is salty, crumbly, and sharply tangy. It is used in popular recipes and as a complement to relaxing meals and snacks of any sort. See FETA.

Mechalla and majdouli are very salty. These cheeses require soaking in warm water before eating.

Melting Cheeses

Kenafa and **sweet cheese** are unsalted, very fresh, soft cheeses that melt easily and freely. They are used to make the popular cheesecake dessert called *kenafa*. They can also be used as a base for other sweet desserts. Originally, these cheeses were made from sheep's or goat's milk and distributed in brine-filled pails. Consumers would boil the cheese in fresh water repeatedly to remove the salt preservative so they could use the cheese in preparing sweet foods. Today, the cheeses are commonly made from cow's milk with no salt and are sold frozen.

Twisted string cheese, chechil panir, husats, or **tel** cheese are Armenian pasta filata cheeses, which are pulled into thin strings and formed in braids. Often they are made with small nigella seeds. The original cheeses were made by direct acidification rather than through addition of cheese culture.

Sulguni (Georgian cheese) is a pasta filata cheese made from raw milk that has been kneaded in hot water and formed in round pieces. See PASTA FILATA.

Hard, Dry Cheeses

Roumy cheese is a dense hard yellow cheese with a very strong smell. It is strong tasting, salty, and crumbles easily. It was common to preserve the cheese in wax. This type of cheese is primarily consumed by Egyptians.

Shanklish is a cheese preserved with a thick coat of herbs and spices. The spices are typically oregano-based, but differ from region to region.

See also EGYPT; IRAN; and TURKEY.

Carr, Sandy. *The Simon & Schuster Pocket Guide to Cheese.* New York: Simon & Schuster, 1981.

Petrosian, Irina, and David Underwood. *Armenian Food: Fact, Fiction, & Folklore.* 2d ed. Bloomington, Ind.: Yerkir, 2006.

Robinson, R. K., and A. Y. Tamime, eds. *Feta and Related Cheeses.* New York: Ellis Horwood, 1991.

Paul Scharfman

military rationing of cheese and cheese products has occurred throughout history, because cheese provides a portable source of protein, calcium, and pleasure. Some of the first records of cheese being used as a military ration come from references to "aged soldier cheese" on Hittite tablets, written in second-millennium B.C.E. Anatolia. The cheese scientist and historian Paul Kindstedt believes that these references imply the creation of an aged hard-rind cheese, which would likely have been coagulated by rennet—an early innovation in cheesemaking. Through the era of Roman conquest, cheese continued to play an important role in military rationing, both in peacetime and during wars. Archaeologists have found ceramic cheesemaking molds at Roman-era military encampments around Europe, and the poet Virgil wrote that the daily ration for Roman soldiers would include an ounce of sheep's milk cheese. See VIRGIL.

The Bible mentions cheese only twice, once in direct reference to a military supply. In the first book of Samuel in the Old Testament, David, who was later called upon to defeat the Philistine giant Goliath, was told by his father, Jesse, to bring "ten cheeses" to the Israelite army commander. Jesse was a farmer who owned sheep, so we can assume the cheeses were made from sheep's milk, though we have no information about their age, coagulation, or size. See BIBLICAL REFERENCES.

In modern times, cheese continued to be an important component of military fare. During World War I, Camembert gained prominence as France's national cheese because of its role on the war front: "It was in the trenches that grassroots France became familiar with Camembert," according to the French sociologist and historian Pierre Boisard (2003, p. 102). Although Gruyère was more popular with the army because of its durability—in 1916, a quarter of all Gruyère was sent to the troops—Camembert, championed by the Normandy cheesemakers' syndicate responsible for its production and marketing, became an important part of soldiers' diets. When the war ended with an upsurge of patriotism, the smell of Camembert became synonymous with the smell of victory, and thus the cheese became symbolic of the republic's strong new national identity. See CAMEMBERT DE NORMANDIE.

In the United States during World War I, the military relied on a new style of processed cheese made by James Kraft, who had recently invented a shelf-stable cheese using emulsifying salts. The US Army placed orders for 25 million tins of Kraft's cheese product. That number expanded exponentially during World War II, when cheese was included in some K-rations, the daily rations given to combat soldiers, as a snack alongside bread or crackers. According to US Army documents, the surgeon general ordered that cheeses meant for military personnel were to be kept in quartermaster depots for at least 60 days to reduce the incidence of brucellosis among troops, a precursor to the 1949 law regulating cheese aging that is still on the books today. Cheese was also used on military bases as a cooking ingredient, mostly in a tomato-based macaroni and cheese dish. The US Army worked to devise a cheaper way of storing and shipping cheese, ultimately coming up with a dried, dehydrated cheese cake. This product, incidentally, was repurposed after the war by the Frito Company to become Cheetos, the popular snack. See 60-DAY AGING RULE and KRAFT FOODS.

Today, cheese remains a popular ration for militaries around the world. Napoleon famously quipped that "an army marches on its stomach," and it is no less true now than it was then. According to unclassified American military documents, cheese "has been a highly popular and coveted item by the US Army and Marine Corps Warfighters for use as a spread on crackers and bread and as a seasoning to many entrees" (Nattress et al., 2009, p. 3) Cheese also appears in the military rations of France, the United Kingdom, Australia, Saudi Arabia, Greece, and many more—a testament to its importance on the battlefields of the world.

See also WORLD WAR I and WORLD WAR II.

Boisard, Pierre. *Camembert: A National Myth.* Translated by Richard Miller. Berkeley: University of California Press, 2003. English translation of *Le Camembert: Mythe national* (Paris: Calmann-Lévy, 1992).

Kindstedt, Paul. *Cheese and Culture: A History of Cheese and Its Place in Western Civilization.* White River Junction, Vt.: Chelsea Green, 2012.

Marx de Salcedo, Anastacia. *Combat-Ready Kitchen: How the U.S. Military Shapes the Way You Eat.* New York: Current, 2015.

Nattress, Daniel et al. "Improved Storage Stability of Meal Ready-To-Eat Cheese Spread Under Heat-Stressing Conditions." Technical Report Natick/TR-10/003, US Army Natick Soldier RD&E Center, 2009.

United States Army Medical Department. *Preventive Medicine in World War II.* Vol. 4: *Communicable Diseases,* by S. B. Hays et al. Washington, D.C.: Office of the Surgeon General, Department of the Army, 1958.

Sam Chapple-Sokol

milk is the white fluid produced by female mammals after giving birth, to nourish the young until weaning. Its composition closely matches the needs of individual mammalian species in any land or water environment. Humans are unique in having learned to consume the milk of other species, chiefly goats and sheep (starting in western Asia, the Near East, and parts of the Mediterranean), water buffaloes (especially in India), and cows (throughout northwestern Europe and the industrialized West).

Composition

Mammals' milk is among the most complex and most imperfectly understood of foods. It comprises three chemical "phases" or mechanically separable forms:

1. An aqueous (water-based) solution called "serum" or "whey." Among the dissolved substances are lactose (the principal milk sugar); mineral elements including sodium, potassium, and calcium; and several water-soluble proteins, principally lactoglobulin and lactalbumin. In fluid milk whey is the "continuous phase," or that in which the others are dispersed. See WHEY.
2. An "emulsified phase" of microscopic fat globules, all containing huge assortments of triglycerides (each composed of a glycerol molecule with three separate fatty acid molecules attached) and other lipid substances, and surrounded by a thin but resistant globule membrane. Fatty acid molecules are built around architectural units of carbon linked to hydrogen, strung out in longer or shorter chains identified by the number of carbon atoms and the relative positions of the hydrogen atoms. Milk can contain several hundred different fatty acids; its flavor and "mouthfeel" are chiefly deter-mined by relative amounts of short-chain, medium-chain, and long-chain acids. The emulsion has a lower specific gravity than the whey solution. In species whose milk contains large fat globules, especially cows and water buffaloes, the emulsified milk fat tends to form a cream layer at the top. Mechanical agitation of such milk or cream under the right conditions produces a "phase inversion," driving off most of the other two phases as buttermilk and converting the previously emulsified fat globules into a continuous phase called "butter," with tiny droplets of buttermilk dispersed throughout a solid mass. See FAT and BUTTER.
3. A "suspended phase" of particles known as "casein micelles" containing most of the protein in milk, especially ruminants' milk. These microscopic structures (varying in size and configuration among species but always much smaller and denser than fat globules) are made up of many different amino acid chains linked to phosphate ions, which in turn bond with calcium ions to act as an adhesive holding together the entire particle. This phase is the foundation of cheesemaking. Either increased acidity (lowered pH), enzymatic action, or a combination of both can overcome the slight negative electric charge that causes casein micelles to repel each other, allowing the neutrally charged particles to gather into clumps large enough to "precipitate" (literally fall out of the whey suspension) as a coagulum, or "curd." See CASEIN and COAGULATION OR CURDLING.

Each phase contains still-unmeasured complexities, and each is powerfully affected by such factors as stage of lactation and the mother's nutritional status.

The Role of Ruminants

Virtually the only animals whose milk humans use for cheesemaking are ruminants (cud chewers). The size and configuration of casein micelles in most ruminants' milk allows easier precipitation than that of most other creatures, including humans. The fatty acid composition of cow's, goat's, sheep's, and water buffalo milk fat results in cheese flavors particularly pleasing to people in cheese-loving regions of the world. Relative amounts differ greatly by species; sheep's and goat's milk is distinctively flavored by short-chain fatty acids including butyric, capric, caproic, and caprylic acid. With lesser amounts of these, the flavor of cow's milk is the blandest of any ruminant milk.

Ruminants are by definition hoofed herbivores that "ruminate" by chewing a cud of swallowed and regurgitated grass or other vegetation, initiating a complex digestive process involving several digestive chambers. The first two, the very large "rumen" and the smaller adjacent "reticulum," contain trillions of bacteria that break down cellulose and other fibers in the food before it travels through the abrading folds of the "omasum." Only then does food reach the true stomach, or "abomasum," the only chamber of the system that directly secretes hydrochloric acid and digestive enzymes as does a human stomach. In infant ruminants, the reticulo-ruminal chambers are undeveloped. The mother's milk is shunted straight through to the abomasum, where chymosin, an enzyme formerly known as "rennin," aids in digesting casein. See RENNET and RUMINANTS.

Effects of Domestication

Throughout the mammalian class many intricacies and subtleties of milk still defy exact analysis. Any animal's milk will be noticeably influenced by factors including climate, environment, diet, and heredity. In the case of domestic ruminants, all of these have been strongly shaped by human intervention since the start of domestication.

Sheep and goats were first domesticated in southwestern Asia, possibly as early as 9000 B.C.E. Cattle domestication probably occurred in the same general area at about the same time or a few centuries later as that of dairy-type water buffalo, by about 5000 B.C.E. in the Indus Valley (embracing parts of today's Pakistan and India). In all cases humans soon introduced the animals to environments far from the original site of domestication, while substituting more or less restricted pasturage for their original grazing territories.

Only in the last two centuries have people worked purposefully to increase the milk output of dairy stock through what are often called "feeding-and-breeding" strategies. The chief targets of attention have been cows, whose breeding and lactation cycles are more flexible than those of goats, sheep, or buffaloes. In the English-speaking world, cow's milk cheeses have always been more economically important than other kinds.

Milk and Microbes

Mammal's milk, as secreted by a nursing mother and ingested by a nursing infant, remains within a fairly sterile nipple-to-mouth system without encountering the microbial environment of the outside world. As with the placental blood that milk replaces after birth, its sole biological role is life support. Once exposed to the open air, however, it is an ideal growth medium for bacteria that work immediate changes on milk. This is especially true during the warmest months of the year—until very recently the only time at which the animals' seasonal breeding cycles permitted milking. Luckily the most easily attracted bacteria in hot, dry climates are harmless thermophilic members of the *Lactobacillus* and *Streptococcus* genera that quickly begin fermenting this desirable food supply, changing lactose to lactic acid. See STARTER CULTURES. The lowered pH of the resulting soured milk tends to inhibit dangerous pathogens that prefer less acidic environments, affording a certain limited defense against milk-borne contagions while making it a more suitable food for adult humans who lack the nursling's ability to digest lactose. See PH MEASUREMENT and LACTOSE INTOLERANCE.

In the earliest milking regions, milk was most often consumed as products resembling yogurt; as simple fresh cheeses made through acid coagulation, rennet curdling, or a combination of both methods; or—the least perishable form—brined cheeses. A combination of sheep's and goat's milk was generally used for all these purposes, though cow's milk was also a frequent source. See ORIGIN OF CHEESE.

Fresh soured forms of milk and simple cheeses produced by mesophilic rather than thermophilic organisms accompanied the northwestward spread of dairying into Europe before 5000 B.C.E. In the cooler temperatures of northwestern and, to an extent, Alpine regions, cows (comparatively heat-intolerant) became the predominant dairy animal. Where they went, two fairly durable milk derivatives eventually followed: butter and fairly large ripened cheeses. (Ripening, which involved successive stages of colonization by several different bacterial species over extended periods of time, was impossible in warm climates before mechanical refrigeration.) Goat's and sheep's milk cheeses, usually younger and smaller in size, remained more important in southern Europe. Farther north sheep were more valued for wool than milk, and goats seldom furnished cheese milk except in harsh environments where they were considered the "poor man's cow."

Fluid Milk Versus Cheese

Europe's bovine dairying strongholds were also the regions where industrialization, land enclosures, urbanization, and the development of advanced agricultural economies most rapidly reshaped farming after the seventeenth century C.E. Simultaneously the same regions acquired a commanding global role in scientific research and medical theory. Nutritional doctrines that took root in England and the United States during the nineteenth and twentieth centuries placed an unprecedented emphasis on cow's milk in fresh, drinkable form as an indispensable dietary requirement for children after weaning and a valuable priority for adults.

As a result the fluid milk market came to consume an increasing share of a greatly expanded cow's milk supply now maintained throughout the year. This in itself was a crucial break with earlier seasonally limited grazing practices that had dictated the uses of milk for all purposes including cheese. As priorities shifted, many industrialized countries saw shrinking demand for farmhouse cheeses that bore the individual character of seasonally produced milk from local pastures or local dairy breeds.

In major cow-dairying areas, cheese did not share the new nutritional éclat of drinkable milk. It was long considered "strong" and indigestible in genteel British circles. During the nineteenth century a general movement took place toward factory-scale cheesemaking concentrated on a shrinking number of fairly bland varieties. But in England and even more in France, metropolitan consumers formed a limited but loyal market for one-of-a-kind cow's milk cheeses from farmhouse makers in rural districts. Connoisseurs everywhere also became familiar with a certain international cast of cow's milk stars including Cheshire, Stilton, bloomy-rind types like Brie, and of course the perpetually treasured Parmesan. Roquefort was the only sheep's milk outlier in the usual assortment.

Very different patterns of milk production and consumption prevailed in countries bordering the Mediterranean. The fluid milk market was negligible; sheep and goats remained the preferred dairy animals. Local cheeses made on a small scale with little technological innovation were slower to disappear.

Eventually outsiders took notice. Toward the turn of the twentieth century, a small coterie of English and American epicurean writers sang the praises of rustic southern European cheeses from goat's or other non-bovine milk, as well as pungent-smelling washed-rind cow's milk cheeses.

Science and Cheese

Dairy microbiology began to emerge as a scientific discipline by about 1900. For the first time the three phases of dairy animals' milk could be visualized under a microscope. So could the microorganisms responsible for both an array of different cheese cultures and many food-borne epidemics. That both familiar and out-of-the-way cheeses depended on the qualities of milk, whether bovine or non-bovine, was now scientifically demonstrable. So were the reasons behind traditional customs like bringing the milk for some cheeses to a certain temperature before adding a starting ferment and rennet, or combining batches from the evening and morning milking. Researchers also learned to propagate standardized starters of desired organisms in the laboratory and add them to the milk in exact amounts depending on precise analysis of crucial factors.

The microbiological revolution also encouraged early twentieth-century cheesemaking experiments based on pasteurized milk, which was already altering the fluid milk market. But hopes of producing a wide range of first-class cheeses from pasteurized milk—a goal still imperfectly realized today—were hobbled by a gap-ridden understanding of milk chemistry and biochemistry. Makers of Cheddar-type cheeses (the standard-bearers of the North American cheese market) were not alone in finding that changes in the bacterial flora and enzymatic makeup of pasteurized milk bafflingly inhibited the action of both starters and rennet. See PASTEURIZATION.

The nineteenth-century tuberculosis epidemic, which was just beginning to yield some clues to early researchers by about 1900, gave a spur to milk pasteurization when dairy cows and their milk were recognized as a major route of transmission. Goats, however, seemed to be relatively immune. Goat dairying to supply a purportedly more healthful alternative to fluid cow's milk soon experienced a surge in milk-drinking countries. Dairy goat herds gained a following throughout the United States; California had become an important center before 1920, though it would be another sixty years before the milk started to be used for cheesemaking.

Throughout the twentieth century technological breakthroughs in producing and distributing fluid cow's milk on a gigantic industrial scale had the effect of making fresh drinkable milk progressively less like any kind of milk fit for cheesemaking. This was especially true in the United States, the world leader of modern dairying and supposedly an educational example to Third World nations. Homogenization, higher-temperature pasteurization methods, and new feeding strategies to maintain cows year-round on computer-calculated rations interposed successive barriers to consumers' understanding of the basic substance. See HOMOGENIZATION.

New Directions

Fluid milk production on an agribusiness scale did not directly figure in the 1960s and 1970s countercultural reaction against mass-marketed, industrially processed food. But the backlash later helped prepare the ground for an American cheesemaking renaissance that began around 1980 with a few small California goat's milk cheese ventures. The idea struck a chord with back-to-the-land nonconformists who had acquired experience milking a cow or a handful of goats to supply a commune. Some underwent a post-hippie transformation to small, idealistic entrepreneurs. Thus it happened that a radical vanguard of restaurateurs seeking locally produced ingredients of strictly vetted provenance came on the scene at the right moment to forge ties with some goat's milk cheese pioneers. Timely reinforcement from a completely different direction arrived in 1983 with the founding of the American Cheese Society, which shortly became a clearinghouse of professional knowledge about milk chemistry and microbiology for hopeful cheesemaking neophytes. See COUNTERCULTURE; AMERICAN "GOAT LADIES"; and AMERICAN CHEESE SOCIETY.

The "Mediterranean diet" vogue that began in the late 1980s helped young, fresh goat's milk cheeses (both domestic and imported) find an audience beyond exclusive gourmet circles. Within a couple of decades some were appearing on supermarket shelves. It was many middlebrow American consumers' first clue to the existence of cheese from non-bovine milk. US sheep's milk cheese production has also enjoyed rapid growth after tiny beginnings at around 1990, and domestic buffalo milk mozzarella is now being produced at a handful of farmstead operations.

The US cheese revolution has also given some cow dairyists profitable alternatives to fluid milk produced under the cumbersome federal milk marketing system. Unlike the mainstream fluid milk system, artisan cheesemaking has a real place for milk from cow breeds with distinctive individual qualities. In 2000 the USDA's Agricultural Marketing Service division, belatedly recognizing the growing importance of cheese milk, revised the schedule for basic milk prices guaranteed to farmers to allow "multiple component pricing" of Class III milk—that is, milk used to make hard cheeses—with milk fat, protein, and non-protein solids factored in. Milk with good protein content, crucial to most hard and aged cheeses, has been a major beneficiary.

At the same time other farmers have opted to create or contribute to independent fluid milk operations in which the original character of cow's milk from small pasture-raised herds is preserved as faithfully as possible through low-temperature pasteurization methods without homogenization. Often sold in cheese stores, these local brands—ideal for home experiments in making a few simple fresh cheeses—offer an opportunity to educate consumers about the links between good milk and good cheese.

See also COW; GOATS; and SHEEP.

Du Puis, E. Melanie. *Nature's Perfect Food: How Milk Became America's Drink*. New York: New York University Press, 2002.

Jensen, Robert G., ed. *Handbook of Milk Composition*. San Diego: Academic Press, 1995.

Mendelson, Anne. *Milk: The Surprising Story of Milk through the Ages*. New York: Knopf, 2008.

Valenze, Deborah. *Milk: A Local and Global History*. New Haven, Conn.: Yale University Press, 2011.

Wong, Noble P., et al. *Fundamentals of Dairy Chemistry*. 3d ed. New York: Van Nostrand Reinhold, 1988.

Wylie, Andrea. *Re-imagining Milk*. New York and London: Routledge, 2011.

Anne Mendelson

A **milk boiler** is a cooking pot fitted with a specialized perforated lid that prevented rich, frothy sheep's milk from boiling over during the production of ricotta cheese. Ceramic milk boilers came into use in Italy during the second millennium B.C.E., around the same time that shepherd cheesemakers from the lowlands began to systematically access pastures in the Apennine Mountains during the summer for transhumant grazing. See TRANSHUMANCE. The lids were of two different designs. In southern Italy, the lid consisted of a shallow bowl, with a large circular hole in the center surrounded by a collar. During heating, milk would rise through the central hole as bubbles, which would then burst and drain back down into the pot through small perforations in the bottom of the bowl. In northern Italy, the lid took the form of an inverted funnel containing a ring of small holes around its base. The funnel rested on a special pot that contained an internal ledge to support the device.

Although they were evidently used widely in Italy during the second millennium B.C.E., milk boilers virtually disappear from the archeological record of the first millennium B.C.E. The apparent decline in sheep's milk ricotta making may have been related to the abrupt rise in hard pecorino cheesemaking around the same time. Hard pecorino cheeses, with their superior durability, transportability, distinctive piquant flavors, and versatile grating and cooking properties, became extremely popular throughout the northern Mediterranean during the first millennium B.C.E. See PECORINO SARDO. Nevertheless, shepherds in the Apennines have continued to use versions of milk boilers into modern times.

See RICOTTA and SHEPHERD.

Barker, Graeme. *Landscape and Society: Prehistoric Central Italy.* London: Academic, 1981.
Kindstedt, Paul. *Cheese and Culture. A History of Cheese and Its Place in Western Civilization.* White River Junction, Vt.: Chelsea Green, 2012.
Trump, David. *Central and Southern Italy Before Rome.* New York: Praeger, 1966.

Paul S. Kindstedt

milkmaids

See DAIRYMAIDS.

milk marketing boards have been set up in various countries to help regulate the market for milk and dairy products, promote the sale of milk products through advertising, and provide support for dairy research. In the United States the National Dairy Promotion and Research Board (NDB) was formed under USDA authority in May 1984 to conduct coordinated dairy promotion and research to help increase demand for and expansion of domestic and international markets for dairy products. The NDB funds Dairy Management Inc. (DMI) to manage the national dairy checkoff program. Dairy farmers pay 15 cents and dairy importers pay 7.5 cents for every 100 pounds (45 kilograms) of milk sold or imported, into a dairy product promotion fund that is managed by DMI along with state and regional promotion groups. That money, under USDA oversight, is used to fund programs designed to promote dairy consumption and to enhance the image of dairy farmers, dairy products, and the dairy industry.

The UK board was established in the 1930s to provide a reasonable price for dairy farmers producing milk. It guaranteed to buy the milk and then placed it to processors. When milk was plentiful all processors had enough milk for their needs, but in the late summer and autumn milk supply could be limited and processors making butter, cheese, and milk powder had no milk. This was because priority was given to fresh milk, cream, and yogurt producers. There was also no direct contact between farmers and processors because the board could send the milk anywhere in the United Kingdom where needed. Butter and milk powder stocks would rise during periods of good supply and this led to "butter mountains" being produced. Political action was needed across Europe to deal with this issue.

This all changed in 1994 when the board was deregulated and then disbanded in 2002. This paved the way for processors to bid directly for the volume of milk they needed and establish commercial relationships with farmers. This led to greater "ownership" of the milk, and improved quality standards for both composition and microbiological content. In particular there has been a renaissance in cheesemaking with a wide range of exciting new varieties.

Perhaps the most famous new cheese produced in the United Kingdom, Lymeswold, was developed by the board in the 1970s. Due to overwhelming demand, production was under pressure and quality was compromised, resulting in its demise. Dairy Crest still owns the brand name, so perhaps Lymeswold will be revived at some point. Most recently with global prices down there has been a call to return to some system of guarantee for producers.

See also MILK.

Dairy Crest. http://www.dairycrest.co.uk/who-we-are/
our-history.aspx.
FarmingUK. http://www.farminguk.com.
Rance, Patrick. *The Great British Cheese Book*. London:
Pan Macmillan, 1988.

John Pearson

Milleens

See COUNTY CORK and STEELE, VERONICA.

milling is the cutting of slabs of curd to small pieces for cooling, for further drainage of whey, for distributing salt over the increased surface area, and for preparing the curd to be pressed into molds. Curd particles smaller than a gram in size retain three times the salt of curds larger than twenty grams. Smaller particles result in less mechanical openness in the cheese and an increase in the retention of salt; therefore, less salt is needed.

Mills may be operated by hand or mechanically. A mechanical mill is advised if the amount of curd is substantial. All mills should have safety cutout attachments and cut the curd quickly, cleanly, and without crushing or squeezing. Most of the hand mills available today are of the peg mill type. For small-scale manufacture there are three types of mills available:

- Chip mills, used mainly for Cheddar types, produce 1–2-inch pieces of curd. To produce a 1.7 percent salt concentration in the final product, 2.5 percent salting on the curd is required. Chip

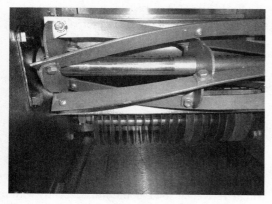

The lower cutting edge of a chip mill, which is used primarily to mill Cheddar-type cheeses. © VAL BINES

mills are more complicated in their design and therefore more difficult to clean. See CHEDDAR.
- Large-toothed peg mills, used for Cheddar, produce pieces of curd with an irregular shape due to their tearing action. With a larger surface area, salt is more readily absorbed and therefore less salt is required.
- Small-toothed peg mills, used traditionally for Cheshire, produce small, crumb-like pieces of curd, with a very large surface area. The large-toothed mill has largely replaced this, through which curd may be passed twice to obtain smaller pieces. See CHESHIRE CHEESE (U.K.).

The milling operation takes place when the pH of the curd reaches 5.4 or lower or with an acidity of 0.45 percent lactic acid, and the temperature of the curd is 98.6°F (37°C). The curd may be milled into the vat or the cooler; the mill is placed at one end of the vat or cooler and the curd moved away, so that there is space under the mill. The curd slabs or blocks are then cut so that they will pass smoothly through the mill, and the pieces are stirred with a stainless fork to prevent them from knitting together again. Salt may be applied at this point in even quantities and until milling is completed. The curd must be continually stirred to ensure the mixing of the salt and to prevent clumping of the curd. If curd becomes clumped, a fault known as "green spot" may occur. These areas of reduced salt have a grey color and distinctive "off" flavor caused by lactobacilli growing in localized clumps. Training and education of staff will help to eliminate this problem. The curd is ready to be molded when the temperature is between 80–86°F (27–30°C); higher than this encourages "early blowing" caused by the growth of non-starter lactic acid bacteria.

See also CURD MILL; MOLDING; SALT; and STIRRING.

Maddever, K. D. *Farmhouse Cheddarmakers' Manual.*
Thames Ditton, U.K.: Milk Marketing Board, 1988.
Van Slyke, Lucius L., and Walter V. Price. *Cheese*. Revised
and enlarged edition. Atascadero, Calif.: Ridgeview,
1992. First published in 1932 by Orange Judd.

Val Bines

Mimolette. There are few cheeses as striking as a mature Mimolette, with its slightly flattened sphere shape, electric-orange interior, and dusty, pitted moon-like surface. At first glance a wedge of this French

Mimolette's dusty, pitted, moon-like exterior is due to the action of microscopic cheese mites that are allowed to burrow into its rind, creating tiny holes and pockmarks that promote ripening and make for a special aroma.
© CHRIS WAITS

cow's milk cheese looks like a slice of ripe summer cantaloupe.

The origin of Mimolette is also unique. During the Franco-Dutch War (1672–1678), French trade with the Netherlands was cut off, stopping shipments of the popular Dutch pressed cheese Edam, which left a shortfall in cheese supplies to feed the population and French army. So French finance minister Jean-Baptiste Colbert commissioned cheesemakers in northern Flanders to create a knock-off of Edam, but with a bright color that would easily distinguish it from the Dutch original. The name Mimolette derives from *demi-mollet*, a term that means partly soft or supple, describing its texture when young. The cheese is also known as Boule de Lille, referring to the city of Lille where the cheese was first matured. (Allegedly Mimolette was the favorite cheese of the late French president Charles de Gaulle, who was born in Lille.) It is still mostly produced in the Flanders area of Pas-de-Calais, but some production is also based in Calvados and Loire-Atlantique. See EDAM.

Like Edam, Mimolette belongs to the category of washed-curd cheeses. After ripening pasteurized milk with lactic bacteria and rennet coagulation, the vat is vigorously stirred to render tiny grains of curd. They're partially drained of whey and steeped, or "washed," in hot water to yield a cheese with a smooth, creamy body and sweeter, less acidic taste. Mimolette curds are then colored with annatto, a natural plant-based pigment, before being pressed for twenty-four to thirty-six hours and brined in a salt bath. See ANNATTO. Weights range from 5 to 8 pounds (2.3–3.6 kilograms). The Dutch cheese Commissiekass is a similar orange-hued, washed-curd tomme, though its rind is coated in orange paraffin whereas Mimolette has a natural rind.

Sold at various stages of maturity, many industrial versions of Mimolette are eaten young, between six weeks and three months of age. They're mild and pleasant, yet unremarkable. But at the other end of the spectrum is Mimolette *très vieille* (extra aged), ripened for eighteen to twenty-four months. As the cheese matures affineurs test its stage of ripeness by using a wooden mallet to "sound" the cheese. See MARTELLETTO. During this prolonged rest in the aging room, the cheese is transformed; its color deepens, the paste becomes dense and waxy, its aroma hints of butterscotch, and the flavor takes on complexity with fruity, nutty, and caramel qualities.

This transformation occurs partly through the action of microscopic cheese mites that are allowed to burrow into the rind of Mimolette, creating tiny holes and pockmarks that promote ripening and make for a special aroma. The mites also leave a characteristic patina of gray dust as they burrow. Wheels of aging Mimolette are continually brushed to prevent mite colonies from becoming too invasive, damaging the cheese under the rind. The presence of mites in Mimolette, though traditional, caused the US FDA to temporarily ban the cheese from import between 2013 and 2014 as mites are deemed an allergen. Mimolette is a favorite served on cheese plates as it pairs well with beer, lighter reds, and dessert wines.

See also CHEESE MITES and WASHED-CURD CHEESES.

American Cheese Society. "Ask Dr. Cheese: Washing Curd." http://www.cheesesociety.org/ask-dr-cheese-washing-curd/.

Fletcher, Janet. *Cheese & Wine*. San Francisco: Chronicle Books, 2006.

McCalman, Max, and David Gibbons. *Cheese: A Connoisseur's Guide to the World's Best*. New York: Clarkson Potter, 2005.

McNaughton, Neville. "Gouda, Edam and Other Washed Curd Cheese: The Original Washed Curd Cheeses." *Cheese Reporter*, 25 January 2002. http://www.cheesereporter.com/Neville/neville.jan.25.htm.

Michelson, Patricia. *Cheese: Exploring Taste and Tradition*. Layton, Utah: Gibbs Smith 2010.

"Mimolette—Extra Vielle." *Culture*. http://culturecheesemag.com/cheese-library/Mimolette--Extra-Vielle.

Président. "Mimolette." http://www.president.uk.com/french-cheese/mimolette#.

Elaine Khosrova

Mish

See EGYPT.

mites

See CHEESE MITES.

Mizithra

See ANARI; LOR; RICOTTA; and XYNOMYZITHRA KRITIS.

modernist cooking techniques, which incorporate methods, ingredients, and tools from the laboratories of chemists and physicists, started to be applied to cheese both in homes and in restaurants around the turn of the twenty-first century. One of the most widespread applications, popularized by Nathan Myhrvold in his book *Modernist Cuisine*, is the use of emulsifying salts in the melting of cheese for products such as macaroni and cheese, queso, and nacho cheese. This technique, first patented by James Kraft in the early twentieth century, utilizes an emulsifying salt, usually sodium phosphate or sodium citrate, which attaches to both the dairy fats and the water in the cheese. When heat is applied to melt the cheese, the result is a homogenous solution rather than heterogeneous separation. The process, which led to the popularization of melting cheeses such as Velveeta and of products such as Kraft Macaroni and Cheese, has been reclaimed by culinary modernists to make sauces, dips, and dishes out of a range of cheeses. See KRAFT, JAMES L.; VELVEETA; and MAC AND CHEESE.

The traditional cheese sauce is the Mornay, a béchamel sauce consisting of butter, flour, and milk, to which cheese has been added. The advantage to using emulsifying salts instead of the roux-based Mornay sauce is that dishes can taste intensely of cheese, instead of being masked by the milk, butter, and flour. Myhrvold's recommendations for home cooks to make "constructed cheeses" include an aerated "easy cheese" using Gruyère and nitrous oxide, a concentrated Cheddar soup, and slices of "American cheese" using a blend of Swiss and Cheddar cheeses, emulsifying salts, and seaweed derivatives.

Chefs in the fine-dining world have begun applying modernist techniques to cheese, many of which require advanced equipment and ingredients that are generally unavailable to the home cook. The world-renowned Spanish chef Ferran Adrià of the former modernist restaurant elBulli created a variety of dishes featuring cheese. A 2007 menu featured Parmesan Water, a separation and clarification of Parmesan whey, served in a champagne flute alongside tomato couscous as a sort of sipping cheese. Adrià also created a Munster tempura, a Gruyère waffle, and a Gorgonzola bonbon. José Andrés of Minibar, a twelve-seat restaurant in Washington, DC, created the Idiazabal Cheese Egg using xanthan gum, calcium salt, and a vacuum to create a spherification of Idiazabal cheese reminiscent of a soft-boiled egg. Finally, Grant Achatz of Chicago's Alinea created balloons of mozzarella, which he filled with a cheese curd foam, resembling a modernist Burrata.

Achatz, Grant, and Nick Kokonas. *Alinea.* Berkeley, Calif.: Ten Speed, 2008.
Adrià, Ferran, and Albert Adrià. *elBulli 2005–2011.* London: Phaidon, 2014.
Myhrvold, Nathan, et al. *Modernist Cuisine: The Art and Science of Cooking.* Vol. 4: *Ingredients and Preparations.* Bellevue, Wash.: Cooking Lab, 2011.

Sam Chapple-Sokol

Mohant is a semisoft PDO (protected designation of origin) cheese made from cow's milk. It is produced by local farmers and small dairies in the Bohinj Valley, located in Slovenia's Julian Alps.

Traditionally, Mohant was made from raw milk of the autochthonous Cika cattle breed on several mountain farms and in villages surrounding Lake Bohinj. Since the red-colored Cika breed was not the best choice for intensive meat and milk production, it has largely been replaced by other breeds. Morning milk is mixed with ripened and partially skimmed evening milk. Curd formed by the addition of rennet is cut into small pieces and scalded. The curd is then drained, salted, and moved to wooden or plastic containers called *deže*, where it is covered with cheesecloth or plastic film and a wooden lid. Rocks or weights are used to press the covered cheese and attain a deoxygenated environment. Ripening takes place in three stages: (1) an initial cold ripening at a temperature of 54–61°F (12–16°C) for 15 to 20 days, followed by (2) a warm ripening at 66–73°F (19–23°C) for 15 to 20 days, completed by (3) a final maturation at 54–61°F (12–16°C) again for up to two months. Finally, the mature cheese is kneaded well and packed in glass or plastic jars.

The typical Mohant is a light-yellow, soft cheese; the consistency is dense but spreadable and creamy. The flavor is tangy, sharp, and can be slightly bitter as the result of proteolysis and lipolysis, but the cheese is mostly known by its distinctive, strong smell. Gourmets say that "the best Mohant is the one that could flow by itself from the mountain to the valley," since with longer maturation it becomes softened and shiny. Usually, Mohant is served spread on bread or with boiled potatoes.

Ravnik, Monika. *Specifikacija za Mohant* [Specification for Mohant]. 2012. http://www.mkgp.gov.si/ fileadmin/mkgp.gov.si/pageuploads/podrocja/Varna _in_kakovostna_hrana_in_krma/zasciteni_kmetijski _pridelki/Specifikacije/MOHANT_SP_EU.pdf.

Petra Mohar Lorbeg and Andreja Čanžek Majhenič

moisture can be defined as the percentage of water in the finished product or as the mass of water per unit mass of dry material. The cheesemaking process mainly consists of removing moisture and concentrating the total solids of the milk (casein, fat, and more or less minerals and lactose). For removing moisture from a rennet gel, the moisture removal process is termed syneresis. See SYNERESIS.

The Code of Federal Regulations (CFR) classifies cheeses by their maximum moisture and minimum milk fat using the nomenclature hard cheeses, soft-ripened cheeses, and semisoft cheeses in 21CFR133 (2014). These are the standards of identity required for specific standardized cheeses and related products. The CFR outlines the legal limits of moisture and milk fat in cheeses and cheese products as follows:

- Hard cheeses: They must not contain more than 39 percent moisture and solids, not less than 50 percent of milk fat.
- Semisoft cheeses: They contain more than 50 percent of moisture and their solids contain not less than 50 percent of milk fat.
- soft-ripened cheeses: Interestingly, the CFR does not establish any moisture targets for soft cheese, only their solids must contain not less than 50 percent of the milk fat.

Moisture content in cheese has a major effect on the quality of the finished product. Moisture affects flavor development, body, ripening, and cheese yield. In hard cheeses like Cheddar, the amount of yield is directly proportional to the amount of moisture. A 1 percent increase in moisture can increase the yield over 1.5 percent. Moisture also dictates the shelf life and stability of the product. It impacts the microbial, chemical, and enzymatic activity.

Diverse microbial growth can be the result of increased moisture allowing for development of off flavors such as bitterness and whey taint in hard cheeses such as Cheddar, ammonia and sulfur in cheese such as blue cheese, and unwanted surface molds in cheese such as Brie. See DEFECTS.

Accelerated ripening is caused by the enzymatic reaction in high moisture cheese. A weak body product is one of the outcomes of this process. This also has a detrimental effect on the ease with which the cheeses can be sliced and shredded. The product becomes pasty and will stick to the slicing and shredding knives. Conversely, low moisture products tend to be crumbly and not have the typical creaminess of the standardized product. The cheese will fall apart when cut or sliced. See ACCELERATED RIPENING.

The basic principle of moisture analysis is the measurement of the sample of cheese before and after drying. There are many different choices for moisture analysis, with the most common methods being the vacuum oven, microwave oven, and near infrared spectroscopy.

Kosikowski, Frank V., and Vikram V. Mistry. *Cheese and Fermented Milk Foods*. 3d ed. 2 vols. Westport, Conn.: F. V. Kosikowski, 1997.
McClemens, D. Julian. "Determination of Moisture and Total Solids." http://people.umass.edu/mcclemen/ 581Moisture.html.
United States National Archives and Records Administration. *Code of Federal Regulations*. Title 21. Food and Drugs, 2014.
Wehr, Michael, and Joseph F. Frank. *Standard Methods for Examination of Dairy Products*. 17th ed. Washington, D.C.: American Public Health Association, 2004.

May M. Leach

molding involves putting the milled salted curds into a uniform container to give the cheese its final shape and even size. Usually made from food-grade plastic or stainless steel, molds come in different shapes and sizes, depending on the type of cheese and the cheesemaker, and contain holes to allow the whey to drain. Presses are inserted into the top of the molds to apply uniform pressure to the curds and contribute to drainage. Molds have traditionally been cylindrical for artisanal cheeses and rectangular for factory-produced cheeses. The cylindrical mold may be tapered or not depending on how it is to be pressed.

Rectangular molds have three parts: a top, a collar, and a base with pins that are removed to allow the collar to slide down during pressing.

For hard-pressed Cheddar cheeses, the molds are usually lined with cloth, which helps form a close, smooth rind and prevents the curd from blocking the drainage holes. Rectangular molds require two cloths, one to fold into the long side and one for the short side. Some cheesemakers prefer the traditional muslin cloths, which require a dedicated washer and dryer, since damp cloths will allow the growth of mold. There are now blue disposable cheesecloths available, but often cheesemakers use them more than once, which means that these also must be washed and dried. The disposable cloths have a smooth side, which goes next to the curd, and a coarser side, which helps drain whey from the outside of the curd. The Laude company makes cheese molds that do not require cloth liners because of the honeycomb finish on their internal surface. Yet even though they do not need to be lined, the molds themselves require more careful cleaning.

Once the mold is lined with cloth, the curd is weighed or measured by volume into the mold to give a uniform size to the finished cheese. The curd is then pressed into place. With cylindrical molds, the curd must be pushed into the edges of the mold with as few air spaces as possible. The cloth is gently pulled up to remove creases, and a lid, or "follower," is added. At this point, the cheeses are prepressed by standing one on top of the other and rotating their positions, and then they are placed in the press under light pressure (20 psi). After a period of 2 to 3 hours, they are removed from the press and from their molds, and the cloths gently pulled out from any places where they may have been caught in the curd. The cheeses are then returned to their molds, where a higher pressure (40 psi) is applied to them for 12 to 16 hours. Next, the cheeses are bathed in water for 10 to 15 seconds in their original cloth at 140°F (60°C). The cloth is then replaced, and the cheese is returned to the press for an additional 24 hours. Finally, the cheeses are "larded," or coated with fat, and then a "bandage" of muslin, a cover of Plasticoat, or a coating of wax may be applied. If the cheeses are to be bandaged, they are pressed once again before the bandage is put on.

See also CHEESECLOTH; CLOTHBOUND CHEESES; FORMS OR MOLDS; and PRESS.

Maddever, K. D. *Farmhouse Cheddarmakers' Manual*. Thames Ditton, U.K.: Milk Marketing Board, 1988.
Van Slyke, Lucius L., and Walter V. Price. *Cheese*. Revised and enlarged edition. Atascadero, Calif.: Ridgeview, 1992. First published in 1932 by Orange Judd.

Val Bines

molds

See FILAMENTOUS FUNGI and HYPHAE.

monastic cheesemaking. Cheese has for centuries played an important role in Catholic monastic life, and monastic agriculture and enterprise have had a profound influence on the development of a diverse array of cheeses. Among the cheeses scholars believe were started or stimulated by monastic enterprise are Maroilles, Chaource, Époisses, Comté, Bleu de Gex, Cantal, Munster (a corruption of the French word for monastery), Roquefort, and Parmigiano Reggiano. Cheeses made to this day at monasteries include the famed cheeses of the abbeys of Tamié in the Savoie, Cîteaux in Burgundy, Belloc in the Pyrénées-Atlantiques, and Scourmont in Belgium, where Chimay is made. See MAROILLES; CHAOURCE; ÉPOISSES; COMTÉ; BLEU DE GEX; CANTAL; MUNSTER; ROQUEFORT; and PARMIGIANO REGGIANO.

The monastic orders most closely associated with cheesemaking are the Benedictines, the Cistercians, and the Cistercians of the Strict Observance, better known as the Trappists. These orders follow the Rule of St. Benedict, or Regula Monachorum, a set of rules written by Benedict of Nursia in the sixth century to guide the spiritual life of monks and the administration of their monasteries, including their structure and location, the garments and diets of their inhabitants and the hour and manner of their prayer. See SAINT BENEDICT.

In Chapter 48 Benedict wrote, "Idleness is the enemy of the soul. The brethren, therefore must be occupied at stated hours in labor" and "for then are they truly monks when they live by the labor of their hands." Religious scholars cite these passages as the foundation of the Benedictine and Cistercian culture of the dignity and godliness of manual labor alongside prayer and study. According to these precepts, monasteries were organized as self-contained, self-reliant enclosed communities, which subsisted where possible on the fruits of their own labors.

Monastic life is ideally suited to cheesemaking, with its rigorous and repetitive daily routines and scientifically minded monks adept at the commerce of agriculture. Cheese preserved and added value to the monastery's large quantities of milk—monasteries acquired over the centuries vast land holdings and herds that often numbered in the thousands—and was an important source of protein in a diet in which meat was generally forbidden (for the rule restricts the consumption of the meat of four-footed animals).

Monastic cheeses can take many forms. The Benedictine monks of the Abbaye de Notre Dame de Belloc in the Basque Country of southern France make a celebrated firm sheep's milk cheese. The brothers of the Abbaye de Saint-Benoît-du-Lac in Quebec make Bleu Benedictin. The sisters of Our Lady of the Angels in Virginia's Blue Ridge Mountains make an Edam-like ball of cheese dipped in crimson wax.

But the kind of cheese most closely associated with the Benedictines and Cistercians is the so-called "smear-ripened" or "washed-rind." These cheeses rely for their ripening on the action of bacteria cultivated on their surface through repeated "washings" or "smearings" of the young cheeses with a diluted brine solution sometime mixed with bacteria-rich scrapings from older cheeses. Often these cheeses are flavored with further washings in wine, beer, or distilled spirits. They are typically, often emphatically, pungent.

Some bacteria-ripened cheeses are very high in moisture and bacteria are encouraged to grow thick and damp on their surface. They are short lived, strong smelling, and prone to running. Examples include Époisses, Vacherin Mont d'Or, and Jasper Hill Farm's Winnimere. See ÉPOISSES and WINNIMERE.

But the style of washed-rind or smear-ripened cheeses most closely associated—even synonymous—with monastic production is the so-called Trappistes: plump, gray-tinged rosy wheels of various sizes with a typically semifirm, supple, creamy paste dotted here and there with little holes. The bacteria on their surface are restricted through washings and brushings, so they do not develop quite the intense aroma of the softer style. The most famous Trappiste is the original—though not current—Port Salut, named for the Abbaye de Notre Dame du Port-du-Salut in the French Maine, where the cheese was invented. The monks of Port-du-Salut sold the cheese and its name long ago to a French industrial cheese company, but passed its recipe to several of its daughter and sister houses. It exists today as the Véritable Trappe of the Abbaye de la Coudre in the Mayenne, and, among others, in the cheeses of the Abbaye de Notre Dame de Timadeuc in Brittany, the Abbaye Notre Dame de Bonne Espérance in Echourgnac, the Belgian Abbaye Notre Dame de Scourmont where Chimay is made, as well as Munkeby made by Cistercian monks north of Trondheim in Norway since 2008.

Scholars offer a theory as to why this style might have developed in monasteries. Smear-ripened or washed-rind cheeses must be made with very "sweet" milk, that is, milk that contains few harmless lactic acid-producing bacteria. The population of these bacteria grows as the milk sits until it is made into cheese. Peasant farmers, with only a cow or two, would have had to combine milk of several milkings to make enough cheese to make the effort worth their while, so these bacteria would have time to flourish. Acidic milk like this favors the growth of acid-tolerant molds, as in "bloomy-rind" cheeses like Brie or Camembert, but restricts the growth of bacteria. The monasteries, however, thanks to their large herds and available labor force, would have had access to fresh milk more or less straight from the cow. There was no need to combine the milk of several milkings so the surface bacteria so critical to this classic monastic style of cheese would have flourished. Scholars further surmise that as cheese became an important source of income to the monastery, the monks would have experimented with larger lower-moisture cheeses that could travel better and have a longer "shelf life," hence the Trappist style so famous today.

See also ABBAYE DE TAMIÉ; JERVAULX ABBEY; and WASHED-RIND CHEESES.

Berman, Constance Hoffman. *Medieval Agriculture, the Southern French Countryside and the Early Cistercians.* Philadelphia: American Philosophical Society, 1986.

Kinstedt, Paul. *American Farmstead Cheese: The Complete Guide to Making and Selling Artisan Cheese.* White River Junction, Vt.: Chelsea Green, 2005.

Kinstedt, Paul. *Cheese and Culture: A History of Cheese and Its Place in Western Civilization.* White River Junction, Vt.: Chelsea Green, 2012.

Rance, Patrick. *The French Cheese Book.* London: Macmillan, 1989.

Matthew Rubiner

Mongolia is a landlocked country in East Asia where cheese is an integral part of the larger category of *tsagaan idee* (white foods—dairy products). There are essentially three fundamental types or styles of Mongolian cheese, although there is regional variation, which can at times be substantial. They also differ substantially from Western-style cheeses, being neither made with rennet nor salt, and not aged. The three types of cheese are byaslag, eezgii, and aaruul. Byaslag is closest to what in this context we can loosely think of as a European-style cheese. The word itself is translated as "cheese," although it is not uncommon to specify imported European cheeses with the Russian word *syr*. Mongolian cheese can, in theory, be made from almost any milk, although in practice, cow's milk is the most common. Sheep and goats are rarely, if ever, milked in Mongolia. In some parts of the country, yak milk, which has a notably higher fat content, is used instead of cow's milk. Rather than using rennet, Mongolian cheese relies on production via a type of yogurt.

Tsgaan idee is indeed an expansive category, including airag (fermented mare's milk, not used in cheesemaking), öröm (a type of clotted cream), and tarag (yogurt). *Tsagaan idee* is co-produced with cheese to make fullest use of the milk. Given Mongolians' traditionally nomadic lifestyle, cheeses are not aged, but rather either eaten fresh, or sliced and dried to preserve them. While there is some commercial production of Mongolian cheeses, and aaruul in particular, it remains very much a local product, produced by most herding families. *Tsagaan idee* are most traditionally eaten in the largest quantities during the summer, when meat is eaten less often. However cheeses may be eaten throughout the year, often with milky tea, and make up a standard part of any holiday or festive eating.

Byaslag is usually eaten fresh, and spoils relatively easily, making it not as common as other cheeses. It is also the cheese with the least regional variation. It is a rather mellow (some might say bland) cheese, somewhat akin to mozzarella when fresh, and when dried, perhaps something akin to Edam or Gouda. Milk is allowed to sour, and then the curds are separated from the whey and pressed and allowed to dry. Traditionally this is done by placing them between two pieces of wood, which are then weighted down. Eezgii in the early stages is made similarly to byaslag. However, rather than separating the solids from the whey, it is heated and dried.

Aaruul are dried curds, and if Mongolia can be said to have a cheese most associated with it, it is aaruul. After pressing, they are dried, usually on the roof of the *ger* (the Mongolian round felt tent) in the summer. Many versions of aaruul can be bitter, depending on the cream content, and in its dried form can last almost indefinitely.

It is among aaruul that you find the most regional variation, and recognition of such. Although there is no formal classification system (such as the French AOC), different regions are recognized as producing distinct versions of aaruul. One *aimag* (district), Bayanhongor, is known for thick, soft, brown aaruul, while the neighboring *aimag* of Arhangai produces a white one, which may be sweetened with sugar and have flour added. To complicate matters, each family will make different versions of aaruul for different reasons (sales, guests, long-term preservation). Aaruul thus is the most expansive category, varying by taste, texture, richness, and so forth depending on where and by whom it is made.

Since the mid-1990s there have been a few joint ventures in Western-style cheesemaking with European partners. The most successful of these involved making a European-style cheese (as a large, round wheel) with yak milk.

See also YAK.

"Butter and Cheese." Mongolfood. http://www .mongolfood.info/en/recipes/cheese.html
"Byaslag." Cheese.com. http://www.cheese.com/byaslag.

Christopher Kaplonski

MonS Fromager-Affineur is synonymous with fine cheese, not only in France but around the world. In 1964, Hubert Mons and his wife, Rolande, began selling cheeses at the markets in and around Roanne, in the Loire department of the Rhône-Alpes region. As their business grew, so did their expertise, which inspired their eldest son, Hervé, to work for some of the greatest cheesemongers in Paris. In 1983, he returned to set up the family's first permanent shop and maturing room in the Halles Diderot, in the Roanne city center. This combination of retail and affinage became a hallmark of the MonS brand.

Their younger son, Laurent, took over the family shop in Roanne in the 1990s, and Hervé focused on the affinage, adding another large maturing room designed specifically for cooked-curd mountain cheeses. The entrepreneurial Hervé next set his sights on export opportunities, and the MonS business now trades with more than twenty countries, including the United States, Japan, and Australia.

In 2010, a disused railway tunnel in nearby Saint-Haon-le-Châtel was converted into a dedicated affinage facility to mature tommes and other uncooked, hard cheeses such as Salers, Cantal, and Laguiole. In 2012 MonS opened an affinage center in Perpezat dedicated to maturing Saint-Nectaire cheeses within the PDO (protected designation of origin) zone of production. In addition to these regional cheeses, Hervé travels all over France to source the best cheeses from producers who still work with traditional methods, then carefully matures them in the MonS cellars.

More than eight retail stores in France, including three in Lyon, showcase the fine French cheeses matured in the MonS cellars. There is also a retail outlet at the Borough Market in London, UK, and a boutique in Neufchâtel, Switzerland.

Over the years MonS has partnered with creameries to produce branded products, and in 2016 launched two creameries. One is at its headquarters in Saint-Haon-le-Châtel, France. In Wisconsin, MonS has partnered with François Kerautret and Arnaud Solandt to establish Creamery 333, which launched with a natural-rind goat tomme aged by Crown Finish Caves in Brooklyn.

See also FRANCE and MATURING.

MonS Fromager-Affineur. http://www.mons-fromages.com/en.

Sonia Cousins

Montasio is an ancient Alpine cooked-curd, cow's milk cheese from the northeastern-most part of Italy. It is named for the Jôf di Montasio (Montasio Massif), the peak of which is the second-highest in the Julian Alps. Montasio cheese has been made from sheep's, goat's, and cow's milk in huts in this mountain range for about a thousand years and for nearly that long in the Benedictine monastery of Moggio Udinese. The first written records of Montasio are price lists from the town of San Daniele del Friuli, dated 1775. From its earliest days, Montasio was sold at a premium: its consumers paid about double the price of other local cheeses.

Montasio was protected by government decree in 1955; it received its Italian DO (denominazione

di origine) in 1986 and its European PDO (protected designation of origin) in 1996. The Montasio consortium (Consorzio per la Tutela del Formaggio Montasio) was founded in 1984; its members include farms with thirteen hundred stalls certified for Montasio milk; forty-three creameries, and seventeen *stagionatori* (agers).

Montasio PDO's production zone encompasses the entire region of Fruili-Venezia Giulia as well the provinces of Belluno and Treviso, and parts of the provinces of Padua and Venice in the eastern Veneto. Its production regulations uphold the traditional eighteenth-century recipe, strictly define milk standards, and stipulate the following: Wheels are a maximum of 3 inches (8 centimeters) high, between 12–14 inches (30–35 centimeters) in diameter, and weigh 13–18 pounds (6–8 kilograms); maximum moisture content is initially 37 percent and fat in dry matter (FDM) a minimum 40 percent. Montasio's semihard paste, elastic when young, is cream-colored with occasional small eyes and becomes increasingly straw-colored and yellowish with age. With age the paste gradually dries and hardens, turning crumbly and eventually hard enough to grate. Meanwhile its flavors evolve from mild, creamy, and fruity to fuller, more savory and piquant, with hints of spice.

Montasio is sold at four different stages: *Fresco* (young or fresh), 60 to 120 days; *mezzano* (semi-aged or medium), from 120 days to 10 months; *stagionato* (aged), 10 to 18 months; and *stravecchio* (extra aged), over 18 months. Each wheel is stamped with its production date and producer's identification number. After one hundred days all wheels passing inspection are fire-branded with the consortium's official logo. Additionally wheels made in mountain creameries receive the PDM (prodotto della montagna) label. In 2009 there were just under 1.05 million wheels made; in 2014 that figure dropped to around 950,000. Most Montasio is sold in northern Italy; about 4 percent is exported. When young, Montasio is a popular sandwich and family snacking cheese. It is layered with apples and fried in a famous regional dish, frico. Aged, it is often grated onto pasta dishes or into soups.

See also ALP CHEESEMAKING; ALP-STYLE CHEESES; FRICO; and SOUPS.

Disciplinare di Produzione del Formaggio "Montasio" D.O.P. G.U. no. 301 del 28.12.2005 (Montasio PDO Production Regulations).

Luigi Guffanti. http://www.guffantiformaggi.com.
Montasio. http://www.formaggiomontasio.net.

David Gibbons

Montbéliarde is a French cattle breed registered as pure since 1889 that originated in the mountainous area of Franche-Comté; it has now been introduced across all of Europe, North America, Australasia, and Asia. The breed has been developed for its milk to be used in cheese production, with an ideal butter-fat-to-protein ratio for cheese. The Montbéliarde is also a very healthy, long-lived, hardy breed that is easily managed. This in itself leads to very hygienic, low-somatic-cell-count milk ideal for the making of all types of cheese.

Many of the cows in the Comté region of France are exclusively fed hay to reduce the risk of late blowing in the cheese. This hay diet leads to lower yields but higher milk prices, thus enabling the small herds (average size, thirty cows) to remain profitable. These family farms all sell to the many small local cooperative dairies.

There are nine AOC (appellation d'origine contrôlée), or controlled designation of origin, cheeses in France that name the Montbéliarde breed as part of their requirements, including Comté, Morbier, Mont d'Or, Bleu de Gex, Reblochon, Abondance, Tome des Bauges, Bleu du Vercors-Sassenage, and Cantal. More than sixty thousand tons of these cheese varieties are made using Montbéliarde milk in France each year.

Along with the many positive attributes of Montbéliarde milk for cheese, the breed is also very good for beef; as a result, the bull calves and cull cows have greater value than they might have had otherwise.

See also BREEDING AND GENETICS; COMTÉ; COW; and FRANCE

"Organisme de Sélection de la Race Montbéliarde"
    http://www.montbeliarde.org.
Procross. http://www.creativegeneticsofca.com/
    procross.htm.

Ian Sharman

Montchevré is the leading producer of goat cheese in the United States. Located in Wisconsin, which has earned the appellation "America's Dairy-land," this specialty producer makes more than 18 million pounds of goat cheese annually. Its story is rooted in France, the birthplace of its president, Arnaud Solandt, and its master cheesemaker, Jean Rossard.

A tragic accident propelled Arnaud Solandt into the cheese business at a young age. In 1986, a few years after he and his family had moved to the United States, his father was killed in an accident on his way home from a cheese show. The twenty-year-old Solandt dropped out of school to run his father's sales office for a few months, but ended up making cheese his life's work. Although his father had been marketing imported French cheese, tax threats and international trade disputes prompted the younger Solandt to suggest producing cheese in the United States. He found a small, vacant cheese plant in Preston, Wisconsin, with a supply of goat's milk from the nearby Mount Sterling cooperative. There, he and Jean Rossard started Montchevré (from the French words for mountain and goat), where they began making Blue, a traditional blue cheese made from goat's milk, and Cabrie, a soft-ripened goat's milk cheese. Since its creation, Montchevré has been extremely innovative and receptive to market needs, and led the trend in flavored goat cheeses. For example, in 1994 Montchevré introduced fresh goat cheese rolled in candied cranberries. In 1995 Montchevré started crumbling fresh goat cheese for salad and pizza applications. Those innovations have become staples in supermarkets and grocery stores across the United States.

Today located in Belmont, Wisconsin, Montchevré transforms 1.5 million pounds of milk into cheese every week. Their team trains and works with 350 family dairy farms across 5 neighboring states: Wisconsin, Iowa, Illinois, Minnesota, and Missouri. With this level of supply, Montchevré can offer a palette of more than 50 different goat cheeses. Its success lies in the high quality of its milk, its French expertise in making goat cheese, and its ability to innovate and adapt flavors to the American palate.

See CHEVRÉ and WISCONSIN.

Hurt, Jeanette. *The Cheeses of Wisconsin: A Culinary Travel Guide*. Woodstock, Vt.: Countryman, 2008.

Gersende Cazaux

Mont d'Or, also called Vacherin du Haut-Doubs, is a lightly pressed soft cheese with a washed rind, made with raw cow's milk, not to be confused with Switzerland's Vacherin Mont d'Or cheese, which is

Mont d'Or, an unctuous washed-rind cheese made with raw cow's milk in the Jura Mountains, has a PDO label that requires that it be aged in spruce boxes. COURTSEY OF THE INTERPROFESSIONAL UNION OF MONT D'OR

made with heat-treated milk. See SWITZERLAND. Mont d'Or is produced in the Jura Mountains; more precisely in Doubs Department at an altitude of roughly 700 meters minimum. Milk from Montbéliarde and Simmental cows is used. See MONTBÉLIARDE. Mont d'Or has had a PDO (protected designation of origin) label since 1996. Around 5,000 metric tons of Mont d'Or cheeses are produced each year, by ten dairies and one farm producer.

Mont d'Or is a flat wheel strapped with strips of spruce bark and marketed in round boxes of various diameters, also made of spruce. The weight, including the box, is between 17 ounces (480 grams) and 7 pounds (3.2 kilograms); the height of the box is 2½–3 inches (6–7 centimeters) and the diameter is 4–13 inches (11–33 centimeters). Mont d'Or cheese has a white or ivory body and a washed rind on which molds eventually appear. The color of the rind is yellow to light brown, slightly corrugated and pleated—not unlike the Jura Mountains themselves.

The origins of Mont d'Or are hard to trace, but as early as the thirteenth century it is recorded that cheeses were being made in Haut-Doubs regions that were encircled in wood. One thing that is certain is that Mont d'Or was regularly present at the table of Louis XV in the eighteenth century. Then, it was recorded in letters from Jean-Jacques Rousseau to Antoine-Augustin Parmentier in 1799. In the past it was made in the winter months when the cows came down from alpage (mountain pastures) and there was not enough milk to make Gruyère (now Comté) cheese. At present Mont d'Or is produced

only between mid-August and mid-March and sold between 10 September and 10 May.

Only raw cow's milk, from a mixture of morning and the previous evening's milk, is used to make Mont d'Or. Starters used are composed of *Streptococcus thermophilus* and *Lactobacillus delbrueckii* subsp. *bulgaricus* (yogurt cultures). The use of these starters leads to a slow acidification during Mont d'Or manufacture. *Geotrichum candidum*, which will play a role in the maturation of Mont d'Or during ripening, is also added to the milk before renneting. See LACTOBACILLUS; STARTER CULTURES; and GEOTRICHUM CANDIDUM.

After molding the curd is slightly pressed for five to ten minutes. After unmolding (around one hour after molding), the curd is encircled with strips of spruce bark (which give the cheese a typical resinous flavor) to avoid collapsing. After three to four hours of acidification, cheeses are salted in brine for forty-five minutes to one hour (for medium size). During ripening cheeses are held at 52–55°F (11–13°C) and at a relative humidity of 95 percent on spruce planks. During this period, around fifteen days, cheeses are regularly turned and rubbed with brine. After washing the cheeses are squeezed into their characteristic spruce boxes, then aged for a minimum of twenty-one days and a maximum of sixty days.

Mont d'Or can be eaten raw, using a small spoon, at the end of the meal, for example, or baked (called "Mont d'Or chaud" or "boîte chaude"). To make it: 1) Preheat the oven to 400°F (210°C); 2) Wrap the Mont d'Or cheese box with aluminum foil, making sure to enclose it so the foil goes up to the top of the outside of the container, but leave the top exposed.; 3) With the tip of a knife, make a small hole in the center of the cheese. Pour dry white wine (¼ cup [60 milliliters] of white Jura wine for example) into the hole. Sprinkle with pepper; 4) Bake in the oven (around thirty minutes for a medium-size cheese); 5) Serve immediately by placing the box directly on the table, accompanied by boiled potatoes still warm and saucisse de Morteau.

See also BARK-WRAPPED CHEESES.

Lanquetin, Didier. "Le Mont d'Or ou Vacherin du Haut-Doubs A.O.C." *Revue des ENILS* 252 (2002): 42–44.
Millet, Jean. "Mont d'Or ou Vacherin du Haut-Doubs, vingt-cinquième fromage d'Appellation d'Origine." *Technicien du lait et de ses dérivés* 996 (1985): 31–39.
Mont d'Or. http://www.mont-dor.com.

Eric Beuvier

Monte Enebro is a Spanish goat's milk cheese made exclusively at Queserias del Tietar, in the town of Avila, southwest of Madrid. The cheese was invented in 1995 by Rafael Baez, who had spent the majority of his working life as an engineer, but at the age of sixty-three fulfilled his lifelong desire to make cheese, particularly a style of cheese that was not traditional to the area. Although he died in 2012, his daughter Paloma, who had worked with him for many years, took over the running of the dairy.

The name "Monte Enebro" translates as Juniper Hill, owing to the abundance of juniper plants growing in the vicinity of Baez's house and dairy. The cheese is easily recognizable by its shape, nicknamed "Pata de Mulo"—a slightly flattened, bottom-heavy log—and by its charcoal-colored rind. Contrary to popular belief, the cheeses are not ash coated, but are sprayed with a solution of *Penicillium roqueforti* after two days in molds, after which they are matured for an additional thirty days. See PENICILLIUM.

Monte Enebro has a smooth, dense, and creamy texture, with a bold, goaty aroma, a distinct tang, and pleasing spice notes imparted by the *Penicillium roqueforti* rind. Monte Enebro has won many awards in various international cheese competitions and was voted as one of the hundred Best Food Products of Spain. It is delectable eaten as is, although serving it deep fried with blossom honey is a particularly pleasing combination. Baez himself enjoyed eating it with caramelized onions. Sweet white wines are the perfect match for Monte Enebro.

See also SPAIN.

Harbutt, Juliet, and Martin Aspinwall. *World Cheese Book.* New York: Dorling Kindersley, 2009, p. 158.
McCalman, Max, and David Gibbons. *The Cheese Plate.* New York: Clarkson Potter, 2002, pp. 208–209.

Emma Young

Monterey Jack

See JACK.

Monte Veronese

Monte Veronese is an Italian PDO (protected designation of origin) cheese made with cow's milk in the area north of Verona and east of Lake Garda, which includes the regional park of the Lessini Mountains and Monte Baldo. It is a sparsely inhabited area with glorious pastures providing plentiful, high-quality forage. The dairy potential of the area became apparent in 1287, when the bishop of Verona, Bartolomeo della Scala, granted a group of Cimbri, a Germanic people already settled in the Asiago plateau, the exploitation of the mountain land and resources.

In 1996 Monte Veronese was awarded PDO status for both of its variants: Monte Veronese whole milk PDO, to be enjoyed young, with a soft texture, regular eyes, and sweet flavor, yet full of character, thanks to the prized pastures, and Monte Veronese PDO *d'allevo* (thoroughbred), made with semi-skim milk and suitable for aging from a minimum of six months to well over two years. This latter variant has a compact texture and a more intense flavor that can become almost tangy as the aging process goes on.

Although Monte Veronese is an excellent cheese, it is not yet well known outside its production area. Its unique marking consists of its name repeated all along the rind. One of the sides of the cheese wheel is labeled with "Monte Veronese" and the name of the dairy that produced it; the label is green for the whole milk young cheese and blue for the aged cheese, d'allevo. Wheels produced in the highest pastures bear an extra "M" (for mountain product) next to the markings of the consorzio di tutela (producers' association).

See also ITALY.

Monte Veronese Formaggio DOP. http://www .monteveronese.it.

Erasmo Gastaldello

Montgomery's Cheddar

See CHEDDAR.

Monty Python,

Monty Python, a British comedy troupe, first showed their iconic sketch "The Cheese Shop" on 30 September 1972, in episode 33 of the BBC series *Monty Python's Flying Circus*, entitled "Salad Days." It was one of several Monty Python "across the counter" sketches, a frequently used premise that also includes such famed sketches as "The Dead Parrot," "The Ministry of Silly Walks," and "The Argument Clinic."

In "The Cheese Shop," a man identified in the script as Mr. Mousebender, played by John Cleese, enters a cheese shop—Ye Old Cheese Emporium—to negotiate the "vending of some cheesey comestibles."

There he encounters the cheesemonger, Mr. Wensleydale, and a bazouki band, whose presence is not explained. No cheese is visible. Mr. Mousebender attempts without success and with increasing frustration to order several cheeses. Each request is met with a response ranging from a simple "no" to "the van broke down," "never at the end of the week," and "the cat's eaten it." He orders a total of forty-two cheeses, including the fictional Venezuelan Beaver Cheese, although this number did change slightly in later performances. One final desperate query reveals that the shop has no cheese at all and results in the exasperated Mr. Mousebender drawing a pistol, shooting Mr. Wensleydale in the head, and, in a nonsequitor ending typical of Monty Python sketches, donning a 10-gallon hat and riding off into the final scene of a Western movie, *Rogue Cheddar*.

"Cheese Shop" sketch (Episode 33, "Salad Days"). *Monty Python's Flying Circus*. Aired 30 November 1972; recorded 7 January 1972. https://www.youtube.com/watch?v=B3KBuQHHKx0.

Matthew Rubiner

The **moon** is made of green cheese. At least, that is what dupes believe in a proverb written by the English playwright and epigrammatist John Heywood (1546):

Ye fetch circumquaques to make me believe,
Or thinke, that the moone is made of greene cheese.
And when ye have made me a lout in all these,
It seemeth ye would make me goe to bed at noone.

The conceit here is that a simpleton, seeing the moon's reflection in water, could mistake it for a green cheese—not the color green, but rather an unaged, luminous milky-white wheel of fresh cheese. See GREEN CHEESE.

There is no evidence that anyone actually believed the moon to be made of cheese; it was simply a proverb that poked fun at the extreme credulity of the ignorant. Other English scholars and wits penned variations on the same theme. Richard Shacklock's *Hatchet of Heresies* (1565), a translation into English of a Latin text written by the Polish cardinal Stanislaus Hosius, includes the line "Whilst they tell for truthe Luther his lowde lyes, so that they may make theyr blinde brotherhode and the ignorant sort beleve that the mone is made of grene cheese." In his lengthy discourse *The Discovery of a World in the Moone* (1638), the natural philosopher John Wilkins deploys the proverb to bemoan the scientific illiteracy of the common man. Wilkins speculates that the moon may actually be habitable (or already inhabited), and yet ignorance and superstition about the moon give equal weight to absurd premises: "You may as soon persuade some Country Peasants that the Moon is made of Green Cheese (as we say) as that 'tis bigger than his Cart-wheel."

Some class snobbery aside, the association between the moon and cheese is both ancient and cross-cultural, particularly within the beast fable tradition. A Serbian fable tells the tale of a wily fox that tricks a wolf into thinking the moon's reflection in water is actually cheese; the wolf bursts when it attempts to drink all the water to get at the "cheese." A more elaborate Hebrew version of this same tale, told by the French scholar Rabbi Raschi (1040–1105), goes that a fox encourages a wolf to join a Jewish household as it prepares for the Sabbath meal. When the wolf approaches the family it is beaten away with sticks, and the wolf angrily returns to the fox demanding an explanation. The fox answers that the family was angry because the wolf's father stole choice meat from a prior Sabbath banquet, but that if the wolf follows him he will still be fed. The fox leads the wolf to a well, above which hang two counterbalanced pails: the fox steps into the first pail, descends to the bottom, and urges the wolf to step into the other pail. The hungry wolf, seeing the "cheese" (i.e., moon) reflected in the bottom of the well, steps in, and the lighter fox ascends and steps out from the well. When the wolf asks how he in turn will get out of the well, the fox replies "the righteous is delivered out of trouble and the wicked cometh in in his stead. Is it not written, Just balances, just weights?" The lesson presumably being that justice ultimately prevails on earth—though this particular wolf might not see it that way. Other stories with the moon/cheese element can be found in the fifteenth-century Scottish poem "The Fox, the Wolf, and the Husbandman" and in Aesop's fables.

In the modern era the idea that the moon is made of cheese gets mostly playful, often literal treatment. Norton Juster had fun with it in his 1961 novel *The Phantom Tollbooth*, when the Spelling Bee, showing off the "half-bakery" to Milo, munches on some "half-baked" ideas: "He picked up a long one that stated 'THE MOON IS MADE OF GREEN CHEESE' and hungrily bit off the part that said 'CHEESE.' 'Now THERE's a half-baked idea,' he said, smiling." In the cartoon *Tom and Jerry* short "O-Solar Meow" (1967), Tom sends Jerry to the moon by stuffing him into a powerful cannon; Jerry is last seen happily dining on prodigious quantities of cheese. And in the *Wallace and Gromit* clay animation "A Grand Day Out," finding no cheese in the kitchen to eat with their crackers, the pair builds a spaceship to partake of the moon's bounty. Once there Wallace slices a bit of moon cheese for them both to try, and, after hopefully speculating that it might be Wensleydale or Stilton – theories Gromit emphatically rejects – Wallace concludes that "it's like no cheese I've ever tasted..." See WALLACE AND GROMIT.

More recently, in the early days of Google Moon (a sister project to Google Earth), zooming in on the moon beyond the highest available image resolution would turn it yellow and display a Swiss cheese eye pattern on the moon's surface. And in 2014 a Washington State–based company called nutra DRIED began selling a line of "Moon Cheese," removing the moisture from cheese in order to create crunchy snacks. The dehydrated, no-refrigeration-required cheese comes in three flavors: Cheddar, Gouda, and Pepper Jack. They vaguely resemble asteroids.

See also APHORISMS AND SAYINGS and LITERATURE OF CHEESE.

Cashford, Jules. *The Moon: Myth and Image.* New York: Four Walls, Eight Windows, 2003.
Heywood, John. *The proverbs of John Heywood: Being the "Proverbes" of that author printed 1546,* edited by Julian Sharman. Folcroft, Pa.: Folcroft Library Editions, 1972.
McKnight, George Harley. "The Middle English Vox and Wolf." *Publications of the Modern Language Association of America* 23 (1908): 497–509.
Park, Nick, dir. *Wallace and Gromit: A Grand Day Out.* Perf. Peter Sallis. Aardman Animations, 1989. https://www.youtube.com/watch?v=T0qagA4_eVQ.
Wilkins, John. *The Discovery of a World in the Moone; Or, A Discourse Tending To Prove That 'Tis Probable There May Be Another Habitable World In That Planet.* London: Printed for EG by Michael Sparke and Edward Forrest, 1638.

Max P. Sinsheimer

The **moose,** as it is known in North America, or elk, as it is known in Eurasia (not to be confused with the American elk, which is a different creature), is the largest living member of the deer species. Preferring temperate and subarctic habitats in the Northern Hemisphere—particularly forested areas near bodies of water—moose (scientific name *Alces alces*) are recognizable for their large size, long muzzles, bell (a flap of skin beneath the throat similar to a turkey's wattle), and huge palmate antlers in the bulls (meaning the antlers look like an open hand with fingers extended). Moose in the wild can become aggressive if startled, but moose that have been around humans since birth, and have imprinted on their human handlers, are much tamer, to the point where they may be milked—as they are on commercial farms in Russia and on one dairy farm in Sweden, The Elk House, which makes the world's only moose cheese.

The Elk House (Älgens Hus) in Bjursholm, Sweden, is a 59-acre (24-hectare) moose dairy run by Christer and Ulla Johansson. They own three milk-producing moose, Gullan, Haelga, and Juna, along with a number of non-lactating moose that draw tens of thousands of tourists annually. Three weeks after they are born the calves are moved completely over to milk replacer, allowing the Johanssons to hand milk the still-lactating animals, yielding about 1 gallon (4.5 liters) per day.

A milkmaid with her favorite moose cow at Kostroma Moose Farm in Russia. The farm ranches their moose, allowing them to wander the woods for most of the year, and then return when calving to find shelter and oats.
© ALEXANDER MINAEV

This is far stingier than cows (which give around 8 gallons [36 liters] per day, depending on the breed), and also requires more exertion; milking sessions last anywhere from thirty minutes to two hours, if a loud noise causes the skittish animals to dry up. The resulting salty milk is exceptionally high in butterfat (10–12 percent, compared to around 5 percent for Jersey cow milk), protein (8–12 percent), and minerals (having values as high as 358 mg/100 g for calcium, 158 mg/100 g for sodium and 150 mg/100 g for phosphorus, as well as considerable amounts of iron, aluminum, selenium, and zinc). The milk is difficult to turn into cheese because the high fat, protein, and solid content make the cheese harden too quickly. Still, the Johanssons have perfected a formula to produce three styles of cheese: a rind style, a blue style, and a feta style. About 660 pounds (299 kilograms) of the cheese are sold annually, served in the Johanssons' own restaurant, at upscale Swedish hotel restaurants, and for export, fetching as much as $400 or more per pound.

The Johanssons credit moose milk dairies in Eastern Russia for the idea to start their own, though no Russian dairy makes moose cheese. In Russia moose milk is marketed medicinally, as a (largely unverified) treatment for everything from peptic ulcers to radiation lesions. Kostroma Moose Farm, just east of the city of Kostroma, sells the milk to a nearby sanatorium for people suffering from gastrointestinal diseases. The animals are not entirely domesticated, but rather ranched; the moose roam the surrounding forest free for much of the year but return when calving in late May or June, knowing they will be fed oats. By September the lactation period is over.

See also REINDEER.

Kostroma Moose Farm. http://www.moose-farm.ru/e040.htm.

LeBlanc, Tyler. "Moose Milking in Russia." *Modern Farmer*, 30 April 2014. http://modernfarmer.com/2014/04/moose-milk-mother-natures-antacid.

Medhammar, Elinor, et al. "Composition of Milk from Minor Dairy Animals and Buffalo Breeds: A Biodiversity Perspective." *Journal of the Science of Food and Agriculture* 92, no. 3 (2012): 445–474.

"Moose Milking." NPR News, 28 June 2003. http://www.npr.org/templates/story/story.php?storyId=1313736.

"Swedish 'Dairy' Thrives By Milking Moose." *Farm Show Magazine* 28, no. 5 (2004). http://www.farmshow.com/a_article.php?aid=17083.

Max P. Sinsheimer

Morbier is an uncooked pressed raw-milk cheese from the Jura Massif, an Alpine mountain range north of the Western Alps. Morbier takes its name from its village of origin, Morbier, which is today a small town in the Haut-Jura, France. Under its thin beige to orangey-pink rind is a smooth and tender cheese that is easy to recognize with its horizontal black ash line down the middle of the paste.

The milk for Morbier comes from Montbéliarde and Simmental cows. See MONTBÉLIARDE. Their feed comprises grazing grass and hay. No fermented feed is allowed. The grazing areas must be at least equal to 2.5 acres (1 hectare) per milking cow. The cows are milked twice a day at regular times. The transportation of the milk and the cheesemaking are done on a daily basis. The cheese is matured in cellars for a minimum period of forty-five days. Morbier requires 63–74 quarts (60–70 liters) of milk to make a wheel weighing on average 15 pounds (7 kilograms), and measuring 12–16 inches (30–40 centimeters) in diameter and 2–3 inches (5–8 centimeters) in height.

The existence of Morbier is recorded from the end of the eighteenth century. In 1795 the earliest documents recorded the existence of a "fat" cheese weighing 18–22 pounds (8–10 kilograms) called "Petit Morbier." In 1799 the description of this new cheese in documents became more specific, evoking the manufacture "of cheeses made like gruyères giving a more fat paste without holes and veined by a black line." At this time the peasants in the Franche-Comté delivered the cow's milk to the village cheesemaker to be made into Comté. See COMTÉ. The very harsh climate sometimes made these journeys impossible, which encouraged the milk producers to make their own cheese. To protect the curds obtained from the evening milking, they sprinkled a layer ash over them. In the morning they then covered this first part of the cheese with the curds from the second milking. This resulted in a delicious cheese weighing 13–18 pounds (6–8 kilograms) with an ash line in the middle. Today this dark line is made using charred vegetable matter.

Forgotten about for a long time, Morbier was left to industrial structures that produced a pasteurized cheese lacking in flavor. After a ten-year battle before the Conseil d'Etat, the producers of Morbier were able to bring Morbier back to its original territory by obtaining a PDO in 2002. The PDO prevented dairies outside the region from producing their generic versions in the Morbier name after a five-year time period. By 2007 no more generic versions were allowed to use the Morbier name; be warned, though, as copies of this famous cheese that do not bear the PDO label still exist. Today about forty cheesemakers produce nearly 10,000 tons of Morbier each year. In 2016 some two thousand farmers were able to produce the milk that complies with the requirements of PDO Morbier.

The current success of Morbier is not just an increase in the volume and its wider celebrity. Firmly established in a network of numerous dairies, it creates value and plays a significant part in the local economy, in parallel with the other regional PDO dairies. In August each year a festival is organized in Morbier, with a competition to judge the best cheese. It attracts around three thousand visitors.

Morbier can be eaten all year round. It should be left at room temperature for at least thirty minutes before being eaten so that it can reveal all its aromas, with fruity, yogurt, vanilla, milky, and even fudge being the most notable. Morbier is ideal on a cheese platter. It is a mild cheese that goes well with a number of ingredients. It also features in different recipes and is quite surprising when melted and warm, on a pizza or in a raclette. It can also accompany fruit and a white wine from the Jura.

See also ASH.

Vernus, Michel, and Thierry Petit. *Le Morbier, le Bleu de Gex—Une histoire.* Pontarlier, France: Editions du Belvédère, 2010.

Florence Arnaud

morbiflette

See TARTIFLETTE.

morge is a very important part of defining the outside croute (rind) of a hard cheese. Basically, it is the rubbing of coarse salt over the cheese and then with a wet cloth spreading the wet salt over the cheese surface. What happens next is a brown sticky film forms on the surface of the cheese that encourages proteolytic bacteria—in particular *Brevibacterium linens*—and a host of other lactic acid bacteria to grow on the crust, which, over time and continued rubbing with a brine-soaked cloth, turns the outside crust brown. See BREVIBACTERIUM LINENS and LACTIC ACID BACTERIA.

There are many reasons for this process for hard cheeses like Beaufort, Comté, and Gruyère. It is not just about inhibiting the growth of unwanted thick molds; it is to encourage beneficial bacteria on the surface of the cheese to slowly work their way into the cheese and naturally combat negative microorganisms present in the fermentation by promoting the positive bacteria. It is also plays a very key part in the development of flavors and textures. Lactic acid bacteria are hugely important groups of microorganisms used in food fermentation whether dairy, vegetable, bread, or wine; they inhibit bacteria that would spoil the food by promoting healthy flora.

The early process of morge on young cheeses is vital as there are an abundant host of bacteria, which are allowed to multiply within this high salty solution, such as coryneform bacteria and micrococcaceae with the Gram-negative bacteria almost nonexistent even after thirty days. *Moraxella* shows up toward the end of the thirty days but is overshadowed by all the other positive bacteria, with the coryneform being the dominant organisms at the end of the thirty days. It is important to start the morge at the dairy where the cheese is made and within the same time frame to capture the bacteria on the batch of cheese—which will be maybe only six or eight in a small Comté Fruitier or just two in a Beaufort Chalet Alpage mountain dairy—and to activate the high acidity in these bacteria onto their fresh, fragile rind and encourage their growth. These freshly made cheeses, rubbery and soft to the touch, have been made with milk heated in copper pans—another vital element to encourage the curdling but also the wealth of flora in the milk. Heating the milk and measuring the acidity levels on a constant basis during the curdling process while monitoring the grain size of the curd are not only methods of evaluating the transformation of the milk, but also help define the texture and taste of the cheese. It may be an age-old process in the world of hard cheese making, but when you have a handmade cheese given such a measured approach right from the start you will be admirably rewarded.

During this eight- to fifteen-day period of morge treatment, the levels of bacteria reached on the surface can be the same as the inside of the cheese; an important and vital start to promote the flavor, aroma, and character of the cheese. By introducing this fast-acting rind deacidifying treatment to allow bacteria to multiply, not only are microflora encouraged to grow but the positive flora are allowed to out-compete and combat the negative. Once the cheeses are transferred into the main ripening rooms, the natural atmosphere with abundant flora floating in the air, humidity at 95 percent, and the spruce wood boards all contribute to the onward maturing process along with the regular brushing and rubbing over of brine.

The wooden boards are another element to the flavor profile of the cheeses. They have to be regularly scrubbed with water and a hard bristle brush to keep mites at bay. However the wood is porous and its temperature is ambient to the room, allowing the cheese sitting on the board to obtain air all around the surface evenly. The cheeses are checked, brushed, and turned every day, and as time passes and the crust forms, the process is reduced. See WOODEN SHELVES.

It is also important to note that with a high mountain cheese like Beaufort Chalet d'Alpage, the cattle are grazing on a very specific pasture that is only used in the summer by the farmers and cannot be given any form of treatment other than the natural fertilizer provided by the animals. The grass and wild flora enjoyed by the cattle contain a multitude of microorganisms and bacteria that will, when the milk is transformed into curds in the first part of fermentation, produce an acidity and unique flavor characteristics that will be further enhanced and influenced once the morge treatment is started and thereafter by the ongoing morgeage or ripening period.

See also BRINING; DRY SALTING; SALT; and MATURING.

ARIATT (Association Régionale de l'Industrie Agro-alimentaire et de Transfert de Technologie). http://www.ariatt.fr.
Fromage Beaufort. http://www.fromage-beaufort.com.
Profession Fromager. http://www.professionfromager.com.

Patricia Michelson

morphology is used to describe the physical characteristics of the organism. With regard to microbial cells, morphology includes both the shape and the arrangement. Typical cell shapes include cocci (spherical), bacilli (rod), vibrio (comma shaped), and spiral (corkscrew). A practical utilization of

morphology would be a cheesemaker who wishes to add the starter cultures in the correct balance to produce an Italian style cheese. This is done by adding the starter in the correct rod to coccus ratio. See STARTER CULTURES.

Common descriptions of the arrangement of cells may include unicellular (made of one cell), diploid (two cells per unit), tetrad (four cells per unit), and sarcina (eight cells). When describing the arrangement of cells one may also utilize the terms "staph" meaning "grapelike clusters" or "strep" meaning "chains." Thus if we were to use a microscope to observe the common yogurt culture *Streptococcus thermophilus* we would see spherical cells arranged in a chain, not unlike what we would observe when viewing a string of pearls.

See TAXONOMY.

Mullan, W. M. A. "Microbiology of Starter Cultures." Dairy Science and Food Technology, 2001. http://www.dairyscience.info/index.php/cheese-starters/49-cheese-starters.html.

Todd Pritchard

Motal Paniri is a traditional Iranian cheese produced in the Azerbaijan region as well as in Ardabil, Meshkin Shahr, Mooghan, Kordestan, Damghan, and the north of Khorasan. In these three latter regions, it is called Panire Khiki or Panire Pousti. Motal Paniri seems to be one of the oldest cheeses in the world, considering the ancient method of its preparation, which requires the use of sheep skins as natural containers for its ripening and storing. Motal and Khik are local names of sheep- or goat-skin pouches used for cheese storage during the maturation period and beyond. Before use, the skin is thoroughly cleaned, washed, and salted. Then, the skin of the front and rear legs is tied together, and the skin is blown to ensure that there are no holes.

Both ewe's and cow's milk can be used for manufacturing Motal Paniri. Traditional rennet is used for coagulation of the milk. After the fresh cheese is prepared, it is salted and transferred to the ripening rooms, which are cold and moist, for about 8 to 10 days. Then the cheese is broken into small pieces of about 4–6 inches (10–15 cm) in diameter, which are packed into the sheep skin through the neck opening. The pouch is then obstructed and kept in a cold, moist place such as a basement or storehouse for 2 to 3 months to be well ripened. Once it has ripened, Motal Paniri can be stored in cold and dry places for about 7 to 8 months.

In some regions Motal Paniri is prepared from salted Shor, which is ripened and kept in the sheep skin for several months. A traditional dairy product from the Azerbaijan region of Iran, Shor is prepared from Ayran, buttermilk that is separated from yogurt during butter making by shaking it in traditional instruments such as the Tulugh and the Nehra.

Motal Paniri is a semihard cheese with a dry appearance. It is characterized by its white color, salty and acidic taste, specific pleasant aroma, and brittle texture. It is usually consumed as a table cheese.

See also IRAN; KUPA PANIRI; LIGHVAN PANIRI; and SHEEP- AND GOAT-SKIN CHEESES.

Lame, H., and M. Hekmati. "Etude de quelques caractéristiques d'une variété fromagère traditionnelle iranienne appelée'Fromiage en outre.'" *Le Lait* 547 (1975): 418–423.
Najafi, A., et al. "Microbiological Changes of Pousti Cheese During Ripening." *Food Technology and Nutrition* 8 (2011): 85–91.
Shafiei, Yahya. "Jortan and Shor, Two Traditional Dairy Products Which Are Produced in Azerbaijan Region of Iran." *Special Issue of International Dairy Federation* 1201 (2011): 66–69.
Shafiei, Yahya. "Iranian Traditional Cheeses." *The 1st Conference of Iranian Traditional Dairy Products.* Khoy, Iran, 2013. Manuscript No.: O.124. In Persian.

Yahya Shafiei Bavil Oliaei

mozzarella is a fresh pasta filata ("spun paste") style cheese, originating in Italy and now made and consumed worldwide. See PASTA FILATA. Used today mostly as a term for a fresh cow's milk cheese, mozzarella was originally made with 100 percent water buffalo milk and currently has DOP (denominazione di origine protetta) status as Mozzarella di Bufala Campana. The name mozzarella is derived from *mozzare*, meaning "to separate," a word of the Neapolitan dialect in Campania referencing the stretching process of production.

The history of mozzarella cheese is closely tied to the water buffalo. There are competing speculations about the breed's arrival in Italy, but general consensus is that water buffalo have been in Italy since the seventh century. Eastern Mediterranean and Middle Eastern migrants most likely introduced cheeses made with buffalo milk to Italy in the twelfth century. Buffalo milk mozzarella gained popularity in the eighteenth century, specifically in and around Campania. During World War II the Nazis destroyed southern Italy's water buffalo herds; consequently, production of mozzarella shifted to cow's milk and that version is what arrived in the United States (to New York City, initially) and launched the incredible popularity of mozzarella cheese in America. After World War II water buffalo from India were brought to Italy to repopulate the original herds and production of Mozzarella di Bufala returned to the south. See WATER BUFFALO.

Mozzarella di Bufala was granted a DOP on 12 June 1996. This protection stipulates that the cheese must be made from 100-percent water buffalo milk and only in the provinces of Caserta, Salerno, and parts of Benevento, Naples, Frosinone, Latina, and Rome (all located in south-central Italy). The Consortium for the Protection of the Buffalo Cheese of Campania has been designated by Italian law as the entity "responsible for the protection, surveillance, promotion and marketing" of Mozzarella di Bufala Campana cheese. True Mozzarella di Bufala must have a wrapping printed with the name "Mozzarella di

Laverstoke Park Farm in Hampshire, England, produces an organic fresh buffalo mozzarella, shown here floating in water. COURTESY OF LAVERSTOKE PARK FARM

Bufala Campana," the logo of the association, and the relevant legal information and authorization number.

Water buffalo milk is noteworthy in its differences from cow milk, resulting in a completely different type of mozzarella when used. Water buffalo milk has twice the fat (approximately 21 percent) of average cow's milk, but less than half the cholesterol. The flavor is also more pronounced: when making mozzarella from water buffalo milk the cheese should have a mossy, grassy aroma and a slightly tangy (though never sour) flavor. When made with cow's milk, mozzarella simply tastes milky and sweet. Though mozzarella made with water buffalo milk is the original, most consumers today only know the cow's milk mozzarella, a cheese much more prevalent worldwide and often referred to as Fior di Latte in Italy. Versions of cow's milk mozzarella range in most markets from industrial, dry and rubbery cheese (mostly made for high-volume use on pizza) to locally made, higher moisture cheeses made for eating fresh.

Mozzarella is generally made in five steps, with variations based on the target texture and flavor:

1. Ripening the milk: Traditional forms of mozzarella are inoculated with a starter culture made from the whey from the previous day's cheesemaking. Most industrial and commercial mozzarella today is made using a commercial starter culture.
2. Renneting the curd: Calf's rennet is traditionally used as a coagulant to separate the curd from the whey. Microbial rennet is fairly common as well.
3. Cutting the curd: The curd is usually cut or milled into 1-inch (2.5-centimeter) cubes.
4. Heating the curd: The curd (still suspended in the whey, or sometimes after draining the whey and replenishing with water) is heated. This softens the curd and also increases its acidity.
5. Stretching the curd ("filatura" or "spinning"): This is the signature step for pasta filata style cheeses, and involves stretching and pulling the curd mass after it has softened from the heating. Some producers have elaborate methods for stretching the curd, and some versions of this style are braided, tied (Scamorza, Caciocavallo) or stretched into rope-like shapes (queso Oaxaca). Sometimes a wooden stick is used to stretch the curd, often it is done by hand even at high temperatures. In larger-scale production the process is automated with machinery.

Mozzarella can be salted during the stretching process, or put to marinate in a salt brine. Smoked mozzarella is also a popular variation of the classic method, with smoking done at the end of the cheesemaking process. See BRINING and SMOKED CHEESES.

Mozzarella cheese is ideally eaten fresh, but can also be used as an ingredient in many Mediterranean dishes. The most popular way to consume mozzarella cheese is on pizza. See PIZZA. It is also featured in pasta and vegetable dishes, as a stuffing in breads and in Italian specialties such as eggplant and chicken parmigiana. In the classic Italian Caprese salad it is served fresh with tomatoes, basil, and olive oil. American restaurants often include mozzarella on pressed panini sandwiches, and fried mozzarella "sticks" can be found at pizzerias and at many chain restaurants throughout the United States. Variations on the typical 10–12-ounce (284–340-gram) format of the mozzarella ball are used in appetizers and salads: Bocconcini (2-ounce [57-gram] balls), Ciliegini (half-ounce [14-gram] balls) and Ovoline (4-ounce [113-gram] balls) lend themselves to different applications.

Mozzarella producers in Italy are known locally, with limited amounts of Mozzarella di Bufala exported out of the country. Cow's milk mozzarella is made for export out of Italy, but mass production for food service and retail is dominated by a small number of global companies. Two of the largest producers and distributors of mozzarella cheese worldwide are Leprino Foods ($3 billion in yearly revenue; based in Denver, Colorado) and Saputo Inc. ($9.62 billion in yearly revenue; based in Montreal, Canada). In the United States regional producers of cow's milk mozzarella include Point Reyes Farmstead Cheese and DiStefano on the west coast, Lioni Latticini and Calabro on the east coast. The state of Wisconsin alone produces an average of 650 million pounds (295 million kilograms) of mozzarella per year.

South America has emerged recently as a potential market for water buffalo milk cheeses, specifically mozzarella made with water buffalo milk as in the traditional Mozzarella di Bufala Campana. Annabella Buffalo Cheeses in Colombia has seen recent success and is currently the only producer in the world making 100-percent grass-fed water buffalo milk mozzarella.

See also MOZZARELLA DI BUFALA CAMPANA.

Consortium for the Protection of the Buffalo Cheese of Campania. "Campania Buffalo Mozzarella Cheese." http://www.mozzarelladibufala.org/allestimento.htm.

Harbutt, Juliet. *World Cheese Book.* New York: DK Publishing, 2009.

Rubino, Roberto, et al. *Italian Cheese: A Guide to Its Discovery and Appreciation.* Bra, Italy: Slow Food Editore, 2005.

Elena Santogade

The **Mozzarella Company** was founded by Paula Lambert in 1982, when she returned home to Dallas, Texas, after studying Italian in Perugia, Italy. Surveying the locally available cheeses, she concluded that if she wanted to continue to eat the luscious mozzarella she had enjoyed as a student, she would have to make it herself. Traveling back to Italy, Lambert persuaded the cheesemaker Mauro Brufani, head of the *caseificio Brufani* in Assisi, Italy, to teach her how to make mozzarella. After a three-week internship, she returned to Texas and found factory space in Dallas's artsy suburb of Deep Ellum. With help from the Italian food scientist Giovanni Marchesi to design her own *caseificio*, Lambert, backed by two partners, hoped to make a hundred pounds of mozzarella weekly, using raw milk delivered daily and pasteurized in-house. Her plan was to sell largely to retailers and restaurateurs.

Unfortunately, the Dallas market was not yet ready for artisanal mozzarella, and the fresh cheeses languished on retailers' shelves. Lambert thought diversifying her product line might be the solution, and on another trip to Italy, she perfected recipes for ricotta, caciotta, scamorza, and other young cheeses. She entered them in the 1985 American Cheese Society competition and won several awards. These plaudits, coupled with her efforts to personally promote her cheeses to restaurateurs and chefs at the time when Americans were starting to pay greater attention to artisanal foods, ensured the company's success after a difficult launch.

Today, the Mozzarella Company makes more than five thousand pounds each week of cow's and goat's milk cheeses of diverse kinds. It does a brisk online and wholesale business, boasts a cheese-of-the-month club, and offers classes in cheesemaking and pairing beer or wine with cheese. The Mozzarella Company's cheeses continue to win accolades in national competitions.

Lambert, Paula. *The Cheese Lover's Cookbook and Guide: Over 150 Recipes with Instructions on How to Buy, Store, and Serve All Your Favorite Cheeses.* New York: Simon and Schuster, 2000.

Mozzarella Company. http://www.mozzco.com.

Cathy K. Kaufman

Mozzarella di Bufala Campana, widely acknowledged as the king of pasta filata (pulled curd) cheeses, is highly prized, versatile, and considered gastronomically and nutritiously superior to other types of mozzarella. It is the largest-selling PDO (protected designation of origin) food in south-central Italy and third among Italian cheeses overall. Mozzarella di Bufala Campana hails from Campania, a region whose main geographic features are the Piana del Vulturno in the Caserta area and the Piana del Sele, encompassing Salerno, Eboli, and Paestum. Like many of the world's finest cheeses, its quality and character are attributable not only to a very specific zone and method of production but to the milk of a particular breed of animal, the Italian Mediterranean buffalo.

Used as draft animals in Greek and Roman times, water buffalo may have been brought in greater numbers to Sicily toward the end of the first millennium C.E. by Saracen conquerors from North Africa. Scant references exist from the late Middle Ages thorough the Renaissance. In the tenth and eleventh centuries the so-called *impaludamento* (swamping) of these areas invited farmers to employ water buffalo. Just as this magnificent animal is particularly suited to the soggy, fertile soil of these floodplains, so its milk, which is higher in protein, fat, and calcium than a cow's, is optimal for making mozzarella-type cheeses. In the twelfth century the monks of San Lorenzo in Capua, near Caserta, offered rations of buffalo mozzarella to pilgrims. Records from the Reggia di Carditello, the Bourbon dynasty's royal estate also near Caserta, in the late eighteenth century indicate the presence of a large herd of water buffalo and sales of mozzarella. In the latter half of the nineteenth century a central market called the Taverna grew up in the nearby town of Aversa; from there, buffalo mozzarella's popularity began to spread throughout a newly unified Italy and beyond.

Mozzarella di Bufala Campana was awarded its Italian DOC (denominazione di origine controllata, or controlled designation of origin) in 1993 and European PDO in 1996. Its zone comprises the entire provinces of Caserta and Salerno as well as selected municipalities in the provinces of Naples and Benevento, and in the regions of Lazio, Puglia, and Molise. The Consorzio di Tutela di Mozzarella

Campana (Consortium for the Protection of Mozzarella Campana) is the official body for enforcing PDO requirements, regulating breeders and dairies, and promoting the product. The PDO's rules specify traditional animal husbandry and cheesemaking practices. There are about 1,500 officially sanctioned *allevamenti* (breeders) and 107 *caseifici* (cheesemaking dairies) under its tutelage.

According to the consortium approximately 84 million pounds (38 million kilograms or between 41,000 and 42,000 tons) are produced each year, about 57 percent from the province of Caserta and 33 percent from Salerno. Domestic sales account for 75 percent of production. France is the top foreign market, with roughly 28 percent of exports, followed by Germany (18 percent), Spain (12 percent), the United Kingdom (11.5 percent), and Switzerland and the United States (about 9 percent each).

Buffalo mozzarella appears porcelain white in color, due to the milk's characteristic lack of carotenoids. The cheese has a smooth, shiny surface and a rind merely 0.04 inch (1 millimeter) thick. Soon after the cheese is made, both its internal striations and somewhat elastic consistency begin to meld and soften. The fresh tastes and aromas of cow's milk mozzarella are intensified in its buffalo incarnation. The flavors are lightly acidic and creamy, with notes of lactic fermentation and possible hints of musty or barnyardy aromas.

Mozzarella di Bufala Campana is labeled with the circular PDO logo featuring the black silhouette of a water buffalo head, the producer's authorization number, a reference to the governing EU laws, and the European Union PDO logo. Similar cheeses labeled "mozzarella di bufala" or "buffalo mozzarella," but without these guarantees, are not the genuine PDO articles.

Connoisseurs of buffalo mozzarella often prefer cheeses from the areas around Battipaglia, Caserta, and Paestum for their terroir and authenticity. Recommended producers include Granato, Rivabianca and Vanullo in Capaccio-Paestum; Casa Madaio in Eboli; and Battaglia in Capua. The selector-affineur Guffanti, located in northern Italy near Milan, also carries select PDO mozzarellas.

See also ITALY; MOZZARELLA; PASTA FILATA; and WATER BUFFALO.

Consorzio Tutela Mozzarella di Bufala. http://www
  .mozzarelladop.it.
DiPalo, Lou, and Rachel Wharton. "Mozzarella
  (Burrata)." In *DiPalo's Guide to the Essential Foods of
  Italy*, pp. 34–35. New York: Ballantine, 2014.
La Mozzarella di Campania DOP. http://www
  .mozzarelladibufala.org.
Ministero delle Politiche Agricole Alimentari e Forestali.
  "Modifica del disciplinare di produzione della
  denominazione 'Mozzarella di Bufala Campana,'
  registrata in qualita di denominazione origine protetta
  in foraa regolamento CE n. 1107 dale 12 giugno
  1996." http://www.mozzarelladop.it/disciplinare_
  mozzarella_2008.pdf.
Rubino, Roberto, et al. *Italian Cheese: A Guide to Its
  Discovery and Appreciation*. Bra, Italy: Slow Food
  Editore, 2005.

David Gibbons

Mucor is a diverse fungal genus comprising fifty-eight known species, including a few species found in cheeses. *Mucor* species are known to have different morphological or functional characteristics than higher fungi (i.e., Basidiomycetes and Ascomycetes). In terms of their appearance, contrary to higher fungi, septa are absent from their hyphae apart from septa isolating reproductive structures as well as old or damaged hyphae. Some *Mucor* species (e.g., *M. circinelloides*) have been reported as dimorphic, meaning that these species can occur in a filamentous form, developing hyphae on the cheese surface, or a unicellular form called yeast form, particularly at low oxygen concentrations such as in cheese cores. See FILAMENTOUS FUNGI; FUNGI; and HYPHAE.

Hyphal growth in *Mucor* is much faster than in other species commonly found in cheese with an often aerial mycelium that rises off the cheese surface. See MYCELIA. *Mucor* species also produce abundant asexual spores that are formed in a bag-like structure called sporangia. They may also produce spores resulting from sexual reproduction called zygospores that are formed after hyphal fusion from two compatible individuals. However, these latter are usually absent in cheeses. See SPORES.

Contrary to most food-borne fungi, *Mucor* does not tolerate low moisture environments. In natural habitats *Mucor* species are present at an early stage, rapidly colonizing substrates by exploiting easily accessible nutrients. They also produce high spore numbers in order to spread and colonize new surfaces, prior to being replaced by higher fungal species that have the ability to metabolize more complex sources of energy.

Mucor isolates are found in environmental samples such as soil, air, and dust, as well as raw materials and processed foods and feeds. The genus includes technologically useful species as well as contaminant species. Indeed, their ability to break down fats and proteins may improve texture, flavor, and the nutritional quality of foods. See ENZYMES. *Mucor* species can be used as adjunct cultures in food fermentations, especially in fermented Asian soybean- or rice-based products (e.g., sufu, a fermented soybean paste from China and Vietnam) and in uncooked hard cheeses such as French Tommes, Saint-Nectaire, and Italian Taleggio. See ADJUNCT CULTURES; TOMME; SAINT-NECTAIRE; and TALEGGIO. Interestingly, several *Mucor* species are known to produce high quantities of carotenoid pigments (e.g., beta-carotene) which can play a role in the visual aspect of chesses. As contaminants, they are responsible for defects including the so-called "cat-hair" defect observed on soft cheeses, where they can develop rapidly. See DEFECTS. Some adjunct culture producers offer *Penicillium* strains with anti-*Mucor* activities that may help to outcompete *Mucor* and suppress its growth. Contrary to other frequent cheese contaminants such as some *Penicillium* species, *Mucor* have never been reported as mycotoxin producers. See MYCOTOXINS.

Only a few species are a matter of interest or concern when it comes to cheesemaking. *M. fuscus* and the recently described *M. lancelolatus* are considered the useful *Mucor* species, while *M. racemosus* (which may also be used as an adjunct), *M. circinelloides* or *M. brunneogriseus* and *M. spinosus* (sometimes also known as *M. plumbeus*) are the most common contaminant species. Morphological and physiological differences exist among these various species, but they are easily differentiated using molecular methods. Unlike other fungal species used for cheesemaking, useful *Mucor* strain inoculation often occurs from the spores present in the cheesemaking environment rather than from artificial inoculation.

Hermet, A., et al. "Molecular Systematics in the Genus *Mucor* with Special Regard to Species Encountered in Cheese." *Food Microbiology* 116 (2012): 692–705.

Hoffmann, K., et al. "The Family Structure of the *Mucorales*: A Synoptic Revision Based on Comprehensive Multigene-Genealogies." *Persoonia-Molecular Phylogeny and Evolution of Fungi* 30 (2013): 57–76.

Walther, G., et al. "DNA Barcoding in *Mucorales*: An Inventory of Biodiversity." *Persoonia-Molecular Phylogeny and Evolution of Fungi* 30 (2013): 11–47.

Jean-Luc Jany

Munster is a semisoft cheese with a dense texture and a rind washed with a saltwater solution, which, by fostering the growth of fungi and bacteria including *Brevibacterium linens*, leaves the cheese with a sticky and highly aromatic orange coating. Munster is made from cow's milk from the Vosge pastures primarily in Alsace, but stretching to Lorraine and Franche-Comté. The Alsatian side of the Vosge valley call the cheese Munster, and the Lorraine side call it Gerome, but essentially it is the same style of cheese, and the AOC (appellation d'origine contrôlée) protecting it have combined the two into Munster-Gerome.

Munster dates back to the seventh century, when monks made the cheese from milk from the local *marcaires* (milkers), a French word that describes humble farmers. Tradition has it that on St. Urbain's day, 25 May, the marcaires leave their valley farms for the higher pastures (alpage, or, to keep it regional, *chaumes*) to allow the cattle to enjoy the open air and untreated grasses. This also allowed them to grow the grass on their farmland that they then cut and dry in the barns for feed during the colder months when the cattle had to stay indoors. See ALPAGE; MONASTIC CHEESEMAKING; and TRANSHUMANCE.

One of the stipulations in the making of Munster-Gerome is that only grasses and no other feed is given to the herds to ensure the purity of the milk and taste of the cheese. The Vosgian cattle breed is a robust walker and adaptable to weather changes and mountain paths; it is patched black and white with scattered spots and a white stripe can be seen from head to tail but the head is mostly white or spotted or a soft ashen hue. The ears are black as are the horns, nostrils, and hoofs. The Vosgian valleys are gently undulating with stubble fields and open meadows with pine and beech trees and weather patterns during the summer are normally very good, enabling hayfields to be kept going from May through to early July. In the small farms the grass is still cut with a long scythe and gathered up by hand. The grasses are stored in the rafters of the barns to dry out over summer and then brought down bit by bit during the harsher winter months to feed the cattle. See FERMIER.

Munster attained its AOC in 1969. The Confrérie Saint Grégoire du Taste-Fromage de la Vallée de Munster is a professional society created in 1987 with over five hundred members. Their striking robes resemble the monk's habit from the Munster Abbey and each member has a bronze medal with the shield of the village of Munster in the center and round the sides smaller shields of the fifteen other towns of the district.

To make Munster, morning milk or the first milking is mixed with the skimmed milk of the previous day and warmed in a copper cauldron (*kessel*) to 90°F (32°C), when rennet is added. The curds are then cut one hour later. It is important that a copper pan is used, as it imparts flavor to the cheese. The curds are placed into molds, salted, and turned frequently before going to the high humidity cold cellars for aging. The cheeses are hand rubbed every two days in a saltwater solution in the typical monastic style to encourage *Brevibacterium linens* and other microbes. This, together with the humidity, turns the outside sticky and orange-red and allows the cheese to remain soft and supple. Affinage is at least four to six weeks for the larger versions, and more commonly two to three months. The resulting cheese is 5–8 inches (13–19 centimeters) in diameter and 1–3 inches (2.4–8 centimeters) high and weighs between 1–3 pounds (450 grams–1.5 kilograms). A 1-pound (450-gram) cheese uses about 5 quarts (5 liters) of milk, with a fat content of 45–48 percent. There are also smaller versions. The fermier cheeses made with unpasteurized milk within a very restricted area account for about 5 percent of the overall production.

Munster has a strong, gamey smell and a heightened bite, yet a subtle, mellow, creamy finish. This is a perfect cheese to enjoy with rye bread or biscuits with cumin seeds, white wines like Riesling or Gewurztraminer, or a blond beer.

See also FRANCE and WASHED-RIND CHEESES.

Office de Tourisme de la Vallée de Munster. "The Vosgian Cow." http://www.vallee-munster.eu/en/terroir/vache-vosgienne.htm.
Rance, Patrick. *The French Cheese Book*. London: Macmillan, 1989.

Patricia Michelson

Murazzano is a fresh PDO (protected designation of origin) cheese in the Robiola family, produced in about fifty towns in the Piedmont region in northern Italy. Traditionally it is made from full-fat, raw ewe's milk, to which up to 40 percent cow's milk is added. About 21 tons are produced every year. The origin and center of production of this cheese is Murazzano, a small town located in the Alta Langa, an Alpine area of Piedmont, where, on market day, the women sold their Murazzano cheese (typically called "tuma") to the shopkeepers of the towns on the plains, including Turin. A fresh cheese produced with ewe's milk in the area where the Celtics, an old Italic population, once lived, it is mentioned by Pliny the Elder in his *Naturalis Historia*, but there is no evidence that this is the same cheese. See PLINY the elder.

The ewe's milk used for Murazzano mostly comes from the native Pecora delle Langhe, an endangered breed of sheep. After coagulation, the curd is cut to the size of a hazelnut and drained for 24 hours in molds called *fascelle*, which in the past were made of wood or aluminum. See FASCÈRA. The cheese is dry-salted, then left to ripen for 4–10 days. Murazzano is cylindrical and flat, about 4–6 inches (10–15 centimeters) wide and 1.2–1.6 inches (3–4 centimeters) high, with a weight of 0.7–0.9 pounds (300–400 grams). When fresh, Murazzano has no rind, but later forms a yellowish film. The paste is soft and white or ivory-white with a few small holes. The odor is pleasant, with milk and cream characteristics, while the taste is sweet for fresh products (after 7–10 days) and more savory and intense in cheeses aged for up to 2 months.

See also ITALY and ROBIOLA DI ROCCAVERANO.

Assopiemonte DOP & IGP. http://www.assopiemonte.com.
Ministero dell'Agricoltura e delle Foreste. *DOC Cheeses of Italy: A Great Heritage*. Milan: Angeli, 1992.
Ottogalli, Giorgio. *Atlante dei formaggi*. Milan: Hoepli, 2001.
AAVV. Formaggi d'Italia. Bra: Slow Food, 2005.

Giuseppe Zeppa

Murcia and Murcia al Vino cheeses are made in the Murcia region of southeastern Spain, using goat's milk from the Murciano-Granadina breed. In 2001, the European Union awarded both varieties PDO (protected designation of origin) status. These PDOs protect 186 livestock farms, which have 66,000 milking goats that produce 4.9 million gallons (18.6 million liters) of milk per year. One-seventh of that milk—about 700,000 gallons (2.6 million liters)—is transformed into nearly 90,000 pounds (41,000 kilograms) of Murcia cheese and 666,000 pounds (302,000 kilograms) of Murcia al Vino cheese.

To make Murcia cheese, pasteurized milk, after the addition of a starter culture, is coagulated at 86–93°F (30–34°C) for 45–60 minutes using animal rennet. The cheese can be consumed fresh, or ripened after an aging period of 21 days at a temperature of 48–55°F (9–13°C) and a relative humidity higher than 80 percent. Murcia al Vino cheese is manufactured in the same way as Murcia ripened cheese, but it is soaked in red wine ("vino") to give the rind its characteristic color and aroma. Murcia al Vino is soaked in red-wine baths four times: the first time before starting the ripening process, for 30 minutes; the second time after 7 days of ripening, for 15–30 minutes, depending on the state of the rind; the third time after 14 days of ripening, for 15–30 minutes; and the fourth time (optional, depending on the state of the rind) after 21 days of ripening, also for 15–30 minutes.

Murcia al Vino is mostly known in the international market as "The Drunken Goat." This name is registered by Forever Cheese for the United States and by Central Quesera Montesinos (a Murcia-based company founded in 1978) for the rest of the world. This trademark refers to the company's PDO Murcia al Vino cheese. Even though it is exported to multiple countries, it is in the United States that this Spanish cheese has become particularly recognized. Since 1997, the US market has been responsible for 85 percent of Montesinos's Drunken Goat exports— approximately 518,000 pounds (235,000 kilograms) of cheese per year.

Murcia and Murcia al Vino ripened cheeses have a cylindrical shape and are sold in three different sizes, 1.1, 2.2, and 3.3 pounds (0.5, 1, and 1.5 kilograms). The smallest of the three sizes is sold after 30 days of ripening, while the other two are sold after a ripening period of 45 days. The cheeses have a smooth, thin rind that becomes red-violet in the Murcia al Vino variety; the interior is firm and compact, with a creamy and elastic texture. Its taste is pleasantly acidic and slightly salty, with a delicate goaty aroma.

See also MURCIANA and SPAIN.

López, M. B., et al. "Physicochemical Study of Murcia al Vino Cheese." *Small Ruminant Research* 106 (2012): 154–159.

Martínez, Sidonia, et al. "The Spanish Traditional Cheeses: Characteristics and Scientific Knowledge." In *Handbook of Cheese, Production, Chemistry, and Sensory Properties*, edited by Enrique Castelli and Luiz Du Vale, pp. 123–167. Hauppauge, N.Y.: Nova Science, 2013.

Smith, Adrienne. "Spanish Cheese Makers Get Their Goat!" Foods and Wines from Spain. http://www.foodswinesfromspain.com/spanishfoodwine/global/products-recipes/products/more-about-products/4754076.html.

Javier Carballo

Murciana is a hardy, handsome breed of milking goat that originated in the mountainous areas of northwestern Murcia and northeastern Granada, in the southeast of Spain. The breed's official name is Murciano Granadina; its Latin name is *capra aegagrus hircus* and it is also referred to as Royal Murciana, Murciane, and Murcian. Spain's principal milking goat breed, with an estimated 500,000 head spread throughout the land, its milk is used to make many regional cheeses, including Murcia Curado PDO, Murcia Fresco, and Murcia al Vino.

In the mid-1970s, the Spanish Ministry of Agriculture officially merged the ancient Murciano and Granadina breeds that had been increasingly crossbred throughout the 1960s. A molecular-genetic study published in 2010 ("Is the Murciano Granadina a Single Goat Breed?") concluded that while a single herd book could be maintained, individual characteristics of two separate genetic groups persisted.

Murciana goats have been chronicled since the fifteenth century. They were brought to the Americas by Spanish colonizers beginning in the sixteenth century. Distinct lineages exist in the Latin American countries as well as in North Africa. The breed was brought to other European countries more recently. The US milking breed LaMancha is also in part descended from the Murciana. See LAMANCHA.

Murcianas are uniform black to mahogany in color, with erect ears, short hair and no spots (a disqualifier for purebreds). The females have large, accessible udders and weigh 88–121 pounds (40–55 kilograms), while the males weigh 110–154 pounds (50–70 kilograms). They are known as efficient foragers; ready migrators, particularly well-adapted to the dry, arid conditions of their native territory; and easy milkers, producing an average of 560 quarts (530 liters) over a lactation period of 210 days, or about 5 pints (2.5 liters) per day. Exceptional individuals have yielded nearly two and a half times that much. Their milk's protein content is 3.6–3.8 percent and its fat content 5.6–5.8 percent. For production and quality, these numbers compare favorably to all other European breeds employed in cheese-making.

The Asociación Española de Criadores de Cabras de Raza Murciano-Granadina (ACRIMUR), the Spanish Association of Breeders of Murciano-Granadina Goats, was founded in 1979. It counts among its members fifty-two breeders in the Murcia region, and a total of fifty-nine in sixteen other regions of Spain.

See also GOAT and MURCIA.

ACRIMUR. http://www.acrimur.es.
Department of Animal Science, Oklahoma State University. http://www.ansi.okstate.edu.
Engle, Amy. "Murciana Goats." *Culture*, 24 February 2014. http://www.culturecheesemag.com/farm-animal/murciana-goats.
Murcigran. http://www.murcigran.es.

David S. Gibbons

Murray's Cheese on Bleecker Street in New York's Greenwich Village is one of the city's best-known purveyors of great domestic and imported cheeses. Founded in 1940 by Murray Greenberg, a Jewish veteran of the Spanish Civil War, the shop was located originally on Cornelia Street, where it sold butter and eggs, and later, blocks of cheese to Village residents. In the 1970s, Greenberg sold the store to his clerk, Louis Tudda, from Calabria, Italy, who imported cheeses, olive oil, and other items to sell to his Italian neighbors.

In 1991 Rob Kaufelt, a longtime customer, overheard Tudda say he lost his lease and would close the business. Kaufelt had worked for years in his family's New Jersey supermarkets and also owned several specialty food shops himself, and so, because of this chance encounter, he bought the cheese shop from Tudda. Moving the store to the corner of Cornelia and Bleecker Streets, he sold an array of American and imported cheeses in a space not much bigger than a closet. But when there is demand for the product, the size of the shop doesn't matter.

The timing of Kaufelt's ownership coincided with the renaissance of American artisan cheese and an explosion of consumer interest in great-tasting products. In 2004, outgrowing the corner store, the business moved across Bleecker Street. Kaufelt built underground caves to properly age cheese, opened a satellite store in Grand Central Station, and part-nered with the Kroger Company to establish in-store cheese shops. The excellent products sold by Murray's Cheese, combined with a tradition of personal customer service, contributed to the growth of American artisan cheese and a worldwide reputation for outstanding quality.

Hook, Raymond. "Hooked on Cheese: Interview with Murray's Rob Kaufelt." *The Daily Meal*, 22 May 2014. http://www.thedailymeal.com/hooked-cheese-rob-kaufelt/52214.
Wharton, Rachel. "Murray's Cheese." *Edible Manhattan*, 6 March 2012. http://www.ediblemanhattan.com/magazine/murrays-cheese.

Jeff Roberts

The myceliam (pl. **mycelia**) is the vegetative part of filamentous fungi consisting of a net of interlaced and sometimes interconnected hyphae. See HYPHAE and FILAMENTOUS FUNGI. While hyphae are microscopic structures, the dense net of the mycelium forms a visible structure. After spore germination, the first hypha or germ tube emerges from the spore, grows, and branches to form the mycelium. Due to the apical growth of hyphae, which can colonize substrates in every direction, mycelial growth is radial and individual mycelia are disk-shaped. Mycelia can be more or less raised from the surface, have different textures, and display different colors, depending on the pigments (e.g., carotenoids or melanins) that they synthesize.

Interactions between the mycelium and the substrate (cheese) vary. Some growing hyphae spread on the cheese surface while others penetrate the substratum or grow upward into raised structures that support the release and spread of spores. See SPORES. In cheeses, enzymes are mainly secreted by the mycelium to degrade milk proteins and lipids into peptides and fatty acids that in turn may be transported into the hyphae to support mycelial growth. This breakdown also directly contributes to the ripening process See MATURING and ENZYMES.

Mycelia play an important role in the appearance of mold-ripened cheeses. For example, the dense white coat observed on the surface of Camembert-type cheeses mainly results from *Penicillium camemberti* mycelium growth whereas the surface of uncooked hard cheeses such as French tommes is covered with different colored mycelia produced by different species, including some *Mucor* species.

See *MUCOR*; CAMEMBERT DE NORMANDIE; TOMME; and *PENICILLIUM*.

Chamba, J. F., and F. Irlinger. "Secondary and Adjunct Cultures." In *Cheese: Chemistry, Physics and Microbiology*, edited by P. F. Fox, et al., pp. 191–206. New York: Elsevier Academic Press, 2004.

Gow, N. A. R., and G. M. Gadd. *The Growing Fungus*. London: Chapman & Hall, 1995.

Jean-Luc Jany

mycotoxins are compounds produced by fungi that can be harmful to humans or livestock. The health impacts of these compounds vary depending on the concentration and specific mycotoxin, but can range from short-term problems such as diarrhea and dehydration to more severe problems such as immunosuppression, cancer, and death. Originally described in the mid-1900s following several large-scale outbreaks in livestock, mycotoxins are produced by a variety of widely distributed fungi including *Penicillium*, *Aspergillus*, and *Fusarium*. See PENICILLIUM and OUTBREAKS.

All these fungal groups can be found growing in cheeses and some researchers have demonstrated the ability of isolates of fungi from cheese to produce mycotoxins in the lab. However negative human health impacts due to mycotoxins in cheese have rarely been reported. The most dangerous mycotoxins that have been detected in cheese are ochratoxins and aflatoxins. These can be present in cheese products either due to the growth of contaminant molds on the surface or interior of cheeses or due to growth on feed used for livestock. The levels of these toxins in cheese products and reported in the literature are generally well below maximum levels set by regulatory agencies in the United States and Europe.

Some strains of the mold *Penicillium camemberti*, widely used in the production of Camembert and other bloomy-rind cheeses, can produce the mycotoxin cyclopiazonic acid. The mold *Penicillium roqueforti*, used in the production of blue cheeses, can produce the mycotoxins roquefortine C and mycophenolic acid. Industrial strains of both these molds that are inoculated into cheeses are generally selected to produce very little or none of these mycotoxins.

See also FUNGI and PATHOGENS.

Hymery, Nolwenn, et al. "Filamentous Fungi and Mycotoxins in Cheese: A Review." *Comprehensive Reviews in Food Science and Food Safety* 13, no. 4 (2014): 437–456.

Benjamin Wolfe

Naboulsi

See MIDDLE EAST.

nachos are a dish of tortilla chips covered in cheese, sometimes in combination with savory toppings such as peppers, chicken, and refried beans. There is no one definition of nacho cheese; it varies from a cheese-flavored sauce to a flexible flavor blend of cheeses. All, however, stem from the relationship between cheese and tortilla chips consumed together. According to historical accounts, maître d' Ignacio Anaya, known by his diminutive "Nacho," first served his eponymous dish, "Nachos Especiales," in 1943 at the Victory Club in Piedras Negras, Mexico. A dozen women whose husbands were stationed at Fort Duncan Air Base were on a shopping trip and stopped at the Victory Club for a meal. When they arrived, the chef was absent and Anaya served them tortilla chips with cheese melted over them—probably Wisconsin Cheddar—and jalepeños. See CHEDDAR.

A recipe for nachos appears in the 1949 cookbook, *A Taste of Texas*. Decades later, in 1976, Frank Liberto of Rico's Products Co. Inc. first introduced nachos at a Texas Rangers baseball game. In order to shorten the time between ordering and receiving one's food, he used a cheese sauce poured over the nachos instead of melting the cheese over the nachos. Today Rico's uses a blend of cheese whey, partially hydrogenated soybean oil, and Cheddar cheese, among other ingredients, to make their sauce. In 1972 Frito Lay introduced Nacho Cheese Flavored Doritos, which use both Cheddar and Romano. Yet, perhaps in part because the FDA does not define or standardize the term, Pringle's uses a blend of Cheddar, Romano, and Parmesan and Old El Paso uses Cheddar and blue for their "nacho cheese" flavor.

Orr, Adriana P. "Nachos, Anyone?" OED Online. http://public.oed.com/aspects-of-english/word-stories/nachos-anyone.
Wong, Venessa. "There's No Such Thing as Nacho Cheese." *Bloomsburg Business*, 29 January 2015. http://www.bloomberg.com/news/articles/2015-01-29/there-s-no-such-thing-as-nacho-cheese.

Beth M. Forrest

naming cheese is an economic, political, and cultural issue. The possibilities for and stakes of naming cheese vary from country to country. When the European Union released its geographical indication (GIs) registry in the mid-1990s, this raised the question of possible restrictions on the use of popular cheese names by New World cheese producers. Indeed the European Union has taken steps to ban the use of names that might be considered GIs with historical ties to Europe, such as "Brie," "feta," and "Gruyère." But while GIs receive extensive protection within the European Union, the United States has not yet developed a framework of protections. The political nature of cheese naming illuminates the complex relationship between European and New World cheesemakers competing over the status of what names qualify as protected or generic.

Geographic indication controls the naming of an agricultural product, limiting it to a specified geographical region and method of production. This type of protectionist trade barrier defending regional products dates back to 1891, when the French began protecting sparkling wine produced in Champagne by legally barring producers of similar sparkling wines from using the term "champagne." Such protection was greatly expanded in 1951, when European countries gathered at the Stresa Convention to create the first international agreement on cheese naming. At the Stresa Convention, Italy, France, Denmark, Austria, the Netherlands, Belgium, Sweden, and Norway all participated in granting protected status to such cheeses as Roquefort, Pecorino Romano, and Parmigiano Reggiano. See STRESA CONVENTION.

While within Europe GIs and protected designation of origin (PDO) status protect and politicize the interconnection between place of production and cheese naming, some small batch producers feel that regulations have missed the mark in defining these traditional, historically established cheeses. For example, some producers feel that geographic denominations cover areas that are too big and have too broad, or even unsuitable, definitions. For example, some Bitto cheese producers in Italy have been banned from calling their cheese by its proper name because they refuse to conform and compromise to standards constructed by bureaucratic naming regulations. These dissenting cheesemakers have formed an independent, alternative association to preserve their traditions. See BITTO. Although GIs attempt to preserve tradition, they also create a level of commodification and standardization, which can sometimes redefine distinctions in local identity.

North American dairy producers, cheesemakers, and food companies have fought the extension of European GI protections that would force them to rebrand many of their products. In 2014 the American Cheese Society (ACS), which represents fifteen hundred cheesemakers, sent out a press release calling for an approach to cheese naming in which "common sense should prevail over nationalism and protectionism." According to the ACS, the history of cheesemaking in the United States stems from immigrants who came to the New World from Europe with recipes and traditions, as well as the names they brought from Europe. Over the course of generations, cheeses such as Brie, Havarti, Cheddar, Parmesan, and ricotta, have become generic terms in the perception of American consumers. Under US law, a term is considered generic when it is so widely used that consumers view it as designating an entire category of all the goods of the same type, rather than a geographic origin. See AMERICAN CHEESE SOCIETY.

Nonetheless, some North American producers have taken steps to work with the European Union to protect classic cheese names. For example, in 2013 Canada agreed to recognize the geographical indications of five cheeses (feta, Asiago, Fontina, Gorgonzola, and Munster) as part of the Canada-European Union Comprehensive Economic Trade Agreement (CETA). Any new cheeses made in these styles in Canada are required to be labeled with qualifiers, such as "-kind," "-type," "-style," or "imitation." The European Union also succeeded in incorporating GI protection into trade deals with countries such as South Korea, which prohibited the sale of feta made outside of Greece, and Asiago, Fontina, and Gorgonzola made outside of Italy.

Controversy over naming cheese has stood in the way of international trade agreements between the United States and the European Union. In 2015 negotiators met to create a trade agreement deal that would eliminate tariffs on at least 97 percent of goods traded across the Atlantic, but US and EU regulators could not agree on what legally qualified as "feta." The European Union believes that protecting the authenticity of these names also protects European intellectual property. Although the United States does claim to protect Geographic Indications through a subset of trademark law and the US Trademark Act, it does not protect geographic terms or signs that are deemed "generic."

In the growing artisanal cheese sector, North American producers avoid controversy by creating novel names for their cheeses. Creative names that establish new cheeses can draw from local inspiration, such as regional geographical features or the name of a particular farm. A name might also refer to a cheese's production process, such as mode of aging or ingredients. Including the kind of milk (cow's, sheep's, goat's, etc.) used in production is a popular practice when naming cheese. Unrestrained by regional artisanal traditions, American cheesemakers invent cheeses by mixing varieties of milk, adding flavorings, and playing with bacterial cultures. Naming new products can play a major role in distinguishing them on the market, while also conveying something to consumers about particular characteristics of the cheese. Although some cheesemakers take poetic license in naming a cheese, without familiar classificatory categories they run the risk of being confusing and insufficiently descriptive. With consumers becoming increasingly interested in where the food they eat comes from and how it is made, artisanal cheese producers can successfully promote and distinguish their cheeses from Old World varieties. See ARTISANAL.

See also GEOGRAPHICAL INDICATION.

American Cheese Society. "What's in a Name? Actually, a Lot." 13 March 2014. http://www.cheesesociety.org/wp-content/uploads/2011/02/ACS-Common-Cheese-Names.pdf.

Dalton, Matthew. "Salty Issue in U.S.—European Trade Talks: Feta Cheese." *Wall Street Journal*, 19 October 2015.

Goler Solecki, Sarah. "A Tale of Two Cheeses: Parmesan, Cheddar, and the Politics of Generic Geographical Indications (GGIs)." PhD diss., LUISS Guido Carli, 2015. http://eprints.luiss.it/1395.

Melkonan, Raffi. "The History and Future of Geographical Indicators in Europe and the United States." Third-year paper, Harvard University, 2005. https://dash.harvard.edu/handle/1/8852204.

United States Patent and Trademark Office. "Geographical Indication Protection in the United States." http://www.uspto.gov/sites/default/files/web/offices/dcom/olia/globalip/pdf/gi_system.pdf.

West, Harry G., et al. "Naming Cheese." *Food, Culture & Society* 15, no. 1 (2012): 7–41.

Marissa Sertich Velie

Nanoški sir (Nanos cheese) has been a PDO (protected designation of origin) cheese since 2011. The name *Nanoški* comes from the plateau Nanos in Vipava Valley, in southwestern Slovenia, where the first cheese production was mentioned by land registers of the Vipava manor as early as the sixteenth century. Originally this cheese was made with sheep's milk, but sheep breeding as well as cheese-making diminished in the years after World War II. In 1986 the production of Nanos cheese was revived by Vipava dairy, using milk of the autochthonous Slovenian Brown cow breed. The milk from this area is distinguished for its high content of beta-carotene, which gives the cheese an intense yellow color, and for a high content of minerals, especially calcium. See YELLOW VS. WHITE.

To make Nanoški sir, raw milk is first thermized or partially pasteurized, which means that it is heated to a temperature of 135–154°F (57–68°C) for at least fifteen seconds. Then it is partially skimmed, cooled, and left overnight to ripen. After warming to 89–93°F (32–34°C), the milk is inoculated with thermophilic starter culture and coagulated by the subsequent addition of rennet. The curd cutting, stirring, and scalding result in pea or corn-size granules. Once the curds have been drained, they are placed into molds. After a few hours of pressing and frequent turning, the cheeses are removed from their molds and brined for three days. Ripening at 83–88 percent relative humidity and 57–61°F (14–16°C) follows for at least sixty days.

Finished Nanos cheese is of a hard type, with wheels 3–4 inches (8–10 cm) high, 13.4 inches (34 cm) in diameter, and weighing about 17–22 pounds (8–10 kilograms). The rind is smooth, firm, and dry, with a yellow to brick-red color. The interior of the cheese is yellowish to intense yellow, flexible, and waxy, with no visible fractures, although a few scattered pea-size eyes are allowed. During the cheese's maturation the wheels are located in a ripening depot in the upper part of the wine-growing district of Vipava Valley, at about 500 meters above sea level. A characteristic piquant and slightly nutty taste is given to Nanos cheese by the specific microflora of the wine-growing district of Vipava Valley and by the famous north wind, called *vipavska burja*. Extended maturation of 12 months gives rise to a stronger flavor and a harder texture.

Nanoški sir GIZ. *Nanoški sir Specifikacija* [Specification for Nanos cheese]. 2013. http://www.mkgp.gov.si/fileadmin/mkgp.gov.si/pageuploads/podrocja/Varna_in_kakovostna_hrana_in_krma/zasciteni_kmetijski_pridelki/Specifikacije/NANOSKI_-_spec._junij_2013.pdf.

Andreja Čanžek Majhenič
and Petra Mohar Lorbeg

natural-rind cheeses are a category of cheeses that have self-formed rinds that develop during the aging process. The molds and microflora that develop on natural-rind cheeses are generally obtained naturally from the raw milk and aging environment used during their production. Natural-rind cheeses present the best of the cheeses for those who claim that the rind has a more intense and rich flavor than the core. On small cheeses such as Livarot, Époisses, and Munster, rinds impact the entire flavor of the cheese. Their classifications as washed, smear, hard, semihard, and mold-ripened are important features that characterize these cheeses. Diversity, density, and dynamics of their microbial communities ensure multifunctionality—flavor, color, appearance, and barriers against undesirable microorganisms. See WASHED-RIND CHEESES and BLOOMY-RIND CHEESES.

The natural cheese rind is an open ecosystem and consequently the origin of natural microbial populations is a very complex subject. Use of raw milk, traditional practices in cellar care (old-young smearing, brines, ripening of wood shelves, washing with salt water) and cellar environments (aerosols), play key roles in maintaining the natural microbial diversity. It is still a challenge to understand how the microbial community forms in these reservoirs, how they are transferred on the rinds, and why they are well adapted to the cheese rind.

More than 130 bacterial species have been inventoried in natural-rind cheeses, including lactic acid bacteria (34), Gram positive catalase bacteria (51), and Gram negative bacteria (35), in addition to yeast (31) and mold (20). This was done by combining culture dependent and high throughput sequencing technologies on cheeses including hard, semihard, soft, and, blue veined cheeses all around the world. Diversity is also assessed by the genomic diversity intraspecies, by the number of species present on one rind, and the balance between them. Density is an important feature because yeasts can reach population levels of 8 log cfu/ cm^2 and ripening bacteria more than 10 log cfu/cm^2, which has been shown on the rinds of smear-ripened and mold-ripened cheeses. Dynamic shifts qualify the rind because the balance between microbial populations changes throughout the ripening period. It is driven by the shift in environmental factors including oxygen availability, salt content increase, temperatures lower than 12°C, relative humidity change, and by microbial interactions. See MICROBIAL FLUX AND SUCCESSION and PHENOTYPIC VARIABILITY.

Lactic acid bacteria are detected throughout the ripening of cheeses. Not only starter cultures, but organisms such as Vagococcus, Carnobacterium and some halophilic bacteria such as Marinilactibacillus and Facklamia are also found in Gorgonzola blue veined cheese, soft (Havarti-type), semisoft (Tomme de Savoie), semihard (Dunbo-type, mimolette, Saint-Nectaire, Tilsit-like) and semi-dry cheeses (Raclette, Tilsit). At the beginning of ripening of Reblochon,

Gubbeen or later for Camembert, Limburger, Raclette-type cheese, Saint-Nectaire, and Tilsit cheeses, the strong growth of yeasts (Debaryomyces, Yarrowia, Candida, and Geotrichum) contributes to deacidification of the surface. This allows for the growth and control of the acid-sensitive and salt-resistant bacteria called ripening bacteria: Staphylococcus (S. equorum), Brevibacterium, and Arthrobacter. Gram negative bacteria (Proteus, Pschychrobacter) are also good colonizers with high aromatic potential on cheeses such as semihard cheeses (Gubbeen, Tilsit) and soft cheeses (Camembert, Livarot, Munster). Molds (Penicillium, Asperigillus, Mucor, Scopurialopsis) can strongly colonize the rind and are decisive for the appearance of hard cheeses (Cantal) or semihard (Reblochon Saint-Nectaire), and various Canadian cheeses. This yeast-bacteria-mold community found on most cheeses has a high metabolic activity of proteolysis, lipolysis, amino acid catabolism and fatty acid oxidation, and acts in synergy for the production of aromatic compounds. For example, volatile sulfur compounds responsible for the characteristic flavor of smear-surface ripened cheeses such as French smear cheeses (Livarot, Epoisses, Munster) results from the synergy between yeasts (Yarrowia lipolytica), Geotrichum candidum, and ripening bacteria (Brevibacterium linens).

Microbial strains have been selected for adjunct cultures to make pasteurized or raw-milk cheeses. See ADJUNCT CULTURES. But commercially selected bacterial strains added to brine or smear solutions, or spread onto the surface, are often less competitive than indigenous bacteria for colonizing the rind. Their number and diversity cannot match that of microorganisms naturally present, generating more richness and diversity in sensory properties.

See also FUNGI; MICROBIAL COMMUNITIES; and RINDS.

Irlinger F., S. Layec, S. Hélinck, E. Dugat-Bony. "Cheese Rind Microbial Communities: Diversity, Composition and Origin." FEMS Microbiology Letters 362, no. 2 (2015): 1–11.

Montel M. C., S. Buchin, A. Mallet, C. Delbes-Paus, D. Vuitton, N. Desmasures, and F. Berthier. "Traditional Cheeses: Rich and Diverse Microbiota with Associated Benefits." International Journal of Food Microbiology 177 (2014): 136–154.

Wolfe B. E., J. E. Button, M. Santarelli, and R. J. Dutton. "Cheese Rind Communities Provide Tractable Systems for In Situ and In Vitro Studies of Microbial Diversity." *Cell* 158, no. 2 (2014): 422–433.

Marie-Christine Montel

Neal's Yard Dairy is a London-based company that is widely credited with the revival of British and Irish farmhouse cheese that has taken place since the early 1980s. Founded in Neal's Yard in Covent Garden in 1979, in its early years "the Dairy" made yogurt, ice cream, and soft cheeses. Randolph Hodgson, a recent dairy science graduate brought in to manage the production, bought the business within its first year. See HODGSON, RANDOLPH.

Within a short time Hodgson had his great epiphany: that Neal's Yard Dairy was perfectly placed to bridge the gap between the last remaining British farmhouse cheesemakers and a market starved for authenticity and flavor. At the time small-scale producers of classic British cheeses were on the brink of extinction, undervalued by supermarkets that prized consistency, low prices, gimmicky flavors, and overdesigned labels. Hodgson made it the mission of the Dairy to bring British farmhouse cheeses to a wider audience and to sell them in a way that allowed customers to buy based on flavor. He traveled to farms to meet with cheesemakers and select the best batches, then conveyed those cheeses directly to his customers, offering samples to taste and helping people understand and appreciate them.

The company's work continues in much the same way to this day, and still includes selection at the farm and an emphasis on selling based upon flavor, whether in the shops or over the phone to customers around the world. Through its work as a sounding-board and a conduit for feedback to producers, the company has facilitated the development of a new generation of British cheeses including Tunworth, St. Jude, Riseley, Baron Bigod, Innes Log and Brick, Stawley, and Stichelton. See STICHELTON.

In addition to a shop around the corner from its original location in Covent Garden, Neal's Yard Dairy now has two other shops in London and a large cheese maturation facility based near Tower Bridge, from which cheeses are dispatched to a host of domestic and international customers.

See also CHEESEMONGER; CHESHIRE CHEESE (U.K.); and UNITED KINGDOM.

Neal's Yard Dairy. https://www.nealsyarddairy .co.uk.

Francis Percival

Neal's Yard Dairy cheesemongers giving customers samples of the British and Irish farmhouse cheeses on display at their Borough Market shop in London. © NEAL'S YARD DAIRY

needles are implements used in the process for making blue cheese. At the beginning of the cheese's aging period—and sometimes again later during the aging—wheels are pierced throughout with needles. This step in the cheesemaking process is commonly referred to as needling, piercing, or skewering. This process allows air to flow into the wheels to encourage the growth of *Penicillium roqueforti* or other similar mold that gives a "blue cheese" its characteristic blue veining. The piercings also create pathways for carbon dioxide to be released. See CARBON DIOXIDE and PENICILLIUM.

Piercing needles generally range from 2 to 5 millimeters in diameter. Smaller cheesemakers and home hobbyists will often pierce wheels by hand using single needles. For larger volume cheesemaking, automatic piercing machines are employed. The diameter of the needles and the number and frequency of piercings vary depending on the cheese being made.

The famous French blue Roquefort is only pierced once, approximately one week into its aging period. Gorgonzola is traditionally pierced twelve days after production and then again at twenty days. Stilton is first pierced at four weeks, nearly halfway into its aging process, and is pierced both vertically and horizontally (as opposed to cheeses that are only pierced from top to bottom). Danish Blue and Maytag Blue are each pierced within one to three days of production.

See also BLUE CHEESES.

Caldwell, Gianaclis. *Mastering Artisan Cheesemaking.* White River Junction, Vt.: Chelsea Green, 2012.
Tunick, Michael H. *The Science of Cheese.* New York: Oxford University Press, 2014.

Elena Santogade

Neolithic

See EARTHENWARE POTTERY and ORIGIN OF CHEESE.

The **Netherlands,** a country in Western Europe, is characterized by its very low position, even below sea level, in the delta of several large rivers. This geographical situation with fertile soils and a mild climate has made the Netherlands, especially its coastal regions of Holland and Friesland, a pro-

pitious location for keeping cattle. Archaeological evidence from these regions indicates a perennial tradition of cheesemaking, dating back either to 6000 or 4000 B.C.E. One of the first written accounts can be found in Julius Caesar's *De bello gallico* (ca. 57 B.C.E.).

Cheese Leaders in Terms of Productivity and Transport Expertise

For centuries Dutch cows were internationally known to be by far the most prolific in terms of milk production. Dutch livestock farming including dairy production consequently became, as early as the Middle Ages, an export product that propelled agriculture in adjacent regions, such as Denmark, Britain, and Schleswig-Holstein. Since the twelfth century the constant overflow of Dutch dairy produce was canalized via local markets. The emergence of weigh houses showed that butter and cheese were not considered as mere byproducts but as big business. Soon Dutch butter and cheese began to conquer foreign markets. In the sixteenth century the Dutch cheese trade already supplied markets in Norway, southern Netherlands, the German and Baltic regions, France, and the Iberian peninsula. By 1567 the Florentine merchant Lodovico Guicciardini in his travel account *Description of the Low Countries* waxed lyrical on the advanced state of agriculture in the Netherlands and the vital importance of dairy for its economy.

Again its geographical position in a densely populated and wealthy region at the crossroads of European trade, combined with the dense canal network in Holland and Friesland, facilitating efficient transport, substantially favored the Netherlands in becoming "the cheese storeroom of Europe." But what did the Dutch cheese tableau actually look like at the time its reputation was already established? The Netherlands was and still is known for the production of hard or semihard cheeses, based on fullcream cow's milk. The reason for this renown was quite simple: In early modern times only hard cheeses were somewhat transportable. It was the hard rind, rubbed with vinegar, beer, or salt, that made Edam cheese roll, quite literally, in impressively growing quantities onto distant markets. Local producers and politicians soon got wind of this business opportunity and pursued a strategy of upscaling by pushing the impoldering of two vast inland seas. Production

Polders are areas of the Netherlands reclaimed from the sea by draining. The soil is very fertile due to saline deposits, and the flat land is fantastic for grazing. This is Beemster Polder, a UN World Heritage Site renowned for its dairy farming. © KATE ARDING

had by that time spread far outside of Edam but the spherical cheese was already carved into collective memory. Its reputation can also be deduced from its higher taxation rate during the sixteenth century: Edam cheese was clearly more prestigious or had a bigger market volume than Gouda and Leiden cheese. In the course of the eighteenth century Edam cheese had already gone global. A special treatment based on an extract of Pernambuco wood, imported from Brazil, not only enabled transatlantic transport but en passant also bestowed a second unmistakable identifying mark. The legend of the "Dutch red balls" was born and would, allegedly, even inspire French cheesemakers to develop an orange-colored rival, the mimolette. See EDAM; GOUDA; and MIMOLETTE.

However transportability and thus omnipresence were not the only aspects that characterized pre-modern Dutch cheese culture. Quite typically Dutch cheesemakers also added spices or herbs, resulting in cumin cheese from Leiden, clove cheese from Friesland, or various green cheese types, enriched with parsley, horseradish, or even with sheep's droppings

extract. Enriching could, depending on the period, have different functions. Sometimes color served as an official hallmark to distinguish cheese qualities, but additives could also stimulate bacterial activity or, in pre-refrigeration times, enhance preservability or mask the loss of flavor, especially with skimmed cheese. Another typically Dutch habit was to export the best dairy products and to import second-choice dairy for domestic consumption. This system, which perplexed foreign observers, could only persist as long as the Dutch operated as global dairy hegemons, exporting about 11–22 million pounds (5–10 million kilograms) of cheese yearly. That was the case far into the eighteenth century, although changes in the air would soon urge the Dutch to reconsider their market strategy.

Cheese Leaders in Terms of Mass Marketing

In the course of the eighteenth century Dutch farmers already began to face a series of internal and external problems, such as rinderpest (cattle plague), trade embargos, and the rise of Gouda and Edam producers abroad. Statistics show that cheese production in North Holland continued to grow steadily between 1767–1804. However the new era confronted the Dutch peasantry with two issues: The first was how to address inconsistencies in fat content, while the second concerned the growing distinction between artisanal and industrial production. Both problems spread deep discord and were symptomatic of an inward-looking Dutch peasantry losing its momentum. See FAT; ARTISANAL; and INDUSTRIAL.

Up to 1830 both Gouda and Edam were full-cream cheeses and therefore produced twice a day by women in highly labor-intensive processes. But from 1830 onward producers increasingly switched for various reasons to the production of skimmed cheese. In addition, the first cheese factories arose in the 1870s, producing predominantly skimmed cheese. But not all producers (whether artisanal or industrial) could resist selling skimmed cheese as full-cream cheese. This triggered the so-called cheese conflict, which was only resolved by ministerial decrees between 1913 and 1919, stipulating that fat content should be measured and indicated and that only hallmarked cheese was suitable for export.

But there was a second major issue, namely that of former "apprentice" countries like Denmark, Britain, and Schleswig-Holstein, which were progressively outdoing the Dutch in terms of dairy productivity and quality. Unlike the Netherlands, butter and cheese production in those regions had already been professionalized and largely industrialized. Within just a few decades the Dutch share of the British cheese market sank from an overwhelming 63.5 percent (1860) to a startling 6.5 percent (1929).

Only in the post–World War I period would the Netherlands regain its previous position. Two factors were decisive in making Dutch cheese attractive and competitive again. An educational offensive, essentially drawing from numerous grassroots initiatives—self-supportive as peasants are—helped in identifying arrears and in defining solutions. But local and national governments turned out to be highly instrumental as well by providing the necessary infrastructure (legislation, hallmarks, hygiene standards, education and research programs, etc.).

The centralized and highly systematic marketing offensive that laid the foundations for the postwar performance was essentially conceived in the 1930s. Both the establishment of the Dutch Dairy Office

and its launch of the rather penetrant icon of the cheese maid in historical costume significantly contributed to making Dutch cheese ever more popular at national and international levels. Gouda and Edam had conquered the people's minds by morphological and chromatic virtue; the cheese maid corroborated the rock-solid reputation even more by appealing to its artisanal production (quod non). Both cheeses received a protected geographical indication (PGI) in 2010 and still form the backbone of Dutch cheese export, Gouda now representing 65 percent of Dutch production and 45 percent of its export share. However ongoing innovation also paved the way for new commercial cash cows, such as the holey cheese Maaslander, produced since the 1980s, and different types of spread cheese. Cheese based on seaweed, invented by Wageningen University in 2015, could be a future trend.

Despite such commercialization the Dutch cheese landscape still offers real jewels to attentive explorers. The farm-produced versions of Gouda and Leiden cheese or Kernhem, a reinvention of the legendary high society Meshanger (knife-sticker) dessert cheese from the nineteenth century; Rommedoe full-cream cow's milk cheese from Limburg; and sheep's milk cheese from Texel with its unique "merroir," to mention just a few examples, all testify to an increasing awareness of artisanal cheese heritage. Explorers who are keen on experiencing cheese should focus on the region Woerden-Gouda-Leiden. It is the only region where the production of farmer cheese still prevails. See FARMER CHEESE. Woerden not only hosts a historical cheese market but also provides storage to arguably the non plus ultra among Dutch cheeses. Reypenaer cheese (est. 1906) obtains its inimitable flavor during a long natural ripening process (up to two and a half years) in a unique microclimate. Last but not least the family-owned factory Boska (est. 1896) in nearby Bodegraven offers virtually all cheese tools. One could, by way of conclusion, argue that the Dutch at least learned their lesson: Today they earn a fortune by exporting their worst cheese types, which enables them to keep the best for their own consumption.

See also HOLSTEIN.

Argeloo, Marc. *Hoe de Edammer de wereld veroverde: de geschiedenis van een rond kaasje* [How Edam Cheese Conquered the World: The History of a Round Cheese]. Hoorn, Netherlands: Uniepers, 2011.

Bieleman, Jan. *Five Centuries of Farming: A Short History of Dutch Agriculture, 1500–2000.* Wageningen, Netherlands: Wageningen Academic Publishers, 2010.

Meulen, Hielke van der. *Traditionele streekproducten: gastronomisch erfgoed van Nederland* [Traditional Specialty Products: Dutch Gastronomical Heritage]. Doetinchem, Netherlands: Elsevier, 1998.

Vernooij, Aad. *Hard van binnen, rond van fatsoen: geschiedenis van de Nederlandse kaascultuur* [Hard Inside, Round Form: History of Dutch Cheese Culture]. Wormer, Netherlands: Inmerc, 1994.

Rengenier C. Rittersma

nettle (*Urtica dioica*) is a plant that was once used to create vegetarian rennet for fresh ripened (unaged or slightly cured) cheese. The rennet is made by boiling nettle in water and then stirring salt into the mixture until it dissolves. The salt releases the coagulating enzyme from the nettle, and the strained liquid becomes the rennet. Since the strength of the rennet varies from one batch to the next, it is unsuitable for commercial production. Nevertheless, the prevalence of Internet recipes for it attests to its continued use in home cheesemaking, at least for fresh cheeses. Because of its salt content, rennet made from nettle will inhibit the ripening characteristics of aged cheeses. It is used mostly as an herbal surface wrap for cheeses like St Pat from Cow Girl Creamery, in Petaluma, California, and Cornish Yarg, from Lynher Dairies Cheese Company, in Truro, West Cornwall.

St Pat is a seasonal cheese commemorating the arrival of spring and St. Patrick's Day. It is a double-cream, bloomy-rind cheese made from organic Jersey milk and finished by wrapping the cheese in wild nettle leaves from Fresh Run Farms in Bolinas, California. The leaves are frozen prior to wrapping and impart an artichoke flavor with hints of mushroom. The Cornish Yarg recipe is inspired by a thirteenth-century cheese recipe and gets its name from the maker's surname, Gray, spelled backward. The cheese is wrapped in stinging nettles, brined for eighteen hours, dried for two days, and then aged for six weeks. Its flavors are tangy and buttery with notes of citrus and mushrooms. The rinds of both St Pat and Cornish Yarg are edible and vegetarian friendly.

Nettle may do more than contribute flavor to cheese. An interesting Polish study (Kraszewski et al., 2004) showed an improvement in the nutrient intake of Holstein-Friesian dairy cows that were fed nettles combined with other herbs. The study also found improvements in milk composition, in the technological properties of milk for cheesemaking processes, and in the rheological properties of rennet-induced gels among cows fed

Cornish Yarg is an unusual nettle-wrapped cheese made by Lynher Dairies in West Cornwall, England. The nettles are not only aesthetically pleasing, they also attract naturally occurring molds and impart a mushroomy taste to the cheese as it matures. © LYNHER DAIRIES

the nettle mixture. The study concluded that herbal additives in dairy cows' food could improve feed intake, composition of milk, and technological properties for cheesemaking.

Kraszewski, J., A. Strzetelski, and B. Niwińska. "Effects of Dietary Herb Supplements for Cows on Feed Conversion, Milk Yield, and Technological Quality of Milk." Poster presentation at the European Association for Animal Production, Session C6.9, Bled, Slovenia, 8 September 2004.
"St Pat." Cowgirl Creamery. https://www.cowgirlcreamery.com/library-of-cheese/st-pat.

David Gremmels

Neufchâtel is a soft white cheese with a molded rind from the village of Neufchâtel-en-Bray in Normandy. It is one of the oldest cheeses in France as it was first mentioned in a charter in 1037. Legend has it that its famous heart shape originated during the Hundred Years' War (1337–1453), when young farm girls who befriended the English occupiers decided to send heart-shaped cheeses to England to show their love for the English soldiers. In 1936 a decree for the first time defined the acceptable sizes and formats of Neufchâtel cheese. Among them are mentioned the "bonde," "double bonde," the "briquette," and "square," but the "heart" was rare in the early twentieth century. It became more common later, and especially at the beginning of the twenty-first century when it was the emblematic shape for Neufchâtel.

A lactic soft cheese with surface mold and the flavor of raw cow's milk, Neufchâtel has been an AOC (appellation d'origine contrôlée) traditional product since 1969 and obtained the PDO (protected designation of origin) label in 1996. The production process includes a specific curd-draining phase prior to molding. Curd is put in cloth bags and drained between twelve to twenty-four hours, then mixed with salt and molded in the shape of the six authorized shapes (bonde, double bonde, square, briquette, heart, big heart). While it is still young (twelve to fifteen days) it can accompany cider or white wine, while its slightly salty taste means it can be paired with numerous sweet and savory combinations. Between one to three months spent maturing in a ripening room will develop a more mature and stronger taste profile, enhancing the flavors of more powerful wines. The rind will develop red stains, and texture will evolve and become creamier. Ideal in a sauce, Neufchâtel also enhances tarts and desserts.

See also CAMEMBERT DE NORMANDIE; CREAM CHEESE; and NORMANDY.

Janier, Christian. *Le fromage.* Lyon, France: Editions Stéphane Bachès, 2014.

Jean-Louis Bloquel

New York State saw the introduction of dairy farming and cheesemaking in the early seventeenth century, when Dutch settlers began claiming Native American lands in the Hudson, Connecticut, and Delaware River valleys—a region they called New Netherland. The first shipment of cattle (which are not indigenous to the Americas) arrived in 1625; by 1631 milk, butter, and cheese were being produced in Rensselaerswyck Manor (near present day Albany); and a 1656 edict lists cheese as a principal commodity brought to market in the capital, New Amsterdam (now New York City). The city also hosted regular livestock fairs, facilitating trade and cross-breeding with other European cattle varieties, including Devons from Connecticut and Massachusetts, which were considered ideal for breeding with the local Holland bulls. Production was handled primarily by farmstead women, who made Schmierkase or pot cheese as well as spheres compressed by hand, aged, and sliced into thin rounds that were eaten with bread.

English-style cheesemaking became predominant after the British took control of the region in 1664, and production remained artisanal through the eighteenth century. A cheese press was first used in Hindsdale, New York, in 1807; by the 1820s, Herkimer County gained recognition for its distinctive Herkimer method of production, which was openly shared with any who sought to learn it. Stressing order and cleanliness, its widespread adoption resulted in superior-quality cheeses while promoting the concept of standardization. See CHEESE PRESS and STANDARDIZATION.

By 1851 New York was producing 50 million pounds of cheese per year, all on individual farms; that same year, the world's first cheese factory opened in Rome, New York, featuring innovative techniques and machinery (willfully never patented) while supporting a system of associative dairying. See WILLIAMS, JESSE. Milk from numerous local farms was collected and blended to produce consistent, more marketable large wheels; farmers were repaid in shares of cheese equal to their milk contribution, with a share also going to the factory. Within fifteen years New York had 425 cheese factories. A renowned Monday market established in Little Falls, New York, in the 1860s attracted buyers from as far as Boston, Baltimore, and Philadelphia and set prices for the entire Northeast. A good part of the state's production was exported to England well into the nineteenth century.

Multiple small factories throughout New York once produced a distinctive, widely appreciated, old-style sharp Cheddar also known as "Yankee cheese" or "store cheese"; every grocer in the Northeast kept a wheel of it, unrefrigerated, on the counter where it was cut and sold by the pound. After World War II its production declined and eventually ceased as small factories were pushed out of business by corporations. Today, the state remains a leading producer of industrial dairy products, including yogurt, cream cheese, ricotta, mozzarella, and other "old world" traditions brought by European immigrants. Artisanal production, including the use of sheep and goat milk, was revived in the 1980s by a handful of farmstead dairies; by 2014 New York could count more than forty small-scale makers who are cognizant of terroir and favor raw milk as the vehicle for expressing geographic variation.

See also UNITED STATES.

Behr, Edward. *Looking for Old-Fashioned Cheddar.* Theme issue, *The Art of Eating* 39 (1996).
DeVoe, Thomas F. *The Market Book.* New York: Printed for the author, 1862.
Stamm, Eunice R. *The History of Cheese Making in New York State.* Endicott, N.Y.: E. R. Stamm, 1991.

Robert LaValva

Njeguški

Njeguški is a Montenegrin autochthonous full-fat hard cheese. The original production area is the peripheral areas of the Lovćen mountains and the Adriatic Sea coastline. The center of production historically and today is the village Njeguški, where mountain and Mediterranean climates collide. This collision has an effect on the herbal composition of pastures, milk quality, and ripening conditions, which gives the cheese its piquancy.

During the Roman Empire, Rome was supplied with the cheese Caseus doclestes. Since Doclea was an old state that existed in what is present-day Montenegro, it is assumed that this cheese is an ancestor of Njeguški cheese. Heinrich Stieglitz, in his travelogue *Ein Besuch auf Montenegro* (1841), commented that he was served with extremely tasty cheese during his visit to Njeguški.

The original Njeguški cheese is produced from sheep's milk. Rennet is added to the fresh milk after milking, at a temperature of 90–95°F (32–35°C). Coagulation is forty-five to sixty minutes. After forming, the curd is cut to the size of walnuts, and after five minutes of resting, to the size of corn grains. Cheese curd is formed in gradually heated whey up to 113°F (45°C). The curd has to be formed by hand in the whey until it gains a globular shape. This phase lasts fifteen to twenty minutes. Formed curd is placed in cheesecloth, then in a cheese mold and pressed. Pressing is carried out with a wooden circular plank with a stone added on top. After twenty-four hours of pressing, the cheese is removed from the mold, salted with dry salt, and placed in a wooden box. The cheese stays in this box for two days and is salted two to three times, then it ripens on dry wooden shelves. Ripening on the shelves lasts at least four weeks, and after that the cheese is ready for consumption. See WOODEN SHELVES.

Ripened Njeguški cheese may be exposed to smoke for a few days or dipped into olive oil where it matures from 90 to 150 days. Longer ripening and ripening in olive oil gives the cheese a more piquant taste. The finished product has a low cylindrical shape, a weight of 2 to 7 pounds (1–3 kilograms), compact surface, golden-yellow crust, closed structure with a few eyes, and a pleasant, slightly sour-milky and moderately salty aroma.

Adžić, N., et al. "Higijenska ispravnost njeguškog sira" [Hygenic Quality of Njeguški Cheese]. *Agriculture and Forestry* 41, nos. 1–4 (1995): 99–104.
Dozet, N., et al. *Autohtoni mlječni proizvodi* [Autochthonous Dairy Products]. Belgrade, Serbia: Poljoprivredni institut Podgorica, SILMIR-Beograd, 1996.
Mirecki, S., et al. "Mikrobiološki i hemijski kvalitet njeguškog sira" [Microbiological and Chemical Quality of Njeguški Cheese]. *Agriculture and Forestry* 43, no. 3 (1997): 117–125.

Slavko Mirecki

non-starter lactic acid bacteria

non-starter lactic acid bacteria (NSLAB) are spontaneous, lactic acid bacteria that are not deliberately added but are commonly present in cheese. They are detected in high numbers in most ripened cheeses, including some pasteurized milk cheeses. NSLAB may come from milk, especially when raw milk is used, but also from the environment of dairy plants. They are thus "natural" contaminants of cheese. It is difficult to eliminate them by hygienic measures because some NSLAB strains can survive milk pasteurization, whereas others survive in the cheese plant and contaminate milk after pasteurization. Even at the laboratory scale, it is a challenge to manufacture experimental cheeses without NSLAB. The best way to prevent the growth of "natural" NSLAB is to inoculate the cheese with adjunct cultures that can exert a barrier effect against them. See ADJUNCT CULTURES and HYGIENE.

NSLAB grow during the ripening phase, even in the absence of residual lactose, and the substrates they use as carbon and energy sources are still debated. Some NSLAB use milk citrate, and others use the ribose that may be released from nucleic acids when starters die and lyse. Amino acids can also be used as carbon sources. The main NSLAB species are mesophilic facultatively heterofermentative lactobacilli, members of the group of *Lactobacillus casei* or *lactobacillus paracasei,* and *lactobacillus rhamnosus.* Many other NSLAB species, however, have been described in cheese, including other facultatively heterofermentative species of lactobacilli (*L. plantarum, L. pentosus, L. curvatus,* etc.), some obligately heterofermentative species of lactobacilli (*L. fermentum, L. buchneri, L. parabuchneri, L. brevis,* etc.), and species of *pediococci* and *enterococci.*

When present in high numbers, NSLAB can participate in cheese ripening because of their enzymatic activities. They can exert a positive or negative effect on cheese flavor, or have only a neutral presence, as shown in many research works that have led to apparently conflicting results. The impact of NSLAB on cheese properties depends on their population level—below a million cells per gram of cheese, they will hardly have any influence, but this depends also on the type of cheese and the species and strains present. They can contribute to the main biochemical reactions occurring during cheese ripening, such as proteolysis and the conversion of the peptides and amino acids produced by proteolysis into flavor compounds, thus increasing cheese flavor. The presence of NSLAB that have a heterofermentative metabolism and produce ethanol as end products of fermentation is often associated with changes in the flavor in hard and semihard cheeses because of a concomitant increase of the formation of ethyl esters. These flavor compounds can be associated with expected or undesirable "fruity" or "fermented" flavors, depending on the variety of cheese. Heterofermentative NSLAB produce carbon dioxide and can be responsible for undesirable formation of holes or slits. The metabolism of some NSLAB such as *enterococci* can also result in the formation of biogenic amines in cheese, impairing cheese quality. Finally, NSLAB may exert indirect effects on cheese quality via interactions with other cheese microorganisms. For example, the growth of NSLAB in Swiss cheese has been shown to slow the growth of *Propionibacterium freudenreichii,* a species used as a ripening culture to form the typical holes present in this type of cheese.

See also FLAVOR; LACTIC ACID; and LACTIC ACID BACTERIA.

Beresford, Tom. "What Are Non-Starter Lactic Acid Bacteria and How Do They Affect Cheese Quality?" In *Cheese Problems Solved,* edited by P. L. H. McSweeney, pp. 124–130. Cambridge, U.K.: Woodhead, 2007.
Settanni, Luca, and Giancarlo Moschetti. "Non-Starter Lactic Acid Bacteria Used to Improve Cheese Quality and Provide Health Benefits." *Food Microbiology* 27 (September 2010): 691–697.

Anne Thierry

Noord-Hollandse Edammer

See EDAM.

Noord-Hollandse Gouda

See GOUDA.

The **Normande** is a breed of cow developed in Normandy, France, with a distinctive hide of cream, rust-brown and dark-brown spots, and (ideally) "glasses," dark rings around the eyes. The breed emerged in the late nineteenth century by crossing regional Cotentine and Augeronne breeds (themselves crosses of cows from Brittany, Jersey, Guernsey, the Netherlands, and Great Britain) with the meaty Durham breed. The resulting hardy, multipurpose

Normande thrives on rough forage while producing top-quality milk for cheesemaking and a good carcass yield with well-marbled meat (not to mention being a work animal before tractors). The breed averages 14,000 pounds (6350 kilograms) of milk per lactation, 4.4 percent fat and 3.6 percent protein; the high percentage of beta and kappa caseins in their milk improves curdling rates and, in combination with other attributes, contributes to a 15 percent higher yield per volume compared to average milk.

Normande milk was historically the primary milk for cheesemaking in Normandy. Pressures to increase productivity and "modernize" farms in the latter half of the twentieth century pushed Normandes into a minority (40 percent of dairy cows in Normandy in 2010), obliging the cheese producers' associations to make Normande milk an explicit requirement for appellation d'origine contrôlée (AOC) cheese production in the early 2000s. See APPELLATION D'ORIGINE CONTRÔLÉE. These requirements are to be phased in to give farmers time to gradually convert their herds from more productive and socially valued breeds: Livarot will be made with 100 percent Normande milk by 2017, Pont L'Evêque must be 50 percent by 2017, Camembert de Normandie 50 percent by 2020, and Neufchatel must be at least 60 percent Normande milk.

See also CAMEMBERT DE NORMANDIE; COW; LIVAROT; NEUFCHÂTEL; and NORMANDY.

Bertaux, Jean-Jacques, and Jean-Marie Levesque, eds. *La Vache et L'Homme*. Caen, France: Musée de Normandie—Editions Maît'Jacques, 1997.

Juliette Rogers

Normandy

Normandy is a lush, flat, maritime region of northern France where cows graze beneath apple trees on nutritious and abundant grasses. Their milk is rich, the cheeses made from them even more so, making Normandy the premier French region for soft cheeses, butter, and cream production. Fifteen percent of the milk in France is produced and transformed in Normandy.

Normandy has long been a premier dairy region—the first mention of dairy activity in Normandy was recorded in 911 B.C.E. The following Norman cheeses, which were first recorded in the eleventh century, all have protected designation of origin status, and are required to be made with milk from the Norman cow. See APPELLATION D'ORIGINE CONTRÔLÉE and NORMANDE.

- Camembert de Normandie: Marie Harel, a country cheesemaker who lived near the town of Camembert, is the reputed inventor of the Camembert in 1791, though historical evidence that she actually did so remains elusive. See CAMEMBERT DE NORMANDIE and HAREL, MARIE.
- Livarot, made in and around the town of Livarot, is also called "le colonel" for the five bands of raffia that encircle each cheese. See LIVAROT.
- Pont-l'Évêque, made in and around the town of Pont l'Évêque, follows the same fabrication procedures as Livarot, except that it is made in a square mold. See PONT L'ÉVÊQUE.
- Neufchâtel is the most distinctive Norman cheese, and the oldest on record, dating to well before the Hundred Years' War. It differs from the other Norman cheeses in that the curds are whipped before being put in molds, giving it a more firm, less elastic and creamy texture. See NEUFCHÂTEL.

See also FRANCE.

Androuet, Pierre. *The Complete Encyclopedia of French Cheese (and Many Other Continental Varieties)*. New York: Harper's Magazine Press, 1976.
Rance, Patrick. *The French Cheese Book*. London: Macmillan, 1989.

Susan Herrmann Loomis

Norway

Norway, a Scandinavian country, has a food culture that has been closely associated with the civilization of milk and butter since the time of the Vikings (around 1000 C.E.), in contrast to the culinary centrality of wine and oil in the south of Europe. In the twenty-first century dairy products, especially cheese, still play a major role in Norwegian food habits. Norwegian cheese is divided between industrially made and traditional farmhouse-made cheeses. Industrially made hard cheeses are standardized and predominate and are well integrated into the structure of everyday meals, especially breakfast and lunch. While traditional farmhouse cheeses are making a comeback they are mostly eaten during the weekend or on special occasions.

This Gamalost, a pungent Norwegian sour skimmed-milk cheese, was made by Maria Ballhaus of Sogn Jord og Hagebruksskule. It won the gold medal at the 2009 National Farmhouse Cheese Show in Mære, Norway. OVE FOSSÅ

Since the Middle Ages traditional cheesemaking in the region produced whey cheeses made from the skimmed sour milk of cows. Since the end of the nineteenth century, however, modern industrial cheesemaking has produced standardized cheeses that have definitively been the favorite of Norwegian eaters, with a per person annual consumption of such cheese in 2015 of around 31 pounds (14 kilograms). The everyday cheeses commonly consumed by Norwegians today include hard yellow cow's milk cheeses, such as Norvegia or Jarlsberg, and "brown cheese," a caramelised whey cheese made from goat's or cow's milk. See CONCENTRATED WHEY CHEESE. They are the fruits of the consolidation and standardization of the dairy system in Norway after World War II, when milk was no longer used on the farm but sent to the national cooperative. From that period, the consolidation of numerous local brands and products to a very few national brands eventually offered Norwegian consumers mass-produced cheeses. The most widely consumed cheese today is an industrial hard cheese inspired by Dutch Gouda and produced in Norway since the end of the nineteenth century, called Norvegia. As reflected in its name, this is has been "the" archetype of Norwegian cheese for more than a century.

A number of economic structures, quotas, and regulations made the production of farmhouse cheese almost impossible until the 1990s, when the new agricultural landscape encouraged emphasizing quality over quantity, giving farmhouse cheeses a newly added value. As elsewhere across Europe and the Americas, since the beginning of the twenty-first century there has been a renaissance, or even a "naissance," of Norwegian farmhouse cheeses as well as increasing importation and consumption of foreign cheeses (still under 11 pounds [5 kilograms] per person in total). Both Gamalost frå Vik and Skjørost fra Røros were traditional artisanal whey cheeses made until the middle of the twentieth century, when they were centralized in one local dairy. They received protected geographical indications a few years after a 2002 Norwegian law was passed on the protection of geographical indications and designations of origin for agricultural products and foodstuffs. See GEOGRAPHICAL INDICATIONS.

While the central industrial dairy Tine still dominates the dairy market both in distribution and production with more than 1,542 million quarts (1,460 million liters) of milk a year, today's farmhouse cheesemakers have organized together through the Norsk Gardsost (Norwegian Farm Cheese), a nationwide organization for Norwegian craft and farm dairy founded in 1997. The reintroduction of speciality food products into the market is no simple task, however, and so relatively few artisanal cheeses are currently produced, marketed, and consumed in Norway, despite twenty years of governmental support for them. The Sognefjord Artisanal Geitost, a caramelised brown cheese of raw goat's milk, became a Slow Food Presidium in 2005, emphasizing the struggle between farmstead cheesemakers and authorities about the forbidden use of raw milk. See SOGNEFJORD ARTISANAL GEITOST and SLOW FOOD.

In November 2015 the headline, "White Mould cheese 'Mild Master' from the farm dairy Tingvollost Nordmøre, won one of the most prestigious awards at the World Cheese Awards in the UK," was a media sensation for Norwegian cheese lovers, as this type of award was both new and unfamiliar in the land of standardized cheeses. Today there are more than one hundred farm cheesemakers in

Norway, producing several hundred types from the most traditional to the most innovative, including the Tingvollost that in 2015 was named "best in the world" by the World Cheese Awards in the United Kingdom. Norwegian cheeses are entering a new era, when both "old" and "new" farmhouse cheeses are becoming increasingly visible and progressively more culturally and economically significant.

See also DENMARK; JARLSBERG; and SWEDEN.

Anderson, Nina. "Mild Mester til topps blant verdens beste oster." *VG Forbruker*, 30 November 2015.
Amilien, Virginie, and Erling Krog. *Den kultiverte maten* (The Cultivated Food). Bergen, Norway: Fagbokforlaget, 2007.
Flandrin, Jean-Louis, and Massimo Montanari. *Histoire de l'alimentation*. Paris: Editions Fayard, 1996.
Fosså, Ove. "How Old Is Old Cheese? Gamalost in Coffin-shaped Boxes and Eccentric Jars." In *Milk: Beyond the Dairy*, edited by Harlan Walker. Totnes, U.K.: Prospect, 2000.
Matmerk. About Protected Designations. http://www.matmerk.no/no/beskyttedebetegnelser/om-beskyttede-betegnelser.
Opplysningskontoret for Meieriprodukter. Dairy statistics 2015. http://www.melk.no/melk-og-meierifakta/meieristatistikk.
Slow Food. "Sognefjord Artisanal Geitost." http://www2.slowfood.no/docs/geitost_ENG.pdf.

Virginie Amilien

Nostrano Valtrompia is a medium-fat and very hard Italian PDO cheese, produced throughout the year from raw cow's milk with the addition of saffron. The milk comes from the Brown Swiss breed for at least 90 percent of the total production. See BROWN SWISS. The remaining 10 percent can come from other breeds or hybrids. The summer production represents about 10 percent of the total production. The weight of the cheese varies from 18 to 40 pounds (8–18 kilograms), and it has a cylindrical shape with flat sides, a diameter between 12 and 18 inches (30–45 centimeters), and a height of 3–5 inches (8–12 centimeters). The minimum aging period is twelve months, at the end of which the side of the cheese is marked by fire brand for identification. The rind and texture are hard and the interior color is straw yellow tending toward yellowish green.

In the first days after manufacture, the dry salting is done by hand on the entire cheese and during the aging the cheese is routinely turned over, and the sides are rasped and rubbed with linseed oil. The addition of saffron in small quantity during the coagulation improves the color and texture of the cheese; otherwise, for reasons having to do with the partial skimming of milk and the cows' diet, it would tend toward greener shades. The production and aging area includes the municipality of Brescia Province in the Trompia Valley and Gussago, the hamlet of Quarone and Civine.

Cheese production in the Trompia Valley is documented as early as 1484 and continues today, with the practice of transhumance from the valley to the mountain pastures. It is a continuation of a centuries-old tradition, characteristic of a lifestyle that developed in regions with irregular and difficult terrain, where the only way to survive was to exploit the resources of the mountain, the subsoil, forests, meadows, and pastures, and medium and high mountains. Cheese was the basis for the creation of mountain communities that succeed in overcoming seemingly insurmountable difficulties caused by isolation and poverty of resources. See TRANSHUMANCE.

Today just under fifty dairy farms arrayed on twenty mountain pastures produce Nostrano Valtrompia, with a total production of around 130 quintal of cheeses. These dairy farms also produce Nostrano in the bottom of the valley.

See also ITALY.

"Censimento Alpeggi anno 2000 Regione Lombardia / Comunità Montana Valle Trompia." Author: AA.VV. Editor: Cassa Rurale ed Artigiana di Bovegno Editore, 2000.
Production Specifications. http://www.nostrano-valtrompia.it/file/disciplinare.pdf

Carlo Fiori

The **Nubian** dairy goat descends from Asian, African, and European ancestors and was first imported into the United States in 1906. The Nubian has an exotic look due to its convex nose and long ears that hang wide, pendulous, and well below its mouth. Its hair is short and glossy and comes in every color, solid and patterned. Nubians are one of the largest breeds of dairy goats, standing 30 inches (76 centimeters) at the withers (shoulders) and weighing

The Nubian dairy goat has an exotic look due to its convex nose and long ears that hang wide, pendulous, and longer than the nose. © REDWOOD HILL FARM

134 pounds (61 kilograms) or more. Today the Nubian is one of the most popular breeds of dairy goats in the United States, with the highest number of animal registrations held by the American Dairy Goat Association (ADGA).

Nubian milk is prized for cheesemaking because of its high butterfat and solids content, which results in a higher cheese yield, even though the average milk volume per animal is lower than it is from other goat breeds. Many farmstead cheesemakers use Nubians for their cheese production because they do well in smaller herds and are renowned for their pet-like personalities. As a whole, they tend to be able to breed and kid with greater flexibility within the typical seasonal calendar of dairy goats. Nubians are also the most prolific in their offspring, with three to four kids per gestation not uncommon.

See also GOAT.

Considine, Stephen. "The Straight Scoop on Nubians." *United Caprine News*, April 2010.
Pegler, Henry Stephen Holmes. *The Book of the Goat.* London: "The Bazaar" Office, 1884.

Jennifer Bice

O'Banon

See AMERICAN "GOAT LADIES"; CAPRIOLE; and LEAF-WRAPPED CHEESES.

odor-active compounds are volatile substances that contribute to aroma and therefore flavor. Although hundreds of volatiles have been identified in cheese, only a few dozen at most play a role in the flavor of any particular variety.

Gas chromatography-olfactometry is the technique commonly used in the laboratory to determine the identities of odor-active compounds as well as the aromas that correspond to them. In this method, volatiles are released from a specimen and directed into the instrument (a gas chromatograph), where they are separated, detected, and finally sniffed by a researcher as they exit. Classes of compounds that contain odor-active volatiles found in cheese include alcohols, aldehydes, esters, fatty acids, methyl ketones, other ketones, lactones, nitrogen- and sulfur-containing compounds, and terpenes. The volatile compounds of Cheddar cheese have been extensively identified. Cheddar has been found to contain the ketones acetone (odor of wood pulp), 2-butanone (butterscotch), 2-pentanone (orange peel), 1-octen-3-one (analogous to the alcohol 1-octen-3-ol, with an odor of mushroom), beta-damascenone (applesauce), 2,3-butanedione (butter), p-cresol (cow or barn), butanal (pungent), and acetoin (sour milk), among hundreds of other active compounds. The fatty acids that contribute to Cheddar flavor (along with their odor descriptors) include propionic (burnt), butyric (cheesy), valeric (various odors), isovaleric (Swiss cheese), caproic (various odors), caprylic (sweaty), capric (stale butter), lauric (soapy), and phenylacetic (rosy) acids. Aldehydes are commonly perceived as smelling like cut grass, malt, or soap. Esters provide floral, fruity, and sweet notes, and lactones impart coconut and peach aromas. Nitrogen-containing compounds are responsible for earthy and barn-like odors, and sulfur-containing compounds convey onion and garlic aromas. Milk from animals on forage often contains terpenes that contribute pine and floral odors to cheese. Nearly all odor-active compounds are soluble in fat but not in water, so the higher the fat content of the milk, the more flavorful the cheese is likely to be.

See also AROMA; FAT; and FLAVOR.

Curioni, P. M. G., and J. O. Bosset. "Key Odorants in Various Cheese Types as Determined by Gas Chromatography-Olfactometry." *International Dairy Journal* 12 (2002): 959–984.

Singh, T. K., M. A. Drake, and K. R. Cadwallader. "Flavor of Cheddar Cheese: A Chemical and Sensory Perspective." *Comprehensive Reviews in Food Science and Food Safety* 2 (2003): 166–189.

Michael Tunick

Odyssey

See HOMER.

oil-marinated cheeses use oil to preserve the cheese while adding flavor from different oil types—olive oil, grape seed, and sunflower—and infusions of dried flowers, herbs, vegetables, or spices.

Thousands of years before refrigeration, in the ancient lands of Greece, olive oil was used to protect cheese from spoilage. The most recognized example is the mixed goat's and sheep's milk or pure sheep's milk Ladotyri cheese. The translation of the name of this regionally protected cheese is "oil cheese," and it is produced only on the islands of Lesvos in the northern Aegean Sea and Zakynthos in the Ionian Sea. The key difference between Lesvos and Zakynthos Ladotyri production is that Lesvos is dipped in oil as it ages, while Zakynthos is submerged in olive oil during the full ripening period. See LADOTYRI MYTILINIS.

Another excellent cheese submerged in oil is the Italian fresh cow's milk cheese Piedmontese Tomini. Tomini is a creamy white cheese that has clean lactic acid flavor that is mellowed through submersion in safflower or sunflower oils and herbs. Traditionally used in antipasto dishes, you will find this cheese layered into large glass bowls that are showcased on top of store counters.

When entire pieces of cheese are marinated in oil, the oil will soak into every crevice. As the cheese marinates and ages, the flavor will increase, creating a unique blend of flavor and texture. Oil acts as a natural preservative that creates a barrier from oxygen, delaying spoilage and oxidation. Oil-marinated cheeses must be properly stored in a cool dark storage area in order to prolong shelf life; refrigeration is recommended for food safety preservation. Food grade oils can last from a few months to a few years in an airtight container, preferably of tinted glass to protect the oil-marinated cheese from light oxidation.

Creating your own personalized, marinated cheese in oil is easy. First obtain a sterile, rubber-sealed canning jar, then select your favorite cheese and couple it with food grade oil that has good taste, color, and viscosity and is free from impurities. Place the cheese in the oil, along with your choice of seasonings. Make sure all ingredients are fully submerged under the top layer of oil for proper preservation. Lastly let your oil-marinated cheese rest for at least three days for optimal flavor development, in the refrigerator for food safety. After refrigeration the oil will congeal; let your marinade warm to room temperature before serving. It's important to note that oils flavored with various ingredients may become rancid and oxidize sooner than oil with no other additives. Cheese preserved in good food grade oil with no other additives will have a longer shelf life. Favorite dishes to crown with oil-marinated cheeses include pastas, risottos, pizzas, eggs, popcorn, chips, and french fries.

"How Long Does Oil Last?" Eat By Date. http://www.eatbydate.com/other/condiments/how-long-does-oil-last/.

Kochilas, Diane. "Ladotyri," 12 March 2013. http://www.dianekochilas.com/ladotyri-cheese-preserved-in-olive-oil.

Jill E. Allen

Oldways Preservation and Exchange Trust

(Oldways) is a nonprofit food and nutrition educational organization with a mission of inspiring good health by promoting culinary traditions and lifestyles. Founded in 1990 by K. Dun Gifford, Oldways has been a prominent advocate for traditional cuisines, sustainable agriculture, and nutritional science. Some of its signature accomplishments include developing the well-known Mediterranean Diet Pyramid in 1993 with the Harvard School of Public Health; developing healthy-eating guides reflecting Latin American, Asian, African, and vegetarian culinary traditions; founding the Chefs Collaborative to bring chefs together in support of local foods and sustainable farming; forming the Whole Grains Council and developing the Whole Grain Stamp, which as of 2015 was found on more than ten thousand food products in forty-five countries; and organizing the Cheese of Choice Coalition.

The Cheese of Choice Coalition (CCC) was founded in 1999 to protect American consumers' rights to consume, and producers' rights to sell, cheese made from unpasteurized milk. At that time, US regulatory challenges threatened to outlaw this staple of many European cuisines. A collaboration among Oldways, the American Cheese Society, the Cheese Importers Association of America, and Whole Foods Market, the CCC successfully defended this time-honored style of cheese. After a decade of dormancy, the CCC was revitalized in 2014 in response to an unfavorable regulatory climate that continues to challenge the legal status of raw-milk cheese and other traditional cheesemaking practices in the United States. Through a combination of advocacy, education, consumer outreach, and community engagement, the CCC continues to support consumers' rights to enjoy their cheese of choice.

Gifford, K. Dun, and Sara Baer-Sinnott. *The Oldways Table: Essays and Recipes from the Culinary Think Tank.* Berkeley, Calif.: Ten Speed, 2007.

Oldways Whole Grains Council. "Whole Grains Statistics." http://wholegrainscouncil.org/newsroom/whole-grain-statistics.

Bradley M. Jones

The **olha** is a pastoral institution in the French Basque province of Soule in southwestern France. In Basque, *olha* denotes both a mountain hut and a cheesemaking syndicate of shepherds who use the hut during the period of summer transhumance. Until recently, syndicate members combined their flocks of sheep in late May, took them to the high pastures along the Franco-Spanish border, and made cheese in the hut until mid-September. In the 1970s, the hut was an exclusively male domain, and cheesemaking was a male activity. The number of active shepherds in the ten syndicates operating in one mountain community (Sainte-Engrâce) varied from four to eighteen. Their amalgamated flocks ranged from 300 to nearly 1,400 ewes. Shepherds rotated between the hut and their farms in the valley. The order of their rotation was fixed so that each shepherd spent the same number of days in the hut and made exactly the same number of highly prized "mountain cheeses." The olha and its cheesemaking practices provided an institutionalized, egalitarian domain for male camaraderie. No syndicates still operate in the traditional way, however, owing to rural depopulation and apathy among young men for the vocation of their fathers and forefathers. No one in Sainte-Engrâce makes mountain cheese any longer. Certain striking transformations have taken place. One household now has exclusive use of the pasturage belonging to its olha, in which no other members remain active. With four hundred ewes on separate lactating cycles, the household uses the hut as a resting place but makes cheese in the farmhouse during eleven months of the year. Contrary to local tradition, the principal cheesemaker is female. She will inherit the house and business enterprise. The olha, as an institution, has fallen into disuse. Boar hunting has taken its place as the focus of male camaraderie.

See also BASQUE; GENDER; and TRANSHUMANCE.

Ott, Sandra. *The Circle of Mountains: A Basque Shepherding Community*. Reno: University of Nevada Press, 1993.

Sandra Ott

Ontario, Canada's most populous province, is its second-largest cheese-producing region after neighboring Quebec, accounting for about a third of the country's overall cheese production by weight. Specialty cheeses (a category that excludes Cheddar, mozzarella, processed, cottage, and pizza cheese) make up almost half of Ontario's production—a larger proportion than any other province—while Cheddar alone represents roughly 35 percent of the total cheese. See CHEDDAR and SPECIALTY CHEESE.

Ontario's cheesemaking dates from the arrival of European settlers, who brought livestock with them from Europe. While French colonists typically made softer, creamier cheeses, the British brought their traditional Cheddar-making techniques with them to the New World. The high quality of available pastures and agricultural land encouraged the establishment of a strong dairy tradition, especially in the southern part of the province. In the middle of the nineteenth century the devastation caused by the wheat midge as well as a drop in wheat markets encouraged numerous farmers to convert to dairy operations. As there was neither refrigeration nor rapid transportation for fluid milk, much of the milk produced was destined to become farmstead cheese, a more stable and often safer product than fresh milk. See FARMSTEAD.

Canada's first cooperative cheese factory, The Pioneer, was founded in 1864 by entrepreneur Harvey Farrington in Ontario's southern county of Oxford. Two years later a "Mammoth Cheese" weighing 7,300 pounds (3,311 kilograms) was created in nearby Ingersoll to celebrate the county's growing industry. More than 2,400 cows worked to produce the required 35 tons of milk. After three months of aging, the colossal cheese was shipped to New York State, then to England and Europe, to showcase the region's expertise in industrial dairying.

Hundreds of commercial operations opened their doors during the following decades, a sign that cheesemaking was definitively moving from the farmstead to the factory. Southern Ontario became a major exporter of cheese—mainly Cheddar—with 234 million pounds (106 million kilograms) shipped abroad in 1904. Cheddar was the province's second most important export product after timber, and accounted for close to 70 percent of the British Empire's import demand. As the 1,200 factories operating at the turn of the century refined their technology and patented new methods, the region (and Canada more generally) became mainly associated with industrial cheeses. Through most of the twentieth century this reality was embodied perhaps most eloquently in the increasing popularity of processed products and Kraft Dinner macaroni and cheese, the brainchildren of Ontario-born James Lewis Kraft's eponymous corporation. The young entrepreneur, who grew up on an Ontario dairy farm close to the American border before launching his business in Chicago, was the first to obtain a patent for processed cheese in 1916. Half a century later, at the height of its power, Kraft Foods Inc. controlled close to 50 percent of the total production of Canadian cheese. See INDUSTRIAL; KRAFT FOODS; PASTEURIZED PROCESS CHEESES; and MAC AND CHEESE.

However, toward the end of the twentieth century, a renewed interest in artisanal cheeses paved the way for the establishment of small-scale operations. Capitalizing on the trend, in 2006 the professional organization Dairy Farmers of Ontario launched an Artisan Cheese Program (later renamed the Artisan Dairy Program to reflect its broadening focus) to encourage the resurrection and diversification of the artisanal cheese sector and to assist small-scale producers using traditional methods. Today a large variety of artisanal cheeses are crafted in Ontario; the Canadian Dairy Information Center lists over a hundred farmstead or artisan cheeses produced throughout the province. Sixteen percent of artisanal cheeses are made from raw milk. Ewe's milk products account for about 40 percent of the entries, followed by goat's milk cheeses and then cow's milk cheeses, which constitute close to a quarter of entries. Inversely the vast majority of the 190 cheeses registered as industrially produced are made using cow's milk. Five of them, manufactured by Quality Cheese Inc. and commercialized under the brand Albert's Leap, use buffalo milk. See ARTISANAL.

Ontario cheeses are regularly acclaimed in competitions at home and abroad. In 2013 the Lankaaster Aged Loaf, a Gouda-type cheese crafted by Glengarry Fine Cheese, was named Supreme Global Champion at the Global Cheese Awards. The same dairy's Celtic Blue Reserve was crowned Best of the Show at the 2015 American Cheese Society Judging and Competition. Many domestic and international cheese events are also held in the province. The British Empire Cheese Show, hosted by the Central Ontario Cheesemaker Association, is Canada's oldest cheese convention; The Great Canadian Cheese Festival, held in Picton since 2010, claims to be the largest artisan cheese show in North America. Over 150 artisanal cheeses from throughout the country are represented annually, along with a variety of local foods, wines, and craft beers. The Canadian Amateur Cheesemaking Awards, showcasing homemade cheeses from across the country, were held conjointly with The Great Canadian Cheese Festival for the first time in 2015. Many winners hailed from Ontario, indicating that artisanal cheesemaking is on the rise both domestically and commercially.

See also CANADA and QUEBEC.

Canadian Dairy Information Centre. http://dairyinfo.gc.ca/index_e.php.
Guidi, Kathy. *Canadian Cheese: A Guide*. Richmond Hill, Ont.: Firefly, 2014.
Menzies, Heather. *By the Labour of Their Hands: The Story of Ontario Cheddar Cheese*. Kingston, Ont.: Quarry Press, 1994.

Laura Shine

An **opportunistic pathogen** is a microorganism that is normally found in the host environment but typically does not cause disease. Opportunistic pathogens are often commensal organisms or members of the normal microbial community of a host that under normal conditions do not cause disease. Opportunistic pathogens are distinguished from primary or obligate pathogens in that the latter require the host for long-term survival. Today, most foodborne pathogens found in cheese or dairy products are opportunistic pathogens. Examples include *Escherichia coli*, *Listeria monocytogenes*, and *Staphylococcus aureus*. These organisms are able to survive and replicate in the environment or as nonpathogenic commensals on a host in the absence of disease. Practicing good hygiene is often the key to successful control of contamination of food products by opportunistic pathogens.

See also HYGIENE and PATHOGENS.

Falkow, Stanley. "Host-Parasite Relationships." In *Sherris Medical Microbiology: An Introduction*, 4th ed., edited by Kenneth J. Ryan and C. George Ray, pp. 149–172. New York: McGraw-Hill, 2004.

John Barlow

Opus Caseus is a French education center that offers professional development programs for cheesemakers, retailers, and affineurs, in courses that alternate theory classes and hands-on practicums. Courses have been offered at Mons headquarters in St. Haon le Chatel, France, as was well as in the United States and the United Kingdom. Programs are for cheese professionals only, and admission is by application. The Academie Opus Caseus was the first cheese school accredited as an Approved Educational Center by the American Cheese Society to offer preparation for the ACS Certified Cheese Professional™ Exam. See AMERICAN CHEESE SOCIETY.

Opus Caseus training programs evolved out of the expertise developed within MonS Fromager-Affineur over two generations. It covers everything a cheesemonger needs to be successful. The French iteration of this professional development school grew out of a partnership with French grocery retailer Casino, wherein MonS cheese counters were established within their stores; in order to support such a high-end product line, counter staff had to be thoroughly trained. Laurent Mons wrote the curriculum, and demand grew over time to the extent that he has developed much of the training curriculum for the French CQP (Professional Qualification Certificate) Fromager program nationwide. In 2012 the American Sue Sturman was invited to join Laurent Mons and together they developed an Anglophone program known as Academie Opus Caseus.

See also ACCREDITATIONS and MONS FROMAGER-AFFINEUR.

Academie Opus Caseus. http://academie-mons.com.

Kathy Guidi

organic certification guarantees federally established agricultural and downstream food processing methods for preserving the environment, avoiding the use of pesticides and antibiotics, and supporting animal health and welfare.

Consumer demand for organic cheese currently outstrips supply in the United States. In 2014 organic cheese sales reached US $396 million, up 19.5 percent from 2013 sales. There is greater demand for organic milk and dairy products than ever before. This larger dairy category grew 10.9 percent in 2014 to reach US $5.5 billion, placing it second in terms of US sales of organic foods after fresh fruits and vegetables. These recent strong growth trends are not anomalies. The organic food category has seen double-digit growth every year since the 1990s when the organic movement was officially set in motion with the formation of the US Organic Foods Protection Act.

While impressive, growth rates could be higher still if supply was not constrained by a shortage of organic grains and feed—conversion of farmland into organic pastures has not kept pace with consumers' appetite for organic foods. Apart from raising prices, feed shortages make it difficult to increase the dairy supply to meet demand. Smaller organic cheese producers are further challenged sourcing organic milk from diaries since most have contracts to supply larger processors.

Federal certification and stringent labeling guidelines are generally regarded as positive contributions to the organic movement. As knowledgeable consumers demand authenticity, producers are constantly challenged to prove that their source ingredients are organic.

There are four levels of USDA organic labeling. The first and most stringent is "100% organic" in which any product must be made entirely from certified organic ingredients and methods. The second-level category "Organic" is available to any product containing at least 95 percent certified organic ingredients (excluding salt and water). Both categories are allowed to use the USDA organic seal while listing the organic ingredients on the information panel. The third USDA organic category "Made with organic ingredients" must contain at least 70 percent organic ingredients, three of which can be listed on the product's front packaging. The fourth and final distinction is "Contains organic ingredients" for products with less than 70 percent organic ingredients (excluding salt and water). In this case organic ingredients can be listed in the ingredient list but not on the product's front packaging and they cannot use the USDA organic seal.

While artisan cheesemakers will often use organic ingredients in production, it's worth noting that the term "artisan" itself does not indicate an organic product. The potential for consumer confusion is high with goat's and sheep's milk cheeses that are often sold in smaller artisan markets. Quality organic goat's and sheep's milk are harder to source as these dairies have had a harder time making the transition to organic. Their specialist needs, capacity constraints, and the similar challenges of sourcing reliable organic feed make them expensive operations. This situation is bound to change if demand remains high and the organic industry continues to mature.

The high consumer demand is driven in part by the belief that organic food is nutritionally superior to conventional foods. Interestingly these beliefs persist despite numerous inconclusive studies on the superior nutritional value of organic foods. The exception to this are organic dairy-product studies which have shown organic milk does indeed provide an enhanced nutritional profile with higher protein and omega-3 fatty acid levels—a beneficial fat thought to provide a wide range of health benefits.

See also ARTISANAL.

Chang, Kenneth. "Organic Food vs. Conventional Food." *New York Times*, 4 September 2012.

Greene, Catherine, and William McBride. "Consumer Demand for Organic Milk Continues to Expand—Can the U.S. Dairy Sector Catch Up?" *Choices*, 1st Quarter 2015. http://choicesmagazine.org/choices-magazine/theme-articles/theme-overview/consumer-demand-for-organic-milk-continues-to-expandcan-the-us-dairy-sector-catch-up.

Matt, Darja, et al. "Quality of Organic vs. Conventional Food and Effects on Health." Estonian University of Life Sciences, September 2011.

Meyers, Courtney, and Katie Abrams. "Feeding the Debate: A Qualitative Framing Analysis of Organic Food News Media Coverage." *Journal of Applied Communications* 94, nos. 3 and 4 (2010): 22.

United States Department of Agriculture Organic Regulations, 7 C.F.R. Part 205 (2015).

Domenic Venuto

The **origin of cheese** is an intriguing and elusive topic. When, where, and why did cheesemaking begin? Did cheese have a single point of origin, from which the know-how then spread and evolved into the great diversity of geographically dispersed cheeses today; or, alternatively, did cheese originate independently in multiple places and times throughout the course of history? Such questions are central to understanding the role that cheese played in the larger story of human development since the Neolithic.

To probe the origin of cheese is to leave the world of definitive certainty behind and enter the netherworld of evidential-based reasoning. Until recently the lines of evidence available to support reconnaissance missions into the deep past have not been robust enough to dispel the fog that shrouds ancient prehistory. However in recent decades remarkable advances in many scientific and scholarly fields, such as archaeology and anthropology, archaeochemistry, archaeobiology, archaeogenetics, and genetic modeling, have generated new lines of evidence that enable credible forensic probing to extend back for ten thousand years or more. Equipped with this new evidential base, the scientist and scholar can now, for the first time, begin to build a case for the origin(s) of cheese and its dispersal through time and across continents.

An abundance of ancient written accounts that have been translated with a high degree of confidence provide some of the earliest and the most secure evidence for cheesemaking in antiquity. Writing originated for the first time during the early third millennium B.C.E. in Sumer, the great civilization of city-states that arose in southern Mesopotamia beginning in the fourth millennium B.C.E.. The development of cuneiform writing furnished a powerful new record-keeping tool to support the increasingly complex bureaucratic and religious functions of the Sumerian city-states. Cheese is well represented in those first clay cuneiform tablets, many of which have survived intact in the archaeological record these past five thousand years, and which confirm that dairying and cheesemaking had already attained a remarkable degree of sophistication by the third millennium B.C.E. Even earlier evidence for dairying and dairy processing in Sumer has been dated to the late fourth millennium B.C.E., as evidenced in proto-cuneiform tablets that were the antecedents to cuneiform writing. In light of the overwhelming evidence that cheesemaking know-how was already widely practiced at the dawn of Sumerian civilization, it seems likely that the origin of cheese occurred sometime prior to Sumer, somewhere in the distant past of prehistory. In the absence of written records, however, other lines of evidence are needed to examine that possibility.

Since the 1980s new analytical methodologies have made it possible to identify the foods that were contained in many ancient unglazed pottery vessels at the time of their use. The approach involves extracting lipid residues preserved within the fabric of ancient pottery sherds recovered from the archaeological material record. Amazingly the identities of the sources of extracted lipids (e.g., plant or animal source; porcine or bovine source; carcus fat or milk fat source) can often be determined based on the stable carbon isotope (C12 and C13) contents contained within the residues. Using this approach, archaeo-chemists have identified milk fat residues in numerous ancient pottery sherds, the oldest of which, recovered from western Anatolia, date all the way back to the seventh millennium B.C.E., at the dawn of the Neolithic pottery era. The implications of these findings are clear: Neolithic peoples sometimes used ancient pots as containers for dairy products, demonstrating definitively that milk production occurred as early as the seventh millennium B.C.E. in western Anatolia.

The presence of milk fat residues in ancient potsherds does not necessarily constitute evidence of cheesemaking, only that the original pot contained milk in some form at the time of use. However controlled laboratory studies of unglazed potsherds, designed to simulate conditions of archaeological pottery, have strongly suggested that the presence of milk fat residues in ancient potsherds constitute telltale signs of concentrated dairy products such as butter and cheese, rather than of liquid milk, which failed to deposit permanent measurable milk fat residues into the fabric of the experimental pottery sherds.

More direct evidence to support the hypothesis that Neolithic cheese curds deposited permanent milk fat residues into ancient pottery has accrued from recent analyses of sherds that originated from Neolithic ceramic sieves. Remnants of Neolithic sieves, dated to the sixth millennium B.C.E. have been abundantly recovered from northeastern and northwestern Europe; other sieve remnants have been found in the archaeological material record from the Bronze Age of central Italy, the Balkans, and the Indus River region of Pakistan. It has long been suspected that these ancient pottery sieves were used to separate curds from whey during cheesemaking, based on modern peasant ethnography that has documented the widespread use of similar sieves in central Italy, central Europe, the Balkans, and the Middle East. Recent analyses of Neolithic sieve shreds from the sixth millennium B.C.E. definitively identified milk fat embedded within the pottery fabric. The presence of milk fat residues in these sieve remnants almost certainly means that Neolithic cheesemakers used such sieves in cheesemaking some seven thousand years ago in much the same way as is still practiced today in some traditional societies. As for the even older pots containing milk fat residues that have been

dated to the seventh millennium B.C.E. from western Anatolia, it is now plausible to posit that those pots contained soft acid coagulated or acid-heat coagulated cheeses, placed there by Neolithic cheesemakers, which deposited milk fat into the pottery fabric. Indeed the packaging of soft cheeses in clay pots remains a common practice among traditional cheesemakers in the Anatolian peninsula to this day.

Using this analytical approach and applying the assumption that the presence of milk fat residues constitutes a telltale sign of butter or cheese, it is possible to track the ancient practice of milk production and cheesemaking through time and space by analyzing the pottery remnants left behind by migrating Neolithic peoples. For example, various lines of evidence indicate that migrations of Neolithic peoples out of Southwest Asia into Europe took place near the end of the seventh millennium B.C.E. Among the evidence for Neolithic migration around this time is a portfolio of potsherds recovered from the Balkan peninsula that chronicles the spread of dairying as migrating Neolithic farmers transported their pottery-making technology and dairy subsistence strategy with them. From there these Neolithic farmers continued their migration into central, eastern, and southern Europe by the sixth millennium B.C.E., reaching the British Isles by the fifth millennium B.C.E., and the western Baltic region, Scandinavia, and Finland by the fifth–fourth millennium B.C.E., leaving behind a trail of potsherds containing milk fat residues. Indeed by the time Sumerian scribes were documenting the use of cheese in religious rites during the third millennium B.C.E. using their newly invented technique of writing, Neolithic peoples in England were employing cheese in cultic practices performed near Stonehenge, as inferred from the abundance of potsherds containing milk fat residues that were laid down at Durrington Walls in the vicinity of Stonehenge during the third millennium B.C.E. Thus it appears that Neolithic farmers meticulously conserved dairying and cheesemaking as a component of their subsistence strategy, even as they migrated vast distances, sometimes under conditions of great environmental duress. Similar analyses have also confirmed the occurrence of dairying and cheesemaking as early as the fifth millennium B.C.E. in northern Africa, and the second millennium B.C.E. in the steppe zone of Central Asia, though it remains to be determined whether these practices arrived for the first time with migrating Neolithic peoples from the Near East or, alternatively, arose independently in these regions.

Based on the above findings, it now seems plausible to push the origin of cheese back to at least the seventh millennium B.C.E. in Anatolia. It also appears plausible to follow the dispersal of cheesemaking from its apparent point of origin in Southwest Asia to Europe, and perhaps Africa and Asia, by migrating Neolithic peoples. Unfortunately, however, the trail of pottery sherds ends in the seventh millennium B.C.E. because the Neolithic discovery of ceramic technology occurred around this time. Prior to this there were no pots in which to store cheese or butter. Therefore if dairying and cheesemaking preceded pottery, other lines of evidence are needed to probe farther back in time to fill in the details.

The advent of dairying (that is, the harvesting of milk from other mammals by humans) is now fairly well established. Advances in techniques to analyze skeletal and dental remains of the animals kept by Neolithic peoples for vital diagnostic characteristics, along with advances in ethnographic interpretive frameworks, have led to breakthroughs in the ability to detect the emergence, and track the spread, of livestock domestication and dairying. Indeed recent archaeozoological and archaeogenetic findings clearly demonstrate the occurrence of sheep and goat domestication in the upper Fertile Crescent region of Southwest Asia around the middle of the ninth millennium B.C.E. Similarly cattle were also domesticated in the Middle Euphrates basin slightly later. Evidence of Neolithic dairying quickly followed in the same region, commencing around the end of the ninth millennium B.C.E.

When did these Neolithic dairy farmers begin to make cheese for the first time? Presumably the answer lies somewhere between the onset of dairying in the ninth millennium B.C.E. and dawn of pottery in the seventh millennium B.C.E. Recent archaeogenetic analyses and genetic modeling studies suggest that cheesemaking may have originated shortly after the onset of dairying in the ninth millennium B.C.E., based on the following reasoning. Genetic evidence indicates that lactase persistence, the ability of adult humans to tolerate the consumption of the milk sugar lactose, did not develop for the first time in human populations until the sixth millennium B.C.E. in central Europe. Therefore from the onset of dairying in the ninth millennium B.C.E. to the sixth millennium B.C.E. Neolithic peoples meticulously

conserved dairying as a component of their subsistence strategy, even though the adult population could not drink milk because of the prohibitive effects of lactose intolerance. What then provided the incentive for these peoples to cling tenaciously to dairying? Within this context it is plausible to posit, though it is by no means proven, that simple acid-coagulated cheesemaking, and later the more complex acid-heat and rennet-coagulated cheesemaking, provided the means for the adult population to tap into the life-giving reservoir of nutrients in milk, even though they could not drink milk, by making cheeses available with greatly reduced lactose contents. Cheesemaking thus would have provided a compelling incentive for Neolithic farmers to conserve dairying, which in turn would have also furnished a regular supply of milk for their very young children, as a supplement to mother's milk. Continual exposure of young children beyond weaning to milk could have thus contributed to the selection pressure that ultimately led to the genetic selection for lactase persistence several millennia later.

So in the end, what can one say about the origin of cheese? Frankly, nothing with certainty, but much with qualified caution. Cheesemaking almost certainly stretches back to the seventh millennium B.C.E., based on the abundant presence of milk fat residues in Neolithic potsherds. Less certain, but still plausible, is the hypothesis that cheesemaking extends all the way back almost to the beginning of dairying itself; perhaps to the early eighth millennium B.C.E. Indeed it seems possible that cheesemaking helped to make dairying a subsistence strategy worth conserving for thousands of years until adult populations eventually developed the genetic capacity to consume liquid milk.

See also ANCIENT CIVILIZATIONS; ARCHAEOLOGICAL DETECTION; EARTHENWARE POTTERY; and LACTOSE INTOLERANCE.

Evershed, R. P., et al. "Earliest Date for Milk Use in the Near East and Southeastern Europe Linked to Cattle-herding." *Nature* 455, no. 7212 (2008): 528–531.

Itan, Y., et al. "The Origins of Lactase Persistence in Europe." *PLoS Computational Biology* 5, no. 8 (2009): 1–13.

Kindstedt, P. S. *Cheese and Culture: A History of Cheese and Its Place in Western Civilization.* White River Junction, Vt.: Chelsea Green, 2012.

Kindstedt, P. S. "Introduction: The History of Cheese." In *Global Cheesemaking Technology: Cheese Quality and Characteristics.* Hoboken, N.J.: Wiley, 2016.

Vigne, Jean-Denis, and Daniel Helmer. "Was Milk a 'Secondary Product' in the Old World Neolithisation Process? Its Role in the Domestication of Cattle, Sheep and Goats." *Anthropozoologica* 42, no. 2 (2007): 9–40.

Paul S. Kindstedt

Orkney cheese is a lactic, crumbly, semifirm cow's milk cheese of a type typically made in the more remote farming communities of the British Isles, such as England's Yorkshire Dales and the valleys of South Wales. These simple cheeses were made for household consumption in locations that lacked the rich pastures and advanced cheesemaking technologies of Britain's intensive dairying regions like Cheshire and Somerset. The size of the cheese was determined by the amount of milk available, often resulting in cheeses around 4½–9 pounds (2–4 kilograms) and therefore smaller than most commercial British varieties.

Orkney itself consists of around seventy islands located off Scotland's northeast coast and farming can be traced back to Neolithic times yet, despite its northerly location, the islands benefit from a relatively mild climate and level land with fertile soil when compared to much of the Scottish mainland. During World War II the islands were the site of a Royal Naval base, which with sixty thousand garrisoned troops, led to an increase in local food production. The subsequent postwar closure of the base left Orcadian dairy farmers with a large surplus of milk and, consequently, a creamery was established to manufacture a Cheddar-style cheese that could be shipped and marketed to the Scottish mainland. Orkney Scottish Island Cheddar is now produced in a multimillion pound facility in Orkney's capital, Kirkwall, and was granted protected geographical indication (PGI) status by the European Parliament in November 2013.

The Seator family of Grimbister Farm, near Kirkwall, is the only current producer of a traditional Orkney cheese, which they make by hand from the unpasteurized milk of their small herd of Friesian cows. Known as "Grimbister," or "Seator's Orkney," the cheese's fresh character and limited production restricts wider distribution outside of Scotland.

See also UNITED KINGDOM.

Rance, Patrick. *The Great British Cheese Book*. London: Macmillan, 1983.

Towrie, Sigurd. Orkneyjar. http://www.orkneyjar.com.

Chris George

Oscypek is a raw ewe's milk cheese, traditionally made by shepherds in the Tatra Mountains of Poland. Milk for Oscypek comes from the Zackel sheep, an ancient breed thought to have been introduced by nomadic farmers arriving from Walachia in Romania. Oscypek is almost unknown outside the country's borders even though its origins date back to the fourteenth century. It has been in continuous production ever since, even surviving (in reduced quantities) Poland's Communist era.

Production of Oscypek takes place in traditional mountain shepherd huts known as *bacówka*, between May and September. During this time, a fire is kept burning constantly inside the hut, providing heat for both cooking and cheesemaking, while the smoke is used to preserve and flavor the cheeses. Milk from the morning or from the previous day's milking is left to ripen at room temperature until it can be mixed with milk from the latest milking in a large wooden vat. Liquid calf rennet is added, and once the curd has formed, it is cut and mixed with hot water. The curd is worked slowly by hand for at least an hour. During this time, the cheesemaker stretches and softens the curd, gently forming it into a shape resembling a spindle.

A carved wooden band is then placed around each cheese, imprinting a beautiful, intricate decoration of geometric patterns onto its surface. The design is

The beautiful geometric designs on the rinds of Oscypek, a Polish raw sheep's milk cheese, are imprinted by carved wooden bands. The design is unique to each cheesemaker, thereby allowing the identification of the origin of each cheese. © REYTAN

unique to each cheesemaker, like a brand, thereby allowing the identification of the origin of each cheese. Cheeses are finished by bathing them in salt before suspending them over the rafters of the hut above the fire to be smoked for four or five days.

Oscypek cheeses weigh between 21 and 28 ounces (600–800 grams) and measure 3 to 3½ inches (8–9 centimeters) in diameter. The interior paste is compact and firm, with a clean, gently smoky aroma and flavors of milk and chestnuts. Oscypek is excellent grilled or consumed with wine, vodka, or beer.

Today fewer than forty shepherds still make traditional Oscypek because of increasing competition from less expensive cow's milk versions of the cheese that are, confusingly, also labeled Oscypek. In an effort to preserve and secure production of traditional Oscypek, Slow Food International has included the cheese in its Presidia. In 2008, Oscypek was the first Polish product to be granted protected designation of origin (PDO) status.

See also POLAND; SLOW FOOD; and SMOKED CHEESES.

"Juliet Harbutt: A Life through Food." Interview by Sheila Dillon. *Food Programme*. Podcast. BBC Radio 4. 14 December 2015. http://www.bbc.co.uk/programmes/b06rwgcx.
Slow Food Foundation for Biodiversity. "Ark of Taste." http://www.fondazioneslowfood.com/en/what-we-do/the-ark-of-taste.

Kate Arding

Ossau-Iraty is an uncooked and pressed cheese made from ewe's milk. It is made exclusively in the Béarn and Basque Country (Pyrénées-Atlantiques), and in three communes in the Hautes Pyrénées, the terrain being mainly mountainous and characterized by high humidity, ideal conditions for lush and varied grass to grow. Cylindrical in shape with a straight or slightly convex heel, Ossau-Iraty has a natural smooth rind that can vary between orange and gray in color and a cream-colored homogeneous center. It comes in two versions: dairy (traditional or industrial dairies) or farm (made in farmsteads, using raw milk), this milk coming either from the farm (in the valleys) or the pastures (mountains in the summer). This traditional cheese received appellation d'origine contrôlée (AOC) status in 1980 and protected designation of origin (PDO) status in 1996. Ossau-Iraty comes in two sizes: small (4–7 pounds

[2–3 kilograms]) and large (8–11 pounds [4–5 kilograms]).

The name "Ossau-Iraty" refers to the two "countries" sheltering the shepherds and their flocks and the cheesemakers: "Ossau" for the Pic du Midi d'Ossau, the celebrated summit in the Béarn, and "Iraty" for the magnificent beech forest of Iraty in the Basque Country. The breeding of dairy ewes from the three local breeds (Manech black-faced, Manech red-faced, and Basco-Béarnaise) enables the steep grassy slopes in this region to be exploited and maintained during the summer transhumance and through the grazing in the valleys. See TRANSHUMANCE.

The first written proof of a commercial activity involving ewe's cheese in the Pyrenees dates from the fifteenth century. Since then making pure ewe's milk cheese has continued to be a major activity for the Basco-Béarnaise pastoral population. Ossau-Iraty now groups milk producers, dairies, farmstead producers, and cheese maturers whose practices are governed by a PDO specifications document.

The minimum period for maturing Ossau-Iraty is between 80 and 120 days depending on the format. The milk must come exclusively from the local breeds, and it must be used whole, at most forty or forty-eight hours after the last milking (in other words at most every four milkings). (Forty hours in farmstead transformation.) The identification of each PDO Ossau-Iraty cheese at the time of its making is mandatory: the rind of each cheese is marked by a ewe's head (facing head-on) for farm Ossau-Iraty cheeses and a ewe's head (in profile) for dairy Ossau-Iraty cheeses. The fat and dry matter levels in the cheese are fixed (50 percent and 58 percent minimum, respectively).

Ossau-Iraty cheese production is around 3,700 tons per year, of which 640 tons are raw milk (50 percent farmhouse and 50 percent dairy), and involves 1,400 farmers and some 20 enterprises or cooperatives. Ossau-Iraty is an obvious choice on any cheese platter but is also used in cooking and snacking.

See also BASQUE COUNTRY and IDIAZABAL.

Delfosse, Claire. "La France fromagère, 1850–1990." PhD diss., University of Provence, 2007.
Lassalle, Danielle. *Berger basque, berger pyrénéen: À la croisée des chemins*. Bayonne, France: Editions Elkar, 2015.
Ossau-Iraty. http://www.ossau-iraty.fr.

Céline Barrere

outbreak is a term referring to two or more cases of a similar illness from the same source. Dairy-related outbreaks of illness date back to antiquity, centuries before Louis Pasteur developed the process of pasteurization, when typhoid, scarlet fever, diphtheria, and tuberculosis predominated. See PASTEUR, LOUIS. While raw milk was responsible for most of these outbreaks, various types of cheese prepared from raw milk were also sometimes implicated. In one such example from 1923, an outbreak involving over fifty cases of typhoid fever was traced to an infected cheesemaker with this cheese consumed shortly after manufacture. Implication of Cheddar, Colby, and various cheeses in outbreaks of illness during the 1940s led to the current sixty-day minimum aging requirement at not less than 35°F (2°C) for a range of cheeses including Parmesan, Cheddar, Gouda, Gruyère, Gorgonzola, and Asiago. See 60-DAY AGING RULE.

While raw-milk cheeses are highly prized for their complex aroma and taste resulting from naturally occurring bacteria in the cheese during fermentation and aging (similar to fine aged wines), current evidence from outbreaks and experimental cheesemaking trials suggests that some important milk-borne bacterial pathogens including nontyphoid *Salmonella*, enterohemorrhagic *Escherichia coli*, and *Listeria monocytogenes* can persist in the finished cheese at infectious levels. Widespread adoption of pasteurization after World War II coupled with major advances in dairy sanitation, milk handling, and animal husbandry practices have now relegated typhoid fever, scarlet fever, diphtheria, and milk-borne tuberculosis to scourges of the past, being replaced now by *Salmonella*, enterohemorrhagic *Escherichia coli*, *Listeria monocytogenes,* and *Brucella*, in particular. See SALMONELLA and LISTERIA.

From 1973 to 1992, a total of thirty-two cheese-related outbreaks were responsible for about seventeen hundred cases of illness in the United States. Of these outbreaks, eleven were attributed to the use of raw and improperly pasteurized milk or post-pasteurization contamination, with these same outbreaks responsible for 1,238 cases of illness, most of the hospitalizations, and all fifty-eight fatalities. The deadliest and now infamous outbreak, which included fifty-two fatal cases of listeriosis traced to queso fresco Mexican-style soft cheese that was commercially produced in southern California from a mixture of raw and pasteurized milk with postprocessing contamination also involved. See POST-PROCESS CONTAMINATION. *Salmonella* was responsible for three of these eleven outbreaks and two-thirds of all cases. Two of these outbreaks were traced to cheese containing less than two *Salmonella* cells per gram, thus reinforcing the highly infectious nature of certain strains. Of the remaining outbreaks, three were due to illegally imported queso fresco Mexican-style soft cheese containing *Brucella melitensis* (which causes undulant fever), two to *Streptococcus* species in cheeses prepared from raw or improperly pasteurized milk, and one each from *Staphylococcus aureus* and a pathogenic strain of *Escherichia coli*.

In a more recent survey, ninety outbreaks from 1998 to 2011 attributed to cheese in the United States were responsible for a total of 1,882 illnesses, including 230 hospitalizations and six deaths. Thirty-eight (42 percent) were traced to raw-milk cheese, forty-four (49 percent) to cheese prepared from pasteurized milk, with the remainder of uncertain status. Consumption of raw-milk cheese led to 168 hospitalizations as opposed to only sixty-one for cheeses prepared from pasteurized milk with 39 percent of the outbreaks from pasteurized milk cheese traced to norovirus, which typically has a low hospitalization rate. Among the eighteen identified cheese varieties, queso fresco prepared from raw milk was responsible for eighteen outbreaks followed by "homemade" cheese from raw milk (seven outbreaks), and other raw-milk Mexican-style cheeses (five outbreaks) with mozzarella, Cheddar, and Swiss (all prepared from pasteurized milk) responsible for three outbreaks each. In terms of pathogens, *Salmonella* accounted for the highest number of outbreaks from raw-milk cheese (thirteen outbreaks) followed by *Campylobacter* (ten outbreaks), *Brucella* (five outbreaks), and enterohemmorhagic *Escherichia coli* (four outbreaks). In contrast, norovirus was the leading cause of outbreaks from pasteurized milk cheese (thirteen outbreaks), followed by *Listeria monocytogenes* (eight outbreaks), and then *Salmonella* (six outbreaks). Leading cheese/pathogen combinations included unpasteurized queso fresco (or other Mexican-style cheese) and *Salmonella* (ten outbreaks), pasteurized queso fresco (or other Mexican-style cheese) and *Listeria monocytogenes* (six outbreaks), unpasteurized "homemade" cheese and *Campylobacter* (four outbreaks), unpasteurized queso fresco (or other Mexican-style cheese) and *Listeria monocytogenes* (three outbreaks), and unpasteurized queso fresco (or other Mexican-style cheese) and *Brucella* (three outbreaks). While twenty-seven of the thirty-eight outbreaks involving raw-milk cheese were traced to questionable milk sources or manufacturing errors, it is important to recognize that thirty of forty-four (68 percent) outbreaks from cheese prepared using pasteurized milk were linked to various commercial settings including restaurants, delis, and banquets where the cheese was likely contaminated during slicing or by the food handler. Thus, not all cheese-related outbreaks are the result of the manufacturer. This is particularly true for norovirus, which is spread by infected food handlers and remains the leading cause of food-borne illness overall. Thus, due diligence is needed from both cheesemakers and retailers to curb the incidence of cheese-related outbreaks of illness, particularly in regard to soft Mexican-style cheeses.

See also HYGIENE; PATHOGENS; RAW-MILK CHEESES; and MEXICAN CHEESES.

Altekruse, S. F., B. B. Timbo, J. C. Mowbray, et al. "Cheese-Associated Outbreaks of Human Illness in the United States, 1973 to 1992: Sanitary Manufacturing Practices Protect Consumers." *Journal of Food Protection* 61, no. 10 (1998): 1405–1407.

Gould, L. H., E. Mungai, and C. B. Behravesh. "Outbreaks Attributed to Cheese: Differences between Outbreaks Caused by Unpasteurized and Pasteurized Dairy Products, United States, 1998–2011." *Foodborne Pathogens and Disease* 11, no. 7 (2014): 545–551.

Ryser, E. T. "Public Health Concerns." In *Applied Dairy Microbiology*, 2d ed., edited by E. H. Marth and J. L. Steele, pp. 397–545. New York: Marcel Dekker, 2001.

Ryser, E. T. "Incidence and Behavior of *Listeria monocytogenes* in Cheese and Other Fermented Dairy Products," In *Listeria, Listeriosis, and Food Safety*, 3d ed., edited by Elliot T. Ryser and Elmer H. Marth, pp. 405–501. Boca Raton, Fla.: Taylor & Francis, 2007.

Elliot Ryser

packaging is the principal means by which cheese is protected from contamination or damage during storage, transport, and display to the customer or consumer. Whole soft cheese and cheese that has been cut to expose its internal surfaces clearly need protection against chemical, physical, and microbiological contamination, by wrapping in paper or plastic film, or by sealing the cheese inside bags, pouches, trays, or jars. However, less obvious is the need to protect whole, hard cheese such as truckles of Cheddar for which the packaging is integral to the cheese; for these cheeses, "packaging" may take the form of a cloth binding and applying a layer of lard or vegetable fat that develops into an impenetrable rind as the cheese matures. See TRUCKLE and CLOTHBOUND CHEESES. An alternative is plastic coating that is painted onto the cheese.

Packaging can therefore take a number of different forms that, in addition to protecting the cheese, may control the rate of maturation, by limiting or permitting the exchange of water vapor, carbon dioxide, and other gases between the cheese and the environment. Loss of moisture in cheese during maturation or shelf life results in weight loss, which is a major economic factor but, perhaps more importantly, moisture loss also increases the concentration of salt in the moisture, which is one of the factors that determine the growth of pathogens and spoilage organisms against the flourishing of desirable microbes. Desirable microbes not only include organisms that contribute to flavor and texture but also surface bacteria, yeasts, or molds whose growth can provide an attractive presentation, both visual and aromatic, when the cheese is in a retail or catering display. Thus the choice of packaging can play a major role in successfully developing a cheesemaker's chosen market sector. See MOISTURE; PATHOGENS; and NATURAL-RIND CHEESES.

Most commercial supply chains require three layers of packaging to achieve product protection throughout all stages of supply. Each layer has different functional requirements so the properties of packaging materials and processes must generally achieve a number of criteria.

Primary Packaging

Primary packaging is in direct contact with the food and must be free from chemical contaminants (e.g., pesticides or preservatives) and foreign bodies (e.g., shards of broken glass); it must also be of a good hygienic standard. These criteria also apply to the gases used for aerobic or modified atmosphere packs. Primary packaging materials used in a vacuum pack or modified atmosphere applications may need to be impervious to the exchange of gases.

Secondary Packaging

Secondary packaging is generally designed to group small numbers of retail packs for shelf display or consumer convenience; it may therefore be required to provide the customer with promotional and compositional labeling, and the retailer with stock control information (e.g., barcoding). Examples of secondary packaging include shrink-wrap, "mother" bags, and shelf display trays.

Tertiary Packaging

Tertiary packaging can take diverse forms, from cardboard outer cartons to plastic pallet wrap. Principally

Women at a Wisconsin dairy wrap slabs of cheese in foil for distribution. WISCONSIN HISTORICAL SOCIETY

it provides product protection, identification, traceability, and storage instructions during transport and warehouse storage, but where temperature control is a requirement and active refrigeration is not available (e.g., for some mail order services), it may also provide insulation that prolongs the efficacy of ice packs placed in the unit to maintain the cheese at a low temperature. Tertiary packaging must be robust enough to maintain security against accidental, and possibly malicious, damage or contamination.

Packaging Technologies

Primary packaging materials and their modes of use can range from the very simple to the very sophisticated but these variants can broadly be placed into five categories.

Simple primary packaging

Simple primary packaging generally begins with a simple process on fresh or early-maturing curd, for example, rubbing up of Stilton wheels using a knife to smooth the surface, or larding of cloth bound Cheddar truckles using a hot iron to create a continuous, even rind. At cutting, either before dispatch to a business customer or sale to a retail consumer, the cut portion is loosely wrapped in a non-rigid film wrap or in waxed paper. White mold ripened cheese may be wrapped in perforated Brie paper, which is a laminate of oriented polypropylene (OPP) and paper that allows oxygen exchange but retains moisture; the number, size, and density of perforations is varied according to the barrier required. Numerous laminate combinations of paper with cellulose, plastic, or aluminum coatings are possible.

Liquid coatings

Liquid coatings, comprising either molten wax or polyvinyl acetate (PVA), are applied directly to the surface of whole cheese at the start of maturation and often a second time several weeks later, either by dipping the cheese in wax or by painting PVA onto the cheese. Both coatings may contain color or the antifungal agent, pimaricin (also known as natamycin).

Gas atmosphere composition

The gas atmosphere composition to which cheese is exposed during its shelf life can have a considerable effect on the presentation and the longevity of the product. If a cheese is simply packed in an aerobic atmosphere, its appearance may deteriorate rapidly due to undesirable mold growth; nevertheless, packing soft cheese in permeable film wrap or in the aerobic atmosphere of a semi-rigid container may remain the only cost-effective option for many small businesses.

Vacuum packaging

Vacuum-packed cheese may exhibit an extended shelf life, since most of the molds that cause their spoilage fail to grow in an atmosphere that contains less than 1 percent oxygen; however, the blue color of blue-veined cheese rapidly deteriorates in the absence of oxygen and can only be restored by exposing the cheese to air for about one hour before serving.

Modified-atmosphere packing

Modified-atmosphere packing (MAP) has been developed to effect a compromise between packing in air or under vacuum. As with vacuum packing, MAP requires either the use of gas-impermeable bags or pouches, or semi-rigid trays and laminate films that can ensure a hermetic seal. MAP requires the use of complex packing equipment and a high level of staff training, which is a major investment for many small businesses.

Other Attributes

Businesses that purchase packaging materials should hold detailed packaging specifications, for their primary packaging as a minimum. In the European Union (EU), these documents should include evidence of compliance with the Materials and Articles in Contact with Food legislation, which ensures that no toxic substances can migrate into the cheese. Other relevant EU legislation covers the reuse and recycling of packaging waste, including energy recovery, composting, and biodegradation.

All packaging materials should be stored in a clean, dry, hygienic location, well segregated from other materials such as food ingredients, maintenance lubricants, or pest control poisons; the premises should be adequately pest-proofed and subject to regular pest control inspections.

See also WAXING AND COATING.

Research Information Ltd. *Food Packaging Bulletin.*
   http://www.researchinformation.co.uk/fpbu.php.
Robertson, G. L. *Food Packaging: Principles and Practice.*
   3d ed. London: CRC Press, 2012.
Schneider, Y., et al. "Packaging Materials and
   Equipment." In *Technology of Cheesemaking*, edited by
B. A. Law and A. Y. Tamime, 2d ed., pp. 413–439.
   Oxford: Wiley-Blackwell, 2010.

Paul Neaves

pairing

See BEER PAIRING; BREAD PAIRING; CHEESE ACCOMPANIMENTS; and WINE PAIRING.

Palmero is a Spanish cheese from the island of La Palma, in the Canary Islands, made exclusively from raw goat's milk from the Palmera breed. Palmero cheese has been protected with a designation of origin (DO) since 2001. The history of the Palmero cheese begins with the introduction of the pre-Hispanic goats by the first inhabitants of the island (of Berber origin). Since the incorporation of the island of La Palma to the Crown of Castile in 1493, there has been written information on the importance of the cheese industry in this territory. In this way, there is evidence of exports in the mid-sixteenth century to the ports of San Juan de Puerto Rico and Santo Domingo, and to the islands of Cape Verde.

The DO protects thirty-one livestock farms, which have 4,613 milking goats (head) that produce 413,410 gallons (1,564,929 liters) of milk per year that are transformed into approximately 523,218 pounds (237,328 kilograms) of cheese. Milk is coagulated at 80–91°F (27–33°C) during forty-five minutes, using animal (commercial calf or artisanal kid) rennet. For generations, cheesemakers have used kid rennet preparations as coagulant, which seems to be an essential element for the development of the typical taste and texture of Palmero cheese. The cheese is pressed by hand (most popular) or with pneumatic presses.

After salting (dry salt method), the cheese is often smoked (approximately 80 percent of the producers smoke the cheese following traditional methods). The smoking process for Palmero protected designation of origin (PDO) cheeses uses four different materials: almond shell (*Prunus dulcis*), segmented prickly pear cactus (*Opuntia ficus indica*), pine needles, and wood of canary pine (*Pinus canariensis*), which generate four distinct categories of smoked cheese. Pine needle is the most used material followed by almond shells. Cheeses can be consumed fresh or ripened (after more than eight days of ripening). Ripened Palmero cheese has a cylindrical shape and is commercialized in sizes varying from 2 to 33 pounds (0.75–15 kilograms). The rind is smooth, yellow, or brown (when smoked). The mass is ivory-white in color, with little mechanical holes. The taste is slightly acid and moderately salty.

See also SPAIN.

Fresno, M., A. Rodríguez, A. Escuder, et al. "Production System of Palmero PDO Cheese." In *Changes in Sheep and Goat Farming Systems at the Beginning of the 21st Century: Research, Tools, Methods, and Initiatives in Favour of a Sustainable Development*, edited by F. Pacheco and P. Morand-Fehr, pp. 265–268. Zaragoza, Spain: CIHEAM, 2009. http://om.ciheam.org/article.php?IDPDF=801159.

Martínez, Sidonia, Juan A. Centeno, Inmaculada Franco, et al. "The Spanish Traditional Cheeses: Characteristics and Scientific Knowledge." In *Handbook of Cheese, Production, Chemistry, and Sensory Properties*, edited by Henrique Castelli and Luiz du Vale, pp. 123–167. New York: Nova Science, 2013.

Javier Carballo

paneer, sometimes spelled "panir," is a semisoft cheese made from cow's or buffalo's milk that is a common ingredient in the cuisine of northern India and Pakistan, but not widely used elsewhere in the Indian subcontinent. Its origins are uncertain; according to the United Nations' Food and Agricultural Organization, paneer may have been introduced into northern India by Persian and Afghan invaders in the thirteenth and fourteenth centuries. Traditionally the cheese was produced in Indian homes where the milk was brought to a boil and the curds were formed by adding vinegar, lemon juice, yogurt, or buttermilk.

The curds are called *chhana* in Hindi. When drained and kneaded to make a smooth mixture, they are mixed with sugar, ghee, and flavorings to create sweets, especially in Bengal. Chhana is the basis of such famous Bengali sweets as *sandesh* (little fudge-like sweetmeats formed into decorative shapes and often flavored with spices, flower essence, and even chocolate) and *rosogolla* (balls soaked in sugar syrup). In other parts of India, most sweets are made with khoya, or thickened milk.

To make paneer, the curds are stirred and drained in a muslin cloth. For firmer paneer, the curds are pressed under a weight or between two plates. Commercially, the curds are drained in large, round pans with holes in the bottom and pressed under weights. The slabs of cheese are cut into rectangles and immersed in chilled water for several hours to make them firm.

The freshly made curds have a mild, slightly milky taste but after draining and pressing, the paneer has a bland flavor and very little aroma, so that it absorbs the flavors of the sauce it is cooked in. Paneer is sold fresh or frozen in Indian grocery stores. In North Indian cuisine, the cheese is used as a substitute for meat in vegetarian dishes. Fried cubes of the cheese can be added to rice and mixed with peas, tomatoes, and nuts to make an elegant *pullao*. A wide variety of curries are made with paneer, including *paneer kofta* in which the paneer is mixed with spices, shaped into balls, and served in an onion and tomato-based gravy and *mattar paneer*, a stew of fried paneer and peas in a spicy tomato gravy. Squares of paneer can be threaded on to skewers and grilled to make paneer kabobs. One of the most popular dishes in Indian restaurants in the west is *palak* or *saag paneer*—chopped or pureed spinach prepared with fried paneer and a thick gravy.

Paneer is very rarely used in South Indian cuisine, although today South Indian restaurants may include *palak paneer* or, a more recent creation, paneer 65 (a very hot dry curry) on their menus since these are popular with their customers. Most restaurants use commercially produced frozen paneer.

See also INDIA.

Bladholm, Linda. *The Indian Grocery Store Demystified.* Los Angeles: Renaissance, 2000.

Sen, Colleen Taylor. *Feasts and Fasts: A History of Food in India.* London: Reaktion, 2015.

Colleen Taylor Sen

Parmesan

See PARMIGIANO REGGIANO.

Parmigiano Reggiano is an ancient and revered cheese from the Emilia-Romagna region of Italy. Often referred to as "the king of cheeses," Parmigiano Reggiano is among its country's greatest gastronomic products and a major export. Nearly 35 percent of the roughly 3.3 million wheels made

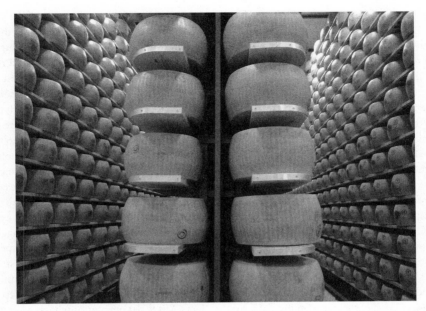

Wheels of Parmiggiano Reggiano aging in Giorgio Cravero's caves in the town of Bra, Italy. Giorgio Cravero is the fifth generation of *raffinatores* (cheese agers) in his family. © KATE ARDING

each year are sold abroad. Of that export total, approximately 20 percent go to France, 20 percent to Germany, about 17 percent to the United States, and an equal amount to the United Kingdom.

History

Written references to Parmigiano Reggiano types date back to Roman times, when cheeses were first shipped beyond their localities and given place-names: Columella, Marziale, and Varrone all mention *caseum paramensis* (cheese from Parma). The Benedictine and Cistercian monks of the Po Valley likely made very similar cheeses in the Middle Ages; it is often said the recipe hasn't changed for nearly nine hundred years. See MONASTIC CHEESEMAKING. Other notable documentation dates from 1254, when a Genoese noblewoman traded her house for a yearly guarantee of cheese; from 1351, when Bocaccio, in his *Decameron*, imagined denizens of the wonderland Bengodi perched atop a mountain of grated cheese, making maccheroni and ravioli—the first mention of Parmigiano's epic marriage with pasta—and from Samuel Pepys's seventeenth-century diary, wherein he recounts securing his stash of Parmigiano from the Great Fire of London. Around the same time, Molière, seeking longevity, was said to have limited his diet to a daily ration of Parmigiano, a regimen reflecting its superior nutritional value and digestibility. Parmigiano Reggiano has been prized for these traits—and for its culinary versatility—ever since.

Contrary to a popular misconception, "Parmesan" is not an Anglicization but rather a French contraction of "Parmesano," from Renaissance times when there were numerous alliances between powerful French and Italian families. By the late nineteenth century, with Italian unification, specific place-names became more commonplace and producers from around Reggio Emilia began to refer to their cheeses as Reggiano. In 1934, efforts begun at the dawn of the twentieth century culminated in local producers forming a consortium called the Consorzio del Grana Tipico, *grana* (grainy) cheeses being a more general category. In 1954 the consortium's name was changed to the Consorzio del Formaggio Parmigiano-Reggiano, and the cheese's modern double name became official. See CONSORZIO DEL FORMAGGIO PARMIGIANO-REGGIANO.

PDO and Production Zone

Parmigiano Reggiano's PDO (protected designation of origin) is among the most stringent of all. Put in place by the European Union in 1996, it stemmed from earlier Italian government declarations and laws. In 2008 an EU high court ruling confirmed that the denomination "Parmesan" was also protected; this protection does not extend beyond Europe, however, so producers elsewhere may use the name with impunity.

Parmigiano Reggiano's PDO mandates that it be made from the unadulterated raw milk of cows raised in its delimited zone, which includes the provinces of Modena, Parma, and Reggio Emilia as well as the section of the province of Bologna left (or north and west) of the Reno River and that of Mantova right (or south) of the Po River. The milk must be delivered to the creamery within two hours of each milking.

The PDO specifies the following: wheels weighing at least 66 pounds (30 kilograms), 14–18 inches (35–45 centimeters) in diameter, 8–10 inches (20–26 centimeters) high, with slightly convex sides and a rind just under ¼ inch (6 millimeters) thick; straw- or light straw-colored paste with a grainy, flaky consistency; minimum fat in dry matter of 32 percent; and a minimum of 12 months aging within the production zone. Cows employed for Parmigiano Reggiano production must consume no more than 50 percent dry feed, 75 percent of which must be from within the zone; silage is not permitted. The rules permit Parmigiano to be sold grated or portioned, as long as these operations are also performed within the zone.

How It's Made

While most Parmigiano Reggiano is made from Holstein-Friesian milk, some is made exclusively from the milk of other breeds, including the Bruna Alpina (Brown Swiss), and the traditional local Vacca Bianca Modenese (Modenese white cow) and the Vacche Rosse (red cows), or Reggiana. The former sub-category is called Solo di Bruna (only from the brown); the latter two now have their own organizations, a Slow Food Presidium for the white Modenese and the Consorzio Vacche Rosse for the red. There are approximately 350 sanctioned producers of Parmigiano Reggiano, ranging from small farms or creameries that manufacture just a few wheels per day to much larger co-ops and dairies capable of turning out scores of them daily. That number once hovered closer to seven hundred but difficult times in the Italian economy during the early twenty-first century forced the industry to contract.

A wheel of Parmesan is made of the whole milk from a morning's milking combined with the skimmed milk from the previous evening's milking. The milk is acidified with fermented whey and coagulated with calf rennet. The curds are cut and cooked at a temperature of 131°F (55°C) in large copper vats, then drained. Each batch eventually yields two wheels of cheese. Once formed, the cheeses are brined for about twenty-four days then brought to their aging rooms. A matrix is inserted into the molds used to form the wheels and it imprints "Parmigiano Reggiano" in pin-dot lettering around their sides as well as the producer's identification number and the month and year of production, with the month abbreviated—for example, "Mag" for Maggio (May).

At twelve months each wheel is inspected visually and given the so-called hammer test: A consortium inspector called a *battitore* (drummer) taps it with a small metal mallet to check for structural defects. Up to 10 percent of wheels are rejected. All wheels deemed acceptable are graded and fire-branded with the official consortium stamp. After eighteen months a producer or *stagionatore* (ager) may request further inspection. The finest cheeses are then marked "Extra," which qualifies them for export. Some producers x-ray all their wheels to detect irregularities.

Aging and Flavor

Among Parmigiano Reggiano's signature traits is prodigious umami. In fact, it has some of the highest levels of free glutamates, the amino acids responsible for the fifth taste, of any food. At 1,200 milligrams per 100 grams, it is second only to Roquefort (1,280 milligrams) among cheeses. Aged Parmigiano Reggianos have been known to go as high as 1,600 milligrams. They offer complex, long-lasting flavor profiles, featuring lactic (fermented milk), sweet (fresh cream, melted butter), fruity or citrusy notes (apricot, banana, dried fruits, lemon, pineapple), balanced by savory nutty (hazelnut, walnut) and meaty ones. Some producers make the extra effort of producing organic cheeses or exceeding legal minimums for standards such as the cows' feed, which they believe enhances their organoleptic qualities. See FLAVOR.

Beginning at about eighteen months, crystals of the denatured cheese protein tyrosine form in the paste and are often visible as small white spheres. These "crunchies" offer a pleasant contrast to the cheese's generally semihard yet moist consistency;

they also contribute bitter notes, balancing the sweet and salty ones. See CRYSTAL. With age a Parmigiano becomes harder, saltier, and more concentrated; bitter notes continue to emerge. Export-quality cheeses are sold beginning around twenty-four months and may be enjoyed up to thirty-six months, at which point some may be more suitable to grating over pasta than savoring as stand-alone table cheeses.

Sophisticated connoisseurs may highlight nuances of seasonality and terroir, maintaining that cheeses from different microclimates or made at different times of the cows' lactation cycle exhibit subtle distinctions. Cheeses from the hills around Reggio, for example, may possess more acidity while Parma's have more butterfat, meaning their crystal pockets will take longer to develop. Regardless, any well-aged Parmigiano Reggiano is a benchmark cheese, the pride of Italy and coveted by turophiles the world over.

See also ITALY.

Consorzio Vacche Rosse website. http://www
.consorziovaccherosse.it.
DiPalo, Lou, and Rachel Wharton. "Grana Padano and
Parmigiano-Reggiano." In DiPalo's Guide to the
Essential Foods of Italy. New York: Ballantine, 2014.
Ministere delle Politiche Agricole Alimentari e Forestali
website. http://www.politicheagricole.it.
Parmesan.com. http://www.parmesan.com.
Parmiggiano Reggiano website. http://www
.parmigianoreggiano.com.

David Gibbons

Paški sir is a sheep's milk cheese that is produced throughout the 177-square-mile (284-square-kilometer) Croatian island of Pag, which is located along the eastern part of the Adriatic Sea. The production of a Paški cheese similar to the one that is known today is presumed to have started in 1870, when farmers crossed a local domestic sheep breed with Merino Negretti rams to obtain the more milk-productive Paška sheep breed adapted to the specific environment of Pag. The oldest available document that describes the production of Paški cheese was written in 1925 in the book *Cheesemaking According to the Newest Science and Practice*.

The Island of Pag has a karst area, meaning a rocky pasture consisting of a range of quality pastoral species. Climatically, the island is exposed to strong storms that cause sea salt to cover the very limited vegetation. The climate is mild and dry, typically Mediterranean. The botanical composition of the meadows and pastures is characterized by intense, aromatic, and healthful herbs. Six hundred farmers breed Paška sheep on Pag, potentially producing up to a hundred tons of Paški cheese annually. Paški cheese is produced on local farms, as well as in three dairy plants (Gligora Kolan, MIH Kolan, and Paška sirana Pag). Gligora's Paški cheese was ranked number one in the category of hard sheep cheeses at the World Championship Cheese Contest, which took place in Madison, Wisconsin, in 2014.

The number of sheep on the island of Pag varies between twenty-five thousand and twenty-eight thousand. Paška sheep are smaller in size than other Croatian sheep. The sheep lamb in January and February. For milking purposes, lambs only suckle their mother for one month. The yield of milk varies between 21 and 40 gallons (80–150 liters) per lactation. Typically, Paška sheep stay out to pasture year round. In addition to pasture, Paška sheep are fed with hay and corn, especially during lactation.

The quality of Paška sheep's milk has been well investigated and is characterized by a high total solids content, as well as a large amount of fat and protein, which make it desirable for cheesemaking. Only natural rennet should be used for coagulation. The coagulum is first cut into 2–3 inch (5–7 centimeter) squares and later broken into rice-size grains using wooden tools. The grains are heated to 106°F (41°C) and allowed to settle to form the cheese body. The cheese is then molded and pressed. Over the next forty-eight hours it is salted three times with medium-size sea salt grains rubbed onto the surface. Paški cheese should be ripened for a minimum of two months. For cheese of the best quality, ripening will be extended up to five months, at a temperature of 61°F (16°C) and a relative humidity of up to 90 percent.

Cylindrical in shape with a flat surface, Paški cheese has a diameter of 7–9 inches (18–23 centimeters), a height of 2.8–3.5 inches (7–9 centimeters), and a weight that varies between 4.5 and 9 pounds (2–4 kilograms). The rind of the cheese is hard, with a yellowish color that can vary to reddish or brown. Paški cheese is slightly elastic and easy to cut, with older cheese having a more granular texture. On the cut surface, a few eyes can be noticed. The cheese melts in your mouth, releasing an intense flavor, typical of sheep cheeses. Nutritionally, Paški cheese is rich in minerals.

See also CROATIA and SHEEP.

Filipović, S. *Cheesemaking According to the Newest Science and Practice.* Zagreb, Croatia: St. Kugli, 1925. In Croatian.

Kitonić, T., and Lj Tratnik. "Influence of Cow Milk in Mixture with Sheep Milk on the Quality of Cheese Produced with the Paski Sir Cheesemaking Technology." *Milchwissenschaft* 53 (1998): 20–22.

Matutinovic, S., et al. "Effects of Flock, Year, and Season on the Quality of Milk from an Indigenous Breed in the Sub-Mediterranean Area." *Small Ruminant Research* 100 (2011): 159–163.

Rogosic, J. *Management of the Mediterranean Natural Resources.* Mostar, Bosnia and Herzegovina: Skolska Naklada, 2000, pp. 112–127. In Croatian.

Samaržija, D. *Paški Cheese—Protection of Geographical Indications (Specification).* Zagreb, Croatia: University of Zagreb, Faculty of Agriculture. In Croatian.

Samaržija, D., et al. "Mineral Value of Croatian Artisanal Hard Sheep Cheeses in Terms of Geographical Indication." *Milchwissenschaft* 60 (2005): 158–161.

Samir Kalit

pasta filata, literally "spun paste," refers to a family of Italian cheeses whose paste is stretched or pulled during cheesemaking. It includes roughly a dozen cheeses ranging from fresh (mozzarella) to extra-aged (provolone), primarily from the regions of Campania, Basilicata, and Puglia. *Filata* derives from *filo* meaning "string" or "thread," thus the popular supermarket cheese known as string cheese. The most common pasta filata cheese, mozzarella, is, the second most popular cheese (after Cheddar) in the United States. The name derives from the Italian word *mozzare,* meaning to tear or break up. See MOZZARELLA; MOZZARELLA DI BUFALA CAMPANA; and STRING CHEESE.

Pasta filata cheeses are made by cutting up the curd, more accurately known as coagulum, and melting it in very hot water (approximately 170°F [77°C]) to the point that it can be stretched and pulled into long wide ribbons. On an artisanal scale, a large wooden or metal spatula is used to assist in the stretching. Once the curd has been sufficiently worked, the paste is formed into a variety of round or oval shapes from *cilegieni* (little cherry-size orbs) to very large braids known as *treccione,* which can weigh 10 or more pounds (4.5 or more kilograms). Frequently these cheeses are also smoked. In recent years another pasta filata cheese, burrata, a cream-enriched mozzarella from Puglia, has become popular on restaurant menus. Burrata can be made from buffalo milk or cow's milk. Today a number of burratas are made around the United States from cow's milk that is enriched with cow's cream. See BURRATA.

The provolone family—a subfamily of the pasta filata family—comprises cheeses of varying degrees of ripeness and pungency and includes provolone dolce (two to three months old) and provolone piccante (aged for a year or more). Provolone is more

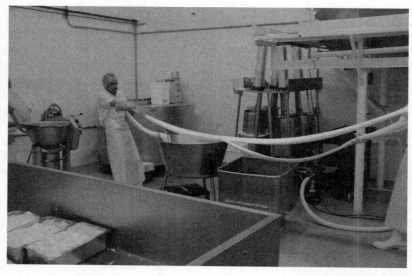

Hand-stretching is extremely physical and requires deftness and care. Here cheesemakers at Ochoa's Quesaria in Albany, Oregon, work the curd. © GIANACLIS CALDWELL

This beautiful skein is the result of the Ochoa's Quesaria cheesemakers laboriously hand-stretching the curd.
© GIANACLIS CALDWELL

or less a mozzarella that has had its surface rubbed with a brine, bound with a twine or rope (depending upon its weight), and then hung up to age. During the curing, or ripening process, a rind develops that turns golden yellow and the paste of the cheese becomes dense and turns an ivory color. Some producers will apply a light wax to the developing rind to prevent undesirable molds from forming and also to prevent the aging cheeses from drying out. Some provolones resembles melons in size and weight, while others are torpedo-shaped and can weigh up to 200 pounds (91 kilograms). The name derives from the word *prova*, meaning "globular" in the Campanian dialect. See PROVOLONE VALPADANA; PROVOLONE DEL MONACO; and PROVOLA DEI NEBRODI.

Scamorza, too, is a spun paste cow's milk cheese, originally from Basilicata. Today the center of export production of that cheese is in Lombardy in the north of Italy. Like a provolone, it can be pear-shaped, but it is also available in many other shapes (including animals and birds) and sizes. Semisoft with a texture similar to that of a firm, dry mozzarella, scamorza can be found throughout Apulia and in some parts of Campania and Molise. In general the cheese is made from pasteurized cow's milk but may be made from a mixture of cow's and sheep's milk. At the end of the cheesemaking process, which involves pulling the curd as for mozzarella, the cheeses are hung together on strings to ripen for about two weeks. The process of ripening the cheese has given scamorza its name, which in southern Italian slang means "beheaded." Scamorza can also be smoked, in which case it is known as scamorza affumicata.

Caciocavallo is another pasta filata cheese. Its name means "cheese on horseback" and derives from the manner in which the cheese is suspended (sawhorse style) over a wooden board to drain and then age. Its look is quite similar to a provolone. The cheese can be made from sheep's or cow's milk, and it is produced throughout southern Italy and the Balkans. See CACIOCAVALLO.

Pasta filata cheeses vary greatly in taste and texture due to varying aging times as well as size and weight. They can be enjoyed as is at room temperature or used in pasta dishes and for pizza making.

Di Palo, Lou. *Di Palo's Guide to the Essential Foods of Italy.* New York: Ballantine, 2014.
Jenkins, Steven. *Cheese Primer.* New York: Workman, 1996.
Sardo, Piero, et al. *Formaggi d'Italia: Guida alla Scoperta e alla conoscenza.* Bra, Italy: Slow Food Editore, 1999.

Alexandra Leaf

Pasteur, Louis (1822–1895), was a French scientist who, with his collaborators, made pivotal discoveries in the nineteenth century. Above all he laid the foundation for a new discipline, microbiology. His work demonstrated first the role of microorganisms in the distribution of infectious diseases, and he subsequently developed vaccines against several diseases (rabies, for example). His work also demonstrated the role of microorganisms in fermentation, as well as in defects appearing during fermentation. Perhaps most influential for dairying and cheesemaking, he invented the pasteurization process, which is still used all over the world. All his work led to better hygiene practices, in different fields: body hygiene, medicine (saving many lives), and food hygiene. The impact of his research was so important that a commemorative tablet was placed in the front of his native house in Dole (Jura) in 1883: "Louis Pasteur, bene-factor of humanity."

Interestingly Pasteur did not begin his career by studying germs or diseases, but rather he was a chem-ist and worked on tartrate crystals, and its racemic acid, the paratartrate. Both have similar atomic com-position and are impossible to distinguish visually. The only method is to apply a ray of polarized light, which is diverted or not according to the nature of the crystal. Pasteur decided to solve this mystery and reached his first scientific success. Very early in his career Pasteur founded a new branch of science, stereochemistry. Due to his discovery of tartrate crystals, he traveled throughout Europe with the conviction that science must contribute not only to knowledge but to concrete applications. He never hesitated to go out of his laboratory to explore *in situ*, understand, and demonstrate. He even made his students visit industries, which was at the time revolutionary.

In 1854, after several years of research in Dijon and Strasbourg, Pasteur left for Lille, which was a flourishing and active economic area. Napoleon III, the new emperor of France, decided to create in Lille the first university dedicated to science and tech-nology. Originally the faculty had been hired at least in part to solve the practical problems of the indus-tries of the region; for example, the production of alcoholic drinks. Indeed, many distilleries and brew-eries were located near Lille, along with beet sugar production facilities. Pasteur was named dean of the faculty, which gave him the opportunity to enter into the study of fermentation processes, and particularly beers and wine.

The idea that yeast plays a certain role in wine and beer production was not new, but Pasteur showed that the production of alcohol was due to these mi-croorganisms. He also demonstrated that the appear-ance of substances like lactic acid or acetic acids, leading to excessive acidification of the product, was due to bacteria. This acidification of wine and beer was a major economic problem and Pasteur found that a moderate heat treatment could eliminate bac-teria and solve the problem without damaging the overall quality of the product. The process of "pas-teurization" was born. He applied the same strategy for milk before bottling, eradicating progressively tu-berculosis propagation by raw milk. He also studied also butyric fermentation, but as far as we know, not cheese. However it is obvious that without Pasteur's discoveries, cheese microbiology would not have started so early, in 1865–1870.

Pasteur's personality was exceptionally determined. He fought against the scientists of his time concern-ing spontaneous generation. The origin of microor-ganisms was the subject of a vast debate and to deny the spontaneous generation theory (the spontaneous appearance of germs under particular physicochem-ical conditions) was to deny divine creation. Passion-ate debates occurred in the Academy of Science in Paris and finally through Pasteur's demonstrations he was able to convince the assembly that germs were indeed alive and everywhere in the air.

Pasteur's research with regard to rabies vaccina-tion was so crucial that a dedicated institute called the Pasteur Institute was founded in Paris in 1888. It is still considered one of the leading international centers for the study of infectious diseases. Pasteur was the director until he died in 1895. As a national hero, a national burial was organized in Notre Dame Cathedral, and his body was placed in the crypt of the Pasteur Institute that is open to visitors.

All of his life was dedicated to science. His wife, Marie, supported him every day to make it possible for him to devote more of his time to science. Thanks to his fierce battle against pathogens, many newborns and their mothers did not die after delivery, which had been a frequent cause of death in the nineteenth century. By a cruel irony of destiny, Louis and Marie still lost three of their four young children to infec-tious diseases. Sometimes a short anecdote can give a good idea of a person's character. When Pasteur was traveling, he wrote to Marie every day, and ended each letter with the same sentence: "To you and to science for life, Louis."

See also PASTEURIZATION.

Besson, André. *Louis Pasteur: un aventurier de la science.* Monaco: Editions du Rocher, 2013.
Orsenna, Erik. *La vie, la mort, la vie: Louis Pasteur 1822–1895.* Paris: Edition Fayard, 2015.

Sylvie Lortal

pasteurization is the application of mild heat to foods to facilitate the destruction of microorgan-isms. Historically pasteurization was employed for two purposes: to achieve public health protection through destruction of pathogenic microorganisms, and to facilitate the extension of product shelf life through destruction of spoilage microorganisms. The famous French scientist Louis Pasteur (1822–1895) pioneered the concept of pasteurization. Working in the 1860s he discovered that subjecting grape juice to mild heat treatment could eliminate spoilage organisms and ensure the production of wine of consistent high quality. This concept was later applied to achieve public health protection. Pasteurization of milk was first proposed in 1886 by the German scientist Franz Ritter von Soxhlet to improve the safety of bottled milk fed to infants.

The application of pasteurization to milk and dairy products has resulted in major public health advances worldwide and has had a profound positive impact on the safety of dairy products. Milk-borne diseases, including tuberculosis, diphtheria, scarlet fever, typhoid fever, Q fever, brucellosis, anthrax, and foot and mouth disease were prevalent prior to the adoption of milk pasteurization. Typhoid fever caused by *Salmonella typhi*, scarlet fever due to *Streptococcus pyogenes*, and diphtheria due to *Corynebacterium diptheriae*, were the leading causes of milk-borne disease in the United States between the years 1900 and 1939. Between 1912 and 1937, 65,000 deaths were recorded in England and Wales alone due to tuberculosis contracted from milk consumption.

Pasteurization is accomplished at specific heating temperatures and holding times to achieve destruction of the most resistant vegetative pathogen of public health concern. *Mycobacterium tuberculosis* was the original target for milk pasteurization, when minimum time/temperature parameters of 30 minutes at 142°F (61°C) were established. These parameters were later revised when milk pasteurization time/temperature parameters—30 minutes at 145°F (63°C) for vat pasteurization; 161°F (72°C) for 15 seconds for high temperature, short time pasteurization (also known as HTST)—were established to ensure destruction of *Coxiella burnetti*, an intracellular bacterium that is the causative agent of Q fever.

Historically application of pasteurization to milk intended for cheesemaking was found to have a number of benefits. Pasteurization of milk was found to assure the consistency and quality of cheeses. If raw milk used for cheesemaking was of inferior quality, cheese made from pasteurized milk resulted in improved flavor, yield, uniformity, shelf life, and simplification of the cheese manufacturing process. Pasteurization was also found to extend the shelf life of some cheeses for shipment across great distances, such as Brie, which was first imported to the United States in 1936. Pasteurization was used to facilitate export because of the need to find a stable and safe way to distribute cheese. See SHELF LIFE.

In the United States the Food and Drug Administration (FDA) is the agency that regulates the safety of milk and dairy products produced in, or imported to, the United States. US regulations that govern the use of raw, heat-treated, and pasteurized milk for cheesemaking were promulgated in 1949. To assure the safety of cheese cheesemakers can either pasteurize milk utilized in cheesemaking; or they can hold cheese at temperatures of not less than 35°F (2°C) for a minimum of sixty days. See FOOD AND DRUG ADMINISTRATION and 60-DAY AGING RULE.

A number of considerations must be made when deciding whether to employ pasteurization or to utilize aging of sixty days or longer to achieve cheese safety. The type of cheese being produced dictates whether pasteurization or sixty days of aging can be legally applied. The US Code of Federal Regulations (21 CFR, Part 133) provides specific requirements for cheeses by category. Further considerations include food safety implications, the quality and sensory characteristics desired, costs of capital investment in pasteurization equipment, and the cheesemaker's level of control over milk quality and consistency. The return of artisan cheesemaking and the widespread demand for artisan cheese products has resulted in a global reexamination of the safety of traditional artisan cheeses. Efforts have been underway in North America to examine a regulatory change requiring mandatory pasteurization of all milk intended for cheesemaking. The pathogens of concern to cheesemakers today, including *E. coli* O157:H7, *Listeria monocytogenes*, *Salmonella typhimurium* DT 104, and *Staphylococcus aureus*, were not the same pathogens of concern in 1948. In 1997 the US Food and Drug Administration requested that the National Advisory Committee for the Microbiological Criteria for Foods review the rules in place regulating raw-milk cheese production. Concern was expressed that aging alone may be insufficient to provide an adequate level of public health protection. At the same time, in 1996, a proposed amendment in Canada would have required all cheeses to be made from pasteurized milk or the equivalent. Health Canada ultimately withdrew this amendment because a Scientific Expert Committee stated that the technical requirements could not be met in the manufacturing process by small scale cheesemakers.

Pasteurization of milk intended for cheesemaking is a contentious issue. In order to facilitate global trade, the concept of Appropriate Level of Protection (ALOP) was established in 1994 by the World Trade Organization through the Sanitary and Phytosanitary (SPS) Agreement. The United States and Europe have remained divided over approaches to achieve the ALOP for cheeses. In 1997, at a Codex Committee on Food Hygiene meeting, a draft outline was prepared by the United States, France, and the International Dairy Federation on development of a milk code. The committee agreed to stop work on the "Proposed Draft Code of Hygienic Practice for the manufacture of un-ripened cheese and ripened soft cheese." In this Draft Code, the United States had proposed "Pasteurization, or an equivalent measure approved by the official agency having jurisdiction, shall be used in order to achieve the ALOP." France objected, noting "common hygiene provisions provide adequate health protection without pasteurization." The United States maintained the position that "raw milk and raw milk products are potentially hazardous foods that support growth of pathogens such as *Listeria*, *Salmonella*, *E. coli* and others. Cheese poses a particularly high health risk because it is usually ready-to-eat (RTE) and will not be cooked before consumption. Scientifically accepted processes control the threat. These can include pasteurization, heat treatment, sterilization of milk; aging of cheese and new technologies not yet developed." The US position is counter to that of the EU Commission, which states: "Consumer safety is protected when strict veterinary and sanitary practices are followed from production to consumption including: using raw milk from herds in good health with regular veterinary inspections, subject to sanitary controls; using milk that is collected, transported and transformed within a short period of time applying strict hygiene; and educating consumers about proper storage and shelf life."

Curiously the United States amended the legal definition of pasteurization in the 2002 Farm Bill. Title X, subtitle I, Section 10808(b) of the Farm Security and Rural Investment Act broadened the definition of pasteurization by mandating that Section 403(h) (Misbranded Food) of the Federal Food, Drug and Cosmetic Act (FFDCA) be amended to include a definition for pasteurization. The new US

working definition became: "Any process, treatment, or combination thereof, that is applied to food to reduce the most resistant microorganism(s) of public health significance to a level that is not likely to present a public health risk under normal conditions of distribution and storage."

This definition aligns with Codex, which states that "from raw material production to the point of consumption, dairy products produced under this Code should be subject to a combination of control measures, and these control measures should be shown to achieve the appropriate level of public health protection." Codex defines pasteurization as "a microbiocidal heat treatment aimed at reducing the number of any pathogenic micro-organisms in milk and liquid milk products, if present, to a level at which they do not constitute a significant health hazard. Pasteurization conditions are designed to effectively destroy the organisms *Mycobacterium tuberculosis* and *Coxiella burnettii*."

European Community Directives contain regulations for the production and marketing of milk and milk-based products. These regulations establish hygienic standards for raw-milk collection and transportation that focus on issues such as temperature, sanitation, and microbiological standards, enabling production of milk of the highest quality. EU microbiological criteria laid out in Commission Regulation (EC) No 2073/2005 for cheese are risk-based and differ depending upon whether cheese has been made from heat-treated or raw milk. In cheese made from heat-treated milk, limits have been established for *Staphylococcus aureus* (as a food safety index), along with targets for *E. coli* (as a hygienic indicator). The application of *E. coli* limits provides a scientifically meaningful standard in cheese made from heat-treated milk as *E. coli* does not survive heat treatment, thus its presence in cheese made from heat-treated milk indicates post-pasteurization contamination. For cheeses made from raw milk, if levels of coagulase-positive *Staphylococcus aureus* are found to exceed 10^5, the batch must be tested and absence of enterotoxin demonstrated. The stage of cheesemaking where the criterion applies is "at the time during the manufacturing process when the number of staphylococci is expected to be the highest." Action required in the case of unsatisfactory results includes "improvements in production hygiene and selection of raw materials. If values of $>10^5$ cfu/g are detected, the cheese batch has to be tested for staphylococcal enterotoxins." The EU microbiological criteria for cheese also include standards for *Listeria monocytogenes* (which must not exceed 100 cfu/g at end of shelf life), *Salmonella* (ND in 25g), and *E. coli O157* (ND in 25g). It is notable that no limits were established for *E. coli* in raw-milk cheese. *E. coli* does not offer a meaningful hygienic index in raw products as its presence is expected, consistent with guidance from ICMSF.

Food Standards Australia New Zealand (FSANZ) has applied the concept of equivalence to assess the safety of cheeses. See FOOD STANDARDS AUSTRALIA NEW ZEALAND and EQUIVALENCE OF PASTEURIZATION. Comprehensive risk assessments conducted by FSANZ demonstrated that raw-milk hard Swiss cheese varieties, including Emmentaler, Gruyère, and Sbrinz, and extra-hard grating cheeses, including Parmigiano Reggiano, Grana Padano, Romano, Asiago, and Montasio, had a level of microbiological safety equivalent to cheeses made from pasteurized milk due to manufacturing and aging parameters. In the United States, a petition would need to be filed, and the FDA would need to approve the manufacturing parameters as equivalent in order to use the labeling term "pasteurized."

Cheeses made from milk subjected to a sub-pasteurization heat treatment (or thermization) are legally classified as raw-milk cheeses. Thermization is beneficial for milk that has been transported and stored under refrigeration or when there will be a delay in milk utilization prior to cheese manufacture. The use of thermization helps to reduce the growth of psychrotrophic bacteria that cause quality defects in cheese. Much of the milk used in the United States for raw-milk cheesemaking is subjected to some form of heat treatment, generally thermization. As a rule, this treatment consists of heating at 131°F (55°C) for a period ranging from two to sixteen seconds. Pasteurization alone will not ensure the safety of cheeses. For pathogens such as *Listeria monocytogenes*, contamination primarily results from post-pasteurization environmental recontamination of cheese. In fact numerous studies have shown a higher incidence of *Listeria* in cheeses made from pasteurized milk versus raw milk.

See also *LISTERIA*; PASTEUR, LOUIS; PATHOGENS; RAW-MILK CHEESES; and THERMIZED MILK CHEESES.

Donnelly, C. W. "The Pasteurization Dilemma." In *American Farmstead Cheese*, edited by P. S. Kindstedt, pp. 173–195. White River Junction, Vt.: Chelsea Green, 2005.

National Advisory Committee on Microbiological Criteria for Foods. "Requisite Scientific Parameters for Establishing the Equivalence of Alternative Methods of Pasteurization." *Journal of Food Protection* 69, no. 5 (2006): 1190–1216.

Catherine Donnelly

pasteurized process cheeses are dairy products produced by the continuous blending with heat, of a mixture of natural cheese and other ingredients to form a stable, homogeneous mass. This hot, liquid "melt" is then discharged to a form or package, where it cools and hardens. Three factors are critical in producing pasteurized process cheese. The first is agitation or shear. Bulk natural cheese is ground or shredded before being added to the mixture, while the mixture itself is subjected to shear that varies from gentle to intense, depending on the final product desired. The second factor is heat, which is required along with agitation to obtain adequate hydration and blending of the ingredients. The third factor is the addition of emulsifying salts (trisodium citrate and/or sodium phosphates). These factors are required for two reasons. The first is to chelate cross-linking calcium from the cheese protein, allowing these proteins (caseins) to dissolve into the melt. The free caseins act to stabilize fat and moisture in the final product. The second reason is that emulsifying salts are added to poise the pH of the product in the proper range of between 5.6 and 6.0. Above pH 6.0, the product has less shelf stability and an unpleasant, "soapy" flavor. Below pH 5.6, the product tends to be brittle, and releases excessive free oil.

In the initial processing step the ingredients (ground cheese, dairy powders, stabilizers, emulsifiers, salt, flavors, colors, preservatives, fillers, and water) are blended in the process cheese cooker. The mixture is heated, with continuous agitation, by either direct steam injection, indirect heating (with steam or water), or a combination of both methods. During this process, the emulsifying salts dissolve and chelate calcium, allowing the release of casein molecules. The milk fat melts and is dispersed into smaller droplets with casein molecules deposited on their surfaces. Moisture is also worked into smaller droplets by agitation, and is dispersed uniformly throughout the melt. The process cheese melt is held at a maximum temperature of approximately 165–195°F (74–91°C) with continuous agitation for several minutes or more, depending on the product to be made, then is discharged to forms or the final package. During cooling of the melt, the casein forms a solid three-dimensional network with fat and water droplets embedded within it.

Pasteurized process cheese flavor, texture, and functionality vary based on the amount of natural cheese used, the moisture content, and the amount and type of emulsifying salts added. In the United States there are three standards of identity for pasteurized process cheese: pasteurized process cheese, pasteurized process cheese food, and pasteurized process cheese spread. All of these products have specific standards of identity listing the minimum natural cheese and fat, maximum moisture, and allowed ingredients. Pasteurized process cheese has the highest required natural cheese and fat percentages and the lowest allowed moisture and number of additional ingredients. Pasteurized process cheese sauce, which has no standard of identity, generally contains the lowest natural cheese content, highest moisture content, and widest variety of ingredients.

See also FUNCTIONAL PROPERTIES; INDUSTRIAL; INDUSTRIALIZATION; and PASTEURIZATION.

Tamime, A. Y. *Processed Cheese and Analogues.* Oxford: Wiley-Blackwell, 2011.
United States, Code of Federal Regulations, Title 21, Part 133: Cheeses and Related Cheese Products, Section 133.169: Pasteurized Process Cheese; Section 133.173: Pasteurized Process Cheese Food; Section 133.179: Pasteurized Process Cheese Spread.
Zehren, V. L., and D. D. Nusbaum. *Process Cheese.* Madison, Wis.: Cheese Reporter, 2000.

Dana D. Wolle

pastoralism refers to a social form of subsistence based on tending large herds or flocks of livestock, usually ruminants that produce milk. It can be taken to refer both to long-range tribal nomadism ("pastoral nomadism") and to smaller-range, semi-sedentary patterns of movement that shepherds employ mainly to find fresh grass and seasonal resources, such as water and pasture land for their flocks. Pastoral peoples may tend not only sheep but also goats, cattle, and dromedaries.

Potentially crossing multiple regional and national borders, transit routes for pastoral herders have historically served as pilgrimage or trade routes, but also as routes for trafficking and smuggling. This helps to explain why a number of normalizing forces, from colonial bureaucracies to wage employment, have actively discouraged pastoral practices, resulting in the economic and social marginalization of former pastoralist peoples. The sedentarization of pastoralists is often connected to larger geopolitical circumstances, such as colonization or the creation of post-colonial nation-states, as well as to economic and demographic factors, such as the expansion of metropolitan areas and increased dependence on cash economies as a result of the introduction of factory jobs and a market economy. Pastoralism as a way of life is in decline throughout the world.

Classic pastoralist sites encompass the regions of the Middle East and North Africa (Chatty 2006), vast arid regions spanning the borders of Afghanistan, Pakistan, and Iran; the mountainous areas of Hindu Kush, Tibet (Jones 1996), and sub-Saharan Africa (used, for example, by the Nuer of Anglo-Egyptian Sudan, famously described by the anthropologist E. E. Evans-Pritchard, 1940), as well as Western Europe (see, for example, the ethnographic films produced by David MacDougall with Sardinian shepherds in Italy, 1992, and with Jie cattle breeders in Uganda, 1973). Pastoralism as a mode of living is sometimes also used to describe the tending of undomesticated or semi-domesticated animals, such as the pigs in Papua New Guinea and the reindeer-corralling seasonal activities of the Saami of northern Europe.

Pastoralist societies share important elements of seasonality, mobile abodes, cyclical movement between camps and homestead, careful balancing of herd numbers and human demographics, self-sustenance through excellent knowledge of local natural resources and self-sufficiency skills, as well as extensive trade networks connected with their habitual trails and stations. From livestock they derive an extensive range of foodstuffs, raw and clothing materials, means of transportation, and draft animals. Pastoral societies are noted for their will to maintain self-rule within often authoritarian nations and for their reluctance to give in to large centralized administrative structures and obligations (such as travel documents and taxation), as well as for the diversity of their social arrangements, including segmentary tribes that conduct alliances by lineage, chiefdoms, and the egalitarian ethos of pastoral peasants.

The categories of nomadism, pastoralism, and transhumance are sometimes used in interchangeable ways, which can create some confusion. Braudel provides a clear and historically grounded distinction between transhumance and nomadic pastoralism as "two Mediterranean ways of life" (1995, pp. 85–102).

See also SHEPHERD and TRANSHUMANCE.

Braudel, Fernand. *The Mediterranean in the Age of Philip II.* Vol. 1. Translated by Siân Reynolds. Berkeley: University of California Press, 1995. English translation of *La Méditerranée et le monde méditerranéen à l'époque de Philippe II*, Vol. 1 (Paris: Colin, 1949).

Chatty, Dawn, ed. *Nomadic Societies in the Middle East and North Africa: Entering the Twenty-first Century.* Leiden, The Netherlands: Brill, 2006.

Johnson, Douglas L. "The Nature of Nomadism: A Comparative Study of Pastoral Migrations in Southwestern Asia and Northern Africa." University of Chicago, Department of Geography, Research Paper 118, 1969.

Evans-Pritchard, E. E. *The Nuer: A Description of the Modes of Livelihood and Political Institutions of a Nilotic People.* Oxford: Clarendon, 1940.

Jones, Schuyler. *Tibetan Nomads: Environment, Pastoral Economy, and Material Culture.* London: Thames and Hudson, 1996.

MacDougall, David. *To Live with Herds.* London: Royal Anthropological Institute, 1992. DVD, 90 min.

MacDougall, David. *Tempus de Baristas* [Time of the Barmen]. San Francisco: Kanopy Streaming, 1973. e-Film, 100 min.

Salzman, Philip Carl. *Pastoralists: Equality, Hierarchy, and the State.* Boulder, Colo.: Westview, 2004.

Cristina Grasseni

pasture, the foundation of every great cheese, is ideally composed of all the wide mix of grasses, wildflowers, herbs, and other broad-leafed plants, as many as seventy-five or one hundred, that may inhabit a section of permanent grazing land. The forage plants, consumed fresh or dried as hay, are the chief traditional food of dairy animals. European cheese appellations commonly mandate forage as the foundation of the animals' diet. (Feeding silage, because of the risks of inferior flavor and of conveying certain pathogens to cheese, is often forbidden. See SILAGE.) Allowing animals to spend their days outdoors is more humane, with the benefit to them and the farmer that they are healthier. And permanent pasture especially suits hilly and mountainous areas with generous rainfall, where plowing would cause erosion. Compared with feeding grain, milk from animals on pasture has a higher proportion of polyunsaturated fat, which makes the cheese softer and also healthier for the consumer. In addition to the grasses and legumes found in temporary pastures, which are periodically plowed and replanted, permanent pastures contain many broad-leafed plants that contribute aroma to dairy products. Pasture can be an essential component of the taste of terroir of a cheese. See AROMA and TERROIR.

Within a permanent pasture, the many different organisms form an ecological community. Soil itself is sometimes called a "living organism," because it is filled with plant roots, worms, insects, and various microorganisms, especially bacteria and fungi. The microorganisms, concentrated in the top inch (two or three centimeters) of soil, digest organic matter, making nutrients available to plants. In permanent pasture, they are protected by a thatch of dead plant material just above the surface that slows evaporation and keeps the soil moister and cooler. A permanent pasture also contains many more mycorrhizal fungi, which are symbiotic with the plants; they live on or in plant roots and help to supply mineral nutrients and water.

Unlike conventional agriculture, which relies on large expenditures on fertilizer, herbicides, pesticides, and machinery, agriculture that relies heavily on pasture requires only low inputs of labor and capital. Permanent, rotationally grazed pasture can offer strong economic advantages beyond more fertile soil. Plowing and replanting are eliminated. It also takes less time to move animals into fresh pasture than it does to feed them in confinement. There's less harvesting and hauling of food, less handling of manure, less barnyard runoff to pollute streams, less erosion, less need for fertilizer, and less call for herbicides and pesticides, for those who use them—permanent pasture is highly sustainable. The savings in labor, materials, and equipment generally results in a higher net income per animal.

The Options of Plowing and of Confining Animals

Plowing, in addition to requiring time, equipment, and fuel, has other drawbacks. It disrupts soil structure and the life in the soil, particularly fungi. And the weight of the machinery compacts it, so less water infiltrates it and more runs off, carrying nutrients with it. The soil, being less porous, contains less air, so roots are deprived of much of the oxygen and nitrogen they need. Besides, when pasture is plowed and replanted, the number of species is limited, affecting the aroma of cheese, and plant roots don't have time to reach deep for water and nutrients. Long-term yields are lower.

Yet some farmers do periodically plow their pastures, because that immediately releases nutrients that boost growth for a year or two and because plowing gives an opportunity to replant with species, such as legumes, chosen for high nutritional value. Plowing and replanting of pasture can also occur as part of a crop rotation with cereals, such as corn (maize) or barley, which a farmer may grow as feed for the animals.

Despite all the advantages to pasture, not every dairy farmer uses it. In areas of high-cost agricultural land, for instance, a farmer may worry about the damage to forage from animals trampling with their hooves. For maximum productivity, a farmer may confine the animals, clip the fresh plants by machine, and then deliver the forage to the animals. The most profitable methods depend on the variables of the individual farm—the skills of the farmer, how much land is available, its fertility and cost, and the distance from the pasture to the place where the animals are milked.

Managing Pastures

The greatest nutritional value in the plants lies in the first centimeters of growth. As plants reach roughly 10 inches (25 centimeters), they put their energy into reproduction: buds, flowers, and seeds. The quality of the forage promptly declines and growth ceases. In temperate climates with plenty of rainfall, a length of about 8 inches (20 centimeters) represents the best compromise between quality and yield. When the animals eat the pasture down to about 4 inches (10 centimeters), the farmer moves them into a fresh area. The old grazier's rule of thumb is: "Take half, leave half." That's a useful guide, although different species have different growing habits and respond differently to being grazed. Most important is that if the animals eat the plants too close to the soil, growth both above and below ground is reduced and

recovery is delayed. Continuous overgrazing causes erosion.

The best way to maintain and improve a pasture is simply to graze it regularly, each time letting it regrow before grazing it again. During the height of spring growth, the pasture may be ready again in as little as twenty days. It helps to fertilize, if a soil test shows particular needs, though the rules for some cheese appellations specifically limit or prohibit synthetic nitrogen fertilizer, because in too great quantity it favors faster-growing species that eventually eliminate slower-growing ones. A more long-term solution to increasing nitrogen in a poorly maintained pasture is to overseed with legumes, such as clover or alfalfa (lucerne), whose roots, if the right bacteria are also supplied, fix the nitrogen from the air within soil.

To allow a steadier pattern of growth-grazing-regrowth, intensively managed pasture is divided into small paddocks using lightweight, easily moved fencing, and the animals are shifted frequently into fresh plots. That may occur every couple of days, even every day or every twelve hours with very small plots, depending on the rate of growth during that period and the number of animals in relation to the area. The idea is to stock the space densely enough that the animals eat everything more or less evenly.

But an animal does have preferences, and in a lightly populated permanent pasture she will choose her diet from among the plants growing there. Less desirable species, even poisonous ones, can spread. The solutions are denser stocking, cutting the pasture now and then by machine, and, for instance, eradicating troublesome thistles by hand. In contrast a dairy farmer who pursues non-pasture intensive methods supplies a ration that gives complete control over what each cow eats, apart from quantity. See TOTAL MIXED RATION.

The precise plant species within a permanent pasture, and their number, reflect the particular soil and rock, altitude, exposition, precipitation, and the treatment by the farmer. See BIODIVERSITY. The number of species remains stable from year to year (barring only the effects of a rare, extreme dry spell), although the abundance of each may vary. Proportions are more stable in more diverse pastures, and the greatest diversity occurs not in warm, fertile plains but in mountain pastures, especially at high altitude. See ALPAGE. The *cahier des charges* for AOP Beaufort, in the Alpine region of eastern France, cites studies showing a total of 250 to 300 species for the appellation.

The catch with intensive use of pasture, if the goal is a complex aged cheese from a biodiverse pasture, is that dense stocking with animals and frequent grazing reduces the number of plant species. The faster-growing, more competitive plants overshadow the slower-growing ones, which never have time to catch up. The number of animals must be limited and there must be a longer delay before regrazing, so that all the plants have the time they need to grow.

During the course of the year, the milk changes in response to the state of the pasture and the immediate weather, so each day the cheesemaker must make adjustments. The biggest change in milk comes in fall and spring, during the gradual transition from pasture to hay and back again. Where lush summer plants may be 85 percent or more moisture, hay is the reverse. And while turning fresh forage into hay makes it less nutritious, some hay is much higher quality than other.

The most nutritious hay—the best for milk for cheese—naturally comes from plants that are at their peak moment for grazing. That means spring and to a lesser extent early fall. During those periods, when there is rapid growth and more forage than the animals can eat, the excess is made into hay. Quality is better preserved by faster drying, whether outdoors by the sun or indoors with the aid of a machine. That leaves a greener color from chlorophyll, as well as a little more carotene, which shows up in slightly yellower cheese even in winter. Although winter cheeses can be outstanding, summer cheeses with their yellower color from fresh forage, are generally superior. See COLOR.

The Link of Pasture to Flavor in Cheese

The romantic idea that herbs and wildflowers, compared with grasses, legumes, and concentrated feeds, lend important aromas to cheese has support from multiple scientific studies. Although the overwhelming majority of cheese aromas come from proteins, fats, and sugars, certain distinctive aromas come from the terpenes in broad-leafed pasture plants. Terpenes are organic compounds that are the distinguishing components of the essential oils of plants. In nature their role is to repulse predators, such as herbivores, and to attract pollinators. Studies suggest that half the species in a mountain pasture may contribute terpenes

that affect the flavor of cheese. Greater diversity doesn't give stronger flavor than grasses or corn do, but it does give more complex flavor. The terpenes may also have an indirect effect. They are antimicrobial, and researchers theorize they modify the way microorganisms act inside a cheese during aging, and in that way influence flavor, although this has not yet been confirmed by study. For the most biodiverse pastures to have their full effect on cheese flavor, the milk must be raw, because pasteurization alters the terpenes and other important compounds, such as native enzymes and microorganisms, and mutes their impact. See FLAVOR AND RAW-MILK CHEESES.

The quantities of terpenes from humid mountain climates aren't enough for tasters to detect in young cheeses, only in more aged ones. Examples of aromatic plants that influence AOP Saint-Nectaire from high in the central French region of Auvergne include creeping thyme, yellow gentian, spignel (*fenouil des Alpes*), yarrow, and alpine clover (*trèfle des Alpes*). For the mixed-milk cheese DOP Robiola di Roccaverano, from the Italian region of Piedmont, they include wild carrot, sage, rue, creeping thistle, spike lavender, various species of thyme, and a wild rose.

At an extreme from well-watered mountain pastures are the warm, dry, wild or semi-wild shrublands associated especially with the Mediterranean. There the quantities of terpenes are strong enough to be detected even in fresh cheese and milk. Sheep and cattle are raised in some areas of shrubland, and goats happily browse higher-growing, woodier plants, preferring the tender tips. In California the broad name for these landscapes is chaparral, originally Spanish, from *chaparro*, scrub oak. In Europe the different kinds of shrubland draw their names from different languages—*macchia* (Italian) or *maquis* (French), *garrigue* (French), *matorral* (Spanish), and *phrygana* (Greek). These categories have been finely subdivided into numerous ecological habitats. Each, as in permanent pastures elsewhere, has its community of plants that reflects its geology and climate.

The diverse aromatic forage plants in permanent grazing land may be responsible for the difference between a merely good cheese and an exceptional one. Pasture provides an essential link between cheese and place.

Claps, Salvatore. "Un mondo di aromi." In *Il caciocavallo podolico e la Manteca*. Potenza, Italy: ANFOSC, 2001.
Martin, B., et al. "How Do the Nature of Forages and Pasture Diversity Influence the Sensory Quality of

Dairy Livestock Products?" *Animal Science* 81 (2005): 205–212.

Murphy, Bill. *Greener Pastures on Your Side of the Fence.* 4th ed. Colchester, Vt.: Arriba, 1998.

Ormeño, E., et al. "Production and Diversity of Volatile Terpenes from Plants on Calcareous and Siliceous Soils: Effect of Soil Nutrients." *Journal of Chemical Ecology* 34, no. 9 (September 2008): 1219–1229.

Réseaux d'Élevage pour le Conseil et la Prospective, Collection References. "Caprins fromagers spécialisés avec pâturage et en circuits courts." Paris: Institut de l'Elevage, 2011. http://www.pep.chambagri.fr/mydms/pep_caprins/file_506af38cc3a41.pdf.

Van Soest, Peter J., et al. *I Pascoli naturali: Metodologia di campionamento e valutazione nutrizionale delle essenze spontanee dei pascoli del Ragusano.* Ragusa, Italy: Consorzio Ricerca Filiera Lattiero-Casearia di Ragusa, 2001.

Voisin, André. *Grass Productivity.* New York: Philosophical Library, 1959. Originally published as *Productivité de l'erbe* (Paris: Flammarion, 1957).

Edward Behr

pâte molle cheeses

See SOFT-RIPENED CHEESES.

pathogens are organisms that cause disease. In the context of cheese production and consumption, pathogens are microorganisms (e.g., bacteria and viruses) associated with food safety concerns. In the broader context, pathogens include any organism that is able to cause disease in a host species. Some of the most important pathogens of dairy animals are those that cause infections of the mammary gland. With a few exceptions, most bacteria that cause mammary gland infections are opportunistic pathogens. See OPPORTUNISTIC PATHOGEN. Common bacterial pathogens that cause mastitis in dairy animals include: *Escherichia coli*, *Klebsiella pneumoniae*, *Streptococcus agalactiae*, *Streptococcus dysgalactiae*, *Streptococcus uberis*, *Staphylococcus aureus*, and a number of other *Staphylococcus* species.

Some obligate pathogens of dairy animals are shed in the milk of infected animals, including *Mycobacterium bovis*, the causative agent of bovine tuberculosis; *Brucella abortus*, the causative agent of brucellosis; and *Coxiella burnetii*, the causative agent of Q fever. These organisms are also examples of zoonotic pathogens, organisms that can be transmitted from animals to humans and can cause disease in humans.

Pasteurization conditions were originally developed to prevent human exposure to these three zoonotic pathogens through consumption of milk and dairy products from infected animals. Although many regions have controlled bovine tuberculosis and brucellosis, these diseases persist globally and human exposure through unpasteurized fluid milk remains a concern. Pasteurization also reduces contamination of fluid milk with other potential human pathogens. See PASTEURIZATION.

Pathogenic organisms that contaminate food sources are described as food-borne pathogens. Other examples of potential food-borne pathogens that may contaminate milk and cheese include the bacterial species *Escherichia coli*, *Listeria monocytogenes*, and *Staphylococcus aureus*. These organisms can be shed in the milk of infected animals, but they may also contaminate milk from other sources. For example, *Escherichia coli* is an opportunistic pathogen commonly found in feces (i.e., a fecal-borne pathogen) and thus manure contamination of teat and udder skin or milking equipment can lead to milk contamination during harvest. While a majority of *E. coli* strains are nonpathogenic (i.e., do not cause disease), *E. coli* is one of many enteric pathogens causing gastrointestinal illness in people. Further, some *E. coli* strains may cause urinary tract infections. Hemolytic uremic syndrome is a severe, potentially life-threatening disease, caused by shiga toxin-producing *Escherichia coli* (STEC) infections and has been associated with unpasteurized fluid milk consumption in a number of cases worldwide. *Listeria monocytogenes* can be found in the dairy farm environment or in the cheese processing environment, and thus may contaminate milk during harvest or dairy products before or after processing. See LISTERIA and POST-PROCESS CONTAMINATION.

Pathogens may cause disease by a number of mechanisms, but generally the steps in establishing an infection include (1) exposure of the host to the pathogen, (2) attachment or adhesion to the host cells, (3) entry into the host cells or tissue, and (4) multiplication in the cells or tissue space. Infectious disease is typically a manifestation of the cellular or tissue damage associated with this pathogenic process, although signs and symptoms of disease may result from the host's immune system response to pathogen invasion. In some infections there may be no obvious outward clinical signs and the infection may be described as asymptomatic or subclinical.

At one extreme of asymptomatic infections, the host may successfully mount an immune response and clear the pathogen before manifesting any clinical signs. At the other extreme, a pathogen may persist in the host and cause a chronic subclinical infection. Here, the host may be described as an asymptomatic carrier of the pathogen. For example, *Staphylococcus aureus* frequently causes subclinical mastitis in dairy cattle, and may go unrecognized in infected cattle by dairy farmers. The infected cattle can be a source of this pathogen for other cattle in the herd. Subclinical mastitis of dairy cattle is an example of an asymptomatic disease state that is associated with signs of inflammation such as an elevated white blood cell count. This distinguishes a subclinical infection from colonization by normal commensal microorganisms. In addition to causing tissue damage through cellular destruction, many pathogens release toxins that are responsible for the signs of disease. Many pathogens produce proteins or molecules that play a role in the ability of the organism to adhere to cells and invade tissue sites. These molecules are described as virulence factors when they contribute to the ability of the pathogen to survive in the host and cause disease. Some virulence factors are intrinsic to the species or strain of bacteria, encoded in the core chromosomal genes—while other genes encoding virulence factors are found on mobile genetic elements and may be transferred between species and strains of bacteria.

The genes that encode for the increasing problem of antibiotic resistance in bacteria are both chromosomally encoded and found on mobile genetic elements. The latter case makes it possible for antimicrobial resistance to be transferred between different strains and species of bacteria contributing to the spread and emergence of antibiotic resistance among bacterial pathogens. Some virulence factors are secreted molecules that behave as toxins in the host. In some cases the bacterial pathogen may multiply in a food product like milk or cheese resulting in accumulation of the bacterial toxin in the food product. When the food is consumed it is the preformed toxin that causes illness, and not infection and multiplication of the bacterial pathogen in the host. For example, the *Staphylococcus* enterotoxins are a cause of food poisoning where gastroenteritis results from consumption of foods (including milk and cheese) that contain these toxins. See STAPHYLOCOCCUS AUREUS. Finally, with reference to the rhyme based on lines in a poem by Jonathan Swift, "big fleas have little fleas that bite 'em, and little fleas have smaller fleas, ad infinitum," some pathogenic bacteria may also have their own pathogens. In cases where viruses cause destruction (lysis) or slow growth of a bacterial host it is reasonable to describe these viruses as pathogens of bacteria. See BACTERIOPHAGES.

Kousta, M., M. Mataragas, P. Skandamis, et al. "Prevalence and Sources of Cheese Contamination with Pathogens at Farm and Processing Levels." *Food Control* 21, no. 6 (2010): 805–815.
Zottola, E. A., and L. B. Smith. "Pathogens in Cheese." *Food Microbiology* 8, no. 3 (1991): 171–182.

John Barlow

patrimony, with regard to cheese, is the expectation that dairy traditions have cultural value, and moreover that food heritage is a resource deserving of valorization. The significance of the notion of patrimony for geographical indications and other forms of quality certification lies in its capacity to add symbolic value to commodities for marketing purposes. See GEOGRAPHICAL INDICATION. Patrimony is a direct translation of *patrimoine, patrimonio, patrimoni* in Latin languages. Unlike the related concept of "heritage," *patrimony* is not commonly used in English.

"Patrimonialization" concerns the value-adding processes that invest something (whether material culture, natural resources, or ritual practices) with a heritage status. As folklorist Barbara Kirshenblatt-Gimblett writes, "heritage is a new mode of cultural production in the present that has recourse to the past" (1995, pp. 369–370). Her insight that "heritage produces the local for export" (p. 373) can be usefully applied to food heritage.

To consider a cheesemaking technique, a historical cheesemaking locale, or even a certain breed of dairy animals as a form of patrimony is a cultural, economic, and political decision. It needs to be argued for and is typically contested owing to conflicts of interest. In general, claims to patrimony require that dairy farmers, cheesemakers and affineurs—but also public administrators, consumers' associations, and tourist entrepreneurs—cooperate to identify, describe, study, safeguard, extol, reproduce, and market specific items of tangible and intangible heritage (i.e., cultural, natural, or material) in relation to one or more specific cheesemaking traditions.

Patrimony is often described as a commonwealth handed down from generation to generation, and thus pertains to autochthonous populations or at least to a community of craft practitioners that identifies itself as unique and largely unchanged over time. Such claims have been criticized as they lead to defining both products and producers in terms of a static, sedentary imaginary of authenticity. In reality, populations and cultures are always dynamic and changing.

What this means is that "patrimonialization" is a negotiated process rife with frictions and debates. Some of these contests may include the identification of the borders for specific production areas as with many geographical indications, or the limitations imposed on production protocols (regarding, for instance, the use of starter cultures or animals' diet) as well as other aspects of the dairy production cycle (such as the standardization of maturing environments, curdling and cutting tools, and the increasing reliance on high-yield breeds for milk production). See BITTO. There is no solid consensus on what constitutes patrimony. The concept of patrimony is sometimes cast in the language of "tipicity" or "tipicality" (in Italian *tipicità*) or with recourse to the French *terroir*.

Nevertheless, vast cheesemaking regions across Western Europe share a cultural notion of place-based foods that, over time, has been articulated in specific policies and appellations. The notion of food heritage and particularly its anchorage in the idea of designation of origin (DO) is enduring in Europe, and marks a clear contrast with American food cultures (see Trubek, 2008; Paxson, 2013; West, 2013).

See also DESIGNATION OF ORIGIN and TERROIR.

Bessière, Jacinthe, and Laurence Tibère. "Editorial: Patrimoines Alimentaires." *Anthropology of Food* 8 (2001). http://aof.revues.org/6782.

Grasseni, Cristina. *The Taste of Heritage*. Oxford: Berghahn, 2016.

Paxson, Heather. *The Life of Cheese: Crafting Food and Value in America*. Berkeley: University of California Press, 2013.

Kirshenblatt-Gimblett, Barbara. "Theorizing Heritage." *Ethnomusicology* 39, no. 3 (Autumn 1995): 369–370.

Trubek, Amy. *The Taste of Place: A Cultural Journey into Terroir*. Berkeley: University of California Press, 2008.

West, Harry G. "Appellations and Indications of Origin, Terroir, and the Social Construction and Contestation of Place-Named Foods." In *The Handbook of Food Research*, edited by Anne Murcott, Warren James Belasco, and Peter Jackson, pp. 209–228. London: Bloomsbury, 2013.

Cristina Grasseni

Pavé d'Affinois is a French soft cheese from the Côte du Rhône region (near Lyon) with a fine bloomy rind, a delicate flavor, and a silky-smooth texture. This cheese—which is also a brand name—was created in 1981 using a technology based on ultrafiltration, patented by J. L. Maubois et al. in 1969. The innovation was to concentrate first the milk fats and proteins by ultrafiltration, removing the water and very small solutes in the permeate, leading to a viscous "pre-cheese" called "retentate." Starters and rennet are then added to this retentate before it is molded directly. This intensive technology increases cheese yield by at least 20 percent and leads to a cheese with high calcium content and more whey proteins per gram than traditional cheese. Indeed, the whey proteins are fully retained by ultrafiltration. Frank Kosikowski concluded his 1985 paper on the topic by saying, "it is an interesting new cheese." See WHEY and ULTRAFILTRATION.

Initially produced in a characteristic 6-ounce (160-gram) cube shape from pasteurized cow's milk, it is now made in many shapes, with herbs or other natural additives and from either goat's or sheep's milk. The cheese contains 45 percent fat in dry matter and 40 percent moisture. Its ripening time is short, about two weeks and the Pavé d'Affinois is very stable. Pavé d'Affinois is produced by only one company, Guilloteau, in the Côtes du Rhone region.

See also BRIE DE MEAUX and FRANCE.

Fromagerie Guilloteau. http://www.pavedaffinois.com.

Kosikowski, Frank. "Ultrafiltration of Milk on French Farms and in the Making of a New Specialty Cheese Industry." *Journal of Dairy Science* 68 (1985): 2403–2410.

Maubois, J. L., G. Mocquot, and L. Vassal L. "A Method for Processing Milk and Dairy Products." French patent no. 2.052.121, 1969.

"Pavé d'Affinois." Cheese.com. http://www.cheese.com/pave-daffinois.

Sylvie Lortal

Paxton and Whitfield is the United Kingdom's oldest cheesemonger. It first opened in 1797 on Jermyn Street, London, when Sam Cullen, who had had a cheese stall in Aldwych market since 1742, could afford to move to permanent premises nearer to his wealthy customers. He took on two partners, Harry Paxton and Charles Whitfield, whose names the shop still bears. The business grew steadily, gaining its first royal warrant as cheesemonger to Queen Victoria by the mid-nineteenth century.

As factory creameries replaced independent farmers in cheese and butter production in the late nineteenth century, and the well-to-do turned their interest to European cheeses rather than British, times became difficult. It was not until after World War II and the end of rationing that butter, eggs, and cheese became widely available again, and Paxton's renewed contacts with traditional British and Irish cheesemakers and started to import from Europe. See WORLD WAR II and MILITARY RATIONING.

Today Paxton's works in partnership with Androuët in Paris, selling British cheeses to them, and importing their French ones. See ANDROUËT. Cheeses from other countries are sourced through specialist wholesalers in London. The Jermyn Street shop stocks about 150 artisan cheeses, roughly 65 percent British and Irish, 25 percent French, and 10 percent Spanish, Italian, and Dutch. The most popular are Stilton, Cheddar, and Brie, although in winter, when Vacherin Mont D'Or comes into season, there is great demand for that too. See STILTON; CHEDDAR; and BRIE DE MEAUX.

Paxton's remains a family business and now holds two royal warrants to supply cheese to the queen and to the Prince of Wales. In recent years the company has expanded to include two maturing rooms, four shops, a wholesale business supplying top restaurants, trade customers in the United Kingdom and overseas, and significant online sales. One of the company's most innovative ideas has been the launch of bespoke cheese wedding cakes.

See also UNITED KINGDOM.

Rista, Christine, ed. *The Essential Guide to London's Best Food Shops*. London: New Holland Publishers, 2000.

Jill Norman

Pecorino di Filiano is a PDO (protected designation of origin) hard cheese made from sheep's milk in the northwest of the Basilicata region of southern Italy, an area dominated by the massive castles of Federico II, Melfi and Lagopesole. The origin of this cheese dates back many centuries, as reported in many texts since 1600. In fact, the name of the village, Filiano, probably comes from the great quantity of wool spun (Italian *filare*) by the women; this indicates the presence of a lot of sheep farms in the area.

To make Pecorino di Filiano, raw milk is filtered and reheated in a traditional copper boiler. When the temperature reaches 97–104°F (36–40°C), goat or lamb rennet is added (from animals raised in the production area). Salt can be added as a dry rub or brine. The ageing occurs in cool, well aerated natural limestone caves with a temperature of 54–57°F (12–14°C) and a relative humidity of 70–80 percent. Pecorino di Filiano is produced by small farmers using local and Mediterranean sheep breeds: Gentile di Puglia and Lucania, Leccese, Comisana, Sarda, and their cross-breeds, but production also occurs in small and medium-size dairies. It is mostly sold at local markets, but occasionally can be found abroad.

Pecorino di Filiano is used as a table cheese or grated. *Semistagionato*, semi-aged, indicates a cheese aged for about two to five months; *Stagionato*, aged, indicates a cheese aged for more than six months. The rind is typically marked by the "fuscella" (mold); it is golden yellow, verging on dark brown in older cheeses. Cheeses aged for sixty to ninety days have a sweet and delicate taste, which becomes stronger and more savoury with longer aging.

See also ITALY; PECORINO DI PICINISCO; PECORINO ROMANO; PECORINO SARDO; PECORINO SICILIANO; and PECORINO TOSCANO.

Istituto Nazionale di Sociologia Rurale. *Atlante dei prodotti tipici: i formaggi*. Milan: F. Angeli, 1990.

Pecorino di Filiano is a PDO hard cheese made from sheep's milk in the Basilicata region of southern Italy.
© ROCCO LUCIA

Pizzillo, Michele, et al. "T-Cheese. Med Basilicata Cheese: Pecorino di Filiano Cheese." In *New Technologies Supporting the Traditional and Historical Dairy in the Archimed Zone*, pp. 172–183. Edited by E. Cosentino. Ragusa, Italy, 2008.

Salvatore Claps

Pecorino di Picinisco

Pecorino di Picinisco is a hard, uncooked cheese produced in the Comino Valley in Frosinone province (Lazio), Italy. The cheese is cylindrical in shape with straight sides and a straw-colored, thin, and rough rind. Each wheel is 2.8–4.7 inches (7–12 centimeters) high and 4.7–10 inches (12–25 centimeters) in diameter and weighs 1.5–5.5 pounds (0.7–2.5 kilograms) for the *scamosciato* (chamois-like) type or 1.1–4.4 pounds (0.5–2.0 kilograms) for the *stagionato* (matured) type. Both types of cheese have a compact interior paste with some holes. The paste of the scamosciato cheese is white to straw yellow in color, with a moisture content of less than 45 percent, while that of the stagionato type is straw colored but has a moisture content of less than 35 percent. The scamosciato cheese has a marked aroma of mountain pasture and a mild flavor, while the stagionato type has a similar, marked aroma and a strong flavor.

Pecorino di Picinisco cheese is made using ewe's milk from the Sopravissana, Comisana, and Massese breeds or crossbreeds, with an optional inclusion of up to 25 percent goat's milk from the grey Ciociara, white Monticellana, Capestrina breeds or crossbreeds. The raw milk is coagulated at 97–100°F (36–38°C) using lamb or kid rennet paste. After coagulation, the curd is cut into rice-size pieces, transferred into molds, and manually pressed. The cheese can also be cooked in whey for 2 to 5 minutes. Cheeses are dry-salted for 12 to 24 hours, depending on the dimensions of the wheel. Ripening takes from 30 to 60 days for the scamosciato type and 90 days for the stagionato type in fresh rooms. During the ripening time, the rind may be rubbed with olive oil and wine vinegar to prevent mold growth and to give aroma to the cheese.

See also PECORINO DI FILIANO; PECORINO ROMANO; PECORINO SARDO; PECORINO SICILIANO; and PECORINO TOSCANO.

Formaggio.it. http://www.formaggio.it.
Ministero delle Politiche Agricole. "Disciplinari di produzione prodotti DOP e IGP riconosciuti: Formaggi." https://www.politicheagricole.it/flex/cm/pages/ServeBLOB.php/L/IT/IDPagina/3340.

Marta Bertolino

Pecorino Romano

Pecorino Romano is a rennet-coagulated cheese made with ewe's milk and matured for five to eight months (or longer), depending on if it is intended for table or grating use. The result is a hard cheese with a white interior and a pale yellow to brown or black exterior, protected by a DOP (denominazione di origine protetta) since 1996. It is produced in wheels of roughly 49–71 pounds (22–32 kilograms), 12–13 inches (30–33 centimeters) high, and 11–12 inches (28–32 centimeters) wide. The first half of this cheese's name is an adjective whose root comes from the Italian word for sheep, *pecora*. The second half refers to the countryside that surrounds Rome, where this cheese has been made almost nonstop since antiquity.

Bronze cheese graters discovered in tombs dating to the first millennium B.C.E. suggest that hard, rennet-coagulated cheeses such as pecorino were consumed at least that long ago. Virgil, writing in the first century B.C.E., discussed the inclusion of 1-ounce (28-gram) portions of pecorino cheese as a basic ration for Roman soldiers. Writing in the same era, Marcus Terentius Varro identified pecorino as not just an important military meal, but something that was crucial for the success of armies in the field as it provided salt, fat, and protein for soldiers in need of both energy and endurance, as well as the valued logistical trait of being a cheese that would last on long marches See VIRGIL and VARRO, MARCUS TERENTIUS.

Pecorino Romano is often discussed in the same breath as its more expensive cousin Parmigiano Reggiano. By comparison, Pecorino Romano has more salinity and a sharp flavor that make it excellent for cooking, but challenging for some to eat raw. These same qualities, however, are valued by connoisseurs from the locales in which it is made. At its best Pecorino Romano exhibits a paste that, while compact, crumbles nicely and settles on the palate with bright, tangy notes that balance sheepy sweetness with lashes of salinity. The crunch of the cheese is another appealing aspect. The compact nature of its paste and its naturally hard texture makes it a favorite for home and restaurant cooks, in Italy and abroad, to grate over pasta dishes, meat sauces, and even sautéed and roasted vegetables.

Pecorino Romano flavor can fluctuate according to the milking season. Winter, summer, and spring reveal unique aspects and variants of sweet and salty, which reflect the lactation and grazing matter of the ewes from which each cheesemaker draws milk. Hallmarks of Pecorino Romano include a fat content in the 36 percent range; a paste that has fine, hard granules from cooking and pressing; aging for eight months in cellars whose air is dry and cool; and a rind that is brushed with olive oil to finish.

Today Pecorino has achieved a mass popularity and is produced en masse in the province of Lazio, in Sardinia and in Grosseto, Tuscany. Much of Pecorino Romano, in fact, does not originate in its traditional area of Rome, but from those places, using the traditional recipe.

See also ITALY; PARMIGIANO REGGIANO; and PECORINO SARDO.

Androuet, Pierre. *Guide to Cheese.* Henley-on-Thames, U.K.: Aidan Ellis, 1993.
Dalby, Andrew. *Cheese: A Global History.* London: Reaktion, 2009.
Formaggio.it. http://www.formaggio.it.
Harbutt, Julie. *The World Cheese Book.* London and New York: DK, 2015.
Kindstedt, Paul. *Cheese and Culture: A History of Cheese and Its Place in Western Civilization.* White River Junction, Vt.: Chelsea Green, 2012.
McCalman, Max. *Cheese: A Connoisseur's Guide to the World's Best.* New York: Clarkson Potter, 2005.

Robert McKeown

Pecorino Sardo is a firm sheep's milk cheese from the Italian island region of Sardinia. It is made in two distinct styles: *dolce* (sweet) and *maturo* (matur).

Pecorino Sardo Dolce is a straw-colored wheel, 2.5–4 inches (6–11 centimeters) tall and 6–7 inches (16–18 centimeters) in diameter, with rounded edges and slightly convex sides. It is aged for twenty to sixty days. Dolce's paste is pale yellow and firm but springy and elastic, and often scattered throughout with small irregular holes. It is mild and sweet, with aromas of sheep's milk and hay.

Maturo cheeses are taller, approximately 5 inches (12 centimeters) high and 6–8 inches (16–20 centimeters) in diameter with straighter sides and sharper edges. They are aged for at least sixty days and often longer. Their rind color ranges from pale yellow to mahogany; their texture is hard and grainy, more or less, depending on age, and their flavor is more piquant and pronounced in salt.

While the legal designation Pecorino Sardo is modern—Pecorino Sardo was awarded DOC (denominazione di origine controllata) status in 1991 and granted PDO (protected designation of origin) protection in 1996—the history of pecorino-type cheeses in Sardinia and throughout the Mediterranean region is certainly ancient. Homer described Pecorino-type cheese in the *Odyssey*. Virgil lists Pecorino among the standard rations of Roman soldiers. Medieval tax records show exports of Sardinian cheeses to Pisan merchants. See HOMER and VIRGIL.

The initial steps in the making of Dolce and Maduro cheeses are the same: pasteurized or thermized sheep's milk is coagulated with calf rennet at 95–102°F (35–39°C). Coagulation is achieved in thirty-five to forty minutes. Once set, the curd is "cooked" to a temperature not above 109°F (43°C), a process that further expels whey and contributes to the final texture of the cheese.

The curd of Dolce is cut into large pieces, roughly the size of a hazelnut, which preserves moisture and results in a softer cheese. Curd for Maduro is cut smaller, to the size of a corn kernel, which facilitates greater whey expulsion and results in a drier, more age-worthy cheese. Both styles may be either brined or dry-salted. They may be smoked, although this practice is rare.

Pecorino Sardo is often confused with another Sardinian sheep's milk cheese, Fiore Sardo. Though the two cheeses are similar, they differ in several key respects: Fiore Sardo is made of raw sheep's milk exclusively of the Sarda breed and is coagulated with goat or sheep rennet. It has more bulging, rounded sides and is in practice more likely to be smoked.

See also FIORE SARDO; SARDA; and SARDINIA.

Associazione Formaggi Italiani D.O.P. http://www.afidop.it/en/dop-igp-cheeses/pecorino-sardo-dop.
Consorzio per la Tutela del Formaggio Fiore Sardo D.O.P. http://formaggio.it/formaggio/fiore-sardo-d-o-p.
Kindstedt, Paul. *Cheese and Culture: A History of Cheese and Its Place in Western Civilization.* White River Junction, Vt.: Chelsea Green, 2012.
Sardegna Agricultura. http://www.sardegnaagricoltura.it.

Matthew Rubiner

Pecorino Siciliano is a raw, hard PDO (protected designation of origin) cheese produced with whole sheep's milk taken from ewes raised in Sicily. It is one of the oldest cheeses in Europe, and its origins are legendary. It is cited in many writings, among which the most notable is *The Odyssey* in which Homer tells about the sheep's cheeses produced by the giant Cyclops Polyphemus. It also appears in *Naturalis Historia* by Pliny the Elder. It is historically linked to the sheep farms of hills and semi-arid areas where ewes of autochthonous breeds are fed diets mainly based on natural pasture. In such farming systems, this cheese is manufactured with artisanal procedures using wooden tools, typical of the Sicilian dairy tradition. See HOMER; PLINY THE ELDER; and WOODEN VATS.

Lambs' rennet is used for coagulation and the separation of the curd from the whey is made by hand using traditional equipment to obtain the cheese curd. Afterward the curd cheese is placed into a bulrush basket. Dry salting is manually performed and the cheeses are then placed on a wooden workbench to mature at least four months.

Pecorino Siciliano has a cylindrical shape with slightly convex faces and a rind color ranging from white to light yellow. The paste is hard and compact, white or straw-colored, with few aeration holes. The weight varies from 9 to 26 pounds (4–12 kilograms); cheeses with greater weight are aged longer from six to over twelve months. The aroma and flavor of Pecorino Siciliano PDO varies according to the degree of aging, from fresh and floral, to a more pronounced taste of fruity, and spicy for aged cheeses. The annual production of the certified PDO cheese amounts to 40 tons, and the sales market is mainly regional.

See also SICILY; PECORINO DI FILIANO; PECORINO DI PICINISCO; PECORINO ROMANO; PECORINO SARDO; and PECORINO TOSCANO.

Todaro M., et al. "Effect of Different Salting Technologies on the Chemical and Microbiological Characteristics of PDO Pecorino Siciliano Cheese." *European Food Research and Technology* 233 (2011): 931–940.

Settanni L., et al. "Selected Lactic Acid Bacteria as a Hurdle to the Microbial Spoilage of Cheese: Application on a Traditional Raw Ewes' Milk Cheese." *International Dairy Journal* 32: 126–132.

Massimo Todaro

Pecorino Toscano

Pecorino Toscano is a sheep's milk PDO (protected designation of origin) cheese produced in the whole region of Tuscany and some municipalities of Umbria and Lazio. It comes in two types: *pasta tenera* (soft) and *pasta semidura* (semihard).

Pecorino Toscano is made using whole ewe's milk from breeds typical of the area (Sardinian, Comisana, Massese, Appenninica, and Langhe are the principal ones). Raw or pasteurized milk, inoculated with autochthonous or selected starter, is coagulated at 91–100°F (33–38°C), using calf rennet, within twenty to twenty-five minutes. For the "pasta tenera" type, after coagulation the curd is cut into pieces the size of hazelnuts and then transferred into molds and manually pressed. Cheeses are brined and ripened for at least twenty days in cool (41–54°F [5–12°C]) rooms with a relatively humidity of 75–90 percent and during ripening the rind can be rubbed with anti-mold products. For "pasta semidura" type, after coagulation the curd is cut into pieces the size of corn kernels and then transferred into molds and manually pressed. Ripening lasts four months in cool (41–54°F [5–12°C]) rooms with a relatively humidity of 75–90 percent and during ripening the rind can be rubbed with anti-mold products.

The cheese is cylindrical with straight or slightly convex sides and a straw-colored rind. It is 3–4 inches (7–11 centimeters) high, 6–9 inches (15–22 centimeters) in diameter, and weighs from 15 ounces to 8 pounds (0.7–3.5 kilograms). The interior of the *pasta tenera* cheese is white to white straw–colored, compact with a fat content of at least 40 percent while the *pasta semidura* cheese is straw-colored, compact, hard when cut, and with a fat content of at least 45 percent and a fragrant flavor. It can be used as table or grating cheese.

Ministero delle Politiche Agricole. "Disciplinari di produzione prodotti DOP e IGP riconosciuti: Formaggi." http://www.politicheagricole.it/flex/cm/pages/ServeBLOB.php/L/IT/IDPagina/3340.

Pecorino Toscano official website. http://www.pecorinotoscanodop.it.

Pirisi, A., et al. "Sheep's and Goat's Dairy Products in Italy: Technological, Chemical, Microbiological, and Sensory Aspects. *Small Ruminant Research* 101 (2011): 102–112.

Marta Bertolino

pelle à brie

pelle à brie is the traditional perforated ladle used for molding traditional Bries such as Brie de Meaux and Brie de Melun, two French AOP (appellation d'origine protegée) cheeses.

Bries are soft cow's milk cheeses named after Brie, the French region from which they originate (roughly corresponding to the modern department of Seine-et-Marne). A Brie may be produced from whole or semi-skimmed milk. The curd is obtained by adding rennet to raw milk and warming it to a maximum temperature of 99°F (37°C). In artisanal cheese-making, the cheese is then cast into molds with the traditional perforated ladle called pelle à brie. The 8-inch (20-centimeter) mold is filled with several thin layers of cheese and drained for approximately eighteen hours. The cheese is then taken out of the molds, salted, inoculated with cheese mold (*Penicillium candidum* or *Penicillium camemberti*) or *Brevibacterium linens*, and aged in a cellar for at least four to five weeks.

The role of the pelle is to protect the fragile texture of the curd, which will drain slowly. A crumbled curd would result in draining too quickly, giving dry and tight pastes, far from the soft texture that is expected. See DRAINING.

The pelle à brie has a diameter of 12 inches (30 centimeters) and an inversed handle. They were initially tinned iron with a wooden handle, but then were made from stainless steel. In the twenty-first century, titanium is increasingly being used, as its lightness allows a more precise movement and decreases the hardness. A pelle à brie in titanium is worth about $570 (500 euros). However, industrial Brie's processes now use decurdling tools such as knives or blades for cutting curd after coagulation and then molding curd by gravity transfer without the traditional pelle à brie. See CHEESE KNIFE and CUTTING.

See also BRIE DE MEAUX.

Harbutt, Juliet. *World Cheese Book*. London: DK, 2009.

Gilles Garric

Peluso, Franklin

Peluso, Franklin (1945–), is a California cheesemaker known primarily for production of Teleme, a young cow's milk cheese. As the former proprietor of the Peluso Cheese Company with his father, Frank, Peluso is credited with broadening the audience for this soft, tangy, stracchino-like cheese, formerly sold largely to Greek and Italian immigrants. But the family's Teleme trail leads back to Peluso's grandfather, Giovanni, an immigrant from southern Italy, who settled in Los Banos, California, and made his first commercial Teleme in 1927.

Giovanni was likely influenced by a similar cheese made at the time by a Greek family in Pleasanton, east of San Francisco. To protect the moist, floppy squares in their packaging, Giovanni coated them with a light dusting of rice flour. When his son and grandson revived Teleme production at their four-year-old Peluso Cheese Company in 1980, they maintained the floury signature. In 2005 the Pelusos sold their company and rights to the family name. Franklin Peluso briefly moved his family to Maine to try cheesemaking there but returned to California in less than a year. He subsequently launched the Mid Coast Cheese Company to resume production of the six-pound Teleme. Now made in a rented facility in Hanford, California, and marketed as Franklin's Teleme (to distinguish it from Peluso Cheese Company Teleme, which is still in production), Franklin Peluso's buttery cheese is produced with pasteurized Holstein milk and relies on the technique of curd washing to minimize acid development. See HOLSTEIN WASHED-CURD CHEESES. Released after about ten days of ripening, it has a supple texture and a sour-cream fragrance; with additional age, it becomes runny and develops a mushroom aroma. In 2012 the creamery debuted Franklin's Washed-Rind Teleme, a more pungent, month-old cheese produced by washing the squares repeatedly with *Brevibacterium linens* and brine. See BREVIBACTERIUM LINENS and BRINING.

Davies, Sasha. *The Guide to West Coast Cheese: More than 300 Cheeses Handcrafted in California, Oregon, and Washington*. Portland, Ore.: Timber, 2010.

Janet Fletcher

Penicillium

Penicillium is a group of molds (filamentous fungi) that includes some of the most widely distributed fungi in the production and aging of cheese. Only two of the approximately three hundred described species in the genus, *Penicillium roqueforti* and *Penicillium camemberti*, are commonly used as inoculants in cheese production. These fungi contribute to the distinct appearance and taste of some of the largest groups of cheeses, such as blue cheeses and white mold-ripened cheeses. Most *Penicillium* species reproduce asexually, leading to the production of characteristic green or blue spores. *Penicillium* species grow in a remarkable diversity of habitats, including in soils, on plants, in aquatic environments, and even occasionally on or in humans. Those species that grow on cheese have adapted to live in a high-salt, proteinaceous, high-fat, and cold environment.

Several *Penicillium* species are purposefully grown in the cheesemaking environment and are either inoculated onto the surfaces of cheeses or added to the milk used for cheesemaking. *Penicillium roqueforti* is used in the production of blue cheeses and creates their characteristic blue veins. Spores of the fungus are inoculated into the milk used for cheesemaking, and the fungal spores rest inside the curd until the cheese is aerated by spiking (or needling) it from the outside. The oxygen that enters the cheese when it is spiked encourages the fungus to grow, creating the veining pattern. See NEEDLES.

Penicillium camemberti is the white mold that colonizes bloomy-rind cheeses such as Brie and Camembert. Spores of the fungus are either added to the milk used for cheese production or sprayed onto the surface of the cheese. This mold is white, but wasn't always so. The wild relatives of this mold have greenish-blue spores. As scientists began to industrialize microbes used in cheese production, white mutants of this mold spontaneously appeared, and these mutant strains have been used ever since. See BRIE DE MEAUX AND CAMEMBERT DE NORMANDIE.

Undesirable *Penicillium* species can commonly contaminate cheeses, leading to both aesthetic and flavor defects, but also to potential mycotoxin contamination. One of the most widespread contaminant species is *Penicillium commune*. This is thought to be the wild ancestor of the white *Penicillium camemberti*. Other common cheese contaminants include *P. palitans*, *P. solitum*, and *P. crustosum*. In order to combat these invasive molds, cheesemakers must go to extreme measure to make sure their production and aging environments are incredibly clean, or they must choose starter cultures that prevent the growth of these molds. Some yeasts and a few strains of *Penicillium camemberti* can reduce colonization by contaminant *Penicillium* species. Some cheese producers that do not want any fungal growth on their cheeses may add the antifungal agent natamycin to inhibit, in particular, *Penicillium* growth.

Identification of *Penicillium* species is challenging because many species that occur in the cheesemaking environment share similar morphological characteristics (spore color, growth rate, etc.). It is impossible to know just by looking at a mold with the naked eye what species it belongs to; accurate identification relies on the use of DNA sequencing combined with morphological studies. Because of the challenges associated with species identification, the taxonomy of this group is still in flux and can cause confusion for cheese producers who buy cultures under certain scientific names. For example, *Penicillium album* and *Penicillium candidum* are commonly used names for white molds used in cheesemaking, but the distinction between these two molds is no longer scientifically valid, because scientists have found them to be the same as *Penicillium camemberti*. See TAXONOMY.

See also BLUE CHEESES; BLOOMY-RIND CHEESES; FILAMENTOUS FUNGI; and FUNGI.

Gillot, Guillaume, et al. "Insights into *Penicillium roqueforti* Morphological and Genetic Diversity." *PLOS ONE* 10 (June 2015): e0129849.
Ropars, Jeanne, et al. "A Taxonomic and Ecological Overview of Cheese Fungi." *International Journal of Food Microbiology* 155 (April 2012): 199–210.

Benjamin Wolfe

Pepper Jack

See JACK.

peptidases are enzymes that hydrolyze a peptide bond in short peptide substrates producing shorter peptides and/or amino acids as products. Peptidases do not act on large protein substrates. Peptidases are essential for the ripening of many hard cheese varieties as they are the enzymes that liberate free amino acids from casein-derived peptides. These amino acids in turn are broken down to many volatile flavor compounds during amino acid catabolism.

Peptidases are microbial enzymes produced in the curd during manufacture or ripening. While some peptidases may be produced by the bacteria, yeasts, and molds characteristic of the ripening of some varieties, the most important peptidases in cheese are from starter and non-starter lactic acid bacteria (LAB). Peptidases of LAB are intracellular enzymes that are released into the cheese matrix following cell death and lysis. LAB produce a number of oligoendopeptidases (that act on internal peptide bonds in short peptide substrates), di- and tripeptidases (that hydrolyze the peptide bond in dipeptides and the N-terminal peptide bond in tripeptides, respectively), and a range of amino peptidases (that remove the N-terminal amino acid from the substrate), but apparently LAB lack a carboxypeptidase. Peptides containing the amino acid proline are often degraded slowly by peptidases.

Since the caseins are rich in proline, LAB also possess a family of proline-specific peptidases (proline iminopeptidase, X-prolyldipeptidylaminopeptidase, prolinase, prolidase, aminopeptidase P) that efficiently degrade such peptides. Peptidases of LAB are capable, at least in theory, of hydrolyzing every peptide bond in the casein system.

See also CASEIN; ENZYMES; FLAVOR; and LACTIC ACID BACTERIA.

Sousa, M. J., et al. "Advances in the Study of Proteolysis in Cheese during Ripening." *International Dairy Journal* 11 (2001): 327–345.

Upadhyay, V. K., et al. (2004). "Proteolysis in Cheese during Ripening." In *Cheese: Chemistry, Physics and Microbiology*, vol. 1, *General Aspects*, 3d ed., edited by P. F. Fox, et al., pp. 392–433. Amsterdam: Elsevier Applied Science, 2004.

P. L. H. McSweeney

Petite, Marcel (1901–1983), was born in Grand Combe Chateleu, near Monteaux, France. The son and the grandson of a cheesemaking family, he continued on with the tradition and passed it to his two sons Louis and François in 1966. In 1975 Louis left the organization and François continued running the family business. Marcel's father was the cheesemaker in Grand Combe Chateleau where he produced Gruyère de Comté. In 1928 Marcel followed his father's footsteps and produced cheeses in three different fruitieres (cheesemaking location/house of each town): La Gauffre, Mont de Grand Combe, and Les Gras. His debut at maturing cheese started in 1934 when he took over the caves of Bernandines, an old convent near Pontarlier. After World War II he continued cheesemaking and maturing, which led him to his discovery of Fort Saint Antoine in 1966; he started affinage (the art of maturing cheese) in this underground fort with 12,000 wheels of Comté. His pioneering act was the slow and cold affinage and to support and engage the company in organic farming at a time, the 1960s, when it was not popular. His uncanny ability to predict the right amount of time needed for aging each batch of wheels to their optimal flavor profiles was famed. He passed away in 1983 at the age of eighty-two. His passion for terroir, organic farming, and full usage of natural ambiance of the Fort Saint Antoine caves are still guiding his son Lionel and his grandson. Today there are thirty-six Marcel Petite fruitieres. On the company website they indicate, "When selecting Comté, the Marcel Petite cellar Master considers four key criteria: Delicacy, subtlety, intensity and depth of flavor. The ripening age is an indicator, but not the main criterion of selection."

See also COMTÉ; FORT SAINT ANTOINE; GRUYÈRE; and ORGANIC.

Comté Marcel Petite. http://www.comte-petite.com.

Ihsan Gurdal

phenotypic variability is a technical term applied to cheese microbes that characterizes their aptitude for variations in their physical traits. Those physical traits are determined by their genetics, and by expressed genes submitted to environmental influences and to random genetic variations. Phenotypic variability encountered includes growth and biochemical characteristics, antigens, and phage susceptibility.

The phenotype is a key criterion for the identification of microorganisms. Indeed a microbial species is described by a specific phenotype, shared by all of the strains belonging to that species. Considering a microbial species as a whole means consideration of its pan-genome, that is, the sum of multiple genomes of the strains representing the species. The pan-genome includes the "core genome" containing genes present in all strains, related to functions linked to basic biology and phenotype of the species, and the "dispensable genome" containing genes present in some but not all strains. Thus the core genome is responsible for the phenotypic characteristics and specifics of the species, and the dispensable genome is responsible for the intraspecies diversity that results in phenotypic variability of strains inside the species. This variable part of the phenotype is linked to minor variations of the genotypes (the difference of only one nucleic acid in the genome sequence can be responsible for the modification of the phenotype). It is generated by mechanisms allowing the microorganism to adapt to a randomly fluctuating environment.

The phenotypic variability, even if concerning a very small part of the genome, can have major impacts on cheesemaking. Most, if not all, technological properties are strain-dependent and can induce functional variations in cheese. Indeed, this phenotypic variability of strains can affect a large range of technological properties, as for example the capacity of a strain to produce aroma compounds, antifungal components, and exopolysaccharides, and to resist various concentrations of salts or extremes of pH. Such is the case for lipolysis during cheese ripening, which is involved in flavor formation due to release of free fatty acids, that are important flavor compounds in most cheeses. Abeijon et al. (2014) in a study of twenty-one strains of *Propionibacterium freudenreichii*, the main agent of lipolysis in Swiss-type cheeses, underlined the high strain dependency of the ability of the strains to produce free fatty acids. In a model medium supplemented with an emulsion of milk fat, nineteen strains out of the twenty-one tested released free fatty acids, whereas two strains did not display any detectable lipolytic activity. The production of exopolysaccharides (EPS) by microorganisms is another phenotypic feature that may vary between strains. EPS affect the texture of numerous dairy products and can be used to improve the texture of low-fat cheese or to reduce syneresis in fermented milk. Twenty-eight EPS-producing strains of *Lactobacillus* (fourteen *L. plantarum* strains, nine *L. kefiranofaciens* strains, and five *L. paracasei* strains) were studied in fermented milks. The analysis of the EPS produced showed high strain-dependence between strains in terms of concentration and molecular weight of the EPS produced resulting in fermented milks with different rheological properties. The strain dependence can also impact the safety of cheese when it concerns the inhibitory potential of some microorganisms toward undesirable or pathogenic varieties. Then the ability of dairy-related bacteria to exert antifungal activities is now well established. These properties are generally multifactorial and result from the production of different metabolites by bacteria, such as organic acids, H_2O_2, CO_2, ethanol, and proteinaceous compounds (peptides, cyclic dipeptides) being most of the time strain-dependent. Thus, for five strains of *Lactobacillus casei*, Cortés-Zavaleta et al. (2014) observed up to 75 percent variation between strains for their potential to inhibit the growth of four spoilage molds targeted.

As strain-dependent phenotypic variability can deeply impact the final properties of cheeses, it must be kept in mind for the selection or development of starter cultures. Indeed, starters are generally chosen for specific functionality regarding cheese: acidification, specific flavor notes, de-bittering properties, characteristic flavor and color of smear-rind cheeses, phage susceptibility, and generation of holes in Swiss-

type cheeses. The choice of a selected strain, according to its phenotypic specificity, is then a trigger to modulate cheese properties and for cheese technology innovation. The huge impact of phenotypic variability between strains belonging to the same species on the final quality of cheeses underlines the importance of proper management and conservation of related microbial resources. Microbial species (bacteria, yeast, and fungi) are described with respect to a single type strain, which is the reference strain and must be available in at least two official bacterial collections. Nevertheless, taking into account the phenotypic variability of microorganisms, the type strain of a given species does not encompass by itself all the potential variation of the expressed physical traits. Thus it is crucial to maintain and enrich collections of microorganisms with high diversity of strains of technological interest, with these collections being major actors for innovation in the dairy industry. By understanding that greater phenotypic variability of strains for a given species will be reachable to the users (cheesemakers, starter producers), the greater the possibility for discovery of new strains—and, thus, more diverse cheeses will be produced and sustained.

See also BIODIVERSITY; MICROBIAL COMMUNITIES; STRAINS; and TAXONOMY.

Abeijon Mukdsi, M. C. et al. "The Secreted Esterase of *Propionibacterium freudenreichii* Has a Major Role in Cheese Lipolysis." *Applied Environmental Microbiology* 80 (2014): 751–756.

Cortés-Zavaleta, O., et al. "Antifungal Activity of Lactobacilli and Its Relationship with 3-Phenyllactic Acid Production." *International Journal of Food Microbiology* 173 (2014): 30–35.

Hamet, M. F., et al. "Selection of EPS-producing Lactobacillus Strains Isolated from Kefir Grains and Rheological Characterization of the Fermented Milks." *LWT–Food Science and Technology* 63 (2015): 129–135.

Tettelin H., et al. "Comparative Genomics: The Bacterial Pan-genome." *Current Opinion in Microbiology* 12 (2008): 472–477.

Florence Valence

philosophies of taste. Defining and explaining "taste" is a complex endeavor because to taste is never simply a biological response to certain stimuli. Tasting a piece of cheese and appreciating the sensory experience involves both the mind and the body, requiring considerations of value, context, custom, affect, and much more. Remaining in the realm of biology, although clearly crucial to both the making and consuming of cheese, certainly limits understanding. Take the Merriam-Webster definitions of "taste": "to perceive or recognize as if by the sense of taste"; and "cheese": "a food consisting of the coagulated, compressed, and usually ripened curd of milk separated from the whey." On this view to taste cheese is for an individual to perceive through sensation a piece of coagulated, compressed, and ripened curds. Yes, but also, no. In order to fully comprehend the experience of tasting, recognizing, and appreciating cheese, other definitions and expectations must also be incorporated—literally and figuratively.

Such definitions and expectations frame the sensory experience, making the dictionary accurate but not compelling when it comes to tasting and evaluating cheese. In the Western tradition different theories of taste inform such frames. Those most relevant to traditions of cheese (making and eating) involve: aesthetics and taste, psychology and taste, and cultures of taste.

Aesthetics of Taste: Preference versus Judgment

The Western philosophical tradition of aesthetics defined the five senses as sight, sound, touch, taste, and smell. In traditional aesthetics there is a long tradition of privileging the "intellectual senses"—sight and sound—over the bodily senses of touch, taste, and smell. To have bodily pleasures, in this theory, was not to have a transcendent aesthetic experience. Rather the ability to be discerning in the aesthetic evaluation of an object is crucial. Enlightenment philosopher Immanuel Kant's first premise about aesthetics is that it should be grounded in a notion of disinterestedness. Thus an aesthetic appreciation must be "only directed at the experience, of the object appreciated" (Sweeney, 2012, pp. 53–54). The problem with food, in this line of reasoning, is that it satisfies base desires; our biological need for food trumps our pursuit of beauty and pleasure. Kant thought pleasure should be a consequence of our sensory engagement but not simultaneous. In this understanding of food, art, and aesthetics, the process of making the food is irrelevant; instead what is crucial are the material properties of the food as an object to be appreciated and savored. Kant's charac-

terization helped lead to a heightened focus on the visual aesthetics of food when people intend food to transcend the quotidian. Thus the sensory experience of eating a remarkable piece of aged blue cheese could not easily be defined as beautiful or transcendent, although a still life painted by Raffaelle Peale of cheese and crackers or by Pablo Picasso of blue cheese and wine certainly could. See ART.

Recently more attention has been paid to the possible aesthetics of the bodily senses. In this line of argument, artistry comes from sensations understood to have aesthetic dimensions. For example, philosopher Emily Brady queries the traditional Western philosophical distinction of higher and lower orders of pleasures. She thinks that smells and tastes can be incorporated into traditional forms of aesthetic theory and argues that the neglect in aesthetic theories of food is due to the predominance of the visual. Tastes and smells bring experience inside the corporeal body, and thus for philosophers of aesthetics exist in the "realm of the crude" (Brady, 2012, p. 72). As the same time, Brady thinks that "smells and tastes have a place in our more ordinary aesthetic responses" (p. 69). She argues that people make sensory discriminations all the time during everyday processes of cooking and eating. Here the issue at hand lies in the limits of the Kantian requirement of disinterested judgment. Individuals can create preference through judgment: "One aroma is lovely, another stinks, one taste is vibrant, another dull. That we make and defend judgments like these indicates our capacity for aesthetically appreciating different smells and tastes" (p. 75). In this philosophy of taste, there can be an everyday aesthetic that has a corporeal base. An individual may eat a piece of cheese or paint that cheese and in either case demonstrate aesthetic judgment.

Taste as a Cultural Process Shared by Individuals

Another means for framing taste is to consider an individual's sensory experience within a larger context. How do we *know* the tastes of food? How are tastes related to judgments? What makes us think that some tastes are desirable? Problematic? When humans taste food or drink, when the bite or sip rests in the mouth and then moves into our bodies, culture, biology, and nature are integrated; this is a universal process. At the same time, taste is ultimately subjective, a sense that can never truly be physiologically shared. The body (or at least the mouth, nose, and brain) always mediates between food and drink as an external social object and an internal sensory subject. Taste can not be understood or explained only at the individual level; our cultural tastes ultimately shape our physiological taste experiences. However an individual human body never lives (or tastes) in complete isolation. Thus, as David Howes (2003, p. xi) puts it: "Sensation is not just a matter of physiological response and personal experience. It is the most fundamental domain of cultural expression, the medium through which all the values and practices of society are enacted." Once the food or drink enters the human body, sensing taste also requires talking taste. Sharing this particular sensory experience requires oral communication, a shared vocabulary and dialogue with others. The complexity of discerning taste, therefore, lies in how that dialogue develops, and what factors shape both the conversation and the final sensory evaluation. Physiology, context, perception, and experience constantly interact as we chew, sip and swallow. Taste is both intrinsic and extrinsic to the object—the wheel of Brie, the slice of Manchego, the hunk of Cheddar.

Focusing on the taste experience as a dialogue between biological taste and cultural tastes, an interaction between the natural world and social relations expands upon the Western philosophical tradition focusing on aesthetics and taste. When inner and outer worlds intersect sensory meanings are created. One powerful frame involves the tastes of food and drink and the ascription of certain aesthetic sensibilities to these tastes in relation to social standing and social hierarchy. Such a sociological theory of taste is long-standing, articulated by Georg Simmel in the nineteenth century and by Pierre Bourdieu almost a century later. These analyses of taste rely on a theory of consumption based on the social significance of the decision to eat a certain type of cheese or wine. This is based on a fundamental assumption (in this case anthropologist Mary Douglas): "An individual's main object in consumption is to help create the social universe and to find in it a creditable place" (1982, p. 26). When it comes to the social goals for a good, she did not see a distinction between goods ascribed to "subsistence/survival, thus necessities versus goods that move beyond subsistence," into luxuries or treats (p. 17). For Douglas any and all classifications of food and drink are socially created with ultimate ends of placing a person within a social standard or hierarchy. In such a theory of taste soft, hard, creamy, and tangy are secondary to what the piece of cheese signifies about the producer or consumer of that cheese.

Another way to bring cultural context to a definition to taste is to consider the relationship between people and their environment. Terroir, or the taste of place, values the ways in which foods can reflect the natural environment, the intersection of that nature with human production practices, and the cultural context in which production decisions are made, often carrying on the practices of generations (Trubek, 2008). Terroir has long been valued in France as a mode of sensory evaluation while also helping to frame engagements with the agrarian landscape. This can extend to cheese made in any manner of locale, from Comté in the foothills of the French Alps to Ragusano in southern Sicily to Bayley Hazen Blue in northern Vermont. Terroir (if the intersection of natural products with human practices remains central) helps to explain the sensory qualities of a cheese, taking into account the particular physical environment it comes from as well as the cultural traditions and aspirations of the people who created it and continue to eat and savor it.

See also TASTE and TERROIR.

Bourdieu, Pierre. *Distinction: A Social Critique of the Judgement of Taste*. New York: Routledge Classics, 1979.

Brady, Emily. "Smells, Tastes and Everyday Aesthetics." In *The Philosophy of Food*, edited by David M. Kaplan. Berkeley: University of California Press, 2012.

Douglas, Mary. *In the Active Voice*. London: Routledge, 1982.

Howes, David. *Sensual Relations: Engaging the Senses in Culture and Social Theory*. Ann Arbor: University of Michigan Press, 2003.

Simmel, Georg. *Sociological Theory*. 7th ed. New York: McGraw-Hill, 2008, pp. 158–188.

Sweeney, Kevin. "Hunger Is the Best Sauce: The Aesthetics of Food." In *The Philosophy of Food*, edited by David M. Kaplan. Berkeley: University of California Press, 2012.

Trubek, Amy. *The Taste of Place: A Cultural Journey into Terroir*. Berkeley: University of California Press, 2008.

Amy B. Trubek

pH measurement is a measure of the acidity or alkalinity of a substance. The term pH specifically relates to the concentration of hydrogen ions in the water phase of the material. By definition, an acid is a molecule that is capable of releasing a positively charged hydrogen ionto the surrounding aqueous environment. Hydrogen ions are extremely reactive to both organic and inorganic compounds; therefore, one can think of the freed hydrogen ion as the business end of the acid molecule. Hydrogen ions are the driving force behind the multifaceted changes that are triggered by acidification and de-acidification during cheesemaking and ripening, respectively. Thus, pH measurements furnish invaluable diagnostic information during cheesemaking and ripening.

The measurement of pH is performed using a specialized electrochemical probe called a pH electrode that is fitted with a glass membrane that permits positively charged hydrogen ions from the surrounding aqueous environment to accumulate within sites at the membrane surface. Therefore, when a pH electrode is immersed in a sample of milk, whey, or cheese curd, the electrode membrane will acquire an excess of positively charged hydrogen ions on the exposed side of the membrane, the extent of which will depend on the concentration of hydrogen ions within the water phase of the test sample. This, in turn, forces positively charged ions to be displaced from the inside surface of the glass membrane to the solution inside the electrode, essentially creating a weak electrical current across the membrane that is modulated by the hydrogen ion concentration in the test sample. This creates a potential difference between the pH electrode and a reference electrode, which are coupled to one another via the pH meter. The pH meter detects this difference in electrical potential between the electrodes.

The external reference electrode possesses a constant known electrical potential, which enables the pH meter to be calibrated so that it can translate the potential difference, measured in millivolts, to the hydrogen ion concentration present in the test sample. The specific relationship between hydrogen ion concentration in the test sample and the potential difference is logarithmic in nature, meaning that a tenfold change in hydrogen ion concentration in the test sample causes a onefold change in electrical potential difference. As a practical matter, this means that a one-pH-unit change corresponds to tenfold change in hydrogen ion concentration; a two-pH-unit change

corresponds to a $10 \times 10 =$ hundred fold change in hydrogen ion concentration, and so forth. Furthermore, pH is expressed using a negative logarithmic scale, meaning that a one-unit decrease in pH corresponds to a tenfold increase in hydrogen ion concentration. Thus, relatively small decreases in pH correspond to large increases in acidity. For example, the typical two-unit decrease in pH that occurs during cheesemaking from that of the starting milk (near pH 7) to that of the final cheese (near pH 5) represents about a hundred fold increase in hydrogen ion concentration.

The concepts of pH and its measurement are central to cheesemaking during three successive stages. First, the pH of the milk profoundly influences the coagulation step at the start of the manufacturing process. During acid coagulation, it is the production of lactic acid by lactic acid bacteria, and the resulting accumulation of hydrogen ions to high concentrations (corresponding to pH values around 4.6), that cause casein micelles to interact among themselves and separate from the water phase of the milk, thereby triggering coagulation. In rennet coagulation, the pH of the milk influences both the rate at which rennet enzymes transform the surfaces of casein micelles in preparation for coagulation and the rate at which micelles interact among themselves and separate from the water phase of the milk, once the enzymatic transformation is complete. In acid-heat coagulation the pH of the milk must be carefully balanced with the heating conditions in order to induce casein micelles, along with whey proteins, to interact among themselves and separate from the water phase as flocculated curds.

Second, throughout the various cheesemaking steps that follow coagulation in the making of rennet coagulated cheeses, the levels to which hydrogen ions accumulate due to the fermentation of lactose to lactic acid by lactic acid bacteria modulate curd shrinkage and the concomitant release of whey from curd particles, referred to as syneresis, as well as the release of calcium phosphate from curd to whey. Cheesemakers control this process by measuring the pH and adjusting the rate of pH change, in order to produce cheese with the correct moisture and mineral contents and pH level, all of which are critical for the proper ripening of aged cheeses.

Third, during the ripening of certain aged cheeses, the neutralization of hydrogen ions by microflora that proliferate internally or at the cheese surface may trigger cascades of physico-chemical changes and microbial progressions that transform such cheeses into finished products with extraordinary sensory characteristics.

Finally, the microbiological safety of cheese throughout cheesemaking and ripening is influenced by the pH.

See also ACIDIFICATION and DEACIDIFICATION; CALCIUM PHOSPHATE; LACTIC ACID; LACTIC ACID BACTERIA; and SYNERESIS.

Fox, Patrick F., Timothy P. Guinee, Timothy M. Cogan, et al. *Fundamentals of Cheese Science.* Gaithersburg, Md.: Aspen, 2000.

Paul S. Kindstedt

Piacentinu Ennese

Piacentinu Ennese is a traditional Sicilian hard-pressed ewe's milk cheese produced exclusively in the province of Enna. In 2011 the Piacentinu Ennese received PDO (protected designation of origin) status. The traditional technology and tools used to make the cheese are similar to those used to make PDO Pecorino Siciliano; the distinctive difference is the addition of saffron (*Crocus sativus*) to the milk for Piacentinu Ennese. See PECORINO SICILIANO and SAFFRON.

A legend reports that in the eleventh century Roger I, the Norman count of Sicily, requested that a local cheesemaker create a cheese to cure the depression of his beloved wife, Adelasia. Saffron has been considered an energizing and antidepressant spice since ancient times, so the cheesemaker added it to a traditional pecorino cheese, creating a cheese unique to Sicily. "Piacentinu," from the Sicilian dialect word *piacenti*, means "what you like." Piacentinu Ennese PDO is made using raw sheep's milk, artisanal rennet, and no starter culture, and adding locally grown saffron and black pepper grains. The saffron contributes to the deep yellow color and, with its unique group of volatiles, including safranal and a set of cyclohexenones, may also have antitumoral properties.

Piacentinu Ennese has a compact texture and presents a strong characteristic smell. The pairing of spices, black pepper, and saffron, and the raw milk impart the characteristic aroma properties of the cheese. Piacentinu cheeses are cylindrical, range from about 8–10 pounds (3.5–4.5 kilograms) and are generally consumed at two to four months for semi-aged and over four months for aged. The aging process occurs in cool and slightly ventilated rooms.

See also SICILY.

Carpino, S., et al. "Volatile Fingerprint of Piacentinu Cheese Produced with Different Tools and Type of Saffron." *Small Ruminant Research* 79 (2008): 16–21.
D'Auria, M., et al. "Volatile Organic Compounds from Saffron." *Flavour and Fragrance Journal* 19 (2004): 17–23.

Stefania Carpino

Piave

Piave is a hard cow's milk cheese sold throughout Europe and the United States at five different ages, from Piave Fresco (aged twenty to sixty days) to Piave Vecchio Riserva (aged over eighteen months). The protein chains in Piave will form crunchy deposits of tyrosine crystals when aged, adding to the character of the cheese. See CRYSTAL.

This cheese's namesake is the Piave River, the source of which is found in the Dolomite Mountains, in the northernmost part of Veneto, Italy. Piave has been protected by a DOP (denominazione di origine protetta) since 2010 and is produced exclusively by Cooperative Lattebusche, a dairy cooperative in Veneto. Piave is a descendant of Bellunese cheesemaking traditions, and is made from pasteurized cow's milk collected in two milkings, one of which is skimmed.

The paste of Piave is white in its early ages, turning a light beige as the cheese matures into Vecchio. It is dense and crystalline in texture, without holes. It has a nutty, sweet taste and tropical fruit undertones that intensify with aging. The rind is soft and clear when fresh, becoming hard and brown as it ages, and is impressed vertically at the base with the name of the cheese. Aged over twelve months, Piave works well as a grating cheese, shaved over salads or pasta, paired with figs, honey, and quince paste, or enjoyed with a glass of Barolo or amber ale.

See also ITALY.

Associazione Formaggi Italiani. "Piave PDO." http://www.afidop.it/en/dop-igp-cheeses/piave-pdo.
Di Palo, Lou. *Di Palo's Guide to the Essential Foods of Italy: 100 Years of Wisdom and Stories from Behind the Counter.* New York: Ballantine, 2014.

Kate Demase

Pichtogalo Chanion, also called Chaniotiki Mizithra, is a Greek, soft, spreadable PDO (protected designation of origin) cheese (granted in 1994) named for the Greek words *pichto* (thick) and *gala* (milk). It is exclusively produced in the county of Chania on the Greek island of Crete from sheep's or goat's milk, or both. The milk used is fresh or pasteurized, deriving from animals fed only by the rich endogenous vegetation of the local area.

Pichtogalo Chanion has a white color, no holes, no shape or skin, and a sweet and acid, fresh and pleasant taste. Its aroma is characteristic and is similar to yogurt. It has a maximal moisture content of 65 percent, minimum dry fat content of 50 percent, 16 to 20 percent protein, and salt content around 1 percent. Its production is very simple and is still performed traditionally: Within forty-eight hours after milking, the milk is filtered and coagulated at 64–77°F (18–25°C) in two hours using natural rennet. The addition of calcium chloride or starters is permitted only if the milk used is pasteurized. The curd remains in the cauldron for another twenty-four hours for acidification. Without being cut, it is afterward filtered using cheesecloth. After the addition of 1 percent salt, the cheese is ready for consumption. It is put in containers, preserved at 39°F (4°C) and consumed within two to three months.

Pichtogalo Chanion is used in traditional Cretan recipes, as Dakos, Bougatsa, Boureki, and Kalitsounia, as well as the pies of Sfakia and a Cretan meat pie called *tourta*. It has been produced for hundreds of years from the Chania people in low quantities, but its production has increased recently. In 2012, 45 tons were produced. It has been exported only to Germany in minimal quantities.

See also GREECE.

Chatzikokolakis, Kostas. "Kissamos-Kisamos (Values of)." Personal blog, 30 May 2012. http://hatzikos. blogspot.gr/2012/05/blog-post_30.html.

Marina Georgalaki

Cheese brought to **picnics** is named or unnamed. The pattern was set by two doggerel poems for children, "The Happy Courtship, Marriage, and Pic Nic Dinner of Cock Robin and Jenny Wren" (1806) and "The Mice and Their Pic Nic" (1809). In the former, Magpie and Little Mary each contribute a generic cheese to the birds' "pic nic"; in the latter, Epicure Mice "pic nic" on Cheshire cheese in the pantry of a London townhouse.

Gourmands are usually particular about naming their cheese. Jean Anthelme Brillat-Savarin is fond of Gruyère or Roquefort for a hunter's lunch in the field, and W. C. Fields packed Swiss, Liederkranz, and Camembert for a three-day motor trip binge. The dessert at Ford Madox Ford's "Banquet at Calanques," is sweet-cream cheese with a sauce made of marc and sweet herbs. Rex Stout names Wisconsin cheese as Nero Wolfe's favorite in *Too Many Cooks* and *Death of a Dude*. But it's unclear which of Wisconsin's six hundred cheeses Wolfe prefers, maybe all.

Food writers are often ambivalent about the type of cheese brought to picnics. Isabella Beeton's staggering "Bill of Fare for Picnic of Forty Persons" in *The Book of Household Management* calls only for "some cheese." Linda Hull Larned calls for unnamed "Deep Fried Cheese Cutlets" in the first picnic cookbook, *One Hundred Picnic Suggestions*. Similarly May E. Southworth's *The Motorist's Luncheon Book* advises apple pie with generic cheese. James Beard's *Menus for Entertaining* has it both ways. For "An Elegant Picnic for the Beach," he suggests Emmentaler and a Roquefort loaf, but commits only to cheese for "A Festive Country or Beach Picnic." Elizabeth David suggests a dessert of dried figs with either a "homemade sour milk cheese, very slightly salted, or a little French cream cheese" in *Summer Cooking*, but Parmesan in a Tian in *Mediterranean Food*. Alice Waters's *Chez Panisse Menu Cookbook* suggests a marinated goat cheese with olives and whole garlic. For skiing,

This illustration is from the children's poem "The Happy Courtship, Merry Marriage, and Pic Nic Dinner of Cock Robin and Jenny Wren" (1806). It contains the first use of "pic nic" to designate an outdoor picnic.

in the Alps or anywhere, Joan Hemingway and Connie Maricich's *The Picnic Gourmet* names Gruyère or Appenzeller.

Named and unnamed cheeses are sometimes (oddly) associated with love. A little block of Stilton is part of the elegant and expensive array of food designed for seducing the eponymous heroine in Mary Elizabeth Braddon's *The Doctor's Wife*. When the teamster Billy Roberts courts the laundress Saxon Brown in Jack London's *The Valley of the Moon*, he packs Swiss. Less successful is Dick Diver, who eats Bel Paese and Mortadella while trying to attract a Hollywood starlet in F. Scott Fitzgerald's *Tender Is the Night*. Edith Wharton, a foodista who knows better, links only unidentified cheeses to unhappy love affairs in *Summer* and *Hudson River Bracketed*. The family on the grass in Hyde Park eating cheese-stuffed chapatis in Monica Ali's *Brick Lane* seems ordinary except that the wife is thinking about her lover. Rupert Birkin and Ursula Brangwen pack some cheese for their lovemaking in Sherwood Forest in D. H. Lawrence's *Women in Love*. Ian McEwan's *Enduring Love* begins with a disastrous picnic as Joe and Clarissa Rose unpack fresh mozzarella, purchased at a posh London shop, they never get to eat.

Authors allude to cheese at various locations. On a prairie where in Illinois Charles Dickens feasted on buffalo tongue and unnamed cheese in *American Notes*. On the grass where Martin Booth's Mr. Butterfly in *A Very Private Gentleman* packs 2 ounces (50 grams) of pecorino, and 3½ ounces (100 grams) of prosciutto. This precision is telltale for an expert gunsmith. On the side of the road where Water Rat serves the Sea Rat wine, a yard-long baguette, sausage, and some unnamed "cheese which lay down and cried" in Kenneth Grahame's *The Wind in the Willows*. In Prospect Park where Sophie Zawistowska, struggling to overcome her demons, shops for salami and Swiss on pumpernickel at a Brooklyn deli in William Styron's *Sophie's Choice*. In Yorkshire where in *Possession*, A. S. Byatt is partial to creamy-white Wensleydale because it's from Yorkshire, her native region. On a train where Constance Spry remembers the cost of the picnic lunch basket on her first solo ride in her *Cookery Book*, but not the name of the cheese. On a sailboat where James Ramsay intently watches as his father slices "cheese into thin yellow sheets" with his penknife in Virginia Woolf's *To the Lighthouse*. In the woods where Osbert Sitwell prefers goat cheese because it's earthy in "Picnics and Pavilions." At the

beach where Sylvia Plath confided in her journal that she gorged on generic cheese and ham sandwiches with mustard, coleslaw, and tomatoes. In a cow pasture where pieces of "salad and cheese were disgustedly spat out on the grass" in Martin Amis's *Dead Babies*. The most oddball is when Alex Thomas asks Iris Chase for a cheese sandwich, she hands him hard-boiled egg, instead. The missing cheese is part of the subterfuge in Margaret Atwood's *The Blind Assassin*. And finally, the most sardonic: William Goldman's *The Princess Bride*, Vizzini and the Man in Black would rather drink poisoned wine than eat cheese.

See also ART; CHILDREN'S LITERATURE; and LITERATURE.

Beard, James. *Menus for Entertaining*. Rev. ed. New York: Marlowe & Company, 1997.
Beeton, Isabella. "Bill of Fare for a Picnic of 40 Persons." In *The Book of Household Management*. London: S. O. Beeton, 1861.
Brillat-Savarin, Jean Anthelme. *The Physiology of Taste, or Meditations on Transcendental Gastronomy* (1825). Trnslated by Anne Drayton, New York: Penguin, 1994.
David, Elizabeth. *Summer Cooking*. London: Penguin, 1965.
David, Elizabeth. *A Book of Mediterranean Food*. 2d rev. ed. New York: New York Review of Books, 2002.
Hemingway, Joan, and Connie Maricich. *The Picnic Gourmet*. New York: Random House, 1975.
Levy, Walter. *The Picnic: A History*. Lanham, Md.: Rowman & Littlefield/AltaMira, 2014.
Taylor, Robert Lewis. *W. C. Fields: His Follies and Fortunes* Garden City, N.Y.: Doubleday, 1949.

Walter Levy

Picodon

See CAILLÉ DOUX AND CAILLÉ ACIDE.

piercing

See NEEDLES.

pimento cheese is a cheese spread synonymous with the southern United States. In its purest form, pimento cheese is made by combining grated Cheddar (or a creamy, farmers' style cheese), mayonnaise, and pimento peppers. The pimento, pimiento, or cherry pepper is the apex of flavor in the time-honored mixture. First cultivated in the United

States in the early 1900s, pimentos boast an intensely aromatic, sweet, rounded chili flavor.

Recipes for pimento cheese vary regionally, with salt, pepper, hot sauce, minced onions, Worcestershire sauce, paprika, cayenne pepper, and pickles serving as popular additions. For many southerners, pimento cheese represents the halcyon days of their youth. A toothsome pimento cheese sandwich on white bread with the crusts cut off is symbolic of cultural heritage, regional identity, and hospitality.

The precise debut of pimento cheese is somewhat unclear, though a cookbook published in 1867, alludes to its creation. *Mrs. Hill's Southern Practical Cookery and Receipt Book* contends: "To protect fresh cheese from flies, mix red pepper with butter with which it [the cheese] is greased." George Reigel of the Pomona Products Company further massaged the proliferation of the recipe by distributing canned pimentos as early as 1916. At its origin, pimento cheese spread was a working-class culinary practice that capitalized on the increasing availability of cheaply priced commodity cheese and bountiful southern crops of pimento peppers.

Today pimento cheese is available in mass-produced formats, but homemade recipes continue to be passed down through generations, especially in the southern United States.

Claiborne, Craig. "Food News: Bright Note of Pimentos." *New York Times*, 12 February 1960.

Myers, Kendra. "Pimento Cheese." In *The New Encyclopedia of Southern Culture*, Vol. 7: *Foodways*, edited by John T. Edge. Chapel Hill: University of North Carolina Press, 2007.

Smith, Annabella P. *Mrs. Hill's Southern Practical Cookery and Receipt Book*. 1867. Columbia: University of South Carolina Press.

Tess McNamara

dipped them in hot water, and hung them for aging. As the cheeses matured, the netting cut diamond-shaped patterns into them that resembled the exterior of a pineapple. Norton then shellacked his cheeses (to keep the oily residue from seeping out) and eventually sold them in 2-, 4-, and 6-pound (1-, 2-, and 2.7-kilogram) sizes. He patented his process in 1810.

Although these specialty cheeses commanded slightly higher prices, they proved very popular. In 1844 Norton built a factory next to his house to keep up with the market demand for pineapple cheese. By the end of the nineteenth century the family began purchasing nearly 1 million gallons (4.5 million liters) of milk per year to maintain production. The popularity of pineapple cheese led to the production of similar products throughout New York, southern Michigan, and the Pacific Northwest. The Norton family remained in the business for ninety-five years until the Kraft Cheese Company purchased the Norton trademark and discontinued the sale of its products in 1931.

See also SPECIALTY CHEESE.

Gold, C. L. "Pineapple Cheese: First Made in Goshen More Than a Century Ago." *Hartford Courant*, 22 February 1937.

"Goshen Loses One of Its Leading Men." *Hartford Courant*, 27 December 1907.

Kurau, Florence W. "His Cheeses Made History in Goshen: In 1800s Lewis Norton Manufactured Product Famed Throughout the Country." *Hartford Courant*, 7 January 1951.

"'Pine Cheese Farm' Sold." *Hartford Courant*, 19 March 1906.

State of Connecticut. "Twenty-Second Annual Report of the Secretary of the Connecticut Board of Agriculture." Hartford: Press of the Case, Lockwood & Brainard Company, 1888.

Gregg Mangan

pineapple cheese is a curd or milk cheese molded into the shape of a pineapple—the traditional symbol of hospitality in early America.

The first pineapple cheese made in America came from West Goshen, Connecticut. There Louis Norton, inspired by a cheese sample an uncle brought back from Europe, began making pineapple-shaped cheeses at the start of the nineteenth century. Using the milk of approximately fifty cows from his farm, Norton pressed curds in pineapple-shaped molds made of wood. He then placed the cheese in heavy cord nets,

Piophila casei, the cheese fly, is—along with molds and mites—a well-known colonizer of cheese. *Piophila casei* lays its eggs on the fresh surface of a cheese. A member of the Piophilidae family, it is also called the "cheese skipper" (or "ham skipper") due to the ability of its larvae to jump through the air.

Eggs hatch within thirty-six to forty-eight hours of being laid and larvae reach their development in about eight days, while more than two weeks is needed for larvae to become pupae and then adult insects. The duration of the life cycle depends on

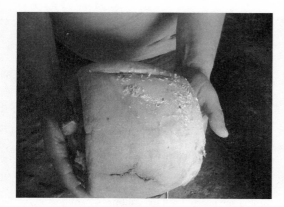

Piophila casei, the cheese fly, lays its eggs on the fresh surface of a cheese. The larvae penetrate the cheese and digest the paste, which becomes creamy and spicy. This photo was taken at a dairy farm in San Basilio, Sardinia, a region where "maggot cheeses" are an (illegal) delicacy. © ALESSANDRA GUIGONI

environmental conditions: a temperature of around 68–72°F (20–22°C) (or slightly higher) is ideal for larvae development.

The flies are detritivores, feeding on decaying matter. The larvae move with distinctive saltatory movements and penetrate the cheese by means of enzymes present in the saliva, causing digestion of the cheesy paste, which becomes creamy and spicy. Some cheeses containing the larvae of *Piophila casei* (i.e., maggots) are well known and considered a delicacy in some regions of Mediterranean, such as Piedmont, Lombardy, and Corsica: consumers love their pungent taste. Maggot cheese is linked especially to Sardinia, where it is called casu marzu (or casu fràzigu), or "rotten cheese." Andrew Zimmern's television program *Bizarre Foods* may have contributed to casu marzu's worldwide reputation. See SARDINIA.

Casu marzu is one of the 183 traditional Sardinian agricultural and food products that are officially acknowledged by the Ministry of Agricultural, Food and Forestry Policies (MIPAAF). It can be obtained both from long-ripened ovine milk cheese and from cow's milk cheese (like *pirittas*). This cheese with live maggots may be consumed in a variety of ways: one can put in the refrigerator for some hours to stun the maggots with the cold, or the creamy cheese may be ground with a food mill to kill most of the maggots, or the cheese is placed in a plastic or paper bag to suffocate them. But many people eat the cheese as is, with living insect larvae.

It is considered dangerous to consume the cheese if it contains larvae that have been dead for some time or have already become pupae. If when opening the cheese, larvae are found dead, Sardinians assume that something went wrong during the process. When the maggots have already become pupae the process of proteolysis is too advanced. The cheese paste is liquefied and ammonia and carbon dioxide have been produced, with a consequent bad smell and taste.

Casu marzu is clearly in defiance of European Union rules on food hygiene and its commercial sale is illegal. Nonetheless, although initially the production of casu marzu was a fortuitous occurrence, in recent years it has been done intentionally because those who prize it are known to buy it on the black market at a high price.

See also CHEESE MITES.

Overstreet, Robin M. "Flavor Buds and Other Delights." *Journal of Parasitology* 89, no. 6 (2003): 1093–1107.
Regione Autonoma della Sardegna, and ERSAT. "Casu fràzigu." http://www.sardegnaagricoltura.it/documenti/14_43_20070607153029.pdf.
"Sardinia." *Bizarre Foods with Andrew Zimmern*, season 6, episode 14. Aired 5 July 2011.
University of Florida, Department of Entomology and Nematology. "Piophila casei." http://entnemdept.ufl.edu/creatures/urban/flies/cheese_skipper.htm.

Alessandra Guigoni

pitching is a cheesemaking term that is used in the making of English cheeses that are traditionally scalded (cooked) and drained in the vat, such as Cheddar and Double Gloucester. See CHEDDAR and GLOUCESTER. Pitching refers to the practice that occurs near the end of scalding, when the cheese-maker ceases to stir the curd-whey mixture and allows the curds to settle at the bottom of the vat in preparation for whey drainage (also known colloquially as "whey-off"). The amount of time allotted to pitching before the start of draining may be increased, decreased, or eliminated altogether depending on the rate of acidification during scalding. For example, when acid production occurs too rapidly, necessitating a reduction in the scalding time, the curds may experience excessive mineral (calcium phosphate) loss and retain too much whey, increasing the risk of producing an overly moist and acidic cheese. In this situation, the cheesemaker may dispense with pitching altogether by stirring the curd-whey mixture continuously throughout draining in order to encourage additional curd shrinkage and release of whey. At the other extreme, when acid production occurs too slowly, resulting in a longer scalding time, the curds may retain too much calcium phosphate and lose too much whey, increasing the risk of producing a cheese that lacks the proper acidity and moisture content. In this case, the cheesemaker may extend the time that the curd is pitched before commencing draining in order to reduce the release of whey and lactic acid from the curds. Intermediate to these extremes would be to pitch the curd shortly before draining.

See also CALCIUM PHOSPHATE; DRAINING; and SCALDING.

Scott, R., R. K. Robinson, and R. A. Wilbey. *Cheesemaking Practice*, 3d ed. Gaithersburg, Md.: Aspen, 1998.

Paul S. Kindstedt

pizza is a humble Italian flatbread whose modern version is linked with the city of Naples. It is made from leavened dough, stretched and slapped into a flat, round base, scattered with assorted toppings, and then baked in a very hot oven. Pizza can be sold either whole or in slices. Modern pizza toppings commonly include tomatoes and cheese, although the addition of meats and vegetables is also popular. It was not until Italian immigrants brought pizza to America, at the end of the nineteenth century, that the dish began its path toward global domination. Indeed, what began as a regional Italian specialty had to take a detour to the New World before returning and gaining national popularity on its home soil. It increased in prominence in the rest of Italy after World War II but took until the 1960s to spread to the north of the nation. Its low cost and ready appeal to local tastes have allowed pizza to become a circular superstar of international cuisine and one of the world's most popular fast foods.

Pizza is one of several flatbreads to be found throughout the world. Many ancient cultures, from the Etruscans to the Greeks, adopted the custom of having one's meal or snack on an edible plate, whether for the sake of economical necessity or mobility. Whatever the nature of the actual dish, the word "pizza" has been around in some form or other for more than a millennium. Burton Anderson (1994) notes that its first use, as *picea* or *piza* in a Neapolitan

dialect, may have been as early as 977 C.E. at Gaeta, a port between Rome and Naples.

Neapolitan pizza, *la pizza napoletana*, is the prototype of the dish we know today. This flatbread, along with boiled pasta and deep-fried dough, was one of the street foods that allowed Naples's urban poor to survive. A key to the dish's success as a humble form of nourishment was the ovens' powerful heat, which expanded a small amount of dough into a seemingly larger amount of food. This was a blessing for those with a limited budget because it provided an inexpensive, satisfying meal.

Pizza came in a variety of flavors; common toppings included lard, garlic, salt, olive oil, oregano, fish, and cheese. The addition of tomatoes to pizza may not have occurred until the first half of the nineteenth century, after the New World fruit was introduced to Europe and was no longer suspected of being poisonous. The original pizza was sold whole as well as in slices; customers paid for the size they could afford. The dish, hawked by street vendors, grew in popularity throughout Naples in the eighteenth century. It was not until 1830, however, that the first pizzeria, Antica Pizzeria Port'Alba, opened its doors. Local pizzerias ultimately installed tables, which allowed their customers to sit down and dine, attracting a more respectable audience. In time, even the upper classes could not resist the lure of this local specialty.

National lore asserts that the Italian king Umberto I traveled to Naples with his queen, Margherita of Savoy, in 1889 and sought out the regional dish. To honor the royal visit, the pizza maker Raffaele Esposito served the couple an assortment of pizzas including one topped with green basil, white mozzarella, and red tomatoes, which echoed the newly unified country's tricolor flag. This pizza, which particularly delighted the queen, was named Margherita in the queen's honor and is considered the archetype of contemporary pizza.

In 1984 the True Neapolitan Pizza Association (Associazione Verace Pizza Napoletana or AVPN) was formed in Naples in order to promote and protect the authenticity of the local specialty. It recognizes only two varieties, the Marinara (tomato, oil, oregano, and garlic) and the Margherita (tomato, oil, mozzarella, grated cheese, and fresh basil). The supremacy of Neapolitan pizza is a result of the superiority of local products as well as highly regulated production techniques, specifically the making of the fermented dough. The AVPN's guidelines require the use of highly refined Italian wheat flour, type "00," which is low in protein and yields a product that is soft and easily stretched. The pizza must be cooked on the stone surface of a wood-fired oven at 905°F (485°C) for 60–90 seconds in total, which produces a soft, foldable crust with the flavor of well-prepared, baked bread. The underside is crisp, speckled with char, and softens once the pizza is cut and the juices flow. This crust, underlining a perfect balance between bread and toppings, is a signature of Neapolitan pizza. The dish should be consumed immediately, straight out of the oven, in the pizzeria.

AVPN pizza makers use mozzarella—either the firmer mozzarella fior di latte, made from cow's milk, or the tangy and creamy mozzarella di bufala, made from the milk of the water buffalo. Hard, grated cheese is also permitted. In contrast, the generic, global pizza industry relies on a mass-produced, machine-folded pasta filata cheese, also known as mozzarella. This mozzarella, however, is overpasteurized, kneaded, and pulled until most of its butterfat is removed, yielding an easily shredded, rubbery cheese with a lengthy refrigerated shelf life.

See also ITALY MOZZARELLA; MOZZARELLA DI BUFALA CAMPANA; and PASTA FILATA.

Anderson, Burton. *Treasures of the Italian Table: Italy's Celebrated Foods and the Artisans Who Make Them.* New York: Morrow, 1994.
Associazione Verace Pizza Napoletana. "Regulations for Obtaining Use of the Collective Trade Mark 'Verace Pizza Napoletana' (Vera Pizza Napoletana)." http://www.pizzanapoletana.org/public/pdf/disciplinare%202008%20UK.pdf.
Helstosky, Carol. *Pizza: A Global History.* London: Reaktion, 2008.

Allison Radecki

plakous was an ancient Greek food usually translated as "cheesecake." No Greek recipe survives, but an allusive description by Antiphanes, quoted in his fourth century B.C.E. comedy *Deipnosophists*, gives the main ingredients: "The streams of the tawny bee, mixed with the curdled river of bleating she-goats, placed upon a flat receptacle of the virgin daughter of Zeus, delighting in ten thousand delicate toppings—or shall I simply say cheesecake?" In other words, plakous consisted of a cereal base topped with a filling of goat cheese sweetened with

honey; there is indeed some resemblance to modern cheesecake.

In the second century B.C.E., there is evidence of a Latin equivalent, *placenta*. Curiously, this name was borrowed from *plakounta*, the accusative case of the Greek word, which suggests that the speakers' knowledge of Greek was limited. For this Latin cheesecake, a very detailed recipe survives in Cato's handbook *On Farming* (chapter 76; for reconstructed modern recipes see the bibliography). It, too, had a cereal base with cheese and honey above; it was baked, and it was tasty enough that slave waiters were accused of licking it on its way to the dining room (Lucilius, *Satires* fragment 585 Marx). See CATO, MARCUS PORCIUS.

The Latin term survives in modern Romanian *plăcintă* as the name for a much smaller, but still cheesy, cake. In Austria and the western Balkans, the same name emerges again, in forms such as *Palatschinke* and *palacsinta*, for a pancake with sweet toppings among which sweetened quark or cottage cheese may be included. See QUARK and COTTAGE CHEESE.

See also ANCIENT CIVILIZATIONS and CHEESECAKES.

Dalby, Andrew, and Sally Grainger. *The Classical Cookbook.* 2d ed. London: British Museum Press, 2013, pp. 113–115.
Grant, Mark. *Roman Cookery: Ancient Recipes for Modern Kitchens.* London: Serif, 1999, pp. 104–106.

Andrew Dalby

plant-derived coagulants are enzymes harvested from plants that can bring about coagulation of milk and thereby serve the same purpose in cheesemaking as animal- or microbial-derived rennet. See ENZYMES and RENNET. These coagulants may be commonly referred to as "thistle rennet," as many of the plants from which the coagulating enzyme can be extracted are related to thistles.

The two most common sources of plant-derived coagulants are the cardoon and the globe artichoke, but fig leaves and sap, nettles, safflower, and other plants have also been used. Enzymes derived from the thistle, cyprosin and cardosin, work similarly to animal-based chymosin to cause milk curdling. See CHYMOSIN. The enzyme may be accessed either by steeping the plant in water to make a "tea" and adding it to the cheese milk, or by adding the plant directly to the cheese milk for a period of time during the cheesemaking process. Plant-derived coagulants yield less predictable results than, and are not as widely available as, animal and microbial rennet, making cheeses in this style relatively uncommon today.

Thistle-coagulated cheeses are most commonly found in the Iberian peninsula, but can also be found in parts of France and Italy. The southwestern region of the Iberian peninsula that includes Extremadura and Andalusia is particularly well known for these cheeses. See SPAIN and PORTUGAL. Thistle-coagulated cheeses developed because of the abundance of requisite plant material in the area and the ability of sheep's milk, the primary milk source in these regions, to coagulate effectively with this enzyme. Azeitão, Serra da Estrela, and Torta del Casar cheeses, which are still available and exported globally, are among the most popular examples of cheeses made in this style. See AZEITÃO; SERRA DA ESTRELA; and TORTA DEL CASAR. Historically thistle-rennet (*hierba cuajo*, Spanish for grass or herb rennet) cheeses were made across a broader region, but many cheesemakers working within traditions that may have originally used plant-derived coagulants have moved to animal or microbial rennet. The use of thistle rennet has dwindled both because of the inconsistency in enzyme concentration within the plants, which yields unpredictable results in the final cheese product, and variable wild thistle availability in these cheesemaking regions. Nowadays commercial and therefore standardized thistle rennet is widely used for the cheeses in question.

Cheeses coagulated with plant enzymes were popular among, and possibly developed by, Iberian Jews following strict kosher dietary laws that forbade mixing milk and meat. Within this community, the rennet derived from animals' stomachs was considered a type of meat product, and was forbidden from being consumed at the same time as milk. Spanish Jews therefore sought out processes for making cheese that would allow them to avoid mixing a meat product into milk. Jews had arrived in Spain as early as the first century B.C.E., and evidence of thistle-coagulated cheesemaking generally follows their migration patterns as they moved around the peninsula seeking safety and economic self-determination depending on the social pressures of the subsequent centuries. Even in settled areas of conversos, "secret" Jews who maintained elements of their culture but officially converted to Christianity during the Inquisition, the practice of making cheese with plant-derived coag-

ulants carried on. See DIETARY LAWS (RELIGIOUS). To this day vegetarian cheese consumers often seek out these cheeses or cheese coagulated with microbial rennet because they consider the use of an animal-derived rennet to render a cheese non-vegetarian.

Beyond these benefits to the Jewish community, thistle- and other plant-derived coagulants provided additional qualities sought by traditional cheesemakers. Wild thistle and fig sap were available year-round, whereas animals that provided a source of rennet were slaughtered only in the spring, leading to rennet shortages much of the rest of the year. Some also preferred the taste and texture of thistle-coagulated cheeses, which are known for their buttery, molten paste and were considered to be less bitter than other cheeses. With the advent of commercially available animal and microbial rennet, however, thistle rennet's traditional advantages have largely been surpassed. Plant-derived coagulants therefore play a relatively minor role in today's cheesemaking landscape.

See also COAGULATION OR CURDLING.

Arding, Kate, and Elaine Khosrova. "Rennet's Role." *Culture: The Word on Cheese*, 2 December 2011. http://culturecheesemag.com/cheese-iq/rennets-role.
Donnelly, Catherine W., ed. *Cheese and Microbes.* Washington, D.C.: ASM Press, 2014.
Tovar, Rosa. "Spanish Thistle-Bloom Cheese." *Gastronomica* 2, no. 2 (Spring 2002): 77–82.

Jessica A. B. Galen

plasmin is the most predominant indigenous proteinase in mammalian milk (e.g., bovine, caprine, buffalo, camel, equine) used for human consumption. In mammalian systems, plasmin is secreted as its zymogen, plasminogen. Also present in the mammalian system are inhibitors and activators of plasmin and plasminogen that act in a cascade system.

The concentration/activity of plasmin in milk is influenced by various factors, including stage of lactation, age of cow, and disease state (mastitis). The concentration of plasminogen in fresh milk is approximately 0.8–2.8 micrograms/milliliter; that of plasmin is approximately 0.1–0.7 microgram/milliliter. The concentration of plasminogen decreases during storage as plasmin concentration increases, due to the action of plasminogen activators. Plasmin is very heat-stable; it fully survives pasteurization and partially survives ultra-high-temperature (UHT) treatment of milk. The activity of plasmin in milk increases after pasteurization because of inactivation of its inhibitors, which are heat labile. It is active over a broad range of pH and temperature but optimally active at pH 7.5–8.0 and 99°F (37°C). At the normal pH of milk, plasmin is exclusively associated with the casein micelles. Plasmin dissociates from the casein micelles when the pH of milk is reduced suggesting that plasmin activity in cheese is influenced by the pH of whey drainage. The activation of plasminogen coupled with inactivation of plasmin inhibitors by heat affects the relative activity of plasmin in cheeses. Hence, plasmin activity is relatively higher in high-temperature cooked cheeses such as Swiss cheese—which contains 1.5 to approximately 3 times that in low-temperature-cooked cheeses such as Cheddar.

Casein proteolysis by plasmin in cheese influences texture and flavor of cheeses especially in Swiss-type cheeses, which have high plasmin activity. Plasmin has been considered experimentally as an added enzyme to improve ripening and flavor development of cheese. The presence of whey proteins in cheese is thought to inhibit plasmin activity.

See also MILK.

Bastian, Eric D., and Rodney J. Brown. "Plasmin in Milk and Dairy Products: An Update." *International Dairy Journal* 6, no. 5 (1996): 435–457.

Farkye, Nana Y., and Patrick F. Fox. "Observations on Plasmin Activity in Cheese." *Journal of Dairy Research* 57, no. 3 (1990): 412–418.

Farkye, Nana, and Patrick F. Fox. "Contribution of Plasmin to Cheddar Cheese Ripening: Effect of Added Plasmin." *Journal of Dairy Research* 59, no. 2 (1992): 209–216.

Ismail, B., and S. S. Nielsen. "Invited review: Plasmin Protease in Milk: Current Knowledge and Relevance to Dairy Industry." *Journal of Dairy Science* 93, no. 11 (2010): 4999–5009.

Nana Y. Farkye

Pleasant Ridge Reserve, made by the Uplands Cheese Company, is an unpasteurized cheese crafted from May through October from the milk of pastured cows near Dodgeville, Wisconsin. Inspired by the French Alp-style cheese Beaufort, and named after the rolling hills of Uplands Farm, Pleasant Ridge Reserve is crafted in ten-pound wheels, washed several times a week with a brine solution, and ripened in special cheese-aging rooms built on the farm. Wheels are typically sold at less than one year of age, but batches of year-old, or "extra aged" cheese are available in the fall and early winter.

Pleasant Ridge Reserve was created in 2000 by two farming couples, Mike and Carol Gingrich and Dan and Jeanne Patenaude, with the help of the Center for Dairy Research in Madison, Wisconsin. In 2001 the cheese vaulted to fame after winning the coveted Best of Show award at the annual American Cheese Society competition. It repeated the honor in 2005 and again in 2010, and earned the US Champion Cheese title in 2003. Pleasant Ridge Reserve is the only cheese to win the American Cheese Society Best of Show three times, and is the only cheese to win both American cheese competitions. See COMPETITIONS.

In 2013 the Gingriches and Patenaudes retired and sold the farm and creamery to Andy Hatch, a cheese-maker who has crafted Pleasant Ridge Reserve since 2007, and Scott Mericka, a dairy herdsman at Uplands Farm since 2010. With their wives, Caitlin Hatch, and Liana Mericka, they continue the Uplands cheese tradition of crafting award-winning seasonal cheese.

See also BEAUFORT WISCONSIN.

"Pleasant Ridge Reserve." *Culture: The Word on Cheese.* http://culturecheesemag.com/cheese-library/pleasant-ridge-reserve.

Uplands Cheese. http://uplandscheese.com.

Jeanne Carpenter

Pliny the Elder (full name Gaius Plinius Secundus: 23–79 C.E.), Roman general and historian, is often referred to as "the Elder" to distinguish him from his nephew, author of a collection of letters. Pliny died in the eruption of Vesuvius: he had led a fleet across the Bay of Naples to rescue the people of Pompeii, saving many lives, but unwisely stayed behind to observe the volcano at close hand.

Pliny was not only a man of action but also a tireless reader and note taker. His one surviving work, the *Natural History* in thirty-seven books, is an ambitious survey of the natural world, its products, and their uses to man. It was a popular text in medieval Europe and is still mined by scholars in many disciplines. Pliny rarely names sources for individual details in his work, and for this reason their reliability is sometimes hard to judge.

Food historians focus on books 8–11 (animals), 12–19 (plants), and 20–32 (substances used in medicine and diet). Cheese finds a place in book 11, as a product of milk, and in book 28 where its dietary effects are discussed.

Pliny gives an interesting list, probably from personal knowledge, of the best cheeses on sale in Rome in his time, beginning with "those which come from the provinces: best is that of the Nîmes region (especially the districts of Lozère and Gévaudan) but only briefly, when fresh-tasting." These are the districts that now produce Cantal, Salers, and Laguiole. Pliny recommends two provincial cheeses from high mountain pastures, one from Tarentaise in the French Alps, now the source of Beaufort, and the other from Dioclea, modern Montenegro, still proud of its cheese. He then lists Italian cheeses, from Liguria, Umbria, Vestinum close to Rome, noting also the cheeses of Luna on the borders of Liguria and Tuscany, "remarkable for their vast size, a single cheese weighing as much as a thousand pounds." Like other Roman connoisseurs he likes smoked goats' milk cheese and prefers the kind that was made elsewhere but smoked in Rome. Pliny mentions only one "transmarine" cheese from Rome's eastern provinces: "that of Bithynia is usually considered the first in quality."

See also ANCIENT CIVILIZATIONS.

Pliny the Elder. *Pliny: Natural History*. 10 vols. Translated by H. Rackham, W. H. S. Jones, and D. E. Eichholz. Cambridge, Mass.: Harvard University Press, 1938–1962. See Volumes 3 and 8.

Andrew Dalby

Pljevlja cheese is the most popular and widely produced Montenegrin traditional cheese. It is a white, brined, soft to semihard, fatty cheese. Traditionally Pljevlja cheese is made from sheep's milk, but lately more and more is produced from cow's milk and mixed cow's milk and sheep's milk. The production area is in northern Montenegro, in the municipality of Pljevlja. Historical data show that Pljevlja was an important item in trade between this region and Dubrovnik and the Venetian Republic.

Most of the cheeses are produced in households, but also in three small-scale dairy plants. After milking, the milk is filtrated through a cheesecloth and rennet is added at a temperature of 82–90°F (28–32°C).

Traditionally Pljevlja cheese was produced using domestic rennet prepared from the stomachs of young ruminant animals (calf, lamb, goat kid). Today, for the production of Pljevlja cheese, industrial liquid rennet is used. The optimal duration of coagulation is sixty minutes. Coagulated curd is cut into three-quarter-inch (2-centimeter) cubes. After settling at the bottom of the vessel, the curd is stirred slowly and, if necessary, additionally cut. The whole process takes ten to twenty-five minutes. Then the curd is collected into a cheesecloth and hung for whey separation by self-pressing. After twenty-five to thirty minutes of self-pressure, the curd is placed on a table and pressed with a circular wooden plank. The final whey separation is carried out by additional loading of the wooden plank with stones of different sizes. After six hours, the cheese is cut into slices. It is desirable that slices have a shape that best fits the form of wooden tubs used for ripening. Thus, the space between slices is reduced and provides anaerobic ripening conditions. Slices are stacked into wooden tubs, salted during stacking, and immersed in brine. Cheese ripens in brine for four to eight weeks. Periodically the surface of brine should be cleaned, or, if necessary, completely replaced with fresh brine.

Dozet, N., et al. *Autohtoni mlječni proizvodi* [Autochthonous Dairy Products]. Belgrade, Serbia: Poljoprivredni institut Podgorica, SILMIR-Beograd, 1996. Autochthonous dairy products from Bosnia and Herzegovina, Montenegro, and Serbia are presented in the book. In addition to technology recorded directly in the field, the quality of the raw material (milk), the finished product, byproducts, and sensory and microbial analysis are presented in detail. The book is a valuable source of scientific data about autochthonous dairy products from this area.

Pljevlja is the most popular and widely produced traditional Montenegrin cheese. The sliced cheese is salted and stacked into wooden tubs and immersed in brine for four to eight weeks before serving. © SLAVKO MIRECKI

Mirecki, S., and Z. Konatar. "Technology and Quality of Pljevlja Cheese—Traditional Montenegrin Dairy Product." *Journal of Hygienic Engineering and Design* 6 (2014): 208–214.

Slavko Mirecki

The **Point Reyes Farmstead Cheese Company** is a farmstead dairy and creamery in Point Reyes, California. The original dairy operation was begun by Bob and Dean Mae Giacomini in 1959 and the cheesemaking operation was founded in 2000 by their four daughters—Karen, Diana, Lynn, and Jill—as their father neared retirement. Bob and Dean Mae ran the dairy farm for 40 years on 720 acres with approximately 450 Holstein cows. In 1997, they sold a portion of their land to the Point Reyes National Seashore for preservation, and the family downsized their herd for the capital investment to launch the cheese company. As a farmstead operation, Point Reyes Farmstead Cheese Company milks around 330 cows in its dairy facility and turns 90 percent of that fluid milk into cheese on site; the remaining 10 percent of milk is sold to Clover Stornetta, a nearby dairy farm.

Having turned the dairy into a farmstead cheese company and invested in the operations to produce California's first blue cheese, on 1 August 2000 Point Reyes sold the first batches of Point Reyes Original Blue, a rindless, raw-milk cheese aged for five months. Point Reyes Farmstead Cheese sold only its raw-milk Original Blue for nine years until the company hired cheesemaker Kuba Hemmerling in 2009, and he developed a Gouda-like pressed and brined cheese named Toma, their washed-rind Bay Blue, and a fresh mozzarella using pasteurized milk.

The Point Reyes Farmstead Cheese Company prides itself on being a farmstead operation, with control over the raw ingredients including its cows' diets and subsequent fluid milk, which imparts a unique flavor to their cheeses. Its Bay Blue, Original Blue, and Toma have won top honors from the American Cheese Society, and the Specialty Food Association's Specialty Outstanding Food Innovation award.

See also CALIFORNIA and FARMSTEAD.

Paxson, Heather. *The Life of Cheese: Crafting Food and Value in America.* Berkeley: University of California Press, 2013.
Point Reyes Farmstead Cheese Company. http://www.pointreyescheese.com.

Stephanie Maroney

Poland, a country in central Europe, is the sixth-largest cheese producer in the world according to the Food and Agricultural Organization (FAO) of the United Nations. Poland's important role as a cheese producer is possibly due to the diversity of its agricultural structure, which is based on small, family farms as well as on large, highly specialized farms. Cattle breeding is mostly concentrated in the Podlasie, Masovia, Masuria, and Greater Poland regions, whereas sheep breeding is more intensive only in the mountainous regions of southern Poland.

The earliest evidence for cheesemaking in Poland comes from the sixth millennium B.C.E. and was discovered by investigating organic residues preserved in pottery sieves. Cheesemaking in Poland was developed by Cistercian abbeys and various monasteries that have been established since the medieval period. See MONASTIC CHEESEMAKING. The art of cheesemaking was popularized by Protestant minorities from Germany, the Netherlands, and Switzerland. Production of cheeses was also influenced by Napoleon's army and three partitions of Poland. For centuries, dairy production was based on household manufacture for individual use. The most important period in the history of Polish cheesemaking dates back to the end of the nineteenth century, when the first Polish dairies were established as private projects, landowning companies, or dairy cooperatives. The output of Polish dairies suffered severely during the two World Wars. During the postwar era, dairying was restored, but it was primarily focused on industrial production.

Poland's cheese consumption is dominated by fresh cheeses. See FRESH CHEESES. The most popular dairy product in this category is Twarog. This traditional fresh cheese is made by the acidification of cow's milk. It is produced in most Polish dairies and is often manufactured at home. Other fresh Polish cheeses include cream cheeses—natural or with sophisticated ingredients—and cottage cheeses, which were introduced to the Polish market by the Regional Dairy Cooperative in Piatnica, a producer from northeastern Poland. See COTTAGE CHEESE and CREAM CHEESE. A range of fresh goat cheeses is offered by Agro-Danmis, a Polish company whose 1,200 goats form the largest herd in Bukowiec, in the Greater Poland region.

The second place in the Polish cheese market belongs to hard cheeses, which are predominantly used in food service for preparing various types of casseroles. Currently, the production of high-quality, matured, hard cheeses based on traditional recipes and with the use of the best ingredients, is being restored. Old Poland is the finest Polish brand of long-maturing cheeses, such as Bursztyn, Rubin, Grand Radamer, and Grand Gouda. These excellent dairy products are produced by the Spomlek Dairy Cooperative in the town of Radzyn-Podlaski, in eastern Poland. Less than 20 percent of the Polish cheese market is shared by processed (melted) and mold-ripened cheeses.

Many regional cheeses are manufactured by small artisanal producers. In these local products, the use of sheep's and goat's milk is common. Some Polish cheeses are protected by European Union law as regional products. In 2007 Bryndza podhalanska became the first Polish product to be awarded the PDO (protected designation of origin) label. This cheese, from the Podhale region, is produced from at least 60 percent raw sheep's milk. The PDO certificate was also granted to two other cheeses from this region of Poland: Redykolka, also composed largely of sheep's milk, and Oscypek, a scalded, smoked cheese similar to the Italian Provolone Affumicato, but made from cow's and sheep's milk and presented in a decorative spindle shape. See OSCYPEK.

Two Polish cheeses were recently awarded the PGI (protected geographical indication) designation: Korycinski homemade cheese, a hard, yellow cheese made from cow's milk, which is named after the town of Korycin in eastern Poland, and Wielkopolska fried cheese from the Greater Poland region. The PGI designation means that at least one of the stages of production must take place in the area of origin.

Alegría, Ángel, et al. "Biodiversity in Oscypek, a Traditional Polish Cheese, Determined by Culture-Dependent and -Independent Approaches." *Applied and Environmental Microbiology* 78 (March 2012): 1890–1898.

Lipińska, Melania. "Historia nie tylko mlekiem pisana [History Written Not Only by Milk]." National Association of Dairy Cooperatives Revisory Association, March 2004. http://www .mleczarstwopolskie.pl/menu-2/polska-spoldzielczosc -mleczarska/historia-nie-tylko-mlekiem-pisana.

Salque, Mélanie, et al. "Earliest Evidence for Cheese Making in the Sixth Millennium BC in Northern Europe." *Nature* 493 (January 2013): 522–525.

Wielicka, Anna, and Elżbieta Goryńska-Goldmann. "World and Poland per Capita Cheese Consumption." *Roczniki Akademii Rolniczej w Poznaniu* 367, Ekonomia 4 (2005): 157–166. http://www.jard.edu.pl/pub/ 17_4_2005.pdf.

Magdalena Kowalczyk

politics of cheese. The most pressing international political issues facing the cheese industry are in the areas of (1) international trade, concerning disputes over name protections or geographical indications as well as tariffs, and (2) health and safety regulations that have prompted disagreements about milk processing and acceptable techniques of aging cheese.

International Trade

In trade negotiations, the European Union (EU) has pushed the governments of Latin America, Canada, and the United States to commit to enforcing European protections on rural products that have been granted geographical indication (GI) status by the European Commission. See GEOGRAPHICAL INDICATION. The export of artisanal foods, such as meats, condiments, wines, liquors, oils, and beers, helps maintain a balance in the trade deficit of Europe. Cheese is another value-added product that European legislators consider central to maintaining a robust agricultural industry. European cheese exports to the rest of the world amounted to 721,000 tons in 2014; Germany led production with 2,298 tons, followed by France and Italy producing 1,828 tons and 1,176 tons, respectively. Exports slowed during the first half of 2014 and may continue to do so, owing to political conflicts with trading partners, specifically a Russian ban on some agricultural foods and American changes in health and safety regulations.

In recent trade negotiations, after the 2008 collapse of the Doha Development Round of the World Trade Organization's efforts, Latin American governments have been willing to enact safeguards for Europe's name protections as they seek preferential treatment for their own exports to enter the EU market. Canada similarly agreed to protect European geographical indications under the auspices of the Canada-EU Comprehensive Economic and Trade Agreement (CETA). In the United States, similar demands have met resistance from larger producers. In negotiations over the Transatlantic Trade and Investment Partnership (TTIP) between the United States and the European Union, trade representatives from Europe have raised the possibility of including protection measures in the agreement to limit the use of GI names by American producers. This could affect producers of Parmesan-type and other Italian-style cheeses made in Wisconsin and California, for example, and has sparked a response from several

US cheesemakers, who claim they could lose up to $4 billion in revenue if such measures were imposed on them.

Tariffs and quotas are another domain where regional political differences have emerged over the commercialization, import, and export of cheeses. In 2009 the outgoing Bush administration set high duties for Roquefort and other European products in retaliation for the longstanding ban on American beef raised with hormones. The extra tariffs were eventually eliminated by the Obama administration in exchange for greater access to the European Union's hormone-free beef market. In the late 1990s, a similar conflict caused political upheaval between the United States and France when elevated tariffs were set for some French agricultural products.

Health and Safety Regulations

Regarding standards for food safety regulation, the pasteurization of milk for cheesemaking continues to be a contentious topic around the world. While many artisanal makers prefer to use raw milk, state health regulators have been increasingly demanding that all milk intended for human consumption be pasteurized, especially for cheese transported from thousand of miles away. The United States, Canada, and Mexico, along with many countries in South America, require that all imported cheese be made with pasteurized milk if it is aged for fewer than sixty days, while at the same time they have refused to allow exports of unpasteurized cheeses. See 60-DAY AGING RULE and RAW-MILK CHEESES. Canada heavily controls the sale of raw milk cheeses across provincial borders. European multinational corporations that pursue the export market have adapted recipes of traditional cheeses to meet these requirements. However, because of the changes in the recipes, those cheeses cannot be marketed as the original name-protected originals. Camembert sold outside of Europe cannot bear the French AOC label or the new European Union PDO labels. In Europe, the issue has become a point of contention between traditional producers and dairy conglomerates. Smaller producers denounce the change of recipes as an infringement on their denominations of origin, while conglomerates appeal that the changes would allow for more trade. Both camps are inveighing upon national governments, as well as upon the European Union, to draft clear rules that do not threaten commercialization.

Currently the US federal government is undertaking a review of the 60-day rule on unpasteurized milk cheeses. Cheesemakers on both sides of the Atlantic have lobbied the regulating agencies, such as the Food and Drug Administration (FDA) in the United States, to reconsider current limits on the use of raw milk in traditional cheesemaking. Distributors and retailers fear that a change in rules may adversely impact the production processes of hundreds of cheesemakers, as well as the commercialization of unpasteurized cheeses, with possible market loss.

Along with expressing concerns over the potential contamination of unpasteurized cheeses, North American health regulators have recently challenged the use of wooden boards in cheese aging as possible sources of harmful bacteria, as well as the maximum allowed count of non-toxigenic E. coli. Aging on wood is standard in artisanal European cheesemaking. Many commercially made cheeses are often aged on metal or plastic shelving. Other cheeses are aged inside vacuum-sealed, Cryovac bags. According to traditional cheesemakers, these practices are not desirable, since those inert surfaces may negatively affect the development of flavor and texture. See MATURING; PACKAGING; and WOODEN SHELVES.

In response, artisanal trade associations, along with large artisanal cheese distributors in the Americas and Europe, have presented complaints to health regulators and have lobbied legislators to limit the impact of changes on artisanal cheese production. Although Europeans consume the most cheese per capita, the United States is rapidly becoming an important consumer by volume. According to the European Union's official data source, Eurostat, Greece tops the list of cheese consumption per capita at 68 pounds a year, while in 2012 US consumers bought 33.5 pounds annually. However, according to the Wisconsin Milk Marketing Board, Americans will consume 36.5 pounds by 2024. By 2014, the United States was already producing more than 11 billion pounds annually, an increase of almost 25 percent in just ten years. This increase in overall production and consumption is occurring at the same time as Americans' consumption of processed cheese is declining. Research from the University of Wisconsin–Madison shows that in 2012, Americans consumed 3.69 pounds of processed cheese per capita, down from 5.45 pounds in 1995. See PASTEURIZED PROCESS CHEESES.

Social movements, such as Slow Food and farm-to-table, and changes in consumer preferences for organic, non–genetically modified food products, are opening avenues for artisanal cheeses to resurface in the market. A demand for freedom of consumer choice and knowledge of ingredients has emerged as a rallying cry for consumers worried about processed foodstuffs. In response, some food conglomerates and retailers have lobbied legislators to change regulations that benefit shelf-stable products at the expense of those that may be healthier although more perishable.

See also FOOD AND DRUG ADMINISTRATION; GENETICALLY MODIFIED ORGANISM; and SLOW FOOD.

CLAL.it. "European Union: Dairy Sector." http://www.clal.it/en/?section=stat_ue15.

Clarke, Toni, and Krista Hughes. "U.S. FDA Moves to Dampen Fears It Will Ban Cheese Aged on Wood." *Reuters*, 10 June 2014. http://www.reuters.com/article/2014/06/10/us-fda-cheese-idUSKBN0EL2IV20140610.

Eurostat. "Milk and Milk Product Statistics." http://ec.europa.eu/eurostat/statistics-explained/index.php/Milk_and_milk_product_statistics.

Johnson, Renée, and Charles Hanrahan. "The US-EU Beef Hormone Dispute." Congressional Research Service Report R40449, 14 January 2015. https://www.fas.org/sgp/crs/row/R40449.pdf.

McNeal, Gregory S. "FDA May Destroy American Artisan Cheese Industry." *Forbes*, 9 June 2014. http://www.forbes.com/sites/gregorymcneal/2014/06/09/fda-may-destroy-american-artisan-cheese-industry/.

Wisconsin Cheese. "Cheese Statistics." http://media.eatwisconsincheese.com/dairyimpact/statistics/cheeseStatistics.aspx.

Carlos Yescas

Poncelet Punto Selecto is a unique operation, with two restaurants, a store, and an affinage center in Spain. Jesus Pombo, founder and owner, opened the first retail location in Madrid in 2004, and expanded his operation to include wholesale and maturing rooms in 2009, a restaurant in Madrid in 2011, and a market stall in Seville and a restaurant in Barcelona in 2014. Their restaurants in Madrid and Barcelona have in-house maturing rooms where the cheeses are carefully looked after until the moment of service. The menus at these restaurants are cheese-centric with a large selection of wines and other Spanish delicacies.

Since setting up their affinage center, the company has become one of the most important distributors of Spanish cheese around the world. They provide Spanish cheeses for export and bring in selected wheels of French, Swiss, English, Italian, and American cheeses. Perhaps the most important contribution to the industry is the consolidation and careful curation of Spanish cheeses, including those from

Poncelet Punto Selecto, in Madrid, is one of the most important distributors of Spanish cheese around the world. Pictured here is their retail shop; they also have two restaurants and an affinage center. © KATE ARDING

the Canary Islands, as well as those made on the mainland.

Pombo has worked with producers all over Spain sourcing some of the most iconic cheeses from his country. As of 2016 Poncelet carried approximately 150 Spanish cheeses, including such staples as Manchego and Idiazabal as well as new inventions by a burgeoning artisanal community of local cheesemakers. See MANCHEGO and IDIAZABAL. Felipe Serrano Ruiz is Maître Fromager and responsible for overseeing the cheese selection and careful maturation in their aging facility in the outskirts of Madrid. Pombo and his team are frequent speakers at gastronomic events and promote cheese connoisseurship in classes at their two restaurants, becoming an integral part of the revolution of Spanish food, and working closely with some of the most renowned chefs in selecting cheeses and producers.

See also CHEESEMONGER and SPAIN.

Anglés, Maria. "Cheese Bar abre en Barcelona." *Expansión*, 21 October 2014. http://www.expansion.com/2014/10/21/directivos/rincon-gastronomico/1413916697.html.
Poncelet Cheese Bar. http://www.ponceletcheesebar.es.
Poncelet Punto Selecto. http://www.poncelet.es.

Carlos Yescas

Pont-l'Évêque is a soft, washed-rind cow's milk cheese from Normandy, France, that has had an AOC (appellation d'origine contrôlée) designation since 1976. Its classic format is about 4.3 inches (11 centimeters) square and about an inch (3 centimeters) high, but it also comes in smaller and larger formats. Its rind is a mix of white and reddish-orange resulting from the mix of surface microorganisms—the *Brevibacterium linens* (orange) found along its edges and any protruding parts kept in check by the white *Geotrichum candidum*, which prevents the stickiness common to many other washed-rind cheeses. The paste runs from ivory to straw yellow, and usually has a few small openings that may disappear with age. Flavors should be mild: herbaceous, milky, and creamy; and its aromas can be intense: barnyardy, fungal, and perhaps a little smoky, but ammonia is not welcome.

Pont-l'Évêque is widely believed to be the cheese formerly known as Augelot or Angelot, developed by Cistercian monks in the twelfth century. See MONASTIC CHEESEMAKING. Cheeses going by these names are mentioned in the *Roman de la Rose* and other sources through the seventeenth century, when the name Pont-l'Évêque appeared for a cheese from the same area (most likely because nonlocals discovered them at the market town of Pont-l'Évêque). Production was initially quite local, but soon spread as its commercial value grew. Historians say that the cheese's square shape was adopted in the late eighteenth century to set it apart from other regional cheeses less valued at the time. Present at the Paris wholesale market in the early nineteenth century, it conquered Paris as a luxury cheese by mid-century, aided by the new railway. Émile Zola devoted a passage to it in *The Belly of Paris*, and production reached 1.8 million in 1877. It would gradually lose ground to Camembert, which stole its market share and its milk supply as the end of the century approached. See CAMEMBERT DE NORMANDIE.

Pont-l'Évêque was one of many cheeses whose AOC rules were made stricter in the early 2000s, with the revised criteria becoming law in 2010. All milk production, fabrication, and affinage must take place within designated areas of the administrative departments of Manche, Calvados, Orne, and western Eure. By 2020, 50 percent of its milk must be from Normande breed cows, which must be at pasture at least six months of the year and have hay available all winter. See NORMANDE. Milk may undergo thermal treatments or microfiltration, or may be used raw. After renneting, the curd is cut, stirred, and partially drained before molding and final draining. Cheeses are salted for four days after renneting, left to drain, and rubbed down before they are moved to an aging room; during aging they may be brushed or washed (in a solution of water and salt, with the possible addition of cultures) to help the surface microbial ecosystem develop in balance. Cheeses may leave the dairy (and the production zone) eighteen days after renneting.

Production of Pont-l'Évêque is declining, dropping by 30 percent between 2002 and 2012, when annual production was 2,361 metric tons; it has since increased to 2,750 metric tons, of which 16 percent is made with raw milk. It has retained a good number of farmer-producers, although their production quantity is low. The AOC brands (and their dairy parent groups) as of 2014 were Isigny Ste-Mère (Cooperative Isigny Ste-Mère); Lanquetot (Société Fromagère d'Orbec, Lactalis group); St. Hillare, Gillot (Laiterie de

Saint Hilaire de Briouze, Fléchard group); Graindorge, La Perelle, Père Eugène (Fromagerie Graindorge); Fromagerie de la Houssaye (Triballat group); and Domaine du Plessis. The farmstead producers are Domaine Saint Hippolyte, Ferme de l'Oraille (Houlet family), Ferme de la Moissonnière (Françoise family), Ferme des Bruyères (Martin family), and Spruytte (Spruytte family).

See also NORMANDY and WASHED-RIND CHEESES.

Fromages AOP de Normandie. http://www.fromage
-normandie.com/fr/anglais.

Juliette Rogers

Portugal is located on the western coast of the Iberian Peninsula, bordered by the Atlantic Ocean to the west, the Mediterranean Sea to the south, and Spain to the north and east. The country also comprises the islands of the Azores, which lie around 700 miles (1,100 km) west of Lisbon, and the archipelago of Madeira, which sits just north of the Canary Islands to the west of Morocco. Approximately half of the country is used for agricultural activities, with cheesemaking and wine production among the most important of those. Artisanal cheeses, many of which have been given a protected designation of origin (PDO), are a big part of the Portuguese diet. Although the country is home to high-output multinational dairy companies, the most famous Portuguese cheeses are, for the most part, still produced in small local dairies.

Climate and Geography

Continental Portugal is crossed by several rivers, the most important of which are the Minho, Douro, Mondego, Tagus, and Guadiana. The country, one of the warmest in Europe, has a Mediterranean climate, with annual average temperatures in the mainland varying from around 54–55°F (12–13°C) in the north to 63–64°F (17–18°C) in the south. However, extreme temperatures can occur in the northeastern mountains in the winter, where they may fall to 5°F (−10°C), particularly in the higher peaks of Serra da Estrela, a popular area for skiing, and in southeastern parts in the summer, often exceeding 113°F (40°C). Autumn and winter can be rainy and windy, with average rainfall amounts varying from less than 24 inches (60 centimeters) in the southern parts of Alentejo to more than 118 inches (300 centimeters)

in the mountains to the north. Portugal as a whole is among the sunniest areas in Europe, with around 2,500–3,200 hours of sunshine a year, with an average of 4–6 hours of sunlight a day in the winter and 10–12 hours a day in the summer.

The northern part of the country is rugged, mountainous, and dotted with vineyards, and after the slopes of the central regions and the fertile and lowlands of Ribatejo, the vast plains of the Alentejo region stretch south of Lisbon, with a range of mountains dividing the Alentejo from the Algarve, whose wide sandy beaches and attractive bays run along the southern coast. The Azores archipelago includes nine volcanic islands with fertile soil, a moderate, humid climate, and consistent rainfall throughout the year; while Madeira is typically warm and sunny.

Portugal's geography and climate are especially well suited to raising a wide variety of cattle. Dairy cattle farming in particular can be traced as far back as the Roman Empire.

Dairy Farming

The presence of three diverse climatic systems in Portugal resulted in the development of three types of livestock production. The first is an Atlantic system corresponding essentially to regions of hydric (water) richness, which led to a predominance of autochthonous bovine breeds (Barrosã, Maronesa, and Arouquesa). The second is a Mediterranean system with a different level of water abundance that led to the presence of different types of livestock, from the cold Planalto Mirandês and Beira Alta (bovine, ovine, caprine), to the Serra da Estrela regions (ovine) the flatlands (Lezíria) of Ribatejo (bovine and equine), to the lowlands of Alentejo (bovine and caprine) and the hot and driest region of Algarve (caprine). The third system in the Azores islands is a temperate climate with steady rainfall and fertile soils, creating conditions that are ideal for dairy farming (mainly bovine Holsteins) year-round. Close to 90 percent of the useful agricultural land of the Azores is used for pasture, either for dairy cattle or for beef cattle. Moreover, the islands produce more than a third of all the milk produced in Portugal, most of which is transformed into cheese.

Livestock raising in Portugal frequently utilizes transhumance (*transumância*), a seasonal movement of the herds (usually ovine) to places with better climate conditions (i.e., pasture) during specific seasons, a common practice in many mountainous regions of Europe. Thus, in many parts of Portugal, livestock grazing is traditionally of the extensive type, with the herds, usually relatively small, feeding freely on pasture during a part of the year, and taken to the mountainous area at the beginning of spring. See TRANSHUMANCE.

Recently, Portugal's extensive milk production has declined throughout the country as a result of changes in legislation and market conditions that allowed larger companies to incorporate smaller ones, as well as the traditional or specialty cheeses they produced. Today, close to a hundred medium-to-large dairy companies operate in Portugal, with the French multinational Bel fromagerie located in the Azores. See BEL GROUP.

Cheese Production

Portugal produces a variety of cheeses from bovine (cow's), ovine (sheep's), or caprine (goat's) milk. The most emblematic of these are from raw milk, many of which bear the PDO distinction and are known by the name of the region where they are produced. Those made from sheep's milk are produced by coagulating the milk with an aqueous extract of the cardoon plant (*Cynara cardunculus*). See PLANT-DERIVED COAGULANTS. More than fifteen ovine raw-milk cheeses (ten of which bear the PDO distinction) and three caprine (one PDO) types are recognized in mainland Portugal, while in the Azores, more than five raw cow's milk cheese varieties (two PDO) are officially recognized. Although these may dominate the gourmet or specialty cheese market, uncountable varieties of so-called *queijo fresco* (fresh cheese) produced in many small dairies, as well as "industrial" cheeses, must also be considered. See FRESH CHEESES and INDUSTRIAL.

The consolidation of the dairy industry is increasing, with more than 80 percent of all milk collected by the ten largest companies (Agros, Danone Portugal, Fromageries Bel Portugal, Insulac, Leicarcoop, Lacticoop, Proleite, Racoop, Unicol, and Unileite). There are many industry associations, the largest of which is ANIL (National Association of the Dairy Industry), as well as associations of companies dedicated to particular types, varieties, or regions of cheeses. Lactaçores is an association devoted to marketing cheeses in the Azores from such dairies as Unileite (São Miguel), CALF (Faial), Uniqueijo (São Jorge), and Lactopico (Pico Island).

Famous Portuguese raw-milk cheeses include Azeitão, Serpa, and Serra da Estrela (sheep's milk), Queijo de cabra transmontano (goat's milk), and São Jorge and Pico cheeses (cow's milk).

- Azeitão is a PDO raw ewe's milk cheese produced exclusively in the municipalities of Setúbal, Palmela, and Sesimbra in southwestern Portugal. The milk is coagulated using a wild thistle flower (*Cynara cardunculus*) with high proteolytic activity. The final cheeses have a cylindrical shape and an acidic, salty, somewhat bitter and very spicy (*picante*) flavor, with grassy and nutty aromas. See AZEITÃO.
- Serpa is a PDO artisanal cheese produced in a demarcated area of Serpa and Beja in Alentejo. Serpa cheese is made using raw ewe's milk and an aqueous extract of dried cardoon flowers (*Cynara cardunculus*), a wild plant that grows naturally in the region, as a coagulant. The resulting cylindrical cheeses have a semisoft texture and buttery yellowish paste, with a distinctive flavor that tastes almost fermented, with balanced sweet and bitter notes. See SERPA.
- Serra da Estrela is probably the most famous of the traditional PDO Portuguese cheeses. It is produced mainly from November to March, exclusively with milk from the Bordaleira sheep breed. Ewe's milk is coagulated with an extract of cardoon flowers. Serra da Estrela cheese has a cylindrical shape and is extremely soft, with an almost spreadable texture. The paste can be white or slightly yellow in color with a few small holes and has a rich, slightly acidic taste. See SERRA DA ESTRELA.
- Queijo de cabra transmontano is a PDO cheese made with caprine milk from the Trás-os-Montes e Alto Douro in the northeastern region of Portugal. It is a hard cheese, ripening on average for sixty days, with a paste showing a few eyes, and with a *picante* bouquet.
- São Jorge is a semihard, traditional PDO cheese that is manufactured from raw cow's milk on the island of São Jorge in the Azores. The cheese is firm but supple, with small holes inside the paste and a natural rind. As it ages, the cheese develops a mild, mouth-puckering sour aftertaste while becoming more crumbly. See SÃO JORGE.

The list of popular and typical Portuguese cheeses is too long to include all of them here. Such cheeses as Pico, Terrincho, Rabaçal, Castelo Branco, and many others excluded from this discussion are also representative of the Portuguese cheese market. See CASTELO BRANCO.

Consumer Culture

Today most cheeses in Portugal are sold through supermarkets, although many specialty and traditional cheeses are still sold directly from the producer to the consumer or by independent retailers. Another way of selling specialty cheeses is through farmers' markets, which are very common in Portugal, especially during the summer. Cheese is a common staple of the Portuguese diet, and varieties such as São Jorge are experiencing an increase in popularity as well as market share in both Europe and North America. The dairy industry is the most important source of living in the Azores, guaranteeing a sustained growth of the local economy.

Fernandes, J. P., et al. "Caracterização e cartografia dos sistemas extensivos de pastoreio em Portugal continental." In *Actas do X Colóquio Ibérico de Geografia, Évora*, September 2005. http://www .apgeo.pt/files/docs/CD_X_Coloquio_Iberico_ Geografia/pdfs/098.pdf.
Freitas, C., and F. X. Malcata. "Microbiology and Biochemistry of Cheeses with Appélation d'Origine Protegée and Manufactured in the Iberian Peninsula from Ovine and Caprine Milks." *Journal of Dairy Science* 83 (2000): 584–602.
Kongo, J. Marcelino. *São Jorge: The Cheese and the Island, 500 Years.* Ponta Delgada, Portugal: University of Azores, 2009.

J. Marcelino Kongo and F. Xavier Malcata

Posavec is a semihard, full-fat cheese in block form. Its production is geographically restricted along the Sava River area, the longest river that flows through Slovenia, where more farmers make their livelihood from cattle breeding than from agriculture. Here cheese has complemented the peasant lifestyle for many centuries as an indispensable part of meals prepared for farmworkers, as well as a way to market surplus milk. Feed from different seasons and cultivation of fodder in the uplands of the central Slovenian hills alongside the Sava River contribute to Posavec's mild, clean taste and typical aromatic notes. Today Posavec's popularity is declining.

The base material for Posavec is cow's milk that has been standardized at 2.9 percent milk fat and pasteurized (heated to 165°F [74°C] for 15 seconds). The milk is ripened overnight by the use of *okisovalec*, skimmed and sterilized milk that has been fermented with mesophilic homofermentative lactococci, heterofermentative lactococci, and *Leuconostoc*. The addition of a chymosin (rennin) and pepsin mixture to the warm (90°F [32°C]), acidified milk produces a firm gel in 30 to 40 minutes; calcium chloride (0.05 percent) and sodium nitrate (0.02 percent) may be added as well. The curd is cut into hazelnut-size pieces, and 25–30 percent of the whey is replaced with fresh water heated to 108–122°F (42–50°C) in amount of about 15 percent of the total volume of milk so that the temperature of the vat content rises to 97–100°F (36–38°C). A prolonged holding and stirring at later temperature follows until the grain is firm and pea-sized. The complete cheese mass is pressed for about 10 minutes, and then portioned, molded, and pressed for another 90–120 minutes. Over the next two days, the cheeses are brined, and then after draining and surface drying, they are wrapped and ripened for 25–35 days at 55–59°F (13–15°C).

The final block cheese is about 9 inches (23–24 centimeters) long by 9 inches (23–24 centimeters) wide by 2.8–3.5 inches (7–9 cm) high, and weighs 10–11 pounds (4.5–5.5 kilograms). The large surfaces are flat, the ends are slightly convex, and all the edges are nicely rounded. The rind is smooth and dry, and yellow in color. The interior is elastic, flexible, and usually bright to pale yellow in appearance. A few pea-size, well-defined eyes are often evenly scattered throughout the cheese, although small fissures are also tolerated. The taste and smell are mild, clean, and aromatic.

Perko, Bogdan. *Slovenski avtohtoni siri—siri z geografskim poreklom: Zgodovina, področje, tehnološki postopki* [Slovenian Autochthonous Cheeses—Cheeses with Geographical Origin: History, Region, Technological Processes]. Rodica, Slovenia: Biotechnical Faculty, 2003.

Andreja Čanžek Majhenič and Petra Mohar Lorbeg

post-process contamination is the unintended recontamination of a food product with microorganisms after a processing step has been used to remove or kill them. In the dairy industry it is most often applied when microorganisms capable of causing harm to product quality or safety are found in pasteurized milk or cheeses made from pasteurized milk. It is therefore also referred to as post-pasteurization contamination.

Cheese is not made in a sterile environment; consequently contamination with microorganisms is inevitable. Nevertheless most microbial contaminants are not harmful and in fact in some aged cheeses can even be helpful to the cheese. But extra care must be given to prevention of post-pasteurization contamination with spoilage bacteria, yeast, and mold or with disease causing bacteria (pathogens).

The source of contaminants includes any contaminated surface that the cheese or milk may come into contact with; for example, packaging materials, contaminated water splashing from the floor, air, aerosols, clothing, people. Once a cheese or milk is contaminated it can itself be the source of contamination of equipment and other cheeses.

Preventative measures consist of proper design and construction of the building and processing equipment, air filtration, thorough cleaning and sanitation of product contact and environmental surfaces, including equipment, and adherence to hygienic practices of personnel and good manufacturing practices (GMPs). The latter includes training of personnel on GMPs, keeping personnel free of contaminants (e.g., clean clothing, clean footwear, use of hand sanitizers), and prevention of people who have possibly been in contaminated areas from entering the manufacturing and packaging areas without first thoroughly following strict hygienic protocols.

Not all undesirable microorganisms are killed with pasteurization and those that survive can either form or can become part of an established biofilm on any surface that the milk or cheese comes into contact with. Biofilms are often the major source of contamination and sites where they may have established are often inconspicuous. Biofilms are microbial communities that are formed when microorganisms stick to surfaces and produce an extracellular substance called an exopolysaccharide. This material confers an increased resistance to the microorganisms against cleaners, sanitizers, and heat. A biofilm could consist of a single strain of bacteria or multiple types of microorganisms, but once established they might not be completely removed by conventional cleaning protocols but will continue to slough viable contaminants.

See also BIOFILMS; EXOPOLYSACCHARIDE; PASTEURIZATION; and PATHOGENS.

Oliver, S. P., B. M. Jayarao, and R. A. Almeida, 2005. "Foodborne Pathogens in Milk and the Dairy Farm Environment: Food Safety and Public Health Implications." *Food-borne Pathogenic Disease* 2, no. 2 (Summer 2005): 115–129.

Mark E. Johnson

pot cheeses are a group of ripened cheeses that are produced from ewe's, goat's, or cow's milk and matured in an earthenware pot that is buried underground for four to six months. This earthenware pot, which is called *kupa* (*küpə*) or *koozeh* in Iran and *carra* (*jarra*) or *testi* in Turkey, has a larger opening compared to the conventional pot.

The preparation of pot cheeses varies across regions and countries. Sometimes the earthenware pots are coated with a lacquer layer; glazed pots are preferred because they are better able to keep moisture in the cheese. Their capacity ranges from 0.26–1.32 gallons (1–5 liters). The openings of pots are finally closed by grapevine leaves and a sheet of paper or clean cloth, or both of them. Then they are obstructed by clay and stored in underground caves for four to six months. The prepared pots are lowered into deep pits about 5.5–6.6 feet (5–6 meters) below the ground surface. There they are placed, upside down, in holes containing washed and wet sand, so that their bottom is barely flush. Potting usually starts in late June to early July, when milk is abundant and white cheese is cheap.

The famous pot cheeses of Iran are Kupa Paniri, Jajikhli Panir, Ziraly Panir, and from Turkey, Carra or Testi Peynir.

• Kupa Paniri (Küpə Pəniri) or Panire Koozeh is a traditional cheese produced by the Turkish and

Çömlek peyniri, or pot cheese, is a Turkish cheese from the Central Anatolia region made in earthenware pots and kept in natural caves.

Kurdish tribes in the northwest and western regions of Iran. Typically, it is made from raw milk of various origins. Kupa Paniri is a semihard cheese with a very pleasant flavor. It is consumed as a table cheese and characterized by its dry appearance, yellowish-white color, salty taste, specific pleasant aroma, and brittle texture. See KUPA PANIRI.

- Jajikhli Panir (Cacıxli Pənir) has been produced by Kurdish and Turkish tribes in rural areas of the northwest and west of Iran. It is produced in the Ghotoor (Qotur) area in Khoy city. Jajikhli Panir is a semihard brined cheese mainly produced from raw ewe's, goat's, and cow's milk. Jajikh is a regional term meaning vegetable and herbs. Herbs or vegetables are added to the curd or cheese before filling the pots. See JAJIKHLI PANIR.
- Ziraly Panir is produced similarly to Jajikhli Panir, but traditionally the curds are blended with cumin seeds instead of herbs. See ZIRALY PANIR.
- Carra or Testi Peynir is a type of traditional pot cheese produced from goats' milk in Hatay, southern Turkey. It is a semihard or hard cheese with a spicy flavor resulting from the herbs added to the curd. Skim milk or partially skim milk, as well as cow's, sheep's or goat's milk or mixtures of them, are used for its manufacture. The block of curd is sliced into pieces measuring about 1.5–1.9 inches (4–5 centimeters) thick, and coarse salt is sprinkled between the slices and held for two to three days. The Carra curds, along with those of another cheese called cokelek (a low-fat cheese produced from ayran), which is salted at 4 percent and contains 5 percent black cumin and 5 percent thyme, are placed as layers in earthenware jugs. Then the jugs' openings are covered with a piece of cloth and sealed with a peculiar mixture consisting of wood ash, salt, olive oil, and water. After this mixture has been dried, the jugs are tightly covered with another piece of cloth. Then, the jugs are buried underground during the ripening period, which lasts for at least four to five months.

Some other pot cheeses produced in Turkey (including their production areas) are Kup (Nigde, Sivas, Bitlis, Isparta, Trabzon, Artvin, and Tokat), Kupecik (Cankiri), Ayas (Ankara), Canak (Yozgat), and Comlek (Kayseri, Cankiri, Nevsehir, and Kirsehir).

See also IRAN and TURKEY.

Hayaloglu, Ali A., and Patrick F. Fox. "Cheeses of Turkey: 3. Varieties Containing Herbs or Spices." *Dairy Science and Technology* 88 (2008): 245–256.
Kirdar, S. S., and I. Gün. "The Goat's Cheeses of Turkey: Mediterranean Region." Paper presented at the IDF International Symposium on Sheep, Goat, and Other Non-Cow Milk, Athens, Greece, 16 May 2011.
Lame, H., M. Hekmati, and M. Moharramkhani. "Contribution à l'étude du 'fromage en pot' de l'Iran." *Le Lait* 53 (1973): 163–168.
Shafiei, Y. "Iranian Traditional Cheeses." Paper presented at the 1st Conference of Iranian Traditional Dairy Products, Khoy, Iran, 24 February 2013. In Persian.

Yahya Shafiei Bavil Oliaei

poutine Quebec's popular street food, began in the late 1950s at two fast-food restaurants in rural Quebec, specifically the south-central region east of Montreal. Although the combination of french-fried potatoes, fresh Cheddar cheese curds, and gravy spent the next half century sweeping North America and spreading around the world, no chef played a part in its original recipe. The inventors were customers at two modest food counters. They would order "frites," and help themselves to the cheese curds offered on the counter like a condiment, dropping them among the steaming hot potatoes, initially in a small paper bag. The final touch came later—a topping of the sauce that was simmering on the stove for hot chicken sandwiches.

At its best, the dish is a cousin to cheese fondue, the crisp, hot potatoes causing the cheese curds to melt so that each fry can be lifted, dripping with cheese and accented with gravy. Quebec loves fries, and as a major dairy region, is a big cheese curd producer and consumer. It was, according to Montreal poutine researcher Charles-Alexandre Théorêt, "the inevitable meeting." The two originating restaurants, each later claiming to have launched poutine, were the Café Idéal, later named Le Lutin Qui Rit ("the laughing leprechaun"), in Warwick, where it was first served in 1957, and Le Roy Jucep drive-in in Drummondville, where it was offered beginning in 1958, and added to the menu around 1964, initially under the name "fromage-patate-sauce." The name has been traced to Europe's potato dumplings, sometimes made with a mixture of freshly grated potatoes and mashed potatoes; Acadians have a "poutine râpée" of grated potatoes stuffed with pork.

In the 1970s larger fast-food establishments started selling poutine, varying it with spaghetti sauce, Montreal smoked meat, mozzarella cheese, and other trimmings. By the late 1980s, even the giant chains Burger King and McDonald's offered it, but connoisseurs have always claimed that the best versions are served at small roadside stands, where the cheese curds are more likely to have the rubbery texture of freshness and melt readily. Appearing in Montreal in the late 1980s, poutine soon moved from its cup to a wide dish in which the fries nearly drown in gravy—still the prevailing style. Commercial mixes appeared, canned or dehydrated, allowing home cooks to make the dish with ease. After the millennium, chefs took up the cause of varying the popular dish, even adding luxury ingredients such as duck foie gras or lobster sauce. Since 2013, Montreal restaurants have staged Poutine Week each February; as many as forty chefs compete with ethnic variations of the dish, even including a vegan version. For the full story, including cartoons, songs, and recipes, Théorêt's little book *Maudite Poutine!* is an entertaining read. The website for Montréal Poutine adds additional flavor.

See also FONDUE and QUEBEC.

Montréal Poutine. http://www.montrealpoutine.com.
Théorêt, Charles-Alexandre, and Patrice Lamoureux. *Maudite Poutine! L'histoire approximative d'un plat populaire.* Montreal: Héliotrope, 2007.

Julian Armstrong

pregnancy advice on cheese eating is distributed to women by a range of authoritative resources including the Food and Drug Administration (FDA), Centers for Disease Control and Prevention (CDC), Food and Agriculture Organization/World Health Organization (FAO/WHO), obstetricians and professional obstetric organizations such as the American College of Obstetrics and Gynecology, and popular resources, including websites and well-known books (e.g., *What to Expect When You're Expecting*). These entities have an interest in communicating to women about cheese consumption during pregnancy because of the risks associated with exposure to *Listeria monocytogenes*, a harmful pathogen that has historically been associated with dairy in general and cheese in particular. Because *Listeria monocytogenes* can cross the placental barrier, pregnant women and

fetuses are particularly vulnerable to listeriosis, the infection associated with the pathogen. Listeriosis infection during pregnancy can result in miscarriage, stillbirth, fetal infection, and premature labor. See LISTERIA.

Public health entities and other authorities tasked with advising pregnant women on safe cheese consumption do not communicate clearly to consumers about risks and safety. Current advice is inconsistent and confusing, is based on outdated studies of pathogenic risks in cheese, and ignores the track record of the most common causes of *Listeria* outbreaks in cheese. While most resources generally agree that pregnant women should not eat soft cheese unless they can confirm it is pasteurized, the recommendations only provide a smattering of examples of soft cheese, leaving ambiguous the definition of "soft"; pregnant women, who likely encounter a growing diversity of cheese options no matter where they live, must therefore try to interpret this vague term on their own. The statement that soft cheese is safe as long as it is pasteurized also signals to pregnant women that pasteurization is necessary and sufficient to protect against *Listeria*. The history of *Listeria* outbreaks in cheese, however, reveals that these outbreaks often originate in soft cheeses that were illegally manufactured in unlicensed facilities, or that were contaminated with *Listeria* via post-pasteurization recontamination from the processing environment, which negates any potential benefits of heat treatment. This headline likewise leaves open to interpretation the safety of cheese that is unpasteurized but is not soft, which is mentioned in some publications but not addressed consistently in terms of likely risks. See OUTBREAK AND POST-PROCESS CONTAMINATION.

Public health entities should rectify both the insufficient microbiological basis of current recommendations and the incoherent communication of risks of cheese consumption during pregnancy. Recommendations would be improved if informed by an analysis of historical *Listeria* outbreaks in cheese as well as a study of *Listeria*'s likelihood of survival to the point of consumption when it is introduced at various stages of production, and in a variety of microbial environments that we call cheese. These studies should assess cheeses based on characteristics such as water content, aging, acidity, pasteurization, and other factors that could influence whether or not a cheese is likely to provide a hospitable environment for *Listeria*. Data from such studies could then be channeled into a coherent, unambiguous set of recommendations that would allow women to make better-informed decisions. This work is more essential now than ever before: as artisanal cheese increases in popularity, particularly across the United States, pregnant women will be faced with a growing range of cheese options to meet their nutritional, culinary, and dietary preferences during pregnancy.

See also FOOD AND DRUG ADMINISTRATION; HYGIENE; PASTEURIZATION; and PATHOGENS.

American College of Obstetricians and Gynecologists. "Frequently Asked Questions." https://www.acog.org/-/media/For-Patients/faq103.pdf?dmc=1&ts=20150401T1226191129.

Centers for Disease Control. "Listeriosis (Listeria) and Pregnancy." http://www.cdc.gov/pregnancy/infections-listeria.html.

Donnelly, Catherine. "Growth and Survival of Microbial Pathogens in Cheese." In *Cheese: Chemistry, Physics, and Microbiology*, edited by Patrick F. Fox, et al., pp. 541–560. London: Elsevier, 2004.

Food and Drug Administration. "Preventing Listeriosis—Attention Pregnant Women: Some Cheeses Could Harm Your Unborn Baby!" http://www.fda.gov/Food/ResourcesForYou/HealthEducators/ucm106913.htm.

Interagency Food Safety Analytics Collaboration. "Foodborne Illness Source Attribution Estimates for *Salmonella, Escherichia coli* O157 (*E. coli* O157), *Listeria monocytogenes* (*Lm*), and *Campylobacter* using Outbreak Surveillance Data." February 2015. https://www.cdc.gov/foodsafety/pdfs/ifsac-project-report-508c.pdf.

Paxson, Heather. *The Life of Cheese: Crafting Food and Value in America*. Berkeley: University of California Press, 2013.

Jessica A. B. Galen

prematuration, also known as pre-ripening, refers to an optional step in cheesemaking during which raw milk, usually with a small amount of lactic acid culture added, is allowed to ripen at temperatures ranging from 46–61°F (8–16°C) for up to twenty-four hours. During this period a small amount of acid is produced, thanks to the growth of the native raw milk lactic acid bacteria or the added culture, and a slight drop in pH, usually of only about 0.1 unit, is achieved. The milk might then be combined with fresh, warm milk and either pasteurized or continue on through the cheesemaking steps. The practice is used most frequently in France for the manufacture of soft-ripened cheeses, such as Camembert and Reblochon, and some hard styles as well. See SOFT-RIPENED CHEESES.

Prematuration is thought to have several useful effects on cheese milk including the limitation of the growth of cold-loving psychrotrophic microbes; the improvement of rennet activity, and possible increased amino acids (protein pieces) that might be helpful to the cheesemaking process. During refrigeration and storage, psychrotrophic microbes, such as yeasts and molds, can grow leading to spoilage, off-flavors, and the presence of undesirable enzymes. The limitation of their growth in the prematured milk is due to the increased populations of harmless lactic acid bacteria, which have the competitive advantage at those temperatures and therefore outgrow the cold-loving microbes. Coagulation time (also called rennet clotting time) is improved since coagulants perform better in more acidic conditions. The freeing of some amino acids from the milk proteins provides fuel for starter cultures used after prematuration, facilitating the continued acid production throughout cheesemaking. See COAGULATION OR CURDLING.

When prematured milk is pasteurized, the raw-milk bacteria and the added starter culture bacteria, both of which will have increased in population during the prematuration period, are reduced, or particularly in the case of pathogenic bacteria, destroyed. This means that the milk can then be recultured with a desired bacterial blend that is different from the original pre-ripening culture. The earlier stated benefits will still be experienced and the new culture can define the flavor and ripening profile. For example, if a cheese is to be made using thermophilic bacteria and prematured milk is used, if it is not pasteurized after prematuration, the mesophilic bacteria will grow rapidly, until the temperature of the milk exceeds their toleration, thus out-competing the more recently added cultures. Not only will this potentially limit the acid production that is meant to occur after draining and during pressing, but will change the entire character of the finished cheese.

See also LACTIC ACID and LACTIC ACID BACTERIA.

Fox, Patrick, et al. *Fundamentals of Cheese Science*. Gathersburg, Md.: Aspen, 2000, p. 16.

Lane, Cait, et al. "Effect of Prematuration Conditions on the Proteolytic and Rheological Properties of Cheesemilk." *Le Lait* 81, no. 3 (2001): 415–427.

Gianaclis Caldwell

A cheese **press** is often used near the end of cheese-making to expel the final amount of whey from the curd. The cheese press helps the curd knit together by holding the curds under pressure for a specified amount of time—usually a number of hours, and often at increasing amounts of pressure. The cheese press also serves to shape the curd into its final form before brining, wrapping, and aging. From a simple homemade press to a large-scale piece of equipment the components do not vary much; the curd is put into a perforated mold (also referred to as a hoop or frame, they can be either adjustable or a set shape and size) lined with cheesecloth and a follower is placed on top (circular or rectangular, based on the shape of the cheese). The press then applies pressure to the follower, spreading it over the wheel's top surface area. A drip tray below funnels whey away from the wheel as it is expelled.

Only some of the many cheeses made in the world require the use of a cheese press. Smaller format, soft, and blue cheeses are drained under the pressure of their own curd and gravity and do not get additionally pressed. Cheeses requiring the use of a press usually start at around two pounds (one kilogram)—such as many tomme-style cheeses. Cheddar, Gouda, Gruyère, and other large format, hard-aged cheeses are usually put in the press. The smaller the curd is milled, the more pressure the cheese needs in order to knit the curds back together. See TOMME.

In many cheeses fermentation is still actively happening during pressing. It is therefore very important that the temperature and humidity conditions of the room are controlled so the curd reaches the target rate of acidification. The goal is to keep the curds warm enough that they can properly knit together, but not so warm that the fat separates and leaks out. Like many steps in cheesemaking, much is learned from trial and error, and the sharing of information through generations of experimentation. The amount of pressure is also a key factor. Recipes often identify pressure in pounds per square inch (psi) or in kilopascals (a standard metric unit of pressure); these measurements are helpful if using a pneumatic or hydraulic press—both of which customarily have programmable gauges. Cheesemakers using mechanical presses most often define their own parameters for pressure based on the cheese style and wheel size they are making.

Historically the cheese press was pieced together with whatever materials were available to the cheesemaker, and many small producers and home hobbyists still employ this method; cheesemakers have been known to press the curd with rocks and timber. Today most commercial cheese presses are made of

Students studying agricultural sciences at Hampton Institute in Hampton, Virginia, in 1900 practice operating cheese press screws. UNIVERSAL HISTORY ARCHIVE / UIG / BRIDGEMAN IMAGES

stainless steel, and use pneumatic or mechanical systems to create pressure.

Four primary styles of cheese presses are used today: A-frame, horizontal, vertical, and mechanical. Each has unique benefits depending on the size of the cheesemaking space, the style of cheese made, and the budgetary constraints of the operation. A horizontal press usually consists of two trays at about waist height, on which wheels of cheese are placed on their curved sides so that the bottom of one wheel is pressed against the top of the next. This design is physically easier on the cheesemaker (it eliminates bending and heavy lifting), easier to clean, and more affordable. The vertical-style cheese press uses less floor space. Cheeses are stacked one on top of another and pressed down with pressure from above. The A-frame style takes the vertical concept and tilts the stacks at a slight angle, providing better drainage in comparison to the completely vertical press. Mechanical presses are less expensive and less costly to maintain, since they use levers and weights as opposed to electricity and digital pressurized systems. The lever-style press is also referred to as a Dutch-style press, as this model gained popularity in the Netherlands, and older models are often made of wood. They are not as efficient for higher volume cheesemaking however, since they usually don't have the capacity to press multiple wheels at once. While used or refurbished commercial cheese presses can be bought for $5,000 to $10,000, new presses run upward of $50,000, depending on the size and style. For hobbyist cheesemakers, tabletop mechanical presses run from $150 to $300, and there are many do-it-yourself guides to making mechanical presses for less than $25.

See also FORMS OR MOLDS; HOOPS; and PRESSED CHEESES.

Kindstedt, Paul. *American Farmstead Cheese*. White River Junction, Vt.: Chelsea Green, 2005.
Tunick, Michael H. *The Science of Cheese*. New York: Oxford University Press, 2014.

Elena Santogade

pressed cheeses refers to a family of cheeses that employ the application of external pressure to complete the fusion of cheese curds into the final shape and form of the cheese. The amount of pressure applied to pressed cheeses may be: very limited, as when a small weight is placed on the top of the draining curds to make certain smear-ripened cheeses; quite substantial (e.g., up to 59 pounds per square inch [0.41 megapascals]), as in the making of large Cheddar cheeses that employ high-pressure presses; or between these two extremes.

The vast majority of pressed cheeses are rennet coagulated types because rennet curds exhibit a remarkable capacity to contract, expel whey, and fuse together in response to applied pressure. Pressing, therefore, is one of the tools that cheesemakers use to modulate the moisture content of rennet coagulated cheeses over wide ranges (i.e., from around 30 to 65 percent), depending on the variety. Pressing modulates mainly moisture content among the curd grains (intergranular moisture). The moisture content of the curd grains per se (intragranular moisture) is modulated in the vat, before pressing. The development of pressing technologies represented important milestones in the history of cheese because they enabled the production of drier, more durable aged cheeses, and they created new opportunities for the making of larger ripened varieties. See MOISTURE.

Acid coagulated cheeses are notably absent from the pressed family because acid curds lack the capacity to contract, expel whey, and fuse together under pressure. Instead, the curds flow when compressed and tend to squeeze out through the openings in the press mold that would normally allow for the removal of whey. In contrast, acid-heat coagulated cheeses, like those coagulated with rennet, can be pressed and fused to form varieties with lower moisture contents. Therefore, the pressed family of cheeses includes a few examples of acid-heat coagulated types, such as queso blanco and paneer. However, because of their high starting pH values, acid-heat coagulated cheeses are unsuitable for ripening, therefore the pressed family includes only fresh cheeses made by acid-heat coagulation. See MEXICAN CHEESES and PANEER.

The first definitive evidence of pressing in cheesemaking derives from the Roman period. Columella noted that pressing was employed to produce dry aged cheese and, consistent with this, perforated ceramic press molds for cheesemaking have been abundantly recovered from many Roman archeological sites. Presumably, pressing also arose early in antiquity in the development of the mountain cheeses of central Europe, and in the massif central of France, in parallel with the making of larger cheeses produced from large volumes of milk from transhumant communal herds. However, the precise timing is unknown. See ANCIENT CIVILIZATIONS and COLUMELLA, and LUCIUS JUNIUS MODERATUS.

During the latter Middle Ages, demesne cheese-makers on English manors began to produce larger cheeses, which undoubtedly inspired innovations in pressing. See MANORIAL CHEESEMAKERS. The trend to larger cheeses in England continued and accelerated during the sixteenth through eighteenth centuries, prompting the development of very high-pressure pressing techniques that have come to characterize the family of English pressed cheeses. Around the same time the Dutch were perfecting their pressed cheeses for the international market, Gouda and Edam being the most famous varieties. See GOUDA and EDAM. In modern industrial practice, pressing is often performed in mechanized pneumatic presses, in large towers that are held under a slight vacuum and filled with curds that press under their own weight, or in hydraulic presses that are followed by treatment in a vacuum chamber.

See also PRESS.

Kosikowski, F. V., and Vikram V. Mistry. *Cheese and Fermented Milk Foods.* 3d ed. 2 vols. Westport, Conn.: F.V. Kosikowski, 1997.

Paul S. Kindstedt

Preveli (Dry Cheese) is a semihard Croatian cow's milk cheese that looks like a loaf of bread, with a diameter of approximately 6 inches (14 centimeters) and a height of approximately 2 inches (4 centimeters). It belongs to the group of acidic dried cheeses that are obtained from acidic coagulum. This cheese is mainly produced along the river Sava (from Zagreb to Moslavina) in Croatia.

Cheesemakers in the past produced Preveli by salting and drying fresh sour cheese to extend its shelf life. It is not clear when this cheese first appeared, but it is known as a traditional breakfast for farmers (grass cutters) working in the fields, given the fact that it is well preserved (dry and salty). Moreover, Preveli is traditionally served to guests as an appetizer, together with bacon. Preveli has an acidic, fresh, and salty taste and a laminated texture on the cut surface. Quite frequently this cheese is preserved by smoking; therefore it appears to be white or smoky in color. See SMOKED CHEESES.

The production procedure of Preveli cheese is still not standardized. Fresh raw milk is used, which is fermented at a room temperature of approximately 77°F (25°C) for a period of forty-eight hours. Cream,

which is separated on the surface of the coagulum, is skimmed, the acid coagulum is cut into big sheets, and then heated up to 131°F (55°C) for two hours to initiate syneresis. See SYNERESIS. Sheets of coagulum are removed and transferred into perforated molds for draining purposes. After draining the cheese is air dried by the wind or above a traditional wood-burning stove during the winter season. If Preveli cheese is smoked it develops a fatty surface and phenolic compounds preserve the cheese.

See also CROATIA.

Andrić, J. "Cheese and Form." In *Cheese: Tradition and Heritage,* edited by Ž. Obad. Zagreb, Croatia: Pučko Otvoreno Učilište, 2003. In Croatian.
Kalit, Samir. and Iva Dolenčić Špehar. "Preveli sir: Protection of Geographical Indications." Zagreb, Croatia: University of Zagreb, Faculty of Agriculture, 2012. In Croatian.

Samir Kalit

Prgica

See CONE-SHAPED CHEESES.

primary cultures

See STARTER CULTURES.

propionibacteria

See DAIRY PROPIONIBACTERIA.

propionic acid is a volatile three-carbon organic acid that is very effective at inhibiting the growth of molds. In cheese, propionic acid along with acetic acid and carbon dioxide may be produced through the fermentation of lactate by *Propionibacterium freudenreichii*. Propionic and acetic acids produced in this way contribute to the flavor and aroma of Alp-style cheeses such as Emmentaler. Both the concentrations of propionic and acetic acid and their balance are influenced by the metabolism of the specific propionibacteria strains present in the ripening cheese, which in turn influences both the intensity and character of cheese flavor and aroma. For example, strains that possess strong aspartase activity generally grow to higher populations, ferment lactate more intensively, and produce more intense flavor in the cheese during ripening than strains with weak aspartase activity. Furthermore, the fermentation of lactate becomes coupled to the fermentation of aspartic acid when aspartic acid accumulates during ripening due to proteolysis, which causes a shift in lactate fermentation toward the production of more acetic acid and carbon dioxide and less propionic acid. *Propionibacterium freudenreichii* strains are sensitive to high salt concentration and low pH, and normally are unable to ferment lactate to propionic acid, acetic acid, and carbon dioxide in cheeses such as Cheddar, unless the cheese is abnormally low in salt and high in pH.

See also ACETIC ACID; ALP-STYLE CHEESES; CARBON DIOXIDE; and DAIRY PROPIONIBACTERIA.

Fox, P. F., et al. *Fundamentals of Cheese Science.* Gaithersburg, Md.: Aspen, 2000.
McSweeney, P. L. H., ed. *Cheese Problems Solved.* Cambridge, U.K.: Woodhead, 2007.

Paul S. Kindstedt

protected designation of origin

See DESIGNATION OF ORIGIN and GEOGRAPHICAL INDICATION.

proteins in the milk of ruminants are composed mainly of caseins and whey proteins. The amounts vary with species and breed, but typically the total amount of protein (nitrogen × 6.28) is 1–1.2 ounces per quart (30–35 grams per liter) of which about 80 percent is casein. During cheesemaking caseins coagulate to form a three-dimensional matrix that traps fat globules and serum (water and soluble milk components) forming a gel. Subsequent steps in cheesemaking remove more or less serum creating higher and lower moisture cheese varieties. Whey proteins as the name implies remain in the serum, which in popular language is called whey. See WHEY.

Proteins and Coagulation

Caseins are present in milk as spherical particles of about 10–300 nanometers called micelles that consist of four main types of caseins. Casein micelles are hydrophobic, meaning that they are not soluble in water; however micelles remain dispersed in their native watery milk environment due to net positive surface charges and a stabilizing casein fraction called kappa-casein on their surfaces. During cheesemaking coagulation can be induced in three ways. First, enzymatic or rennet coagulation is initiated when rennet cleaves the stabilizing kappa-casein allowing the micelles to stick together or aggregate. Second acid or lactic coagulation occurs when lactic acid bacteria convert lactose to lactic acid and reduce the pH of milk from 6.7, its near neutral native condition, to a pH of less than 5 where the net surface charge on the micelles is reduced to near zero. Acidification also disrupts the native micelle structure, but the net result is that the caseins aggregate forming a gel. Third heat-acid coagulation occurs when milk or whey or blends of milk and whey are heated to temperatures above 176°F (80°C) and then acidified with an organic acid such as vinegar. Heat-acid coagulation has the advantage that native whey proteins are soluble at low pH, but if the globular structure of the whey proteins is first unfolded by heating above 176°F (80°C), then subsequent acidification causes both caseins and whey proteins to aggregate together forming not a gel as in rennet or acid coagulation but clumps of curd that either fall to the bottom of the vat or float on the surface. Of course, recovery of whey proteins in addition to caseins increases yield, especially considering that denatured whey proteins have excellent water-holding capacity. See COAGULATION OR CURDLING and CASEIN.

Milk Protein and Health Benefits

Milk is a rich source of proteins and peptides with demonstrated physiological functionality, nutritional and immunotropic activities that may promote human health. Peptides derived from caseins and whey proteins including opioid peptides, antihypertensive peptides, casein phosphopeptides, α- and β-lactorphins, and albutensin have been shown to possess various bioactive properties. Whey protein has the highest biological value of any protein and also is one of the richest sources of leucine, an essential amino acid that triggers initiation of muscle protein synthesis.

Other milk proteins also exhibit a wide range of bioactive properties. For example, caseinophosphopeptides, glycomacropeptides, and lactoferrin help reduce the risk of dental caries. Casein derivatives are applied, in addition, in the dry mouth syndrome. Lysozyme is routinely used for food conservation and in pharmaceutical products. Lysozyme was also used in infected children as an antimicrobial agent showing synergistic effects in combination with different antibiotics. Proline-rich polypeptide (PRP) was introduced to therapy for Alzheimer's disease patients. The therapeutic value of PRP was proved in several clinical trials and supported by studies on its mechanism of action.

Proteins and Cheese Functionalities

Milk proteins have nearly perfect amino acid balance for humans and display an astounding range of functionalities, which have been used for everything from glues to paper sizing to billiard balls. During cheesemaking the cheesemaker is essentially manipulating conditions to obtain the desired functional responses from the proteins. Consider several examples. First, increased temperature during cooking strengthens the hydrophobic interactions of the caseins causing them to contract and squeeze out whey like squeezing water out of a sponge; this process is called syneresis. See SYNERESIS. Second, extensive demineralization (removal of calcium and phosphorus) of the micelle, as occurs during acidification of soft-ripened cheeses to a pH of less than 5, creates the firm, brittle texture of feta cheese. It also allows for development of the soft creamy texture of bloomy cheeses as yeasts and molds on the surface consume the lactic acid and raise the pH. See DE-MINERALIZATION. Third, managing the extent and rate of acid development allows the cheesemaker to manage cheese stretchability and meltability. Minimal acid development with a final pH above 6 in Latin American fresh cheeses, such as panela, prevents melting so they can be used in stir fries. Melting and stretching of most ripened cheeses is effected by a final pH in the range of 5.3–5.2; and, interestingly, meltability increases and stretchability decreases as the caseins are broken down into smaller fragments during ripening. Finer tuning of stretching can be obtained, for example, by draining mozzarella at a lower pH than the traditional 6.3. Reducing the pH at draining extracts more calcium from the curd, which weakens the casein structure and allows it to stretch at a higher pH. See FUNCTIONAL PROPERTIES and PH MEASUREMENT.

Proteins and Flavor

Proteins are also important to flavor development. Enzymes (which are also proteins) are present in all cheese either because they are a natural component of milk, or because they are added either by rennet addition or by microbial production. See PLASMIN and ENZYMES. Enzymes degrade proteins, creating peptides and free amino acids, which impart a great variety of flavors to ripened cheese. For example, some hydrophobic peptides are well known to cause bitterness. Amino acids produced by protein hydrolysis also act as substrates for secondary catabolic reactions leading to a large variety of compounds which contribute flavors and aromas. See FLAVOR and AROMA.

See also MILK.

Artym, Jolanta, et al. "Milk-Derived Proteins and Peptides in Clinical Trials." *Postepy Higieny Medcyny Doswiadczaine* 67 (2013): 800–816.
Fox, Patrick F., and Paul L. H. McSweeney. *Advanced Dairy Chemistry*. Vol. 1: *Proteins, Parts A and B*. 3d ed. London and New York: Kluwer Academic/Plenum, 2003.
Goff, Douglas. "Milk Proteins." In *The Dairy Science and Technology Ebook*. https://www.uoguelph.ca/foodscience/book-page/milk-proteins.
Shah, Nagendra P. "Effects of Milk-Derived Bioactives: An Overview." *British Journal of Nutrition* 84, suppl. 1 (2000).

Arthur Hill and Mary Ann Ferrer

proteolysis. The ripening process of cheese—through which bland, flavorless curd is converted to the mature product—is biochemically very dynamic. Three major biochemical events occur during ripening: (1) metabolism of residual lactose, and of lactate and citrate; (2) lipolysis and metabolism of fatty acids; and (3) proteolysis followed by amino acid catabolism. Proteolysis—the breakdown of the casein matrix of the curd to a range of peptides and ultimately to free amino acids—is generally considered to be the most important and most complex of these events. Proteolysis contributes to the softening of cheese by breaking down its structure and by providing new charged groups to which water can bind. Proteolysis contributes to flavor through the peptides formed and, more importantly, by providing amino acids which are further broken down to a wide range of volatile flavor compounds.

The enzymes that catalyse proteolysis—proteinases and peptidases—originate from six major sources.

The Coagulant

Most of the enzymes in rennets used to coagulate milk (e.g., chymosin) are lost in the whey but a small proportion remain trapped in the curd during cheesemaking. Residual coagulant is the major proteolytic agent in many cheeses, except those that are cooked or heated to high temperatures during manufacture (e.g., Parmigiano Reggiano, Emmentaler, or pasta filata varieties). See COAGULATION OR CURDLING and RENNET.

The Milk

Milk contains a number of indigenous proteinases, the most important of which is plasmin, a blood enzyme that leaks into milk. Plasmin is quite heat-stable and is of most significance in cheeses that are cooked or heated during manufacture. Somatic cells (white blood cells) are present in high numbers in mastitic milk and contain many proteinases that may be of significance under certain circumstances. See MILK and PLASMIN.

The Starter

Lactic acid bacteria (LAB) are auxotrophic for many amino acids. Put more simply, they are unable to synthesize many amino acids and must get them preformed from their environment. Milk is rich in proteins, but relatively poor in free amino acids, so LAB have evolved a wide range of enzymes to release the amino acids they need from the caseins. The principal proteinase in LAB is the cell envelope-associated proteinase (CEP, or lactocepin), which is loosely attached to the cell surface and which acts directly on the caseins when the cell is growing in milk. However during cheese ripening the CEP appears to act mainly on intermediate-size peptides produced by chymosin and plasmin. LAB contain a large number of intracellular peptidases that can break down short peptides, ultimately to free amino acids. The amino acid proline—which has an unusual structure—is commonly found in the caseins and many peptidases are unable to degrade proline-containing peptides. LAB have thus evolved a number of specialized peptidases that allow them to use such peptides. Starter LAB are generally not metabolically active in cheese during ripening as the conditions are hostile to their growth. However they contribute to ripening through their enzymes, which are released

on lysis after cell death. See LACTIC ACID BACTERIA and STARTER CULTURES.

Non-starter LAB

Non-starter lactic acid bacteria (NSLAB) are a wild secondary flora that grow during the ripening of many cheeses and which can contribute to proteolysis. Their enzyme systems appear to be generally similar to those of starter LAB. See NON-STARTER LACTIC ACID BACTERIA.

Secondary Starter

Many cheese varieties are characterized by the growth of a secondary microflora during ripening. For example, *Propionibacterium freudenreichii* grow during the ripening of Swiss-type cheeses to produce its eyes; a complex Gram-positive bacterial flora grows at the surface of smear-ripened varieties; and the molds *Penicillium camemberti* and *P. roqueforti* grown on Camembert and blue cheese, respectively. Many of these organisms are strongly proteolytic and contribute significantly to proteolysis in varieties where they grow. See DAIRY PROPIONIBACTERIA and *PENICILLIUM*.

Exogenous Enzymes

Exogenous (or added) enzymes have attracted much academic interest regarding accelerating ripening but are not used commonly in industry. See ACCELERATED RIPENING

The relative importance of enzymes from these six sources depends very much on the variety. However, in general, residual coagulant and plasmin act on intact caseins during ripening to form long and intermediate-size peptides that are then acted upon by the CEP of the starter, producing shorter peptides, which, in turn, are degraded to free amino acids by starter peptidases. Only a proportion of the caseins are broken down fully to amino acids during ripening—in Cheddar cheese, perhaps 75 percent of the caseins remain as intact proteins or large polypeptides. However, a long-ripened cheese such as Cheddar contains a very large number of peptides that can be studied by urea polyacrylamide gel electrophoresis, liquid chromatography, and mass spectrometric techniques.

The direct contribution of proteolysis to cheese flavor is now thought to be relatively minor as its products—peptides and free amino acids—are generally not strongly flavored. However the amino acids produced by proteolysis are of great importance to flavor as they are degraded to a range of important volatile compounds through a complex biochemical process known as amino acid catabolism. For most amino acids, this involves enzymatic transfer of its amino group to an acceptor molecule, and the resulting alpha-keto acid is then degraded enzymatically or chemically to a number of flavor compounds. The sulfur-containing amino acid methionine is degraded by various enzymes that act upon its side chain, producing strongly flavored volatile sulfur compounds such as methanethiol.

See also CASEIN; ENZYMES; LIPOLYSIS; and PEPTIDASES.

Ardo, Y., et al. "Proteolysis in Cheese during Ripening." In *Cheese: Chemistry, Physics and Microbiology*, Vol. 1, *General Aspects*, 4th ed., edited by P. L. H. McSweeney, et al. Amsterdam: Elsevier, forthcoming.
Upadhyay, V. K., et al. "Proteolysis in Cheese during Ripening." In *Cheese: Chemistry, Physics and Microbiology*, Vol. 1, *General Aspects*, 3d ed., edited by P. F. Fox, et al., pp. 392–433. Amsterdam: Elsevier Applied Science, 2004.

P. L. H. McSweeney

Provola dei Nebrodi

Provola dei Nebrodi is a pear-shaped hard pasta filata cheese made from raw cow's whole milk, sometimes with sheep's and/or goat's milk mixed in. The Provola dei Nebrodi is the only Sicilian "provola" that is aged. It originated in the area of Floresta in northeastern Sicily, but spread to the surrounding areas.

Provola dei Nebrodi is made by mixing 99°F (37°C) heated evening milk with the morning milk. The milk coagulates in a wooden vat called a *tina* by adding farmhouse kid's or lamb's rennet paste. See TINA. Lamb paste, rich in lipases, contributes to the production of free-fatty-acids (FFA) and the characteristic flavor of this cheese. The curd is broken and left to drain on a wooden table, starting a natural process of acidification, after which it is cut and stretched using hot water or hot whey from ricotta production. See WHEY and RICOTTA.

Finally the curds are shaped like a ball and worked by hand to obtain a pear shape. After the molding, the "provola" is salted in saturated brine for twenty-four hours for every 2 pounds (1 kilogram) of cheese and then hung up for one to four months for aging. Ripening is done in cool and ventilated premises called *maaseni*, where the cheeses are hung in pairs over wooden poles attached to the ceilings.

The rind is thin, with a straw-yellow color tending toward yellow-amber as the aging process advances. The interior is white with a tendency toward a straw-yellow color. The texture is soft and compact. It has fruit notes, and is reminiscent of warm milk and butter. It tastes sweet and slightly sour when fresh, savory and strong when aged. The weight varies from 2 pounds (1 kilogram) when made for fresh or semi-aged consumption, but varies from a minimum of 7 pounds (3 kilograms) to a maximum of 15 pounds (7 kilograms) when the cheese is made for aging.

See also PASTA FILATA and SICILY.

Campo, P., and G. Licitra. *Historical Sicilian Cheeses*. Ragusa, Italy. CoRFiLaC, 2006.
Concurso, C., et al. "Free Fatty Acids in 'Provola del Nebrodi,' a Historical Sicilian Cheese." *Italian Journal of Food Science* 18, no. 2 (2006): 151–162.
Food in Italy. http://www.foodinitaly.com.

Margherita Caccamo

Provolone del Monaco

Provolone del Monaco is a semihard pasta filata cheese produced in some municipalities in the Metropolitan City of Naples, Italy. It received the European recognition of protected designation of origin (PDO) in 2010.

Traditionally Provolone del Monaco was produced in the Monti Lattani (Sorrento peninsula) and marketed in the nearby city of Naples. Due to land

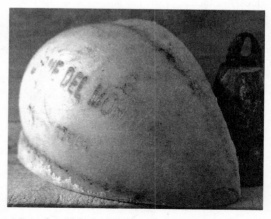

A Provolone del Monaco from La Verde Fattoria in Vico Equense, Italy. © VINCENZO SPIONE

imperviousness of the Monti Lattari and the Sorrento peninsula the best way to reach Naples was by sea. The farmers, in order to shelter from the sea and the night humidity, covered themselves with the large cape-like robes worn by monks. In Naples the people who worked in the market at the port began to call the carrier the "Monaco," and his cheese "Provolone del Monaco."

Provolone del Monaco is pear-shaped (without the neck) or melon-shaped and presents longitudinal coves that divide the cheese into six wedges because of the raffia laces used to support the cheese during the ripening period. It has a thin and smooth pale-yellow-colored rind and weighs 6–18 pounds (2.5–8 kilograms). The interior paste is cream colored, compact with eyes (5 milimeters) that may increase in size (12 milimeters) toward the center. The cheese has a fat content of at least 40 percent on a dry matter basis and a sweet and buttery aroma with a pleasant spicy taste.

The cheese is made with raw whole cow's milk with at least 20 percent coming from the local Agerolese breed. The raw milk is coagulated using kid rennet paste or calf liquid rennet or a combination of both (with a minimum of 50 percent kid rennet paste). The curd is then kneaded in water at 185–203°F (85–95°C) and stretched, and the cheese ripened at least six months. During this period the rind could be rubbed with Penisola Sorrentina—PDO extra virgin olive oil.

De Angelis, M., and M. Gobbetti. "Pasta-Filata Cheeses: Traditional Pasta-Filata Cheese." In *Encyclopedia of Dairy Sciences*, 2d ed., edited by J. W. Fuquay et al., pp. 745–752. Boston: Elsevier, 2011.

Ministero delle Politiche Agricole. "Disciplinari di produzione prodotti DOP e IGP riconosciuti: Formaggi." https://www.politicheagricole.it/flex/cm/pages/ServeBLOB.php/L/IT/IDPagina/3340.

"Provalone del Monaco." Cheese.com. http://www.cheese.com/provolone-del-monaco.

Marta Bertolino

Provolone Valpadana

Provolone Valpadana is a semihard, DOP (denominazione di origine protetta) pasta filata cheese. It is produced in two varieties: "Dolce" (mild) and "Piccante" (sharp). The sweet variety is aged for two to three months, and the sharp variety, for a minimum of three months to more than a year. Both varieties, sweet and sharp, also come smoked. Provolone Valpadana received the DOP certification in 1996, with an area of origin in the following regions of the Po Valley in Italy: Lombardy, Veneto, Emilia-Romagna, and the province of Trento.

Provolone Valpadana was born in the Po Valley in the second half of the nineteenth century, after the unification of Italy (1861), which made it possible to overcome the barriers between the different areas of the peninsula and, therefore, the establishment of entrepreneurs from the south. They brought with them the culture and tradition of "pasta filata," or stretched, cheeses. The name "provolone" appears in the literature for the first time in 1871 in Eugenio Canevazzi and Francesco Marconi's *Vocabolario di agricoltura*.

Production of Provolone Valpadana takes place throughout the year, using whole, raw cow's milk collected in the origin area fewer than sixty hours after the first milking. The sweet variety of cheese is fully pasteurized (heated to 161°F [71.7°C] for 15 seconds), while the sharp variety is thermized (heated to 149°F [65°C] for 15 seconds). The starter cultures used in processing must be natural acidified whey, left over from previous cheesemaking. The milk is coagulated at a temperature of about 97–102°F (36–39°C), and depending on the specific variety of provolone, the type of coagulant used is different. The sweet variety is made with calf rennet (a small percentage of lamb or kid rennet is also allowed), while the sharp variety is coagulated only with kid or lamb rennet. After a double breaking of the coagulated gel in order to obtain curd granules of the correct dimensions for the different type of cheeses to be produced, the curd is cooked at about 126–127°F (52–53°C). Next it is laid on tables, where it is left until it naturally reaches the acidification (pH 4.7 to 5.2) suitable for the stretching phase of provolone, which is done using boiling water and the experience of the cheesemaker. See ACIDIFICATION and STRETCHING.

Provolone Valpadana presents a greater variety of shapes and weights than any other dairy product. The shaping is carried out manually or with the aid of special molds. See FORMS OR MOLDS. There are distinguishable official shapes: salami (cylindrical), melon, truncated conical, tangerine, and pear topped by a small spherical head (flask). The outer surface can have small inlets determined by the passage of support ropes. The different shapes have weights that range from about 1 pound to more than 220 pounds (0.5 kilogram to more than 100 kilogram). The cheese thus obtained is placed in cold water or cooled for firming.

The salting of the cheese takes place in brine with a salt concentration up to 22°Bé (Baumé degrees), for a variable period of time in relation to the weight of the cheeses—from a few hours up to thirty days. See SALT and BRINING. Once pulled out of the brine, the cheeses are washed in cold water, dried, and tied. The "binding" of the cheeses with suitable ropes is a special touch given by the cheesemakers, another old tradition that has not been lost.

The aging period can vary depending on the weight of the cheese as well as the variety. If the cheese is smoked, paraffin use is allowed. See SMOKED CHEESES. The rind is smooth, thin, and light yellow, golden, or sometimes yellow-brown. The sweet variety can also be rindless if it will be cut into portions and packaged. The paste is generally compact and may have slight and rare holes; some flaking (peeling) is permitted in cheese at an early age, while a more marked exfoliation is allowed in long-aged cheese. The flavor is delicate for sweet cheeses and with short aging but becomes pronounced with longer maturation and in the sharp cheeses.

See also ITALY and PROVOLONE DEL MONACO.

Canevazzi, Eugenio, and Francesco Marconi. *Vocabolario di agricoltura* [Vocabulary of Agriculture]. Rocca San Casciano, Italy: Cappelli, 1871.
Ministero delle Politiche Agricole, Alimentari e Forestali. http://www.mipaaf.it.
Consorzio Tutela Provolone Valpadana. http://www.provolonevalpadana.it.

Carlo Fiori

pultost

See SOUR SKIMMED-MILK CHEESES.

Puritans, who emigrated from England to America around 1620–1640 and colonized the lands of indigenous peoples, did little cheesemaking. The cheesemaking that did occur was on a very small scale, for home production, and was part of an oral tradition passed down from mothers to daughters. For this reason there is very little written documentation of the processes. We do know that the cheesemaking undertaken by Puritan women mimicked the regional styles of their homelands in England.

The majority of Puritans living in what would come to be called New England could not afford to keep a cow. For the few households that did have a cow, milk production was limited by seasonal breeding, supplies of animal feed, and access to salt, cheese hoops, and press. See SALT; HOOP; and PRESS. Rennet, the enzyme used to coagulate milk, is derived from the stomach lining of suckling ruminants. See RENNET. Cheesemaking was most commonly begun by soaking a piece of dried cow stomach, or maw, in heated milk. While it is possible that immigrants brought dried maws with them from England, continuous cheesemaking required a steady supply of rennet, which meant slaughtering calves. The few cows that survived the voyage were incredibly valuable as farming tools. Therefore the need for meat and rennet was in direct competition with plow-pulling and milk production.

If a seventeenth-century New England household was in possession of a cow, and that cow calved and survived the birthing process, and if the household had sufficient feed stored to enable milk production to continue, then there was a chance that cheesemaking would occur. During the sixteenth and seventeenth centuries in England, a shift in cheesemaking occurred that the Puritans then continued in New England: making cheese from skim milk. As the desire for butter increased, cheesemaking transitioned from a process in which the entire milking was used in making cheese, to a several-stepped process where milk was settled and skimmed, before butter was made from the cream and cheese was made from just the milk.

Puritan members of the Massachusetts Bay Colony replicated the hard cheeses that became namesakes in the region of East Anglia. Cheshire and Somerset were developed by scalding skim milk and pressing the cheeses for longer periods of time to produce drier, harder products that had lower moisture content, making them easier to transport in comparison to softer cheeses. Cheesemaking in New England followed the tradition of creating round, hard cheeses in the style of East Anglia up through the nineteenth century.

While female heads of household in Puritan New England did engage in cheesemaking, it was on a very small scale, undertaken only by the few who had cattle. The majority of cheese consumed in seventeenth-century America was imported, until cattle stocks became larger and more stable. Cattle served not only as a source of dairy foods and meat, but also as a tool used to displace indigenous people. Puritans would intentionally graze cattle on lands they wanted to control, often decimating native crops and erecting fences to claim "ownership."

See also UNITED STATES.

Jenkins, Steven, *Cheese Primer*. New York: Workman, 1996.
Kindstedt, Paul, with the Vermont Cheese Council. *American Farmstead Cheese: The Complete Guide to Making and Selling Artisan Cheese*. White River Junction, Vt.: Chelsea Green, 2005.

Kristina Nies

Puzzone di Moena (or Spretz Tzaorì) is a semihard and semicooked cheese produced in the Fassa, Fiemme, and Primiero valleys of Trento province and in the municipalities of Anterivo and Trodena of Bolzano province in Italy. It received the European recognition of PDO (protected designation of origin in 2014.

The first time that the term "Puzzone di Moena"—which literally means "big stink of Moena"—was used was during a radio broadcast in the summer of 1974, referring to a smeared-rind cheese produced by the cheesemaking company of Moena. The alternate name, Spretz Tzaorì, means "flavorful cheese" in Latin. Both names refer to the strong taste described as salty or spicy and slightly bitter, and to its high, penetrating, and slightly ammonia odor. The aromatic characteristics were appreciated by the poor mountain people due to their ability to increase the flavor of ordinary dishes such as potato and cornmeal mush.

Puzzone di Moena is cylindrical with straight or slightly convex sides, and a rind that can be smooth or rough, oily, and ocher to tan-reddish colored. It is 4–5 inches (9–12 centimeters) high, 13–17 inches (34–42 centimeters) in diameter, and weighs 20–29 pounds (9–13 kilograms). The interior paste is white to yellow colored, soft, elastic, with small eyes and a fat content of at least 45 percent.

The cheese is made with raw cow's milk obtained from herds fed with at least 60 percent of local forage. The milk obtained from two milkings could be partially skimmed and then is coagulated using bovine rennet. The curd is semi-cooked at 111–118°F (44–48°C) for fifteen to thirty minutes. During the first two to three weeks of ripening a solution of lukewarm water and salt is smeared on the rind two times a week, decreasing to once a week thereafter until the end of the ripening (a minimum of ninety days).

Caseificio Sociale di Moena. http://www.puzzonedimoena.com.
Ministero delle Politiche Agricole. "Disciplinari di produzione prodotti DOP e IGP riconosciuti: Formaggi." https://www.politicheagricole.it/flex/cm/pages/ServeBLOB.php/L/IT/IDPagina/3340.

Marta Bertolino

quark is a soft, nonaged and unsalted fresh cheese traditionally made by draining coagulated sour milk, most often cow's milk. It is widespread in the German-speaking and Slavic countries as well as in northern Europe. The German term in English is often translated either as farmer's cheese, cottage cheese, or ricotta, none of which is entirely accurate. Traditionally, quark is made from soured, thickened milk; in contemporary commercial production a very small amount of rennet is added to facilitate curdling. The curd is cut and left to drain in bags, or on a larger commercial scale today centrifuges are used to separate the whey from the solids, with the resulting cheese being much creamier in texture and containing more water—by law, at least 73 percent in the dry matter.

Quark is an essential ingredient when making a German-style cheesecake and for improved results when baking, the cheese should be pressed dry using a cloth before use; Austrian Topfen and Polish Twaróg in general contain less whey. Arguably the best commercially available quark in Germany comes from the cooperative dairy of the small town Asendorf in Niedersachsen. It is called *Schichtkäse*, layered cheese, as the good ladies in the white frocks working there ladle the fresh curd into small square molds in alternating layers with different fat content (the luxury version has some whipped cream added). Quark's longstanding roots in Germanic and Eastern European history may go back to Roman times. Historian Tacitus (ca. 55–115 C.E.) reports in his *Germania* about the wild tribes in the far north in the first century C.E. who, according to him, survived on meat, wild berries, ale, and *lac concretum* (solid milk). Recently this has been corroborated by archaeological findings of seven-thousand-years-old earthenware sieves in central Poland on which traces of milk fat were found. See ANCIENT CIVILIZATIONS and EARTHENWARE POTTERY.

They are further witnessed by a multitude of regional names for it, such as Weißkäse (literally white cheese, north Germany), Glumse (east Germany), Bibbeleskäs (southwest Germany), Topfen (Bavaria/Austria), twaróg or ser biały (Poland), tvorog (Russia), and Schmierkaes (Pennsylvania Dutch). It further proves Germanic predilection for quark that even its connection with times of hardship haven't cast any lasting shadows. From nineteenth century pauperism to Nazi propaganda for food rationing, quark was recommended as a cheap, more abundant and filling substitute for butter. After World War II, although margarine consumption went down in favor of butter and the consumption of full-fat cheese shot up with Schmelzkäse, spreadable processed cheese, being a favorite—quark consumption also rose considerably, almost tripling. Across the national borders quark is used in all kinds of sweet and savory dishes. For a quick dessert it is mixed with various fresh fruit; while a popular lunch is quark seasoned with finely cut fresh herbs (mainly parsley, dill, and chives), a little onion, and served with baked potatoes. Traditional Slavic influence sees quark served with linseed (flaxseed) oil while Russian Easter is incomplete without "paskha," a dessert consisting of quark, egg yolks, sugar, and candied fruit, traditionally drained in square, obelisk-shaped wooden molds, but today often made in plastic flower pots. Quark is an essential ingredient in many variants of pierogi, pancakes, strudel, and cakes, but features much less in Roman cultures, although the French have fromage blanc or frais (with the related Petit

Suisse as well as cervelle de canut and claquebitou). In German cheese parlance *quarkig* is also used to describe the crumbly tangy white core of a cheese that has yet to fully ripen.

See also FARMER CHEESE and FRESH CHEESES.

Heinzelmann, Ursula. *Beyond Bratwurst: A History of Food in Germany*. London: Reaktion, 2014.
Salque, Mélanie, Peter I. Bogucki, Joanna Pyzel, Iwona Sobkowiak-Tabaka, et al. "Earliest Evidence for Cheese Making in the Sixth Millenium BC in Northern Europe." *Nature* 493, (2013): 522–525.

Ursula Heinzelmann

Quartirolo Lombardo is a square-shaped PDO (protected designation of origin) cow's milk cheese produced in the northern Lombardy region of Italy, with a long history dating to the tenth century. It was originally produced at the end of the summer when the cows were brought back down from the mountain pastures and fed with the fourth and last cut of grass, *erba quartirola* in Italian. Now it is produced according to the PDO rules established in 1993 by thirty-one cheese factories in the area between the Po River plain and the pre-Alpine valleys between Bergamo and Lecco.

There are two types of Quartirolo Lombardo: the fresh one matures for at least five days, and the aged one, for more than thirty days. It is produced with full-fat, or less frequently, with part-skimmed cow's milk, with the addition of starter and calf rennet. The curd is broken down twice into small granules the size of a hazelnut and transferred into

Fresh (left) and ripened (right) versions of Quartirolo Lombardo, an Italian cow's milk cheese. COURTESY OF THE CONSORTIUM FOR THE PROTECTION OF QUARTIROLO LOMBARDO

traditional molds. Then it is kept in warm rooms with a high humidity for a maximum of twenty-four hours.

Salting is done dry or in brine, and the cheese is aged at a temperature of 36–46°F (2–8°C) and a relative humidity of 85–90 percent. The final product has a square shape measuring 7–8.7 inches (18–22 cm) wide and 1.6–3.1 inches (4–8 cm) high, with an average weight ranging from 3.7–7.7 pounds (1.7–3.5 kilograms). The paste is white and firm, with a fine, granular texture that softens during ripening, and occasionally has small, irregular holes. Initially rindless, the cheese develops a pinkish rind with prolonged aging. The taste is distinctive, slightly sour, and aromatic in the fresh cheese, becoming more intense as the cheese ages.

See also ITALY and LOMBARDY.

Mucchetti, Germano, and Erasmo Neviani. *Microbiologia e tecnologia lattiero-casearia, Qualità e sicurezza*, pp. 566–569. Milan, Italy: Tecniche Nuove, 2006.

Milena Brasca

Quebec is Canada's largest province and a pioneer in Canadian production of fine and artisanal cheeses. Although a large portion of the hundreds of Quebec's cheeses available in shops today are offspring of the "renaissance" movement that sprung up during the 1980s, cheeses have been made in Quebec for many centuries. French settlers brought cows with them as early as Jacques Cartier's third voyage in 1541. As more boats arrived in the beginning of the seventeenth century, starting with explorer Samuel de Champlain's in 1608, they transported colonists and cattle mainly from Brittany and Normandy. Early on, settlers established around Quebec City, on Île d'Orléans and in the Saint Lawrence River plains started making fresh, creamy cheeses. Some families also produced lightly aged fromage Raffiné, a deformation of the French word affiné, or "matured"; the cheese is related to Burgundy's Soumaintrain. The Paillasson, still made today (albeit with pasteurized milk) and said to be North America's oldest cheese, took its name, meaning "doormat," from the small reed mat on which it was placed to dry. Most of these cheeses were made for domestic consumption, but records show that some were already being sold outside the household as well. By the end of the seventeenth century, vigorous cattle herds were to be found in many parts of the province. The Canadienne, the only dairy cow bred on the American continent, was eventually developed to tolerate harsh winters. Today, a very limited number of purebreds remain, making the breed an object of conservancy efforts; a few of Quebec's cheeses, including the famous Pied-de-vent from the Magdalen Islands and Fromagerie Charlevoix's 1608, are produced with Canadienne milk.

Following the British conquest and the strengthening foothold of Anglo-Saxon culture, many French cheesemaking traditions were abandoned as Cheddar production gradually took the lead. By the mid-nineteenth century, a push for the industrialization of what was essentially a household activity led to the creation of the first commercial dairies in the Anglophone region of the Eastern Townships, southeast of Montreal. The first cheesemaking schools opened a few years later, sowing seeds for the development of standardized production methods in step with technological innovations. In the small agricultural town of Saint-Hyacinthe, a government-funded dairy institute studied and refined centrifugal and curdling processes and conducted chemical, bacteriological, and nutritional research; in fact, Canada was among the first nations to promote pasteurization and enforce sanitary laws regulating milk collection and cheesemaking. See PASTEURIZATION. In 1890, the Fromagerie Perron was founded in the Lac-Saint-Jean region; still operating today, it is Quebec's oldest dairy. Toward the end of the nineteenth century, it was one of the largest producers of the millions of cases of Cheddar shipped every year to the British Isles; indeed, cheese was one of the colony's major agricultural exports. See CHEDDAR.

Although Cheddar prevailed, one other type of cheese was widely embraced and celebrated. Oka, created in 1893 by Trappist monk Marie-Alphonse Julien as a local rendition of Brittany's Port-Salut, is a small, round semisoft cow's milk cheese covered in a copper-orange hand-washed rind and aged on planks of South Carolina cypress. Although it has become a highly industrialized product, it remains one of the province's historically emblematic cheeses. In later years, monasteries were instrumental in the development of Quebec's cheese scene. In the 1930s, the Sisters of Mont-de-la-Rédemption were the first women to raise goats and produce goat's milk cheese, although in 1943, the province's first

blue cheese, l'Ermite, was developed in the Abbey of Saint-Benoît-du-Lac. But from 1950 to 1970, artisanal cheesemaking was gradually displaced by industrial production and large dairy conglomerates such as Agropur, an agricultural mega-cooperative founded in 1938, which now includes more than 3,550 farmers and transforms 1.4 billion gallons (5.4 billion liters) of milk every year, and Saputo, which from humble beginnings in Montreal in 1954 became one of the ten largest dairy processors in the world.

Standardized, pasteurized and highly processed cheeses were the norm until the late 1970s, when back-to-the-landers and European immigrants launched a new wave of artisanal production. Their curiosity piqued by these curious cheeses and their palates, in many cases, refined by travels abroad, Quebecois and Canadians alike embraced this new trend. Over the next decades, the offer of fine cheeses expanded dramatically. Today, more than four hundred different cheeses are made in Quebec; many have won significant awards nationally and abroad, and often take home the majority of prizes at the Canadian Cheese Awards, the country's largest cheese contest. Specialty shops have sprung up in every part of the province; tourists and locals can meander along the Route des Fromages (The Cheese Route) to taste local delicacies made of cow's, goat's, or sheep's milk. Often strongly linked to Quebec's distinct cultural identity, many are named after significant historical figures and events—Le Riopelle de l'Isle, Le 1608, Le Rébellion 1837, Le Curé Labelle—or iconic geographical landmarks—Le Trois-Pistoles, Le Péribonka, Le Pont Tournant. Quebecois parlance is also an endless source of inspiration: Le Placoteux, Le Diable aux Vaches, Le Pied-de-Vent, Le Skouik! Skouik!, or Le Ratoureux evoke the province's linguistic idiosyncrasy.

The distinctive cultural character of Quebec cheeses is fiercely guarded by producers and consumers alike and became a highly charged political issue when the federal authorities attempted to ban the sale of raw-milk cheese in 1996. The unrelenting uproar from Quebec caused the government to amend the proposed legislation. In 2008, Quebec became the only jurisdiction in North America to allow the production of raw-milk cheeses aged less than sixty days. But just a few weeks after the controversial decision was announced, an outbreak of Listeria caused many to point fingers at the still-rejoicing raw-milk cheese producers. During a highly mediatized blitz through the province's most reputable cheese shops, sanitary authorities destroyed more than 27 tons (24 metric tons) of cheese in a single day. Close to 10 more tons (9 metric tons) were subsequently seized in dairies found to be contaminated with the specific *Listeria* strain involved in the death of two people and at least thirty-eight cases of food-borne illness. Although it eventually transpired that the culprits were more likely pasteurized products, the hype surrounding the outbreak caused an irremediable blow to the nascent industry. Facing a newly sceptical public and ever-tightening regulations, many cheesemakers traded raw milk for its pasteurized or thermized counterparts. As of 2016, out of approximately 110 Quebec dairies, only some 15 craft a raw-milk cheese, down from over 30 before the listeriosis outbreak. See *LISTERIA*; OUTBREAK; RAW-MILK CHEESES; and THERMIZED MILK CHEESE.

Another considerable challenge for the Quebec cheese industry pertains to the prohibitive prices that have become the norm in grocery stores and specialty shops. While cheesemakers mention small production volumes, high milk costs, and distribution expenses as contributing factors, restrictive prices mean that, for many consumers, Quebec specialty cheeses are reserved for special occasions. Nonetheless, with many new specialty cheeses being developed every year, continued high turnouts at local cheese festivals, and a dynamic industry that strives to create unique and diversified products for a curious and enthusiastic public, fine cheeses remain one of Quebec's flagship foods.

See also CANADA.

Ferland, Catherine. "Fromages du Québec." *Encyclopédie du patrimoine culturel de l'Amérique française*. http://www.ameriquefrancaise.org/fr/article-640/Fromages_du_Qu%C3%A9bec.html#.U9VlPq15PaN.

Hornsby, David J. "Multilevel Governance in Domestic Regulatory Conflict: Raw-Milk Cheese in Canada." Paper presented at the Canadian Political Science Association Annual Meeting, Waterloo (Canada), 18 May 2011. http://ssrn.com/abstract=1905406.

Lambert, Michel. *Histoire de la cuisine familiale du Québec*, Vol. 4: *La plaine du Saint-Laurent et les produits de la ferme traditionnelle* [*A History of Household Cooking in Quebec*, Vol. 4: *The Saint-Lawrence Plain and the Products of the Traditional Farmstead*]. Quebec: GID, 2011.

Les Producteurs de lait du Québec. *Our Cheeses.* http://www.ourcheeses.com/.

Turgeon, Laurier. "Les produits du terroir, version Québec." [Terroir Products in Quebec] *Ethnologie Française* 40, no. 3 (2010): 477–486.

Laura Shine

queso Oaxaca

See MEXICAN CHEESES.

queso panela

See MEXICAN CHEESES.

R

Raclette is a semisoft washed-rind cow's milk cheese with a smooth supple texture and excellent melting characteristics. It is produced in a wheel format ranging from 14 to 15 inches (35 to 38 centimeters) in diameter, approximately 3 inches (8 centimeters) in height and weighing between 15 to 18 pounds (7 to 8 kilograms). Raclette is also the name of a traditional dish made with this cheese, melted over various cooked and pickled accompaniments. The moisture content, combined with its young age of three to four months when ripe, gives this cheese a silky smooth quality with a low level of fat separation when heated gently. Traditionally this would be done with the paste of a halved wheel exposed to an open flame until a molten layer of cheese can be scraped directly over potatoes, pickled onions, or cornichons to name a few of the many possibilities. The name Raclette is derived from the French verb *racler*, meaning "scrape." Today there are many devices sold for the purpose of melting Raclette cheese.

Both the cheese and the meal have their origins in the Alpine regions of Switzerland and France where cheesemaking and transhumance have been intertwined for many centuries. Like many other traditional cheeses, climate and other environmental conditions have had more to do with its origin than modern national boundaries. That said, the appellation d'origine contrôlée (AOC) designation for this style is located in French-speaking Switzerland. Traditionally made at certain times of the year in Alpine regions, this cheese is now made year round in other parts of Europe and around the world.

AOC Raclette du Valais

AOC Raclette du Valais is made exclusively in the Swiss canton (state) of Valais with the exception of the area of Kandersteg in the canton of Bern. This is some of the steepest and most beautiful agricultural land in the world where nature clearly has the upper hand and people have developed methods of farming strictly tied to seasonal rhythms over many centuries. There are 174 fromageries registered to produce this cheese in adherence to strict guidelines that maintain traditional practices, according to the Swiss Federal Office for Agriculture (Office Fédéral de l'Agriculture). AOC regulations require raw milk from no more than two milkings, and that the cows be fed non-ensiled, non-GMO feed, among other stipulations. See SILAGE. The milk must be less than twenty-four hours old and is heated in copper vats to a temperature of 90°F (32°C) before adding rennet (animal rennet required). After coagulation and cutting, the curd can be heated to between 97–113°F (36–45°C). This range of heat for the final cooking of the curd allows the cheesemaker to decide how to reach the final moisture target for the finished cheese. The AOC specifications for the moisture content are between 36–44 percent, which is a large range. Cheese in the lower moisture range is often aged for longer than six months and would not be considered a melting cheese after this point.

Among the breeds of cow used for producing the milk for this traditional production is the Eringer. These stout, rugged animals are beloved by Alpine herdsmen and are adorned with very expensive and decorative collars from which their bells are hung.

Eringer cows, a breed whose milk is used in the production of Raclette cheese, are adorned with decorative collars from which bells are hung. In this photo they are seen engaging in posturing and head-butting tussles to establish a herd hierarchy. © JEREMEY STEPHENSON

During certain times of the year their milk production drops as the cows engage in posturing and head-butting tussles to establish a herd hierarchy. There will always be one at the head of the herd known as the "fighting queen." This cow, during her reign, will lead the herd in and out of the milking barn. At the end of the alpage season the cows are moved down to the lower altitudes and the herds are split up to reside in smaller groups with their respective owners. Before this, however, there is a festival during which all the fighting queens are brought together and allowed to lock horns and tussle for the top position among all the herds of the alpage. This ritual is not harmful to the cows but rather celebrates their natural characteristics of strength and endurance. It is emblematic of the same characteristics required of the Alpine peoples in many countries who have cared for livestock and made cheese over the centuries in the harsh and spectacular Alpine landscape. See ALPAGE and ALP CHEESEMAKING.

Raclette Outside the AOC Production Area

Raclette-style cheese has been traditionally made in Alpine regions of France near modern Switzerland, during the spring and fall when the cows were kept in smaller herds. This was before and after their seasonal movement into the alpage for the production of larger cheeses such as Beaufort. During this period less milk was collected from cows and was used to produce smaller cheeses such as Raclette. Large scale production of non-AOC Raclette-style cheese has developed in France and other countries, with the use of milk from large stationary herds with feed regimens far different from the traditional AOC requirements.

In the United States and other countries there are an increasing number of smaller artisanal producers and some larger companies producing Raclette-style cheese as awareness of this cheese grows among consumers. In 2015 the American Cheese Society introduced a new category to its Cheese Judging and Competition called TR: "Raclette-Style—Aged Over 45 Days—All Milks." Outside the AOC region the cheese can have a wide range of flavor profiles due to the many combinations of breed, feed, make room procedures, equipment, and not least of all, methods of affinage. The organoleptic qualities described in the Swiss AOC specifications are worth keeping in mind when looking for good examples of this cheese. Descriptors such as "slightly lactic" or "milky," "mildly acidic," "fresh butter," "floral," and sometimes "vegetal" reflect characteristics that result from the best manufacturing practices. Cheese with "off," "unclean," or bitter flavors should not be mistaken for a good representation of this cheese, which can be excellent as a flavorful table cheese and in its melted form can be transcendent.

Flammer, Dominik, and Fabian Scheffold. *Swiss Cheese: Origins, Traditional Cheese Varieties and New Creations.* 3d ed. Zurich: Shoppenkochen, 2010.

Kindstedt, Paul. *Cheese and Culture.* White River Junction, Vt.: Chelsea Green, 2012.

Maison du Lait. http://www.maison-du-lait.com/fr.

Swiss PDO-PGI Association. http://www .aop-igp.ch.

Jeremy Stephenson

Ragusano, a raw cow's milk stretched-curd cheese made with natural animal rennet (lamb and/or kid), is one of the oldest Sicilian cheeses.

Ragusano, a Sicilian stretched-curd cheese, in the maturing rooms at La Fromagerie in London. © KATE ARDING

Since the sixteenth century this cheese has been the object of a thriving commerce beyond the boundaries of the Kingdom of Sicily. Ragusano is produced in the entire province of Ragusa and the townships of Noto, Palazzolo Acreide, and Rosolini in the province of Siracusa. Ragusano was given a PDO (protected designation of origin) designation in 1996.

Ragusano is still produced using traditional utensils. Milk from the Modicana breed is coagulated in a wooden vat (*tina*), and the curd is cut with a wooden staff (*ruotula*); a small round container made of copper or wood (*staccio*) and a wooden staff (*manuvedda*) are used for the stretching process; and a wooden table (*mastredda*) is used for the final shaping of the cheese. Ragusano has the shape of a rectangular block with rounded corners. The rind is smooth, thin, and compact, with a golden or straw-yellow color that tends to turn brownish as the aging process continues; in some cases it is brushed with olive oil. The interior color of the cheese is white tending toward straw-yellow with aging, and the texture is compact with widely spaced holes. The semi-aged cheese has a pleasant, sweet, and piquant delicate taste; it becomes savory and tending toward spiciness with prolonged aging. The weight varies from 22–35 pounds (10–16 kilograms). The PDO-certified cheeses show a clear, distinctive "Ragusano" fire stamped on one side.

See also CACIOCAVALLO; PASTA FILATA; TRADITIONAL EQUIPMENT; SICILY; and TINA.

Trasselli, Carmelo. *Da Ferdinando il cattolico a Carlo V. L'esperienza siciliana (1475–1525)*, vol. 1. Soveria Mannelli, Italy: Rubbettino, 1982.

Stefania Carpino

Rance, Patrick (1918–1999), was an English cheesemonger, author, and champion of British farmhouse cheese. The son of a vicar, he was born on England's Essex coast and developed a love for cheese at a young age.

After serving in World War II and spending a brief spell with the Conservative Party Central Office as a public opinion researcher, Rance, with his new wife, Janet, fulfilled an ambition to run a grocer's shop when they took over the business at Well's Stores in the village of Streatley, Berkshire. In this tiny shop, Rance began a crusade to bring traditional British cheeses to the attention of the wider public, and rallied against the multitude of bland, mass-produced imitations that had gradually saturated the UK market throughout the middle and latter part of the twentieth century.

To this end, Rance traveled the length and breadth of the British Isles seeking out traditional cheeses, in particular those utilizing raw milk, in a bid to counter what he described as "the follies of witless pasteurization." Not only did he strive to bring the best of British cheese to his small shop counter, but he inspired existing farmhouse cheesemakers to continue their trade (even going so far as to purchase cheese in advance with blank checks), as well as offering encouragement and advice to new or aspiring cheesemakers.

In 1982 Rance published *The Great British Cheese Book*, a detailed survey of the United Kingdom's surviving farmhouse cheeses and a homage to those that had been lost, followed in 1989 by *The French Cheese Book*. Both books, intensively researched and drafted in Rance's passionate and unassuming style, were met with critical acclaim and remain required reading for cheese enthusiasts decades after publication.

His dedication fueled a new generation of British cheese professionals and helped lay the foundations for a resurgence in the British farmhouse cheese industry. As Rance stated in *The Great British Cheese Book*, "Good cheese has been almost killed by lack of understanding and care.... It can only be raised back to health by a professional, indeed a vocational, attitude in those who wish to put things right and make a living by doing so" (p. 155).

See also FARMSTEAD; RAW-MILK CHEESES; and UNITED KINGDOM.

McCalman, Max, and David Gibbons. *Mastering Cheese: Lessons for Connoisseurship from a Maître Fromager.* New York: Clarkson Potter, 2009.
Rance, Patrick. *The Great British Cheese Book.* London: Macmillan, 1982.
Rance, Patrick. *The French Cheese Book.* London: Macmillan, 1989.

Chris George

Raschera is an Italian semihard, pressed, medium fat or fat PDO (protected designation of origin) cheese produced from cow's milk with the possible addition of small quantities of ewe's and/or goat's milk. Raschera today may be produced anywhere in the province of Cuneo, but it is a typical and historical product of the Monregalese valley and is named for the Alpe Raschera, a pasture at the foot of Monte Mongioie in the village of Magliano Alpi. About 720 tons of Raschera PDO are produced every year.

Raschera PDO cheese can be named "d'Alpeggio" when it is produced in the summer in mountain pastures over 900 meters above the sea level. After coagulation, the curd is cut to produce granules the size of hazelnuts. The curd is then collected, drained in muslin for ten to fifteen minutes, and finally put into cylindrical (called "fascele") or quadrangular (called "conca") forms where it is pressed at least twelve hours. The cheese is dry salted with or without a brine and ripened for at least one month (per disciplinare). Cylindrical Raschera has a diameter of 12–16 inches (30–40 centimeters), a convex edge of 3–4 inches (7–9 centimeters), and a weight of 15–20 pounds (7–9 kilograms) while the square shape has a side of 12–16 inches (30–40 centimeters), a straight edge of (5–6 inches) (12–15 centimeters), and a weight of 18–11 pounds (8–10 kilograms). The rind is thin, elastic, and regular, reddish-gray with red patches. The paste is white or ivory with small and sparse eyes, elastic, and consistent. The fresher cheeses have a fresh and delicate odor with milk and cream characteristics, while for the aged cheeses the odor is spicy, savory, and persistent.

See also ITALY.

Assopiemonte DOP & IGP. http://www.assopiemonte.com.
Consorzio del Raschera Tutti. http://www.raschera.com.
Ministero dell'Agricoltura e delle Foreste. *DOC Cheeses of Italy: A Great Heritage.* Milan: Franco Angeli, 1992.
Ottogalli, G. *Atlante dei formaggi.* Milan: Hoepli Editore, 2001.
Rubino, Robert, et al., eds. *Italian Cheese: A Guide to Its Discovery and Appreciation.* 6th ed. Bra, Italy: Slow Food Editore, 2009.

Giuseppe Zeppa

raw-milk cheeses are made from milk that has not been pasteurized. See PASTEURIZATION. Within the United States, no other processing technique is considered to be equivalent to pasteurization by the US Food and Drug Administration (FDA). Therefore the use of milk subjected to thermalization, microfiltration, high pressure, electro-shock, or sonication to reduce the microbiota of raw milk would still legally result in a raw-milk cheese.

However others embrace a stricter definition, maintaining that in order to be a true raw-milk cheese, the milk must not be subjected to any treatment severe enough to damage the milk's native bacteria and enzymes. In some cases this includes the temperature used during the curd cooking step during cheese manufacture.

The two most often debated issues surrounding raw-milk cheese are safety and flavor. Some regulatory authorities recommend pasteurization of milk for cheesemaking because it results in the complete destruction of all known pathogens in the milk at that early stage and represents a convenient and effective "critical control point" in HACCP systems. See HAZARD ANALYSIS AND CRITICAL CONTROL POINT AND PATHOGENS. While it does not sterilize milk—so-called "thermoduric," or heat-insensitive, microbes remain viable—it also destroys most of the bacteria, yeasts, and mold spores present.

From a flavor perspective pasteurization was initially advocated for cheesemaking in the early twentieth century because it resulted in decreased variability in cheese quality. At the time bacterial counts in milk often exceeded 2 million colony-forming units per milliliter of milk, over one hundred times what we find today in hygienically produced milk. See COLONY-FORMING UNIT. The microbial species present in milk have a significant influence on the development of flavor in cheese, both desirable and undesirable. Strong evidence is accruing that the diversity of species present in the milk is crucial to flavor development. Pasteurization decreases the diversity of the milk by destroying the majority of the species present.

In the production of raw-milk cheese, it is critical to have controls in place over the milk production and handling that keep pathogens from getting into the milk in the first place. This necessitates a meticulous approach to keeping milk from any diseased animals carefully segregated and strict attention to proper cleaning and sanitation of the teats, equipment, and people that the milk comes into contact with up to the point that it enters the vat. It also requires that attention be paid to the way the milk is handled, as prolonged refrigeration can favor the growth of cold-loving ("psychrotrophic") bacteria that would be destroyed by pasteurization, but can subsequently cause spoilage in a raw-milk cheese.

A second approach to controlling pathogens is to ensure that the cheese has a sufficient set of physicochemical characteristics (high acidity and low water activity) that pathogens will not grow even if the milk is contaminated. Cheeses that meet these conditions if made properly include hard and long-aged cheeses such as Parmigiano Reggiano. Needless to say, cheeses with low acidity and high water activity do support the growth of pathogenic bacteria if they are present. This characteristic is a more relevant indicator of its potential risk than whether or not it is made with raw milk. Cheeses that have high moisture and low acidity can support the growth of any pathogens present in the milk, but for the same reasons they also are more susceptible to post-pasteurization contamination, whose effects can be just as dangerous. Soft high moisture cheeses have been implicated in almost all the cheese recalls due to the presence of pathogens, regardless of the heat-treatment status of the milk. See POST-PROCESS CONTAMINATION.

Regardless of the type of cheese being produced, attempting to rely on the characteristics of the cheese to control the growth of pathogens rather than the hygiene of the raw materials is contrary to the tenets of responsible cheesemaking. To be of high quality all cheeses require the use of carefully produced raw materials; raw-milk cheese require them to be impeccable. Producers who cannot consistently produce milk that is free of pathogens and spoilage bacteria must incorporate downstream controls such as pasteurization to control those risks effectively.

An important issue for advocates of raw-milk cheese is flavor quality. Most of the flavor in cheese is the result of a combination of microbial metabolism and the activity of enzymes both deliberately added and naturally present in milk. The loss of microbial species and native enzymes as the result of pasteurization may result in a loss of flavor elements that give raw-milk cheese the special complexity so cherished by consumers. Whether this complexity results in desirable cheese flavor or not will be dependent on the types of bacteria in the raw milk, the cheesemaker's level of technical control over the physical characteristics of the cheese (salt, moisture, acidity), and ultimately the taste of the individual consumer.

Consumers value raw-milk cheese both for the assurance they provide about the quality of the milk used to make them (there is no option for carelessness or corner-cutting when there is no pasteurization step downstream in the process), and for the extra complexity and length of flavor that they can deliver when made carefully and sensitively. It is entirely possible to make raw-milk cheeses that are awkwardly acidic and bitter as the result of misuse of starter and rennet during the cheese make, just as it is for pasteurized cheeses. In fact, in American cheese competitions the most common flavor faults cited with cheeses made from either raw or pasteurized milk are exactly those. Poorly made raw-milk cheese may taste "animal"-like or dirty, even if they do not contain pathogens. Most judges of cheese and cheese consumers alike would consider these to be defects, even if they are enjoyed by a few. Conversely the most often cited criticism of pasteurized cheeses is that they lack flavor complexity (also known as tasting "flat"), even if they also taste "clean." See DEFECTS. To increase desirable flavor notes in pasteurized milk cheeses the addition of specific flavor-producing bacteria and enzymes to the milk is often relied upon in the form of adjunct cultures. See ADJUNCT CULTURES. Not surprisingly, many raw-milk cheese also add the same bacteria and enzymes to alter the flavor profile of their cheeses.

See also EQUIVALENCE OF PASTEURIZATION; FOOD AND DRUG ADMINISTRATION; and 60-DAY AGING RULE.

Bouton, Y. "Incidences du niveau de flore d'un lait de fabrication sur la qualité d'un fromage à pate pressée cuite." Les Nouvelles du Comté 30 (2000): 1–4.
Code of Hygienic Practice for Milk and Milk Products. http://media.wix.com/ugd/76ddc6_0dcf14d581c44dc6a808dc4411d5b52e.pdf.
D'Amico, Dennis. "Microbiological Quality and Safety Issues in Cheesemaking." In Cheese and Microbes, edited by Catherine Donnelly, pp. 251–309. Washington, D.C.: ASM Press, 2014.
Donnelly, C. W. "The Pasteurization Dilemma." In American Farmstead Cheese, edited by Paul S. Kindstedt, pp. 173–195. White River Junction, Vt.: Chelsea Green, 2005.
European Commission. Commission Regulation (EC) no. 1441/2007 5 December 2007 amending regulation (EC) No. 2073/2005 on microbiological criteria for foodstuffs. Official Journal of the European Commission L322 (2007): 1–29.

Mark E. Johnson and Bronwen Percival

Reblochon, or Reblochon de Savoie, is a semi-hard cheese made with raw whole cow's milk in the Haute-Savoie and Savoie departments in the Alpine regions located in the eastern part of France. It is a flat disc-shaped cheese with a diameter of 5 inches (13–14 centimeters), around 1½–2 inches (3–3.5 centimeters) high, weighing 16–19 ounces (450–550 grams). A smaller version of Reblochon cheese also exists, having a diameter of 3 inches (9 centimeters) and weighing 8–10 ounces (240–280 grams). It has an ivory-colored and a creamy and supple body, and a yellow-orange rind covered with a thin white mold. Reblochon cheese has a protected designation of origin (PDO) label, obtained in 1958. Around 15,300 metric tons of Reblochon cheeses are produced each year, of which about 2,000 tons are fermier (farm-produced). See FERMIER.

Reblochon is produced in dairies or cooperatives (Reblochon laitier), or on farms (Reblochon fermier). The milk comes from Montbéliarde, Tarine (also called Tarentaise), or Abondance cows. See MONTBÉLIARDE and ABONDANCE. The cooperative- or dairy-produced Reblochon is made once a day, from a blend of the milks from several different farms. Some operations are mechanized; it has a red casein disc as a label. The farm-produced Reblochon is made twice a day directly after milking and from the milk of a single herd. Its production is entirely manual (curd cutting, stirring, molding, and turning of the cheeses); its label is a green casein disc. Each year most of the farm producers return, from the end of May to September, to high mountain pastures with their cattle. Farm-produced Reblochon always carries the farm-produced logo "Reblochon fermier" on its packaging.

The name Reblochon derives from the patois term reblocher which means "to pinch the cow's udder a second time." In the thirteenth century the farmers of the Thônes valley in Haute-Savoie were taxed by landowners (monks or nobles) according to the amount of milk their herds produced. When farmers were controlled by the inspector, they would not fully milk their cows until the yield was measured; thus they paid less tax to the landowners. After the control they milked the cows a second time (pinched their udder) and immediately used this milk, rich in fat, to manufacture a cheese that became known as Reblochon. The cheese was secretly eaten only by the family of the farmer. At the beginning of the twentieth century, only

Reblochon, a semihard cheese made with raw whole cow's milk in the Haute-Savoie and Savoie departments of France. COURTESY OF COOPÉRATIVE DU REBLOCHON FERMIER

40 tons of Reblochon were produced. However, with the development of railways, tourism, and winter sports, Reblochon's fame rapidly increased across France.

Only raw whole cow's milk is used. Starters used are composed of *Streptococcus thermophilus* and *Lactobacillus delbrueckii* subsp. *bulgaricus*; sometimes *Lactococcus lactis* strains are also used. Thermophilic starters (streptococci and lactobacilli) come from yogurt cultures or from strains isolated in the past from Reblochon fermier wherein no commercial starters were used. See STARTER CULTURES. Milk is curdled in less than an hour through the addition of natural rennet. After molding cheeses are slightly pressed using a weight (2–4 pounds [1–2 kilograms]) on them for a few hours, allowing the excess whey to drain off. After brining cheeses are held in a pre-ripening cellar (*séchoir*) at 57–61°F (14–16°C) for four to seven days; this step allows the growth of yeasts, important for the maturation of Reblochon cheeses. Then cheeses are placed in a ripening cellar at 54°F (12°C). In these two cellars cheeses are regularly turned and rubbed with brine. The optimal period of Reblochon cheese ripening is four to five weeks. Reblochon is an ingredient in one of the best loved Alp dishes, tartiflette.

See HAUTE-SAVOIE and TARTIFLETTE.

Froc, Jean. *Balade au pays des fromages: Les traditions fromagères en France*. Versailles, France: Editions Quae, Inra, 2006.

Lanquetin, Didier. "Le Reblochon de Savoie A.O.C." *Revue des ENILs* 266 (2002): 34–36.

Martin, Bruno, and Jean-Baptiste Coulon. "Facteurs de production du lait et caractéristiques des fromages. II. Influence des caractéristiques des laits de troupeaux et des pratiques fromagères sur les caractéristiques du reblochon de Savoie fermier." *Le Lait* 75 (1995): 133–149.

Reblochon de Savoie. http://www.reblochon.fr.

Eric Beuvier

Red Hawk is a small, triple-cream (75 percent fat in dry matter), washed-rind cow's milk cheese manufactured by Cowgirl Creamery in Marin County, California. Red Hawk is made with pasteurized, organic milk and cream from the nearby Straus Family Creamery using vegetarian rennet. Each round weighs about 10 ounces. During its maturation of approximately four weeks, the cheese is regularly washed with brine to encourage bacterial growth on the rind. Red Hawk is only produced in Cowgirl Creamery's Point Reyes Station facility, near Tomales Bay and the Pacific Ocean, which the lead cheesemaker, Maureen Cunnie, believes lends the aging room a unique microbial environment, filled with a cocktail of marine bacteria.

Red Hawk is a soft, creamy cheese with a pungent, fruity, and slightly beefy flavor. It takes its name from the red-tailed hawks that are frequently seen in the area around Point Reyes. Red Hawk won Best in Show accolades at the American Cheese Society conference in 2003.

See also CALIFORNIA and COWGIRL CREAMERY.

Cowgirl Creamery. https://cowgirlcreamery.com.

Davies, Sasha. *The Guide to West Coast Cheeses: More than 300 Cheeses Handcrafted in California, Oregon, and Washington*. Portland, Ore.: Timber, 2010.

Anne Saxelby

Red Leicester, or "Leicester" (pronounced "lester"), is a hard British cow's milk cheese originating from the English county of Leicestershire. Although flatter and broader than many of its English counterparts, Red Leicester's traditional cylindrical form is similar to other British "territorial" cheeses such as Cheddar or Double Gloucester, and is made using the same manufacturing methods (e.g., scalding, cheddaring, pressing, cloth binding). See TERRITORIAL. A finished cheese would be around 6 inches

Sparkenhoe Red Leicester, made by David and Jo Clarke at their small dairy farm in the southwest Leicestershire countryside, is the only traditional Red Leicester as of 2016. This cheese gets its distinct reddish-orange color from the addition of annatto, a natural colorant extracted from dried seeds. © KATE ARDING

(15 centimeters) deep, 20 inches (51 centimeters) across, and weigh approximately 44 pounds (20 kilograms). However, currently, the vast majority of Red Leicester consumed is produced in a rindless, industrial block format, which is stored and prepackaged in plastic.

In all forms, Red Leicester has a distinct reddish-orange color derived from the addition of annatto, a naturally occurring food colorant. See ANNATTO. Historically this practice became common for a number of British cheeses, the vivid color being reminiscent of the exclusive high fat, pasture-grazed cheeses, which were available to the affluent members of seventeenth- and eighteenth-century society.

Leicestershire has been a cheese producing region for several hundred years and a permanent cheese market was established in the town of Leicester in 1759. The majority of the Red Leicester produced within the county was consumed locally but a proportion reached farther afield, including London, most likely along the same distribution channels as Leicestershire's most famous cheese, Stilton. As a hard pressed cheese, Red Leicester had a longer shelf life than Stilton, and it is likely the two varieties were made side by side allowing producers greater flexibility in the market place. See STILTON.

The first factory-produced Red Leicester was made in 1875 and farmhouse production, unable to compete, consequently fell into steep decline. During World War II food rationing was implemented in Britain and the majority of cheese production shifted to large centralized creameries. In addition, the use of food coloring was banned, resulting in the loss of Leicester's distinctive red hue. Postwar, use of coloring returned and the prefix "Red" was added to distinguish the cheese from the inferior, "white" wartime variety. However, by this time, farmhouse production of Red Leicester had ceased entirely.

In 2006, David and Jo Clarke of Sparkenhoe Farm, Leicestershire, began production of the only current traditional Red Leicester. The cheese is made by hand, using unpasteurized milk from their herd of 150 Friesian-Holsteins, and comes in the traditional clothbound format.

Cheke, Val. *The Story of Cheese-Making in Britain.* London: Routledge & Kegan Paul, 1959.
Rance, Patrick. *The Great British Cheese Book.* London: Papermac, 1988.

Chris George

Redwood Hill Farm and Creamery is one of America's most influential goat dairies and cheesemakers. Begun in 1968 in Sebastopol, California, the dairy was acquired in 1978 by Jennifer Bice, daughter of the original owners, and her husband, Steven Schack. Along with other pioneering California goat cheese makers, they helped popularize goat's milk and cheese among chefs and natural food store customers. See AMERICAN "GOAT LADIES." Although they have expanded their production from chèvre to soft-ripened cheeses, as well as Cheddar, feta, and kefir, they have stopped selling raw goat's milk. In 2015 they were producing about a hundred thousand pounds of cheese per year.

Arguably, their greatest accomplishments have come with their breeding of goats. Redwood Hill currently has 300 goats in a herd made up of Alpine, LaMancha, Nubian, and Saanen breeds. See ALPINE; LAMANCHA; NUBIAN; and SAANEN. They have won Best in Show at the American Dairy Goat Association (ADGA) for each of these breeds. Redwood Hill

Farm has been named "Premier Breeder" at the ADGA six times. In addition, Jennifer Bice has served as a Board of Directors member of the American Cheese Society (ACS) and was inducted into the ACS Academy of Cheese (a kind of cheese Hall of Fame) in 2011 as one of the founding women of American goat cheese. See AMERICAN CHEESE SOCIETY.

In 2005 Humane Farm Animal Care designated Redwood Hill as the nation's first certified humane goat dairy. Many cheese companies and dairies use the word "sustainable" in their marketing, but Redwood Hill has lived up to this goal, fully powering their farm with renewable solar energy, as well as 90 percent of their creamery, warehouse, and offices. Redwood Hill is also well known for their yogurt, which is one of the few goat's milk yogurts available nationally. In 2010 they started producing the Green Valley Organics line of lactose-free organic dairy products made from the cow's milk of a neighboring farm. Redwood Hill Farm, while owned solely by Jennifer Bice (Schack died in 1999), includes five family members among the fifty-seven people it employs.

In December of 2015, Bice announced that the Swiss-based Emmi company would acquire Redwood Hill Farm, which would continue as an independent subsidiary, with Bice, the company's leadership, and all of its employees continuing in their current jobs.

See also CALIFORNIA.

Lentz, Helen. "Redwood Hill Farm & Creamery Acquired by Farmer-Owned Swiss Dairy Maker Emmi." Redwood Hill Farm Blog, 1 December 2015. http://www.redwoodhill.com/news/7261.
Redwood Hill Farm Artisan Dairy. http://www.redwoodhill.com.
Roberts, Jeffrey. The Atlas of American Cheese. White River Junction, Vt.: Chelsea Green, 2007, p. 368.

Gordon Edgar

reindeer (*Rangifer tarandus*) are a hardy but unlikely milk source for cheese given the animal's low yield of 1½ cups per day. Nonetheless, the reindeer-herding Sami people of northern Scandinavia, who utilize every part of the animal, have perfected making cheese from reindeer milk.

Spanning four countries (Finland, Norway, Russia, and Sweden), the Samis have occupied this harsh Arctic region for more than five thousand years, with reindeer husbandry an important part of their culture. Building on their prowess at hunting, they mastered the art of nomadic reindeer herding more than three hundred years ago.

Reindeer milk is exceptionally rich, with a butterfat content of 22.5 percent, which is more than six times higher than the average cow's milk. The milk is also high in protein (10.3 percent) and low in lactose (2.4 percent). To make cheese, the milk is curdled, drained, and pressed into a flat wooden dish, in which it was traditionally "cooked" over an open fire, giving the cheese its distinctive speckled-brown appearance.

Considered a fresh cheese, Sami reindeer cheese has an earthy flavor and a firm, chewy texture that produces a distinctive squeak against the tooth. The cheese can also be dried and stored for several years, which creates a rock-hard cheese that must be softened over heat before it can be eaten.

Reindeer cheese can be found in Finland, where it is called Leipäjuusto (bread cheese) or Juustoleipä (cheese bread). Elsewhere, including the United States, Leipäjuusto or Juustoleipä (as in Wisconsin) is made from cow's milk. Although this "Finnish squeaky cheese" has the same appearance and texture as the original, including its squeakiness, it has a much milder taste than the cheese traditionally made from reindeer milk. Customarily, Leipäjuusto is sliced and served with coffee as a substitute for cream, or it is fried in butter and served with cloudberry jam.

Ciletti, Barbara J. Making Great Cheese at Home: 30 Simple Recipes from Cheddar to Chèvre plus 18 Delicious Cheese Dishes. New York: Lark, 1999.
Harbutt, Juliet, and Martin Aspinwall. World Cheese Book. New York: Dorling Kindersley, 2009.

Domenic Venuto

relative humidity (RH), expressed as a percentage, refers to the ratio of partial water vapor pressure in the air to the saturation water vapor pressure (i.e., the maximum quantity of water that the same air can hold). In other words, RH is a relative measure of how much moisture is held in the air of a space, whether that space is a maturing room, a creamery, or the great outdoors. All things being equal, air temperature and RH have an inverse relationship. As air temperature rises, its capacity to hold moisture increases and its RH decreases at given moisture content.

As an example, a room with a dry bulb temperature of 59°F (15°C) will register at a lower RH than a room held at 50°F (10°C) for the same amount of moisture in the air. Conversely, as temperatures increase at constant moisture content, RH will decrease. The dew point is the air temperature at which water vapor condenses into liquid, and will read as 100 percent RH. If temperature and pressure are held constant, higher relative humidity means being closer to reaching the dew point and condensation. While RH can be influenced by the introduction of water vapor via steam or atomizing humidification systems, other factors must be taken into consideration when attempting to achieve a desired RH. Dry bulb temperature (T), dew point, room pressure, air renewal rates, volume of cheese, and type of cheese can all impact the RH in a production or maturing space. A hygrometer is used to measure RH, the simplest of which is a psychrometer.

Relative humidity has been found to impact the microbial growth of cheese, and its physical characteristics, such as the thickening of the cheese under rind. For example, Camembert is typically stored at 90 percent RH, while Cheddar is stored at 85 percent RH. If Camembert is stored at Cheddar's 85 percent RH, it will end up drying out and not ripening correctly. If it is stored at 98 percent RH, sporulation of *Penicillium camemberti* will occur too quickly, and the rind will be too runny. That is why affineurs take care to precisely control the relative humidity during cheese ripening.

See also MOISTURE.

Leclercq-Perlat, M. N., et al. "Temperature and Relative Humidity Influence the Ripening Descriptors of Camembert-type Cheeses Throughout Ripening." *Journal of Dairy Science* 95 no. 8 (2012): 4666–4682.

"Ripening & Aging Guidelines." *Artisan Cheese Making at Home.* http://www.artisancheesemakingathome .com/cheesemaking-ripening.html.

"What Is Relative Humidity?" Environdata. http:// environdata.com.au/faqs/what-is-relative- humidity.

Adam Smith

rennet is a natural coagulant used in cheese manufacture. It is a blend of enzymes, mainly chymosin and pepsin, extracted from the abomasum, the fourth stomach cavity of young ruminant animals, such as milk-fed calves. See CHYMOSIN. Rennet aids in the digestion of milk by these animals, probably by delaying its discharge into the intestine and thereby increasing the efficiency of its digestion. There is a myth that before recorded history, humans stored and transported milk in bags made from the stomach cavities of young animals and that they observed its overnight clotting and separation into curds and whey. By this process, they inadvertently found the means to remove water from milk and thereby extend its shelf life. See ORIGIN OF CHEESE.

Rennet from calves is rich in chymosin, the coagulant of milk, while rennet from adult cows contains more pepsin. As a result of its proteolysis, or breakdown of proteins, pepsin is thought to contribute to the development of bitterness in cheeses. Consequently, rennet from calves is preferred to that from adult cows. See PROTEOLYSIS.

Three isoenzymes A, B, and C, have been identified for chymosin and six for pepsin. Enzymatic action occurs in two phases. In the primary phase, chymosin cuts the Phe_{105}-Met_{106} bond in the protein kappa-casein and produces two peptides. One peptide, the caseinomacropeptide (CMP), or the glycomacropeptide (GMP), which is negatively charged because of its sialic acid content, is highly soluble and transfers to the whey. The other peptide, the para-kappa-casein, is insoluble and stays bound to the multi-molecular casein micelle. After about 80 percent of the kappa-casein has been cut, the casein micelle becomes totally insoluble. The milk begins to clot, and a gel of increased firmness is formed. Most of the clotting activity is lost in the whey, but the small part that remains in the curd will act as a proteolytic agent during cheese ripening. Then, in the secondary phase, the residual rennet will contribute to general proteolysis in the cheese as it continues to ripen.

In the traditional preparation, the abomasum is cleaned, air-dried, and soaked in whey. In some countries, cheesemakers perform this task themselves, using the abomasum both to clot milk and as a source of thermophilic lactic acid bacteria starters. In the modern approach, the abomasum is incubated in industrial vats together with an enzyme extraction solution made of salt, acid, and preservatives. Depending on the incubation period, rennet of controlled strength is extracted, then flocculated and filtered. In 1872 the first standardized rennet was produced by Granday, a French family company. In 1874 Christian D. A. Hansen, a Danish pharmacist, first sold standardized rennet to be used directly by cheesemakers. HANSEN, CHRISTIAN D.A. The commercial rennets are actually available in liquid or powder forms from many companies and with different appellation. Rennet extract or "rennet 520," which contains 520 mg/l of chymosin and 92 mg/l of pepsin—was previously called 1/10,000, meaning that ⅕ teaspoon (1 ml) is able to clot 2.6 gallons (10,000 ml) of milk at a temperature of 95°F (35°C) in about 40 minutes. Concentrated rennet extract contains 700 mg/l of chymosin. Each type of rennet has controlled chymosin/pepsin ratios and strengths, allowing a better control of milk clotting and quality of cheese.

Animal rennet is still used for the production of high-quality traditional cheeses, and PDO (protected designation of origin), PGI (protected geographical indication), and TSG (Traditional Specialty Guaranteed) cheeses. Animal rennet may be used in halal, organic, and genetically modified organism-free products, but is not suitable for kosher or vegetarian products. See DIETARY LAWS (RELIGIOUS).

The rennet Naturen from Denmark's Chr. Hansen company, which is purified from abomasal extract from calves, adult bovines, or lambs, is mainly developed for traditional cheesemaking. It is available in different chymosin/pepsin ratios in liquid or powder forms. Carlina is produced by Danisco-DuPont for all cheese types and for traditional cheesemaking. Rennet extracts can contain 0.5 percent to 1 percent sodium benzoate, or E211, for preservation. See CULTURE HOUSES.

Because of a worldwide scarcity of abomasa in the early 1960s as well as the high cost of rennet production from calf material, rennet substitutes are now available, as are other animal sources such as lamb rennet, in addition to bovine, porcine, and chicken pepsin. Moreover, some nonanimal sources for coagulants are proposed for lacto-vegetarians: chymosin produced by fermentation with GMOs, rennet produced from non-GMO microbial sources, and vegetable coagulants. They differ for their cost, quality, and effects. The European Union (EU) did not regulate the use of enzymes in food prior to 2009; but since that time, enzyme producers must submit applications for the use of enzymes in foods, and now the European Food Safety Authority (EFSA) carries out safety evaluations. France and Denmark were the only EU members that had their own regulations; yet, although both countries permit the use of chymosin produced by fermentation with or without GMOs, neither allows the use of vegetable coagulants. See GENETICALLY MODIFIED ORGANISM and FERMENTATION-PRODUCED CHYMOSIN.

Lamb Rennet and Bovine, Porcine, and Chicken Pepsin

Bovine, porcine, and chicken pepsin have the same proteolytic activity as chymosin on buffalo's, cow's, and goat's milk, but chicken pepsin is the least suitable for milk clotting. Lamb rennet pastes produced by cheesemakers are used in traditional sheep's milk cheeses like Provolone, Valpadana, Pecorino Romano, and Fiore Sardo in Italy, and in Majorero, Roncal, Idiazabal, and Cabrales in Spain. Lamb rennet contains a lipolytic enzyme that can produce free fatty acids, giving a piquant aroma to cheeses.

Microbial Recombinant Rennet (or Chymosin)

In 1990 the US Food and Drug Administration approved the first rennin (or chymosin) from Pfizer produced by a genetically modified bacterium, Escherichia coli K-12. In this technique, genetic material (ribonucleic acid, or RNA) coding for chymosin is removed from an animal source and inserted via plasmids into a microorganism that will produce it in large amounts when growing in adequate conditions in a fed-batch fermenter. At the end of the fermentation, the microorganism is separated or killed so that no genetically modified organisms remain. Chymosin is recovered from the broth after filtration and/or chromatographic purification and concentration. The chymosin obtained by this process is isolated as pure and is strictly identical to the animal enzyme. Since no pepsin is present in the enzyme, it does not introduce bitterness and yields high-quality cheeses, and therefore is extremely cost-effective.

Chymosin can be produced from the yeast Kluyveromyces marxianus var. lactis, from the mold Aspergillus niger var. awamori, or from the bacteria E. coli, Bacillus subtilis, or Lactococcus lactis. The two main sources of rennet worldwide are produced either by one of the most common molds, *Aspergillus niger*, such as Chy-Max from Chr. Hansen, or by the yeast *Kluyveromyces lactis*, such as Maxiren from the company DSM. Provided that no animal source is used during the fermentation of microorganisms, the enzyme produced by fermentation is suitable for use in vegetarian cheeses, but some questions still arise from the origin of the genetic material, whether natural or synthetic. Some trials have been made to produce a recombinant bovine chymosin by *Lactococcus lactis*, but the enzyme was not excreted because of a possible attachment to the cell envelope. Recombinant chymosins are approved for commercial use in food in many, but not all, countries. They account for 35 percent of the total cheese market.

There are several different types of Chy-Max and Maxiren, and Chr. Hansen has developed an enzyme (FAR-M) from a camel gene as a way to lower enzyme costs, increase cheese yield and shelf life, and improve cheese taste. Enzyme preparations are available in liquid or powder.

A large part of global cheese production is conducted using chymosin produced with GMOs. By 2008, approximately 80 to 90 percent of commercially made cheeses in the United States and Britain were made using fermentation-produced chymosin. One reason may be that chymosin produced by GMOs is about ten times more active than natural rennet. Milk-clotting enzymes produced by a pure-culture fermentation process of *Aspergillus oryzae* modified by recombinant deoxyribonucleic acid

(RDNA) techniques to contain the gene coding for aspartic proteinase from *Rhizomucor miehei var. Cooney et Emerson* may be safely used in the production of cheese according to the US Food and Drug Administration, provided that the generating organism has been removed.

Mold Sources of Rennet

Some molds are able to produce proteolytic enzymes that clot milk. The main molds used in the curdling process are *Rhizomucor miehei*, *Endothia parasitica* (or *Cryphonectria parasitica*) and *Rhizomucor pusillis*. Molds are grown in a fermenter, then concentrated and purified. Microbial rennets are less expensive than pure chymosin produced by fermentation, but more thermostable (able to function at high temperatures). Microbial proteases are able to cut the kappa-casein and other milk proteins and can result in some bitterness in cheeses, especially after long ripening periods and to lower cheese yields. *C. parasitica* proteinase severs the Ser_{104}-Phe_{105} bond of kappa-casein, while that from *R. miehei* breaks the Phe_{105}-Met_{106} bond. Milk-clotting enzymes produced by a pure-culture fermentation process from *Endothia parasitica*, *Bacillus cereus*, *Rhizomucor pusillus*, *Rhizomucor miehei Cooney et Emerson* are regarded as safe by the US Food and Drug Administration, provided that the generating organism has been removed.

Table 1. Properties of commercial microbial proteases

Commercial Name	Microrganism	Company	Properties
Fromase	*Rhizomucor miehei*	DSM	acid protease; pure protease; all types of cheeses
Hannilase L	*Rhizomucor miehei*	Chr. Hansen	acid protease; thermostable; low price; nonindustrial cheeses; liquid and granular forms
Hannilase XP	*Rhizomucor miehei*	Chr. Hansen	thermolabile (unstable when heated); highly purified; industrial cheeses
Marzyme	*Rhizomucor miehei*	Danisco-DuPont	acid protease; low price; fast milk clotting; liquid or powder form
Suparen/Surecurd	*Cryphonectria parasitica*	DSM	high thermolability (very unstable when heated); Swiss-type and hard cheeses
Thermolase	*Cryphonectria parasitica*	Chr. Hansen	endothiapepsin; highly proteolytic; high thermolability (very unstable when heated); Swiss-type and hard cheeses

Vegetable Coagulants

Many plants produce proteases in young stems, buds, leaves, and flowers that have coagulating properties on milk. Some of these include caper leaves, nettles, thistles, mallow, cardoon, ficus, and ground ivy. An aqueous extract that can clot milk can also be obtained from the flowers of the plant *Galium verum*, or yellow bedstraw. In Morocco, shepherds used to add drops of sap from fig leaves to fresh goat's milk in order to clot it. Enzymes from thistle or *Cynara* flowers are used in some traditional cheese production, especially in the Mediterranean. The enzymes called cyprosin, cardosin, and cynarase are aspartic peptidases extracted from the flowers of *Cynara cardunculus* or *Cynara humilis*, which belong to the same genus as the artichoke. Cardosin A and B are remarkably similar to chymosin and pepsin, respectively. Enzymes from *Cynara cardunculus* break the Phe_{105}-Met_{106} bond of kappa-casein. Their proteolytic activity is less specific than chymosin, and due to a pepsin-like activity, they result in lower cheese yields and higher bitterness in ripened cheeses than does calf rennet. The coagulation rate and the curd firmness are also lower, and the curd has more acidity than with chymosin. Vegetable enzymes are used for the production of farm cheeses such as Queso de la Serena, Torta del Casar, Los Pedroches, and Flor de Guía in Spain; Serra da Estrela and Serpa in Portugal; and Caciofiore in Italy. Moreover, the use of vegetable coagulant is essential in the definition and differentiation of the following cheeses: Azeitão, Nisa, Serpa, Evora, Beira Baixa, and Serra da Estrela from Portugal and Queso de la Serena from Spain. See PLANT-DERIVED COAGULANTS.

See also CULTURE HOUSES; COAGULATION OR CURDLING; ENZYMES; and RUMINANTS.

Fox, Patrick F. "Exogenous Enzymes in Dairy Technology." In *Handbook of Food Enzymology*, edited by John R. Whitaker, Alphons G. J. Voragen, and Dominic W. S. Wong, pp. 279–301. New York: Dekker, 2003.

Jacob, Mandy, Doris Jaros, and Harald Rohm. "Recent Advances in Milk Clotting Enzymes." *International Journal of Dairy Technology* 64 (2011): 14–33.

Sousa, Maria J., Ylva Ardö, and Paul L. H. McSweeney. "Advances in the Study of Proteolysis During Cheese Ripening." *International Dairy Journal* 11 (2001): 327–345.

Marie-Hélène Famelart

restaurant dining has played an important role in the popularization of European cheeses, and also in European ways of eating cheese—especially as part of the dessert course—in the United States. Young Americans who visited Paris in the late 1960s and early 1970s discovered fine cheese shops and, in restaurants, exquisite collections of cheese on rolling carts that captured the imagination of tourists and Parisians alike. Androuët, the Parisian cheese shop and cheese-centric restaurant, was an iconic benchmark for a fantasized European and French model for living. See ANDROUËT.

In 1978 a young woman raised on a turkey farm in Santa Rosa, California, returned from a transformative trip to France to start what would become the United States' first enduring business to produce a fresh goat cheese: Laura Chenel California Chèvre. The little rounds of the cheese ended up coated in seasoned bread crumbs and baked, then set on a plate with seasonal salad greens at the soon-to-be legendary restaurant Chez Panisse in Berkeley, California. Thus began a wave of fresh goat cheese on restaurant menus across America. See LAURA CHENEL'S CHÈVRE and AMERICAN "GOAT LADIES."

In the late 1980s and early 1990s, several developments coalesced to propel cheese onto the menus of restaurants across the country. While artisanal cheesemaking in America was advancing by leaps and bounds, historically significant and classical English cheesemaking was also being resuscitated. New ingredients, fine cheeses among them—at first mostly from France and Italy, and later from Spain—were brought to the United States and promoted, and they found favor among chefs who were themselves becoming celebrities and style makers.

An era with great focus on pairing wine with food quickly followed, exposing the country to a broad range of international foods and cheeses, despite evidence that cheese and wine are not always a great match (a University of California, Davis, scientific study found that some of the nuance of a red wine is lost with butterfat in the mouth). Today, one of the bestselling menu items in casual and fairly sophisticated restaurants alike is an artisan cheese plate or a platter (or board or slab of slate), sometimes including hand-cured meats, along with diverse accompaniments. Cheese plates are also popular at artisan brewpubs, and beer is arguably a better match for cheese. See WINE PAIRING; BEER PAIRING; and CHEESE COURSE.

Today many chefs consistently have on hand some Parmigiano Reggiano, an aged Gruyère, and a well-made local goat cheese. Chefs and restaurant workers now need to be familiar with the various families of cheeses to be credible practitioners of the farm-to-table movement so prevalent in contemporary public dining.

Cheese is all over the American menu, from freshly pulled mozzarella on handmade Neapolitan pizzas to upscale, creative grilled cheese sandwiches; from grand luxe macaroni and cheese with shaved black truffles to highly creative tacos sprinkled with the latest or most classical dried, fresh Mexican-style cheese (these cheeses cannot be imported, so they are made in a classical Mexican style). None of this is to be confused with the massive amounts of industrial cheese used in the food service industry.

Fletcher, Janet. *The Cheese Course: Enjoying the World's Best Cheeses at Your Table.* San Francisco: Chronicle, 2000.

Lambert, Paula. *Cheese, Glorious Cheese: More Than 75 Tempting Recipes for Cheese Lovers Everywhere.* New York: Simon & Schuster, 2007.

Wolf, Clark. *American Cheeses: The Best Regional, Artisan, and Farmhouse Cheeses, Who Makes Them, and Where to Find Them.* New York: Simon and Schuster, 2008.

Clark Wolf

The **Richmond Hill Café and Larder** in

Melbourne, Australia, was opened in 1997 by a partnership including renowned cook and restaurateur Stephanie Alexander and cheese importer Will Studd. While neither is still associated with the business, the original concept of a cheese shop and produce store within a neighborhood café and restaurant remains largely unchanged. The Cheese Room was the first walk-in, temperature-controlled fromagerie in Melbourne, and while many in Australia have copied the concept, few have replicated it successfully.

Cheeses are displayed and matured on wooden shelving, tasting is encouraged, and all cheeses are cut and wrapped to order by enthusiastic and knowledgeable staff. The range includes Australian artisan cheeses from small farmstead producers, as well as established local brands and benchmark cheeses from Europe. The cheesemongers work closely with local suppliers and importers to ensure the range changes frequently and is seasonally appropriate. Cheese accompaniments, made in house by the restaurant chefs, are available for sale in the produce store. One of the unique features of The Cheese Room is that cheeses are always showcased on the café and restaurant menu, either incorporated into dishes or simply to enjoy as a cheese platter. An online shop and Cheese Club (offering exclusive cheese selections throughout the year, and discounts on purchases) service cheese lovers Australia-wide, and cheese appreciation events, such as cheese and wine matching workshops, are hosted regularly.

See also AUSTRALIA AND NEW ZEALAND.

Richmond Hill Cafe and Larder. http://www.rhcl.com .au/the-cheese-room.

Sonia Cousins

ricotta cheese is a product of the heat-acid coagulation of proteins in sweet whey. It is white, grainy, soft, moist, sweet, and slightly creamy, depending on how much cream is added to the curd. Perhaps the first reference to ricotta cheese was made during the years 170–230 C.E. by the Greek writer Athenaeus who wrote about a soft Sicilian cheese; however some believe that ricotta was brought to Sicily by Arabs between the years 965 and 1072. An ancient Greek cheese called oxygala is believed to have Persian origins, probably supporting the theory of an Arabic origin of ricotta. The name "ricotta" is derived from the Latin word "recocta," which means recooked or cooked twice. Depending on how the term "cheese" is defined, some people would define ricotta not as a cheese but as a secondary product of cheesemaking.

Ricotta salata curds are drained using a cheesecloth.
© REBECCA SIEGEL

Ricotta di Bufala Campana and Ricotta Romana are popular Italian varieties protected by the European designation of origin (PDO); they are made from buffalo's and sheep's milk whey respectively, and both have a characteristic delicate and sweet flavor. Most Italian ricotta is made from sweet whey derived from the production of pasta filata type cheese such as mozzarella and provolone. See PASTA FILATA.

The procedure for making ricotta includes (1) heating the whey or whey-milk mixture to 176–185°F (80–85°C); (2) adding an acidulant (citric acid, vinegar, or lemon juice); (3) holding the acidified curd at high temperature; and (4) scooping the curd out in a perforated container. Most ricotta around the world is sold fresh while it is perfectly moist and creamy and its flavor is bright and sweet; however a few varieties of this cheese are subjected to further processing to extend the shelf life as in the case of ricotta salata (pressed, salted, and dried) and ricotta affumicata (smoked). Ricotta is a favorite of Italian cuisine where it is used in ravioli, lasagna, cannelloni, and sweet dishes but its use is not limited to this region. All around the world, utilization of whey for cheesemaking has produced ricotta-type varieties in different regions, such as Requesón in Latin America and Romanian Urdă; Anari from Cyprus; Lor from Turkey; and Manouri, Anthotyros (DOC), and Mizithra from Greece. See ANARI; LOR; MANOURI; URDĂ; and XYNOMYZITHRA KRITIS.

See also FRESH CHEESES and RICOTTA INFORNATA.

Farkey, N. Ana. "Acid- and Acid/Rennet-Curd Cheeses Part C: Acid-Heat Coagulated Cheeses." In *Cheese: Chemistry and Microbiology*, vol. 2, *Major Cheese Groups*, edited by Patrick Fox, et al., pp. 343–348. New York: Elsevier, 2004.

Hill, Arthur. "Cheesemaking Technology E-Book." https://www.uoguelph.ca/foodscience/book-page/ricotta-cheese.

Arthur Hill and Mary Ann Ferrer

ricotta infornata historically derives from the need to preserve the perishable ricotta cheese made during the production of Maiorchino cheese produced in northeastern Sicily in the area of the Peloritani mountains. See MAIORCHINO. Because of the difficulty of reaching the inhabitants to sell ricotta to, the housewives, after lightly salting the dried

Ricotta infornata production involves slowly baking a large wheel of ricotta in a stone oven, which causes it to lose a lot of its moisture, resulting in a flatter, less perishable cheese. © JAMESON FINK

ricotta, thought it was a good idea to bake the ricotta cheese in a stone oven in order to reduce the humidity content and thereby preserve it.

Ricotta infornata has a flattened round shape, a compact structure, a dark brown color, and an odor characterized by roasted notes. It is obtained from baking ricotta produced from a mixture of wheys (60 percent goat's milk and 40 percent sheep's milk). Sometimes water with fig latex is added to the whey in order to speed up the coagulation. The day after coagulation, the ricotta is salted and left to drain. It is then placed in a ceramic dish and baked at 480°F (250°C) for thirty minutes. The following day the ricotta is turned upside down in the dish and baked again until the oven cools down. This procedure is repeated as many as five or six times, or until the consistency of the product is soft and compact, with a browned external rind resulting from the high cooking temperatures. The traditional tools used are a copper boiling pot, ricotta foamer, basket, stone oven, and antique ceramic dishes.

See also RICOTTA.

Campo P., and G. Licitra. *Historical Sicilian Cheeses*. Ragusa, Italy: CoRFiLaC, 2006.

Margherita Caccamo

rinds form on the exterior of cheeses that age or ripen naturally—without any applied coating or wrapping such as wax, plastic, or mold inhibitor. Cheese rinds, also called crusts, vary greatly in how they appear and there is a great spectrum of what is considered desirable by the cheesemaker, the affineur, and the consumer.

Types of Rinds

There are three main categories of cheese rinds: bloomy, natural, and washed. Each of these groups has a very distinctive look, microbial population, and effect on the cheese. In addition, some rinds—and the cheeses they form around—are a combination of categories and created using a mixture of affinage techniques.

Bloomy Rinds

White surface mold and yeast-ripened cheeses, such as Crottin, Camembert, and Brie, have a rind that in color may be pure white to creamy or mottled with colors from other fungi. In texture they range from felt-like to thin, moist, and tender. The surface may look smooth, fuzzy, or wrinkled and moist. The aroma of bloomy-rinded cheeses is often mushroomy, earthy, and with a whiff of ammonia (a byproduct of protein breakdown from mold growth and metabolism). Bloomy rinds are developed over a rather intensive series of steps, usually taking 1 to 3 weeks, which encourage the growth of the microflora that help create the rind and discourages the growth of other microflora. The rinds on all these cheeses are edible but will have a very different flavor and texture than the interior, or paste, of the cheese.

The surface ripening yeasts and molds (most commonly *Geotrichum candidium* and *Penicillium camemberti/candidium*) used in making bloomy-rinded cheeses are responsible not only for the transformation of the rind, but their growth also raises the surface pH and gradually the interior of the cheese from a starting acidic pH, usually between 4.7 and 5.1, to sometimes over 7 (alkaline) at the surface—the softer the final cheese, the more likely that the pH is also higher. As the pH increases the moisture content of the interior also rises due to the effect that pH has on the ability of proteins to bind moisture. Both of these factors increase the risks associated with soft-ripened cheeses, whether pasteurized or raw. Once the rind of a bloomy cheese is established, the cheese is usually wrapped to limit further growth and thick-

ening of the rind. Often excess ammonia will accumulate in the rind during the wrapped stage. For that reason these cheeses often benefit aesthetically from being unwrapped many minutes before use to make the rind and cheese more palatable.

See BLOOMY-RIND CHEESES.

Natural Rinds

Natural rinds occur on any semisoft to extra-hard cheese, including blue cheeses, Cheddar, Parmigiano Reggiano, and many others. Typically natural rinds are dry, mottled, and range in color from golden to brown, unless other ingredients with color have been applied during aging. The texture of a natural rind may be dry and flaky, dry and smooth, or slightly moist. The aroma of a natural rind is usually earthy and moldy. Natural rinds are typically developed over many months of affinage. Many things, other than the nature of the cheese, will influence the development of the rind. Cheesemakers may implement many techniques for nurturing a natural rind: brushing or wiping; using a cloth moistened with a solution, such as salt water, to wipe the rind; or rubbing the rind with various herbs or ingredients such oils, colored spices, or cocoa powder. In the case of traditional English Cheddar (also made in other countries), the rind is covered with lard- or butter-slathered cheesecloth, which is pressed into the surface of the rind (called bandaged or clothbound). This coating helps protect the cheese during its long aging and in the past helped support large format cheeses during their first stages of ripening. See CLOTHBOUND CHEESES.

On most naturally rinded cheeses, the rind should be thin, with the interior paste not being affected visually or texturally by the rind treatment (unlike bloomy-and washed-rind cheeses, which experience incredible transformations due to the rind treatment). Dry, naturally rinded cheeses are a common surface for the growth of the mold *Scopulariopsis*, which is known to attract and possibly have a symbiotic relationship with the cheese mite. Together they can transform the rind into a pitted, cratered, flaking surface with a flora-type aroma, not desirable in most cheese types. See CHEESE MITES. Naturally rinded blue cheeses are sometimes wrapped with leaves to help absorb some of the moisture and give a pleasing look to the final product. See LEAF-WRAPPED CHEESES. The surface pH of most naturally rinded cheeses is often higher than the stable pH of the interior, due to the activity of yeasts and molds. The natural rind on most cheeses is considered edible, but is rarely thought of as palatable, due to its texture and strong flavor and aroma.

See NATURAL-RIND CHEESES.

Washed Rinds

Although the rinds of some of the cheeses in the natural-rind category are washed with various substances during aging, a cheese in the category of washed rinds is quite distinctive in texture, aroma, and flavor. Washed-rind cheeses, also known as "stinky cheeses," have a surface that varies in color from tan to reddish-orange and are typically sticky and moist, sometimes with a slightly gritty texture noticeable when eaten. The aroma of washed-rind cheeses is unmistakable—sulfur, dirty socks, sweat— many things not usually associated with fabulous flavor come to mind when smelling these cheeses. The surface-ripening microbes on the rind are responsible for the distinctive odor, as well as the change in texture of the interior of the cheese from firm at the end of cheesemaking to buttery soft at the end of ripening. Some washed-rind cheeses, such as Beaufort and Gruyère, also called mountain- or Alp-style cheeses, also have washed rinds, but the large-scale format of these cheeses limits the effect of the surface-ripening microbes to just the rind—leaving the paste firm to hard. In fact, this category of washed-rind products usually falls more into the natural-rind group. As mentioned earlier, there are many crossovers between interior and exterior cheese manufacturing processes.

The washed-rind cheese usually develops its distinctive characteristics during an aging period of about 4 to 8 weeks. During this time the affineur moistens the surface of the cheese with a mild brine solution usually infused with a culture mix of surface-ripening microbes. Sometimes the practice includes harvesting these microbes from the surface of a cheese near its completion and then washing this mix, sometimes called a morge, on the younger cheeses. See BRINED CHEESES and MORGE. The beautiful orange to reddish color of washed rind cheeses is now believed to be created by pigments produced by yeasts (it was previously attributed to the bacteria *Brevibacterium linens*). Washing usually occurs daily in the early stages of ripening. The surface-ripening bacteria raise the surface pH of the cheese, and eventually affect the interior pH, above a level considered protective, making it easy for pathogens that either survived during the cheesemaking process or are reintroduced through post contamination or spread from cheese to cheese during the washing process to grow. While the rind of these cheeses is completely edible, some advise not eating it due to the associated high food safety risk.

See WASHED-RIND CHEESES.

Rinds as Microbial Communities

For many years, cheesemakers assumed that the microflora—the yeasts, molds, and bacteria—on the surface of the cheese were mainly those present in the raw milk (when used), inoculated into the milk, applied to the surface of the cheese, or known to be present in the environment. But recent research has indicated that many of these purposefully introduced microbes are not present on the final cheese, even though the rind has all of the characteristics that these microbes were thought to be responsible for creating. Instead, incredibly diverse communities of previously unsuspected microbes have been found to be living in harmony, creating unique characteristics as a community. Research conducted by Wolfe and others (2014) has suggested that how you make a cheese is more important than where you make a cheese. Although where milk is collected— the biodiversity of the farm—and where the cheese is made and aged (especially if these steps take place on the farm) "confers essential cheese quality characteristics on their ecosystems" (Demarigny, 2015). Just how those ecosystems—of the environment, in the milk, and in the cheese—influence the rind of the cheese has yet to be completely understood.

See also COOKING WITH RINDS and MICROBIAL COMMUNITIES.

Demarigny, Yann. *The Microbiology of Raw Milk, Section 4: What Variation Is Found in the Milk Ecosystem and Where Does It Come from?* Conseil National des Appellations d'Origine Laitieres and Specialist Cheesemakers Association. London: Bronwen Percival, 2015.
Donnelly, Catherine. *Cheese and Microbes.* Washington, D.C.: American Society for Microbiology, 2014.
Fox, Patrick, et al. *Fundamentals of Cheese Science.* Gathersburg, Md.: Aspen, 2000.
Wolfe, Benjamin, et al. "Cheese Rind Communities Provide Tractable Systems for In Situ and In Vitro Studies of Microbial Diversity." *Cell* 158 (2014): 422–433.

Gianaclis Caldwell

ripening

See MATURING.

ripening cultures, also known as secondary cultures, form the community of molds, yeasts, and bacteria that cause cheeses to mature and evolve during the aging process. Their role is distinct from that of the starter cultures that cause initial fermentation of milk during cheesemaking. Ripening cultures are critical to cheese development, bringing about the tastes, aromas, and textures that characterize each cheese through biochemical action on the curd.

Ripening cultures may be introduced during the cheesemaking process, the aging process, or both. Conduits for their introduction are abundant. Microbes contributing to flavor development may be found in the raw milk in the case of raw cheeses, and can also be added in the form of freeze-dried cultures to cheese milk before it undergoes coagulation. Pasteurization eliminates extant microbial life in the milk; cheese made from pasteurized milk is therefore unlikely to exhibit ripening cultures originating in the milk itself. See PASTEURIZATION. Once the curds are formed and begin the aging process, numerous environmental factors will affect the development of ripening cultures. The cheese itself, based on its acidity level and rate of acid development, moisture level, salt level, and other factors, provides an environment that fosters the growth of some microbes while hindering others. The aging room is also a critical source of microbes; affineurs carefully monitor cave temperature and humidity to encourage optimal culture growth. They may also take steps to cultivate particular microbial growth in the aging room by spraying cultures directly onto cheese or the walls of the cave. Salt, used as a preservative and contributor of flavor in cheesemaking, may also contribute marine microbes that influence flavor development. See MATURING; CAVE; WOODEN SHELVES; and SALT.

Ripening cultures tend to follow an established protocol in their interactions with cheese. These microbes break down proteins and fats in the curd, yielding amino acids, fatty acids, and other components that bring about the flavor and aroma compounds perceived in the final cheese. See PROTEOLYSIS and LIPOLYSIS. These flavors and aromas are the byproduct of the enzymatic activity resulting from the microbes' fulfilling their own nutritional needs. The effects of ripening cultures are often most visibly noticeable on cheese rinds, but they are critical to the development of the paste as well. Although ripened cheeses may tend to be associated with a dominant bacterium or mold, they are in fact the product of diverse communities of microbes. See MICROBIAL COMMUNITIES.

Although ripening takes place because of the work of a community of microbes, the category or style of a cheese is often inextricably linked to its dominant ripening cultures. For example, bloomy-rind cheeses are known for their fluffy white rind thanks to their colonization by the mold *Penicillium camemberti*. The mold works from the outside in, breaking down fats and proteins in the curd to yield a creamy interior. *P. camemberti*, an acid-tolerant mold, is able to inhabit the rind of these cheeses thanks to a relatively rapid drop in pH once the curds are collected. See BLOOMY-RIND CHEESES. Pungent washed-rind cheeses are likewise deeply linked to their ripening cultures. These cheeses begin as high-moisture, low-acidity curds, which form an ideal habitat for the coryneform bacteria that colonize their rinds as they are washed and bring about the strong flavors and aromas that define them. See WASHED-RIND CHEESES. The firm, edible rind on natural-rind cheeses is achieved when sequential waves of microbes cultivated in an aging room inhabit the surface of cheeses, each making the cheese surface a suitable environment for the microbes that will follow. See NATURAL-RIND CHEESES and MICROBIAL FLUX AND SUCCESSION. In most blue cheeses the mold *Penicillium roqueforti* is introduced into the milk at the start of cheesemaking. The affineur pierces the cheese during the aging process, exposing the embedded mold to oxygen so it can grow throughout the paste and create the distinctive blue veining and accompanying aromas. See BLUE CHEESES and NEEDLES.

Historically cheesemakers used ripening cultures that were indigenous to their regions, perpetuating cheesemaking traditions through the protection and proliferation of these cultures. Today most ripening cultures added to the cheese milk and introduced by hand in aging rooms are purchased in a freeze-dried form. These packets of cultures are isolated from traditional cheeses and available for global purchase by cheesemakers seeking consistent flavor and texture outcomes. Wild-type strains of microbes found in raw milk and other ingredients, however, are thought to contribute unique flavor components to cheese. This notion has motivated some artisan producers to seek out locally derived ripening cultures that would yield consistent, reliable results while injecting the concept of terroir into their cheeses. See WILD-TYPE STRAIN and TERROIR. One recent analysis, however, found that the community of microbes present on cheese rinds is generally consistent within cheese styles no matter where the cheese was made, and that the moisture and other characteristics of the cheese itself influences microbial growth much more than geography does. A full understanding of the microbial effects on cheese aging and the mechanisms through which microbes affect cheese flavor is still being developed.

As with most other facets of cheesemaking, the scale and approach of the cheesemaker will govern the selection of ripening cultures. The effects of ripening cultures are particularly complex and variable in the context of artisanal and raw cheesemaking, in which the milk-producing animals may be interacting with a range of food sources and a varied climate that affect the microbiota of the milk. Even cheeses that have been made for years or generations may vary in their ripening trajectory because of the performance of the microbes that interact with the cheeses as they age. Artisanal cheesemakers must pay close attention to cheeses as they ripen, making course corrections throughout the aging process by introducing more or less moisture, for example, to the surface of a washed-rind cheese to cultivate the right conditions for coryneform bacteria. In industrial cheese production, by contrast, ripening cultures perform more predictably because inputs such as animal feed source, milk pasteurization, and aging conditions have been standardized and do not vary from season to season.

See also STARTER CULTURES.

Donnelly, Catherine W., ed. *Cheese and Microbes.* Washington, D.C.: ASM Press, 2014.
Jenkins, Steven. *Cheese Primer.* New York: Workman, 1996.
Kinstedt, Paul, ed. *American Farmstead Cheese: The Complete Guide to Making and Selling Artisan Cheeses.* White River Junction, Vt.: Chelsea Green, 2005.
Miller, Greg "Scientists Uncover a Surprising World of Microbes in Cheese Rind." *Wired,* 31 July 2014.
Paxson, Heather. *The Life of Cheese: Crafting Food and Value in America.* Berkeley: University of California Press, 2013.
Wolfe, Benjamin, et al. "Cheese Rind Communities Provide Tractable Systems for In Situ and In Vitro Studies of Microbial Diversity." *Cell* 158 (17 July 2014): 422–433.

Jessica A. B. Galen

Robiola di Roccaverano is a small, round Italian PDO (protected designation of origin) cheese made entirely from goat's milk or from at least half goat's milk with either ewe's or cow's milk, or both. About 110 tons are produced every year in eleven towns in the province of Asti and nine towns in the province of Alessandria, in Piedmont, Italy.

This cheese belongs to the group of "Robiola," typical fresh cheeses produced in Piedmont and Lombardia, either named for the town of Robbio in the province of Pavia or the Latin word "rubeole" (ruddy) for the color of the ripened product. These cheeses were reported in the *Summa Lacticiniorum* written by Pantaleone da Confienza in the fifteenth century.

After coagulation, the curd is cut into hazelnut-size pieces, then collected in typical molds. The cheese is dry salted and then left to ripen for a minimum of four days. There are two types of Robiola di Roccaverano: *fresco* ("fresh") and *affinato* ("ripened"). The fresco has a ripening time of four to ten days, with a paste that is white or ivory-white without holes. There is no rind. The odor is fine and delicate, the taste acidic. The paste is soft, rubbery, and soluble. After the eleventh day, the Robiola is *affinato*, and the paste is ivory or pale-yellow, soluble and crumbly. The rind is thin with white molds. The odor is intense and pungent, the taste acid and savory. Roccaverano cheese has a round form with a diameter of 4–6 inches (10–14 centimeters), an edge of 1–2 inches (2.5–4 centimeters), and a weight of 8–15 ounces (250–400 grams).

See also ITALY.

Assopiemonte DOC & IGP. http://www.assopiemonte.com.
Ministero dell'Agricoltura e delle Foreste. *DOC Cheeses of Italy: A Great Heritage.* Milan: Franco Angeli, 1992.
Ottogalli, G. *Atlante dei formaggi.* Milan: Hoepli Editore, 2001.

Rubino, Robert, et al., eds. *Italian Cheese: A Guide to Its Discovery and Appreciation*. 6th ed. Bra, Italy: Slow Food Editore, 2009.

Giuseppe Zeppa

Rocamadour is a smooth and creamy PDO (protected designation of origin) goat's milk cheese hidden under a thin velvety skin. It is named for the commune in southwestern France that is at the center of its production area. These small goat cheeses have been appreciated since at least the fifteenth century, when they featured in a monograph by J. Meulet as an acceptable item with which tenant farmers could pay taxes. A bail was drawn up in 1451 between the lord suzerain of the region, the bishop of Evreux, and his vassals that fixed the value of the tithes in cheeses.

Rocamadour belongs to a family of goat cheeses called Cabécous, and obtained its PDO status in 1996. Rocamadour producers must comply with strict farming and production conditions. The milk must come only from Alpine or Saanen goats, and 80 percent of the animals' feed must come from the defined PDO area and be made up of quality fodder and grain. See ALPINE and SAANEN. The Rocamadour PDO area includes all the communes of the Causses du Quercy, whose geology, flora, climate, and limestone terrain are ideal for goat farming.

Rocamadour is made from raw whole goat's milk. The goats are milked twice a day, in the morning and evening. The milk production per goat is roughly 2–3 liters per day for ten months. Rennet and whey are added to the milk, which is left for twenty-four hours while it curdles. The curds are then put into large bags and drained for another twenty-four hours. The drained curds are salted and then placed in molds to form the small Rocamadour cheeses. The cheeses are then immediately removed from the molds and placed on the maturing grills. The cheeses are transferred to the ripening room where they remain for at least six days, turned over each day.

The particularity of this cheese is what the French term *piauler*. Rocamadour is enjoyed by connoisseurs because of the small layer of cream that develops between the skin and the heart of the cheese; at room temperature the thin skin pearls.

Rocamadour is soft and creamy at the end of its short maturing period, when aged between six and ten days. Its rind is then white, soft, and formed and its heart has become smooth. After further maturing it becomes drier with a more dominant flavor, a stronger taste, and a creamy, buttery, and more distinctive goat smell. In 2014, 1,023 tonnes of Rocamadour PDO were made and sold. There are thirty-four farmstead producers and three private enterprises that collect the milk and curds from fifty producers.

See also RAW-MILK CHEESES and ROCAMADOUR PILGRIMAGE.

Froc, Jean. *Balade au pays des fromages: Les traditions fromagères en France*. Versailles, France: Editions Quae, 2007.

Marie-Line Gaudru

Rocamadour pilgrimage—pilgrimage to the cheese-producing commune of Rocamadour, located on and near a 492-foot (150-meter) cliff overlooking the Alzou Canyon in southwestern France's Lot department—probably has ancient, pre-Christian origins. Montaigu and Parkinson Gostling suggest it may have first been dedicated to the pagan goddess Soulivia. But the first mention of religious travel to the cliffside shrine of Rocamadour's Black Madonna was in a Papal Bull written by Pascal II in 1105 C.E. supporting the Tulle abbey's claim to Rocamadour over the competing claim of the Marcilhac monks. With ownership settled, pilgrims began arriving en masse, keen to see such wonders as the body of Saint Amadour, discovered in 1166 C.E. during the burial of a devout local. The mummified remains were declared to have belonged to a saint, probably Zaccheus, the short-statured tax collector mentioned in the Gospel of Luke, who was said to have escaped to France after the crucifixion of Jesus. Whatever the body's true origin, it soon became identified as belonging to Saint Amadour (*amator* meaning "lover" in Latin), and the spelling of the village changed from "Rocamaior" (large cliff) to "Roc Amadour" (Amadour's Rock).

Pilgrims also came to see the Black Virgin of Rocamadour, a wooden sculpture of Mary and Jesus in the *sedes sapientiae* style, carved in dark walnut wood, bathed in incense smoke, and plated in oxidizing silver. Although its veneration predated the discovery of Saint Amadour by several centuries, it was determined by the local clergy that Amadour had carved the statue and taken it to the shelter of the cliff to honor the Virgin Mary in hermetic isolation. The resident monks produced a book in 1172 C.E., *The Miracles of Our Lady of Rocamadour*, which documented supernatural healings, rescues from shipwrecks, and other extraordinary occurrences associated with the site, drawing ever greater numbers of pilgrims. In its golden age, as many as twenty thousand pilgrims arrived at Rocamadour daily, and a series of mills set up along the Alzou River below the cliff were used to make bread to feed the masses. Cheese was probably provided as well.

Although such luminaries as Henri II and Saint Louis were among the medieval pilgrims to Rocamadour, its popularity as a pilgrimage destination waned by the fourteenth century and the ravages of the Hundred Years War (which saw both the body of Saint Amadour and the shrine's archives destroyed) nearly put an end to the site. Efforts to restore the shrine and its pilgrimage were undertaken in the nineteenth century, and pilgrimage began again in earnest. However, by the late twentieth century Rocamadour's appeal was more touristic than religious, with attractions like The Monkey Forest (where tourists may encounter a colony of free-roaming Barbary macaques) and Eagles' Rock (a showcase for local and exotic birds of prey), as well as the beauty of the gravity-defying medieval buildings, enticing the majority of visitors. Pilgrimage continues in the twenty-first century, although most pilgrims now merely pause as they travel along the Way of Saint James, a walking pilgrimage that terminates in Santiago de Compostela, Spain. Some Catholic pilgrims still visit the site specifically to venerate the Black Madonna, although certain "esoteric" pilgrims focus on the site's pagan origins and claim that the location features unusual "energies."

Part of Rocamadour's appeal for pilgrims and tourists alike has always been its cuisine. Restaurants offer walnuts, magret de canard, foie gras lamb, and Rocamadour, a cabecou-style cheese that was first granted appellation d'origine contrôlée (AOC) status (now AOP status) in 1995. Rocamadour cheeses are small flat disks, about 2 inches (5 centimeters) across and weighing about 1 ounce (28 grams) each. The milk used to produce the cheeses comes exclusively from Alpine Chamoisée or Saanen goats, which are well-suited to Rocamadour's scrubby lime-

stone landscape. About thirty-seven farms produce the cheese, which is eaten in its fresh, mild stage, but also as it ages. Older Rocamadour, with its dry rind and creamy interior, develops a strong, distinctive scent, and flavor.

The popularity of Rocamadour cheese gave rise to Rocamadour's annual Fête des Fromages, which has been held on Pentecost Sunday in June every year since 1990. The festival is known for its market, featuring a variety of cheeses from the Lot and beyond, wine tasting, family activities, musical performances, and a plate lunch that typically features a grilled lamb chop, aligot, a Rocamadour salad, and cheesecake or walnut cake. See ALIGOT. Since 2006, Rocamadour's pilgrimage history has been acknowledged during the cheese festival through a formal "Blessing of the Flock" either before or after a troop of goats is marched through the village in an imitation transhumance. After Rocamadour's curate blesses the goats, sprinkling them with holy water and thanking God and the Virgin Mary for Rocamadour's bounty, those assembled turn and follow the goats to the Fête, embarking on a pilgrimage of a devoutly gustatory character.

See also FRANCE and ROCAMADOUR.

Montaigu, Henry. *Rocamadour: Ou, la pierre des siècles.* Paris: Editions S.O.S., 1974. Rocamadour; or The rock of the centuries–not much is written in English on Rocamadour's pre-Christian past.

Parkinson Gostling, Frances M. *Auvergne and Its People.* London: Methuen, 1911.

Rocacher, Jean. *Rocamadour et son pelèrinage: Étude historique et archéologique.* Toulouse, France: Privat; Association les Amis de Rocamadour, 1979. Jean Rocacher is the best-known author on Rocamadour. The title translates as Rocamadour and its pilgrimage; An historical and archaeological study.

Weibel, Deana L. "Of Consciousness Changes and Fortified Faith: Creativist and Catholic Pilgrimage at French Catholic Shrines." In *Pilgrimage and Healing*, edited by Jill Dubisch and Michael Winkelman, 111–134. Tucson: University of Arizona Press, 2005.

Weibel, Deana L., and Katie L. Kujala. "Blessed Goats: On the Melding of Church and Cheese in Rocamadour, France." *Digest: A Journal of Foodways and Culture* 2, no. 2 (2014).

Deana L. Weibel

Rogue Creamery is an artisan cheese company based in southern Oregon that produces award-winning blue cheeses. It was founded in 1933 by a cooperative to pool milk and to make fine cheese and cultured dairy products.

Called Rogue River Valley Creamery at this point, in 1935 it was purchased by the Vella and Viviani families, who were associated with Vella cheese and the Sonoma Cheese factory. See VELLA CHEESE COMPANY. The creamery was originally founded to provide cheese and cultured dairy products for southern Oregon communities; however, the company has reached out beyond southern Oregon its cheeses are now available at Neal's Yard Dairy in London, Laurent Dubois in Paris, Simon Johnson in Australia, and fine cheese shops all over the world.

July 2002 marked its purchase by David Gremmels and Cary Bryant. Gremmels is the former president and chairman of the American Cheese Society and his impressive cheesemaking experience began with working with Ignazio "Ig" Vella, as well as short courses at the University of California, Davis, and several other reputable institutes. David is at the forefront of promoting American cheese, sustainability, and organic agriculture.

Situated along the middle Rogue River and its tributaries in Josephine and Jackson counties, the valley forms the cultural and economic epicenter of southern Oregon. The creamery is named after this Southern Oregon Appellation where it operates, and the names of the cheese varieties all reference local landmarks.

The creamery produces nine varieties of blue cheese and eleven varieties of Cheddar plus two American originals named TouVelle. This is compared to the one style of Cheddar produced in 1933. The creamery produces almost 200,000 pounds of cheese annually. Rogue River Blue was honored twice as the Best in Show winner at the American Cheese Society (in 2009 and again in 2011), one of only two cheeses to win this top honor multiple times.

See also BLUE CHEESES and ROGUE RIVER BLUE.

Wolf, Clark. *American Cheeses*. New York: Simon and Schuster, 2008, pp. 218–219.

Emma Young

Rogue River Blue is one of nine blue cheeses made by Rogue Creamery in southern Oregon.

Rogue River Blue, made by Rogue Creamery in Oregon, is wrapped in local Syrah grape leaves macerated in pear brandy. In 2015 it was awarded First Place Gold for the Blue Veined Cheese Category at the American Cheese Society Awards. © 2016 FRANKENY IMAGES

It is a cow's milk blue cheese wrapped in macerated Syrah grape leaves, making it an extremely distinguishable cheese to the eye and to the palate. It was first made in 2002. Rogue River Blue is predominantly an unpasteurized cheese; however a pasteurized version is also made at present for Australian and some US markets.

Rogue Creamery was established in 1933 under the name Rogue River Valley Creamery, and was purchased in 2002 by its president, David Gremmels, and Cary Bryant. The cheese is named after the river that is adjacent to the creamery's dairy. Many of the Rogue Creamery cheeses are named after geographical locations in the area, such as Oregon Blue, Crater Lake Blue, and Rogue's Mary. Rogue River Blue is an award-winning cheese. It has twice won Best of Show in the American Cheese Society competition (in 2011 and 2009), and in 2015 it was awarded First Place Gold for the Blue Veined Cheese category at the US Championship Cheese Contest.

The milk for Rogue River Blue comes from a combination of Brown Swiss and Holstein cows. The dairy, which also raises milking Shorthorn, Normandy, Montbéliarde, and Jersey cows, is holistically managed and produces organic certified milk. The cows are robotically milked on average three times a day, and each cow produces enough milk to yield approximately 50 pounds (23 kilograms) of cheese daily. The cows are out on pasture for ten months a year, and they graze on organically certified native grasses, supplemented with hay from the farm and certified organic and non-GMO grain from a local cooperative.

The milk is inoculated with starter cultures at the beginning of the make, and *Penicillium roqueforti* mold is added. Renneting comes from organic *Mucor miehei* enzymes and coagulation takes about thirty-five minutes following the addition of starter cultures. Pre-salting occurs in the vat, and twelve hours later, after the cheeses have been in their molds overnight, they are dry-salted by hand. The cheeses are then pierced with stainless steel needles to allow for mold development and wrapped in Cowhorn Vineyard's biodynamic certified Syrah grape leaves, which have been macerating in Clear Creek pear brandy for eight months. The wheels are then aged for twelve to eighteen months.

A plethora of flavors can be discerned in tasting Rogue River Blue; no two experiences are identical. Beneath the leaf wrapping, the cheese has an antique ivory appearance, with an even and present distribution of blue and green caves and veins. On the palate, salty, savory notes initiate, transitioning into ripe fruits, with a finish of sweet cream, balanced by a slight grip from the brandy. This is all carried by a "crunchy-smooth" texture. Rogue River Blue is perfectly paired with a sweet dessert wine, port, Riesling, or bold red.

See also BLUE CHEESES; LEAF-WRAPPED CHEESES; and ROGUE CREAMERY.

Harbutt, Juliet. *World Cheese Book*. London: Dorling Kindersley, 2009, p. 296.

Emma Young

Roncal is a Spanish protected designation of origin (PDO) cheese from Navarra (Roncal Valley), near the border of France. Roncal cheese is made from raw ewe's milk, exclusively from the Lacha and Rasa Aragonesa breeds. Farming in the Roncal Valley is an ancient practice, with existing documentary evidence of this activity since the year 1345. Sheep graze all year in the mountains using the natural pastures. The cheese has been protected with a designation of origin (DO) since 1981. The DO currently protects 220 livestock farms, which have 53,914 milking sheep (head) that produce 635,516 gallons (2,405,691 liters) of milk per year that are transformed into 848,581 pounds (384,910 kilograms) of cheese.

The PDO requires a regulatory council whose main objectives are to promote and control the cheese manufacture, to improve the quality of Roncal cheese through approval and oversight of the dairy laboratories of each company, and to keep a permanent record of both dairies and farmers. An official panel evaluates the sensory quality of the final cheese. Additional quality controls involve physicochemical analysis and milk quality controls by relevant laboratories.

Roncal cheese is manufactured following traditional practices, during the months of December to July. Milk is coagulated at 86–99°F (30–37°C) for forty-five to sixty minutes, using animal rennet and the resulting curd is cut to the size of rice grains. The mixture is beaten by hand to separate the whey from the curds, which are then cut into blocks and placed inside the molds. The cheese is pressed (by hand or using a press) and salted (dry or brine salted) before starting the ripening process. Ripening takes place at 45–54°F (7–12°C) for more than 120 days. Ripened cheeses are yellowish-white to straw colored, cylindrical in shape, and weigh 2–7 pounds (1–3 kilograms). The cheese has a natural hard brown rind and the paste has a hard or semihard texture. The flavor is well developed and pronounced, with buttery and toasted notes, and aromatics of straw, mushrooms, and dried fruit. The taste is slightly spicy and it has a persistent aftertaste.

See also SPAIN.

Larrayoz, Patricia, Carlos Mendia, Paloma Torre, et al. "Sensory Profile of Flavor and Odor Characteristics in Roncal Cheese Made from Raw Ewe's Milk." *Journal of Sensory Studies* 17, no. 5 (November 2002): 415–427.
Martínez, Sidonia, Juan A. Centeno, Inmaculada Franco, et al. "The Spanish Traditional Cheeses: Characteristics and Scientific Knowledge" In *Handbook of Cheese, Production, Chemistry, and Sensory Properties*, edited by Enrique Castelli and Luiz du Vale, pp. 123–167. New York: Nova Science, 2013.

Javier Carballo

Roquefort is a semisoft blue-veined cheese made from sheep's milk and produced in the south of France.

It is made from the raw milk of only one breed, the Lacaune, and aged in the natural Combalou caves of the village of Roquefort-sur-Soulzon. Roquefort received the first ever AOC (appellation d'origine contrôlée) designation in 1925, and a PDO (protected designation of origin) in 1996. The seven Roquefort producers in the world make about 17,000 tons of the cheese annually (about 4,000 tons of which is exported). Of all the French PDO cheeses, the volume of Roquefort is second only to Comté. See COMTÉ.

Historians debate whether Pliny the Elder had in mind Roquefort when he dismissively wrote in *Natural History* (79 C.E.) that "the cheese of this kind which is made at Rome is considered preferable to any other; for that which is made in Gaul has a strong taste, like that of medicine." Whatever Pliny thought, Roquefort was undoubtedly popular in France as early as 1411, when King Charles VI gave rights to the aging of Roquefort to the single village of Roquefort-sur-Soulzon (Aveyron). This ruling was upheld in 1666 by the Parlement de Toulouse, in which merchants selling imitation Roquefort would be fined. See PLINY the elder and CHARLES VI.

The milk for Roquefort must come from Lacaune ewes, which are pregnant for five months before producing milk for seven months. Once their milk comes in, milking takes place twice a day, morning and evening. A Lacaune ewe produces an average of 3 pints (1.2 liters) of milk per day, or some 211 quarts (200 liters) during the entire milking period. The milk is collected daily and transported to one of the dairy plants of the seven Roquefort producers: Carles, Fromageries Occitannes, Gabriel Coulet, Le Vieux Berger, Papillon, Socieété (the largest by far), and Vernières. See LACAUNE.

At each Roquefort dairy, each silo of milk is tested by an on-site lab for its sanitary quality. If anything is detected, the entire batch of milk is thrown out. The milk that passes inspection is heated (from 82–93°F [28–34°C]) and rennet is added. It takes two hours for curds to develop. *Penicillium roqueforti* is either sowed into the milk before curdling, or sprinkled over the curds as they are being cut and mixed. This mold, traditionally multiplied by leaving rye bread to mold in the caves, as two producers still do (Carles and Papillon), will produce the blue-green veins that are characteristic of Roquefort cheese. The curds are then placed in molds and the excess whey drains away as the cheeses are turned over three to five times a day. Each cheese is stamped to ensure the traceability from the milk to the cheese (identification of the dairy and date of the cheesemaking process).

The wheels of cheese are then placed in a tub of dry sea salt for five days. Afterward they are brushed to remove excess salt. The wheels are then pierced with about forty needles from top to bottom, aerating the cheese. Carbon dioxide escapes and oxygen enters, allowing the mold *Penicillium roqueforti* to grow. See NEEDLES.

The wheels are moved to the caves under the village of Roquefort-sur-Soulzon (as per the PDO requirements) and are left for a minimum of fourteen days in 98 percent RH at 46–50°F (8–10°C). These caves are naturally ventilated with cool, humid air from faults in the rocks, called "fleurines." These fleurines guarantee a constant temperature and humidity. See FLEURINES. After their time in the caves, the wheels are wrapped in impermeable foil to slow the growth of the mold, while still allowing the creamy texture to develop. The cheese is then transferred to separate chilled facilities to mature for a total minimum of ninety days and an average of five months. All Roquefort cheeses are distinguished by the INAO label and a logo from the Confederation de Roquefort depicting a red ewe. The labels of the individual producers also appear.

In 2009 the American Secretary of Trade threatened Roquefort with a 300 percent tariff in retaliation for Europe's refusal to import hormone-fed beef. Roquefort producers were forced to considerably reduce the price of their exported cheese in order to sell it in the US market.

Roquefort is moist and very creamy. The milder Roqueforts are buttercream smooth with full flavor. The stronger versions might taste salty and sharp, but this can be lessened by taking the cheese out of the fridge at least one hour before tasting. Roquefort is excellent when paired with a sweet white wine or even a port. The most famous pairing is Sauternes but many connoisseurs prefer other wines such as a Jurançon moelleux. Roquefort is frequently served as part of a cheeseboard, with walnut bread or crumbled atop salads. Fruits (fresh or dry) or fresh vegetables also accentuate Roquefort's flavors.

See also BLEU D'AUVERGNE; BLUE CHEESES; and *PENICILLIUM*.

Bushak, Lecia. "FDA Bans Roquefort, Other French Cheeses Due to Bacteria Levels; Though They're Virtually Harmless." *Medical Daily*, 6 September 2014.

http://www.medicaldaily.com/fda-bans-roquefort-other-french-cheeses-due-bacteria-levels-though-theyre-virtually-301638.

Curnonsky (pseud. of Maurice Edmond Sailland). *Lettres de Noblesse.* Paris: Les Éditions Nationale, 1935.

Da Silva, Élian, and Dominique Laurens. *Fleurines & Roquefort.* Rodez, France: Éditions de Rouergue, 1995.

Rebuffet-Broadus, Christina. "The Secrets of Roquefort." *France Today,* 28 February 2012. https://www.francetoday.com/archives/the_secrets_of_roquefort.

Roman, Gabrielle. "Bon Fromage: Roquefort, the "King of Cheeses." *Culture,* 20 February 2015. http://culturecheesemag.com/blog/bon-fromage-roquefort-king-cheese.

"Roquefort, Wrecker Trucks, Tree Moving." *How Do They Do It?,* season 7, episode 15, 2006. https://www.youtube.com/watch?v=gWM_R2tDOfA.

Mélanie Verdellet

Roumy

See EGYPT.

ruminants are the world's dairy animals. Around 30 million years ago, Earth's moist climate became arid, giving rise to dry grasslands. Ruminants thrived because of their ability to extract nourishment from high-fiber poor-quality plant material otherwise useless to humans. This was possible because they are mammals with a stomach in four parts: rumen, reticulum, omasum, and abomasum. In the first two chambers, rumen and reticulum, food mixes with saliva and separates into solid (cud) and liquid. Cud is regurgitated to be chewed, mixed with saliva, and broken down further. The word "ruminant" comes from the Latin *ruminare*, which means to chew over again. Fiber is broken down in these first two chambers by microbes (bacteria, as well as protozoa, fungi, and yeast) into three volatile fatty acids: acetic, propionic, and butyric. Together these chambers are called reticulorumen. Next is the omasum where water and inorganic mineral elements are absorbed into the bloodstream. Then food travels into the abomasum, which is the direct equivalent of the monogastric stomach. There are about 150 species of ruminants. Wild ruminants number at least 75 million and are native to all continents except Antarctica. Domestic ruminants are greater than 3.5 billion with cattle, sheep and goats accounting for about 95 percent of total population. Goats were domesticated in the Near East circa 8000 B.C.E. Most others were domesticated by 2500 B.C.E. either in Near East or Southern Asia.

See also CAMEL; COW; DONKEY; GOAT; MARE; MILK; MOOSE; REINDEER; SHEEP; WATER BUFFALO; and YAK.

Kamin, Charlotte, and Nathan McElroy. "Types of Rennet." In *A First Course in Cheese.* New York: Race Point, 2015.

McGee, Harold. "Mammals and Milk." In *On Food and Cooking.* New York: Scribner, 2004.

Adam Moskowitz

Saanen goats are a breed of dairy goat whose ancestors come from the Saanen Valley of Switzerland. There were nineteen different importations to North America between 1904 and 1922, primarily to the United States, that provided the genetics for the Saanen breed we know today. Saanens must be all white or cream; a few small spots of color are allowable, but discriminated against. The ears are erect and point forward, and the face is straight or slightly concave. Saanens are one of the largest dairy goat breeds and have a rugged bone structure.

Saanens are excellent milk producers and are known for some of the highest milk production records worldwide, although their levels of milk components such as butterfat and protein are lower than those of breeds such as the Nubian. See NUBIAN. Because of their sweet nature and easygoing personality, Saanens are sometimes called the "gentle giants" of the goat world. They are an excellent choice for milk production with their combination of high milk volume and ease of handling.

See also GOAT.

Rogers, Allan. *Saanen Roots: A History of the Saanen Dairy Goat Breed in the United States.* Scottsdale, Ariz.: Dairy Goat Journal, 1981.

Jennifer Bice

Saanens, one of the largest dairy goats, are excellent milk producers and known for some of the highest milk production records worldwide. © REDWOOD HILL FARM

saffron is a spice obtained from the flower of *Crocus sativus.* The three bright red stigmas—the "female" part of the flower that receives pollen—at the center of each cup-shaped purple bloom are collected and dried to obtain the saffron threads. Saffron has long been considered an energizing and antidepressant spice; it is also added to milk in the production of Piacentinu Ennese cheese.

Crocus sativus is adapted to the Mediterranean maquis shrubland and similarly hot, dry, and semi-arid lands. Yet it is a surprisingly hardy plant, surviving frosts as low as 14°F (−10°C) and even snowfall for short periods. The plants grow best in full sunlight. Planting is mostly done in June. In early autumn the corms (underground bulb-like organs) send up leaves and begin to bud, and by mid-autumn they flower. Time is of the essence when harvesting the threads, since after blossoming at dawn, flowers wilt the same day. Blooms all occur within a one- to two-week window. The reason why this spice has historically been so expensive is because the yield is so small; roughly 150 flowers together yield only 0.035 ounce (1 gram) of dry saffron threads.

Saffron's golden-yellow color is due to alpha-crocin, the chemical that is also responsible for saffron's flavor. The organic compound safranal gives saffron much of its distinctive aroma. Different saffron crocus cultivars result in thread types that are distinct and are often regionally clustered.

In the Sicilian province of Enna, cheesemakers add locally grown saffron and black pepper grains to ewe's milk during Piacentinu Ennese production. The saffron contributes to the cheese's deep yellow color and its delicate aroma.

See also GRANA PADANO; PECORINO SICILIANO; and PIACENTINU ENNESE.

Carpino, S., T. Rapisarda, G. Belvedere, and G. Licitra. "Volatile Fingerprint of Piacentinu Cheese Produced with Different Tools and Type of Saffron." *Small Ruminant Research* 79 (2008): 16–21.

D'Auria, M., G. Mauriello, and G. L. Rana. "Volatile Organic Compounds from Saffron." *Flavour & Fragrance Journal* 19 (2004): 17–23.

Russo, E., M. Dreher, and M. L. Mathre, eds. *Women and Cannabis: Medicine, Science, and Sociology.* New York: Haworth Herbal Press, 2003.

Willard, P. *Secrets of Saffron: The Vagabond Life of the World's Most Seductive Spice.* Boston: Beacon, 2002.

Stefania Carpino

saganaki is a Greek culinary dish of fried cheese served as an appetizer or *meze* (small dish accompanying alcoholic drinks such as tsipouro, ouzo, wine, or beer). *Saganaki* means small *sagani* (from the Turkish word *sahan*), a frying pan with two handles in which the cheese is fried and sometimes served.

To make saganaki, a rectangular slab of cheese of about 0.40–0.80 inches (1–2 centimeters) thick is fried in olive oil or butter. Traditionally in northern Greece pork fat was used for frying the cheese or, by those who could afford it, butter made from goat's and sheep's milk. In southern Greece, however, olive oil was commonly used, and by the end of the twentieth century, its use spread to the rest of the country. In order for saganaki to fit the needs of healthier eating, the cheese is also prepared in nonstick frying pans or it is grilled.

The main idea in the preparation of saganaki is to maintain the shape of the cheese. This is normally achieved by creating a crispy coating that keeps the melting cheese from running and spreading in the frying pan. To that end, the cheese is dipped in cold water (for a richer taste, milk or beaten eggs may be used), coated in flour, and then fried. Saganaki is made with semihard cheeses, such as kasseri, kefalotyri, graviera, and kefalograviera. There are also regional cheese variations ideal for frying, such as Formaella Arahovas from central Greece, and white cheeses with a rubbery texture such as talagani, Mastelo, and the Cypriot Halloumi. These have a higher resistance to heat and do not need to be coated in flour. See KASSERI; GRAVIERA AGRAFON; GRAVIERA KRITIS; GRAVIERA NAXOU; KEFALOGRAVIERA; FORMAELLA ARAHOVAS PARNASSOU; and HALLOUMI.

The fried cheese is served warm with squeezed lemon on top. Outside Greece, some chefs choose to pour brandy, ouzo, or wine over the cheese while it is still hot and bubbling, and serve it flambéed. Other Greek dishes cooked in the saganaki are shrimp saganaki and mussels saganaki, which are made with feta and a spicy tomato sauce.

See also GREECE.

Kochilas, Diane. *The Country Cooking of Greece.* San Francisco: Chronicle, 2012.

Elia Petridou

Saint Bartholomew was an apostle, one of the twelve disciples of Jesus Christ, and thought also to have been referred to in the Gospel of John as Nathaniel. Scholars believe Bartholomew was simply a patronymic identification, translating as "Son of Tolomai." Although sometimes identified as the patron saint of cheesemongers, what can be said with any certainty of Saint Bartholomew's association with cheese, or with cheesemongers, is very little.

Although accounts vary widely as to his life after the death of Jesus, the most widely accepted narrative describes him as a messenger of Christianity, albeit in locations as diverse as Egypt, India, Mesopotamia, Persia, and Armenia. It was in Armenia that Bartholomew is believed to have met his end by the knife, having been both flayed alive and beheaded. Due to the circumstances of this unhappy demise, his emblem is represented in many works of art as the flaying knife. The knife, one can only assume, is the likely link and chief source of an arguably unsavory association with Florentine cheesemongers.

Only a few references make a connection between Saint Bartholomew and the sellers of cheese in Florence; more commonly, he is recognized as the patron saint of tanners and butchers, also professions for which the knife would have been an important tool of the trade. Although it is conceivable that the association with cheesemongers may have originated with medieval Florentine guilds, it is difficult to slice through to the truth of the matter.

Saint Bartholomew's feast day is 24 August. His name can be invoked against twitches and nervous disorders, and he is widely recognized as being the patron saint of tanners, leather workers, and butchers. To a lesser degree, he is associated as a patron of Florentine salt merchants and cheesemongers.

Jones, Alison. *Saints.* Edinburgh and New York: W. & R. Chambers, 1992.

Lisa Trocchia-Baḷḳīts

Saint Benedict

Saint Benedict (480–ca. 547 c.e.) was a Christian monk who lived in Italy during the turbulent times that marked the end of the Western Roman Empire and the beginning of the Middle Ages. He was born in the province of Nursia and educated in Rome, where as a deeply religious young man, he became disillusioned with the vice and temptations of the Eternal City. He left Rome to pursue a life of solitude as a hermit, practicing an extreme form of asceticism in the Eastern monastic tradition of the time. Benedict soon attracted a following and eventually established a new monastery at Monte Cassino.

The *Rule of Saint Benedict*, a written code of laws that governed all aspects of life in Benedict's new monastic community, differed from the prevailing Eastern tradition in ways that profoundly affected cheese history in Europe. Benedict's *Rule* relaxed the extreme ascetic practices of Eastern monasticism, including those governing food and drink. For example, although the *Rule* prohibited the eating of meat, it allowed for two cooked dishes to be served each day, along with a moderate ration of wine (or beer, by extension). These provisions enabled sophisticated food cultures to develop within Benedictine houses, which often drew upon cheese and eggs as meat substitutes. The *Rule* also promoted monastic self-sufficiency, which in turn encouraged both in-house dairying and cheesemaking in many regions of Europe, as well as the careful oversight of cheesemaking operations on external manorial holdings that many Benedictine houses acquired through aristocratic gifts. For nearly 1,500 years, the Benedictine Order and its Cistercian and Trappist reform orders contributed to the evolution of diverse cheese varieties throughout Europe and beyond.

See also MONASTIC CHEESEMAKING.

Daley, Lowrie. *Benedictine Monasticism: Its Formation and Development Through the 12th Century.* New York: Sheed and Ward, 1965.
Kindstedt, Paul. *Cheese and Culture: A History of Cheese and Its Place in Western Civilization.* White River Junction, Vt.: Chelsea Green, 2012.

Paul S. Kindstedt

Sainte-Maure de Touraine

Sainte-Maure de Touraine is a soft goat cheese made in Touraine, a province near the city of Tours in west-central France. It has had PDO status since 1990. The production area is mainly situated in the Indre-et-Loire *département* and cantons bordering the Loir-et-Cher, Indre, and a few cantons and communes around Vienne. A legend on the plateau de Sainte-Maure de Touraine recounts that the cheese originated from the Moorish invasions during the Carolingian era when goat breeding was introduced.

Sainte-Maure de Touraine is made from fresh, raw whole goat's milk. It comes in a log shape and has a gray-blue rind. Depending on the season one cheese (around 9 ounces [250 grams]) is made with from 4–5 pints (2–2.5 liters) of goat's milk. Curdling lasts twenty-four hours and the curds are then manually ladled into truncated conical molds. This is then drained for forty-eight hours before being removed from the molds. This is when the cereal straw is placed in the middle to consolidate the still fragile cheese. This straw has the name of the cheesemaker on it and for the PDO this is a guarantee of its authenticity. The cheese is then dusted with salted ash. Finally the cheese is matured for a minimum of ten days in a cool, humid, and aired ripening room.

Sainte-Maure de Touraine should be eaten at the end of a meal. It can also be served in thin slices with an aperitif or warm on toast in numerous recipes.

See also ASH and LOIRE VALLEY.

Roy, Nathalie. *Le Sainte Maure de Touraine: une histoire, une passion*. Montpelier, France: Éditions Mimosa, 2010.
Sainte Maure de Touraine. http://www .stemauredetouraine.fr.

Cécile Gourinel

Saint-Félicien

See CAILLÉ DOUX AND CAILLÉ ACIDE.

Saint Gall, also known as Gallus, was an Irish missionary said to have first brought cheese to Switzerland. Saint Gall was one of twelve followers of Saint Columbanus and eventually established a hermitage in a mountainous region near Lake Constance in Switzerland. After his death, the hermitage became a monastery, Saint Gallen, where in the eighth century the monks began to make cheese. The monks are claimed to have taught the farmers in the area how to make cheese, but it is more likely that the farmers taught the monks. Alp cheesemaking requires a specific method, which evolved over centuries. The monks had only been in the region for about one hundred fifty to two hundred years. However, they soon became quite adept at the process.

Cheese from Saint Gallen originally came in two sizes, a large wheel called Alp Cheese (*casei alpini*), and a smaller hand cheese. The cheese had a smooth texture with a creamy and nutty flavor. As the reputation of Saint Gallen's cheesemaking spread, the cheeses began bringing in a significant amount of money for the monastery. Soon the practice flourished and the Saint Gall region, which had expanded considerably by the ninth century, became the primary supplier of Appenzeller cheeses. These large rounds of cheese are still made in the region today. Swiss settlers learned the art of cheesemaking and it became a major source of income for the region, bringing it to the attention of other important figureheads, such as the counts of Gruyère.

See also MONASTIC CHEESEMAKING and SWITZER-LAND.

Kindstedt, Paul. *Cheese and Culture: A History of Cheese and Its Place in Western Civilization*. White River Junction, Vt.: Chelsea Green, 2012.
Strabo, Walahfrid, and Maud Joynt. *The Life of St. Gall*. London: Society for Promoting Christian Knowledge, 1927.

Esther Martin-Ullrich

Saint-Nectaire is a semisoft washed-rind PDO cheese from the Massif du Sancy in Auvergne, France. It is a pressed, uncooked cow's milk cheese, mainly from Holstein and Montbéliarde breeds, but sometimes Salers. See HOLSTEIN; MONTBÉLIARDE; and SALERS (cow). Saint-Nectaire has a round and generous shape, a lovely surface mold, a soft and tender texture, and a delicate hazelnut flavor. The milk comes exclusively from the designated area, in the heart of the Sancy volcanic region in the Auvergne, with an area covering 695 square miles (1,800 square kilometers); this is the smallest PDO zone in Europe. Saint-Nectaire is currently ranked fourth in annual production volume among the PDO French cheeses made from cow's milk, and first of the PDO farm cheeses in Europe.

Ninety percent of the grassland of each Saint-Nectaire farm is natural pasture. Grass grows everywhere on this very fertile volcanic soil, producing a richly aromatic pasture containing licorice, wild thyme, gentian, cranberries, meum, and yarrow. This exceptional biodiversity is unquestionably an environmental asset and certainly enjoyed by the cows. The resulting milk is richer and the cheeses better. This is why the specifications document for PDO Saint-Nectaire includes a prominent place for grass in the feed for the cows; the specifications state that the 30,000 cows producing the milk needed to manufacture the Saint-Nectaire cheese must be born and raised in the protected designation area and grazed at least 140 days per year. Similarly the fodder distributed to the animals must have been produced in the PDO area. See PASTURE.

Saint-Nectaire laitier is made in dairies using milk sourced from several producers; it is pasteurized and standardized in fat content. Saint-Nectaire fermier is made from raw whole milk on the farm twice a day, just after the morning and evening milking. As of 2016 Saint-Nectaire is manufactured by a family of 400 milk producers for Saint-Nectaire laitier, 210 cheese producers for Saint-Nectaire fermier, 8 milk collectors, 4 dairy firms, and 22 maturers. Both styles are matured for at least twenty-eight days. They are washed regularly with saltwater at least two times a week in the first three weeks. In addition they are regularly turned over and rubbed once a week.

The delicately nutty flavor of Saint-Nectaire is highlighted by a light and fruity wine of the Côtes-du-Rhône. It will also fit perfectly with a mineral and floral white wine, such as a Côtes d'Auvergne.

See also AUVERGNE.

AOP Saint-Nectaire. http://www.aop
-saintnectaire.com.
Brosse, Anne-Linne. *Fromages d'Auvergne: une histoire
d'hommes et de femmes*. Editions Quelque part sur Terre,
79 avenue Charles de Gaulle, 15000 Aurillac 2014.
Chapacou, Véronique. *Le saint Nectaire—dix façons de le
préparer*. Paris: Éditions l'Épure, 2009.

Marie-Paule Chazal

Saint Uguzo

Saint Uguzo (also known as Lucio, San Lucio,
Saint Uguzon, San Luguzzone, Sant'Uguzo,
Sant'Uguccione, and Uguzo Uguzon) is the patron
saint of Alpine herdsmen and dairymen, and cheesemakers everywhere. Uguzo (or any of his pseu-
donymns) was a thirteenth- or fourteenth-century
shepherd from the Cavargna Valley of the Alps
(Province Como, Region of Lombardy, Italy). There
is no reliable documentation of the precise dates of
his birth or death.

His life is mostly known by legends. All reprise a
version of this story: Uguzo, laboring as a shepherd
and cheesemaker under a master, gave cheeses as
alms to the poor. When his charities were discovered,
he was dismissed from his position. Under his next
employer, another owner of a flock in the same valley,
he continued his good works. As the story goes, with
God's blessing, Uguzo's new master's flock flourished,
his cheeses were prolific and good. The first master,
seized by jealousy, murdered Uguzo.

On the spot of his death gushes a natural foun-
tain whose water is believed to cure illnesses. Uguzo's life is celebrated in Alpine towns on 12 July (believed to be his birthday), and 16 August, also called
the feast of Saint Roch, or San Rocco. Also in
his honor, the Provence-Alpes-Côte-d'Azur–based
International Cheese Guild, founded in 1969 by
Pierre Androuët, is called The Brotherhood of St.
Uguzon. There is a thirteenth-fourteenth-century
chapel and sanctuary called Santuario di San Lucio,
at the San Lucio pass, between the Italian Cavargna
Valley and Swiss Colle Valley. Saint Uguzo is a popular saint, not granted a position in the Roman mar-
tyrology.

See also GUILDE INTERNATIONALE DES FROMAGERS.

Giovio, Benedetto. *Opere scelte di Benedetto Giovio
(1471–1545)*. Edited by Francesco Fossati and
Maurizio Monti. Como, Switzerland: Tipografia
Provenciale F. Ostenelli di C.A., 1887.
Stückelberg, E. A. "San Lucio (S. Uguzo) il patrono degli
alpigiani." In *Monitore ufficiale della Diocesi di Lugano*.
Lugano, 1912.
*San Lucio di Cavargna: Il Santo, la Chiesa, il Culto,
l'Iconografia*. Cavargna, Italy: Associazione Amici di
Cavargna, 2000.

Tamar Adler

Salers

Salers is a semihard, uncooked, pressed cheese
made from raw cow's milk in the village of Salers in
the Massif Central, south-central France. This village sits at an altitude of 900–1,200 meters in the
Cantal Mountains of the Auvergne. Salers cheese received an AOC designation in 1961, when its producers decided to leave the Cantal PDO in order to
create a higher degree of typicality. See CANTAL.

The AOC regulations stipulate that Salers can only
be made from one single herd of Salers cow's milk
while they are grazing in the summer pastures in the
Auvergne Mountains. Cheesemakers can only make
Salers during the summer months from 15 April to 15
November, whereas Cantal can be made from the
milk of other seasons. Farmhouse producers of Salers
must wait until the grass has grown sufficiently in the
summer pastures to meet the needs of the cows. The
flora that the cows eat in summer pastures is enriched
by the volcanic soils of the Auvergne Mountains. Flavors from plants such as clover, gentian, anise, licorice,
narcissus, saxifrage, arnica, harebell, and Alpine fennel
give the cows' milk a unique flavor.

The production of Salers begins immediately after
milking both in the morning and in the evening.
The raw cow's milk is whole and unheated and put
directly into wooden vat called a *gerle*. Similar to the
tina, these wooden vats are made from chestnut wood
and are rich with natural bacteria that help to add
flavor to the cheese. See BIOFILMS; WOODEN VATS;
and TINA. The wooden *gerle* and high-quality milk
means that the affineurs do not need to add commercial starters or ferments. Rennet is added to set
the cheese. After the cheese sets it is cut and pressed
into blocks for an hour and a half and turned frequently. The blocks of curd are left to mature for
several hours to allow the development of lactic
acid bacteria in the milk (acidification). The volume
of curd is then milled and salted. It is rested for another three hours before being manually packed into
a wheel mold lined with fine linen. It is then pressed
into a wheel for forty-eight hours. Afterward the

cheese is moved to small ripening caves on the farm. The cheese is matured for a minimum of three months and up to forty-five months in cave temperatures of between 43–54°F (6–12°C) in the caves. The final wheel has a diameter of 18 inches (45 centimeters) and weighs 88 pounds (40 kilograms).

Traditional farmhouse Salers producers are becoming increasingly scarce. There are fewer than one hundred producers of Salers today, as the cheese-making process is very labor-intensive and subject to stringent AOC regulations. A wheel of Salers cheese can be identified by the imprint of Salers-Salers on one of the faces and a red plate on the side of the wheel. Salers is a strong-tasting cheese with a thick gray crust and a firm paste and yellow interior color. The flavors combine hints of plant and fruit with peppery and even smoky flavors.

See also SALERS (COW).

Bérard, Laurence, et al. "Salers PDO: The Diversity and Paradox of Local Knowledge." http://www.ethno-terroirs.cnrs.fr/IMG/pdf/Salers_IFSA_2008.pdf.

Brosse, Anne-Linne. *Fromages d'Auvergne, une histoire d'hommes et de femmes*. Aurilac, France: Editions Quelque part sur Terre, 2014.

Le Fromage AOP Salers. http://www.aop-salers.com.

Swinscoe, Andy. "Salers du Buron Traditional, an Ancient Way of Making Cheese." 17 July 2013. http://www.thecourtyarddairy.co.uk/blog/meet-the-producer-salers-de-buron-traditional-an-ancient-way-of-making-cheese.html.

Yves Laubert

Salers (cow) is an ancient breed of cattle named after the town of Salers, in the department of Cantal, in the Auvergne region of south-central France. The milk of Salers cows is the raw material for two of France's great PDO cheeses, Cantal and Salers, and also, to a lesser extent, Saint-Nectaire.

Cattle resembling Salers are depicted in the 17,000-year-old Lascaux cave paintings of southwestern France. Likely descended from the "red cattle" of northern Africa and the Middle East, Salers are reddish brown or mahogany in color and have large lyre-shaped horns. Cows weigh 1,430–1,870 pounds (650–850 kilograms) and are around 57 inches (145 centimeters) tall; bulls weigh 2,200–2,640 pounds (1,000–1,200 kilograms) and are around 61 inches (155 centimeters) tall. Bloodlines of black and also polled (hornless) Salers have been developed, particularly in Britain.

Salers, "considered to be one of the oldest and most genetically pure of all European breeds" (Salers Cattle Society of UK), possess many attractive characteristics: Sturdy and hardy, they are able to forage in rugged terrain, are well-suited to transhumance and can tolerate temperatures ranging from 5 to 86°F (-15–30°C). Salers are also fertile and breed relatively frequently; the cows calve easily and are capable of producing 6,600–8,800 pounds (3,000–4,000 kilograms) of milk per year. They have strong maternal instincts, so strong in fact that they will not give any milk unless their calf begins suckling first, to be gently removed and replaced by a human or machine milker with a collection bucket.

In the 1850s Ernest Tyssandier d'Escous (1813–1889), a native of Salers, politician and agronomist, emerged as the father of the modern breed, improving local purebred herds and renaming the breed—formerly known as Auvergne—after his hometown. In 1906, based on detailed standards and descriptions, the Salers herd book was initiated and it continues, supervised by Groupe Salers Evolution, a nonprofit founded in 1992.

Salers is an ancient and hardy breed of cattle, named after the town of Salers in the Auvergne region of south-central France. © BRONWEN PERCIVAL

The breed's spread was briefly stalled in the 1960s by industrialization and mechanization and in the 1970s by outbreaks of the bacterial infection brucellosis. It bounced back, however, and is now represented in ninety departments of France as well as in thirty countries on five continents. There are approximately 210,000 head of Salers in France, about 9 percent of which are employed for cheese milk production, the rest for beef.

See also CANTAL; COW; SALERS; and SAINT-NECTAIRE.

American Salers Association. http://www.salersusa.org.
Groupe Salers Evolution. http://www.salers.org.
Salers Cattle Society of the UK. http://www.salers-cattle-society.co.uk.
"Salers Tradition." *Culture: The Word on Cheese.* http://www.culturecheesemag.com/cheese-library/Salers-Tradition.

David Gibbons

Salmonella is a genus of facultatively anaerobic Gram-negative rod-shaped pathogenic bacteria that can contaminate milk and cheese. Beyond the species level, *Salmonella enterica* are further subdivided into over twenty-five hundred serotypes including the noteworthy Enteritidis, Javiana, Heidelberg, Typhimurium, Newport, and Typhi. Despite this diversity, all salmonellae are considered a health concern producing illness in animals and humans alike. Severity and duration of symptoms of nontyphoidal salmonellosis in humans depends on the type and amount of organisms consumed as well as host susceptibility but most often presents as mild fever, chills, and abdominal pain, sometimes resembling acute appendicitis, followed by diarrhea lasting between two and six days. Septicemia and subsequent localized tissue infections can also occur in certain cases especially those involving individuals with compromised immune systems. Analysis of cheeses implicated in several outbreaks have approximated contamination levels at less than ten organisms per 4 ounces (100 grams) suggesting a low oral infectious dose.

Salmonella spp. can infect dairy cattle and other ruminant animals ranging from subclinical infections to obvious or clinical disease resulting in symptomatic or asymptomatic shedding in feces and milk. Raw milk, even from healthy cows, occasionally

contains *Salmonella*, including those resistant to one or more antimicrobials, with reported incidence rates ranging from 0 percent to approximately 9 percent varying with geographic location among other factors. Data on incidence of *Salmonella* spp. in cheese is limited but appears to be quite low in the United States and is often linked to imported soft or soft-ripened cheeses produced in Mexico or Central America.

Nontyphoid salmonellae were first recognized as food-borne pathogens in the 1880s, where typhoid fever caused by *Salmonella typhi* accounted for the majority of milk-related illnesses through the first half of the twentieth century. Following a decline in the incidence of milk-borne typhoid with the adoption of pasteurization and the modernization of milk production practices, the gastroenteritic form of nontyphoid salmonellosis was eventually associated with the consumption of raw milk in the 1940s and cheese in 1976. Documented outbreaks of nontyphoidal salmonellosis have been linked to the consumption of raw, inadequately pasteurized, and pasteurized milk and milk products including several varieties of cheese. Follow-up investigations have traced contamination back to mastitic cows, infected dairy herds, and fecal shedding, as well as inadequate sanitation practices, and cross-contamination by employees and animals. Most recent outbreaks have been attributed to the consumption of high-risk Mexican-style cheeses that are often produced in the home and other unlicensed facilities. See MEXICAN CHEESES.

Minimum temperatures allowing for growth range from approximately 43–45°F (6–7°C) depending on serotype but foods held below 41°F (5°C) do not generally support the growth. The minimal pH in which growth is observed also varies with reports as low as pH 3.7. Salmonellae are also quite salt tolerant with the ability to grow in the presence of 8 percent salt. With that, salmonellae have been shown to survive the manufacture and aging of several cheeses. Based on numerous challenge studies it is likely that pathogen growth and survival is heavily and positively influenced by higher moisture and pH values. Persistence of *Salmonella typhi* in Cheddar cheese is believed to be the basis for the curing requirements allowed as an alternative to pasteurization of certain cheese varieties. Despite several outbreaks and reports of extended survival in cheese, most cheeses appear to pose a minimal food safety risk with respect to *Salmonella*.

See also OUTBREAK and PATHOGENS.

Marth, E. H. "Salmonellae and Salmonellosis Associated with Milk and Milk Products: A Review." *Journal of Dairy Science* 52, no. 3 (March 1969): 283–315.

Ryser, Elliot T. "Public Health Concerns." In *Applied Dairy Microbiology*, 2d ed., edited by Elmer H. Marth and James L. Steele, pp. 397–546. New York: Marcel Dekker, 2001.

Dennis D'Amico

salt is a mineral used in the making of nearly all cheeses. It consists of crystallized sodium chloride along with low levels of mineral impurities such as magnesium, potassium, and calcium salts, the concentrations of which may vary considerably depending on the type and source of the salt. Salt is extracted from two principal sources. Rock salt is mined from the earth and is generally highly refined (recrystallized) into nearly pure sodium chloride for food grade use. Sea salt and solar salt, produced through the evaporation of water from the ocean and salt lakes, are often less refined and contain higher levels of salts other than sodium chloride. Commercial forms of food grade salt range in particle size from coarse and flakey to very fine.

Salt is typically incorporated into cheese near the end of the initial cheesemaking process through dry-salting, brine salting, or a combination of both. Salt dissolves into the water phase of cheese as a stable solute, and the resulting brine concentration, or salt-in-moisture content, shapes the chemical environment at the surface and within the body of the cheese, thereby influencing the quality and safety characteristics of nearly all cheeses. In fresh (unripened) cheeses made by acid coagulation or acid-heat coagulation, salt has the fairly uncomplicated function of "seasoning" the cheese (enhancing the perception of delicate flavors originating from the milk and lactic fermentation), and providing a mild preservative effect by slightly slowing the growth of spoilage microbes that quickly render fresh cheeses inedible. See FRESH CHEESES. However the role of salt in rennet-coagulated cheeses that undergo ripening is far more complex and multifaceted, affecting the microbiological, enzymatic, and physicochemical processes that transform newly made and rather bland rennet curd into the stunning array of fully ripened cheeses with diverse flavor, texture, and visual characteristics that have been developed over the centuries in so many regions around the world. A few examples will help to illustrate the interplay of salt with ripening phenomena.

Of primary interest is the capacity of salt to influence the metabolism, growth, and survival of bacteria, yeast, and molds that are deliberately added during cheesemaking as starter cultures and adjunct cultures, as well as those microbes that originate from the milk and cheesemaking environment. See STARTER CULTURES; ADJUNCT CULTURES; and MICROBIAL COMMUNITIES. Different cheese varieties require different levels of salt to promote the peculiar microbial progression that enables each variety to ripen normally. Swiss-type cheeses, for example, generally require salt-in-moisture levels of less than 3 percent so that the salt-sensitive *Propionibacterium* species, which are essential for the production of eyes and typical nutty flavor, are not inhibited in their fermentation of lactate to carbon dioxide, and propionic and acetic acids. See EYES; CARBON DIOXIDE; DAIRY PROPIONIBACTERIA; PROPIONIC ACID; and ACETIC ACID. In contrast, the moderately salt-tolerant mesophilic starter lactococci used in Cheddar cheesemaking perform best during ripening when salt-in-moisture levels fall in the range of about 4–6 percent, with an optimum level of around 5 percent. Below this range the lactococci tend to survive too long during ripening, whereas above this range they die off too quickly. In either case, the critical contribution of starter lactococci to the proteolytic cascade that is necessary to produce typical Cheddar cheese flavor is disrupted, resulting in inferior flavor. At the high end of the salt spectrum, the high salt-in-moisture levels that gradually develop within blue cheeses during ripening as a result of the inward diffusion of salt from the surface, accommodates and modulates the growth of *Penicillium roqueforti* mold, which dominates the characteristic ripening of blue cheeses. See CHEDDAR; BLUE CHEESES; and PENICILLIUM.

Salt also influences enzymatic processes such as proteolysis and lipolysis, which serve as drivers of ripening. See PROTEOLYSIS and LIPOLYSIS. Salt accomplishes this indirectly through its accommodation and modulation of microbes that secrete extracellular enzymes that participate in ripening, such as the yeasts and smear bacteria that colonize the surface of washed-rind cheeses, and through its effects on microbes that contribute intracellular enzymes that are released when the cells die and lyse (burst open), such as in the above example of starter lactococci in Cheddar cheese ripening. Furthermore salt exerts direct effects on enzymatic activities. For example, the activity of residual coagulant toward alpha-s- and beta-caseins, which mediates the first steps in the proteolytic cascades that underpin texture and flavor development in most cheeses other than the highly cooked types, is strongly influenced by the salt-in-moisture content. See FLAVOR and TEXTURE.

Finally, salt helps to define the physicochemical environment within the cheese by modulating interactions between casein and calcium, and casein and water; these interactions have important implications for ripening. For example, during the early stages of Cheddar and mozzarella ripening, salt that is dissolved in the water phase of the cheese triggers decreases in casein-calcium crosslinking, and increases in casein-water interactions. The resulting enhancement of casein solvation contributes directly to desirable textural changes, and may potentially influence proteolytic changes as well. See CASEIN.

The above examples illustrate only a few of the many ways that salt content, in concert with moisture content and acidity (pH), sculpt the ripening phenomena of cheese. The bottom line is that salt occupies a position in the chemical landscape of a ripening cheese that is virtually irreplaceable, which explains why cheese scientists have encountered a myriad of challenges during numerous attempts throughout the past four decades to develop low-salt versions of ripened cheeses that traditionally contain higher salt contents.

See also BRINING and DRY SALTING.

Drake, S. L., and M. S. Drake. "Comparison of Salty Taste and the Intensity of Sea and Land Salts from Around the World." *Journal of Sensory Studies* 26 (2011): 25–34.
Fox, Patrick F., et al. *Fundamentals of Cheese Science.* Gaithersburg, Md.: Aspen, 2000.

Paul S. Kindstedt

Salva Cremasco is a soft washed-rind and square-shaped cow's milk cheese produced in northern Italy using traditional techniques, protected by a PDO since 2011. It was originally produced to preserve excess milk in late spring or summer when milk production was most abundant; its name comes from the Italian word *salva* ("save"). Fewer than ten dairies in the production area (the provinces of Bergamo, Brescia, Cremona, Lecco, Lodi, and Milan)

make the cheese according to the strict PDO specifications.

Salva Cremasco is produced from whole raw or pasteurized cow's milk with the addition of autochthonous starter cultures isolated from Salva Cremasco and calf rennet. The curd is cut and left to rest for fifteen to nineteen minutes and further broken down to pieces the size of a hazelnut, then transferred to molds and kept at a temperature of 70–84°F (21–29°C) for eight to sixteen hours before being moved to maturing cellars. The cheese is kept on wooden boards at a temperature between 36–46°F (2–8°C) and 80 to 90 percent of humidity, being regularly washed or brushed with brine for at least seventy-five days, by which time the cheese has acquired a unique flavor and an optimal texture.

The final cheese is square-shaped in two sizes weighing 3 and 9 pounds (1.5 and 4 kilograms), respectively. The natural rind is thin and wrinkled, pinkish in color and molds can be present. It ripens from the outside in, with a pale yellow creamy layer just under the rind. The paste is ivory. The texture is compact, granular, with irregular thin eyes. It has a pleasant mild, fruity, and rich flavor, more intense with ripening.

See also ITALY.

Carminati, D. "Il Salva Cremasco." *Latte-Milano* 28, no. 8 (2003): 60–63.

Milena Brasca

Salva Cremasco is a dense, cube-shape cow's milk cheese from northern Italy. COURTESY OF THE CONSORTIUM FOR THE PROTECTION OF SALVA CREMASCO

San Michali is a Greek cheese produced on the island of Syros. The traditional cheese produced from cow's milk was given protected designation of origin (PDO) recognition in 1994. San Michali has a 40 percent maximum moisture content and a 36 percent minimum dry fat content. It is a hard, cylindrical cheese with a white or off-white color and a salty and peppery taste. Its mass is compact, with many very small irregular holes and an external rind that is often covered with paraffin. During cheese manufacturing, the addition of rennet, lipase, starter lactic acid bacteria, and calcium chloride (up to 20 grams per 100 kilograms of milk) is allowed.

For the production of San Michali cheese, cow's milk is skimmed and pasteurized. After coagulation at about 90–93°F (32–34°C), the curd is cut into particles the size of corn kernels, heated to 118.4–122°F (48–50°C), partly salted, transferred to molds, and placed under strong pressure. For a period of twelve days, the cheese is salted by immersion in brine at a temperature of about 50–57°F (10–14°C) with a density of 18–20 Bé. The cheese is then placed in maturation rooms at 57–61°F (14–16°C) and 85 percent relative humidity, where it remains for at least four months. In 2012 the production of PDO San Michali cheese was eight tons.

See also GREECE.

Anifantakis, Emmanuel M. *Greek Cheeses: A Tradition of Centuries*. Athens: National Dairy Committee of Greece, 1991, p. 87.
"San Michali." CheeseNet.gr. http://www.cheesenet.gr/english/cheeses/sanmichali.htm.

Maria Kazou and Konstantinos Papadimitriou

São Jorge is a traditional (PDO) semihard Portuguese cheese, manufactured from raw cow's milk on the island of São Jorge (Azores archipelago). The manufacture of the cheese arose from the need to address the lack of food experienced by the first settlers on the island, and later as a means to overcome the disappearance of the few crops due to an infestation by the insect *Phylloxera*.

References to São Jorge cheese date back to as early as 1574, and it is believed that its manufacture was started by a Flemish settler, Wilhelm van der Haegen (later renamed Guilherme da Silveira), originally from the Netherlands, who brought cheese knowhow to the islands that are situated in the middle of the Atlantic Gulf Stream, having a mild, damp climate and a fertile volcanic soil that supports abundant pasture accessible to cattle all year-round. Around the 1870s a wave of cattle-raising occurred, which led to more than 80 percent of the arable land being converted to pasture, with a low density of animals per area that still remains true today. By the end of the nineteenth century, the dairy industry was the most important economic activity on São Jorge island.

The cheese is made from raw milk heated at 86°F (30°C), which is mixed with whey from the previous batch, followed by addition of animal rennet. The curds are cooked at 97–99°F (36–37°C), and, after draining, are milled, salted, and pressed into molds, followed by ripening for three to nine months, resulting in cheeses of 18 to 26 pounds (8 to 12 kilograms). At the end of the ripening period, members of the association Confraria do Queijo de São Jorge grade the cheeses according to the developed aroma and taste. The highest-quality cheeses are then labeled and marketed with the PDO seal and the name São Jorge printed on the cheese wheel surface.

Studies have shown that lactobacilli, followed by enterococci, are the dominant bacteria in the cheeses after three months of ripening, with the most frequently isolated species being *Lactobacillus paracasei*, *L. rhamnosus*, and *Enterococcus* spp. At the end of the ripening period the cheese is firm but supple, with small holes inside in the paste, which is pale gold in color; the natural rind has a deeper gold color. Sao Jorge has a peppery, grassy aroma and taste. As it ages it develops a mild, mouth-puckering sourness aftertaste and becomes more crumbly. Cheeses ripening for more than four months have a musty flavor or aroma, which can be described as earthy or barnyardy.

São Jorge may be enjoyed as a table cheese, as a dessert accompanied with a slice of banana or jam, or used in cooking. After more than five hundred years, São Jorge cheese remains an important source of income for the islanders, and a highly priced product in such markets as the European Union, United States, and Canada.

See also PORTUGAL.

Kongo, J. M., et al. "Characterization of Dominant Lactic Acid Bacteria Isolated from São Jorge Cheese, Using Biochemical and Ribotyping Methods." *Journal of Applied Microbiology* 103 (2007): 1838–1844.
Kongo, J. M., and F. X. Malcata. "Azorian Traditional Cheesemaking: A Case Study Pertaining to a Unique

Food Chain." In *Food Chains: New Research*, edited by Melissa A. Jensen and Danielle W. Mueller. New York: Nova Science, 2012.

Souza, J. P. C. S. "Os lacticinios na região açoriana ocidental." Dissertation, Insituto de Agronomia. Lisbon, 1887.

J. Marcelino Kongo and F. Xavier Malcata

Sarda is an autochthonous (local) sheep breed of Sardinia, a Mediterranean island and autonomous region of Italy. It developed and adapted over a long time for local environments and needs, and probably originated from the large Asian stock. It was introduced to the island by populations coming from North Africa and its first illustration dates from the Proto-Sardic art of 2000 B.C.E. Traditionally Sardinian sheep were divided into three varieties by size: small (mountain variety), medium (hill variety), and large (lowland variety). Breeding started in 1927 with the establishment of the herd book in order to improve milk yield but also to fix morphological traits such as the white color and the polled trait (without horns). Now the Sardinian sheep is a medium-size animal, with a live weight of 132–176 pounds (60–80 kilograms) for males and 99–121 pounds (45–55 kilograms) for females. Its udder is well-developed with a large bag and teats of medium size.

Due to its remarkable milk production level and its capacity to exploit different environmental conditions fairly well (from marginal areas, in the highlands and mountains, to flat irrigated lowlands), the total breed stock has increased since the 1980s. Nowadays it is the largest Italian sheep breed (about 50 percent of the national sheep stock) with about 4 million head, of which about 3 million are bred in Sardinia.

Sheep graze almost exclusively on natural pastures in the uplands and on shallow non-plowable soils, and either on natural pastures or forage crops on the lowlands and the moderate hill slopes. From March to June the ewes have plenty of good pastures and supplementation is not usual. In autumn and in winter the animals usually get supplements in the form of hay and concentrates. Under these conditions daily milk yield and composition are strongly affected by seasonal variations of feed availability. Trends of seasonal effects usually show a spring peak for milk production and fat and protein yields.

See also SARDINIA and SHEEP.

ASSO.NA.PA. *Le razze ovine e caprine*. Rome: ASSO. NA.PA, 2002. http://www.assonapa.it/pubblicazioni/razze-ovine-caprine-italia/razze_ovine_caprine_italia.pdf.

Addis, M., et al. "Milk and Cheese Fatty Acid Composition of Sheep Fed Different Mediterranean Forages with Particular Reference to Conjugated Linoleic Acid *cis*-9, *trans*-11." *Journal of Dairy Science* 88, no. 10 (2005): 3443–3454.

Cabiddu, A., et al. "Managing Mediterranean Pastures in Order to Enhance the Level of Beneficial Fatty Acids in Sheep Milk." *Small Ruminant Research* 59, nos. 2–3 (2005): 169–180.

Antonio Pirisi

Sardinia, the second largest island in the Mediterranean, is the most important region in Italy for dairy sheep breeding, accounting for about 45 percent of the total animals raised. Consequently many of the traditional cheeses in this region are sheep's milk cheeses.

Sardinia has a typical Mediterranean climate with rainfall concentrated between autumn and spring. In Sardinia the sheep industry is exclusively based on the local dairy sheep breed (Sarda) and its production accounts for 30 percent of the total rural income of the region. See SARDA. The typical flock management has evolved over the twentieth century. In the past the problem of a winter shortage of herbage was solved by transhumance. Flocks were moved, under the shepherd's control, for long distances (often more than 31 miles [50 kilometers]) from the uplands to the lowlands in winter, and vice versa at the beginning of the hot season. In the 1960s, following the progressive setting aside of lands previously cropped with winter cereals and the favorable trend of the sheep cheese market, most shepherds increasingly became landowners and the sheep farm started to settle on the arable plateaus and lowlands. Nowadays transhumance has lost its meaning and is limited to short walks from one part to another of the farm or of the collective pastureland. See TRANSHUMANCE.

The products of the sheep milk industry have always been important in Sardinia, although, in the past, activities were based on direct processing of milk on the farm into typical traditional cheeses. It began to grow in importance when factories in another region of Italy, the Latium, started to take an interest in milk from Sardinia, due to the insufficiency of their regional dairy production. The earliest cheese factories were established at the end of the nineteenth century to increase the output of Pecorino Romano for export to North America. Consequently sheep farms freed themselves from direct milk processing, hence the opportunity to devote themselves more actively to sheep husbandry. Further momentum was gathered by shepherds' cooperatives organized in Sardinia, from before World War I until after the 1950s with the support of the regional government established during that period. Over the past few years the sheep's milk yield has amounted to about 300,000 tons per year resulting in 54,000 tons of cheese.

The main use of sheep's milk is for cheesemaking, although a small amount of milk is consumed directly or transformed into yogurt. The transformation of sheep's milk into cheese is carried out mainly in the factories at industrial levels, of which roughly half are cooperatives and half privately owned, although a significant amount of this milk is processed in small dairies by the breeders themselves. Forty-five percent of the total milk is processed into Pecorino Romano PDO cheese, which is a hard grating or table cheese made exclusively from sheep's milk; its manufacture is, by law, restricted to Sardinia, the Latium region, and the province of Grosseto (Tuscany) in Italy. In 1996 it was recognized as PDO cheese. The sensory features, particularly the piquant taste of ripened (five to eight months at least) Pecorino Romano, depend mainly on lipolysis due to the use of lamb rennet paste for the milk coagulation. Most of it is exported to the United States and Canada. See PEC-ORINO ROMANO.

Other traditional PDO sheep milk cheeses are Fiore Sardo and Pecorino Sardo. The first one is mainly manufactured on the farm by processing raw milk without any addition of starter culture and using lamb or kid rennet paste. Lipolytic enzymes of lamb rennet contribute to the typical piquant aroma of the ripened cheese. Pecorino Sardo is mainly manufactured in factories with heat-treated milk. Due to the large amount of sheep's milk produced, the dairy factories located in Sardinia also produce different varieties of hard, semihard, and soft cheese such as Canestrato, Pepato (flavored with peppers), Caciotta, Bonassai, and fresh and ripened whey cheeses called ricotta. See FIORE SARDO; PECORINO SARDO; and RICOTTA.

See also ITALY and SHEEP.

Associazione Formaggi Italiani D.O.P. http://www .afidop.it/en.

Pirisi A., and T. Cubeddu. *I formaggi della Sardegna.* Potenza, Italy: Caseus Editions, 2004.

Pirisi A., et al. "Sheep's and Goat's Dairy Products in Italy: Technological, Chemical, Microbiological, and Sensory Aspects." *Small Ruminant Research* 101, nos. 1–3 (2011): 102–112.

Antonio Pirisi

Sartori Cheese is a fourth-generation cheese company headquartered in Plymouth, Wisconsin. Founded by an Italian immigrant, Paolo Sartori, and his business partner, Louis Rossini, in 1939, the then-called S&R Cheese Company produced Italian-style cheeses including mozzarella and provolone. Paolo's son Joe Sartori helped grow the company and in 1953 joined forces with his neighbor Louis Gentine to form the Sargento Cheese Company. Sartori later sold his interest in Sargento, and in 1970 became the first exporter of cheese to Japan and Italy under the Sartori label. In 1986 Paolo's grandson and the current CEO, Jim Sartori, took the reins and in 1996 changed the name of the company to Sartori Foods.

Sartori owns three cheese plants in Plymouth and one in Antigo, Wisconsin. The Plymouth facilities are used to produce cheeses for food service and retail, while the Antigo facility is dedicated to the production of Sartori's so-called reserve cheeses, including SarVecchio Parmesan, Asiago, Fontina, and a unique cheese they created called Bellavitano. This twenty-pound aged cow's milk cheese pays a nod to the Sartori family's Italian roots, but with a decidedly American twist owing to the many rubs used to coat all but the original cheese, called BellaVitano Gold. Cognac BellaVitano, Chai BellaVitano, and Cinnamon BellaVitano are some of the more unusual flavorings.

The company's flagship cheese, SarVecchio Parmesan, was created prior to Sartori's ownership of the Antigo plant. The original cheesemaking facility was owned by J. L. Kraft and was used to produce Parmesan among other cheeses. When employees of the plant got word that Kraft was planning to close it, they banded together and bought it. See KRAFT, JAMES L. Already experienced in making Parmesan, they created the cheese they named Stravecchio. When the Sartoris bought the plant in 2006, they changed the name to SarVecchio. Today, three of Sartori's four Master Cheesemakers are Masters in SarVecchio.

Given the company's familial lineage, it should come as no surprise that the fourth generation also reports to work at Sartori. Bert Sartori works in a broad capacity for the company and his sister Maria is the brand ambassador. Because Sartori is a private company, sales and production figures are closely held secrets, but it is safe to say that many millions of pounds of cheese, and presumably millions of dollars, come rolling off their combined lines each year.

See also WISCONSIN.

Umhoefer, John. "An Interview with Jim Sartori." WCMA Perspectives. *Cheese Reporter*, 3 February 2012. http://www.cheesereporter.com/Umhoefer/umhoefer.february3.2012.htm.

Laura Werlin

Savencia Fromage & Dairy (formerly Bongrain SA) is the second largest producer of cheese and cheese products in France, and the fifth largest worldwide. It has employees in 29 countries and its products are sold in 120 countries. In addition to cheese, the company is known for its butter, cream, and other value-added dairy products. Savencia sells products at the retail, food service, and industry levels.

The company now known as Savencia was founded by Jean-Noël Bongrain, who sought a new and innovative course for his family's creamery in Illoud, in the east of France. In 1956 he introduced the Caprice des Dieux ("whim of the gods"), which deviated dramatically from the established models of French cheese. The cheese was distinctive not only for its oval shape and colorful label, but also for its name, meant to evoke a sense of elevated gastronomy. These innovative features allowed Bongrain to distinguish his product from traditional French cheeses, which were nearly all round and most often named for a local village or saint. Moreover, this cheese was also technologically innovative, utilizing a short acidification process at high temperature by thermophilic starters as well as early draining. This technology has since been employed in the production of many Savencia cheeses. Thanks to its unctuous texture, Caprice des Dieux is still appreciated and sold sixty years after its creation.

Savencia manufactures a number of its cheeses in the regions in which they will be distributed, especially in the case of specialty cheeses such as Époisses Berthaut (Burgundy) and Etorki (Basque region). See ÉPOISSES DE BOURGOGNE. The same is true outside of France: Savencia's most popular product in the United States is Alouette, a spreadable cheese made in Lancaster, Pennsylvania. Alouette's range of flavors, including Flame-Roasted Red Peppers and Smoky Jalapeño, speaks to the company's ongoing interest in developing novel cheese products. In 2015 Bongrain officially changed its name to Savencia Fromage & Dairy, eliminating the Bongrain name from its public identity to improve name recognition and ease of pronunciation for an increasingly global audience.

See also FRANCE.

"La Brebiou." *Culture: The Word on Cheese*. http://culturecheesemag.com/cheese-library/Le-Brebiou.
"Savencia." *I Love Cheese*. http://ilovecheese.be/bongrain-fr.
Savencia Fromage & Dairy. http://www.savencia-fromagedairy.com/en.

Jessica A. B. Galen

Saxelby Cheesemongers is a cheese shop that operates from a market stall in the historic Essex Street Market in New York City's Lower East Side. In 2006, at the age of 25, Anne Saxelby singlehandedly opened her eponymous counter. As the shop's sole staff member she worked tirelessly, driven by an ethos to support local and regional small-scale cheesemakers.

Arriving initially in New York City to attend art school, Saxelby discovered as a postgraduate that she didn't like spending time in galleries as much as she enjoyed working hands-on with cheese. Before opening her shop, she gained formative experience working as a cheesemonger and apprenticing with American and French cheesemakers and affineurs. Entrenched in some of the world's most renowned cheesemaking regions, Saxelby claimed cheese as her new art medium.

Saxelby Cheesemongers is best known for curating a unique selection of American farmstead and artisanal cheeses and trumpeting about their producers in the process. At its inception, the shop focused on the northeastern United States and in recent years expanded to include Midwest and mid-Atlantic producers. In 2007, Saxelby partnered with Benoit Breal.

Together the two have grown the business to include a successful wholesale department, selling to well over one hundred New York City restaurants and smaller businesses. To satisfy the demands of chefs, Saxelby reached out to mentor and friend, French affineur Hervé Mons, for a line of his exceptional cheeses. To meet increasing distribution needs, Saxelby and Breal also opened a cave-aging facility in Red Hook, Brooklyn, in 2011.

See also NEW YORK.

Witchel, Alex. "Making New Yorkers Say Cheese, Smile or No." *New York Times*, 26 July 2011.

Tess McNamara

Sbrinz is an AOP (appellation d'origine protégée) Swiss cheese with many strict requirements and limitations surrounding its production. This includes the areas in which Sbrinz can be produced, the nutrition of the animals, the treatment of the meadows, the way of storing and handling the milk and the cheese, and every step in the production of the cheese, including its maturation and declaration (the stage at which the cheese may legally be named Sbrinz). Thus, it is not surprising that now only about two dozen dairies still produce just shy of twenty tons of Sbrinz each year, of which one ton (5 percent) is alpage. See ALPAGE. Sbrinz is made in the Luzern, Schwyz, Obwalden, Nidwalden, and Zug cantons, in the Muri district (Aargau canton), in three villages in the Bern canton, and in three dairies of the St. Gallen canton.

Sbrinz is exclusively made from whole, raw cow's milk—mixing with thermized (partially pasteurized) milk is forbidden. It is shaped like a drum and has a diameter of about 18–26 inches (45–65 centimeters) and a height of 5.5 to about 7 inches (14–17 centimeters). It can weigh 55–99 pounds (25–45 kilograms) and must be aged for at least sixteen months before it can be moved out of its original production and aging facility and be sold. Up to eleven months, just before the first evaluation of the cheese happens (covering holes, paste, aroma, taste, appearance, and maturing capability), the wheels are called Spalen and often sold as a cheaper version of Sbrinz. More traditionally minded cheesemakers, however, never release their wheels before they have been aged three years.

It is mostly the water content (33 percent) and the salt content (1.3 percent) that differentiate Sbrinz—and its unique texture and taste—from other hard cheeses, including the somewhat-related Berner Oberländer Hobelkäse or Parmigiano Reggiano, to which it is often compared (although the latter is made with skim milk). See PARMIGIANO REGGIANO. Throughout its entire production process, Sbrinz releases more water than do other cheeses. This begins with a very fine cutting of the curd, into pieces about the size of rice grains. The curd is then heated to about 135°F (57°C), which expels more liquid. Lastly, the cheese spends at least fifteen days in a salt bath, as opposed to the usual twenty-four to forty-eight hours, before it is transferred to the aging shelves. There, it will slowly form a rind that will release some fat that is toweled off weekly.

Although we can assume that Sbrinz was already being made during the Middle Ages in central Switzerland as well as in parts of the Bern canton, nobody really knows where its name comes from. The most plausible explanation is based on the name of the Bernese town Brienz, from which the cheese was brought southbound, over massive mountains, into northern Italy, where it became a very popular product. Another theory is centered on the expression *Brenza*, which in some regions of Italy means sheep's milk cheese. Since cheeses from Switzerland were already exported to Italy at a time when they were primarily made with goat's and sheep's milk, this is a plausible theory too.

See also SWITZERLAND.

Flammer, Dominik, and Fabian Scheffold. *Swiss Cheese: Origins, Traditional Cheese Varieties, and New Creations.* Zurich: Shoppenkochen, 2010.
Sbrinz Switzerland AOP. http://www.sbrinz.ch.
Swiss PDO-PGI Association. http://www.aop-igp.ch.

Caroline Hostettler

scalding or cooking is the process during which the curds and whey are stirred continuously and maintained in particulate form to enable even heating and controlled moisture expulsion. See SYNERESIS.

Scalding normally begins around fifteen minutes after cutting, once the curds have had the chance to begin the healing process. See CUTTING. During this stage the condition of the curd will change from soft to firmer particles. Heating involves the introduction of steam or hot water into the jacket of the vat; steam is preferable if available, as it may be quickly shut off without any further rise in temperature. All things being equal, lower scalding temperatures leave more moisture, and therefore more lactose in the curd and produce a softer cheese in which the acidity develops rapidly during a short maturation period. High scalding temperatures produce a drier, firmer curd suitable for a long-keeping, slow-maturing cheese. The curd must at all times be prevented from forming a mat due to inefficient stirring.

The rate at which the temperature is raised during the scalding process is important. The scalding should proceed slowly at first and then more quickly. Failure to do this will cause "case hardening," in which the curd particle develops a skin on its surface, which locks in the whey, and increases moisture retention. It is important not to heat the curds and whey over 109°F (43°C) when using a mesophilic culture, though in thermophilic mountain-style cheeses the scalding temperatures can reach 131°F (55°C) or more.

See also STIRRING.

Ministry of Agriculture, Fisheries and Food. *Cheesemaking*. London: Her Majesty's Stationery Office, 1959 (out of print).
Scott, R., R. K. Robinson, and R. A. Wilbey. *Cheesemaking Practice*. 3d ed. Gaithersburg, Md.: Aspen, 1998
Van Slyke, Lucius. L., and Walter V. Price. *Cheese: A Treatise on the Manufacture of American Cheddar Cheese and Some Other Varieties*. Rev. and enl. ed. Atascadero, Calif.: Ridgeview, 1992.

Val Bines

Scamorza

See MOZZARELLA; MOZZARELLA COMPANY; and PASTA FILATA.

Schmid, Willi,

Schmid, Willi, was born in Krummenau, Switzerland (St. Gallen canton) in 1961 as the fourth son of a farming family. He felt drawn to farm work early on but realized that there would be no space for him on the parental farm where his brothers were already working. Instead he decided to become a cheesemaker, working at several dairies before opening his own Städtlichäsi (the dairy of the small town) in the town of Lichtesteig.

There Schmid gets the raw product for his cheeses, the milk, from only eight herds. He exclusively works with farmers who, like himself, respect animals and meadows and refuse to use chemicals, producing the cleanest, healthiest, and tastiest milk. Schmid pays up to 50 percent more per quart (liter) than other producers do, and in return he expects consistency and honesty.

Schmid uses the milk of cows, sheep, goats, and buffalo. Each milking from each herd is transformed into an individual batch of cheeses; not mixing milks helps Schmid create cheeses that taste different from each other and reflect the character of each farm. He has a keen sense of taste and scent, and a deep knowledge of the chemistry of cheesemaking, which helps him approach his craft in an unusually spontaneous way. At the beginning of each day he first sniffs, then tastes each of the delivered milk batches. According to his impressions he decides what cheese to make out of each one. His most successful cheeses are Millstone, Jersey Blue, Bergfichte, and Bergmatter.

Flammer, Dominik, and Fabian Scheffold. *Swiss Cheese: Origins, Traditional Cheese Varieties and New Creations*. Zurich: Schoppenkochen, 2010.
Willi Schmid—Städtlichäsi Lichtensteig. http://www .willischmid.com.

Caroline Hostettler

Scopulariopsis is a genus of the filamentous fungi that has worldwide distribution and diverse habitats, including soil, animal, and plant materials and wood, paper, and cellulose. It has a teleomorph, or sexual form, named *Microascus*. *Scopulariopsis* can grow on the coats of soft, mold-ripened, or bloomy-rind cheeses and can also colonize the rinds of natural, mold-ripened hard cheeses. In the United Kingdom, *Scopulariopsis* is mostly noted for its prevalence on the coat of Stilton cheese, where it can produce an attractive, orange color; however, it is more often associated with a less appealing brown discoloration. See STILTON.

Twenty-two species of *Scopulariopsis* have been described, though few have a strong association with cheese. Although it remains relatively uncommon, *Scopulariopsis brevicaulis* has been recorded as an occasional member of the cheese spoilage microflora. Where spoilage occurs in proteinaceous foods, including cheese, *Scopulariopsis brevicaulis* is notable for its production of ammonia, which characterizes the strong, distinct aroma of many ripening rooms. *Scopulariopsis fusca* and *Scopulariopsis candida* have also been isolated from cheese and related products.

Scopulariopsis spp. are mesophilic organisms, showing no growth at 41°F (5°C) and slow growth at 99°F (37°C). They are considered to be xerophilic, tolerating environments with low available water; the minimum water activity for growth is a_w 0.85 to 0.90. At pH 5.5, *Scopulariopsis brevicaulis* is capable of growth in the presence of the chemical preservative sorbate, at a concentration of 4,700 micrograms per kilogram. Mycotoxin production among *Scopulariopsis* spp. has not been reported.

See also FILAMENTOUS FUNGI and FUNGI.

Pitt, John I., and Ailsa D. Hocking. *Fungi and Food Spoilage.* 3d ed. New York: Springer, 2009.
Samson, R. A., et al. *Introduction to Food-borne Fungi.* 5th ed. Baarn, Netherlands: Centraalbureau voor Schimmelcultures, 1996.

Paul Neaves

secondary cultures

See RIPENING CULTURES.

Selles-sur-Cher is a soft cheese made from whole goat's milk, produced in the Sologne region of north-central France. It obtained PDO status in 1975. It has a characteristic cylindrical shape, with a diameter of 4 inches (10 centimeters), 1–1.5 inch (2–3 centimeters) thick, and beveled edges, and a vegetable carbon ash–coated rind that gives the cheese a light to dark ash color. The texture is both fine and firm, the interior is chalky-white and homogenous, and the fresh taste is highlighted by the rind, which should not be removed on eating. About 500 tons are produced each year.

Selles-sur-Cher is a commune in the Loir-et-Cher, a mosaic of moor and heath and pastures between the Sologne, Touraine, and Berry regions. Characterized by poor soil, the terroir is ideal for goats. The sandy and sandy-clay terroirs of western Sologne and the Cher Valley, coupled with the climate of this region, impose special fodder systems based on the production of hay. This hay production has enhanced the value of grasslands and pastures of little value for agriculture such as those in the Sologne, Nahon, and Fouzon regions. The particularity of this feed for the goats and an ancestral savoir-faire account for the specificity of the Selles-sur-Cher cheese.

Selles-sur-Cher is obtained from whole goat's milk and the addition of a small amount of rennet. The curds are then placed in cylindrical molds. After draining for twenty-four hours, the cheeses are removed from the molds and salted and ash coated using a mix of vegetable carbon then salt that will enhance the maturing. The maturing time in the area

is ten days minimum, which allows the light blue mold to develop on the rind. The cheese is soft, white, very fine, and with a hazelnut taste and a slight scent of goat. Its early fresh goat smell develops toward hints of mushroom and goat near the end of maturing.

Excellent on any cheese platter, Selles-sur-Cher can also be sampled in thin slices with an aperitif or used in numerous recipes. It pairs well with a freshly baked baguette or granary bread and wines from the same terroir, white or red, whether from the Loire Valley or the coteaux du Cher (Cheverny red or Chenin de Touraine). Selles-sur-Cher is best eaten at room temperature with its rind to appreciate fully all its flavors and aromas.

See also ASH.

Froc, Jean. *Balade au pays des fromages: Les traditions fromagères en France.* Versailles, France: Editions Quae, 2007.

Benoit Foisnon

sensory analysis includes a variety of tools to measure human responses to foods and other products. Selection of the appropriate methodology and data analysis is always critical to accomplishing successful results. The most basic sensory test is cheese grading, where quality is judged by an expert (grader) who assigns scores based on defects observed. The results are quickly obtained but are not scientific enough to be used in research since they do not employ experimental design and statistics. The sensory analyses used by researchers may be classified as effective (or analytical) tests and affective (or hedonic) tests. The people who participate in these tests are considered to be panelists, and they comprise a sensory panel or taste panel. For statistical validity, all samples should be evaluated by each panelist at least twice. See CHEESE GRADING.

Several types of tests are used in effective and affective analyses. The simplest are discrimination tests, where a panelist has to determine if there is a difference between three cheeses. In a triangle test, the panelist is presented with three unknown samples, two of which are identical, and has to choose which one is different. In a duo-trio test, one sample is known (a control) and the panelist decides which of the two unknowns is identical to the control. The ABX test has two different controls and the panelist determines which one corresponds to the unknown.

A variation of discrimination tests is the directional difference test, where the panelists are informed of the difference being tested, such as salt level.

Another type of analytical sensory test is the threshold test, where the lowest detectable concentration of an odor-active compound is measured. See ODOR-ACTIVE COMPOUNDS. Panelists have to determine the minimum level that a compound is detected or recognized. At least seventy-five panelists and constant environmental conditions are required to produce reliable data. The other common analytical test is descriptive analysis, which requires panelist training. Generally only six to twelve panelists are needed, but they have to undergo many hours (often more than one hundred) of instruction and tasting.

Ideally references (food or chemical examples) are also provided in addition to attribute definitions to aid panelists in training and attribute identification and scale usage. Lexicons of cheese flavor descriptors have been developed so that panelists have definitions on which to base their responses. For Cheddar, the lexicon developed by researchers at Mississippi State University and Sensory Spectrum, Inc. includes the five basic tastes (bitter, salty, sour, sweet, and umami) along with brothy, catty, cooked, cowy, diacetyl, fatty acid, feed, fruity, milkfat, nutty, sulfur, and whey. Each attribute has a reference; for example, the reference for umami is one gram of monosodium glutamate in 100 milliliters of water and the reference for sulfur is a boiled egg or a freshly struck match. Additional descriptors for other cheese varieties include ammonia, animal, astringent, biting, buttery, caramel, creamy, decaying animal, fresh fish, goaty, mushroom, pineapple, pungent, rancid, sauerkraut, smoky, soapy, soy sauce, sweaty, and toasty. Intensity impressions of each component are marked on a scale from 0 to 7. Panelists do not swallow the cheeses and they cleanse their palates between samples with water and unsalted crackers. See CHEDDAR.

Affective sensory analyses are performed with at least fifty untrained volunteers and include several types of tests. In preference tests, people are presented with cheese samples and asked to rank them from most to least preferred (even if they do not like any of them). In acceptance tests, also called degree of liking tests, people rate cheese one at a time using a nine-point hedonic scale ranging from like extremely to dislike extremely. These tests are sometimes used with fewer points or, in the case of children or non-

English speakers, smiling and frowning faces. In qualitative tests, consumers are interviewed individually in depth or participate in an interactive group discussion guided by a moderator. The latter, known as a focus group, lasts up to two hours and may be recorded for later analysis and observed by company representatives behind a two-way mirror.

When cheese producers wish to obtain information on the sensory qualities of their products, they must decide on which tests should be performed based on their objectives. Difference tests are selected for analyzing factors such as product improvement, processing changes, and quality control. Affective tests are employed to find preferences and acceptability. Descriptive analyses can be used to describe and measure the overall quality of the cheese (including both positive and defective attributes); it can also be used to correlate sensory with instrumental measures and study the effect of cheesemaking and aging conditions on the final sensory quality of the product.

See also AROMA; COLOR; DEFECTS; FLAVOR; FLAVOR WHEEL; TASTE; and TEXTURE.

Drake, Mary Anne. "Sensory Analysis of Dairy Foods." *Journal of Dairy Science* 90 (2007): 4925–4937.
Meilgaard, Morten C., et al. *Sensory Evaluation Techniques.* 4th ed. Boca Raton, Fla.: Taylor & Francis, 2007.

Michael Tunick

A **separator** is a mechanical centrifuge that is designed to separate fat globules in the form of cream from milk. The separator consists of a stack of conical disks that form a series of narrow channels mounted on a revolving bowl. Milk is pumped through a central axis, and centrifugal force generated by the revolving bowl drives fat globules and milk serum down the parallel channels that separate the disks. Openings in the disks located close to the central axis allow the less dense fat globules (cream) to exit the channels early and collect in the cream discharge line, whereas the heavier milk serum (skim milk) traverses the entire length of the channels and collects in the skim discharge line.

In traditional cheesemaking, gravity separation of cream is used in the making of some cheese varieties that are produced from partly skim milk, such as Parmigiano Reggiano. In large-scale industrial production of cheese from partly skim milk, cream is

first separated from the milk using a cream separator, and then a portion of the cream is recombined with the skim milk to attain a target fat percentage or casein-to-fat ratio in the cheese milk in a process known as standardization. Milk separation or standardization to a target casein-to-fat ratio is widely practiced in cheesemaking to ensure that cheeses conform to the relevant standards of identity with respect to fat in dry matter content, to produce cheese with consistent chemical composition and quality, and to maximize economic returns. Separation or standardization is also employed in the making of low-fat versions of some cheese varieties.

See also FAT; MILK; and SKIMMING.

Law, Barry A., and Adnan Y. Tamime, eds. *Technology of Cheesemaking.* 2d ed. Oxford: Wiley-Blackwell, 2010.
Walstra, Pieter, Jan T. M. Wouters, and T. J. Geurts. *Dairy Science and Technology.* Boca Raton, Fla.: CRC/ Taylor & Francis, 2006.

Paul S. Kindstedt

Serbian white brined cheeses

Serbian white brined cheeses are the most widely produced and consumed cheeses in Serbia, amounting to about 60 percent of the country's total cheese consumption. There are many different types of Serbian brined cheeses, which are named according to their production regions, such as Sjenica cheese, Zlatar cheese, Svrljig cheese, and Homolj cheese. Although these cheeses share similarities, they can also be rather different in respect to type of milk, region of production, manufacturing protocols, composition and sensory properties. Some of the white brined cheeses are recognized as products with geographical indications, but only at the national level of protection.

Traditionally, Serbian white brined cheeses were usually made from raw sheep's and goat's milk, but today they are produced mainly from raw or pasteurized cow's milk, because non-cow's milk represents only about 1–2 percent of Serbia's total milk production. After coagulation, the cheese curd is cut into cubes measuring 0.4–2 inches (1–5 centimeters) on a side, and the whey is drained using little or no pressure. Cheeses are salted with dry salt or in brine. The shapes of the final cheeses vary and may be rectangular or cylindrical, weighing from 0.5 to just over 2 pounds (250–1,000 grams), depending on the final packaging. The primary characteristic of this cheese

group is its ripening in brine with a salt concentration of 6–8 percent w/v. The cheeses have no rind and no gas holes, but small mechanical openings are expected. They belong to the soft to semihard group and have a smooth, crumbly texture that becomes brittle as the cheese gets old. The taste is acidic, salty, and very piquant, especially in mature cheeses. The specific sensory properties of the cheeses are primarily a result of natural microflora, mesophilic lactococci, lactobacilli, and enterococci originating from raw milk and the environment of the production region.

See also BRINED CHEESES.

Dozet, Natalija, et al. *Autohtoni mlječni proizvodi* [Autochthonous Dairy Products] Podgorica, Montenegro: Poljoprivredni Institut, 1996.

Zorica Radulović and Jelena Miočinović

Serpa is a traditional Portuguese cheese with a protected designation of origin (PDO). It is manufactured in a legally bounded area of Serpa and Beja counties, in Alentejo, the largest and driest province of inland Portugal. Serpa is one of the most genuinely crafted and high-quality cheeses from Portugal, although nowadays some cheese is also produced on a semi-industrial scale.

The origin of this unique cheese is lost in time, but it is believed to have started when shepherds moved to Alentejo from nearby regions, as part of a search for fresh pastures for their sheep flocks. Like Serra de Estrela cheese and other traditional Portuguese cheeses, Serpa cheese is obtained from raw ewe's milk to which an aqueous extract of dried cardoon flowers (*Cynara cardunculus L.*) has been added as coagulant. In artisanal processing, fresh milk is heated to 95°F (35°C) and filtered through white wool blankets to remove any foreign materials. Then 32 ounces salt/13 gallons milk (approximately 900 grams salt/50 liters milk) and vegetal coagulant are added under gentle stirring. The resulting curd is stirred vigorously, with the help of a wooden stick, to produce a smooth grainy mass—that is pressed by hand, molded, and left to rest for some time before being placed in a maturation room. Cheeses are carefully unmolded on the following day, and turned every day for eight to ten days—besides washing with warm milk whey. A white cotton cloth is then placed around the cheese to avoid degradation of the rind and the delicate texture, and the cheese is transferred to a warmer and drier room for an extra thirty to forty-five days of ripening.

Serpa cheese possesses a pleasant semisoft texture, buttery, yellowish paste, and a distinctive flavor, almost fermented, with balanced sweet and bitter notes. The cheese is cylindrical, and may be marketed in four regular sizes, ranging from 4–12 inches (10–30 centimeters) in diameter. Their rich adventitious microflora is dominated by such genera as *Leuconostoc* and *Lactococcus*—known for their strongly proteolytic features.

Serpa cheese may be enjoyed both as a dessert or as an appetizer, and may be served with red wines or Flemish beers and artisanal wheat bread.

See also PORTUGAL.

Freitas, Cristina, and F. Xavier Malcata. "Microbiology and Biochemistry of Cheeses with Appélation d'Origine Protegeé and Manufactured in the Iberian Peninsula from Ovine and Caprine Milks." *Journal of Dairy Science* 83, no. 3 (March 2000): 584–602.
Roseiro, Luisa, R. Andrew Wilbey, and Manuela Barbosa. "Serpa Cheese: Technological, Biochemical, and Microbiological Characterisation of a PDO Ewe's Milk Cheese Coagulated with Cynara Cardunculus L." *Le Lait* 83, no. 6 (2003): 469–480.

J. Marcelino Kongo and F. Xavier Malcata

Serra da Estrela

Serra da Estrela is the most famous of Portuguese cheeses, and evidence exists of its manufacture dating back to Roman times. The cheese is named after the highest mountains of Portugal, the Serra da Estrela. These mountains possess a special microclimate that supports the growth of natural pastures used throughout most of the year to feed the flocks. Serra da Estrela cheese has a protected designation of origin (PDO) designation and is produced from November to March, using raw milk of the Bordaleira sheep breed coagulated with an aqueous extract of dried cardoon flowers (*Cynara cardunculus L.*), an endemic wild plant. After coagulation, ideally at 81–84°F (27–29°C) for approximately sixty minutes, salt is added, and curd is hand pressed to aid in syneresis. It is then ripened for a minimum of thirty days, under low temperature, and high humidity. The rich local pasture appears to be a major contributor to the aroma and texture of Serra da Estrela cheese, as well as the proteolytic quality of the vegetable rennet and the pattern of manual curd cutting.

Serra da Estrela is often so soft that it may be spread on a piece of bread; commercial cheese is usually cylindrical in shape, with weight ranging from 2–4 pounds (0.7–2 kilograms). Its texture varies from very soft when young, to hard but sliceable when old. The paste can be white or slightly yellow in color, with a few small holes; and it exhibits a unique rich, slightly acidic taste. While quite varied at its early stages, ripening becomes eventually controlled by wild strains of *Lactococcus lactis*, *Enterococcus faecium*, and *Leuconostoc mesenteroides*.

Serra da Estrela is an excellent complement of a gourmet meal, and has increasingly been used as ingredient in nouvelle cuisine.

See also PORTUGAL.

Freitas A. C., A. C. Macedo, and F. X. Malcata. "Review: Technological and Organoleptic Issues Pertaining to Cheeses with Denomination of Origin Manufactured in the Iberian Peninsula from Ovine and Caprine Milks Revisión: Aspectos Tecnológicos y Sensoriales de Quesos con Denominación de Origen Elaborados en la Península Ibérica con Leche de Oveja y de Cabra." *Food Science and Technology International* 6 no. 5 (2000): 351–370.
Freitas, Cristina, and F. Xavier Malcata. "Microbiology and Biochemistry of Cheeses with Appélation d'Origine Protegeé and Manufactured in the Iberian Peninsula from Ovine and Caprine Milks." *Journal of Dairy Science* 83, no. 3 (March 2000): 584–602.
Macedo, Angela C., F. Xavier Malcata, and Jorge C. Oliveira "The Technology, Chemistry, and Microbiology of Serra Cheese: A Review." *Journal of Dairy Science* 76, no. 6 (June 1993): 1725–1739.

J. Marcelino Kongo and F. Xavier Malcata

sexual imagery

sexual imagery has surrounded dairying and cheesemaking since ancient times. A product of animal lactation, cheese has often been associated with women in general and breasts in particular. By association with its appearance and its manual extraction, milk has also long been associated with semen, sex, or both. By extension the milkmaid is often described as a sexually available or desirable woman. The milkmaid in a bawdy seventeenth-century broadside ballad suggests that she "had rather stroak a Man, than draw a Cow's Teat." Long after the disappearance of milkmaids from the rural landscape the sexy milkmaid remains a familiar trope in the twenty-first century.

Sexually attractive young women have been called "cheese" and "cheesecake" in English, while in Australian slang "old cheese" is a dubious term of endearment for an older woman, especially a mother or wife. In a sexual context cheese is rarely used to describe parts of the human anatomy.

At the same time there are a number of modern cheeses that through design or accident resemble female breasts and are marketed accordingly. The most famous breast-shaped cheese is tetilla ("Tetilla" is a local name for nipple or teat) a cow's milk cheese from the Galicia in northwestern Spain. Other breast-named cheeses include sein de nounou (wet-nurse's breast), a raw-milk goat's milk cheese from central France, sein d'Hélène ("Helen's breast"), a modern cow's or ewe's milk cheese from Quebec, and Zizzona di Battipaglia ("zizza" is an Italian slang term for breast), an Italian buffalo milk mozzarella variant.

In historical literature the imagery of the coagulating action of rennet on milk was commonly used as an analogy to describe the role of semen in the "setting" of the fetus in the uterus. This analogy is alluded to in the Old Testament in Job's plea to God, "Did you not pour me out like milk, And curdle me like cheese" (10:10) and used by Aristotle in the fourth century B.C.E. in "On the Generation of Animals." See BIBLICAL REFERENCES. The survival of this imagery into the modern era is seen in use of the Basque verb gatzatu, "to curdle," which can refer to both the formation of milk curds and conception.

In addition to milk and cheese, the cheese grater is used in the context of sexual imagery. Perhaps because of the repetitive, rhythmic manner in which it is used, a "cheese grater" can refer to a physical object, a synonym for "vagina" or a sexual act (both modern and ancient). Aristophanes's 411 B.C.E. play Lysistrata mentions a sexual position called "the lioness on the cheese-grater" (although the exact nature of this sexual position remains a subject of scholarly debate). The Englishman John Florio's seventeenth-century Italian and English dictionary describes a gratuggia (a grate or grater) as "a womans quaint," whereas the sixteenth-century Italian playwright Pietro Aretino's lustful abbess wants to grate a young man's cheese ("formaggio") on her grattugia.

See also CURDLING, CULTURAL THEORIES OF.

Williams, Gordon. A Dictionary of Sexual Language and Imagery in Shakespearean and Stuart Literature. London: Athlone, 1994.

Adam Balic

Sfela is a semihard white brined local cheese, produced exclusively in the region of Messinia and Laconia in South Peloponnese, Greece. Although it resembles feta cheese, it also borrows some of the production technology of hard cheese, notably the reheating. This is why it is often called "feta of fire." See FETA.

In the past Sfela, a pastoral cheese from raw sheep's milk or in combination with goat's milk, was produced by shepherds exclusively from herds of ewes traditionally raised and adapted to the particular region, whose diet was based on the local vegetation. Each pastoral family had its own particular production technology. That ensured unique taste and quality nurturing the flavors of their natural habitat, so both milk and technology reflected the region, the climate, the culture, and the experience of the local people. However, Sfela has been protected and regulated by a PDO since 1996.

Milk coagulation takes place at 86–90°F (30–32°C) with traditional rennet. The curd is reheated to 100–104°F (38–40°C), then is drained, lightly pressed, and cut into slices that look like slices of loaf bread, traditionally called "sfelides"; most probably this is where the name of the cheese comes from. The sfelides are salted and left until the next day when they are packed in wood barrels or tin cans with heavy brine (salt content 20 percent). Barrels or tins are kept at room temperature for a few days and then in cold rooms of 39–43°F (4–6°C) until consumption.

Sfela's chemical characteristics make it harder than feta cheese, with an excellent aroma and unique personality. It is consumed locally, but also used in modern gastronomy for a variety of dishes, as an appetizer, grilled, in sophisticated recipes, or accompanying fine meats or strong vegetables.

See also BRINED CHEESES and GREECE.

Anifantakis, Emmanuel. Greek Cheeses. Athens: National Dairy Committee of Greece, 1991.
Ministerial Decision no. 313056, 1994. http://www.wipo.int/edocs/lexdocs/laws/el/gr/gr067el.pdf.

Eugenia Manolopoulou

sheep are even-toed ruminants, members of the order *Artiodactyla*, the family *Bovidae*, and, with goats, comprise the subfamily *Caprini*. In the wild, sheep inhabit high elevations, often migrating seasonally. Under conditions of domestication, their adaptability across climate and conditions is fabled. The terminology associated with sheep under domestication

The first milking of the day in the Sicilian countryside with fifth-generation shepherd Filipo. The fresh ewe's milk will be brought to his small cheesemaking room and made into ricotta, pecorino, and tuma. © HALEY POLINSKY

is of a variety often bewildering to the novice. Its diverse linguistic roots (Old and Middle English, ancient and prehistoric German, Dutch, Latin, and Old Norse) in the English language alone is testimony to the history of pastoral diffusion throughout Indo-European cultures and societies. Female sheep are called ewes; male sheep are called rams; castrated males wethers; animals not yet weaned lambs; and those between the age of weaning and first shearing are hoggets.

All domestic breeds of sheep in existence today belong to the same species, *Ovis aires*, and are descendants of a single common ancestor, the mouflon (*O. orientalis*). The western branch of an evolutionary expansion centered on the southern Himalayas, mouflons are found today in the mountainous regions of the Caucasus, Anatolia, northeastern Iraq, and northwestern Iran, although their range was originally more extensive. Remnant populations of very early domesticated sheep that strongly resemble the mouflon (and until relatively recently were believed to be a separate species) can be found in Corsica and Sardinia. Related species like the North American Bighorn (*O. canadensis*), the Urial (*O. vignei*), and Argali

(*O. ammon*) have never been subject to domestication.

Archaeological remains from northeastern Iraq and Jericho offer strong evidence that by 7000 B.C.E. early pastoralists had domesticated sheep, likely through a combination of taming (hand-rearing young animals) and early forms of herding believed to have evolved as an extension of ancient hunting practices. Neoteny, or the retention of juvenile characteristics into adulthood (including behavioral traits like docility), is a hallmark of domestication. Morphological evidence of neoteny, including hornless ewes and shortened limb bones, found in these sites suggest that domestication was well-advanced by this point, although it is highly likely that the process began much earlier, leaving little trace in the archaeological record.

Sheep are gregarious animals that hew to a home range in hefts, or groups of related females; rams associate in age cohorts, interacting with females only during the rut, or mating season. The social structure of sheep—which includes deference to a single, dominant leader, and strong bonds between individuals—as well as relatively weak territorial instincts (unlike deer, sheep will not defend their home range), likely facilitated the process of domestication. A human herdsman could be substituted for a dominant animal, and as sheep are neither particularly fast-moving nor nervous compared to other wild ungulates (such as red deer or gazelles), flocks could thus be controlled by human herders. So managed, early domesticates would have constituted an important and reliable source of protein.

With their wooly fleeces and edible flesh, sheep are quintessential multipurpose livestock, but their earliest uses would have been for meat, milk, hides, and bones, not for their signature coverings. Wild species are hairy, not wool-bearing: the fleece of domestic sheep is a product of anthropogenic selection brought to bear on what originally served these animals as a seasonal undercoat. Both wild sheep and primitive breeds, like the Soay sheep of Scotland, support this contention: their coats are composed of kemp fibers, or hair, and they shed their undercoats seasonally. By 6000 B.C.E. sculptural evidence of wool-bearing sheep exists from Iraq, and by 4000 B.C.E. textile evidence from Babylonia suggests that people wore cloth spun of wool.

The importance of wool in the history of human societies is well-known, if not always well-remembered, today. (The seat of the Chancellor of the Exchequer, for instance, in the British Parliament, remains a wool sack, in recognition of this article's foundational role in establishing the nation's wealth and economy since the Middle Ages.) Wool fibers, spun into yarn and woven into fabric, provided warmth and protection in the form of clothing and sometimes shelter, as in Mongolia, where yurts composed of felted wool provide moveable domiciles for nomadic peoples. The need to process wool has spurred technological change, from the simple spindle to the steam-powered looms of the industrial age, while historically, evolving technologies induced breeders to select for different characteristics in their flocks' wool, particularly with respect to the length and diameter of fiber.

Once domesticated, sheep spread rapidly through western Asia, southern Europe, Southeast and East Asia, and North Africa. A tremendously plastic organism, local and regional types proliferated, from the fat-tailed sheep of Persia and Central Asia (known for their milking abilities) to the intensely coveted Spanish Merino, descended from medieval North African importations and prized for its superfine wool. New, and newly potent, methods of selection and husbandry accelerated the transformation of regional kinds into recognizable breeds beginning in the eighteenth century so that domestic breeds today number in the hundreds, globally.

Among Anglophone cultures, sheep are not widely reputed for their milk or cheesemaking abilities, but this was not always the case. In the British Isles, for example, sheep's milk, cheese, and butter were important articles of consumption during the Middle Ages. Only with the growing significance of wool production to the late-medieval and early modern economy did this usage decline. Preference for cow's milk grew in the thirteenth and fourteenth centuries, and with this latter species' ability to produce greater quantities of milk (cows produce approximately ten times the yearly output of sheep), by 1800 the cow's dominance in the dairy was complete. Specialization in breeding contributed to this shift. Breeds bearing particular kinds of wool (long, short, or middle) were increasingly distinguished, and new breeds oriented toward meat production, like the Southdown, gained a following.

Despite the spread of dairy cows, breeding sheep and goats has not only been economically important historically, but also today. This is because in many cases, with the exception of Australia and New Zealand, sheep and goat breeding is practiced in disadvantaged areas, where cattle have difficulty settling. The great ability of sheep and even more of goats to use foraged resources and shrubs in inaccessible areas, as well as their ability to adapt to climates, make these species an integral part of a balanced exploitation of the territorial resources system.

Elsewhere, though, the role of sheep in dairy cultures evolved quite differently. Sheep's milk, in fact, lends itself well to cheesemaking. With twice as much fat and 70 percent more protein than cow's milk, the solid yield from fluid milk is much higher. Only 4 pounds (2 kilograms) of sheep's milk (as opposed to 8 pounds [3.5 kilograms] of cow's milk) is required, on average, to produce 1 pound (450 grams) of cheese, which will have the added virtue of more calcium than cow's milk cheese. These traits help account for the continued value of milking breeds elsewhere in Europe. Throughout the Mediterranean and northern Europe, milking breeds and the signature cheeses they produce, from Roquefort to feta, remain important elements of the pastoral economy. The French Lacaune breed, German Oldenburg, Spanish Manchega and Churra breeds, Greek Chios, Italian Comisana and Sarda, to name just a few, are all important ovine producers in the global cheese economy, while the Dutch East Friesian enjoys wide popularity in Britain, Australia, New Zealand, and much of North America. See EAST FRIESIAN (SHEEP); LACAUNE; LATXA; and SARDA.

Under the aegis of European imperialism, sheep were transported from their evolutionary and cultural points of origin in Eurasia to every other continent (except Antarctica), where they often evolved, adapted, and were selected into novel breeds, like the Navajo-Churro, which originated with Spanish sheep brought to the Americas in the sixteenth century, but was transformed by Navajo pastoralists and weavers. In the nineteenth century sheep dominated grassland economies in Australia, New Zealand, the American west, and Patagonia. As cotton and then synthetic fibers rose to dominance, wool's share of the global textile markets subsided, and with it, the number of sheep to be found in many parts of the world. *O. aires* remains important to many pastoral societies, however, and among small-scale farmers, many of whom are part of a pendulum-swing back from the industrial-scale agricultural practices of the twentieth century. With their renewable harvests of milk and wool, their terminal value as meat producers, and their small size and easy handling, compared to other kinds of livestock, it is likely that they will continue to be part of human societies, cultures, and ecologies for some time to come.

See also COW and GOAT.

Clutton-Brock, Juliet. *A Natural History of Domesticated Mammals*. Cambridge, U.K.: Cambridge University Press, 1999.
Dohner, Janet Vorwald. *The Encyclopedia of Historic and Endangered Livestock and Poultry Breeds*. New Haven, Conn.: Yale University Press, 2001.
Ryder, M. L. *Sheep and Man*. London: Duckworth, 2007.
Trow-Smith, Robert. *A History of British Livestock Husbandry*. 2 vols. London: Routledge and Kegan Paul, 1959.

Rebecca J. H. Woods

sheep- and goat-skin cheeses

sheep- and goat-skin cheeses refers to a group of traditional cheeses ripened in bags or casings prepared from sheep's or goat's whole skins. These types of cheeses are undoubtedly the oldest cheeses in the world, and their history of production is tied to the history of cheese discovery, which likely occurred by accident when a traveler carried his milk supply in a pouch made from a sheep's stomach, over four thousand years ago. Some examples of cheeses in this group are Motal Paniri, Panire Khiki or Panire Pousti, and Panire Tavalesh and Assalem of Iran and Tulum Peyniri of Turkey. See MOTAL PANIRI and TULUM. These types of traditional cheeses accomplish their ripening period in sheep's or goat's skin bags, stored in a cold and moist place for two to three months.

The style of preparing sheep's or goat's whole skin casings varies by region. In the goat skin bags, which are prepared in Turkey for storing and ripening Tulum Peyniri, the hairless side of the skin is on the inside; but, in Iran the woolly or hairy side is usually turned to the inside. Before use, the skin is thoroughly cleaned, washed, and salted. Then, the skin of the front and rear legs is tied together, and air is blown in to ensure that there are no holes; the existence of a hole even the size of a pinhead will cause the cheese to deteriorate. Then, cheese chunks are put into the skin pouch through the neck opening for storage.

Ewe's, goat's, and cow's milk can be used for manufacturing these types of cheeses. Traditional rennet is usually used for coagulation of the milk. After fresh cheese is prepared, it is salted and transfered to the ripening rooms for ten to thirty days. Then the ripened cheeses are broken into small pieces of 3.9 to 5.9 inches (10–15 centimeters), poured into the sheep's or goat's skin bags, and kept in cold, moist places like basements and storehouses for two to three months to be well ripened.

The literature reports that tulum cheese ripened in goat's skin bags has unique chemical, microbiological, and sensorial properties compared to cheeses ripened in other packaging materials. It was reported that the use of goat's skin bags for cheese ripening causes a greater decrease in the moisture content of cheeses because of its porous structure, as well as lower microbial counts in comparison with cheeses ripened in plastic containers. Also, goat's skin bags are preferred over sheep's skin as a packaging material for cheese because of their stronger structure.

Results of a study conducted on the effect of rennet type (commercial and traditional rennet) and container type (goat skin or plastic containers) on microbial and chemical properties of local kordish cheese showed that the type of rennet and the type of container had no significant effect on microbial properties, whereas some chemical properties such as dry matter, ash, acidity, and pH of the cheeses were significantly affected by the type of container. The type of rennet used also had a significant influence on dry matter, ash, and the ratio of fat on dry matter.

See also IRAN; TRADITIONAL EQUIPMENT; and TURKEY.

Gün, I., et al. "Some Properties of Goat Skin as a Packaging Material for Tulum Cheese." Paper presented at the IDF International Symposium on Sheep, Goat, and Other Non-Cow Milk, Athens, Greece, 16 May 2011.

Hashemi, M., et al. "Evaluation of Rennet Type and Container Influences on Physicochemical and Microbial Properties of Local Kurdish Cheese." Paper presented at the IDF International Symposium on Sheep Goat and other Non-Cow Milk, Athens, Greece, 16 May 2011.

Hayaloglu, Ali A., et al. "Microbiology, Biochemistry, and Volatile Composition of Tulum Cheese Ripened in Goat's Skin or Plastic Bags." *Journal of Dairy Science* 90 (2007): 1102–1121.

Lame, H., and M. Hekmati. "Etude de quelques caractéristiques d'une variété fromagère traditionnelle iranienne appelée 'Fromiage en outre.'" *Le Lait* 547 (1975): 418–423.

Shafiei, Y. "Iranian Traditional Cheeses." Paper presented at the 1st Conference of Iranian Traditional Dairy Products, Khoy, Iran, 24 February 2013. In Persian.

Yahya Shafiei Bavil Oliaei

shelf life, or durability, of ripened cheese begins when maturation ends; but the moment when this transition occurs can be difficult to identify accurately. Unlike nonfermented foods, the organoleptic qualities of cheese evolve continuously from the day the curd is made, through maturation and shelf life, to the day the cheese is consumed. Whereas the sensory quality of nonfermented food remains unchanged until the food suddenly spoils, the flavor and texture of cheese vary continuously, appealing to different palates at different stages of ripeness. Some like Camembert mild and firm, others like it strong and runny, so the end of life is variable—the two dates could be a month apart.

"Cheese" is but a single word, yet it represents innumerable varieties, with widely differing compositional characteristics. A combination of salt content, moisture content, and pH value, together with competition from the complex microflora of most cheeses, determines whether a variety can safely be stored at room temperature or must be refrigerated and whether the shelf life is one week or one year. See AMBIENT STORAGE. In part, the durability of a cheese is determined by the fate of pathogens. All serogroups of *Salmonella* can die during the maturation of hard

cheese, so farmhouse Cheddar may become safer the longer it is stored. Conversely, *Listeria monocytogenes* may grow in mold-ripened cheeses, so it may be necessary to restrict their shelf life to prevent the numbers of *Listeria* from achieving high levels. See PATHOGENS and LISTERIA.

During maturation of hard cheeses, protease and lipase enzymes gradually increase the depth of flavor, so mild Cheddar may be ripened for just a few weeks, whereas Parmesan is matured for at least twelve months. See PROTEOLYSIS and LIPOLYSIS. British territorial cheeses and Dutch-style, washed-curd cheeses may be eaten either fresh or matured. See TERRITORIAL and WASHED-CURD CHEESES. The pH value of mold-ripened cheese rises to neutral during maturation and shelf life because molds produce ammonia, which is strongly alkaline and neutralizes the lactic acid that developed during curd formation. See AMMONIA; LACTIC ACID; and PH MEASUREMENT. Fresh, soft cheese (e.g., lactic or cream cheese) is usually not ripened; most varieties remain stable throughout their shelf life. See FRESH CHEESES.

Thus, the biochemical processes that take place during cheese storage vary widely from one style to another. So, what restricts the shelf life of cheese? Some may argue that for hard cheese it is simply strength of flavor; there comes a point when the cheese is simply too strong for most palates. But for most cheeses, the visible growth of undesirable or unintended molds is probably the main cause of shelf-life limitation.

So, when does maturation end and shelf life begin? The answer is: at a point somewhere between the cheesemaker and the retailer, determined by the type of cheese and the required strength of flavor. What can be said, however, is that when a whole cheese has been cut, especially if portioned for retail, it has ceased to mature and its durability is limited.

See also MATURING.

Goyal, Sumit, and Gyanendra Kumar Goyal. "Machine Learning Models for Predicting Shelf Life of Processed Cheese." *International Journal of Open Information Technologies* 1 (2013): 28–31.

Law, Barry A., and Adnan Y. Tamime, eds. *Technology of Cheesemaking.* 2d ed. Oxford: Wiley-Blackwell, 2010.

Specialist Cheesemakers Association. *Shelf Life of Ready to Eat Food in Relation to L.* monocytogenes— *Guidance for Food Business Operators.* Kettering, U.K.: Chilled Food Association, 2010. http://www .specialistcheesemakers.co.uk/tech_committee/ publications/shelf_life_of_rte_foods_in_relation _to_lm_final_18_3_10.pdf.

Lynher Dairies in West Cornwall, England, makes an unusual nettle-wrapped cheese called Cornish Yarg. Apart from lending the cheese a latticed beauty, the nettles attract naturally occurring molds and impart a mushroomy taste as it matures. © LYNHER DAIRIES

Juliansplatte is a classic Alp dairy in the Allgäu region, which straddles the border between Bavaria and Austria. © KATE ARDING

A Brown Swiss cow munching hay in northern Italy. The milk of this docile breed is particularly suited to making hard, Alp-style cheeses. COURTESY OF CONSORZIO DI TUTELA DEL FORMAGGIO ASIAGO

The Alkmaar auction is the most famous of the five traditional cheese markets that flourished in the Holland countryside from the late Middle Ages. Here spectators watch as workers carry sleds of Edam cheese. © PAULO OLIVEIRA SANTOS

While Mexico is perhaps known for its fresh young cheeses, there are approximately sixty types of cheese currently produced in Mexico that range from fresh, soft, firm, and hard cheeses to pulled-curd and aged cheeses. PHOTO BY JORGE FERNANDO GÓMEZ CARBAJAL

Various types of caciocavallo, southern Italy's beloved "cheese on horseback," a stretched-curd cousin of mozzarella and provolone. © VINCENZO SPIONE

Gorwydd Caerphilly, made by the Trethowan family, is considered the modern standard-bearer for Caerphilly, a semifirm cow's milk cheese that originated in Wales. Here it is being sold from a small stall in Borough Market, London's oldest food market. © VISITBRITAIN

La Fromagerie, owned by Patricia Michelson, is a London-based cheese seller and maturer with a particular focus on French cheeses. There are two locations: one in Marylebone and the other in Highbury & Islington. The shops feature climate-controlled display facilities, including walk-in "cheese rooms" that allow customers to fully immerse themselves in the experience of tasting and selecting. © KATE ARDING

Humboldt Fog is a soft-ripened pasteurized goat's milk cheese, notable for the thin line of ash running through it. To form the cheese, half the curds are ladled into molds, and vegetable ash is applied to the surface. The second layer of nascent curds is then poured on top of the ash to form a layer cake–like cheese.

Rush Creek Reserve, made by Uplands Cheese in Wisconsin, is a spruce bark–wrapped raw cow's milk cheese. It is modeled after a Vacherin Mont d'Or, another cheese best eaten with a spoon. © KATE ARDING

Poutine, Quebec's popular street food, is a combination of French-fried potatoes, fresh Cheddar cheese curds, and gravy. Connoisseurs have always claimed the best versions are served at small roadside stands, where the cheese curds are more likely to have the rubbery texture of freshness and melt readily. PHOTO BY CHARLES O'BRIEN

Specialist Cheesemakers Association. *Shelf Life of Ready to Eat Food in Relation to* L. monocytogenes—*Worked Example—Brie with Garlic and Herbs.* http://www .specialistcheesemakers.co.uk/tech_committee/ publications/lm_and_shelf_life_brie_example _technical_final.pdf.

Paul Neaves

The **shepherd,** for thousands of years, has had an indispensable job wherever open land was grazed or browsed. With a staff and a dog, and aimed small stones (that land beside the animals, to make a sound), he or she guides the herd to the best food, leads the animals to water, and in hot weather to shade, and protects them from predators, including, particularly in the past, wolves. In contrast to the repeated grazing of modern, closely managed pasture, with its small enclosures, easily moved fencing, and frequent rotation and regrowth, the animals guided by a shepherd might graze a spot of open land just once or twice a year. The shepherd, a word that commonly embraces cowherd and goatherd, sometimes milks the animals and sometimes makes cheese. Where the grazing land was close to home, animals often used to be tended by children. But a shepherd might be away for days at a time, or in the case of transhumance, for the whole of summer. Those shepherds who spend long periods alone have a reputation for not being the most socially integrated people.

For millennia, the effort or expense of dividing large areas of open land with stone walls or wooden fences has been as a rule prohibitive, or those divisions weren't or aren't allowed. But in the late nineteenth century, after the invention of inexpensive barbed-wire fencing and then other kinds, the practice of shepherding dairy animals diminished steadily in the cheese-producing countries of the West, until by the end of the twentieth century it had all but disappeared. Hardly more than a handful of traditional shepherds are left in southern Italy, although some migrants from poorer countries work there as shepherds. Farther east, in the major cheese-producing country of Greece, shepherding remains current.

See also PASTORALISM; PASTURE; and TRANSHUMANCE.

Andrews, Kevin. *The Flight of Ikaros: A Journey into Greece.* Boston: Houghton Mifflin, 1959.
Merwin, W. S. "Shepherds." In *The Lost Upland: Stories of Southwest France.* New York: Alfred A. Knopf, 1992.

Edward Behr

A fifth-century Byzantine mosaic from the emperor's palace in Istanbul, depicting a young shepherd carrying a basket of cheese. DE AGOSTINI PICTURE LIBRARY / M. SEEMULLER / BRIDGEMAN IMAGES

The **Shorthorn,** also called Dairy Shorthorn or Milking Shorthorn, is a cattle breed developed during the late eighteenth century, and then regarded as the model of purposeful livestock improvement through systematic mating. It was created by several landowners in northern England including the brothers Robert and Charles Colling in County Durham and Thomas Bates of Kirklevington, Yorkshire. Working with large local cattle apparently of mixed English and Dutch ancestry, they employed "close breeding" of selected individuals, with a carefully chosen outcross or two, to perpetuate desirable traits in a purebred lineage. The resulting sturdy reddish- or roan-coated stock was a sensation in the British Isles. A few representative animals were brought to the United States, often as "Durhams," in the 1780s and 1790s by progressive breeders. The breed briefly enjoyed a commanding position in American livestock farming during the early nineteenth century.

Shorthorns were initially promoted as a dual breed, equally good for meat and milk production. In fact owners tended to manipulate the stock in one or the other direction. Meanwhile leading agriculturalists who saw specialization as the key to efficient production began advocating a sharp differentiation between beef and dairy breeds. In the long run more breeders chose to manage Shorthorns for beef than milking purposes. Owners who took Shorthorns' dairy possibilities seriously often believed that breed improvement programs unduly concentrated on weight gain for beef production, leaving milking as a neglected stepchild.

As newer dairy breeds appeared, Shorthorn milk had difficulty competing, perhaps for lack of systematic focus on marketing needs. It was often not rich enough for the lucrative butter market but not copious enough in amount to suit the rapidly growing fluid milk market. It was not a great favorite with cheesemakers; Shorthorn milk is now known to usually lack the beta variation of kappa-casein, a factor in speed and completeness of curd formation.

Attempts to maintain the Shorthorn's dual-purpose qualities proved difficult. In Great Britain the Shorthorn Cattle Society now has a "Beef Shorthorn" and a "Dairy Shorthorn" wing. In the United States the two camps eventually went their separate ways. The American Shorthorn Breeders' Association (later the American Shorthorn Association), founded in 1872, now represents only beef breeders. The American Milking Shorthorn Society, which decisively split off in 1948, maintains a secondary emphasis on meat as a "salvage" purpose for cows at the end of their productive milking life.

Though not now ranked among major dairy cattle breeds, Shorthorns still have their proponents, including some small-scale cheesemakers. They may also have promise in the genetic outcrossings now often recommended by breed-health experts as a necessary corrective to shrinking gene pools among breeds that supply the most cheese milk.

See also COW.

Becker, Raymond B. *Dairy Cattle Breeds: Origin and Development*. Gainesville: University of Florida Press, 1973.
Porter, Valerie. *Cattle: A Handbook to the Breeds of the World*. London: Christopher Helm, 1991.

Anne Mendelson

shredding is a common machining step used for the size reduction of various cheeses. Cheese is shredded by manufactures and converters as well as at home by consumers. Shredded cheese has increased surface area and allows for faster melting compared to other forms of size reduction such as slicing and cubing. Cheese is also shredded in order to allow for uniform mixing and maximum coverage with a minimum amount of product.

The quality of shredded cheese is determined by a number of factors including the amount of fines, shred length uniformity, shred shape uniformity, presence of matting/clumps, adhesiveness to equipment, ease of shredding, and others. The so-called "shreddability" of cheese can be affected by many intrinsic and extrinsic factors. The composition of cheese has dramatic effects on shreddability. Often cheeses with high moisture content and high fat content (e.g., Havarti) will confer a softer/pastier cheese and will therefore have a propensity to gum up and clog shredding equipment. Cheeses that are very dry and firm (e.g., Cotija) will often crumble into small particles and form excessive fines when shredded. Age of cheese can also play a role. Many cheeses have an optimal window in which shreddability is at a maximum. Mozzarella, for example, is typically shredded approximately five days after production. Any earlier and the free moisture causes low-quality shreds. Shredding cheese later results in further ripening of the cheese and softening of the structure, also leading to low-quality shreds.

Commercial shredding lines usually consist of a cutter to first reduce the size of cheese blocks before being fed into the shredder. Many common shredders fall into two main categories: modified hammer mill style and "squirrel cage" disintegrators. The former consists of rotating knives that force cheese through various gratings to produce shreds. The latter has rotating cylindrical cages lined with knife blades that spin in opposing directions subjecting the cheese to centrifugal forces and forcing cheese through knife blade slots producing shreds. The shreds then move to final processing and packaging.

Most commercially shredded cheeses will have "anti-caking" or "free-flowing" agents added to the shreds prior to final packaging. Common anti-caking agents include microcrystalline cellulose, powdered cellulose, potato starch, and other starches. These compounds are typically used in concentrations ranging from 0.5 percent to 2 percent by weight. Anti-mycotic agents (e.g., natamycin) are often added to the anti-caking agents in order to prevent mold growth on shredded cheese.

Many shredded cheeses are preserved by a combination of anti-mycotic agents and modified atmosphere packaging. Carbon dioxide and/or nitrogen are flushed into the packages of shreds prior to sealing in order to displace ambient air that was present. Nitrogen is thought to have minimal effects on cheese flavor due to its inert nature. Carbon dioxide can have effect on flavor either directly (dissolving in trapped water forming carbonic acid) or indirectly by affecting microbial activity in the cheese.

See also CHEESE GRATER; CHEESE KNIFE; CUTTING; FUNCTIONAL PROPERTIES; and MELTING.

Apostolopoulos, C., and R. J. Marshall. "A Quantitative Method for the Determination of Shreddability of Cheese." *Journal of Food Quality* 17 (1994): 115–128.

Fellows, P. J. *Food Processing Technology: Principles and Practice.* 3d ed. New York: CRC Press, 2009.

Kindstedt, P. S. "Factors Affecting the Functional Characteristics of Unmelted and Melted Mozzarella Cheese." In *Chemistry of Structure-function Relationships in Cheese,* edited by E. L. Malin and M. H. Tunick, pp. 27–41. New York: Plenum Press, 1995.

United States Department of Agriculture. "USDA Specifications for Shredded Cheddar Cheese." https://www.ams.usda.gov/sites/default/files/media/shreddedcheddar.pdf.

Pat Polowsky

Sicily's dairy culture has a tradition going back thousands of years, meticulously described both in classical literature—abounding of mythological characters—and in folkloristic narrations of the pastoral world.

Cheese was known by the ancients as a natural method of preserving milk, a primary and precious good, which maintained its nutritional characteristics intact, even after its transformation. Diodorus Siculus ascribes to Aristaeus, mythical son of Apollo and grandchild of Zeus, the invention of cheese. Supposedly Aristaeus was fed by the nymphs with some cheese, and learned from them the art of cheesemaking (Diod. IV, 81, 2). See ARISTAIOS. And in a famous passage of *The Odyssey* (IX), Homer narrates in rich detail the primitive procedure that took place in Polyphemus's cave in (supposedly) Sicily for the production of sheep's milk cheese, probably an ancient form of Sicilian Pecorino. See HOMER. The diverse manufacture techniques and the variety of tools are integral to the sociocultural context of the Sicilian peasantry, as well as to its language and its popular beliefs.

Even more than Italy, Sicily presents an orography with 61.4 percent of hill areas, 24.4 percent of mountain, and only 14.2 percent of flat areas. The limited flat areas and hilly parts at lower altitude are used for high-income agriculture: greenhouse, citrus and grape cultivation, and horticulture. Animal husbandry is relegated to the mountain areas and the high hills (extensive production systems), with the exception of the province of Ragusa, where settled intensive animal production systems have developed.

In Sicily some 335,000 cattle are bred, of which about 170,000 belong to the so-called "milk line," which produce 190,000 tons of milk per year. The province of Ragusa produces about 70 percent of the total dairy cow milk production of Sicily, mainly for fluid milk consumption. Only a small percentage of this milk, coming from the marginal areas of the same territory, is used to produce the Ragusano PDO. See RAGUSANO. The Sicilian sheep and goat population is around 1 million head (the second Italian region after Sardinia) and the annual milk production is about 35,000 tons.

In summary, the Sicilian dairy sector moves in two directions: one industrial, to produce fluid milk, fermented milk (yogurt), and standardized dairy products made by processes of industrial transformation (pasteurization, use of starter cultures, steel equipment); the other toward traditional methods where, despite the reduced milk production, there is a significant variety of types, shapes, and different production and aging technologies. See INDUSTRIAL and TRADITIONAL EQUIPMENT.

About 6 million people live in Sicily, and the production of milk and cheese is able to satisfy less than 20–25 percent of the regional consumption. As a consequence Sicily is forced to import about 80 percent of its milk and cheese to satisfy the requirements of Sicilian consumers. Despite the low level of self-supply, the animal production sector in Sicily is still very important, mainly due to the presence of more than fifteen thousand farmers (even if in the last thirty years the number of farmers has been reduced by more than half). Almost all of them are family farmers with an average of about 35 dairy cows or 130 sheep and goats. They are very small farmers who practice extensive agriculture, maintaining diverse mixed production systems and products even with scarce resources. They are located, usually, in an agriculturally unsuitable environment (hills, mountains) that would otherwise be abandoned, where livestock and farming are often the only way to use the land.

To be small and settled in less-favored areas has some drawbacks: fragmentation and greater variability of the products and relatively low quantity produced per unit of Sicilian dairy family farmers; pulverization of the marketed products with the consequence of weak contractual power; and difficulties in reaching high-profile markets.

Fortunately the Sicilian dairy family farmers, like many other rural marginal areas of Europe, have very important strengths regarding sustainable agriculture and food security. They use natural resources as production factors, so they are defined, most of the time, as agro-ecological and sustainable food producers. They play a role as guardians of the environment due to their protection of natural resources: reducing soil erosion, reducing deforestation and desertification, and keeping animal and vegetal biodiversity. They are custodians of the important sociocultural heritage of rural communities including ancient knowledge of the art of producing cheese and using traditional methods and tools. The quality of the final products is strongly linked to the territory due to many biodiversity factors, forming part of the production system and of cheese processing. Small family farmers contribute 70 percent of the world's food, assuring food security to the worldwide population, especially in rural areas. These production systems cannot be considered only from the business point of view, but must be evaluated on their socioecological merits. It will be necessary to increase public awareness of the importance of the settlement of small family farmers in less favored areas, not only as producers of high-quality and safe food, but above all as a testimonial of sustainable agriculture, in defense of biodiversity and respect for the territorial environmental resources, and recognizing the human presence in the role of the guardian of the environment and as custodian of rural cultural heritage.

Sicilian cheese varieties are in part related to the countless people who have dominated Sicily over the centuries (Greeks, Romans, Arabs, Normans, Swabians, Bourbons, etc.) and in part to the climatic conditions of the island. Sicily is, in fact, the region in which the stretching of cheese (pasta filata) is widespread, a process that allowed a longer shelf life of the product in historical periods in which producers did not have modern technology. See PASTA FILATA.

Sicily has four PDO cheeses recognized by the European Commission: Ragusano PDO (stretched cheese from cow's milk), Pecorino Siciliano PDO (pressed cheese from sheep milk), Vastedda della Valle del Belice PDO (stretched cheese from sheep's milk), and Piacentinu Ennese PDO (pressed cheese from sheep's milk). See PECORINO SICILIANO; VASTEDDA DELLA VALLE DEL BELICE; and PIACENTINU ENNESE. Other important historical cheeses produced include Provola dei Nebrodi (stretched cheese), Provola delle Madonie (stretched cheese), Provola Iblea (stretched cheese), Palermitano (stretched cheese), Tuma Persa (pressed cheese), Fiore Sicano (pressed cheese), and Maiorchino (pressed cheese). See PROVOLA DEI NEBRODI; PALERMITANO; TUMA PERSA; FIORE SICANO; and MAIORCHINO.

One of the most famous dairy products in Sicily is ricotta, produced from the whey after cheese-making. There are different varieties of ricotta depending on: the species producing the milk (cows, sheep, goats, buffalo) and the technology used (addition of 5–10 percent of milk in the whey, use of acidification elements, etc.). Fresh ricotta is, mainly, targeted for direct consumption; it is a key raw material for the many recipes in Sicilian cuisine; it is the queen of ingredients in Sicilian pastry. Furthermore fresh ricotta, in different and specific areas of Sicily, is processed and converted into baked (ricotta infornata) or salted ricotta. See RICOTTA and RICOTTA INFORNATA.

The total production of Sicilian cheeses is estimated at around 9,000 to 10,000 tons per year. The largest portion is Pecorino cheese, with over 6,000 tons, of which only a small percentage is produced for certification as Pecorino Siciliano PDO. Ragusano, Palermitano, and Provola dei Nebrodi cheese all exceed 500 tons per year. The remaining dairy products are produced in small quantities with the exception of ricotta, which is produced in industrial quantities.

See also ITALY.

Campo, Patrizia, and Giuseppe Licitra. *I Formaggi Storici Siciliani*. Ragusa, Italy: CoRFiLaC Press, 2006.
PSR Sicilia 2007/2013—Analisi delle principali filiere regionali—Filiera Lattiero—Casearia, Palermo,

November 2012. http://www.issm.cnr.it/progetti/
agroalimentare/analisi_sicilia.pdf.
"Ragusano." Cheese.com. http://www.cheese.com/
ragusano.

Ivana Piccitto

silage is green forage that has been preserved
through acidification of the plant mass by anaerobic
microorganisms, which prevents spoilage as well as
the proliferation of potentially toxic microorganisms.

Preservation by silage is a very old technique
(historical documents date back to 1500 B.C.E.) and
consists of the storage of plant mass in special closed
containers (traditional silos) or in outdoor silos. The
result is a feed easy to introduce in rations for animal
breeding because it is palatable and chemically stable
throughout the year, by replacing, in whole or in
part, the green (grass) and dried (hay) forage. By
isolating the plant mass from the outside environment, the silos prevent the plants and any aerobic
bacteria present from consuming oxygen during the
first period of maturation. In the very early days, in
fact, the acetic aerobic fermentation lowers the pH
to between 4.5 and 5. The acidification of the silo
leads to the development of lactic acid bacteria that
cause lactic fermentation, bringing the pH to values
even lower than 4.

Completely mechanized forage harvesters cut the
plants into small pieces so that the fodder can be layered and compacted in the silos in order to reduce
the presence of air in the mass. When the operation
of storage and compaction ends, the silage is covered with plastic film and carefully sealed to prevent
the entry of air.

All fodder plants may be preserved using silage.
A silage is good when its acidity is lower than pH 4,
has no mold, is not hot, and will not overheat in contact with air. Silage feeding is not recommended for
the production of certain cheese varieties, such as
Gruyère, Comté, and Emmentaler, because of microbiological problems that can arise.

See also PASTURE and TOTAL MIXED RATION.

"Quality and Feeding." Corn Agronomy, 20 November
2015. http://corn.agronomy.wisc.edu/Silage/S006
.aspx.
"Silage Making." UK Agriculture. http://www
.ukagriculture.com/crops/silage_making.cfm.

Rosario Petriglieri

Single Gloucester

See GLOUCESTER.

sir iz mišine is one of Croatia's traditional cheeses,
produced on family farms in central Dalmatia, and is
very well known and regarded as a regional product.
Historically, the production of sir iz mišine ("cheese
in a sack") in the Croatian territory started when
the Illyrians and the Thracians grazed their sheep in
the pastures of the mountain called Dinara. They
used a lamb skin for storage and transport of cheese
from the mountain to the valley because of a lack of
wood for packaging and shipping the cheese.

Sir iz mišine is manufactured from sheep's milk.
Evening milk is cooled, depending on the farm, to
44.6–53.6°F (7–12°C) and mixed with morning milk
before cheesemaking. Commercial liquid microbial
coagulant is used, and the temperature of the milk
at renneting is 89.6–98.6°F (32–37°C). When coagulated (setting time is between thirty and fifty
minutes depending on the farm), the curd is cut, by
scoop, into irregularly shaped small pieces, or by
knife, into cube-shaped pieces approximately a square
inch (3 square centimeters) on each side. Curd
grains are stirred by hand or by scoop and heated to
a temperature of 93.2–104°F (34–40°C). The curd
is cooked for twenty to thirty minutes, depending
on the farm, and afterward the whey is drained.
Rough curd is shaped by hand, and then scooped
and drained through a cloth under its own weight.

Sir iz mišine (cheese in a sack) is a traditional Croatian
sheep's milk cheese. After the whey is drained the cheese
curd is cut into pieces, dry-salted, and put in a lambskin
sack for ripening. © SAMIR KALIT

After the whey is drained, the cheese curd is cut into pieces approximately 4 × 4 × 2 inches (10 × 10 × 5 centimeters) in size, dry-salted with large-grain sea salt, and then put into a skin sack. The average weight of the cheese in the sack, depending on the size of the lamb skin, is 44 pounds (20 kilograms).

To prepare the lamb skin, the lamb is slaughtered, and the skin gently removed. To avoid tearing the skin, meat and fat residues on the skin are carefully scraped off, and the skin is cleaned with water and then sun-dried and smoked. Prior to use, the skin is submerged in whey or hot water. All openings are closed except the neck, through which the curd is filled. Cheese is ripened in the lamb skin sack for sixty days at a temperature of 61–64°F (16–18°C) and a relative humidity of 65–80 percent.

Because the cheese is ripened in an animal-skin sack, lipolysis is the predominant biochemical change leading to the accumulation of medium- and long-chain free fatty acids, such as palmitic, oleic, and stearic acids. No research has been done on this specific cheese regarding aroma compounds, but on tulum cheese, which is a similar cheese to sir iz mišine, the following predominant aroma compounds were found: short-chain fatty acids, 2-butanone, diacetyl, and primary alcohols, including ethanol. See AROMA and TULUM.

See also CROATIA and SHEEP- AND GOAT-SKIN CHEESES.

Hayaloglu, Ali A., et al. "Microbiology, Biochemistry, and Volatile Composition of Tulum Cheese Ripened in Goat's Skin or Plastic Bags." *Journal of Dairy Science* 90 (2007): 1102–1121.
Tudor Kalit, Milna, et al. "Changes in the Composition and Sensory Properties of Croatian Cheese in a Lamb Skin Sack (Sir iz mišine) During Ripening." *International Journal of Dairy Technology* 67 (February 2014): 255–264.

Samir Kalit

The **60-day aging rule** for cheese was established in 1949 in response to outbreaks of brucellosis, salmonellosis, and staphylococcal poisoning linked to Cheddar cheese (Ryser, 2001). Boor (2005) cites the 1946 work of Gilman and colleagues on survival of *Brucella abortus* in Cheddar cheese as the origin of the 60-day holding rule, although it was known at that time that pathogens such as *Salmonella* could survive beyond sixty days of holding in Cheddar cheese (D'Amico, 2014). Since that time, however, we've discovered pathogens such as *Listeria monocytogenes*, *Campylobacter*, *Salmonella*, and toxic forms of *E. coli* that may survive aging and remain present, especially in raw or unpasteurized milk cheeses.

In the United States, there are over seventy cheeses defined in the Food and Drug Administration (FDA) Code of Federal Regulations (CFR) Title 21 Section 133. The FDA allows a few of these cheeses to be made with raw milk from cow, goat, sheep, or buffalo but due to pathogen concerns, these cheeses must be aged at a temperature of 35°F (2°C) for not less than sixty days in order to be considered safe and wholesome for sale.

The 60-day aging rule is not enforced for all cheeses. For example, ricotta, feta, chèvre, quark, cottage cheese, cream cheese, Mexican-style cheeses, provolone, and Italian style mozzarella, do not fall under the 60-day aging rule and these cheeses must be made from pasteurized milk. The 60-day rule does not apply to processed cheese spreads.

There are many factors during the cheesemaking process that may affect pathogen survival and growth, including the following:

- pH
- moisture
- salt content
- acidity
- temperature
- starter cultures

For those cheeses that do fall under the 60-day rule, they must be manufactured under good hygienic practices (GHP), good manufacturing practices (GMP), and have a food safety plan in place regardless of whether the cheese is raw/unpasteurized or pasteurized. The American Cheese Society (ACS) also recommends attending a food safety education workshop, having an existing environmental monitoring program in place, maintaining accurate documentation/records, participating in a review by a third party, and working with local regulators to produce a safe and wholesome raw/unpasteurized milk cheese. The cheesemaker may also need to consider testing both the raw milk and finished product.

In 2009, the FDA began an assessment of the 60-day aging rule. The assessment has been completed and is awaiting approval. What will the FDA recommend after their assessment of this 60-day aging rule? A number of scenarios are possible. One scenario would be to ban all raw milk/unpasteurized cheeses. That is highly unlikely, but possible. Another scenario would be to change the 60-day aging rule to a longer time frame based on scientific literature. A third scenario would be to consider using the European (France and/or Germany) way with an intense look at hygienic practices and animal health. The last scenario would be that the FDA does nothing at all and leaves the 60-day rule as is. Only time will tell which way the FDA decides to go.

The United States may need to look at other safety measures instead of the 60-day aging rule because this rule does not apply to all cheeses. Other countries such as France and Germany rely on animal health, hygienic milk collection, storage, accelerated cooling, and microbiological criteria for their raw/unpasteurized milk cheeses.

See also FOOD AND DRUG ADMINISTRATION; POLITICS OF CHEESE; and RAW-MILK CHEESES.

Boor, K. J. "Origin of the 60-Day Minimum Holding Period Requirement for United States Cheeses Made from Sub- or Unpasteurized Milk." *Food Protection Trends* 25, no. 10 (2005): 767–770.

D'Amico, Dennis J. "Microbiological Quality and Safety in Cheesemaking." In *Cheese and Microbes,* edited by Catherine W. Donnelly, pp. 251–310. Washington, D.C.: American Society for Microbiology, 2014.

D'Amico, D. J., and C. W. Donnelly. "Microbiological Quality of Raw Milk Used for Small-Scale Artisan Cheese Production in Vermont: Effect of Farm Characteristics and Practices." *Journal of Dairy Science* 93, no. 1 (2010): 134–147.

Knoll, Lauren P. "Origins of the Regulation of Raw Milk Cheeses in the United States " (2005 third-year paper). Unpublished manuscript. http://nrs.harvard.edu/urn-3:HUL.InstRepos:8852188.

Ryser, E. T. "Public Health Concerns." In *Applied Dairy Microbiology,* 2d ed., edited by E. H. Marth and J. L. Steele, pp. 397–545. New York: Marcel Dekker, 2001.

Marianne Smukowski

skimming refers to an adjustment of milk fat content realized either naturally by migration to the surface of fat globules or industrially by use of a centrifugal force. Milk fat accumulates in spherical globules ranging in size from 0.2 to 15 micrometers. Its content and its composition vary according to the cow's breed, lactation stage, and feeding. Cheesemakers know that optimum organoleptic qualities (taste, aroma, and texture) of a specific cheese variety are linked to a precise fat content, which is generally expressed by the ratio of fat to dry matter. To achieve a consistent ratio in the cheese, the fat content of the milk used to make it must be adjusted. That is done by either gravitational or centrifugal skimming. Traditional, simple gravitational methods of skimming involve allowing the milk to stand for an hour before removing the layer of milk fat that has risen to the surface. This process is very efficient when freshly obtained warm milk is used; refrigeration of milk decreases separation efficiency.

Centrifugal skimming, on the other hand, is generally accomplished in the processing plant by centrifugation in a piece of equipment known as a separator. See SEPARATOR. Whole milk, heated to 104–122°F (40–50°C), and often pasteurized, is continuously submitted to a centrifugal field (around 6,000 × g) for two to three seconds in a rotating bowl containing a stack of tronconic disks. The disks create thin channels in which the cream and skim milk are separated, according to Stokes's law, because of the lower density of milk fat. Since greater centrifugal force is exercised on the heavier skim milk, it moves to the outside of the bowl, where it passes through an outlet. Today, industrial separators are fully hermetic to avoid air introduction and subsequent foam formation. Usually the cream flow is 10 percent of the entering milk flow. In cheese plants, fat content is then adjusted by mixing whole milk with skim milk, either in a cheese vat or with a special device immediately after centrifugal separation, or by mixing whole milk with cream for high-fat cheeses. Centrifugal skimming is never complete. Fat in skim milk accounts for approximately 0.5 gram per liter and consists of small globules of less than 1 micrometer in diameter. Separators also concentrate gross milk impurities in their bowls; automatic discharge of this sediment is triggered by a timer.

See also FAT; MILK; and STANDARDIZATION.

Bylund, Gösta. *Dairy Processing Handbook.* 3d ed. Lund, Sweden: Tetra Pak, 2015.

Pointurier, Hubert, and Jacques Adda. *Beurrerie industrielle: Science et technique de la fabrication du beurre.* Paris: La Maison Rustique, 1969.

Jean Louis Maubois

skorup is an extra-fatty dairy product produced in the mountainous parts of Montenegro. It contains more than 80 percent fat in dry matter and 8–10 percent proteins. By its composition, it is located between cheese and butter, but it is neither cheese nor butter.

Through the centuries, skorup was, and is, primarily produced in households. Organized production began in 1908 with the establishment of the Livestock Institute in Nikšić and construction of a dairy plant. Two years later, skorup won the high score in sensory evaluation at the Food Fair in London. It is mostly produced from mixtures of cow's and sheep's milk. Fresh milk is filtered, poured into the pot, and gradually heated to boiling. When the milk starts to boil, it is kept at the same temperature for thirty minutes to increase the total solids in the milk; the higher the content of solids, the better the skorup quality. Milk is then poured into wide, shallow wooden or metal vessels. In the vessels, the milk is gradually cooled, whereby the formation of skorup starts as fatty globules and other ingredients rise to the surface of the milk. Formation of skorup lasts from one to three days. Most often, skorup is collected from milk after two days. After collection, skorup is placed in wooden tubs, layer by layer. Each layer is dry-salted. At the bottom of the tubs, there is a hole through which excess milk is discharged. When the tub is filled and skorup is drained, skorup is transferred from the tub into specially prepared sheep skins. Air in the skin must be avoided because ripening conditions for skorup should be anaerobic. See SHEEP-AND GOAT-SKIN CHEESES.

Skorup can be consumed immediately after it is collected from milk (young skorup), after a month of ripening in the tubs (mature skorup), and after six to twelve months of ripening in sheep skin (old skorup). There are dairies in Montenegro that produce skorup in an industrial way, but they focus on young skorup. Production of old skorup can only be done in the traditional way.

Dozet, Natalija, et al. *Autohtoni mlječni proizvodi.* [Autochthonous Dairy Products] Podgorica, Montenegro: Poljoprivredni Institut, 1996.

Slavko Mirecki

škripavac is a soft cheese that is produced in Lika, Gorski Kotar, and Kordun, mountainous regions of Croatia. Due to the specificity of this mountainous climate, characterized by short summers and long cold winters, soft cheese is mainly used for domestic consumption in this area. For the production of

škripavac raw cow's milk and rennet is used. Milk used for škripavac is produced from cows that are fed rich hay and a small amount of concentrates. Hay is harvested from the natural mountainous meadows, which gives the milk a unique composition high in fat content, but low in protein.

The make involves heating the curd to a temperature of 113°F (45°C). The size of the curd grains is similar to that of a hazelnut. Heating these grains gives škripavac cheese a rubbery taste. (In Croatian, "škripiti" means rubbery.)

Škripavac cheese has a cylindrical shape, a diameter of approximately 6 inches (15 centimeters) and a height of approximately 2 inches (6 centimeters). The weight of the cheese can vary between 2–4 pounds (900–1,200 grams). This cheese does not have a rind and it is milky in color. The cut surface is closed with a few holes remaining due to whey retention in the cheese body. The taste of the cheese is mildly sweet and a little salty.

See also CROATIA.

Magdić, Višnja, et al. "Sir škripavac—Technology and Quality." *Stočarstvo* 60 (2006): 121–124. In Croatian.

Samir Kalit

skyr

See ICELAND.

Sleight Farm is located near the village of Timsbury in Somerset, England, and is known for its raw goat's milk cheeses, as well as its pork and kid meat, which it supplies to some of London's best restaurants. It is owned and managed by Mary Holbrook, who was destined for a career in academia but instead settled with her husband—himself a distinguished professor of molecular biology—at his inherited family farm.

In the late 1970s she began keeping a few goats, experimenting with styles resembling Coulommiers and feta and selling them to local shops. See COULOMMIERS and FETA. She also developed her signature lactic cheese, a mold-ripened pyramid called Tymsboro (an archaic name for the nearby village). In the early 1980s, when she was in London for an archaeological meeting, she visited the famous department store Harrods to take stock of the competi-

Slovenia

See KRAŠKI KOZJI SIR and KRAŠKI OVČJI SIR.

Slow Food,

it is often said, was established as a direct response to the opening of a McDonald's restaurant in the center of Rome. In fact its antecedents are more interesting with roots in a culture of convivial wine and song, proto-environmentalism as well as left politics and the enjoyment of typical foods. Its predecessor was Arci Gola, a gastronomical group that grew out of a national association of societies under the auspices of the Italian Communist Party (PCI). With its heart increasingly centered on the Langhe region of Piedmont, Carlo Petrini emerged as the leader of this group of gastronomes dedicated to promoting a philosophy of taste and enjoyment alongside an enhanced understanding and knowledge of food and wine. Yet the foundation of Arci Gola in 1986 coincided with the scandal of methanol-contaminated wine—which also originated in the same region—that had serious repercussions for the entire Italian wine industry. The opening of a McDonald's in Piazza di Spagna in Rome was therefore considered another episode in the continuing threat to Italian culinary tradition, one that triggered a response by Arci Gola's membership with a manifesto published in the group's magazine in 1987 and signed by a host of well-known Italian intellectuals and artists. As an argument against the quickening pace of life in general and a consequent deterioration in the quality of food and eating in particular, it set forth a case for fast food's antithesis. Using a snail as its symbol the Slow Food concept thus became the basis of an international movement for "the defense of the right to pleasure," and was formally launched in Paris in November 1989.

Given its mission to inform, to educate, but above all to enjoy, it was natural that taste workshops were a vital way of bringing both producers and gastronomes together. Besides the large professional trade fairs such as Vinitaly, the growing network of *condottes*, local Slow Food associations, served to provide lay members with opportunities to learn about high-quality specialty products. Ultimately this process was to lead to the first international Salone del Gusto held over four days at the end of November 1996. The event was held, as it has been biennially ever since, in the Lingotto building, the iconic Fiat car factory

Sleight Farm near Bath, England, is known for its excellent fresh goat's milk cheeses. Mary Holbrook, the owner, has a mixed herd of more than 140 goats, some of which are seen here. © KATE ARDING

tion. A "dear old Cockney biddy" behind the counter suggested that Holbrook show her wares to their buyer; soon she was supplying numerous customers in London, including the young Neal's Yard Dairy. See NEAL'S YARD DAIRY.

Mary Holbrook eventually acquired a herd of dairy sheep, as well; her sheep's milk cheeses included soft, mold-ripened Little Ryding and cooked-curd Tyning. The sheep were sold in the early 1990s, but Holbrook continues to make a range of goat cheeses that are notable for their bold and complex flavors. These include Tymsboro, fresh Sleightlett, aged Old Ford, and cardoon-stamen-coagulated Tilleys along with its washed-rind sibling Cardo, which is matured in the ripening rooms of Neal's Yard Dairy, where Holbrook works alongside the maturation team one day per week.

Timsbury Community Website. http://www.timsbury.net/history.

Bronwen Percival

on the south side of Turin and today it attracts hundreds of thousands of Italian and international visitors, swelled by the addition of the Terra Madre event that runs alongside. The Salone del Gusto is, however, more than a series of taste workshops, though these are a vital part of the program. Above all, it serves to showcase those products regarded as endangered by global market forces and which have been recognized as worthy of inclusion in the Ark of Taste. While this project is designed to catalogue high-quality products (over 2,700) tied to a specific territory and threatened with extinction, a more carefully defined set of criteria were developed to identify products worthy of inclusion in a Presidium. The word literally means a garrison, or defensive structure, yet it is not only the product that is being defended but the knowledge, craftsmanship, and even the identity of its producers. Today there are more than 460 Presidia across the world each with a set of producers using methods and local materials that have been described within an agreed protocol. The objective of such codification is to maintain the integrity of the product, raise awareness among consumers, and make it more visible in today's market. Coordinating the work of the Ark and the Presidia is the Slow Food Foundation for Biodiversity, inaugurated in 2003.

As one of the most endangered types of indigenous foods under the particular scrutiny of food safety regulations are products derived from milk, it was appropriate that Slow Food should choose to hold a fair under the banner of "Cheese." Held on alternate years to the Salone in Carlo Petrini's home town of Bra (and where the headquarters of Slow Food are located), the event was first held in 1997. Further reinforcing this center of gravity of the movement, in 2004 the University of Gastronomic Sciences was established in the old Roman town of Pollenzo, just 4 miles (7 kilometers) from Bra. The university runs a three-year undergraduate program in gastronomic science and a master's in food culture and communication. Bra also hosts Slow Food Editore, dedicated to producing guides to fine wines and good local restaurants.

There is little doubt that Slow Food has made a major contribution to international discourse on gastronomy and on the need to protect high-quality products, including cheese, under the banner of "good, clean and fair." Yet despite its extraordinary innovation and energy, the sustainability of the organization appears to rest heavily on the longevity of its founder and president, Carlo Petrini.

See also FAIRS AND FESTIVALS.

Petrini, Carlo. *Slow Food Revolution: A New Culture for Eating and Living*. New York: Rizzoli, 2005.
Slow Food International. http://www.slowfood.com.
University of Gastronomic Sciences. http://www.unisg.it.

Colin Sage

Smelly Cheese Shop, The, is located in the iconic Central Market in Adelaide, South Australia. It was opened by Peter Heaney in 2001 as a sister store to Say Cheese, which had been operating in the Central Market since 1995. Say Cheese was already a strong business, but it offered a fairly conventional range of cheeses, similar to that of other delicatessens and gourmet food stores at the time. Specialized cheeses such as washed rinds, goat's milk varieties, and cheeses made from mixed milk were under-represented, but more Australians were gaining a taste for their complex flavors. The Smelly Cheese Shop became a showcase for cheeses with bolder flavors, including artisan Australian varieties from small producers.

A crucial feature of the business's success is the direct relationships it has with cheesemakers in Europe, the British Isles, and the United States, through Peter's partner, Valerie Henbest. French-born Valerie regularly visits producers overseas, and all the cheeses she sources are freighted by air, resulting in products of a higher quality than those available from many other Australian importers. Another unique feature of the business is the maturation room (which is overseen by a full-time French-trained affineur), where hard cheeses from Australia and Europe are carefully matured before sale. The Smelly Cheese Shop also has a wholesale division (which distributes cheeses to restaurants and other retailers in all Australian states), an online store and cheese club servicing customers Australia-wide, and hosts regular cheese appreciation events for members of the public.

See also AUSTRALIA AND NEW ZEALAND and CHEESEMONGER.

The Smelly Cheese Shop. http://www.smellycheese.com.au.

Sonia Cousins

smoked cheeses are cheeses that have been deliberately exposed to smoke or smoke derivatives to enhance the storage potential or sensory properties of the cheese. Exposing perishable foods such as meat and fish to vaporous smoke is one of the oldest forms of food preservation, and the practice of smoking cheeses probably also originated as a means to prevent spoilage. Smoking serves to preserve cheese in two ways: (1) partially dehydrating the product, especially at the surface, and (2) depositing vaporous acidic compounds and compounds that have antimicrobial and antioxidant properties on the cheese surface, which render the cheese more hostile to the growth of dangerous microorganisms. Smoking also affects the taste and appearance of cheese through the absorption of flavorful compounds and through reactions of smoke components with cheese proteins to form a brown color. By the time of the Roman Empire, some smoked cheeses had acquired considerable fame for their superior flavor, especially those smoked at the Velabrum in Rome, as noted by the writers Pliny the Elder and Martial. See ANCIENT CIVILIZATIONS and PLINY THE ELDER.

In modern practice, the smoking of cheese is usually performed to enhance the sensory properties and appeal to niche markets. However, smoking is not without controversy. Concerns have been raised about possible health risks posed by the transfer to some food products of carcinogenic polycyclic aromatic hydrocarbons, which may be present in smoke at high levels depending on the conditions used to generate the smoke. However, in the case of cheese, the "cold smoking" conditions typically used to treat cheese seem to obviate this risk. An alternative to natural smoking is the application of liquid smoke, which is prepared by passing smoke through water.

Gilbert, J., and M. E. Knowles. "The Chemistry of Smoked Foods: A Review." *Journal of Food Technology* 10 (June 1975): 245–261.

Riha, W. E., W. L. Wendorff, and S. Rank. "Benzo(a)pyrene Content of Smoked and Smoke-Flavored Cheese Products Sold in Wisconsin." *Journal of Food Protection* 55 (1992): 636–638.

Paul S. Kindstedt

soft-ripened cheeses, also called pâte molle cheeses, are a type of cheese whose texture softens during aging through the action of secondary starter cultures, or ripening cultures, of molds, yeast, and bacteria. Because these microorganisms are aerobes, they grow on the surface of the cheese and transform it from outside to inside. See RIPENING CULTURES.

This type of cheese is usually small and has a high ratio of surface to volume with a high moisture content of 50–60 percent. For the growth of secondary starter cultures, the aging room should have a high humidity of 85–98 percent and a well-controlled temperature. The aging process takes two to six weeks. The soft-ripened cheeses can be divided into two groups: bloomy rind, with a furry white or beige coat, and smear or washed-rind, with a pinkish red- to orange-colored sticky surface. See BLOOMY-RIND CHEESES and WASHED-RIND CHEESES.

The bloomy-rind cheeses such as Camembert, Brie, Chaource, and Neufchâtel are ripened by the white-rind-forming molds of *Penicillium camemberti* and *Geotrichum candidum*. In the nineteenth century, the gray-colored molds *P. album* and *P. glaucum* were widely used, but the customers preference for white rind made *P. candidum* (the trade name of *P. camemberti*) more common in the twentieth century. The cultures are added to milk or sprayed on the surface of the new cheese after unmolding and the initial drying. The washed-rind cheeses, including Livarot, Époisses de Bourgogne, Fromage de Herve, Langres, Munster, Limburger, and Reblochon, are commonly ripened by *Brevibacterium linens* and other coryneforms. See PENICILLIUM; GEOTRICHUM CANDIDUM; and BREVIBACTERIUM LINENS.

For either type of soft-ripened cheese, a sweet rennet curd or an acid curd can be used. The fragile curd is ladled directly into the molds to hold the maximum moisture or, for larger-size cheeses, the curd is cut into small pieces before molding. The curd is seldom cooked, and a light pressing can be applied to achieve the desired moisture content and acidity. The cheese is removed from the molds and dry-salted or brined before being dried. The role of the white molds and the smear bacteria in aging has been intensely studied, but the mechanisms are not yet perfectly understood. The pH of the curd reaches 4.6–4.7 by the primary lactic acid–producing culture, and the yeasts and *Geotrichum candidum* take up the surface followed by a fast growth of *Penicillium camemberti* for bloomy-rind kinds. These microorganisms consume lactose and metabolize amino acids to produce ammonia, so the surface acidity decreases and ammonia diffuses into the center of the cheese. As a result lactate and soluble calcium phosphate move toward the surface increasing the pH of the interior.

Increased pH and proteolysis by residual rennet and the secondary starter culture gradually soften the interior of the cheese. For a smear-ripened cheese, washing with brine encourages the proliferation of *Brevibacterium linens* and suppresses mold growth. The high proteolytic acidity of *B. linens* induces similar softening effects on the interior of the cheese. In addition to the soft texture, the other important characteristics of soft-ripened cheese are distinctive aromas and flavors. These secondary starter culture and non-starter microorganisms in the air produce countless volatile compounds such as aldehydes, short-chain fatty acids, ketones, lactones, and sulfur compounds through extensive proteolysis and lipolysis in the cheese. See PROTEOLYSIS and LIPOLYSIS.

Production of high-quality soft-ripened cheese demands from the cheesemaker a profound knowledge of the microbial ecology of the cheese surface as well as knowledge of how to balance the microflora to arrive at the optimum flavor and texture. Unlike the production of hard cheeses, soft-ripened cheese production is highly market–driven. Hard cheeses were developed out of necessity as an effective way of preserving seasonal milk and making a durable form for transportation, but soft-ripened cheeses are fragile. Before refrigeration was widely available, the production was near the metropolitan areas, where they were sold and consumed. In this sense the soft-ripened cheese is an indulgence food.

Fox, P., et al. *Cheese, Chemistry, Physics and Microbiology.* London: Elsevier, 2004.

Law, Barry, and A. T. Tamime. *Technology of Cheesemaking.* 2d ed. New York: Wiley-Blackwell, 2010.

Tunick, Michael. *The Science of Cheese.* New York: Oxford University Press, 2014.

Soyoung Scanlan

Sognefjord Artisanal Geitost is a traditional Norwegian condensed whey cheese made from goat's milk whey. It is recognized as a Slow Food Presidium cheese. See SLOW FOOD. The production takes place in and around Undredal and Aurland along the innermost branches of the Sognefjord, much of it within the UNESCO World Heritage Site of Nærøyfjorden. The area has a centuries-old tradition of producing white and brown cheese from raw goat's milk on summer mountain farms. The white cheese was originally unsalted, and often eaten with salt meats for dinner. The brown geitost, or brimost as it is known locally, is inseparable from the production

The first presentation of Sognefjord Artisan Geitost at the Slow Food Cheese festival in Bra, Italy, in September 2005. One of the producers, Pascale Baudonnel, is at right. From left are the daughters of three producers: Brita Underdal, Anna Elise Borlaug, and Maria Baudonnel Underdal. OVE FOSSÅ

of the white cheese. The whey from the white cheese is boiled over an open fire for 8–10 hours to concentrate and brown it. A little goat's milk and cow's cream is added to the whey to make a smoother, tastier product.

During the twentieth century the industrialization and centralization of dairies in Norway nearly wiped out farmhouse cheesemaking. But thanks to stubborn *budeier* (dairymaids) on remote mountain farms, traditions were kept alive. In the 1990s the food safety authorities tried to shut down the last producers of traditional raw-milk cheeses, but did not succeed. The producers in Undredal fought the authorities, and won. In 2003 they received authorization to make raw-milk cheese and that sparked a revival of raw-milk cheesemaking in Norway.

Within the Presidium, there are at present four producers, one of them a cooperative of three families. The home of the cooperative and one other producer is the tiny village of Undredal, which has a population of eighty people and five hundred goats.

See also CONCENTRATED WHEY CHEESE and NORWAY.

"Sognefjord Artisanal Geitost." Slow Food Foundation. http://www.fondazioneslowfood.com/en/slow-food-presidia/sognefjord-artisan-geitost.

Ove Fosså

Sombor cheeses are traditionally produced from raw sheep's milk in the northern part of Serbia (around the city of Sombor) and are highly appreciated for their unique nutty flavor as well as for their mushroom shape. The earliest historical record of Sombor cheeses, which describes their position in the local market dates back to 1748. Today these cheeses are still produced by a few small craft manufacturers, usually using cow's milk.

Sombor cheese production is characterized by two specific processes: the addition of water to the milk (15–20 percent of the total volume) and the washing of the cheese curd to prevent intense acid development. Blocks of cheese are usually dry-salted and put together in special wooden molds called *kačica*, where ripening takes place. During pressing, the molds are turned upside down, and the next day the upper part of the cheese is formed by mounding a mass of curd approximately 4–5 inches (10–15 centimeters) above the mold's upper edge, forming a shape resembling a mushroom. The cheese is wrapped in cloth and left to ripen for one month at 59–68°F (15–20°C) and 80 percent relative humidity. Owing to Sombor cheese's specific shape and differential ripening, the upper and lower parts of the cheese are characterized by different properties. The upper parts have a strong skin, yellow color, and semihard texture, while the lower parts are characterized by a white color, soft texture and higher acidity (similar to brined cheeses). Characteristic flavors are the result of complex biochemical changes during ripening, mostly owing to autochthonous microflora activity.

Dozet, Natalija, et al. *Autohtoni mlječni proizvodi* [Autochthonous Dairy Products]. Podgorica, Montenegro: Poljoprivredni Institut, 1996.

Zorica Radulović and Jelena Miočinović

A **soufflé,** minus an accent over the final letter, is, according to the 1913 edition of *Webster's Revised Unabridged Dictionary*, "a murmuring or blowing sound." With the diacritic marked, it is also, in both sweet and savory forms, an egg-based baked foam that effects an apparently miraculous rise from frothy batter to a puffed, crusty balloon when baked.

A soufflé is made of beaten egg whites folded into a sauce base and baked in a ramekin or other high-sided dish. The rise of the crust is due to a few scientific principles, beginning with the soufflé's main ingredient: egg whites. As the egg whites are beaten, their proteins bond to each other, creating bubble walls. Then as the soufflé is baked, the heat from the oven heats the batter and some of its liquid is converted to gas, further expanding the bubble walls.

Sweet soufflés are made with a base of fruit and sugar, or of cocoa powder or melted chocolate. Savory soufflés have a base of béchamel sauce and usually contain shredded cheese, commonly Gruyère, Comté, Parmesan, or a combination. In the United States Cheddar is a regular substitute.

The first recipe for a baked egg foam resembling today's soufflé is found in Vincent La Chapelle's 1742 *Le Cuisinier Moderne*, for his "Crème à la Sultane," which instructs: "Once it's pushed up, sprinkle with sugar towards the end. Serve warm." Sweet soufflés were served by the Parisian chef Antoine Beauvilliers at the end of the eighteenth century. He offered recipes for them in his 1814 *L'Art du Cuisiner*. Other early soufflé recipes appeared in Louis Ude's 1813 *The French Cook*. The most technical, detailed soufflé recipes of the nineteenth century appeared in Antoine Carême's *Pâtissier Royal Parisien*, which also made them seem much more finicky and difficult than they are.

Cheese soufflés gained popularity soon after the sweet kind, with one of the oldest and best recipes for a Parmesan soufflé coming from Antoine Escoffier's encyclopedic 1903 *Guide Culinaire*. Soufflés of sweet and cheese varieties came into great vogue in the United States in the 1960s.

Davidson, Alan. *The Oxford Companion to Food*. Oxford: Oxford University Press, 1999.
Escoffier, Antoine. *The Complete Guide to the Art of Modern Cookery*. Translated by H. L. Cracknell and R. J. Kaufmann. New York: John Wiley, 1997.
Goldstein, Darra. *The Oxford Companion to Sugar and Sweets*. Oxford: Oxford University Press, 2015.
McGee, Harold. *On Food and Cooking*. New York: Scribner, 2004.

Tamar Adler

Cheese **soups** are popular in the cheesemaking mountain regions of Europe: the Alps, the Jura, Auvergne, extending from France to Switzerland, Austria, southern Germany, and northern Italy. The soups are filling, rustic, with some based on milk and flour, or egg, others on bread or rice and vegetables. Piemontese rice soup is made with winter vegetables and rice, finished with egg beaten with grated Parmesan and parsley. Swiss cheese soup has cubes of bread, Sbrinz, and onions cooked in butter, all put into soup plates and hot beef bouillon poured over. For Auvergnat cheese soup onions cooked in butter are added to vegetable stock. A soup tureen is filled with alternate layers of bread and finely sliced Cantal, the boiling broth poured over and the soup is cooked in the oven until a layer of melted cheese forms on top. Gruyère, Emmentaler, and Comté are used in similar soups in the Jura and Savoie. Cheese and beer soup is popular in Germany. Onions and garlic are cooked in butter, flour is added, then chicken stock and beer; and handfuls of grated Emmentaler or Gruyère are stirred in to finish. Two Italian soups combine eggs and Parmesan: for zuppa pavese, poached eggs and small pieces of fried bread topped with grated cheese are put into soup plates and chicken stock is poured over; Stracciatella is made by whisking a mixture of egg, Parmesan, and semolina into chicken stock until threads appear.

Many soups are finished with croûtes topped with grated cheese browned in the oven. The best known is mahogany-colored French onion soup. Cheese has a place in many other vegetable soups; pea and Stilton, spinach and Parmesan, pumpkin and Fontina are more recent recipes.

Graham, Peter. *Classic Cheese Cookery*. Harmondsworth, U.K.: Penguin, 1988.
Grigson, Sophie, ed. *The Soup Book*. London: Dorling Kindersley, 2009.

Jill Norman

sour skimmed-milk cheeses (Sauermilchkäse, in German) designates a family of mostly northern European cheeses with very ancient roots, made from skim sour milk (most often cow's) without the use of rennet. Historically a byproduct of sour cream (especially in Norway) and butter, the most lucrative dairy commodity of a farm in these regions, it prevented the rather large amounts of skim milk from spoiling. This milk was still rich in protein but, before modern centrifuges and cooling systems, undoubtedly had already been allowed to develop a sour tang in the attempt to get as much cream off it as possible. For the simplest, smallest forms of Sauermilchkäse, the skim milk is left to thicken (possibly with lactic acid bacteria added to hasten the process), cut, slightly warmed, cut again, left to drain in bags, and finally pressed and broken into big crumbs. This quark, which is much drier and tastes more sour than what is conventionally sold

Pultost is a Norwegian sour skimmed-milk cheese flavored with caraway seeds. This Pultost was made by Tom Seter of Lage Vigdal, and was the Gold medal winner at the National Farmhouse Cheese Show in Oslo, Norway, October 2005. OVE FOSSÅ

under the name, is thoroughly mixed with salt and sodium bicarbonate (baking soda), sometimes flavored with caraway seeds, and left to ferment at room temperature. It is then shaped into small rounds, sticks, or loaves, traditionally using very simple devices ranging from human hands to small wooden molds and woven baskets, and left to ripen again. Depending on local traditions and the bacterial cultures present, these small cheeses may develop either white mold or the more pungent and sticky washed rind with *Brevibacterium linens.* In contemporary commercial production both are sprayed on the fresh cheeses. As the cheeses ripen from the outside, the white curd gradually turns yellow and becomes almost translucent, or speckig ("glassy"). All these cheeses have a very low fat content (1 to a maximum 10 percent FDM) and are very rich in protein (around 30–50 percent). See QUARK.

In Germany traditional varieties include Hessischer Handkäse (a PGI, protected geographical indication), Harzer Käse, Nieheimer (PGI and Ark of Taste), Mainzer Käse, Korbkäse, Stangenkäse, and Olmützer Quargel, with Würchwitzer Milbenkäse (Ark of Taste) traditionally left to mature in small boxes with mites. Handkäse is typically eaten "with music" (Handkäs' mit Musik), that is, with chopped onions, oil, and vinegar. Kochkäse (from Franken and Hessen) is heated, often with cream or butter, to make it soft and spreadable.

The Norwegian gamalost (old cheese) is infamous for its strong taste and smell. Francis Merrick Wyndham describes his encounter with gamalost in Norway in 1859 like this: "When we visited the dairy, I had the imprudence to venture into the cellar beneath, and to look into a coffin-shaped box where the *Gammel ost* was kept, and whence issued such an odour, that I quickly let go the lid and scrambled up the stairs again." The modern industrial Gamalost frå Vik (PGI) is a younger and milder cheese, but it can look quite fearsome at the stage in ripening when it is covered in a thick lawn of *Mucor* molds. The brown, 4-pound (1.7-kilogram) wheels of gamalost mature in just two weeks.

Pultost from Hedmark and Oppland (Slow Food Presidium) is recognized by its grainy consistency. It is not pressed into molds or shaped in any way, but the separate grains of a young cheese gradually "melt" together as it ripens and becomes stronger in taste. Most often it is flavored with caraway. The whitish-yellow pultost is traditionally eaten with

bread, or with boiled potatoes. Kokost is pultost heated with cream to make it smooth and spreadable.

Olomoucké tvarůžky (PGI) is a Czech cheese similar to German Handkäse. It is also known and produced in Germany as Olmützer Quargel, and in Austria simply as Quargel.

Sour milk cheesemaking used to occur everywhere in the eastern Alps. Much has disappeared, but a number of local varieties are still found in Switzerland, Austria, and Italy.

Werdenberger Sauerkäse, Liechtensteiner Sauerkäse, and Toggenburger Bloderkäse share the same protected designation of origin in Switzerland and Liechtenstein, and are distinguished mostly by the production area, providing a taste of terroir. Bloderkäse is a young cheese up to twenty days old. After thirty days it becomes known as a Sauerkäse (sour cheese). Quite different from other sour milk cheeses is the Swiss Schabziger from the Glarus region. It is hard and dry, shaped as a small cone, colored green, and flavored with blue fenugreek (*Trigonella caerulea*). It is primarily used in grated form to flavor dishes. Sold in the United States as Sap Sago, in Switzerland the oldest brand is Schabziger, in existence since 1463.

Aurina Valley Graukäse from Alto Adige (southern Tyrol) in Italy is a Slow Food Presidium cheese. The drained white curds are molded into wheels of up to 9 pounds (4 kilograms). The cheese ripens for two to three weeks, turning "glassy" like German Handkäse or even becoming soft and jellylike. It is closely related to the Tyrolean Graukäse (PDO) from Austria.

Other Austrian sour milk cheeses are Montafoner Sura Kees and Innviertler Abgereifter (both in the Ark of Taste), Murtaler Steirerkäse, Ennstaler Steirerkäse, and Glundner Käse from Kärnten.

Fosså, Ove. "How Old Is Old Cheese? Gamalost in Coffin-Shaped Boxes and Eccentric Jars." In *Proceedings of the Oxford Symposium on Food and Cookery 1999*. Totnes, U.K.: Prospect, 2000, pp. 144–160.
Gudheim, Helge. *Kinning, bresting og ysting i Valdres.* Ulnes, Norway: Mat og Kultur AS, 2013.
Heinzelmann, Ursula. *Erlebnis Käse und Wein*. Frankfurt: Scherz, 2009.

Ove Fosså and Ursula Heinzelmann

South Africa is seeing a twenty-first-century florescence of cheesemaking. In spite of wide-open spaces suitable for dairying as well as culinary and cultural influences from the cheese-loving Europeans and English, cheese production and diversity in South Africa was fairly minimal until the late twentieth century. Annual per capita consumption of cheese in South Africa as of 2015 was 4 pounds (1.9 kilograms), up from 2 pounds (1 kilogram) in 1995.

A lack of refrigeration in many areas, indigenous diets with minimal dairy consumption, and the challenges of logistics and regulations for importing livestock were important factors. From the late nineteenth to the early twentieth centuries, Department of Agriculture moves designed to put the wheels in motion for dairy business in fact threw up roadblocks to cheesemaking. The government urged cooperation among farmers to produce quality dairy products and cultivate markets. Jerseys, Guernseys, Ayrshires, Shorthorns, Herefords, Devons, and other cattle breeds were imported for cross-breeding; Friesland cows were especially used to improve the milk supply. The legacy of that cooperative effort, geared toward standardization and economies of scale, proved inhospitable to farmstead cheesemakers. Jane Selander, who runs Constantia's Cheesery south of Capetown, told *Culture* magazine in 2012 that Dairy Board control from 1918 to 1998 meant farmers who wanted to make cheese had to buy their milk back from the board.

An interest in diverse, sophisticated cheese has been on the rise since 1995. It is attributable to a number of factors, including a generation of young consumers with greater knowledge of food and wine thanks to magazines, cookbooks, and cooking shows; an increase in dining out; and the maturity of the South African wine industry, on the tails of which farmstead and artisanal cheesemaking is following. Commercial food service has accounted for a 50 percent growth in demand for processed cheese alone. Once considered a luxury, cheese is finding a place at the table for many occasions. European-style bloomy, washed-rind, brushed-rind, brined, blue, and raw-milk cheeses are growing among the ranks of South African cheese.

Two separate annual events organized by Agri-Expo and its various partners and sponsors have fueled demand for these cheeses and bolstered the efforts of artisan cheesemakers. Launched in 2002, the annual South African Cheese Festival is now the country's premier outdoor food festival and has been attended by some thirty thousand cheese lovers in recent years. The South Africa Dairy Championships, held since 1833, showcase South African cheeses, inspire improved cheese quality, and elevate its profile among consumers. More than half the 879 entries at the 2015 championships were cheese, which is the event's largest category. In 2016, 895 dairy products (including raw-milk cheese, which was added as a category in 2013) were entered from 85 producers.

Historian Sir Charles Prestwood Lucas, who wrote in 1913 that South African cheeses were as yet "only imitations of the Dutch, Cheddar, and Stilton types," would scarcely recognize the present selections, many with creative names that proudly proclaim their national origin. Examples include Kwaito, a mild and creamy cow's milk Gouda-style (plain or flavored); the name is slang in the Isicamtho language for "cool," and also a term for a popular genre of South African music. Highvelder is a full-flavored, semihard goat's milk cheese from the Greater Benoni area. Langbaken Karoo Crumble from the Northern Cape is a crumbly, mature Jersey milk hard cheese with a tangy and slightly fruity aftertaste.

Some South African cheesemakers today are crafting cheese as homage to international influences. Award-winning Dalewood Fromage Huguenot, a semihard, brushed-rind, pasteurized Jersey milk estate cheese from the Western Cape, is aged six months to two years; Swissland Brie is made from goat's milk in a Swiss-style chalet in KwaZulu-Natal. Boerenkaas, a farmer's cheese that is akin to Gouda and originally developed in the Netherlands, is produced at the foot of the Zuurberg Mountains in the Eastern Cape. Award-winning, small-batch Healey's handmade bandaged Cheddar, made with raw milk from grass-fed Friesian cows and aged eight to twenty-four months in the Cape Winelands, follows a 150-year-old recipe. On the north side of Paarl, artisanal mozzarella produced by Buffalo Ridge according to Italy's DOC standards from the milk of water buffalo imported from Campagnia is one of the most exotic European-origin cheeses in South Africa.

Sustainability is another contemporary approach being embraced by some South African cheesemakers. Examples include Wegraakbosch Farm, in the mountains of Magoebaskloof in Limpopo province, a solar-powered eco-friendly dairy that produces Mutchli, Emmentaler, Havarti, and Tilsiter with milk from Brown Swiss cows and a few Saanen goats. Dragonfly Farm in Napier (Overberg) produces an organic Alp-style goat cheese.

Clarke, Jim. "Legends of the Magic Cape." *Culture*, Summer 2012.

"15 South African Cheeses Everyone Should Try." Eat Out, 24 April 2013. http://www.eatout.co.za/article/15-south-african-cheeses-everyone-should-try.

Lucas, Sir Charles Prestwood. *South Africa: History to 1895*. Capetown: Clarendon, 1913.

"Slow Cheese: South Africa." Slow Food Foundation. http://slowfood.com/slowcheese/eng/104/south-africa.

South African Cheese. http://www.cheesesa.co.za.

"South Africa's Cheese-makers." http://www.southafrica.net/za/en/articles/entry/article-south-africas-cheesemakers1.

Robin Watson

Cheese in **Spain** richly reflects, in both production and consumption, the country's culturally diverse history and its equally diversified geographic regions. With more than one hundred recognized types of cheese, those made with sheep's milk remain the most common, but goat's milk, cow's milk, and mixed milk cheese are produced in forms of fresco (fresh), pressed, curado (aged one year), añejo or viejo (aged for more than one year), and blue-veined.

History

Archaeological evidence suggests that cheese was made and consumed in ancient Spain. Vessels and straining implements date rudimentary cheese-making back to the fourth millennium B.C.E. More advanced methods had been established prior to the Roman occupation, including a pressed sheep's milk cheese. For Romans cheese remained a prominent part of their diet, even when in Hispania, eating it as part of *ientaculum*, or breakfast.

With subsequent cultures gaining and losing power from the fifth century through the next millennium, cheese production and consumption remained. Isidore of Seville, in his sixth century *Etymologies*, when writing of salt wrote: "Indeed, even sheep, cattle, and oxen are especially incited to their fodder by salt, and their milk is more bountiful and their gift of cheese more gratifying." He also discusses a *fiscella*, a small basket for straining curd, and explains that cheese, or *caseum*, is named so as it "lacks whey" which was "completely removed so it might be firmed in its bulk." The medieval sheep ranchers in Castile

wielded considerable power in the semi-arid plains, where the region was dominated by sheep and goat farming, as it is today, responsible for the globally known Manchego. See MANCHEGO.

The Catholic church, particularly the Benedictine monasteries, and later the Cistercians, known for their agricultural production and record keeping, extended cheesemaking practices throughout not just Spain, but much of western Europe. For example, Cóbreces, a cow's milk cheese, is both named after and produced by Cistercian nuns in the Cantabrian region. Along the northern swath of Spain, devoted pilgrims—including shepherds—along the Camino de Santiago, consumed cheese and brought with them knowledge of cheese production. This is also where one finds the Picos de Europa, the mountain range rich with damp limestone caves used to age blue cheeses like the emblematic Cabrales. See CABRALES and MONASTIC CHEESEMAKING.

Not only Christians, but Muslims and Jews also played a role in cheese production and consumption. One of the more unique continuations of Spanish cheese traditions is its "thistle" cheese, which uses wild thistle's pistils (*Cynara cardunculus* L. and *Cynara lumilis* L.) as a coagulant rather than animal rennet. This tradition of using the thistle, still in use in Catalonia, Extremadure, and the Balearic Islands (as well as Portugal), appears in the 1513 treatise *Obra de agricultura*, by Gabriel Alonso de Herrera. In it he notes that this improves the end product, not making it bitter as rennet or fig sap does, but rather the cheese "becomes flavorful, for perfection of taste…which is sweet." Chef Rosa Tovar asserts that it was the Jewish prohibition on mixing meat and milk that necessitated the substitute that continued the practice. The tradition was later introduced to the Spanish borders and islands when Jews were forced to convert and later expelled from Spain. Today, because the thistle plant can lack the enzymes to properly coagulate the milk, synthetic products (fermentation-produced chymosin) are sometimes used, but several traditional cheeses are made protected by DO status, including Torta del Casar and Las Hurdes, which uses the milk from the black retinta goats. Two other popular thistle cheeses include Serrat, a sheep's milk cheese in Catalonia, and its relative, Tupi, a fresh, soft curd cheese sold in small pots and eaten for dessert. Additionally it may have been the disdain for the Jewish separation of meat and cheese that Christians began grating cheese on their meat dishes. See PLANT-DERIVED COAGULANTS; FERMENTATION-PRODUCED CHYMOSIN; TORTA DEL CASAR; and DIETARY LAWS (RELIGIOUS).

The Muslim influence on agriculture and cuisine also remained even after the Christians began reconquering Spain and medieval cookbooks from the Islamic areas of Spain—the east and south—incorporate the ingredients, many of which use cheese. Moorish eggplant, which calls for grating cheese over eggplant, is one of the recipes in Rupert de Nola's 1520 *Libre de Coch* and the earlier fourteenth-century Catalan cookbook *Sent Soví*, which was heavily influenced by Arabic foodstuffs, includes recipes for garlic cheese, two-cheese sauces, slices of cheese cooked with a fritter batter, cheese fritters, and cheese cream. Spanish dishes with cheese even traversed Europe; "squash in the Catalan Style," is included in the *Libro de Arte Coquinaria*, a mid-fifteenth-century cookbook by Martino de Como, a dish of squash mixed with saffron, sugar, sweet spices, and verjuice, and finished with egg yolks and aged cheese.

In the sixteenth century, when Spain was expanding its power in the Americas and enjoying its Golden Age of literature, cheese became a signifier of good taste—even poorer homes could usually procure a bit of cheese for guests. In the 1554 picaresque novella *Lazarillo de Tormes*, the title character, who is continuously searching for food, laments that one of his masters locked up all of the food and there was not even "cheese lying on a shelf" like one would find normally and resorts to eating the cheese rinds from a mouse trap. Sancho Panza, too, in Cervantes's epic 1605 novel *Don Quixote*, spent many pages nibbling on Manchego and Troncon cheeses and washing them down with local wines. In both books and in reality, cheese was the food that Spaniards expected to have on hand, poor and rich alike. The quality, however, might differ. It is at the wedding of the wealthy Camacho where Sancho Panza swoons; cheese was served with plenty of bread and wine and appeared again at dessert, in *la flaona*, fritters filled with hard and soft cheeses, lightened with whipped eggs, sweetened with sugar, and flavored with mint and rosewater, served with honey.

In Minorca the English introduced Friesian cows after its occupation (1713–1763), a breed used in Mahón, a cheese now with denominación de origen protegida (PDO) status. See MAHÓN-MENORCA. By the nineteenth century, however, and throughout much of the twentieth century, the quality of Spanish cheese was questioned. Travelers to Spain were ambivalent, at best, regarding cheese. One traveler, Robert Mccoun, reported in 1852 that it was the cheese and bread that were the only parts of the meal that saved the diner from the "uncivilized" cuisine of Spain, while his contemporary Richard Ford wrote,

> The Spanish loaf has not that mysterious sympathy with butter and cheese as it has in our verdurous Old England, probably because in these torrid regions pasture is rare, butter bad, and cheese worse, albeit they suited the iron digestion of Sancho, who knew of nothing better: none, however, who have ever tasted Stilton or Parmesan will join in his eulogies of Castilian *queso*, the poorness of which will be estimated by the distinguished consideration in which a round cannon-ball Dutch cheese is held throughout the Peninsula.

Spain, economically, lagged behind much of western development for much of the last two centuries but since the mid-1980s has enjoyed some prosperity—both of which affected cheese. After the Spanish Civil War, World War II, and during the authoritarian rule of Francisco Franco, attempts were made to make Spain efficient and self-sufficient. A 1960s quota mandated that dairies fulfill a minimum of 10,000 liters of milk per day, a practice that industrialized cheesemaking to the extent that many traditional cheeses stopped being produced entirely or went underground. Since the 1980s when this legislation was repealed, artisanal Spanish cheese has had a renaissance, with some traditional cheeses, including Garrotxa, being rediscovered. See GARROTXA. The government began promoting Spain as "the land of 100 cheeses." In 1981 the Spanish Ministry of Agriculture, Fisheries and Food first designated Roncal, a sheep's milk cheese made from the Lacha breed in the Navarra mountains, protected by denominación de origen (DO). Since then Spain's National Designations of Origin Institute (INDO) continues to regulate cheese with either DO, currently twenty-eight, as does the European Union with appointing denominación de origen protegida (PDO) status.

Varieties

Spanish cheeses reflect the geographic diversity of the country along regional divisions. The verdant and mountainous north produces cheese from cow's and mixed milks. Arzúa-Ulloa, Tetilla, and the smoked San Simón are popular cow's milk cheeses from Galicia. Asturias, el Pais de los Quesos (the land of cheeses), and Cantabria include the cow's and mixed milk blues Cabrales and Picón Bejes-Tresviso, as well as Afuega'l Pitu, Casín, and the smoked Gamoneú and Liébana. The Basque and Navarre enjoy Idiazábal, a pressed sheep's milk cheese that pairs well with the cider, and is frequently served as part of a cider house meal. To the east Tronchón is a sheep's-goat's milk cheese from Aragon and Formatge de l'Alt Urgell i la Cerdanya is a soft cow's milk cheese from Catalonia. See ARZÚA-ULLOA; AFUEGA'L PITU; and IDIAZABAL.

Along the periphery Valencia cannot currently boast any PDO cheeses, but several goat's milk cheeses, including Blanquet, remain popular. Murcia, just to the south offers Queso de Murcia, made from the Murcian breed of goats, and the similar Queso de Murcia al Vino, the rinds of which are soaked in red wine (a.k.a. Drunken Goat). To the east, in addition to Mahón the Baleric islands are also known for the blended milk Queso Mallorca, aged for a range of times. Along the south the Alpujarra Mountains give name to the eponymous goat cheese, marked with flowers and grasses to reflect the local flora. Extremadura showcases the La Serena and Torta del Casar, both of which are made with Merino sheep's milk and curdled with thistle, and the goat's milk Ibores. The Canary Islands boast three PDO cheeses: goat cheese Majorero, the mixed milk Flor de Guía, and frequently smoked goat's milk Palmero. See MURCIA; LA SERENA; and PALMERO.

In the interior regions of Spain, cheese production is dominated by the sheep and goats of the plains. Rioja celebrates the goat's milk Camerano, often served with honey as dessert. Castile-León offers a range of styles, from the aged sheep's milk Zamorano, rubbed with olive oil, to Valdeon, a blue wrapped in maple or chestnut leaves, to fresh cheeses including Burgos. Finally Castile La Mancha offers the most well-known of Spanish cheeses, Manchego. See ZAMORANO and VALDEON.

In Spain cheese is commonly served in tapas in the cafes and bars. Cheese may also be eaten by itself, as a table cheese, in main dishes, with desserts, or with accompaniments such as cured meats, fresh bread, fresh fruits or the characteristic *membrillo* (Spanish quince paste).

See also LA MANCHA.

Canut, Enric. *Cheese * Landscape*. Barcelona: Udyat DL, 2008.

European Commission of Agricultural and Rural Development. DOOR list. http://ec.europa.eu/agriculture/quality/door/list.html.

Nadeau, C. *Food Matters: Alonso Quijano's Diet and the Discourse of Food in Early Modern Spain*. Toronto: University of Toronto Press, 2016.

Roden, Claudia. *The Food of Spain*. New York: Ecco, 2011.

Tovar, Rosa. "Spanish Thistle-Bloom Cheese." *Gastronomica* 2, no. 2 (Spring 2002): 77–82.

Beth M. Forrest

Specialist Cheesemakers Association

(SCA) is an organization founded in the United Kingdom in 1989 as an alliance of cheesemakers, retailers, wholesalers, and others interested in cheese. The association was established to defend the right to make cheese from unpasteurized milk, in opposition to a government proposal to enforce compulsory pasteurization of milk in order to control *Listeria monocytogenes*. See PASTEURIZATION and LISTERIA. Today, the SCA offers an opportunity to share ideas and increase sales of specialist cheeses by providing a forum for its members to air their views on commercial, technical, and legislative matters to a worldwide audience.

In 2008 the SCA established a Technical Committee (SCA/TC) to utilize the available knowledge and expertise to publish technical articles, organize conferences, symposia, and training courses, and actively participate in the work of external organizations. The SCA/TC is responsible for maintaining and revising the SCA Assured Code of Practice (ACOP), which has become an international benchmark for good cheesemaking procedures. The code also forms the basis of a customized version of the Safe and Local Supplier Approval (SALSA) audit standard, known as SALSA *plus* CHEESE, which provides a management framework to enable cheesemakers, wholesalers, and retailers to attain third-party approval, demonstrating to their customers their commitment to quality, safety, and legality. The ACOP has legal status in England that enables the Primary Authority Co-ordinated Partnership (a UK government initiative intended to promote consistent interpretation of food law in different regions of the UK) to provide a "level playing field" across the country. The patron of the SCA is HRH the Prince of Wales.

See also HODGSON, RANDOLPH and UNITED KINGDOM.

SALSA: Safe and Local Supplier Approval. http://www
.salsafood.co.uk.
Specialist Cheesemakers Association. http://www
.specialistcheesemakers.co.uk.

Paul Neaves

specialty cheese is a retail category, as well as a marketing term, that distinguishes products considered "special" in comparison to the most popular varieties of industrially manufactured block, or commodity, cheese. The American Cheese Society defines specialty cheese as "cheese of limited production, with particular attention paid to natural flavor and texture profiles. Specialty cheeses may be made from all types of milk (cow, sheep, goat) and may include flavorings, such as herbs, spices, fruits and nuts."

Specialty cheeses may include international styles (in the United States, for example, Parmesan, Gouda, feta); cheeses with added flavorings, such as herbs, spices, peppers, fruits, and nuts; cheeses that are individually wrapped or specially packaged; and cheeses made in small quantities for niche markets, whether manufactured by hand or using industrial methods. Examples include pieces of Cheddar cut into the shape of Wisconsin or Vermont and coated in wax, an herbed cheese such as Boursin, and any farmstead cheese. Whereas all artisanal cheeses are specialty cheeses, not all specialty cheeses are artisanal. See FARMSTEAD and ARTISANAL.

Specialty cheeses are value-added products, largely distinguished by how they are marketed. Whereas commodity cheese is sold as a staple good, in precisely weighed, Cryovaced "grab-and-go" pieces in the dairy case of a supermarket, alongside gallons of milk and pounds of butter, specialty cheese is often displayed in the deli section of a supermarket in hand-wrapped random-weight pieces, alongside salami and olives. By the 2010s American supermarket chains such as Wegman's, Whole Foods, and Kroger's offered service dairy departments where imported and domestic specialty cheeses are promoted by sampling and cut and wrapped to order. See ADVERTISING AND PROMOTION.

Consumer demand for specialty cheese has grown steadily since 2000, largely unscathed by the economic downturn of 2008. Cheese leads the US specialty food industry as a whole, with $3.71 billion of specialty cheese sales in 2014, up 8 percent from 2012.

See also INDUSTRIAL.

Sowerwine, Alyssa. "Demand for Specialty Cheeses Grows in Deli, Dairy Retail Cases." *Cheese Market News*, 8 June 2012. http://www.cbs-global.com/article/demand-for-specialty-cheeses-grows-in-deli-dairy-retail-cases.
"US Specialty Food Sales Top $100 Billion; Cheese Still Top Category." *Cheese Reporter* 139, no. 42, 10 April 2015. http://npaper-wehaa.com/cheese-reporter/2015/04/s2/#?article=2489261.
Werlin, Laura. *The New American Cheese: Profiles of America's Great Cheesemakers and Recipes of Cooking with Cheese.* New York: Stewart, Tabori & Chang, 2000.

Heather Paxson

spino

See CHEESE KNIFE.

spores are unicellular or pluricellular structures encountered in different prokaryotic and eukaryotic organisms. Bacterial spores are formed by some Gram-positive bacteria belonging to the phylum Firmicutes. These spores facilitate survival in unfavorable conditions for extended periods and are resistant to chemical and physical treatments. Originating from various substrates, they may contaminate milk and pose problems in cheeses even when subjected to heat treatments. The resistance and toxigenic capacities of some spore-forming bacterial species make spores a concern for the cheese industry. Aerobic spore-formers, such as some *Bacillus* species, are commonly associated with heat-treated milk spoilage, whereas anaerobic spore-formers, such as some *Clostridium* species, may cause gas defects (e.g., "late blowing") in Beaufort, Comté, Emmentaler, or Gouda cheeses. See DEFECTS.

Fungal spore production is considered to be a method of reproduction and dissemination. It may result from: (1) hypha fragmentation or sporogenesis (spore production) within specialized structures for molds and (2) single-cell budding or scission) for yeasts. See HYPHAE and FILAMENTOUS FUNGI. In turn, sexual spore production involving meiosis is more dependent on environmental conditions and is usually rarer. In cheeses, asexual spores are most abundant and are formed by technological or contaminant molds and yeasts. In higher fungi such as

Penicillium or *Geotrichum* species, asexual spores are named conidiospores or conidia. See CANDIDUM; GEOTRICHUM; and PENICILLIUM. Conidia from *Penicillium roqueforti* are famous for giving their unique color to the veins in blue-veined cheeses. In *Mucor* species belonging to lower fungi and encountered in cheeses such as the French Tomme or Saint-Nectaire, asexual spores are produced in bag-like structures named sporangiospores. See MUCOR.

In spore-forming bacteria, spores are produced when subjected to environmental stresses such as nutrient limitation, osmotic pressure, or temperature deviations; whereas, germination occurs when conditions become suitable again for growth. In fungi, endogenous molecules like diterpene conidiogenone, nutritional factors, or certain light wavelengths are known to positively or negatively affect the production of spores. Fungal germination is activated by spore rehydration when colonizing a substrate and may also be influenced by environmental factors or by volatile compounds such as 1-octen-3-ol (a.k.a. "mushroom alcohol"). This molecule may be involved in quorum sensing, inhibiting spore germination when spore concentration is high, and thus favoring new substrate colonization.

Fungal spore germination is at the origin of mycelium development and represents an earlier step before fungal colonization of cheeses. See MYCELIA. Traditionally, fungal cheese colonization occurs from the spores present in the milk, on cheesemaking utensils, or in the cheese factory environment. In modern industrial cheesemaking, colonization requires better control and standardization and relies on deliberate spore inoculation during manufacture. Spores can be directly inoculated into milk or sprayed onto the cheese surface. In order to produce spores, strain cultivation on solid or liquid media can be used. Interestingly, different Roquefort cheese producers still use the ancestral method of inoculating sterilized rye and wheat bread with lyophilized *P. roqueforti*, which is left to grow for three weeks before being dried and sprayed into the milk. Different companies commercialize fungal adjunct cultures in the form of lyophilized spores. See ADJUNCT CULTURES and ROQUEFORT.

See also FUNGI.

Chamba, J. F., and F. Irlinger. "Secondary and Adjunct Cultures." In *Cheese: Chemistry, Physics, and Microbiology*, 3d ed., Edited by P. F. Fox et al. Vol. 1: *General Aspects*, pp. 191–206. Oxford: Elsevier, 2004.

Doyle, C. J., et al. "Anaerobic Sporeformers and Their Significance with Respect to Milk and Dairy Products." *International Journal of Food Microbiology* 197 (March 2015): 77–87.
Gow, N. A. R., and G. M. Gadd. *Growing Fungus*. New York: Chapman & Hall, 1995.

Jean-Luc Jany

Spressa delle Giudicarie

Spressa delle Giudicarie is an Italian cheese made from partially skim raw cow's milk produced in the Giudicarie, Chiese, Rendena, and Ledro Valley municipalities. The cows roam the mountains of the Alps and are fed only on hay, except during the summer months (July–September) when the cheese is not made. Producers allow for the cream to rise naturally. Spressa delle Giudicarie obtained PDO (product of designated origin) status in 2003.

According to some sources, this cheese has been made since the thirteenth century and was originally produced as a byproduct of butter, making it low in fat content. Spressa delle Giudicarie cheese is produced between September and July; the cows are milked twice per day to create this cheese. First the producer adds bovine liquid rennet at 91–99°F (33–37°C) to curdle the milk. Next the producer waits between twenty to fifty minutes before cutting the curd and mixing it for a further thirty-five to sixty-five minutes before removing it from the whey liquid and putting it into cylindrical molds. Then the curd rests for twenty-four hours after which it is salted in brine for four to six days or dried for eight to twelve days. Finally ripening occurs at 50–68°F (10–20°C) and 80–90 percent humidity over three months.

The finished cheese is semihard with a dark brown or yellow crust, a pale yellow paste, and small holes spaced sparsely throughout the paste. The taste can vary from light and sweet to robust and piquant depending on its age. This cheese is molded into a flat cylindrical shape with a diameter of 12–14 inches (30–35 centimeters). In Italy Spressa delle Giudicarie can be eaten fresh, melted for polenta dishes, or paired with dark red meats.

Zeppa, Giuseppe, et al. "Technological and Chemical Characterization of PDO Cheeses of Italy." In *Handbook on Cheese: Production, Chemistry, and Sensory Properties*, edited by Luiz Du Vale and Henrique Castelli, pp. 64–65. New York: Nova Science, 2013.

Megan A. Schraedley

Squacquerone di Romagna is a fresh, soft PDO cheese produced in all municipalities of Ravenna, Forlì-Cesena, Rimini, and Bologna provinces of Italy and in the municipalities west of the Porettana road in the Ferrara province. It received the European recognition of protected designation of origin in 2012. It takes its name from the Emilia-Romagna dialect, where "squacquaron" means "rich in water."

The first documented traces of Squacquerone production go back to 1800 in an epistle dated 15 February between Cardinal Bellisomi—who was in Venice for the conclave where Gregorio Chiaramonti was elected as Pope Pius VII—and the vicar of Cesena. Bellisomi was asking about a Squacquerone lot that he had ordered and that was produced by the cheesemaker Domenico Bazzocchi.

Squacquerone di Romagna is made with whole cow's milk obtained from a herd feeding on at least 60 percent of local forage rich in fiber. The milk is pasteurized and autochthonous starters are used to obtain the typical acidity of the cheese (pH 4.95–5.3). The milk is coagulated using calf liquid rennet and the curd is cut into walnut-size pieces. The curd is molded and then left at 59°F (15°C) for twenty-four hours. The cheese ripens for one to four days at 37–43°F (3–6°C). The resulting cheese is rindless and takes the shape of the mold (usually round) where it is formed. The interior paste is white to pearly colored, soft, creamy with a fat content of 46 to 55 percent on the matter and moisture content of 58 to 65 percent. It has a sweet or slightly acid taste and an herbaceous aroma.

Squacquerone di Romagna is eaten with an IGP flat bread called "Piadina Romagnola," produced in all municipalities of Ravenna, Forlì-Cesena, Rimini, and in some municipalities of Bologna province.

Ministero delle Politiche Agricole:. "Disciplinari di produzione prodotti DOP e IGP riconosciuti: Formaggi." https://www.politicheagricole.it/flex/cm/pages/ServeBLOB.php/L/IT/IDPagina/3340.

Marta Bertolino

standardization is the process of adjusting milk composition. It is necessary in order to produce any lower fat cheeses such as cottage, low-moisture part skim mozzarella, or Parmesan cheese—or to produce cheeses higher in fat such as creamy Havarti or double cream Camembert. Standardization is also helpful in reducing variation in milk composition that occurs due to seasonality, including major changes in the environment such as temperature and humidity. The US Food and Drug Administration (Code of Federal Regulations, Title 21, Part 133) has also set legal requirements for many (but not all) cheeses in the proportion of fat in the solids portion of a particular cheese variety (referred to as fat on a dry basis [FDB]). Standardization of milk before cheesemaking ensures that the cheese will meet these requirements. The ratio of fat to total solids content in a cheese is determined by the ratio of casein to fat in the milk from which it is made. Standardization is the adjustment of this ratio and is accomplished by removal of cream, or addition of cream, addition of casein by incorporation of nonfat dry milk, skim milk, condensed milks, or milks separated by membrane processing (ultrafiltration). See ULTRAFILTRATION.

Most large cheese factories use standardization to increase cheese yield by increasing the total amount of fat and casein in the milk albeit in the desired ratio. This is referred to as fortification and is often accomplished through the use of concentrated whole or skim milk. Fortification increases the productivity of the cheese plant; that is, more cheese is made per vat of milk without an increase in production time or vat size.

Many large factories have developed rigorous standardized manufacturing schedules for each type of cheese produced and there is little allotted time to fit in changes to the schedule once the cheesemaking process has begun. Standardization of milk to a consistent composition decreases the potential that a change in schedule would be necessary and results in cheese of consistent composition and acidity, which results in consistent sensory and performance attributes. Large factories receive entire truckloads of milk from one large milk producer and this milk will generally have a consistent composition from one truckload to another. However, another large producer might have a milk composition quite different from it. Since the amount of milk going into an individual vat to be made into cheese might come from one of these large producers, there could be large variation in milk composition between vats. Standardization of milk eliminates this variation.

See also MILK; FAT; and SKIMMING.

Guinee, T. P., B. T. O'Kennedy, and P. M. Kelly. "Effect of Milk Protein Standardization Using Different Methods on the Composition and Yields of Cheddar

Cheese." *Journal of Dairy Science* 89, no. 2 (2006): 468–482.

Johnson, Mark. "Preparation of Cheese Milk." In *Encyclopedia of Dairy Sciences*, 2d ed., edited by J. W. Fuquay, P. F. Fox, and P. L. H. McSweeney, pp. 544–551. 4 vols. Amsterdam: Academic Press, 2011.

University of Guelph. Food Science Department. "Standardization of Milk for Cheese Making." http://www.uoguelph.ca/foodscience/book-page/standardization-milk-cheese-making.

Mark E. Johnson

standards of identity are definitions and standards for food established by the US Food and Drug Administration (FDA) to maintain the integrity of food products and to ensure they meet consumer expectations under the Food, Drug, and Cosmetic Act (FDCA). The FDA currently has about three hundred identity standards in twenty categories of food. Located in the Code of Federal Regulations (Title 21 Part 133), the Standards of Identity for Cheeses and Related Cheese Products were developed by the FDA in the late 1940s to ensure uniform standards for cheese and cheese products in interstate commerce. The standards contain definitions, methods of analysis, and requirements for specific standardized products by identifying major varieties of cheese and describing their manufacturing procedures, allowable ingredients, and composition with regard to moisture and fat. In addition to defined standard names (Cheddar, Gouda, etc.), general categories are included encompassing products defined by moisture and percent of milkfat contained in the solids (hard, hard-grating, semisoft, etc.). Though pasteurization of all milk and milk products in final package form for direct human consumption entered into interstate commerce is mandatory in the United States, alternative procedures to pasteurization are provided for certain cheese varieties. As defined by each individual standard, select cheeses can be manufactured from raw or heat-treated milk so long as they are cured for a specified amount of time at a defined temperature, typically no less than sixty days at a temperature greater than 35°F (2°C). Currently, more than thirty standardized natural cheese varieties can be legally made from raw milk in the United States provided that they are sufficiently aged.

See also FOOD AND DRUG ADMINISTRATION and 60-DAY AGING RULE.

United States Food and Drug Administration. *Code of Federal Regulations*. Title 21. Part 133. "Cheeses and Related Cheese Products". http://www.accessdata.fda.gov/scripts/cdrh/cfdocs/cfcfr/CFRSearch.cfm?CFRPart=133.

Dennis D'Amico

Staphylococcus aureus is an important opportunistic pathogen of humans and many animal species. The genus *Staphylococcus* currently contains seventy-one species or subspecies, most of which are nonpathogenic. *Staphylococcus aureus* is a major pathogenic species. However, *S. aureus* is often isolated from humans and animals in the absence of signs of disease and, therefore, it is also described as part of the normal commensal bacteria of skin or other surfaces of humans and other animals. For example, *S. aureus* is isolated from the nares (nose) of approximately 30 percent of humans but is also commonly found from swabs of the perineum (genital area), axillae (armpits), and groin. Similarly, *S. aureus* can be isolated from the skin (e.g., teat and udder, perineum, hocks) and nares of cattle and other domestic species. In humans, *S. aureus* can cause minor superficial skin infections, as well as more severe infections including abscesses, endocarditis, osteomyelitis, and mastitis. Similar diseases are observed in domestic animals. In dairy animals, especially cattle, *S. aureus* is a major cause of mastitis, which reduces milk quality and production. Interestingly, the strains of *S. aureus* that cause mastitis in ruminants appear to be genetically distinct from those commonly isolated from humans or companion animals such as cats, dogs, and horses. Antibiotic resistant *S. aureus*, especially methicillin resistant *S. aureus* (MRSA), is a major human health concern. *S. aureus* is also a food-borne pathogen.

Staphylococcal enterotoxins are a cause of food poisoning, which results from consumption of foods (including milk and cheese) that contain these toxins. The toxins are preformed during the growth of *S. aureus* in the contaminated food and thus gastroenteritis can occur due to exposure to the toxins in the absence of a *S. aureus* infection in the affected individual. *S. aureus* also forms biofilms in the dairy production environment.

See also BIOFILMS; OPPORTUNISTIC PATHOGEN; and PATHOGENS.

Hermans, K., L. A. Devriese, and F. Haesebrouck. "Staphylococcus." In *Pathogenesis of Bacterial Infections in Animals*, 4th ed., edited by C. L. Gyles,. et al., pp. 75–87. Ames, Iowa: Blackwell, 2010.

John Barlow

Star Provisions is a cheese shop located in Atlanta's Buckhead neighborhood. Chefs Anne Quatrano and Clifford Harrison opened the expansive store at the front of their Bacchanalia restaurant in 2000. It functions as a specialties market and features numerous sections selling cheese, pastries, fish, and meats, as well as kitchenware. There is also a small café with tables serving breakfast and lunch.

Since opening, Star Provisions has become a destination for food lovers in the southern United States. Tim Gaddis, who began carrying cheeses made in Georgia and Tennessee before other retailers, headed the cheese department until 2014, when he started working for Many Fold Farm in Palmeto, Georgia. His work behind the cheese counter and in the selection of cheeses for the service cart at Bacchanalia helped galvanize support for artisan cheesemakers in the region, with Star Provisions carrying the largest selection of cheeses made in the southeastern United States, alongside European and other American cheeses. The cheese section of the store features a wall-length refrigerator and a smaller counter unit styled as a New York deli, displaying hundreds of cheeses and charcuterie.

Quatrano and Harrison have continued to support local producers at their store and at their other restaurants in the city of Atlanta. They have been recognized for their work and nominated for multiple awards. Anne Quatrano won the James Beard Foundation Best Chef award in the Southeast region in 2003.

Star Provisions. http://www.starprovisions.com.

Tanner, Ron. "Atlanta's Star Provisions: A Chef-Owned Specialty Shop." *Specialty Food Magazine*, 18 February 2003. https://www.specialtyfood.com/news/article/atlantaatms-star-provisions-a-chef-owned-specialty-shop.

Carlos Yescas

starter cultures, also called primary cultures, are batches of microorganisms used in the manufacture of fermented foods such as cheeses. As suggested by their name, they are used to "start" the transformation of milk into cheese. The most common starter cultures are lactic acid bacteria (LAB). See LACTIC ACID BACTERIA. Starter LAB cultures generally grow at a population of a billion cells per gram of cheese during the first stages of cheese manufacture, then their viable population decreases during ripening. LAB owe their name to their ability to ferment sugars into lactic acid. In cheesemaking, their major function is to ferment the sugar present in milk, lactose, into lactic acid, thus lowering the pH of the milk.

Ripening cultures, also called secondary cultures, are sometimes also referred to as starter cultures, although they grow during the ripening phase and are thus not technically "starters." They include bacteria, yeasts, and filamentous fungi. See RIPENING CULTURES and FILAMENTOUS FUNGI. Ripening cultures provide specific characteristics to each variety of cheese, such as flavor, texture, and character. For example, filamentous fungi form the velvety white rind of Brie cheese and the blue veins of Roquefort cheese, whereas propionibacteria are responsible for forming the characteristic holes in Swiss-type cheeses. See DAIRY PROPIONIBACTERIA.

The production of lactic acid from lactose by LAB has several beneficial consequences. It contributes to the transformation of milk into a coagulum (also called curd), along with the action of the coagulant. See COAGULATION OR CURDLING. By lowering the pH of the milk, the lactic acid helps prevent the development of pathogenic bacteria. In addition to acidifying the milk, starter LAB also contribute to changes in cheese texture and flavor, both during their growth in the milk and later, during the ripening of the cheese. In general, the texture of the cheese softens, while the flavor becomes more complex and intense. LAB have a complex proteolytic system that hydrolyzes milk proteins into smaller molecules, peptides, and amino acids, resulting in flavors such as umami. LAB also produce many volatile flavor compounds such as diacetyl, known for its butter-like flavor, through the fermentation of citrate and lactose. The conversion of amino acids by LAB during the ripening process can result in a variety of flavors, including nutty, fruity, chocolaty, and even garlic. Some of these reactions also occur after LAB death and lysis, because of the activity of some of their intracellular enzymes, in particular, peptidases, which are released and remain active in the cheese. See FLAVOR.

An early example of a commercial lactic acid bacteria (LAB) starter culture, sold by Chr. Hansen's Laboratory, Inc. of Little Falls, New York. COURTESY OF ERIC JOHANSEN / CHR. HANSEN A/S

In modern times, starter cultures are intentionally introduced in most cases, especially for all industrial-scale fermentations. Many forms of commercial starter cultures are available, in the form of frozen or freeze-dried cultures, or more recently, spray-dried cultures. In the 1900s to the 1930s, starters were undefined mixtures of LAB that originated from successful artisanal cheesemaking processes and were propagated by back-slopping practices. Then a more rational strategy of strain isolation and assembling was initiated to ensure better consistency in product quality. These defined starter cultures are manufactured mixtures of several strains. They are less resilient than undefined starter cultures and, in particular, more susceptible to bacteriophage predation. However, some traditional starter cultures containing undefined multiple strains still exist and are difficult to replace, such as the famous "Flora Danica" culture. See BACTERIOPHAGES and STRAINS.

The LAB species used as starter cultures are chosen according to their characteristics (optimum growth temperature, metabolites produced) and for the particular cheese manufacturing process. Mesophilic (thriving at moderate temperatures) LAB species have an optimum growth temperature of 68–86°F (20–30°C) and are involved in the manufacture of most cheese varieties, including soft cheeses such as Brie, semihard cheeses such as Gouda, and hard cheeses such as Cheddar. The main mesophilic species is *Lactococcus lactis* (*L. lactis*), used alone or in combination with *Leuconostoc* spp. See LACTOCOCCUS LACTIS. The so-called thermophilic (thriving at high temperatures) LAB species, with optimum growth temperatures of around 104–113°F (40–45°C), are used in the manufacture of cheeses in which the curd is heated, such as Swiss-type cheese varieties (e.g., Emmentaler) and Italian cheeses (e.g., mozzarella and Grana). The main species of thermophilic LAB are *Streptococcus thermophilus*, *Lactobacillus helveticus*, and *Lactobacillus delbrueckii*. See LACTOBACILLUS. Mesophilic and thermophilic starter cultures can be used in combination. For example *L. lactis* is frequently associated with *S. thermophilus* in the manufacture of Cheddar and mozzarella cheeses. LAB are also classified according the end products they form. Homofermentative (single end product) LAB such as *Lactococcus* and *Streptococcus* produce lactic acid as the sole product of glucose and lactose fermentation, whereas heterofermentative (multiple end products) LAB such as *Leuconostoc* produce other end products, such as carbon dioxide, ethanol, and acetic acid, in addition to lactic acid. Within a given LAB species, the choice of a strain or a combination of strains is important, because many properties are strain dependent. For example, not all strains of *L. lactis* are capable of acidifying milk. This is the case for many plant-derived strains of *L. lactis*, which are not able to ferment lactose or to grow in milk. Among the acidifying strains chosen for use in cheesemaking, the acidification rate varies from strain to strain. Similarly, the strains of thermophilic lactobacilli used in cheesemaking are all capable of hydrolyzing milk proteins, but the level and specificity of proteolytic activity is strain dependent. Strains also differ in their ability to adapt to the environmental conditions prevailing during cheese-making, as well as in their ability to produce amino-acid-derived flavor compounds. To perform all the functions required (acidification, proteolysis, aromatization, etc.), several strains are combined, such as acidifying LAB strains and flavor-generating adjunct strains. See ADJUNCT CULTURES.

In the manufacture of traditional artisanal cheeses, starter LAB can also be acquired through traditional practices. Back slopping is defined as a practice where a new batch of food to be fermented is inoculated by using a sample from a previous batch of fermented food. It is applied in the manufacture of some traditional cheeses, where whey from the previous batch is used to prepare natural whey cultures. Another example is the natural inoculation that results from the use of wooden vats for the manufacture of some traditional protected designation of origin (PDO) cheeses, for example, the "tina" and the "gerle" used in the manufacture of Ragusano cheese in Sicily and Salers cheese in France, respectively. See RAGUSANO; SALERS (COW); TINA; and WOODEN VATS. The biofilm of LAB present on these wooden vats constitutes a natural and efficient inoculation system for the milk, making the deliberate addition of starters unnecessary. The presence of acidifying LAB can also simply derive from a spontaneous contamination of raw milk at the milking stage.

See also COAGULATION OR CURDLING.

Johnson, Mark E. "Mesophilic and Thermophilic Cultures Used in Traditional Cheesemaking." In *Cheese and Microbes*, edited by Catherine W. Donnelly, pp. 73–94. Washington, D.C.: ASM, 2014.

Lortal, Sylvie, Giuseppe Licitra, and Florence Valence. "Wooden Tools: Reservoirs of Microbial Biodiversity in Traditional Cheesemaking." In *Cheese and Microbes*, edited by Catherine W. Donnelly, pp. 167–176. Washington, D.C.: ASM, 2014.

Parente, Eugenio, and Timothy M. Cogan. "Starter Cultures: General Aspects." In *Cheese: Chemistry, Physics, and Microbiology*, 3d ed., edited by Patrick F. Fox et al., Vol. 1: *General Aspects*, pp. 123–147. London: Elsevier, 2004.

Anne Thierry

Steele, Veronica, is credited with the development of modern Irish artisanal cheese. In the early 1970s, she and her husband, Norman, a lecturer in philosophy at Trinity College Dublin, decided to leave the city and the academic life in favor of raising a family on a small farm. Veronica first experimented to provide an alternative to processed cheese for her family and to preserve the excess milk from their one cow. She eventually evolved a soft and pungent washed-rind cheese called Milleens. It was a great success and by 1981 was selling in shops and restaurants throughout Ireland and as far away as London and Paris.

Steele was also inspired by cheesemaking as a route to viability for a rural area struggling with high unemployment. "There's nothing involved which isn't in your home kitchen," she told the *Irish Farmers Journal* in an interview, stressing the importance of starting small and experimenting freely. Supported by a grant from an Irish development agency, she taught a series of home cheesemaking classes around her kitchen table and gave seminars in Lavistown House, a center for traditional skills education. Her original experiments inspired the women she taught, who went on to make other iconic Irish cheeses such as Durrus, Cashel Blue, St. Tola, Ardrahan, and Gubbeen. See CASHEL BLUE. Today, Veronica and Norman's son Quinlan carry on the tradition of making Milleens, but all of Ireland owes Veronica Steele a debt of gratitude for her vision and generosity of spirit.

See also COUNTY CORK and IRELAND.

Campbell, Susan. "More Home-Made Cheese Please." *Irish Farmers Journal*, 8 August 1981.

Bronwen Percival

Stelvio (or Stilfser) is a semihard and semi-cooked PDO cheese produced in six districts of the province of Bolzano, in Italy: Venosta Valley, Burgraviato, Salto-Sciliar, Pusteria Valley, Isarco Valley, and Bolzano municipality. It received the European recognition of protected designation of origin in 2007. It takes its name from the Stelvio municipality of Bolzano province (Stilfser is the German translation of Stelvio).

Stevio cheese production goes back to 1914, when documents from the Stilfs (Stelvio) dairy factory describe the production of the cheese. At the same time the documented traces of cheese production in the six districts mentioned above date back to the *Bergbauernbuch* of the Tyrolean historian Hermann Wopfner, where the cheese is well established in the dietary habits of Tyrolean people. Furthermore, in the land registers of the thirteenth and sixteenth centuries it is reported that the farmers paid taxes of the Schwaigen—the Alpine farm—to landowners in the form of cheese.

Stelvio is made with whole cow's milk that may be partially skimmed. The milk is pasteurized and an autochthonous starter is used. The milk is co-agulated using calf liquid or powdered rennet made locally using traditional methods. The curd is cut into corn-size particles, which are semi-cooked using hot water at 97–104°F (36–40°C) and then pressed. Ripening lasts at least sixty days at 50–57°F (10–14°C) and 85–95 percent of humidity. During ripening the rind is smeared twice a week with a brine solution. During the first two to three weeks of ripening a strain culture made of *Arthobacterium* ssp., *Brevibacterium* ssp., and eventually yeasts—produced locally—are added to the brine to smear the rind with a red color and to give a characteristic flavor to the cheese.

The final product is cylindrical in shape with straight or slightly convex sides and a yellow-orange to orange-brown rind. It is 3–4 inches (8–11 centimeters) tall, 13–15 inches (34–38 centimeters) in diameter, and weighs 18–22 pounds (8–10 kilograms). The interior paste is pale yellow to straw colored, compact, elastic with small irregular eyeholes, it has a fat content of at least 50 percent on a dry matter basis, a moisture content below 44 percent, and a boiled milk, butter, and mature hay smell and taste typical of the mountain cheeses. Stelvio is consumed as a table cheese combined with speck, or as an ingredient in cornmeal mush or cereal soups typical of Tyrolean meals.

Consorzio Formaggio Stelvio: http://www.stilfser.it/en.
Ministero delle Politiche Agricole. "Disciplinari di produzione prodotti DOP e IGP riconosciuti." https://www.politicheagricole.it/flex/cm/pages/ServeBLOB.php/L/IT/IDPagina/3340.

Marta Bertolino

stewing consists of subjecting cheese to controlled temperatures and humidity for a period of time that changes according to the type of cheese subject to the process. It is part of the process of cheesemaking, used to stimulate the acidification of the curd and the completion of the whey syneresis.

The stewing can take place in: a steel tray with a cover in which steam is insufflated, located in the cheesemaking room; in conventional cells; or in special temperature- and humidity-controlled rooms dedicated to stewing (called *locale di stufatura* in Italy).

In traditional cheesemaking similar results may be reached by immersing the cheese in hot whey (*scotta*). The overall goal is to raise the temperature of the curd, as mentioned, to enhance the fermentation and the syneresis.

Stewing is a common practice for soft cheeses with short or medium aging, before salting, but is also used in many varieties of cheeses with longer maturation periods. For example, stewing of stracchino occurs at a temperature of 75–82°F (24–28°C) for six to ten hours, while Camembert stews at 82–86°F (28–30°C) for fifteen to twenty hours with relative humidity maintained at about 90 percent and up to 95 percent. In the traditional production of Pannerone Lodigiano, the curd is stewed for four to five days at temperatures of 82–86°F (28–30°C), so as to achieve the formation of the distinctive holes. For Pecorino Toscano, stewing temperatures exceed 104°F (40°C). Gorgonzola DOP utilizes two rounds of stewing: The first is for a few hours, to develop the right acidity. After a brief period in a cold storage, the cheese is removed from the mold and dry-salted on the entire surface. The second stewing process happens in rooms called *camerino* (or "purgatory") where the process of stewing lasts from twenty-four to forty-eight hours at a temperature of 68–75°F (20–24°C) in order to restart the fermentations of yeasts. These yeasts, by producing gas, open the texture and promote the growth of molds.

In Castelmagno cheesemaking, after about twenty-four hours of hanging in dry cloth or placed in molds, the curd is cut into blocks and left under the whey for forty-eight hours or more, so as to maintain a sufficient temperature to allow a prolonged lactic fermentation. It is important to achieve a strong acidification of the curd (pH of less than 4.8) to obtain the characteristic crumbly and brittle texture. Other examples relate to the traditional processes of Ragusano DOP and Pecorino Siciliano DOP, where the curd is immersed in *scotta* after the ricotta production for about two to three hours.

See also ACIDIFICATION and SYNERESIS.

Agrarian Research. http://www.agrarian.com.
Kosikowski, Frank Y. *Cheese and Fermented Milk Foods.* Westport, Conn.: F. Y. Kosikowski, 1997.
Ottogalli, Giorgio. *Atlante dei formaggi: Guida a oltre 600 formaggi e latticini provenienti da tutto il mondo.* Milan: Ulrico Hoepli Editore, 2001.

Carlo Fiori

Stichelton is a raw-milk, full cream English blue cheese that has been in production since 2006.

Located at Collingthwaite Farm on the Welbeck Estate in Nottinghamshire, Stichelton Dairy was set up by Randolph Hodgson and cheesemaker Joe Schneider. Although they draw on the principles of traditional farmhouse raw-milk Stilton production, the cheese cannot legally be called Stilton as Stilton's PDO stipulates the use of pasteurized milk. Instead Stichelton bears the Old English name for the town of Stilton. The dairy has requested an amendment to the PDO to include raw-milk Stilton. Results of the latest request in 2013 were still pending at the time of publication.

Stichelton is made to a Stilton recipe. The raw milk used comes from Collingthwaite Farm's herd of Holstein-Friesian cows, and is pumped directly from the milking parlor into the dairy. Stichelton is made with traditional animal rennet and the same liquid starter (MT36) that Colston Bassett, the last raw-milk Stilton producer, used before switching to pasteurized milk in 1989. Both are used in small quantities to ensure slow acidification and curdling. The delicate curds are hand-ladled from the milk vat to the drainage table so that they retain their shape and fat content. Cheeses are matured slowly (around twelve weeks, with piercing at weeks six and seven) and judged individually for readiness. The process is third-party audited annually to the Safe and Local Supplier Approval (SALSA) plus the Specialist Cheesemakers Association (SCA) Standard. See SPE-CIALIST CHEESEMAKERS ASSOCIATION.

The finished cheese has a complex flavor and rich, creamy texture that varies by season. Peak production is in the autumn with highest sales during the Christmas period. Around fifty-five tons are produced each year and sold internationally. Neal's Yard Dairy is its largest distributor.

See also BLUE CHEESES; HODGSON, RANDOLPH; NEAL'S YARD DAIRY; and STILTON.

Schneider, Joe, interviewed by Celia Plender, 31 March 2014, Nottinghamshire U.K. An Oral History of Neal's Yard, British Library Sound Archive, London, C1649.

West, Harry G. "Thinking Like a Cheese: Towards an Ecological Understanding of the Reproduction of Knowledge in Contemporary Artisan Cheesemaking." In *Understanding Cultural Transmission in Anthropology: A Critical Synthesis*, edited by Roy Ellen, et al., pp. 320–345. Oxford: Berghahn, 2013.

Mukta Das, Celia Plender, and Harry G. West

Joe Schneider, the cheesemaker at Stichelton Dairy, taking a core sample of Stichelton cheese with an iron to check on its development. Stichelton is made to a Stilton recipe, but cannot be legally called Stilton because Stichelton uses raw cow's milk, and Stilton must use pasteurized cow's milk. Stichelton is the Old English name for the town of Stilton. © KATE ARDING

Stilfser

See STELVIO.

Stilton is a cow's milk cheese made in the English counties of Nottinghamshire, Leicestershire, and Derbyshire. Although there is a white variety, Stilton is most commonly known as a blue cheese. Since 1936 Stilton has been overseen by the Stilton Cheese-makers' Association, an organization set up to safe-guard and promote the interests of the Stilton cheese industry. In 1966 the Association was granted a Certification Trademark for Blue Stilton. This gave the cheese legal protection within the United Kingdom, restricting the region of its manufacture to the three counties. Further protection was afforded when in 1996 it was awarded protected designation of origin (PDO) status, thereby eliminating imitation or abuse of its trademark name anywhere in the European Union (EU). Today there are six dairies licensed to make white and blue Stilton (a further dairy is licensed to produce white Stilton only). Together they produce over 8,000 tons (7,247 metric tons) of cheese per year.

Origins

Stilton cheese came to prominence in the early eighteenth century. In 1722 William Stukeley, in his *Itinerarium Curiosum,* wrote, "Stilton...is famous for cheese, which they sell for 12d per pound, and would be thought equal to Parmesan, were it not so near us."

The village of Stilton was a staging post on the Great North Road—the main route from London to Edinburgh. Travelers would spend the night at one of the inns and sample the local fare. Daniel Defoe, one such traveler during the reign of Queen Anne (1702–1714), wrote of being served the local cheese, which was "brought to table with the mites, or maggots round it, so thick, that they bring a spoon with them for you to eat the mites with, as you do the cheese."

The cheese likely eaten by Defoe was one known locally as Quenby. It is thought this was made, or at least overseen, by Elizabeth Scarbrow, housekeeper at Quenby Hall. According to Patrick Rance, Quenby had been supplying the Bell Inn in Stilton with cheese during the first two decades of the eighteenth century. When Scarbrow left Quenby to get married, she continued making cheese. Somewhere between 1720 and 1730 cheese production at Quenby stopped and soon Scarbrow was the main supplier to the Bell Inn. Scarbrow's daughter Frances took up cheesemaking and is credited, along with her husband, William, and the charismatic owner of the Bell and Angel Inn at Stilton, Cowper Thornhill, with turning a popular local cheese into one known throughout the land.

When William Marshall visited the Midlands toward the end of the eighteenth century Frances was still alive. By then Stilton was made "in almost every village, in that quarter of Leicestershire, as well as in the neighboring villages of Rutlandshire" (Marshall, 1790).

The Make

Although in the many accounts of how the early Stilton was made there is much divergent detail, most agree that Stilton was an unpressed "cream" cheese made between May and September. In his *General View of the Agriculture of the County of Leicestershire*, 1794, John Monk gives us a typical account:

> Take the night's cream, and put it to the morning's new milk, with the rennet; and when the curd is come, it is not to be broke, as is done with other cheeses; but take it out with a soil-dish [a dish-like ladle] altogether, and place it in a sieve to drain gradually; and as it drains; keep gradually pressing it till it becomes firm and dry; then place it in a wooden hoop.

Once in the hoops (molds) the cheeses were put on dry wooden boards, turned, and bound tightly with cloth. The cloth was to help create a crust and was changed every day until the crust was properly formed. After this the cheeses were rubbed and brushed for upward of two months. Monk was informed that Stilton was best eaten when it had aged for one year. Writing twenty years later, Joseph Twamley reckoned Stilton not "sufficiently mellow for cutting, until it is two years old; and is not saleable unless it is decayed, blue, and moist." Though the maturation style might have differed wildly between Monk and Twamley's times, the method for Stilton making in the Edwardian era would have been recognizable to them both. However, the early years of the twentieth century would witness huge changes to the Stilton industry.

In 1875, the first factory-made Stilton appeared. Stilton factories were cooperatively run creameries set up by local farmers. Their advantage was the pooling of milk for greater productivity and efficiency. The likes of Mrs. Musson, a farmhouse cheesemaker who produced only two cheeses a day around 1900, would find it difficult to compete. In 1895 the Midland Dairy Institute at Sutton Bonington was opened with courses on how to make Stilton. These shifts in production method and the emphasis on training and professionalization signaled the end of the farmhouse Stilton cheesemaker. When World War I began in 1914 all cheese production was limited to long-keeping hard cheeses and the farmhouse Stilton sector all but collapsed.

Since World War II, when Stilton production was suspended again, much has changed: Stilton is no longer made with raw milk, blue mold cultures are added to the milk, most cheese is made with vegetarian rennet, and production has increased greatly. But the transition from the old to the new has been gradual. Cloth "scrimms" to tie up the curd were still in use as late as the 1960s. No blue culture was routinely added to the milk until the 1970s. And Colston Bassett Dairy still ladle their curd by hand from the vat to the cooling trolley, much as Stilton makers would have done in the 1700s.

See also STICHELTON and STILTON CHEESEMAKERS' ASSOCIATION.

Defoe, Daniel. *A Tour through England and Wales*, Vol. 2. London: Dent, 1928.
Hickman, Trevor. *The History of Stilton Cheese*. Stroud, U.K.: Sutton, 2005.
Marshall, William. *Rural Economy of the Midland Counties*. 2 vols. London: printed for G. Nicol, 1790.
Twamley, Joseph. *Essay on the Management of the Dairy*. London: J. Harding, 1816.

Dominic Coyte

The **Stilton Cheesemakers' Association** (SCMA) was founded in June 1936 by the producers of Stilton cheese in Leicestershire, England. Its goals were to improve quality, to promote the cheese to consumers and to the trade, and to represent the cheesemakers to the government and other bodies.

Today, its prime objectives remain the same, with the additional responsibility of managing and policing correct use of the name "Stilton." In 1962 the SCMA applied for a Certification Trade Mark (CTM) for Stilton in the United Kingdom, which it eventually gained in 1969. Under the terms of the CTM, only producers in the three counties of Derbyshire, Nottinghamshire, and Leicestershire, using milk from a defined area and following a defined recipe, were allowed to use the name on their cheese. Subsequently trademark protection was sought and gained in all of the major overseas markets for Stilton, so that today the name is protected in seventeen different countries. The protection of the name Stilton was extended in 1996 when the European Commission granted Blue Stilton cheese and White Stilton cheese protected designation of origin (PDO) status. Today

the certification Trade Mark and the PDO require that the cheese can only be made in the three counties, in a cylindrical shape, and from locally produced milk that has been pasteurized before use. Milk can be purchased from the surrounding countries during times of shortage, which is also stipulated in the PDO. The cheese must never be pressed; it must be allowed to form its own coat; and the blue cheese must exhibit the classic veining radiating from the center of the cheese.

See also DESIGNATION OF ORIGIN; GEOGRAPHICAL INDICATION; STICHELTON; STILTON; and UNITED KINGDOM.

Stilton: Britain's Historic Blue. http://www.stiltoncheese.com.

Nigel White

Stinking Bishop has become an icon of the modern British cheese movement because of its slightly risqué name, with its amusing double entendre, and also because it is an excellent cheese. It is an eccentric cheese created by an equally eccentric English gentleman.

Like many modern cheesemakers, Charles Martell created his own unique cheese. Launched in 1994 it is a washed-rind cheese whose style dates back to the Cistercian monks who once settled in Gloucestershire where the cheese is made. To give it a regional character it is regularly washed and rubbed with perry, a local specialty made by fermenting pear juice. The perry used to wash the cheese is made from a rather innocuous local variety of pear called "Stinking Bishop," after a rather dastardly nineteenth-century farmer called Frederick Bishop. The rind becomes sticky and pink, with a pungent, almost meaty aroma, while the interior is velvety smooth and almost spoonable. It is bound with a strip of beechwood, which also imparts its own woody notes to a cheese that is farmyardy, but not as strong as its smell, or its name, would suggest. Committed to promoting and preserving local foods and traditions, Martell also farms Gloucester Old Spot pigs and Gloucester cattle, distills his own apple and pear spirits, and makes a number of other cow's and ewe's milk cheeses.

See also ALCOHOL and WASHED-RIND CHEESES.

Charles Martell & Son. http://www.charlesmartell.com.

Juliet Harbutt

stirred curd

See STIRRING.

stirring is the practice of using a paddle or other utensil to mix the curd particles and whey that are formed as a result of cutting. Stirring usually commences soon after cutting and continues in more or less unbroken fashion until close to the time of draining or dipping. See CUTTING and DRAINING.

The purpose of stirring is threefold. First and foremost, stirring encourages syneresis (whey expulsion from the curd) and thereby influences the moisture content of the final cheese. See SYNERESIS. The curd particles created by cutting are very responsive to even small increments of external pressure, such as occur when curd particles collide with one another or with the walls of the cheese vat during stirring. Because such collisions promote whey expulsion from the particles, vigorous stirring is generally practiced in the making of low-moisture cheeses such as Italian Grana types and Swiss types. In contrast, the making of high-moisture cheeses such as the bloomy-rind types generally requires little or no stirring during the period between cutting and dipping. Stirring also prevents curd particles from matting together excessively into large aggregates between cutting and dipping or draining. Large curd aggregates impede syneresis of the particles because of their reduced surface area relative to their volume, and so their formation increases the risk that pockets of higher moisture will develop within the final cheese. Finally, for cheeses that are cooked, stirring promotes uniform heating of the curd particles, thus helping to minimize variation in the rates of syneresis and acidification among particles, which could lead to pockets of variable moisture content and acidity within the final cheese.

Stirring may also refer to the continuous mixing of curd particles during and after draining, which promotes syneresis and more rapid and complete drainage of the whey from the curd. In this process, known as stirred-curd cheesemaking, the mass of drained curd is not allowed to remain still and mat together into fused slabs, as it does during the cheddaring process. Instead, the drained curds are stirred continuously to prevent matting until the cheese is salted, such as in the making of stirred-curd Cheddar cheese, or until further processing such as stretching is performed, such as in stirred-curd mozzarella production.

See also CHEDDARING.

Johnson, M. E., and B. A. Law. "The Origins, Development, and Basic Operations of Cheesemaking Technology." Chapter 2 in *Technology of Cheesemaking*, 2d ed., edited by Barry A. Law and Adnan Y. Tamime. Oxford: Wiley-Blackwell, 2010.

Paul S. Kindstedt

St Pat

See COWGIRL CREAMERY and NETTLE.

stracchino

See LOMBARDY; QUARTIROLO LOMBARDO; ROBIOLA DI ROCCAVERANO; and TALEGGIO.

Strachitunt is an ancient cheese produced in the Val Taleggio in northern Italy, above 700 meters altitude, protected by a PDO since 2014. In this valley valuable cheese production is documented since 1200, and at the beginning of the twentieth century an encyclopedia called *Nuova Enciclopedia Italiana* described the method of production. It is a blue-veined cheese made with full-fat raw milk from Bruna Alpina cows. Strachitunt is named after its round shape, the local idiom *tunt* meaning "round."

Guglielmo Locatelli, a well-known cheesemaker, strove to ensure the survival of this cheese threatened by extinction in the 1970s. Today it represents a niche product made by artisan dairies according to the traditional process. Natural or autochthonous (isolated from Strachitunt) starter cultures and bovine rennet are added to the milk. The "warm curd" made from the morning milk and the curd made the previous evening (commonly named "cold curd") are layered and drained for at least twelve hours in a cloth. The layering of the curds furthers the development of yeast and molds.

The cheese is dry-salted and after thirty days pierced with a needle to help the molds to penetrate and grow. Molds are not inoculated and their presence is strictly related to their presence in the cheese factory environment. Strachitunt is aged for more than seventy-five days at 39–50°F (4–10°C) at the right moisture level for certain molds to develop on the surface and inside the cheese. The final cheese is a wheel of 10–11 inches (25–28 centimeters) in diameter and 6–7 inches (15–18 centimeters) in height with an average weight of 9–13 pounds (4–6 kilograms). It has a thin, wrinkled, yellowish rind, turning gray with ripening. The creamy paste, softer under the rind, is pale to deep yellow, with green-blue molds mostly along the piercing. The flavor is sweet and fruity. Its mild taste intensifies during ripening, from sweet to sharp and tangy.

See also ITALY.

Belotti E., et al. "Un formaggio tradizionale delle valli bergamasche: lo Strachitunt." *Scienza e Tecnica Lattiero-Casearia* 54 (2003): 391–416.
Besana C. "Caseificio Scienza e Tecnologia." In *Nuova Enciclopedia Italiana*. Turin, Italy: Unione Tipografia-editrice Torinese, 1923.

Milena Brasca

strains of microorganisms can be compared to breeds of animals. Genetic variants of microorganisms develop naturally over time through DNA transfer, sexual recombination processes, and accumulation of mutations. Members of a strain are descendants of a common ancestor, sharing features not necessarily found in all individuals of the species and thus displaying minor differences from other strains. When significant variations accumulate over time, a new species may develop. Strains can be differentiated by their genotype (genetic material) or their phenotype (expression of the genotype in observable traits such as acidifying capacity or bacteriocin production). See PHENOTYPIC VARIABILITY. By adapting to the environmental conditions, strain variants can occur naturally in the wild and in the laboratory by applying selective environmental conditions, or they can be designed by genetic engineering techniques. See WILD-TYPE STRAIN. For example, strains of *Lactococcus lactis* can vary naturally in their ability to break down lactose, the major sugar of milk, to produce lactic acid or in their capacity to break down milk proteins. See LACTOCOCCUS LACTIS.

Mutations in the DNA sequence of genes can thus influence the function of proteins, changing their capacity to recognize a substrate or to carry out their activity, such as breaking a peptide bond in milk proteins in order to release peptides or amino acids.

In addition to accumulating mutations, bacterial strains may acquire DNA from the environment by transformation, from bacterial viruses by transduction, or from other bacteria by conjugation. When incorporated into the bacterial genome, this DNA can be expressed and the genes decoded into new proteins that the bacteria did not make previously. Thus, microbial strains can be selected by how they can make a contribution to the optimal processing or to the sensory quality of cheese. Some changes in the genetic makeup of microbial strains can negatively influence cheese quality through unwanted metabolic activities such as biogenic amine production. See DEFECTS. Strain diversity of complex starters contributes to the ability of the microbial community to adapt to processing stresses such as bacteriophage attack. See BACTERIOPHAGES and MICROBIAL COMMUNITIES.

See also TAXONOMY.

Erkus, O., et al. "Multifactorial Diversity Sustains Microbial Community Stability." *The International Society for Microbial Ecology* 7 (2013): 2126–2136.
Holzapfel, W. H., and B. J. B. Wood. *Lactic Acid Bacteria: Biodiversity and Taxonomy*. London and New York: Wiley, 2014.
Spus, M., et al. "Strain Diversity and Phage Resistance in Complex Dairy Starter Cultures." *Journal of Dairy Science* 98, no. 8 (2015): 5173–5182.
Vos, M. "Why Do Bacteria Engage in Homologous Recombination?" *Trends in Microbiology* 17, no. 6 (2009): 226–232.

Gisèle LaPointe

The use of rye **straw mats** as part of the process of cheese maturation is known to have been in existence in France, and specifically the Auvergne region, for centuries. Although the exact origins of the practice are uncertain, Sister Noella Marcellino in the book *Cheese and Microbes* relates that in the context of Saint-Nectaire in the Middle Ages, "rye grain was used to make bread in communal ovens…and rye straw was placed under the ripening cheeses." See AUVERGNE and SAINT-NECTAIRE.

High-moisture cheeses release a considerable amount of whey during the early stages of maturation and this needs to be wicked away in order for a rind to develop properly. If wet cheese is placed directly on a shelf, there is no opportunity for air to circulate underneath. This can cause a detrimental buildup of moisture, which not only inhibits rind development but also provides an ideal environment for pathogens to grow.

Rye is preferred above other varieties such as wheat straw. This is due to its high silica content, which makes it more rigid and less liable to degradation in a humid environment, and naturally resistant to mold and bacteria—especially *Pseudomonas*. Equally rye straw has a superior capacity for absorption of moisture and is considered to impart preferred organoleptic qualities to the cheese it comes into contact with.

As a result rye straw became traditionally associated with the ripening process for cheeses across many regions of France and farther afield. In addition to Saint-Nectaire which, up until the seventeenth century, was known as "rye cheese," Pouligny Saint-Pierre, Brie de Meaux, and Coulommiers all traditionally use straw mats for maturing. However one cheese in particular, Sainte-Maure de Touraine, utilizes rye straw in a different way than the mats. To prevent this fragile, elongated goat cheese from breaking as it ages, a single rye straw is inserted lengthwise into the cheese, effectively acting as a skeleton to support the paste of the cheese surrounding it. See SAINTE-MAURE DE TOURAINE.

The rye straw used for cheese production is generally harvested between May and early June each year. One of the largest areas of production is around Gimel-les-Cascades, in the Corrèze department in central France. Today one company in particular remains famous for its production of straw mats on a commercial scale: Monteil.

The Monteil family has specialized in rye straw production since the mid-1940s, growing an ancient variety of rye that reaches a height of about 6 feet (2 meters) and is particularly suited to their purpose. They have honed their skills over three generations to become one of the largest producers of straw mats in France, introducing a HACCP quality-control system in 2007 and ensuring that every batch of straw is recorded with a batch number as part of their traceability program. See HAZARD ANALYSIS AND CRITICAL CONTROL POINT.

After being cut the rye straw is bound in bundles and stored until needed. Next it is thoroughly combed and brushed before being sterilized to prevent any cross-contamination from pathogens such as *Listeria* or *Salmonella*. The straw is then cut to equal lengths and sewn together by hand using either jute or white-colored yarn.

In recent years many cheese producers have opted to replace rye straw mats with modern synthetic plastic straw mats arguing that they are more sanitary and easier to clean. However traditionalists counter that real straw imparts a particular taste and quality to the cheese that is simply not possible with the synthetic version. For this reason, many PDO cheesemakers still prefer to use rye straw.

Donnelly, Catherine. *Cheese and Microbes*. Washington, D.C.: ASM Press, 2014.
Monteil et Fils. http://www.paillon-monteil.com/en.

Kate Arding

The **Stresa Convention,** officially the International Convention for the Use of Appellations of Origin and Denominations of Cheeses, signed in Stresa, Italy, on 1 June 1951, was the first attempt to create a form of international recognition for cheese names and styles. It was ultimately signed by Austria, Denmark, France, the Netherlands, Norway, Sweden, and Switzerland, and went into effect in September 1953. It was administered by the Italian government, but has become obsolete with more recent texts.

Signatories agreed to reserve use of specific names for cheeses whose characteristics matched expectations of cheese, to "protect their originality" and "inform the consumers." The text defined two categories of names to be protected, "appellations of origin" and "denominations." Appellations must be "manufactured or matured in traditional regions, by virtue of local, loyal, and uninterrupted usages" (language clearly inspired by the French appellation d'origine contrôlée [AOC]). See APPELLATION D'ORIGINE CONTRÔLÉE. Only four cheeses were classified as appellations of origin, with production limited to a specific geographical zone, and their names were protected from misleading use including use of such qualifiers as "type," "kind," or "imitation." The list of denominations was much longer; considered generic, their names were protected by customary physical traits without a geographical component. Denomination cheeses could be made anywhere and bear these names so long as the cheese was recognizably what it claimed to be. Participating countries agreed to enforce and respect use of the protected names.

Outline of the Stresa Convention

Article 1: Convention enforcement; applies to "false" provenance or characteristic information.

Article 2: Defines cheese ("fresh and matured products obtained by draining after the coagulation of milk, cream, skimmed or partially skimmed milk, or a combination of these"); requires suppression of misuse of word "cheese" (later clarifies nonapplication to terms like "head cheese" with no risk of confusion with dairy).

Article 3: Defines "appellation of origin" (elaborated in Annex A) and bans use of qualifiers alongside the appellation.

Article 4: Defines "denominations," generic cheese types whose characteristics (type, shape, size, color) are to be respected (Annex B); cheeses in Annex B may not be moved to Annex A.

Article 5: Allows signatories to add additional cheeses; states procedure.

Article 6: Lists labeling requirements for export.

Article 7: Requires word "processed" appear on products containing melted cheese, which cannot resemble the original cheese; "processed" may be used in conjunction with "appellation of origin" so long as it only concerns one appellation-bearing cheese.

Article 8: Labeling for processed cheeses.

Article 9: Procedures for resolving unforeseen issues.

Article 10: Modalities for taking effect.

Article 11: Withdrawal from the convention.

Protocol: Specifies several details, including some curious provisions in Article 3—its provisions only apply to non-cow's milk cheeses, although the cow's milk cheeses listed in Annex A also benefit from "appellation" protection within all signatory countries; these "appellation" names may still be used on cheeses for export to nonsignatory countries.

Annex A, "Appellations of origin": gorgonzola, Parmigiano Reggiano, Pecorino Romano, Roquefort.

Annex B, "Denominations": Camembert, Brie, Saint Paulin, Fontina, Fiore Sardo, Asiago, provolone, caciocavallo, Emmentaler, sbrinz, Gruyère, Gudbrandsdalsost, Nokkeost, Samsöe, Maribo, Danoe, Svecia, Herrgards, Pinzgauer Berkäse.

The Stresa Convention was modified by the July 1951 Hague Protocol, mostly concerning signatories' preconditions for adhesion. Annex B was modified: "Danoe" became "Danbo," and Gouda, Edam, Leyde, Frise, Fynbo, Elbo, Tybo, Havarti, Danablu, Marmora, and Adelost were added.

See also DESIGNATION OF ORIGIN.

Echols, Marsha. *Geographical Indications for Food Products: International Legal and Regulatory Perspectives*. Alphen aan den Rijn, The Netherlands: Klewer, 2008.

Gangjee, Dev. *Relocating the Law of Geographical Indications*. New York: Cambridge University Press, 2012.

Juliette Rogers

stretching refers to the traditional method for making a pasta filata cheese, such as mozzarella, by immersing the cheese in hot water and then, as the cheese warms and softens, kneading it by hand or mechanically until it becomes a homogeneous mass that can be formed into the desired shape. When curd has reached optimum calcium content (usually when curd pH is between 5.2 and 5.3), it is cut or milled. If the curd contains too much calcium, it will be too rubbery to stretch; if it has too little calcium bound to the caseins, it will be too "soupy" when heated. See CALCIUM PHOSPHATE and CASEIN. If the curd is made by acidifying milk using citric acid rather than adding a starter culture, then it can be ready for stretching at a higher pH (~pH 5.6–5.8). See ACIDIFICATION. The curd pieces are immersed in hot water (or a 5–10 percent brine) and mixed to plasticize and stretch the curd. Traditionally this was performed by hand, using wooden tools. On an industrial scale, the curd is fed into a cooker/stretcher for plasticization. During this stretching process, the internal structure of the cheese becomes fibrous as the renneted caseins in the curd become aligned into fibers with fat globules packed together and accumulating in the channels between the protein strands. See FAT and PROTEINS. This allows long strings of cheese to be pulled from the hot cheese. When the stretching process takes place in a single- or twin-screw cooker, the inlet hopper of the cooker is filled with water heated to 149–158°F (65–70°C) so that as curd is heated, it undergoes mixing and stretching while being pushed down the barrel of the cooker/stretcher by the rotating screw(s). Cheese exits the cooker at 131–149°F (55–65°C) as a smooth plastic mass and is then forced under pressure into chilled molds.

See also COAGULATION OR CURDLING; FUNCTIONAL PROPERTIES; PASTA FILATA; and STRING CHEESE.

Kindstedt, Paul, M. Caric, and S. Milanovic. "Pasta-Filata Cheeses." In *Cheese: Chemistry, Physics, and Microbiology*, 3d ed., edited by Patrick F. Fox et al., Vol. 2: *Major Cheese Groups*, pp. 251–277. London: Elsevier, 2004.
McMahon, Donald, and Craig Oberg. "Cheese: Pasta-Filata Cheeses: Low-Moisture Part-Skim Mozzarella (Pizza Cheese)." In *Encyclopedia of Dairy Sciences*, 2d ed., edited by J. W. Fuquay, P. F. Fox, and P. L. H. McSweeney, Vol. 1, pp. 737–744. San Diego, Calif.: Academic Press, 2011.

Donald McMahon

string cheese is a natural semihard, milk-tasting, stretched-curd cheese with a fibrous texture. Traditional string cheese products, such as Armenian string cheese, Syrian jibneh mshalalleh, Mexican queso Oaxaca, and Slovakian korbáčiky are retailed in various shapes including knots, balls, or braids formed by intertwining, twisting, and folding strings of varying thickness together. In Western Europe and the United States, string cheese is sold mainly as individual sticks—typically approximately 0.4–0.8 inches (1–2 centimeters) in diameter, approximately 4–5 inches (10–12 centimeters) long.

The distinguishing characteristic of all string cheese is its ability to be peeled into strands with the simul-

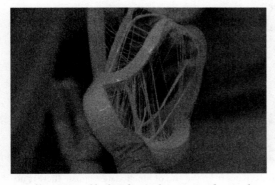

Fine fibers created by hand-stretching an Asadero-style cheese at Ochoa's Queseria in Albany, Oregon. © GIANACLIS CALDWELL

taneous formation of very fine flexible filaments or threads (between the main string and peeled strand), when torn and peeled in a direction parallel to the fibers.

These characteristics are attributable to the plasticization and molding steps of the manufacturing process, which respectively result in the formation of fibers of relatively high tensile strength from the milk protein (calcium phosphate paracasein) and their alignment. Plasticization typically involves heating the curd at the desired acidity (approximately pH 5.2) to approximately 135–140°F (57–60°C), while heating, kneading, and stretching in hot water or diluted brine (e.g., 5 percent NaCl) at approximately 172°F (78°C), or by direct steam injection. The hot molten plasticized curd mass may be manually pulled into long sheets or strands of varying thickness and width that are twisted, intertwined, and folded into various shapes as in traditional string cheeses. Alternatively, the plasticized curd may be extruded through die plates into cylindrical strings that on exiting the extruder are typically conveyed into cold brine, which allows the extruded cheese strings to cool and harden before cutting into sticks of desired length and packaging. Critical parameters in the ability of string cheese to form minute threads when peeled include protein concentration, the level of nonsoluble calcium that cross-links the paracasein molecules constituting the fibers, curd acidity at plasticization that regulates the proportion of soluble to nonsoluble calcium, the proportions of fat and protein in the curd, and degree of fiber alignment.

See also FUNCTIONAL PROPERTIES.

Kindstedt, P., M. Carić, and S. Milanović. "Pasta-Filata Cheeses." In *Cheese, Chemistry, Physics, and Microbiology*, 3d ed., edited by P. F. Fox, P. L. H. McSweeney, T. M. Cogan, et al., Vol. 2: *Major Cheese Groups*, pp. 251–277. Oxford: Elsevier Academic, 2004.

Timothy P. Guinee

Svježi sir (fresh Zagreb cheese) is produced throughout Croatia, most commonly around the capital city of Zagreb. This cheese is produced by local farmers who sell it at the farmer's market. The production process is quite simple: fresh, whole, raw cow's milk is fermented at a temperature of approximately 77°F (25°C) for a period of 24 to 48 hours. During the natural fermentation process, non-starter lactic acid bacteria create acid coagulum, which is covered with sour cream. The sour cream is removed, and the coagulum is cut into squares about the size of 2 × 2 inches (5 × 5 centimeters). The cut coagulum is placed into perforated molds or cheesecloths so it can drain. Occasionally, acid coagulum is heated to a temperature of 104–122°F (40–50°C) to enhance the whey removal. The cheese texture is clumpy (sometimes layered), soft, and fine with a yellowish-white color. The aroma is evident but pleasant, and the taste is full, acidic, and milky. This cheese is also extensively factory-produced from pasteurized milk, with slight modifications in method.

Svježi sir is traditionally consumed for breakfast. It is mixed with sour cream and eaten with traditional smoked bacon. It is also commonly used as a cooking ingredient in the making of traditional pastries such as *šrudle, štrukle,* and *burek.*

See also COTTAGE CHEESE and FRESH CHEESES.

Ćosić, Katica. "The Production of Fresh Cheese in Dairy Biogal d.o.o." BSc thesis, University of Zagreb, 2004. In Croatian.

Samir Kalit

In **Sweden,** a Scandinavian country in northern Europe, the elaboration of dairy products has always played an important role in people's food conservation strategies. Dairy products in general and cheese in particular are central elements in Swedish food culture to this day. Cheese is consumed both for everyday and special occasions and hard cheeses are the most popular products. Swedes also enjoy flavored spread cheese.

The oldest known Swedish cheese was the so-called skörost (acid cheese). Skörost was a grainy mass that was obtained by draining sour skim milk in leaf baskets (in earlier times) and in pieces of cloth (in later periods). Production did not require rennet, therefore it is believed that skörost might have been around already before the Christianization of Sweden (1000–1200 C.E.). A second product that could be obtained from the whey left after producing skörost was whey cheese, a brown thick, sweet paste that could be dried for long-term storage. Whey cheese production requires that the whey be reduced by slowly boiling it for a long time. Therefore it is only in areas where access to firewood is plentiful that it could be produced. Whey cheese is a central product in the

Myhrbodarna Summer Farm, in the County of Jämtland, is only in use from the end of June to late August. There is no electricity or running water, offering visitors a sense of what farmstead life was like in the nineteenth century. Some of the cheesemaking is done outdoors; in this picture you can see the separator and a large pot for cooking whey butter in the foreground, and a wood-fired stove in the background. © PAULINA RYTKÖNEN

Scandinavian transhumance system. See CONCEN-TRATED WHEY CHEESE and TRANSHUMANCE.

Sweden has two dairy traditions, the first is based on the Scandinavian transhumance system, in which elaboration of cheese and other products with milk from goats, cows, and sheep is a food conservation strategy that takes advantage of the rich mountain pastures around summer farms. By the end of the twentieth century this tradition became the foundation for the modern artisan cheese trade. The second is the production of sötmjölksost (sweet milk cheese) based on the use of rennet and curdling with fresh cow's milk, which was introduced to Sweden by Catholic monasteries in the tenth and eleventh centuries and from which industrial cheese production was born in the late nineteenth century.

Olaus Magnus, a Roman Catholic bishop in Sweden, offered in 1555 a glimpse of his perception of the historical geography of Swedish cheese. Hard cow's milk cheese was the main product in Västergötland (southwestern Sweden), while in Östergötland (southeastern Sweden) and "Upper" (northern) Sweden cheese was made with sheep's milk. In Finland (which then was part of Sweden) smoked goat cheese was the dominant product, while in Hälsingland (mideastern Sweden) and Norway (which then owned what is now the Swedish province of Jämtland)

Skärvången Bymejeri, one of Sweden's best-known artisan dairies, specializes in soft cheese from cow's and goat's milk. This label promotes the dairy's "Jämtland," or "slow food" ethos. PHOTO BY PAULINA RYTKÖNEN, WITH PERMISSION FROM SKÄRVÅNGEN BYMEJERI AB

people preferred to consume a worm-eaten cheese with a rind so hard that it was used for soldier's shields. This cheese was likely produced with milk from Scandinavian goats and Alpine cows.

Cheesemaking was part of the daily activities of households, but on special occasions such as weddings of prominent people, or tithes payment, women gathered to make cheese, some of which were square shaped and could weigh up to 220 pounds (100 kilograms). The largest cheeses were kept together by inserting small pieces of sun-dried cheeses into the fresh curd, using them as a plaster. Similar versions were also made by summer farmers in the northern regions and were used to pay taxes. Most cheeses (large and small) were pressed in carved forms from which they got various patterns. An important tradition until today is the production of hard cheeses.

The first dairies were established in large manors already in the seventeenth century, but technical innovations such as the separator and a rising demand for butter in the British market fueled the industrialization of the dairy sector. See SEPARATOR; BUTTER; and INDUSTRIALIZATION. Butter was the most important product and in 1890 butter exports accounted for a total of 10 percent of Swedish exports; therefore the modernization of the dairy industry became a matter of national interest. The success in butter exports created positive spin-off effects on other dairy products. When rennet production was industrialized in the 1870s, it became possible to produce cheese on a larger scale. During the same period dairy schools were established and knowledge was gathered from other countries to support industrial cheese production.

In 1913 exports of butter had fallen to 5 percent of total exports. Eventually this led to a severe economic crisis, which in the 1930s triggered a process of self-regulation in the industry in exchange for government protection. Thereafter the number of industrial dairies declined from around 1,600 in 1932 to a handful by the end of the twentieth century. Industrial cheese production includes basically two types of cheeses, hard cheeses and spread cheese. The latter is often flavored. During the last decades Swedish industrial cheese production has fallen. Between 2010 and 2015 production fell from 103,144 tons to 88,122 tons, while annual per capita consumption remained steady at 22 pounds (20 kilograms).

Industrial production aside, there are today around 160 artisan cheese dairies across Sweden. See ARTI-

SANAL. This is a relatively new trade that arose as a result of a rescue operation to preserve goat farms initiated by the County Board Administration in Jämtland in the 1970s. The infrastructure created for that purpose comprises education, the promotion of producer networks, field visits to farmstead dairies in other countries, and a proactive promotion for the start of artisan dairies all over the country. The stressful market situation for dairy farmers has meant that many have chosen to start their own artisan dairies. Much of the inspiration for product development was initially brought from abroad, leading to the production of mainly French style soft cheeses. But in the last few years traditional cheese recipes have come into use once again. Some examples are the revival of the (medieval) white cheese, which is a cellar stored, brick-shape goat cheese from Jämtland; Wrångebäck, a 22-pound (10-kilogram) round hard cheese with large holes that was invented at a manor dairy in Skaraborg in the late nineteenth century; and Koggost, a spherical Edamer-style cheese that was developed in Gotland, Sweden's largest island, in 1958.

The majority of the artisanal cheese is sold to tourists at the production site and in local markets. Since the late 1990s the National Center for Artisan Food has encouraged artisan cheese production through the national championship in artisan food, courses, and study visits abroad. Since 2014 an annual cheese festival has been organized at the Nordic Museum in Stockholm. The cheese festival is the largest public cheese market in Sweden.

See also DENMARK and NORWAY.

Lindqvist, Nils. "En bit ost—ett stycke kulturhistoria." *Svenska Mejeritidningen*, 1968.
Magnus, Olaus. *Historia om de nordiska folken.* Hedemora, Sweden: Gidlunds Förlag, 2010.
Ragnar, Martin. *Svensk ostkultur i recept och formspråk, ett arv att förvalta.* Stockholm: Carlssons, 2013.
Ränk, Gustav. *Från mjölk till ost: Drag ur den äldre mjölkhushållningen i Sverige.* Stockholm:, Nordiska Museet, 1966.
Staffansson, Jan-Åke. *Svenskt smör: Produktion, konsumtion och utrikeshandel 1861–1913.* Lund, Sweden: Lund University Press, 1995.

Paulina Rytkönen

Swiss cheese is the American-born generic term for a category of cheeses, manufactured and sold primarily in the United States, but also in Finland, France, Norway, and other countries. What makes the cheeses "Swiss" is that they all derive from the same basic recipe and have similar organoleptic characteristics as Switzerland's Emmentaler. See EMMENTALER.

The antecedents to Swiss cheese began when cheesemakers emigrated from Switzerland beginning in the early nineteenth century. Among the first of the non-Swiss Emmentaler types is Allgäuer Emmentaler, originally brought to the Allgäu region of Bavaria by Josef Aurel Stadler in 1821. Another is Norway's Jarlsberg, which was launched in the 1850s. Emmentaler (alternative spelling, "Emmenthaler") is protected by a Swiss appellation d'origine protégée (AOP) but not by a European protected designation of origin (PDO), since Switzerland is not a member of the European Union. See SWITZERLAND and JARLSBERG.

Innovation and Marketing

Starting in the mid-twentieth century, US companies hoping to sell more Swiss cheese began introducing mass-market innovations. By the late 1930s, the Chicago-based Kraft company had already become the world's largest producer of so-called Swiss cheese. In 1943 James Bryan ("Doc") Stine, the chief chemist in Kraft's research lab, created a process for efficient mass production of large blocks of rindless Swiss. Within three years, Kraft had tripled its annual sales in the category to 60 million pounds (27 million kilograms). Stine's process received a US patent in 1950. Although Kraft guarded it as a valuable trade secret, by the mid-1950s other companies were able to emulate the process, and Swiss cheese became an affordable dairy staple in supermarkets and delicatessens across the United States. See KRAFT FOODS.

In 1955 Leonard Gentine, one of the founders of Wisconsin-based Sargento Cheese Company, contributed two more inventions that facilitated the mass-marketing of Swiss cheese and other widely popular types: vacuum-sealed plastic packages and individually sliced portions. In 1960 Kraft was awarded a patent for "modified-atmosphere packaging." Other consumer-oriented innovations included Baby Swiss, a smaller-format type; Lacey Swiss, a cheese with smaller holes and a Havarti-like texture; thinner-sliced or "ultra-thin" Swiss; and reduced-fat variations. See PACKAGING.

The story of Baby Swiss begins with Alfred Guggisberg (1914–1985), who learned cheesemaking as a teenager in his native Switzerland. In 1947 Guggisberg and his wife, Margaret, moved to the United States, eventually making their home in the Doughty Valley of Ohio, where Amish farms supplied milk to the local cheese factory. In the 1960s, Guggisberg created a smaller Emmentaler type he felt would be more accessible to the American palate. Margaret christened it Baby Swiss, and it became a paradigm. The factory was renamed Guggisberg, and the company is still run by family members.

While its most notable trait is its holes, or eyes, Swiss cheese shares several other traits with its European ancestor: a very smooth consistency; a semi-hard, somewhat elastic texture; a flavor profile that includes sweet, nutty notes balanced with mildly sour flavors of lactic fermentation (in longer aged versions, there may be some pleasantly barnyard-like notes); and good melting properties. A true Swiss cheese profile can be difficult to achieve; it requires a great deal of skill and control on the part of the cheesemaker—perhaps more than any other type of cheese. See EYES.

To appeal to a broad demographic, modern Swiss cheese is often marketed as soft and easily melted, while highlighting its buttery and creamy flavors. Connoisseurs of fine table cheeses might criticize it as "industrial," rubbery, or bland. Nevertheless, it can easily liven up a grilled cheese or Reuben sandwich, or even a cheeseburger.

International brands of Swiss cheese include Coon from Australia, Finlandia from Finland, Kerrygold from Ireland, Leerdammer from Holland, and Mainland from New Zealand. The aforementioned Jarlsberg, from Norway, is perennially the best-selling imported cheese in the United States. Other Emmentaler types include Fol Epi from France's Loire Valley; Guldgreve (a.k.a. Swedish Baby Swiss) from Sweden; and Lappi, a Finlandia brand, so called because it was developed in Lapland. See FINLANDIA.

American brands include Alpine Lace (from Land O'Lakes), Amish Country, Edelweiss Creamery, Kraft, Sargento, Swiss Valley, and Tillamook. Large US supermarket chains such as Safeway and Kroger carry these national brands while also offering their own in-house brands. Kraft Swiss cheese slices have about a 20 percent US market share in their category and in turn account for about 30 percent of that company's natural (as opposed to processed) slice offerings. See LAND O' LAKES and TILLAMOOK.

US Production

From a low of about 206 million pounds (93.4 million kilograms) in 1998, US Swiss cheese production increased steadily to 314.5 million pounds (142.5 kilograms) in 2006 and then showed slight declines before climbing to its all-time high of 336.5 million pounds (152.5 million kilograms) in 2010. In 2014 297.8 million pounds (135 million kilograms) of Swiss cheese were produced in the United States, an increase of about 3.3 million pounds (1.5 million kilograms) from 2013. Ohio and Wisconsin each had thirteen plants making Swiss cheese, with the former producing 138 million pounds (62.6 million kilograms) in 2014, compared to 22.7 million (10.3 million) for the latter. Swiss cheese accounted for 5.9 percent of all cheese produced in the United States in 1978; this share declined steadily from 4.4 percent in 1984 to 3.1 percent in 2008 and 2.6 percent in 2014. During that same period, by contrast, shares of total production increased for both Cheddar and mozzarella.

Despite its own production, the United States continues to import Swiss cheese from abroad. The US Department of Agriculture reported Swiss cheese imports of 27 million pounds (12.3 million kilograms) in 2014 and 31.9 million pounds (14.5 million kilograms) in 2015. Norway led the way, providing 13.8 and 12.3 million pounds (6.3 and 5.6 million kilograms) for each year, followed by Finland and Germany, with 7.7 and 8.8 million pounds (3.5 and 4.0 million kilograms), and 7.3 and 9.2 million pounds (3.3 and 4.2 million kilograms), respectively. Switzerland, ironically, supplied only the fourth-largest amount of Swiss cheese to the United States, with about 7.7 million pounds (3.5 million kilograms) imported in each of those years.

Bucher, Anne, and Melanie Villines. *The Greatest Thing Since Sliced Cheese: Stories of Kraft Foods Inventors and Their Inventions.* Northfield, Ill.: Kraft Food Holdings, 2005, pp. 22–23, 24–27.

Guggisberg. https://www.babyswiss.com.

Igourmet.com. www.igourmet.com.

"Cheese Production 2014: Percentage by Type." *Cheese Reporter, Dairy Production Extra,* 15 May 2015, p. 9. http://www.cheesereporter.com/DPE20-202015.pdf.

"Market Indicators: 2008 Cheese Production by Type," 5 June 2009, p. 11. http://www.cheesereporter.com/archive/DPE.pdf.

Sargento. www.sargento.com.

"Swiss Cheese Production Rises, as Does Output of Cream,

Hispanic, Blue, Feta, and Muenster." *Cheese Reporter, Dairy Production Extra*, 15 May 2015, p. 14 http://www.cheesereporter.com/DPE%20-%202015.pdf.

"Swiss, Cream Cheese Production Fall." Cheese Reporter, Dairy Production Extra, ." *Cheese Reporter, Dairy Production Extra*, 5 June 2009, p. 17. http://www.cheesereporter.com/archive/DPE.pdf.

United States Department of Agriculture, Foreign Agricultural Service. "Licensed Cheese Imports: January–December, 2014–2015." *Dairy Monthly Imports*, pp. 14–17. http://www.fas.usda.gov/sites/default/files/2016-01/circular_2015.pdf.

University of Wisconsin–Madison Center for Dairy Research. http://www.cdr.wisc.edu.

David Gibbons

The **Swiss Cheese Union** (Schweizerische Käseunion) was a government-sanctioned cartel that controlled the production and marketing of Swiss cheeses both at home and abroad; it was established in 1914 and disbanded in 1999. The organization's birth the same year that war broke out in Europe is no coincidence. Concerned about their prospects in wartime, Swiss milk producers, cheesemakers, and exporters joined forces to ensure that the nation's dairy industry would not collapse. For the eighty-five years of its life, the Swiss Cheese Union determined milk prices paid to dairy farmers as well as the prices paid to cheesemakers for their wheels. The union also established production quotas for cheese factories and, at least initially, restricted production to Switzerland's three dominant cheeses: Emmentaler, Gruyère and Sbrinz. See EMMENTALER; GRUYÈRE; and SBRINZ.

Under this system exporters never actually owned the cheese—the Swiss Cheese Union did—but they were compensated for warehousing, aging, and cutting wheels. The Swiss Cheese Union also managed promotional and export programs—their efforts devoted, of course, to the trio of permitted cheeses. One highly successful campaign focused on popularizing fondue, formerly a regional dish. Over many decades advertisements and slogans promoted the wholesomeness of fondue and associated fondue parties with stylish living. The organization showcased the cheesy dish at festivals and trade fairs and marched it onto menus for the Swiss military in the 1950s. In 1964 Americans encountered fondue at the Swiss pavilion's chalet-style restaurant at the New York World's Fair. The strategy succeeded beyond imagining. Fondue prepared with grated Emmentaler and Gruyère is now enjoyed far beyond Switzerland's

borders and retains a reputation as the Swiss national dish. See FONDUE.

The Swiss Cheese Union's efforts to stabilize the country's dairy industry did not come without costs, however. While Swiss farmers, cheesemakers, and exporters enjoyed guaranteed customers and margins, the Swiss taxpayer had to make up the difference when revenues did not cover costs. Following World War II the union struggled to sell Swiss cheeses at a profitable price, compelling the government to subsidize the gap. By the time the Swiss Cheese Union disbanded, its deficit approached half a billion Swiss francs.

By focusing all its efforts on three cheese types, the Swiss Cheese Union also discouraged innovation. Cheesemakers who could not get quotas or who made other styles of cheeses were forced underground or out of business. Producers of Appenzeller and Tête de Moine eventually developed their own organizations to counter the weight of the Swiss Cheese Union. See APPENZELLER.

The death knell rang for the Swiss Cheese Union in the late 1990s, when new global trade agreements restricted export subsidies. The Swiss government was compelled to eliminate funding for the Swiss Cheese Union and the organization collapsed. Validating the view that the Swiss Cheese Union had quashed creativity, Swiss cheesemakers almost immediately began devising new recipes and debuting wheels of their own invention.

See also SWISS CHEESE.

"Fondue History and Tradition." Alpenwild. https://www.alpenwild.com/swiss-tours/fondue-history-and-tradition.

National Public Radio. "The Fondue Conspiracy." *Planet Money*, episode 575, 10 October 2014 http://www.npr.org/sections/money/2014/10/10/355177578/episode-575-the-fondue-conspiracy.

Raboud-Schüle, Isabelle. "Comment la fondue vint aux suisses (en passant par Neuchâtel)? Petits histoire du'n mets emblématique." http://www.club-44.ch/?a=7&archive=171576.

"Some Exotic Swiss Recipes for World's Fair." Lodi (California) *News Sentinel*, 16 January 1964.

Janet Fletcher

Switzerland covers little ground on the world map, yet it cradles diverse cultural traditions. The mountains, including the Alps, have long separated groups of people from each other and left them to further nurture the habits they were brought up with. Such diversity is also reflected in the Alp cheeses and the rituals related to them.

Bernese Alps

This region, comprising around 550 Alps (or high mountain pastures), is home to two unique Alp-style cheeses: Berner Oberländer Hoblekäse and, although only in a limited area, Sbrinz. Both are made of whole, raw cow's milk. The Berner Oberländer Hobelkäse weighs between 11 and 33 pounds (5 and 15 kilograms) and, starting in the sixteenth century, probably resulted from the popularity—in Switzerland, but even more so in northern Italy—of the other long-matured and hard-textured cheese, Sbrinz. See SBRINZ.

The name Hobelkäse refers to the fact that, after a maturation of two years, the cheese is shaved (*hobeln*) into paper-thin layers rather than cut. The wheels do not mature lying flat on wood planks but are aged on their sides in wooden racks. Hobelkäse is aged in relatively warm and dry conditions of up to 59°F (15°C) and up to 95 percent humidity. About 800 tons are produced each year.

The farmers and cheese producers from the Bernese Alps have a reputation for working together and, whenever possible, sharing labor and responsibilities. An effort by the Bernese to trademark Hobelkäse cheese, however, was not joined by producers from the upper Valais region bordering the Bernese Alps, where Hobelkäse is also produced. Consequently the Bernese producers eventually succeeded in securing AOP status for the more restricted designation of Berner Oberländer Hobelkäse.

Central and Northeast Switzerland

Reaching from the Entlebuch-Luzern region on its western end, through Toggenburg, Appenzell, and even into the St. Gallen area in the east, this is the largest and least standardized of all Alp zones. With its diverse geography—from rolling hills to steep, bare mountains—this region has brought many different cheeses onto the market, including Appenzeller, Tilsiter, Toggenburger, Sbrinz, and countless Alpkäse. See APPENZELLER and TILSITER.

Central Switzerland used to be under the influence of Allemanic communities and started to make sour cheeses only, and much earlier than other regions did. The people from this area were said to have a sense for trade early on, and they were of the first ones crossing the high mountains southbound in order to sell their cattle, and, after they had adapted to producing rennet cheeses, also their wheels of cheese. Depending on the place and the circumstances, during the summer months farmers in this area either moved their whole family to only one single mountain pasture (Alp) for the entire high-altitude grazing season or they moved upward in stages, bringing only the most necessary goods besides themselves and the animals.

Jura

The Jura is a mountain chain crawling along the northern part of the Swiss-French border. It is not considered part of the Alps, but people there practice transhumance on their mountains. See TRANSHUMANCE. The Jura Mountains have lower altitudes than the Alps; as opposed to averages of 1,500–2,200 meters above sea level and extremes of even over 3,000 meters, the houses of the Jura are usually situated at only 1,300–1,500 meters. This does not necessarily make life and work there easier. While the farmers of the Jura might be able to go back to their regular homes more often and enjoy a little luxury, they often have to deal with water scarcity, since the Jura consists of very porous limestone that absorbs water.

Besides Gruyère, two cheeses in particular have made this region famous: Tête de Moîne and Vacherin Mont d'Or. The first, meaning "monk's head," is one of the oldest cheeses made in Switzerland. The monks of the Bellelay Abbey invented the cheese in the twelfth century. This cheese, weighing less than 2 pounds (1 kilogram), used to be available only for royals and bishops. The cheese is not cut but, using a tool called Girolle, shaved into pretty-looking rosettes. Tête de Moîne is an AOC cheese and produced using whole, raw cow's milk.

Vacherin Mont d'Or also occupies a spot on the list of AOP cheeses. Swiss Vacherin Mont d'Or has to be made from raw cow's milk—heated to a maximum temperature of 119°F (49°C) for at most fiifteen seconds. Vacherin Mont d'Or is a seasonal cheese produced throughout the winter months only. Wheels are encircled with pine bark and packed into wood boxes. Vacherin Mont d'Or is the only cheese of Switzerland where the packaging is officially part of the product and thus included in the price. Its maturation lasts three to four weeks. The Vacherin Mont d'Or comes in various sizes: 12 ounces, 17 ounces, and 7 pounds (350 grams, 500 grams, and 3 kilograms). Its paste is runny and is best eaten with a spoon.

Graubünden

The eastern tip of Switzerland, bordering Liechtenstein and Austria, is particularly rugged and mountainous, making access and management difficult. In terms of its cheese history, the region was influenced by the Romans and produced rennet cheese early on. This is partly because its rough mountains did not allow much planting, so raising cattle and crafting cheeses were a matter of survival.

There is no big name or prestige cheese from Graubünden, although this does not mean that farmers there do not produce great cheese. Quite the opposite: small production wheels can be found in the local dairies and on the Alps above the valleys. There are all kinds of Alpkäse, most of which are still made of raw milk, and this region more than in other areas of Switzerland is known for its production of sheep and goat milk. Within the Alpine communities of Switzerland, the people from Graubünden are respected as an unofficial authority for all things financial. When it comes to paying seasonal employees or buying a piece of land, the people in Graubünden lead the way in setting value.

Pays d'Enhaut

Meaning the "land above," Pays d'Enhaut is a small region tucked between the Gruyère area to the east, the Bernese Alps to the north, and Valais to the south. Fabulous Gruyère is ubiquitous, and so is L'Etivaz, a usually smaller size (33–77-pound [15–35-kilogram]) raw cow's milk cheese produced only during the summer when the animals graze up in the Alps of Pays d'Enhaut (Vaud canton). See GRUYÈRE. L'Etivaz has an AOP appellation. It is aged at least one year; after a maturation of three years it is usually shaved rather than cut and called L'Etivaz Rebibes.

Even more impressive than the cheeses of Pays d'Enhaut is the sense of independence and collaboration of its inhabitants. They have consistently refused to be guided by the mandates of the Swiss Cheese Union, a governmental institution put in place to control and market the cheese industry. See SWISS CHEESE UNION. Instead, they have functioned as a coop, built a communal aging facility for L'Etivaz and promoted the cheese—and many other authentic food products from the region—efficiently. Production is steadily growing; currently there are between 400 and 450 tons of L'Etivaz crafted every year, or around 19,000 wheels.

Ticino

Ticino not only defines a region in the southeast, it represents an entire canton. Ticino was always isolated from the rest of Switzerland, especially before tunnels were built through the mountains making "the south" and Italy more accessible. This isolation is reflected in the cheese culture: Ticino functions independently.

In Ticino transhumance happens in a cooperative way. Shepherds and farmers are hired for the summer and move, via a stop at the lower Alp in the spring and fall, to the high Alp, bringing animals from several farms. At the end of the season, each farmer receives the amount of cheese that matches the ratio of his animals.

There are many different cheeses produced on the roughly two hundred Alps and locally all of them are distinctively named. However, since 2002 the official—and AOP approved—name is Formaggio d'Alpe Ticinese. The individual name of each cheese usually refers to the place it was made, and is engraved on the side of the wheels. The vast majority of cheeses are made from raw cow's milk and they often have grayish, velvety rinds due to aging in moist cellars. They weigh 7–22 pounds (3–10 kilograms) and are never aged over a year.

Valais

The geographic circumstances of the Valais are a bit comparable to Ticino. This region and canton in the southwestern part of Switzerland used to be separated from the rest of the country due to its massive mountain ranges. Dairy production has always been crucial to this region, and it has always been complicated. Even today, this canton practices a unique way of passing on assets from one generation to the next. The total of what a person owns and passes on to others as inheritance is not evenly divided by the number of descendants, but is instead divided by type of goods. So one descendent might inherit all the animals, one the house, one all the stables, etc. This results in constantly changing situations of businesses, landscapes, and relationships.

Even though Valais produces countless types of cheese (that rarely leave the region), the Raclette du Valais AOP is by far the most important one. It is made of raw milk from Eringer cows, a sturdy, small breed that is famous for the fights the females like to get into. It is not exactly clear when Raclette was invented—and if this happened in Valais—but it is known that by the Middle Ages, shepherds liked a meal of cheese melted on an open fire. The name Raclette was declared officially during a Valais wine fest in 1909. See RACLETTE.

See also ALP CHEESEMAKING and ALP-STYLE CHEESES.

CasAlp. http://www.casalp.ch.
Flammer, Dominik, and Fabian Scheffold. *Schweizer Kaese.* AT Verlag: Baden, 2009.
Raclette du Valais. http://www.raclette-du-valais.ch.
Swiss PDO-PGI Association. http://www.aop-igp.ch.
Vacherin Mont d'Or. http://www.vacherin-montdor.ch.

Caroline Hostettler

symbiotic relationship refers to the interactions that occur between the species present in an ecosystem, for example the microbial species present in fermented food ecosystems such as cheeses. Microbial interactions are complex and mediated through a variety of molecular and physiological mechanisms, which have only partially been explained. They occur not only at the species level but also at the strain level and are most often not predictable. See STRAINS and PHENOTYPIC VARIABILITY. They are determinants of the quality of the final product, making this topic one of the most challenging in microbiology. Symbiotic relationships are divided into different classes, depending on which microorganism will benefit from the interaction: mutualism, where both organisms derive benefits; commensalism, where one benefits and the other is unaffected; amensalism, where one is harmed while the other is unaffected; parasitism, where one benefits while the other is harmed; and competition, where both organisms can be harmed. A few examples of the main symbiotic relationships studied in cheese are given below.

A nice example of mutualism is the interaction between the two bacterial species used in yogurt production, *Streptococcus thermophilus* and *Lactobacillus bulgaricus*. It results from the production by each species of a range of metabolites that stimulate the growth of the other species. In addition, many cases of commensalism have been described in cheese. For example, the thermophilic lactobacilli used as starters in Swiss cheese favor the growth of propionibacteria by providing them with peptides and free amino acids required by these bacteria, which are not able to directly use cheese proteins as a nitrogen source. See DAIRY PROPIONIBACTERIA and SWISS CHEESE. On the rind of washed cheeses, the growth of yeasts aid in the development of surface bacteria by deacidifying the cheese surface. Commensalism also occurs at the strain level within a species. This is the case for protease-positive strains of *Lactococcus lactis*, which stimulate the growth of protease-negative strains of the same species.

See also ECOSYSTEM and MICROBIAL COMMUNITIES.

Smid, Eddy J., and Christophe Lacroix. "Microbe-Microbe Interactions in Mixed Culture Food Fermentations." *Current Opinion in Biotechnology* 24 (April 2013): 148–154.

Anne Thierry

syneresis is the phenomena in which gels formed from milk by renneting or lactic acidification naturally contract with time, expelling liquid (whey). Under quiescent conditions, a rennet-induced gel may lose two-thirds of its volume, and up to 90 percent or even more, if external pressure is applied. Syneresis is one of the most important processes in cheesemaking because it directly affects cheese yield, ripening, and quality through its effect on the moisture, mineral, and lactose content of the curd.

During rennet coagulation, the gel assembly process happens because of changes in solubility, rearrangement, and shrinkage of casein particles. These changes represent the active phase of syneresis.

While the gel is being formed, three new kinds of bonds are also formed. Hydrogen bonds are created first and are numerous but have no structuring effect. Then calcium binding happens and it is the most important bond for the structure of the gel. Then at the end disulfide bonds are created allowing the decisive contraction of curd.

The key factors affecting syneresis are classified into two groups: direct and indirect. Direct factors include the size of curd particles, stirring, heating during stirring, and removal of lactose transfer, molding, pressing, and returning. Indirect factors include heat treatment, protein and milk fat content, maturation, addition of calcium chloride, pH, and rennet concentration.

In other dairy products created from acidification, such as yogurt, sour cream, and fresh cheeses, a slight spontaneous syneresis can occur at the surface of the product. This is called passive syneresis, due to acidification, and is considered a defect. However this liquid contains minerals as well as highly nutritional whey proteins and can be consumed.

See also COAGULATION OR CURDLING and WHEY.

Fox, P. F., et al. *Fundamentals of Cheese Science.* Gaithersburg, Md.: Aspen, 2000.

Gilles Garric

synergistic effects refer to the effects of several combined factors, for example two factors A and B, for which the effect of the combination of A and B has a greater effect compared to a simple additive effect (effect of A+B > effect of A + effect of B). These factors can be abiotic (temperature or pH, for instance) or biotic (microorganisms). For example, two microorganisms may have a synergistic effect on the formation of cheese flavor if each of them has a specific contribution in the series of reactions leading to the production of flavor compounds. Let's take the example of the synthesis of ethyl esters in cheese. They are common cheese flavor compounds associated with expected or undesirable "fruity" flavors. Their formation results from a reaction between an acid and an alcohol such as ethanol, catalyzed by enzymes called esterases. The formation of esters in hard cheeses is markedly favored by the synergistic association of an ethanol-producing strain and a strain with a high esterase activity. Another example is the association of a strain with a high proteolytic activity, which produces free amino acids in cheese, and a second one with specific amino acid-converting activities, which will produce flavor compounds from the amino acids produced by the first strain. Abiotic factors can also have synergistic effects (stimulation or inhibition) on microorganisms. For example, the combination of a low pH and a high salt concentration inhibits microbial growth more than the addition of the individual inhibitory effect of each of these factors.

"Synergist." In *Oxford Dictionaries.* http://www .oxforddictionaries.com/definition/english/ synergyist.

Anne Thierry

Taleggio is a soft cow's milk cheese named after Val Taleggio, the mountain valley in northern Italy where it originated. The first documents mentioning this square-shaped stracchino cheese date from the year 1200 C.E. The term "stracchino" is an etymological derivative of the regional word "stracche" (tired) and refers to cheese that was made at the end of summer, when the cows came back fatigued from the transhumance. See TRANSHUMANCE. Originally made by farmers to preserve excess milk when the herd came down from the Alpine pastures at the end of September, it is now produced on a larger scale all year round throughout the Po Valley. However, an important part of its production still takes place outside the dairies, in the natural caves of Valsassina, where the cheese is ripened in the traditional way on wooden planks. Taleggio has been protected by a PDO (protected designation of origin) since 1996 and is one of Italy's best known and most popular cheeses.

Taleggio is a creamy, soft washed-rind cheese produced according to traditional practices. Whole raw or pasteurized milk is heated to a temperature of about 90–95°F (32–35°C). Calf rennet and a lactic starter culture of *Streptococcus thermophilus* and *Lactobacillus delbrueckii* subspecies *bulgaricus* are added at the same time. After coagulation, the curd is broken up in two stages to the final size of a hazelnut, then placed into square molds and kept in warm rooms with a high humidity for eight to sixteen hours.

The cheese is either dry-salted or brined and then ripened on wooden shelves in modern chambers or in traditional caves for at least 35 (up to 50) days at a temperature of 36 and 43°F (2–6°C) and a relative humidity of 85 and 90 percent. During ripening, the cheese is washed once a week with brine to keep it moist. The combination of temperature and salt concentration select and promote the growth of a complex surface microbiota, including different bacteria, yeast, and mold species. These give the cheese its appealing red color and characteristic aroma. The rind pigmentation, texture, and sensory characteristics are in fact strictly correlated with the biochemical modifications occurring during the ripening process from the surface of the cheese to the inside, called "centripetal maturation."

This square cheese is 7–8 inches (18–20 centimeters) wide, about 1.5–3 inches (4–7 centimeters) high, and weighs 3.7–4.8 pounds (1.7–2.2 kilograms). The rind is soft and thin with a natural pinkish-red color, and may have irregular spots of gray-green mold. The number of the dairy plant is impressed on one side. Inside, Taleggio is white to straw yellow, with irregularly spaced tiny holes. The paste is soft and, because of proteolysis, slightly melting under the rind, while being firmer and more crumbly towards the center at the end of ripening. The fragrance is herbaceous and aromatic, and the taste is sweet, delicate, and slightly sour. With time, the taste intensifies and becomes more complex, sometimes tangy and mildly pungent.

Taleggio is a popular table cheese but is also much used in rice and pasta dishes, particularly in the Lombardy region, because of its exceptional melting qualities.

See also ITALY.

Feligini, M., et al. "Identification of Microbiota Present on the Surface of Taleggio Cheese Using PCR-DGGE and RAPD-PCR." *Journal of Food Science* 77 (2012): M609–M615.

Gobbetti, M., et al. "Microbiology and Biochemistry of Taleggio Cheese During Ripening." *International Dairy Journal* 7 (August–September 1997): 509–517.

Milena Brasca

tartiflette is a French dish from the department of Haute-Savoie, in the French Alps. Sliced, cooked potatoes are mixed with onions, *lardons fumés* (little rectangles of smoked salt pork), white wine, and often crème fraîche (slighted soured thick cream), topped with Reblochon AOC cheese, and then put in the oven until the cheese melts and browns (*gratiné*). Morbiflette, a regional adaptation from the department of Jura to the north, showcases local Morbier cheese and often replaces the *lardons* with smoked Morteau sausage from the Jura Mountains. See RE-BLOCHON and MORBIER.

The dish's exact origins are debated by its enthusiasts. Despite its homely and ancestral image, tartiflette per se is a relatively recent creation, the brainchild of Reblochon producers with too much mature cheese on their hands. In the 1980s, in an effort to boost declining sales, *péla*, a traditional regional recipe in which potatoes, onions, and scraps of local Reblochon cheese are cooked in a long-handled pan, was enhanced by the addition of *lardons* and white wine. Most observers say the producers' union launched the updated dish as a marketing tool, while the union itself claims it merely publicized a local restaurateur's version. Either way, the new tartiflette was a resounding success that dramatically lifted Reblochon sales and popularized the dish throughout the country.

Since 2014, commercially produced tartiflettes can aspire to obtain the quality assurance of a Label Rouge, which stipulates that they must contain at least 20 percent Reblochon cheese (and no other) as well as 10 percent wood-smoked *lardons*, 6 percent full-fat crème fraîche, and 6 percent onions. The final dish must also be browned in an oven. See LABEL ROUGE.

See also HAUTE-SAVOIE.

Androuët. "Tartiflette au Reblochon." http://androuet.com/Tartiflette-au-Reblochon-685-recette.html.
Millau, Christian, and Alain Bouldouyre. *Dictionnaire amoureux de la gastronomie*. Paris: Plon, 2008.

Laura Shine

taste is the sensation produced by the interaction of certain molecules with receptors found mostly in the oral cavity. Although the number of chemicals we can taste ("tastants") is quite large, they are all registered by a very small set of receptor types found in the taste buds on the tongue and soft palate. Generally it is held that there are only five basic taste sensations: salty, sour, umami (savory), sweet, and bitter.

The correspondence between this relatively limited palette of tastes and the huge range of sensations that foods can elicit is explained by two facts. First, although colloquially "taste" and "flavor" are used interchangeably, the latter is a broader, integrative sensation comprising taste, aroma, touch, chemical irritation, and even visual and auditory cues—thus, flavor is a "bigger tent" than taste. Second, both taste and flavor are psychological responses to nervous system sensations produced by chemical stimulation of biological receptors; in other words, these sensations are not strictly chemical properties of the foods we eat, but rather learned responses modulated by our individual biological variations. See PHILOSOPHIES OF TASTE.

Cheeses, which in general are beloved for their complex flavors, are capable of offering all the basic taste sensations. Salt is a fundamental ingredient of cheese and plays an important role in ripening. While the main sugar found in milk—lactose—is only sparingly sweet, a few peptides produced by ripening and some residual carbohydrates can lend slight to pronounced sweetness to cheeses. Protein hydrolysis produces abundant free glutamate—responsible for savory taste—in ripened cheeses, while also producing potentially bitter (and potentially unpleasant) short-chain peptides. See PROTEOLYSIS. Finally, lactic acid and other fermentation products can lend cheese a distinct sourness. In general taste in cheeses develops with aging: while saltiness is added mostly in processing and sweetness may decrease during aging as sugars are fermented, both umami and sourness are direct products of aging, as, often, is bitterness—desirable or not. This can be directly observed by comparing, for example, the tastes of fresh mozzarella and the aged pasta filata cheeses; the former is fresh, sweet, and bland, while the latter, produced in the same basic way but aged, are savory, salty, and complex. See MOZZARELLA and PASTA FILATA.

Taste sensation begins with the activation of taste receptors, which are located in the mouth in "taste buds" on the tongue and the soft palate, by tastants. These taste receptors are the functional elements of specialized skin cells that are in turn connected to the nervous system. Current research indicates that each taste receptor cell registers a particular basic taste, but that the infamous "tongue map" indicating that different regions of the tongue register different tastes is incorrect: the taste buds in general all contain receptor cells for each of the five basic tastes. The way these receptor cells work and the molecules they receive are quite distinct.

Salty Taste

Of the five tastes, saltiness is at once the simplest and the least understood. It appears that small, positively charged ions (cations) are the main vector of salty taste: the prototypical salty taste comes from the sodium ion, but lithium ions, although toxic, also produce a clean saltiness. Other small cations, such as potassium and magnesium, produce salty sensations, but usually accompanied by other, difficult to categorize sensations, often described as "metallic" or "soapy." Furthermore the negatively charged ion in the salt (the anion) can modify the salty perception of the cation: while sodium chloride (table salt) is a clean saltiness, sodium citrate is considerably less salty, and sodium salts of fatty acids are not at all salty. See FAT. Humans require sodium and potassium for neurotransmission, as well as a host of other biological functions, and evolutionary biology would have it that this explains our preference for salty foods; this preference, in modern Western diets, is now thought to lead to an overconsumption of sodium-heavy foods. Unfortunately reducing sodium content in cheeses leads to quality differences in the end product because of sodium chloride's functional as well as taste properties. Sodium chloride assists with both cheesemaking and preservation; while the effective saltiness of cheese may be complicated by sodium's interaction with other anions, saltiness is a fundamental aspect of cheese flavor. Saltiness increases as a cheese ages and dries. See DRY SALTING and SALT.

Sour Taste

Like saltiness, sourness is caused by the presence of a positively charged ion, but in this case it is a very specific cation: a hydrogen ion. Those who retain high school chemistry will recall that hydrogen ions dissolved in an aqueous environment (such as most foods or the mouth) are an indicator of acidity, and, indeed, sourness appears to depend fundamentally on the acidity level of the food. However, as in salt perception, the relationship is not simple: different acids with the same pH are not necessarily sour to the same degree—once again anions appear to modulate the taste response. In cheeses the major sources of acidity—and thus sourness—are small organic acids, including lactic and citric (from general fermentation of the milk), and volatile organic acids, most commonly acetic, propionic, and butyric.

Umami Taste

Sweet, bitter, and umami tastes are mechanistically different from saltiness and sourness: they depend on the detection of molecular features by complicated receptor proteins, instead of ionic "gradients" detected by cellular channels. Of these, umami—which is the Japanese word for "deliciousness" and is generally rendered as "savory" in English—shows the greatest specificity for molecular triggers: for humans umami seems to be produced exclusively by the amino acid derivatives monosodium glutamate (the infamous MSG) and monosodium aspartate. In addition certain nucleotides (inosine and guanosine monophosphates) enhance umami. Since these amino acids and nucleotides are usually found in protein-heavy foods, it is thought that humans like umami because it indicates a rich source of nutrients. Because of its association with MSG umami is sometimes controversial; MSG has been demonized as a food additive, although current thinking clears it of any real responsibility for so-called "Chinese-Restaurant Syndrome." Many unprocessed and traditional foods in fact contain significant quantities of MSG and aspartate. Cheeses are some of the most naturally umami foods because their abundant proteins are heavily hydrolyzed during processing and aging into small fragments including MSG and aspartate; thus, just-coagulated cheeses are mild and bland, while long-aged cheeses tend to be delightfully—often irresistibly—savory. See PROTEINS.

Sweet Taste

Humans are thought to have a natural affinity for sweetness because common simple sugars—sucrose, fructose, glucose, maltose—are ready sources of energy. While that is probably correct to some degree, sweetness as a sensation in vivo is not so easily corralled: a number of non-nutritive and even toxic substances are also sweet, including chloroform. While research in recent years has succeeded in identifying the receptors for sweet taste, exactly how they function is still unknown, meaning that predicting which molecules will activate these proteins is not yet possible. In fact some small proteins, while bearing little chemical resemblance to simple sugars, are up to twenty thousand times as sweet on a molecular basis. The basic constituent of cheese—milk—is sweet due to lactose, a simple sugar which is distinctly less sweet than table sugar. As cheeses age, this and other sugars are microbially fermented, leading to a decrease in sweetness. However, in a number of aged cheeses—most notably the Alp-style, Cheddar, and Gouda families—protein breakdown and other aging mechanisms generate new sweet compounds and aroma molecules, which lead to a perception of sweetness. In particular a few amino acids (proline, glycine) that become more abundant in these cheeses have been reported to potentially elicit sweet tastes, especially in combination with calcium and magnesium ions, which are naturally present. It is also possible that sweet impressions are created by volatile compounds evolving from the proteolysis, most notably furanones and pyranones, which have burntsugar, maple, and pineapple aromas.

Bitter Taste

Bitterness and sourness are often confused: sourness is the mouth-puckering perception elicited by acidic foods like lemons or vinegar, whereas bitterness is the complex sensation familiar to consumers of coffee. In fact bitterness sensation is closely related to sweetness: the receptors for these molecules are very similar and seem to be activated by related molecular features, which may explain why many chemicals and foods are both bitter and sweet. Of all the taste sensations humans have the most kinds of receptors for bitterness—more than thirty distinct receptors, leading to a broad variety of bitter sensations: chocolate and endive are not bitter in the same way. Whereas the other four taste sensations are generally thought to be either positive or at worst equivocal, bitterness is usually held to be thoroughly negative. Since many natural plant toxins

and protein-decay indicators are bitter, it is often claimed that bitterness detection and aversion is a natural defense against ingesting these compounds; however, this view is complicated by human preferences for many bitter foods, including coffee, tea, alcohol, and chocolate, and the apparent health benefits of many bitter chemical compounds. In cheeses bitterness is often considered a defect; it develops mostly from protein decomposition during aging, and usually is an indication of either over-aging or improper aging—for example, at higher temperatures to accelerate other chemical reactions. However mild bitterness can be a desirable quality for the balance of a cheese (as in older Goudas or Cheddars), and even pronounced bitterness can be appropriate in some cheeses, such as the extremely proteolyzed Portuguese thistle-rennet cheeses.

See also AROMA; FLAVOR; FLAVOR WHEEL; SENSORY ANALYSIS; and TEXTURE.

Brady, J. W. *Introductory Food Chemistry*. Ithaca, N.Y.: Cornell University Press, 2013.
Chandrashekar, J., et al. "The Receptors and Cells for Mammalian Taste." *Nature* 444, no. 7117 (2006): 288–294.
Drake, M. A. "Invited Review: Sensory Analysis of Dairy Foods." *Journal of Dairy Science* 90, no. 11 (2007): 4925–4937.
Lindsay, R. C. "Flavors." In *Fennema's Food Chemistry*, edited by S. Damodaran et al., pp. 639–688. Boca Raton, Fla.: CRC Press, 2008.
McGee, Harold. *On Food and Cooking*. New York: Scribner, 2004.
McSweeney, P. L. H. "The Flavour of Milk and Dairy Products: III. Cheese: Taste." *International Journal of Dairy Technology* 50, no. 4 (1997): 123–128.

Jake Lahne

tattoos are a form of body art dating to the fourth millennium B.C.E., in which ink is inserted under the skin to change its pigment. After its re-introduction in Europe in the eighteenth century, tattooing experienced oscillating periods of social prejudice and tolerance, but by the early 2000s it had lost much of its stigma, becoming a mainstream form of expressive culture in North America and Western Europe. The popularity of food culture and the ascent of chefs to stardom have given rise to a noticeable increase in food-related tattoos. It should be no surprise, then, that cheese lovers have become keen followers of the practice as well.

Whereas some chefs choose to have their signature dishes inscribed on their skin, cheesemongers and aficionados select cheese-related iconography as an identifier and a sign of their personal commitment to cheese. So pervasive has this become that *Culture* magazine featured a photo spread of cheese tattoos in its June 2011 issue. The profile features the cheesemonger Sheri La Vigne, who commemorates her lifelong dream of owning a cheese shop with a "sacred wedge" of cheese tattooed on her left arm. Having pledged her commitment by captioning her tattoo "Cheese for life," she quips, "No turning back now!" The author and cheesemonger Gordon Edgar puts it this way: "I decided that no matter what happened in the rest of my life, my relationship with cheese—professional and personal—was significant enough to merit a permanent mark on my body."

The most popular cheese-themed tattoo image is a wedge of hard cheese, sometimes enhanced by blue veins or the "eyes" of a Swiss-style cheese. Other popular tattoos represent foods featuring cheese as the core ingredient: pizza slices, cheese melts, tacos, and cheeseburgers. Among professionals, cheesemongers' knives with their distinctive culinary history and unique shapes have become an aesthetically and symbolically appealing image. Dave Puchta says of his tattoo, a trio of cheese knives: "The traditional Parmigiano Reggiano knives are a representation of the heritage that's developed with cheese during its thousands of years of existence."

Cows, mice, and even the word "milk" are also popular in cheese-related tattoos. Perhaps the ultimate expression of one aficionado's love of cheese, though—and, perhaps, brand loyalty as well—is the tattooed image of the Parmigiano Reggiano DOP stamp.

Miller, Laurel, et al. "Body of Work." *Culture: The Word on Cheese*, 3 June 2011. http://culturecheesemag.com/photo-essay/body-of-work.

Paula Arvela

taxonomy allows us to attribute an identity to living organisms; it is the science of biological rank–based classification and undergirds how we scientifically categorize organisms important in cheesemaking. It encompasses the classification (arrangement of organisms into groups called taxa), the nomenclature (assignment of name to taxa), and identification (determination of taxon to which an isolate belongs). The taxonomy places organisms into meaningful groups, with accurate names, thus facilitating scientific communication, and is essential for accurate identification of microorganisms.

The bases of classification were established by Carl von Linné in 1735 as a binary nomenclature where each species has to be assigned to a genus. In this nomenclature each organism has two Latin names, the genus name (italicized and capitalized) and the species epithet (italicized but not capitalized) as for example *Lactococcus lactis*. Classification encompasses eight major taxonomic ranks: life, domain, kingdom, phylum, class, order, family, genus, and species. The work of Woese et al. (1990) on the rRNA data distributed life into three domains: eukaryotes, bacteria, and archaea. These three domains come together on the evolutionary tree where all living organisms come from a common ancestor depicted by the root. Bacteria and archaea are both prokaryotic; the archaea being considered the most primitive are linked to extreme habitats in terms of pressure, temperature or pH. Archaea share common features with bacteria but also share similarities with eukaryotes.

Taxonomy is crucial in cheesemaking in order to guarantee the identity of the microorganism strains used as starter cultures. Indeed, species must be clearly identified, since to be used as cheese ripening agents, they must belong to the list of agents recommended for Qualified Presumption of Safety (QPS) by the European Food Safety Authority (EFSA) or Generally Recognized As Safe (GRAS) from the US Food and Drug Administration. See GENERALLY RECOGNIZED AS SAFE. In addition to these regulatory requirements concerning the starters, the correct identification of strains associated with cheese is a key element to selecting the appropriate species in regard to a specific technology or to distinguish the "positive" strains from the "negative" ones (pathogen or spoilage flora) for the safety warranty and the quality of cheese.

Two different approaches can be used in taxonomy for classification: the phenetic and the phylogenetic. The phenetic classification, based on mutual similarity of phenotype (i.e., expressed physical traits), is convenient to compare as many attributes as possible thanks to the associated numerical taxonomy. The phylogenetic classification is based on the phylogeny, that is, the evolutionary development of a species. It is achieved by direct comparison of the genetic material and of gene products, and it includes all the characters allowing the establishment of the evolutionary history of the considered organisms. Characters used in taxonomy belong to two categories: classical characters (morphology, physiology, metabolism, ecology, etc.) and molecular characters (nucleic acid base compositions, nucleic acid hybridization and sequencing). When a new species has to be described, it is crucial to consider as many as characters as possible, the classical characters as well as molecular ones, in order to have an exhaustive description of the microorganism supported by the phenetic and phylogenetic characteristics as accurately as possible.

The species is an essential rank to determine as it is considered as the basic unit of taxonomy. Eukaryote (including filamentous fungi and yeast) species definition is based on interbreeding, in contrast to prokaryote (bacteria and archaea), which are asexual, and so the definition based on interbreeding can't be used. Thus bacterial strains (genetic variants or sub-types of a microorganism, descended from a single organism or pure culture) are considered as belonging to the same species if they share many stable properties (core housekeeping genes or 16S rRNA sequences, G+C percent), having 70 percent or greater DNA: DNA relatedness. If DNA-DNA hybridization is unequivocally the "gold standard" for identification of new bacterial species, it is time-consuming, labor-intensive, and expensive to perform and is now neglected in favor of other techniques. For bacteria, in order to have a clear and accepted definition of the species, a committee composed of specialized taxonomists for prokaryotes has established various recommendations regarding the species definition in the light of developments in methodologies available to systematists. The committee encourages researchers to base a species description on more than a single strain, to apply DNA profiling, and highly recommend combining several identification methods. To date several systematic manuals of bacteria and fungi are available; among the best known, the *Bergey's Manual of Systematic Bacteriology* (for bacteria and archaea) and the *Ainsworth and Bisby's Dictionary of Fungi* can be cited. In summary, bacterial strains belong to the same strain if they are very close in terms of genome sequence and typical characteristics and fungal or yeast strains belongs to the same species if they are able to breed.

Methods for Microbial Identification

Methods for microbial identification are numerous and the choice of ones to implement is strongly related to the domain (prokaryote or bacteria) and to the alleged species. As explained above, the species is an essential rank to determine. Thus, for microbial identification, methods must be able to determine with certainty the species of the microorganisms studied. Since Louis Pasteur, after a century of discovery in microbiology, identification of microorganisms remains a hot topic even if it has considerably evolved with the advent of molecular biology.

Identification methods can be divided into two main categories: phenotypic and molecular. The phenotypic methods are based on expressed characters by strains: morphology, capacity to use specific carbon sources, nutritional requirements, optimal temperature growth, cell wall composition, etc. These methods are more or less discriminating but their major disadvantage is not being easily automated as well as time-consuming. More recently new phenotypic methods were developed, usable for bacteria and fungi, having the major advantage of being automated. Fourier Transform Infrared spectroscopy and a promising high-throughput identification method, matrix-assisted laser desorption/ionization-time-of-flight mass spectrometry (MALDI TOF-MS), have recently been introduced in taxonomy. Both methods are based on the species-specificity of the generated spectra.

Molecular methods (based on the genomic sequence) can be used as complementary or in place of the phenotypic ones. For identification at the species level, methods based on the comparison of the genome of microorganisms by sequencing of species-specific sequences as for example 16S rRNA for bacteria or the non-transcribed intergenic regions ITS1 and ITS2 of the genes encoding the 18S and 28S ribosomal RNA for fungi are commonly used. These methods are currently used in most microbiology laboratories and the reference sequence data allowing the identification are freely accessible in public databases. To date, more than 14,000 species of bacteria with their 16srRNA respective sequence and more than 31,000 species of fungi are available on the Genbank database (http://www.ncbi.nlm.nih.gov/Genbank/). Molecular methods are numerous, more or less discriminating with regard to the species of microorganisms considered. Most of the time they require DNA replication achieved by Polymerase Chain Reaction (PCR), a technique that has revolutionized molecular biology in general and identification of microorganisms in particular. PCR is based on a thermostable enzyme, the DNA polymerase, which is able to replicate a huge number of copies of DNA from of a single copy. Thus from a weak quantity of microbial DNA, it is possible to have enough DNA material in order to perform one or several molecular identification methods at the species but also the strain level.

Independent of the chosen methods, phenotypic and molecular, the key factor for species identification methods relevance is the context. Are microorganisms to identify already isolated, or are they enclosed in a complex matrix associated in a complex ecosystem such as cheese? Thus two main strategies must be considered: cultivable and uncultivable. The first one requires the isolation and the culture of the microorganism prior to the identification step. Cultivable procedures are used principally when the criteria for identification are phenotypic, when recovery of the isolates from the analyzed product is necessary. Cultivable procedures do not prevent, once the strains are isolated, the use of molecular methods for species identification. The bias of these procedures is the cultivability of the strains since some strains may be viable but not cultivable, and the choice of the culture medium for microorganisms, which can be more or less selective toward some species of microorganisms. The uncultivable strategy does not require the culture and isolation of microorganisms prior to identification. It is based on molecular methods by extracting the DNA directly from the matrix or from the environment where the microorganisms grew (cheese, milk, biofilms, etc.). In this case, all the microorganisms are considered, alive, dead, or alive but not cultivable. Among these methods we can mention the molecular fingerprint methods such as Temporal Temperature or Denaturing Gradient Gel electrophoresis (TTGE and DDGE) allowing rapid identification of a broad range of microbial species within dairy products. By using these technics, Ogier et al. (2004) described the bacterial diversity of various cheeses differing in their technology and microbial composition. Nevertheless these methods only allow the identification of the dominant flora and they require complementary methods to identify species present at low levels in cheese. Another method not requiring cultivation

prior to identification is metagenomic, and is based on the direct sequencing of the total microbial DNA. Initiated in the 1980s, this method was first dedicated to the characterization of complex environments such as oceans and soil. The word "metagenomic" was first used by Handelsman (2004). The technique was made possible thanks to next-generation sequencing technologies and is now increasingly used in food research to identify microorganisms in fermented foods ecosystems. It has been recently applied with success to cheese by Almeida et al. (2014). These authors have created a dairy reference genome catalog including 137 different species of dairy microorganisms. Additionally they have validated their metagenomic approach to identify microorganisms present in cheese by analyzing the microbial composition of the surface of two smear cheeses and one blue-veined cheese.

Whatever the methods implemented, based on cultivable or uncultivable strategies, once the species are determined, the strains must be characterized since each strain is unique inside the species. Thus, after having determined the species, even if it is the basic unit of taxonomy, an ultimate step of strain typing is required.

Strain Typing

Strain typing is the last level of identification and characterization of a microorganism. This allows determination of the characteristics and the potential of the strains for one given species. Strain typing is particularly relevant in cheese technology since most, if not all, of the technological properties are strain-dependent. For one species, there are an infinite number of characters that share the same major properties (same morphology, same capacity to use specific nutrients, same optimal growth temperature, etc.) but can vary for accessory functions (production of specific vitamins, exopolysaccharide, pH or salt sensitivity, etc.) Thus it is crucial to have specific methods to discriminate these strain to strain variations and establish for each strain an "ID card." In addition, to provide the characteristics of the strains, this ID card ensures the traceability of strains and is a key element for the intellectual properties of strains used as starters in cheese technology.

As for microbial identification, for strain typing we can use phenotypical or molecular methods.

Phenotypical methods, based on expressed physical traits, are usually considered as weakly discriminating for species determination, but they can be very useful to characterize specific technological properties, for example the capacity of the strains to produce specific components or to use specific substrates. Phenotypic characteristics are also useful to check the safety of the strains, for example by validating their GRAS status by the absence of antibiotic resistance and production of biogenic amines. The molecular methods, which consist of discriminating strains based on their genetic content, are also of a great interest as they result in identification of unique fingerprints, a kind of barcode for microorganisms. These methods are also called fingerprint methods and can be classified into three categories: DNA banding patterns, DNA hybridization-based methods, and DNA sequencing. DNA banding methods are based on the digestion of total DNA by restriction enzymes and/or amplification of the DNA-specific sequences. One of the most discriminant methods is pulse field gel electrophoresis (PFGE). PFGE consists of the separation of large DNA fragments (10–20kb) generated by restriction enzymes, inside a gel matrix, by applying to the gel an electric field that periodically changes direction (Schwartz and Cantor, 1984). PFGE is currently considered the gold standard technique for epidemiological studies but is very time consuming and requires technical expertise. DNA hybridization-based methods, such as restriction fragment length polymorphism (RFLP), like PFGE, are techniques that involve fragmenting a sample of DNA by a restriction enzyme. This technique was one of the first DNA profiling techniques but is now abandoned in favor of new DNA sequencing technologies. The sequenced-based methods rely on sequencing of specific DNA fragments generally chosen for their representativeness, for example multi-locus sequence typing (MLST). It consists of the typing of multiple loci (specific DNA sequences) of housekeeping genes, that is, constitutive genes that are required for the maintenance of the basic cellular function of the microorganism being considered. MLST requires the sequencing of about six to ten fragment loci (400–600 bp), and can be used for the bacteria and also for fungi. The MLST data are freely accessible in dedicated databases and allow, besides the typing of strains, an estimate of the degree of relationship between strains and thus can be used for phylogenic studies. Another major advantage is its low cost and speed. In the future and thanks to the new technologies of sequencing, in addition to the drastic reduction of their cost, the sequencing of the whole genome of microorganisms could be a response to the molecular typing of the strains.

Most of the above cited methods, phenotypic and molecular, are complementary. The precise choice of methods for identification must be determined according to the level of identification required: species (the basic unit of identification) or strain (the basic unit of typing). The accuracy of the methods is closely related to the microorganisms considering that some microorganisms are more difficult to identify than others. The choice of the strategy, cultivable or not cultivable, will be dictated by the necessity, or not, to recover the strains at the end of the process of identification. Moreover, for strain typing the choice of the method will be dictated by the purpose: screening to find strains with specific properties, to establish the ID card of the strains or to determine the phylogenetic links between strains. Methods for microbial identification and strain typing continually evolve and may, in some cases, result in taxonomic reshuffles. This makes taxonomy a dynamic field that is constantly evolving.

See also FUNGI; MICROBIAL COMMUNITIES; PHENOTYPIC VARIABILITY; and STRAINS.

Almeida, M., et al. "Construction of a Dairy Microbial Genome Catalog Opens New Perspectives for the Metagenomic Analysis of Dairy Fermented Products." *BMC Genomics* 15 (2014): 1101.

Garrity, G. M., et al., eds. *Bergey's Manual of Systematic Bacteriology*. 2d ed., vol. 1. New York: Springer Verlag, 2001.

Handelsman, J. "Metagenomics: Application of Genomics to Uncultured Microorganisms." *Microbiology and Molecular Biology Reviews* 68 (2004): 669–685.

Kirk, P. M., et al. *Ainsworth & Bisby's Dictionary of the Fungi*. 10th ed. Wallingford, U.K.: CABI Publishing, 2008.

Linnaeus, Carl. *Systemae Naturae, sive regna tria naturae, systematics proposita per classes, ordines, genera & species*. Originally published in 1735, with many editions since.

Maiden Martin, C. J. "Multilocus Sequence Typing of Bacteria." *Annual Review of Microbiology* 60 (2006): 561–588.

Ogier, J.-C., et al. "Molecular Fingerprinting of Dairy Microbial Ecosystems by Use of Temporal Temperature and Denaturing Gradient Gel Electrophoresis." *Applied and Environmental Microbiology* 70, no. 9 (2004): 5628–5643.

Saiki, R. K., et al. "Primer-directed Enzymatic Amplification of DNA with a Thermostable DNA Polymerase." *Science* 239, no. 4839 (1988): 487–491.

Schwartz, D. C., and C. R. Cantor. "Separation of Yeast Chromosome-sized DNAs by Pulsed Field Gradient Gel Electrophoresis." *Cell* 37, no. 1 (1984): 67–75.

Stackebrandt, E., et al. "Report of the Ad Hoc Committee for the Re-evaluation of the Species Definition in Bacteriology." *International Journal of Systemic Evolutionary Microbiology* 52 (2002): 1043–1047.

Woese, Carl R., et al. "Towards a Natural System of Organisms: Proposal for the Domains Archaea, Bacteria, and Eucarya." *Proceedings of the National Academy of Sciences USA* 87, no. 12 (1990): 4576–4579.

Florence Valence

Teleme

See PELUSO, FRANKLIN.

territorial refers to a group of British cheeses that were officially defined and codified in the late nineteenth and early twentieth centuries. Before it was a tradable commodity, cheese was first and foremost a way to provision farming families throughout the winter. As the historian Val Cheke noted, for the original cheese producers and consumers of early modern Britain, "Cheese was merely good or bad, thick or thin, new or old, rich or flet [skimmed]." Cheeses that left their area of manufacture were often referred to by their place of origin, but cheeses made in the same county (and thus carrying the same name) could have very different characteristics. Conversely, cheeses made far from one another could be quite alike in style. Late eighteenth-century and early nineteenth-century texts are rife with references to Marlborough, North Wiltshire, and Warwickshire cheese, among many others. These were not specific types or styles, but simply referred to cheeses that had been made in those places. Ultimately, it was all just "cheese," though perhaps "some possessed a better reputation than others, generally because a localized maker had made a special name for quality" (Cheke 1959, p. 124).

Progressive English cheesemakers of the late nineteenth century, faced with an onslaught of imported factory cheeses from the New World, recognized the need to embrace scientific methods and to systema-tize cheese production. This process was led by the new dairy schools, which were responsible for gradually standardizing the production of the various cheeses. Through their work, these schools "incorporated the best points of specific varieties, suited them to market requirements, and manufactured a regulated type of cheese which assumed its position as the county farm-house cheese" (Cheke 1959, p. 226). This process, and the demand for standard types of cheese that could be sold at a distance, along with the increasing demand for liquid milk, led to the disappearance of older and more marginal varieties and methods in the early part of the twentieth century. The older varieties were replaced by a handful of "official" British cheeses, among them Cheddar, Stilton, Leicester (or Leicestershire), Wensleydale, Cheshire, Lancashire, Gloucester, and Caerphilly. These are the British territorials.

See also CAERPHILLY; CHEDDAR; CHESHIRE CHEESE (U.K.); GLOUCESTER; LANCASHIRE; STILTON; UNITED KINGDOM; and WENSLEYDALE.

Cheke, Val. *The Story of Cheese-Making in Britain.* London: Routledge & Kegan Paul, 1959.

Twamley, Josiah. *Dairying Exemplified, or the Business of Cheese-Making.* London: J. Sharp, 1787. Facsimile reproduced by the British Library (ECCO edition) in 2010.

Bronwen Percival

terroir is a French term used since the mid-twentieth century to refer to a more or less defined geographical space with a particular combination of environmental properties, agricultural species, and technical practices that have become established over time. These factors are said to give particular characteristics to foods historically made in this area, conferring the taste of their terroir. Commonly cited terroir vectors for cheese include the breed of dairy animal, the indigenous plant life they graze, and soil mineral or microbial composition.

In contemporary French usage, this is but one of several meanings of terroir, which can also refer to a piece of land of any kind, "country" or "land" (as in "apple country," "the land of wild salmon"), or a rural area and everything typical of it (sociocultural practices, landscape, regional character traits, agricultural crops). Derived from Latin *terra* (earth), its first documented use in the thirteenth century referred to a plot of farmland; sixteenth-century references use it to indicate that something or someone is typical of its place of origin, from peasant dialects to wine. Until the early twentieth century, wine and viticultural experts scorned wines with a perceptible terroir for being unrefined rustic *plonc*, not fit for refined urban palates that esteemed "noble" wines from higher-status producers that managed to transcend the soil.

However, leaders of the movement to legally protect use of winemaking place names in the first third of the twentieth century appropriated the term in a positive way, using terroir to explain why Algerian grapes could never make a real Burgundy, regardless of how they were grown or fermented. French soil scientists took it up in the 1930s to refer to agricultural microenvironments, and it became the defining principle of the nascent French AOC system. See APPELLATION D'ORIGINE CONTRÔLÉE.

This interpretation of terroir was largely focused on higher-prestige wines and spirits until the late twentieth century. The Institut National de l'Origine et de la Qualité (INAO) has enforced and defended the French alcoholic beverages sector since 1935, and its economic clout facilitated research to characterize the impact of production conditions on the final product. Cheeses and other foods received AOC protection under the same legal framework, but without benefit of the same attention from tastemakers, researchers, or bureaucrats.

Cheeses would remain relative outsiders to terroir status until INAO was made responsible for all AOCs in 1990. Because the idea of terroir had been developed exclusively in the context of winemaking and distilling, cheeses and other foods were initially criticized for not abiding by the same standards. INAO requested that many dairy AOC associations revise their production rules to conform to the institutional vision of terroir, which did not always mesh with time-honored practices in dairy. Further adding to tensions, in 1992 the European Union created an EU-wide program of geographical indications (GIs) necessitating that all member states adjust their national systems to conform. At the same time, the worldwide legitimacy of GIs was challenged in World Trade Organization intellectual property rights negotiations. See GEOGRAPHICAL INDICATION and DESIGNATION OF ORIGIN. Skepticism voiced by other EU member states and global trading partners created an urgent need to "defend" the idea of terroir. Research

and theoretical writing to this end has proliferated in disciplines as diverse as economics, geography, marketing, and sociology, often financed by public or dairy industry funds. Some of the same actors also work to introduce the terroir concept in other countries, especially as a means of economic development in poorer countries, hoping to raise respect for the notion worldwide.

Researchers have been working on understanding just how production conditions influence cheese to prove that terroir is "real" and demonstrate how it is transmitted. Agronomists study feeds, breeds, and farm environments to quantify their qualitative differences. More recently, some explore how production practices respecting the terroir might be justifiable under recent policy imperatives for biodiversity and respect for the environment. See BIODIVERSITY.

Microbiologists working on terroir face a double challenge. Their research mainly aims to understand the complex world of microbes originating in bovine feeds, digestive tracts, and milking systems that contribute to milk's fermentation and ripening, resulting in a cheese's distinctive flavors, aromas, textures, and appearance—an indisputable pathway for quantifying the relationship between a natural environment and a distinctive cheese. While some argue that pasteurization is antithetical to the expression of terroir, in the early 1990s, food safety concerns at the international, European Union, and French levels put the future of raw milk into doubt. (Such concerns were prompted by a few high-profile cheese recalls in France, EU food safety directive negotiations, and the draw of lucrative export markets in countries that perceive raw milk as risky.) Though not all French AOC cheeses require raw milk (sixteen out of forty-four do not), raw milk is widely seen as preferable for making a cheese that best reflects its terroir by maintaining the presence of as many native microbes as possible alongside any cultures added to ensure predictable development. The challenge is to learn how to balance the two concerns, allowing the cheese to best reflect its origins while minimizing microbiological risk. See RAW-MILK CHEESES.

Meanwhile, the definition of terroir has continued to change and be debated by researchers trying to make it more useful for producers. Although the legal criteria for AOCs have long required a circumscribed zone and time-honored techniques ("human factors"), until recently the word "terroir" only referred to geographical place. For some theorists this remains the case, but others have worked to insert locally developed human knowledge into the very definition of terroir, which they see as resulting from a constant to and fro between farmers and food artisans and their natural and agricultural environment. Expanding "terroir" to conform to legal language was partly motivated by efforts to make INAO's approach to terroir more inclusive for non-alcohol products.

France is not the only country where people associate particular foods with specific places, nor is the notion new. Pliny the Elder is famed for his minitreatise comparing the cheeses of the Roman world; seemingly every village in Japan is known for some sort of pickle, sweet, or dried fish; and maple aficionados debate the relative merits of New Hampshire, Vermont, and Quebec syrups. But the French have a word for it, and that word is making its way into usage far from home, taking on new implications and meanings in the hands of activists and food producers.

The microbial aspect of terroir has had particular salience in countries where raw milk is controversial; for example, some artisan cheesemakers in the United States draw on the concept of terroir to articulate how they might craft micro-local cheeses that sit apart from mass-produced cheese, both substantively and symbolically. And among makers of English Stilton, dominant large-scale producers have come to rely on trucked-in milk and the convenience of pasteurization (mandatory for the GI) while a lone farmstead producer appeals to terroir in his struggle to use the Stilton name for his otherwise eligible raw-milk cheese. See STICHELTON. Terroir's adoption and adaptations follow the spread of geographical indications and local food movements more generally, as a way for small-scale producers of "traditional" foods to raise consumer awareness and respect for their products in markets that are dominated by industrialized goods and food chain globalization.

Bérard, Laurence, and Philippe Marchenay. *Les produits de terroir: Entre cultures et règlements*. Paris: CNRS, 2004.

Laithier, Cécile, ed. *Microflore du lait cru: Vers une meilleure connaissance des ecosystems microbiens du lait et de leurs facteurs de variation*. Paris: CNAOL, 2011. A state-of-the-art research report on cheese microbiology and terroir. Available online at http://www.rmtfromagesdeterroirs.com/actions-1/ecosystemes-microbiens.

Paxson, Heather. *The Life of Cheese: Crafting Food and Value in America*. Berkeley: University of California Press, 2012.

Rogers, Juliette. "Enseigner le terroir: La difficile appropriation d'une idéologie par des producteurs de lait dans deux syndicats AOC." *Politix* 103 (2013): 149–172. By the only researcher working on how French dairy farmers are taught about terroir by AOC professionals.

Juliette Rogers

Tête de Moîne

See SWITZERLAND.

Texel Sheep Cheese, originating in Texel, the largest of five islands in the north of the Netherlands, is considered a regional specialty that is now included in Slow Food's Ark of Taste to help protect it for future generations. See SLOW FOOD and NETHERLANDS.

During the ice age, this area consisted of a landscape that was formed of clay and rocks. Over time and as a result of the prolonged effect of tidal movements, sand shaped the islands further, providing a salty, sandy landscape that was ideal for herding and grazing sheep. Though remains of the mid-Stone Ages can still be found, the eternal battle against water still means that the area undergoes changes. The islands are known as the "Walking Isles" because the north increases the land mass by depositing sand washed ashore, while the south slowly loses land. Beginning around 1500 C.E., a considerable amount of farmer-produced cheese was made here. However, from 1850 onward, this decreased to the point of almost disappearing completely after World War II.

As of 2016 there are just two farmers producing sheep's milk cheese on Texel. One farm is called Wezenspyk. Here, farmer Anton de Witte buys milk from another farmer to make cheese and because the milk comes from another farm, they made the decision to pasteurize the milk for production. The other farm is called De Waddel. The family Bakker has their own herd of sheep and makes a raw-milk sheep's cheese.

Texelaar is the name of the breed of sheep from which the milk comes. A sturdy breed, built to survive the harsh life on the windy isles, their milk production is very low. Whereas Friesian sheep produce 3 quarts a day, the Texelaar averages only 1 quart. However, the high level of fat and protein contained within the Texelaar milk results in 5 quarts of milk yielding

2 pounds (1 kilogram) of cheese, whereas for the Friesian it would take 7 quarts.

Aside from the differences between raw and pasteurized milk, the production process is almost identical. The milk is warmed to 82–86°F (28– 30°C) and starter and animal rennet are added. After about thirty minutes the curd is then cut to about the size of a pea. At this stage, water at a temperature of 140°F (60°C) is added to warm up the curd. After draining, the cheeses are pressed. Depending on the size, this will be for a maximum of three hours.

The raw-milk cheeses are dry-salted for between one to three days, again depending on the size, which can range from 18 to 105 ounces (500–3,000 grams). These cheeses have a natural rind. Further maturation takes place for at least fourteen days for the small cheeses and up to three to four months for the larger ones.

The pasteurized cheeses are put in brine for forty-eight hours, and are then coated afterward to protect them during aging. The maturation for these cheeses takes longer, because the milk is pasteurized and, therefore, has less flavor. The season for production of the raw-milk cheese is from May until October. The pasteurized sheep's milk cheeses are produced all year around.

Slow Food Foundation. "Texel Sheep Cheese." http://
www.fondazioneslowfood.com/en/slow-food-
presidia/texel-sheep-cheese.

Betty Koster

texture plays a vital role in the enjoyment of cheese. Although people first think of flavor when discussing cheese quality, the texture may be considered just as important. If a piece of cheese does not produce the expected sensation when breaking off a piece and chewing it, consumers will reject it. Texture of cheese also affects flavor perception and is important when cheese is used as an ingredient in another food. The cheese on a cheeseburger, for instance, must not be rubbery or tough, or else the consumer will object.

The texture of cheese, or any food, is the sensory manifestation of its structural, mechanical, and surface properties, and is detected through vision, sound, and especially touch. It encompasses kinaesthesis, the ability to feel movement, and somesthesis, the sensations of pressure, temperature, and pain. In 2008

the International Organization for Standardization defined food texture as "all of the mechanical, geometrical, surface, and body attributes of a product perceptible by means of kinaesthesis and somesthesis receptors and (where appropriate) visual and auditory receptors from the first bite to final swallowing." The organization also defined mechanical attributes as those related to the reaction of the product to stress; geometrical attributes as those related to the size, shape, and arrangement of particles within a product; surface attributes as those related to the sensations produced in the mouth by moisture and/ or fat in and near the surface of the product; and body attributes as those related to the sensations produced in the mouth by moisture and/or fat in the substance of the product and the way in which these constituents are released. See FAT and MOISTURE. Clearly, texture is a complicated subject.

Texture is a sensory property, an opinion-based interaction between people and food, so instruments cannot describe it properly. Sensory analysis is used for this purpose, and cheese grading provides information on textural defects. See CHEESE GRADING; DEFECTS; and SENSORY ANALYSIS. However, scientists have successfully correlated the mechanical attributes mentioned above with sensory attributes, as well as the chemistry of the cheese. Mechanical attributes of cheese include the following:

- Hardness, defined as the force required to compress cheese between molars. The descriptors are soft, firm, and hard.
- Cohesiveness is the structural strength of the cheese, and includes fracturability (or brittleness) and chewiness. Fracturability is the force with which cheese crumbles, cracks, or shatters, and is described as crumbly, crunchy, or brittle. Chewiness is the work required to masticate the cheese until it can be swallowed, and the descriptors are tender, chewy, and tough.
- Springiness or elasticity is the degree to which cheese returns to its original shape once it has been compressed between the teeth. Elastic and plastic are the descriptors.
- Adhesiveness is the force required to remove the material that adheres to the palate during eating. The descriptors are sticky, tacky, and gooey.

The primary instrumental technique for characterizing the texture of cheese (and many other foods) is texture profile analysis (TPA), which was developed in the 1960s. The test is performed on a universal testing machine or a texture analyzer. A cylinder of cheese perhaps $1/3$–$2/3$-inch (10–20 millimeters) in diameter and equally tall is placed on a flat plate and a second plate comes down, compresses the sample by a certain amount, comes up, and repeats the action. This test imitates the act of chewing a piece of cheese twice and produces a graph of force versus time that resembles a tall, thin mountain peak followed by a shorter peak. The first peak represents the amount of force required to compress the sample in the first "bite" and is designated the hardness. The height the sample recovers before the second bite is the springiness, and the cohesiveness is the ratio of the area of the second peak to that of the first. If the cheese is sticky, the force required to pull the upper surface off the sample is the adhesiveness. If the cheese is brittle, the force at which it breaks during the first bite is the fracturability. The hardness, springiness, and cohesiveness values are multiplied to obtain chewiness, which is the work required to take two bites. Researchers use these numbers to compare cheeses as objectively as possible. Compression uniaxial is another instrumental test largely used to characterize the mechanical properties of cheese and correlate texture with the sensory and chemical characteristics of the product. This interdisciplinary approach has been successfully used to characterize the quality of European PDO (protected designation of origin) cheeses, like Parmigiano Reggiano or Comté.

The texture of cheese is affected by several factors. Cheese texture is known to be highly influenced by ripening, but milk and cheesemaking conditions have also been shown to influence the final quality of the cheese especially for their direct effect on pH. When the pH of cheese is below 5.0, as in feta or Cheshire, the casein molecules become more compact and the cheese is more brittle and grainy, and less cohesive and stretchable. Around pH 5.2–5.4, cheese may be plastic and springy like Gouda and Swiss. Mozzarella has an optimum pH around 5.25, where stretching is at a maximum. Cheese becomes less adhesive and more crumbly at pH levels above 5.4. Non-melting Mexican cheeses have a pH above 6.0, where the curd particles do not fuse together. The texture becomes softer when the moisture content is high, harder if the calcium phosphate level is elevated, and less stretchable when the fat content is low, because the protein network is denser. As cheese ages, the bonds within and between casein molecules break down as a result of proteolysis, causing the cheese to soften while becoming easier to fracture and less stretchable. See CASEIN; PH MEASUREMENT; and PROTEOLYSIS.

Cheese varieties may be classified by texture. The major categories are generally considered to be hard (such as Parmigiano Reggiano), semihard (Colby), semisoft (Havarti), and soft (Brie). Other categories could include brittle (Cantal), crumbly (Caerphilly), elastic (Provolone), spreadable (cream cheese), and sticky (Munster). Like texture itself, classes of texture are a matter of opinion.

See also AROMA; COLOR; and FLAVOR.

Gunasekaran, Sundaram, and M. Mehmet Ak. *Cheese Rheology and Texture*. Boca Raton, Fla.: CRC Press, 2003.
International Organization for Standardization. "Sensory Analysis—Vocabulary." ISO 5492 (2008). https://www.iso.org/obp/ui/#iso:std:iso:5492:ed-2:v1:en
Lawrence, R. C., et al. "Texture Development During Cheese Ripening." *Journal of Dairy Science* 70 (1987): 1748–1760.
Tunick, M. H. "Rheology of Dairy Foods that Gel, Stretch, and Fracture." *Journal of Dairy Science* 83 (2000): 1892–1898.
Zannoni, Noel M., and E. A. Hunter. "Texture of Parmigiano Reggiano Cheese: Statistical Relationships between Rheological and Sensory Variates." *Lait* 76 (1996): 243–254.

Michael Tunick

thermized milk cheeses

thermized milk cheeses are cheeses made from milk that has been thermized, meaning they have been heated to a temperature and time combination less than that stipulated by law for compliance with pasteurization requirements. Thermized (or heat treated) milk cheeses are still considered raw-milk cheeses, although in Europe and especially for particular consumers and cheesemakers in the United States there is a clear distinction between cheeses made from raw-milk and cheeses made from thermized milk. There is no legal definition in terms of temperature and time of heat treatment for thermization although it has been recommended that a minimum of 149–151°F (65–66°C) for sixteen to eighteen seconds be used. This suggestion is based on the temperature-time combination likely to kill all *Listeria, Salmonella, E. coli, Campylobacter, Staphylococci,* and *Yersinia*. These are the pathogens of highest probability to be found in raw milk and that potentially pose the greatest threat to the safety of cheese. Thermization also greatly reduces the numbers of spoilage microorganisms such as *Pseudomonas* and coliforms but has less overall impact on beneficial microorganisms such as coryneforms, micrococci, and lactobacilli that can enhance flavor development. Thermization does destroy most of the native lipoprotein lipase, an enzyme believed to positively influence flavor development in cheese by releasing free fatty acids from fat. It is for these reasons that some cheesemakers and consumers feel that thermization is still too similar to pasteurization and will not subscribe to its potential benefits at the cost of potential harm to desired flavor attributes. However, almost all large cheese plants making raw-milk cheeses (particularly aged Cheddar) use thermization as a means to reduce or eliminate the presence of pathogens in raw milk and reduce the potential that they would be found in their cheeses. Thermization, if used, is used in cheeses that are generally aged for six or more months.

It is common practice in some countries for cheesemakers to use thermization when milk will be stored for more than two days at the receiving plant. It is rarely used on farms even though milk may not be picked up for two days or longer.

Thermization has very little impact on whey protein denaturation and does not destroy immunoglobulins. Thermization can activate the germination of spores of psychrophilic aerobic spore formers such as *Bacillus cereus* and *Paenibacillus sp.* but it takes several hours after heat exposure for the spores to actually germinate. Once germinated the viable cells can be killed by pasteurization and if not killed they can multiply and potentially sporulate. Given the low level of these bacteria that can eventually cause a decrease in milk quality, physical removal of spores is the more prudent choice to reduce their numbers. This is done through the use of bacterial removal systems such as centrifuges and microfiltration.

See also PASTEURIZED PROCESS CHEESES and RAW-MILK CHEESES.

Hickey, D. K., K. N. Kilcawley, T. P. Beresford, etc. "Lipolysis in Cheddar Cheese Made from Raw, Thermized, and Pasteurized Milks." *Journal of Dairy Science* 90, no. 1 (2007): 47–56.
Johnson, E, J. H. Nelson, and M. Johnson. "Microbiological Safety of Cheese Made from Heat-Treated Milk, Part 2. Microbiology." *Journal of Food Protection* 53, no. 6 (1990): 519–540.

Mark E. Johnson

A **thermometer,** a device used to measure temperature, is indispensable in cheesemaking. Temperature influences several critical parameters during manufacturing, including: the growth of microorganisms in milk, curd, and whey; the production of lactic acid by starter culture bacteria; and the syneresis and de-mineralization of the curd. Temperature also influences microbial, enzymatic, and chemical changes during ripening. It is necessary to control temperature precisely to avoid unwanted variations in cheese composition, enzymatic activities, and microbial populations that (if they're unwanted variations) lead to inconsistent cheese quality.

Three types of thermometers are used commonly in cheesemaking. Liquid-in-glass thermometers, based on the thermal expansion of a liquid such as mercury or alcohol in a graduated glass capillary, are suitable for laboratory use, but they should not be used in the production area because of the danger of breakage and product and environmental contamination. Bimetal dial thermometers, which utilize the thermal expansion of metallic solids to measure temperature, are a safe, inexpensive, and durable alternative. Thermocouple thermometers, which consist of two lengths of dissimilar metals, joined at one end to form a measuring junction that produces a temperature-dependent electric voltage, are popular for general use. The working thermometers in a cheese facility should be calibrated regularly against a standard thermometer certified by the National Institute of Standards and Technology (NIST traceable) or one of equivalent accuracy. Calibration should be performed using a water bath at around the same temperature that measurements are normally performed.

Wehr, H. M., and J. F. Frank, eds. *Standard Methods for the Examination of Dairy Products.* 17th ed. Washington, D.C., American Public Health Association, 2004.

Paul S. Kindstedt

thistle

See PLANT-DERIVED COAGULANTS.

Tibet has essentially one method of cheesemaking, from which two cheeses are produced—a soft ricotta-like product, called churaloenpa, and its hard, dried sister, churakampo. Neither of these cheeses would have come into being were it not for Tibet's avid

Churakampo, meaning "hard dried cheese," is a Tibetan cheese made from the curds left over after boiling yak buttermilk. The cooked curds are left out in the sun to dry, and sometimes strung like beads and eaten as a snack food while traveling.

consumption of butter made by the yak-herding nomads who populate the Qinghai-Tibetan Plateau of the Himalayas. For centuries these highland dairy folk have churned butter from the fresh or fermented milk of *dri* (the female of the ruminant species; only the males are called yaks), and boiled down the leftover buttermilk into a thick paste of cheese curds. Soured milk or yogurt is generally added to the simmering pot of buttermilk to acidify the mixture and aid in coagulation. Because whole milk, rather than just the separated cream, is used in Tibetan buttermaking, the herders' buttermilk has a high proportion of protein and solids for making cheese curds. The freshly cooked curds, churaloenpa, are eaten warm or fried, often with sugar and salt added. Otherwise, they are spread on a cloth and dried in the sun to make hard pieces of churakampo. This durable style of cheese is also crafted by draining the cooked curds through a basket or cloth, packing them into a wooden mold, and pressing them overnight with stones. Once compacted, the cheese is cut into thin slices and left to dry for a week or more; often the cheese slices are threaded onto a string and then hung inside a tent to dry or over a fire to be smoked. Tibetans often chew churakampo as a snack while traveling or serve it mixed with melted butter and sugar. It is also ground into a cheese powder and used as a cooking ingredient.

Over the past decade, dairy development initiatives in Tibet have brought training in simple Western-style cheesemaking to some of the nomadic communities. The result has been new kinds of yak cheese, but these are generally expensive novelties made for export to Western markets.

See also YAK.

"Yak Cheese." Cooksinfo.com. http://www.cooksinfo.com/yak-cheese.
Food and Agriculture Organization of the United Nations. "Ten Products from Yak and Their Utilization." FAO.org. http://www.fao.org/docrep/006/ad347e/ad347e0l.htm.
Wangdu, Lobsang. "How Well Do You Know Your Tibetan Food?" Yowangdu.com. http://www.yowangdu.com/tibetan-food/tibetan-food.html.
Wu Ning. "Twelve Social, Cultural, and Economic Context of Yak Production." FAO.org. http://www.fao.org/docrep/006/ad347e/ad347e0v.htm.

Elaine Khosrova

Tillamook cheese is produced by The Tillamook County Creamery Association (TCCA). Headquartered in Tillamook, Oregon, the company is known primarily for its Cheddar cheese, which it produces in a variety of flavors and ages. The TCCA also makes a variety of other styles of cheese including Monterey Jack and Colby; total cheese production is over 180 million pounds (82 million kilograms) per year. Working with outside partners, TCCA also sells additional Tillamook branded products including butter and yogurt.

Tillamook, a small town on the central Oregon coast, was first settled by Europeans during the mid-nineteenth century. Dairying, butter making and cheesemaking provided a living for the area's early pioneers. Entrepreneur T. S. Townsend started the area's first commercial cheese factory in 1894. He hired Canadian-born cheesemaker Peter McIntosh to run his operation, and McIntosh is often credited with jumpstarting the area's cheese industry by introducing a reliable Cheddar cheese recipe to the region's dairy farmers.

The TCCA was organized as a dairy cooperative in 1909. Much of the cooperative's early success can be attributed to salesman Carl Haberlach, who encouraged the area's dairy farmers to produce a standardized cheese that would fetch a premium price. During the early decades of the twentieth century, Tillamook-brand Cheddar cheese became popular with consumers up and down the West Coast of the United States.

In 1949, TCCA debuted a new state-of-the-art cheesemaking facility. The flagship plant, still located along US Highway 101 in Tillamook, remains a favorite stop for visitors who enjoy sampling fresh cheese curds and ice cream produced on site. In 2001, TCCA opened a second plant in Boardman, Oregon, near the Idaho border; today the majority of the company's cheeses are produced there.

Bell, Jon. "Tillamook Cheese Factory's Transition." *Oregon Business*, 28 January 2013. http://www .oregonbusiness.com/article/archives-2006-2009/ item/14352-tillamook-cheese-factorys-transition.

Collins, Dean. *The Story of Tillamook: The Little County that Became the Big Cheese*. Portland: Oregon Journal, 1961.

Tami Parr

Tilsiter (or Tilsit) is a cow's milk cheese that takes two distinctive forms, one in the German and Baltic north and one in Switzerland. In its northern incarnations it is a semisoft to semifirm rectangular washed-rind cheese, made both from raw and pasteurized milk. See WASHED-RIND CHEESES. Weighing 8–10 pounds (1.8–2.2 kilograms), at its best it has a pungent aroma, but is surprisingly balanced on the palate (especially if the sticky rind is removed). However, in the northern cantons of Switzerland, Tilsiter comes in round, pressed wheels with small round eyes, as opposed to the unpressed small slit holes in the northern version due to the curd being poured into the molds with the whey. It is brought to market with a dry rind and a strong taste, but has a sweetness that firmly points toward Alp cheesemaking traditions. See ALP CHEESEMAKING and EYES.

Although today the two cheeses seem hardly to resemble one another, they are historically connected. Tilsiter started as a round cheese, in the 1820s in the East Prussian town of Tilsit (today called Sowjetsk and part of the Russian enclave of Kaliningrad, between Poland and Lithuania). There a young cheesemaid, Frau Westphal, née Klunk (born 1790 and in some sources declared to be of Swiss origin), documented and standardized existing cheesemaking practices, giving it some new, distinctive features. It may have evolved from local variants in the Limburger style (Ragnitzer, Woriener, Brioler), affected by moving into new aging facilities with higher humidity (and therefore more prolific growth of *Bacterium linens* mold). See BREVIBACTERIUM LINENS and LIMBURGER. The East Prussian dairy industry was influenced both by Dutch (Friesian and Flemish) Mennonites, religious refugees invited by the Polish king as colonists and dike builders in the

sixteenth century, and Swiss economic refugees. The latter were invited to resettle the land after a pest epidemic of 1709–1710 and mostly worked as herdsmen and milkers.

Until the mid-nineteenth century Tilsiter was made and consumed only in East Prussia. At the end of the century two Swiss dairy workers returning to the Alps, Otto Wartmann and Hans Wegmüller from Holzhof near Biseg/Thurgau, started making Tilsit back home, the latter sometimes credited with writing down the Swiss Tilsit recipe in 1870 in Felben near Frauenfeld. At the same time as production was moving west from Tilsit along the Baltic, expanding to Schleswig-Holstein, it was also spreading from Switzerland into the Allgäu, where it is documented in the very early 1900s. In 1928 a school opened in Tilsit dedicated to the town's most successful export. In 1934 the first German cheese regulation mentions it and in 1948 it became state-regulated in Switzerland.

In addition to the Dutch influence, Tilsiter was also influenced by Swiss cheesemaking practices: reheating the curd and the use of a cheesecloth to extract the curd from the vat are documented from nineteenth-century East Prussia. Tilsiter's defining role in the north of Germany (where it came to stand for cheese as such, as opposed to being just one of many types in the south) also has historical reasons. In the 1800s the duchies of Schleswig and Holstein were renowned for their cattle. On the marshes of the west coast, along the North Sea, cattle were raised and fattened for meat, whereas on the gentle hills on the Baltic coast the main interest was butter, a valuable commodity internationally traded in competition with Ireland and the Netherlands. Dairies were described as "butter factories." Here cheese was a byproduct of butter making and it was well known that the same factory could not produce good quality in both (in the literature of the time cheese from Schleswig-Holstein is described as very lean, dry, and tasteless; "leather cheese"). Cheese was not a commodity, but everyday staple fare. Today, northern Tilsiter is still meant to be consumed young (around three months) and is often flavored with caraway seeds.

Following the division of Germany, in 1961 East German authorities changed the cheese's name from Tilsiter to Tollenser, after a lake in Mecklenburg, to avoid any East Prussian patriotic nostalgia. Swiss authorities reinstated the name Tilsit in 1981 (since 1993 Tilsiter Switzerland has been trademarked). In 2007 the town of Tilsit was officially founded in

Switzerland, on the location where Otto Wartmann is said to have made the first Swiss Tilsit cheese in 1893; in 2009 it partnered with its Russian pendant, Sowjetsk. Since 1995 Tollenser has been protected by a PDO (protected designation of origin), linked to a designated production area in Mecklenburg. Many Allgäu dairies produce block-shaped Tilsiter, but it is rarely an exciting cheese. Since 2013 Holsteiner Tilsiter is protected by a PGI (protected geographical indication). At its best it can achieve an amazing depth in taste and aroma, especially when extra-aged (Hauke Koll at Ostenfelder Meierei being the best source), although it is rarely included in sophisticated cheese selections in Germany.

See also GERMANY and SWITZERLAND.

"Frau Westphal." Milch und Kultur Rheinland & Westfalen e. V. http://www.verein-milch-und-kultur .eu/westphal.html.
Roeb, Frank. "Käsebereitung und Käsespeisen in Deutschland seit 1800." PhD diss., Mainz University, 1976, pp. 99–104, 121.

Ursula Heinzelmann

A **tina** is a traditional wooden vat specifically used in the production of Ragusano, a Sicilian PDO (protected designation of origin) cheese. In the manufacture of this pasta filata style cheese, raw milk is directly placed in the tina. The lactic acid necessary for production is generated by desirable milk flora naturally present in the biofilm that almost entirely covers the surface of the wood inside the tina. Therefore no starter culture is needed. See BIOFILMS and STARTER CULTURES.

Pieces of wood from a tina observed under a scanning electron microscope showed the tina's biofilm was entrapped in a matrix that almost entirely covered the surface of the wood. The confocal microscopy and bacterial-specific staining showed the biofilm had a complex ecosystem consortium (cocci, bacilli, yeasts, and molds) and the occurrence of a polysaccharide layer. See CONFOCAL MICROSCOPY and ECOSYSTEM.

Thus the tina's use is crucial, especially for raw milks with low initial counts of lactic acid bacteria. The amount of yeasts, molds, and enterococci detected is extremely variable from one tina biofilm to another. This means that each tina has its own microbial profile, and an individual piece of Ragusano cheese can be traced using its microbial profile

back to a specific tina and farm from within the PDO territory.

It has been demonstrated that *Salmonella*, *Listeria monocytogenes*, and *E. coli* O157:H7 were totally absent in the fifteen tinas studied, which represented 80 percent of the active tinas in the Hyblean region of Sicily. Moreover, even at the end of the summer period, when the cheese is not produced, a microbial biofilm still survives on a tina's wooden surface. These results strongly reinforce the idea of the crucial role and safety of the wooden vat system.

See also RAGUSANO; RAW-MILK CHEESES; TRADITIONAL EQUIPMENT; SICILY; and WOODEN VATS.

Licitra, G., et al. "Variability of Bacterial Biofilms of the 'Tina' Wood Vats Used in the Ragusano Cheese-Making Process." *Applied Environmental Microbiology* 73 no. 21 (2007): 6980–6987.
Lortal, Sylvie, et al. "Tina Wooden Vat Biofilm: A Safe and Highly Efficient Lactic Acid Bacteria Delivering System in PDO Ragusano Cheese Making." *International Journal of Food Microbiology* 132, no. 1 (2009): 1–8.

Stefania Carpino

titratable acidity measurement. One of the primary functions of converting fluid milk to cheese is the work of a proven dairy culture that can effectively convert the milk sugar (lactose) to lactic acid. Without a successful conversion, considerable amounts of residual lactose may be left in the final cheese, which often leads to a high moisture cheese and potential late fermentation during the aging process, resulting in a defective cheese with poor texture and off-flavors. Improper or incomplete acidification may also lead to fermentation by harmful non-dairy bacteria. Proper acidification profile (time and intensity) plays a major role defining both the final quality of the finished product as well as the general characteristics of a specific cheese variety. The success of this lactose to acid conversion can be observed through the senses (i.e., taste, smell, and even sight and touch because acid production directly affects visual and mechanical textural properties), but can only be precisely monitored by the measurement of the acid being produced. See ACIDIFICATION.

The degree of acid production can be expressed as a pH value or titratable acidity (TA). A pH value is as direct measurement of the concentration of hydrogen ions most commonly done with a pH meter and indicating the relative alkaline or acid state. The pH indicates the strength of the acid condition. TA indicates a measurement of the amount of lactic acid present. TA measures the total acidity, but does not measure the strength of the acids. Both TA and pH values offer complementary valuable information of the cheesemaking process; however TA can only be used on liquid samples (milk and whey) but it is not adapted for solid samples (curd). See PH MEASUREMENT.

In cheesemaking the preferred tool for measuring titratable acidity is the acidometer, a kit to measure acid development during the cheesemaking process. The testing procedure used is called titration. Cheesemakers will use this information to determine when to make control changes in the process such as rennet addition, cut and stir times, whey removal, etc. Each specific style of cheese tends to follow a very specific acid profile in its production to assure a common character from batch to batch.

The procedure for using the acidometer requires three additional components:

- The solution to be titrated (analyte) with an unknown percentage of acid.
- An alkaline titrant prepared as a standardized solution.
- An acid-base indicator solution to mark the endpoint of the test with a specific color change.

The acidometer used in cheesemaking is constructed of a long glass tube with an accurate milliliter measure etched on its face to an accuracy 0.2 milliliters divisions, usually beginning with "0" at the top and "10" at the bottom. It also contains a stopcock at the bottom to easily control small additions (drops) of the titrant to neutralize the analyte. The better instruments also have a simple squeeze-bulb mechanism to automatically refill the tube to "0" before each new test.

The acidometer is prepared by filling it to the "0" mark with the titrant. The titrant of choice for milk and whey is sodium hydroxide (NaOH), which is alkaline and has specific strength depending on the type of units used to express the acidity. The NaOH solution should be frequently remixed to strength because the solution can become neutralized from air contact (CO_2), thus giving inaccurate readings.

Titratable acidity can be expressed in several units: percent lactic acid (%l.a.), degree Soxhlet Henkel (°SH), degree Dornic (°D), or degree Thörner (°TH). Each of these units corresponds to a specific procedure used to titrate dairy products. Percent lactic acid

(%l.a.) is the unit frequently used in the United States (as well as the United Kingdom, Canada, Australia, and New Zealand). Different countries use different procedures, differing basically on the amount of milk (or whey) to be used as sample and their equivalent normalities for NaOH solution.

The titration begins with preparation of a specified amount of milk or whey (analyte), ideally placed in a shallow beaker. Just prior to conducting the titration testing, about three drops of indicator solution are added to the milk or whey being tested. The indicator solution most commonly used in testing for dairy is phenolphthalein, which will be clear when mixed into the testing solution but will change the milk or whey to a magenta pink color as the endpoint has been reached. This endpoint is the point at which the acid (analyte) and alkaline (titrant) are balanced and the factor on which this titration is based.

The acid titration is run by slowly adding the sodium hydroxide titrant a drop at a time into the milk or whey analyte being tested, while steadily stirring. When the indicator color appears and remains at a just-perceivable level and remains visible for at least twenty seconds, the endpoint is reached. The actual percentage of acid is then determined by dividing the number of milliliters of NaOH used by ten (simply done by moving the decimal to the left by one number). For example, fresh milk often tests with about 1.6–1.8 milliliters of titrant being used and thus indicating the acid level of 0.16–0.18 percent acid (most of which is lactic acid).

The normality of the NaOH solution defines the amount of test liquid to be used. For example, an acidimeter in the United States uses a N/10 NaOH solution and the beaker or test tube must be filled with exactly 9 milliliters of sample (milk or whey). The table below explains the amount of sample to be used and their equivalent normalities for NaOH solution:

| | ml of sample | NaOH normality |
Degree	A	B
%l.a.	9 mL	N/10 (1/10=0.10)
Soxhlet Henkel	25 ml	N/4 (1/4=0.25)
Dornic	10 ml	N/9 (1/9=0.11)
Thörner	9 ml	N/10 (1/10=0.1)

Note: The results expressed in one degree can be easily converted into any other unit value by consulting a conversion chart.

Fox, P. F., et al. *The Fundamentals of Cheese Science*. Gathersburg, Md.: Aspen, 2000.

Kindstedt, Paul. *American Farmstead Cheese*. White River Junction, Vt.: Chelsea Green, 2005.

Kosokowski, F. V., and V. V. Mistry. *Cheese and Fermented Milk Foods*, vol. 2. Westport, Conn.: F. V. Kosokowski, 1999.

Jim Wallace

Tolminc is a hard PDO (protected designation of origin) cheese produced only in the strictly defined area around Tolmin, which is located in the foothills of the Slovenian Alps near the Italian border. It is made by local farmers in small dairies, and, in the summertime, on the alpine pastures. The specific alpine flora represent an important part of the feed for the milking cows on the pastures, and influences the cheese aroma and flavor together with natural milk microbiota. The first written records about cheesemaking in the Tolmin region date back to the thirteenth and fourteenth centuries, when cheese was used to pay taxes to the aristocracy. The name Tolminc cheese (Formaggio di Tolmino-Tominski sir) was first written in 1756 in a cheese price list in the town of Videm, in Italian Udine.

Tolminc is traditionally made from whole or partly skim raw cow's milk. The rennet is added to the mixture of ripened evening and fresh morning milk for the formation of a firm coagulum. The coagulum is cut to the size of hazelnuts and scalded during stirring to around 113°F (45°C). Dried curd is transferred using cheesecloth into the molds and pressed for six to twelve hours at room temperature. Cheeses are salted in brine and then moved to the wooden shelves in a cold place for ripening for at least two months.

Tolminc is a hard, flat, round cheese weighing 7–11 pounds (3–5 kilograms). Each cheese is 10–12 inches (25–30 centimeters) in diameter and 3–4 inches (8–9 centimeters) thick, with a smooth and pale yellow rind. The body is yellow, semifirm, and smooth, with a few eyes the size of lentils. Young cheeses have a sweet and milky aroma that with longer maturation become more intense, sweet but tangy, and slightly nutty.

Cimerman, Polona, and Alenka Miklavžin, eds. *Slovenian Protected Agricultural Products and Foodstuffs*. Ljubljana: Ministry of Agriculture, Forestry and Food of Slovenia, 2015. http://www.mkgp.gov.si/fileadmin/mkgp.gov .si/pageuploads/publikacije/Zasciteni_proizvodi_ SLO_ANG/Zasciteni_brosura_ANG_SPLET.pdf.

Perko, Bogdan, and Davorin Koren. *Sirarsko društvo Tolminc*. [Specification for Tolminc], 2012. http:// www.mkgp.gov.si/fileadmin/mkgp.gov.si/pageup-loads/podrocja/Varna_in_kakovostna_hrana_in_ krma/zasciteni_kmetijski_pridelki/Specifikacije/ TOLMINC_januar_2012.pdf.

Petra Mohar Lorbeg and Andreja Čanžek Majhenič

Tölzer Kasladen is a cheese store in Munich and one of the pioneers of artisan cheese in Germany. The Hofmann family has long been an authority on cheese. The founder's great-grandmother was an Alp dairymaid in the Lake Tegernsee region, and her son worked as a cheesemaker. In 1972 Wolfgang Hofmann opened Tölzer Kasladen, in Bad Tölz, a spa town about 50 kilometers south of Munich, with the intention of marketing his own dairy products directly. He has continuously expanded his selection to include numerous raw-milk cheeses from all over Europe. The construction of cheese caves next to his shop was the next logical step for Hofmann, and through this he was able to attract the most demanding customers of the top gastronomic sphere.

Wolfgang's two children have continued the business since the early 1980s according to their father's philosophy. Susanne Hofmann is one of the very few female Maître Fromager globally. She regularly travels through Europe, expanding her network, improving cheese quality together with local producers, and optimizing logistics. Her brother Wolfgang, the Professional Fromager Affineur, is responsible for the cellars, where he stocks and matures over 150 types of raw-milk cheese. All cheeses are directly supplied from small artisan producers from ten European countries.

In order to pass on their extensive knowledge, the Hoffmann family founded Käseakademie in 2009. Here professionals and amateurs alike are trained in cheesemaking, selling, and tasting. Käseakademie is a unique institution working to preserve cheese culture throughout Germany. As of 2016 Tölzer Kasladen had five branches in several Bavarian towns, including a tiny outpost at Munich's famous Viktualienmarkt.

Käseakademie. http://www.kaeseakademie.de.

"Käse und Wein: Interview mit Susanne Hofmann." WeinKenner.de, 15 February 2011. http://www .weinkenner.de/2011/kaese-und-wein-interview-mit-susanne-hofmann-12251.

Tölzer Kasladen. http://www.toelzer-kasladen.de.

Theresa Malec

Toma Piemontese is an Italian PDO (protected designation of origin) cheese produced from cow's milk throughout the provinces of Cuneo, Turin, Biella, Vercelli, Novara, and Verbania and in some towns in the province of Asti. About a thousand tons are produced every year. Toma Piemontese is the most widespread and probably the oldest cheese of the Piedmont region, where the production of cheese and its consumption by common people were first documented in the eleventh century. The cheese had its origins in the mountain pastures of the Piedmont Alps, but throughout the centuries its production has gradually come down to the valleys.

Toma Piemontese is produced with whole or partially skimmed milk. After a double curd cutting, the cheese is put into molds (typically named *fascere*), pressed for 24–72 hours, and salted, traditionally by hand or in brine, for 24–48 hours. See FASCÈRA. The ripening time is 15 days for the small size, which has a diameter of about 6–10 inches (15–25 centimeters) and weighs about 4–8.6 pounds (2–6 kilograms), and 60 days for the large size, which has a diameter of about 8–12 inches (20–30 centimeters) and weighs about 13–17.6 pounds (6–8 kilograms).

There are two types of Toma Piemontese. The first type, Toma Piemontese PDO, is produced with whole milk and has a dough-white or ivory-white appearance with small and sparse holes. This cheese has an elastic texture, a mild odor with milk and cream characteristics, and a delicate, sweet taste. The second type, Toma Piemontese semigrassa PDO, is produced only in a large size with semi-skim milk. Its appearance is yellowish with small and sparse holes. This cheese is characterized by a consistent texture, a strong and persistent odor, and a very savory, salty flavor.

Toma Piemontese is probably the oldest cheese of the Piedmont region of Italy, shown here in both its whole fat and semi-fat versions. © GIUSEPPE ZEPPA

See also ALP CHEESEMAKING; ITALY; and TOMME.

Assopiemonte DOP e IGP. http://www.assopiemonte .com.

Ministero Agricoltura e Foreste. *DOC Cheeses of Italy: A Great Heritage.* Milan: Angeli, 1992.

Ottogalli, Giorgio. *Atlante dei formaggi.* Milan: Hoepli, 2001.

Rubino, Roberto, et al., *Italian Cheese: A Guide to Its Discovery and Appreciation.* Bra, Italy: Slow Food Editore, 2005.

Giuseppe Zeppa

Tomme is a generic term used to describe a round flat cheese with a grayish natural rind. The name most likely derived from the Greek word *tomos* or the Latin *tomus*, meaning a cut, slice, or section of a book. The Merriam-Webster dictionary defines "tome" as a large or weighty book. The use of this term in describing a cheese most likely came from someone asking for a large slice or piece of cheese, but later the term was applied to the entire wheel.

While there are no official rules defining what makes a cheese a Tomme, they are often named after their place of origin such as the famous Tomme de Savoie made in the French Alps, which is typically made from skim cow's milk after the cream is taken for butter production. This pressed cheese was produced and consumed in high mountain pastures; its peasant origins and direct consumption explain its rustic appearance. Tommes were made famous in France and Switzerland, but have declined and are now commonly made throughout the United States. If you ask cheese professionals to define Tomme, some will likely suggest that a Tomme is essentially a "farmer's cheese" made and consumed on the farm. See FARMER CHEESE. Others may tell you that a Tomme is made during summer months while cows are eating fresh, green grass, and others will say that Tommes are only made by professional cheesemakers.

The most common similarities that Tommes share are their shape and size. They are bigger and rounder than they are thick. They can range from 6–40 inches (15–100 centimeters) around and are typically 3–4 inches (7–10 centimeters) thick. Grayish natural rinds tend to be a common characteristic as well, but this rind color is not as consistent a characteristic as the size and shape. The majority of Tommes go through a low heat treatment of the curds resulting in a creamy, pliable texture. They are also allowed to age in cellars that promote the natural microflora giving them the characteristic gray or brownish rind we associate with Tomme.

The flavors of a Tomme can vary greatly and there is no common flavor profile. You can find a Tomme cheese made with a variety of milk types and aging techniques that provide a wide variety of flavors. Some other well-known Tommes in addition to Tomme de Savoie are Tomme de Grosse-Île, Tomme de Manigodine, Crayeuse, Old Kentucky Tomme, Toma Piemontese, Tomme de Abondance, Peekville Tomme, and Thomasville Tomme.

See also TOMA PIEMONTESE and TOMME DE GROSS-ÎLE.

Hazard, Jessica. "Tomme-Style Cheeses." *Culture Magazine*, 9 December 2013. http://culturecheesemag.com/cheese-iq/tommes.
Jenkins, Steve. *The Cheese Primer*. New York: Workman, 1996.
Masui, Kazuko, and Tomako Yamada. *French Cheeses*. New York: DK Publishing, 1996.

Tim Gaddis

Tomme de Grosse-Île

Tomme de Grosse-Île is a semisoft, mixed rind, artisan cheese made with the non-pasteurized milk of Brown Swiss cows from a single island farm. See BROWN SWISS. It is made by Fromagerie Île-aux-Grues in Isle-aux-Grues, Quebec. The recipe for Tomme de Grosse-Île was re-created in the late 1990s from an old island cheese factory recipe, which used milk from cows fed the local marsh hay.

Well known to birders, Isle-aux-Grues is French for "island of cranes." It is the only inhabited island of the twenty-one islands that make up the Isle-aux-Grues archipelago, 65 kilometers east of Quebec City, in the middle of the St. Lawrence River, and is a national historic site that serves as a memorial to the rich Canadian immigration history of Grosse-Île in the early 1900s.

The cows have a diet that includes the geographically unique marsh hay called "foin de batture," a grass collected at low tide that has evolved to grow in the brackish water of the Great Lakes and the Atlantic. Instead of being dried like most silage, it is sealed in plastic bags when damp to deepen the flavor, moisture, and nutrients. Tomme de Grosse-Île is an excellent example of how terroir influences a cheese.

If the cows were not fed their specific marsh hay or if the cheese was made elsewhere, the end result would be a vastly different product.

After ripening three to six months, the straw-colored paste with scattered pinholes is encased in a thin, mottled, ocher-colored crust achieved after frequent brushings with brine. The cheese presents a musty, damp grass aroma. The flavor is complex and layered with hints of cream and fruit, hazelnut and earthy vegetables (especially broccoli or Brussels sprouts), while being slightly acidulous. The profile changes by season; from buttery and nutty in winter, to musky hay in spring, and to sweet and vegetal in summer and fall. This remarkable cheese has won many awards, including Gold in the semisoft category at the World Cheese Awards in 2015–2016.

See also QUEBEC and TOMME.

Fromagerie Île-aux-Grues. http://www.fromagesileauxgrues.com.

Kathy Guidi

Torta del Casar

Torta del Casar is an ancestral and unique PDO (protected designation of origin) Spanish cheese from Extremadura, in the very western part of the country, abutting the border of Portugal. Extremadura is a land that lives up to its name of extremes: hot dry summers and cold winters, and mountain ranges separated by vast flat plains where little grows beyond low grasses and cork oaks. With much of the area not being suited for crops, it instead provides a home for foraging pigs to make the famous Iberian hams and herds of sheep and goats that supply milk for the region's cheese.

Torta del Casar evolved from this region of extremes and is named for its city of origin, Casar de Cáceres. It is truly a unique cheese in the way it has evolved and continues to be produced in this region today. For centuries this flat open land has been best utilized as grazing land most suited to sheep and goats, and for this cheese specifically, the hearty breeds of Merina and Entrefina sheep. The flocks are not known for a high production of milk but for their wool and meat. Nevertheless, the local shepherds milked and made cheese from these flocks for their personal consumption and to supplement their earnings.

The cheese is made from fresh raw sheep's milk using a specific process to retain a high amount of moisture in the finished cheese. A short ripening time of about two months produces a dry but slightly sticky rind. The heart of the cheese, however, is reduced to a very soft and spreadable paste. The cheese is often so soft that a traditional band of cloth was wrapped and fastened around it to hold the shape and keep it from losing its form. The cheese is most commonly served with the top removed so that the fondue-like paste can be scooped out and spread on bread. The flavor and texture is primarily a factor of the rich raw milk, the high moisture of the resulting cheese, and the unique method of coagulation. This process involves the use of the cardoon flower (a thistle-like plant) as a coagulant, instead of the normal source of rennet obtained from the lamb. Most raw milk undergoes a coagulation phase using the rennet enzymes extracted from a specific ruminant, however the custom in this region was to sell the lambs and not slaughter them when young. Many years ago a substitute for lamb rennet, the pistils of a wild thistle (*Cynara cardunculus*), was were discovered to work quite well and is still used today as part of the certification process for this cheese. The enzymes from the cardoon flower reduce the protein structure, hence the soft paste and slightly bitter flavor for this cheese. See PLANT-DERIVED COAGULANTS.

In the past the milk was acidified with a natural culture derived from the previous day's whey held over. The cheese was formed very slowly and patiently in a beautiful strap of hand-plaited grass, gradually coaxing excess moisture from the curd, but never losing excessive moisture. The salt was laid out to dry over many days. It all made a difference. Today the cheese is made in modern dairies with laboratory-derived bacteria cultures to convert the milk sugars, and use of plastic forms to drain the cheese. Salting is also usually performed by brining, rather than the time-consuming dry salting of the past.

The use of these general laboratory derived cultures is brought into question today due to the apparent loss of traditional flavors. Currently research is being done in order to develop a more traditional blend of natural cultures to bring the Torta del Casar more in line with what has been common practice in the past.

Traditional use of the cardoon flower for coagulation must still be observed to be a certified PDO cheese and bear the name Torta del Casar. According to the PDO regulation, Torta del Casar cheese must have a minimum of 50 percent fat in total solids, a minimum of 50 percent total solids, pH 5.2–5.9, and a maximum of 3 percent salt.

See also SPAIN.

Delgado, Francisco-José, Joaquín Rodríguez-Pinilla, José González-Crespo, et al. "Proteolysis and Texture Changes of a Spanish Soft Cheese ('Torta del Casar') Manufactured with Raw Ewe Milk and Vegetable Rennet during Ripening." *International Journal of Food Science & Technology* 45, no. 3 (March 2010): 512–519.
Jenkins, Steven. *Cheese Primer*. New York: Workman, 1996.
McCalman, Max, and David Gibbons. *Cheese: A Connoisseur's Guide to the World's Best*. New York: Clarkson Potter, 2005.

Jim Wallace

total mixed ration (TMR) is a technique for feeding dairy cattle that combines all the nutrients the animals require in a twenty-four-hour period and prevents the animals from selectively eating only certain parts of the feed. It is also referred to as the "constant ration technique."

The use of this method, which was developed in the 1960s, has increased for a number of reasons, including improved animal nutrition and increased profits. It involves weighing the individual ingredients in order to provide a balanced nutrient supply determined on the basis of production and the reproductive requirements of the animals. The ingredients are subsequently mixed in order to avoid selection by the animals, and the resulting mixture is provided daily for the cows to eat at any time.

The TMR can be produced manually by placing all the feeds in the ration on the edge of the manger, mixing and dampening them, and then pushing them into the feeding trough. The physical energy expended in manually producing a TMR is so great, though, that mixer wagons were invented to minimize the labor involved as well as to more accurately measure the feeds and nutrients required by the cows.

To produce a TMR, feeds in the daily ration are loaded into the mixer wagon, which is often equipped with scales and knives. The scale is used for weighing the correct amount of feed to be supplied to the group of animals, and the knives grind the longer, coarse particles into smaller pieces of about an inch to an inch and a half (2–4 centimeters) long, the minimum allowed length for the proper functioning of the rumen.

The proper implementation of total mixed ration requires not only the proper ingredients, but also adequate preparation of the ration so that the animals cannot select the feeds to ingest. Although cutting and mixing the feed is part of this process, it is also necessary to use wet food "binders" (corn or grass silage) or to add water to increase the TMR moisture up to 42–45 percent.

In addition to simplifying the operation of feeding animals, the TMR technique facilitates increased ingestion in animals, with the potential for increased milk production. Furthermore, the provision of a "complete" food allows the animals to ingest in every bite the appropriate amount of fiber, starch, protein, sugars, and mineral salts, resulting in proper synchronization of the digestive process.

Another great benefit of adopting this feeding technique is the reduced competition between animals, since each one of them has access to food at any period during the day or night and always gets the same nutritional components and the same ration. The inability to "separate" feeds, in order to choose the more pleasant (but not always healthier) components also improves animal welfare, thus potentially increasing productive and reproductive performance. Finally, this feeding system can help reduce the "fluctuation" of feed digestibility in the rumen, greatly reducing the risk of disease.

This mode of administering feeds, therefore, can modulate rumen fermentation in an optimal way and maximizes the intake of energy and nutrients. On the basis of significant research, it has been shown that a fractional (twenty-four-hour) ingestion of the diet helps maintain the pH of the rumen fluid at higher, and especially, more constant values than ingestion of feed just twice a day. Moreover, the continuous and balanced availability of substrates used by the microorganisms favors an increase in the ratio between acetic acid and propionic acid, as well as an increase in the quality of protein synthesized in the rumen. See ACETIC ACID; PROPIONIC ACID; and PROTEINS. The result of this method is, in short, not only increased ingestion but also better animal welfare and a quantitative and qualitative improvement in milk production.

In addition to the positive effects on the digestive and metabolic activity of the animals, the TMR technique, if properly practiced, can favorably influence the quality and characteristics of the milk used for cheesemaking. From some research studies, it seems that milk produced by cows fed with the TMR method presents fewer spores, is more acidic, has superior characteristics for cheesemaking, and is able to provide cheese with better aging profiles compared to that produced with milk from cows fed using the traditional technique.

Despite the many benefits of TMR, the technique does have limitations, however. In order to be applied in a cost-effective manner, TMR requires the farmer to group cows according to their physiological stage and production levels, and it requires the availability of stalls that allow easy handling of mixer wagons and that are located far enough away from the milking parlor to limit the effects of microbial environmental pollution.

See also BREEDING AND GENETICS; MILK; RUMINANTS; and SILAGE.

Kmicikewycz, A., and J. Heinrichs. "Total Mixed Rations for Dairy Cows: Advantages, Disadvantages, and Feeding Management." Penn State Extension, March 2015. http://extension.psu.edu/animals/dairy/nutrition/nutrition-and-feeding/diet-formulation-and-evaluation/total-mixed-rations-for-dairy-cows-advantages-disadvantages-and-feeding-management. A revision of "Use of Total Mixed Rations (TMR) for Dairy Cows" by B. P. Lammers, A. J. Heinrichs, and V. A. Ishler.

Rosario Petriglieri

total viable count

See INDIGENOUS MICROORGANISMS.

Tounj cheese is a semihard, full-fat, smoked cheese shaped like a loaf of bread. It is produced in a small area around the village of Tounj, which is located in a hilly area close to the Mala Kapela Mountains in the middle part of Croatia. According to local legend Tounj cheese was brought to Vienna for the emperor of the Austro-Hungarian Empire during the time when the local railway that connected Rijeka with Zagreb and Budapest was being built. The first professional written document about Tounj cheese was written by Baković and Blagojević Požar (1971) who mentioned that this cheese appeared in the literature by Zdanovski much earlier than 1947.

To make Tounj cheese, cow's morning milk is filtered and poured into a vat that contains milk from

the previous evening's milking. The evening milk is usually skimmed and heated to 86–95°F (30–35°C). For milk coagulation homemade rennet was used in the past. The coagulation time varies from thirty to fifty minutes. The coagulum is cut into pieces usually the size of a nut. This cut coagulum is allowed to settle in the vat for sixty minutes at a temperature of around 104°F (40°C) for acidification purposes. The coagulum is removed from the vat and a cheese body is formed, and pressed by hand in a specific mold (shaped like bread), taking care not to allow the cheese to cool. During this process the whey is removed. The cheese is dry-salted and smoked for two to three days using dense and cold smoke in a traditional smoking chamber.

The color of the cheese is a golden yellow. The cut surface is fatty, bright yellow, and may contain about twenty equally distributed eyes with a size of $1/16$–$1/8$ inch (2–4 millimeters). The taste of the cheese is moderately acidic and salty with a typical flavor obtained from the smoking of the cheese using wood from fruit trees (hazelnut, plum, cherry, and sour cherry). The first weeks after Tounj cheese is manufactured it rubs between the teeth during eating; after that it changes to an elastic and easily chewed texture. The average weight of the cheese is 25 ounces (700 grams), varying between 18–35 ounces (500–1,000 grams). Its diameter is 5½–6 inches (14–16 centimeters), and its height is 2–2½ inches (4–6 centimeters).

Tounj cheese was originally eaten by farmers but due to its attractive flavor has now become popular in local greenmarkets among urban consumers and foreign tourists. The cheese is eaten as is without removing any of the smoked rind and is served as an appetizer along with traditional cured meats and bread.

See also CROATIA and SMOKED CHEESES.

Baković, D., and D. Blagojević Požar. "Tounj Cheese." *Mljekarstvo* 21 (1971): 266–270.
Kalit, Samir, et al. "Proteolysis and Optimal Ripening Time of Tounj Cheese." *International Dairy Journal* 15, nos. 6–9 (2005): 619–624.ment>

Samir Kalit

Trachanas is a fermented milk and wheat product that becomes hard by air drying. It has a sour, milky taste and is served as a traditional soup in Cyprus, with the addition of Halloumi cheese pieces. See HALLOUMI.

Trachanas is customarily produced by spontaneous fermentation of a small quantity of goat's milk, which is then inoculated into a larger quantity of milk. The process is repeated as required in order to ferment the desired quantity of milk. The fermented milk is heated to 194°F (90°C), and then finely crushed wheat is continuously mixed with the milk until a wheat-to-milk ratio of 1:2 is achieved. The mixture is left to cool and "rest" for a couple of hours, and then manually cut into small pieces, placed on perforated trays, and left to dry in the sun for five to seven days covered by a net in order to minimize environmental contamination. Traditionally, Trachanas is produced during the summer months of June through September.

There are a few differences in the technology involved when Trachanas is produced on an industrial basis: (a) pasteurized milk is inoculated with yogurt (live cultures of *Streptococcus thermophilus* and *Lactobacillus bulgaricus*) and left to ferment, (b) the Trachanas is cut into pieces mechanically, and (c) the cheese is dried in chambers under controlled temperature conditions (108°F [42°C]) for three days.

Research on Trachanas by Carpino et al. has shown that the cheese's aromatic profile is more diverse when it is air dried than when it is dried mechanically. The microbial ecology of the fermented milk is dominated by lactic acid bacteria (*Lactobacillus plantarum*) and yeasts (*Kluyveromyces marxianus*).

Carpino, S., et al. "Effect of Dehydration by Sun or by Oven on Volatiles and Aroma Compounds of Trachanas." *Dairy Science and Technology* 90 (2010): 715–727.ment>

Photis Papademas

trade (historical). Trade, which encompasses the exchange of goods for currency, credit, or other goods or services, has been a recurring theme in the history of cheese. Cheese has probably been bartered locally for almost as long as it has been made. However, in many places and at many times from antiquity to the present, cheese has also been a significant item of trade that sometimes involved considerable distances. Indeed, long-distance trade shaped the evolution of some cheese varieties because of the demands imposed by transportation, distribution, and marketing. Characteristics such as durability and long shelf life, ease of handling and storing, compatibility with available shipping containers and transportation modes, and the ability to command high prices in the marketplace to offset the expense and risk involved in trade had to be tailored to the needs of the place and time in order for a particular local cheese to succeed in the world of extended trade.

Where and when did the first trade in cheese take place? Ancient Mesopotamia (modern Iraq) would seem to be the perfect candidate. During the third millennium B.C.E., the great city states of Sumer, in southernmost Mesopotamia, boasted impressive cheesemaking capacities that routinely supplied various temple deities with cheese for bloodless sacrifices, the details of which were documented on clay cuneiform tablets by temple scribes. Sumer also developed extensive trade networks, and Sumerian merchants maintained detailed commercial records on cuneiform tablets. Nevertheless, references to cheese are notably absent from the items of trade recorded by Sumerian merchants. It is possible that an active cheese trade may not have developed this early in human history because rennet had not been discovered yet. The complex combination of characteristics that rendered cheese a good candidate for trade in antiquity—durability, large size, superior flavor, etc.—could only be achieved in rennet-coagulated cheeses; thus, it can be said that the discovery of rennet (animal and plant derived) opened the door for cheese to be traded far beyond the confines of the local market. There is no compelling archeological evidence to suggest that Sumerian cheeses included rennet-coagulated types. See also COAGULATION OR CURDLING.

Bronze Age Cheese Trade

The first definitive evidence for cheese in commerce occurs at the end of the Bronze Age (ca. 1200 B.C.E.). By then, rennet had been discovered and rennet-coagulated cheesemaking was well established in the Hittite civilization of Anatolia (modern Turkey). The earliest written evidence of a commercial trade in cheese comes from the Hittite vassal city of Ugarit on the Mediterranean coast (modern Syria). Ugarit was a strategic trading center at the crossroads of major land and maritime routes that linked the eastern Mediterranean and Aegean regions with Egypt and southwest Asia. As such, this prosperous city

supported a large administrative staff that maintained cuneiform archives of trade shipments. Among the cuneiform tablets recovered from Ugarit are records of maritime shipments of cheese received from the Canaanite city of Ashdod in the southern Levant (modern Israel). By this time the Canaanites had developed specialized, rugged, ceramic jars that enabled them to excel in maritime trade, and that were used to ship high-value food products such as olive oil, wine, and honey. Though it is impossible to say for certain, it seems likely that the Canaanite jar served as the shipping container for the transport of cheeses from Ashdod to Ugarit.

It is also impossible to say for certain what these cheeses were like because no description of them has been found. However, some form of white-brined sheep's or goat's milk cheese is the most likely candidate. White-brined cheeses, with their ability to withstand the hot, dry environment of the eastern Mediterranean, their compatibility with shipping and storage in clay jars, packed in a protective bath of brine, and their robust piquant flavor that was bound to please an aristocratic market in search of exciting new flavors, likely became the cheeses of choice in the eastern Mediterranean during the Bronze Age, as they have been ever since. The use of ceramic jars for shipping and storing white-brined cheeses eventually became ubiquitous in this part of the world, and their use continued well into the nineteenth century when wooden barrels and, eventually, metal containers replaced them.

Greek and Roman Cheese Trade

Following the collapse of the Bronze Age, no evidence of cheese in trade can be found until the rise of Classical Greek civilization. From that point on, numerous written references to cheese in long-distance trade can be found in Greek and Roman literature. For example, cheeses produced on the islands of Cythnos, Rhenaea, and Chios in the Aegean Sea were exported to distant markets and acquired considerable notoriety. Those from Chios were shipped as far as Egypt, where they were subjected to a 25 percent tariff before being offered for sale in the Egyptian marketplace. The considerable expense and risk involved in such long-distance maritime trade and the imposition of tariffs meant that these cheeses must have commanded very high prices in the marketplace and were likely sold as luxury products to the aristocratic class. Thus, cheese as a gourmet item of trade was coming of age as a regular feature of Western food culture by this time.

Nowhere was this more evident than in Sicily, which became the premier supplier of acclaimed cheeses to Athens and beyond during the Classical Greek period. The more temperate and humid environment of Sicily, compared to the hot, dry Adriatic and eastern Mediterranean, enabled Sicilian cheesemakers to perfect hard, aged, rennet-coagulated pecorino cheeses that were durable, long-lived, flavorful and ideal for grating and for use as an ingredient in cooking. Sicilian cheeses became the perfect condiment for an increasingly affluent Mediterranean world that craved spices, seasonings, and flavorful ingredients, and numerous Greek writers made mention of the cheeses from Sicily. By the fourth century B.C.E., Sicily had developed a sophisticated food culture that elevated the status of Sicilian cheeses and transformed the monotony of daily food preparation and cooking into an art. The use of grated cheese in cooking became so pervasive by the late fourth century B.C.E. that Archestratus, a renowned Sicilian chef and cookbook author who has been dubbed the "father of western gastronomy," ridiculed what he considered to be the indiscriminate overuse of cheese sauces to smother fish and certain meat dishes. See ARCHESTRATUS OF GELA The extensive trade in hard grating pecorino and caprino cheeses set the stage for these cheeses to become a Roman staple. By the time of the Roman Empire, the bronze or iron cheese grater had become an essential tool of the Roman kitchen.

As the Romans expanded their empire north of the Alps, they encountered cheesemaking in many of the conquered Celtic lands. Cheeses produced over a wide geographic area, from the arc of the Alps that circumscribed northern Italy, to Toulouse in southern France, to the Massif Central of central France, to the Atlantic coast of northwest Europe, were exported to the great city of Rome. The Rhone River served as a major transportation link to the Mediterranean Sea for many northern cheeses en route to Italy. Cheeses produced in various regions of the Italian peninsula were also very popular in Rome. The first-century C.E. poet Martial featured four of them in Book 13 of his Epigrams, titled *Xenia*, his guide to gourmet foods that served as perfect presents for the gift-giving traditions that took place during the annual celebration of Saturnalia, around the time of the winter solstice. Aristocratic Roman families held lavish dinner parties during Saturnalia, when it was expected of the host to provide the guests with presents of fine foods. The inclusion of cheeses in Martial's gourmet food guide speaks to the luxury status of these Italian-produced cheeses.

English Cheese Trade

The Romans were prolific cheesemakers who brought their sheep and their technology for making small cylindrical pecorino cheeses with them as they established military outposts and country villas throughout the provinces north of the Alps. After the fall of the Western Roman Empire, the Anglo-Saxon conquerors of England inherited the abandoned Roman villas along with Roman cheesemaking technology. Anglo-Saxon nobility continued to make small cheeses on their manors, apparently with few changes, for five centuries. During this time the manor lords used cheese as a form of currency to fulfill their tax obligations to the king and to compensate their manorial servants. When the Normans invaded and wrested control of England from the Anglo-Saxons during the eleventh century, they continued cheesemaking on their newly acquired manors and soon began exporting cheeses across the channel to their former home in Normandy, as well to Flanders. Under the influence of this thriving cheese trade to the Continent, English manorial cheeses became larger in size over the next few hundred years. At the same time, the manors progressively shifted away from using sheep's milk to cow's milk for cheesemaking so that the sheep could be dedicated exclusively to the production of wool to capitalize on the lucrative wool trade with Flanders.

By the time the English feudal manorial system began to break up in the sixteenth century, the shift from sheep's milk to cow's milk cheesemaking in England was nearly complete, and much manorial cheesemaking had become oriented around commercial trade, setting the stage for the yeoman cheesemakers to follow. The yeoman dairymaids of the sixteenth through eighteenth centuries transformed the manorial cheeses of the Middle Ages into the great family of English pressed cheeses, and driving that transformation was the ever-expanding city of London. The London market, along with the London cheesemongers who held a monopoly over market access and whose demands for ever larger cheeses progressively influenced dairymaids in the east, north, and west of England, inspired the development of regionally distinctive cheeses, such as Cheshire, Gloucester, and Cheddar. See TERRITORIAL.

Cheese Trade in Switzerland, Italy, and Holland

Elsewhere in Europe, the reestablishment of overland and maritime trade routes during the Renaissance, following centuries of isolation during the early Middle Ages, created other opportunities for cheese to enter the world of long-distance trade. In western Switzerland, the mountain cheeses from the Gruyère region of the canton of Fribourg acquired such a reputation for their durability and quality by the end of the fourteenth century that they attracted the attention of Bern, Gruyère's powerful neighbor to the north. Bern eventually wrested control of the Gruyère highlands from the counts of Gruyère, which enabled the powerful canton to gain control over the highland cheese trade, and also to recruit some of the Gruyère cheesemakers to its Emmental lowlands, who went on to invigorate cheesemaking there.

The Alp-style cheeses of Gruyère developed a following in the prosperous region of Lake Geneva, located to the south and accessible only by footpath over steep mountain passes. From Lake Geneva, the cheeses from Gruyère began to be shipped down the Rhone River to the Mediterranean Sea, opening up ever-distant markets for these mountain cheeses. In response to the demands of transporting the cheeses by foot to Lake Geneva, and shipping the cheeses in barrels from Lake Geneva southward, cheesemakers in Gruyère progressively increased the size of their cheeses, resulting in the development of the large wheels—about 20 inches (50 centimeters) in diameter and 44–77 pounds (20–35 kilograms) in weight—that are still enjoyed today.

Meanwhile, across the Alps to the south, Benedictine and Cistercian monks were transforming the swampy backwater of the upper Po River Valley of Italy into lush agricultural fields and pastures for dairy cows. By the fourteenth century, large cheeses from the Parma region, suitable for grating and probably of monastic origin, were growing in fame and penetrating ever more distant markets around the Mediterranean and beyond. Parmesan cheese, made by a technology very similar to that of the large Alp-style cheeses but possessing a higher salt content, was ideally suited for trade. Its large, compact barrel-shaped geometry was well proportioned for storage and handling; its tough rind and almost limitless shelf life enabled it to withstand the most abusive rigors of travel.

Far to the north and west, in Holland, Dutch dairy farmers were developing cheeses for export destinations that would include the Mediterranean, even as Parmesan cheese was finding its way into markets as far north as England. Holland was a relative latecomer to cheesemaking in Europe and did not become a major producer until a sinking landscape, brought on by the relentless draining of boglands for three centuries, combined with rising sea levels caused by episodic global warming, triggered catastrophic failures of the wheat crop that the Dutch had so painstakingly developed. No longer able to grow wheat and faced with a crisis, Dutch farmers began to progressively shift into dairying and cheesemaking during the fourteenth century, tailoring their cheeses to the demands of maritime trade, at which the Dutch were beginning to excel. The result was the development of Edam and Gouda cheeses, brilliantly adapted to the rigors of shipping in wooden barrels and brightly colored and preserved with coatings of turnsole and saffron, respectively. The cities of Alkmaar, Rotterdam, and Amsterdam all became major exporters of cheese, and the city of Hoorn came to be known as the "cheese provisioner of all of Europe." Dutch cheeses were exported around the globe, and continue to be to this day. See ALKMAAR AUCTION.

Cheese Trade in America

Cheesemaking in the British colonies of the New World was oriented toward long-distance trade from the very beginning. The New England colonies along the North Atlantic coast became the cheesemaking center of the original 13 American colonies up to the time of the American Revolution. New England established a thriving cheese trade with the islands of the West Indies during the second half of the seventeenth century, which continued for 150 years. The West Indies were being developed intensively as sugar plantations at the time, and they were dependent on food imports to sustain their large enslaved labor force, kidnapped from Africa. New England cheesemakers sent large quantities of Cheshire-style cheese to the West Indies, indirectly helping to sustain the institution of slavery until the slave trade and slavery itself was abolished in the West Indies in the early nineteenth century.

After the Revolutionary War, cheesemakers from New England moved progressively westward through New York State to the southern shores of the Great Lakes, establishing dairy farms and cheesemaking in a broad band stretching from New England to Wisconsin by the middle of the nineteenth century. Much of the vast amounts of Cheddar-style cheese that came to be produced in the northern United States during this period was destined for long-distance trade: to the southern states, where cotton plantations were transforming the economy and tragically breathing new life into the institution of slavery in America; to the growing cities of the East Coast; and eventually to England. America would ultimately lose the English market to cheesemakers in Canada, and then Australia and New Zealand.

Long-distance trade continues to profoundly influence cheesemaking in the twenty-first century. With the advent of free-trade agreements and the proliferation of global trade in food products, many traditional cheeses that sustained communities for centuries or longer are in danger of extinction as a result of competition from lower-priced products, made in the same style, from afar. Yet at the same time, many well-known traditional cheeses, such as Parmigiano Reggiano Gruyère, Comté, feta, Roquefort, and Pecorino Romano, rely on long-distance exports to lucrative foreign markets to support and sustain their traditional practices, ways of life, and working landscapes.

See also ANCIENT CIVILIZATIONS.

Kindstedt, Paul. *Cheese and Culture: A History of Cheese and Its Place in Western Civilization*. White River Junction, Vt.: Chelsea Green, 2012.
Birmingham, David. *Switzerland: A Village History*. New York: St. Martin's, 2000.
De Vries, Jan. *The Dutch Rural Economy in the Golden Age, 1500–1700*. New Haven, Conn.: Yale University Press, 1974.

Paul S. Kindstedt

traditional equipment used in cheesemaking and aging consists of instruments, utensils, and devices traditionally handmade of different materials such as wood, clay, animal skin, stone, and metal developed to facilitate the preparation, maturation, and storing of specific cheeses. Traditional equipment has been utilized in cheesemaking from ancient times to the present.

The various types of traditional cheeses produced around the world include more than a thousand varieties, and specialized traditional equipment is specified for use in their manufacture. We can still find historic equipment in artisanal cheesemaking plants and rural homes. The earliest proposed dates for the origin of cheesemaking range from around 8000 B.C.E., when sheep were first domesticated. Since then animal skins and inflated internal organs have provided storage vessels for foodstuffs. The earliest evidence of cheesemaking in the archaeological record dates back to 5500 B.C.E., in what is now Kujawy, Poland, where pottery strainers containing milk fat molecules were found. Perhaps the oldest device that was accidentally discovered to prepare cheese was a bag made of a sheep's stomach, used for storing and carrying the milk supply, resulting in the milk being turned to curd and whey by the rennet from the stomach, over four thousand years ago. Today similar traditional utensils are still used for cheesemaking, such as the motal and tulum, which are traditional containers made of a whole sheep or goat skin and used for aging and storing special cheeses. See ORIGIN OF CHEESE and SHEEP- AND GOAT-SKIN CHEESES.

Differences in cultures, traditions, tastes, and styles in various areas of the world have led to the large variety of traditional cheesemaking styles and the type of equipment used. Generally we can classify the traditional cheesemaking equipment based on the types of cheese for which they are used; the stage of cheesemaking when they are used and their

Some of the traditional equipment used by a feta cheesemaker in the village of Peleta on the southeastern Peloponnese peninsula in Greece. The metal bowls, spoon, and wood stirrer in the foreground, and vat in the background are used for milk collection; heating, renneting, and coagulation; and curd cutting and stirring.
© VINCENZO SPIONE

application; their significance in the cheesemaking process and specificity, whether they are specific cheesemaking instruments or more general instruments; or based on the material, shape, and size.

Traditional equipment can be used at different stages of the cheesemaking process including: milk collection; milk straining and measuring; milk preparation, heating, renneting, and coagulation; curd cutting and stirring; curd collecting and whey drainage; curd milling, texturing, and cheddaring; curd molding or ladling, and pressing; cheese salting; cheese maturation and molding by storing in natural caves or cellars; cheese testing; cheese polishing, brushing, and washing; waxing and coating; packaging; and cutting and slicing.

Throughout the world containers of different shapes, sizes, and materials are used for milk collection. These containers may be made of clay, wood, or metal. In the rural areas of the Azerbaijan region of Iran, two special containers are used for this purpose named *bayda* and *tiyancha* (tiyəncə). The bayda is a long cylindrical container with a wider top than bottom, and a capacity of 11–22 pounds (5–10 kilograms), made of copper and used for milk collecting and processing. The tiyancha is a bulgy container similar to a small cauldron, which is made of copper and used for milk cooking and processing. The *bidon* is another container used for transporting milk that is usually made of aluminum or galvanized metal. The size of bidons ranges from small 1-liter vessels to large 55-liter containers, usually with an attached or independent lid. Milk measures are used to pick up a certain amount of milk. A traditional measure used in the Azerbaijan region of Iran is called *siya-tutar* (siyə-tutar). It is a copper bowl with a capacity of about 1 liter. Sometimes it is constructed with a handle like a ladle. Milk straining is done before the cheesemaking process to remove any potential dirt and waste particles in the milk. For this purpose a cloth or metal mesh strainer can be used.

Heating, renneting, and coagulation of milk are stages that are performed in a cheese vat. Various traditional vats constructed of wood, earthenware, metal, and copper are used in the production of different artisanal cheeses. They differ in shape and size, from small to large, from circular and semicylindrical to rectangular, and from vertical to horizontal. See VATS. The most common traditional cheese vats are made with wood or copper materials. Wooden barrels may be used as cheese vats in the manufacture of some traditional cheeses such as Gouda. Specially made wooden vats are important for the development of a microbial biofilm that acts as a natural starter culture. However the use of wooden vats is prohibited in many countries. Copper vats are used in the production of famous cheeses such as Grana Padano, Parmigiano Reggiano, and Swiss Gruyère. It is believed that the copper imparts elements of flavor to the finished cheese; however the released copper ions in food can raise the risk of oxidation. Some copper vats are shaped much like an inverted bell. These vats are tapered to a narrow bottom are about 9 feet (2.7 meters) deep. This specific shape can facilitate curd separation. When the curd is cooked, it sinks and forms a compact mass at the bottom simply due to its own weight. This type of vat is widely used in the processing of Parmigiano Reggiano cheese. Another smaller bell-shaped vat is used in processing Bitto cheese in the mountains above Lake Como, Italy. They are sometimes used with wood fires and probably originated in a less mechanized time when smaller amount of cheeses were produced. See COPPER VATS and WOODEN VATS.

Handmade wooden or metal instruments were used for cutting and stirring the curd, and for working the curd before pressing or stretching, such as the spino, a long-handled instrument used in producing Parmigiano Reggiano and the other similar cheeses, for cutting and stirring the curd. It was made from the branches of the biyancospino (hawthorn tree) by monks in the twelfth century. Nowadays metallic horizontal and vertical knives are the most common traditional instruments used for cutting the coagulum into curd particles of a defined size, for example, 1/3–2/3 inch (1–2 centimeters). The cutting of the coagulum is very important and influences the rate of acid development and texture of the cheese. In some cases milling the curd mechanically or by hand is needed to break up the curd into small pieces and enable it to be salted evenly. See CUTTING and CURD MILL.

Different utensils were used for curd collection, such as bowls and a springy metal grill with the cloth folded on it. Cheesecloth, muslin cloth, or fine mesh cloth are terms applied to the specific types of cloths that are used to remove the whey from the cheese curds. Cheesecloth is a loose-woven gauze-like cotton cloth used primarily in cheesemaking and cooking. It is available in at least seven different grades, from open to extra fine weave. See CHEESECLOTH.

Various types of handmade baskets and molds are used for the manufacture of various cheeses. These molds may be cylindrical, conical, or square and may be made from wood or metal. The size and shape of the baskets and molds are determined by the variety of cheese being made. A peculiar basket-type mold is used for the manufacture of two Nigerian white cheeses called Wara and Woagachi. Woagachi cheese is larger than Wara cheese due to the size of the basket-type mold that is used. See FORMS OR MOLDS.

Different types of mechanical cheese presses are available. The traditional stone or wooden press devices working with leverage or screw mechanisms are used for cheese pressing in the production of hard and semihard cheeses. Pressing the curd in the molds assists in some whey removal and compacts the curd pieces into the shape of the mold. The amount of weight to use can be determined through experience. Too much pressure will result in loss of fat in the expressed whey, giving reduced yield and a poorly textured cheese. If too little pressure is used the curds do not mat properly and this will give a cheese with poor body and texture. Barbara Gilmour's cheese press is an ancient stone cheese press that was used for the first time in 1760 for the manufacture of Dunlop cheese. This device can still be seen today at The Hill Farm in East Ayrshire, Scotland. It has a heavy lintel stone with a screwed shaft passing through it attached to a frame, allowing the dead weight of the stone to be lowered progressively onto the cheese. Another old stone cheese press can be found in Strathspey, Scotland. See PRESS.

In the Haj Hasan Almasi artisanal cheese plant located in Kohneh Shahr, Salmas, Iran, leverage wooden press devices, carved stone weights, and metal molds are used in the manufacture of a hard cheese called Ghirmizi Panir (Qırmızı Pənir) or Panire Ghermeze Salmas. In the storehouse multistory wooden shelves are used for keeping and storing the cheese and other types of hard or semihard and moldy cheeses. See WOODEN SHELVES. The cheeses are placed on these wooden shelves and stored at cold and humid conditions to be ripened and molded, for about two months, followed by salting in brine. The cheeses are dry-salted in this step and periodically turned upside down, allowing for maturation and mold formation on all sides of the cheese to be evenly accomplished. The microbial flora of these wooden shelves, besides the air microflora, play an important role in the final completion of the maturation of cheese. Sometimes a wooden ring similar to that used in Gorgonzola production is wrapped around the cheeses. This ring helps dry the surface by absorbing moisture, and leads to the growth of the gray molds on it, covering its surface.

Some specific cheese varieties are placed for maturation in pouches prepared from whole sheep's or goat's skins and stored at cold and moist conditions for about two to three months. The sheep's skin bag, which is produced in Ardabil, Iran, is called a *motal* and is used for the manufacture of Motal Paniri. For manufacture of the motal the skin is throughly cleaned, washed, and salted. Then the skin of the front and rear legs is tied together and the neck opening is used to fill in the cheese. In a motal the woolly or hairy side is placed inside. See MOTAL PANIRI. It is known as khik in Khorasan, Iran and used to produce Panire Khiki, as well as Panire Assalem and Tavalesh in northern Iran. Tulum and touloumi are the same traditional containers often made of goat's skin and used to produce Turkish Tulum Peyniri and Greek Touloumitiri, respectively. Tulum is mainly made of goat's skin and the hairless side of the skin is placed inside. See TULUM.

Another traditional container is a specific earthenware similar to a pitcher, but having a larger mouth, called *kupa* (küpə), *koozeh*, or *jarra* (carra) in different regions of Iran and Turkey. It is used for the manufacturing and storing of a group of cheeses that spend their maturation period in a pot. Kupa are used in the manufacture of a peculiar cheese called Kupa Paniri (Küpə Pəniri), which is produced in northwestern Iran. It is named *koozeh* in the other regions of Iran and the produced cheese is called Panire Koozeh. The capacity of kupe or koozeh ranges from 1 to 5 liters and is sometimes coated with a lacquer layer. Lacquered pots are preferred as they retain cheese moisture better. The cheese is shredded and packed in the pot using a metal pestle. The pots are closed using grapevine leaves or a clean cloth and clay. The pots are then buried underground, upside down, for four to six months. These containers are also used for the production of other Iranian traditional cheeses such as Jajikhli Panir (Penjarli Panir) and Zirali Panir and the Turkish traditional cheeses Testi Peynir or Carra Peynir (Jarra Peynir). See JAJIKHLI PANIR; KUPA PANIRI; POT CHEESES; and ZIRALY PANIR.

Some cheeses such as feta and Sfela cheese are traditionally matured and kept in wooden barrels. Oak barrels are mainly used for this purpose. Each barrel has about a 110-pound (50-kilogram) capacity with a hole in its wooden lid that is closed tightly with a cork; from time to time the hole is opened very quickly to allow the escape of the gases that evolve due to microbial activity during the maturation period. See FETA and SFELA.

For maturation of the white brined cheeses such as Lighvan Paniri, Telems (Telema), Beyaz Peynir, Batzos, and Kalathaki Limnou cheeses, they are placed in tin containers including brine (10–16 percent) and cold stored for at least two to three months. Some of them, such as Lighvan Paniri, stored in natural caves at 50°F (10°C) for about two to four weeks to pass the pre-maturation period. Brined cheese is the main type of cheese produced and eaten in the Middle East and Mediterranean areas. See BRINED CHEESES; LIGHVAN PANIRI; and MIDDLE EAST.

A large group of cheeses including blue cheeses are stored in natural caves during their maturation period, as well as Roquefort, Taleggio, Gorgonzola, and Stilton. Cheeses such as Taleggio are placed on trays made of saturated pine and covered with moist hemp cloth, which helps the fresh Taleggio retain its moisture and prevents it from getting crushed during transport along mountain paths for storage in the caves. See BLUE CHEESES; CAVE; and TALEGGIO.

Some of the mold-ripened cheeses after aging should be washed and brushed before waxing. Waxing is a common step in the production of many hard cheeses such as Edam, Gouda, and Panire Ghermeze Salmas. Cheese wax helps prevent unwanted mold growth while retaining moisture in the aging cheese. It is prepared using a combination of paraffin, microcrystalline wax, and food-grade coloring. The waxing can be done by two methods: dipping in melted wax, or brushing the wax onto the dried cheese with a natural-bristle brush. For dipping, an instrument that is a metallic bar with a ring bent at the end is used. Cheese is placed inside the ring and immersed in melted wax for a short time and then removed. See BRUSHING and WAXING AND COATING.

A cheese trier, also called cheese iron, can be used for testing the maturity of hard cheeses without cutting them open. It is a semicircular grooved blade made of stainless steel. When inserted into the cheese a sample core is removed and evaluated for taste and texture. Then the piece is returned to the cheese so the aging process can continue. The trier needs to be sanitized well before use and the opening around the plug also needs to be sealed with a smear of the cheese sample to prevent mold from entering the cheese body. See CHEESE IRON.

Various types of traditional instruments, including cheese knives, cheese cutters, cheese wires, and cheese slicers, are used for cheese cutting and slicing. Different cheeses require different knives, according to hardness. Hard cheeses require a tough blade that will not be damaged by the hard cheese, such as a Parmesan cheese knife, which is short, thick, and rough. But soft cheeses require a sharp knife that is serrated and often has holes in the blade to prevent the cheese from sticking to it. Some knives also have a ridged and forked end, which helps separate and serve the cheese slices.

The cheese slicer is used usually to cut semihard and hard cheeses. See CHEESE WIRE. The wire cheese cutter is used for cutting adhesive and soft cheeses. It has a fine gauge stainless steel or aluminum wire stretched across a supporting frame and cuts through a cheese block with hand pressure. A modern cheese slicer, also called a cheese plane, is similar to a carpenter's plane and is very common in Nordic countries, the Netherlands, Belgium, Germany, and Switzerland. See CHEESE SLICER. The other device is the girolle, which is used to scrape Tête de Moine Swiss cheese into the form of rosettes that resemble chanterelle mushrooms. This cheese was traditionally scraped with a knife.

Anifantakis, E. M., and G. Moatsou. "Feta and Other Balkan Cheeses." In *Brined Cheeses*, edited by A. Tamime. London: Blackwell, 2006.

Hayaloglu, Ali A., et al. "Cheeses of Turkey: 1. Varieties Ripened in Goat-skin Bags." *Le Lait* 87 (2007): 79–95.

Lame, H., et al. "Contribution à l'étude du "fromage en pot" de l'Iran." *Le Lait* 53 (1973): 163–168.

New England Cheesemaking Supply Co. "A Parma Style Cheese." http://www.cheesemaking.com/Parma2.html.

O'Connor, C. *Traditional Cheesemaking Manual*. Addis Ababa, Ethiopia: ILCA International Livestock Centre for Africa, 1993.

Shafiei, Y. "Iranian Traditional Cheeses." Paper presented at the 1st Conference of Iranian Traditional Dairy Products, Khoy, Iran, 24 February 2013. In Persian.

Yahya Shafiei Bavil Oliaei

traditional speciality guaranteed (TSG)

is a European Union (EU) label that "highlights traditional character, either in the composition or means of production" of a food. Unlike designation of origin (DO) and geographical indication (GI), a TSG has no geographical component, but is based entirely on following the "recipe" correctly. See DESIGNATION OF ORIGIN and GEOGRAPHICAL INDICATION. The label assures use of specific ingredients and particular time-honored techniques to make a food in the "old-fashioned" way, but the product may be made anywhere in the world (although if made outside of the EU, there is no obligation to put the seal on the package).

In 2015 only a few cheeses carried the TSG label: boerenkaas from the Netherlands, mozzarella (Italy), hushållsost (Finland), and ovčí salašnícky údený syr (Slovakia). Cheese lovers may run across cheese-friendly products that also bear the seal, such as *tortas de aceite de castilleja de la cuesta* (Spanish olive oil crackers), cured meats including jambon serrano and several kinds of salami, and several Belgian beer styles.

Council Regulation (EC) no. 509/2006 of 20 March 2006 on agricultural products and foodstuffs as traditional specialities guaranteed. http://europa.eu/legislation_summaries/agriculture/food/l66043_en.htm.

Juliette Rogers

transhumance refers to the specific pastoralist practice of short-range seasonal movement between lowlands and adjacent highlands and includes a cyclical, recurrent, and seasonal commuting between different "stations"—usually a village in the flatland and a number of makeshift mountain abodes in the highlands, or a mountain village and lowland stations. Many take "transhumance" to refer to the equivalent of the French *alpage*, or the Italian *alpeggio* or *monticazione*, to describe the practice of taking sheep, cattle, and goat herds to higher grounds in the summer months to graze upland pastures and thus free the village pastures from the pressure of cattle and flocks, so that hay can be made and preserved for the winter. Transhumance, however, differs from those practices in important respects.

Transhumance is based on three primary characteristics: "the existence of a permanent village base, associated agriculture, and the seasonal movement of livestock" (Jones 2005, p. 358). Not to be confused with nomadic pastoralism, transhumance is compatible with growing crops and orchards, managing forests, and permanent abodes. Fernand Braudel defined transhumance as "simply one form of the Medi-terranean pastoral way of life" (1995, p. 87). In the sixteenth century, transhumant flocks followed trails between the Camargue and the Crau to the Oisans in France, between Navarre and Aragon in Spain, or between the Abruzzi and Apulia in Italy. Castilian transhumance and Merino sheep were at the heart of Europe's textile economy, politics, and finance in the Renaissance.

A division of labor as well as an example of ecological savviness, this specialized seasonal activity might be carried out in a couple of different ways. In one, upland pastureland might be held undivided by an entire community, thus saving on labor to tend cattle and flocks. In this case, the village youth would usually be sent to spend the summers tending cows and goats uphill, while experienced cheesemakers would take turns transforming the milk into cheese in collective dairies. This consorted or cooperative cheesemaking tradition was present in both the eastern and the western Italian Alps, with varying proportions of the cheese production devoted to market sales, as in the case of Val d'Aosta, with its Fontina of the Gruyère family. Another approach was for the high pastures to be held separately by individual households or leased by the municipality to the highest bidder for the grazing season (Viazzo and Woolf, 2002).

Summer transhumance is still practiced in southern Europe, particularly in the French, German, Ladin, and Italian-speaking Alps, as well as in the French, Spanish, and Basque Pyrenees. Such seasonal movement is considered very important to a number of local traditions of cheesemaking. Since milk obtained from cows and herds on higher pastures is difficult to refrigerate or distribute commercially, it is most commonly made into cheese, and often matured at least partially on site. In central Italy and in the Lombard mountains, cheese is matured and kept cool in natural caves or cellars that are close to or that even span streams, as in the *caselli* of Val Taleggio, floorless buildings that straddle the creeks. Similarly, cheese can be matured underground in pits, as in the case of Formaggio di Fossa (lit. "cheese of the pit") of Italy's Emilia-Romagna region. See FOSSA.

A related notion is that of the *alpage* (or *alpeggio* in Italian). Similar to transhumance, alpage is a form of seasonal grazing practiced by dairy farmers that for the rest of the year live stably in their mountain villages. According to the historian Charles Parain, the alpage involves a mountain community and a territorial basin, usually a valley, in which winter storage of animal manure is instrumental for crop production, and the livestock (especially cattle) only move at fixed seasonal times under the care of selected operators in order to exploit the summer pastures and thus consume extra grass at no additional cost. In contrast to this practice of summer high-pasture grazing, transhumance *proper* would designate longer-term, long-distance movement of livestock all year round (and would, for instance, be typical of sheep flocks led by male shepherds). "Transhumant" trails can extend over several regions, and occasionally across national borders, for up to hundreds of miles, and entail a much longer period of mobility for both shepherds and flocks. A further distinction is made between the alpage—the vertical movement of cattle that belong to the community and use the municipal lands of the upper pastures (whether communally or on an individual basis, family by family)—and the *estivage* hosting of herds that do not belong to the local village but rather come from farther away (because of breeding concerns of the lowlands, for example). These are usually young heifers that do not require milking and thus do not contribute to the local cheesemaking economy. Their owners pay rent to the local herders, who tend them over the summer.

Dairy production has historically been one of the main resources for alpine societies relying on transhumance, both in terms of its importance in the local diet and in terms of commerce. Trading, inventorying, and even paying taxes with prestigious, long-matured, and highly priced fat upland cheeses are practices that have been historically documented since the fourteenth century. The "gold of the uplands," as it has been described, would in fact seem to be cheese.

See also ALPAGE and PASTORALISM.

Braudel, Fernand. *The Mediterranean in the Age of Philip II.* Vol. 1. Translated by Siân Reynolds. Berkeley: University of California Press, 1995. English translation of *La Méditerranée et le monde méditerranéen à l'époque de Philippe II.* Vol. 1. Paris: Colin, 1949.

Grasseni, Cristina. *Developing Skill, Developing Vision: Practices of Locality at the Foot of the Alps.* New York: Berghahn, 2009.

Jones, Schuyler. "Transhumance Re-examined." *Journal of the Royal Anthropological Institute* 11 (June 2005): 357–359.

Ott, Sandra. *The Circle of Mountains: A Basque Shepherding Community.* Reno: University of Nevada Press, 1981.

Parain, Charles. "Esquisse d'une problématique des systémes européens d'estivage à production fromagére." *L'Ethnographie* 62–63 (1968): 3–28.

Pitte, J. R. "L'or des alpages," *L'Alpe* 11 (2001): 13–27.

Viazzo, Pier Paolo, and Stuart Woolf, eds. *Formaggi e mercati:Economied'alpeggio in Valle d'Aosta e Haute-Savoie.* Aosta, Italy: LeChateau, 2002.

Cristina Grasseni

Trappist cheeses

See MONASTIC CHEESEMAKING and SAINT BENEDICT.

Travnik

See VLAŠIĆ.

Trichothecium roseum

See FLOWER OF THE MOLDS.

trier

See CHEESE IRON.

triple-cream cheeses (triple crème) are a type of cheese produced from milk enriched with cream; the finished product should have a minimum of 75 percent fat content in dry matter. This type of cheese is a relatively modern French invention to maximize a "rich and creamy" flavor. Most of the aged triple-cream cheeses belong to the bloomy-rind type, whose surface is covered with *Penicillium candidum* or *Geotrichum candidum*. See GEOTRICHUM CANDIDUM and PENICILLIUM. Compared with traditional bloomy-rind cheeses such as Brie and Camembert, which contain about 45 percent fat in dry matter and develop strong flavors during a long, slow aging process, triple-cream cheese is designed to have a subtler flavor and to be consumed as a fresh curd or young cheese, just one to four weeks old.

The added fat hinders the formation of a strong protein network during coagulation; the final curd, retaining over 50 percent moisture, is fragile. Thus, with a few exceptions, this type of cheese is made in small sizes of up to a pound (half a kilogram) per piece. The fresh curd is often used to make different-flavored cheeses, with additions of dried herbs, spices, and dried fruits such as raisins. The texture is soft and smooth as a result of the high fat and moisture content, and its pleasantly lactic and buttery taste appeals to a broad range of consumers. In texture, triple-cream cheese responds to temperature changes less like regular cheese than like butter. Compared with cream cheese, well-made triple-cream cheese has a lighter and more airy mouthfeel, somewhat similar to ice cream; moreover, it should not have any oily feeling.

Most triple-cream cheeses are produced industrially; major production areas in France are Île-de-France, Normandy, and Burgundy. The most famous triple-cream cheese is Brillat-Savarin, which was re-branded in the 1930s from the earlier invention and named after the legendary late eighteenth-century food writer. Lucullus and Grand Vatel are also named after famous connoisseurs. The popular triple-cream cheese Explorateur was created in the 1950s and named in honor of the Explorer, the first US satellite. Also popular are Pierre Robert and Saint-André. Two newcomers, Délice de Bourgogne and Crémeux de Bourgogne, are from Burgundy. A few US artisanal cheese producers make New World–style triple-cream cheeses, including Mt Tam and Red Hawk, from the Cowgirl Creamery in California. See BRILLAT-SAVARIN and RED HAWK.

Many cheese lovers consider triple-cream cheese to be a somewhat dull entry-level cheese because of its mild flavor and light texture. However, triple-cream cheese is different from cream cheese, which is eaten only fresh as a spread or used as an ingredient in sweet or savory recipes. When you let triple-cream cheese age a little longer, it develops a melting texture as well as a nutty, mushroom-like aroma. Then the cheese's fatty nature and light texture are a perfect companion to Champagne and other sparkling wines. Its pleasant acidity and rich taste of cream also pair beautifully with Bordeaux-style red wines. The most seductive part of triple-cream cheese, however, is the luxurious feeling in your mouth.

See also BLOOMY-RIND CHEESES and CREAM CHEESE.

Dalby, Andrew. *Cheese: A Global History*. London: Reaktion, 2009.
Masui, Kazuko, and Tomoko Yamada, eds. *French Cheeses*. 3d ed. London: Dorling Kindersley, 2004.
Tunick, Michael. *The Science of Cheese*. New York: Oxford University Press, 2014.

Soyoung Scanlan

Trnič is a hard cheese traditionally made by the herdsmen on Velika Planina, a plain in the Slovenian Alps. It was widely made in the nineteenth and early twentieth centuries, but only a few individuals preserve the knowledge of Trnič making today. Traditionally Trnič was made by herdsmen in the summer months, during the grazing season. Cheeses were always made in pairs as its shape symbolizes women's breasts. At the end of the grazing season, a herdsman kept one cheese and gave its pair to his beloved as a proof of his love and fidelity, and sometimes as an engagement symbol.

Trnič is a dried cheese in a cupped shape with a nipple on the top and decorated with relief ornaments. It is made from cow's milk, which is left at room temperature to sour. The cream is removed and the coagulum is heated to about 136°F (58°C). After that the mass is drained, salted, shaped by hand into its distinctive form, and decorated using a relief-carved wooden seal called a "pisava." Trnič is then left at room temperature for about four weeks to dry. The size of the cheese depends on the size of the cheesemaker's hands and usually is 2½ inches (5–6 centimeters) in height and 2 inches (4–5 centimeters) in diameter. The color is pale or dark yellow to brownish. It is hard, dry, and crumbly with a salty and slightly acidic taste, which can be slightly piquant.

Young Trnič can be grated on risotto, pasta, and salad, or cut into slices and served with the addition of honey, pepper, and olive or pumpkin-seed oil. Trnič is also recognized as an authentic souvenir from Velika Planina since it can be kept unchanged for years without preservation.

Slovenian Ministry of Culture. "Description of Cultural Heritage." 2014. http://www.mk.gov.si/fileadmin/mk.gov.si/pageuploads/Ministrstvo/Razvidi/RKD_Ziva/Rzd-02_00033.pdf.

Petra Mohar Lorbeg and Andreja Čanžek Majhenič

truckle is the English word used to describe a cylindrical wheel of cheese. Truckles may be described as "barrel-shaped," meaning the cheese cylinder is taller than it is wide. Truckles can vary in size, shape, and weight, and the word is especially used when referring to Cheddar. "Truckle" comes from Old French *trocle* and from Latin *trochlea*, meaning "sheave of a pulley." The sheave of a pulley refers to the grooved wheel that holds a belt, wire rope, or rope. The current usage is thought to date from the early nineteenth century.

See also CHEDDAR.

"Truckle." *Oxford English Dictionary*. http://www
.oxforddictionaries.com/us/definition/American_
english/truckle.

Megan A. Schraedley

tulum is a Turkish cheese named for the handmade dried goatskin or sheepskin sack in which it traditionally has been aged. One of five groups of native cheeses designated by Turkish culinary culture, tulum is made from raw sheep's, goat's, cow's, or mixed milk. tulums vary by region as well as by traditional family recipes. Some prominent tulums include the following:

- Erzincan Tulum Peynirl is made from raw Akkaraman sheep's milk and produced by eastern Turkey's Savak tribe. Aged for three to six months, it is fatty with a white paste, and has a pungent, buttery, and acidic flavor. It is Turkey's most popular tulum.
- Divle Obruk Tulum is named for Divle, the deep natural cave in central Turkey in which it ages at a constant 39°F (4°C). Made from Akkaraman and Morkaraman sheep's milk and a small percentage of goat's milk, production is highest in April or May. The cheese ages four to twelve months and becomes covered with distinctive reddish molds from the cave's natural microflora. It is considered ready to eat when those molds begin to fall off. The paste is a Cheddar-like yellow, the aroma evokes pasture grasses and animal notes, and the flavor is sharp. Divle tulum production is small, so cheese lovers should be wary of fraudulent, artificially colored knockoffs.
- Izmir Tulum Peyniri, produced in the Aegean region, is Turkey's second most popular tulum, and the only one salted in brine. The milk used may be raw sheep's, mixed sheep's and goat's, or cow's. It ripens about fourteen months (best at twelve), steeping in brine and its own whey in a goatskin tulum or perforated nylon bag in a metal drum. The cheese curds absorb some brine; the rest leaks out through the bag. Izmir Tulum is salty, firm, and must contain small holes (1 inch [2–3 centimeters]) or it is considered defective. Cow's milk Izmir Tulum is mild; the sheep's milk version is richer and more aromatic. Both are high in fat.
- Kargı Tulumu is produced in central Anatolia. This creamy tulum is made with autumn milk, ages about six months, and its aroma is reminiscent of wine. It is considered among the best tulums.
- Bez Tulum Peyniri is ripened for two to three months, and usually sold in 26–30-pound (12–15-kilogram) pillars wrapped in a woven PVC casing. This yellowish tulum is chewy, crumbly, and somewhat mealy, with very little salt. The flavor has been called "stimulating."

Longer-aged tulums are made in spring after the birth of kids and lambs, when the milk is richest. The goatskin bags (typical capacity is 22 pounds [10 kilograms]) in which tulums age are permeable by air and water. Commercially produced tulums (made with pasteurized milk) are usually aged in plastic barrels and may be sold in plastic tubs. They're more uniform than tulums from small regional producers. These tulums are ripened beneath a nylon cloth in hard plastic barrels. Scientific research confirms that tulums aged in plastic differ from those aged in goatskin, so the nature of this cheese may change.

In the United States the Wisconsin Sheep Dairy Cooperative produces a mixed sheep's and cow's milk tulum ripened for eight to nine months as a 40-pound (18-kilogram) block inside a plastic bag in a box. This extremely sharp and tangy high-moisture tulum is soft and crumbly.

See also SHEEP- AND GOAT-SKIN CHEESES and TURKEY.

Martino, Francesco. "Turkey: The Treasure in the Cave at Divle." Osservatorio Balcani e Caucaso, 31 December 2013. http://www.balcanicaucaso.org/eng/Regions-and-countries/Turkey/Turkey-the-treasure-in-the-cave-at-Divle-144918.
Slow Food Foundation. "Divle Cave-Aged Cheese." http://www.fondazioneslowfood.com/en/slow-food-presidia/divle-cave-aged-cheese.
"Tulum (Wisconsin Sheep Dairy Coop)." Culture. http://culturecheesemag.com/cheese-library/Tulum-Wisconsin-Sheep-Dairy-Coop.

"Turkish Cheeses." MyMerhaba.com. http://www
.mymerhaba.com/turkish-cheese-in-turkey-1771.html.
"Turkish Roquefort Cheese Owes Its Flavor to Caves."
Daily Sabah, 28 October 2015. http://www
.dailysabah.com/food/2015/10/29/turkish
-roquefort-cheese-owes-its-flavor-to-caves.

Robin Watson

Tuma Persa is a unique cheese produced by only one cheesemaker in the countryside of Castronovo di Sicilia, a town in the area between Agrigento and Palermo in Sicily, Italy. This cheese was produced in many places in Sicily in the eighteenth century. Researchers have found references to it in the early nineteenth century under a variety of names, depending on the area of production, including cacio buffalo, cacio turc, and toma perduta. The meaning of *persa* is "lost."

Legend has it that a cheesemaker had forgotten (lost) one pressed cheese in a corner of the aging room. After a few weeks, he discovered it, and it was full of mold. After dusting the mold, he decided that the cheese was no longer good; but he left the cheese in the same place, intending to throw it out. When he returned a few weeks later, he found the cheese still full of mold; but, before throwing it out, he decided to open it. With wonder, he found that the cheese inside smelled good, looked good, and tasted good—so good that he decided to repeat his accidental discovery.

Around 1990 one Sicilian producer, aware of this historic cheese, decided to try to reproduce it. Today the cheesemaking technology of Tuma Persa is well defined: it is an uncooked, pressed, semihard cheese made from thermized whole cow's milk, using kid rennet. The unique technology comes, just as the legend says, in the ripening phase. The Tuma goes through two fermentation stages before it is salted. In the first, the cheese is set in shape and then not touched for about a week. Then it is washed and left to ferment for an additional ten days, at the end of which it is washed, brushed, and finally, salted. The cheese is brine-salted for a few days to reach a maximum 2 percent salt concentration in the final product; rarely, but if necessary, it may also be dry-salted periodically on wooden shelves and turned regularly. The aging takes place for eight months in thick-walled limestone structures that are partially built into the ground.

Tuma Persa has a cylindrical shape with flat sides, measures about 4–4.7 inches (10–12 centimeters) high and 11–12 inches (28–30 centimeters) in diameter, and weighs 15.4–17.6 pounds (7–8 kilograms). The ochre-color rind becomes dark after the surface is rubbed with a mixture of olive oil and ground pepper. The white to straw-yellow interior is tender and compact, with sparse holes and dough shells. The taste is sweet and spicy, but never salty or bitter, with a long-lasting and peculiarly aromatic aftertaste, an excellent balance between the flavors of the mold, and a thread of wild maturation.

See also SICILY.

Campo, Patrizia, and Giuseppe Licitra. *Historical Sicilian Cheeses*. Ragusa, Italy: CoRFiLaC, 2006.
Consiglio Nazionale delle Richerche (National Research Council of Italy). "I prodotti caseari del Mezzogiorno." 1992. http://www.isa.cnr.it/PRODTIP.
Istituto Nazionale di Sociologia Rurale. *Atlante dei prodotti tipici: I formaggi*. Milan: Angeli, 1990.
Vizzardi, Mario, and Piero Maffeis. *Formaggi italiani: Storia—tecnologia e microbiologia lattiero-casearia*. Bologna, Italy: Edizioni agricole, 1999.

Ivana Piccitto

Turkey's diverse cheese culture reflects its location at the crossroads of Asia and Europe, varying geographical and climatic conditions, and multilayered history. Turkey's national territory extends from Iran and the Middle East to the Balkans, with coasts on three seas, mountainous terrain, and highland

Divle Tulum is a style of pleasantly moldy tulum made in Karaman in Central Anatolia and Kargı Tulum in Çorum (inner Black Sea region). *Tulum* is a Turkish word meaning a whole animal skin; these cheeses are typically aged in a goatskin casing, hairy side out.
© HALEY POLINSKY

plateaus. Turkish cheeses differ from those of Western Europe but share some similarities with the Balkans, especially Greece and Bulgaria. See BULGARIA and GREECE. The Turkish word for cheese is *peynir*, from the Farsi *penîr*, whence also the Hindi *paneer*. See PANEER. Turkish cheeses have roots in Central Asian nomadic pastoralist culture and the agrarian culture that developed in Mesopotamia, also home to the first domestication of animals. In his eleventh-century Turkish dictionary, Mahmut of Kaşgar describes cheese poetically as "sleeping milk."

Traditional Anatolian cheeses are most commonly made of sheep's milk, followed by goat's milk. Nowadays cow's milk dominates commercial cheese-making.

Cheese is an essential Turkish breakfast food, and it is also widely used in cooking, especially as a filling in baked or fried savory pies and breads. Fresh unsalted cheese is used in a number of traditional sweet dishes, particularly cheese halva (*peynirli helva*), and as a filling for *kadayıf* as in the famous dessert *künefe*.

Rennet is the main curdling agent in traditional cheesemaking, but others include cardoons, fig sap, dried figs, chickpeas, and artichokes. Commercial rennet is now widely used even by home cheesemakers and artisanal dairies. Turkish cheeses can be classified as fresh curd cheeses (lor, çökelek, sepet peyniri); brined cheeses (beyaz peynir, teleme, teneke tulum); yellow semi-matured or fully matured dry-salted cheeses (kaşar, kaşkaval, gravyer); and pressed curd cheeses in goatskins or earthen jars (tulum peyniri, çömlek peyniri, küp peynir). Curd cheeses, tulum, and a number of other regional cheeses are made from the whey remaining after churning yogurt to make butter.

Beyaz peynir is the most common cheese in Turkey, a brined cheese very similar to Greek feta, Bulgarian sirene, and Romanian teleme. See FETA and SERBIAN WHITE BRINED CHEESES. Although it is produced in many parts of the country, the best comes from the western provinces of Edirne, Kırklareli, Tekirdağ, and Çanakkale. The district of Ezine in Çanakkale is synonymous with high quality white cheeses. Beyaz peynir is matured in brine for a minimum of six months, giving it a tangy taste and slightly crumbly texture. It is consumed at any meal, often paired with tomatoes and has an affinity with parsley and fresh dill. It is an essential accompaniment to *rakı*, the anise-flavored distilled grape spirit.

Mihalıç is a hard cheese similar to white cheese, but saltier and way stronger in flavor.

Kaşar peyniri is the second most popular cheese, first recorded in 1471 as a cheese served to Sultan Mehmed II. See KASSERI. It is a pulled-curd cheese, formed into big wheels and dry-salted by rubbing, aged for up to two years, but also consumed when young. Turkey's northwestern provinces and Kars in eastern Turkey are famous for Kaşar. It is always present at breakfast and used in many dishes. Young Kaşar is indispensable for the ubiquitous *kaşarlı tost* (grilled cheese sandwiches) made at street corner kiosks and in school canteens. Other yellow cheeses include Kaşkaval and Gravyer. In Kars Gruyère cheese, known as Kars gravyeri, has an interesting connection with the Alps, made by Swiss families who settled in Kars when it was occupied by the Russians in the late nineteenth century.

Tulum peyniri is the most typical cheese of the nomadic Yörük culture, completing the top trio of Turkish cheeses. A pungent cheese with a crumbly texture, it is made in a *tulum*, a Turkish word meaning a whole animal skin used as a casing; known as touloumi in Greece. See TULUM. Salted curd cheese is pressed into a goatskin casing (tulum), hairy side out, and the aging process usually takes place in caves. Tulum cheeses are still predominantly made by Yörüks, semi-nomadic Turkish tribes in the mountainous regions of Anatolia, and to some extent in the Balkan peninsula. The name Yörük or Yürük derives from the verb *yürümek*, meaning to walk, referring to the wandering Turcoman (Türkmen) tribes. The most famous tulum is made in Erzincan in eastern Turkey, followed by the pleasantly moldy Divle Tulum made in Karaman in Central Anatolia and Kargı Tulum in Çorum (inner Black Sea region). In the Aegean region a type of tulum cheese matured in brine is made, the most noted being that of the Bergama region.

Apart from this top trio (Beyaz peynir, Kaşar peyniri, and Tulum peyniri), the most common cheeses are simple whey cheeses. Lor is a sweet whey cheese either unsalted or lightly salted, eaten as a dessert or breakfast treat with sour cherry or mulberry preserves or honey. See LOR. Çökelek is made from the whey remaining from making fatty cheeses. Both Lor and çökelek (sometimes called ekşimik, kesik) are widely used in flat bread wraps and *gözleme* (griddle pies). The crumbly blue cheese Konya küflü peyniri is a moldy version of çökelek and one of the best known of Turkey's relatively few blue cheeses.

String cheeses constitute another popular group, dil peyniri ("tongue cheese") being the most common. This mildly salted cheese has a milky taste with great melting properties. String cheeses of eastern Turkey such as Çeçil or Türkmen Saçağı are extremely salty and are soaked in warm water before eating; the latter is visually striking, resembling a cloud of tangled wires. The cheeses of the southeast are made by boiling the curd and then shaping it into balls, flat disk, or braids (in Turkish, örgü) in the southeastern region and are usually named after the province, such as Antep peyniri (Gaziantep), Urfa peyniri, Diyarbakır örgü peyniri, and Siirt örgü peyniri. Hellim of northern Cyprus belongs to the same category.

Eastern and, to a lesser extent, southeastern Turkey are home to salty herb cheeses, the most famous being Van otlu peyniri; made each spring with foraged greens, wild garlic, and chives. Smoked cheeses are rare, the most famous being isli peynir of Circassian origin.

See also KUPA PANIRI; LIGHVAN PANIRI; and MOTAL PANIRI.

Hayaloglu, Ali A., et al. "Cheeses of Turkey: 1. Varieties Ripened in Goat-Skin Bags." Le Lait 87, no. 2 (2007): 79–95.
Hayaloglu, Ali A., et al. "Cheeses of Turkey: 2. Varieties Ripened under Brine." Dairy Science Technology 88 (2009): 225–244. http://www.dairy-journal.org/articles/dst/pdf/2008/02/dst0733.pdf.
Hayaloglu, Ali A., and Patrick F. Fox. "Cheeses of Turkey: 3. Varieties Containing Herbs or Spices." Dairy Science Technology 88 (2008): 255–256. http://www.dairy-journal.org/articles/dst/pdf/2008/02/dst0734.pdf.
Swan, Suzanne. The Treasury of Turkish Cheeses. Istanbul: Boyut, 2004.
Ünsal, Artun. Süt Uyuyunca-Türkiye Peynirleri. Istanbul: Istanbul 1997.

Aylin Öney Tan

turning refers to the practice of turning over cheeses during their various stages of production and maturation. How often a cheese is turned, and when, is wholly dependent on the type of cheese in question. All cheeses have their associated turning "schedules" that aid drainage, promote fat and protein distribution, and help keep the cheeses symmetrical in shape. If a cheese is to be brine-bathed or dry-salted it will be turned during the process to ensure even salt distribution throughout.

Softer mold-ripened or washed-rind cheeses will be turned more than harder cheeses as they age due to their higher moisture content. This begins every hour or so when the cheeses are still fresh in their molds, gradually increasing to once every two or three days as they age. Mold-ripened cheeses will be rubbed and patted to inhibit extreme mold growth and help prevent the cheeses sticking to surfaces, a problem when aging such cheeses on mats or steel racks. Although less likely to stick to surfaces than their bloomy counterparts, washed rinds will be turned to allow for even rind development and to reduce the risk of the rind becoming too wet or "rotten."

Harder pressed cheeses require less attention and past a certain age will generally be turned weekly, although "wet bottoms" can still be an issue if a cheese is neglected. Most farmstead cheeses are turned by hand, which, despite being labor-intensive, allows cheesemakers and affineurs to keep a close eye on how a cheese is developing. For larger operations turning machines are now available to turn anything, from racks of small, soft cheeses to pallets of block Cheddar, and even robots that can care for vast maturing rooms of Gruyère, Comté, or Parmigiano Reggiano.

See also MATURING.

Kindstedt, Paul. American Farmstead Cheese: The Complete Guide to Making and Selling Artisan Cheese. White River Junction, Vt.: Chelsea Green, 2005.

Chris George

turnsole was a plant-based dye that was used to illuminate medieval manuscripts and was also used in Holland during the nineteenth century and earlier to color the rinds of Edam cheese red. It was prepared by pressing the juice out of the berries of the Chrozophora tinctoria plant and dipping linen rags into the juice until the rags became saturated. After the rags were dried in the sun, they were hung over a tub filled with a solution of a small amount of lime dissolved in urine (preferably urine obtained from a healthy man who had been drinking wine). Ammonia vapors rising from the urine turned the turnsole pigments in the rags to violet. The plant Chrozophora tinctoria was raised in southern France, where the turnsole rags were prepared and then exported to Holland. Edam cheeses were rubbed with turnsole rags repeatedly until they acquired a glowing red color. The red color of the turnsole did not penetrate into the cheese but remained on the rind, where it imparted a very distinctive appearance that made Edam cheese instantly recognizable in the marketplace. The dye also provided a measure of resistance to insects, helping to maintain the integrity of the rind.

During the twentieth century, wax coatings, and later latex coatings, that were used to protect the surface of Edam cheese were colored with red dye, no doubt to mimic the familiar red color of the traditional turnsole-rubbed Edam. Edam is still colored red to this day.

See also EDAM and NETHERLANDS.

Kindstedt, Paul. *Cheese and Culture: A History of Cheese and Its Place in Western Civilization*. White River Junction, Vt.: Chelsea Green, 2012.

Paul S. Kindstedt

Turoš

See CONE-SHAPED CHEESES.

twarog

See POLAND.

typing

See TAXONOMY.

tyrophile denotes a person who is fond of cheese or who holds cheese dear. From the ancient Greek *tyros,* or cheese, and the Greek suffix *-phile*, the term literally translates as "cheese lover." The most commonly understood contemporary meaning of this term denotes cheese aficionados, cheese critics, or, in negative terms—cheese snobs. Tyrophiles, sometimes spelled "turophiles," are individuals invested in cheese appreciation for personal or professional motivations. These producers, purveyors, and consumers are important in the development of cheese connoisseurship.

Tyrophile interests center on sensory and quality enjoyment of cheese and expand to include cheese and dairy technology, history, and politics. These pursuits involve describing the organoleptic facets of cheese as well as taking interest in the legislation and regulations affecting cheese production and sales. Such legal curiosities include the assignment of protected designations of origin (PDO) and government restrictions on raw-milk cheese production. These enthusiasts recognize cheese as a cultural touchstone and testament to agricultural traditions and technology.

Tyrophile culture manifests in celebrity cheese personalities as well as various media. An extensive network of Internet databases and blogs focus on cheese and draw the interest of novice and expert devotees. Cheese lovers congregate within cheese guilds and national and international organizations, under the auspices of which they produce competitions and celebrations observing the importance and pleasures of cheese. The cannon of tyrophilic literature includes scientific as well as cultural-historical writing exemplified by Patrick Rance, a British cheese purveyor, writer, and enthusiast.

Rance, Patrick. *The Great British Cheese Book*. London: Macmillan, 1982.

Brent A. Wasser

A **tyrosemiophile** is a person who collects the round, colorful labels affixed to wooden boxes of Camembert cheese. These labels are about 4 inches (11 centimeters) in diameter, slightly larger than a beer coaster, and sell at antique stores and flea markets for prices that range from a euro each to upward of a hundred euros, depending on their rarity.

The earliest Camembert labels date to around 1887, and the hobby of collecting them was described as early as May 1914 in the *Bulletin de Vieux Papier*. At some point in the first half of the twentieth century collectors gave themselves the donnish name tyrosemiophiles ("tyro" meaning cheese in Greek, "seme" meaning sign, and "phile" meaning lover). In 1951 avid collectors formed the Société de Tyrosémiophilie, with the Club Tyrosémiophile de l'Ouest (Western Tyrosemiophile Club) following in 1960, and its sister organization the Club Tyrosémiophilie de France in 1969. Thomas Pynchon's 1963 novel *V.* mentions the hobby in

Camembert cheese labels are famously eclectic, colorful, and collectible. In this label Pierrot, a stock character of pantomime typically depicted as a naïve and foolish clown, thinks he can reach the moon on a ladder. In the background is Gitonnière Castle, in Touraine. PHOTO © PVDE / BRIDGEMAN IMAGES

chapter 15, where "a group of Tyrosemiophiles (collectors of labels on French cheese boxes)" mingle at a Washington, D.C., party with an inventor celebrating his seventy-second patent rejection.

While the hobby of collecting any cheese label does have a name—laclabphily—Camembert labels overwhelmingly capture the interest of collectors. What is the particular appeal of these labels, stuck on the poplar wood pillboxes of a pungent Normandy cheese? Perhaps it is the extraordinary variety of scenes they capture. There are the expected images of dairymaids, shepherds, and Normande cows that tie Camembert to an idealized pastoral France. But then there are the unexpected and the outright curious: scenes of the launch of Sputnik and man's first steps on the moon, the Concorde in supersonic flight, the Le Mans car race, Mother Goose and the three blind mice, Romeo presenting Camembert to his Juliet, King Kong baring his teeth and protectively

clutching a Camembert box, and even a cubist homage to Picasso. One 1970s label showed a nude woman strategically covered by the name of the producer, Fromince; it stirred up enough controversy that later versions clothed her. Taken together, the Camembert labels are a fascinating study of twentieth-century world history, national (and local) French pride, popular culture, changing social mores, and the enduring power of myths and fairy tales.

But the colorful Camembert labels also belie a sad story about the decline of Camembert production. In the early twentieth century there were hundreds of Camembert producers in Normandy, all selling their cheese into the same export markets, particularly the United States. How did they differentiate their products? In part through kitschy and memorable labels. When the United States banned young raw-milk cheeses for import in 1949, American companies soon flooded the market with pasteurized, mass-produced "Camembert." See 60-DAY AGING RULE and RAW-MILK CHEESES. The number of traditional Camembert producers quickly dwindled, and today 90 percent of Camembert cheese is produced using pasteurized milk, without the AOP (appellation d'origine protegée) label of origin. The reality is that groups like the Club Tyrosémiophile de France, which maintains a quarterly bulletin and a membership that regularly meets to compare and exchange labels, collect evidence of the golden age of Camembert.

See also CAMEMBERT DE NORMANDIE and TYRO-PHILE.

Boisard, Pierre. *Camembert: A National Myth.* Berkeley: University of California Press, 2003.
Camembert Museum. http://www.camembert -museum.com.
Club Tyrosémiophile de France. http://club -tyrosemiophile.fr/actus.
Le Tyrosémiophile. http://www.letyrosemiophile .com.
Pynchon, Thomas. *V.* Philadelphia: Lippincott, 1963.

Max P. Sinsheimer

ultrafiltration (UF) is a macromolecular siev-
ing technique in which hydrostatic pressure forces
milk across a membrane, separating the fat, protein,
and insoluble salts in the milk from the soluble salts,
nonprotein nitrogen, and much of the water. Its development in dairying started at the end of the 1960s
both in the United States, to find a solution to the
pollution caused by the discharge of cheese whey into
rivers, and in France, to improve the cheesemaking
process. Indeed, making cheese from milk requires
three major steps: coagulation, specific concentration
of fat and proteins, and biotransformation of milk
components through acidification and ripening. Differential concentration of fat and proteins is traditionally done by drainage of a heterogeneous mixture of
solids (curd particles) and liquid (whey), which leads
to cheeses with variable composition, size, and quality.
Innovations proposed by Maubois et al. (1969) made
it possible to achieve different concentrations of fat
and proteins in the cheese milk through the use of a
UF membrane with a molecular cut-off weight between 20,000 and 100,000 Da. The aqueous phase
of milk (water, lactose, and soluble mineral salts) is
separated, and the liquid retained by the membrane,
named liquid pre-cheese (LPC), has, progressively,
a composition similar to fresh, soft, and then semihard cheese. The addition of rennet coagulates the
LPC, and the resulting curds are ready for the ripening step. This process has spread throughout the
world because of its numerous advantages: an 18
percent yield increase due to the retention in cheese
of whey proteins, recovery of the curd-forming
ability of sterilized milk, savings of rennet and other
cheese aids, and ease of mechanization and even
robotization of molding equipment.

See also MICROFILTRATION.

Kosikowski, Frank V. "Cheesemaking by Ultrafiltration."
    Journal of Dairy Science 57 (1974): 488–491.
Maubois, J. L., G. Mocquot, and L. Vassal. Procédé de
    traitement du lait et de sous-produits laitiers. French
    Patent 2,052,121, filed 18 July 1969, and issued
    9 April 1971.
Maubois, J. L., G. Mocquot, and L. Vassal. Manufacture
    of Cheese from Ultrafiltered Milk. US Patent
    3914435-A, filed 5 January 1973, and issued 21
    October 1975.

Jean Louis Maubois

The **United Kingdom** has given the world some
of its most renowned cheeses—cheeses that have
evolved dramatically over their long history and continue to do so. Although the classic British cheeses,
from buttery-textured Stilton to crumbly Cheshire,
may be superficially quite distinct from one another,
they share certain basic elements in their production. To varying degrees, all incorporate both curd
drainage and acidification before molding, making
them relatively high in acidity and friable compared
with their Continental cooked and pressed cousins.
Modern versions are also generally curd-salted, a technique that involves the even mixing of salt through
chopped or ground-up ("milled") curd before it is
transferred to the molds, helping to ensure even distribution of salt throughout these bulky cheeses.

Early History

The first evidence of British cheesemaking dates
back to the Roman occupation almost two thou-

One of the more unusual annual traditions in England is the Cooper's Hill Cheese-Rolling and Wake in Gloucester. A 7–9-pound (3–4-kilogram) Double Gloucester cheese is rolled down Cooper's Hill, and the competitors race down after it. The first person to the bottom of the hill wins the wheel of cheese. © PAUL TOWNSEND

sand years ago. For the Romans and the Saxons, cheese was an important food, and documentary evidence shows that rennet from various ruminant sources, as well as vegetable coagulants, were used to make cheeses during the summer months.

Much of the early cheese, particularly in the more rugged northern regions of Britain, was made from ewe's milk. Within the manorial system, production was centralized, with agricultural laborers such as dairymaids and herdsmen playing an important role in the overall productivity of the estate. Cheese was also made within priories and monasteries, whose members are thought to have brought expertise in cheesemaking with them from France. Very little trade in cheese existed; most was consumed for sustenance within its area of production. See MANORIAL CHEESEMAKERS and MONASTIC CHEESEMAKING.

By the seventeenth century, sheep had largely given way to cows as the dominant choice for dairying, particularly in areas whose lush pastures and flatter landscape could support larger herds. Progressively more cheese was sent from farms to supply new and distant urban markets, and cheeses such as Cheshire, which was sent to London by sea and canal, grew rapidly in production to feed the burgeoning demand. In the mid-1680s there were more than four thousand individual producers of Cheshire, with an average size of only five cows per herd, each making one moderate-size cheese per farm per day. In other regions, particularly the Southwest, dairy farmers from a village would combine their cows' milk to make much larger cheeses of up to 120 pounds, the largest of which could be kept for up to five years.

Although cheesemakers in the richer and more accessible regions oriented themselves toward larger-scale production and distant markets, in more isolated rural areas cheeses such as Wensleydale and Caerphilly continued as subsistence foods made on every farm. See WENSLEYDALE and CAERPHILLY.

The United Kingdom is renowned for its large, hard cheeses, but soft cheeses, also known as "cream cheeses," were also part of the classic English repertoire. These could be made either with or without added cream, and involved the slow drainage of sweet curd within a cloth-lined mold. They were made throughout the country, from York to Bath, but the best-known was a cheese called Slipcote, which a 1935 chronicler described as "small, and when mature rather like a Camembert, . . . its name derived from the ease with which its coat or rind detached itself from the mellow ooziness within" (Burdett 1935, p. 30). The name "cream cheese" was often also applied to blue-veined cheeses such as Stilton and Cotherstone, the latter of which, according to an 1861 article in the *Journal of the Royal Agricultural Society*, "more than any other English cheese . . . resembles the foreign

Rochefort [Roquefort]" (Voelcker 1861, p. 39). See CREAM CHEESE.

Codification and Industrialization

From the mid-seventeenth to the early nineteenth century, Cheshire was the predominant English cheese, consumed in vastly larger quantities than Cheddar. However, by 1896, when James Long and John Benson wrote their guide to cheese and cheese-making, Cheddar reigned supreme. Its rise during the mid-to-late nineteenth century was largely due to the work of a generation of scientific innovators, including Joseph Harding, Theodore Candy, and Henry and Edith Cannon. These cheesemakers and teachers worked to standardize and codify Cheddar making, to improve the overall standard of production, and to spread the gospel of consistency and improvement. See HARDING, JOSEPH.

Cheddar itself traveled well, and so did its method of production, which spread to the United States, Canada, New Zealand, and Australia. By the end of the nineteenth century, aided by decreasing transport costs, cheap imported Cheddar from factories in the United States and the British dominions was being imported into the United Kingdom in volumes far greater than that produced domestically. In 1913 fully 82 percent of the cheese consumed within the United Kingdom was imported. British farmhouse cheesemakers were under tremendous economic strain, which was further exacerbated by a labor shortage caused by migration from the countryside to fulfill demand for industrial workers in the cities. Farm cheesemaking gave way to liquid milk production, both to supply local cheese factories with milk for processing and to provide an expanding urban labor force with fresh milk for their tea. Better cash flow also offered an enticement to abandon farmhouse cheesemaking in favor of liquid milk production.

If the economic changes of the early twentieth century were difficult for farmhouse cheesemakers, the two World Wars and the British Ministry of Food's program of rationing, which ran from 1940 to 1954, were devastating. Production, maturation, and distribution of cheese were all brought under government control. Every dairy farm was required to sell its liquid milk to the government, whose objective was to process this valuable resource into edible cheese as efficiently as possible. If resources were wasted, the nation might starve, so cheese production was standardized. The production of soft or "luxury" cheeses, including Stilton, became illegal, and loose-textured cheeses, which were difficult to cut without wastage, were tightened up. This cheese industry played an important part in feeding a country at war, but it almost destroyed indigenous British cheeses in the process. See WORLD WAR I; WORLD WAR II; and MILK MARKETING BOARDS.

British Cheese Today

In the decades that followed, pressure from supermarkets for cheap, uniform cheeses not unlike those made during the era of rationing pushed the few who had returned to farmhouse cheese production closer and closer to the brink. In *The Great British Cheese Book,* published in 1982, Patrick Rance, a retired Army major and a shopkeeper, began to awaken British consumers to a great cheese tradition on the verge of extinction. He exhorted his readers, "Your clamorous protests alone can save our Real Cheese from being lost forever in the rising flood of plastic-smothered insipidity" (Rance, p. vi). Gradually other merchants also began to search out and celebrate the few remaining British cheeses of integrity. See RANCE, PATRICK.

Today farmhouse cheese production in the United Kingdom is experiencing a renaissance. As in the United States and Australia, new entrants are experimenting with the production of a wide range of cheeses beyond the original styles, ranging from lactic goat's cheeses to soft bloomy-rind and washed-rind styles. These producers are experiencing great success, not only among Britons eager to support local food production, but also in export markets ranging from continental Europe to North America and the antipodes.

Furthermore, a new generation of British cheesemakers is beginning to recognize the riches bequeathed to them by their ancestors, who have left tantalizing evidence of the fascinating and unique range of cheeses once produced in the United Kingdom. This next wave is beginning to explore the techniques of their predecessors and to reconsider the essential nature of cheeses that have until recently been taken for granted. Much remains to be rediscovered.

See also CHEDDAR; CHESHIRE CHEESE (U.K.); CLOTHBOUND CHEESES; GLOUCESTER; HODGSON,

RANDOLPH; LANCASHIRE; MILLING; NEAL'S YARD
DAIRY; STICHELTON; STILTON; and TERRITORIAL.

Burdett, Osbert. *A Little Book of Cheese*. London:
    G. Howe, 1935.
Cheke, Valerie. *The Story of Cheese-Making in Britain*.
    London: Routledge & Kegan Paul, 1959.
Foster, Charles F. *Cheshire Cheese and Farming in the
    North West in the 17th & 18th Centuries*. Northwich,
    U.K.: Arley Hall, 1998.
Long, James, and John Benson. *Cheese and Cheese-
    Making, Butter and Milk*. London: Chapman and
    Hall, 1896. Facsimile reprinted by Applewood
    Books (2007).
Rance, Patrick. *The Great British Cheese Book*. London:
    Macmillan, 1982.
Voelcker, Augustus. "On the Composition of Cheese,
    and on Practical Mistakes in Cheese-Making." *Journal
    of the Royal Agricultural Society of England* 22 (1861):
    29–69.

Bronwen Percival

The **United States** has a fascinating four hundred year history of cheese. From the seventeenth century beginnings in New England to the rise of industrial production in the mid-to-late nineteenth-century to the late twentieth century renaissance of artisan cheese, the country experienced wide-ranging changes in scale, quality, and practices.

America's cheese roots trace back to Britain's East Anglia, an area renowned for its dairies and cheese-making. East Anglian cheesemakers produced large, hard-pressed, firm cheeses to sell in London. Transported by wagon, the cheeses could withstand the rough journey to urban markets.

In 1623, Pilgrims from East Anglia brought the first dairy cows to Plymouth Colony to make butter and cheese. After establishing the Massachusetts Bay Colony in 1629, East Anglian Puritans arrived, often with wheels of aged cheeses. See PURITANS. These settlers, with experience in cheesemaking and marketing, made butter and cheese valuable components of the local economy and Massachusetts became the nation's cheese hub. New England farm women, instilled with their East Anglian ancestors' excellent technical and marketing skills, produced cheese in their kitchens for regional consumption and export. Boston merchants shipped hard-pressed farmstead cheeses to the Caribbean; by 1800, nearly 1 million pounds (453,592 kilograms) of New England cheese reached the islands annually.

English settlers introduced wheat cultivation that characterized southern New England farms for decades. However, without proper management, wheat exhausts soil nutrients and leaves behind depleted land. Dairies replaced wheat in New England and growing good grass became the foundation for excellent milk. The region expanded its cheese-making, while production remained focused on small farms.

Over time, as wheat cultivation moved west and impacted soils, dairies followed. Production of pressed cheeses often replaced the former wheat farms. During the eighteenth century, New England cheesemakers established dairies in New York and Vermont, where they replicated the pressed, firm wheels from their former homesteads.

Eighteenth- and early nineteenth-century American cheesemakers, following technological and production changes in England, modified their procedures to make what became known as Cheddar. To prevent cheeses drying out during aging and becoming unduly affected by temperature differences and longer travel distances, cloth-wrapped and waxed Cheddar cheese became the norm in the United States. By 1850, the nation produced nearly 100 million pounds (45 million kilograms) of cheese with New York 50 million pounds (23 million kilograms), Ohio 21 million pounds (10 million kilograms), and Vermont (9 million pounds (4 million kilograms) the top three producers. Remarkably, the entire output came from small farms. See CHEDDAR.

While much of America's immigration and subsequent movement across the country was an east to west phenomenon, Spain's earlier conquest of Central America and the Pacific Coast introduced cows and goats to these regions. In the eighteenth century, Britain's Hudson's Bay Company brought similar animals to the Pacific Northwest and British Columbia. Throughout the nineteenth century, goat milk was prevalent along the West Coast and by the early twentieth century, goat cheese appeared.

The 1850s marked a high point of handmade cheese from small farms. In 1851 Jesse Williams, a skilled cheesemaker, opened the nation's first cheese factory in Rome, New York. Williams bought milk from neighboring farms and developed a rapid process for making large, pressed wheels. The factory gained an immediate reputation for quality cheese and fair prices to local farmers. It spawned dozens, then hundreds, and finally thousands of small to medium size factories across the country making an array of Cheddar-style cheeses. See WILLIAMS, JESSE.

By 1890, farmstead cheese was a memory. A further outcome was both direct and cultural; farm women cheesemakers could no longer compete with large-scale production and most small-scale kitchen enterprises disappeared. Moreover, Americans viewed physical work in cheese factories as incompatible for women and consequently, despite their skills, they were unwelcome. See GENDER.

During the nineteenth and early twentieth centuries, millions of European immigrants arrived in America. While most stayed in cities, many German, Swiss, and Italian farmers and dairymen settled in Wisconsin, Minnesota, and California. They created familiar cheeses from Europe like Liederkranz and Brick (Limburger), Swiss (Emmentaler), and dry Monterey Jack (Italian Tomme). See BRICK; SWISS CHEESE; and JACK.

The early twentieth century saw the advent of processed cheese, an invention of J. L. Kraft and Brothers. During World War I, huge amounts of Kraft cheese packed in cans went to Europe to feed American troops. After World War II, large manufacturers dominated the market with such pasteurized milk cheeses as Brie, Cheddar, cream cheese, Gouda, mozzarella, and Velveeta. Industrial cheese production drove most remaining small to medium factories out of business. See INDUSTRIAL; KRAFT FOODS; PASTEURIZED PROCESS CHEESES; WORLD WAR I; and WORLD WAR II.

The renaissance of American handmade, artisan cheese coincides with fundamental cultural, economic, and social changes often started by the Baby Boom generation. Beginning in the late 1960s, the landscape of food began to evolve as young people, traveling to Europe, enjoyed new foods, returned home, and looked for similar American-made products, most of which didn't exist. Considerable opportunities for farmers and consumers emerged out of soaring demand for unique products and organic foods, the arrival of new immigrants that fueled an expansion of ethnic products and tastes, and the greater levels of disposable income. Since the 1990s, national food trends have embraced a diversity of regional and locally grown fresh foods. Consumers demanded good tasting, healthy food from small-scale, often family farm enterprises that practiced sustainable agriculture. Public pressure compelled large, multichain supermarkets all the way down to small retail shops to change their buying practices. Artisan

cheese with distinctive flavors, perceived health benefits, and connections to land and animals attracted considerable consumer interest. See ARTISANAL.

Many artisan companies based their first efforts on European types; American cheesemakers went to England, France, or Italy to learn from traditional craftsmen. With growing experience and skill, American cheeses evolved and today compare favorably to their European counterparts. Product names also changed. For decades, large manufacturers and artisan producers used well-known European names like Gouda, Gorgonzola, Parmesan, and Munster. Today, most American cheesemakers identify their products by location, historical context, or other unique identity. Examples include Humboldt Fog from Cypress Grove Chèvre; Bayley Hazen Blue from Jasper Hill Farm; Claire de Lune from Pure Luck Dairy; or Timber Coulee Reserve from Hidden Springs Creamery. See HUMBOLDT FOG and CELLARS AT JASPER HILL.

Beginning in 1980, America's artisan cheese community experienced explosive growth in the number of producers and products with corresponding transformation and improvements in quality and safety. In the late 1970s, approximately 48 artisan producers existed, including a handful with roots in the nineteenth century. By 1990, the number increased to 89 and by 2000 stood at 173. Six years later, artisan businesses grew dramatically to 402. Between 2006 and 2012, the number of cheesemakers more than doubled to 826; in some states, artisan cheese companies doubled or tripled in number (Roberts, 2007).

During this period, cow creameries accounted for nearly 60 percent of all cheese companies and goat dairies, playing an important role in the expansion, registered between 40–44 percent. Sheep milk cheesemakers comprise the remainder (Roberts, 2007).

The overall growth is astounding, especially during the recession of 2008–2013, when hundreds of new businesses opened. While assuming some were planned before 2008, small value-added dairies offered a viable alternative for farmers and new entrepreneurs during a difficult economy. Since 2006, the rate of business growth indicates on average approximately eighty new cheese businesses opened annually. Concurrently, at least forty companies closed since 2000, a reminder that competition, quality standards, consistency, and distribution are critical factors to success or failure.

While states like Vermont, Wisconsin, and California have many artisan cheesemakers and receive well-deserved attention, New York and Pennsylvania count for nearly a hundred producers each and rank number one and two nationally. Maine ranks third with more than seventy producers. Beyond this group, North Carolina, Virginia, Texas, and Washington stand out as important centers for artisan cheese.

In 1983, Cornell University's Dr. Frank Kosikowski, together with dozens of artisan producers, founded the American Cheese Society as a national grassroots organization to educate small cheesemakers, while promoting great cheese to consumers. See AMERICAN CHEESE SOCIETY and KOSIKOWSKI, FRANK. Equally important, since the 1990s, a wealth of books, magazines, and other media attention propelled American artisan cheese to the forefront of the contemporary food movement.

The renaissance also reflects a return of women to the cheese room. Beginning with such 1970s artisans as California's Laura Chenel; Maine's Marjorie Lupien (Mystique Cheese) and Barbara Brooks (Seal Cove Farm); and Washington's Sally Jackson, women established new and very successful farmstead cheese businesses. Many of these pioneers raised goats and introduced Americans to chèvre and other goat's milk cheeses. Their presence and leadership created a welcoming environment for women in agriculture and contributed to the rapid expansion of new enterprises after 1980. By 2006, women owned or operated more than half the country's artisan cheese businesses. As the artisan cheese community grew, women cheesemakers stepped into leadership roles in local and national advocacy and trade organizations. See AMERICAN "GOAT LADIES."

Over the past decade, another critical element driving new businesses expansion is the movement of young people into farming and food production with many young entrepreneurs making cheese and other value-added dairy products. Artisan cheese continues to experience growth in consumer demand at state, regional, and national levels. Beyond local retail and direct retailers, supermarkets like Wegmans, Whole Foods Markets, and Trader Joe's, and even conventional chain supermarkets sell artisan cheese.

See also CALIFORNIA; ILLINOIS; NEW YORK; VERMONT; and WISCONSIN.

Chenel, Laura, and Linda Siegfried. *America's Country Cheese: Cooking with America's Specialty and Farmstead Cheeses*. Reading, Mass.: Addison-Wesley, 1989.
Jenkins, Steven. *Cheese Primer*. New York: Workman, 1996.
Kindstedt, Paul S. *American Farmstead Cheese: The Complete Guide to Making and Selling Artisan Cheeses*. White River Junction, Vt.: Chelsea Green, 2005. See pp. 1–37.
Kindstedt, Paul S. *Cheese and Culture: A History of Cheese and Its Place in Western Civilization*. White River Junction, Vt.: Chelsea Green, 2012. See pp. 183–226.
McCalman, Max, and David Gibbons. *The Cheese Plate*. New York: Clarkson Potter, 2002.
McCalman, Max, and David Gibbons. *Mastering Cheese: Lessons for Connoisseurship from a Maître Fromager*. New York: Clarkson Potter, 2009.
Parr, Tami J. *Pacific Northwest Cheese: A History*. Corvallis: Oregon State University Press, 2013.
Paxson, Heather. *The Life of Cheese: Crafting Food and Value in America*. Berkeley: University of California Press. 2013.
Rahmer, Frederick A. *Jesse Williams Cheesemaker*. Rome, N.Y.: F. A. Rahmer, 1971.
Roberts, Jeffrey P. *The Atlas of American Artisan Cheese*. White River Junction, Vt.: Chelsea Green, 2007.
Werlin, Laura. *The New American Cheese: Profiles of America's Greatest Cheesemakers and Recipes for Cooking with Cheese*. New York: Stewart, Tabori & Chang. 2000.
Wolf, Clark. *American Cheeses: The Best Regional, Artisan, and Farmhouse Cheeses, Who Makes Them, and Where to Find Them*. New York: Simon & Schuster, 2008.

Jeff Roberts

The **United States Department of Agriculture** (USDA) is the US federal executive department responsible for developing and executing federal policy on farming, agriculture, forestry, and food. In 1862, President Abraham Lincoln signed into law an act of Congress establishing the USDA. At a time when almost half of all Americans lived on farms, Lincoln would later refer to the USDA as "the People's Department" with the vision of touching the lives of every American, every day. Today, the USDA continues to support the agricultural economy in the United States through efforts to strengthen rural communities; protect and conserve natural resources; and to provide a safe, sufficient, and nutritious food supply.

The USDA is composed of several agencies responsible for marketing; consumer dietary guidance; food safety; foreign markets; conservation; risk management; rural development; and the health and care of plants, animals, and forests and grasslands, among others. The department also conducts and invests in research, development, and outreach with the goals of mitigating animal and plant diseases as well as increasing productivity, sustainability, and product quality and safety. While the Food and Drug Administration (FDA) is responsible for ensuring that the bulk of the nation's food supply is wholesome, safe, and properly labeled, the Food Safety and Inspection Service under the USDA is primarily responsible for meat, poultry, and processed eggs.

The Dairy Programs of the Agricultural Marketing Service (AMS) of the USDA develop quality grade standards for agricultural commodities, administer marketing regulatory programs, as well as marketing agreements and orders thereby facilitating the efficient marketing of milk and dairy products. The AMS also purchases a variety of domestically produced and processed commodity food products thereby providing a domestic outlet for surplus products through the delivery to schools, food banks, and households throughout the United States. Cheese and cheese products with commercial item descriptions (CID) for use in the commodity program include reduced fat Cheddar, pizza cheese blends, lite mozzarella, queso blanco, as well as cottage, cream, Neufchatel, and related products. The CIDs include commodity specifications as well as container and packaging requirements. Under this program, cheese and its constituent ingredients delivered to the government, must be manufactured in plants inspected and approved by the Dairy Grading Branch of AMS. See COMMODITY CHEESE.

The AMS Dairy Grading Program offers the dairy industry marketing tools to provide buyers and sellers with an impartial assessment of product quality. Dairy product grade standards are official descriptions that measure quality based on characteristics important to the consumer, such as taste, texture, or appearance. Graded products meeting these standards are eligible to bear official grade shields. For dairy products not covered by a grade standard, quality specifications establish minimum acceptable requirements. Products meeting the requirement of the specification may bear an official quality shield to serve as a guide to quality for consumers. Inspection and grading services through the AMS are offered to the dairy industry on a voluntary basis. Once an inspection shows that a plant has successfully met the requirements outlined in USDA's General Specifications for Approved Dairy Plants the facility can qualify for commodity pro-

grams as well as other services including grading, sampling, testing, and certification of its product.

United States Department of Agriculture. http://www .usda.gov.

Dennis D'Amico

unripened cheeses

See FRESH CHEESES.

Urdă is a traditional cheese that is made during the summer in Greece, mainly in North Pindos (region of Konitsa, community of Aetomilitsa, height 1,500 meters) from sheep or goat whey. Whey cheeses are produced in many eastern Mediterranean countries under various names. Urdă cheese produced in Greece has many similarities with mizithra cheese, but it is creamier, with a delicate texture, and has superior sensory qualities. The surface of the mature cheeses is yellowish, the shape is spherical, and the weight is about 1.8 pounds (800 grams). Its high quality, special taste and firm texture make it hugely popular among the regional consumers. Currently, this cheese with ancient roots—there are written reports of Urdă cheese from 1830 to 1831—are manufactured chiefly on the farm level, although an increasing fraction has been associated with small industrial dairies.

To manufacture Urdă, a hard or semihard cheese is first made with a procedure that includes "beating"

Urdă, a traditional Greek cheese made during the summer months, being washed with brine to inhibit the growth of molds. © ELENI PAPPA

the coagulum in order to fortify the whey with fat. As a consequence, the whey obtained by this technique is especially rich in fat. The sheep's or goat's whey is filtrated and is heated gradually under continuous stirring to 131°F (55°C). At this temperature, sheep's or goat's milk is added to the whey. The heating under stirring is continued, and at 158°F (70°C) salt is added. The heating is continued again under gentle stirring up to 176°F (80°C). When small curd particles of whey proteins appear, stirring is stopped. The curd is cooked at this temperature for twenty minutes and then transferred to pierced stainless steel molds with cheesecloths inside them. The cheesecloths are tied up, and the cheesecloths with the cheeses inside them are removed from the molds. The cheeses are left to drain in the cheesecloths at about 66°F (19°C) and 70–75 percent relative humidity (RH) until the next day, when the cheeses are washed with brine and then dry-salted. Then the cheeses are left to ripen on wooden shelves at about 66°F (19°C) and 70–75 percent RH. During ripening they are turned over daily, and when necessary, their surface is brushed with brine to inhibit the growth of molds. After twenty-five days, the cheeses are transferred to a 41°F (5°C) storage area, where they are kept for 360 days.

Urdă cheese can be consumed from the first day of its manufacture (the flocculated curd is eaten fresh, preferably when still warm), or it can be preserved for up to a year (for use as a grating cheese in the summer), without losing its well-accepted organoleptic characteristics. Otherwise, it can be cooked in a frying pan and eaten with honey as a dessert. The main biochemical characteristics of Urdă cheese vary depending on the level of maturation (ripening). At 90 days, Urdă contains on average 30 percent moisture, 44.5 percent fat, 20 percent protein, and 3.5 percent salt.

See also GREECE and WHEY.

Alichanidis, E., and A. Polychroniadou. "Characteristics of Major Traditional Regional Cheese Varieties of East-Mediterranean Countries: A Review." *Dairy Science and Technology* 88 (2008): 495–510.

Anifantakis, E. M. *Greek Cheeses: A Tradition of Centuries.* Athens: National Dairy Committee of Greece, 1991.

Eekhof-Stork, N. *The World Atlas of Cheese.* New York: Paddington, 1976, p. 136.

Thesprotos, K., and A. Psalidas. *Geography of Albania and Epirus.* Ioannina, Greece: Society of Epirot Studies, 1964.

Zygourias, N. *The Milk Industry.* 2d ed. Athens: Greek Ministry of Agriculture, 1952. In Greek.

Eleni C. Pappa

Vacherin du Haut-Doubs

See MONT D'OR.

Vacherin Mont d'Or

See MONT D'OR and SWITZERLAND.

vacuuming is a technique used during the maturation of many long-aged natural-rind cheeses as a means of removing cheese mites and their eggs from the cheese and the aging environment. This technique is especially common in the maturation of "bandaged" or clothbound Cheddars and other cheeses that are not brine washed. Historically many producers of clothbound Cheddars and other natural-rind cheeses used methyl bromide, an agricultural pesticide, as a tool in controlling cheese mites in aging rooms. However, most countries have now banned this practice, leaving producers of these cheese styles more manual approaches to mite control.

Vacuuming involves the use of a powerful vacuum attached to a hose with an attached brush that is used to dislodge mold and mites from the rind of a cheese. Alternately "down draft" tables employ cyclonic vacuums to create a draft that pulls mold, dust, and mites down through slats in a work surface. These are collected and contained, removed from the ripening rooms, and disposed of. The use of vacuums is an effective means of limiting the populations of cheese mites in a ripening room but must be done on a routine basis in order to properly disrupt the reproduction cycle by reducing the population of mature cheese mites. While vacuuming may be an effective

means of limiting the total population of cheese mites in a ripening room, it is not a means of eliminating cheese mites from the aging environment.

See also CHEESES MITES and CLOTHBOUND CHEESES.

Carpenter, Jeanne. "On Location: Fighting Cheese Mites at Quickes Dairy." *Cheese Underground*, 3 April 2014. http://cheeseunderground.blogspot.com/2014/04/on-location-fighting-cheese-mites-at.html.
Donnelly, Catherine W. "Mold Ripened Cheese." In *Cheese and Microbes*, pp. 111–113. Washington, D.C.: ASM Press, 2014.

Mateo Kehler

Valdeon is a PDO (protected designation of origin) Spanish blue cheese from Posada de Valdeón in the Picos de Europa Mountains of northern Spain. This is a region particularly known for its blue cheeses. Valdeón is a semifirm blue cheese. Each wheel is wrapped in sycamore leaves. Although this natural covering does not give any additional flavor to the cheese it allows the rind to breathe and prevents off flavors.

Valdeón is made from predominantly cow's milk, as are most of the blue cheeses in the region; however it also has an addition of 5 percent goat's milk which adds a touch of acidity to the cheese. Valdeón also uses a small amount of ewe's milk at certain times of the year. The cow's milk comes from the Parda breed, and the goat's milk comes from the Florida breed, both of which are kept outdoors for seven months of the year. The milk used may be either pasteurized or raw.

Valdeón is dry-salted with rock salt, and cave-aged between two and four months before being wrapped in foil in most cases; however some are wrapped in sterilized sycamore leaves called "plageru," a traditional practice that aids in handling. The cheeses have blue, and occasionally green, veins from the presence of *Penicillium roqueforti* and the paste is an ivory color with a buttery texture, gentle spice, and a good balance of salt. Valdeón eats well alone, although it can also be used as a welcome addition in cooking. It is best paired with a sweet white wine, for example a Muscatel.

See also BLUE CHEESES and SPAIN.

Harbutt, Juliet. *World Cheese Book*. London: Dorling Kindersley, 2009, p. 166.

McMalman, Max, and David Gibbons. *The Cheese Plate*. New York: Clarkson Potter 2002, pp. 211–212.

Emma Young

Valençay is a soft goat's milk cheese with a square-base flattened pyramid shape and a thin ash-covered rind that obtained PDO (protected designation of origin) status in 1998. Originating from the province of Berry in central France, the Pyramide de Valençay is characterized by its harmonious shape, its regular, light gray to blue-gray thin rind, and a smooth and homogeneous porcelain white interior. Centered on the Indre department, the PDO area also includes a few communes in the Indre-et-Loire, Cher, and Loir-et-Cher. With countryside specificities, alternating woodland and crop growing, this terroir gives the Valençay all of its organoleptic qualities.

Legend has it that the shape of the cheese is due to the Prince de Talleyrand. Originally the Valençay was tall and pyramid-shaped. To avoid reminding the emperor Napoleon of his defeat in Egypt, Talleyrand cut the tops off the cheeses, and ordered the shape of the molds to be changed. Today the flattened cheeses weigh 8 ounces (220 grams), and also come in a Petit Valençay version weighing 4 ounces (110 grams).

Valençay is made from raw whole goat's milk. After a maturation phase, a small amount of rennet is added to obtain lactic curds. The molding comprises one or more successive operations. The draining is spontaneous with no pressure put on the curds for a minimum period of twenty hours. This may be followed by a curd regularizing process. Next comes the surface salting and ash coating of the cheese on all its sides. The maturing involves a draining phase that is carried out in the cheesemaking room or the dryer. The air temperature in the maturing room is greater than or equal to 50°F (10°C). The cheeses can be sold from the eleventh day if there is a rind with the presence of superficial mold on the entire surface of the cheese. This is where the art of the cheese master comes into play, enabling a thin rind with surface mold to develop.

Valençay has a slight aroma of goat and undergrowth, accompanied by floral hints. On the palate the cheese is surprisingly firm and supple. Its lactic flavor, ranging from fresh nuts to dried fruit, is accompanied by hints of fruit and hay. Fresh, its texture is fine and creamy. With further maturing it becomes slightly crumbly. Perfect on a cheese platter, the distinct flavors of undergrowth and hazelnut ensure it goes well with all aperitif snacks, gratins, and tarts. Diced, the more mature cheeses will accompany mixed salads. Note too that the ash-covered rind can be eaten and used in cooking.

See also ASH and FRANCE.

Froc, Jean. *Balade au pays des fromages: Les traditions fromagères en France*. Versailles, France: Editions Quae, 2007.

Morgane Dumont

Valle d'Aosta Fromadzo is a classic, low-fat Alpine cow's milk cheese from the autonomous Valle d'Aosta region of northwestern Italy. This area is best known for its Fontina, but Fromadzo is also considered a symbolic expression of the land and culture of this mountain-flanked region. The name Fromadzo derives from local dialect for "formaggio," or cheese, and is a shortening of the term "fromadzo meigro," dialect for low-fat cheese. Historically its low fat content prolonged freshness, providing a good source of protein in times of scarcity.

Pantaleone da Confienza, in his 1477 treatise *Summa lacticinorum*, describes a cheese from the Valle d'Aosta that is "compact and firm, even if not very nutritious," confirming that a low-fat cheese, distinct from Fontina, was already being produced in the valley by this time. The cheese remained popular through the ensuing centuries, appearing frequently on market lists from the sixteenth century on. Valle d'Aosta Fromadzo obtained denominazione di origine controllata (DOC) status in 1995; denominazione di origine protetta (DOP) status followed in 1996.

Production of Fromadzo is closely regulated. While the cheese is made primarily from cow's milk, the addition of a small quantity of goat's milk is permitted. The milk (from at least two milkings) is left to stand for twelve to twenty-four hours for a semi-fat version (containing 20–35 percent fat), or at least thirty-six hours for the lower fat version (with less than 20 percent fat in the finished product), then skimmed, heated, and inoculated with calf's rennet. Once it has coagulated, the curd is cut, heated, and placed in cheese hoops, called "féitchie," then pressed and turned three to four times a day. The rounds are then dry-salted or brined. The cheeses are matured for a minimum of sixty days up to ten months.

The outer rind is straw-yellow in the young cheese, shading toward gray with a reddish cast as it matures. The cheese itself is initially ivory-colored, deepening to yellow after aging, with a firm texture and small or medium-size eyes. Weighing 2–15 pounds (1–7 kilograms), Valle d'Aosta Fromadzo is cylindrical in shape, about 6–12 inches (15–30 centimeters) in diameter and 2–8 inches (5–20 centimeters) high. The mild flavor of the young cheese becomes more pronounced, pungent, and lightly salty with aging. Valle d'Aosta Fromadzo has a milky fragrance, enhanced by the aroma of mountain flowers and grasses if produced in summer months. DOP regulations permit flavoring with plant aromatics such as juniper berries, cumin seeds, or wild fennel.

When young, Fromadzo is eaten as a table cheese, with rye bread or polenta; aged, the cheese is usually grated over soups or pasta. Valle d'Aosta Fromadzo pairs well with young, medium-bodied red wines.

See also FONTINA VAL D'AOSTA and ITALY.

Ministero delle Risorse Agricole, Alimentari e Forestali. "Valle d'Aosta Fromadzo D.O.P." *Gazzetta Ufficiale della Repubblica Italiana*, Serie generale, n. 246, 20 October 1995. https://www.politicheagricole.it/flex/cm/pages/ServeBLOB.php/L/IT/IDPagina/3340.
Rubino, Robert, et al., eds. *Italian Cheese: A Guide to Their Discovery and Appreciation*. Bra, Italy: Slow Food Editore, 2006.
Sacchi, Luisa, ed. *Formaggi Italiani dalla A alla Z*. Milan: Fabbri Editore, 2002.
"Valle d'Aosta Fromadzo D.O.P." Formaggio.it. http://www.formaggio.it/formaggio/valle-daosta-fromadzo-d-o-p.

Meryl S. Rosofsky

Valtellina Casera is an Italian semihard, large, round cow's milk cheese originally produced when cattle returned from the mountain pastures at the end of summer. Nowadays it is made all year round in the province of Sondrio and protected by a PDO (protected designation of origin) since 1996. "Valtellina" refers to the homonymous valley in which the cheese is produced while the local idiom "casera" (deriving from the Latin *caseus*) refers to the place in which the cheesemaking occurred and where the cheese was ripened.

The partially skimmed milk from two or more milkings is coagulated with calf rennet, and the curd is cooked at 104–113°F (40–45°C) for about thirty minutes, then cut to the size of corn kernels. The curd is transferred into molds and lightly pressed for eight to twelve hours; salting is dry or in brine for about forty-eight hours. It is ripened for at least seventy days at 43–55°F (6–13°C) and at a relative humidity above 80 percent. The final wheel is 14–18 inches (35–45 centimeters) wide and 4 inches (9 centimeters) high, with an average weight of 15–26 pounds (7–12 kilograms). The natural rind is hard and thin and the color varies from ivory to pale yellow as the cheese matures; the paste has irregular small holes and quickly begins to dissolve in the mouth, giving a creamy sensation, with flavors changing from milk to hay and nutty.

Valtellina Casera is an excellent table cheese and also plays an important role in traditional northern Italian dishes such as *pizzoccheri* (buckwheat tagliatelle with vegetables, melted butter, and cheese), *sciatt* (cheese dipped in buckwheat batter and deep fried), *tarozz* (mashed potatoes with green beans, onions, butter, and cheese), *chisciöi* (buckwheat pancakes stuffed with cheese), and *polenta taragna* (a combination of corn and buckwheat flour with melted butter and cheese).

See also ITALY.

Morandi, S., et al. "E. Tecnologia di produzione e caratteristiche microbiologiche del formaggio Valtellina Casera." *Scienza e Tecnica Lattiero-Casearia* 55 (2004): 299–317.

Milena Brasca

Varro, Marcus Terentius (116–27 B.C.E.) was a Roman author and antiquarian. He played a role in Roman politics in the last years of the Republic, taking the side of Pompey against Caesar. Ignoring this, the victorious Caesar, sixteen years younger than Varro, commissioned this respected scholar to create a public library of Greek and Latin books, the first in Rome.

Varro wrote in prose and verse on many subjects but most of his works are lost. One that survives is *Farming* (Latin title *Res Rusticae*), a readable introduction to the subject, written at the age of eighty and dedicated to Varro's much younger wife, Fundania, who is said in the preface to have just inherited a farm. It is written as a conversation in which real Roman landowners, friends of Varro, take part alongside fictional characters. In spite of this unusual format Varro's *Farming* is much more systematic than Cato's earlier *On Farming* and was a major source for Columella's more comprehensive work *On Agriculture*.

Varro's discussion of milk and cheese constitutes a subsection of the discussion of sheep, implying that, naturally enough for central Italy, sheep's milk cheese is what he has in mind. He begins with the timetable: "They make cheese between the spring rising of the Pleiades and the summer Pleiades." If the last phrase means "the summer setting of the Pleiades," this places the cheesemaking season between early May and early September, agreeing with other Roman sources. He continues:

> In spring they milk early for cheese-making, in other seasons around midday, though owing to geography and to differences in food it is not the same everywhere. To coagulate two congii [6½ litres] of milk they add an olive-sized amount of rennet. Hare's or kid's rennet is better than lamb's; other people, though, use the milk from a fig branch and vinegar as rennets, and various other substances, all of which are classed as "sap" or "tear" in Greek.

Returning to the use of fig sap as vegetable rennet, Varro suggests that this is the reason why a fig tree flourished in Rome beside the ancient shrine of the goddess Rumina, honored by shepherds. He concludes with the observation that "those who add salt prefer rock to sea salt."

See also ANCIENT CIVILIZATIONS.

Varro, Marcus Terentius. Marcus Porcius Cato on Agriculture; Marcus Terentius Varro on Agriculture. Translated by William Davis Hooper and Harrison Boyd Ash. English translation of *Res Rusticae*. Cambridge, Mass.: Harvard University Press, 1934. See pp. 413–415.
White, K. D. "Roman Agricultural Writers I: Cato and Varro." In *Aufstieg und Niedergang der römischen Welt*. Part 1, vol. 4, edited by H. Temporini, pp. 439–497. Berlin: De Gruyter, 1973.

Andrew Dalby

Vastedda della Valle del Belìce

Vastedda della Valle del Belìce is an Italian PDO (protected designation of origin) pasta filata cheese obtained from raw whole sheep's milk from the Valle del Belice breed. It represents a rare stretched pasta filata cheese made from ewe's milk. The PDO area covers some municipal areas in the districts of Agrigento, Trapani, and Palermo in Sicily.

To make Vastedda della Valle del Belìce, the milk from one or two milking's is processed within forty-eight hours. It is filtered, heated at 100°F (38°C) and coagulated in a wooden vat employing lamb rennet. The curd obtained has to be broken up through the so-called *rotula* in order to form lumps the size of a rice grain, which have to rest for five minutes before being taken and put, without pressing, in bulrush baskets. After twenty-four to forty-eight hours the curd is sliced and put in a wood container called a *piddiaturi*, where it is covered with whey or hot water (176–194°F [80–90°C]) for three to seven minutes until the mass becomes compact and can be spun. Then, out of water, the cords formed are folded and shaped in braids, from which the spheres will be made. These last are put in ceramic soup plates and hand worked until achieving the typical shape of Vastedda. After cooling, the molds are salted in salt brine for one to two hours and after twelve to forty-eight hours they are ready for consumption.

Vastedda della Valle del Belìce has a typical truncated conical shape, with a diameter of 6–7 inches (15–17 centimeters) and a weight of 17–24 ounces (500–700 grams). It is free from rind and the surface is ivory white in color. The flavor is typical of fresh sheep's cheeses, lightly sourish but not spicy. The annual production of certified PDO cheese amounts to 25 tons; the sales market is mainly regional.

See also PASTA FILATA and SICILY.

Mucchetti, G., et al. "Influence of Cheese-making Technology on Composition and Microbiological Characteristics of Vastedda Cheese." *Food Control* 19 (2008): 119–125.

Massimo Todaro

vats vary in shape and size depending on their application, but all are storage or processing vessels made from a range of materials and designed to heat, cool, or mechanically agitate their contents. An open steel pan set over a wood fire in the production of an acid-set cheese represents primitive vat technology. A sealed steam-jacketed drum that mechanically incubates milk, sets curd, and manipulates the curd to the hooping stage exemplifies advanced vat design.

Vats manipulate cheese milk with temperature, agitation, and pressure. Simple temperature-controlled vessels are used for storing milk for pre-ripening periods or for vat pasteurization. These vats include the necessary ports for recording and indicating thermometers. Other vat designs are the locus of the transformation of milk into cheese. In these, milk acidifies and sets into curd, and the curd is manipulated until the desired acidity, texture, and moisture content are achieved. Vats may be round, like the traditional copper vats of the French Jura or Swiss Alps, or may be square, like some designs of wide, shallow, and pitched-bottomed cheddaring tables. Vat shapes include the two joined rounds of double-O vats, the long, rounded-end, deep-cook vats employed in large-scale production, and conical vats with steeply sloping sides that place pressure on the curd as it settles to the bottom. Small-scale producers sometimes use a double-walled steam kettle as a cheesemaking vat.

Vats that heat and cool milk require consistent agitation. The intense and concentrated heat of vats fired directly with burning wood or gas are now less common than the more uniform heat of steam, circulating hot water, or electrical resistance. Most vats include some type of agitator, which may be fixed on a motor above the center of the vessel, or may travel on a track that extends the vat's length. In vats used for transforming milk into cheese, the agitator paddles may be exchanged for curd knives. Cheesemaking vats often include piping for spraying scalding water over the vat's contents, as is the practice with washed-curd cheeses. See WASHED-CURD CHEESES. Most, but not all, vats have outlets near their bases. Some vats have no outlet valve and must instead be emptied by hand or pumped empty over the top of the vessel using a hose.

Vat materials vary depending on the application and the cheesemaking tradition. Vats are most commonly made of copper or stainless steel. Copper is prized for its conductivity as well as its influence on organic acid production and proteolysis in the maturing cheese; however, copper is a reactive metal, causing some cheesemakers and regulators to instead favor stainless steel. Stainless steel is unreactive and durable, making it the standard material for dairy equipment. Some round Dutch vats may include an outer layer of insulative, as well as decorative, teak slats over the double-wall construction common to many vat types. Vat outlets are often controlled by stainless steel ball or check valves. Past valve designs have also employed dairy metal, an alloy now avoided in dairy processing due to its lead content. Vat sizes range dramatically, from 15-gallon (57-liter) micro-dairy pasteurizers to very large, several-thousand-liter vessels.

See also CHEESE KNIFE; COPPER VATS; THERMOMETER; and TRADITIONAL EQUIPMENT.

Kammerlehner, Josef. *Cheese Technology*. Freising, Germany: J. Kammerlehner, 2009. See pp. 260–271.
Mato Rodriguez, L., T. Ritvanen, V. Joutsjoki, et al. "The Role of Copper in the Manufacture of Finnish Emmental Cheese." *Journal of Dairy Science* 94 (2011): 4831–4842.

Brent A. Wasser

The **Vella Cheese Company** in Sonoma, California, is one of the longest running and most honored cheesemakers on the West Coast. Founded by Tom Vella in 1931, it is currently a fourth-generation cheesemaking operation. Through the work of Ignazio (Ig) Vella, who took over in 1981, the Vella Company has been seen by many as a standard of artisanal cheese production that helped influence the wave of artisanal cheesemaking that has flourished in California and the rest of the country since the end of the twentieth century. See ARTISANAL.

Vella is best known for its Dry Monterey Jack, although Vella did not invent it. Dry Jack was a style made by many as many as sixty California cheesemakers in the early 1900s through the 1930s. Aged from seven months to four years, it is a hard-textured but buttery-tasting cheese, rubbed with cocoa and oil, which is most commonly used as a substitute for grating cheeses such as Parmigiano Reggiano. Indeed, legend holds that Dry Jack gained its initial popularity well before Vella Cheese existed, out of the necessity of finding a substitute for Italian grating cheeses during World War I. The only two remaining California producers of Dry Jack are the Vella Cheese Company and the Rumiano Cheese Company in Crescent City, California. Dry Monterey Jack has been honored in the Slow Food "Ark of Taste," which recognizes regionally important traditional foods that are facing extinction. See SLOW FOOD. Vella's Special Select brand of Dry Jack has won numerous awards including Best of Show at the American Cheese Society in 1994 and US Cheese Champion in 1995–1996. See AMERICAN CHEESE SOCIETY. The company's Habañero Jack received a gold medal at the 2014 Los Angeles International Dairy Competition, where its Halapeño Jack, Pesto Jack, and Mezzo Secco cheeses received gold medals in 2015. Vella also makes high-moisture Jack, Cheddar, and traditional Italian styles like Asiago. All milk is sourced from the nearby Merten's Dairy.

As well as starting Vella Cheese, Tom Vella founded Rogue Creamery in Oregon in the 1930s and began producing blue cheese in 1954. After his death in 1998, the family sold Rogue Creamery to David Gremmels and Cary Bryant, although until his death Ig Vella continued to work with them to help create their award-winning blue cheeses. See ROGUE CREAMERY and ROGUE RIVER BLUE.

Ig Vella's influence on innumerable young cheesemakers earned him the first Lifetime Achievement Award bestowed by the American Cheese Society and a History of Excellence Award from the California Artisan Cheese Guild. The town of Sonoma has even named a bridge in his honor. After Vella's death in 2011, his wife, Sally, became president of the company, and his daughter Chickie Vella took over the day-to-day operations.

See also CALIFORNIA and JACK.

Roberts, Jeffrey. *Atlas of American Cheese*. White River Junction, Vt.: Chelsea Green, 2007.

Vanderveen, Sarah Koops. "Dry Monterey Jack Cheese: What's Old Is New Again." *San Francisco Chronicle*, 27 September 1995.

Vella Cheese Company. http://www.vellacheese.com/index.html.

Gordon Edgar

Velveeta is a highly visible processed American cheese product, packaged and sold as a rectangular-sized loaf tucked inside an iconic, yellow cardboard box. Standing as an American brand for nearly a century, Velveeta is perhaps best known as "liquid gold" for its unusual melting properties. When heated, Velveeta remains fully integrated, pooling evenly into a smooth texture that holds as much cultural significance as it does spreadable appeal. See FUNCTIONAL PROPERTIES.

Velveeta is made from pasteurized cow's milk, whey, milk protein concentrate, salt, and various stabilizers and preservatives. By law, Velveeta is sold as a "cheese product" as opposed to a "cheese food," because it contains milk protein concentrate, which is not permissible according to the US Food and Drug Administration's classification of "food."

Although highly processed cheese is often a point of social and political contention today, at its inception Velveeta was perceived as accessible, durable, and novel. American households fell for its easy melt, mild flavor, and versatility, especially in the vein of dips, spreads, and macaroni and cheese dishes.

The Swiss-American cheesemaker Emil Frey created Velveeta in 1918, under the umbrella of the Monroe Cheese Company in Monroe, New York. The impetus underpinning the development of the foodstuff was to repurpose broken wheels of cheese by mixing them together with cheesemaking by-products (namely, whey) to make a cohesive product. Frey experimented for more than two years on his stovetop before releasing a product with velvety consistency that could be melted and reheated with ease. He coined his recipe Velveeta. The original Velveeta box was tin and adorned with the slogan "a triumph in cheese making." The success of the product led to a spin-off, and the Velveeta Cheese Company was formed as an independent entity in 1923.

Kraft Foods acquired the Velveeta Cheese Company and the trade name "Velveeta" in 1927, at which point Frey returned to work as an employee of the Monroe Cheese Company. In 1928 Kraft applied the brand name to its new internally developed processed cheese product, funded through research efforts focused on the nutritive value of whey. Initially Kraft aggressively advertised the cheese product for its nutritional benefits, asserting that the addition of whey elevated the vitamin and mineral content. In 1931 the American Medical Association gave Velveeta its seal of approval on the basis that the product contained the necessary nutritional components to "build firm flesh." See WHEY.

Throughout the decades, Kraft propelled Velveeta into the pop culture spotlight through the release of memorable jingles, commercials, and marketing campaigns. Standout slogans such as "It's all in this little yellow box," and "I'm just a hunka, hunka, melting love," solidified Velveeta's ubiquity among American households.

Today, the Velveeta brand is worth more than 500 million dollars and spans twelve product categories, including Velveeta Shells & Cheese and casserole kits. Its reach includes international markets, but Americans constitute the bulk of Velveeta's consumer base. Approximately 50 million US households purchased at least one Velveeta brand product in the past year.

See also INDUSTRIAL; KRAFT FOODS; and PASTEURIZED PROCESS CHEESES.

Crowell, Susan. "FDA Warns Kraft About Using MPCs in Cheese Products." *Farm and Dairy*, 9 January 2003. http://www.farmanddairy.com/news/fda-warns-kraft-about-using-mpcs-in-cheese-products/123.html.
Geiling, Natasha. "There Is No Shortage of History When It Comes to Velveeta." Smithsonian.com, 15 January 2014. http://www.smithsonianmag.com/arts-culture/there-is-no-shortage-history-when-it-comes-velveeta-180949312/?no-ist.
Levine, David. "Where Does Velveeta (and Liederkranz) Cheese Come From? Monroe, NY, of Course!" *Hudson Valley Magazine*, April 2013. http://www.hvmag.com/Hudson-Valley-Magazine/April-2013/Where-Does-Velveeta-and-Liederkranz-Cheese-Come-From-Monroe-NY-Of-Course.
Tunick, Michael. *The Science of Cheese*. New York: Oxford University Press, 2014.

Tess McNamara

Venissimo Cheese is a San Diego cheese store founded by Gina Freize and her husband, Roger. They opened Venissimo in the Mission Hills area of San Diego in 2004 with a vision to bring great cheeses from around the world to people in Southern California. Freize's upbringing visiting family in Europe made her very aware of the quality that existed around the world. The Freizes built their business around the philosophy of making cheese comprehensible to people willing to try it, and also educating the consumer. They are quoted as saying: "we want to make Camembert as well-known as cappuccino."

As of 2016 there are four retail locations in the San Diego area. The stores have a large selection of European and American cheeses, including some of the most renowned Californian cheeses. The décor is simple with slated boards and well-stocked cases. The store in North Park is inside a craft brewery, while their fourth retail location is in the new San Diego Liberty Public Market. In 2009 their focus on consumer education led them to inaugurate the Academy of Cheese (AOC). The AOC runs weeknight and weekend classes in their stores in Del Mar and North Park, as well as in the greater San Diego area. Robert Graff, a long-term employee with a passion for cheese, teaches most of the classes. Mr. Graff coordinates educational programming based on his own self-taught learning experience, bringing classes that are suitable for all types of learners. In late 2015 Venissimo launched a cheese mobile app to allow their customers to maintain a log of previous purchases, as well as to provide information on cheeses and pairing recommendations.

See also CALIFORNIA.

Venissimo Cheese. http://www.venissimo.com.

Carlos Yescas

Vermont, a small state in the northeastern corner of the United States, has a long history of dairying and cheese production. Puritans from East Anglia brought cows and English dairying techniques with them, and as the Revolutionary War worsened, many relocated to the relatively peaceful mountains of Vermont. See PURITANS. As Boston and New York grew into large industrial cities, Vermont—whose economy would remain agricultural—became the largest supplier of milk to the Northeast's urban centers. The United States' first statewide dairy association formed in Vermont in 1869, and by World War I only Wisconsin could claim more milk cows per farm. Between 1920 and 1963 Vermont had more cows than people, and by 1930 no state in the country had a higher percentage of its population dependent on dairy for its income. Even today, the dairy industry makes up three quarters of Vermont's agricultural income.

Despite this proud history, dairying in Vermont has severely declined in recent years. Between 2004 and 2012, Vermont lost 309 dairy farms, roughly 23 percent of its dairies. Still, the state boasts a wide array of award-winning cheesemakers, including Vermont Creamery, Jasper Hill Farm, Vermont

Shepherd, Consider Bardwell Farm, Maplebrook Farm, and Grafton Village. Cabot Creamery Cooperative, now owned by Agri-Mark Inc., is headquartered in Methuen, Massachusetts. This cooperative is made up of more than 1,200 farmers in New York and six New England states. Cabot Creamery is one of the largest dairies in Vermont. Partnering with Jasper Hill (one of the smallest dairies), Cabot has become famous for its clothbound Cheddar, which has won numerous awards including Best of Show at the 2006 American Cheese Society Awards. See CABOT CREAMERY; CELLARS AT JASPER HILL; GRAFTON VILLAGE CHEESE; VERMONT CREAMERY; and VERMONT SHEPHERD.

Vermont does not boast a specific style of cheese or a regional specialty. Instead, Vermont dairies borrow basic recipes from across Europe, tailoring them to their specific conditions and tastes. Maplebrook Farm, for example, is famous for its mozzarella and burrata, while Vermont Creamery is known for its French-style aged goat's milk cheese, Bijou, and Jasper Hill Farm is known for its raw cow's milk cheese, Bayley Hazen Blue. Vermont's cheeses range from British-style Cheddars to Greek-style fetas without an overriding similarity of milk type, process, or taste. Vermont's claim to regional distinction in cheese thus relies on history, locality, and landscape, rather than on the specific products it yields. Vermont's dairy industry has shaped the state's identity: herds graze on the Green Mountains, and picturesque barns dot the countryside, attracting tourists and boosting the local economy.

Today, as industrial pressures have forced smaller dairies out of business, Vermont is relying on its cheeses to protect this identity. The "working landscape" (as it is named in Vermont) of grazing cattle, sheep, and goats, as well as small dairies and local distributors, functions both to support successful cheese producers and to protect Vermont's traditional landscape. Rather than the land's imparting special characteristics to the cheese (in the French model of terroir), here, as Heather Paxson (2013) suggests, the cheese ensures the continued maintenance of agricultural land and landscapes. Although in 2013 Vermont produced only 1.3 percent of the United States' total fluid milk, its identity as a dairy state endures, with cheese tourism flourishing at festivals and through visits to farms and dairies across the state.

See also UNITED STATES and VERMONT CHEESE COUNCIL.

Morrissey, Charles T. *Vermont: A Bicentennial History.* New York: Norton, 1981.
Paxson, Heather. *The Life of Cheese: Crafting Food and Value in America.* Berkeley: University of California Press, 2013.
United States Department of Agriculture. *Milk Production.* 22 January 2016. http://www.usda.gov/nass/PUBS/TODAYRPT/mkpr0116.pdf.

Sara Harrison

The **Vermont Cheese Council** is an advocacy group that promotes and publicizes Vermont cheese producers. Through cheesemaking workshops, cheese festivals, and educational seminars, the Vermont Cheese Council works to educate food professionals and the public about the process and the artistry of cheesemaking while also connecting consumers to its member cheese producers. The council's membership includes voting members (representing licensed cheesemaking companies), nonvoting associate members (representing retailers or suppliers), corporate sponsors, and individual (consumer) sponsors. Member cheesemakers pay a fee to be represented on the council's website, on its blog, and in its newsletter. Founded in 1996 with nineteen members, the council has grown considerably since then, welcoming its fiftieth member in 2015.

The Cheese Council organizes group visits to local cheese producers and has created the Vermont Cheese Trail. Although the trail has no specific route, the trail map provides the locations of the council's members throughout the state and indicates whether each farm or dairy is open to the public, open with an appointment, or closed to visitors.

The Vermont Cheese Council's largest public event is the Vermont Cheesemakers Festival, begun in 2008. Fodor's Travel rated the festival one of the "ten best US summer food festivals" in both 2014 and 2015. Hosted every summer at Shelburne Farms in Shelburne, Vermont, the festival features a wide-ranging array of workshops, cheesemaking demonstrations, artisanal foods and beverages, and over forty cheese producers.

See also VERMONT.

Bivins, Tom. "Vermont Cheese Council Signs 50th Member." Farm to Plate, 1 June 2015. http://www.vtfarmtoplate.com/announcements/vermont-cheese-council-signs-50th-member.

Marx, Rebecca Flint. "Driving Vermont's Very Tasty Cheese Trail." *Wall Street Journal*, 24 July 2014.
Vermont Cheese Council. http://www.vtcheese.com.

Sara Harrison

Vermont Creamery,

Vermont Creamery, formerly known as the Vermont Butter and Cheese Company, was started in 1984 by business partners Bob Reese and Allison Hooper. Inspired by her time on a goat farm in Brittany, France, Hooper settled in Vermont and became one of the first American cheesemakers to introduce chèvre and crème fraiche—then still exotic fare—to the American market. The creamery, located in Websterville, Vermont, has since expanded its offerings to include a wide range of products from cultured butter to aged goat's milk and mixed milk cheeses, as well as feta and fromage blanc. Vermont Creamery's cheeses have garnered numerous awards and consistently place among the top European goat cheeses at the World Cheese Awards. Its Bijou, a *Geotrichum*-rinded, French-style, aged goat cheese won gold at the 2014 World Cheese Awards, and its fromage blanc, feta, and coupole—another aged goat cheese—as well as its fresh goat cheese all consistently rank in the top three in international and domestic competitions.

Vermont Creamery purchases all of its cow's milk from the St. Albans Cooperative Creamery in northern Vermont. Finding enough goat's milk, however, has remained a persistent problem. The creamery currently gets goat's milk from farms scattered across Vermont, New Hampshire, and Ontario, Canada, but would like to purchase all of its milk from farms near its Vermont facility. To this end, the creamery has started Ayers Brook Goat Dairy, a combination working dairy and educational model dedicated to promoting goat farming in Vermont.

See also VERMONT.

Lynam, Julia. "The Curd Dimension." *Business People— Vermont*, February 2009. http://www.vermontguides.com/2009/02-feb/vtbutter_cheese.html.
Pasanen, Melissa. "Cheese Company Leads Way for Goat Dairies." *Burlington Free Press*, 18 April 2014.
Vermont Creamery. "A Tale of Two Tables: Our Story." http://www.vermontcreamery.com/our-story-of-cheesemaking.
World Cheese Awards. "Results 2014." http://www.worldcheeseawards.com/results/2014.

Sara Harrison

Vermont Shepherd (formerly known as Major Farm) is a 250-acre sheep dairy located in Westminster West, Vermont. Vermont Shepherd is one of the oldest sheep farms in Vermont and is the oldest sheep dairy in the United States. The Major family has had sheep on the farm since 1965 and has run a sheep dairy since 1987. The farm is now run by the Major and Ielpi families and is home to more than ewes.

Vermont Shepherd was also the name of the farm's signature cheese—a Pyrenees-style sheep's milk cheese that won Best in Show at the American Cheese Society's annual competition in 2000. Vermont Shepherd's 100 percent sheep's milk cheese is now called Verano (Spanish for summer) because the cheese is only produced during the summer months. The farm also produces an aged mixed-milk cheese called Invierno (Spanish for winter) using a blend of their sheep's milk and raw cow's milk from the nearby Putney School, as well as a fresh ricotta—Ricotta Lana—during the summer months. Cheeses are produced in a small cheese house on the farm in batches of ten to thirty wheels and aged on the farm in a man-made cave covered by four feet of earth. The wheels are matured on wooden boards for a minimum of sixty days to allow their natural rinds to grow and for the flavor of the cheese to develop. Vermont Shepherd won two conservation awards (in 2002 and 2006) for the quality of its farming work, including improving soils, pastures, and water resources.

See also VERMONT.

McCalman, Max, and David Gibbons. *The Cheese Plate*. New York: Clarkson Potter, 2002.
Vermont Shepherd. http://vermontshepherd.com.
Werlin, Laura, and Martin Jacobs. *The New American Cheese*. New York: Stewart, Tabori & Chang, 2000.

Anne Saxelby

Virgil (full name: Publius Vergilius Maro, 70–19 B.C.) was a Latin poet whose unfinished narrative poem, the *Aeneid*, saved from burning at his death on the orders of the emperor Augustus, became Rome's national epic. His earlier works are the *Eclogues* (or pastoral poems) and the *Georgics* (a poetic handbook on farming). The *Georgics* briefly depicts shepherds making hand-pressed cheeses,

What they milk at sunrise and in daylight hours, they press at night. What they milk at dusk and sunset they either carry to market in wicker baskets at daybreak—if the shepherd is off to town—or else tinge sparingly with salt and set aside till winter.

Similar cheeses recur in the first *Eclogue*, "rich cheeses pressed for the ungrateful city" by Tityrus before the land confiscations of the Civil War. Tityrus may well stand for Virgil himself.

A collection of miscellaneous shorter poems, probably written during Virgil's lifetime and sometimes attributed to him, includes two short pieces on country life. *Moretum* is a day in the life of a peasant, including details of the preparation of a fiery garlic, herb, and cheese mix that he will eat with bread for lunch. Too long to quote here, the recipe has been often recreated. *Copa* describes the welcome awaiting a tired traveler at a rustic tavern somewhere in Italy. Among its homemade delicacies, served by its Syrian bar girl, the "copa Surisca" of the poem's first line, are "little cheeses dried in a rush basket."

See also ANCIENT CIVILIZATIONS.

Dalby, Andrew, and Sally Grainger. *The Classical Cookbook*. 2d ed. pp. 104–105. London: British Museum, 2012. See pp. 104–105.

Kenney, E. J., ed. and trans. *Moretum: The Ploughman's Lunch, A Poem Ascribed to Virgil*. Bristol, U.K.: Bristol Classical, 1984.

Paschalis, Michael. "Tityrus and Galatea (Virgil, *Eclogue* 1): An Expected Relationship." 5 *Dictynna*, 2008. http://dictynna.revues.org/401.

Virgil. *Eclogues* 1.33–35, *Georgics* 3.400–403, *Moretum, Copa*. Translated by H. R. Fairclough and G. P. Goold. 2 vols. Cambridge, Mass.: Harvard University Press, 1999–2000.

Andrew Dalby

Vlašić (or Travnik) cheese belongs to the group of soft white pickled ewe's milk cheeses which are dominantly produced in the Mediterranean countries. The technology of producing white pickled cheeses was brought to Bosnia and Herzegovina by nomadic cattlemen (Arnauts) from the east in the mid-nineteenth century. The production center of this cheese is the Vlašić Mountain (1,933 meters), with a seasonal production from May to October. In this period, sheep (the autochthonous breed Pramenka) feed only on pastures of the Vlašić Mountain, which give specific properties to the milk and cheese.

The production technology of Vlašić cheese is simple and adapted to limited mountain conditions. Immediately after milking the milk is strained, then rennet is added and so the milk coagulates. Local natural calf rennet from one factory close to Vlašić Mountain is primarily used. Then the curd is poured into cheesecloth and strained to form a cheese ball which is then cut into wedges. The wedges are placed into wooden barrels and simultaneously salted. Cheese ripening happens in the salted whey, where exchange of ingredients between the salted whey and the cheese mass happens constantly. A solution of salt in water (brine) is poured as needed. The cheese ripens at a temperature of 55–59°F (13–15°C) for a minimum sixty days. A whole series of complex physical, chemical, microbiological, and biochemical processes take place during the ripening, with results that effect the formation of a characteristic aroma.

The color of the cheese is prominently white with several small holes in the cross section. The consistency is solid but not too hard, easily fracturable and spreadable. The smell is pleasant, of sheep's milk. The taste is milky sour, moderately salty, and pleasant without foreign material. The size of the cheese wedge ranges between 1–3 pounds (500 grams–1.5 kilograms), with an average of 2 pounds (1 kilogram).

This cheese can be used to prepare a traditional plate called "pita" or eaten as a side dish along with the main course. Vlašić is also traditionally served in Bosnia and Herzegovina together with bread, smoked meat, and domestic plum brandy.

Dizdarević, Tarik, et al. "Determination of Sensory Characteristics and Volatile Components Content in Traditional Travnik Cheese." Proceedings of the 6th IDF Symposium on Cheese Ripening, Madison, Wisconsin, 2012.

Doane, Francis, and Willis Huron. *Varieties of Cheese: Descriptions and Analyses*. Rev. ed. Washington, D.C.: U.S. Dept. of Agriculture, Bureau of Animal Industry, 1934.

Sarić, Zlatan, et al. "Quality Aspects of Travnički Cheese Made from Raw and Pasteurized Cow and Goat Milk." *Milchwissenschaft* 57 (2002): 631–634.

Zlatan Sarić and Tarik Dizdarević

Wabash Cannonball

See AMERICAN "GOAT LADIES" and CAPRIOLE.

Wagashi cheese, also known as Woagachi, is produced across much of the Sahel region of Africa, including in Benin, Nigeria, Togo, Ghana, Mali, and Burkina Faso. It is made by Fulbe herders, produced most often by women. The Fulbe (as they call themselves), Fulani (in English), or Peul (in French) are a Muslim pastoral people living across a wide area of sub-Saharan West Africa, from Mauritania to Cameroon, numbering as many as 20 million.

Wagashi cheese is made from cow's milk. The men milk the animals and distribute milk to their wives who transform the surplus milk after consumption or sale. Wagashi is characterized by a very solid form of aggregation of all the proteins present in milk caused by an alkaloid present in the latex of *Calotropis procera*. Parts of this plant, such as leaves and stems, are dipped in warm milk for a few minutes. Then milk is heated on the fire to 190–194°F (88–90°C). At these temperatures the toxic alkaloid of *C. procera* is inactive and milk proteins begin to aggregate, solidify, and appear on the surface.

This curd is separated from the whey and put in a *tamis* (a natural fiber or plastic colander). The resulting white, compact cheese is made in small (12–16-ounce [350–450-gram]) and large (26–30-ounce [750–850-gram]) sizes. It can be sold and utilized fresh as a soft cheese, or it can be left to dry. In some areas of Benin the cheeses are dried on the thatched roofs of paillottes, the typical houses of the camp. Here, too, dried cheeses may be colored a deep red by dipping them in warm water containing sorghum leaves and stems. Any unsold cheese at market is boiled again for hygienic reasons. Wagashi cheese is consumed fried or cooked in sauces, but rarely consumed fresh, as it is, without being cooked. It is considered "the meat of the poor," being a major source of protein.

See also FULBE.

Fox, P. F. *Cheese: Chemistry, Physics and Microbiology*. Vol. 2: *Major Cheese Groups*. Gaithersburg, Md.: Aspen, 1999.
O'Connor, Charles. *Traditional Cheesemaking Manual*. Addis Ababa, Ethiopia: International Livestock Centre for Africa, 1993.

Rosario Petriglieri

Wallace and Gromit is a classic British claymation comedy series created by Nick Park of Aardman Animations. The main protagonist, Wallace, is a charming, absentminded inventor with an insatiable appetite and enthusiasm for cheese and crackers. Wensleydale is his favorite cheese.

Wallace can usually be found dressed in brown trousers, a green sweater vest, and a red tie. His best-known invention is a pair of automated trousers and a bed that tips him into them. English actor Peter Sallis is the genial voice for Wallace. Nick Park has admitted that he only thought to widen Wallace's mouth and further pronounce his smile upon hearing Sallis expressively say "cheese" for the first time.

Wallace's best friend and companion, Gromit, is a silent yet intelligent anthropomorphic dog who communicates through pantomime-like expressions.

Gromit knits, plays chess, reads the newspaper, and appeases Wallace's cheese obsession.

Wallace and Gromit debuted in a stop-motion animation short film, "A Grand Day Out," in 1989. Three more short films and one feature-length film round out the series. Widespread fanaticism has prompted the translation of each release into twenty languages across the globe. The universally iconic duo has a strong following in the United States, United Kingdom, and Japan, and has won more than sixty awards, including three Oscars and six Baftas. DVD sales have exceeded 1.8 million, and Facebook fans total over 900,000. The success and popularity of the series has subsequently inspired comics, video games, TV spin-offs, charities, and books, including *Wallace & Gromit's Cheesy Cookbook*. It should also be noted that the leading producer of Wensleydale cheese, Hawes Creamery, has seen a considerable rise in the popularity of the cheese as a direct result of *Wallace and Gromit*, and has even gone so far as to print *Wallace and Gromit* images on some of its packaging.

Farndale, Nigel. "Wallace and Gromit: One Man and His Dog." *Telegraph*, 18 December 2008.
Wallace and Gromit official website. http://www .wallaceandgromit.com.

Tess McNamara

washed-curd cheeses are a significant family encompassing everything from the famous Dutch Goudas, to Edam and Havarti, to washed-rind cheeses such as Reblochon from France and Gubbeen from Ireland. See GOUDA; EDAM; HAVARTI; and REBLOCHON. Washed-curd cheeses range from semisoft to hard, and their rinds can be waxed or left to develop naturally; beautiful molds can be cultivated on their surfaces, or they can be surface-washed to develop hues that range from brownish-orange to red to pink.

The defining feature of washed-curd cheeses is that their acidity is lowered during the cheesemaking process by removing whey, which has a large amount of lactose (milk sugar) in it, and replacing it with water of varying amounts and temperatures depending on the type of cheese. See DEACIDIFICATION and WHEY. Curd washing takes places after the curd is cut, either immediately or after a predetermined period of time, during which the curd and whey mixture may be stirred. Whey may be removed either by draining it from a valve at the bottom of the vat through a screen or by using a bucket or a pump to remove the whey from the top of the vat. As an example, 30 percent of the whey might be removed, and water added back to the vat at 20 percent of the total volume. This removal of the lactose reduces the food source of the lactic acid bacteria, thus controlling subsequent acidity and directly determining the development of texture, taste, and color characteristics.

Both the acidity and the temperature influence moisture expulsion from the curd. During the washing step, the temperature of the vat is typically increased, with the water typically added at a temperature of about 130°F (54°C), depending on the parameters of the particular cheesemaking process. If very hot water is added, care is needed to make sure that the curd does not become plasticized, or melted and hardened. Plasticized curds have the texture of a hard-boiled egg white, and their structure is irredeemably altered. Stirring the vat while slowly adding the water to evenly distribute it helps avoid this problem. However, curd washing always makes the cheese slightly more elastic, plastic, and firm, because as the pH increases so does the mineralization of the curd as well as the total amount of calcium in the cheese. See PH MEASUREMENT and CALCIUM PHOSPHATE.

By controlling the pH, the addition of water helps produce sweeter-tasting curds and cheese, but it may also reduce their overall flavor. As the cheese ages, the flavors that develop are gentle and not too acidic because the pH has been controlled very significantly during the manufacturing process and because washing the curd raises the final moisture content of the cheese. The added water also has an effect on the final color of the paste, since the color of the cheese is directly affected by the pH of the cheese. The more acidic (lower pH) the cheese, the whiter the paste. See FLAVOR; MOISTURE; and COLOR.

See also WASHED-RIND CHEESES.

Scott, R. *Cheesemaking Practice*. 3d ed. Boston: Springer, 1986.

Giana Ferguson and Brian Schlatter

washed-rind cheeses (aerobic-bacteria ripened) are generally known for their pronounced odor. The cheese that fills a room, sometimes referred

Époisses cheese is given a Marc de Bourgogne (pomace brandy) wash at La Fromagerie in London. The wash encourages the growth of *Brevibacterium linens*, a bacterium that is valued for its attractive creamy-white to yellow-orange pigmentation and its characteristic earthy aroma, which comes from its production of sulfur compounds. © KATE ARDING

to as pungent and reminiscent of the odors of autumn, barnyards, and sometimes locker rooms, is often referred to as smear-ripened or washed-rind. However the basic difference between these two is that the smear-ripened is often an unpressed, soft, surface-ripened cheese and the washed rind is made by heating the curd and pressing it into a firmer cheese. Both cheeses are complex in character and flavor, the rinds often tacky or slick, and the paste is soft and oozy in soft smear-ripened and layered with texture and cream in semisoft washed rinds. The benefit of the washed rinds is they are lower in moisture, firmer in texture, and have a longer shelf life. Characteristic examples of smeared rind cheeses include Limburger, Munster, Maroilles, Port Salut, and Herve cheeses, while Fontina, Beaufort, Abondance, and the family of Gruyères fall in the category of washed-rind cheeses. See LIMBURGER; MUNSTER; MAROILLES; FONTINA VAL D'AOSTA; BEAUFORT; ABONDANCE; and GRUYÈRE.

On the surface of a washed-rind cheese bacterium-like *Brevibacterium linens*, coryneform bacteria, and others like micrococci are often found. These bacteria require a pH of 5.8 or greater to grow. Surface yeast and other microorganisms like *Geotrichum* help facilitate the deacidification of cheese surface, attribute to increasing pH and growth of the bacterium creating the reddish orange washed flora that enhances its flavor. See BREVIBACTERIUM LINENS; GEOTRICHUM CANDIDUM; and DEACIDIFICATION. The bacterium is washed with diluted salt brine to

create the distinctive pungent odor and sweet savory flavors for which this cheese is known. Alsatian monastic cheesemakers evolved this process and began cooking and pressing cheeses with lower moisture to produce a washed-rind cheese, Munster, as early as the seventh century. These were firmer, thus having longer life until reaching peak for sale. See MONASTIC CHEESEMAKING.

In the nineteenth century the process of washing rinds was referred to as "putrefactive fermentation" (Decker, 1905). It is the introduction of a bacteria culture to the surface of fresh cheese curds. The process in Limburger curing can last up to six weeks at a humidity of 95 percent and temperature between 58–63°F (15–17°C). Affineurs will add cider, beer, wine, and spirits like brandy to the dilution, creating a distinctive and regional flavor and experience. Presence of *Brevinobacterium* (often called "red bacteria") and high salt levels (greater than 2 percent) are the main characteristics of the soft smeared-rind cheeses; however the acidification profile is very similar to the family of bloomy-rind cheeses (also called mold-ripened cheeses). In fact cheesemakers often use the same starters and production process to make the two varieties and then differentiate the products based on the salting and ripening conditions. See BLOOMY-RIND CHEESES.

Ardrahan Cheese (Ireland), Red Hawk (United States), and Munster or Munster Gerome (France) are examples of washed-rind cheeses. Munster or Munster Gerome from Alsace-Lorraine, is believed to be the earliest documented washed-rind cheese. It is a semisoft cheese made from cow's milk in copper cauldrons or vats from either raw or pasteurized milk. The rind is shiny and slick orange to red color and has a distinctive intense autumn smell with parallel odors of dirty laundry. Its flavors are subtle, buttery, and creamy, and there are sharp notes at the rind. Its size varies from 5–7 inches (13–19 centimeters) in diameter and 1–3 inches (2.4–8 centimeters) in height and weighs nearly 1–3 pounds (450 grams–1.5 kilograms). It's aged between two and three months. Ardrahan Cheese, produced by Ardrahan Dairy Products Ltd. in Duhollow, Cork, Ireland, is made from Friesian cows' pasteurized milk. The paste is yellow and slightly crumbly, and the rind golden to earthy. Its flavors are butter, savory, and slightly acidic and the aroma is pungent and earthy. It matures in four to eight weeks. Wheels are available in small and large sizes 11 ounces to 3 pounds (300 grams to 1.5 kilograms).

Red Hawk, produced by Cowgirl Creamery in Point Reyes Station, California, is made from pasteurized organic milk and cream. Each round weighs about 10 ounces (284 grams) and matures for about four weeks. Soft and creamy, Red Hawk has a pungent, fruity, and slightly beefy flavor. See RED HAWK.

See also BRINING; BRUSHING; and WASHED-CURD CHEESES.

Almena-Aliste, Montserrat, and Bernard Mietton. "Cheese Classification, Characterization, and Categorization: A Global Perspective." In *Cheese and Microbes*, edited by Catherine W. Donnelly. Washington, D.C.: ASM Press, 2014.

Decker, John W. *Cheese Making: Cheddar, Swiss, Brick, Limburger, Edam, Cottage, Etc.* Columbus, Oh.: n.p., 1905.

Kindstedt, Paul. *American Farmstead Cheese*. White River Junction, Vt.: Chelsea Green Publishing, 2005.

McCalman, Max, and David Gibbons. *Mastering Cheese*. New York: Clarkson Potter, 2009.

Studd, Will. *Chalk and Cheese*. South Melbourne, Australia: Purple Egg, 1999.

David Gremmels

water buffalo. There are some 170 million domestic water buffaloes in the world, with more than 95 percent in Asia. The countries with the largest buffalo populations are India and Pakistan, which are the world's largest buffalo milk producers and where buffaloes collectively produce more milk than cattle. The three next-largest populations of buffalo are in China, Egypt, and Nepal. Dairy buffaloes

Murrah buffaloes in the Philippine Carabao Center at its Central Mindanao University facility in Maramag, Bukidnon. This breed of water buffalo has been used by the Philippine government to upgrade the dairy industry of the country. © KLEOMARLO

outnumber dairy cows in Pakistan, Egypt, and Nepal. In developing countries buffaloes are kept mostly by small-scale producers who raise fewer than five animals in mixed crop–livestock systems. Research institutes devoted solely to water buffalo are located in Hisar, India; Nanning, China; and Nueva Ecija, Philippines.

Domesticated water buffaloes are classified into two subspecies: swamp (*Bubalis carabenesis*) and river (or riverine) (*Bubalus bubalis*). Both are descendants of wild water buffalo (*Bubalus arnee*), which is now an endangered species in South Asia. The swamp subspecies has forty-eight chromosomes and the river subspecies has fifty; they can be crossbred and will produce offspring with forty-nine. Over one hundred breeds exist today. Domesticated swamp buffaloes are smaller than their river counterparts, have lower milk yields (only 1–1.5 liters per day, which is a sixth of the river buffalo yield), and are mainly used in Eastern Asia as beasts of burden, especially in rice cultivation. The Carabao is a breed of swamp buffalo developed in the Philippines and sometimes used for milk production.

Approximately 70 percent of the global water buffalo population consists of river buffaloes. Well-known specialized dairy buffalo breeds in India and Pakistan include Jaffarabadi, Kundi, Mehsana, Murrah, Nagpuri, Nili-Ravi, and Surti, of which Murrah is the most important. Caucasian breeds are found in the Caucasus region, Beheri in Egypt, Carpathian and Danubian in Romania, and Bulgarian Murrah and Italian Mediterranean buffaloes in those countries. River buffalo are dark gray or black with coiled or straight horns. The optimal lactation period for Murrah ranges from 260 to 295 days, with the highest milk yield after five to six weeks. Buffalo usually produce 6–7 liters of milk per day and 1,000–2,100 liters per lactation, and the most milk is produced during the fourth lactation. Commercial buffalo milk production is affected by their late age at first calving (forty to sixty months, as opposed to twenty-four to thirty months for cattle), their long calving interval (fifteen to eighteen months, versus twelve to thirteen months for cattle), and their long dry period (sixty to two hundred days, compared with sixty to ninety days for cattle). Holstein cows are generally culled after three lactations, but healthy water buffalo have long productive lives with nine to ten lactations. See HOLSTEIN and LACTATION.

Some of the shortcomings of the water buffalo milk supply are countered by the fact that the solids level in the milk is high. Buffalo milk averages 4.2–4.5 percent protein, 7–8 percent fat, and 5–6 percent carbohydrate, compared with 3.1–3.9 percent protein, 3.4–5.1 percent fat, and 4.6–5 percent carbohydrate for raw cow's milk. As a result only 11 pounds (5 kilograms) of buffalo milk are needed to make 2 pounds (1 kilogram) of cheese, as opposed to 18 pounds (8 kilograms) of cow's milk. Unlike cattle buffaloes do not transfer carotenoids to milk, making their cheese white. Buffalo milk contains 80 percent less cholesterol and 60 percent more calcium than cow's milk.

Some water buffalo are raised in Italy, where the milk is used for Mozzarella di Bufala. See MOZZARELLA DI BUFALA CAMPANA. In North America farms are located in California, Florida, Texas, Wisconsin, Quebec, and other places for the same purpose. In other countries hard and soft cheese varieties are made from buffalo milk. In Bulgaria a hard white brined cheese is produced through the use of starter cultures and enzymatic coagulant, and a similar cheese, Braila, is manufactured in Romania. The most popular Egyptian variety, Domiati, is a soft cheese, and Egypt's primary hard cheese, Roumy (or Ras), is made from a buffalo—cow's milk mixture and is aged two to three months at 54–4°F (12–18°C). It is similar to Pecorino Romano. See DOMIATI and PECORINO ROMANO. Egypt also has Karish and Mish soft cheeses that are naturally acidified for up to three days and then acid coagulated. In Syria, Alghab is a soft cheese that is naturally acidified for three to four hours and coagulated for the same length of time. Alkarish is made from the whey generated from Alghab manufacture, in the same manner that ricotta is derived from mozzarella. Akkawi is a hard Middle Eastern cheese made from milk containing 10–12 percent salt and ripened in brine. See MIDDLE EAST. Vladeasa is a soft cheese made in Romania using starter cultures and enzymatic or acid coagulation. High fat and low fat types are sold. Madhfor is a soft Iraqi cheese that is lightly acidified before coagulation and brined for two months. A semihard (40–45 percent moisture) cheese, Beyaz Peyner, is made in Turkey. It is manufactured using starter cultures and rennet, coagulated for one and a half to two and a half hours, and aged in brine for four to six months. See TURKEY.

See also COW; GOAT; MILK; and SHEEP.

Borghese, Antonio. *Buffalo Production and Research*. Rome: Food and Agriculture Organization of the United Nations, 2005.

Engle, Amy, and Vermont Water Buffalo, Inc. "Water Buffalo." *Culture*, 24 Feb. 2014. http://culturecheesemag.com/farm-animal/water-buffalo.

Santosh Thomas, C. *Efficient Dairy Buffalo Production*. Tumba, Sweden: DeLaval International, 2008.

Michael Tunick

waxing and coating are strategies, first developed in the late nineteenth century, to protect cheese from contamination such as mold, to help control moisture loss, to control oiling off, and to make the cheese easier to handle and more attractive. Before wax and coatings, cheeses were covered in butter, lard, olive oil, and honey. Moisture does diffuse through the wax but at a much lower rate than if the cheese was not waxed. The wax does allow gases such as carbon dioxide and hydrogen sulfide to diffuse through the wax.

Cheese wax is melted by heating it to 169–181°F (76–83°C). Wax is flammable so care should be taken not to overheat it. If the wax is smoking it is too hot. If dipping cheese by hand, lower half the cheese into the wax and hold for five seconds. Raise the cheese out of the wax and hold above the wax for ninety seconds to allow the excess wax to run off and the wax layer to harden. Turn cheese and repeat with the unwaxed portion of the cheese. Repeat the process until several thin coats of wax are applied. Several thin coats are better than a few thick coats. Typically three to four layers are applied. Once all layers are applied place on waxed paper and allow the wax to harden completely.

There is a risk of the cheese beginning to melt if the cheese is in the wax for more than five seconds. If the cheese begins to melt there may be a problem of oiling off. Manufacturers with a lot of cheese to wax place cheese on a rack and lower it into a vat of melted wax. The rack is raised, the excess wax runs off, and the wax layer allowed to set. This process is repeated until the desired number of layers are added. Spots on the cheese that did not get covered with wax can be painted with wax using a soft natural bristle brush. A nylon brush may melt in the hot wax. Wax can also be painted on the cheese using a soft natural bristle brush. Apply several thin coats allowing the wax to harden between coats.

Wax comes in several different colors. The color has no significant meaning. Darker colors such as black and red may help to control light exposure, which could prevent oxidation of the cheese. Cheese coatings, sometimes called cream wax, are used for the same reason as cheese wax. The coating is a polymer and is similar in appearance and texture to school glue. The cheese coating forms an elastic, transparent protective film on the cheese after drying. The coating is painted on the dry cheese with a soft brush or wiped on with a soft rag. As with the cheese wax, two to three thin coats are applied. The coating should be allowed to dry between coats, which may take several hours. The cheese coating is applied to half of the cheese, allowed to dry, flipped, and applied to the other side. There is also a cheese coating application machine available for manufacturers needing to cover large amounts of cheese.

The cheese should be dry, either by air drying or patting dry with a towel before waxing or coating. Any moisture will cause the wax not to stick to the cheese, which could leave an air pocket or void under the wax that could allow mold to grow. Using gloved hands to handle the cheese will help control contamination of the cheese and will keep oil from the hands off the cheese. These oils can affect how the wax adheres to the cheese. Cheese coating may or may not contain color. It also may or may not contain natamycin. Natamycin is a mold inhibitor that is used to control mold in food. The wax and cheese coating should be removed from the cheese prior to consumption as it is not edible.

See also PACKAGING.

Kosikowski, F. V. *Cheese and Fermented Milk Foods.* 2d ed. Brooktondale, N.Y.: F. V. Kosikowski, 1982.

Peters-Morris, Margaret. *The Cheesemaker's Manual.* 3d ed. Winchester, Ont.: Winchester Print and Stationary, 2003.

Sandy Speich

Welschland is a no-frills cheese shop in Zurich, Switzerland. Laurent Houriet and Jürg Steiner opened this store in 2005, in response to a lack of diversity of food in their adoptive town. They are both second-career entrepreneurs who love food. Houriet comes from Romandie (also known as Welschland), a French-speaking region of Switzerland, and maintains a working relationship with producers there.

Welschland carries a wide selection of cheeses, meat products, accessories, and bread made in house. The store is known for its artisan cheeses from the French-speaking regions of Switzerland, as well as a small but interesting selection of French cheese and other specialties from around the country, including liquors and craft beers. Customers positively review their fresh fondue mix. The store prepares its own blend of cheeses shredded at their premises and prepackages them for sale. Their organic cheese selection is also highly sought after.

See also FONDUE; ORGANIC; and SWITZERLAND.

Welschland. http://www.welschland.com.

Carlos Yescas

Welsh rabbit is a dish of melted cheese on toast. According to the *Oxford English Dictionary*, the name was first recorded in 1725. John Byrom remarks in his *Literary Remains* from that year, "I did not eat of the cold beef, but of Welsh rabbit and stewed cheese." The alternative name, "Welsh rarebit," was recorded in 1785, as an etymological refinement of "rabbit." The Welsh name, *caws wedi' i bobi*, or *caws pobi* translates literally as cooked cheese; *pobi* is Welsh for "oven." The physician Andrew Boorde wrote in his *Fyrst Boke of the Introduction of Knowledge* (1542), "I am a Welshman, I do love cause boby, good roasted cheese." There is some contention, however, that the name of the dish did not originate with the Welsh, but rather that "Welsh" was used disparagingly by the English for anything substandard, such as the substitution of cheese for meat.

In 1747 Hannah Glasse published a recipe for Welsh rabbit in *The Art of Cookery Made Plain and Easy*: "Toast the bread on both sides, then toast the cheese on one side, lay it on the toast, and with a hot iron brown the other side. You may rub it over with mustard." She also included recipes for Scotch (virtually identical) and English (soaked in red wine) rabbits. Charlotte Mason copied all three in her *Lady's Assistant* of 1786. By 1823, Mary Eaton specified the use of Gloucester cheese for Welsh rabbit in *The Cook and Housekeeper's Dictionary* and followed the same method of preparation. In her *Book of Household Management* (1861), Mrs. (Isabella) Beeton recommended Gloucester or Cheshire and gave instructions to lay the cheese "on the toasted bread in a cheese-toaster...and let it be equally melted. Spread over the top a little made mustard and pepper and serve very hot, on hot plates."

During the eighteenth and nineteenth centuries, Welsh rabbit was considered a tavern dish. Now it is mostly eaten at home. In addition to cheese and mustard, traditional recipes include ale or milk, Worcestershire sauce, paprika, or cayenne pepper. Jamie Oliver's (2007) recipe for "Welsh rarebit with attitude" includes egg yolks, crème fraîche, and chili jam. A buck rabbit is a Welsh rabbit with a poached egg on top. Ale or beer was the usual drink to accompany Welsh rabbit; this is still often the preferred drink, although sometimes red wine is served instead.

Ayto, John. *The Diner's Dictionary*. 2d ed. New York: Oxford University Press, 2012.
Oliver, Jamie. *Jamie at Home: Cook Your Way to the Good Life*. New York: Hyperion, 2007.

Jill Norman

Wensleydale is a pressed cow's milk cheese that originates from the eponymous Yorkshire dale in northern England. Modern Wensleydale cheese has a creamy white color and a firm and crumbly

Wensleydale, one of the United Kingdom's oldest cheeses, saw its popularity rise dramatically when it was featured in the *Wallace and Gromit* shorts "A Grand Day Out" and "A Close Shave." © KATE ARDING

texture, and it is typically consumed when it is one to four months old, at which stage it has a fresh, lemony tang and milky, honeyed flavors.

As one of the United Kingdom's oldest cheese varieties, its origins lie in the Norman Conquest of England and the subsequent establishment of Cistercian monastic estates in the Yorkshire Dales in the eleventh and twelfth centuries. The French monks brought their cheesemaking skills to bear on the local sheep's milk, making an unpressed, open-textured, naturally blue cheese, perhaps not dissimilar to Roquefort in style. See ROQUEFORT. Similar cheeses were made throughout the Dales, each taking its name from the particular valley, including Swaledale, Teesdale (Cotherstone), Coverdale, and Nidderdale.

The dissolution of the monasteries in the sixteenth century saw the making of cheese pass to local farmers. In Wensleydale they continued to make the cheese in the same style until the seventeenth century, when cow's milk started to replace the use of sheep's milk in the area. Up until the early part of the twentieth century this cow's milk Wensleydale existed solely as a blue cheese and was held in great regard. It was to be found on the most esteemed epicure's table and was said by some to be better than a prize Stilton: creamy and rich with a delicate blue flavor.

During the mid-twentieth century advances in science and changes in cheesemaking techniques spread by dairy advisors saw the introduction of a new style of "white Wensleydale." Production of white Wensleydale involved the introduction of starter bacteria, greater amounts of pressing, and a standardization of cheese recipes and grading. This "new" cheese held greater commercial attraction because it needed less aging, was faster to make, suffered from less shrinkage, and could be brought to market quickly.

The major producer at the time was Wensleydale Creamery in Hawes, which remains the largest producer of the cheese to this day. It was formed in 1897 by provision merchant Edward Chapman, who set up a factory creamery, collected milk from the farms, and made the cheese himself. The factory almost went out of business in the 1930s but was saved by local man Kit Calvert, who went on to fight for the continuing production of Wensleydale even through the lean "war years."

During those war years, Wensleydale became even more standardized and developed from a moderately acid, moister, softer white cheese into the firm, crumbly, and drier white cheese known widely today.

Production of traditional blue Wensleydale effectively ceased during World Wars I and II and became lost forever when the final farmhouse stopped producing it in 1957.

Today a large amount of Wensleydale is made outside Yorkshire; only cheese labeled "Real Yorkshire Wensleydale" (it holds a protected geographical indication [PGI]) is certified to be made within the dale. In fact, production in the dale almost ended when the creamery at Hawes was threatened with closure in the early 1990s, but a management buyout, followed shortly after by welcome publicity in the animated series *Wallace and Gromit*, ensured new fame and success. See WALLACE AND GROMIT. The cheese has since become a firm favorite in the United Kingdom and is exported all over the world.

Modern variants of the cheese have also been developed, which include various flavorings blended into the cheese before sale (e.g., Wensleydale with cranberries).

Wensleydale cheese is often served as part of a cheeseboard or "ploughman's lunch" with chutney. In the north of England it is often served with fruitcake or apple pie.

Calvert, T. C. *The Story of Wensleydale Cheese*. Lancaster, U.K.: Dalesman, 1946.

Cheke, V. *The Story of Cheese-making in Britain*. London: Routledge and Kegan Paul, 1959.

Council Regulation (EC) 510/2006. "On the Protection of Geographical Indications and Designations of Origin for Agricultural Products and Foodstuffs: Yorkshire Wensleydale." *Official Journal of the European Union* (2013) 231/20.

Davis, J. G. *Cheese*. Vol. 3: *Manufacturing Methods*. Edinburgh: Churchill Livingstone, 1976.

Rance, P. *The Great British Cheese Book*. London: Macmillan, 1982.

Andy Swinscoe

Westcombe Dairy

See CHEDDAR.

whey is a byproduct of cheesemaking, the liquid portion resulting when milk is coagulated by rennet or acid. It is categorized as sweet whey and acid whey depending on how the milk protein (casein) is coagulated. Sweet whey is the serum produced from rennet-induced milk coagulation, such as occurs during the process of Cheddar, mozzarella, and Swiss cheese manufacturing. Acid whey comes from the serum separated from acid-coagulated curds (i.e., cottage cheese, Greek yogurt, and acid casein). Sweet whey usually has a pH around or above 6.0 and a slightly sweet taste, while acid whey's pH is around or below 5.0.

Acid whey and sweet whey also differ in composition and functionality. Acid whey is usually considered more problematic compared with sweet whey because of the higher acid and ash content than sweet whey. The acids are either naturally fermented (i.e., lactic acid from cottage cheese or Greek yogurt production) or manually added (i.e., inorganic acid from acid casein manufacturing), which makes acid whey very sticky and hygroscopic when it is dried or concentrated. The higher ash content in acid whey may limit some of its applications, such as use in infant formula. The Greek yogurt boom in the United States has created an excess of acid whey in recent years, which drives innovations of acid whey applications, such as utilization as a mineral-rich functional ingredient, and bone health products.

Sweet whey is the more commonly and widely used form of whey. When 1 pound (453 grams) of cheese (rennet coagulated) is made, about 9 pounds (4 kilograms) of sweet whey will be produced. Sweet whey had been directly disposed of or used in animal feed and fertilizer for thousands of years until the value was steadily unveiled decades ago. Liquid sweet whey contains about 1.6–1.8 ounces per quart (44–52 grams per liter) of lactose, 0.21–0.28 ounce per quart (6–8 grams per liter) of whey protein, and 0.09–0.25 ounce per quart (2.5–7.2 grams per liter) of minerals. Today a variety of products, like lactose, sweet whey powder, whey cheeses, whey protein concentrate, and whey protein isolate, can be fractioned to fulfill a variety of applications in the pharmaceutical, food, chemical, and animal feed industries.

Lactose is the most abundant component in whey. It is usually a byproduct of whey protein manufacturing, which is crystallized and refined from sweet whey permeate, while whey proteins are recovered by the microfiltration process. Lactose is a disaccharide consisting of one molecule of galactose and one molecule of glucose connected by beta-1-4 glycosidic linkage. Lactose has many nutritional and functional attributes that are different from sucrose, such as less sweetness, low cariogenicity (dental caries–producing effect), Maillard browning, prebiotic effects, and promotion of mineral absorption in the diet. Lactose is widely used in infant formula, bakery, confections, salad dressings, sauces, and pharmaceutical formulations.

Whey proteins are a group of globular proteins including beta-lactoglobulin (beta-Lg), alpha-lactoalbumin (alpha-La), glycomacropeptide (GMP), bovine serum albumin (BSA), immunoglobulins, lactoperoxidase, lactotransferrin, and other minor proteins. Whey proteins are rich in essential amino acids, and are some of the highest quality proteins with many functional and nutritional properties. Beta-Lg composes about 50 percent of whey protein and approx. 0.3 percent of the total bovine milk, and it contributes most of the functionality of whey protein, for example, heat stability, gelling, foaming, and emulsifying properties. Alpha-La is the second most abundant protein in whey (approximately 18 percent), and it is a calcium-binding protein. Bovine alpha-La shows similarity to over 70 percent of the amino acid sequence of human alpha-La, which is the most abundant protein in breast milk. GMP (approximately 15–20 percent of whey protein) is part of kappa-casein and cleaved by rennet and left in the whey solution during cheesemaking. GMP is a protein naturally found without phenylalanine, and can be used as a special dietary protein source for phenylketonuria patients who cannot metabolize phenylalanine properly. BSA (approximately 8 percent of whey protein) is the protein leaked to milk from bovine blood. The contents of minor proteins (immunoglobulins, lactoperoxidase, and lactoferrin) are very low, but have high biological values. Acid whey protein is similar to sweet whey protein except for the absence of GMP, because the cleavage of one third of kappa-casein from its C-terminal only occurs in rennet-induced casein coagulation.

Infant formula and sports nutritional products are the two major applications in functional foods for whey products. Human milk contains higher lactose levels and whey-casein ratios than bovine milk, thus lactose and whey proteins are often used for bovine milk-based infant formula to mimic human milk chemistry. Whey protein is rich in branched amino acid (BCAA), which makes up approximately 20 percent of the whey protein amino acid sequence. BCAA plays a key role in providing energy and muscle building during or after exercise.

Beyond nutritional applications, whey is used to produce a wide variety of cheeses such as Mysost, ricotta, and Ziger. Mysost cheese is made from cheese whey, mainly in Norway, Sweden, Denmark, and in a few states in United States. If using goat's milk cheese whey, a similar cheese is named Gjtost. If sweet whey is used, the whey is normally cultured and then heated to coagulate the whey proteins. The chemical composition of Mysost cheese may vary depending on the manufacturer, location, and manufacturing methods used. The moisture content of Mysost is normally around 13 percent, and fat-in-solids is between 10 to 20 percent. Ricotta cheese is considered an Italian cheese since it originated in Italy. Ricotta cheese is sometimes called whey cheese, albumin cheese, or Ziger. In the United States, to improve its body and flavor, ricotta cheese is made using sweet whey with 5–10 percent whole milk or skim milk added for fresh ricotta and dry ricotta, respectively. Ricotta cheese is made by heating the whey to 185°F (85°C) or higher to coagulate the whey proteins and/or adding acidulents, for example, citric acid, recovering and dipping the curd, adding starter cultures after cooling the curd, salting, packaging, and pressing (dry ricotta cheese).

See also COAGULATION OR CURDLING; CONCENTRATED WHEY CHEESE; HEALTH PROPERTIES; RICOTTA; and WHEY POWDER.

Alsaed, A. K., et al. "Characterization, Concentration and Utilization of Sweet and Acid Whey." *Pakistan Journal of Nutrition* 12, no. 2 (2013): 172–177.

Fox, P. F., and P. L. H. McSweeney. *Dairy Chemistry and Biochemistry*. London: Blackie Academic & Professional, 1998.

U.S. Agricultural Research Service. *Cheese Varieties and Descriptions*. Alexandria, Va.: U.S. Department of Agriculture, 1978.

U.S. Dairy Export Council. *Reference Manual for U.S. Whey and Lactose Products*. http://usdec.files.cms-plus.com/PDFs/2008ReferenceManuals/Whey_Lactose_Reference_Manual_Complete2_Optimized.pdf.

Mingruo Guo and Guorong Wang

whey powder results when liquid whey, the byproduct of cheese manufacture, is dried to form a variety of powdered products with different compositional profiles. Four common whey powders, listed in order of increasing protein content, are as follows: (1) sweet whey powder (SWP), (2) whey protein concentrate 34 (WPC34), (3) whey protein concentrate 80 (WPC80), and (4) whey protein isolate (WPI). All of these products have US federal standards of identity.

The initial steps in production are the same for all whey powders. First, liquid whey collected from cheesemaking is filtered to remove curd particles and then centrifuged to remove fat. The clarified whey is pasteurized, to halt culture activity and prevent further acidification. Caustic may be added at this point to increase the pH, and the whey may be bleached with benzoyl peroxide or hydrogen peroxide if it was generated from colored cheese.

To produce SWP, the clarified, pasteurized whey is spray dried. SWP contains approximately 12.5 percent protein, 73 percent lactose, and 8.5 percent minerals, and is generally used as an inexpensive ingredient in a variety of food products. The fat level is approximately 1 percent, increasing to 4–6 percent in the higher-protein products.

The production of higher-protein whey powder requires additional processing steps to remove lactose and minerals. First, pasteurized, clarified whey is concentrated, either by evaporation or by ultrafiltration (UF). In UF processing, protein is retained on one side of the UF membrane, while smaller dissolved compounds such as lactose and minerals permeate through the membrane. The UF processing generates a liquid "retentate" with a higher protein content and lower lactose and mineral content than the original feed liquid. This liquid concentrate is either spray dried to produce WPC34 (34 percent protein, 52 percent lactose, 9 percent minerals) or it is additionally processed to further increase the protein content prior to spray drying. The WPC34 is used as a higher-protein, more functional alternative to SWP in foods.

The process of increasing the protein content in concentrated liquid whey is referred to as "diafiltration." An initial UF concentrate containing high protein, lactose, and minerals is diluted with water. The diluted liquid is reconcentrated, using a UF membrane with pores large enough to allow lactose and minerals to pass through, while retaining protein. This second concentrate is rediluted and reconcentrated as needed, with each step increasing the protein and decreasing the lactose and mineral contents. WPC80 (80 percent protein, 9 percent lactose, 4 percent minerals) and WPI (90 percent protein, 2 percent lactose, 3 percent minerals) are produced by this method.

Whey protein powders are susceptible to oxidation and browning reactions on extended storage, particularly if they are exposed to light, oxygen, or heat. These oxidation reactions limit shelf life to a period ranging from a few months to approximately a year. The solubility of whey powder decreases with increasing protein, necessitating additional time, temperature, and/or shear to fully hydrate them.

Higher-protein whey powders require more processing and are more expensive to produce, but are also more functional as food ingredients. Whey protein acts as an efficient thickener, water binder, and foaming agent in a variety of food matrices. The nutritional value of whey protein is also utilized in muscle building and sports recovery drinks.

See also ULTRAFILTRATION and WHEY.

Huffman, Lee M., and Lilian de Barros Ferreira. In *Dairy Ingredients for Food Processing*, edited by Ramesh C. Chandan and Arun Kilara, pp. 179–198. Ames, Iowa: Wiley-Blackwell, 2011.

Smith, K. *Dried Dairy Ingredients*. Madison: Wisconsin Center for Dairy Research, 2008. http://future.aae .wisc.edu/publications/dried_dairy_ingdients.pdf.

U.S. Code of Federal Regulations Title 21, Part 184: Direct Food Substances affirmed as Generally Recognized as Safe, Subpart B-Listing of Specific Substances Affirmed as GRAS, Sec. 184.1979 Whey; Sec. 184.1979c: Whey protein concentrate.

Dana D. Wolle

wild-type strain is a term generally used in contrast with genetically modified organisms or with domesticated strains. It refers to the phenotype of the typical form of a species as it occurs in nature. See TAXONOMY and PHENOTYPIC VARIABILITY. Strains naturally present in raw milk and recovered in cheese most often come from the environment. They are not subjected to any modification of their genetic material nor adapted toward technological or starter production stresses. The wild-type strain makes reference to the "ancestral" strain originally associated with the cheese being considered.

As the first traditional cheeses were made without the use of additional starter cultures, the fermentation process was dependent on wild-type strains present in raw milk or those coming from the environment during cheese processing. See STARTER CULTURES. As soon as a wild-type strain becomes associated with a specific technology it can be submitted to an adaptive process, via, for example, horizontal gene transfer, in order to adapt to its new environment. For microbiologists the mechanism of adaptation responsible for phenotypic changes is a fundamental question in evolutionary biology. It concerns bacteria, yeasts, and filamentous fungi used in the production of cheese. The first adaptation of microorganism to milk probably followed the appearance of mammals between 65 and 23 million years ago, but domestication of starters likely coincided with the first archaeological evidence for cheesemaking dating back to 6000 B.C.E. in northern Europe. Like all other domesticated organisms, starters evolved from wild ancestors and studies of food-related microorganisms on comparative genomics reveal that the genomes in these microorganisms were streamlined and accompanied by a loss in parallel to gene acquisition events.

There are evolutionary studies focusing on specific microorganisms, for example, *Lactococcus lactis* for bacteria, *Yarrowia lipolytica* for yeasts, and *Penicillium* for filamentous fungi. These species have developed dynamic metabolic adaptations to survive within the cheese ecosystem. For *Lactococcus lactis*, strains frequently used for cheesemaking are very different from the strains isolated from a vegetal ecosystem in terms of genetic characteristics and subsequent technological properties. Thus, for that species, Passerini et al. (2010) suggested a new classification based on ecological separation between "environmental" strains, and "domesticated" strains, subject to recent genetic bottlenecks. *Lactococcus lactis* strains now associated with cheesemaking are probably derived from an "ancestral" wild-type strain through contamination of raw milk from the environment, most likely from plants. This adaptation responsible for the divergence between wild-type strains and the starter strains currently used in cheesemaking is probably accelerated by the design of the starter, based on the functional selection of strains, mainly considering properties such as acidification, proteolysis, and production of aroma compounds. Considering filamentous fungi, Cheeseman et al. (2014) report multiple recent gene transfers of a huge genomic island, called Wallaby, between *Penicillium* spp. found in the food environment. The widespread occurrence of Wallaby in cheese species (including species never found in other environments, such as *Penicillium camemberti*) together with the identity of the sequence, indicate that these transfers occurred in cheese and were, therefore, very recently promoted by human activity.

The genetic adaptation leading a wild-type strain toward a domesticated strain (and which can be very slow for macroscopic species), can be extremely fast for microorganisms. Thus the opportunity to access the wild-type strain of a species can be often uncertain and difficult.

See also GENETICALLY MODIFIED ORGANISM and STRAINS.

Cheeseman, K., et al. "Multiple Recent Horizontal Transfers of a Large Genomic Region in Cheese Making Fungi." *Nature Communications* 5, no. 2876 (2014): 1–9.
Papadimitriou, K., et al. "How Microbes Adapt to a Diversity of Food Niches." *Current Opinion in Food Science* 2 (2015): 29–35.
Passerini, D., et al. "Genes but Not Genomes Reveal Bacterial Domestication of *Lactococcus lactis*." *PLoS ONE* 5, no. 12 (2010).

Florence Valence

Willard, Xerxes Addison (1820–1882), authored the eight-volume work, *Practical Dairy Husbandry*, in 1872; it was the primary nineteenth-century sourcebook on dairy farms, milk, and the manufacture of butter into cheese. Although Willard started his career in law in Little Falls, New York, he gave up law to purchase a farm from his maternal grandfather. Here he engaged his scientific interests by conducting his own experiments on milk. He started the Farmers' Club in Little Falls, one of the earliest of its kind in the state. As his knowledge on dairy farming grew, he edited the *Herkimer County Journal*, wrote for the New York State Agricultural Society on New York dairies, and in 1864 became the editor of the *Utica Morning Herald*, where he established the agricultural department for the paper. Willard helped organize and led the American Dairymen's Association.

The Association sent Willard as a US representative to visit and study dairies around Europe, including dairies in England, Scotland, Ireland, France, and Switzerland. The research from his travels contributed to his *Practical Dairy Husbandry* volumes and the *Practical Butter Book* (1875). Besides being a leader of the American Dairymen's Association, Willard also established the Dairy Boards of Trade and the New York State Dairymen's Association.

Willard gained and maintained a positive reputation among agricultural associations and societies in Europe and in the United States. He spent his later years giving lectures at universities on the East Coast including Cornell University and Maine State Agricultural College, among others.

See also INDUSTRIALIZATION and NEW YORK.

Reddy, William. *First Fifty Years of Cazenovia Seminary, 1825–1875: Its History—Proceedings of the Semi-Centennial Jubilee General Catalogue.* Cazenovia, N.Y.: Nelson & Phillips, 1877.
Willard, Xerxes A. *Willard's Practical Dairy Husbandry: A Complete Treatise on Dairy Farms and Farming—Dairy Stock and Stock Feeding—Milk, Its Management and Manufacture into Butter and Cheese—History and Mode of Organization of Butter and Cheese Factories.* New York: D. D. T. Moore, 1872.

Megan A. Koch

Williams, Jesse

Williams, Jesse (1798–1864), was a farmer and cheesemaker who opened the first American cheese factory in 1851 in Rome, New York, 35 miles east of Syracuse. Cheese had been made in North America since the arrival in the early seventeenth century of the Puritans, many of whom came from established English dairy regions like Suffolk, Essex, and Norfolk and were experienced at crafting Cheshire and Cheddar. They practiced their skill after arriving in the colonies, but for the first two centuries cheesemaking remained on a small scale.

Jesse Williams, whose family had been farming along the Mohawk River near Rome since after the Revolutionary War, believed dairy farming had the chance to be wildly profitable and devoted himself accordingly. Williams's biographer, Frederick A. Rahmer, reports that after a year spent with his wife touring New York dairies to learn about cheesemaking, "Jesse Williams had become by far the best cheesemaker in this country and perhaps the world" (1971, p. 8). Williams's desire to institutionalize the process was the result of some family drama involving his worries that his son George would not be able to continue to produce cheese of the same quality. Williams's solution was a communal project that would pool milk from area farms at a central location and produce a uniform cheese product from the milk. Motivated by efficiency and idealism, the Williams Cheese Factory was soon collecting the milk of between three hundred and four hundred New York cows and producing a hundred thousand pounds of cheese in its first year—more than five times the amount produced by the typical farmstead—earning Williams the appellation "the father of factory cheese." Fifteen years later, New York State had some five hundred cheese factories.

See also INDUSTRIALIZATION and NEW YORK.

Bradley, Grant. "Real Cheese Product—Jesse Williams: The Father of Factory Cheese." *Culture*, 17 January 2014. http://culturecheesemag.com/blog/real-cheese-product-jesse-williams-the-father-of-factory-cheese.
McMurry, Sally. *Transforming Rural Life: Dairying Families and Agricultural Change, 1820–1885.* Baltimore, Md.: Johns Hopkins University Press, 1995.
Rahmer, Frederick A. *Jesse Williams: Cheesemaker.* Rome, N.Y.: F. A. Rahmer, 1971.

Kelly Alexander

wine pairing

wine pairing with cheese is something that has been going on since Nestor returned from the Trojan War, recovering from his exertions with a cocktail of Pramnian wine, grated goat's milk cheese, and barley meal. Whether or not he worried about which goat cheeses went best with his wine is something Homer didn't record, but, knowing the discerning appetites of the ancient Greeks, it wouldn't be surprising.

In fact, it's highly likely that wine, like beer, was the go-to beverage to match with cheese far earlier than that. After all, wine, like cheese, began as little more than an effort to conserve something that was highly perishable—especially in warm areas such as the Tigris-Euphrates River Basin, where the ancient Sumerians and Mesopotamians had organized a dairy industry as early as 7000 B.C.E.

While beer may have been the go-to pairing for these early cheesemakers, it wasn't too long before wine was on the menu as well: Herodotus describes shipments of wine flowing down the Tigris or Euphrates rivers in the fifth century B.C.E. By the Uruk period (4000–3200 B.C.E.), diners had even developed preferred methods for drinking each: cylinder seals show people imbibing beer from jars with straws, while wine drinkers sipped from cups.

At that time—and for the vast majority of history—the cheese to pair with one's wine was more about availability than choice. It wasn't until the latter half of the twentieth century that choosing what to drink with a cheese became an issue to consider. As David Natt, a UK-based food and wine educator, wrote in his contribution to Sarah Freeman's *The Real Cheese Companion* (2003): "The combination of cheese and wine has changed from 1960s cliché to 1990s conundrum."

While the rise of food as entertainment and socially acceptable obsession certainly has something to do with the increased concern about "proper" pairings, the confusion also has to do with the head-spinning number of cheeses and wines available in urban centers today. Rules are a convenient method to make boundless choice more manageable, and modern cheese guides are rife with pairing guidelines.

Common Approaches

The most common piece of wine and cheese pairing advice—and, arguably, most useful—is to heed the adage "what grows together goes together." Think of Loire goat cheese and the region's sauvignon blancs, both grassy and tangy; consider Époisses de Bourgogne and Burgundian chardonnay, the duo a match in power and richness. France's Jura provides both Comté and its classic wine matches; Tuscany produces both Pecorino Toscano and Chianti. These combinations grew up together, their felicity part nature (climate, geology, landscape) and part nurture (human desire to have appealing food and drink).

Another approach is to look for pairings that complement or contrast in flavor and texture. Take Époisses, for instance: A white Burgundy could make a sumptuous, rich on rich pairing, while a Champagne also works well, the high-acid, bubbly wine a dynamic, refreshing counterpoint to the oozing cheese.

That said, the contrast approach has its limits: Most big reds will obliterate a cheese; a pungent washed-rind cheese may likewise punish a light, frisky white. A few guidelines are useful here:

- Match weight. A light, fresh cheese wants a light, fresh wine; a lustily-flavored Cheddar wants something just as robust.
- Pad those tannins. Tannins, astringent compounds found primarily in red wines, bind to proteins, so the best matches for tannic wines are dense, rich cheeses without too much salt.
- Play salt off sweet. Salt accentuates tannins and alcohol, so salty cheeses like Parmigiano Reggiano and blues tend to do well with dessert wines.
- Watch for rinds. They can pack a punch of funk that will throw off any wines— when this happens, just cut it off.
- When in doubt, reach for white wines. Most have no tannins and little oak, the toughest elements to deal with when it comes to cheese.

- Respect your elders. If it's an old, special bottle, opt for a fairly simple cheese, just to keep the competition to a minimum.

A Scientific Approach

Québécois sommelier François Chartier takes a scientific approach to matching wines and foods, charting the volatile molecules of different foods—including cheeses—in order to better understand their pairing potentials. For instance, in his book *Taste Buds and Molecules: The Art and Science of Food, Wine, and Flavor* (2012), he points out that cheeses with fresh herb and floral notes—such as some summer milk cheeses—are rich in terpenes, like linalool—as are grape varieties such as Gewürztraminer, muscat, and Riesling. These chemical similarities make them ideal pairings. Likewise, blues tend to have a high level of thiols, which he points to as the "major aromatic signature" of Sauvignon Blanc—thus explaining why the classic match of Sauternes (a sweet wine made with a high percentage of Sauvignon Blanc) works so well with Roquefort.

His approach also allows for flexibility when the desired wine and cheese are not a natural fit. To make a bloomy-rind cheese match well with a red, he suggests cutting it in half and sprinkling the cut surface with cloves. After wrapping up the cheese and letting it sit for a few days, the eugenol in the cloves will have permeated the paste, readying the cheese for big reds such as Zinfandel or Rioja that have spent time in charred oak barrels (which are also high in eugenol). Use black olive paste instead of cloves for syrah, or sundried tomato puree for New World Pinot Noir.

Of course, Chartier's approach requires a fair amount of dedication to master, but his work highlights a couple handy points: when in doubt, reach for Swiss, Mimolette, and Parmigiano, which, because of their chemical makeup, work well with a wide variety of wines. Or, if the cheese has already been ordered, fino sherry is always a good bet: "With its 307 identified volatile compounds, like manzanilla, its royal companion, fino offers a very wide palette of aromas that can complement a vast array of ingredients," he writes. (p. 69).

Method

Generally, most sommeliers and cheesemongers agree that three to five cheeses on a plate is plenty;

any more than that can be overwhelming (physically as well as mentally).

On the wine front, one wine is enough, but opening three or four bottles at once will allow more opportunity to compare and contrast the wines and their reactions with the cheeses.

To assess the felicity of a match, try the wine(s) first: Swirl the glass so you can really smell the wine (after all, what we register as flavor mostly originates as scent). Take a sip and roll it around in your mouth; think about what you taste and feel. Is it smooth and rich, or light and lively? Does it taste like fruit or more like earth? Does it taste like something you would want to eat with your cheese?

If you're tasting multiple wines, taste all of them before you move on to the cheese, making notes as you go.

When it's time to taste the cheese, approach it like wine: smell, then taste, noting not just the initial flavors but also the notes that linger. When you're ready to combine cheese and wine, begin with cheese, then follow with wine, as the acidity and tannins in the wine will help ready the palate for the next bite. When your palate needs a break, reach for a cracker or a slice of bread.

And if the pairing doesn't work out as well as hoped, know that there's not an expert in history who's claimed to always get it right. As each vintage of wine and batch of cheese is different, and each continues to evolve until the moment it is consumed, it's impossible to always get it right. That's the beauty of the pairing of wine and cheese.

See also BEER PAIRING.

Chartier, François. *Taste Buds and Molecules: The Art and Science of Food, Wine, and Flavor.* Hoboken, N.J.: Wiley, 2012.

Dalby, Andrew. *Cheese: A Global History.* The Edible Series. London: Reaktion Books, 2009.

Freeman, Sarah. *The Real Cheese Companion: A Guide to the Best Handmade Cheeses of Britain and Ireland.* London: Time Warner. 2003.

Kindstedt, Paul S. *Cheese and Culture: A History of Cheese and Its Place in Western Civilization.* White River Junction, Vt.: Chelsea Green, 2012.

McCalman, Max, and David Gibbons. *The Cheese Plate.* New York: Clarkson Potter, 2002.

Rosengarten, David, and Joshua Wesson. *Red Wine with Fish: The New Art of Matching Wine with Food.* New York: Simon & Schuster, 1989.

Tara Q. Thomas

Winnimere is a raw cow's milk cheese made by Jasper Hill Creamery in Greensboro Bend, Vermont. Inspired by cheeses such as Vacherin Mont d'Or, Winnimere is a farmstead, soft-ripened, washed-rind cheese wrapped in spruce bark weighing 24 ounces (680 grams) per piece. See MONT D'OR. Forty-five Ayrshire cows feeding on hay during the winter months create rich milk that is both high in fat and protein. During peak production, Winnimere is made twice per week with approximately four hundred wheels made per batch. Traditional animal rennet is used in the making of it. The day after production Winnimere is wrapped in strips of spruce cambium (the tree's flexible inner layer) harvested from Jasper Hill's local woodlands. While being aged Winnimere is washed with cultured salt brine several times per week, depending on the need of individual cheeses, to promote even rind development.

After it is aged for sixty days, Winnimere is properly eaten by peeling off the top layer and scooping it with a spoon. One of the finest (if not decadent) features of this cheese is its velvety, creamy texture. This is accomplished through minimal handling of the curd, creating a high moisture cheese. Tasting notes include bacon, sweet cream, mustard, and spruce—think campfire. A suggested beverage pairing is a smoky, meaty red wine or a porter-style beer. The name of the cheese comes from a street on the edge of Caspian Lake, where the grandfather of the cheesemaking brothers Mateo and Andy Kehler enjoyed an ice fishing shack. In 2013 this cheese won the American Cheese Society's Best in Show award.

See also BARK-WRAPPED CHEESES; CELLARS AT JASPER HILL; and VERMONT.

Darlington, Tenaya. "Vixens." In *Di Bruno Bros. House of Cheese: A Guide to Recipes, Wedges, and Pairing,* p. 112. Philadelphia: Running Press Book, 2013.

McCalman, Max, and David Gibbons. "Taking the World Stage." In *Mastering Cheese: Lessons for Connoisseurship from a Maître Fromager,* p. 271. New York: Clarkson Potter, 2009.

Adam Moskowitz

Wisconsin leads the United States in cheesemaking, producing more than 3 billion pounds (1.4 billion kilograms) of cheese annually as of 2015. Known as "America's Dairyland" because of its history of milk and cheese production since the 1850s, Wisconsin is today transitioning from a

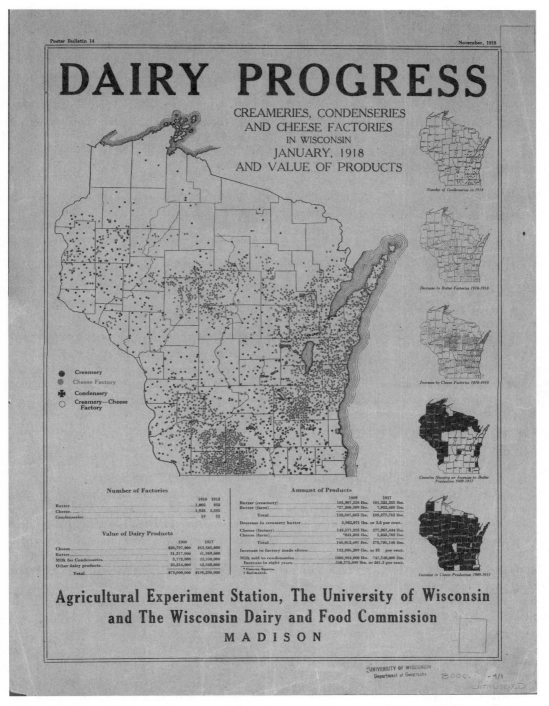

This map illustrates creameries, condenseries, and cheese factories in Wisconsin as of January 1918. Five smaller maps in the margin show changes in production and in the number of factories from 1909 to 1918. WISCONSIN HISTORICAL SOCIETY

commodity to specialty cheese production state. More than 45 percent of all specialty cheese in America is produced in Wisconsin, accounting for six hundred types, styles, and varieties.

Wisconsin is the only state to require its cheesemakers be licensed, a lengthy process requiring attendance at multiple university courses, hundreds of hours of apprenticeship with an existing licensed cheesemaker, and a written test. Veteran cheesemakers making one type of cheese for at least ten years may apply to become a Master Cheesemaker, a program administered by the Wisconsin Center for Dairy Research at the University of Wisconsin-Madison. Masters-in-training spend three years in university courses and advanced training to become certified as a master in one type of cheese. Only about fifty master cheesemakers are certified in Wisconsin, compared with twelve hundred licensed cheesemakers. See WISCONSIN'S CHEESEMAKER LICENSING PROGRAM.

About ten thousand dairy farms dot the Wisconsin landscape, each with an average of 125 dairy cows. More than one-quarter practice a style of farming known as intensive rotational grazing, with cows grazing on fresh pasture at last nine months of the year. As 90 percent of all Wisconsin milk is turned into cheese, grass-based cheese is on the rise in the state, with an increasing number of cheesemakers crafting seasonal and artisan cheeses. For example, Pleasant Ridge Reserve, the most awarded cheese in the nation, is made in Wisconsin May through October from the milk of pastured cows. See PLEASANT RIDGE RESERVE.

In national cheese contests, such as the American Cheese Society competition and the US Championship Cheese Contest, Wisconsin often dominates with the number of awards earned. See COMPETITIONS. While the state has long been renowned for its commodity Cheddar and mozzarella production, more than 75 percent of all cheese factories today make at least one type of specialty cheese, a growing trend since 2004. This increase in bolder, more flavorful production of high-quality specialty cheese is the direct result of demand from American chefs and consumers, who increasingly request more sophisticated flavors.

Dairying and cheese production is actively supported by the University of Wisconsin, which carries a rich history of promoting the industry. In 1890, Professor Stephen Babcock developed the first test for butterfat content in milk, allowing the manufacture of consistently higher quality butter and cheese.

Since the 1880s, the university has offered agricultural and cheesemaking "short courses" in Madison to educate dairy farmers and cheesemakers on the latest technology available. The state is renowned for its "Wisconsin Idea," a principle that the university system should improve people's lives beyond the classroom, taking the latest information and research to farms through outreach and public service. This concept resonates through every aspect of the Wisconsin dairy industry.

See also UNITED STATES.

Janus, Edward. *Creating Dairyland: How Caring for Cows Saved Our Soil, Created Our Landscape, Brought Prosperity to Our State, and Still Shapes Our Way of Life in Wisconsin*. Madison: Wisconsin Historical Society, 2011.
Wisconsin Milk Marketing Board. http://www.eatwisconsincheese.com.

Jeanne Carpenter

The **Wisconsin Cheese Makers Association,** one of Wisconsin's oldest continually operating trade associations, was formed in 1893 as advocates of quality cheesemaking in the state rallied against "undue competition from deceitful and dangerous imitations," as stated in its founding articles. Cheesemakers, cheese buyers, marketers and suppliers to the industry joined to create an organization driven by the desire to produce consistent, quality cheese for US and international markets.

Within a decade of WCMA's formation, Wisconsin was the nation's second-largest cheesemaker and by 1909 had surpassed New York State, opening a lead in production that Wisconsin has not surrendered to this day. The number of Wisconsin cheese manufacturers peaked in the 1920s with more than 2,000 small factories. As of 2015, 130 factories in Wisconsin, large and small, produce 3 billion pounds of cheese, more than seven times the production of 1925.

Through the decades, the association has advocated for state-of-the-art practices, from proper sanitation to a scientific approach to cheesemaking. Professors from the Dairy School at the University of Wisconsin have lectured at WCMA meetings, and today the Wisconsin Center for Dairy Research on the University campus is a key WCMA partner.

Through advocacy, workshops, and seminars, WCMA continues to address quality cheesemaking, effective regulation, and the education of its members.

The cheese competition initiated by WCMA in 1893 has become the World Championship Cheese Contest, the largest technical cheese and butter competition in the world. The association hosts, in alternating years, the International Cheese Technology Expo and the Wisconsin Cheese Industry Conference.

See also WISCONSIN.

Apps, Jerry. *Cheese: The Making of a Wisconsin Tradition.* Amherst, Wis.: Amherst, 1998.

Janus, Edward. *Creating Dairyland.* Madison: Wisconsin Historical Society Press, 2011.

John Umhoefer

Wisconsin's cheesemaker licensing program

is unique, since Wisconsin is the only state that requires all cheesemakers to be licensed. This license is administered by the Wisconsin Department of Agriculture, Trade and Consumer Protection (WDATCP). In January 1915 the Wisconsin Cheese Makers Association asked the legislature to pass a law requiring the licensing of cheesemakers. The law, signed by Governor Emanuel L. Philipp the same year, required anyone seeking a license to have twelve months of cheesemaking experience. At that time, a license cost one dollar, and along with it, the cheesemakers received a copy of current dairy laws, a list of licensing rules and regulations, and instructions for operating a cheese factory.

The Wisconsin Cheese Makers Association took the job of creating the first regulations for cheesemaking very seriously. As the Wisconsin dairy regulator E. L. Aderhold explained, "We had to make them comprehensive, we had to make them adequate so as to get good results, and we had to make them reasonable" (Wisconsin Cheese Makers Association, pp. 40–41). A century later, the cost of a license is $75, the necessary experience and education has increased, and a written exam is required of all new applicants. But the aim of the licensing program remains the same: to standardize Wisconsin cheese production, to raise both the quality of Wisconsin cheese and the safety of its cheesemaking facilities, and finally, to promote the Wisconsin "brand." According to John Umhoefer, the executive director of the Wisconsin Cheese Makers Association in 2015, "E. L. Aderhold would be proud."

See also WISCONSIN and WISCONSIN CHEESE MAKERS ASSOCIATION.

Umhoefer, John. "100 Years of Success." *Cheese Market News*, 15 February 2015. http://www.cheesemarketnews.com/guestcolumn/2015/06feb15.html.

Wisconsin Cheese Makers Association. *Proceedings of the Wisconsin Cheese Makers' Association Annual Convention: 1916–17–18.* Madison, Wis.: Democrat Printing Company, 1918. http://hdl.handle.net/2027/wu.89044369783.

Wisconsin Department of Agriculture, Trade and Consumer Protection Administrative Code, Chapter ATCP69. Buttermakers and Cheesemakers. Register July 2011 No. 667. http://docs.legis.wisconsin.gov/code/admin_code/atcp/055/69.

Marianne Smukowski

witchcraft

See MAGICAL THINKING.

wooden shelves

are used to store and ripen cheeses in cellars in many countries, including the United States. In France, for example, about 350,000 tons of cheese are ripened on wooden shelves; their use is even mandatory for some famous PDO (protected designation of origin) cheeses such as Comté, Beaufort, Reblochon, and Roquefort. Spruce wood is frequently used to make the shelves. See COMTÉ; BEAUFORT; REBLOCHON; and ROQUEFORT.

Wooden shelves have two main roles: the first is related to the microbial ecology of the cheese surface, as a microbial biofilm rapidly covers the shelves and positively interacts with the cheese. The other one, very important from a technological point of view, is to regulate hydric exchange between the cheese curd and the cellar air humidity. By using wood with various levels of hygrometry (10 to 19 percent humidity) cheesemakers modulate, with an ancestral empirical knowledge, the kinetics of cheese drying, which has a key influence on the correct setup of the microbial rind and more broadly the whole ripening process.

Cheesemakers are very careful in choosing the wooden shelves from sawmills. The wood must be correctly dried, which might require several months. A shelf that is too humid favors mold defects on the surface of the cheese, and some pseudomonas, for example. If too dry, wood favors the development of thick, strong rinds and red defects. There is much empirical know-how of cheesemakers by touch. Analytical tools like the pin-type moisture meter exist to confirm the cheesemaker's estimation.

A huge amount of empirical knowledge but little scientific literature exists about shelves and cheese. The microbial ecology and safety of wooden shelves used for the ripening of Reblochon de Savoie is one of the cases extensively studied. This smear-ripened cheese is most often made from raw milk. Microbial biofilms explored on fifty shelves, from different farms and different seasons, were shown to be mainly composed of *micrococci, corynebacteria*, sometimes *leuconostocs, lactobacilli, enterococci*, coagulase-negative *staphylococci*, and *pseudomonads*, plus yeasts and molds. This composition is very stable over time and was similar to that of the cheese surface, supporting the claim of cheesemakers that wooden shelves represent a valuable source of microbial flora for the rind. The colonization of the wood occurs about in the first $1/16$ inch (2 millimeters) of depth. The wood has a neutral pH, high water availability, and low salt content. Despite these favorable conditions of growth, from ninety shelves explored for safety assessment, neither *Listeria* nor *Salmonella* spp. were found and less than 10 cfu/ cm^2 for *S. aureus* and *E. coli,* indicating the strength of the local positive biofilms. The wood itself can release antimicrobial compounds toward pathogens. No food-borne disease outbreak has ever been attributed to the use of wood. However, as with wooden vats, more scientific studies, cleaning, and general guidelines for wooden shelves management would certainly be welcomed by regulatory authorities and will allow cheesemakers to keep this natural material with exceptional virtues in cheesemaking.

See also BIOFILMS; RIPENING CULTURES; and WOODEN VATS.

Lortal, S., et al. "Wooden Tools and Microbial Biodiversity in Traditional Cheesemaking." In *Cheese and Microbes*, edited by Catherine W. Donnelly, pp. 167–176. Washington, D.C.: American Society for Microbiology, 2014.

Mariani, C., et al. "Biofilm Ecology of Wooden Shelves Used in Ripening the French Raw Milk Smear Cheese Reblochon de Savoie." *Journal of Dairy Science* 90 (2007): 1653–1661.

Sylvie Lortal

wooden vats in different forms have been used for centuries by farmers and cheesemakers all over the world to collect and transform milk. Unfortunately, as wood is a biodegradable material in contrast to ceramic, there are very few historical artifacts to date this use. It is likely as old as cheesemaking itself. Wood from many tree species can be used, such as oak, spruce, pine, chestnut, beech, and walnut, depending on the region and altitude. What matters is that no chemical preservative treatment has been applied to the wood before contact with milk. Douglas fir and chestnut are the most common woods used for making cheese vats.

For some PDO (protected designation of origin) cheeses, such as Ragusano in Sicily and Salers in France, the use of wooden vats is mandatory, with specific names for the vats, respectively *tina* and *gerle*. See RAGUSANO and SALERS. Each cheesemaker has its own tina or gerle. Both have been deeply explored by microbiologists recently. Wooden vats in daily contact with raw milk are covered by a thick biofilm composed of a rich microbial ecosystem entrapped in a thick polysaccharide matrix. Molecular exploration revealed within the biofilm the predominance of lactic acid bacteria, in particular *S. thermophilus*, thermophilic lactobacilli, lactococci, and leuconostocs, whereas other species like coryneform bacteria can also be present. Variable but usually low levels of molds and yeasts were detected. See BIOFILMS; MICROBIAL COMMUNITIES; and LACTIC ACID BACTERIA.

For lactic acid bacteria, several strains of the same species coexist, leading to a very robust biodiverse system. Interestingly, the lactic acid bacteria strains found in this wooden biotope forms unique genomic clusters when compared to all other collection strains of the same species. The biofilm is a very efficient system of lactic acid bacteria delivery when raw milk is put in the vat, inoculating the milk like a starter culture addition would do. Indeed, for example, between 100,000 and 1 million of total count is found in a sterile milk after ten minutes of contact with a tina or a gerle vat. In this way wooden vats are a source of valuable microbial diversity and contribute to the subsequent acidification step. In the tina like in the gerle, pathogenic species like *Listeria, Salmonella* or *E. coli* were never found and wooden vats have never been involved in any food-borne disease outbreak to date.

Wooden vats are thus a natural, safe, free, and efficient starter inoculation system. Despite all these qualities, and because wood is a porous material difficult to clean, the *Codex Alimentarius* does not approve the use of wood in contact with food, including milk or cheese. See CODEX ALIMENTARIUS. In Europe as well as in the United States, use of wood, which has a positive consumer image as a natural material, is still allowed. The only mandatory aspect is to guarantee the efficiency of cleaning toward pathogens. More research about cleaning and the writing of guidelines would be very useful to definitively reassure safety authorities. Until now each cheesemaker has, on the same basis, his own procedure to clean wooden vats. See HYGIENE and PATHOGENS.

See also TINA and WOODEN SHELVES.

Lortal, S., et al. "Wooden Tools and Microbial Biodiversity in Traditional Cheesemaking." In *Cheese and Microbes*, edited by Catherine W. Donnelly, pp. 167–176. Washington, D.C.: American Society of Microbiology, 2014.

Scatassa, M.-L., et al., 2015. "Transfer, Composition and Technological Characterization of the Lactic Acid Bacteria Populations of the Wooden Vats Used to Produce Traditional Stretched Cheeses." *Food Microbiology* 52 (2015): 31–41.

Sylvie Lortal

The **World Trade Organization** (WTO) provides a forum for governments to negotiate trade agreements and to settle trade disputes to facilitate the liberalization of trade. WTO agreements provide the legal framework for international commerce, essentially binding governments to keep their trade policies within agreed limits. In pursuit of harmonization, the Agreement on Sanitary and Phytosanitary Measures (SPS) utilizes the *Codex Alimentarius* as the benchmark against which national measures and regulations related to food are evaluated and in the settling of trade disputes. While member countries are encouraged to use international benchmarks, the agreement allows countries to use different standards and different methods of inspecting products. If an exporting country can demonstrate that the measures it applies to its exports achieve an equivalent level of health protection as in the importing country, then the importing country is expected to accept the exporting country's standards and methods.

See also CODEX ALIMENTARIUS and GENERAL AGREEMENT ON TARRIFS AND TRADE.

World Trade Organization. "Understanding the WTO." 5th ed. Geneva, Switzerland, 2011. https://www.wto.org/english/thewto_e/whatis_e/tif_e/tif_e.htm.

Dennis D'Amico

World War I, a conflict of unprecedented scope and magnitude with more than 70 million men in arms, produced casualties on a scale the world had never known. The conflict was also unique in the severe challenges that the war's sheer scale imposed on its participant nations to provision their troops in the field while avoiding privation on the home front. Scholars have argued that victory or defeat in World War I depended as much on the capacity of combatant nations to feed their populations and their troops as on the production of weaponry and other war materiel. Indeed, the denial of that capacity to the enemy through blockades and attacks on shipping was a major strategy on both sides of the conflict. Food production, agriculture, and government policy related to food were all transformed in the process. And cheese, as a compact, caloric, preservable, transportable food—a mainstay of traditional diets throughout Europe, and an important military ration throughout history—was no exception.

Among the first impacts of the war on its participants' capacity to produce sufficient food were acute labor shortages, as young men enlisted or were conscripted by the millions. The agriculture sectors were particularly hard hit, as unskilled agricultural workers were disproportionately liable to be conscripted. By 1915, a year into the conflict, 16 percent of British agricultural workers had joined the armed forces.

During World War I even the famously colorful and whimsical labels of Camembert abandoned their pastoral scenes of milkmaids and monks for subjects of a more martial nature, like this Camembert "Le Poilu d'Argonne," which depicted French troops charging through the barbed wire of no man's land. © JEAN-MARIE BIDAUX

In France farmers left for the front just as the harvest of 1914 was getting under way. Many farmstead cheese operations were forced to close and never reopened. This hemorrhage of able-bodied men also had a profound impact on the demographic of farming and cheesemaking as women took on the labor and management of many cheesemaking operations.

The impact of World War I on each combatant nation's ability to feed itself and its troops differed considerably. In the early years of the war, food supplies in Britain, for example, were little affected. The country was heavily dependent on imports for its food supply, a legacy of free trade policies and a long-held confidence in the British Navy to protect Britain's access to foreign sources of supply, even in the event of war. Much of Britain's grain, butter, lard, ham, and bacon, and three-quarters of its cheese were imported. The German U-boat campaign to disrupt supplies to Britain did not yet constitute a sufficient menace, but later in the war would have a significant impact on food supplies.

During the war Britain sent more than 3 million tons of food to its more than 5 million soldiers fighting in France and Belgium and other theaters of the war. These rations, per person per day, included (at least on paper) 20 ounces of fresh or frozen meat, or 1 pound of salt meat; 4 ounces of bacon; 20 ounces of bread or 16 ounces of flour or 4 ounces of oatmeal; 3 ounces of cheese; 4 ounces of butter or margarine; 1 ounce of tea; 4 ounces of jam or dried fruit; pepper, mustard; 8 ounces fresh vegetables or tenth of a gill of lime juice; half a gill of rum or pint of porter; and 2 ounces of tobacco. However as the war settled into a horrific quagmire of bloody trench warfare, and as the U-boat campaign against Allied transport shipping intensified, the British government was forced to step in to regulate food supply and pricing. By January 1918 sugar was rationed, followed in April by restrictions on meat, butter, margarine, and cheese. See UNITED KINGDOM.

The French experience was different. Though much of the war's bloodiest battles took place on French soil, the French people, at least those not under German occupation, did not suffer the severe food shortages experienced by the Central Powers, or even Britain. There were no food riots and the standard of living of its citizenry never fell to insufficient levels. And although there were acute agricultural labor shortages, and shortages of milk and other inputs to cheesemaking such as rennet and packaging materi-

als, and occasional controversies over the diversion of milk from the general population to be made into cheeses for France's millions of troops at the front, neither citizen nor soldier lacked for the cheeses that were and remain such an important part of the French diet. French soldiers, the "Poilu," were provisioned with one-quarter of the national output of Gruyère, or Cantal when Gruyère fell short, and Camemberts by the millions. Even the famously colorful and whimsical labels of Camembert abandoned their pastoral scenes of milkmaids and monks for subjects of a more martial nature, like Camembert Les Poilu des Argonnes, which depicted brave French troops charging through the barbed wire of no-man's-land, or the Camembert des Allies celebrating the camaraderie of Allied forces, or the more extreme Camembert National depicting Kaiser Wilhelm, shot from his boots by French artillery, hastily retreating on a donkey from the bucolic French countryside to a charred German hellscape, strewn with skeletons and lit by burning castles. See FRANCE.

The United States was a late entrant to the war, at least as a combatant, and its commitment of troops was far smaller than that of its European Allies. Still the challenge of feeding its troops as well as contributing to the provisioning of Allied soldiers' efforts while avoiding shortages at home caused many of the same social stresses, if less severe, as in European countries. Nonetheless, President Woodrow Wilson sought to avoid mandatory, government-regulated rationing programs, preferring instead to promote voluntary "conservation" programs as well as "Meatless Mondays" and "Wheatless Wednesdays." See UNITED STATES.

One notable effect of US participation in the war was a backlash in the States against products of German origin or tradition, including beer, cheese, and sauerkraut. Another example was the transformation of the popular Californian cheese, Monterey Jack, into a harder, more aged Dry Jack to satisfy the American Italian community's hunger for hard Italian cheeses, which were no longer imported. See VELLA CHEESE COMPANY and JACK. Another example of the transformation of the American cheese industry during this time was the invention by James Kraft, among others, of process cheese, an amalgam of melted cheese and emulsifying salts that could better withstand warm temperatures and protracted storage and transport, making it ideal for shipping to soldiers in Europe. See KRAFT, JAMES and PASTEURIZED PROCESS CHEESES.

See also MILITARY RATIONING and WORLD WAR II.

Boisard, Pierre. *Camembert: A National Myth.* Berkeley: University of California Press, 2003.

Marx de Salcedo, Anastacia. *Combat-Ready Kitchen: How the U.S. Military Shapes the Way You Eat.* New York: Current, 2015.

Rance, Patrick. *The Great British Cheese Book.* London: Macmillan 1982.

Richardson, Matthew. *The Hunger War: Food, Rations & Rationing, 1914–1918.* Barnsley, U.K.: Pen & Sword Military, 2015.

Stearman, Laura. *World War One: The Few that Fed the Many.* Warwickshire, U.K.: National Farmers Union. https://www.nfuonline.com/assets/33538.

Matthew Rubiner

World War II was truly a global war. Virtually all nations of the world participated or were affected. Vast Allied and Axis armies, navies, and air forces operated in often distant theaters of war, far from sources of food and supplies. Agricultural workers, including, of course, dairy farmers and cheesemakers, left their farms for the front or to work in rapidly expanding war-related industries. All these factors combined to strain each participant nation's capacity to feed its troops and its citizenry, and the troops and citizenry of many allied nations. Cheese, as a concentrated, preservable, and transportable source of nutrition would serve an important role throughout the war as a military ration—as it had for millennia—and the circumstances of cheese production would be altered forever as countries sought to realign their agriculture and food-producing industries to meet the demands of war.

In the early years of the war Great Britain, heavily dependent on imports of food including cheese and other dairy products as well as meat, grains, and other foodstuffs, and with an agriculture capacity inadequate to feed its people, faced near-strangulation by the devastatingly effective German submarine campaign against Allied shipping. The Soviet Union, whose agricultural heartland was devastated by German invasion and with few accessible warm water ports, was also dependent on food imports and suffered shipping losses, of as high as 20 percent, to German attack.

In response to its growing food crises, the British government established programs to restrict consumption at home through rationing food staples. Basic items such as butter, bacon, and sugar were rationed in 1940, and cheese and meat would follow in 1941.

The British government also instituted agricultural reforms that would have profound effects on the British cheese industry and accelerate a trend away from farmstead production of traditional British cheese toward the industrial production of a few cheeses deemed critical to the war effort. A Ministry of Food established in 1939 redirected all milk destined for cheese to the production of "National Cheese," a hard, long-lasting Colby-like cheese, at the expense of other less sturdy cheeses such as Stilton, Lancashire, and Caerphilly. This policy, combined with the mass displacement of farmers and cheesemakers to the war and to the industries that supported it, resulted in a dramatic reduction in traditional British cheesemaking that has only in recent decades seen a reemergence. See UNITED KINGDOM.

Britain also turned to the colonies and Commonwealth nations of the vast British Empire to support its food needs and the needs of its troops and sailors. New Zealand, for example, increased its exports of cheese to Britain from 80,000 tons in 1938 to more than 132,000 tons by 1942. And Canada's food exports also provided an essential lifeline to Britain, accounting for 24 percent of its cheese imports by the war's end.

French agriculture, under German occupation since its fall in 1940, experienced severe shortages of agricultural workers, which had a strong effect on its famed cheese industry. More than 400,000 agricultural workers left the farms for the front, many of course not to return. Even among the 2 million French prisoners of war held by the Germans, more than 50,000 were sent to work on German rather than French farms. Shortages of horses, tractors, fuel, fertilizer, and pesticides led to sharp declines in yields, especially in the meat and dairy sectors. The French cheese industry also suffered from Occupation restrictions on its cheeses' fat content, to divert cream and butter to the German war effort. Camembert makers, for example, were forbidden to produce cheese with a fat content higher than 30 percent, well below the traditional 45. See CAMEMBERT DE NORMANDIE and FRANCE.

The United States on the other hand, with its vast agricultural and industrial capacity—dormant after a decade of economic depression—and under no real

military threat to its homeland, was the only country in World War II to experience significant agricultural and industrial growth, and was able to meet
the food requirements of its servicemen with relative ease. The American soldier and sailor were the
"best fed in the world," according to historian Lizzie
Collingham. A typical ration, she writes, included
"3,000 calories a day including veal for breakfast,
Spam for lunch and dried sausage for dinner. In each
ration there was also a fruit bar, crackers, cheese, a
bouillon cube, malt-dextrose tablets, and a packet
of lemon crystals to dissolve in water." See UNITED
STATES.

The United States was not only able to provide its
enormous army and civilian population with plentiful quantities of food; it was also able to feed the
soldiers and civilians of its allies Soviet Union, China,
and Great Britain.

While in the United States rationing programs
were put into place to reduce domestic consumption
of important foods and other commodities critical
to the war effort, including metals and rubber, and
to spread shortages fairly across the population, rationing in the United States had less impact on its
civilian population than similar programs in other
countries. Collingham cites a 1943 opinion poll that
found that rationing and wartime food shortages had
barely made any impact on American meals. Two-
thirds of the women surveyed asserted that their
diet had changed very little since the introduction of
rationing, and three-quarters of the women acknowledged that the size of their meals had stayed the same.

American industrial ingenuity during the war also
led to advances in processed and dehydrated cheeses
that would become fixtures in the American diet. In
1941 the US Congress passed the Lend Lease Act,
which resulted in the purchase of 150 million pounds
(68 million kilograms) of US Grade 1 Cheddar cheese.
The purpose of the purchase was to supplement the
diets of US armed forces. This higher production
volume meant increased numbers of unskilled workers, use of obsolete equipment, improper temperature control/holding time, and a lack of quality control. These practices are often cited as the cause of
typhoid outbreaks linked to Cheddar cheese during
the mid-twentieth century. Further outbreaks of brucellosis, salmonellosis, and staphylococcal poisoning
were linked to cheese consumption in the years surrounding World War II. In response, in 1949 the FDA
published two options for producing safe cheese

products, which led to the 60-day aging rule and use
of pasteurization of milk intended for cheesemaking.
In 1944 alone, the US Quartermaster Corps requi-
sitioned more than 100 million pounds (45 million
kilograms) of canned processed cheese, as well as
500,000 pounds (226,800 kilograms) of processed
cheese spread.

See also INDUSTRIALIZATION; MILITARY RATIONING;
OUTBREAK; 60-DAY AGING RULE; and WORLD WAR I.

Boisard, Pierre. *Camembert: A National Myth.* Berkeley:
University of California Press, 2003.
Collingham, Lizzie. *The Taste of War: World War II and
the Battle for Food.* New York: Penguin, 2012.
Marx de Salcedo, Anastacia. *Combat-Ready Kitchen: How
the U.S. Military Shapes the Way You Eat.* New York:
Current, 2015.
Rance, Patrick. *The Great British Cheese Book.* London:
Macmillan 1982.
Wright, Katherine. *Rationing in the Second World War:
Spuds, Spam and Eating for Victory.* Gloucestershire,
U.K.: The History Press, 2007.

Matthew Rubiner

The **World-wide Traditional Cheese
Association** (WwTCa) is a nonprofit scientific
association that proclaims sociocultural aims concerning the discovery, qualification, and enhancement of traditional dairy products all over the world.
Founded in 2009 by a group of French and Italian
researchers, the association aims to develop an international scientific network that allows researchers
working in universities and research centers in the
field of dairy production to interact and integrate their
actions and knowledge in order to scientifically characterize and safeguard the traditional products present
all over the world, for which scientific and technical
information is available. The main goal of the association is to help define "from cheesemakers to
consumers" chain-like models of interaction and integration between the scientific research community
and the world of production, in order to concretely
use the most advanced technical and scientific knowledge. Exchanging knowledge and training on multidisciplinary research on food safety, technology,
chemical-physical properties, health, aromatic and
sensorial properties, and biodiversity protection of
traditional cheeses is the scientific core of the association thanks to the expertise of its members who
represent universities and research centers. From the

consumers' point of view, WwTCa contributes to defining any activity able to qualify and enhance world traditional dairy products, giving the guidelines for experimental marketing strategies for traditional dairy products, and setting up communication plans to correctly provide consumers with scientific information on their properties. WwTCa interacts as well with national and international governmental authorities in order to scientifically document the peculiarities of traditional production methods and related products.

WwTCa. http://www.wwtca.org.

Catherine Donnelly

Xygalo Siteias (or Xigalo Siteias) is a spreadable cheese that is produced exclusively in the Sitia region of Crete from raw goat's or ewe's milk or a mixture of both, from native breeds around Sitia. The word "xygalo" is connected to the ancient Greek word "oxygala," meaning "acid" plus "milk." It has been protected by a PDO (protected designation of origin) since 2011.

Ancient references to oxygala are found in Pliny's *Natural History*, where it is described as a kind of salted cream cheese produced from goat's milk. Dalby (2003) reports that oxygala was yogurt or something close to it, and that a cheese named oxygalaktikon was made from oxygala. Plutarch as well as Polyaenus said that oxygala was a food of the ancient Persians. It was likely the kind of cheese that needs souring of the milk, and from which the whey is always removed.

The region of Sitia has been connected with developed animal and cheesemaking traditions from the Minoan years up to today. There are written agreements from 1347 to 1450 c.e. on frequent loading of cheeses from the harbor of Sitia to Venice, Egypt (Alexandria), Cyprus, and elsewhere. Sitia is referred to as one of the seven regions of Crete in which sheep and goat farming dates to the thirteenth and fourteenth centuries. The production of Xygalo Siteias occurred mainly in the hot summer months.

In the 1970s the first modern dairy plant in the region of Sitia was created. Today in Sitia there are two dairy plants with an approved installation code for the production of traditional milk and dairy products. The main points in the particular acidification technology used for Xygalo Siteias production include fat standardization to obtain a low fat product, the addition of salt before acidification, two stages of acidification-maturation, a first for seven to ten days at 59–68°F (15–20°C) and a second for about one month at 50–59°F (10–15°C), and no stirring of the product during this time so that the desirable microbial flora from the environment necessary for the natural fermentation can develop.

Xygalo Siteias is white in color, spreadable, and grainy in texture, and without any rind. It tastes fresh, slightly acidic, and mildly salty. It is similar in density to Galotyri and Katiki Domokou cheeses but is less salty. It is eaten as a spread on bread, but also used in pies, salads, etc. In Greece it may be found on supermarket shelves and in restaurants in eastern Crete, and increasingly Athens and Thessalonica; the network CONCRED (Conserving Cretan Diet), which certifies restaurants that offer dishes according to the traditional Cretan diet, has chosen it as a characteristic Cretan appetizer.

See also GALOTYRI; GREECE; and KATIKI DOMOKOU.

"The Cheeses of Crete." Destination Crete. http://www.destinationcrete.gr/en/to-tiri/ta-tiria-tis-kritis.

Commission Implementing Regulation (EU) no. 766/2011 of 29 July 2011 entered a name in the register of protected designation of origin and protected geographical indications (Xygalo Siteias/ Xigalo Siteias) (P.D.O.).

Dalby, Andrew. *Food in the Ancient World from A to Z*. London and New York: Routledge, 2003, p. 218.

Kurmmann, J. A., et al. *Encyclopedia of Fermented Fresh Milk Products: An International Inventory of Fermented Milk Products*. New York: Springer, 1992.

Tunick, Michael H. "Laws, Regulations and Appellations, Xygalo Siteias." In *The Science of Cheese*, p. 203. New York: Oxford University Press, 2014.

Aikaterini Georgala

Xynomyzithra Kritis is a Greek PDO cheese produced on the island of Crete from sheep's and goat's milk whey, or a combination of both. According to the legislation, the milk must be exclusively from Crete, from traditionally raised animal herds whose diet is based on local plants. The name comes from the Greek whey cheese Mizithra (a similar cheese is known as Anari in the island of Cyprus) that is turned sour ("xyno" means sour). The origins of Xynomyzithra Kritis can be traced back to the seventeenth century and its history is rooted in the ancient sheep-rearing activity on the island. It is a soft, creamy, white, and shapeless cheese with grains in its mass and with no cuts or external rind. It has, as its name implies, a sour and a bit acidic and sweetish taste. Its production has increased in recent years to 38 tons as of 2012.

In older times this type of cheese was produced only in small quantities and was mainly referred as the cheese of "kouroupa" (a *kouroupa* is a clay container with a narrow mouth). Cheese was placed in these containers, covered with grape leaves, and buried under the earth for three to six months to ripen. During the ripening period the *kouroupa* are turned upside down and their lids are kept loose in order to facilitate the removal of the superfluous whey. The gradual removal of the whey favors the ripening process of the cheese.

Today, for large-scale production, filtered whey is heated and constantly stirred at 190–198°F (88–92°C) for approximately thirty minutes. Full fat milk is added (maximum 15 percent) when the temperature reaches 154–158°F (68–70°C). Under these circumstances, a fat layer of curd is formed on the top. It is allowed to rest for thirty minutes and then transferred to molds to drain for three to five hours. After drainage salt is added (1.5–2 percent), followed by careful mixing. The mixture is placed in cloth bags and pressed for about one week. Acidified cheese is placed in barrels with a filling procedure gradually carried out by hand so as to avoid gaps in the cheese mass. The barrels are transferred and kept upside-down in a room of 41–50°F (5–10°C) for at least two months to fully ripen.

Xynomyzithra Kritis is one of Crete's most well-known and acclaimed cheeses and it is generally consumed either as table cheese or in traditional pies. The famous Greek salad *ntakos*, also known as *koukouvagia* ("koukouvagia" means owl) contains in some cases Xynomyzithra rather than feta or Mizithra cheese owing to its special taste. Xynomyzithra cheese is also used in the small cheese pies called *kalitsounia* and a famous Cretan pie named *boureki* that is made with zucchini and potatoes. As a dessert, it is commonly served with honey.

See also ANARI and GREECE.

Anifantakis, E. M. *Greek Cheeses. A Tradition of Centuries.* Athens: National Dairy Committee of Greece, 1991.
"Xynomyzithra Kritis." Cheesenet.gr. http://www.cheesenet.gr/english-html/cheeses/xynomyzithra.htm.

Georgia Zoumpopoulou

The **yak,** a huge, arch-backed, black or white, hairy, noisy Asian relative of our common cattle that thrives in cool summers and severely cold winters, is an animal essential to the way of life of the Tibetan herder, providing meat and milk, wool, leather, and even dung for fuel.

The wild yak (*Bos mutus*) is found in the Himalayan mountains of Tibet and their surroundings at elevations of 14,000 feet, and in fact cannot live below 12,000 feet in elevation for any length of time. Over thousands of years, wild yak bulls have interbred with various cattle breeds at lower altitudes, and their offspring eventually became the domesticated Tibetan yak (*Poephagus grunniens* or *Bos grunniens*: "grunting bovine").

Although yaks produce significantly less milk (*dri*) than do cows, the fat content of yak's milk is more than twice that of cow's milk. This means that the fat can be skimmed off to make butter—the principal product and a staple food of the local people—while still leaving sufficient solids to make yogurt and the traditional cheeses of Bhutan, Nepal, and Tibet.

In 1952, in an attempt to help the Nepalese people earn cash incomes, the Food and Agriculture Organization of the United Nations (FAO) helped set up

A yak in the Annapurna mountain range of central Nepal. In 1952 the Food and Agriculture Organization of the United Nations (FAO) helped set up dairies in Nepal to convert yak milk into Swiss mountain-style cheeses.

dairies to convert yak's milk into Swiss mountain-style cheeses. Production is very seasonal and remains under government control, but a few private enterprises have been set up and European-style yak cheese is now made across a wide region for export to the West. But projects like these must be managed with care, because the balance of nature, human survival, and commercialism is fragile at best in this region. In Nepal and some other areas, social change has led to a great reduction in yak numbers, and it is likely that yak herding may diminish in the future as transportation and communications improve and traditional values are eroded.

See also TIBET.

Bishop, N. H. "From Zomo to Yak: Change in a Sherpa Village." *Human Ecology* 17 (1989): 177–204.
Li Yifang. *Past, Present and Future of Milk Industry in China*. Beijing: China Agriculture Press, 1999.
Miller, D. J. "The Importance of China's Nomads." *Rangelands* 24 (2002): 22–24.
"Tibet." Cheese.com. http://www.cheese.com/tibet.
Xu Guifang, and Wang Zhigang. "Present Situation and Proposal for Future Development of Yak Industry in China." *Forage and Livestock*, Supplement (1998): 6–8.

Juliet Harbutt

yeasts

See FUNGI and FILAMENTOUS FUNGI.

yellow vs. white.

Color in cheese is either an inherent color or an added color. Even though milk is white, most cheeses range from pale yellow to orange. White versus yellow is an important attribute influencing the consumer's perception of cheese quality and an important characteristic determining consumer choice.

Cheese that is orange and therefore made with added color typically uses annatto as the favorite color of choice. Annatto is a natural food coloring made from the achiote tree. Seeds from the tree's flowers have a bright red pulp. Extract is made from the ground pods. To produce a yellow or orange cheese, annatto is added directly to the milk. In order to measure the shade of the finished product's color, the National Cheese Institute provides a reference color standard that represents the color ranges in the marketplace. The scale range is one to eleven. This tool allows the cheesemaker to maintain the color consistency for their product specifications. See ANNATTO.

Cheese that is produced with milk from grass-fed cows has a deeper yellow color due to the beta-carotene in the grass. There is a marked difference between this cheese and cheese made when the cows are fed hay. This occurrence is most evident in the spring months. See MILK.

Even though sheep's milk has a high butterfat content, due to converting beta-carotene to vitamin A, sheep cheese has an off-white color. In contrast, the low butterfat milk from goats produces a white-colored cheese.

Aged artisanal cheeses also have a deeper yellow color due to the loss of moisture during the aging process creating a more concentrated color.

See also COLOR.

Aubrey, Allison. "How 17th Century Fraud Gave Rise to Bright Orange Cheese." *National Public Radio*, 7 November 2013. http://www.npr.org/blogs/thesalt/2013/11/07/243733126/how-17th-century-fraud-gave-rise-to-bright-orange-cheese.
Davies, Sasha, and David Bleckman. *The Cheesemaker's Apprentice: An Insider's Guide to the Art and Craft of Homemade Artisan Cheese, Taught by the Masters*. Beverly, Mass.: Quarry Books, 2012.
Kosikowski, Frank V., and Vikram V. Mistry. *Cheese and Fermented Milk Foods*. Vol. 1: *Origins and Principles*. 3d ed. Westport, Conn.: F. V. Kosikowski, 1997.

May M. Leach

yield

is the amount of cheese produced from a given quantity of milk and is usually given as a percentage. The main contributors to yield are the casein and fat content of milk, how much of each are recovered as cheese, and the moisture content of the cheese. The more fat and casein in the milk the higher the cheese yield; likewise, the more moisture in the cheese, the greater the cheese yield. See CASEIN; FAT; and MOISTURE.

Some fat and casein loss is inherent in the process of making cheese, but excessive agitation or pumping of milk can result in additional fat loss. Improvements in the mechanization of the cutting process have substantially reduced the fat and casein losses in the large commercial vats. Fat losses in rennet-set cheeses generally range between 7 and 10 percent for cow's milk and 12 to 18 percent for sheep's and goat's milk. The reason for the increased fat losses with goat's and sheep's milk has not fully been elucidated, but it may be in part due to a larger number of smaller fat globules in their milk compared to cow's milk. Fat losses for traditionally manufactured "pasta filata" cheeses such as mozzarella can be as high as 12–20 percent due to the heating and stretching process that the cheeses undergo, which churns fat out of the molten curd. The fat and casein not recovered as cheese ends up in the whey. The fat can be recovered as whey cream, which is used to make butter and ice cream. The defatted whey is further processed to produce various whey products. See PASTA FILATA; STRETCHING; and WHEY.

Casein losses are around 5–6 percent for all milks. The initial clotting of the casein involves about a 4 percent loss in casein due to the hydrolysis of ƙ-casein that is necessary to form the coagulum, and additional loss of casein occurs as the result of cutting the coagulum into small pieces called curds and subsequent initial stirring of the curds. If the curds break or shatter because of excessive agitation, it can result in very small pieces of curd called fines. Fines are not captured with the rest of the curds on whey removal and end up in the whey. Some can be filtered out of the whey but are generally not added back to the curds. Instead, they are sold separately to companies making processed cheeses and sauces, but at a much reduced price compared to the remaining cheese and they are typically higher in moisture and lower in fat.

As with casein loss, most of the fat loss also occurs at the cutting step and the subsequent stirring of the curds in whey. See CUTTING and STIRRING. The knives first expose the fat at the surface of the curd and it "pops out" of the curd. Subsequent excessively rough stirring may shatter the curd exposing new surfaces. Additional fat loss occurs during milling and salting of Cheddar cheese curds, pressing of cheese into forms, and a very small amount of the loss is due to the brining of cheese. Generally only 2–4 percent of soluble solids (e.g., lactose, serum proteins) of milk are recovered as cheese. The amount recovered is dependent on their content in milk with more of these components recovered with a higher moisture content of the cheese.

See also COAGULATION OR CURDLING.

Fox, Patrick F., Timothy P. Guinee, Timothy M. Cogan, et al., eds. "Cheese Yield." In *Fundamentals of Cheese Science*. Gaithersburg, Md.: Aspen, 2000. See pp. 169–205.

Guinee, T. P., E. O. Mulholland, J. Kelly, et al. "Effect of Protein-to-Fat Ratio on the Composition, Manufacturing Efficiency, and Yield of Cheddar Cheese." *Journal of Dairy Science* 90, no. 1 (2007): 110–123.

Mark E. Johnson

Zamorano is a Spanish sheep's milk cheese from the province of Zamora, in the Castile-León region, made using milk from Churra and Castellana breeds. This geographical area has a strong pastoral and cheese-making tradition. The first evidence of cheesemaking in this area dates from the Bronze Age over 4,000 years ago, and consists of clay pots with holes where the cheese was left to drain. There are also multiple traces and written records on the activities of sheep grazing and cheesemaking during the Roman Empire and the Middle Ages. Cistercian monasteries had a major role in the conservation of cheesemaking traditions from their origin in the twelfth century until their demise in the nineteenth century. Currently, the artisans combine traditional manufacturing methods with modern systems and protocols of quality control.

The cheese has been protected with a designation of origin (PDO) since 1993 (Commission Regulation [EC] No. 1107/96). Today, the PDO protects seventy-nine livestock farms that have 39,696 milking sheep (heads) that produce 465,134 gallons (1,760,727 liters) of milk per year transformed into approximately 794,958 pounds (360,587 kilograms) of cheese. Milk is coagulated at 82–90°F (28–32°C) for thirty to forty-five minutes, using animal rennet. Salting can be performed using dry salt or by submerging the cheese in brine for a maximum of thirty-six hours. Ripening takes place under 59°F (15°C) and at 75–95 percent relative humidity for more than one hundred days, during which the cheese is turned and rubbed with olive oil.

Zamorano cheese has a cylindrical shape, a distinctive zigzag pattern on the sides, and a pale yellow to dark gray colored rind. Usually, it weighs more than 9 pounds (4 kilograms). The texture of the mass is firm and compact. The flavor is intense, but not overpowering, very nutty and buttery, and slightly piquant.

See also SPAIN.

Ferrazza, R. E., J. M. Fresno, J. I. Ribeiro, et al. "Changes in the Microbial Flora of Zamorano Cheese (P.D.O.) by Accelerated Ripening Process." *Food Research International* 37, no. 2 (March 2004): 149–155.
Martínez, Sidonia, Juan A. Centeno, Inmaculada Franco, et al. "The Spanish Traditional Cheeses: Characteristics and Scientific Knowledge." In *Handbook of Cheese, Production, Chemistry, and Sensory Properties*, edited by Enrique Castelli and Luiz du Vale, pp. 123–167. New York: Nova Science, 2013.

Javier Carballo

Ziraly Panir is a type of pot cheese that is produced in the northwestern region of Iran as well as in Khoy city, particularly in the Ghotoor (Qotur) area by Turkish and Kurdish tribes. The production method of this type of cheese is similar to Jajikhli Panir, except that Ziraly Panir uses cumin seeds instead of herbs. See JAJIKHLI PANIR. Ziraly Panir is a semihard brined cheese mainly produced from raw ewe's milk. However, milk of other species such as goat and cow or a mixture of milks can be used. There is no heat treatment in the processing of this traditional cheese. It is characterized by a hard and brittle texture, a white or darker color (depending on the

Ziraly Panir is a traditional Iranian sheep's milk pot cheese that contains cumin seeds. © YAHYA OLIAEI

cumin-seed content) with gray traces of cumin-seeds, a slight salty and acidic taste, and a fermented aroma combined with cumin-seed flavor. The essential oils and the main constituent aroma compounds of cumin seeds, cuminaldehyde and cuminic alcohol, give the cheese its strong, warm aroma. See AROMA.

In the Mediterranean region of Turkey, similar traditional cheeses containing cumin seeds are produced, such as Carra or Testi Peynir, which mostly contain black cumin or garden thyme. Another example is Leyden cheese, a yellow cumin-spiced hard cheese produced in Leiden, Netherlands, from partly skimmed cow's milk. It is believed that cumin seeds can enhance appetite, taste perception, digestion, lactation, and vision strength. Moreover, they are beneficial for treating and reducing the symptoms of some diseases, such as heart disease, chronic fever, diarrhea, vomiting, abdominal distension, edema, and puerperal disorders.

See also IRAN; POT CHEESES; and TURKEY.

Hayaloglu, Ali A., and Patrick F. Fox. "Cheeses of Turkey: 3. Varieties Containing Herbs or Spices." *Dairy Science and Technology* 88 (2008): 245–256.
Shafiei, Y. "Iranian Traditional Cheeses." Paper presented at the 1st Conference of Iranian Traditional Dairy Products, Khoy, Iran, 24 February 2013. In Persian.

Yahya Shafiei Bavil Oliaei

APPENDIX

CHEESE MUSEUMS

Cheese museums throughout the world appear to be relatively rare, given that cheese is produced as a means of preservation almost everywhere there are animals whose milk is consumed by humans. Although in our very commercialized world the term *museum* is often confused with such activities as factory tours, showcases, tasting rooms, or other means of enticing retail customers, the museums listed below all are characterized by an actual physical building or space, and a collection and/or demonstration of a process, rather than serving as only a virtual or online museum.

These twenty-five cheese-related sites are scattered over thirteen countries, almost all of which are in Western Europe or North America. Four countries, France, Switzerland, the Netherlands, and the United States account for thirteen of the twenty-five; of the other nine countries, each has only one or two museums. Each museum listing includes its name in English, its name in its native country's language, its city and postal code, its telephone number, its web address, and a brief description. The host countries and names of the museums within each country are in alphabetical order. Because internet information is so fluid and subject to rapid change, the information for each listing often has had to be derived from several sources or databases.

Some of the museums have opened their doors relatively recently; others have been established for years. But they all seem to share at least two common attributes: frequent changes in the information that is available on their websites, and times and dates of openings and closings that usually vary by season. This may be due to budget constraints that govern staffing, acquisitions, and maintenance of the physical plant as well as of the collections. Even the missions of museums change over time and sometimes quite suddenly.

Please be aware: before planning a visit to one of the museums, take care to use the telephone number and web address offered here to ascertain the current days and times of opening and closing and of any special events that might be scheduled.

Austria

Alpine Dairy Farming Museum (Alpsennereimuseum Hittisau)
http://www.vorarlbergmuseen.at/museen/alpsennereimuseum-hittisau/
Platz 370, 6952 Hittisau, Austria
Tel: +43(0)5513/620 950

In western Austria near 120 mountain pastures, the museum exhibits authentic dairying implements with a kitchen that documents 300 years of cheesemaking experience focused on Bregenzerwald cheeses.

Belgium

Old Cheese Factory Museum (De Oude Kaasmakerij)
http://www.deoudekaasmakerij.be
Graventafelstraat 48 A, 8980 Passendale, Belgium
Tel: +32 (0)51 77 70 05

Sited in a cheese factory closed in 1963, this re-created 1930s Belgian creamery presents classic cheesemaking processes, from combining the culture with the milk, through to the molding and aging of the cheese.

Canada

Cheddar Museum: The Old Perron Cheese Factory (La vielle fromagerie Perron)
http://www.museecheddar.org
148 Avenue Albert-Perron, Saint-Prime, Quebec
G8J 1L4, Canada
Tel: (418) 251-4922

Recently this rare hundred-year-old cheese factory in Quebec was restored and opened as a museum to commemorate the importance of artisanal cheesemaking in the area. Old equipment and tools are exhibited.

Ingersoll Cheese & Agricultural Museum
http://www.Ingersoll.ca/visitors/cheese-and
-agricultural-museum/cheese-agricultural-museum
290 Harris Street, Highway 119, Ingersoll, Ontario
N5C 2V5 Canada
Tel: (519) 485-5510

Sited in several buildings, including a replica of a nineteenth-century Canadian cheese factory, this museum tells the story of how early dairying and cheesemaking shaped the growth of the small town of Ingersoll in the late 1800s.

Finland

Dairy Museum (Meijerimuseo)
http://www.meijerimuseo.fi
Hyvelänraitti 6, Saukkola 09430, Finland
Tel: +358 (40) 549 3515

Occupying an early 1900s dairy building in Nummi-Pusula in southwest Finland, the museum's mission is to show the long tradition of dairy farming in the area from before dairies were founded in the late nineteenth century until the mid-twentieth century. Old equipment and utensils for processing and packaging, and a dairy lab of the 1930s and 1940s all contribute to the story of the local industry until the 1960s.

Nakkila Cheese Museum (Nakkilan kotiseutumuseo)
http://aikamatkasatakunnassa.fi/kohteet/nakkilan
-kotiseutumuseo/
16 Pakkalantie, 29250 Nakkila-Seura, Finland
Tel: +358 (44) 209 1717

With the claim of being the first cheese/dairy museum in western Finland, its mission is to show the importance of the local dairy industry that made traditional Finnish cream cheese and buttermilk cheese. Featured is the original equipment used in its operation from the 1920s to 1963.

France

Museum of Camembert Cheese (La Maison du Camembert)
http://www.maisonducamembert.com
61 le Bourg, 61120 Camembert, France
Tel: +33 02 33 12 10 37

A restored old farmstead features the history of one of France's most important cheeses, the stories of some of the cheesemaking families who produced it, and how it has been advertised and marketed. Illustrated with an extensive collection of old labels, a film, and a sound-and-light show.

Museum of Cheeses of Auvergne (Maison de la Fourme d'Ambert et des fromages d'Auvergne)
http://www.maison-fourme-ambert.fr
29 rue des Chazeaux, 63600 Ambert, France
Tel: +33 04 73 82 49 23

Sited in a fourteenth-century nobleman's house, a large collection of old dairy and cheesemaking equipment and implements and a film tell the history of the Auvergne AOP cheeses.

Manoir de l'Isle and Museum of Normandy Cheeses (Le Manoir de l'Isle et et le Musée du Fromage)
68 rue Marcel Gambier, 14140 Livarot, France
Tel: +33 02 31 63 34 31

The museum includes a reconstructed farm dairy, a former cheese factory, videos of bygone cheesemaking processes, and a large collection of labels of cheeses made in the area: Livarot, Neufchâtel, Camembert, and Pont-l'Évêque.

Roquefort Cheese Producers' Museum and Caves (Société des Caves et Producteurs réunis de Roquefort)
http://www.visite-roquefort-societe.com/fr
Avenue François Galtier, 12250 Roquefort-sur-Soulzon, France
Tel: +33 05 65 58 54 38

One of the largest Roquefort producers presents guided tours through the underground caves. A sound-and-light show, tasting room, and exhibit room demonstrate how specific microclimates contribute to Roquefort's unique characteristics.

Germany

Bernbeuren Dairy Museum (Das Bernbeuren Molkereimuseum)
http://www.kaeskueche-bernbeuren.de
Füssener Str. 24, 86975 Bernbeuren, Germany
Tel: +49 8860 8480

Until 1968 Bernbeuren was a small cheese factory producing the soft, washed-rind cheeses Romadur and Limburger. Now a part of the Käsküche health resort, which offers classes on how to make cheese, yogurt, and quark, the museum exhibits cheesemaking objects of yore.

Endingen Cheese Museum (Das Käserei Museum)
http://www.kaeserei-museum.de
Rempartstrasse 7, 79346 Endingen am Kaiserstuhl,
Germany
Tel: +49(0)7642 9289520

From 1901 the building served as a cheese dairy and,
later, filled other purposes before being given to the
town of Endingen. After a gift of 200 objects and all
equipment for cheesemaking from a cheese master, it
opened as a museum with a German cheese kitchen.
Now run by Martin Buhl, owner of Monte Ziego and a
leading purveyor of organic artisanal cheese.

Italy

**Parmigiano Reggiano Cheese Museum (Museo del
Parmigiano Reggiano)**
http://www.parmigianoreggiano.com/where/museum/
default.aspx
Corte Castellazzi, Via Volta 5, 43019 Soragna (Parma),
Italy
Tel: +39 0524 596 129

Material was collected from all five provinces where
Parmigiano Reggiano is produced, and objects from the
mid-1800s to the mid-twentieth century are arranged
chronologically. The use of cheese in gastronomy and its
history, as well as the processes of cheesemaking, are
explored. Sited in the historic cheesemaking facility of
Castle Meli-Lupi of Soragna.

Japan

Megmilk Snow Brand Museum
http://www.fleemy.com/megmilk-snow-brand-museum/
Naebocho 6-chome 1-1, Higashi-ku, Sapporo 065-0043,
Japan
Tel: +81(0)11 704 2329

Opened to observe the fiftieth anniversary of the 1933
founding of the first factory in Japan that specialized in
cheese production, the museum deals with dairy farming
history on the island of Hokkaido and uses miniature
models to show how manufacturing is carried on today
in the Sapporo factory.

Netherlands

Amsterdam Cheese Museum
http://www.cheesemuseumamsterdam.com
Prinsengracht 112, 1015 EA Amsterdam, Netherlands
Tel: +31 20 331 6605

This museum, although smaller than the one in Alkmaar,
and primarily a cheese store, showcases an impressive
variety of Dutch cheeses and is only a block or so from
the Anne Frank House. Additional exhibition space was
under construction in early 2016.

**Bodegraven Cheese Museum (Kaasmuseum
Bodegraven)**
http://www.kaasmuseum.org
Julianastraat 4, 2411CV Bodegraven, Netherlands
Tel: +31(0)172-65 09 09

The museum uses hundreds of objects, pictures,
documents, and videos to tell of Bodegraven's history as
an important cheese center and to show everything
about farmhouse cheese making and such related
activities as warehousing and the cheese market.

Dutch Cheese Museum (Het Hollands Kaasmuseum)
http://www.kaasmuseum.nl
Waagplein 2, 1811 JP Alkmaar, Netherlands
Tel: +31(0)72 515 55 16

Renovated in 2014, the museum is installed on two
floors of an old cheese weigh house still in use in
Alkmaar, an important Dutch cheese market. It shows,
with a collection of cheese presses, equipment, and
utensils, how cheesemaking developed, and explains the
difference between making farmhouse cheese and
factory cheese.

Gouda Cheese Museum (De Goudse Waag)
http://www.goudsewaag.nl
Markt 35, 2801 JK Gouda, Netherlands
Tel: +31(0)182 529996

Sited in a former cheese weigh house dating from 1668,
the museum focuses on the development of the dairy
industry, Gouda cheese, and other aspects of the Gouda
region, enhanced by dioramas of dairy farming and
cheesemaking. The place of cheese in human nutrition
and the Dutch economy is emphasized.

Slovenia

Alpine Dairy Museum (Plansarski muzej)
http://www.bohinj.si/en/attractions/alpine_dairy_
farming_museum
Stara Fužina 181 4265 Bohinjsko jezero, Slovenia
Tel: + 386(0)45 770 156

An abandoned village cheese factory is now home to an
Alpine dairy hut interior with other objects, photographs,
and documents showing high Alpine dairy farming.
Originally all Bohinj cheese was made in summer
mountain pastures until a co-op opened the cheese
factory that existed from 1883 until 1967. The collection
was renovated in 1990.

Switzerland

Appenzeller Cheesemaking Demonstration Center (Appenzeller Schaukäserei)

http://www.schaukaeserei.ch/en/adventures/
guided-tours.html
Dorf 711, CH-9063 Stein AR, Switzerland
Tel: +41(0)71 368 50 70

Audiovisuals, exhibits, and tours are employed to demonstrate how the famed Appenzeller cheese is manufactured, stored, and aged to acquire its special qualities.

The House of Gruyère (La Maison du Gruyère: Fromagerie de Demonstration)

http://www.lamaisondugruyere.ch/homepage-en/
Place de la Gare 3, CH-1663 Pringy-Gruyères,
Switzerland
Tel: +41(0)26 921 84 00

To demonstrate the production of Gruyère cheese and bolster its claim that it came into being in the Gruyère region in 1115, there is a multi-sensoral tour with an audio guide as well as printed brochures in many languages.

National Dairy Museum (Nationales Milchwirtschaftliches Museum)

http://www.museumkiesen.ch
Gurtengasse 6, CH-3629 Kiesen, Switzerland
Tel: +41(0)31 781 28 46

The emphasis here is on how Swiss cheese is made, how regional cheesemakers have produced Emmentaler and Tilsiter, and also how they have influenced cheesemaking worldwide. There is an authentic and complete cheesemaking kitchen dating from 1815, when Emmentaler was first produced down in the valley. The museum celebrated its 200-year existence in 2015.

United Kingdom

Wensleydale Creamery, Visitor Center and Museum

http://www.wensleydale.co.uk/cheese-making-and
-museum

Gayle Lane, Hawes, North Yorkshire DL8 3RN,
United Kingdom
Tel: +44(0)1969 667664

Old cheesemaking implements and a renovated farmhouse kitchen and dairy illustrate how the production of genuine Yorkshire Wensleydale has evolved through the centuries using traditional methods: cutting, stirring, "pitching," and salting.

United States

Cuba Cheese Shoppe and Museum

12 West Main Street, Cuba, NY 14727, United States
Tel: (585) 968-3949

A relatively recent museum, focused on the western New York State milk and cheese industry, which grew in the 1850s after dairying replaced wheat farming that had shifted westward to the Great Plains.

Henning's Wisconsin Cheese Store and Museum

http://www.henningscheese.com/cheese_store_
museum.html
20201 Point Creek Road, Kiel, WI 53042, United States
Tel: (920) 894-3032

Sited in a cheese factory, a collection of early 1900s cheesemaking equipment is part of the currently operating factory. Visitors can visit the museum, see videos of Cheddar and string cheese production, and watch cheese being made.

National Historic Cheesemaking Center and Museum

http://www.nationalhistoriccheesemakingcenter.org
2108 6th Avenue, Monroe, WI 53566, United States
Tel: (608) 325-4636

In the 1870s after wheat farming had left the area, migrants from New York State convinced their Green County Swiss and Dutch immigrant neighbors to follow New York's lead and shift to dairying. The center and museum now offer cheesemaking demonstrations and access to hundreds of video and audio recordings of interviews with early cheesemakers.

Shirley Cherkasky

DIRECTORY OF CONTRIBUTORS

Nancy Jones Abeiderrahmane
Engineer and Entrepreneur, Private Dairy Plant; Author, *Camel Cheese*, Brentford, United Kingdom

Alexis Marie Adams
Writer (alexismadams.com), Leonidio, Greece, and Red Lodge, Montana

Tamar Adler
Author, *An Everlasting Meal: Cooking with Economy and Grace* and *Something Old, Something New*; Contributing Writer, *The New York Times Magazine*; Contributor, *Vogue* magazine

Anastasios Aktypis
Food Science and Human Nutrition, Agricultural University of Athens, Greece

Kelly Alexander
Former Senior Editor, *Saveur* magazine; Writing Instructor at the Center for Documentary Studies, and Doctoral Student in Cultural Anthropology, Duke University, Durham, North Carolina

Voula Alexandraki
Laboratory of Dairy Research, Agricultural University of Athens, Greece

Darina Allen
Ballymaloe Cookery School, Shanagarry, County Cork, Ireland

Gary Allen
Food Writer, Kingston, New York

Jill E. Allen
Corporate R&D and Sensory Manager, Tillamook County Creamery Association, Tillamook, Oregon

Montserrat Almena-Aliste
Cheese Technologist and Sensory Consultant, and Director of Animal Product Development at FoodScience Corporation, Shelburne, Vermont

Valente Alvarez
Professor and Director, CFAES Department of Food Science and Technology, The Wilbur A. Gould Food Industries Center, Ohio State University, Columbus, Ohio

Virginie Amilien
Research Professor, SIFO - Consumption Research Norway, and Akershus University College of Applied Sciences, Oslo, Norway

Rania Anastasiou
Department of Food Science and Human Nutrition, Agricultural University of Athens, Greece

Anders Andrén
Professor Emeritus, Department of Food Science, Swedish University of Agricultural Sciences, Uppsala, Sweden

Jonathan Shapiro Anjaria
Assistant Professor, Department of Anthropology, Brandeis University, Waltham, Massachusetts

Kate Arding
Operations Manager, Talbott & Arding Cheese and Provisions, Hudson, New York

Julian Armstrong
Food Writer, *Montreal Gazette*, and Author, *Made In Quebec: A Culinary Journey*, Montreal, Canada

Florence Arnaud
Interprofessional Union for the Defense of Morbier, Poligny, France

Paula Arvela
Honorary Post-Doctoral Research Associate with the Faculty of Law, Humanities and the Arts, School of Humanities and Social Inquiry, University of Wollongong, New South Wales, Australia

Volker Bach
Independent Scholar and Translator, Hamburg, Germany

Barbara Backus
Founder and Owner, Goat's Leap Cheese, St. Helena, California

Owen Baily
Cheese Maturer, Neal's Yard Dairy, London

Deirdre Baker
Children's Book Reviewer, *Toronto Star*, and Assistant Professor, Department of English, University of Toronto

Adam Balic
Independent Scholar, Edinburgh, Scotland, United Kingdom

John Barlow
Associate Professor, Department of Animal and Veterinary Sciences, University of Vermont, Burlington, Vermont

Céline Barrere
Union for the Defense and Management of AOC Ossau-Iraty Cheese, Ostabat-Asme, France

Scott Alves Barton
PhD, Food Studies, New York University, New York, New York

Nina Bauer
Independent Researcher, Copenhagen, Denmark

Janice Beaton
Owner, Janice Beaton Fine Cheese and Mabou Cheese + Bar, Calgary, Alberta, Canada

Edward Behr
Editor, *The Art of Eating* magazine, and Author, *The Food and Wine of France: Eating and Drinking from Champagne to Provence*, St. Johnsbury, Vermont

David R. Benson
Professor, Molecular and Cell Biology, University of Connecticut, Storrs, Connecticut

Marta Bertolino
Department of Agricultural, Foresty and Food Sciences, University of Turin, Italy

Eric Beuvier
Dairy Technology and Analysis Research Unit, French National Institute for Agricultural Research (INRA), Poligny, France

Jennifer Bice
Founder and Managing Director, Redwood Hill Farm & Creamery, Sebastopol, California

Val Bines
Cheese Technologist, Reading, United Kingdom

Winifred Bird
Independent Journalist and Japanese-to-English Translator and Editor, Oregon, Illinois

Jean-Louis Bloquel
Union of Neufchâtel, Neufchâtel-en-Bray, France

Renata Blumberg
Assistant Professor, Nutrition and Food Studies, Montclair State University, New Jersey

Richard K. Blundel
Department of Public Leadership and Social Enterprise (PuLSE), The Open University Business School, Milton Keynes, United Kingdom

Adriana Bonanno
Department of Agriculture and Forestry Science, University of Palermo, Italy

Despina Bozoudi
Laboratory of Food Microbiology and Hygiene, Faculty of Agriculture, Aristotle University of Thessaloniki, Greece

Milena Brasca
Institute of Sciences of Food Production, National Research Council of Italy, Milan, Italy

Molly Browne
Monger Liaison, Cellars at Jasper Hill, Greensboro, Vermont

Jay Butcher
Export Team, Neal's Yard Dairy, London

Margherita Caccamo
Research Coordinator, Consorzio Ricerca Filiera Lattiero-Casearia (CoRFiLaC), Ragusa, Italy

Gianaclis Caldwell
Author, *Mastering Artisan Cheesemaking* and *Mastering Basic Cheesemaking*, and Cheesemaker and Co-owner, Pholia Farm Creamery, Rogue River, Oregon

Javier Carballo
Food Technology Department, University of Vigo, Spain

Jeanne Carpenter
Wisconsin Cheese Originals, Oregon, Wisconsin

Stefania Carpino
Research Director, Consorzio Ricerca Filiera Lattiero-Casearia (CoRFiLaC), Ragusa, Italy

Ricki Carroll
Founder, New England Cheesemaking Supply Company, South Deerfield, Massachusetts

Gersende Cazaux
Cheesemonger at MonS Fromager-Affineur, Toulouse, France

Juan A. Centeno
Food Technology Area, Faculty of Science, University of Vigo, Spain

Sam Chapple-Sokol
Research Consultant, Culinary Diplomat, and PhD Candidate, American University School of International Service, Washington, DC

Marie-Paule Chazal
Saint-Nectaire Cheese Union, Besse-et-Saint-Anastaise, France

Shirley Cherkasky
Independent Scholar, Alexandria, Virginia

Salvatore Claps
Director in Charge, Council for Agricultural Research and Analysis of Agricultural Economics, Research Unit for Extensive Animal Husbandry, Muro Lucano, Italy

Carly Cody
Mission Cheese, San Francisco, California

Sue Conley
Co-founder, Cowgirl Creamery, Point Reyes Station, California

Bénédicte Coudé
Wisconsin Center for Dairy Research, Madison, Wisconsin

Sonia Cousins
Independent Consultant and Cheese Educator, Newcastle, Australia

Dominic Coyte
Borough Cheese Company, London

Dennis D'Amico
Department of Animal Science, University of Connecticut, Storrs, Connecticut

Andrew Dalby
Linguist, Translator, and Historian; Author of *The Classical Cookbook*, Saint-Coutant, France

Amr Daoud
Abu Daoud for Dairy and Trading, Alexandria, Egypt

Tenaya Darlington
Author, *Di Bruno Bros. House of Cheese: A Guide to Wedges, Recipes, and Pairings*, and Associate Professor, English Department, Saint Joseph's University, Philadelphia, Pennsylvania

Mukta Das
Anthropology and Sociology Department, School of Oriental and African Studies (SOAS), University of London

Christine de Sainte Marie
French National Institute for Agricultural Research (INRA), Ivry-sur-Seine, France

Carol Delaney
Carol Delaney Consulting, Montpelier, Vermont

Dominique Delugeau
Senior Vice President of Speciality Cheese, Saputo Cheese USA; President, Cheese Importers Association of America, Milwaukee, Wisconsin

Kate Demase
Store Team Leader, Whole Foods Market, Arlington, Massachusetts

Peter H. Dixon
Owner, Dairy Foods Consulting, and Artisan Cheesemaker, Parish Hill Creamery, Putney, Vermont

Tarik Dizdarević
Faculty of Agriculture and Food Sciences, University of Sarajevo, Bosnia and Herzegovina

Catherine Donnelly
Editor of *Cheese and Microbes*, and Professor, Nutrition and Food Science, University of Vermont, Burlington, Vermont

Morgane Dumont
Union of Valençay, Valençay, France

Fuchsia Dunlop
Author and Cook, London

Bronwyn Dunne
Food Writer and Director of *In the Kitchen with Bronwyn* Culinary Website, South Burlington, Vermont

Gordon Edgar
Rainbow Grocery Cooperative, San Francisco, California

Anastasia Edwards
Independent Food Historian and Writer/Editor, London

Francisco José Perez Elortondo
University of the Basque Country (UPV/EHU), Vitoria-Gasteiz, Spain

Mireille Faguet
Union of Crottin de Chavignol, Sancerre, France

Marie-Hélène Famelart
French National Institute for Agricultural Research (INRA), Rennes, France

Nana Y. Farkye
Professor Emeritus, Dairy Products Technology Center, Dairy Science Department, California Polytechnic State University, San Luis Obispo, California

Giana Ferguson
Gubbeen Farmhouse Products Ltd., County Cork, Ireland

Mary Ann Ferrer
Food Science, University of Guelph, Ontario, Canada

Elizabeth Field
Independent Scholar, Canaan, New York

Hunter Fike
Merchandising and Category Manager, Di Bruno Bros., Philadelphia, Pennsylvania

Matteu Filidori
Union for the Defense and Promotion of PDO Brocciu, Aléria, France

Carlo Fiori
Affineur, Luigi Guffanti Formaggi 1876, Arona, Italy

Janet Fletcher
Food Writer, Publisher of the *Planet Cheese* blog, Napa, California

Benoit Foisnon
Leader, Union for the Defense and Promotion of Selles-sur-Chur, Loir-et-Cher, France

Beth Forrest
Professor of Liberal Arts, Culinary Institute of America, Hyde Park, New York

Ove Fosså
President of the Norwegian Slow Food Ark of Taste Commission, Sandnes, Norway

Olívia Fraga
Food Writer, São Paulo, Brazil

Paul Freedman
Professor, Department of History, Yale University, New Haven, Connecticut

Tim Gaddis
Many Fold Farm, Chattahoochee Hills, Georgia

Jessica A. B. Galen
Graduate, Food Studies MA, New York University, and Former General Manager, Lucy's Whey, Brooklyn, New York

Jean-Louis Galvaing
Bleu d'Auvergne Union, Auvergne, France

Gilles Garric
French National Institute for Agricultural Research (INRA), Rennes, France

Janvier Gasana
Professor of Environmental & Occupational Health, Epidemiology, and Medicine, Department of Environmental & Occupational Health, Kuwait University Faculty of Public Health, Jabriya, Kuwait

Erasmo Gastaldello
Independent High-Quality Cheese Shop Keeper, Schiavon (VI), Italy

Marie-Line Gaudru
Union of Rocamadour Cheese Producers, Cahors, France

Aikaterini Georgala
Agriculturist and Biologist, Researcher-Laboratory Teaching Staff, Laboratory Dairy Research, Department of Food Science and Human Nutrition, Agricultural University of Athens, Greece

Marina Georgalaki
Department of Food Science and Human Nutrition, Agricultural University of Athens, Greece

Chris George
Cheesemonger, Online Shop Manager, Mons Cheesemongers; Educator, Neal's Yard Dairy, London

Efstathios Giaouris
Department of Food Science and Nutrition, Faculty of the Environment, University of the Aegean, Myrina, Lemnos Island, Greece

David Gibbons
Co-author of *Mastering Cheese*, and Cheese Columnist for *Wine Spectator* magazine, East Hampton, New York

Craig Gile
Cabot Creamery Cooperative, Cabot, Vermont

Cécile Gourinel
Interprofessional Committee of Sainte-Maure de Touraine, Chambray-lès-Tours, France

Cristina Grasseni
Cultural Anthropology, Utrecht University, Netherlands

David Gremmels
Rogue Creamery, Central Point, Oregon

Stephan Gruber
Department of Biomedical Imaging and Image-Guided Therapy, High Field MR Center, Medical University of Vienna, Austria

Kathy Guidi
Author, *Canadian Cheese: A Guide*, St. John, Virgin Islands

Alessandra Guigoni
European Institute of Design (IED), Cagliari, Italy

Timothy P. Guinee
Department of Food Chemistry and Technology, Teagasc Food Research Centre Moorepark, Fermoy, County Cork, Ireland

Katy Gunn
Neal's Yard Dairy, London

Ming Guo
Professor, Department of Nutrition and Food Sciences, University of Vermont, Burlington, Vermont

Ihsan Gurdal
Owner, Formaggio Kitchen, Cambridge, Massachusetts

Cherry Haigh
The Dialogue Agency, London

Juliet Harbutt
Cheese Consultant, Speaker, Trainer, and Writer, Havelock North, New Zealand

Sara Harrison
Gammelgården Creamery, Pownal, Vermont

Magdalini Hatzikamari
Department of Food Science and Technology, School of Agriculture, Aristotle University of Thessaloniki, Greece

Ursula Heinzelmann
Food and Wine Writer and Author of *Beyond Bratwurst: A History of Food in Germany*, Berlin, Germany

Stefan Helmreich
Professor and Elting E. Morison Chair, Head, Anthropology, Massachusetts Institute of Technology, Cambridge, Massachusetts

Jessica Hendy
Postdoctoral Researcher, Department of Archaeology, University of York, United Kingdom; Max Planck Institute for the Science of Human History, Jena, Germany

Elodie Herninelle
Union Members of Maroilles, La Capelle, France

Arthur Hill
Professor and Chair, Department of Food Science, University of Guelph, Ontario, Canada

Caroline Hostettler
Quality Cheese, Fort Myers, Florida

Chrystelle Hustache
Interprofessional Union of Bleu du Vercors, Lans-en-Vercors, France

Christine Hyatt
Cheese Chick Productions, Portland, Oregon

Shari Jacobson
Associate Professor of Anthropology, Department of Sociology and Anthropology, Susquehanna University, Selinsgrove, Pennsylvania

Alexandra Jacquot
Interprofessional Union of Langres, Langres, France

Jean-Luc Jany
Laboratory of Microbial Ecology and Biodiversity, University of Western Brittany, Plouzané, France

Mansi Jasani
The Cheese Collective, Mumbai, India

Mark E. Johnson
Assistant Director, Wisconsin Center for Dairy Research, Madison, Wisconsin

Bradley M. Jones
Graduate Student in Cultural Anthropology, Washington University in St. Louis, Missouri

Graham M. Jones
Anthropology Program, Massachusetts Institute of Technology, Cambridge, Massachusetts

Samir Kalit
Faculty of Agriculture, Dairy Science Department, University of Zagreb, Croatia

Christopher Kaplonski
Division of Social Anthropology, University of Cambridge, United Kingdom

Mary Karlin
Author of *Artisan Cheese Making at Home* (http://www.artisancheesemakingathome.com), Superior, Arizona

Cathy Kaufman
President, Culinary Historians of New York, and Educator, New York, New York

Maria Kazou
Laboratory of Dairy Research, Department of Food Science and Human Nutrition, Agricultural University of Athens, Greece

George Keen
United Kingdom Representative of Farmhouse Artisan Cheesemakers European (FACE) Network

Mateo Kehler
Founder, Cellars at Jasper Hill, Greensboro, Vermont

Alan Kelly
School of Food and Nutritional Sciences, University College Cork, Ireland

Elaine Khosrova
Founding editor, *Culture* magazine, and Author, *Butter, A Rich History*, Chatham, New York

Paul S. Kindstedt
Professor, Nutrition and Food Sciences, University of Vermont, and Author of *Cheese and Culture: A History of Cheese and Its Place in Western Civilization*, Burlington, Vermont

J. Marcelino Kongo
Institute of Technological Innovation, University of the Azores, Ponta Delgada, Portugal

Betty Koster
Owner, L'Amuse Fromagerie, Ijmuiden, Netherlands

Magdalena Kowalczyk
Institute of Biochemistry and Biophysics, Polish Academy of Sciences, Warsaw, Poland

Jake Lahne
Assistant Professor, Department of Culinary Arts and Food Science, Drexel University, Philadelphia, Pennsylvania

Gisèle LaPointe
Dairy Farmers of Ontario Professorship in Dairy Microbiology, Department of Food Science, University of Guelph, Ontario, Canada

Yves Laubert
Interprofessional Committee of Cantal and Salers Cheese, Aurillac, France

Robert LaValva
Founder, New Amsterdam Market, New York, New York

May M. Leach
Q. A. and New Product Development Manager (Retired), Cabot Creamery, Cabot, Vermont

Alexandra Leaf
Independent Scholar and Assistant Professor, The New York City College of Technology

Eric LeMay
Author, *Immortal Milk: Adventures in Cheese*, Athens, Ohio

Walter Levy
Independent Scholar, Accord, New York

Giuseppe Licitra
Professor, Animal and Food Sciences, University of Catania, Italy

Didier Lincet
Union of Chaource Cheese Defense, Chaource, France

Evanthia Litopoulou-Tzanetaki
Laboratory of Food Microbiology and Hygiene, Faculty of Agriculture, Aristotle University of Thessaloniki, Greece

Susan Herrmann Loomis
Journalist, Author, and Publisher, *On Rue Tatin* (http://susanloomis.com), Louviers, France

Petra Mohar Lorbeg
Institute of Dairy Science and Probiotics, University of Ljubljana, Domžale, Slovenia

Sylvie Lortal
Research Director, French National Institute for Agricultural Research (INRA), Rennes, France

John A. Lucey
Professor of Food Science, Director of Center for Dairy Research, University of Wisconsin–Madison

Dan Macey
Food Stylist; Board Member, Historic Foodways Society of the Delaware Valley, Philadelphia

James MacGuire
Contributor, *The Art Of Eating*; Guest Instructor, King Arthur Flour Baking Education Center; and Co-translator, *The Taste of Bread*, Montreal, Canada

Andreja Čanžek Majhenič
Chair of Dairy Science, University of Ljubljana, Domžale, Slovenia

F. Xavier Malcata
Laboratory of Process Engineering, Environment, Biotechnology and Energy, Department of Chemical Engineering, University of Porto, Portugal

Theresa Malec
Cheese Expert, Berlin, Germany

Gregg Mangan
Independent Author and Historian, New Fairfield, Connecticut

Alexandra O. K. Mannerings
Freelance Science Writer, Centennial, Colorado

Eugenia Manolopoulou
Laboratory of Dairy Research, Department of Food Science and Human Nutrition, Agricultural University of Athens, Greece

Sister Noella Marcellino
Abbey of Regina Laudis, Bethlehem, Connecticut

Stephanie Maroney
Cultural Studies, University of California, Davis

Charles Martell
Charles Martell & Son Ltd., Dymock, Gloucestershire, United Kingdom

Esther Martin-Ullrich
Gastronomy, Boston University Metropolitan College, Boston, Massachusetts

Jean Louis Maubois
Director of Research, French National Institute for Agricultural Research (INRA), Rennes, France

Baltasar Mayo
Institute of Dairy Products of Asturias (IPLA-CSIC), Asturias, Spain

Cristina Mazzoni
Department of Romance Languages and Linguistics, University of Vermont, Burlington, Vermont

Max McCalman
Author of *The Cheese Plate, Cheese: A Connoisseur's Guide to the World's Best, Mastering Cheese, Lessons for Connoisseurship from a Maître Fromager*, and *Max McCalman's Swatchbook of Wine and Cheese Pairings*; Maître Fromager, Artisanal Bistro, New York

Anne E. C. McCants

Department of History, Massachusetts Institute of Technology, Cambridge, Massachusetts

R. K. McGuffey

Independent Author, Indianapolis, Indiana

Robert McKeown

Institute for Comparative Studies in Literature, Art and Culture (ICSLAC), Carleton University, Ottawa, Canada

Donald J. McMahon

Western Dairy Center, Utah State University, Logan, Utah

Tess McNamara

Director of Retail & Operations, Lucy's Whey, and Freelance Food Writer, Brooklyn, New York

P. L. H. McSweeney

Professor, School of Food and Nutritional Sciences, University College Cork, Ireland

Agnès Meilhac

Interprofessional Union for the Defense of Brie de Meaux, Melun, France

Anne Mendelson

Co-founder, Culinary Historians of New York, and Author, *Milk: The Surprising Story of Milk through the Ages* and *Chow Chop Suey: Food and The Chinese American Journey*, North Bergen, New Jersey

Patricia Michelson

Owner, La Fromagerie London, and Author, *Cheese: The World's Best Artisan Cheeses* and *Cheese: Exploring Taste and Tradition*, London

Nicholas Millard

Holden Farm Dairy, Ceredigion, Wales

Diana Mincyte

Assistant Professor, New York City College of Technology

Jelena Miočinović

Associate Professor, Faculty of Agriculture, University of Belgrade

Slavko Mirecki

Biotechnical Faculty, University of Montenegro, Podgorica, Montenegro

Vikram Mistry

Professor and Department Head, Dairy Science, South Dakota State University, Brookings, South Dakota

Gina L. Mode

Assistant Coordinator, Cheese Industry and Applications Group, Wisconsin Center for Dairy Research, Madison, Wisconsin

Marie-Christine Montel

Research Director, Cheese Research Unit, French National Institute for Agricultural Research (INRA), Center Auvergne Rhône Alpes, France

James Montgomery

Montgomery's Cheddar, Somerset, United Kingdom

Thomas Moschakis

Assistant Professor, Department of Food Science and Technology, School of Agriculture, Aristotle University of Thessaloniki, Greece

Adam Moskowitz

Founder, Cheesemonger Invitational, Brooklyn, New York

Paul Neaves

Proprieter, Williams & Neaves, The Food Microbiologists, Surrey, United Kingdom

Kristina Nies

Independent Scholar, Cambridge, Massachusetts

Meredith T. Niles

Assistant Professor, Department of Nutrition and Food Sciences, University of Vermont, Burlington, Vermont

Jill Norman

Former Editor of the Penguin Food and Wine List, Author of *Herbs and Spices: The Cook's Reference* and *The New Penguin Cookery Book*, Editor of *The Cook's Book*, and Literary Trustee of the Elizabeth David Estate, London

Yahya Shafiei Bavil Oliaei

Assistant Professor, Department of Food Science and Technology, Faculty of Agricultural Sciences and Natural Resources, Khoy Branch, Islamic Azad University, Khoy, Iran

Garrett Oliver

Brewmaster, The Brooklyn Brewery; Author, *The Brewmaster's Table*; Editor-in-Chief, *The Oxford Companion to Beer*, Brooklyn, New York

Barbara Orland

Senior Scientist, Affiliated to the Pharmazie-Historisches Museum, University of Basel, Switzerland

Sandra Ott
William A. Douglass Center for Basque Studies, University of Nevada, Reno, Nevada

Don Otter
Senior Outreach Specialist, Center for Dairy Research, University of Wisconsin–Madison

Photis Papademas
Department of Agricultural Sciences, Biotechnology, and Food Science, Cyprus University of Technology, Limassol, Cyprus

Konstantinos Papadimitriou
Laboratory of Dairy Research, Department of Food Science and Human Nutrition, Agricultural University of Athens, Greece

Eleni C. Pappa
Hellenic Agricultural Organization "DEMETER," General Directorate of Agricultural Research, Institute of Technology of Agricultural Products, Dairy Research Department, Ioannina, Greece

Tami Parr
Author, *Artisan Cheese of the Pacific Northwest* and *Pacific Northwest Cheese: A History*, Portland, Oregon

John A. Partridge
Department of Food Science and Human Nutrition, Michigan State University, East Lansing, Michigan

Aurélie Passel
Union of Fourme de Montbrison, Montbrison, France

Heather Paxson
Professor of Anthropology, Massachusetts Institute of Technology, and Author of *The Life of Cheese: Crafting Food and Value in America*, Cambridge, Massachusetts

John Pearson
Technical Consultant, London

Luisa Pellegrino
Department of Food, Environmental, and Nutritional Sciences (DEFENS), University of Milan, Italy

Bronwen Percival
Buyer and Quality Assurance Manager, Neal's Yard Dairy, and Co-founder, MicrobialFoods.org, London

Francis Percival
Food Editor, *The World of Fine Wine*, and Co-founder, London Gastronomy Seminars

Karl J. Peterson
Blogger (The Dairy Free Traveler) and Contributor to *Savoring Gotham*, New York, New York

Elia Petridou
Department of Social Anthropology and History, School of Social Sciences, University of the Aegean, Mytilini, Greece

Rosario Petriglieri
Consorzio Ricerca Filiera Lattiero-Casearia (CoRFiLaC), Ragusa, Italy

Ivana Piccitto
Consorzio Ricerca Filiera Lattiero-Casearia (CoRFiLaC), Ragusa, Italy

Antonio Pirisi
Department for Research in Animal Production and Technology Products of Animal Origin, Agricultural Research Agency of Sardinia, Bonassai, Italy

Celia Plender
Doctoral Candidate, Social Anthropology, School of Oriental and African Studies, University of London

Pat Polowsky
Cheese Research Group, Wisconsin Center for Dairy Research, Madison, Wisconsin

Todd Pritchard
Senior Lecturer, Nutrition & Food Sciences, University of Vermont, Burlington, Vermont

Mary Quicke
Managing Director, Quicke's, Devon, United Kingdom

Allison Radecki
Food Writer and Gastronomic Community Connector, Alumna of the University of Gastronomic Sciences, Pollenzo, Italy

Zorica Radulović
Faculty of Agriculture, University of Belgrade, Serbia

Matt Ranieri
Old Chatham Sheepherding Company, Old Chatham, New York

Vince Razionale
Grafton Village Cheese, Grafton, Vermont

Matthew J. Rippon
School of Geography, Queen Mary, University of London, England

Georges Risoud
Union for the Defense of Époisses Cheese, Époisses, France

Rengenier C. Rittersma
Rotterdam School of Management, Erasmus University, Rotterdam, Netherlands

Kelly Roberson
Writer, Editor, and Project Manager, Kelly Roberson, Inc., Des Moines, Iowa

Jeffrey P. Roberts
New England Culinary Institute, Montpelier, Vermont

Sara Rodgers
Development Editor, Oxford University Press, New York, New York

Juliette Rogers
Centre d'Economie at de Sociologie Appliquées à l'Agriculture et aux Espaces Ruraux (CESAER), Dijon, France

Meryl S. Rosofsky
Department of Nutrition and Food Studies, New York University

Denis Roy
Professor, Department of Food Sciences, Laval University, Quebec, Canada

Matthew Rubiner
Owner, Rubiner's Cheesemongers & Grocers, Great Barrington, Massachusetts

Elliot Ryser
Professor, Department of Food Science and Human Nutrition, Michigan State University, East Lansing, Michigan

Paulina Rytkönen
School of Technology and Environmental Studies, School of Natural Sciences, Södertörn University, Huddinge, Sweden

Colin Sage
Department of Geography, School of the Human Environment, University College Cork, Ireland

Svijetlana Sakić
Faculty of Agriculture and Food Sciences, University of Sarajevo, Bosnia and Herzegovina

George Samouris
Researcher, Veterinary Research Institute of Thessaloniki, Greece

Mary Ellen Sanders
Dairy & Food Culture Technologies, Centennial, Colorado

Elena Santogade
Sales Manager, Grafton Village Cheese, Brattleboro, Vermont

Zlatan Sarić
Faculty of Agriculture and Food Science, University of Sarajevo

Anne Saxelby
Saxelby Cheesemongers, New York, New York

Soyoung Scanlan
Andante Dairy, Petaluma, California

Paul Scharfman
President, Specialty Cheese Company, Inc., Reeseville, Wisconsin

Brian Schlatter
Partner, Black Radish Creamery, North Market, Columbus, Ohio

Megan A. Schraedley
Department of Communication, University of Missouri–Columbia

Marissa Schwoch
Specialist Cheesemakers Association Technical Committee, Wakefield, United Kingdom

Colleen Taylor Sen
Independent Scholar, Chicago, Illinois

Jessica Sennett
Cheese Grotto, Brooklyn, New York

Ian Sharman
Chairman, Montbeliarde UK, Nottinghamshire, United Kingdom

Lynn L. Sharp
Department of History, Whitman College, Walla Walla, Washington

Christy Shields-Argelès
American University of Paris and l'Institut Interdisciplinaire d'Anthropologie du Contemporain (IIAC), Paris, France

Laura Shine
Doctoral Candidate, Humanities, Concordia University, Montreal, Canada

Max Shrem
French Teacher, Chadwick School, Palos Verdes, California

Eirny Sigurdardottir
Búrið Cheese Shop, Reykjavík, Iceland

Valeria Siniscalchi
Associate Professor, École des Hautes Études en Sciences Sociales (EHESS), "Norbert Elias" Research Center, Marseille, France

Max P. Sinsheimer
Editor, Oxford University Press, New York, New York

Adam Smith
Cellars at Jasper Hill, Greensboro, Vermont

Andrew F. Smith
Food Studies Department, The New School, New York, New York

Marianne Smukowski
Outreach Program Manager, Wisconsin Center for Dairy Research, Madison, Wisconsin

Jeremy Snyder
Principal, Science in a Nutshell Productions, Delmar, New York

Sandy Speich
Senior Technical Specialist, Dairy Connection, Inc., Madison, Wisconsin

Sarah Spira
Content Manager, American Cheese Society, Denver, Colorado

Jeremy Stephenson
Cheese Program Director, Spring Brook Farm, Reading, Vermont

Molly Stevens
Cookbook Author, Williston, Vermont

Cathy Strange
New World Chapter President and International Ambassador, Guilde Internationale des Fromagers, and Global Senior Coordinator, Cheese and Specialty, Whole Foods Market, Austin, Texas

Susan Page Sturman
Board of Directors, American Cheese Society, and Director, Academie Opus Caseus, Brookline, Massachusetts

Andy Swinscoe
Owner, The Courtyard Dairy, North Yorkshire, United Kingdom

Mona Talbott
Talbott & Arding Cheese and Provisions, Hudson, New York

A.Y. Tamime
Member of the Publication Committee of the Society of Dairy Technology (SDT), and Dairy Science and Technology Consultant, Ayr, Scotland

Aylin Öney Tan
Food Journalist, Researcher, and Author of *A Taste of Sun & Fire: Gaziantep Cookery*, Ankara, Turkey

Gil Fils Tansman
Doctoral Candidate, Nutrition and Food Science, University of Vermont, Burlington, Vermont

Anne Thierry
STLO (Science and Technology of Milk and Eggs), INRA, Rennes, France

Paul Thomas
Paul Thomas Dairy Consultancy & Training, Salisbury, United Kingdom

Tara Q. Thomas
Executive Editor, *Wine & Spirits Magazine*, and Columnist, *Culture* magazine, Brooklyn, New York

Massimo Todaro
Department of Agriculture and Forestry Science, University of Palermo, Italy

Peter Tomkins
Research Fellow, Sheffield Centre for Aegean Archaeology, Department of Archaeology, University of Sheffield, United Kingdom

Lisa Trocchia-Balķīts
Interdisciplinary PhD Candidate, Social Ecology of Food Systems, Ohio University, Athens, Ohio

Amy B. Trubek
Author, *The Taste of Place: A Cultural Journey into Terroir*, and Associate Professor, Nutrition and Food Sciences, University of Vermont, Burlington, Vermont

Maria Trumpler
Senior Lecturer, Women's, Gender, and Sexuality Studies, Yale University, New Haven, Connecticut

Effie Tsakalidou
Laboratory of Dairy Research, Agricultural University of Athens, Greece

Michael Tunick
Dairy & Functional Foods Research Unit, Eastern Regional Research Center, Agricultural Research Service, USDA, Wyndmoor, Pennsylvania

John Umhoefer
Executive Director, Wisconsin Cheese Makers Association, Madison, Wisconsin

Florence Valence
STLO (Science and Technology of Milk and Eggs), INRA, Rennes, France

Deborah Valenze
Author, *Milk: A Local and Global History*, and Professor of History, Barnard College, Columbia University, New York, New York

Marissa Sertich Velie
Pastry Chef and Food Writer, Poughkeepsie, New York

Domenic Venuto
Independent Food Writer, Brooklyn, New York

Mélanie Verdellet
Confederation of Roquefort, Millau, France

Géraldine Verdier
Union for the Defense of Chabichou du Poitou, Mignaloux-Beauvoir, France

Almut H. Vollmer
Research Assistant Professor, Utah State University, Logan, Utah

Aurélien Vorger
Union of Fourme d'Ambert, Ambert, France

Dominique Angèle Vuitton
Research Unit EA 3181 "Epithelial Carcinogenesis" and WHO Collaborating Centre for Prevention and Treatment of Human Echinococcosis, University of Bourgogne/Franche-Comté, Besançon, France, and Vitagora Pole, Dijon, France

Jim Wallace
New England Cheesemaking Supply Company, South Deerfield, Massachusetts

Guorong Wang
Research Scientist at Leprino Foods, Denver, Colorado

Brent A. Wasser
Former Manager, Sustainable Food & Agriculture Program, Williams College, Williamstown, Massachusetts

Robin Watson
Independent Publishing Professional, Taylor, Michigan

Deana L. Weibel
Associate Professor and Chair of Anthropology, Grand Valley State University, Allendale, Michigan

Susan Weingarten
Visiting Scholar, Oxford Centre for Hebrew and Jewish Studies, University of Oxford, United Kingdom

Nicole Welk-Joerger
History and Sociology of Science, University of Pennsylvania, Philadelphia, Pennsylvania

Laura Werlin
Author and Cheese Educator, San Francisco, California

Harry G. West
Professor of Anthropology, Department of Sociology, Philosophy, and Anthropology, University of Exeter, United Kingdom

Nigel White
Former Secretary, British Cheese Board; Former Secretary, Stilton Cheese Makers' Association, Surrey, United Kingdom

Andrea S. Wiley
Professor of Anthropology, Indiana University, Bloomington, Indiana

Joby Williams
The Kernel Brewery, London

Bee Wilson
Food Writer, United Agents, London

Carol Wilson
Food Writer, Cookbook Author, Heswall, United Kingdom

Clark Wolf
Clark Wolf Company, New York, New York

Benjamin E. Wolfe
Assistant Professor of Microbiology, Department of Biology, Tufts University, Medford, Massachusetts

Dana D. Wolle
Assistant Coordinator, Cheese Industry and Applications Group, Center for Dairy Research, University of Wisconsin–Madison

Rebecca J. H. Woods
Department of History, Columbia University, New York, New York

Carlos Yescas
Co-founder, Lactography, Program Director, Oldways Cheese Coalition, and Graduate Student, and Doctoral Candidate, New School for Social Research, New York, New York

Emma Young
Mons Cheesemongers, London

Giuseppe Zeppa
Associate Professor, Department of Agriculture, Forest and Food Sciences, University of Turin, Italy

Paul Zindy
Counseil National des Appelations D'Origine Laitières (CNAOL), Paris, France

Georgia Zoumpopoulou
Laboratory of Dairy Research, Department of Food Science and Human Nutrition, Agricultural University of Athens, Greece

INDEX

Page numbers in boldface refer to the main entry on a subject. Page number in italics refer to illustrations and tables

with quark, 599
soufflé, **665–666**
soups, **666**
with Svježi sir, 688
sweets made with *chhana*, 538
with Taleggio, 697
tartiflette, 609, **698**
in Turkey, 733
with Valtellina Casera, 747
Welsh rabbit, **760–761**
Cullen, Sam, 554
Culture (magazine), 701
culture and taste, 563–564
culture houses, **207–210**
cultures. *See also* adjunct cultures; ripening cultures;
    starter cultures
DVS (direct vat set), 208
freeze-dried ripening cultures, 620
phage-resistant, 208
cumin seeds, 77, 405, 503, 585, 747, 785
Cunnie, Maureen, 609
cup cheese, 23
curd, assessing the, 170
curd cheeses
in Baltics, 57–58
in Turkey, 733
curdling
cultural theories of, **210–211**, 450
mechanisms of, 171
curd mill, **212**, 343
curd washing/rinsing, 221
Customs of Corbie, The, **212–213**
cutting, *213*, **213–214**
traditional instruments, 727
cyclapiazonic acid, 505
Cyclops Polyphemos. *See* Homer
Cynara cardunculus (cardoon), 276
Cypress Grove Chevre, 22, 108, 116, 194, **214–215**, 741.
    See also Humboldt Fog
Cyprus cheeses. *See* Anari; Halloumi
Cyprus Organization for Standardization, 341
Czech sour milk cheeses, 667

D
Daani, 248
Dacca, 58
dadhanvat, 373
dairy allergy, **217–218**
Dairy Australia, 49
Dairy Board (South Africa), 668
Dairy Business Innovation Center, **218**
Dairy Connection, 207
Dairy Crest, 481
Dairy Farmers of Ontario, 526
*Dairy Farming: Being the Theory, Practice, and Methods of
    Dairying* (Sheldon), 306
Dairy Industry Association of Australia (DIAA), 49
dairy industry/sector
in Iran, 380–381
in Italy, 385
in Portugal, 581–582
USDA and, 743
in Vermont, 751

Dairy Innovation Australia Ltd. (DIAL), 209
dairymaids, **218–220**, *219*, 306
sexual imagery and, 647
Dairy Management Inc. (DMI), 481
dairy propionibacteria, **220–221**, 676
proteolysis and, 593
Dairy Shorthorn. *See* Shorthorn (cattle breed)
Dalby, Andrew, 123, 779
Dale End Cheddar, 196
Dalewood Fromage Huguenot, 668
Dalí, Salvador, 42
Damascus (goat breed), 321
Damdaran, 381
Danablu, 227
Danbo, 227
Danisco, 208
Danisco-DuPont, 613, *614t*
Danish cheeses. *See* Denmark; Havarti
Danlac Canada, 346
Daphne Zepos Teaching Award, 64
David, Elizabeth, 567
Davies, Christie, 165
Davil's Gulch, 200
deacidification, **221**
of surface in washed-rind cheeses, 757
in washed-curd cheeses, 756
Deal, Christian and Josiane, 446
deamination, **221–222**
de aro, 468
De aversatione casei (On the dislike of cheese) (Schoock), 138
Debaryomyces, **222**
De bello gallico (Caesar), 512
Decameron (Bocaccio), 539
de cincho, 469
de cuadro, 468
defects, **222–226**
caused by *Mucor*, 502
in Cheddar, *224–226t*
due to carbon dioxide, 116
fruity flavor, 297
Defoe, Daniel, 681
de Gaulle, Charles, 291
De Generatione Animalium (Aristotle), 210
Deipnosophistae (Athenaeus)
fragments of Archestratus in, 37
on plakous, 572
De Kaaskamer van Amsterdam, **226**
Délice de Bourgogne, 730
del morral, 468
DelvoCheese, 210
demineralization, **226–227**, 234, 592
Denmark, **227–228**
Denominazione di Origine
    Montasio, 489
Denominazione di Origine Controllata (DOC)
    Fontina Val D'aosta, 280
    Gorgonzola, 323
    Pecorino Sardo, 557
    Valle d'Aosta Fromadzo, 746
denominazione di origine protetta (DOP)
    Piave, 566
    Provolone Valpadana, 595
    Valle d'Aosta Fromadzo, 746